Lecture Notes in Computer Science   13530

More information about this series at https://link.springer.com/bookseries/558

Elias Pimenidis · Plamen Angelov ·
Chrisina Jayne · Antonios Papaleonidas ·
Mehmet Aydin (Eds.)

Artificial Neural Networks and Machine Learning – ICANN 2022

31st International Conference on Artificial Neural Networks
Bristol, UK, September 6–9, 2022
Proceedings, Part II

Springer

Editors
Elias Pimenidis (ID)
University of the West of England
Bristol, UK

Chrisina Jayne (ID)
Digital Innovation
Teesside University
Middlesbrough, UK

Mehmet Aydin (ID)
The University of the West of England
Bristol, UK

Plamen Angelov (ID)
Lancaster University
Lancaster, UK

Antonios Papaleonidas (ID)
Democritus University of Thrace
Xanthi, Greece

ISSN 0302-9743   ISSN 1611-3349 (electronic)
Lecture Notes in Computer Science
ISBN 978-3-031-15930-5   ISBN 978-3-031-15931-2 (eBook)
https://doi.org/10.1007/978-3-031-15931-2

Preface

The International Conference on Artificial Neural Networks has entered this year its fourth decade. After two years of disturbance the conference has returned in a hybrid mode with delegates attending on site and remotely via an immersive online space. In 2022 the 31st ICANN was organized under the auspices of the European Neural Networks Society (ENNS) and hosted by the University of the West of England, in Bristol, United Kingdom.

The event attracted a large number and wide range of new and established researchers from five continents and 27 countries in total. The delegates came from Australia, Belgium, Brazil, Canada, China, Czech Republic, Egypt, Finland, France, Germany, Greece, India, Israel, Italy, Japan, Mexico, Morocco, New Zealand, Norway, Portugal, Slovakia, Spain, Sweden, Switzerland, Turkey, UK, and USA.

The research themes explored all innovative pathways in the wider area of Neural Networks and Machine Learning. There were 561 papers submitted. These were reviewed by at least two reviewers with the average number of reviews being 3 per paper. The quality of the submitted work was very high and the program committee chairs had the challenge and delight to be able to select 259 papers in total to be presented orally at the conference. These papers arc included in the four volumes of these proceedings. Out of the selected papers, 255 were regular papers, with an additional four submissions accepted for presentation as extended abstracts. These, despite their short length, represent future concepts that promise very high quality research outputs, and the program committee agreed to offer the authors the opportunity to share their ideas with the delegates of the conference.

The papers included in these four volumes of the Lecture Notes in Computer Science series addressed a variety of topics, representing a wide breadth of research, not just in the area of Artificial Neural Networks but in related AI topics themes too: Deep Learning, Neural Network Theory, Neural Network Models, Recurrent Networks, Reinforcement Learning, Natural Language Processing, Generative Models, Graphical Models, Supervised Learning, Image Processing, CNN, Evolutionary Neural Networks, Unsupervised NN, Relational Learning, Image Processing, Recommender Systems, and Features Based Learning.

The conference delegates benefited from the inspiring keynote speeches by four distinguished invited speakers, details of which are given below.

Agnieszka Wykowska leads the unit Social Cognition in Human-Robot Interaction at the Italian Institute of Technology, Genoa, Italy. Her background is cognitive neuroscience with a Ph.D. in psychology from Ludwig Maximilian University Munich. In 2016 she was awarded an ERC Starting grant for InStance: Intentional Stance for Social Attunement, which addresses the question of attribution of intentionality to robots. She is Editor-in-Chief of the International Journal of Social Robotics. She is the President of the European Society for Cognitive and Affective Neuroscience (ESCAN). She is a delegate to the European Research Area (ERA) Forum, and a member of ELLIS (European Lab for Learning and Intelligent Systems). Her research bridges psychology, cognitive neuroscience, robotics and healthcare. Among other work her team develops robot-assisted training protocols to help children diagnosed with autism-spectrum disorder improve social skills.

Věra Kůrková is a senior scientist in the Institute of Computer Science of the Czech Academy of Sciences. She received a Ph.D. in mathematics from Charles University, Prague, and a Dr. Sc. in theoretical computer science from the Czech Academy of Sciences, from which she received the Bolzano Medal for her contribution to mathematical sciences. Her main interests are the mathematical theory of neurocomputing and machine learning. She has served as president of the European Neural Network Society (ENNS), and she is a member of the editorial boards of the journals Neural Networks, Neural Processing Letters, and Applied and Computational Harmonic Analysis. She has been involved in the organization of many conferences, among them ICANN 2008 and 2001.

The Anh Han is a professor of Computer Science and head of the Centre for Digital Innovation, Teesside University. His research covers several topics in AI and interdisciplinary research, including evolutionary game theory, behavioural and cognitive modelling, agent-based simulations, knowledge representation and reasoning, and AI safety. He has published over 100 peer-reviewed articles in top-tier conferences (AAAI, IJCAI, AAMAS) and journals. He regularly serves in the program committees of top-tier AI conferences, and he is on the editorial boards of several journals (Adaptive Behavior, PLOS One, Frontiers in AI and Robotics, Entropy). He has been awarded prestigious research fellowships and grants from the Future of Life Institute, the Leverhulme Trust Foundation, and FWO Belgium.

Lyndon Smith is a professor in the Centre for Machine Vision, University of the West of England, Bristol. He has over 28 years of research experience in the field of Computer Simulation and Machine Vision, with particular emphasis on 3D analysis of complex surface textures and object morphologies. A strong area of ongoing research is the development of deep learning for vision-based solutions for complex problems, the automation of which had been previously considered intractable. This is leading to strong industrial impact in a number of sectors.

September 2022

Plamen Angelov
Mehmet Aydin
Chrisina Jayne
Elias Pimenidis

Organization

General Chairs

Elias Pimenidis   University of the West of England, UK
Angelo Cangelosi   University of Manchester, UK

Organizing Committee Chairs

Tim Brailsford   University of the West of England, UK
Larry Bull   University of the West of England, UK

Honorary Chairs

Stefan Wermter (ENNS President)   University of Hamburg, Germany
Igor Farkaš   FMPI, Comenius University in Bratislava, Slovakia

Program Committee Chairs

Plamen Angelov   Lancaster University, UK
Mehmet Aydin   University of the West of England, UK
Chrisina Jayne   Teesside University, UK
Elias Pimenidis   University of the West of England, UK

Communication Chairs

Paolo Masulli   ENNS, Technical University of Denmark
Kristína Malinovská   FMPI, Comenius University in Bratislava, Slovakia
Antonios Papaleonidas   Democritus University of Thrace, Greece

Steering Committee

Jérémie Cabessa   Université Versailles Saint-Quentin-en-Yvelines, France
Włodzisław Duch   Nicolaus Copernicus University, Torun, Poland
Igor Farkaš   Comenius University, Bratislava, Slovakia
Matthias Kerzel   Universität Hamburg, Germany
Věra Kůrková   Czech Academy of Sciences, Prague, Czechia

Alessandra Lintas   Université de Lausanne, Switzerland
Paolo Masulli   iMotions A/S, Copenhagen, Denmark
Alessio Micheli   University of Pisa, Italy
Erkki Oja   Aalto University, Finland
Sebastian Otte   Universität Tübingen, Germany
Jaakko Peltonen   Tampere University, Finland
Antonio J. Pons   Universitat Politècnica de Catalunya, Barcelona,
                                      Spain
Igor V. Tetko   Helmholtz Zentrum München, Germany
Alessandro E. P. Villa   Université de Lausanne, Switzerland
Roseli Wedemann   Universidade do Estado do Rio de Janeiro, Brazil
Stefan Wermter   Universität Hamburg, Germany

Local Organizing Committee

Nathan Duran   University of the West of England, UK
Haixia Liu   University of the West of England, UK
Zaheer Khan   University of the West of England, UK
Antonios Papaleonidas   Democritus University of Thrace, Greece
Nikolaos Polatidis   Brighton University, UK
Antisthenis Tsompanas   University of the West of England, UK

Hybrid Facilitation and Moderation Committee

Anastasios Panagiotis Psathas   Democritus University of Thrace, Greece
Dimitris Boudas   Democritus University of Thrace, Greece
Ioanna-Maria Erentzi   Democritus University of Thrace, Greece
Ioannis Skopelitis   Democritus University of Thrace, Greece
Lambros Kazelis   Democritus University of Thrace, Greece
Leandros Tsatsaronis   Democritus University of Thrace, Greece
Nikiforos Mpotzoris   Democritus University of Thrace, Greece
Nikos Zervis   Democritus University of Thrace, Greece
Odysseas Tsonos   Hellenic Open University, Greece
Panagiotis Restos   Democritus University of Thrace, Greece
Tassos Giannakopoulos   Democritus University of Thrace, Greece
Vasilis Kokkinos   Democritus University of Thrace, Greece

Program Committee

Abdelhamid Bouchachia   Bournemouth University, UK
Abdur Rakib   University of the West of England, UK
Abraham Yosipof   College of Law and Business, Israel
Akihiro Inokuchi   Kwansei Gakuin University, Japan

Alaa Zain   Hosei University, Japan
Albert Bifet   LTCI, Telecom ParisTech, France
Alejandro Cabana   Universidad Autónoma de Madrid, Spain
Alexander Claman   University of Miami, USA
Alexander Gepperth   ENSTA ParisTech, France
Alexander Ilin   Aalto University, Finland
Alexander Kovalenko   Czech Technical University in Prague, Czechia
Alexander Krawczyk   HAW Fulda, Germany
Ali Zoljodi   MDU, Sweden
Aluizio Araújo   Universidade Federal de Pernambuco, Brazil
Amit Kumar Kundu   University of Maryland, College Park, USA
An Xu   Donghua University, China
Anastasios Panagiotis Psathas   Democritus University of Thrace, Greece
André Artelt   Bielefeld University, Germany
Andre de Carvalho   University of São Paulo, Brazil
Andrea Castellani   Bielefeld University - CITEC, Germany
Andrea Galassi   University of Bologna, Italy
Angelo Cangelosi   University of Manchester, UK
Anmol Biswas   Indian Institute of Technology, Mumbai, India
Anna Jenul   Norwegian University of Life Sciences, Norway
Annie DeForge   Bentley University, USA
Anselm Haselhoff   Hochschule Ruhr West, Germany
Antisthenis Tsompanas   University of the West of England, UK
Antonio García-Díaz   Université libre de Bruxelles (ULB), Belgium
Antonio Pons   Universitat Politècnica de Catalunya, Spain
Antonios Papaleonidas   Democritus University of Thrace, Greece
Argyris Kalogeratos   CMLA, ENS Cachan, France
Asada   Osaka University, Japan
Asei Akanuma   Goldsmiths College, University of London, UK
Atsushi Koike   Tohoku University, Japan
Baris Serhan   University of Manchester, UK
Barkha Javed   University of the West of England, UK
Benedikt Bagus   Hochschule Fulda, Germany
Benyuan Liu   University of Massachusetts, Lowell, USA
Bernhard Pfahringer   University of Waikato, New Zealand
Bi Yan-Qing   National University of Defense Technology,
                                     China
Binyi Wu   TU Dresden, Germany
Binyu Zhao   Harbin Institute of Technology, China
Bo Mei   Texas Christian University, USA
Boyu Diao   ict, China
Cao Hongye   Northwestern Polytechnical University, China

Carsten Marr	German Research Center for Environmental Health, Germany
Chao Ma	Hong Kong Polytechnic University, Hong Kong, China
Cheng Feng	Fujitsu R&D Center, China
Ching-Chia Kao	Academia Sinica, Taiwan
Chrisina Jayne	Teesside University, UK
Christian Bauckhage	Fraunhofer IAIS, Sankt Augustin, Germany
Christian Oliva	Universidad Autónoma de Madrid, Spain
Christoph Linse	Universität zu Lübeck, Germany
Chuan Lu	Aberystwyth University, UK
Chuang Yu	University of Manchester, UK
Chunhong Cao	Xiangtan University, China
Chun-Shien Lu	Academia Sinica, Taiwan
Claudio Bellei	Elliptic, UK
Claudio Gallicchio	University of Pisa, Italy
Claudio Giorgio Giancaterino	Catholic University of Milan, Italy
Connor Gäde	University of Hamburg, Germany
Constantine Dovrolis	Georgia Institute of Technology, USA
Cornelius Weber	University of Hamburg, Germany
Coşku Can Horuz	University of Tübingen, Germany
Cui Wang	Macao Polytechnic University, China
Dan Fisher	University of North Carolina, Wilmington, USA
Daniel Kluvanec	Durham University, UK
David Dembinsky	German Research Center for Artificial Intelligence, Germany
David Martínez	DataSpartan Ltd., UK
Dayananda Herurkar	DFKI, Germany
Denise Gorse	University College London, UK
Dennis Becker	Lüneburg University, Germany
Dimitrios Bountas	Democritus University of Thrace, Greece
Dimitrios Michail	Harokopio University of Athens, Greece
Diyuan Lu	Frankfurt Institute for Advanced Studies, Germany
D. J. McMoran	University of North Carolina, Wilmington, USA
Domenico Tortorella	University of Pisa, Italy
Dominique Mercier	German Research Center for Artificial Intelligence, Germany
Doron Nevo	Bar-Ilan University, Israel
Douglas Nyabuga	Donghua University, China
Efe Bozkir	University of Tübingen, Germany
Eisuke Ito	Ritsumeikan University, Japan

Elias Pimenidis	University of the West of England, UK
Fabian Hinder	Bielefeld University, Germany
Fanglin Chen	Harbin Institute of Technology, Shenzhen, China
Fares Abawi	University of Hamburg, Germany
Federico Tavella	University of Manchester, UK
Feixiang Zhou	University of Leicester, UK
Feng Wei	York University, Canada
Florence Dupin de Saint-Cyr	IRIT, Université Paul Sabatier, France
Francesco Semeraro	University of Manchester, UK
Francois Blayo	Neoinstinct, Switzerland
Frank Gyan Okyere	Rothamsted Research, UK
Frederic Alexandre	Inria, France
Gang Yang	Renmin University, China
Giannis Nikolentzos	Athens University of Economics and Business, Greece
Gonzalo Martínez-Muñoz	Universidad Autónoma de Madrid, Spain
Grégory Bourguin	LISIC/ULCO, France
Guillermo Martín-Sánchez	Graduate Training Center of Neuroscience, Germany
Gulustan Dogan	University of North Carolina, Wilmington, USA
Habib Khan	Islamia College Peshawar, Pakistan
Hafez Farazi	University of Bonn, Germany
Haixia Liu	University of the West of England, UK
Haizhou Du	Shanghai University of Electric Power, China
Hang Gao	Institute of Software, Chinese Academy of Sciences, China
Haopeng Chen	Shanghai Jiao Tong University, China
Hazrat Ali	Hamad Bin Khalifa University, Qatar
Heitor Gomes	University of Waikato, New Zealand
Hideaki Yamamoto	Tohoku University, Japan
Hina Afridi	NTNU, Norway
Hiroyoshi Ito	University of Tsukuba, Japan
Hisham Ihshaish	University of the West of England, UK
Hong Qing Yu	University of Bedfordshire, UK
Hongchao Gao	South China University of Technology, China
Honggang Zhang	University of Massachusetts, Boston, USA
Hugo Eduardo Camacho Cruz	Universidad Autónoma de Tamaulipas, Mexico
Hugues Bersini	Université libre de Bruxelles, Belgium
Huifang Ma	Northwest Normal University, China
Huiyu Zhou	University of Leicester, UK
Hy Dang	Texas Christian University, USA
Igor Farkaš	Comenius University in Bratislava, Slovakia

Ioannis Pierros	Aristotle University of Thessaloniki, Greece
Iveta Bečková	Comenius University in Bratislava, Slovakia
Jae Hee Lee	University of Hamburg, Germany
James J. Q. Yu	Southern University of Science and Technology, Hong Kong, China
James Msonda	Aberystwyth University, UK
Jan Faigl	Czech Technical University in Prague, Czechia
Jan Feber	Czech Technical University in Prague, Czechia
Jan Kalina	Czech Academy of Sciences, Czechia
Jérémie Cabessa	University Paris 2, France
Jia Cai	Guangdong University of Finance & Economics, China
Jiajun Liu	CSIRO, Australia
Jianhua Xu	Nanjing Normal University, China
Jian-Wei Liu	China University of Petroleum, Beijing, China
Jianyong Chen	Shenzhen University, Shenzhen, China
Jichao Bi	Zhejiang University, China
Jie Shao	University of Science and Technology, Chengdu, China
Jim Smith	University of the West of England, UK
Jing Yang	Hefei University of Technology, China
Jingyi Yuan	Arizona State University, USA
Jingyun Jia	Florida Institute of Technology, USA
Johannes Brinkrolf	CITEC Centre of Excellence, Germany
Jonathan Jakob	Bielefeld University, Germany
Jonathan Lawry	University of Bristol, UK
Jonathan Mojoo	Hiroshima University, Japan
Jordi Cosp-Vilella	Universitat Politècnica de Catalunya, Spain
Jordi Madrenas	Universitat Politècnica de Catalunya, Spain
Joseph Jaja	University of Maryland, USA
Juan Liu	Wuhan University, China
K. L. Eddie Law	Macao Polytechnic University, Macao, China
Kamran Soomro	University of the West of England, UK
Katsiaryna Haitsiukevich	Aalto University, Finland
Kenneth Co	Imperial College London, UK
Koji Kyoda	RIKEN Center for Biosystems Dynamics Research, Japan
Koloud Alkhamaiseh	Western Michigan University, USA
Kostadin Cvejoski	Fraunhofer IAIS, Sankt Augustin, Germany
Kostantinos Demertzis	Democritus University of Thrace, Greece
Kristian Hovde Liland	Norwegian University of Life Sciences, Norway
Kuntal Ghosh	Indian Statistical Institute, India

Larry Bull	University of the West of England, UK
Lei Luo	Kansas State University, USA
Leiping Jie	Hong Kong Baptist University, Hong Kong, China
Lian Yahong	Dalian University of Technology, China
Liang Ge	Chongqing University, China
Liang Zhao	Dalian University of Technology, China
Liang Zhao	University of São Paulo, Brazil
Lingfei Dai	ICT - CAS, China
Linlin Shen	Shenzhen University, China
Lu Wang	Macao Polytechnic University, Macao
Luca Oneto	University of Genoa, Italy
Luca Raggioli	University of Manchester, UK
Luís A. Alexandre	UBI and NOVA LINCS, Portugal
Luis Lago	Universidad Autónoma de Madrid, Spain
Lun-Ing Zhang	China University of Petroleum, Beijing, China
Magda Friedjungová	Czech Technical University in Prague, Czechia
Manon Dampfhoffer	Université Grenoble Alpes, France
Marc Wenninger	Technische Hochschule Rosenheim, Germany
Marcello Trovati	Edge Hill University, UK
Marco Perez Hernandez	University of the West of England, UK
Maria Papadaki	University of Derby, UK
Marika Kaden	HS Mittweida, Germany
Markus Kollmann	Heinrich Heine Universität, Germany
Marta Romeo	University of Manchester, UK
Martin Butz	University of Tübingen, Germany
Martin Ferianc	University College London, UK
Masanari Kimura	ZOZO Research, Japan
Masoud Daneshtalab	Mälardalen University, Sweden
Matthew Evanusa	University of Maryland, USA
Matthias Karlbauer	University of Tübingen, Germany
Matthias Kerzel	University of Hamburg, Germany
Mattias Dahl	Blekinge Institute of Technology, Sweden
Md Delwar Hossain	Nara Institute of Science and Technology, Japan
Mehmet Emin Aydin	University of the West of England, UK
Mihaela Oprea	University Petroleum-Gas of Ploiesti, Romania
Mohammad Loni	MDU, Sweden
Moritz Wolter	University of Bonn, Germany
Mu Hua	University of Lincoln, UK
Muhammad Usama Javaid	Eura Nova, Belgium
Nashwa El-Bendary	Arab Academy for Science, Technology & Maritime Transport, Egypt
Nathan Duran	University of the West of England, UK

Nermeen Abou Baker	Hochschule Ruhr West, Germany
Nikolaos Polatidis	University of Brighton, UK
Oleg Bakhteev	MIPT, Russia
Olga Grebenkova	Moscow Institute of Physics and Technology (MIPT), Russia
Or Elroy	CLB, Israel
Ozan Özdemir	University of Hamburg, Germany
Paulo Cortez	University of Minho, Portugal
Plamen Angelov	Lancaster University, UK
Rafet Durgut	Bandirma Onyedi Eylul University, Turkey
Roman Moucek	University of West Bohemia, Czechia
Roseli S. Wedemann	Universidade do Estado do Rio de Janeiro, Brazil
Ruijun Feng	Zhejiang University of Finance and Economics, China
Saikat Chakraborty	Kalinga Institute of Industrial Technology (KIIT), India
Sajjad Heydari	University of Manitoba, Winnipeg, Canada
Sander Bohte	CWI, Netherlands
Sandrine Mouysset	IRIT, France
Sebastián Basterrech	VSB-Technical University of Ostrava, Czechia
Sebastian Otte	University of Tübingen, Germany
Senwei Liang	Purdue University, USA
Shelan Jeawak	University of the West of England, UK
Shoubin Dong	South China University of Technology, China
Sidi Yang	RI-MUHC, Canada
Song Guo	Xi'an University of Architecture and Technology, China
Songlin Du	Southeast University, China
Stefan Wermter	University of Hamburg, Germany
Steve Battle	University of the West of England, UK
Sven Behnke	University of Bonn, Germany
Takaharu Yaguchi	Kobe University, Japan
Takeshi Ikenaga	Waseda University, Japan
Tang Kai	Toshiba, China
Tetsuya Hoya	Nihon University, Japan
Tianlin Zhang	University of the Chinese Academy of Sciences, China
Tieke He	Nanjing University, China
Tim Brailsford	University of the West of England, UK
Ting Bai	Hefei University of Technology, China
Toby Breckon	Durham University, UK
Varun Ojha	University of Reading, UK

Wenxin Yu	Southwest University of Science and Technology, China
Xi Cheng	Nanjing University of Science and Technology, China
Xia Feng	Civil Aviation University, China
Xian Zhong	Wuhan University of Technology, China
Xiang Zhang	National University of Defense Technology, China
Xiaoqing Liu	Kyushu University, Japan
Xiumei Li	Hangzhou Normal University, China
Xizhan Gao	University of Jinan, China
Xuan Yang	Shenzhen University, China
Yan Chen	Chinese Academy of Sciences, China
Yangguang Cui	East China Normal University, China
Yapeng Gao	University of Tübingen, Germany
Yaxi Chen	Wuhan University, China
Yiannis Aloimonos	University of Maryland, USA
Yihao Luo	Huazhong University of Science and Technology, China
Yipeng Yu	Tencent, China
Yuan Li	Academy of Military Science, China
Yuanyuan Chen	Sichuan University, China
Yuchen Zheng	Shihezi University, China
Yuchun Fang	Shanghai University, China
Yue Gao	Beijing University of Posts and Telecommunications, China
Yuji Kawai	Osaka University, Japan
Zhaoxiang Zang	China Three Gorges University, China
Zhaoyun Ding	National University of Defense Technology, China
Zhengfeng Yang	East China Normal University, Shanghai, China
Zhenjie Yao	CMCC, China
Zhiping Lai	Fudan University, China
Zhiqiang Zhang	Hosei University, Japan
Zhixin Li	Guangxi Normal University, China
Zhongnan Zhang	Xiamen University, China

Contents – Part II

Alleviating Overconfident Failure Predictions via Masking Predictive Logits in Semantic Segmentation

Quan Tang[1], Fagui Liu[1,2](✉), Jun Jiang[1], Yu Zhang[1],
and Xuhao Tang[1]

[1] South China University of Technology, Guangzhou 510006, China
fgliu@scut.edu.cn
[2] Peng Cheng Laboratory, Shenzhen 518055, China

Abstract. Currently, semantic segmentation is formulated to a classification task as image classification with similar networks and training settings. We observe an excessive overconfidence phenomenon in semantic segmentation regarding the model's classification scores. Unlike image classification, segmentation networks yield undue-high predictive probabilities for failure predictions, which may carry severe repercussions in safety-sensitive applications. To this end, we propose manually perturbing the predicted probability distribution via masking predictive logits during training that explicitly enforces the model to re-learn potential patterns, based on the pure intuition that meaningful patterns help alleviate overconfident failure predictions. A direct instantiation is presented that randomly zeroes out the model's predictive logits but keeps their expectations unchanged before computing the loss in the training phase. This instantiation requires no additional computation cost or customized architectures but only a masking function. Empirical results from various network architectures indicate its feasibility and effectiveness of alleviating overconfident failure predictions in semantic segmentation.

Keywords: Overconfidence · Masking logits · Post-dropout · Failure predictions · Semantic segmentation

1 Introduction

Semantic segmentation enables the ability of pixel-level scene parsing, commonly formulated as a pixel-by-pixel classification task and tackled by fully convolutional networks (FCN) [15]. It gains momentum due to the dramatic advances in convolutional neural networks (CNNs) [13]. Despite the growing accuracy on benchmarks, safety remains challenging when deploying segmentation models in safety-sensitive applications such as autonomous driving [22,23], medical diagnosis [25], *etc.*. Models are expected to present a reliable confidence assessment along with the prediction, which helps avoid high-risk errors by triggering backup systems or human involvement.

E. Pimenidis et al. (Eds.): ICANN 2022, LNCS 13530, pp. 1–13, 2022.
https://doi.org/10.1007/978-3-031-15931-2_1

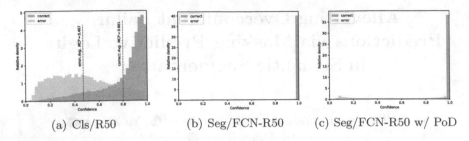

(a) Cls/R50   (b) Seg/FCN-R50   (c) Seg/FCN-R50 w/ PoD

Fig. 1. MCP statistics in different tasks. (a) Classification on ImageNet. (b) Segmentation on Cityscapes w/o (b) and w/ (c) the proposed PoD. FCN-R50 replaces fully connected layers in R50 (*i.e.* 50-layer ResNet) with convolutions to produce dense predictions. Thus they have similar architectures, but the predictive MCP statistics vary tremendously in image classification (a) and semantic segmentation (b), particularly for erroneous samples (*i.e.* failure predictions). Note that distributions of both correct and erroneous samples are plotted in relative density for convenient visualization.

However, studies [14,17] have revealed that deep CNNs are overconfident estimators that yield high-confidence probabilities even for failure predictions, which is also known as confidence miscalibration [7]. The predictive confidence should match the classification accuracy for a well-calibrated model. For example, if a calibrated segmentation network classifies 1,000 pixels as positive with a probability of 0.8 each, we expect 800 pixels to be correctly classified as positive. Overconfident predictive probabilities for failure predictions mean the model is unconscious when making a mistake, which may carry severe repercussions in safety-sensitive applications.

In classification, a natural idea for confidence estimation is taking the maximum class probability (MCP) given by the softmax layer. Hendrycks *et al.* [10] notice a significant difference in MCP values between incorrect and correct samples, which is utilized for failure or out-of-distribution detection. Corbière *et al.* [4] deem that MCP leads by design to high confidence values and is insufficient for distinguishing correct and erroneous predictions. They use the true class probability (TCP) instead to address failure predictions by incorporating an independently auxiliary model. Hein *et al.* [9] theoretically evidence that ReLU networks tend to produce overconfident predictions for abnormal samples.

The works mentioned above address predictive overconfidence in image classification, and that in semantic segmentation is seldom investigated. Although both are formulated as a classification task with similar networks and training settings, we observe excessively overconfident predictions in semantic segmentation compared to image classification, as shown in Fig. 1. For image classification on ImageNet [19] (see Fig. 1(a)), the MCP statistics of correct and erroneous samples show a notable gap. However, for semantic segmentation on Cityscapes [5] (see Fig. 1(b)), a similar model exhibits undue-high classification scores even for error samples (*i.e.* severe predictive overconfidence), which is insufficient to distinguish between correctly and incorrectly classified samples, unfavorable for safety-sensitive applications. See Appendix 6.1 for more examples.

Considering the aforementioned problem regarding deep segmentation networks, we present a pure intuition that perturbing the predicted probability distribution enforces the re-learning of meaningful patterns, which helps alleviate the overconfidence. To this end, we propose an explicit instantiation that randomly zeroes out predictive logits before computing the loss during training. We ensure that logits' expectations remain unchanged so that the model can learn and converge properly. This instantiation is easy to implement by applying a standard dropout operator on the predictive logits, so we call it Post-dropout (PoD)[1]. We note that *we do not intend to improve the segmentation performance of a fine-trained model but rather to improve the prediction quality in terms of model confidence derived from MCP, especially for failure predictions.* The contributions are summarized as follows:

- We observe a huge gap between image classification and semantic segmentation regarding the predictive probability distribution, with the latter yielding a severe overconfidence phenomenon.
- We propose a formally simple method dubbed PoD that masks predictive logits by randomly zeroing to alleviate overconfidence in failure predictions, which requires negligible additional computation cost and no customized architectures. Empirical results evidence the feasibility and effectiveness.

2   Related Work

With growing applications of deep learning-based decision-making systems in real-world scenarios, confidence (or uncertainty) estimation attracts broad interest. Hendrycks *et al.* [10] show strong baseline results for erroneous- and abnormal-sample detection using prediction probability statistics derived from MCP. However, this paper observes an insignificant gap in MCP statistics between correct and incorrect samples in semantic segmentation. Corbière *et al.* [4] propose an advanced target criterion for model confidence based on TCP statistics and introduce an independent subnetwork to predict TCP values at test time. Moon *et al.* [16] propose a novel loss function that explicitly regularizes class probabilities to be better confidence estimates. These works mainly target image classification with semantic segmentation being less explored. We mark an immense difference in predictive probability distribution between image classification and semantic segmentation, which well motivates this work.

It is a consensus that overfitting may lead to predictive overconfidence regarding machine learning models. Overfitting is where the model performs excellently on training samples but fails to generalize on new unseen data, whereas overconfidence is where the model produces overconfident classification scores that do not reflect its actual accuracy (*i.e.* miscalibrated confidence [7]). Overfiting can be tackled with techniques like early stopping, dropout [21], data augmentation or weight regularization. Therefore, modern neural networks are hard to overfit.

---

[1] A dropout layer is commonly used before the classification layer that produces the logits.

This paper observes severe predictive overconfidence in semantic segmentation when the model shows no sign of overfitting. To this end, we present a simple yet effective method to alleviate segmentation overconfidence, particularly in failure predictions.

3   Method

3.1   Preliminary

Let $\mathcal{D} = \{\boldsymbol{x}_i, y_i \mid y_i = 1, 2, \ldots, K\}_{i=1}^{N}$ denotes the training domain in semantic segmentation with N samples and K categories, where $\boldsymbol{x}_i$ represents the ith sample (i.e. pixel) and y_i the corresponding label. We denote $\{\boldsymbol{x}, y\}$ as any training sample for simplicity. A segmentation network outputs a K dimensional logits $\mathbf{L} = \{\ell_1, \ell_2, \ldots, \ell_K\}$ for a given input pixel $\boldsymbol{x}$. The common practice is to apply softmax operation to obtain the predicted probability distribution $\mathbf{P} = \{p_1, p_2, \ldots, p_K\}$, where

$$p_k = \frac{exp(\ell_k)}{\sum_{j=1}^{K} exp(\ell_j)}, k = 1, 2, \ldots, K. \tag{1}$$

Let p_m denotes the maximum class probability (MCP) of sample $\boldsymbol{x}$, defined by

$$p_m = max\{\mathbf{P}\} = max\{p_1, p_2, \ldots, p_K\}, \tag{2}$$

where m is the predicted class. The true class probability (TCP) is p_t where $t = y$ is the ground-truth class. Then standard cross-entropy loss $\mathcal{L}_{CE}$ is calculated during training to minimize the difference between predicted probability distribution and labeled distribution, as shown by Eq. 3.

$$\mathcal{L}_{CE} = -\sum_{k=1}^{K} y_{.,k} log(p_k) = -log(p_t), \tag{3}$$

where $y_{.,k} \in \{0, 1\}$ and $y_{.,k} = 1$ only when the pixel $\boldsymbol{x}$ belongs to class k otherwise $y_{.,k} = 0$.

3.2   Masking Predictive Logits

Based on the observation that semantic segmentation networks yield excessive overconfidence in failure predictions, a natural intuition is to manually perturb the predictive probability distribution to enforce re-learning on error samples that alleviates predictive overconfidence. We thus propose masking predictive logits during training. Specifically, for a given sample $\boldsymbol{x}$ and the corresponding predictive logits $\mathbf{L}$, we define a mask $\mathbf{M} = \{m_1, m_2, \ldots, m_K\}$ and a masking function $\mathcal{F}$ to obtain the masked logits $\mathbf{L}'$, as shown by Eq. 4.

$$\mathbf{L}' = \mathcal{F}(\mathbf{L}, \mathbf{M}). \tag{4}$$

$\mathbf{L}'$ is then used to compute the perturbed predictive probability and the cross-entropy loss. We keep the logits' expectations $\mathbb{E}(\cdot)$ unchanged after the masking operation so that the model can learn and converge appropriately in the training phase, as Eq. 5 presents.

$$\mathbb{E}(\mathbf{L}') = \mathbb{E}(\mathcal{F}(\mathbf{L}, \mathbf{M})) = \mathbb{E}(\mathbf{L}). \tag{5}$$

Based on the aforementioned analysis, we present an instantiation that randomly zeroes out the logits. Concretely, we define a binary mask m_k as:

$$m_k \sim \mathcal{B}(\frac{1}{\delta}, \delta), k = 1, 2, \ldots, K. \tag{6}$$

$\mathcal{B}(\cdot, \cdot)$ means Bernoulli distribution and δ a hyper-parameter that is empirically set to 0.9 in this paper. We then obtain the masked logits $\mathbf{L}' = \{\ell'_1, \ell'_2, \ldots, \ell'_K\}$ following Eq. 7.

$$\mathbf{L}' = \mathcal{F}(\mathbf{L}, \mathbf{M}) = \mathbf{L} \otimes \mathbf{M}, \tag{7}$$

where $\otimes$ means element-wise multiplication. In this way, for any ℓ'_k, its expectation $\mathbb{E}(\ell'_k)$ remains unchanged, as shown by Eq. 8.

$$\mathbb{E}(\ell'_k) = \mathbb{E}(\ell_k \times m_k) = \mathbb{E}(\ell_k) \times \mathbb{E}(m_k) = \mathbb{E}(\ell_k). \tag{8}$$

This instantiation is easy to implement with modern deep learning frameworks by inserting a standard dropout operator after the predictive logits and before the softmax layer, dubbed Post-dropout (PoD), where the dropout probability is $(1 - \delta)$. The advantages are twofold. Firstly, it introduces negligible computation cost, *i.e.* we need to compute just an additional masking function and can obtain improved predictive probability by a single inference. Secondly, it requires no customized architectures or network modifications. Thus it can be effortlessly integrated into any existing segmentation network.

3.3 Differences with Previous Methods

Gal *et al.* [6] propose Monte-Carlo Dropout (MCD) to estimate model uncertainty by interpreting the use of dropout in CNNs as a Bayesian approximation of the Gaussian process. PoD presented in this paper marks two inequalities to MCD. First, MCD applies dropout before the classifier as the usual way dropout is used in CNN, whereas PoD puts it behind for randomly zeroing out predictive logits. Second, dropout behavior varies in MCD and PoD, with the former activating dropout during inference to average several stochastic predictions and the latter disabling dropout and outputting improved probabilities by a single inference.

4   Experiments

This section presents extensive comparisons quantitatively and qualitatively, suggesting that the proposed method effectively alleviates overconfident failure predictions in semantic segmentation.

We conduct extensive experiments on different-scale datasets with varying segmentation networks to verify the generality of the proposed method. The used datasets are Cityscapes [5] and CamVid [2]. We experiment with four segmentation methods, *i.e.* FCN [15], PSPNet [24], DeepLabv3 [3] and AlignSeg [11], where MobileNetv2 [20] or ResNet [8] serves as the backbone network. The mean intersection over union (mIoU) is adopted to evaluate segmentation accuracy. Following prior works [4,14], we use AP-Error (AP-E), AP-Success (AP-S) and AUC to measure the quality of failure prediction. See Appendix 6.2 for more details.

4.1   Comparative Results

The proposed PoD is built on the MCP criterion to alleviate predictive over-confidence in error samples. We implement the competitive MCD [6] that also uses MCP to estimate model uncertainty for comparisons, where the naive use of MCP [10] serves as the baseline. ConfidNet [4] using the advanced TCP criterion is also presented for a sufficient comparison.

Results are summarized in Table 1. MCD [6] improves the quality of confidence estimation by averaging several stochastic feed-forward predictions but results in noticeable accuracy degradation ($\downarrow$). The proposed PoD that requires only a single inference outperforms the baseline and MCD with a large margin in all settings while maintaining the segmentation accuracy, suggesting the feasibility and effectiveness.

Since we intend to improve the prediction quality in terms of model confidence derived from MCP, especially for failure predictions, we should pay more attention to the AP-E metric. Surprisingly, our PoD outperforms the ConfidNet [4] in most settings (6/9), even using the naive MCP criterion. ConfidNet uses the advanced TCP criterion and demands an additional subnetwork requiring independent training, whereas PoD does not modify the segmentation network and can be jointly trained.

4.2   Qualitative Assessments

This subsection provides illustrations on datasets to give more insights into the proposed PoD. As shown in Fig. 2, on the one hand, PoD has almost zero impact on the segmentation accuracy, thus producing similar predictions and errors. On the other hand, it helps the model yield higher confidence scores for correctly predicted pixels and lower ones for misclassified pixels, which is vital for failure detection in safety-sensitive applications.

Table 1. Comparisons of different methods using various segmentation networks and datasets. R means ResNet and Mv2 MobileNetv2. The best results are boldfaced. ↓ denotes significant accuracy degeneration and blue numbers improvement over the baseline.

Network	Dataset	Method	mIoU(%)	AP-E(%)	AP-S(%)	AUC(%)
FCN-Mv2	Citys	Baseline [10]	60.98	21.08	81.51	51.67
		MCD [6]	41.39↓	49.54(+28.46)	73.98	64.44
		ConfidNet [4]	60.98	45.22(+24.14)	**89.98**	72.60
		PoD (ours)	60.72	**51.43**(+30.35)	89.87	**74.84**
FCN-R18	Citys	Baseline [10]	60.52	22.75	81.88	52.93
		MCD [6]	40.29↓	41.03(+18.28)	77.40	66.85
		ConfidNet [4]	60.52	47.17(+24.42)	**91.01**	**75.05**
		PoD (ours)	60.50	**49.46**(+26.71)	89.95	69.78
FCN-R50	Citys	Baseline [10]	67.37	33.20	85.04	59.50
		MCD [6]	49.34↓	47.40(+14.20)	77.92	65.86
		ConfidNet [4]	67.37	**60.20**(+27.00)	**94.67**	**82.53**
		PoD (ours)	67.39	51.37(+18.17)	90.30	74.64
DeepLabv3-R101	Citys	Baseline [10]	79.00	23.13	85.18	54.35
		MCD [6]	56.09↓	35.92(+12.79)	77.94	58.40
		ConfidNet [4]	79.00	**60.15**(+37.02)	**95.87**	**84.09**
		PoD (ours)	78.77	50.88(+27.75)	90.98	73.57
AlignSeg-R101	Citys	Baseline [10]	79.13	24.42	85.45	55.16
		MCD [6]	55.44↓	38.85(+14.43)	75.22	58.44
		ConfidNet [4]	79.13	**54.06**(+29.64)	91.99	76.37
		PoD (ours)	79.03	51.91(+27.49)	**92.43**	**77.71**
FCN-R18	CamVid	Baseline [10]	57.20	29.14	87.83	61.53
		MCD [6]	53.99↓	44.84(+15.70)	91.75	75.93
		ConfidNet [4]	57.20	46.83(+17.69)	**95.49**	82.21
		PoD (ours)	57.25	**49.87**(+20.73)	95.45	**83.54**
FCN-R50	CamVid	Baseline [10]	61.29	21.94	88.07	56.73
		MCD [6]	59.13↓	38.47(+16.53)	91.29	70.99
		ConfidNet [4]	61.29	47.91(+25.97)	**96.09**	83.57
		PoD (ours)	61.23	**48.03**(+26.09)	95.93	**83.81**
PSPNet-R101	CamVid	Baseline [10]	71.06	17.54	89.94	55.13
		MCD [6]	67.43↓	29.04(+11.50)	91.25	64.85
		ConfidNet [4]	71.06	42.65(+25.11)	**98.17**	**87.51**
		PoD (ours)	70.77	**42.67**(+25.13)	95.26	79.06
DeepLabv3-R101	CamVid	Baseline [10]	70.73	18.47	89.93	55.78
		MCD [6]	67.80↓	32.35(+13.88)	91.77	67.64
		ConfidNet [4]	70.73	40.15(+21.68)	**97.99**	**86.16**
		PoD (ours)	71.10	**41.45**(+22.98)	95.09	77.93

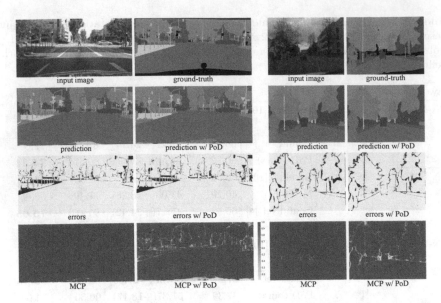

Fig. 2. Comparisons of model predictions, errors (*i.e.* failure predictions, highlighted in black) and MCP maps on Cityscapes (left two columns) and CamVid (right two columns). We ignore pixels belonging to the *void* class when depicting model errors. The model is DeepLabv3-R101. See Appendix 6.3 for more examples.

5   Conclusion

We observe an immense difference in predictive MCP statistics with semantic segmentation against image classification. A strategy dubbed PoD is proposed to alleviate predictive overconfidence on failure predictions in deep segmentation models. Extensive empirical results with varying segmentation networks evidence the feasibility and effectiveness. To our best knowledge, we are the first to explore the effect of this post-dropout operation, although it seems counter-intuitive by taking effect after the classification layer in a classification task, which is commonly believed that this regime may destroy the predicted probability. However, the results presented in this paper somehow suggest a different path and show the great potential of using the naive MCP to address failure predictions in semantic segmentation. In the future, we expect to conduct more theoretical explorations on how PoD affects model learning in the training phase.

6   Appendix

6.1   Observing Overconfidence

We provide error and correct distributions derived from maximum class probability (MCP) based on various-scale datasets and different-complexity networks.

For image classification, we use datasets of MNIST [13], CIFAR100 [12], ImageNet [19] and networks of LeNet [13], R18/50/101 (*i.e.* ResNet) [8]. For semantic segmentation, we use CamVid [2] and Cityscapes [5] datasets and the naive fully convolution network (FCN) [15] with different backbones. Results are presented in Fig. 3. We observe that segmentation models yield excessively overconfident predictions, which seems a common phenomenon with various datasets and networks. The proposed method notably alleviates overconfidence in failure predictions and improves segmentation models' prediction quality.

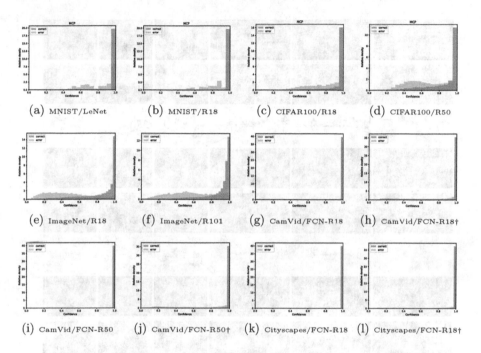

Fig. 3. Error and correct distributions based on MCP statistics in image classification (a)∼(f) and semantic segmentation (g)∼(l). The proposed method (marked with †) notably alleviates predictive overconfidence of failure predictions in semantic segmentation.

6.2   Datasets and Metrics

Datasets. Cityscapes [5] is a large-scale urban scene segmentation dataset containing 2,975 images for training, 500 images for validation and 1,525 images for testing. We train segmentation models on the training set and report performance on the validation set.

CamVid [2] is a relatively small-scale dataset, containing 367 images for training, 100 images for validation and 233 images for testing. We train models on the training and validation sets and report performance on the test set.

Evaluation Metrics. AP measures the area under the precision-recall curve, which shows the relation between precision and recall. AP-Success indicates that the correct predictions are used as the positive class while AP-Error indicates failure predictions as the positive class.

AUC is the area under ROC curve where ROC is the Receiver Operating Characteristic showing True Positive Rate versus False Positive Rate. It can be interpreted as the probability that a positive example has a greater prediction score than a negative example.

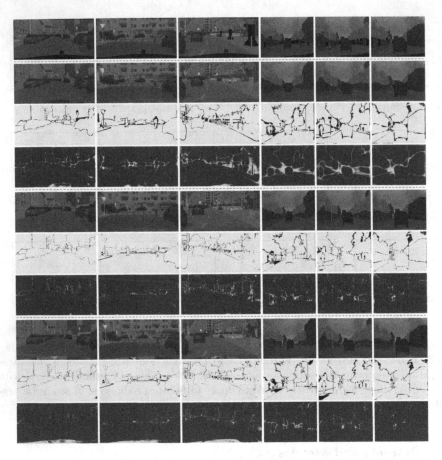

Fig. 4. Examples of model predictions, errors and MCP maps after applying the proposed PoD. **Row 1**: ground-truth. **Row 2 ∼ 4**: results of FCN-R18. **Row 5 ∼ 7**: results of PSPNet-R101. **Row 8 ∼ 10**: results of DeepLabv3-R101.

Implementation Details. Following prior works [3,24], we use standard mini-batch stochastic gradient descent (SGD) as the optimization algorithm with $momentum = 0.9$. We schedule the learning rate as $lr = baselr \times (1 -$

$\frac{iter}{totaliter})^{power}$ where $power = 0.9$ and $baselr = 0.01$. We also set the weight decay to 1×10^{-4} and 5×10^{-4} for Cityscapes and CamVid, respectively, to prevent overfitting. We empirically crop images to 768×768 for Cityscapes and 384×384 for CamVid during training. The training setting remains the same when applying the proposed PoD.

We implement the ConfidNet [4] for a sufficient comparison, following the hyper-parameter setting in the original paper. Note that we omit the fine-tuning process since we observe a slight difference. Thus, the mIoU score remains unchanged after applying the ConfidNet.

Table 2. Results on Weizmann Horses dataset using FCN-R50.

Method	mIoU(%)	AP-E(%)	AP-S(%)	AUC(%)
Baseline(MCP) [10]	80.97	39.15	99.63	94.01
PoD(ours)	81.04	**39.74**	**99.64**	**94.12**

6.3 Supplemental Experiments

Supplemental Qualitative Results. We present more qualitative results on datasets using FCN [15], PSPNet [24] and DeepLabv3 [3]. As shown in Fig. 4, the model's predictive MCP map somewhat matches the model errors after applying the proposed PoD, suggesting that the model yields a lower confidence score for failure predictions, *i.e.* alleviating overconfidence in failures.

Results on Weizmann Horses. We conduct experiments on the relatively simple Weizmann Horses [1] dataset used for binary segmentation. As pointed out by Niculescu-Mizil *et al.* [18] that neural networks typically produce well-calibrated probabilities on binary classification tasks. We verify the proposed PoD in this case and still achieve improvements on metrics, as shown in Table 2.

References

1. Borenstein, E., Ullman, S.: Class-specific, top-down segmentation. In: Heyden, A., Sparr, G., Nielsen, M., Johansen, P. (eds.) ECCV 2002. LNCS, vol. 2351, pp. 109–122. Springer, Heidelberg (2002). https://doi.org/10.1007/3-540-47967-8_8
2. Brostow, G.J., Fauqueur, J., Cipolla, R.: Semantic object classes in video: a high-definition ground truth database. Pattern Recogn. Lett. **30**(2), 88–97 (2009)
3. Chen, L.C., Papandreou, G., Schroff, F., Adam, H.: Rethinking atrous convolution for semantic image segmentation. arXiv preprint arXiv:1706.05587 (2017)
4. Corbière, C., Thome, N., Bar-Hen, A., Cord, M., Pérez, P.: Addressing failure prediction by learning model confidence. In: Proceedings of the 33rd International Conference on Neural Information Processing Systems, pp. 2902–2913 (2019)

5. Cordts, M., et al.: The cityscapes dataset for semantic urban scene understanding. In: Proceedings of the IEEE Conference on Computer Vision and Pattern Recognition, pp. 3213–3223 (2016)
6. Gal, Y., Ghahramani, Z.: Dropout as a Bayesian approximation: representing model uncertainty in deep learning. In: International Conference on Machine Learning, pp. 1050–1059 (2016)
7. Guo, C., Pleiss, G., Sun, Y., Weinberger, K.Q.: On calibration of modern neural networks. In: International Conference on Machine Learning, pp. 1321–1330 (2017)
8. He, K., Zhang, X., Ren, S., Sun, J.: Deep residual learning for image recognition. In: Proceedings of the IEEE Conference on Computer Vision and Pattern Recognition, pp. 770–778 (2016)
9. Hein, M., Andriushchenko, M., Bitterwolf, J.: Why relu networks yield high-confidence predictions far away from the training data and how to mitigate the problem. In: Proceedings of the IEEE/CVF Conference on Computer Vision and Pattern Recognition, pp. 41–50 (2019)
10. Hendrycks, D., Gimpel, K.: A baseline for detecting misclassified and out-of-distribution examples in neural networks. In: International Conference on Learning Representations (2017)
11. Huang, Z., Wei, Y., Wang, X., Shi, H., Liu, W., Huang, T.S.: Alignseg: feature-aligned segmentation networks. IEEE Trans. Pattern Anal. Mach. Intell. **44**(1), 550–557 (2021)
12. Krizhevsky, A., Hinton, G., et al.: Learning multiple layers of features from tiny images (2009)
13. LeCun, Y., Bottou, L., Bengio, Y., Haffner, P.: Gradient-based learning applied to document recognition. Proc. IEEE **86**(11), 2278–2324 (1998)
14. Li, Z., Hoiem, D.: Improving confidence estimates for unfamiliar examples. In: Proceedings of the IEEE/CVF Conference on Computer Vision and Pattern Recognition, pp. 2686–2695 (2020)
15. Long, J., Shelhamer, E., Darrell, T.: Fully convolutional networks for semantic segmentation. In: Proceedings of the IEEE Conference on Computer Vision and Pattern Recognition, pp. 3431–3440 (2015)
16. Moon, J., Kim, J., Shin, Y., Hwang, S.: Confidence-aware learning for deep neural networks. In: International Conference on Machine Learning, pp. 7034–7044 (2020)
17. Nguyen, A., Yosinski, J., Clune, J.: Deep neural networks are easily fooled: high confidence predictions for unrecognizable images. In: Proceedings of the IEEE Conference on Computer Vision and Pattern Recognition, pp. 427–436 (2015)
18. Niculescu-Mizil, A., Caruana, R.: Predicting good probabilities with supervised learning. In: Proceedings of the 22nd International Conference on Machine Learning, pp. 625–632 (2005)
19. Russakovsky, O., et al.: Imagenet large scale visual recognition challenge. Int. J. Comput. Vision **115**(3), 211–252 (2015)
20. Sandler, M., Howard, A., Zhu, M., Zhmoginov, A., Chen, L.C.: Mobilenetv 2: inverted residuals and linear bottlenecks. In: Proceedings of the IEEE Conference on Computer Vision and Pattern Recognition, pp. 4510–4520 (2018)
21. Srivastava, N., Hinton, G., Krizhevsky, A., Sutskever, I., Salakhutdinov, R.: Dropout: a simple way to prevent neural networks from overfitting. J. Mach. Learn. Res. **15**(1), 1929–1958 (2014)
22. Tang, Q., Liu, F., Jiang, J., Zhang, Y.: Eprnet: efficient pyramid representation network for real-time street scene segmentation. IEEE Trans. Intell. Transp. Syst. **23**, 7008–7016 (2021)

23. Yang, K., Bi, S., Dong, M.: Lightningnet: fast and accurate semantic segmentation for autonomous driving based on 3d lidar point cloud. In: 2020 IEEE International Conference on Multimedia and Expo, pp. 1–6. IEEE (2020)
24. Zhao, H., Shi, J., Qi, X., Wang, X., Jia, J.: Pyramid scene parsing network. In: Proceedings of the IEEE Conference on Computer vision and Pattern Recognition, pp. 2881–2890 (2017)
25. Zheng, Y., Chen, Z., Li, X., Si, X., Dong, L., Tian, Z.: Deep level set with confidence map and boundary loss for medical image segmentation. In: 2020 IEEE International Conference on Multimedia and Expo, pp. 1–6. IEEE (2020)

Cooperative Multi-agent Reinforcement Learning with Hierachical Communication Architecture

Shifan Liu[✉], Quan Yuan, Bo Chen, Guiyang Luo, and Jinglin Li

State Key Laboratory of Networking and Switching Technology,
Beijing University of Posts and Telecommunications, Beijing 100876, China
{lsf,yuanquan,czb199871,luoguiyang,jlli}@bupt.edu.cn

Abstract. Communication is an essential way for multi-agent system to coordinate. By sharing local observations and intentions via communication channel, agents can better deal with dynamic environment and thus make optimal decisions. However, restricted by the limited communication channel, agents have to leverage less communication resources to transmit more informative messages. In this article, we propose a two-level hierarchical multi-agent reinforcement learning algorithm which utilizes different timescales in different levels. Communication happens only between high levels at a coarser time scale to generate sub-goals which convey the intention of agents for the low level. And the low level is responsible for implementing these sub-goals by controlling primitive actions at every tick of environment. Sub-goal is the core of this hierachical communication architecture which requires the high level to communicate efficiently and provide guidance for the low level to coordinate. This hierarchical communication architecture conveys several benefits: 1) It coarsens the collaborative granularity and reduces the requirement of communication since communication happens only in high level at a larger scale; 2) It enables the high level to focus on the coordination of goals without paying attention to implementation, thus improves the efficiency of communication; and 3) It makes better control by dividing a complex multi-agent cooperative task into multiple single-agent tasks. In experiments, we apply our approach in vehicle collision avoidance tasks and achieve better performance than baselines.

Keywords: Multi-agent cooperation · Hierarchical architecture · Communication

1 Introduction

Communication is an important way to realize coordination in the field of multi-agent reinforcement learning (MARL) from StarCraft II [20] to autonomous

This work was supported in part by the Natural Science Foundation of China under Grant 61902035, Grant 61876023, Grant 62001054 and Grant 62102041, and in part by the Fundamental Research Funds for the Central Universities.

vehicles control [2]. In the partially observable cooperative multi-agent tasks, communication between agents is vital to transmit local perceptions and behavior intentions so as to gain a better knowledge of the global environment. However, the communication resource is always limited in real-world scenario. At the same time, too much irrelevant information may damage agent's decision-making. So the communication behavior must be improved to accommodate the limited communication channel and transmit valuable information. In state of the art, some methods [5,15,17] attempt to learn better communication protocol to generate more informative messages and extract more useful information from messages, while some other methods [3,9,10,13] attempt to optimize the communication topology to avoid meaningless communications.

However, all these methods focus only on the information of observation and intention at one single moment, meanwhile agents in these methods have to communicate at every tick of environment. Such flat communication architecture have several disadvantages. First, it does not utilize the abstract structure information in the environment and tasks, so that the collaboration is always at the smallest granularity which results in a lot of unnecessary communication. Second, it ignores the consistency and coherence of agents' intention, which causes the similarity of messages between adjacent moments. So a large amount of communication resource is wasted to spread highly repetitive messages. In addition, the joint state action space can be very huge since it grows exponentially with the number of agents, leading to poor scalability.

Thus, we propose a strong explainable hierachical multi-agent communication method where different level operates at different time scales. In our method, agent's policy can be divided into two levels. Communication occurs only in the high level which is also called manager. Every c timestep, each manager encodes its own observation into messages to communicate with other agents and is responsible for providing a sub-goal to the low level which is also called worker. In the next c timesteps, worker have to complete the sub-goal set by manager by controlling primitive actions. Since the sub-goal has a semantics of guidance to the low level, it forces manager to learn more efficient communication to instruct its worker effectively. In this architecture, manager can be seen as the brain of the agent, expressing its intention by setting sub-goals. And worker is equivalent to the nervous system of the agent, it only needs to react according to sub-goals and the environment, without paying attention to other agents' policy.

This hierachical communication architecture can solve the above problems because manager and worker works at different time scales while coordination occurs only at the high level, by obtaining auxiliary information in communication, manager learns to set more effective sub-goals which enable the agent to achieve collaboration without any communication for a period of time, thereby increasing the granularity of collaboration and reducing the need for communication. Meanwhile, the sub-goal contains the intention information of the agent and manager will not carry out the next round of communication until the sub-goal is completed at which time the intention of the agent has already changed, so the similarity of messages between two communication rounds is relatively low. Besides, since collaboration has fully achieved in the high level, the tasks of worker degenerate into single-agent reinforcement learning tasks, the complexity of worker's action space will grow linearly with the number of agents, which brings better scalability. We explore this hierachical communication architecture in simulation environment of Traffic Junction, and compare it with baselines under different difficulties.

The remainder of this paper are organized as follows: First, related work of MARL methods and hierachical reinforcement learning (HRL) methods will be summarized in the next section. Then we will present the details of our method and analyze its characteristics. After that, experimental results will be present to evaluate the performance of our method. In the last part, this article will be concluded and we will give planning for futrue work.

2   Related Work

Reinforcement learning has been proved to be an effective method to realize intelligence. However, due to the instability of the environment, reinforcement learning is hard to be directly extended to the field of multi-agent. QMIX [14] and QTRAN [16] try to optimize the joint value function while MADDPG [12] and COMA [6] takes policy-based MARL methods where an actor-critic framework is adopted to coordinate action generation and action evaluation. Both of them work in the fashion of centralized training and decentralized execution (CTDE) to get the global information in centralized training period.

Utilizing communication to realize coordination povides a more stable and scalable collaborative MARL paradigm. DIAL [5] and CommNet [17] are pioneer works to study whether the communication protocol can be learned using reinforcement learning. However, both of them use a fully connected communication network, which causes serious information overload. To solve this problem, VAIN [8] and TarMAC [4] use attention mechanism to evaluate the importance of the received messages and extract valuable informations. IC3Net [15] uses a gating unit to determine whether a message is deserve to be broadcast. BiCNet [13] and NeurComm [3] endeavor to improve communication efficiency by optimizing communication network topology. BiCNet uses a bidirectional recurrent neural network as a ring communication network to aggregate messages, while NeurComm designs a neighboring communication protocol according to which messages could pass through neighbors over time by cascaded communication. All these methods work in a flat communication architecture where agents have to achieve coordination relying on communication at every timestep.

Hierarchical reinforcement learning has been proposed in [18] which presents temporal abstraction mechanism by posing options. In the last couple of years HRL has achieved great advances due to the increasing success in deep reinforcement learning (DRL). There are two main frameworks in the existing HRL methods. One is option-based methods, such as Option-Critc Architecture [1] and A2OC [7]. By learning options which control agent's policy over a period of time, agents can make temporal extended actions to achieve its target. The other is sub-goal-based methods, such as h-DQN [11], FuN [19], which often has two levels, the high level aims to maximize cumulative rewards by making sub-goals for the low level and the low level is responsible for realizing the sub-goal by generating primitive actions and interacting with environment.

The majority of the existing HRL methods focus on using temporal abstraction to scale up learning or solve sparse rewards problem in reinforcement learning. Considering that hierachical mechanism naturally has the potential to simplify complex tasks and realize control at different scales, and sub-goal has the semantics of temporal extended intentions, we propose a sub-goal based hierachical communication architecture to slove multi-agent coordination problems.

3   Method

In this section, we present a communication enabled approaches of hierachical multi-agent reinforcement learning (H-MARL) to solve cooperative tasks. Figure 1 (a) illustrates the overall design of H-MARL and Fig. 1 (b) describes its dynamics. In our method, each agent consists of two parts: high level and low level, also known as manager and worker. Manager consists of communication module and sub-goal generation module and worker only has an action generation module. In theory, the communication module can be realized using any communication method mentioned above. Here we use a method which is similar to DIAL to generate real-valued messages so as to perform end-to-end training between communication module and sub-goal generation module.

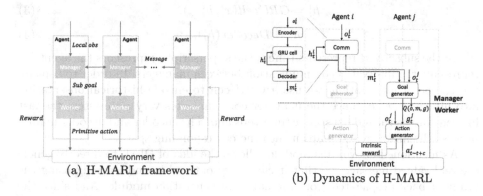

(a) H-MARL framework   (b) Dynamics of H-MARL

Fig. 1. Framework and dynamics of H-MARL. In (a) managers communicate with each other to set sub-goals for workers to maximize reward from environment, workers control primitive actions to complete the sub-goal. In (b) The black line represents the forward propagation process, and the red line represents the back propagation process. (Color figure online)

Every c timestep, each manager encodes its local observation as a message by communication module and sends it to other agents so as to obtain the global perception of environment and intentions of other agents, then a sub-goal is generated relying on aggregated messages and provided for its worker. The action of worker is the primitive action of the agent and it is responsible for realizing the sub-goal in the next c timesteps. In this architecture, sub-goal generated by manager is strongly instructive since it gives guidance to worker for the next period of time, so it is neccessary for manager to communicate efficiently to achieve fully coordination during one communication round. Meanwhile, sub-goal enables worker to operate separately without coordination, so the task of worker can be seen as an independent single-agent reinforcement learning task and communication is not needed for every micro-actions. To improve its policy, worker is given an intrinsic reward which is related to the completion of sub-goals. And when worker's behaviour is ultimately align with the sub-goal, manager can learn to set optimal sub-goals based on worker's ability.

3.1   Communication Module

The communication module is responsible for generating manager's messages by encoding the agent's local observations o into message vectors m:

$$m_t^i = \pi_\psi(o_t^i), \tag{1}$$

where ψ is the parameter of the communication network π_ψ. The forward propagation during message generation can be described by the following formulas:

$$x_t^i = Encoder(o_t^i), \tag{2}$$

$$h_t^i = GRUcell(x_t^i, h_{t-c}^i), \tag{3}$$

$$m_t^i = Decoder(h_t^i), \tag{4}$$

where the subscript t represents time t, the superscript i represents the agent i, c represents the interval of communication between managers. In order to capture the temporal information, we use a GRU cell to encode historical observation into hidden state h. Since the manager communicates very c timestep, the last hidden state is the hidden state c timesteps ago. The encoder and decoder mainly process the message and maps it into the corresponding space.

As mentioned above, this module follows the idea of DIAL to directly generate real-valued messages so that it can carry out end-to-end learning using the gradient back propagated from the sub-goal generation module. And since the instructive semantics of sub-goal, the effective communication can be learned during the process of learning to set appropriate sub-goals.

3.2   Sub-goal Generation Module

The sub-goal generation module adopt actor-critic framework where the actor network takes its local observation and messages received from other agents as input to generate a sub-goal g and Q value is generated by critic network to evaluate this sub-goal:

$$g_t^i = \pi_\theta(o_t^i, m_t^{i-}),\tag{5}$$

$$Q = Q_\omega(o_t^i, g_t^i, m_t^{i-}),\tag{6}$$

where π_θ is the policy network of actor and θ is its parameter, Q_ω is the value network of critic and ω is its parameter, m_t^{i-} represents the concatenation of messages of all agents except agent i.

Sub-goal is the core concept of hierarchical reinforcement learning. For different tasks, sub-goal often has different representation. But generally, it has several properties: 1) it has to give clear guidance to worker's decision in a period of time; and 2) the completion of sub-goal can be precisely measured so as to generate intrinsic rewards to worker. Manager will learn a better sub-goal in the process of maximizing extern reward. In section of experiment, we will present our sub-goal setting under Traffic Junction environment.

A challenge H-MARL faces is the asynchrony between agents. Since the decision process of manager is semi-MDP [18] while the decision process of worker is MDP, the action of different managers may not be synchronized. In the worst case, the hierachical architecture will be invalid. To solve this problem, we force managers to make synchronous decisions. Specifically, we fix c timesteps for worker to execute the sub-goal regardless of when it complete. In order to make this setting reasonable, we add the action of "maintain" (take no action) to the action set of worker if it does not have orignally. In this way, the sub-goal can remain valid within c steps because the agent can finally reach the desired goal at step c by maintaining its state even after completing the sub-goal. In fact, setting a penalty for the agent's "maintain" action can help manager learn to generate sub-goals that can just be achieved in c timesteps, so that the efficiency loss caused by action "maintain" is almost negligible. Experimental results also show that this setting is quite useful.

Another classic challenge is the instability between manager and worker in HRL. When the model is untrained, worker cannot complete the sub-goals set by its manager, making the experience collected at the beginning of the experiment of little help for manager. This problem persists in our method but is not significant. Since worker executes a relatively simple single-agent reinforcement learning task, it can achieve convergence and obtain a stable ability in a short time. Then manager can obtain useful experience based on the ability of workers. To improve the training process, we apply pre-training instead of synchronizated training to relieve this instability and the comparison will be shown in experiment section.

3.3   Action Generation Module

The worker is responsible for completing the sub-goal relying on its observation, so the input of action generation module includes local observation and the sub-goal which is set by its manager and will be maintained in the following c steps. The output of this module is the primitive action of the agent. We choose Policy

Gradient (PG) algorithm for implementation, and the policy of worker can be described as:

$$a_{t+k}^i = \pi_\sigma(g_t^i, o_{t+k}^i), \quad 0 \le k \le c, \tag{7}$$

where π_σ is the policy network of worker and σ is its parameter. Within c timesteps after obtaining the sub-goal, worker have to make its action a_{t+k}^i according to its local observation o_{t+k}^i at each subsequent timestep.

In order to evaluate the actions of worker, an intrinsic reward is needed to measure the degree of sub-goal realization and give worker corresponding rewards. If the sub-goal is defined as the desired state to reach, then the intrinsic reward under this sub-goal can be defined as:

$$r_i = -d(s, g), \tag{8}$$

where the function d is used to measure the "distance" between the reached state and the expected state. Similar to sub-goal, it can also be defined differently for different tasks.

Although the environment is still unstable where an agent's policy will be influenced by other agents, it is reasonable to assume that worker performs a single-agent task in our method. After the policy of worker converges, manager can coordinate based on worker's capabilities to decompose the overall task into multiple sub-tasks which can be completed without any cooperation. And when all workers make actions strictly according to sub-goal, the actions of other agents become "determinated" for each worker, thus worker will not face unstable environment and can be trained using single-agent RL method.

3.4 Learning

This part describes the learning of each module. First of all, noticed that although the entire model is end-to-end trainable, we artificially break the gradient between manager and worker, so that they can be trained using respective rewards. Meanwhile, we make the policy of all agents sharing same parameters.

The object of manager is to learn the optimal communication network π_ψ and sub-goal generation network π_θ to maximize the expected cumulative reward which is also affected by the policy of worker π_σ:

$$E_{\pi_\psi, \pi_\theta, \pi_\sigma} \left(\sum_{i=1}^{n} \sum_{t=0}^{\infty} \gamma^t r_{i,t} | s_0 \right), \tag{9}$$

where i is the number of the agent, t is the number of timestep.

As mentioned above, manager performs end-to-end training, the communication network can be trained using the gradients backpropagated from the sub-goal genaration module. So we update actor-critic framework of sub-goal genaration module with external rewards, the Temporal-Difference (TD) error is:

$$\delta_t = r_{t \sim t+c} + \gamma Q_\omega(o', m', g') - Q_\omega(o, m, g), \tag{10}$$

where o', m', g' respectively represents the observation after c timesteps, as well as the communication message and sub-goal generated by the target policy network, γ is the discount factor. In order to keep the form of formula, we write the cumulative reward $\sum_t^{t+c} r$ as $r_{t \sim t+c}$. The critic of manager will be updated as follows:

$$\theta \leftarrow \theta + \alpha_\theta Q_\omega(o, m, g) \nabla_\theta ln\pi_\theta(g|s, m). \tag{11}$$

The actor of manager will be updated as follows:

$$\omega \leftarrow \omega + \alpha_\omega \delta_t \nabla_\omega Q_\omega(o, m, g). \tag{12}$$

Workers which uses policy gradient algorithm will be updated with intrinsic rewards as follows:

$$\sigma \leftarrow \sigma + \alpha_\sigma \gamma^t G_t \nabla_\sigma ln\pi_\sigma(a|g, o). \tag{13}$$

In the above three formulas, α_θ, α_ω, and α_σ are corresponding learning rate, and $G_t = \sum_{t=0}^{\infty} r_t$.

4   Experiments

Our simulated environment Traffic Junction is shown in Fig. 2 where several vehicles have to go through an intersection by self-coordination without traffic lights scheduling. At each time step, a vehicle will be randomly added into map with a certain probability, and then each vehicle will travel along the designed route to its destination. The observation of each vehicle includes last action, route number, position, and the map information within its observation field. The action of the vehicle includes going ahead and stopping, collision of vehicles will cause a penalty of 20, and the stopping action will generate a cumulative penalty of 0.01. The goal of each vehicle is to avoid penalty as much as possible to reach its destination. In experiment, some properties of the environment such as the size of the map, the maximum number of vehicles, the probability of adding vehicles and the observation range of vehicles can be set manually.

In addition to the cumulative average reward, our evaluation metric also includes the success rate: if there is no collision happened in an episode then we consider the episode to be a success, otherwise it is a failure.

4.1   Details

In this experiment, we set the interval of manager's decision-making $c = 3$, that is manager generates its sub-goal every three time steps. The sub-goal is defined as the location that agent is expected to reach after c timesteps. And Euclidean distance is choosen as a measure to define the intrinsic reward:

$$r_i = d(loc_{t-1}, g) - d(loc_t, g), \tag{14}$$

when the movement of agent is close to sub-goal, it gets a positive reward, and when it moves away from the sub-goal, it gets a penalty. The reward provided for worker can be descried as:

$$r_w = \alpha r_i + (1 - \alpha)r, \tag{15}$$

where worker's reward r_w is the proportional sum of intrinsic reward r_i and extern reward r, and α is a proportional coefficient to control the learning effect. Experiments show that adding a certain proportion of external rewards to the overall reward of workers can encourage worker to perform better.

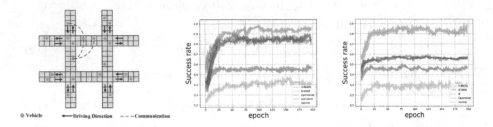

Fig. 2. Traffic Junction   Fig. 3. Easy mode   Fig. 4. Medium mode

4.2 Results

We compare H-MARL with two SOTA communication-based MARL methods: IC3Net and CommNet. At the same time, two ablation experiments, noComm and noHire were performed:

1) noComm—In this controller, each agent works the same as H-MARL except it has no communication. In implementation, we force the message generated to be zero and the gradient will not be propagated to communication module. Since the vehicle cannot obtain auxiliary information after the communication is removed, we adjust the vision of vehicle to 1 rather than 0 to obtain a comparable effect, which means the vision of vehicle in other methods is 0 instead.

2) noHire—In this method, hierachical structure is abandoned. In implementation, we keep the entire structure of the manager and discard the level of worker. And the action of manager is set to be primitive actions directly.

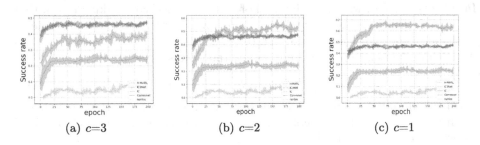

(a) $c=3$ (b) $c=2$ (c) $c=1$

Fig. 5. Hard mode using different intervals

Table 1. Success ratio at different difficulties

Table 2. Communicate ratio

Difficluty	H-MARL	IC3Net	CommNet	noComm	noHire
Easy	0.935	0.844	0.843	0.549	0.411
Medium	0.834	0.565	0.562	0.457	0.286
Hard	0.367	0.464	0.459	0.340	0.052

Methods	ratio
CommNet	1.0
IC3Net	0.683
H-MARL	**0.333**

As shown in Fig. 3, Fig. 4 and the Table 1, H-MARL achieves significant advantages in success rate both in easy and medium mode. IC3Net and Comm-Net perform almost equivalently. In easy mode, our method achieves an improvement close to 0.1. At the same time, two ablation experiments proves that cooperation effect will be greatly reduced whether the communication or the hieracical structrue is removed. Since in noHire we apply a very naive communication network and noComm can obtain an additional vision, the effect of noComm is better and more stable than noHire.

When we adjusted the experiment difficulty to medium, the effect of IC3Net and CommNet sufferd a huge drop which is close to 0.3, while our method only dropped by only 0.1, which means our method has greater advantages in medium mode. However when we continued to increase the experiment difficulty to hard, the success rate suffered a significant drop which is close to 0.5 as shown in Fig. 5 (a), and the effect at this time is worse than IC3Net and CommNet which means the hieracical method is no longer so effective in hard mode.

Results above show that the hierarchical approach where $c = 3$ achieve better effect in easier scenario. In fact, when the task becomes complex, it is hard for agents to agree on the sub-goals to achieve after c steps since the abstract structure of task is difficult to represent clearly at this scale, so it fails in hard mode. In order to adapt our method to more complex environment, we reduce the communication interval c and corresponding results is shown in Fig. 5, when we set $c = 2$, the success rate rises to the level equivalent to IC3Net and CommNet, and when c is reduced to 1, the success rate can be improved by more than 0.1 of baselines. This fact gives us a thought, whether we can use a learnable parameter c rather than a fixed c, so that when the task is easy, manager can choose a larger communication interval, and when the task becomes complex, the communication interval can also be reduced to 1 in which case the hieracical method can also achieve better performance under the same communication frequency.

Table 2 shows the communication rate of H-MARL and baselines where H-MARL has the lowest communication rate. CommNet's communication rate is 100% since it uses fully connected communicate framework, IC3Net uses gating mechanism to reduce the communication rate to 0.69 and the hieracical architecture can reduce the communication rate to $1/c$ by controlling communication interval c.

Experiments show that the hierarchical approach indeed achieve better effect using less communication resources in any scenario, and when the environment becomes complex, using a smaller communication interval c can achieve better performance.

4.3 Training Improvement

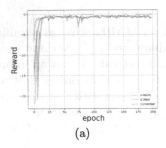
(a)

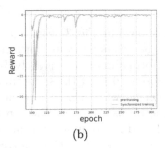
(b)

Fig. 6. Comparison of rewards. (a) Rewards of H-MARL and baseline. (b) Rewards of pre-training and synchronized training.

In the reward curve compared with IC3Net and CommNet as shown in Fig. 6 (a), the change of H-MARL is very unstable in the early stage of training, and there are many sharp drops, which is caused by the instability between the high and low levels mentioned above. Then we implement pre-training instead of synchronized training, specificlly we do not update manager's policy and generate random sub-goals to train workers until the policy of worker converges when the epoch is about 100. After 100 epochs of pre-training, the convergence curve of reward becomes flat and converges quickly, and there is no sudden drop any more, as shown in Fig. 10.

5 Conclusion and Futrue Work

This paper propose a two-level hierachical communication method H-MARL which takes advatage of temporal abstraction to reduce communication and improve coordination. We design synchronization mechanics to ensure the reliability of the hierarchical architecture in MARL and analyze some characteristics of this method. In the simulation environment of Traffic Junction, experimental results show that H-MARL can improve the efficiency of collaboration while reducing the amount of communication. In the futrue, researches about learning an adaptive communication interval to cope with scenario in different complexities will be carried out.

References

1. Bacon, P.L., Harb, J., Precup, D.: The option-critic architecture. In: Proceedings of the AAAI, vol. 31 (2017)

2. Cao, Y., Yu, W., Ren, W., Chen, G.: An overview of recent progress in the study of distributed multi-agent coordination. IEEE Trans. Ind. Inform. **9**(1), 427–438 (2012)
3. Chu, T., Chinchali, S., Katti, S.: Multi-agent reinforcement learning for networked system control. In: Proceedings of the ICLR (2019)
4. Das, A., Gervet, T., Romoff, J., Batra, D., Parikh, D., Rabbat, M., Pineau, J.: Tarmac: targeted multi-agent communication. In: Proceeding of the ICML, pp. 1538–1546. PMLR (2019)
5. Foerster, J., Assael, I.A., De Freitas, N., Whiteson, S.: Learning to communicate with deep multi-agent reinforcement learning. In: Advances in Neural Information Processing Systems, vol. 29 (2016)
6. Foerster, J., Farquhar, G., Afouras, T., Nardelli, N., Whiteson, S.: Counterfactual multi-agent policy gradients. In: Proceedings of the AAAI, vol. 32 (2018)
7. Harb, J., Bacon, P.L., Klissarov, M., Precup, D.: When waiting is not an option: learning options with a deliberation cost. In: Proceedings of the AAAI (2018)
8. Hoshen, Y.: Vain: attentional multi-agent predictive modeling. In: Advances in Neural Information Processing Systems, vol. 30 (2017)
9. Jiang, J., Lu, Z.: Learning attentional communication for multi-agent cooperation. Advances in Neural Information Processing Systems, vol. 31 (2018)
10. Kim, D., Moon, S., Hostallero, D., Kang, W.J., Lee, T., Son, K., Yi, Y.: Learning to schedule communication in multi-agent reinforcement learning. In: Proceedings of the ICLR (2018)
11. Kulkarni, T.D., Narasimhan, K., Saeedi, A., Tenenbaum, J.: Hierarchical deep reinforcement learning: integrating temporal abstraction and intrinsic motivation In: Advances in Neural Information Processing Systems, vol. 29 (2016)
12. Lowe, R., Wu, Y.I., Tamar, A., Harb, J., Pieter Abbeel, O., Mordatch, I.: Multi-agent actor-critic for mixed cooperative-competitive environments. In: Advances in Neural Information Processing Systems, vol. 30 (2017)
13. Peng, P., et al.: Multiagent bidirectionally-coordinated nets: Emergence of human-level coordination in learning to play starcraft combat games. arXiv:1703.10069 (2017)
14. Rashid, T., Samvelyan, M., Schroeder, C., Farquhar, G., Foerster, J., Whiteson, S.: Qmix: monotonic value function factorisation for deep multi-agent reinforcement learning. In: Proceedings of the ICML, vol. 80, pp. 4295–4304 (2018)
15. Singh, A., Jain, T., Sukhbaatar, S.: Learning when to communicate at scale in multiagent cooperative and competitive tasks. In: Proceedings of the IMCL (2018)
16. Son, K., Kim, D., Kang, W.J., Hostallero, D.E., Yi, Y.: Qtran: learning to factorize with transformation for cooperative multi-agent reinforcement learning. In: Proceedings of the ICML, vol. 97, pp. 5887–5896 (2019)
17. Sukhbaatar, S., Fergus, R., et al.: Learning multiagent communication with back-propagation. In: Advances in Neural Information Processing Systems, vol. 29 (2016)
18. Sutton, R.S., Precup, D., Singh, S.: Between MDPs and semi-MDPs: a framework for temporal abstraction in reinforcement learning. Artif. Intell. **112**(1–2), 181–211 (1999)
19. Vezhnevets, A.S., et al.: Feudal networks for hierarchical reinforcement learning. In: Proceedings of the ICML, pp. 3540–3549 (2017)
20. Vinyals, O., et al.: Starcraft ii: a new challenge for reinforcement learning. arXiv:1708.04782 (2017)

Emotion Aware Reinforcement Network for Visual Storytelling

Xin Li, Hanqing Cai, Tianling Jiang, Chunping Liu, and Yi Ji[✉]

School of Computer Science and Technology, Soochow University, Suzhou, China
xli1997@stu.suda.edu.cn, jiyi@suda.edu.cn

Abstract. Visual storytelling is the task of generating a sequence of human-like sentences (i.e. story) for an ordered stream of images. Unlike traditional image captioning, the story contains not only factual descriptions but also concepts and objects that do not explicitly appear in the input images. Recent works utilize either end-to-end or multi-stage frameworks to produce more relevant and coherent stories but usually ignore latent emotional information. In this work, to generate an affective story, we propose an **E**motion **A**ware **R**einforcement **N**etwork for **VI**sual **S**tory**T**elling (**EARN-VIST**). Specifically in our network, lexicon-based attention is leveraged to encourage the model to pay more attention to the emotional words. Then we apply two emotional consistency reinforcement learning rewards using an emotion classifier and commonsense transformer respectively to find the gap between generated story and human-labeled story so as to refine the generation process. Experimental results on the VIST dataset and human evaluation demonstrate that our model outperforms most of the cutting-edge models across multiple evaluation metrics.

Keywords: Visual storytelling · Attention mechanism · Reinforcement learning

1 Introduction

Stories are an integral part of human culture, allowing us to express emotions, share knowledge, and shape our perspective of the world. Recently, increasing attention has been attracted to visual storytelling [4,17,24], since it has the potential to provide scene understanding to visually impaired users. This task aims at generating a human-like story based on a stream of given images. Different from generating caption for an image, visual storytelling is more challenging since it requires the agent to explore the deep meaning of images and understand the relationship between characters in images.

In this field, most mainstream approaches utilize two kinds of frameworks. One is the end-to-end framework [9,10], while the other is multi-stage [8,24]. The common thought behind the end-to-end framework is to use a convolution neural network (CNN) as an encoder to extract high-level image features and

© The Author(s), under exclusive license to Springer Nature Switzerland AG 2022
E. Pimenidis et al. (Eds.): ICANN 2022, LNCS 13530, pp. 26–37, 2022.
https://doi.org/10.1007/978-3-031-15931-2_3

overall image features, then feed the representational vector into a long short-term memory (LSTM) to generate the story. These models can always produce meaningful stories with outstanding performance on the automatic metric. In contrast, known as the plan-write strategy, multi-stage methods advocate dividing the storytelling process into several steps to complete.

Despite the aforementioned remarkable progress, there are still several challenges in generating a natural story. One major drawback is that few models consider emotion when generating a story, which serves as the integral factor in a natural one. In this work, we aim at resolving this challenge in an end-to-end framework. After a careful investigation of natural stories, we find that there are at least two ways to express emotions with natural language. One is to describe emotional states (such as happy) by explicitly using strong emotional words (such as good, nice, smile, great, etc.), the other is to make the emotional tone of the sentences more obvious.

Inspired by the idea, we propose a novel method named as Emotion Aware Reinforcement Network for visual storytelling (EARN-VIST) as in Fig. 1. First, a lexicon-based attention mechanism is applied to encourage the model to pay more attention to emotional words. Second, we propose two emotional consistency rewards using an emotion classifier and commonsense transformer named **Emo-EC** and **Emo-CT** respectively for reinforcement learning. In the story view, Emo-EC attempts to control the emotion phrase alignment from a general perspective, so we only focus on four basic emotions [5], which are anger, fear, happiness, and sadness. We additionally add 'neutral' to account for cases with no strong emotions and define the Emo-EC as an equal probability. Then, the emotion distribution is always hierarchical. For example, the emotion 'happy' can be extended to 'satisfied', 'accomplished', 'excited', 'grateful' etc. Single emotional consistency reward from story-view may fail to effectively control the emotion alignment. Consequently, in sentence-view, for the sake of commanding the emotion trend further and excavating the pluralized emotion, we utilize the commonsense transformer and define the Emo-CT as Levenshtein distance. Besides, we also compute the classic sentence-level BLEU as the BLEU reward to maintain the fluency of the generated sentences. The framework aggregates the aforementioned rewards and optimizes with the reinforcement learning algorithm.

The main contributions in our paper can be summarized as follows:

- We propose lexicon-based attention to encourage the model to pay more attention to emotional words for the purpose of generating affective story.
- We introduce two emotional consistency reinforcement learning rewards to control the emotion alignment between generated story and human-labeled story from both story-view and sentence-view.
- We provide quantitative analysis, human evaluation to demonstrate that EARN-VIST can generate affective story without sacrificing the story quality.

2   Related Work

2.1   Visual Storytelling

Visual storytelling aims to create a subjective and imaginative story with semantic understanding in the scenes. End-to-end based methods [9,10] mainly exploit
the encoder-decoder framework where a convolutional neural network (CNN)
as an encoder to extract high image features and overall image features while
a decoder network takes the vector into long short-term memory (LSTM) to
generate the story. For example, by rethinking what makes a good story, Hu
et al. [9] proposed three assessment criteria which were *relevance, coherence,
expressiveness* based on reinforcement learning to assess the quality of story
generation. Qi et al. [17] introduced a novel latent memory-guided graph transformer with a graph encoding module and a latent memory unit for visual storytelling. Recently, researchers are more inclined to employ multi-stage models
[7,24], known as the plan-and-write strategy. For example, Xu et al. [24] put
forward an imagine-reason-write framework that leveraged an imaginative module to learn the storyline and a relational reasoning module to exploit external
knowledge to enrich the storyline for the story generation. Notably, few previous
works took emotion into consideration when generating a story, which made the
generated story boring and monotonous. Wherefore, we propose lexicon-based
attention and composite emotional consistency rewards to encourage the model
to generate emotional story.

3   Approach

We define the visual storytelling task as follows: the input is a series of images
$I = \{i_1, i_2, \ldots, i_m\}$ and the task is to generate a sequence of coherent sentences
$S = \{s_1, s_2, \ldots, s_m\}$ (i.e., a story), where s_i is a sequence of words depicting
the i-th image. $VB = VB_g \bigcup VB_e$ is a vocabulary, which consists of a generic
vocabulary VB_g and an emotion vocabulary[1] VB_e, and we require that VB_g
$\bigcap VB_e = \phi$. As the emotion category is not one-fold, we divide the VB_e into
several classes VB_e^z, which represents a list of words related to emotion type z.

3.1   Tracking Emotion in Text

To generate an affective story, we are expected to reason about the inner sentiment under texts. Moreover, the emotion distribution in a natural story is
always hierarchical and basic emotion can be extended to more pluralize emotions. Therefore, our model attempts to guide the emotion alignment from story-
view and sentence-view, which inspires us to utilize a coarse-to-fine text emotion
classifier.

---

[1] We build this emotion vocabulary in terms of the NRC Affect Intensity Lexicon
[15]. There are four emotion categories in emotion vocabulary, which are anger, fear,
sadness, happiness.

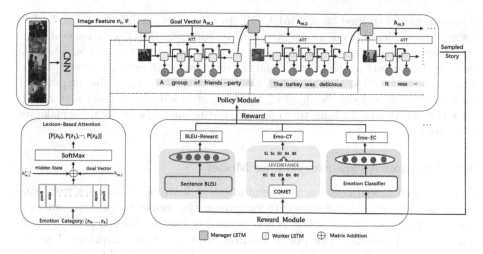

Fig. 1. Overview of EARN-VIST. Our model is an encoder-decoder framework based on reinforcement learning. Image features are obtained by pre-trained CNN and then are put into a hierarchical decoder which consists of manager LSTM and worker LSTM to generate a sample story. Given the goal vector from manager LSTM and hidden state from worker LSTM, lexicon-based attention is applied to encourage the model to generate more emotional words. Once the candidate story is generated, two emotional consistency rewards are put together to guide the emotion phrase alignment. Besides, a classic sentence-level BLEU reward is utilized to control the fluency of the generated story. The dotted line in the figure represents the internal structure of the attention mechanism.

Text Emotion Classifier. Our Emo-EC reward captures the emotion in story text using an emotion classifier. In story-view emotion classification, we just focus on basic emotions and adapt Fast-BERT[2] to train a multi-label classification model on 5 emotions, which are joy, anger, fear, sadness, and neutral. Following [3], We exploit the fully-connected layer on the final hidden representation corresponding to the special classification token ([CLS]).

Since there is currently no excellent dataset that annotates emotion for story-style text, we train the classifier on the SemEval-2018 dataset [14]. Experimental results show that our model's Jaccard accuracy, F1 Marco, and F1 Micro on the validation set are 70.0%, 64.7%, 77.4% respectively, which are the benchmark evaluation metrics in text emotion classification. The performance of the above emotion classifier shows that it is confident to find the underlying emotion in text.

Commonsense Transformer. Our Emo-CT reward is expected to reason about the pluralized and specific sentiment in text from a sentence view. We make use of **commonsense transformer (COMET**[3]) [2], a knowledge base con-

---

[2] https://github.com/utterworks/fast-bert.
[3] https://github.com/atcbosselut/comet-commonsense.

struction model trained on ATOMIC [19] and ConceptNet [20] $Cause - Effect$ knowledge tuples. Given an event and a relation, COMET can generate rich and diverse commonsense inferences about the relation. For example, when the event is 'Eric wants to see a movie' and the relation is $xReact$ (The description of $xReact$ is the reaction that person X would have to the event), the output commonsense inferences can be 'happy', 'excited', etc.. $xReact$, $oReact$ and $xFeels$ have the ability to scrutinize text emotion, but in our experiments, we make use of $xReact$.

3.2 Emotion Aware Storytelling Model

Our proposed model is based on a reinforcement learning framework with composite reward functions designed to encourage the model to generate an emotional, relevant and fluent story. It is composed of two modules: a policy module and a reward module. The policy module takes an image sequence I as the input and performs sequential actions to generate sentences. The reward module receives generated story and calculate the gap between generated story and gold story[4] and then refine the policy model.

Policy Module. Specifically, the policy module is a CNN-RNN architecture. We first feed the image sequences into ResNet [6] and extract their high-level image features. For follow-up needs, we compute the average value of all the image features v_i in (1). Then, the image features and overall image sequences features are sent into decoder.

$$\overline{V} = \frac{1}{n} \sum_i v_i \tag{1}$$

The decoder is hierarchical which involves manager LSTM and worker LSTM [10]. The manager LSTM serves as a supervisor to control the overall flow of the story. To be more specific, when describing i-th image, the manager LSTM should take three kinds of information into consideration in (2), which are: 1) overall information of the image sequence; 2) image information in the i-th image; 3) sentences generated for previous image. The manager LSTM then predicts a hidden state $h_{m,i}$ as the goal vector and passes the vector to the worker LSTM.

$$h_{m,i} = \text{LSTM}_M\left(\left[\overline{V}; v_i; h_{w,i-1}^T\right], h_{m,i-1}\right) \tag{2}$$

The worker LSTM then attempts to complete the generation of word description based on the goal vector. When generating t-th word for the i-th image, the LSTM decoder takes the current image information v_i and word embedding of the previously generated word e_i^{t-1} and goal vector $h_{m,i}$ as input to predict its hidden state $h_{w,i}^t$ in (3). Then, the worker LSTM enforces a linear layer $f(\cdot)$ to approximate the probability of choosing the next word in (4).

$$h_{w,i}^t = \text{LSTM}\left(\left[v_i; h_{m,i}; e_i^{t-1}\right], h_{w,i}^{t-1}\right) \tag{3}$$

---

[4] Note that gold story represents the manually annotated story in VIST dataset.

$$p_\theta\left(y_i^t \mid y_i^{1:t-1}, v_i, \bar{V}\right) = \text{softmax}\left(f\left(h_{w,i}^t\right)\right) \tag{4}$$

After manager LSTM produces goal vector $h_{m,i}$ and worker LSTM produce hidden state $h_{w,i}^t$, lexicon-based attention is applied to encourage the model to pay more attention to the emotional words in the emotion vocabulary.

$$c_{tk} = \text{Sigmoid}\left(\alpha^\top h_{m,i} + \beta^\top h_{w,i}^{t-1} + \gamma^\top \text{Emb}\left(w_k^z\right)\right) \tag{5}$$

$$P(emo(W_t) = Z_k) = \frac{\exp\left(c_{tk}\right)}{\sum_{m=1}^{T_z} \exp\left(c_{tm}\right)} \tag{6}$$

in (5), α, β and γ are trainable parameter, t represents t-th time step, i represents i-th sentence and w_k^z denotes k-th word in emotion vocabulary VB^z. In (6), $emo(W_t)$ represents emotion classification at the t-th time step, Z_k represents the emotion label of k-th word and T_z denotes the total number of words for emotion category Z. For each emotional words w_k^z, the attention score at the time step t is determined by three parts: the goal vector of the manager LSTM, the hidden state of the worker LSTM and embedding $Emb\left(w_k^z\right)$ of the k-th word in VB_e. In this way, such lexicon-based attention gives higher probability to the emotional words that are more relevant to the current image and context.

Reward Module. A quantity of reinforcement learning works have optimized the evaluation measures as rewards. Here, we propose two emotional consistency rewards from story-view and sentence-view, Emo-EC and Emo-CT, to optimize adherence to the gold story's emotion arc.

Emo-EC Reward. This reward tracks the implicit emotion in given text using an emotion classifier which strives to maintain emotional consistency in story view. Since the number of input images and output sentences is always 5, we first divide the generated story and gold story into three segments: beginning, body, ending according to the ration of 1:3:1. For each segment, we use the classifier to obtain the emotion, resulting a sequence of emotion-phrase $a_g = \{e_1, e_2, e_3\}$ and $a^* = \{s_1, s_2, s_3\}$ where a_g and a^* respectively represent generated story and gold story. Moreover, we define the Emo-EC reward as the equal probability between the each segment of a_g and a^* in (7). Here k is the number of tokens in the emotion-phrase.

$$r_{Emo-EC} = \frac{1}{k} \sum_{j=1}^{k} p_{Emo-EC}\left(a_{g,j} \mid a_j^*\right) \tag{7}$$

Emo-CT Reward. This reward dominates the alignment of emotion phrase between generated candidate story and gold story using the COMET, generating two emotion phrase $a_g = \{e_1, e_2, e_3, e_4, e_5\}$ and $a^* = \{s_1, s_2, s_3, s_4, s_5\}$. Similar to Emo-EC reward, this reward requires to find out the gap between the a_g and a^* more accurately. Since the levenshtein distance can find how different two strings are, so we define the reward as a Levenshtein distance between a_g and a^* in (8):

$$r_{Emo-CT} = \text{Levenshtein}\,(a_g, a^*) \tag{8}$$

3.3 Training

By maximizing the given reward (9), reinforcement learning can learn a policy to encourage the model to focus more on those key aspects and then generates more emotional and fluent story. In (9), $\pi \equiv p_\theta\,(y_i \mid \mathbf{v}_i, \overline{\mathbf{v}})$ is the policy and b is the baseline that reduces the variance of the given rewards. In (10), λ, μ and ρ are the weight coefficients.

$$J_{RL}(\theta) = \sum_{Y,V \in D'} E_{y_i \sim \pi_i}[(b - r\,(y_i)) \log \pi_i] \tag{9}$$

$$r\,(y_i) = \lambda r_{Emo-EC}\,(y_i) + \mu r_{Emo-CT}\,(y_i) + \rho r_{BLEU}\,(y_i) \tag{10}$$

During training, we find that optimizing only with the reinforcement learning loss is possible to increase expected rewards, while sacrificing the quality of our generated model. To this end, we first train our model with maximum likelihood estimation(MLE) and then continue to train the model jointly with reinforcement and MLE loss (11). Following [9,18], we always set the $\omega = 0.5$ as it is a good trade-off between reinforcement learning loss and MLE loss.

$$Loss_{\text{mixed}} = \omega Loss_{RL} + (1 - \omega)Loss_{MLE} \tag{11}$$

$$Loss_{\text{MLE}} = Loss_{decoder} + Loss_{emo} \tag{12}$$

$$Loss_{emo} = \sum_{Z,V \in D'} \sum_{i=1}^{N} \sum_{t=1}^{T} -log\,P(emo(W_{i,t}) = Z_{i,t}) \tag{13}$$

$$Loss_{decoder} = \sum_{Y,V \in D'} \sum_{i=1}^{N} \sum_{t=1}^{T} -log\,P(W_{i,t} = Y_{i,t}) \tag{14}$$

4 Experiments

4.1 Dataset

Two datasets are used in this paper: VIST[5] [11] and SemEval-2018 Task1[6] [14] dataset. The SemEval-2018 Task1 dataset is used to train our text emotion classifier. We then train and evaluate our model on VIST dataset. SemEval-2018 dataset offers a training set of 6,857 tweets, with binary labels for the eight

---

[5] https://visionandlanguage.net/VIST/.
[6] https://competitions.codalab.org/competitions/17751.

plunchik categories, plus optimism, pessimism, and love. We keep the Anger, Joy, Fear, Sadness while list other emotions as neutral emotion. We train and evaluate our model on VIST dataset which is the most popular dataset in visual story-telling task. The dataset consists of 10,117 Flicker albums with 21,0819 unique images and is split into training/ validation/ testing sets with 400,98/4,988/5,050 samples.

Table 1. Comparison on BLEU, METEOR, ROUGE, CIDEr between EARN-VIST and other models.

Method	BLEU-1	BLEU-2	BLEU-3	BLEU-4	METEOR	ROUGE	CIDEr
XE-ss [23]	62.3	38.2	22.5	13.7	34.8	29.7	8.7
AREL [23]	63.8	39.1	23.2	14.1	35.0	29.5	9.4
HSRL [10]	–	–	–	12.3	35.2	**30.8**	10.7
RECO-RL [9]	–	–	–	12.4	33.9	29.9	8.3
INet [12]	64.4	40.1	23.9	14.7	35.6	29.7	10.0
SGVST [22]	65.1	40.1	23.8	14.7	35.8	29.9	9.8
IRW [24]	66.7	41.6	**25.0**	**15.4**	35.6	29.6	11.0
LMGT [17]	67.5	41.6	**25.0**	15.1	35.6	29.7	10.0
EARN-VIST	**68.8**	**43.5**	24.3	13.7	**35.9**	29.5	**11.9**

4.2 Quantitative Evaluation

We compare our model with the following baselines: (1) **XE-ss** [23], **AREL** [23]; (2) **HSRL** [10](3) **ReCo-RL** [9] (4)**INet** [12] (5) **SGVST** [22] (6) **IRW** [24] (7)**LMGT** [17]. These approaches achieved either state-of-the-art or competitive results on VIST dataset. In particular, **IRW** [24] is an imagine-reason-write generation framework and **LMGT** [17] is a latent memory-guided graph transformer framework. A group of automatic metrics, including BLEU [16], METEOR [1], ROUGE [13] and CIDEr [21], are used for our quantitative evaluation. In particular, BLEU [16] is a popular metric in text generation task that calculate the word-overlap score between generated sentence and gold-standard sentence. In Table 1, we notice that our EARN-VIST achieves state-of-the-art on the BLEU-1, BLEU-2, METEOR and CIDEr. Specifically, EARN-VIST makes the improvement compared with the previous best model by 1.3% on BLEU-1, 1.9% on BLEU-2, 0.1% on METEOR and 0.9% on CIDEr. Besides, the performance of BLEU-3, BLEU-4 and ROUGE is also competitive. The reason for the excellent performance of EARN-VIST can be attributed to two level decoder extended with lexicon-based attention and composite reward.

Table 2. Ablation experiment results. Note that here B represents baseline model, Att represents lexicon-based attention and the weight coefficient of r_{Emo-EC} and r_{Emo-CT} are both fixed to 0.3.

Model	BLEU-4	METEOR	ROUGE	CIDEr
B [9]	12.40	33.90	**29.90**	8.60
B+Att	12.42	35.36	29.23	11.37
B+(Emo-EC)	13.27	35.70	29.34	11.48
B+(Emo-CT)	13.49	35.76	29.45	11.62
B+(Emo-EC)+(Emo-CT)	13.55	35.82	29.46	11.66
EARN-VIST	**13.64**	**35.90**	29.49	**11.93**

4.3 Ablation Study

In order to analyze the effect of our proposed attention mechanism, Emo-EC reward and Emo-CT reward, we conduct the ablation study and the results are listed in Table 2. Note that our basic model is ReCo-RL [9] which is an encoder-decoder framework trained on reinforcement learning. Since Hu et al. [9] does not provide the result with two decimal places of the baseline, we set the second decimal place to 0 by default. We first add three approaches to the baseline to test their effects separately. As shown in the Table 2, each of the three approaches has a positive effect on our baseline. Specifically, our proposed approaches achieve a 2 to 3 point improvement on the CIDEr metric. Next, we combine Emo-EC reward and Emo-CT reward together into our baseline to see if there will be better results than only one approach into our baseline. It is clear that when Emo-EC and Emo-CT are combined, the metrics are further improved. Among them, BLEU-4 and METEOR achieve a more than one point improvement, and then CIDEr achieves a relatively small promotion. Finally, we add the three approaches proposed in this paper to the baseline, that is, EARN-VIST. It can be seen from the results that it achieves SOTA results on three metrics. At the same time, it should be noted that none of our proposed approaches have improved the ROUGE metric, but the ROUGE metric of our model is still very competitive.

4.4 Effect of the Hyper-parameter λ, μ and ρ

Since λ, μ and ρ (10) are important hyper-parameter for training EARN-VIST, we try to find out the appropriate combination. But if we conduct experiment on three parameters at the same time, the process will be very time consuming and not necessarily efficient. Therefore we take the control variable method and fix $\rho = 0.5$. Then we train the model with different λ and μ. From the results in Table 3, we find that $(\lambda, \mu) = (0.3, 0.3, 0.5)$ and $(0.4, 0.4, 0.5)$ are appropriate value combinations for EARN-VIST. We speculate that above mentioned combinations are better paired with r_{Emo-EC} and r_{Emo-CT} than other combinations.

Table 3. Results of EARN-VIST with different λ and μ.

λ	μ	BLEU-1	BLEU-2	BLEU-3	BLEU-4	METEOR	ROUGE	CIDEr
0.1	0.1	68.55	43.52	24.29	13.55	35.82	29.46	11.46
0.2	0.1	68.69	43.38	24.26	13.60	35.84	29.44	11.86
0.3	0.3	68.88	43.52	24.35	**13.64**	**35.90**	**29.49**	**11.93**
0.4	0.4	**69.00**	**43.63**	**24.37**	13.62	35.87	29.47	11.66
0.5	0.5	68.76	43.31	24.20	13.48	35.83	29.43	11.84
0.6	0.7	68.75	43.34	24.24	13.60	35.87	29.48	11.68

Table 4. Human Pairwise Evaluation between EARN-VIST and other models. For each pairwise comparison, the three columns indicate the percentage that volunteers prefer this story to the other one, and volunteers think both are of equal quality.

Aspects	AREL	EARN-VIST	Tie	PR-VIST	EARN-VIST	Tie
Relevance	21.25%	66.25%	12.50%	34.00%	46.00%	20.00%
Coherence	30.00%	53.75%	16.25%	34.00%	44.00%	22.00%
Emotional Consistency	12.50%	75.00%	12.50%	26.00%	46.00%	28.00%

4.5   Human Evaluation

Previous visual storytelling work [23] has shown that current string-match-based automatic metrics are not the perfect way to prove model's performance. So we further conduct pairwise human evaluation to examine the quality of our model. Specifically, we randomly select 180 sampled stories generated by EARN-VIST and invite 20 well-educated undergraduates and postgraduates to carry on human evaluation. All choices are shuffled before evaluation to avoid bias. In practice, we conduct two sets of human pairwise experiments, which are EARN-VIST vs AREL [23], EARN-VIST vs PR-VIST [8]. For each sample pair, given on photo stream and two stories generated by two models, the volunteer is asked to perform pairwise evaluation based on their relevance, coherence and emotional consistency. We also provide neutral option for the case that volunteers think the two choices are equally good on the particular criterion. **Relevance** evaluates how the story accurately describes what is happening in the image stream. **Coherence** assesses whether the sentence in the story is coherent with the other sentences. **Emotional-Consistency** evaluates whether the emotion is accurately expressed in the story. Table 4 illustrates the results between EARN-VIST and AREL, PR-VIST. We can observe that compared with other outstanding models, in terms of relevance, coherence, emotional consistency, EARN-VIST significantly outperforms others.

4.6   Implementation Details

Following previous works [9,23], we utilize the pretrained ResNet-152 [6] to learn deep image features. The hidden size of manager LSTM and worker LSTM are both set to 512. When training with MLE (12), the batch size is set to 32, learning rate is set to 2e−4. When training with MLE loss and reinforcement learning loss (11), the batch size is set to 16 and learning rate is set to 1e−4. The batch size and learning rate of Fast-Bert are set to 6 and 5e−5 respectively. The sampling algorithm of COMET is top-1. We implement and run our model on a GeForce RTX 2080 Ti with Pytorch.

5   Conclusion

In this paper, we propose a novel emotion aware generation framework for visual storytelling. In order to produce affective story, we first leverage hierarchical decoder extended with lexicon-based attention to generate more emotional lexicon. Then, since our framework is based on reinforcement learning, we propose two emotional consistency rewards from story-view and sentence-view to control the emotion phrase alignment. Extensive experiments on VIST dataset and human evaluation demonstrate that EARN-VIST outperforms most strong baselines. In other words, EARN-VIST can generate more relevant, coherent and emotional stories compared with others. In future work, we will focus our work on the diversification of generated sentences and the transfer of sentence styles.

Acknowledgements. Supported by National Natural Science Foundation of China Nos 61972059, 61773272, 61602332; Natural Science Foundation of the Jiangsu Higher Education Institutions of China No 19KJA230001, Key Laboratory of Symbolic Computation and Knowledge Engineering of Ministry of Education, Jilin University No 93K172016K08; the Priority Academic Program Development of Jiangsu Higher Education Institutions (PAPD).

References

1. Banerjee, S., Lavie, A.: Meteor: an automatic metric for MT evaluation with improved correlation with human judgments. In: Proceedings of the ACL Workshop on Intrinsic and Extrinsic Evaluation Measures for Machine Translation and/or Summarization, pp. 65–72 (2005)
2. Bosselut, A., Rashkin, H., Sap, M., Malaviya, C., Celikyilmaz, A., Choi, Y.: Comet: commonsense transformers for automatic knowledge graph construction. arXiv preprint arXiv:1906.05317 (2019)
3. Brahman, F., Chaturvedi, S.: Modeling protagonist emotions for emotion-aware storytelling. arXiv preprint arXiv:2010.06822 (2020)
4. Chen, H., Huang, Y., Takamura, H., Nakayama, H.: Commonsense knowledge aware concept selection for diverse and informative visual storytelling. arXiv preprint arXiv:2102.02963 (2021)
5. Gu, S., Wang, W., Wang, F., Huang, J.H.: Neuromodulator and emotion biomarker for stress induced mental disorders. Neural Plasticity 2016 (2016)
6. He, K., Zhang, X., Ren, S., Sun, J.: Deep residual learning for image recognition. In: Proceedings of the IEEE Conference on Computer Vision and Pattern Recognition, pp. 770–778 (2016)

7. Hsu, C.C., et al.: Knowledge-enriched visual storytelling. In: Proceedings of the AAAI Conference on Artificial Intelligence, vol. 34, pp. 7952–7960 (2020)
8. Hsu, C.Y., Chu, Y.W., Huang, T.H., Ku, L.W.: Plot and rework: modeling storylines for visual storytelling. arXiv preprint arXiv:2105.06950 (2021)
9. Hu, J., Cheng, Y., Gan, Z., Liu, J., Gao, J., Neubig, G.: What makes a good story? designing composite rewards for visual storytelling. In: Proceedings of the AAAI Conference on Artificial Intelligence, pp. 7969–7976 (2020)
10. Huang, Q., Gan, Z., Celikyilmaz, A., Wu, D., Wang, J., He, X.: Hierarchically structured reinforcement learning for topically coherent visual story generation. In: Proceedings of the AAAI Conference on Artificial Intelligence, pp. 8465–8472 (2019)
11. Huang, T.H., et al.: Visual storytelling. In: Proceedings of the 2016 Conference of the North American Chapter of the Association for Computational Linguistics: Human Language Technologies, pp. 1233–1239 (2016)
12. Jung, Y., Kim, D., Woo, S., Kim, K., Kim, S., Kweon, I.S.: Hide-and-tell: learning to bridge photo streams for visual storytelling. In: Proceedings of the AAAI Conference on Artificial Intelligence, pp. 11213–11220 (2020)
13. Lin, C.Y.: Rouge: a package for automatic evaluation of summaries. In: Text summarization branches out, pp. 74–81 (2004)
14. Mohammad, S., Bravo-Marquez, F., Salameh, M., Kiritchenko, S.: Semeval-2018 task 1: affect in tweets. In: Proceedings of the 12th International Workshop on Semantic Evaluation, pp. 1–17 (2018)
15. Mohammad, S.M.: Word affect intensities. arXiv preprint arXiv:1704.08798 (2017)
16. Papineni, K., Roukos, S., Ward, T., Zhu, W.J.: Bleu: a method for automatic evaluation of machine translation. In: Proceedings of the 40th Annual Meeting of the Association for Computational Linguistics, pp. 311–318 (2002)
17. Qi, M., Qin, J., Huang, D., Shen, Z., Yang, Y., Luo, J.: Latent memory-augmented graph transformer for visual storytelling. In: Proceedings of the 29th ACM International Conference on Multimedia, pp. 4892–4901 (2021)
18. Ranzato, M., Chopra, S., Auli, M., Zaremba, W.: Sequence level training with recurrent neural networks. arXiv preprint arXiv:1511.06732 (2015)
19. Sap, M., et al.: Atomic: An atlas of machine commonsense for if-then reasoning. In: Proceedings of the AAAI Conference on Artificial Intelligence, vol. 33, pp. 3027–3035 (2019)
20. Speer, R., Chin, J., Havasi, C.: Conceptnet 5.5: an open multilingual graph of general knowledge. In: Thirty-first AAAI Conference on Artificial Intelligence (2017)
21. Vedantam, R., Lawrence Zitnick, C., Parikh, D.: Cider: consensus-based image description evaluation. In: Proceedings of the IEEE Conference on Computer Vision and Pattern Recognition, pp. 4566–4575 (2015)
22. Wang, R., Wei, Z., Li, P., Zhang, Q., Huang, X.: Storytelling from an image stream using scene graphs. In: Proceedings of the AAAI Conference on Artificial Intelligence, pp. 9185–9192 (2020)
23. Wang, X., Chen, W., Wang, Y.F., Wang, W.Y.: No metrics are perfect: adversarial reward learning for visual storytelling. arXiv preprint arXiv:1804.09160 (2018)
24. Xu, C., Yang, M., Li, C., Shen, Y., Ao, X., Xu, R.: Imagine, reason and write: visual storytelling with graph knowledge and relational reasoning. In: Proceedings of the AAAI Conference on Artificial Intelligence, pp. 3022–3029 (2021)

Long-Horizon Route-Constrained Policy for Learning Continuous Control Without Exploration

Ruidong Cao[1], Min Dong[1(✉)], Xuanlu Jiang[1], Sheng Bi[1], and Ning Xi[2]

[1] School of Computer Science and Enginneering, South China University
of Technology, Guangzhou, China
hollymin@scut.edu.cn
[2] Faculty of Engineering, The University of Hong Kong, Hong Kong, China

Abstract. Imitation Learning and Offline Reinforcement Learning that learn from demonstration data are the current solutions for intelligent agents to reduce the high cost and high risk of online Reinforcement Learning. However, these solutions have struggled with the distribution shift issue with the lack of exploration of the environment. Distribution shift makes offline learning prone to making wrong decisions and leads to error accumulation in the goal-reaching continuous control tasks. Moreover, Offline Reinforcement Learning generates additional bias while learning from human demonstration data that does not satisfy the Markov process assumptions. To alleviate these two dilemmas, we present a Long-horizon Route-constrained (LHRC) policy for the continuous control tasks of goal-reaching. At a state, our method generates subgoals by long-horizon route planning and outputs actions based on the subgoal constraints. It can constrain the state space and action space of the agent. And it can correct trajectories with temporal information. Experiments on the D4RL benchmark show that our approach achieves higher scores with state-of-the-art methods and enhances performance on complex tasks.

Keywords: Imitation learning · Offline reinforcement learning · Learning from demonstrations

1 Introduction

Reinforcement Learning (RL) has been a widely available solution in the domain of robotic continuous control tasks [10,20,21]. An intelligent agent learns through exploration and exploitation in the environment, where it continuously collects samples and discovers how to obtain rewards based on these samples. With such a mechanism, the agents can learn skills. However, such an online approach of frequent interacting with the environment is not applicable in many scenarios. Firstly, it is dangerous to let the agent interact with the environment frequently in some scenarios such as medical skill learning and work-at-height learning [7].

© The Author(s), under exclusive license to Springer Nature Switzerland AG 2022
E. Pimenidis et al. (Eds.): ICANN 2022, LNCS 13530, pp. 38–49, 2022.
https://doi.org/10.1007/978-3-031-15931-2_4

And secondly, agents such as robots may collide and wear out during learning in realistic scenarios, which increases the cost [11]. To solve the dilemma of online reinforcement learning, learning from demonstrations provides a feasible solution. Agents can learn offline from pre-collected expert demonstrations, reducing costs due to interaction with the environment. Learning in the data is much cheaper than learning in the environment. Some research has shown that offline learning solutions, represented by Imitation Learning (IL) [6,24] and Offline Reinforcement Learning [1,11], can be used as prior skill learning methods to accelerate online learning and multitask learning [22]. Offline learning itself has also shown promising performance in many scenarios. However, with the lack of exploration and exploitation, offline learning is overly dependent on the merits of the expert dataset [15].

The distribution shift between the environment and the demonstrations is the main factor that affects the performance of the Offline RL algorithms [4,8]. When performing online learning, the off-policy RL algorithm collects data into the replay buffer by exploring the environment and then updates the policy based on the replay buffer. As the policy is updated and exploration increases, the data in the replay buffer becomes more and more diverse, and its data distribution gradually approaches that of the realistic environment. Demonstration datasets can be collected from the environments by the other behavioral policy during its training or testing phase or come from human experts and hand-crafted policies. The off-policy RL algorithms can perform offline learning by simply replacing the replay buffer with the demonstration data. However, the possibility of errors increases when an agent has challenged with unexplored states during testing. The agent policy overestimates the Q value of state-action pairs due to the lack of correction opportunities brought by exploration.

Furthermore, datasets collected from RL behavioral policy usually have large-scale data. But the quality of them is not good enough due to the odd states like robotic arm twitching. In contrast, the data distributions of datasets from human experts and hand-crafted policies are more narrow and biased. The datasets are prone to contain subjective and redundant behaviors. It is because the decision process is non-Markovian. But learning directly from human experts is a goal of demonstration learning when applied to the real world in the future. Imitation learning is generally suitable for human demonstration data but limited by the dataset scale. While offline RL is based on the assumption that the decision process conforms to Markov property. Learning in such data will generate additional bias.

We propose a method named Long-horizon Route-constrained Policy (LHRC) to alleviate the above two aspects. Our approach constrains the policy of the agent to reduce the extrapolation error. It performs route prediction according to the current state in the environment by generating multiple subgoal nodes on the route. When conducting a continuous control task, the agent controls the robot along the subgoal. The role of subgoals is similar to placing several markers on a marathon to guide the direction. Meanwhile, the training of the route generative model utilizes temporal information, which is beneficial for learning on non-Markovian demonstration data. We evaluated our approach on a complex domain of a benchmark, and our method ranked ahead in several cases compared to state-of-the-art methods.

2 Related Work

Behavioral Cloning (BC) [18] is a usual offline IL method of learning from expert demonstration datasets to produce a policy that generates action based on the current state. BC is a kind of supervised learning that takes states as input and actions as labels, and its training object is to make the generated actions as close as possible to the actions adopted by experts. Hierarchical Behavioral Cloning (HBC) [13,14] uses hierarchical policies to optimize Behavioral Cloning methods, including high-level and low-level policies. It first adopts a high-level policy to predict a future subgoal state based on the current state. Secondly, it uses a low-level policy to generate a sequence of continuous actions based on the current and the subgoal state. Compared to BC, which uses a single state-action pair as a training sample, HBC is trained based on state-action pair sequences with temporal information. It improves performance on offline tasks. However, such Behavioral Cloning methods are sensitive to the quality of the demonstration data and lack error correction capability during testing.

Off-policy RL methods such as Deep Q-Network (DQN) [16], Deep Deterministic Policy Gradients (DDPG) [12], and Soft Actor-critic (SAC) [5] can perform offline learning. But with extrapolation errors, it is difficult for them to outperform the behavioral policies of the demonstration data. Therefore, Offline RL research has employed mechanisms like policy constraint and value function regularization to alleviate such issues. Batch-Constrained deep Q-learning (BCQ) [4] is a compromise between IL and RL, and it constrains policy when training. BCQ constrains the generated actions to not deviate from the distribution of the demonstration data. Its policy consists of a conditional variational auto-encoder (VAE) [2] for action imitation and a perturbation network that restricts the action space to the neighborhood of action space of behavioral policy. Such constraint reduces the risk of incorrect Q-value estimation to reduce the error accumulation in the Bellman iteration. Similarly, Bootstrapping Error Accumulation Reduction (BEAR) [8] also performs as a policy constraint method. It uses the maximum mean discrepancy between its policy and behavioral policy as a support constraint for action generation instead of perturbing based on imitating behavioral policy. Compared with BCQ, BEAR can learn from suboptimal data, and it trains more stochastic policy with a broader action space. Compared to the policy constraint methods, Conservative Q-Learning (CQL) [9] adds a regularization term to the Q-function as a penalty. It makes the expected value of a policy under this Q-function lower bounds its true value. CQL performs well on complex and multi-modal datasets by learning a conservative Q-function to avoid overestimating out-of-distribution (OOD) state-action pairs. Since Offline RL is hyperparameter-sensitive and unstable, various methods have their own merits under different scenarios and datasets.

3   Problem Statement

The Offline Reinforcement Learning problem for continuous control tasks is formalized within a Markov decision process (MDP). MDP is defined by a tuple $(\mathcal{S}, \mathcal{A}, P, R, \rho_0, \gamma)$, where $\mathcal{S}$ is the state space, $\mathcal{A}$ is the action space, $P(s'|s, a)$ is the state transition distribution, $R(s, a, s')$ is the reward function, ρ_0 is the initial state distribution and $\gamma \in [0, 1)$ is the discount factor. At every step in environment, the agent observes the state s, performs a policy π to generate an action a, and then gets the next state $s' \sim P(\cdot|s, a)$ and the reward $r = R(s, a, s')$. Our approach focuses on goal-reaching tasks, using whole trajectories of horizon T formed as $(s_0, a_0, r_0, s'_0, ..., s_T, a_T, r_T, s'_T)$ for policy learning. The state dimension depends on the environment and the objects, and it contains object position and robotic gesture information. The action dimension depends on the robotic degrees of freedom (DoF). The reward function related to tasks can be either a sparse reward or a dense reward. The sparse reward shows whether has the goal state reached. The dense reward measures the distance to the goal state. The terminal signal of a trajectory is either timeout or the completion of the task. While Offline RL training, we use the general evaluation criterion to train the policy so that the expected cumulative undiscounted returns $J(\pi) = E_{\pi, P, \rho_0}[\sum_{t=0}^{T} \gamma^t R(s_t, a_t, s_{t'})]$ of trajectories become the maximum during testing in the environment.

4   Long-horizon Route-constrained Policy

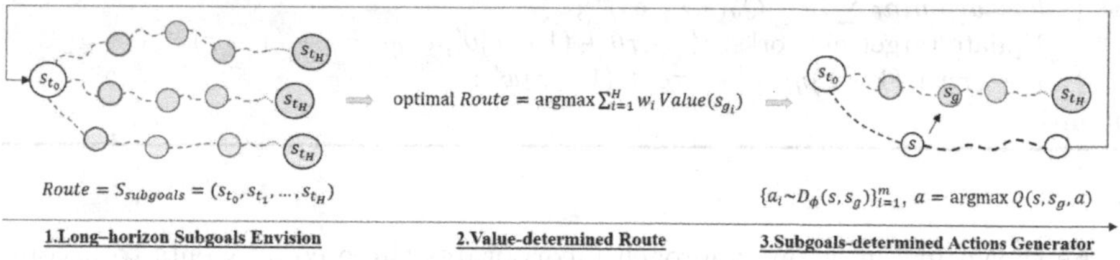

Fig. 1. The overview of the decision process for the Long-horizon Route-constrained Policy.

Our approach divides the entire decision process for goal-reaching tasks into two phases: long-horizon route planning and short-horizon subgoal-constrained action generation. When the system is at state s, the route planner first envisions a long-horizon route containing multiple subgoals. The action generator then generates the action a to reach the next state s' with the first subgoal as a constraint. After several timesteps state transitions, the action generator changes the subgoal until all subgoals have traversed. The route planner then re-predicts a new long-horizon route based on the current state. Nextly the agent follows the above steps in the loop to complete the task.

Algorithm 1: LHRC

---

1 Initialize Subgoals VAE $G_\omega = \{E_{\omega_1}, D_{\omega_2}\}$, Action VAEs $G_\psi = \{E_{\psi_1}, D_{\psi_2}\}$,
$G_\phi = \{E_{\phi_1}, D_{\phi_2}\}$, Q-networks $Q_{\eta_1}(s, a)$, $Q_{\eta_2}(s, a)$, $Q_{\theta_1}(s, s_g, a)$, $Q_{\theta_2}(s, s_g, a)$,
and their networks $G_{\psi'}$, $G_{\phi'}$, $Q_{\eta_1'}$, $Q_{\eta_2'}$, $Q_{\theta_1'}$, $Q_{\theta_2'}$;

2 **for** $i = 1, 2, , ..., n_{iters}$ **do**

3   Sparsely sample batch of N sequences $(s_{t_0}, a_{t_0}, r_{t_0}, s'_{t_0}, ..., s_{t_H}, a_{t_H}, r_{t_H}, s'_{t_H})$
        from the dataset $\mathcal{D}$;

4   Train Subgoals VAE, $S_{subgoals} = \{s_{t_i}\}_{i=1}^H$:

5 $\mu_s, \sigma_s = E_{\omega_1}(s_{t_0}, S_{subgoals})$, $z \sim \mathcal{N}(\mu_s, \sigma_s)$, $\tilde{S}_{subgoals} = D_{\omega_2}(s_{t_0}, z)$

6 $\omega \leftarrow argmin_\omega \sum (S_{subgoals} - \tilde{S}_{subgoals})^2 + D_{KL}(\mathcal{N}(\mu_s, \sigma_s) \| \mathcal{N}(0, 1))$;

7   Batch of NH tuples $(s, a, r, s') \leftarrow \{(s_{t_i}, a_{t_i}, r_{t_i}, s'_{t_i})\}_{i=1}^H$

8   Train Action VAE:

9 $\mu_h, \sigma_h = E_{\psi_1}(s, a)$, $z \sim \mathcal{N}(\mu_h, \sigma_h)$, $\tilde{a} = D_{\psi_2}(s, z)$

10 $\psi \leftarrow argmin_\psi \sum (a - \tilde{a})^2 + D_{KL}(\mathcal{N}(\mu_h, \sigma_h) \| \mathcal{N}(0, 1))$;

11   Sample m actions: $\{a_i \sim D_{\psi_2'}(s')\}_{i=1}^m$

12   Update Q-networks:

13 $y = r + \gamma \max_{a_i} [\lambda \min_{j=1,2} Q_{\eta_j'}(s', a_i) + (1 - \lambda) \max_{j=1,2} Q_{\eta_j'}(s', a_i)]$

14 $\eta \leftarrow argmin_\eta \sum (y - Q_\eta(s, a))^2$;

15   Batch of NH tuples $(s, s_g, a, r, s') \leftarrow \{(s_{t_i}, s_{t_{i+1}}, a_{t_i}, r_{t_i}, s'_{t_i})\}_{i=0}^{H-1}$

16   Train Action VAE:

17 $\mu_a, \sigma_a = E_{\phi_1}(s, s_g, a)$, $z \sim \mathcal{N}(\mu_a, \sigma_a)$, $\tilde{a} = D_{\phi_2}(s, s_g, z)$

18 $\phi \leftarrow argmin_\phi \sum (a - \tilde{a})^2 + D_{KL}(\mathcal{N}(\mu_a, \sigma_a) \| \mathcal{N}(0, 1))$

19   Sample m actions: $\{a_i \sim D_{\phi_2'}(s', s_g)\}_{i=1}^m$

20   Update Q-networks:

21 $y = r + \gamma \max_{a_i} [\lambda \min_{j=1,2} Q_{\theta_j'}(s', s_g, a_i) + (1 - \lambda) \max_{j=1,2} Q_{\theta_j'}(s', s_g, a_i)]$

22 $\theta \leftarrow argmin_\theta \sum (y - Q_\theta(s, s_g, a))^2$;

23   Update target networks: $\theta_i' \leftarrow \tau\theta + (1 - \tau)\theta_i'$, $\phi' \leftarrow \tau\phi + (1 - \tau)\phi'$,
        $\eta_i' \leftarrow \tau\eta + (1 - \tau)\eta_i'$, $\psi' \leftarrow \tau\psi + (1 - \tau)\psi'$;

24 **end**

As shown in Fig. 1, our approach incorporates three components to accomplish the above process. We first train a conditional variational auto-encoder (VAE) to generate r routes $\{S_{subgoals}^i\}_{i=1}^r$ of horizon H, and then adopt a value model to evaluate each route. We calculate the value of a route with the sum of weighted values of subgoals on the route, $V(Route) = \sum_{i=1}^H w_i V(s_{g_i})$. The action generator contains a conditional VAE that takes the current state and the subgoal state (s, s_g) as the input. It samples multiple actions from the VAE and selects the optimal action through a Q-network. The entire train loop is shown in Algorithm 1.

We first train a conditional VAE $G_\omega = \{E_{\omega_1}, D_{\omega_2}\}$ as a subgoals generative model for the long-horizon route planner. Firstly, we sparsely sample a batch of N sequences from the trajectories in the dataset. For each complete demonstration trajectory $(s_0, a_0, r_0, s'_0, ..., s_T, a_T, r_T, s'_T)$, We fix the end of the trajectory and randomly truncate the front half of the trajectory to sample a sequence of random length $(s_t, a_t, r_t, s'_t, ..., s_T, a_T, r_T, s'_T), t \geq 0, (T - t) \geq H$. Then we equate the sequence into $(H + 1)$ segments and random sample a quaternion from each segment to form a route containing sparse subgoals $(s_{t_0}, a_{t_0}, r_{t_0}, s'_{t_0}, ..., s_{t_H}, a_{t_H}, r_{t_H}, s'_{t_H})$. The encoder of Subgoals VAE takes $\{s_{t_i}\}_{i=0}^H$ as input and obtains the μ_s, σ_s of the latent Gaussian distribution through the temporal model Long Short-term Memory (LSTM) network. The decoder samples the latent feature z from the Gaussian distribution $N(\mu_s, \sigma_s)$ and reconstructs the subsequent route $\{s_{t_i}\}_{i=1}^H$ with the initial state s_{t_0}. Update the weights both to minimize the Mean Square Error of the reconstructed states between the original states and make the latent Gaussian distribution approximate the $\mathcal{N}(0, 1)$. The long-horizon route planner samples latent features $z \sim \mathcal{N}(0, 1)$ and generates multiple routes for the current state at testing time. These routes limit the future states for the agent to the experience of the demonstration data, reducing the occurrence of OOD states. The architecture of the subgoals generator has shown as Fig. 2. The encoder and decoder are similar, including a Multilayer Perceptron (MLP) of two layers followed by an LSTM of two hidden layers and the full-connected layers.

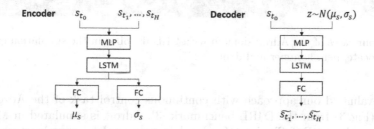

Fig. 2. The architecture of the subgoals generator for long-horizon route planner.

Secondly, for goal-reaching tasks, learning to achieve the goal is more necessary than learning to fit the trajectory, so we calculate the sum of weighted subgoal values for the route. From the last subgoal s_{t_H} to the first subgoal s_{t_1}, the weight of the value decreases evenly. To estimate the value of each subgoal state, we use reinforcement learning methods. First, we train an Action VAE to generate action a with state s as input. We then train a Q-network to evaluate the state-action pair (s, a), sample actions $\{a_i\}_{i=1}^m$ from the decoder of Action VAE, and set the training target y using the optimized Clipped Double Q-learning method from BCQ to reduce the overestimation bias. At testing time, the route planner generates multiple actions for each subgoal and gets the maximum Q value of these state-action pairs. The maximum Q value is the subgoal value, and then we can calculate the route value. In this way, the agent can find a goal-driven route in the environment.

Finally, we train the model that generates action for the current state with a subgoal as a constraint. For the subgoal-constrained Action VAE and its corresponding Q-network, the training process is similar to the previous steps, differing only in taking one more subgoal state as a conditional input. The encoders of both Action VAEs use 4-layer MLP, and the decoders use 3-layer MLP. The critics are consist of 3-layer MLP. We apply the models trained through plenty of steps to the environment. In Sect. 5, our experiments show that our approach is better than benchmark Offline RL algorithms from human demonstrations with non-Markovian processes and performs well in several scenarios.

5   Experiments

5.1   Dataset

Fig. 3. Four cases of the Adroit domain with 24-DoF robot in the simulation environment: relocate, pen, hammer and door.

We evaluated our approach with continuous control task of the Adroit [19] domain (Fig. 3) from the D4RL benchmark [3]. Adroit is simulated in Mujoco, controlling the 24-Dof Shadow Hand robot to complete complex tasks. The Adroit domain contains tasks: aligning a pen with a target orientation (pen), hammering a nail into a board (hammer), opening a door (door), move a ball to a target position (relocate). We experimented with three types of datasets for all scenarios of Adroit. The "human" dataset includes 25 human demonstration trajectories, the "expert" dataset includes 5000 trajectories from an RL policy that solves the task, and the "cloned" dataset includes 5000 trajectories from a mixture of human demonstration trajectories and its behavioral cloned policy data. The narrow data distribution and non-Markovian human demonstration data with the high DOF robots bring challenges to task learning.

5.2   Implementation Details

Evaluation Metric. Our evaluation metric follows the evaluation protocol in D4RL, using the "pen" and "door" datasets of each type as "training" data for hyperparameters tuning, with "hammer" and "relocate" as "evaluation" datasets. Each dataset was trained with 500K gradient steps and tested every 5000 steps (an epoch). We perform the evaluation for the final epoch model in the environment, calculate the undiscounted returns and get the normalized scores.

Experimental Settings. Our code is built on BCQ. We trained and evaluated the model on NVIDIA GeForce RTX 2080 Ti, following the evaluation protocol of D4RL in our experiments and tuning the hyperparameters. With experiments, we found that some hyperparameters such as learning rate, discount factor, τ, and λ have little effect on our model, so we used the default values of 0.001, 0.99, 0.005, 0.75 in order. Trajectory sampling during training needs to divide a demonstration trajectory into $H+1$ segments. It means to predict H subgoals during testing. For the -expert datasets, we used $H=1$, and for the -human and -cloned datasets, we used $H=10$ for the pen and hammer tasks and $H=20$ for the door and relocate tasks. For the batch size N, we found that a smaller size of 20 works better. During the testing phase, our approach also requires a k. The k indicates the step times toward a subgoal before changing to the next subgoal. This hyperparameter is not relevant to training and only used during testing. So we uniformly used $k=5$ for all tasks.

Table 1. Normalized scores on Adroit domain from D4RL, averaged across 3 seeds.

Dataset	BC	BEAR	BRAC-p	BRAC-v	AWR	BCQ	CQL	Ours
pen-expert	85.1	105.9	−3.5	−3.0	**111.0**	**114.9**	107.0	110.8
hammer-expert	**125.6**	**127.3**	0.3	0.3	39.0	107.2	86.7	110.6
door-expert	34.9	**103.4**	−0.3	−0.3	102.9	99.0	101.5	**103.4**
relocate-expert	**101.3**	98.6	−0.3	−0.4	91.5	41.6	95.0	**100.0**
pen-human	34.4	−1.0	8.1	0.6	12.3	**68.9**	37.5	**45.2**
hammer-human	1.5	0.3	0.3	0.2	1.2	0.5	4.4	**6.8**
door-human	0.5	−0.3	−0.3	−0.3	0.4	0.0	**9.9**	3.6
relocate-human	0.0	−0.3	−0.3	−0.3	0.0	−0.1	**0.2**	0.1
pen-cloned	**56.9**	26.5	1.6	−2.5	28.0	44.0	39.2	**52.8**
hammer-cloned	0.8	0.3	0.3	0.3	0.4	0.4	**2.1**	5.5
door-cloned	−0.1	−0.1	−0.1	−0.1	0.0	0.0	**0.4**	2.2
relocate-cloned	−0.1	−0.3	−0.3	−0.3	−0.2	−0.3	−0.1	−0.2
Avg	36.7	38.4	0.5	−0.5	32.2	39.7	**40.3**	**45.1**

5.3   Results

In a nutshell, our approach is a long-horizon route-constrained policy for learning from offline data. To evaluate our method, we need to answer two questions through experiments. 1) Is the temporal constraint of the policy important for non-Markovian demonstration data? Is our approach efficient on non-Markovian data from human experts? 2) Is it efficient for goal-reaching continuous control tasks on different types of offline demonstration datasets, and has it alleviated the dilemma of Offline RL caused by the lack of exploration? We compare our approach with state-of-the-art methods: BC, BCQ, BEAR, behavior-regularized actor-critic (BRAC) [23], advantage-weighted regression (AWR) [17], and CQL. Table 1 shows normalized scores results on the Adroit domain for different types of different tasks, and we have bolded the top 2 methods on each dataset. The results provide obvious evidence to answer the above two questions, and we discuss the following comparisons to analyze the Long-horizon Route-constrained policy.

Comparison for the Temporal Constraint Requirement for Different Type Data. Our optimal model for the -expert datasets used H = 1, which means to predict only one subgoal during route planning, while for the -human and -cloned datasets H¿1. The reason is that the -expert datasets are generated by RL policy. Their decision process is closer to the Markov process. They select the action with the highest Q value at a state. While -human and -cloned datasets are closer to the human expert's decision-making process and involve human habits and subjective consciousness. Figure 4 shows the trajectory characteristics of the -expert data of hammer tasks. The behavioral policy from the -expert dataset tends to choose an action that is most advantageous to reach the goal at the current state. The RL policy prefers to hammer the nail into the board in a single stroke, but it is also easier to produce bad states such as robotic arm twitching. In contrast, the human experts and the IL behavioral policy in the -cloned dataset prefer to hammer the nail with several times. Behavioral policies with different characteristics require the agent with different temporal modeling abilities. The agent policy learning from -expert data should capture less temporal information. Too much temporal information will make the agent fall into the trap that makes the agent treats bad states as goals. Therefore we used H = 1. And our method increased the number of subgoal predictions on the other two datasets. In this way, our policy has not only constrained the state space but also learned the characteristics of human expert demonstrations through temporal information.

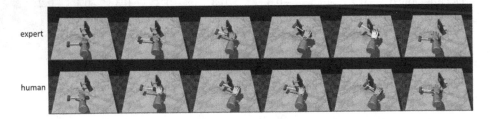

Fig. 4. The hammer trajectory from -expert data and -human data. The behavioral policy in -expert hammers the nail into the board in a single stroke while the human expert hammers several times.

As shown in Fig. 5, the control trajectory characteristics of the agent policy we learned from the -expert data are similar to those of the -expert behavioral

Fig. 5. The trajectories generated by our approach learning from -expert and -human data.

policy, which prefers to hammer in a single stroke. The trajectory characteristics of the agent policy learned from -human data are also similar to its behavioral policy. It means that the agent policy prefers to hammer several times. The agent policy learned from -human data is not efficient due to temporal capture, which generates some redundant states. But it can consequently get back to the correct trajectory from the redundant states.

Comparison with the Baseline. The baseline of our method is BCQ. At a state, BCQ generates actions through a conditional VAE and then selects the action with the highest Q value. And our approach first predicts H subgoals and then takes them as constraints to generate actions. Our approach imitates how the behavioral policy generates actions on the one hand. On the other hand, it constrains the state space at testing close to the demonstration data state space. This double constraint reduces the occurrence probability of OOD data. The results show that on -expert data, our approach is comparable to BCQ, and on other types of data, our approach outperforms BCQ overall. The more disadvantageous performance is in the pen-human dataset. The reason is that the pen task focuses on the orientation of the pen, which has a smaller state space, so in this case, the route-constrained policy is less helpful for learning. The scale of the -human dataset is also smaller, and our method contains two Q-networks, where the dataset scale affects the Q-network training. Nevertheless, we still ranked the top 2 performance on pen-human.

Comparison with State-of-the-art Methods. We also obtained comparable performance compared with SOTA methods on the -expert data. And we gained scores over 100 on all tasks, which means our agent policy outperformed the behavioral policy on the -expert data. Furthermore, our method has a significant advantage on the -human and -cloned data. Neither our method nor SOTA methods can obtain positive scores on relocate-cloned data. It indicates that there is still much room to improve with offline learning from demonstration data. In addition, our method earned the highest average score. These comparisons with IL and offline RL methods show that our long-horizon route-constrained policy alleviates the distribution shift issue and effectively mitigates the dilemma of learning on non-Markovian demonstration data for offline RL.

6 Conclusion

In this paper, we describe the extrapolation error issue and the difficulty of learning from different types of demonstration data. Current Imitation Learning and Offline Reinforcement Learning methods are facing the challenges of these issues. So we propose a Long-horizon Route-constrained policy based on these issues. The policy contains a route planning model, a route evaluation model and a subgoal-constrained action generation model. LHRC can reduce extrapolation error through route constraints. And it is adaptable to non-Markovian demonstration data through temporal modeling. We will discuss the state space and the reward functions for the realistic environment in the future. Moreover, we are looking forward to transferring the model from the simulated environment to the real scene.

Acknowledgements. This research work is supported by Guangdong Province Science and Technology Plan projects (2020A0505100015).

References

1. Agarwal, R., Schuurmans, D., Norouzi, M.: An optimistic perspective on offline reinforcement learning. In: International Conference on Machine Learning, pp. 104–114. PMLR (2020)
2. Doersch, C.: Tutorial on variational autoencoders. arXiv preprint arXiv:1606.05908 (2016)
3. Fu, J., Kumar, A., Nachum, O., Tucker, G., Levine, S.: D4rl: datasets for deep data-driven reinforcement learning. arXiv preprint arXiv:2004.07219 (2020)
4. Fujimoto, S., Meger, D., Precup, D.: Off-policy deep reinforcement learning without exploration. In: International Conference on Machine Learning, pp. 2052–2062. PMLR (2019)
5. Haarnoja, T., Zhou, A., Abbeel, P., Levine, S.: Soft actor-critic: off-policy maximum entropy deep reinforcement learning with a stochastic actor. In: International Conference on Machine Learning, pp. 1861–1870. PMLR (2018)
6. Huang, D.A., et al.: Motion reasoning for goal-based imitation learning. In: 2020 IEEE International Conference on Robotics and Automation (ICRA), pp. 4878–4884. IEEE (2020)
7. Jin, Y., Yang, Z., Wang, Z.: Is pessimism provably efficient for offline rl? In: International Conference on Machine Learning, pp. 5084–5096. PMLR (2021)
8. Kumar, A., Fu, J., Soh, M., Tucker, G., Levine, S.: Stabilizing off-policy q-learning via bootstrapping error reduction. In: Advances in Neural Information Processing Systems, vol. 32 (2019)
9. Kumar, A., Zhou, A., Tucker, G., Levine, S.: Conservative q-learning for offline reinforcement learning. Adv. Neural. Inf. Process. Syst. **33**, 1179–1191 (2020)
10. Levine, S.: Reinforcement learning and control as probabilistic inference: tutorial and review. arXiv preprint arXiv:1805.00909 (2018)
11. Levine, S., Kumar, A., Tucker, G., Fu, J.: Offline reinforcement learning: tutorial, review, and perspectives on open problems. arXiv preprint arXiv:2005.01643 (2020)
12. Lillicrap, T.P., et al.: Continuous control with deep reinforcement learning. arXiv preprint arXiv:1509.02971 (2015)

13. Mandlekar, A., et al.: Iris: implicit reinforcement without interaction at scale for learning control from offline robot manipulation data. In: 2020 IEEE International Conference on Robotics and Automation (ICRA), pp. 4414–4420. IEEE (2020)
14. Mandlekar, A., Xu, D., Martín-Martín, R., Savarese, S., Fei-Fei, L.: Learning to generalize across long-horizon tasks from human demonstrations. arXiv preprint arXiv:2003.06085 (2020)
15. Mandlekar, A., et al.: What matters in learning from offline human demonstrations for robot manipulation. arXiv preprint arXiv:2108.03298 (2021)
16. Mnih, V., et al.: Human-level control through deep reinforcement learning. Nature **518**(7540), 529–533 (2015)
17. Peng, X.B., Kumar, A., Zhang, G., Levine, S.: Advantage-weighted regression: simple and scalable off-policy reinforcement learning. arXiv preprint arXiv:1910.00177 (2019)
18. Pomerleau, D.A.: ALVINN: an autonomous land vehicle in a neural network. In: Advances in Neural Information Processing Systems, vol. 1 (1988)
19. Rajeswaran, A., et al.: Learning complex dexterous manipulation with deep reinforcement learning and demonstrations. arXiv preprint arXiv:1709.10087 (2017)
20. Shao, L., Migimatsu, T., Zhang, Q., Yang, K., Bohg, J.: Concept2robot: learning manipulation concepts from instructions and human demonstrations. Int. J. Robot. Res. **40**(12–14), 1419–1434 (2021)
21. Smith, L., Dhawan, N., Zhang, M., Abbeel, P., Levine, S.: Avid: learning multi-stage tasks via pixel-level translation of human videos. arXiv preprint arXiv:1912.04443 (2019)
22. Wang, X., Lee, K., Hakhamaneshi, K., Abbeel, P., Laskin, M.: Skill preferences: learning to extract and execute robotic skills from human feedback. In: Conference on Robot Learning, pp. 1259–1268. PMLR (2022)
23. Wu, Y., Tucker, G., Nachum, O.: Behavior regularized offline reinforcement learning. arXiv preprint arXiv:1911.11361 (2019)
24. Yu, T., et al.: One-shot imitation from observing humans via domain-adaptive meta-learning. arXiv preprint arXiv:1802.01557 (2018)

Model-Based Offline Adaptive Policy Optimization with Episodic Memory

Hongye Cao[1], Qianru Wei[1], Jiangbin Zheng[1], and Yanqing Shi[2(✉)]

[1] School of Software, Northwestern Polytechnical University, Xi'an 710072, China
`2020204278@mail.nwpu.edu.cn`, `{weiqianru,zhengjb}@nwpu.edu.cn`
[2] College of Information Management, Nanjing Agriculture University, Nanjing 210095, China
`yqs4869@njau.edu.cn`

Abstract. Offline reinforcement learning (RL) is a promising direction to apply RL to real-world by avoiding online expensive and dangerous exploration. However, offline RL is challenging due to extrapolation errors caused by the distribution shift between offline datasets and states visited by behavior policy. Existing model-based offline RL methods set pessimistic constraints of the learned model within the support region of the offline data to avoid extrapolation errors, but these approaches limit the generalization potential of the policy in out-of-distribution (OOD) region. The artificial fixed uncertainty calculation and the sparse reward problem of low-quality datasets in existing methods have weak adaptability to different learning tasks. Hence, a model-based offline adaptive policy optimization with episodic memory is proposed in this work to improve generalization of the policy. Inspired by active learning, constraint strength is proposed to trade off the return and risk adaptively to balance the robustness and generalization ability of the policy. Further, episodic memory is applied to capture successful experience to improve adaptability. Extensive experiments on D4RL datasets demonstrate that the proposed method outperforms existing state-of-the-art methods and achieves superior performance on challenging tasks requiring OOD generalization.

Keywords: Offline reinforcement learning · Constraint strength · Episodic memory

1 Introduction

With the development of reinforcement learning (RL), the application of RL methods to real-world applications has received more attention [10]. Existing RL methods have been applied in the fields of computer vision [17], robotics [5], and natural language processing [16]. However, applying RL to key areas such as healthcare and autonomous driving is difficult [12]. The challenge is to reduce risky, costly trial and error in interacting with the real world. Therefore, researchers propose a learning mode that uses the collected datasets for reinforcement policy learning.

Early research focused on using off-policy methods for policy learning on collected datasets [9]. However, Fujimoto et al. [4] found that off-policy methods incur extrapolation errors caused by the distribution shift between offline datasets and states visited by

E. Pimenidis et al. (Eds.): ICANN 2022, LNCS 13530, pp. 50–62, 2022.
https://doi.org/10.1007/978-3-031-15931-2_5

behavior policy during training. This limitation makes the off-policy methods unstable and divergent. Subsequently, the offline RL method proposes to constrain the policy to the behavioral policy within the dataset to avoid the extrapolation errors [4].

Model-free offline RL methods impose conservative constraints on the value function [8]. This approach results in an overly conservative policy due to the constraints of the value function. Yu et al. [19] proved that model-based methods are well-suited for the batch offline settings. Model-based offline RL methods avoid extrapolation errors by computing model uncertainty to constrain policies within the support region of the offline data. Similar to supervised learning methods, the state-action transition relationships in batch data can be efficiently mined to align with behavioral policies [18]. However, behavioral policies in datasets may not be optimal and these approaches limit the generalization potential of the policy in out-of-distribution (OOD) regions of datasets. Due to the sparse rewards of low-quality datasets and the artificial fixed uncertainty calculation, these methods have weak adaptability to different learning tasks [11].

Hence, Model-based offline Adaptive policy optimization with Episodic Memory (MAEM) is proposed in this work to improve the generalization ability of the policy. Ensemble models are built to capture state-action transition information in the collected dataset and rollout to explore OOD regions. Inspired by active learning [1], constraint strength is proposed to adaptively adjust the trade-off between the return and risk of the model according to the KL divergence [13] in the rollout. The adaptive policy based on constraint strength can balance the robustness and generalization ability. To solve the adaptive convergence and the sparse reward problem, episodic memory [11] is further applied to capture successful policy experience to speed up adaptive policy optimization. Episodic memory stores the best rewards in the past to improve sample efficiency, and the agent can repeat the best results without gradient-based learning. Rollout based on successful experience can safely conduct OOD exploration to adapt to different offline tasks quickly. The main contributions of this paper are as follows:

- We propose the model-based offline adaptive policy optimization with episodic memory. Constraint strength is proposed to adaptively adjust during policy learning to balance return and risk for OOD regions exploration.
- Episodic memory is applied to store successful policy experience to improve sample efficiency and adapt policy to different RL tasks quickly. This adaptive adjustment and experience reuse algorithm improves the generalization ability of the policy.
- Extensive experiments on D4RL datasets demonstrate that the proposed method outperforms existing state-of-the-art (SOTA) methods and achieves superior performance on challenging tasks requiring OOD generalization. Ablation experiments demonstrate the contribution of components in the proposed method.

2 Related Work

2.1 Model-Based Offline RL

Model-based offline RL approaches use supervised learning paradigm to learn dynamic models [19]. The dynamic model can act as a simulator of the environment when the policy is updating. Existing model-based offline RL methods fall into two categories. One is to quantify the uncertainty in the policy optimization of the dynamic model to limit the divergence of the behavioral policy [2]. Another approach is similar to the model-free approach to constrain the state-action function of the policy [18]. However, artificial fixed constraints limit the generalization ability of the policy. Existing methods are less adaptable to different tasks due to sparse rewards on low-quality datasets. Hence, model-based offline adaptive policy optimization with episodic memory is proposed in this paper to improve adaptability and generalization ability of the policy.

2.2 Episodic Memory-Based Methods

Inspired by psychobiology [11], episodic memory-based methods store experiences in a nonparametric table to retrieve past successful strategies quickly when encountering similar states. Episodic RL proposes a framework to retrieve past successful strategies rapidly to improve sample efficiency. Episodic memory stores the best rewards in the past, and the agent can repeat the best results without gradient-based learning. The reuse of successful experience can adapt to different tasks quickly. This approach can deal with the sparse reward of low-quality datasets.

However, for RL agents in continuous state-action space, observing the same state-action pair twice is difficult. Humans can connect and recall similar experiences from different time periods without encountering the same events again [14]. Inspired by this generalized learning ability of humans, Hu et al. [7] proposed generalizable episodic memory, a new framework that integrates the generalization ability of neural networks and the fast retrieval of episodic memory. Hence, to solve the adaptive convergence and the sparse reward problem, episodic memory is further applied to capture successful policy experience to speed up adaptive policy optimization.

3 Preliminaries

In the standard RL framework, an agent interacts with the environment to perform a Markov decision process. The standard Markov decision process (MDP) is defined as $M = (S, A, T, r, \mu, \gamma)$, where S represents the state space, A represents the action space, T $(s'|s, a)$ is the transition dynamic model, μ is the initial state distribution and $r(s, a)$ is the reward function. $\gamma \in (0, 1)$ is the discount factor. The goal of RL is to learn a policy π $(a | s)$ that can maximize the expected discounted return $\eta_M (\pi) := E[\sum_{t=0}^{\infty} \gamma^t r(s_t, a_t)]$. $V_M^{\pi} (s) = E[\sum_{t=0}^{\infty} \gamma^t r(s_t, a_t)|s_0 = s]$ is the expected discounted return under policy π when the state starts from s.

In offline RL, offline reinforcement policy learning is performed through the collected datasets and the model does not interact with the real environment. We define the offline dataset $D_{env} = \{(s, a, r, s')\}$ which contains all the offline collected state-action distributions. In the model-based approach, $\widehat{T}(s'|s, a)$ is the dynamic model estimated from transitions in the D_{env}. The goal is to get a policy that maximizes $\eta_M (\pi)$ with the offline dataset D_{env}.

4 Approach

Existing model-based methods constrain the policy by computing the uncertainty of the model. These approaches limit the generalization potential of the policy in OOD regions. These methods have weak adaptability to different learning tasks due to the sparse rewards of low-quality datasets and the artificial fixed uncertainty calculation. Our goal is to build a model-based policy optimization approach that utilizes data efficiently and enables the safe exploration of OOD regions without extrapolation error.

In this section, constraint strength is first introduced into policy optimization. How to adjust the constraint strength adaptively to balance the return and risk of the model is discussed (in Sect. 4.1). Then, episodic memory is applied to capture successful policy experience to improve adaptability (in Sect. 4.2). Finally, the proposed practical algorithm and implementation details are presented (in Sect. 4.3).

4.1 Adaptive Constraint Strength Optimization

Offline RL methods perform policy learning from offline collected datasets. It is vulnerable to extrapolation error because of no interaction with the environment. We need to add constraints on policy learning to reduce the interference of extrapolation errors [18, 19]. First, uncertainty calculations are introduced into the model to avoid the effects of model extrapolation errors. M and $\widehat{M}$ are the optimal policy MDP and the learned MDP with same reward function, respectively. The estimator error for the true return between the optimal model and the actual model is defined.

$$S_{\widehat{M}}^{\pi}(s, a) := E_{(s,a)\sim\widehat{T}}[V_{\widehat{M}}^{\pi}(s')] - E_{(s,a)\sim T}[V_M^{\pi}(s')], \tag{1}$$

and we can deduce the following equation based on discounted return and state-value function.

$$\eta_{\widehat{M}}(\pi) - \eta_M(\pi) = \gamma E_{(s,a)\sim\widehat{T}}[S_{\widehat{M}}^{\pi}(s, a)]. \tag{2}$$

From the error estimate between two models and the expected discounted return under policy π, the discounted return can be derived as follows.

$$\eta_M(\pi) = E_{(s,a)\sim\widehat{T}}[r(s, a) - \gamma S_{\widehat{M}}^{\pi}(s, a)] \geq E_{(s,a)\sim\widehat{T}}[r(s, a) - \alpha u(s, a)] \geq \eta_{\widehat{M}}(\pi), \tag{3}$$

where α is the constraint strength and $u(s, a)$ is the uncertainty. The error between the two models is determined by the return. Therefore, uncertainty is set for the return between the models. Now, the goal is to learn a policy that can maximize $E_{(s,a)\sim\widehat{T}}[r(s, a) - \alpha u(s, a)]$. Uncertainty $u(s, a)$ is an artificial fixed calculation based on reward function [19]. How to adjust the constraint strength for OOD generalization is important. Inspired by active learning [1], an adaptive optimization is set up during rollout according to the KL divergence to adjust the constraint strength automatically.

The mechanism of adaptive adjustment is that when the model achieves better rollout return results under the current policy, the model can effectively perform OOD exploration [2]. The constraint strength of the model can be relaxed to better improve the scalability of the model. On the contrary, when the model achieves poor rollout return results under the current policy, the model is affected by extrapolation error and is doing harmful exploration. The constraint strength of the model must be strengthened to avoid further interference by extrapolation error and prevent the model from divergence due to the interference of extrapolation error. The exploration in the OOD region and extrapolation error avoidance are effectively balanced through adaptive adjustment of the constraint strength.

KL divergence [1, 13] is used to optimize the constraint strength of the model adaptively. KL divergence $D(P||Q)$ is proposed to measure the difference between probability distributions. It has a clear physical meaning in information theory and is used to measure the number of additional bits required to encode the average of samples from the P distribution using a Q distribution-based encoding. In the trust region policy optimization algorithm [13], the average KL divergence is used to constrain the update of the policy. The average KL divergence is computed as follows.

$$P_{KL} = \frac{1}{N} \sum_{n=1}^{N} D(P_{\theta(n)}||P_N), \tag{4}$$

where

$$P_N(y_i|x) = \frac{1}{N} \sum_{n=1}^{N} P_{\theta(n)}(y_i|x), \tag{5}$$

where $D(P_{\theta(n)}||P_N)$ represents the KL divergence of two probability distributions.

Calculate the KL divergence between the return distribution of the current rollout and the previous rollouts. The KL divergence is normalized to optimize the constraint strength of the model adaptively as follows.

$$\text{norm}\left(KL(M, r_j), K_{model}\right) = log \frac{P_{KL}^M}{\frac{1}{N} \sum_{n=1}^{N} P_{KL}^n}, \tag{6}$$

$$\alpha = (1 + \text{norm}\left(KL(M, r_j), K_{model}\right))\alpha, \tag{7}$$

where K_{model} is the KL set to store the KL divergency. When the KL divergence of the return value of the current policy increases compared to the average KL divergence of the previous policy, the model suffers from greater extrapolation error interference. Therefore, the constraint strength must be increased to constrain the exploration of the OOD region during rollout. When the KL divergence is reduced, the model achieves better results during rollout. Reducing the constraint strength can improve the safe OOD exploration for generalization of the policy.

4.2 Episodic Memory

Constraint strength is proposed to balance the return and risk of the policy. However, due to the adaptive adjustment and sparse reward in low-quality datasets, policy convergence bootstrapping remains challenging over long periods of time. How to use the data better for adaptive policy optimization is extremely critical. Hence, value-based episodic memory [11] is applied to avoid overly optimistic estimates during the policy optimization. For policy learning based on episodic memory, policy can be strictly within offline trajectories to avoid overly optimistic estimates, and the optimality of episodic memory can ensure safe exploration of OOD regions to avoid divergence.

At each step, the larger value between the best return on the current trajectory and Q_β is taken. Q_β is generalized from similar experience and can be defined as a value estimate for counterfactual trajectories [11]. This process proceeds recursively from the last step to the first step, forming an implicit planning scheme in episodic memory that aggregates optimal experiences along and across trajectories. The entire backpropagation process can be written in the following formula.

$$R_t = \begin{cases} r_t & \text{if } t = T \\ r_t + \gamma \max(R_{t+1}, Q_\beta(s_{t+1}, a_{t+1})) & \text{if } t < T \end{cases}, \qquad (8)$$

where t represents the step size along the trajectory, T is the trajectory length, and Q_β generalizes from similar experience. Furthermore, the backpropagation process in Eq. (8) can be expanded and rewritten as follows:

$$V_{t,h} = \begin{cases} Q_\beta(s_t, a_t) & \text{if } h = 0 \\ r_t + \gamma V_{t+1,h-1} & \text{if } h > 0 \end{cases}, \qquad (9)$$

$$R_t = V_{t,h^*}, \ h^* = \arg\max_{h>0} V_{t,h}. \qquad (10)$$

where h represents the length of rollout steps. $Q_\beta(s_t, a_t) = 0$ and $V_{t,h} = 0$ if $t > T$. The best state-value experience will be stored in episodic memory.

4.3 Practical Implementation

We describe a practical implementation of MAEM driven by the above analysis. First, ensemble models are trained on the offline dataset in a supervised mode. The ensemble models can effectively explore the OOD region. Supervised learning mode can efficiently mine all state-action transitions in the data. After obtaining N ensemble models, the model is rolled out to explore the OOD region based on the episodic memory D_{em}. The model is constrained to produce extrapolation errors by computing the uncertainty during model rollout, and the KL divergence is applied to optimize constraint strength for adaptive optimization. In the process of rollout, the uncertainty and KL divergence are calculated to optimize the constraining of the policy learning. Finally, SAC [6] algorithm is used to update policy π with D_{env} and D_{em} until convergence. Meanwhile, the episodic memory is updated with a memory update frequency p.

The goal of designing uncertainty estimators is to capture the epistemic uncertainty and arbitrary uncertainty of real dynamics. The bootstrap ensemble and the learning variance of the Gaussian probability model are combined to perform uncertainty calculations theoretically [19]. The uncertainty estimator is designed as $u(s, a) = max_{i=1}^{N} ||\Sigma_\varphi^i(s, a)||_F$, the maximum standard deviation of the learned models in the ensemble. Algorithm 1 Model-Based Offline Adaptive Policy Optimization with Episodic Memory and Algorithm 2 Update Episodic Memory are listed below.

Algorithm 1 Model-Based Offline Adaptive Policy Optimization with Episodic Memory

---

Require: Offline dataset D_{env}, constraint strength α, rollout horizon h.

1: Train an ensemble of N dynamic models $\{M_i\}_{i=1}^N$ on the dataset D_{env}.

2: Initialize critic network V_θ and actor network π_φ with random parameters θ, φ.

3: Initialize episodic memory D_{em} and KL set K_{model}.

4: **for** $t = 1, 2, 3 \ldots$ **do**

5:     Sample state s_1, action a_0 from D_{env} for the initialization of the rollout.

6:     **for** $j = 1, 2 \ldots, h$ **do**

7:         Sample a transition $(s_j, a_j, r_j, \ s'_j, R_j)$ from D_{em}

8:         Randomly select dynamics M from $\{M_i\}_{i=1}^N$ and sample $s_{j+1}, r_j \sim M(s_j, a_j)$

9:         $r_j \leftarrow r_j - \alpha u(s_j, a_j)$

10:        Feedback (s_j, a_j, r_j, s_{j+1}) to adaptive adjustment

11:        $\alpha \leftarrow (1+\text{norm}\,(KL\,(M, r_j), K_{model}))\,\alpha$

12:        $K_{model} = \{KL\,(M, r_j)\} \cup K_{model}$

13:    **end for**

14:    Use SAC to update critic networks V_θ and actor network π_φ with $D_{env} \cup D_{em}$

15:    **if** $t \bmod p = 0$ **then**

16:        Update Episodic Memory

17:    **end if**

18: **end for**

Algorithm 2 Update Episodic Memory

1: **for** trajectories τ in episodic memory D_{em} **do**

2:     **for** s_j, a_j, r_j, s_{j+1} in reversed(τ) **do**

3:         Compute R_j with Equation (10) and save into episodic memory D_{em}

4:     **end for**

5: **end for**

---

5   Experiment

In the experiments, we aim to study the following questions: (1) How does the proposed method MAEM perform compared with SOTA methods on the standard offline RL benchmark? Moreover, how does MAEM perform on low-quality datasets? (2) Can MAEM achieve good performance on challenging tasks that require the generalization of OOD behavior? (3) What is the performance effect of each component in MAEM?

5.1   Experimental Dataset and Settings

Our method is evaluated on a large subset of datasets in the D4RL [3] benchmark based on the MuJoCo simulator [15], including three environments (halfcheetah, hopper, and walker2d) and four dataset types (random, medium, mixed and med-expert), applying

12 problem settings. The datasets are generated as follows: **random:** roll out a random policy for 1M steps; **medium:** train the policy using SAC, then push it out 1M steps; **mixed:** use SAC to train a policy until a certain performance threshold is reached; **med-expert:** combine 1M rollout samples from a fully trained policy with another 1M rollout samples from a partially trained policy or a random policy.

In all domains, each model in the ensemble is parameterized as a 4-layer feedforward neural network with 200 hidden units. The discount factor is set to 0.99. The constraint strength initialization is initialized between 1 and 5. The epoch length is set to 1000. The rollout length is set between 1 and 5. The frequency p of memory update is set to 10. For the SAC update, we sample a batch of 256 transformations, 5% of which are from D_{env} and the rest from D_{em}.

5.2 Comparative Methods

Comparative experiments are conducted with the following SOTA methods.

- BC. Behavioral policies are imitated through supervised learning and make it the offline version.
- CQL [8]. A model-free offline RL method learns action-value functions through regularization to obtain conservative policies.
- SAC [6]. The method performs typical SAC updates using static datasets.
- MOPO [19]. A model-based offline RL method learns an ensemble model through supervised learning and incorporating uncertainty penalties into the return.
- COMBO [18]. A conservative offline model-based policy optimization method regularizes the value functions of unsupported state-action tuples generated under the learned model.

5.3 Comparative Experiment

The results of the comparative experiments are shown in Table 1. Compared with other offline RL methods, among the 12 tasks, MAEM has the highest value in 8 tasks. Compared with the model-based offline RL algorithms, MAEM is optimal in 8 tasks out of 12 tasks. This result shows that the proposed model-based method outperforms the SOTA model-based methods.

Compared with model-free offline RL methods, MAEM achieves the best value in 10 out of 12 tasks. This outcome shows that MAEM can achieve better results than the model-free methods. The method of policy learning through supervised learning and adaptive adjustment can effectively implement offline RL. Moreover, compared with the offline version of BC, the proposed method has 11 optimal values on 12 tasks. These results demonstrate the superior generalization ability of MAEM.

Moreover, in order to verify the effect of policy optimization on low-quality datasets with sparse rewards, comparison is made with model-based approaches MOPO and COMBO, which explored in the OOD region, on three low-quality, high-complexity datasets. The results in Fig. 1 show that MOPO with artificial fixed uncertainty does not perform well and is prone to divergence. MAEM outperforms MOPO on all three datasets. On the hopper-random dataset, MAEM achieves similar performance to COMBO and performs more stable than COMBO. MAEM outperforms COMBO on the other two datasets. The complexity of the Walker2d-random dataset is high and the task is difficult to perform. The policy learning of MAEM on this dataset is slow but eventually converges stably and outperforms MOPO and COMBO. Adaptive adjustment of constraint strength adapts the policy to low-quality datasets. Crucially, episodic memory stores empirical data for policy optimization to overcome the sparse reward problem of low-quality datasets to ensure safe OOD exploration. Overall, the proposed MAEM method outperforms existing SOTA offline RL methods.

Table 1. Comparative experiment results on D4RL datasets. Each number is the normalized score proposed in [3] of the policy at the last iteration of training, averaged over 3 random seeds. We bold the highest score across all methods.

Environment	Dataset	MAEM	COMBO	MOPO	SAC	CQL	BC
HalfCheetah	random	**42.1**	38.8	35.4	30.5	35.4	2.1
HalfCheetah	medium	46.0	**54.2**	42.3	-4.3	44.4	36.1
HalfCheetah	mixed	**62.2**	55.1	53.1	-2.4	46.2	38.4
HalfCheetah	med-expert	**99.3**	90.0	63.3	1.8	62.4	35.8
Hopper	random	14.2	**17.9**	11.7	11.3	10.8	1.6
Hopper	medium	**97.4**	94.9	28.0	0.8	58.0	29.0
Hopper	mixed	**102.0**	73.1	67.5	1.9	48.6	11.8
Hopper	med-expert	55.4	111.1	23.7	1.6	98.7	**111.9**
Walker2d	random	**21.9**	7.0	13.6	4.1	7.0	9.8
Walker2d	medium	25.4	75.5	11.8	0.9	**79.2**	6.6
Walker2d	mixed	**69.8**	56.0	39.0	3.5	26.7	11.3
Walker2d	med-expert	**116.5**	96.1	44.6	-0.1	111.0	6.4

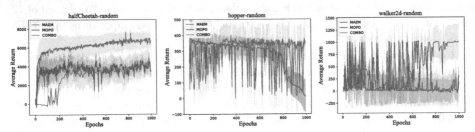

Fig. 1. Learning curves on low-quality datasets. Each number is the averaged return during training, averaged over 3 random seeds and the shadow is the standard error.

5.4 Evaluation on Tasks Requiring OOD Generalization

To answer question (2), two environments are used, halfcheetah-jump (half-jump) and ant-angle, which requires the agent not only to execute the behavioral policy of the dataset but also explore the OOD region to perform tasks that are different from the behavioral policy [19]. The behavioral policy is trained with SAC for 1M steps and takes the full replay buffer as the trajectories for offline dataset. These trajectories were assigned new rewards to motivate cheetah to jump and ant to run toward the upper right corner at a 30-degree angle. Comparative experiments are conducted with model-based algorithms COMBO, MOPO and model-free algorithms CQL, SAC.

Table 2. Average returns of half-jump and ant-angle that require OOD generalization. All results are averaged over 3 random seeds. We bold the highest score across all methods.

Environment	Batch mean	Batch max	MAEM (ours)	COMBO	MOPO	CQL	SAC
Half-jump	-1022.6	1808.6	**5789.1**	5392.7	4016.6	741.1	-3588.2
Ant-angle	866.7	2311.9	**3086.4**	2764.8	2530.9	2473.4	-966.4

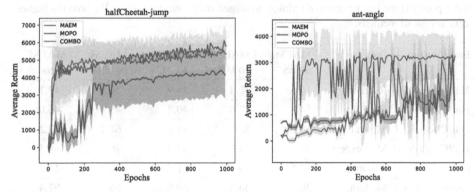

Fig. 2. Learning curves on half-jump and ant-angle tasks. Each number is the averaged return during training, averaged over 3 random seeds and the shadow is the standard error.

The results in Table 2 show that MAEM outperforms other methods on both tasks. Compared with CQL, MAEM improves two tasks by 87.2% and 19.9%. Model-based methods are more suitable for OOD generalization in offline environments. The learning curves of MAEM, MOPO and COMBO in Fig. 2. Show that MAEM has a better and more stable policy learning effect on both tasks. The constraint strength can be adaptively adjusted according to the changes in the policy learning process to balance the robustness and generalization of the policy. Episodic memory can store excellent empirical data to speed up adaptive policy optimization. These results demonstrate that the proposed method can achieve safe and effective generalization in the OOD region.

5.5 Ablation Study

To answer question (3), the following ablation experiments are set up. We denote no ES as the method without ensemble models, no UN as the method without uncertainty, no ACS as the method without adaptive constraint strength and no EM as the method without episodic memory.

The results of ablation experiments are shown in Table 3. The method without ensemble models has the worst results on 12 datasets. This finding shows that exploration process of rolling out the ensemble models is an indispensable and important part of offline RL. The method without uncertainty is prone to extrapolation errors and has a poor performance. Compared with MAEM, the performance of the method without ACS drops significantly on all 12 tasks. This result indicates that the adaptive adjustment of the constraint strength has a greater impact on the generalization ability of the model. The method without EM achieves better results than the three other types of ablation methods but remains inferior to the MAEM method. The method without EM outperforms COMBO in 6 out of 12 tasks and outperforms CQL in 7 out of 12 tasks. This result suggests that episodic memory enables safe exploration in the OOD regions by capturing empirical data, but it also shows that the uncertainty constraints of the model have a greater impact on policy optimization.

Table 3. Ablation experiment results on D4RL datasets. Each number is the normalized score [3] of the policy at the last iteration of training, averaged over 3 random seeds. We bold the highest score across all methods.

Environment	Dataset	MAEM: no ES	MAEM: no UN	MAEM: no ACS	MAEM: no EM	MAEM (ours)
Half Cheetah	Random	16.6	32.3	34.9	30.1	**42.1**
HalfCheetah	Medium	14.1	34.0	40.7	45.9	**46.0**
HalfCheetah	Mixed	18.6	53.1	51.1	61.1	**62.2**
HalfCheetah	Med-expert	33.2	74.6	77.3	98.9	**99.3**
Hopper	Random	3.1	9.3	11.7	9.0	**14.2**
Hopper	Medium	30.9	43.3	29.0	85.0	**97.4**
Hopper	Mixed	34.0	49.5	67.5	101.7	**102.0**
Hopper	Med-expert	12.4	24.7	29.7	43.7	**55.4**
Walker2d	Random	4.1	8.1	13.6	13.3	**21.9**
Walker2d	Medium	4.0	9.0	12.7	20.2	**25.4**
Walker2d	Mixed	10.2	28.9	39.0	68.6	**69.8**
Walker2d	Med-expert	30.5	48.8	50.6	106.8	**116.5**

Moreover, no EM method achieves poor results on low-quality dataset tasks. This finding further shows that episodic memory can effectively improve the policy adaptability on low-quality datasets. Overall, the components in MAEM greatly contribute to improving the adaptability and generalization ability of the policy.

6 Conclusion and Future Work

In this paper, we propose a novel offline RL method, model-based offline adaptive policy optimization with episodic memory to improve the generalization ability. Constraint strength is proposed to balance return and risk adaptively according to the changes during OOD generalization, and episodic memory is applied to improve adaptability and speed up adaptive policy optimization. Experiments on D4RL datasets demonstrate that MAEM outperforms existing SOTA offline model-based and model-free methods. Moreover, MAEM achieves superior performance on tasks requiring OOD generalization. Finally, ablation experiments demonstrate the contribution of the MAEM components. In future work, we will study adjusting the constraint strength better and improve the generalization ability to apply this method to more practical offline RL tasks.

Acknowledgments. The work is supported by the National Social Science Foundation of China under Grant No. 21CTQ024.

References

1. Beygelzimer, A., Dasgupta, S., Langford, J.: Importance weighted active learning. In: Proceedings of the 26th Annual International Conference on Machine Learning, pp. 49–56 (2009)
2. Chen, X.-H., et al.: Offline model-based adaptable policy learning. In: Advances in Neural Information Processing Systems, vol. 34 (2021)
3. Fu, J., Kumar, A., Nachum, O., Tucker, G., Levine, S.: D4RL: datasets for deep data-driven reinforcement learning. arXiv preprint arXiv:2004.07219 (2020)
4. Fujimoto, S., Meger, D., Precup, D.: Off-policy deep reinforcement learning without exploration. In: International Conference on Machine Learning, pp. 2052–2062. PMLR (2019)
5. Garaffa, L.C., Basso, M., Konzen, A.A., De Freitas, E.P.: Reinforcement learning for mobile robotics exploration: a survey. IEEE Trans. Neural Netw. Learn. Syst. **PP**(99), 1–15 (2021)
6. Haarnoja, T., Zhou, A., Abbeel, P., Levine, S.: Soft actor-critic: off-policy maximum entropy deep reinforcement learning with a stochastic actor. In: International Conference on Machine Learning, pp. 1861–1870. PMLR (2018)
7. Hu, H., Ye, J., Zhu, G., Ren, Z., Zhang, C.: Generalizable episodic memory for deep reinforcement learning. arXiv preprint arXiv:2103.06469 (2021)
8. Kumar, A., Zhou, A., Tucker, G., Levine, S.: Conservative q-learning for offline reinforcement learning. arXiv preprint arXiv:2006.04779 (2020)
9. Lange, S., Gabel, T., Riedmiller, M.: Batch reinforcement learning. In: Wiering, M., van Otterlo, M. (eds.) Reinforcement Learning, Adaptation, Learning, and Optimization, pp. 45–73. Springer, Heidelberg (2012). https://doi.org/10.1007/978-3-642-27645-3_2
10. Levine, S., Kumar, A., Tucker, G., Fu, J.: Offline reinforcement learning: tutorial, review, and perspectives on open problems. arXiv preprint arXiv:2005.01643 (2020)
11. Ma, X., et al.: Offline reinforcement learning with value-based episodic memory. arXiv preprint arXiv:2110.09796 (2021)
12. Matsushima, T., Furuta, H., Matsuo, Y., Nachum, O., Gu, S.: Deployment-efficient reinforcement learning via model-based offline optimization. arXiv preprint arXiv:2006.03647 (2020)
13. Schulman, J., Levine, S., Abbeel, P., Jordan, M., Moritz, P.: Trust region policy optimization. In: International Conference on Machine Learning, pp. 1889–1897. PMLR (2015)

14. Shohamy, D., Wagner, A.D.: Integrating memories in the human brain: hippocampal-midbrain encoding of overlapping events. Neuron **60**, 378–389 (2008)
15. Todorov, E., Erez, T., Tassa, Y.: Mujoco: a physics engine for model-based control. In: 2012 IEEE/RSJ International Conference on Intelligent Robots and Systems, pp. 5026–5033. IEEE (2012)
16. Wang, W.Y., Li, J., He, X.: Deep reinforcement learning for NLP. In: Proceedings of the 56th Annual Meeting of the Association for Computational Linguistics: Tutorial Abstracts, pp. 19–21 (2018)
17. Wang, Y., Tan, H., Wu, Y., Peng, J.: Hybrid electric vehicle energy management with computer vision and deep reinforcement learning. IEEE Trans. Industr. Inf. **17**, 3857–3868 (2020)
18. Yu, T., Kumar, A., Rafailov, R., Rajeswaran, A., Levine, S., Finn, C.: Combo: conservative offline model-based policy optimization. arXiv preprint arXiv:2102.08363 (2021)
19. Yu, T., et al.: MOPO: model-based offline policy optimization. arXiv preprint arXiv:2005.13239 (2020)

Multi-mode Light: Learning Special Collaboration Patterns for Traffic Signal Control

Zhi Chen, Shengjie Zhao$^{(\boxtimes)}$, and Hao Deng

School of Software Engineering, Tongji University, No. 1239, Siping Road, Shanghai, China
{chenzhi123325,shengjiezhao,denghao1984}@tongji.edu.cn

Abstract. To alleviate traffic congestion, it is a trend to apply reinforcement learning (RL) to traffic signal control in multi-intersection road networks. However, existing researches generally combine a basic RL framework Ape-X DQN with the graph convolutional network (GCN), to aggregate the neighborhood information, lacking unique collaboration exploration at each intersection with shared parameters. This paper proposes a multi-mode Light model that learns the general collaboration patterns in a road network with the graph attention network and trains simple Multilayer Perceptron for each intersection to capture each intersection's unique collaboration pattern. The experiment results demonstrate that our model improves average by 27.19% compared with the state-of-the-art transportation method MaxPressure and average by 4.57% compared with the state-of-the-art reinforcement learning method Colight.

Keywords: Deep reinforcement learning · Traffic signal control · Multi-agent system · Graph attention network

1 Introduction

Horrible traffic congestion will lead to air pollution and economic loss problems. For alleviating traffic congestion, researchers in the transportation field have proposed various signal control methods to coordinate traffic movements at each intersection, such as Fixed Time [8], Max-pressure [13], GreenWave [9]. The above methods are based on domain knowledge and can not adapt to the dynamic traffic environment, leading to difficulties in giving optimal solutions for traffic signal control. Nowadays, many researchers [1,4,16] have started to exploit reinforcement learning(RL) to design the traffic signal control method, which outperforms conventional deterministic traffic signal control methods in reducing vehicles' driving time.

For traffic signal control in a large-scale multi-intersection road network, the mainstream approaches based on RL nowadays adopt the distributed framework

E. Pimenidis et al. (Eds.): ICANN 2022, LNCS 13530, pp. 63–74, 2022.
https://doi.org/10.1007/978-3-031-15931-2_6

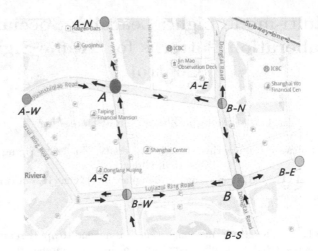

Fig. 1. There are two intersections, A and B, with different neighbors. The agent should give different strategy to control A and B even the states of A and B are indentical.

Ape-X DQN [7], which divides the training process into two separate parts: acting and learning. As for acting, a unified agent is set at each intersection to acquire the samples of the interaction between the environment and the agent and store them in the experience pool. In the learning process, the unified agent is trained with the experience pool. To achieve collaboration among intersections, the unified agent at each intersection observes the traffic conditions of its neighbors [17] and its past behaviors [6]. Although the mainstream methods have effectively alleviated traffic congestion, training the unified agent with shared parameters leads to insufficiency in learning the collaboration patterns of intersections. As Fig. 1 shows, there are two intersections in the road network, intersection A connecting three two-way streets and one-way street, and intersection B connecting two one-way streets and two-way streets. Their collaboration patterns differ, which means their neighbors influence them entirely differently. The agent at intersection A should aggregate information about its neighbors differently from that at intersection B, which the mainstream methods do not consider. The CoLight [15] realizes this problem and uses the graph attention network with a multi-head mechanism to learn more collaboration patterns. However, CoLight [15] still shares parameters so that it is hard to learn all traffic patterns in a large-scale road network. In this paper, we introduce Multi-mode Light method that can explore the collaboration patterns at each intersection so that the agent consider the different cooperation between the target intersection and its neighbors. In particular, our work makes the following key contributions:

Cooperation Through Multi-mode Graph Attention Network. We propose a new graph convolutional network—multi-mode graph attention network, which adds a Multilayer Perceptron to the graph attention network(GAT). The GAT with a multi-head mechanism captures the general collaboration patterns.

The additional Multilayer Perceptron is trained separately at each intersection to decide the unique weights of the multi-head outputs in the GAT to capture the intersection's unique collaboration pattern. In the experiments, we demonstrate that the additional Multilayer Perceptron enhances the agents' recognition of intersections' unique collaboration patterns. Then the agents can give better traffic signal control strategies and reduce the average travel time of vehicles.

Simple Modifications Rather than Complex Designs. In real road networks, the number of intersections is usually hundreds or thousands. The model we study should not be too complex to apply to the large-scale road network. Our model uses Ape-XDQN [7] as the basis and uses Multi-mode Graph Attention Network to aggregate the traffic features of adjacent intersections. Since our specificity module is a simple Multilayer Perceptron, the space-time complexity of the models is linearly realted to the number of intersections.

Experiment on the Large-Scale Road Network. This work conducts experiments on both synthetic and real-world data of different scales. The experimental results demonstrate that our model benefits from the Multi-mode Graph Attention Network, which can recognize intersections' unique collaboration patterns and significantly outperforms the state-of-the-art methods in real-world data in reducing travel time of vehicles.

2   Related Works

2.1   Conventional Traffic Control

The approaches in transportation engineering usually treat the traffic signal control problem as an optimization problem. The Webster method [8] assumes that traffic flow is constant over time and calculates the minimum signal period to meet the traffic demand by solving a specific functional equation. Some use the knowledge of transportation engineering to develop regularized control schemes. The literature [5] introduces a Self-Organizing Traffic Light Control(SOTL) method that controls traffic signals based on some rules that decide the phase when the number of vehicles waiting for a green light is more than a threshold value. The literature [13] introduces the intersection pressure concept and aims to balance the queue length between adjacent intersections by minimizing intersection phase pressure.

2.2   Reinforcement Learning

With the development of research in signal control at single intersections, researchers pay more attention to the signal control problem in multi-intersection road networks. They have tried to coordinate multiple intersections with the strategies in multi-agent reinforcement learning(MARL). The literature [2] divides MARL using in traffic signal control problems into joint-action and independent learners. Independent learners use independent reinforcement learning agents to control traffic signals, where each agent does not communicate explicitly to resolve conflicts between intersections [3]. The learning process often fails to converge to a balanced strategy ont the complex environment. Joint-action learners train a global agent to control all intersections [11], which takes all intersection states as input directly and give joint actions for all intersections. This joint-action method leads to the curse of dimensionality in the agent's state-action space.

Therefore, some use the distributed framework Ape-XDQN [7] as a base framework. And they empower the agents to communicate with each other to achieve collaboration. The researcher [10] assumes that the influence between neighbors is static, then uses the convolutional graph network [12] to model the influence of neighbors. In other words, [15] proposed using Graph Attention Networks [14] to learn the dynamic interactions between the hidden states of neighboring agents and the target agents. However, as described in the introduction, the Apx-XDQN-based approach is not a good solution because they can only learn the general collaboration patterns existing at intersections in large-scale road networks.

3   Problem Definition

In this section, we describe how to model the problem of traffic signal control for multiple intersections as an RL problem. Especially, the traffic signal control problem is viewed as a Markov game and characterized by the following major components $< \mathcal{S}, \mathcal{O}, \mathcal{A}, \mathcal{P}, r, \pi, \gamma >$:

- **System state space** $\mathcal{S}$: We assume that there are N intersections in the road network. The system state space is the set of states of N intersections, such as the signal phases, the number of waiting queues on the approaching lane.
- **Observation space** $\mathcal{O}$: Observation $o \in \mathcal{O}$ refers to the part of the system state space $\mathcal{S}$. In this work, as Fig. 2 shows, we define the observation o_i^t for agent i at time t is the current phase represented by a one-hot vector, the number of vehicles on each approaching lane, and the pressure of the intersection.
- **Set of Action** $\mathcal{A}$: In the traffic signal control problem, an agent i would choose an action a_i^t indicating that this intersection would be in phase a_i^t from time t to $t + \Delta t$. As Fig. 2 shows, the set of actions for the agents is 'East Straight West Straight (ESWS)', 'North Straight South Straight (NSSS)', 'East Left West Left (ELWL)', 'North Left South Left (NLSL)'.
- **Transition probability** $\mathcal{P}$: The transition probability $\mathcal{P}(s^{t+1}|s^t, a^t) : \mathcal{S} \times \mathcal{A}_1 \times \cdots \times \mathcal{A}_N \rightarrow \Omega(\mathcal{S})$ defines the probability distribution of the system state at the next moment $t + 1$ when the state s^t of the traffic system at moment t and the corresponding joint action a^t of all the agents are given, where $\Omega(\mathcal{S})$ denotes the space of state distributions.
- **Reward** r: Each agent can get a reward after giving action. In this work, we want to minimize the travel time of all vehicles, which is hard to measure

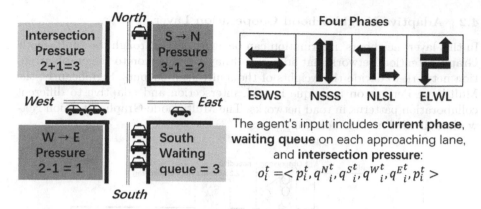

Fig. 2. The definitions of phase, waiting queue, pressure, and intersection pressure. And the agent's observation.

in real-time. Therefore, we use equivalent rewards to determine the learning direction of the agents, which is defined as $r_i^t = -\sum_l u_{i,l}^t$. $u_{i,l}^t$ is the queue length on each approaching lane l at time t.

- **Policy π and discount factor γ:** In this work, we use the action-value function $Q_i(o_i^t, a_i^t; \theta)$ for each agent i at time t to approximate the total reward $G_i^t = \sum_{t=\tau}^{T} \gamma^{t-\tau} r_i^t$, where T is total time steps of an episode and the discount factor $\gamma \in [0, 1]$ distinguishes the importance of historical rewards. The policy π is choosing the action a' according to the action-value function, where a' is $\arg\max_{a \in \mathcal{A}} Q(o_i^t, a; \theta)$.

4   Method

This section introduces our proposed Multi-mode Light, a reinforcement learning neural network for traffic signal control problems. As shown in Fig. 3, Multi-mode Light has three layers: the observation embedding layer, the adaptive neighborhood cooperation layer, and the q-value prediction layer.

4.1   Observation Embedding Layer

In this layer, we embed the k-dimensional observed data to m-dimensional latent layer data by a Multilayer Perceptron:

$$h_i = Embed(o_i^t) = \sigma(o_i W_e + b_e), \tag{1}$$

where $o_i^t \in \mathbb{R}^k$ is the intersection i's observation at time t, $W_e \in \mathbb{R}^{k \times m}$ and $b_e \in \mathbb{R}^m$ are the weight matrix and bias vector to learn, σ is ReLU function. The output of embedding layer $h_i \in \mathbb{R}^m$ represents the current latent traffic state of the i-th intersection.

4.2   Adaptive Neighborhood Cooperation Layer

In this layer, neighbors' information can be aggregated through the Multi-mode Graph Attention Network that adds a Multilayer Perceptron to the graph attention network to decide the weights of the multi-head outputs. Significantly, the Multilayer Perceptron is unique in each intersection and adaptive to different collaboration patterns in road networks. The Multi-mode Graph Attention Network is divided into the following parts:

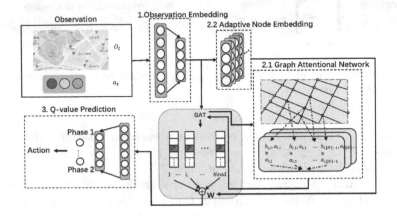

Fig. 3. Framework of the proposed Multi-mode Light.

Graph Attention Network

Observation Interaction: This part learns the importance of the neighbor intersection to the target intersection. First, we embed the representation of these two intersections and calculate the importance e_{ij} with:

$$e_{ij} = (h_i W_t) \cdot (h_j W_s)^T, \tag{2}$$

where $W_t, W_s \in \mathbb{R}^{m \times n}$ are embedding parameters for target intersection and neighbor, respectively.

Attention Distribution within Neighborhood: To normalize the importance of all neighbor intersections for the target intersection and explore the relationships, we adopt the Softmax function as

$$\alpha_{ij} = softmax(e_{ij}) = \frac{\exp(e_{ij}/\tau)}{\sum_{j \in \mathcal{N}_i} \exp(e_{ij}/\tau)}, \tag{3}$$

where $\mathcal{N}_i$ is the neighborhood intersections of the target intersection i and τ is the temperature factor which is a hyperparameter. The general attention score α_{ij} is the final importance score of the neighbor intersection j.

Neighborhooh Aggregation: To aggregate information about neighborhoods and understand their movements, we combine the representation of several neighboring intersections with their importance (the general attention score α_{ij}):

$$hs_i = \sigma(W_q \cdot \sum_{j \in \mathcal{N}_i} \alpha_{ij}(h_j W_c) + b_q), \tag{4}$$

where $W_c \in \mathbb{R}^{m \times c}$ is weight parameters for neighboring intersection embedding, W_q and b_q are trainable parameters.

Adaptive Node Embedding and Multi-head Attention: The neighborhood representation hs_i stands for one type of collaboration pattern with neighboring intersections. To ensure that the attention mechanism covers intersections with different patterns, we use multi-head attention mechanism to learn more general collaboration patterns. Specifically, multi-head attention functions are trained in parallel to generate multiple intersection's neighborhood representation hs_i and average them as hm_i:

$$hm_i = \sigma(W_q \cdot (\frac{1}{H} \sum_{h=1}^{h=H} \sum_{j \in \mathcal{N}_i} \alpha_{ij}^h(h_j W_c^h)) + b_q), \tag{5}$$

where H is the number of attention heads.

Then we add an adaptive node embedding module to each intersection to decide the weights of each head in the multi-head mechanism as

$$w_i = \sigma(W_{ai}h_i + b_{ai}), \tag{6}$$

$$H_i = [\sum_{j \in \mathcal{N}_i} \alpha_{ij}^1(h_j W_c^1), \cdots, \sum_{j \in \mathcal{N}_i} \alpha_{ij}^H(h_j W_c^H)], \tag{7}$$

$$hm_i = \sigma(W_q \cdot (w_i \cdot H_i) + b_q), \tag{8}$$

where the $h_i \in \mathbb{R}^k$ is the output of Observation Embedding Layer, $w_i \in \mathbb{R}^{H \times 1}$ is the weight of the multi-head at intersection i, and the final intersection representation hm_i is weighted sum of the multi-headed output hs_i^h based on the weights w_i. Note that each intersection has its parameters $W_{ai} \in \mathbb{R}^{H \times m}$, and the overall parameters will only increase by $N \times H \times m$.

4.3 Q-value Prediction

In this section, we use Deep Q-Network(DQN) to decide the optimal action with the latent representation hm_i. The DQN accepts the state features of the target intersection i and predicts the score for each alternate action according to Bellman's equation:

$$Q(s_t, a_t) = R(s_t, a_t) + \gamma \max Q(s_{t+1}, a_{t+1}). \tag{9}$$

In this work, we use the action-value function $Q_i(o_i^t, a_i^t; \theta)$ for each agent i at time t to predict the expected reward G_i^t and train the DQN by minimizing the loss:

$$\mathcal{L}(\theta_n) = \mathbb{E}[(r_i^t + \gamma \max_{a'} Q(o_i^{t'}, a_i^{t'}; \theta_{n-1}) - Q(o_i^t, a_i^t; \theta_n))^2], \qquad (10)$$

where θ_n denotes the n-iteration parameter and $o_i^{t'}$ is the next observation for o_i^t.

5   Experiment

We evaluate our Multi-mode Light method on two synthetic datasets and three real-world datasets.

5.1   Settings

We perform experiments on CityFlow, an open-source simulator that can support large-scale urban traffic simulation. CityFlow accepts traffic data and road network, simulates traffic flow, and interacts with agents. We set some limits according to real-world conditions, such as a three-second yellow light time and a minimum switching phase time.

5.2   Datasets

Synthetic Virtual Data: In the experiments, we use synthetic data to test the model's performance under known traffic patterns. The specific synthetic data are presented as follows:

- $Bidirect_{6\times6}$: A 6×6 grid road network structure with two-direction traffic flow. This traffic flow is 300 vehicles per lane in the East→West and West→East direction and 90 vehicles per lane in the North→South and South→North direction.
- $Undirect_{6\times6}$: The road network is the same to the $Bidirect_{6\times6}$. But traffic flow is only 300 vehicles per lane in the West→East and 90 vehicles per lane in the North→South.

Real-world Data: The dataset uses real-world road networks and is extracted from accurate traffic data to reflect the model's performance in the real world.

- $Jinan_{3\times4}$: A public dataset of Jinan city with a 3×4 grid road network structure and a one-hour traffic flow of 6296 vehicles.
- $Hangzhou_{4\times4}$: A public dataset of Hangzhou city with a 4×4 grid road network and a one-hour traffic flow of 2984 vehicles.
- $NewYork_{28\times7}$: A public dataset of NewYork city with a 28×7 grid road network structure and a one-hour traffic flow of 11059 vehicles.

5.3   Compared Method

To validate the effectiveness of the Multi-Mode Light model, we compare some state-of-the-art methods, which have two categories: transportation engineering methods and reinforcement learning methods.

The transportation engineering methods are listed as follows:

- **Fixed-time Control** [8]: This is a method which fixs the traffic signal switching time without consider anything.
- **MaxPressure** [13]: A state-of-the-art conventional traffic method always selects the phase with the highest intersection pressure.

The reinforcement learning methods are listed as follows:

- **Individual RL** [16]: Each intersection trains a reinforcement learning agent that does not consider information about its neighbors.
- **One Model** [4]: A agent acquire empirical samples and train one model uniformly.
- **Neighbor RL** [1]: Neighbor RL is similar to One Model but adds the target intersection's neighboring information to the observation space.
- **Colight** [15]: Colight uses graph attention networks to learn the way of aggregation between target intersection and its neighbors, and train an agent.

5.4   Evaluation Metric

We use the average travel time of vehicles to evaluate the performance of the various methods since lower average travel times respond to better road traffic conditions, which is consistent with the goal we want to optimize (alleviating traffic congestion problems). The average travel time of vehicles is the average difference in time between all vehicles entering the road network and reaching their destination.

Table 1. Performance (average travel time of all vehicles) on synthetic data and real-world data.

Head	$Undirect_{6\times6}$	$Bidirect_{6\times6}$	$Jinan_{3\times4}$	$Hangzhou_{4\times4}$	$NewYork_{28\times7}$
Fixedtime [8]	209.68	209.68	869.85	728.79	1950.27
MaxPressure [13]	186.07	194.96	361.33	422.15	1633.41
Individual RL [16]	314.82	261.60	325.56	345.00	–*
OneModel [4]	181.81	242.63	728.63	394.56	1973.11
Neighbor RL [1]	240.68	248.11	1168.32	1053.45	2280.92
CoLight [15]	176.98	173.69	299.47	317.04	1156.61
Multi-mode Light	176.98	173.64	291.41	293.01	1107.24

"–*" means no result as Individual RL can not scale up to the $NewYork_{28\times7}$ dataset.

5.5   Performance Comparison

In this subsection, we compare the performance of Multi-mode Light with other state-of-the-art methods. Table 1 shows the performance (average travel time of vehicles) on synthetic datasets and real-world datasets, where the performance of Fixedtime [8], MaxPressure [13], Individual RL [16], OneModel [4], Neighbor RL [1] refer to Colight [15]. Multi-mode Light's performance in real-world datasets is the best compared to all other state-of-the-art transportation engineering methods and reinforcement learning methods. The results depict the feasibility of the following design: we use a multi-mode graph attention network to learn intersection collaboration patterns and add the intersection pressure to the observation space.

In the synthetic dataset, Multi-mode Light performs best and improves average 12.16% compared with transportation methods and average 29.15% compared with reinforcement learning methods. However, Multi-mode Light does not improve obviously compared to Colight [15]. Colight learns the collaboration patterns of intersections with graph attention network without Multilayer Perceptron in each intersection compared to multi-mode graph attention network. The collaboration patterns of intersections in the synthetic datasets are fixed and rare. Colight and Multi-mode Light work equally in learning the collaboration patterns in the road network on synthetic dataset.

In real-world dataset, Multi-mode Light performs best because of the various collaboration patterns in real-world. Compared with the state-of-the-art transportation method MaxPressure, we improve average 27.19%. Compared with the state-of-the-art reinforcement learning method Colight, the average improvement is 4.57%. It is intuitive that our model would perform better and better than Colight as the road network complexity increased, and it does. In $Jinan_{3\times4}$, Multi-mode Light improves only 2.69%, while improves 4.27% in $NewYork_{28\times7}$.

5.6   Ablation Experiments

In this experiment, we focus on exploring the effectiveness of multi-mode graph attention network and the necessity of adding intersection pressure to observation space. The results of the ablation experiments are shown in Table 2, where we conduct Multi-mode Light, Multi-mode Light using graph attention network and Multi-mode Light without the intersection pressure on three representative datasets ($Bidirect_{6\times6}$, $Hangzhou_{4\times4}$, $NewYork_{28\times7}$). In particular, if our model removes the specific Multilayer Perceptron in multi-mode graph attention network and intersection pressure in observation space, it turns to Colight [15].

Table 2. Performance (average travel time of all vehicles) of ablation experiments

Head	$Bidirect_{6\times6}$	$D_{Newyork}$	$D_{Hangzhou}$
Multi-mode Light - mlp	176.5(−1.64%)	1224.77(−10.61%)	302.99(−3.4%)
Multi-mode Light - pre	172.18(+0.84%)	1212.90(−9.54%)	295.61(−0.88%)
Multi-mode Light	173.64	1107.24	293.01

All methods have almost the same effect in the $Bidirect_{6\times6}$ because the collaboration patterns in the $Bidirect_{6\times6}$ can be mined with simple observations and graph attention network. Whereas in the small-scale real-world dataset $Hangzhou_{4\times4}$, the multi-mode graph attention network performs better. The graph attention network can only mine the general collaboration patterns, but lacks the specific collaboration patterns for each intersection. Without observing the intersection pressure, the performance degrades only 0.88%. There is a 3.4% performance degradation without multi-mode graph attention network. In the large-scale real-world dataset $NewYork_{28\times7}$, the performance degrades by 9.54% in the absence of intersection pressure observations and by 10.64% in the absence of additional Multilayer Perceptron. We argue that the pattern existing at intersections are more in the large-scale road network than in the small-scale road network. The observation only including the waiting cars in the intersection limit the learning ability of multi-mode graph attention network. The complex traffic make the graph attention network hard to learn the unique collaboration patterns existing in real-world.

6   Conclusion

To alleviate traffic congestion, existing methods use domain knowledge or introduce deep reinforcement learning networks to design traffic signals to coordinate the flow of vehicles at intersections. Specifically, we note that it is necessary to consider the neighbors and collaborate with them when controlling traffic signals. At the same time, since the traffic conditions at each intersection are not the same, the collaboration patterns with neighbors should be different. We propose a multi-mode graph attention network based on this idea to learn the unique collaboration patterns of different intersections. We have conducted extensive experiments using various data types and demonstrated that our proposed approach works better than state-of-the-art methods. Moreover, the simple improvements do not significantly increase network complexity and are only linearly related to the number of intersections. Several critical future directions are pointed as follows. First, traffic conditions are usually cyclical and have different patterns at different times. The mining of temporal patterns should be considered in the future. Second, urban facilities are becoming more and more abundant nowadays, and more urban information should be considered. Using more data to assist in decision-making may help to improve the performance of the model.

Acknowledgement. This work was supported in part by the National Key R&D Program of China 2020YFB2103900, in part by the National Natural Science Foundation of China under Grant 61936014, in part by the Shanghai Municipal Science and Technology Major Project under Grant 2021SHZDZX0100, in part by the Natural Science Foundation of Shanghai under Grant 22ZR1462900 and in part by the Fundamental Research Funds for the Central Universities.

References

1. Arel, I., Liu, C., Urbanik, T., Kohls, A.G.: Reinforcement learning-based multi-agent system for network traffic signal control. IET Intel. Transport Syst. **4**(2), 128–135 (2010)
2. Arulkumaran, K., Deisenroth, M.P., Brundage, M., Bharath, A.A.: A brief survey of deep reinforcement learning. arXiv preprint arXiv:1708.05866 (2017)
3. Casas, N.: Deep deterministic policy gradient for urban traffic light control. arXiv preprint arXiv:1703.09035 (2017)
4. Chu, T., Wang, J., Codecà, L., Li, Z.: Multi-agent deep reinforcement learning for large-scale traffic signal control. IEEE Trans. Intell. Transp. Syst. **21**(3), 1086–1095 (2019)
5. Cools, S.B., Gershenson, C., D'Hooghe, B.: Self-organizing traffic lights: a realistic simulation. In: Prokopenko, M. (ed.) Advances in Applied Self-Organizing Systems. Advanced Information and Knowledge Processing, pp. 45–55. Springer, London (2013). https://doi.org/10.1007/978-1-4471-5113-5_3
6. Ge, H., Song, Y., Wu, C., Ren, J., Tan, G.: Cooperative deep q-learning with q-value transfer for multi-intersection signal control. IEEE Access **7**, 40797–40809 (2019)
7. Horgan, D., et al.: Distributed prioritized experience replay. arXiv preprint arXiv:1803.00933 (2018)
8. Koonce, P., Rodegerdts, L.: Traffic signal timing Manual. Technical report, United States. Federal Highway Administration (2008)
9. McShane, W.R., Roess, R.P.: Traffic engineering (1990)
10. Nishi, T., Otaki, K., Hayakawa, K., Yoshimura, T.: Traffic signal control based on reinforcement learning with graph convolutional neural nets. In: 2018 21st International Conference on Intelligent Transportation Systems (ITSC), pp. 877–883. IEEE (2018)
11. Prashanth, L., Bhatnagar, S.: Reinforcement learning with average cost for adaptive control of traffic lights at intersections. In: 2011 14th International IEEE Conference on Intelligent Transportation Systems (ITSC), pp. 1640–1645. IEEE (2011)
12. Schlichtkrull, M., Kipf, T.N., Bloem, P., van den Berg, R., Titov, I., Welling, M.: Modeling relational data with graph convolutional networks. In: Gangemi, A., et al. (eds.) ESWC 2018. LNCS, vol. 10843, pp. 593–607. Springer, Cham (2018). https://doi.org/10.1007/978-3-319-93417-4_38
13. Cools, S.B., Gershenson, C., D'Hooghe, B.: Self-organizing traffic lights: a realistic simulation. In: Prokopenko, M. (eds) Advances in Applied Self-Organizing Systems. Advanced Information and Knowledge Processing, pp. 27–66. Springer, London (2013). https://doi.org/10.1007/978-1-4471-5113-5_3
14. Veličković, P., Cucurull, G., Casanova, A., Romero, A., Lio, P., Bengio, Y.: Graph attention networks. arXiv preprint arXiv:1710.10903 (2017)
15. Wei, H., et al.: Colight: learning network-level cooperation for traffic signal control. In: Proceedings of the 28th ACM International Conference on Information and Knowledge Management, pp. 1913–1922 (2019)
16. Wei, H., Zheng, G., Yao, H., Li, Z.: Intellilight: a reinforcement learning approach for intelligent traffic light control. In: Proceedings of the 24th ACM SIGKDD International Conference on Knowledge Discovery & Data Mining, pp. 2496–2505 (2018)
17. Xu, M., Wu, J., Huang, L., Zhou, R., Wang, T., Hu, D.: Network-wide traffic signal control based on the discovery of critical nodes and deep reinforcement learning. J. Intell. Transp. Syst. **24**(1), 1–10 (2020)

Pheromone-inspired Communication Framework for Large-scale Multi-agent Reinforcement Learning

Zixuan Cao, Xiujun Ma$^{(\boxtimes)}$, Mengzhi Shi, and Zhanbo Zhao

Key Laboratory of Machine Perception (MoE), School of AI,
Peking University, Beijing, China
{maxiujun,shimengzhi,zhaozb1997}@pku.edu.cn, caozixuan.percy@stu.edu.cn

Abstract. Being difficult to scale poses great problems in multi-agent coordination. Multi-agent Reinforcement Learning (MARL) algorithms applied in small-scale multi-agent systems are hard to extend to large-scale ones because the latter is far more dynamic and the number of interactions increases exponentially with the growing number of agents. Some swarm intelligence algorithms simulate the mechanism of pheromones to control large-scale agent coordination. Inspired by such algorithms, **PooL**, a pheromone-inspired indirect communication framework applied to large-scale multi-agent reinforcement learning is proposed in order to solve the large-scale multi-agent coordination problem. Pheromones released by agents of PooL are defined as outputs of value-based reinforcement learning algorithms, which reflect agents' views of the current environment. The pheromone update mechanism can efficiently organize the information of all agents and simplify the complex interactions among agents into low-dimensional representations. Pheromones perceived by agents can be regarded as a summary of the views of nearby agents which can better reflect the real situation of the environment. Q-Learning is taken as our base model to implement PooL and PooL is evaluated in various large-scale cooperative environments. Experiments show agents can capture effective information through PooL and achieve higher rewards than other state-of-arts methods with lower communication costs.

Keywords: Multi-agent communication · Swarm intelligence · Reinforcement learning

1 Introduction

MARL focuses on developing algorithms to optimize different agents' behaviors that share a common environment [2]. MARL faces two major problems. First, partial observations from different agents as input features cause a curse

Supported by the National Key Research and Development Program of China: Science and Technology Innovation 2030- "New Generation Artificial Intelligence" Major Project under Grant 2018AAA0102301.

E. Pimenidis et al. (Eds.): ICANN 2022, LNCS 13530, pp. 75–86, 2022.
https://doi.org/10.1007/978-3-031-15931-2_7

of dimensionality. Second, it is difficult to consider all possible interactions among agents because the number of possible interactions grows exponentially. In MARL, there are various methods to solve the two problems. These methods can be roughly divided into two categories, Centralized Training Decentralized Execution (CTDE) [14] and multi-agent communication. In the CTDE framework, agents can access global information while training, and agents select actions based on partial observations while executing. But CTDE algorithms are still unable to deal with large-scale agents for the reason that the dimension of global information is still too high to handle even at the training step. Multi-agent communication is another promising approach to coordinate the behaviors of large-scale agents. But designing an effective communication mechanism is not a trivial task.

Swarm Intelligence refers to solving problems through the interactions of simple information-processing units [9]. A representative algorithm is Ant Colony Optimization (ACO). It takes inspiration from the foraging behavior of some ant species and uses a mechanism similar to pheromones for solving optimization problems [4]. The effectiveness of such ACO algorithms depends on the exploration of a large number of units (e.g. robots) and pheromone-inspired indirect communication among them. However, in ACO's settings, units' behaviors are confined by predefined rules, which is unsuitable in MARL environments.

In this paper, inspired by the pheromone mechanism introduced in ACO, an indirect communication framework for MARL is developed. The output of values-based reinforcement learning algorithms is the expected cumulative rewards of actions. These values can be used not only to select actions but also to reflect the agents' views of the environment. These values output by different agents can be organized by a pheromone update mechanism similar to ACO. Therefore, the pheromone information perceived by agents combines the views and knowledge of other agents around them, and can better reflect the real situation of the current agent.

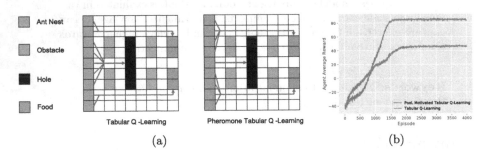

Fig. 1. (a) Demonstration of our motivation. Agents receiving pheromones bypass traps and find better paths. (b) Motivation experiment results. Agents using PooL achieve higher rewards. (Color figure online)

The motivation behind our framework is shown in Fig. 1. In a simple grid maze environment, there are ant nests (blue grid cells), obstacles (grey grid cells), traps (black grid cells), and food (orange grid cells). Agents (i.e. ants) get negative rewards at every time step. Agents will exit from the environment if they fall into traps or find food. Agents who find food get extra positive rewards. If agents take actions dependently, they are very easy to fall into local optimization (fall into traps). But if agents communicate through pheromones, those agents who find the optimal solution will transfer the information of the optimal solution to other agents. As a result, more agents find the optimal solution with the guidance of pheromones. The motivation experiment result is shown in Fig. 1(b). We generate pheromones for each grid cell in every step and use pheromone information to update Q-Table. We will discuss the implementation of PooL in detail in Sect. 4.

Following the intuition above, the pheromone mechanism is extended to the field of Deep Reinforcement Learning (DRL). PooL simulates the process of ant colonies releasing pheromone, feeling the pheromone and the surrounding environment, and making decisions. A pheromone receptor is designed to convert pheromone information to a fixed dimension feature. For each agent, the original reinforcement learning component receives information both from the real world and the pheromone receptor to choose actions and release pheromones. In this way, PooL realizes indirect agent communication and distributed training and execution in MARL. We combine PooL with Deep Q-Learning and evaluate PooL in various settings of MAgent [21] which is further capsuled by Petting-Zoo [16]. Experiments show that PooL can achieve effective communication of local information and get higher rewards.

2   Related Work

2.1   Multi-agent Reinforcement Learning

[5,10,17] are classic MARL algorithms following the framework of CTDE [14]. Such methods suffer from the curse of dimensionality because they still need to handle all agents' features while training. Communication is an effective way to solve this problem. CommNet [15], ATOC [8] and TarMAC [3] are such methods based on communication between agents. But they still assume a centralized controller that can access all communication needed information while training. DGN [7] models agents' interactions with graph structures. In DGN, agents' communication is achieved by the convolution of graph nodes (e.g. agents nearby). Graph convolution can express more complex agent interactions. But its performance and convergence speed are still confined by the number of agents. To make algorithms scale to many agents, MFQ [11] accepts the average action value of nearby agents as extra network input. [22] proposes to approximate Q-function with factorized pairwise interactions.

2.2   Control Algorithms Based on Swarm Intelligence

[1,19] utilize pheromones to achieve multi-agent coordination. However, Swarm Intelligence algorithms like Bird Swarm Algorithm and Ant Colony Optimization

are rule-based, as a result, they can not learn from environments. Phe-Q [13] first introduces the idea of pheromone mechanisms to reinforcement learning. [18] proposes to release the pheromone according to the distance between the agent and the target, and apply the pheromone information to Deep Reinforcement Learning.

Learning-based methods are more and more popular with the success of deep learning in many fields. Most methods mentioned above can not take advantage of deep neural networks. DRL is applied in [18], but the way [18] obtains pheromones is artificially designed based on the specific environment. It will be more appropriate if pheromones are generated based on learning algorithms.

3   Background

3.1   Problem Formulation

The problem for multi-agent coordination in this paper can be considered as a Dec-POMDP game [6]. It can be well defined by a tuple $M = <I, S, \{A_i\}, P, \{R_i\}, \{\Omega_i\}, O, T, \gamma >$, where I is a set of n agents, S is the state space, A_i is the action space for agent i, Ω_i is the observation space for agent i, T is the time horizon for the game and γ is the discount factor for individual rewards R_i. When agents took actions a in state s, the probability of the environment transitioning to state s' is $P(s'|s,a)$ and the probability of agents seeing observations o is $O(o|s,a)$.

For agents in the problem above, their goal is to maximize their own expected return $G_i = \sum_{t=0}^{T} \gamma^t R_i^t$. The achievement of this goal requires the cooperation of agents belonging to the same team.

3.2   Tabular Q-Learning and Deep Q-Learning

Q-Learning is a popular method in single agent reinforcement learning. For agent i, Q-Learning uses an action-value function for policy π_i as $Q_i^\pi(\Omega_i, a) = \mathbb{E}[R_i \mid \Omega_i^t = \Omega, a_i^t = a]$. Tabular Q-Learning maintains a Q-table and update Q-values by the following equation:

$$Q_i^\pi(\Omega_i, a) = Q_i^\pi(\Omega_i, a) + \alpha(R_i + \gamma \max_{a'} Q_i^\pi(\Omega_i', a') - Q_i^\pi(\Omega_i, a)). \qquad (1)$$

For every step, the agent selects its action based on the max value of these actions with an epsilon-greedy exploration strategy.

As Q-Table can not handle high dimensional states, Deep Q-Learning (DQN) uses neural network to approximate Q-function. DQN tries to optimize Q_i^* with back propagation by minimizing the follwing loss function:

$$\mathcal{L}_i(\theta) = \mathbb{E}_{\Omega, a, r, \Omega'}\left[(Q_i^*(\Omega, a \mid \theta) - y)^2\right], \text{ where } y = r + \gamma \max_{a'} \bar{Q}_i^*(\Omega', a'). \qquad (2)$$

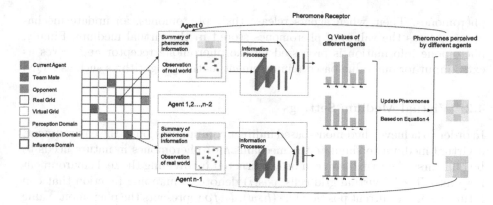

Fig. 2. Overview of PooL. The left part represents agents' environment from the view of our proposed framework. The right part shows how agents process information from two sources (real world observations and pheromones) and release pheromones based on their output.

4   Methodology

4.1   Communication Framework Overview

Figure 2 gives a whole picture of PooL. In the left of Fig. 2, a simple grid world is built as a demonstration. From the view of the grey agent, the black-bordered squares represent the real grid cells of our environment. They are the smallest units to express information in our environment. In order to realize indirect communication based on pheromones, we need to set up a virtual medium, which is represented by the blue-bordered squares. The area near the current agent is divided into three regions: Influence Domain, Observation Domain, and Perception Domain. Agents handle these three regions with different behaviors. **Influence Domain** decides the influence range of pheromones released by agents. **Observation Domain** is the partial observation of the current agent. **Perception Domain** decides the range of pheromones that agents can perceive.

The right part of Fig. 2 shows how PooL processes received information and updates pheromones. PooL consists of three components. The first is the information processor (composed of convolution layers and fully connected layers). Its input feature consists of two parts: real-world observations and a summary of pheromone information. Its output is Q-values, which can be transformed into pheromones. The second is the pheromone update mechanism realized through a virtual medium. Thirdly, a pheromone receptor is used to sense the pheromone information from the surrounding by convolution layers and transform the information into the representation features of the current environment. With the increase of the number of agents, the pheromone information extracted by agents can more accurately reflect the situation of the local environment.

In the following sections, we introduce the realization of our framework in three steps. First, a virtual medium is defined to allow the propagation of pheromones. Then, when agents release their pheromones, an update mechanism updates the values of pheromones stored in the virtual medium. Finally, pheromone information is processed by the pheromone receptor and serves as extra input for our value-based reinforcement learning algorithms such as DQN.

4.2   Virtual Medium Settings

In order to achieve pheromone-based indirect communication in the environment, a virtual medium to simulate the mechanism of pheromones in nature needs to be built first. A virtual map can be constructed by dividing the real environment map into $H \times W$ virtual grid cells. $pos(i)$ denotes a mapping function that can return agent i's current position like (h, w). $Info$ represents the pheromone value stored in the virtual medium whose shape is (H, W, N_A) (N_A is denoted as the number of actions). $N(h, w)$ represents the current number of agents in (h, w). The pheromone released by agent i is denoted as $Phe(i)$. $Phe(i)$ is a vector with N_A dimensions.

4.3   Pheromone Update Rule

Following Q-Learning's idea, pheromones are defined based on the Q-function. As the range of the Q-function's estimated values changes while training, Q-values are standardized as pheromones. For agent i's Q-values Q_i, they are transformed by a z-score normalization function $normalize(Q_i)$. After z-score normalization, values of pheromones obey the standard normal distribution with the mean of 0.0 and the standard deviation of 1.0.

$$Phe(i) = normalize(Q_i), \quad \text{where } Q_i = (Q_i(\Omega_i, a_0), \cdots, Q_i(\Omega_i, a_{N_A-1})). \quad (3)$$

At the beginning of each time step, each agent calculates their Q-values and releases their pheromones on their Influence Domain. We take the mean value of all released pheromones in each grid cell, and update the value of pheromones in each grid cell according to the evaporation coefficient β. For a virtual grid cell, whose position is (h, w), its pheromone value is updated by the following equation:

$$\text{Info}(h, w) = (1 - \beta)\,\text{Info}(h, w) + \beta \sum^{I_{h,w}} Phe\,(i)\,/N(h, w). \quad (4)$$

$I_{h,w}$ is a set of agents where for every $i \in I_{h,w}$, there is $pos(i) = (h, w)$.

4.4   Pheromone Inspired Q-Learning

We illustrates how PooL combines with Tabular Q-Learning and DQN. For Tabular Q-Learning, after calculating Eq. 1 and 4, we can transfer pheromone information to Q-Table of all agents by Eq. 5 below. σ is an update coefficient which is set to 0.01 in our motivation experiment mentioned in Sect. 1. $Info(h, w)[a]$ represents the pheromone value in (h, w) of current action index.

$$Q_i^\pi(s, a) = (1 - \sigma)Q_i^\pi(s, a) + \sigma Info(h, w)[a], \text{ where } pos(i) = (h, w). \quad (5)$$

As for DQN, a pheromone receptor is added to process pheromone information stored in $Info$. Therefore, our PooL-motivated DQN receives information from two sources. Except for the partial observation of the current environment, PooL also receives the information processed by the pheromone receptor. For agent i, the summary of pheromone information processed by agent i is denoted as $Rec(i, Info)$. The optimization goal for pheromone-inspired DQN can be updated to:

$$\mathcal{L}_i(\theta) = \mathbb{E}_{\Omega, Info, a, r, \Omega', Info'}\left[(Q_i^*(\Omega, Rec(i, Info \mid \theta_r), a \mid \theta_p) - y)^2\right],$$
$$\text{where } y = r + \gamma \max_{a'} \bar{Q}_i^*(\Omega', Rec(i, Info'), a'). \quad (6)$$

5 Experiment

In this section, we describe the settings of our experiment environments and show the performance of PooL. We first show the main results compared with other methods in various settings of MAgent [21]. Then, the Battle environment is taken as an example to discuss details about our framework.

5.1 Main Experiments

PooL is mainly evaluated in six multi-agent environments. We first introduce the settings of these environments and our training procedure, and then show the performance of various methods from different aspects (Fig. 3).

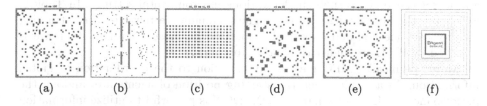

(a)	(b)	(c)	(d)	(e)	(f)

Fig. 3. Demonstration of Pettingzoo MAgent environments. (a) Battle (b) Battlefield (c) Combined Arms (d) Adversarial Pursuit (e) Tiger-Deer (f) Gather

Environment Description. Agents in MAgent [21] settings can get the location of obstacles and the location and HP (Health Points) of other agents within their view range. In our experiment, we use Battle, Battlefield, Combined Arms, Tiger-Deer, Adversarial Pursuit, and Gather as our running multi-agent environments. Details about these environments refer to [16].

Experiment Settings. PooL is compared with DQN [12], MFQ [20] and DGN [7]. DGN is only applied in Battle, Battlefield, Adversarial Pursuit, and Tiger-Deer environments. In these four environments, We use the same settings as DGN in which reborn agents constantly replace killed agents and the total number of agents remains unchanged during the game. But for Combined Arms and Gather, the previous setting goes against the original intention of these two environments. Therefore, we only compare PooL with MFQ and DQN in these two environments. Firstly, DQN models are trained by self-play as our opponents. Then different methods are trained against those opponents.

Hyper Parameters of PooL. The Influence Domain is 1×1 virtual grid cell. The Perception Domain is 3×3 virtual grid cells. The evaporation coefficient β is 0.5 and the virtual map size $H \times W$ is 10×10 for Gather with real-world map size 200×200 and 8×8 for other environments with smaller real-world map sizes. Other key settings are shown in Table 1.

Table 1. Detail settings of Experiment Environment. For Battle and Battlefield, Our agents can be either red or blue. For Combined Arms, each team contains two types of agents: Ranged and Melee.

Environment	Agents to be trained			Agents of opponents		
	Ob. Space	Amount	Role	Ob. Space	Amount	Role
Battle, Battle Field	(5, 7, 7)	80	Red or Blue	(5, 7, 7)	100	Red or Blue
Tiger and Deer	(5, 3, 3)	101	Deer	(5, 9, 9)	20	Tiger
Pursuit	(5, 5, 5)	100	Blue	(5, 6, 6)	25	Red
Gather	(5, 7, 7)	495	Predator	–	1636	Food
Combined Arms	(7, 7, 7)	66,55	Melee, Ranged	(7, 7, 7)	66,55	Melee, Ranged

Main Results. It can be seen from Fig. 4 that our method has a higher reward and faster convergence speed under various environmental settings. In Table 2, we choose the best model with the highest cumulative rewards in the training step for each method and do a final evaluation. In most environments, rewards achieved by PooL are higher than other methods.

More specifically, MFQ pays more attention to the coordination of global information. As a result, when the starting position of agents are random, the performance of MFQ is similar to DQN. DGN is powerful to utilize information from its neighborhood. But as it regards agents as a graph, the convergence speed of training is much slower than other methods. PooL effectively simplifies complex information in the environment, so that the agent trained by PooL can not only converge quickly but also use additional information to find better policies. PooL also has its limitation. The results in Combined Arms show that the current framework can not obtain significant advantages compared with other algorithms when there are heterogeneous agents in the same team.

In order to further demonstrate the advantages of our proposed framework, we use our model trained by PooL against models trained by other methods.

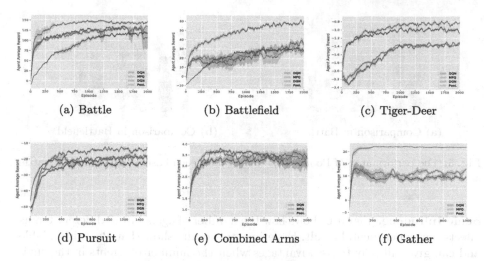

(a) Battle   (b) Battlefield   (c) Tiger-Deer

(d) Pursuit   (e) Combined Arms   (f) Gather

Fig. 4. Main results of experiments. PooL (the green line) achieves higher rewards except in Combined Arms. The experimental results also show that PooL is more stable in repeated experiments. (Color figure online)

Table 2. Evaluation results against fixed trained models. PooL outperforms all other methods except in Combined Arms.

Environment	Average cumulated reward			
	DQN	MFQ	DGN	PooL
Battle	128.7 ± 13.0	124.7 ± 5.4	111.2 ± 7.6	$\mathbf{148.5 \pm 12.6}$
Battlefield	43.7 ± 7.1	39.8 ± 8.2	55.9 ± 7.1	$\mathbf{66.6 \pm 6.6}$
Tiger-Deer	-1.84 ± 0.29	-1.29 ± 0.12	-1.21 ± 0.13	$\mathbf{-0.77 \pm 0.09}$
Pursuit	-18.8 ± 4.6	-17.6 ± 4.1	-18.5 ± 3.0	$\mathbf{-13.5 \pm 5.56}$
Combined Arms: Melee	2.00 ± 0.19	3.14 ± 0.19	–	$\mathbf{4.21 \pm 0.23}$
Combined Arms: Ranged	3.65 ± 0.31	$\mathbf{4.21 \pm 0.24}$	–	3.90 ± 0.30
Gather	3.33 ± 0.88	9.57 ± 1.17	–	$\mathbf{22.0 \pm 0.32}$

Because only Battle and BattleField are completely symmetrical in settings, our comparison experiment is only carried out in these two environments. Figure 5 indicates that PooL not only has better convergence and cumulative rewards during training but also has advantages against other methods. In the comparison, the overall worst performing method is DGN, which is based on graph convolution. This may be due to DGN overfitting the opponent's strategy in environments with large-scale agents. PooL not only achieves higher rewards when fighting against fixed agents trained by DQN but also learns more general strategies than other methods.

5.2 Detailed Experiments in Battle

In this section, we take Battle as an example to discuss the details of our proposed method.

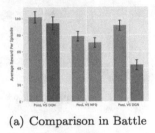
(a) Comparison in Battle

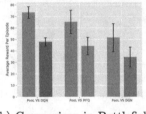
(b) Comparison in Battlefield

Fig. 5. The performance of PooL competing against each baseline algorithm in Battle and Battlefield.

Scale Influence. Figure 6 shows how the number of agents from different teams affects our experimental result. Experimental results show that PooL is scalable and can give full play to its advantages when the number of agents in the environment is different. DQN, however, fails to learn a good policy when the number of agents becomes larger. MFQ suffers from unstable training procedures when there are more agents.

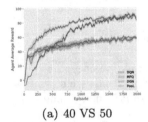
(a) 40 VS 50

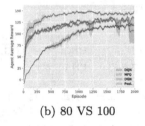
(b) 80 VS 100

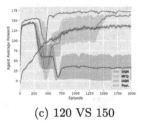
(c) 120 VS 150

Fig. 6. Scale influence

Hyper Parameter Selection. In our proposed method, there are three key hyper parameters to choose: the size of our virtual map, the range of perception, and the evaporation coefficient of pheromones. In Fig. 7(a), models are trained with virtual map sizes 6, 8 and 10 respectively. The result indicates that PooL is not sensitive to this parameter. Figure 7(b) shows a larger perception range (from 1×1 to 5×5) contributes to better performance. Figure 7(c) indicates that when the evaporation coefficient is between 0.1–0.9, the average reward after model convergence is almost the same. A value of 0.1 or 0.9 may slightly reduce the convergence speed of the model. Therefore, we recommend a value of about 0.5 according to the actual environment. If the evaporation coefficient is too large, the model can not effectively extract historical information. If the evaporation coefficient is too small, the information reflected by the pheromone will lag.

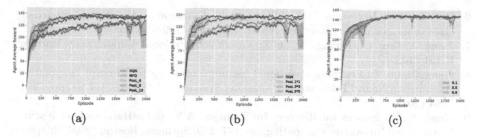

Fig. 7. Hyper Parameters Selection (a) Virtual Map Size has little effect on the performance of PooL. (b) Greater Perception Range leads to better performance (c) A moderate coefficient is conducive to obtaining stable training results.

6   Conclusion

In this paper, we propose PooL, a pheromone-inspired indirect communication framework applied to the MARL cooperation task. Inspired by swarm intelligence algorithms like ACO, PooL inherits the advantage of swarm intelligence algorithms that can be applied to large-scale agent coordination. Q-Learning is taken as an example to realize our framework. In our proposed framework, the information of agents in the environment is organized and dimensionally reduced by the pheromone update mechanism. Therefore, the cost of communication between agents is also very small. PooL is evaluated with different MARL algorithms in various environments with hundreds of agents. Experimental results show that PooL converges faster and has higher rewards than other methods. Its superior performance with low cost in game environments shows that it has the potential to be applied in more complex real-world scenes with a bandwidth limit. PooL's success indicates that rule-based swarm intelligence control algorithms are promising to combine with learning-based models for large-scale agent coordination.

References

1. Bourenane, M., Mellouk, A., Benhamamouch, D.: Reinforcement learning in multi-agent environment and ant colony for packet scheduling in routers. In: Proceedings of the 5th ACM International Workshop on Mobility Management and Wireless Access, pp. 137–143 (2007)
2. Buşoniu, L., Babuška, R., De Schutter, B.: Multi-agent reinforcement learning: an overview. Innovations in Multi-agent Systems and Applications-1, pp. 183–221 (2010)
3. Das, A., et al.: Tarmac: targeted multi-agent communication. In: International Conference on Machine Learning, pp. 1538–1546. PMLR (2019)
4. Dorigo, M., Birattari, M., Stutzle, T.: Ant colony optimization. IEEE Comput. Intell. Mag. 1(4), 28–39 (2006)
5. Foerster, J., Farquhar, G., Afouras, T., Nardelli, N., Whiteson, S.: Counterfactual multi-agent policy gradients. In: Proceedings of the AAAI Conference on Artificial Intelligence, vol. 32 (2018)

6. Hansen, E.A., Bernstein, D.S., Zilberstein, S.: Dynamic programming for partially observable stochastic games. In: AAAI, vol. 4, pp. 709–715 (2004)
7. Jiang, J., Dun, C., Huang, T., Lu, Z.: Graph convolutional reinforcement learning. ICLR (2020)
8. Jiang, J., Lu, Z.: Learning attentional communication for multi-agent cooperation. Advances in Neural Information Processing Systems. NIPS 2018, vol. 31, pp. 7254–7264 (2018)
9. Kennedy, J.: Swarm intelligence. In: Zomaya, A.Y. (ed.) Handbook of Nature-Inspired and Innovative Computing, pp. 187–219. Springer, Boston (2006). https://doi.org/10.1007/0-387-27705-6_6
10. Lowe, R., Wu, Y., Tamar, A., Harb, J., Abbeel, P., Mordatch, I.: Multi-agent actor-critic for mixed cooperative-competitive environments. In: Advances in Neural Information Processing Systems. NIPS 2017, vol. 30, pp. 6379–6390 (2020)
11. Luo, R., Yang, Y., Li, M., Zhou, M., Zhang, W., Wang, J.: Mean field multi agent reinforcement learning. The 35th International Conference on Machine Learning (ICML 2018). PMLR, pp. 5567–5576 (2018)
12. Mnih, V., et al.: Human-level control through deep reinforcement learning. Nature 518(7540), 529–533 (2015)
13. Monekosso, N., Remagnino, P.: Phe-Q: a pheromone based Q-learning. In: Stumptner, M., Corbett, D., Brooks, M. (eds.) AI 2001. LNCS (LNAI), vol. 2256, pp. 345–355. Springer, Heidelberg (2001). https://doi.org/10.1007/3-540-45656-2_30
14. Oliehoek, F.A., Spaan, M.T., Vlassis, N.: Optimal and approximate q-value functions for decentralized POMDPs. J. Artif. Intell. Res. 32, 289–353 (2008)
15. Sukhbaatar, S., Szlam, A., Fergus, R.: Learning multiagent communication with backpropagation. In: Advances in Neural information Processing Systems. NIPS 2016, vol. 29, pp. 2252–2260 (2016)
16. Terry, J.K., et al.: Pettingzoo: Gym for multi-agent reinforcement learning. arXiv preprint arXiv:2009.14471 (2020)
17. Wei, E., Wicke, D., Freelan, D., Luke, S.: Multiagent soft q-learning. In: 2018 AAAI Spring Symposium Series (2018)
18. Xu, X., Li, R., Zhao, Z., Zhang, H.: Stigmergic independent reinforcement learning for multiagent collaboration. IEEE Trans. Neural Networks Learn. Syst. (2021)
19. Xu, X., Zhao, Z., Li, R., Zhang, H.: Brain-inspired stigmergy learning. IEEE Access 7, 54410–54424 (2019)
20. Yang, Y., Luo, R., Li, M., Zhou, M., Zhang, W., Wang, J.: Mean field multi-agent reinforcement learning. In: International Conference on Machine Learning, pp. 5571–5580. PMLR (2018)
21. Zheng, L., Yang, J., Cai, H., Zhou, M., Zhang, W., Wang, J., Yu, Y.: Magent: a many-agent reinforcement learning platform for artificial collective intelligence. In: Proceedings of the AAAI Conference on Artificial Intelligence, vol. 32 (2018)
22. Zhou, M., et al.: Factorized q-learning for large-scale multi-agent systems. In: Proceedings of the First International Conference on Distributed Artificial Intelligence, pp. 1–7 (2019)

Reinforcement Learning for the Pickup and Delivery Problem

Fagui Liu[1,2], Chengqi Lai[1(✉)], and Lvshengbiao Wang[1]

[1] South China University of Technology, Guangzhou 510006, China
201921042012@mail.scut.edu.cn
[2] Peng Cheng Laboratory, Shenzhen 518055, China

Abstract. The pickup and delivery problem (PDP) and its related variants are an important part in the field of urban logistics and distribution, and there are many heuristic algorithms to solve them. However, with the continuous expansion of logistics scale, these methods generally have the problem of too long calculation time. In order to solve this problem, we propose a reinforcement learning (RL) model based on the Advantage Actor-Critic, which regards PDP as a sequential decision problem. The actor based on the attention mechanism is responsible for generating routing strategies. The critic is designed to improve the solution quality during training. The model is trained using policy gradient. The experimental results show that compared with the heuristic algorithms and previous RL approach, the proposed model has obvious advantages in computational time, and it is also competitive in terms of solution quality.

Keywords: Pickup and delivery problem · Reinforcement learning · Attention mechanism

1 Introduction

In recent years, with the popularization and development of the mobile Internet, the logistics industry has also developed rapidly. And the urban distribution has become an important part of the entire logistics industry. In today's society that emphasizes the use of high-tech means to build smart cities, it has become a new challenge to combine the latest software and hardware technologies to improve the efficiency of urban distribution.

The pickup and delivery problem (PDP) is one of the most important research topics in the field of urban distribution, which is mainly divided into the static PDP [1] and the dynamic PDP [2]. Static means that all data is known and will not change before the routes are constructed, while dynamic means that some data can be obtained or the data will change during the process of constructing the routes. In the real world, the PDP often faces many practical constraints. For example, large vehicles are not allowed to drive in cities, goods need to be

© The Author(s), under exclusive license to Springer Nature Switzerland AG 2022
E. Pimenidis et al. (Eds.): ICANN 2022, LNCS 13530, pp. 87–98, 2022.
https://doi.org/10.1007/978-3-031-15931-2_8

picked up or delivered within the time specified by the customer, and mixed loads between different types of goods are not allowed.

In the past few decades, there has been a lot of research on PDPs, and the solutions are mainly exact algorithms and heuristic algorithms. However, as the scale of the problem increases and the complexity increases, the solving time of these algorithms becomes longer and longer, resulting in the inability to obtain satisfactory results within a reasonable time. In order to solve this problem, some researchers have begun to try to introduce some new methods. In recent years, deep learning has performed well in tasks such as image recognition and processing, and reinforcement learning has also achieved very good results, such as AlphaGo. As a result, some researchers began to combine deep learning and reinforcement learning to solve combinatorial optimization problems, and achieved good results. Compared with the traditional exact algorithms and heuristic algorithms, its advantage lies in the rapidity of the solving, even the complex large-scale problems can be quickly solved.

This paper focuses on the characteristics of the one-to-many PDP. Our major contributions are three-fold: Firstly, we design a reinforcement learning model based on the Advantage Actor-Critic. The role of actor is to generate routing strategies, in which the pointer network is used to select at each step of the training process, and will eventually output the constructed routes. The role of critic is to evaluate the quality of the actor generation strategies and guide the actor to iteratively update in the right direction. Secondly, since the training of the model requires a large amount of instances, we generate a large amount of instances for model training based on the Li & Lim benchmark [3] and the characteristics of this problem. Thirdly, we have conducted a lot of experiments to show that our model performs better than the heuristic algorithms and previous RL approach on this problem.

The remainder of this paper is organized as follows. Section 2 summarizes related work. Section 3 gives the definition and specific description of the problem. Section 4 describes the overall structure and concrete realization of the model. Section 5 presents the experimental results and related experimental analysis. Finally, Sect. 6 summarizes the work of this paper and future research directions.

2   Related Work

As a type of classical NP-hard problems in combinatorial optimization, PDPs have received much attention in the past decades. Researchers have proposed many exact algorithms and heuristic algorithms. Among them, exact algorithms include branch and bound method [4], column generation [5], etc. The advantage of these algorithms is that they can obtain the optimal solution to the problems. However, when the problem scale increases, its calculation time will increase exponentially, which is not acceptable. As a result, more researchers have turned to heuristic algorithms. Researchers have proposed a variety of heuristic algorithms such as genetic algorithm [6], artificial immune algorithm [7], tabu search algorithm [8] and so on. Although the results obtained by heuristic algorithms are not necessarily optimal, they can obtain relatively good results in a reasonable time, and are most widely used at present.

In recent years, due to the outstanding performance of reinforcement learning, many scholars have begun to use reinforcement learning to model and solve combinatorial optimization problems. Vinyals [9] improved the sequence-to-sequence model by adding the attention mechanism, proposed pointer network and solved small-scale Travelling Salesman Problem (TSP). However, the training of this network is supervised learning, which is obviously inappropriate for NP-hard problems. Therefore, Bello [10] introduced the concept of reinforcement learning in the pointer network, and used the policy gradient method to train the parameters of the network, and verified the effectiveness of the model on TSP and knapsack problems. On this basis, Nazari [11] believed that the previous network is difficult to apply to complex combinatorial optimization problems, and there is no relationship between the input sequence. Therefore, the encoding process of the pointer network is simplified, so that the model remains unchanged for the input sequence, so that the output of the network will not be affected when the input sequence is changed. Kool [12] made extensive use of the attention mechanism, improved both the model and the training method, and solved various combinatorial optimization problems, including TSP, Vehicle Routing Problem (VRP), Orienteering Problem (OP).

Zhao [13] combined reinforcement learning and heuristic algorithm, took the output of reinforcement learning as the initial solution of the heuristic algorithm, and proposed a two-stage framework to solve VRP and Vehicle Routing Problem with Time Window (VRPTW). In practical applications, Xu [14] proposed a new order scheduling algorithm that not only optimizes the long-term efficiency of the ride-hailing platform, but also satisfies the real-time needs of customers, which is verified in the actual scheduling system of Didi Chuxing. Lin [15] proposed a multi-agent reinforcement learning framework to solve the problem of large-scale vehicle scheduling on the ride-hailing platform. The experimental data comes from the real data of Didi Chuxing. The same multi-agent framework is also used by Lopes [16], who proposed a multi-agent framework using metaheuristics, which verified the feasibility and advancement of the framework on VRPTW. Different from the idea of using pointer network, Dai [17] treated combinatorial optimization problems as weighted graphs, and combined structure2vec and reinforcement learning to solve Minimum Vertex Cover (MVC), Maximum Cut (MC) and TSP.

From the above literature review, it can be concluded that reinforcement learning is a relatively new direction for solving combinatorial optimization problems. Therefore, inspired by the previous research work, this paper will use reinforcement learning to solve the one-to-many PDP.

3 Problem Definition

The classic pickup and delivery problem is one-to-one. But in real scenes, the situation is always different. Sometimes the pickup point in a customer request corresponds to several different delivery points, and the goods at these delivery points must be delivered by the same vehicle. There are two reasons for this situation: 1) Insufficient number of vehicles or insufficient number of drivers. 2) According to customer requirements, mixing of different types of goods is not allowed. For example, tea cannot be packed with other odorous goods. Therefore, for this one-to-many pickup and delivery problem with special requirements, the variables will be explained below. And this problem is static, which means that all data is known before the paths are constructed.

A problem instance contains n requests, each request includes a pickup point and $k \in [2,4]$ delivery points. The set of pickup points is P, and the set of delivery points is D. For the same request, the pickup must precede the delivery, and the vehicles must first pick up all the goods from the pickup point and then deliver them to each corresponding delivery point. For different requests, the pickup and delivery can be crossed. Given depot v_0 and the set of vehicles M, all vehicles must start from the depot and return to the depot after completing their tasks. The type and speed of vehicles are assumed to be the same, with maximum load limits and maximum distance limits, which is to avoid inequality in workload between drivers. The value of each edge is the distance between two points, represented by Euclidean distance. A summary of the above variables and definitions of other variables are shown in Table 1.

Table 1. Variables

Variable	Definition
$G = (V, E)$	graph
$V = v_0 \cup P \cup D$	the set of points
$E = V \times V$	the set of edges
v_0	depot
n	number of requests
$P = \{p_0, p_1, ..., p_n\}$	the set of pickup points
$D = \{d_0, d_1, ..., d_{n*3}\}$	the set of delivery points
$c_i = (x_i, y_i)$	coordinate of point i
q_i	demand of point i
Q	max load of vehicle
Q'	current load of vehicle
H	max distance of vehicle
$d_{i,j}$	distance between i and j
R	solution sequence

Figure 1 illustrates three requests R1, R2, R3 and two routes associated with vehicle V1, V2. For example, the pickup point 1P in R1 is visited by V1, so the delivery points 1D1, 1D2 are also delivered by V1. The same applies for R2 and R3.

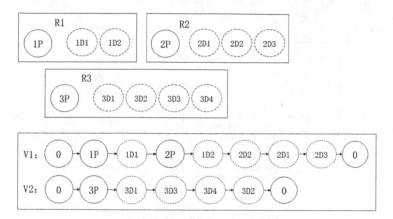

Fig. 1. An example of PDP

In the process of planning the driving route R of the vehicles, our goal is to minimize the total driving distance F.

$$F = \sum_{m \in M} \sum_{i=1}^{|R|-1} \left\| R_{i+1}^m - R_i^m \right\|_2 \tag{1}$$

where $\|\cdot\|_2$ represents the L2 norm, $|R|$ represents the number of nodes in the current route R.

At the same time, the definitions of the three basic elements in the model related to the above variables are given below. 1) Agent: In this problem, a car is an agent. Starting from the initial state, the agent will choose the next action according to the strategy. After each action is completed, the agent will update the strategy according to the data feedback obtained. 2) State: In this problem, the state is divided into static state and dynamic state. The static state is the property that does not change over time, such as the coordinates of each point. The dynamic state is the property that will change with the training process, such as the current load and position of the vehicles. 3) Reward: The training goal of the model is to maximize the reward value, and the goal of Eq. (1) is to minimize the driving distance, so we take $-F$ as the reward value.

4   Reinforcement Learning Model

We use reinforcement learning to regard the one-to-many PDP as a dynamic route generation problem, and the route planning of each vehicle as a decision sequence. The general framework of the model is shown in Fig. 2. The main composition and function of each part of the framework will be described in detail below.

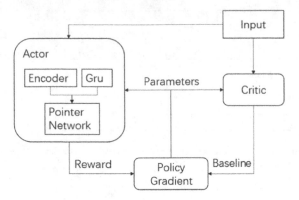

Fig. 2. The proposed model

4.1 Actor Network

Encoder: The encoder produces the embedding of the current graph, making the agent understanding the representation of each point. It is worth mentioning that the static state and the dynamic state are embedded respectively. And the proposed model is insensitive to the order of the input sequence. As shown in Eq. 2 and Eq. 3, the static and dynamic state are embedded into a x-dimensional space. The embeddings will be the input to the pointer network.

$$s_i^r = W^s s_i + b^s \tag{2}$$

$$d_{i,t}^r = W^d d_{i,t} + b^d \tag{3}$$

where s_i means the static state and $d_{i,t}$ means the dynamic state of point i at step t.

Decoder: The decoder uses the embedding of current vehicle information as input, and decodes the present state into x-dimensional hidden state. We use a gated recurrent unit layer to generate hiddden state h_t, which is the query in the attention layer.

Point Network: The network incorporates the outputs of the encoder, the outputs of the decoder and the mask matrix as inputs. It contains attention mechanism, which is used to represent the similarity between the current state and each point. At last, the parameter a_t can be represented as follows:

$$a_t = softmax(v_a tanh(W_a[s_i^r; d_{i,t}^r; h^t])) \tag{4}$$

where $[\cdot; \cdot]$ represents the concatenation operator between vectors.

The network observes a mask matrix to know which points are available. The value of each point is 1 when it is available and 0 otherwise. Given *mask* to be the mask matrix, as shown in Eq. 5, we compute the probability of choosing next point at step t.

$$p(R(t), G) = softmax(a_t + mask_t) \tag{5}$$

4.2   Critic Network

We implement a policy gradient algorithm to train the model. The basic idea is that, instead of letting the model learn from optimal solutions provided by existing algorithms, we use the reward function defined earlier to evaluate the quality of the solutions generated by the model. In each training iteration, we use θ to denote all the trainable variables.

We use Eq. 6 to estimate the gradient of the loss function $L(\theta)$ with respect to the trainable variables θ. The parameter S is the batch size. The critic is set to predict the advantage function, which is exactly the $b(G)$.

$$\nabla_\theta L = \frac{1}{S} \sum_{i=1}^{S} (F(R_i|G_i) - b(G_i)) \nabla_\theta \log p_\theta(R_i|G_i) \tag{6}$$

The critic network is used to map the current graph into a baseline $b(G)$. It contains two modules. The first module is the encoder, which has the same structure as the actor encoder. The encoder is used to embed the information into static state and dynamic state. The second module is the full connection layer, which contains three convolution layers. After the encoder's output are concatenated, it performs convolution and ReLU operations continuously to obtain the baseline. The training steps of the proposed model are illustrated in Algorithm 1.

Algorithm 1. Processing Procedure of the Model

Input: Static state and dynamic state
Output: Solution sequence R

  1: Generate problem instances
  2: Initialize parameters θ
  3: **for** each epoch **do**
  4:     **for** each batch **do**
  5:        Compute embeddings of static and dynamic state by Equation 2 and 3
  6:        Compute the hidden state by Decoder.
  7:        Compute the output probability by 5
  8:        Compute the reward for solution R and the baseline by critic
  9:        Update the parameters through the Adam optimizer
10:     **end for**
11: **end for**
12: **return**

4.3   Update and Mask

During the training process, after each step of selection, the static state still remains the same, but the dynamic state will change. So we design an update function to deal with these changes. Given that the newly selected point is i, there are three main changes:

- the demand of i should be updated to 0.
- the current position of the vehicle should be updated to i.
- if i is the pickup point, the current load of the vehicle should be added with q_i. Otherwise, it should be subtracted by q_i.

During the training process, the vehicle can not reach all points at a certain time. Therefore, in order to speed up the model training, we design a mask function to mask the points that the vehicle can not reach in the next step after the selection is completed. Given that the current vehicle is at point i, point j will be masked when it meets the following three conditions:

- the demand of j is 0, indicating that it has been served.
- j is the pickup point, and its demand exceeds the remaining load of the vehicle.
- j is the delivery point, but the vehicle has not picked up goods from its corresponding pickup point.

5   Experiments

We conduct extensive experiments to test the performance of the model in terms of solution quality and computation time. All experiments are conducted on a desktop computer configured with an Intel(R) Core(TM) i5-9400 CPU and 16GB of memory. The code is implemented in Python and Pytorch.

5.1   Experiment Setting

Data generation: Li & Lim benchmark is commonly used in the pickup and delivery problem, but the number of instances required for reinforcement learning model training is much larger than the number of instances in this benchmark. So we generate a large amount of instances in a random way based on the Li & Lim benchmark. For each instance, it is divided into pickup points and delivery points. The coordinates of each point are perturbed within a certain range to generate new instances, by adding or subtracting a random value. Then $k \in [2,4]$ delivery points are randomly assigned for each pickup point. Dividing the demand of the pickup point into k equal parts and assigning it to the delivery point. Instances can be divided into C, R and RC. C indicates that the points are clustered, R indicates that the points are randomly dispersed, and RC indicates that the points are partially clustered and partially randomly dispersed.

For the parameters of data generation, the perturbation value is a random integer between -5 and 5. The demand q_i of a pickup point is a random integer between 2 and 9. We set the maximize load $Q = 30$ when $n = 50$, $Q = 50$ when $n = 100$, $Q = 70$ when $n = 400$.

For the hyperparameters in the model, the encoder embeds the graph information into a 128-dimension vector. We clip the L2 norm of the gradient to 2.0.

The dropout is 0.1 and the learning rate of the Adam optimizer is 10^{-3}. We set the batch size to 128, and the epochs to 80. All the trainable variables are initialized with the Xavier initialization.

5.2 Baselines

To evaluate the proposed model, we compare the model against different baselines: heuristic algorithms and the Attention Model (AM) presented by [18]. Heuristic algorithms include ant colony optimization (ACO) [19], genetic algorithm (GA) and simulated annealing (SA) [7]. They are all the prevalent methods for solving both constrained and unconstrained optimization problems. And in the testing process, we use greedy and beam search. The beam width is 10.

The running time comparison is also important. Since the model is end-to-end, the training time is not considered when analyzing the performance of the proposed model. The running time of each method is calculated by running a total of 128 instances. All the reported calculation time is in seconds.

5.3 Results

Table 2 shows the performance of each method in different scale test scenarios for the three datasets. Columns with headers "Distance" and "Time" report the average tour distances and total calculation time. RL represents our model. We can draw the following conclusions. In most cases, our model achieves the best performance in terms of solution quality and computational time compared to the other baselines. In addition, no matter our method or AM, the reinforcement learning-based method performs better than the heuristic algorithms. All methods get similar results on the distance for three datasets of small-scale problems. However, as the problem size increased, the gap gradually increased. In a few cases, AM is better than our model in terms of solution quality, but in most cases we are the better one. Secondly, our method is the best in terms of calculation time.

As the size of the problem increases, the running time of the heuristic algorithms increases exponentially with the number of customers due to the NP-hard nature of the problem itself. The heuristic algorithms need to solve the problem from scratch every time, which makes it difficult for the heuristic algorithms to find a good solution at a reasonable time. Our model uses some trained information to greatly reduce the computation and can provide high-quality solutions in tens of seconds.

5.4 Training Pace

During model training, we rely on the critic to guide the actor to update in the right direction. However, the training critic depends on the data generated by the actor, which makes the training process very difficult. Therefore, learning from the training methods of Generator and Discriminator in GAN in image

Table 2. Experimental results comparison

(a) Results for C instances

Method	n = 50		n = 100		n = 400	
	Distance	Time	Distance	Time	Distance	Time
ACO	8.36	212.21	13.69	505.64	45.14	3536.12
GA	8.45	176.93	13.88	446.61	45.66	3021.32
SA	9.11	125.55	14.12	321.52	46.23	2312.15
AM(greedy)	8.17	17.46	13.21	33.78	44.67	120.74
AM(10)	7.98	20.19	**12.96**	38.12	**44.28**	140.74
RL(greedy)	8.09	16.07	13.19	31.56	44.59	124.58
RL(10)	**7.96**	18.56	13.03	35.78	44.35	137.58

(b) Results for R instances

Method	n = 50		n = 100		n = 400	
	Distance	Time	Distance	Time	Distance	Time
ACO	7.36	198.46	11.69	487.60	35.64	3418.96
GA	7.55	164.74	11.98	421.05	36.06	2877.43
SA	7.81	120.12	12.23	311.29	36.43	2251.85
AM(greedy)	7.15	13.60	11.33	27.01	35.57	101.23
AM(10)	7.04	15.19	11.16	30.12	35.13	116.74
RL(greedy)	7.10	13.19	11.28	24.19	35.36	102.58
RL(10)	**6.98**	15.06	**11.07**	29.78	**34.79**	114.58

(c) Results for RC instances

Method	n = 50		n = 100		n = 400	
	Distance	Time	Distance	Time	Distance	Time
ACO	9.46	241.41	14.89	564.35	48.76	4023.14
GA	9.52	197.86	15.08	511.21	49.32	3463.68
SA	10.01	151.24	15.32	403.61	50.13	2775.52
AM(greedy)	9.33	19.34	14.98	39.03	48.67	157.71
AM(10)	**9.22**	22.64	14.76	44.12	48.23	175.44
RL(greedy)	9.30	20.01	14.92	40.12	48.50	155.39
RL(10)	9.24	22.56	**14.65**	43.98	**47.82**	170.69

generation problems [20]. When we train the model, we do not simply train actor for each step of critic, but consciously control the pace of the two network training. For example, first train A steps of critic, and then train B steps of actor. At the beginning of the training, we set A greater than B. As the training progresses, we let A gradually decrease and B gradually increase. At the end of the training, B will be greater than A. As shown in Fig. 3, tested on the R benchmark of $n = 100$, in our model, the training effect is best when A = 4, B = 1 is initially set.

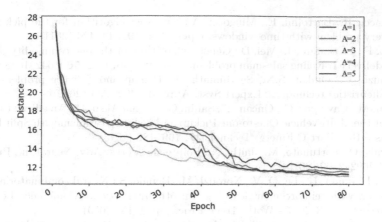

Fig. 3. Results of different training paces

6 Conclusions

This paper proposes a RL model for solving the one-to-many PDP, consisting of an actor to generate routing solutions and a critic to guide the actor to update in the right direction. And we generate massive instances to help the training and evaluation of the model. The experimental results show that the proposed model is better than the heuristic algorithms and other model.

The future research will focus on the following two points. Firstly, we plan to use advanced reinforcement learning methods to improve the performance of the model, such as hierarchical architecture and multi-head attention mechanism. Secondly, we try to combine reinforcement learning with heuristic algorithms.

Acknowledgements. This work is supported by the Major Program of Guangdong Basic and Applied Research under Grant 2019B030302002, the Science and Technology Major Project of Guangzhou under Grant 202007030006, the Engineering and Technology Research Center of Guangdong Province for Logistics Supply Chain and Internet of Things under Grant GDDST[2016]176, the Industrial Development Fund Project of Guangzhou under Project x2jsD8183470.

References

1. Berbeglia, G., Cordeau, J.-F., Gribkovskaia, I., Laporte, G.: Static pickup and delivery problems: a classification scheme and survey. TOP **15**, 1–31 (2007)
2. Berbeglia, G., Cordeau, J.F., Laporte, G.: Dynamic pickup and delivery problems. Eur. J. Oper. Res. **202**, 8–15 (2010)
3. Li, H., Lim, A.: A Metaheuristic for the Pickup and Delivery Problem with Time Windows **12**(02), 173–186 (2003)
4. Wolfinger, D., Salazar-González, J.J.: The pickup and delivery problem with split loads and transshipments: a branch-and-cut solution approach. Eur. J. Oper. Res. **289**, 470–484 (2021)

5. Baldacci, R., Bartolini, E., Mingozzi, A.: An exact algorithm for the pickup and delivery problem with time windows. Oper. Res. **59**, 414–426 (2011)
6. Zhao, F., Li, S., Sun, J., Mei, D.: Genetic algorithm for the one-commodity pickup-and-delivery traveling salesman problem. Comput. Ind. Eng. **56**, 1642–1648 (2009)
7. D'Souza, C., Omkar, S.N., Senthilnath, J.: Pickup and delivery problem using metaheuristics techniques. Expert Syst. Appl. **39**, 328–334 (2012)
8. Şahin, M., Çavuşlar, G., Öncan, T., Şahin, G., Tüzün Aksu, D.: An efficient heuristic for the Multi-vehicle One-to-one Pickup and Delivery Problem with Split Loads. Transp. Res. Part C Emerg. Technol. **27**, 169–188 (2013)
9. Vinyals, O., Fortunato, M., Jaitly, N.: Pointer networks. Adv. Neural Inf. Process. Syst. 2692–2700 (2015)
10. Bello, I., Pham, H., Le, Q. V., Norouzi, M., Bengio, S.: Neural combinatorial optimization with reinforcement learning. In: 5th International Conference Learning Represent. ICLR 2017 - Work. Track Proc., pp. 1–15 (2019)
11. Nazari, M., Oroojlooy, A., Takáč, M., Snyder, L. V.: Reinforcement learning for solving the vehicle routing problem. Adv. Neural Inf. Process. Syst., 9839–9849 (2018)
12. Kool, W., Van Hoof, H., Welling, M.: Attention, learn to solve routing problems! In: 7th International Conference Learning Represention ICLR 2019, pp. 1–25 (2019)
13. Zhao, J., Mao, M., Zhao, X., Zou, J.: A hybrid of deep reinforcement learning and local search for the vehicle routing problems. IEEE Trans. Intell. Transp. Syst. (2020)
14. Xu, Z., Li, Z., Guan, Q., Zhang, D., Li, Q., Nan, J., Liu, C., Bian, W., Ye, J.: Large-scale order dispatch in on-demand ride-hailing platforms: a learning and planning approach. In: Proceedings of ACM SIGKDD International Conference Knowledge Discovery Data Mining, pp. 905–913 (2018)
15. Lin, K., Zhao, R., Xu, Z., Zhou, J.: Efficient large-scale fleet management via multi-agent deep reinforcement learning. In: Proceedings of ACM SIGKDD International Conference Knowledge Discovery Data Mining, pp. 1774–1783 (2018)
16. Lopes Silva, M.A., de Souza, S.R., Freitas Souza, M.J., Bazzan, A.L.C.: A reinforcement learning-based multi-agent framework applied for solving routing and scheduling problems. Expert Syst. Appl. **131**, 148–171 (2019)
17. Dai, H., Khalil, E.B., Zhang, Y., Dilkina, B., Song, L.: Learning combinatorial optimization algorithms over graphs. Advances Neural Information Processing Systems, pp. 6349–6359 (2017)
18. Li, J., Xin, L., Cao, Z., Lim, A., Song, W., Zhang, J.: Heterogeneous attentions for solving pickup and delivery problem via deep reinforcement learning. IEEE Trans. Intell. Transp. Syst., 1–10 (2021)
19. Liang, D., Zhan, Z.H., Zhang, Y., Zhang, J.: An efficient ant colony system approach for new energy vehicle dispatch problem. IEEE Trans. Intell. Transp. Syst. **21**, 4784–4797 (2020)
20. Pfau, D., Vinyals, O.: Connecting Generative Adversarial Networks and Actor-Critic Methods. arXiv preprint arXiv:1610.01945 (2016)

Towards Relational Multi-Agent Reinforcement Learning via Inductive Logic Programming

Guangxia Li[1(✉)], Gang Xiao[2], Junbo Zhang[1], Jia Liu[1], and Yulong Shen[1]

[1] School of Computer Science and Technology, Xidian University, Xi'an, China
{junbzhang,jialiu23}@stu.xidian.edu.cn, gxli@xidian.edu.cn,
ylshen@mail.xidian.edu.cn
[2] National Key Laboratory for Complex Systems Simulation, Beijing, China
searchware@qq.com

Abstract. We present a relational multi-agent reinforcement learning algorithm in which two agents work together to achieve a goal in an environment represented by structured entities and relations. Our proposal takes a hybrid connectionist-symbolic approach, where a classical actor-critic method with an iterative weight update scheme is used to guide the derivation of an agent's policy, which is purely expressed as first-order logic. A recent technique, differentiable inductive logic programming, is applied to integrate these two parts into a trainable system. We tailor the centralized training with decentralized execution framework to meet the symbolic-represented underlying structure. Agents are designed to communicate with one another in terms of logical predicates to alleviate the partially observable problem prevalent in the multi-agent setting. Empirical studies on the classical grid-world task demonstrate that the proposed method can learn close to optimal strategies and has better interpretability than traditional reinforcement learning approaches.

Keywords: Reinforcement learning · Multi-agent · Inductive logic programming

1 Introduction

Owing to the availability of massive amounts of data and computing resources, artificial intelligence (AI) has recently achieved spectacular performance in domains such as vision, language, control, and decision-making. Unfortunately, the holy grail of artificial general intelligence that can learn, reason, and act like human beings remains out of reach. One drawback of modern AI is its lack of capacity to generalize beyond experiences. To fundamentally solve this problem, it is believed that one should avoid learning from a large amount of data's attribute-value representation, but turn to imitating human intelligence, which can compose an infinite number of concepts from a finite set of means [1]. Relational learning advocates the construction of new inferences, predictions, and

E. Pimenidis et al. (Eds.): ICANN 2022, LNCS 13530, pp. 99–110, 2022.
https://doi.org/10.1007/978-3-031-15931-2_9

behaviors from structured representations of entities and relations, using rules regarding how they can be composed.

Common approaches to relational learning include hierarchical models [16], probabilistic programming [7], causal reasoning [12], and graph networks [1]. Inductive logic programming (ILP), a classical symbolic approach, has recently regained considerable attention [11]. ILP uses logic programming as a uniform representation for examples, background knowledge, and hypotheses. Given an encoding of the known background knowledge and a set of examples represented as a logical database of facts, an ILP system can derive a logic program that entails all positive and none of the negative examples. The learned program has an explicit symbolic structure that can be inspected, understood, and verified. However, it cannot deal with noise or mislabeled inputs and is inapplicable to non-symbolic domains where data may be ambiguous. Attempts have been made to integrate symbolic ILP with connectionist learning approaches to overcome these limitations. A representative work in this direction is differentiable inductive logic programming (DILP), which implements an ILP within an end-to-end differentiable model [4]. The use of differentiable models makes DILP trainable via gradient optimizers, which are widely used in artificial neural networks. Thus, a hybrid connectionist-symbolic method with DILP can learn explicit symbolic rules from noisy and ambiguous data.

We are particularly interested in the sequential decision-making task and the corresponding machine-learning paradigm—reinforcement learning (RL). Reinforcement learning concerns how intelligent agents ought to take action in an environment to maximize long-term rewards. It has been regarded as a promising method that can eventually lead to the development of artificial general intelligence [14]. For decades, relational reinforcement learning (RRL) has drawn considerable attention as a subfield of reinforcement learning. Early work in RRL learned first-order logic rules from relational representations of states, actions, and policies in terms of predicate language via logical decision trees [3]. It works on crisp symbolic inputs and cannot handle noise and ambiguity. The state-of-the-art approach replaces the logical decision tree with DILP, making the induction procedure compatible with policy-learning algorithms in RL [8]. Empirical evaluations have demonstrated that RRL has superior interpretability and generalization ability compared with the classical RL approach.

In this study, we take a step further upon RRL by formulating it in a multi-agent setting. Most existing RRL methods are for a single agent, whereas a large number of RL applications involve the participation of more than one agent. Multi-agent reinforcement learning (MARL) is challenging because the environment faced by each agent is no longer stationary as all policies change together. In addition, each agent may have limited access to the observations of others, leading to suboptimal policies. With this in mind, we propose a relational multi-agent reinforcement learning algorithm in which two agents perform hybrid connectionist-symbolic learning via DILP and coordinate their actions using an augmented actor-critic gradient policy. We adopt the centralized training with decentralized execution paradigm because of its popularity in the MARL community. In the training phase, the actor of each agent is trained from its own observation but is guided by a critic who has a global view of all agents. In the execution phase, multiple actors are allowed to communicate with one another in terms of logical predicates to alleviate the partially observable problem. We evaluate our algorithm with the classical grid-world task, where two agents cooperate to reach a goal while trying to prevent collisions. The algorithm successfully generates interpretable policies and outperforms a benchmark that trains the agents independently.

The remainder of this paper is organized as follows. Section 2 reviews related work. Section 3 provides a short introduction to the differentiable inductive logic programming that underlies our work. Section 4 begins with a problem formulation in terms of the MARL. Subsequently, a relational multi-agent reinforcement learning algorithm is presented. Section 5 presents experimental results and discussion. Finally, Sect. 6 concludes the study.

2   Related Work

Interest in relational reinforcement learning has been longstanding [15] and has risen again recently owing to its potential to overcome the drawbacks of the connectionist approach. Early works used predicate-represented states and actions combined with relational regression to learn the action value function [3]. Discrete logic operations are non-differentiable, making it difficult to apply modern gradient-based RL methods. Recent extensions have employed the differentiable inductive logic programming technique [4] so that the RL problem be solved by the policy gradient [8]. Inductive logic programming is not the only method to implement relational learning. Self-attention, for instance, has been used to build relation block which is embedded into neural networks to learn pairwise interactions of entities [17].

One of the challenges in multi-agent reinforcement learning is the so-called non-stationarity problem. There has been no shortage of efforts to address this issue. A class of methods tries to learn communication protocols to coordinate agents' behaviors for cooperative tasks [5]. Other approaches either take the actions, observations, or policies of other agents as inputs [10] or explicitly model the decision-making process of other agents [6]. Among these methods, centralized training and decentralized execution is a commonly used paradigm. In particular, the actor-critic method with centralized critic and decentralized actors is representative of this idea [10].

Relational reinforcement learning has not been fully examined in a multi-agent context. The use of a relational representation of the state space in multi-agent planning and coordination tasks has been proposed [2]. The effect of using relational representation with respect to agent communication has also been investigated [13]. A recent approach utilized a variational auto-encoder to infer the interactions between agents [18]. It is a purely connectionist approach, and cannot solve problems at an abstract level.

3   Preliminary

In this section, we briefly introduce inductive logic programming and its differentiable implementation. Further details can be found in [4,11].

3.1   Inductive Logic Programming

Inductive logic programming (ILP) is a technique for constructing logic programs from examples and background knowledge, such that all positive examples are entailed by the program, while negative examples are not. The constructed logic program is neither a command nor a function but a set of if-then-like rules. As rules have an explicit symbolic structure, it is possible for humans to read, understand, and verify them. However, ILP cannot deal with ambiguous or noisy data and is incompatible with neural-network-based systems.

The basic components of ILP are the atoms and clauses. An atom α is a tuple $p(t_1, \ldots, t_n)$ where p is an n-ary predicate and $t_1, \ldots, t_n$ are terms, either variables, or constants. An atom is ground if it contains no variables. A clause is defined as the rule of $\alpha_0 \leftarrow \alpha_1, \ldots, \alpha_n$, where α_0 represents the head atom and $\alpha_1, \ldots, \alpha_n$ represents the body atom. The head atom is true only when all body atoms are true. We limit the arity of the predicate to at most two, as in [4] to make ILP computationally feasible. The number of body atoms is restricted to two as well. If there are more than two atoms in a clause body, it can be converted into an equivalent logic program with two body atoms.

3.2   Differentiable Inductive Logic Programming

From a machine-learning perspective, the ILP system can be interpreted as implementing a rule-based binary classifier on examples, mapping each example to true or false according to the axioms provided to the system, and inferring the system by training new rules. Differentiable inductive logic programming (DILP) is a reimplementation of ILP in an end-to-end differentiable architecture [4]. It interprets the ILP task as a binary classification problem and minimizes the cross-entropy loss with regard to the ground-truth Boolean labels during training.

Instead of the binary discrete semantics of mapping ground atoms to true or false, DILP uses a continuous representation of the rules that map each atom to a real interval $[0, 1]$. For each predicate, the DILP generates a series of potential clause combinations based on the rule template and assigns trainable weights to clause combinations. It uses forward chain derivation to infer the results of applying rules to background facts. The system can be trained using gradient-based methods through differentiable deduction of continuous values. The loss value is defined as the cross-entropy between the confidence of the predicted atom and ground truth.

4 Methodology

4.1 Problem Setting

We consider a scenario in which multiple agents work collaboratively in an environment to achieve a goal. It can be formally defined as a partially observable Markov game for N agents that contains a set of states S describing the possible configurations of all agents, a collection of observation sets $O_1, \ldots, O_N$ and a collection of action sets $A_1, \ldots, A_N$, one for each agent in the environment [9]. To choose an action, each agent i uses a stochastic policy $\pi_{\theta_i} : O_i \times A_i \mapsto [0, 1]$ that produces the next state according to the state transition function $T : S \times A_1 \times \cdots \times A_N \mapsto S$. A reward $r_i : S \times A_i \to \mathbb{R}$ is then revealed to the agent together with an observation correlated with state $o_i : S \to O_i$. The goal for agent i is to maximize the expected sum of the discounted rewards $\mathbb{E}[\Sigma_{t=0}^{T} \gamma^t r_{i,t}]$, where γ is a discount factor and $r_{i,t}$ is the reward received at time step t by agent i.

Several factors make this problem challenging for reinforcement-learners. One is the aforementioned non-stationary environment problem, as an agent must take action in an environment affected by other agents' actions that are out of its control. The other is the partially observable setting, which restricts the agent from observing the entire state of the environment. Decisions must be made under environmental uncertainty. To address these challenges, we adopt the commonly used centralized training with decentralized execution framework [10]. It allows agents to use global information to ease training, as long as this information is not used at the execution time. We modify the actor-critic reinforcement learning method under this framework so that every agent has a critic trained in a centralized manner and an actor working on local observations. The proposed multi-agent actor-critic algorithm is presented below.

4.2 Partner-Aware Actor-Critic Gradient Policy

We propose a multi-agent actor-critic reinforcement learning algorithm under centralized training with decentralized execution framework. As in [10], each agent is associated with an actor relying on a policy function to generate actions and interact with the environment and a critic that can access the global information to evaluate the actor and guide it during training. As each agent can only access its local observations during execution, a partially observable problem exists that hinders their cooperation. Thus, we perform message transfer among the agents to alleviate this problem. Specifically, we propose a simple extension of the actor-critic policy gradient method, where the critic is augmented using extra information taken from the messages sent by other agents. We do not assume that the communication method between the agents has a specific structure. The message can contain an agent's private observations, which can be applied generally to cooperative games.

We denote the policy of N agents in a Markov game by $\pi = (\pi_{\theta_1}, \ldots, \pi_{\theta_N})$ where $\theta = (\theta_1, \ldots, \theta_N)$ are the trainable parameters. According to the policy gradient theorem, the gradient of the expected return of agent i is

$$\nabla_{\theta_i} J(\theta_i) = \mathbb{E}[\psi_i^\pi(\mathbf{x})\nabla_{\theta_i} log\pi_{\theta_i}(a_i|o_i)]$$

where o_i is the local observation of agent i and $\psi_i^\pi(\mathbf{x})$ is a centralized advantage function derived from the corresponding critic of actor i. It is noteworthy that $\mathbf{x}$ can contain different information during the training and execution phases.

With the gradient of the expected return, we can update the policy parameters of each agent as

$$\theta_i = \theta_i + \alpha\nabla_{\theta_i} J(\theta_i)$$

where α is the learning rate.

The critic uses the advantage function to evaluate the selected action of the agent. In contrast to the local observations of actors, we grant the advantage function full access to the global state information of the environment. We allow $\mathbf{x}$ to consist of the observations of all agents at training time, that is, $\mathbf{x} = (o_1,\ldots,o_N)$, and it could also include additional environmental information if available. However, such a global view is allowed only during the centralized training phase. After the training is completed, only the actors are used in the decentralized execution phase. Therefore, for execution, $\mathbf{x} = (o_i, m_i)$ where m_i is the message that agent i receives from other agents.

The centralized advantage function $\psi_i^\pi(\mathbf{x})$ is defined as

$$\psi_i^\pi(\mathbf{x}) = r_i + \gamma V_i^\pi(\bar{\mathbf{x}}; \omega_i) - V_i^\pi(\mathbf{x}; \omega_i)$$

where r_i is the reward obtained by agent i, ω_i is the parameter of the critic network, and $\bar{\mathbf{x}}$ represents the next joint state of all agents.

Moreover, by replacing the single actor-critic in neural logic reinforcement learning [8] with this multi-agent implementation and describing the message between actors in terms of logic predicates, we arrive at a multi-agent reinforcement learning algorithm driven by DILP. This is discussed in the next section.

4.3   Multi-agent Reinforcement Learning with DILP

Figure 1 shows the architecture of the proposed multi-agent reinforcement learning with DILP. As shown, in the process of centralized training, the critic makes use of the global state information (Fig. 1(a)), whereas in the process of decentralized execution, actors communicate with each other and execute their own policies (Fig. 1(b)). Compared to the ordinary Markov game, there is a state encoder E_i and an action decoder D_i for each agent. These are used to handle the states and actions of the agent.

In a multi-agent environment, an agent does not act independently, but must communicate to complete the cooperative task. This requires the state encoder to map the local observations of an agent obtained from the environment and the communication messages received from other agents onto the valuations of ground atoms. The state encoder of agent i is expressed as follows

$$E_i : (o_i, m_i) \rightarrow [0,1]^{|G|}$$

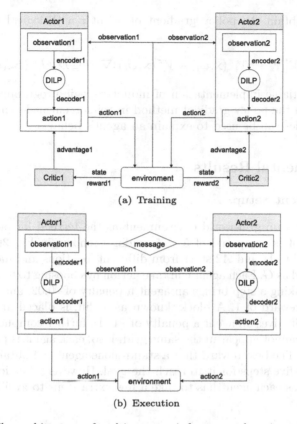

(a) Training

(b) Execution

Fig. 1. The architecture of multi-agent reinforcement learning with DILP.

where G denotes the set of ground atoms.

In addition, it also needs to convert the valuations of the action atoms into action probabilities. The action decoder of agent i is expressed as

$$D_i : [0,1]^{|D|} \rightarrow [0,1]^{|A|}$$

A DILP system represented by f_θ implements differentiable deduction over continuous values by using the information of ground atoms to infer the valuations of action atoms. It can be expressed as

$$f_\theta : [0,1]^{|G|} \rightarrow [0,1]^{|D|}$$

For more details on DILP, please refer to [4].

Finally, we use the state encoder to convert the observation information from the environment and the communication message from other agents into the form of predicates for expression and then use the DILP system to obtain the valuations of action atoms. An action decoder maps values that represent the confidence of the action atoms into action probabilities. Applying the DILP to the actor, we obtain the policy gradient of agent i with logical reasoning as follows

$$\nabla_{\theta_i} J(\theta_i) = \mathbb{E}[(r_i + \gamma V_i^\pi(\bar{\mathbf{x}}; \omega_i) - V_i^\pi(\mathbf{x}; \omega_i))\nabla_{\theta_i} \log D_i(f_{\theta_i}(E_i(o_i, m_i)))]$$

The differentiable implementation of inductive logic programming makes it compatible with the policy gradient method in reinforcement learning, whereby symbols and rules can be used to explain an agent's behavior.

5   Experimental Results

5.1   Experiment Setup

We use a well-known grid-world environment as the testbed for our algorithm. The environment is composed of 5×5 grids, as shown in Fig. 2(a). The two agents denoted by $A1$ and $A2$ start from different locations and move toward a goal, represented as G. Each agent can take action by choosing to move up, down, left, or right. Taking a step brings an agent a penalty of –0.02, and reaching the goal gives it a reward of 1. A block, known as a cliff, is placed at the bottom. Reaching the cliff gives an agent a penalty of –1. To further complicate the task, the two agents cannot appear in the same grid. If so, each agent is punished with a penalty of –1. The best reward that a stand-alone agent can obtain is 0.9 since it takes at least five steps for it to reach the goal. However, this does not apply for two agents, as each agent has to take a few extra steps to avoid collisions.

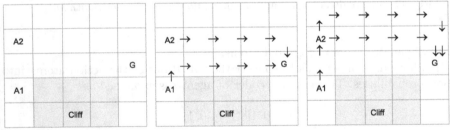

(a) Grid-world environment   (b) Action sequence of MARL-DILP   (c) Action sequence of NLRL

Fig. 2. The 5×5 grid-world environment. MARL-DILP-trained agents take smarter actions than NLRL-trained agents.

The comparison methods include the single-agent RRL method, neural logic reinforcement learning (NLRL) [8], and the proposed multi-agent reinforcement learning with DILP (MARL-DILP). They use the same predicates, rule templates, and hyper-parameters as those defined in [8]. Specifically, an agent's local observation is represented by the predicate $current(x, y)$ and its actions are represented by four direction predicates: $up()$, $down()$, $left()$ and $right()$.

To avoid collisions, MARL-DILP allows the two agents to communicate during the execution phase. Thus, we add an extra predicate $insight(x, y)$ to record the partner-agent coordinates. It is passed between two agents as a message. A DILP can use this predicate message for reasoning and select the most appropriate rules among all clauses related to action predicates.

5.2 Results and Analysis

Performance. Both MARL-DILP and NLRL were trained using 5,000 episodes and tested over 100 further iterations. This procedure was repeated 10 times, the results were averaged and are reported below. The learning curves of the two methods are plotted in Fig. 3 where the horizontal and vertical axes represent the learning episodes and cumulative reward per episode, respectively. As shown in Fig. 3, the learning curve of MARL-DILP starts to converge after 1,000 episodes and is always better than that of NLRL. The average reward and its standard deviation achieved by the two methods during the test phase are listed in Table 1. It is clear that the proposed MARL-DILP outperforms NLRL, as the former receives more rewards. Furthermore, MARL-DILP's reward value of 0.878 approaches 0.9, which is the best reward a stand-alone agent can obtain.

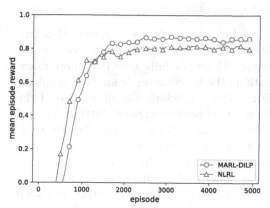

Table 1. The average reward and its standard deviation of MARL-DILP and NLRL.

	Mean	Std.
MARL-DILP	0.878	0.044
NLRL	0.794	0.229

Fig. 3. Averaged variations of the cumulative reward along the 5,000 training episodes.

To provide an in-depth analysis of the learned policies, we further depict the action sequences of MARL-DILP and NLRL in Fig. 2(b) and 2(c), respectively. As shown in Fig. 2(b), because the agent at the bottom of the MARL-DILP communicates through the predicate $insight(x, y)$ to obtain the coordinates of another agent, it can move to the right in time and avoid collisions with the other agent. For the action sequence of NLRL, it can be seen from Fig. 2(c) that the bottom agent always moves up as much as possible. Because the agent cannot obtain the coordinates of another agent, it is punished and chooses other actions once it moves to the right and collides with another agent. This forces the agent to choose a relatively "safe" route to approach the target, which is a suboptimal policy.

Interpretability. We briefly analyze the policies generated by MARL-DILP to demonstrate its interpretability. The human-readable rules derived from the policies of agent $A1$ are as follows. We indirectly express the coordinate information of the grid-world by borrowing auxiliary predicates. The policy first explains the low-level invented predicate, and the target predicate is then interpreted based on the invented predicate. The number preceding each clause indicates the probability that the agent will execute the rule.

$$0.249 : up() \leftarrow zero(X), invented(X)$$
$$0.749 : up() \leftarrow invented(X), zero(X)$$
$$0.781 : invented(X) \leftarrow succ(X, Y), current(X, Y)$$
$$0.825 : right() \leftarrow succ(X, Y), insight(Y, Z)$$
$$0.174 : right() \leftarrow insight(X, Y), succ(Z, X)$$
$$0.149 : down() \leftarrow current(X, Y), last(X)$$
$$0.851 : down() \leftarrow last(X), current(X, Y)$$

The first three clauses relating to predicate $up()$ show that agent $A1$ learns to move upward from its initial position. The following two clauses containing the predicate $right()$ indicate that agent $A1$ successfully uses the communication predicate $insight(x, y)$ which contains the coordinates of another agent $A2$ to move to the right to avoid collisions. When reaching the right edge of the grid, agent $A1$ has only two possibilities for its next movement: hitting the goal directly or moving downward to approach it. As hitting the goal directly completes the game, there is only one situation that deserves a policy. The last two clauses containing the predicate $down()$ correspond to this situation.

Similarly, the rules derived from the policies of agent $A2$ are as follows. It can be observed that agent $A2$ learns to move to the furthest right and then moves down to the goal. Because the clauses related to predicates $left()$ and $up()$ have probabilities no greater than 0.1, they are not listed below. This low probability value verifies that moving left or up is excluded from the optimal policies of agent $A2$.

$$0.246 : right() \leftarrow succ(X, Y), current(X, Z)$$
$$0.754 : right() \leftarrow current(X, Y), succ(X, Z)$$
$$0.988 : down() \leftarrow last(X), current(X, Y)$$

6   Conclusion

In this study, we present a relational reinforcement learning algorithm to solve a multi-agent cooperative task based on inductive logic programming. It extends the existing neural logic reinforcement learning to a multi-agent setting using centralized training with decentralized execution paradigm and an actor-critic method tailored to alleviate the non-stationary environment problem. A predicate-based communication mechanism is employed to improve cooperative behaviors among agents. Empirical studies on the classical grid-world task demonstrate that the proposed method can learn close-to-optimal strategies and has better interpretability than traditional RL approaches. In future work, we wish to extend our method to a more complex multi-agent setting. This involves improving the current memory-intensive DILP for more efficient implementation and designing a more sophisticated mechanism for agent cooperation. In addition, the integration of the proposed model with a deep learning method to learn directly from non-relational data, such as images, deserves further study.

Acknowledgements. This work was supported by the Fund of State Key Laboratory, China under Grant No. XM2020XT1006.

References

1. Battaglia, P.W., et al.: Relational inductive biases, deep learning, and graph networks. CoRR abs/1806.01261 (2018)
2. Croonenborghs, T., Tuyls, K., Ramon, J., Bruynooghe, M.: Multi-agent relational reinforcement learning. In: Tuyls, K., Hoen, P.J., Verbeeck, K., Sen, S. (eds.) LAMAS 2005. LNCS (LNAI), vol. 3898, pp. 192–206. Springer, Heidelberg (2006). https://doi.org/10.1007/11691839_12
3. Dzeroski, S., Raedt, L.D., Driessens, K.: Relational reinforcement learning. Mach. Learn. **43**(1/2), 7–52 (2001)
4. Evans, R., Grefenstette, E.: Learning explanatory rules from noisy data. J. Artif. Intell. Res. **61**, 1–64 (2018)
5. Foerster, J.N., Assael, Y.M., de Freitas, N., Whiteson, S.: Learning to communicate with deep multi-agent reinforcement learning. In: Lee, D.D., Sugiyama, M., von Luxburg, U., Guyon, I., Garnett, R. (eds.) Advances in Neural Information Processing Systems 29: Annual Conference on Neural Information Processing Systems 2016, 5–10 December 2016, Barcelona, Spain, pp. 2137–2145 (2016)
6. Foerster, J.N., Farquhar, G., Afouras, T., Nardelli, N., Whiteson, S.: Counterfactual multi-agent policy gradients. In: Proceedings of the Thirty-Second AAAI Conference on Artificial Intelligence, (AAAI-18), pp. 2974–2982 (2018)
7. Griffiths, T.L., Chater, N., Kemp, C., Perfors, A., Tenenbaum, J.B.: Probabilistic models of cognition: exploring representations and inductive biases. Trends Cogn. Sci. **14**(8), 357–364 (2010)
8. Jiang, Z., Luo, S.: Neural logic reinforcement learning. In: Chaudhuri, K., Salakhutdinov, R. (eds.) Proceedings of the 36th International Conference on Machine Learning, ICML 2019, 9–15 June 2019, Long Beach, California, USA. Proceedings of Machine Learning Research, vol. 97, pp. 3110–3119. PMLR (2019)
9. Littman, M.L.: Markov games as a framework for multi-agent reinforcement learning. In: Cohen, W.W., Hirsh, H. (eds.) Machine Learning, Proceedings of the Eleventh International Conference, Rutgers University, New Brunswick, NJ, USA, 10–13 July 1994, pp. 157–163. Morgan Kaufmann (1994)

10. Lowe, R., Wu, Y., Tamar, A., Harb, J., Abbeel, P., Mordatch, I.: Multi-agent actor-critic for mixed cooperative-competitive environments. In: Advances in Neural Information Processing Systems, vol. 30, pp. 6379–6390 (2017)
11. Muggleton, S., De Raedt, L.: Inductive logic programming: theory and methods. J. Logic Program. **19**, 629–679 (1994)
12. Pearl, J., et al.: Models, Reasoning and Inference. Cambridge University Press, Cambridge, vol. 19 (2000)
13. Ponsen, M.J.V., et al.: Learning with whom to communicate using relational reinforcement learning. In: Babuska, R., Groen, F.C.A. (eds.) Interactive Collaborative Information Systems, Studies in Computational Intelligence, vol. 281, pp. 45–63. Springer, Berlin (2010). https://doi.org/10.1007/978-3-642-11688-9_2
14. Silver, D., Singh, S.P., Precup, D., Sutton, R.S.: Reward is enough. Artif. Intell. **299**, 103535 (2021)
15. Tadepalli, P., Givan, R., Driessens, K.: Relational reinforcement learning: an overview. In: Proceedings of the ICML-2004 Workshop on Relational Reinforcement Learning, pp. 1–9 (2004)
16. Tenenbaum, J.B., Kemp, C., Griffiths, T.L., Goodman, N.D.: How to grow a mind: statistics, structure, and abstraction. Science **331**(6022), 1279–1285 (2011)
17. Zambaldi, V.F., et al.: Relational deep reinforcement learning. CoRR abs/1806.01830 (2018)
18. Zhang, X., Liu, Y., Xu, X., Huang, Q., Mao, H., Carie, A.: Structural relational inference actor-critic for multi-agent reinforcement learning. Neurocomputing **459**, 383–394 (2021)

Understanding Reinforcement Learning Based Localisation as a Probabilistic Inference Algorithm

Taku Yamagata$^{(\boxtimes)}$, Raúl Santos-Rodríguez , Robert Piechocki,
and Peter Flach

Intelligent System Laboratory, University of Bristol, Bristol BS8 1TW, UK
{taku.yamagata,enrsr,r.j.piechocki,peter.flach}@bristol.ac.uk

Abstract. Indoor localisation and tracking in a residential home setting are envisaged to play an essential role in smart home environments. As it is hard to obtain a large number of labelled data, semi-supervised learning with Reinforcement Learning is considered in this paper. We extend the Reinforcement Learning approach, and propose a reward function that provides a clear interpretation and defines an objective function of the Reinforcement Learning. Our interpretable reward allows us to extend the model to incorporate multiple sources of information. We also provide a connection between our approach and a conventional inference algorithm for Conditional Random Field, Hidden Markov Model and Maximum Entropy Markov Model. The developed framework shows that our approach benefits over the conventional algorithms a real-time prediction scenarios. The proposed Reinforcement Learning method is compared against other supervised learning approaches. The results suggest that our method can learn in the semi-supervised learning setting and performs well in a small labelled data regime.

Keywords: Reinforcement Learning · Probabilistic inference ·
Localisation · Semi-supervised learning · Conditional Random Field ·
Hidden Markov Model · Maximum Entropy Markov Model

1 Introduction

Indoor localisation enables the discovery of relevant information about residents' behaviour and preferences, especially those who need long-term monitoring or care [4]. Location-aware applications include surveillance and security, health and sleep monitoring, assisted living for elderly people or patients with disabilities and entertainment.

In this paper, we consider a smart home localisation task where a small amount of labelled data is available at the start, potentially coming from the

This work was supported by SPHERE Next Steps Project funded by the U.K. Engineering, and Physical Sciences Research Council (EPSRC) under Grant EP/R005273/1 and the UKRI Turing AI Fellowship EP/V024817/1.

E. Pimenidis et al. (Eds.): ICANN 2022, LNCS 13530, pp. 111–122, 2022.
https://doi.org/10.1007/978-3-031-15931-2_10

residents themselves. After this first stage, the system receives unlabelled data to predict the current target location and learns a suitable predictive model from them. This is an online task and a special case of the semi-supervised learning paradigm, as labelled data is only available initially.

We propose a reinforcement learning (RL) based approach for semi-supervised online localisation. We build upon prior works [7,10] that formulated the localisation task as a Markov decision process (MDP). Our contributions are in two folds. First, we extend and generalise that framework, providing interpretable reward functions by treating the task as probabilistic inference [6]. We introduce our reward function in Sect. 3.3. As a result, our approach can easily incorporate various sensors and/or combinations of sensors. Second, we also state the connection between the RL based approach and a conventional inference algorithm, namely conditional random fields (CRF) [5] hidden Markov model (HMM) and maximum entropy Markov model (MEMM) [8]. The connection clarifies that our RL approach is advantageous in a real-time prediction scenario, in which the predictions are generated based upon the current and past observations. We show the connections in Sect. 4.

2   Related Work

Much work has already been done for wireless localisation tasks, with many using machine learning techniques. Examples of such methods include localisation using deep neural networks (DNNs) [13], Gaussian process (GP) [2], and HMMs [3,11]. Most of these approaches are based on supervised learning combined with a method to exploit the location's temporal correlation characteristics (e.g., HMM). A RL based approach is not an obvious choice for a localisation task, as it is not usually modelled as an MDP. However, recent works reformulate the localisation task to exploit advanced RL algorithms to learn the location prediction model [7,10]. Our approach builds upon these in formalising the localisation tasks as an MDP, however, their reward function is specific to received signal strengths (RSSs) and also does not have a strong theoretical background for their design; hence it is difficult to incorporate other sensor modalities. In contrast, our reward function is defined as probability distributions (as shown in Sect. 3.3) hence any new sensors can be adopted easily as they become available. While the RL approach is somewhat similar to the CRF approach, there are specific differences that make the RL approach particularly suitable for online prediction. The details of the connection with the CRF and HMM are discussed in Sect. 4.

3   Method

RL is a flexible online learning algorithm that can naturally handle semi-supervised learning settings. To apply RL algorithms to online wireless localisation, we formulate the task as an MDP, which is a four-tuple (S, A, p, r) where S is a set of states, A is a set of actions, p is the state transition probabilities, and r is a reward function. After summarising the problem setting in Sect. 3.1, the detailed description of the MDP setting is shown in Sect. 3.2. We design the reward function following *RL as probabilistic inference* [6], which is described in Sect. 3.3. We follow the prior works [7,10] to formulate the localisation as MDP. However, their reward function is specific to RSSs and does not have a solid theoretical background for their design. In contrast, we propose a reward function defined as probability distributions and allow the incorporation of different sensors.

3.1 Problem Setting

We consider an online room level localisation task for a semi-supervised learning scenario, where the goal is to predict the current target location on a grid while learning the model with labelled and unlabelled data in an online fashion. Our main interests are indoor residential home settings, which have a few access points (APs) installed. These APs communicate with a wearable device worn by the target person and measures RSS. When the engineer installed the APs, a small labelled training data is obtained. Once the deployment is completed, we only receive sequences of unlabelled data afterwards. In this scenario, the prediction model is initially trained with the limited labelled dataset obtained by the engineer and then optimise further from unlabelled data as it arrives.

3.2 MDP Setting

We follow the prior works [7,10] to formulate the localisation as MDP. One way to understand the MDP formulation of localisation is to consider the task of moving a virtual avatar to follow a target based on the RSS information alone without knowing the actual target location. In this setting, the avatar's location is the target's predicted location, and the actions of the MDP are the moves of the avatar. The action at time step t (a_t) can be written as,

$$a_t = \hat{y}_t - \hat{y}_{t-1} \tag{1}$$

where $\hat{y}_t$ and $\hat{y}_{t-1}$ are predicted locations at time step t and $t-1$ respectively. As we assume a room level localisation task, the actions are moving to a certain room (e.g., moving to the kitchen) Hence the above definition of action is a conceptual one. This is useful when we discuss a connection between our RL approach and HMM in Sect. 4. The state at time step t (s_t) is formed by concatenating the current sensor outputs and the previous predicted location.

$$s_t = [\mathbf{x}_t, \hat{y}_{t-1}], \tag{2}$$

where $\mathbf{x}_t$ is RSS information at time step t.

The Agent will learn to generate the best sequence of actions (movement of the avatar) to maximise the sum of rewards. The details of the reward function are described in the following subsection. Note that the location $\hat{y}_t$ is deterministic in terms of the actions; hence deciding the actions is equivalent to deciding the predicted locations.

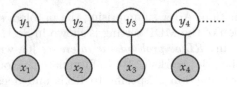

Fig. 1. Graphical model for y_t and $\mathbf{x}_t$, where y_t is a target location at time step t and $\mathbf{x}_t$ is RSS observation at time step t.

3.3   Reward Function

The reward function could be anything as long as it indicates how good the predictions are. In the prior works, the researchers design a specific reward function for a particular sensor [7,10]. It is advantageous to incorporate prior knowledge. However, it does not scale well for a sensor fusion scenario, as it requires manually designing the reward function for each sensor. Furthermore, it is very hard to balance the rewards from all of the sensors. In this work, we design the reward function by getting inspiration from *RL as probabilistic inference*. More specifically, our reward function is designed to maximise the following posterior probability for the optimal sequence of actions (predicted locations $\hat{\mathbf{y}}$).

$$\hat{\mathbf{y}} = \underset{\mathbf{y}}{\mathrm{argmax}}\ P(\mathbf{y}|\mathbf{X}), \tag{3}$$

where $\mathbf{X}$ is a sequence of RSS observations and $\mathbf{y}$ is a sequence of locations. As the rest of this section shows, our reward function is derived by factorising the posterior. It provides a clear meaning of what RL optimises, and we can show the strong connection between our RL approach and the conventional probabilistic inference algorithms (Sect. 4).

We assume that the observation RSS at time step t ($\mathbf{x}_t$) only depends on the target location at the same time step (y_t) as shown in Fig. 1. Then the posterior probability in Eq. 3 can be factorised as follows.

$$
\begin{aligned}
P(\mathbf{y}|\mathbf{X}) &\propto p(\mathbf{y}, \mathbf{x}) \\
&\propto \prod_{t=1}^{T} P(y_t|y_{t-1})\ P(y_t|\mathbf{x}_t)/P(y_t)
\end{aligned}
\tag{4}
$$

where T is the length of the observation sequence $\mathbf{X}$ and the target locations $\mathbf{y}$ and we define $P(y_1|y_0) := P(y_1)$. To make the following discussion simple, we assume the prior $P(y_t)$ has a uniform distribution, then this shows that the posterior can be factorised in two terms one denoting the transition probabilities y_{t-1} to y_t and the other is the location probabilities given the observations. Note that it is not too difficult to consider non-uniform prior for y_t, we can obtain it from a labelled data set.

Instead of maximising the posterior, we consider maximising the log of the posterior, then Eq. 3 can be written as follows.

$$\hat{y} = \operatorname*{argmax}_{y} \sum_{t=1}^{T} \log\left(P(y_t|y_{t-1})\right) + \log\left(P(y_t|\mathbf{x}_t)\right), \tag{5}$$

By defining the reward function as the term inside the summation over time in Eq. 5, the RL algorithm will find $\mathbf{y}$ that maximises the posterior log probability.

$$r_t = \lambda \log\left(P(y_t|y_{t-1})\right) + \log\left(P(y_t|\mathbf{x}_t)\right), \tag{6}$$

where we also introduced a scaling parameter (λ) to control the balance between the two terms. The first term of the reward function is the transition log probability, which can be derived by counting actual transitions on the training labelled data. The second term is the log probability of the location given the RSS information for the time step t, which can be obtained by any discriminative prediction model that produce probabilistic outputs. In our case, we use random frorest (RF) in our experiments. The model is trained to predict the probabilities for all locations with given RSS information.

4   Connection to Inference Algorithm on Graphical Model

This section provides our second contribution. We show what our RL algorithm actually learns as compared to the more conventional probabilistic inference algorithms – the CRF [5] with the Viterbi algorithm. Our intention in this comparison is to make the relationship between our RL algorithm and other non-RL algorithms clear, showing the advantages and limitations of each. First, we show the similarities of our RL algorithm with Q-Learning and greedy-policy to the CRF with Viterbi algorithm. Then, we discuss the connection to the HMM and the MEMM [8] in the following subsection.

4.1   Connection to CRF

We consider a special case of the CRF with the following factor graph (Fig. 2), where f_t are factors for transition probabilities and g_t are factors for the probabilities of y_t given x_t. We use the probabilities for the factors in the graph instead of potentials. The probability factors allow us to train them independently without computing an overall partition function. Assuming we have already obtained these probabilities (factors) from a labelled dataset, the Viterbi algorithm consists of the following two stages. The first stage is deciding a root node, then propagate a message towards the root node. We set y_1 as a root node and consider the message towards y_1. As our graph structure has repetitions of y_t and x_t (dashed-box), we just need to consider messages in/out of the box and then repeat the process of the input to the output backward through time. Following the notation of [1], the message out of the box (red arrow) denoted by

$\mu_{y_t \to f_{t-1}}(y_t)$, is derived from a message from y_{t+1} to f_t which is denoted by $\mu_{y_{t+1} \to f_t}(y_{t+1})$ as follows,

$$\mu_{y_t \to f_{t-1}}(y_t) = \log\left(g_t(y_t, x_t)\right) + \max_{y_{t+1}}[\log\left(f_{t+1}\left(y_t, y_{t+1}\right)\right) + \mu_{y_{t+1} \to f_t}(y_{t+1})]. \quad (7)$$

By adding $\log\left(f_{t-1}\left(y_{t-1}, y_t\right)\right)$ to the both left and right terms, we get the following,

$$\log\left(f_{t-1}\left(y_{t-1}, y_t\right)\right) + \mu_{y_t \to f_{t-1}}(y_t) = \log\left(f_{t-1}\left(y_{t-1}, y_t\right)\right) + \log\left(g_t(y_t, x_t)\right) + \max_{y_{t+1}}[\log\left(f_t\left(y_t, y_{t+1}\right)\right) + \mu_{y_{t+1} \to f_t}(y_{t+1})]. \quad (8)$$

The left hand side of the equation and the inside of the max operator are the same but the time index is shifted by one. We denote them as $Q(s_t, a_t)$ and $Q(s_{t+1}, a_{t+1})$, and also denote $\log\left(f_{t-1}\left(y_{t-1}, y_t\right)\right) + \log\left(g_t(y_t, x_t)\right)$ by $r(s_t, a_t)$, where we used our definition of a_t and s_t (Eq. 1 and Eq. 2). Then we can rewrite Eq. 8 as,

$$Q(s_t, a_t) = r(s_t, a_t) + \max_{a_{t+1}} Q(s_{t+1}, a_{t+1}). \quad (9)$$

This is the same as the Bellman update equation in Q-Learning. The second stage of the Viterbi algorithm is the trace-back stage, which starts from the root node y_1 and selects the next time step y value ($\hat{y}_{t+1}$) recursively by taking argmax of $\log\left(f_{t+1}\left(y_t, y_{t+1}\right)\right) + \mu_{y_{t+1} \to f_t}(y_{t+1})$. By using the notation above, the process can be written as

$$a_t = \underset{a_t}{\operatorname{argmax}} Q(s_t, a_t). \quad (10)$$

This corresponds to the greedy-policy in RL setting.

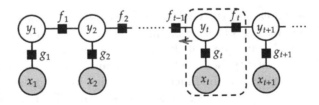

Fig. 2. Factor graph for y_t and $\mathbf{x}_t$, where y_t is a target location at time step t and $\mathbf{x}_t$ is RSS observation at time step t. f_t and g_t are factor nodes.

We now discuss the differences between our RL approach and the Viterbi algorithm. The most prominent difference is that the RL approach predicts in real-time, which means that it predicts $\hat{y}_t$ from data up to the time t ($x_{1:t}$). In the standard Viterbi algorithm we collect all observations ($x_{1:T}$) first, then predict the whole sequence of locations ($y_{1:T}$). 'Viterbi like' prediction without future observations is where the RL approach differs from Viterbi based inference. Let us consider the action-value function (Q) defined in between Eq. 8 and Eq. 9. The action-value function corresponds to a message just before taking maximum within the factor node f_t. Hence, the RL approach learns and predicts the message from future time steps as the action-value function, and uses it to generate predictions. These observations suggest the possibility of adding extra side information to the state (s_t) so that the RL algorithm improves the predictions of the message from the future (action-value function). The side information can be as simple as the just time of day and/or day of the week etc. Evaluating such a scenario is left for future work.

4.2 Connection to HMM and MEMM

So far, we have considered our RL approach as a discriminative model (CRF). Changing it to a generative model (HMM) is straightforward. The HMM considers a joint probability and factorises it as Eq. 11.

$$P(\mathbf{y}, \mathbf{X}) = \prod_{t=1}^{T} P(y_t|y_{t-1})\, P(\mathbf{x}_t|y_t). \tag{11}$$

The corresponding RL reward function becomes,

$$r_t = \lambda \log\left(P(y_t|y_{t-1})\right) + \log\left(P(\mathbf{x}_t|y_t)\right). \tag{12}$$

Compare to our reward function (Eq. 6), the only difference is in the second term. As the observations ($\mathbf{x}_t$) are continuous and the latent variables (y_t) are discrete variables, it is easier to model and train the discriminative model $P(y_t|\mathbf{x}_t)$ than the generative model $P(\mathbf{x}_t|y_t)$.

It is worth discussing a MEMM [8] in comparison to the CRF here. Both of them are discriminative models; hence they start with the probability of $\mathbf{y}$ given $\mathbf{X}$. However, they have different factorisations. The factorisation for MEMM is,

$$P(\mathbf{y}|\mathbf{X}) = \prod_{t=1}^{T} P(y_t|y_{t-1}, \mathbf{x}_t). \tag{13}$$

where we define $P(y_1|y_0, \mathbf{x}_1) := P(y_1|\mathbf{x}_1)$. The factorisation for the CRF is,

$$P(\mathbf{y}|\mathbf{X}) = \prod_{t=1}^{T} \psi_u(y_t, \mathbf{x}_t)\psi_p(y_t, y_{t-1})/Z(\mathbf{X}), \tag{14}$$

where ψ_u and ψ_p are a unary and pairwise potentials respectively, and $Z(\mathbf{X})$ is a partition function, which is defined as follows.

$$Z(\mathbf{X}) = \sum_{y_1}\sum_{y_2}\cdots\sum_{y_T}\prod_{t=1}^{T} \psi_p(y_t, y_{t-1})\psi_u(y_t, \mathbf{x}_t). \tag{15}$$

The MEMM has the probabilities as the factors; hence it can train each factor independently, whereas the CRF has the potentials as the factors and employs the partition function to normalise it. As a result, it is required to look at the entire sequence $(t = 1, 2, \ldots, T))$ to train the factors. The main MEMM disadvantage is a so-called *label bias* [5], which is due to the probability factors. In an extreme case that a certain y_{t-1} has only one possible the next y_t, the observation $\mathbf{x}_t$ does not affect the overall posterior. In another word, the probability of y_t given $\mathbf{x}_t$ does not affect the factor $P(y_t|y_{t-1}, \mathbf{x}_t)$ as it is a probability and is normalised to sum to one. This *label bias* does not happen in the CRF, as each factor is a potential and is not normalised. Now we consider our factorisation (Eq. 4). Because it is using probabilities in the factors, we can train them independently – like MEMM. At the same time, it does not suffer from *label bias* as the probabilities are factorised into the transition probabilities and the discriminative probabilities separately. In summary, our factorisation captures both advantages in the MEMM and the CRF.

5   Evaluation

We empirically evaluate our RL based localisation approach in a semi-supervised learning setting and compared the results with other non-RL based approaches. To demonstrate our RL approach's flexibility to accommodate multiple sensors, we also consider a sensor fusion (RSS and passive infrared (PIR) sensors) scenario. We used a publicly available activity recognition dataset [12], which is described in Sect. 5.1.

5.1   SPHERE Challenge Dataset

The SPHERE challenge [12] is an activity recognition competition where the predictions are made from video, accelerometer, RSS and environmental sensors. The datasets are publicly available. As it also has the target locations, we use the dataset for the localisation task. The location information is room level – nine locations (bathroom, bedroom 1, bedroom 2, hall, kitchen, living, stairs, study, toilet.) There are ten labelled datasets, where each is approximately 30 min long.

5.2   Evaluation Procedure

We use deep Q-Learning (DQN) [9] for our RL agent, which employs DNN to approximate the action-value function $Q(s, a)$ – expected cumulative future rewards starting with state s and action a. It then uses the learned action value function to decide an action to take at time step t by $a_t = \text{argmax}_{a \in \mathcal{A}} Q(s_t, a)$. The DNN has three hidden layers, and each has 256 units with ReLU activation functions except the last layer, which has a linear activation function.

First, we prepared the reward function models: the normalised adjacency matrix and the RF discriminative classification model, which infers the room level location from the RSSs. The RF is trained as a supervised learning model.

The normalised adjacency matrix is obtained by counting room-transitions in the datasets. These models are trained with one SPHERE challenge dataset.

For the sensor fusion scenario, we have access to PIR sensors (as well as RSSs) in each room except the hall. To incorporate the PIR sensors, we compute the log posterior distribution $log(P(y_t|x_t))$, where y_t is the target location and x_t is PIR sensor readings, then add it to the existing reward (Eq. 6.) The posterior distribution is computed as follows. 1) Prepare a vector with the length of number of rooms, and initialised it with 0.05. 2) Add 1 where the PIR sensor becomes active. 3) Normalise the vector by dividing the each element by sum of the all elements. Each element of the vector is the posterior probability for the each room location. We set the hyper-parameter $\lambda = 1/8$ in Eq. 6. It is obtained from our parameter sweep simulations, which evaluate with $\lambda = [0, 1/32, 1/16, 1/8, 1/4, 1/2, 1]$ for the number of labelled datasets are one, two, three and four cases. The results suggest that the performance is not very sensitive to the λ value, but all the results show the best performance between $\lambda = 1/16 and 1/4$. We picked the value between them. The RL agent was trained with five unlabelled datasets. After training the RL agent, we measured its accuracy score with five separated test datasets.

5.3 Baseline Algorithms

We compare the RL performance with three baseline models – type 1 and type 2 RF models and a HMM. The type 1 RF takes a current time window RSS data x_t and predicts the same time window location y_t. The type 2 RF takes two consecutive time slots' RSS $[x_{t-1}, x_t]$ and predicts the later time slot's location y_t. The type 1 RF is the same as the one we used for generating the reward function. Importantly, it does not take into account its temporal characteristics of the target location. The type 2 RF takes into account the temporal characteristics in a straightforward way. The HMM is prepared with its initial state probabilities, transition probabilities and generative model parameters. These are learnt from a labelled dataset. The HMM uses a diagonal Gaussian as its generative model, which assumes the observations are generated by a normal distribution with diagonal covariance matrix.

5.4 Results

Figure 3 shows the accuracy score for the RL approach and the RF models with a different number of labelled datasets with RSS alone. The RL approach outperforms type 1 RF because type 1 RF does not take into account the time correlation characteristics on the locations. The RL approach performs similarly to type 2 RF for two or more labelled datasets; however, it performs better with a single labelled dataset.

The first four rows of Table 1 presents the evaluation results for the two RFs, HMM and RL algorithms. It shows that the RL approach performs better than the RF approaches and is close to the HMM. This is encouraging results because the RL approach predicts the current locations based on the data so far and does

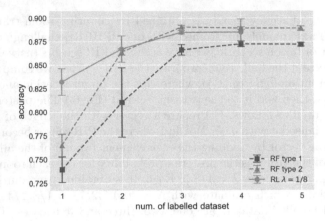

Fig. 3. Comparison against RF models. The plot shows the accuracy score against the number of labelled datasets. The RL approach outperforms type 1 RF because type 1 RF does not consider the time correlation characteristics on the locations. The RL approach performs similarly to type 2 RF for two or more labelled datasets; however, it performs better with a single labelled dataset.

Table 1. Evaluation results summary. Accuracy scores and their standard deviations for two random frorest (RF) models, hidden Markov model (HMM), reinforcement learning (RL) with received signal strength (RSS) as features and RL with RSS & PIR as features.

Model	Feature(s)	Accuracy score	std.
RF type 1	RSS	0.739	0.013
RF type 2		0.765	0.012
HMM		**0.844**	0.003
RL		0.832	0.014
RL	RSS & PIR	**0.867**	0.021

not rely on the future data – *filtering* estimation, whereas the HMM uses all data both past and future to predict the location – *smoothing* estimation. Still, the RL approach achieves similar performance as the HMM, which supports our conclusion in Sect. 4 that the RL learns the message from the future time steps.

The last row of the table shows the results for the sensor fusion scenario (with RSS and PIR sensors.) Although we use very simple models to compute the posterior probabilities for PIR sensors and kept the same hyperparameter settings as other simulations, it shows 3.5% accuracy score gain from the RL with RSS only case.

6   Conclusions

We investigated the use of RL approaches for localisation in a semi-supervised learning setting. We formulated the localisation task as an MDP by introducing the notion of probabilistic inference. This allows us to extend the model to incorporate multiple data sources coherently. We also established a connection between the RL approach and probabilistic inference approaches on a graph such as the HMM, CRF and MEMM, which clarifies their similarities and differences and inspires further improvements for the future.

Our evaluation results suggest that the RL approach allows us to learn in the semi-supervised setting successfully and perform better than the type 2 RF, which takes the current and past data as its input, for the small number of labelled dataset case. Also, it performs close to HMM (1.2% worse in its accuracy score). We see HMM as the upper bound because it uses the entire data sequence to make the prediction (*smoothing*), whereas the RL approach does not rely on future data (*filtering*.) We also evaluated the multiple sensors scenario and demonstrated its ability to incorporate multiple sensors easily. Avenues for future work include enriching the probabilistic mobility model with inertial measurements.

Another area for future work relates to prediction resolution. In this paper, we only dealt with discrete locations. However, we can extend it to continuous location tasks by employing RL algorithms dealing with the continuous state and action space, such as policy gradient algorithms.

References

1. Bishop, C.M.: Pattern Recognition and Machine Learning. Springer, New York (2006)
2. Hähnel, B.F.D., Fox, D.: Gaussian processes for signal strength-based location estimation. In: Proceeding of Robotics: Science and Systems (2006)
3. Kozlowski, M., Byrne, D., Santos-Rodriguez, R., Piechocki, R.: Data fusion for robust indoor localisation in digital health. In: IEEE WCNCW (2018)
4. Kozlowski, M., Santos-Rodriguez, R., Piechocki, R.J.: Sensor modalities and fusion for robust indoor localisation. EAI Endorsed Trans. Ambient Syst. **6**(18), e5 (2019)
5. Lafferty, J.D., McCallum, A., Pereira, F.C.N.: Conditional random fields: probabilistic models for segmenting and labeling sequence data. In: Proceedings of the Eighteenth International Conference on Machine Learning. ICML 2001, San Francisco, CA, USA, pp. 282–289. Morgan Kaufmann Publishers Inc. (2001)
6. Levine, S.: Reinforcement learning and control as probabilistic inference: tutorial and review. arXiv preprint arXiv:1805.00909 (2018)
7. Li, Y., Hu, X., Zhuang, Y., Gao, Z., Zhang, P., El-Sheimy, N.: Deep reinforcement learning: another perspective for unsupervised wireless localization. IEEE Internet Things J. **7**, 6279–6287 (2019)
8. McCallum, A., Freitag, D., Pereira, F.C.N.: Maximum entropy Markov models for information extraction and segmentation. In: ICML (2000)
9. Mnih, V., et al.: Human-level control through deep reinforcement learning. Nature **518**(7540), 529 (2015)

10. Mohammadi, M., Al-Fuqaha, A., Guizani, M., Oh, J.S.: Semisupervised deep reinforcement learning in support of IoT and smart city services. IEEE Internet Things J. **5**, 624–635 (2017)
11. Sun, S., Li, Y., Rowe, W., Wang, X., Kealy, A., Moran, B.: Practical evaluation of a crowdsourcing indoor localization system using hidden Markov models. IEEE Sens.s J. **19**, 9332–9340 (2019)
12. Twomey, N., et al.: The SPHERE challenge: activity recognition with multimodal sensor data. arXiv:1603.00797 (2016)
13. Zhang, W., Liu, K., Zhang, W., Zhang, Y., Gu, J.: Deep neural networks for wireless localization in indoor and outdoor environments. Neurocomputing **194**, 279–287 (2016)

Word-by-Word Generation of Visual Dialog Using Reinforcement Learning

Yuliia Lysa[⊠], Cornelius Weber, Dennis Becker, and Stefan Wermter

Knowledge Technology Research Group, University of Hamburg, Hamburg, Germany
yuliia.lysa@studium.uni-hamburg.de,
{cornelius.weber,dennis.becker-1,stefan.wermter}@uni-hamburg.de
http://www.knowledge-technology.info

Abstract. The task of visual dialog generation requires an agent hold-ing a conversation referencing question history, putting the current ques-tion into context, and processing visual content. While previous research focused on arranging questions to form dialog, we tackle the more chal-lenging task of arranging questions from words, and dialog from ques-tions. We develop our model in a simple "Guess which?" game scenario where the agent needs to predict an image region that has been selected by an oracle by asking questions to the oracle. As a result, the rein-forcement learning agent arranges words to refer to the image features strategically to acquire the required information from the oracle, mem-orizing it and giving the correct prediction with an accuracy well above 80%. Imposing costs on the number of questions asked to the oracle leads to a strategy using few questions, while imposing costs on the number of words used leads to more but shorter questions. Our results are a step towards making goal-directed dialog fully generic by assembling it from words, elementary constituents of language.

Keywords: Visual dialog generation · Deep reinforcement learning · Compositionality

1 Introduction

Deep neural networks have recently led to large progress in image- and natural language processing. Generating meaningful dialogs regarding visual content is required for various applications such as conversations with intelligent robot assistants [7]. One task allowing for research towards conversations is Visual Question Answering (VQA) [10], which consists of a single question-answer pair that is processed individually and, therefore, is limited in modeling complex communication. Visual dialog tasks [3] extend VQA and present sequences of questions, requiring a model to consider the question history and to recognize context. Visual dialogue generation tasks [7], in addition, require a goal-oriented agent to produce sequences of questions, focusing on efficient task completion.

The authors acknowledge support from the German Research Foundation DFG under project Crossmodal Learning (TRR 169). Mengdi Li provided inspiration and feedback on the document.

© The Author(s), under exclusive license to Springer Nature Switzerland AG 2022
E. Pimenidis et al. (Eds.): ICANN 2022, LNCS 13530, pp. 123–135, 2022.
https://doi.org/10.1007/978-3-031-15931-2_11

Question Number	Agent's Actions	Oracle's Answer
1.	"green" + "?"	No
2.	"background" + "light" + "blue" + "?"	No
–	"stop"	–
Agent's Prediction	"2"	

Fig. 1. Left: Example image with the digit in position 2 selected by an oracle, as indicated by the red frame. This position needs to be predicted by the agent. Right: Task of the agent is to generate a suitable question sequence from individual actions, which express words and question marks, to receive answers by the oracle (whether the requested features are present in the selected sub-image; for example, question 1 asks whether it contains green) that allow it to correctly predict the selected position. The questions are created word by word, as the agent selects one new action each round. The agent ends its questions with the "stop" action, which precedes its prediction. (Color figure online)

Examples of visual dialog generation tasks include the description of visual scenes based on question-answer pairs provided in a dataset [9] or the localization of objects in a visual context of the colored MNIST data set [1]. Our objective is to extend the Recurrent Attention Model [8], which has been used in various vision and robotics tasks, to enable the generation of questions using individual words. We will examine compositional questions, which have a stronger resemblance to natural speech patterns instead of a restricted set of questions. Furthermore, the development of an optimal questioning strategy and proper compositional question structure will be analyzed.

Our novel focus is on assembling dialog questions from individual words that refer to image features, thereby generating dialog in a more natural way. Challenges of this task include that the generated language needs to be goal-directed to ask relevant information, needs to be composed of tokens, and these tokens should refer to the visual features of the scene. In order to address those questions, we introduce a simple visually grounded language game (cf. Fig. 1), where the model predicts the location of a digit in the provided image based on a sequence of questions and corresponding answers about its visual attributes.

1.1   Task Definition

The agent is trained on a variation of the MNIST-GuessNumber data set [1] that combines a set of grid images filled with digits and adds the corresponding descriptions for each specific image. The data set is modified to stimulate the generation of compositional questions in which individual tokens refer to distinct features of the images. To this end, the images can be referred to by color words, by attributes "light" and "dark", and by the specifiers "background" and "foreground", or a combination thereof.

One of the digit positions in the grid is selected by an oracle as the target digit. At each step, the agent produces a question from individual tokens and a final end-of-question mark and receives the corresponding question-answer pair as input. They should be based on the attributes of the digits displayed on the currently presented image. Based on the history of question-answer pairs and the learned strategy, the agent selects a new token each round and updates the current question-answer pair. After the agent decides not to ask any further questions by producing a "stop" action, or after a maximum number of questions have been asked, the agent will make the digit prediction. At the end of the task, the agent will receive reward feedback from the environment.

2 Related Work

Deep learning has enabled tasks involving images and text, like image captioning and visual question answering. Visual dialog tasks focus on answering a final question based on visual references and comprehending the relations between a set of given questions and answers. The goal of the task proposed by Hongsuck et al. [6] is to answer a final question about digits' features shown in an image based on a given question & answer history. This model uses supervised learning to investigate *retrieved* attention for visual reference resolution and its combination with *tentative* attention to predict the correct response. These tasks, however, do not require any generation of questions.

2.1 Visual Dialog Generation

The aim of visual dialog generation tasks is to create dialog sequences of question-answer pairs, relating to images. Zhao et al. [1] utilize a modified MNIST data set to generate a grid of differently colored numbers. The task is to identify and locate a specific number on the generated image. The model consists of three networks, "guesser", "answerer" and "questioner", that are pre-trained using supervised learning. Thereafter, only the guesser network is trained using reinforcement learning to learn the correct classification. The vocabulary for the question generation consists of a limited set of attributes that describe each digit, therefore deviating from the natural process of communication.

Vries et al. [9] introduce a GuessWhat game, where two bots hold a conversation about a visual environment, which is represented by an image. One of the bots asks questions and receives binary answers to determine which object was selected. The data set was collected from a series of manually typed questions from a previously conducted study. The questions were later assigned to the corresponding images, therefore providing a static set of questions that the bots choose from.

Das et al. [7] extended on a goal-driven approach for the training of dialog agents. The main objective of the research task is to identify an image by asking questions about its content. The "questioner" and "answerer" bots are trained with supervised learning to ensure that they utilize a common language for communication. Then reinforcement learning is used to improve the performance. This reinforcement learning agent perceives the generated language not as a supervised learning task, therefore attempting to simulate natural human speech. Moreover, the results of this experiment show that the strategy of using reinforcement learning on visual dialog tasks provides better performance than the ones based only on supervised learning [7].

2.2 Compositionality in VQA

Compositional questions are not entirely studied in the context of visual dialog tasks, but there are some novel approaches in the Visual Question Answering field [5,14,15,17]. The following research papers concentrate on multi-hop reasoning. The point of question answering with compositional reasoning is to divide the question into different components and attempt to analyze them separately by considering how the rest of the components will behave [4].

Koushik et al. [5] research compositional reasoning for VQA. They argue that the majority of solutions [10,13,16] exploit statistical properties of the feature distribution to produce a correct answer. Therefore, the models rely on educated guesses instead of reasoning. For their experiments, the CLEVR data set [11] is used to answer corresponding questions about the displayed objects. This is achieved using reinforcement learning methods and a deep LSTM, and additional attention mechanisms in subsequent experiments. While VQA with the attention module yielded satisfactory results, reinforcement learning failed to improve the performance. Nevertheless, it was suggested that the reinforcement learning approach can be further incorporated into tasks with compositional reasoning [5].

3 Methodology

3.1 Data Pre-processing

We generate a collection of colored 28×28 pixel images of MNIST digits arranged on a 2×2 grid[1] This results in four possible positions that can be selected by the oracle as the target, which the agent has to infer. The target number corresponds to the positions in the grid from left to right line by line. The generated images include two primary colors {green, blue}. These colors describe both background and foreground, which can either appear in light or dark. If the background is light, the foreground must be dark, and vice versa, so that the digits are well visible. A rudimentary image preprocessing step extracts the image information and represents the image RGB colors of the background and foreground as a 3×8-dimensional vector.

The generated images allow for eight possible actions that the network can produce form the token set: {"background", "foreground", "dark", "light", "blue", "green", "?", "stop"}. The digits were excluded from the label set due to

---

[1] The dataset and the code of the model implementation are available at: https://github.com/ylysa/Recurrent-Attention-Model.

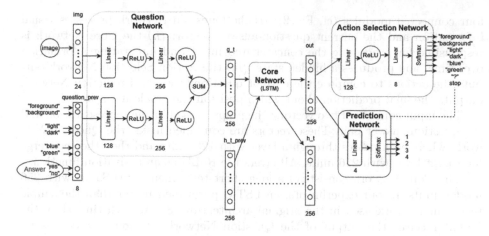

Fig. 2. The model architecture, including layer sizes and activation functions

the lack of compositional combinations with other features. A question includes between one and four actions, selecting one token at a time. For sequentially generating a sequence of tokens, the network receives the previously asked token as input until the "?" token is produced. The question mark concludes the question sequence generation and the model receives the corresponding answer from the oracle. The question sequence and the oracle's answer are combined into an 8-dimensional input vector consisting of two units for "background" or "foreground", two units for "light" or "dark", two units for each color, and two units for the binary answer (yes or no). Each unit is activated when the model has selected the corresponding action or the corresponding answer was received. During the sequence generation, the question token is fed back to the network. An answer to the question is only provided when the sequence is completed with the "?" token or when the limit of four actions has been reached. At the beginning of the next question, or if the generated question structure was invalid, the input vector is reset to a null vector. An answer is given only to valid questions.

For the question sequence, we define a simple grammar that requires a valid question structure that has to fulfill the following pattern: "background" or "foreground" feature followed by "light" or "dark" feature and the color. The order of the selected features must remain identical, but individual features can be omitted. The question must end with a "?" token to be considered valid. A question sequence that consists of only a question mark, without any other words, is invalid.

3.2 Architecture

The utilized model architecture is a modification of the Recurrent Attention Model proposed by Mnih et al. [8]. The agent is initially trained with supervised learning to predict the selected target digit's position and afterward with reinforcement learning to develop a questioning strategy. The agent consists of four connected modules (cf. Fig. 2): *(i)* the Question Network processes visual information and the current question-answer vector; *(ii)* the Core Network is responsible for processing the concatenated input and integrating information over time, and produces a hidden state; *(iii)* the Action Selection Network outputs the actions to compose the current question; *(iv)* the Prediction Network outputs the final prediction about which position the oracle has selected.

The input consists of two vectors: the preprocessed image representation and the question-answer pair. These vectors are combined inside the Question Network, where each passes through a layer with 128 units and then they converge on a joint layer with 256 units. All layers use ReLU as an activation function.

The Core Network consists of a long short-term memory (LSTM) with 256 hidden units. In our experiments, an LSTM performed better than the simple recurrent network used in the original architecture [8]. At each time step, the LSTM receives the output of the Question Network as input, as well as its previous hidden state.

The Action Selection module consists of two layers: one hidden layer with 128 hidden units that receives its input from the Core Network and one output layer with eight outputs corresponding to the eight possible actions. The actions are sampled from a categorical probability distribution created from the output layer's Softmax function. For evaluation, the action with the highest probability is selected.

The Prediction Network has a single output layer, receiving its input directly from the Core Network. The last layer of the Prediction Network uses the Softmax activation function, which predicts the probability of each target. The four outputs correspond to four possible target positions.

3.3 Loss Function

The model parameters are updated using the policy gradient method REINFORCE [12] and portray a partially observable Markov decision process (POMDP) since the underlying states cannot be fully observed (the oracle's selection is unknown). The Question, Prediction, Core, and Baseline Network parameters are trained with supervised loss. The Action Selection module parameters are trained with reinforcement learning, while the weights of the previously trained modules are frozen.

The prediction loss is calculated with negative log-likelihood, where y stands for the ground-truth label from the data set and $log(\tilde{y})$ for the probability distribution over all possible digits generated by the model:

$$L_{pred} = -log(\tilde{y}) \cdot y. \tag{1}$$

A baseline is estimated to approximate the reward function and is used to stabilize the reinforcement learning. The Baseline Network (not shown in Fig. 2) has a single hidden layer with 256 units that maps the output of the Core Network into one output. R_t is the accumulative reward over the entire trajectory and b_t

is the output of the Baseline Network. The baseline loss uses the mean squared error:

$$L_b = \frac{1}{T} \sum_{t=0}^{T} (R_t - b_t)^2. \tag{2}$$

The total reward provided to the model after an episode is $R = r_p + r_l$. The first term is the prediction reward, where the model receives $r_p = 1$ if the prediction was correct and $r_p = -1$ otherwise. The second term is the latency reward [2], calculated as

$$r_l = \frac{1}{T+2}, \tag{3}$$

where T stands for either the episode length or the number of questions in that episode. We conducted experiments for both definitions of the latency reward function. The reward R_t is assigned to an entire trajectory, i.e. dialog, since not a separate question but rather the entire trajectory has to be evaluated.

Empirical sampling over the state-action space in REINFORCE is expressed as $log\pi(a_t \mid s_t)$, the probability of selecting action a_t in state s_t. R_t is the accumulative reward over the whole trajectory and b_t is the output of the Baseline Network. The action loss is defined as

$$L_{act} = \sum_{t=0}^{T} -log\pi(a_t \mid s_t)(R_t - b_t). \tag{4}$$

The baseline and action losses are backpropagated only to the Baseline module and Action Selection module, respectively, but not to the remaining modules. The total loss is the sum of all three components, with equal weights for each component

$$L = L_{pred} + L_b + L_{act}. \tag{5}$$

4   Experiments

The generated images include two colors: green, blue. The four sub-images in the grid are likely to contain identical colors and therefore require complex questions. Overall there exist 1680 unique images; in each image, we ensure that there are no two equal sub-images. This allows to uniquely identify the selected image via a suitable question strategy. Additionally, there are four times as many data samples, since each image consists of four different sub-images that can be selected by the oracle. Only a minority of 300 of the images are used for training, which poses challenges for generalization. The validation data set contains 1000 images, which do not overlap with the training set. The validation set is also used for testing because no hyperparameters are optimized using the validation set. To prevent the predictions from overfitting to the training images regardless of the question sequence, the target sub-image is always selected randomly for each epoch.

4.1   Pre-training

Learning to predict correctly requires question-answer histories that contain sufficient information, while learning the question strategies suffers from noisy rewards resulting from unreliable target predictions. This causes difficulties for the model when learning the predictions and question sequences simultaneously. Therefore, only the Prediction Network is pre-trained using an automatically generated question sequence for each image. During each epoch a different random question sequence is created, to present the model with a large variety of environment states. After the supervised pre-training for less than 20 epochs, the model reaches an accuracy above 90%. After pre-training of the Prediction Network, the Action Selection network is trained using reinforcement learning to learn a correct question generation starting with randomly initialized weights. The model is optimized with Adam Optimizer with a learning rate of 3e-4. Sequences are terminated by the stop action, or after a maximum of 13 time steps, including the initial step with a null vector input. The prediction is derived from the last available state.

4.2   Experiments with Different Time Efficiency Losses

For evaluation of the model, we test multiple implementations of time efficiency constraints, which contribute to the action loss function, and their effect on the resulting behavior.

1. The latency reward defined in Eq. 3 uses the number of selected tokens as the number of required time steps T. The reward function that depends on the number of tokens is referred to as R^{tok}.
2. Time steps T in Eq. 3 are defined as the number of questions posed to the oracle. The reward function that depends on the number of questions is referred to as R^{qu}.
3. The latency reward is applied only if the network predicts correctly, in which case $R = 1 + r_l$, while for false predictions the total reward remains as $R = -1$ regardless of the number of time steps. Here, similar to the second definition of the reward function, T is the number of questions. The corresponding reward function is referred to as R^{qu+lat}.

5   Results

5.1   Accuracy

The model achieves an accuracy above 80% on the validation data (see Fig. 3), where the form of the time efficiency loss does not have a major impact. The model with the R^{qu+lat} loss had the highest accuracy by a small margin at the end. These results demonstrate the generalization capabilities given that only a minority of 300 images from 1680 possible images, were used for training, and utilizing unseen validation images.

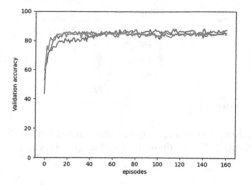
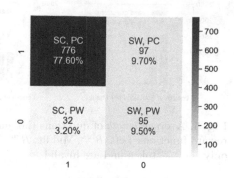

Fig. 3. Validation accuracy with different reward functions (blue: R^{tok}, purple: R^{qu}, red: R^{qu+lat}) (Color figure online)

Fig. 4. Test accuracy of R^{q+lat} (SC: correct question sequence, SW: wrong question sequence, PC: correct prediction, PW: wrong prediction)

For analyzing the models' performance, the generated question sequence and resulting prediction have to be considered. Specifically, if the sequence of questions is considered correct (SC), meaning that it retrieves sufficient information from the oracle for a correct prediction (PC) of the chosen target sub-image. Similarly, the question history can be considered wrong (SW), not asking for sufficient information, possibly resulting in a wrong prediction (PW). The model with the R^{q+lat} reward function provides the best performance in these four criteria and is illustrated in Fig. 4. For most images, the model generates a valid sequence of questions (SC) and the correct prediction (PC). In 9.7% of cases (SW, PC), a correct prediction was partially guessed since an improper question sequence would not guarantee a correct prediction. In 9.5% of cases (SW, PW), the model predicts wrongly given an improper question sequence. In the remaining 3.2% of cases (SC, PW), the model should be capable of predicting the correct sub-image based on the question sequence, however, the Prediction Network predicts the wrong sub-image.

5.2   Question Evaluation

As can be seen in Fig. 5, the average length of the questions for the model with R^{qu} and R^{qu+lat} reward functions is greater in comparison to the model with R^{tok}. The corresponding reward function stimulates longer compositional questions. The majority of questions vary between two and three tokens. For the R^{qu+lat} model, the distribution of question length leans toward three tokens and the number of four tokens questions is the highest among all experiments, which demonstrates the ability of this approach to generate compositional questions.

The average number of valid questions remains under four (see Fig. 6). In the majority of cases, where the sequence is longer than three questions, the

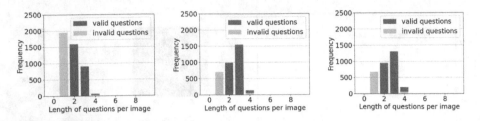

Fig. 5. Average *length* of questions (i.e. number of tokens per question) with different reward functions. Left: R^{tok}; Middle: R^{qu}; Right: R^{qu+lat}. Questions of length 1 contain only the "?" token and are invalid.

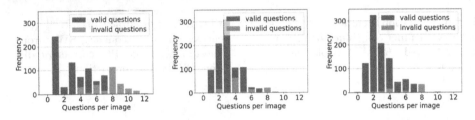

Fig. 6. Average *number* of questions per image with different reward functions. Left: R^{tok}; Middle: R^{qu}; Right: R^{qu+lat}.

remaining questions consist only of question marks. The invalid questions that include some tokens usually do not have the question mark accompanying them.

Upon inspection of the models' generated output, questions often contain a learned bias, such as preferring "dark" over "light", or "background" over "foreground". However, we did not notice any bias for color. These biases do not necessarily degrade performance, since these features are inherently symmetric in the data. It is equally efficient to inquire about a dark background or light background since the same number of digit sub-images is eliminated. The model often does not learn all possible question sequences. The sequences from the R^{qu} and R^{qu+lat} reward functions usually do not include any repetitions beyond the question mark, while we did observe models trained with R^{tok} to repeat questions. We also observed the model to be inefficient in applying the optimal question strategy, when it chose a color that is present only in a single sub-image in its first question, since such a question cannot rule out multiple sub-images.

In typical dialog sequences (see Fig. 7), the questions appear sequentially and with correct structure, the repetitions are avoided and the stop action is selected accordingly. Moreover, the inquired features are all present in the image. The models avoid irrelevant questions and derive a correct prediction based on the question history and the input image. The R^{qu+lat} reward function provides the advantage of generating more complex compositional questions and the number of questions is shorter than those derived by the R^{tok} and R^{qu} reward functions.

a)

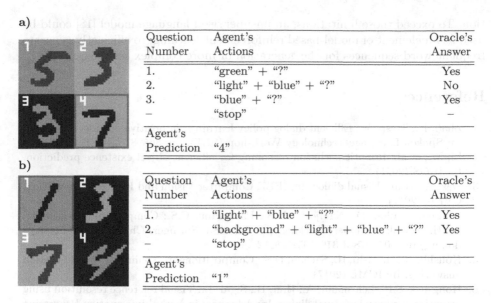

Question Number	Agent's Actions	Oracle's Answer
1.	"green" + "?"	Yes
2.	"light" + "blue" + "?"	No
3.	"blue" + "?"	Yes
–	"stop"	–
Agent's Prediction	"4"	

b)

Question Number	Agent's Actions	Oracle's Answer
1.	"light" + "blue" + "?"	Yes
2.	"background" + "light" + "blue" + "?"	Yes
–	"stop"	–
Agent's Prediction	"1"	

Fig. 7. Two example tasks being solved by the agent. The model in **a)** has been penalized via the number of tokens (R^{tok}), the model in **b)** via the number of questions (R^{qu+lat}) which leads to fewer but longer questions. The display is as in Fig. 1: left, the example image with the oracle's choice in red; right, the generated dialog. (Color figure online)

6   Conclusion

In summary, the Recurrent Attention Model is able to generate questions compositionally from tokens and arrange questions strategically to generate goal-directed visual dialog. The model produces a correct question structure and chooses question tokens sequentially while avoiding repetitions and reducing the total length of the sequence. Further, the model refers to the presented visual content by selecting relevant question sequences for novel image examples that were not shown during the training process. The results show that the learned strategy of the model heavily varies depending on the time efficiency losses used in the reward function. Penalizing the number of questions, instead of the number of words, results in a model that generates fewer questions, but also longer compositional questions. Hence, a suitable reward function may allow generating language of desirable characteristics.

Certain limitations are that the model does not necessarily yield optimal results, often producing correct but less efficient sequences. Future work may involve reinforcement learning algorithms that are more robust to noisy rewards, which promise also to overcome the need for supervised pretraining. Further work may address more complex scenarios and forming longer sentences with grammatical variations. Our model handles only minimal grammar with a small number of words, owed to the sole use of reinforcement learning for word generation. To exceed those limitations, an unsupervised language model [18] could be used as an element of model-based reinforcement learning, to efficiently generate frequent word sequences for the generation of more complex sentences.

References

1. Zhao, R., Tresp, V.: Efficient dialog policy learning via positive memory retention. In: Spoken Language Technology Workshop (SLT), pp. 868–875. IEEE (2018)
2. Li, M., et al.: Robotic occlusion reasoning for efficient object existence prediction. In: IROS (2021)
3. Das, A., et al.: Visual dialog. In: IEEE Computer Vision and Pattern Recognition, CVPR (2017)
4. Giannakopoulou, D., Namjoshi, K.S., Păsăreanu, C.S.: Compositional reasoning. In: Handbook of Model Checking, pp. 345–383. Springer, Cham (2018). https://doi.org/10.1007/978-3-319-10575-8_12
5. Koushik, J., Hayashi, H., Sachan, D.S.: Compositional reasoning for visual question answering. In: ICML (2017)
6. Hongsuck, S.P., Lehrmann, A., Han, B., Sigal, L.: Visual reference resolution using attention memory for visual dialog. In: Advances in Neural Information Processing Systems. NIPS, pp. 3719–3729 (2017)
7. Das, A., et al.: Learning cooperative visual dialog agents with deep reinforcement learning. In: IEEE International Conference on Computer Vision. ICCV, pp. 2970–2979 (2017)
8. Mnih, V., Heess, N., Graves, A., Kavukcuoglu, K.: Recurrent models of visual attention. In: Proceedings of the 27th International Conference on Neural Information Processing Systems (NIPS), vol. 2, pp. 2204–2212 (2014)
9. de Vries H., Strub F., Chandar S., Pietquin O., Larochelle H., Courville A.: Guess-What?! Visual object discovery through multi-modal dialogue. In: IEEE Conference on Computer Vision and Pattern Recognition. CVPR, pp. 4466–4475 (2017)
10. Agrawal, A., et al.: VQA: visual question answering. Int. J. Comput. Vision **123**(1), 4–31 (2016). https://doi.org/10.1007/s11263-016-0966-6
11. Johnson, J., Hariharan, B., van der Maaten, L., Fei-Fei, L., Zitnick, C.L., Girshick, R.: CLEVR: a diagnostic dataset for compositional language and elementary visual reasoning. In: CVPR, pp. 1988–1997 (2017)
12. Williams, R.J.: Simple statistical gradient-following algorithms for connectionist reinforcement learning. Mach. Learn. **8**, 229–256 (1992)
13. Goyal, Y., Khot, T., Agrawal, A., Summers-Stay, D., Batra, D., Parikh, D.: Making the V in VQA matter: elevating the role of image understanding in visual question answering. Int. J. Comput. Vision **127**(4), 398–414 (2018). https://doi.org/10.1007/s11263-018-1116-0
14. Hudson, D.A., Manning, C.D.: GQA: a new dataset for real-world visual reasoning and compositional question answering. In: IEEE/CVF Conference on Computer Vision and Pattern Recognition. CVPR, pp. 6693–6702 (2019)
15. Andreas, J., Rohrbach, M., Darrell, T., Klein, D.: Deep compositional question answering with neural module networks. In: IEEE Conference on Computer Vision and Pattern Recognition. CVPR (2016)
16. Subramanian, S., Singh, S., Gardner, M.: Analyzing compositionality of visual question answering. In: ViGIL@NeurIPS (2019)

17. Agrawal, A., Kembhavi, A., Batra, D., Parikh, D.: C-VQA: a compositional split of the Visual Question Answering (VQA) v1.0 Dataset. CoRR (2017)
18. Radford, A., Jozefowicz, R., Sutskever, I.: Learning to generate reviews and discovering sentiment. arXiv:1704.01444 (2017)

A Novel Approach to Train Diverse Types of Language Models for Health Mention Classification of Tweets

Pervaiz Iqbal Khan[1,2]([✉]) [iD], Imran Razzak[3] [iD], Andreas Dengel[1,2] [iD], and Sheraz Ahmed[1] [iD]

[1] German Research Center for Artificial Intelligence (DFKI), Kaiserslautern, Germany
{pervaiz.khan,andreas.dengel,sheraz.ahmed}@dfki.de
[2] TU Kaiserslautern, Kaiserslautern, Germany
[3] UNSW, Sydney, Australia
imran.razzak@unsw.edu.au

Abstract. Health mention classification deals with the disease detection in a given text containing disease words. However, non-health and figurative use of disease words adds challenges to the task. Recently, adversarial training acting as a means of regularization has gained popularity in many NLP tasks. In this paper, we propose a novel approach to train language models for health mention classification of tweets that involves adversarial training. We generate adversarial examples by adding perturbation to the representations of transformer models for tweet examples at various levels using Gaussian noise. Further, we employ contrastive loss as an additional objective function. We evaluate the proposed method on the PHM2017 dataset extended version. Results show that our proposed approach improves the performance of classifier significantly over the baseline methods. Moreover, our analysis shows that adding noise at earlier layers improves models' performance whereas adding noise at intermediate layers deteriorates models' performance. Finally, adding noise towards the final layers performs better than the middle layers noise addition.

Keywords: Health informatics · Adversarial training · Health mention classification

1 Introduction

Health Mention Classification (HMC) deals with the detection of disease in a given piece of input text. Authorities can use such classification results to monitor the spread of diseases. Further, early detection of health conditions can help in taking preventive measures and efficiently managing resources in emergencies. To train a classifier for HMC, health-related data is collected from social media platforms such as Twitter, Facebook, etc., based on keywords containing

ⓒ The Author(s), under exclusive license to Springer Nature Switzerland AG 2022
E. Pimenidis et al. (Eds.): ICANN 2022, LNCS 13530, pp. 136–147, 2022.
https://doi.org/10.1007/978-3-031-15931-2_12

the names of the diseases such as fever, heart attack, cancer, etc. However, a keyword-based search may result in irrelevant data. For example, "Wow, this is awesome it's like having a depression" is an example of figurative mentions (FM) of disease word *depression*. Another tweet "hearing people cough makes me angry" contains the word *cough* as a non-health mention (NHM). These FM and NHM usage of disease words makes the HMC task challenging. Learning the context of words based on their surrounding words is the key to improving classification results. Transformer models [32] have revolutionized many natural language processing (NLP) tasks [30]. BERT [5] is a transformer model that utilizes the encoder block of the original transformer model and is pretrained on the large unlabelled corpus of text. BERT learns the representations of the words by using two different objective functions, i.e. Masked Language Modeling (MLM) and Next sentence prediction (NSP). RoBERTa [19] is another transformer-based model that has an architecture like BERT, but it uses dynamic masking of tokens instead of static tokens. Moreover, it is pretrained on 1000% more data than BERT. Adversarial training (AT) [6] is used in many tasks as a regularization technique to improve models' robustness against adversarial attacks [23,25]. During AT a small perturbation is added to the original input sample and then the model is trained in parallel with both the original and perturbed sample. Recently, self-supervised methods [3,35] have gained popularity among researchers in the image processing domain. These methods add perturbations to the inputs, and the training objective is to learn similar representations for the pair of clean and perturbed examples while learning different representations for other examples. Barlow Twins (BT) [35] is one such method that works on the principle of redundancy reduction. In this paper, we propose a novel approach of training language models for HMC task on Twitter data that combines the ideas of AT and self-supervised learning. Specifically, we add Gaussian noise as a perturbation to the representations of two language models $BERT_{Large}$ and $RoBERTa_{Large}$ and employ BT as an additional loss for learning the similar representations for a pair of clean and perturbed examples. Experiments show that our proposed approach improves classification results on both $BERT_{Large}$ and $RoBERTa_{Large}$ models over their baselines. The contributions of this paper towards the adversarial training on diverse transformers models for HMC of tweets are manifold. First, it proposes a new training method for the HMC of tweets using adversarial and contrastive learning methods by adding perturbation to hidden representations. Second, it explores the impacts of noise addition on various layer levels. Third, it analyzes the impact of noise amount on adversarial training. Fourth, it leverages explainable AI to understand the importance of words in a Tweet for the classification decision.

The rest of the paper is organized as follows: In Sect. 2, we discuss the related work, whereas, in Sect. 3, we present our method for HMC. In Sect. 4, we give experimentation detail. In Sect. 5, we present the results and analysis of the experiments. Finally, in Sect. 6, we provide the conclusion of the paper.

2 Related Work

2.1 Adversarial Training

AT has shown success in many computer vision tasks [6,29,33]. To generate adversarial examples, perturbations are added using methods such as Gaussian noise and Fast Gradient Sign Method (FGSM) [6]. [23] perturbed word embeddings instead of original input text using FGSM for NLP task. [16,17] added perturbations to the attention mechanism of transformer methods using FGSM. [21] used multi-step FGSM to generate adversarial examples that proved more effective at the cost of computational overhead. [28] proposed a fast method for AT where perturbations and gradients with respect to parameters of the model were calculated and updated in the same backward pass. [36] proposed "Free Large-Batch" algorithm where perturbations were added in the embedding matrix. [23] applied perturbations to the word embeddings of recurrent neural network (RNN) embeddings instead of embedding matrix.

2.2 Self-supervised Representation Learning

The success of supervised deep learning methods depends on the availability of largely annotated data that is costly in practice. Self-supervised learning (SSL) methods have gained popularity where these methods learn representations from unlabeled data. In NLP, many language models [5,19] learned representations from the large unlabelled corpus of text [4,26] by defining proxy tasks such as MLM. Similarly, SSL methods has shown success in computer vision. SimCLR [3] first drastically augmented the images and then trained the model to maximize the cosine similarity between original images and their augmented versions while pushing the other images away from them. Bootstrap Your Own Latent (BYOL) [7] used two versions of the same network called online and target network to learn visual representations. Each network utilized a different augmented version of the original image. The online network aimed to learn representations similar to the target network representations. Barlow Twins (BT) [35] aimed at the principle of redundancy reduction to learn noise-invariant representations.

2.3 Health Mention Classification of Tweets

[12] presented a method "WESPAD" acting as a regularizer for HMC. It partitioned and distorted embedding which helped the model in achieving generalization capability. [11] used non-contextual embeddings for representing the tweets and passed them to LSTMs [8]. Adding LSTM before the classification layer improved the performance compared to the simple SVM, KNN, and Decision Trees. [10] incorporated features from an unsupervised statistical learner for idiom detection, and passed it to CNN based classifier. [2] experimented with both non-contextual embeddings such as word2vec [22] and contextual embeddings such as ELMO [27] and BERT and incorporated sentiment information using WordNet [1], VAD [24], and ULMFit [9] for HMC of tweets. [13] applied

permutation-based pretrained embeddings and finetuned the pretrained model [34] on the HMC dataset to improve classification score. [14] compared the performance of various transformer models on HMC of tweets and showed that RoBERTa$_{Large}$ outperformed other methods.

In this work, we propose a new training approach of language models for the HMC of Tweets that combines the concepts of AT and self-supervised methods. We add Gaussian noise to the hidden representations of BERT$_{Large}$ and RoBERTa$_{Large}$ to generate adversarial examples. We additionally use BT as a contrastive loss.

3 Methodology

3.1 Adversarial Training

Let x be an input and $L \in \{1, 4, 7, 10, 13, 16, 19, 22\}$ be the intermediate layer numbers of the transformer model. Let η denotes a Gaussian noise with mean 'μ' and variance 'σ' given as follows:

$$\eta = N(\mu, \sigma) \tag{1}$$

then, we generate adversarial example x_{adv} by adding η to the representations of one of the layers in L as given below:

$$x_{adv} = E_{L_i} + \eta \tag{2}$$

where L_i denotes i^{th} layer from L, and a E_{L_i} represents the embedding of L_i.

We train the model simultaneously on x, and x_{adv}, and calculate two cross-entropy losses separately on x, and x_{adv}.

3.2 Barlow Twins (BT) Loss

BT loss jointly operates on clean and adversarial inputs. Let E^{clean}, and E^{adv} represent the embeddings of clean and adversarial examples, respectively. E^{clean}, and E^{adv} are fed into neural network f_θ, where θ is a trainable parameter. The outputs of the f_θ for E^{clean}, and E^{adv} are their projections to lower dimensions and centered with mean 0 across batch dimension. BT loss is defined as given below [35]:

$$\mathcal{L}_{BT} = \sum_{i=1}(1 - M_{ii})^2 + \lambda \sum_{i=1}\sum_{j \neq i} M_{ij}^2 \tag{3}$$

where $\sum_{i=1}(1 - M_{ii})^2$, and $\sum_{i=1}\sum_{j \neq i} M_{ij}^2$ are invariance, and redundancy reduction terms respectively, and λ controls the weight of the two terms. M is a square matrix and computes the cross-correlation between E^{clean}, and E^{adv}. M_{ij} is computed as follows:

$$M_{ij} = \frac{\sum_{b=1}^{N} E_{b,i}^{clean} E_{b,i}^{adv}}{\sqrt{\sum_{b=1}^{N}(E_{b,i}^{clean})^2}\sqrt{\sum_{b=1}^{N}(E_{b,i}^{adv})^2}} \tag{4}$$

where i, j, represents the index of the matrix M, and b represents batch samples.

3.3   Adversarial Training with BT Loss for HMC

Figure 1 shows the architecture diagram of the proposed method. First, we pass input tweet through a preprocessing step that removes URLs, user mentions, hashtags, and special characters, and converts emojis to their corresponding text representation. After that, we pass this input to the two transformer models of the same type. The first model directly processes the input example called the clean example, whereas the second model adds Gaussian noise η with $\mu = 0$ and $\sigma = 1$ to one of the hidden states in layer L to generate an adversarial example (discussed in Sect. 3.1). Then, we take the embedding of $[CLS]$ token to extract sentence embedding separately for clean and adversarial input example and pass it to the classification layer. We compute two separate cross-entropy losses for these examples. We also employ BT as a third loss. The inputs to the BT loss are $[CLS]$ token representations from the clean and adversarial examples projected to lower dimensions by a neural network of two layers. Total loss is the weighted average of three losses as given below:

$$\mathcal{L}_{total} = \frac{(1-C)}{2}(\mathcal{L}_{clean} + \mathcal{L}_{adv}) + C\mathcal{L}_{BT} \tag{5}$$

where $\mathcal{L}_{total}$ represents the total loss, $\mathcal{L}_{clean}$ and $\mathcal{L}_{adv}$ represent cross-entropy losses for the clean and adversarial examples, and $\mathcal{L}_{BT}$ represents BT loss. 'C' is the trade-off parameter between three losses.

4   Experiments

4.1   Dataset

We perform experimentation on the extended version of the PHM2017 dataset [2] containing tweets related to 10 diseases, i.e., Alzheimer's, cancer, cough, depression, fever, headache, heart attack, migraine, Parkinson's, and stroke. The dataset contained 15,742 tweets at download time, out of which 4,228 tweets are related to HM, 7,322 tweets are NHM, and 4,192 tweets are FM. For experiments, we follow the same train/validation/test split as in the paper [15]. Further, we combine the FM and NHM tweets in a single class that reduces the task to binary classification.

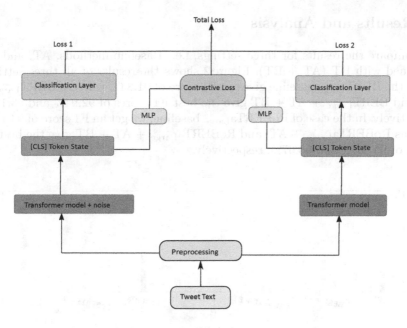

Fig. 1. Architecture diagram of our proposed training approach.

4.2   Experimental Setup

Baseline. We use pretrained $BERT_{Large}$ and $RoBERTa_{Large}$ models and fine-tune them for the classification task as baseline methods for clean examples.

Hyperparameters. For both models, we set the maximum sequence length to 64, and a fixed learning rate of $1e^{-5}$ for all the experiments. For all the experiments, we use AdamW [20] as an optimizer and batch sizes of 16, 24, and 32 and choose the best-performing model on the validation set to evaluate on the test set. In the case of AT combined with BT, we experiment with a $C \in \{0.1, 0.2, 0.3, 0.4\}$ as a trade-off parameter between two cross-entropy and BT losses. However, in the case of adversarial training only, we give equal weights to the two cross-entropy losses. We train both models for 10 epochs and use early-stopping to prevent overfitting of the models. Unlike the original implementation of BT, we project the original embedding dimensions of 1024 to a lower-dimensional space of 300 that is similar to SimCLR and proved more effective in our experiments. The projection network consists of 3 linear layers where the input and output dimensions of the first 2 layers are 1024, whereas the output layer dimensions are 300. The first two linear layers follow 1-d batch normalization and ReLU as an activation function. We set its default hyperparameters values for BT loss.

5   Results and Analysis

We compare the results for three settings, i.e., Baseline methods, AT, and AT combined with BT (AT + BT). Figure 2 shows the results of all three settings where the $BERT_{Large}$ baseline gives an F1 score of 91.84% whereas $BERT_{Large}$ + AT, and $BERT_{Large}$ + AT + BT give the best F1 scores of 92.94% and 93.12%, respectively. In the case of $RoBERTa_{Large}$ baseline, we get an F1 score of 93.13%, whereas $RoBERTa_{Large}$ + AT, and $RoBERTa_{Large}$ + AT + BT give the best F1 scores of 93.73%, and 93.67%, respectively.

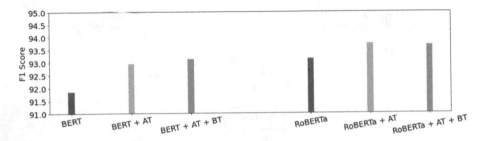

Fig. 2. F1 score of $BERT_{Large}$ and $RoBERTa_{Large}$ baseline methods, their best results using AT on various layers, and best results on AT + BT.

5.1   Effect of Noise on Layers Level of Models

Table 1 shows layer-wise results for the experimental settings of adversarial training, and adversarial training with Barlow Twins as contrastive loss. For $BERT_{Large}$ + AT, adding noise at the 1st layer gives an F1 score of 92.94%. Adding noise after the first layer decreases the performance of the model till the 10th layer. After that starting from layer 13th, Gaussian noise gradually starts increasing the model's performance until we reach the 22nd layer. In the case of $BERT_{Large}$ + AT + BT, adding noise at layer no. 4 gives the highest F1 score of 93.12%, then performance starts decreasing till layer no. 16. However, after layer no. 16, the F1 score again starts increasing. For $RoBERTa_{Large}$ + AT adding noise at layer no. 1 improves the F1 score to 93.64%. After that, model performance varies between layer no. 4 and layer no. 10. Then, at layer 13th, the model gives the highest F1 score of 93.73%. At layer 16th F1 score slightly decreases, and then at layer 19th, layer 22nd F1 score slightly increases. In the case of $RoBERTa_{Large}$ + AT + BT, layer no. 1 gives an F1 score of 93.67% after that model's performance decreases till layer no. 10. Then starting from layer no. 13, the model's performance increases as compared to layer no. 7 and layer no. 10.

Table 1. F1 score of AT, and AT + BT for BERT$_{Large}$ and RoBERTa$_{Large}$ while adding noise at different layers.

Model	L#1	L#4	L#7	L#10	L#13	L#16	L#19	L#22
BERT$_{Large}$ + AT	**92.94**	92.66	92.12	92.03	92.41	92.43	92.40	92.74
BERT$_{Large}$ + AT+ BT	92.64	**93.12**	92.55	92.73	92.16	91.88	92.40	93.03
RoBERTa$_{Large}$ + AT	93.64	93.16	93.41	92.70	**93.73**	93.41	93.46	93.46
RoBERTa$_{Large}$ + AT + BT	**93.67**	93.54	92.88	92.43	93.38	93.62	93.17	93.47

The trend we see in the results is that adding noise to earlier layers increases the model's performance most of the time, then in the middle layers, it degrades the model's performance, then finally model's performance starts rising towards the last layers. The reason for the better performance of noise at earlier layers is, that the model has enough layers to recover the hidden representations, and adding noise at these layers increases the model's generalization capability. Similarly, adding noise at the last layers works better than the middle layers because the model has already learned useful representations, and adding small perturbations doesn't harm the model's performance much. However, adding noise at intermediate layers somehow deteriorates the model's performance because the model hasn't learned useful representations, and adding noise at this stage doesn't allow the model to recover from the damage caused at this stage. BERT$_{Large}$ + AT + BT improves the model's performance as compared to the BERT$_{Large}$ + AT, however, RoBERTa$_{Large}$ + AT + BT performance is sometime slightly worse than the RoBERTa$_{Large}$ + AT during intermediate layers and it is better than RoBERTa$_{Large}$ + AT in earlier and last layers.

5.2 Effect of Noise Amount on Model's Performance

Figure 3 visualizes the effect of noise parameter 'C' on models performance. Figure 3a shows that at $C = 0.4$, layer no. 1 and 4 perform better than other values of 'C', and then at layer no. 22, it gives the best F1 score of 93.03 % for BERT$_{Large}$ + AT + BT. At Layer no. 12, $C = 0.4$ gives the lowest F1 score as compared to other values of 'C' and other layers. $C = 0.1$ performs better than its other values in the middle layers. On $C = 0.2$, and $C = 0.3$ classifier do not perform well as compared to other values. Figure 3b shows the effect of noise amount on RoBERTa$_{Large}$ + AT + BT performance. $C = 0.1$ works well on the initial layers, whereas $C = 0.2$ does not perform well on the initial layers, however, it outperforms other values of 'C' towards layer no. 19, and 22. $C = 0.4$ does not perform well most of the times for RoBERTa$_{Large}$ + AT + BT as compared to other values of 'C'.

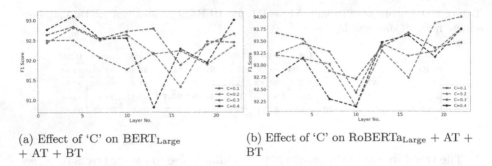

(a) Effect of 'C' on BERT_Large + AT + BT

(b) Effect of 'C' on RoBERTa_Large + AT + BT

Fig. 3. Effect of noise amount parameter 'C' on the performance of both BERT_Large and RoBERTa_Large with AT + BT on test set of PHM2017 dataset.

5.3   Comparison with SOTA

To compare with state-of-the-art (SOTA), we select the best hyperparameters, i.e. layer no. value of 'C', and batch size from the validation set of experiments given in Table 1, and train models 10-fold cross-validation. As shown in Table 2, our propose method for RoBERTa_Large + AT + BT beats the state-of-the-art methods in terms of precision, and F1 score.

Table 2. Comparison of our method with SOTA. Results are the average of Precision (P), Recall (R), and F1 score (F1) on the 10-fold cross-validation of PHM2017 dataset. Our method is directly comparable to methods in [13] and [15] as dataset distribution does not match with other methods.

Method	P	R	F1
Jiang et al. [11]	72.1	**95**	81.8
Karisani et al. [12]	75.2	89.6	81.8
Biddle et al. [2]	75.6	92	82.9
Khan et al. [13]	89.1	88.2	88.4
Khan et al. BERT_Large [15]	93.25	93.75	93.45
Khan et al. RoBERTa_Large [15]	93.95	94.4	94.2
BERT_Large + AT + BT (ours)	93.05	93.4	93.1
RoBERTa_Large + AT + BT (ours)	**94.35**	94.4	**94.45**

5.4   Explaining the Model Decision

To analyze the words that play a significant role in model classification decisions, we utilize a transformer interpret library [18] that is based on *Layer Integrated Gradients* algorithm [31]. For this purpose, we visualize some of the random examples from the test set that are misclassified by the baseline method and correctly classified by our proposed method. Further, we highlight the words supporting the model's decisions as green and words opposing the model's decisions as red. As shown in Table 3, the first tweet in the table is correctly classified by RoBERTa$_{Large}$ + AT + BT and misclassified by RoBERTa$_{Large}$ baseline model. Similarly, the second tweet is a health mention and correctly classified by RoBERTa$_{Large}$ + AT + BT and misclassified by RoBERTa$_{Large}$ baseline model. The third and fourth tweets are non-health mentions and misclassified by RoBERTa$_{Large}$ baseline and correctly classified by RoBERTa$_{Large}$ + AT + BT.

Table 3. Visualization of word importance in classifier decision for random test set examples. Words highlighted with green color supported model prediction, and words highlighted with red color opposed model prediction. In header columns, GT stands for ground truth.

GT	Prediction	Model	Word Importance
HM	NHM	RoBERTa$_{Large}$ baseline	#s I totally forgot mar ia has cancer man fac ep al ming medium skin tone #/s
	HM	RoBERTa$_{Large}$ + AT + BT	#s I totally forgot mar ia has cancer man fac ep al ming medium skin tone #/s
HM	NHM	RoBERTa$_{Large}$ baseline	#s about to take some headache medicine #/s
	HM	RoBERTa$_{Large}$ + AT + BT	#s about to take some headache medicine #/s
NHM	HM	RoBERTa$_{Large}$ baseline	#s i need hollow knight sil ks ong to come out to combat my depression #/s
	HHM	RoBERTa$_{Large}$ + AT + BT	#s i need hollow knight sil ks ong to come out to combat my depression #/s
NHM	HM	RoBERTa$_{Large}$ baseline	#s I just straight ened my hair out of depression wow look at me #/s
	HHM	RoBERTa$_{Large}$ + AT + BT	#s I just straight ened my hair out of depression wow look at me #/s

6   Conclusion

In this paper, we presented a new approach for HMC of tweet examples that combines adversarial training with contrastive loss. We employed Gaussian noise with mean 0 and standard deviation of 1 at various internal representations levels of two transformer models BERT$_{Large}$ and RoBERTa$_{Large}$ and utilized Barlow Twins as a contrastive loss. We evaluated our method on PHM2017 dataset extended version, and the results showed that our proposed approach improved performance over the baseline methods. Further analysis showed that adding noise at initial layers improved models' performance over baseline, whereas noise addition at intermediate layers decreased models' performance. Finally, we observed that adding noise towards the final layers performed better than the noise at the intermediate layers. As a future work, various adversarial example generation methods can be explored for HMC task.

References

1. Baccianella, S., Esuli, A., Sebastiani, F.: SentiWordNet 3.0: an enhanced lexical resource for sentiment analysis and opinion mining. In: LREC, vol. 10, pp. 2200–2204 (2010)
2. Biddle, R., Joshi, A., Liu, S., Paris, C., Xu, G.: Leveraging sentiment distributions to distinguish figurative from literal health reports on Twitter. In: Proceedings of The Web Conference 2020, pp. 1217–1227 (2020)
3. Chen, T., Kornblith, S., Norouzi, M., Hinton, G.: A simple framework for contrastive learning of visual representations. In: International Conference on Machine Learning, pp. 1597–1607. PMLR (2020)
4. Crawl, C.: Common crawl corpus (2019). http://commoncrawl.org
5. Devlin, J., Chang, M.W., Lee, K., Toutanova, K.: BERT: pre-training of deep bidirectional transformers for language understanding. arXiv preprint arXiv:1810.04805 (2018)
6. Goodfellow, I.J., Shlens, J., Szegedy, C.: Explaining and harnessing adversarial examples. arXiv preprint arXiv:1412.6572 (2014)
7. Grill, J.B., et al.: Bootstrap your own latent - a new approach to self-supervised learning. Adv. Neural. Inf. Process. Syst. **33**, 21271–21284 (2020)
8. Hochreiter, S., Schmidhuber, J.: Long short-term memory. Neural Comput. **9**(8), 1735–1780 (1997)
9. Howard, J., Ruder, S.: Universal language model fine-tuning for text classification. arXiv preprint arXiv:1801.06146 (2018)
10. Iyer, A., Joshi, A., Karimi, S., Sparks, R., Paris, C.: Figurative usage detection of symptom words to improve personal health mention detection. arXiv preprint arXiv:1906.05466 (2019)
11. Jiang, K., Feng, S., Song, Q., Calix, R.A., Gupta, M., Bernard, G.R.: Identifying tweets of personal health experience through word embedding and LSTM neural network. BMC Bioinform. **19**(8), 210 (2018)
12. Karisani, P., Agichtein, E.: Did you really just have a heart attack? Towards robust detection of personal health mentions in social media. In: Proceedings of the 2018 World Wide Web Conference, pp. 137–146 (2018)
13. Khan, P.I., Razzak, I., Dengel, A., Ahmed, S.: Improving personal health mention detection on Twitter using permutation based word representation learning. In: Yang, H., Pasupa, K., Leung, A.C.-S., Kwok, J.T., Chan, J.H., King, I. (eds.) ICONIP 2020. LNCS, vol. 12532, pp. 776–785. Springer, Cham (2020). https://doi.org/10.1007/978-3-030-63830-6_65
14. Khan, P.I., Razzak, I., Dengel, A., Ahmed, S.: Performance comparison of transformer-based models on twitter health mention classification. IEEE Trans. Comput. Soc. Syst. (2022)
15. Khan, P.I., Siddiqui, S.A., Razzak, I., Dengel, A., Ahmed, S.: Improving health mentioning classification of tweets using contrastive adversarial training. arXiv preprint arXiv:2203.01895 (2022)
16. Kitada, S., Iyatomi, H.: Attention meets perturbations: robust and interpretable attention with adversarial training. IEEE Access **9**, 92974–92985 (2021)
17. Kitada, S., Iyatomi, H.: Making attention mechanisms more robust and interpretable with virtual adversarial training for semi-supervised text classification. arXiv preprint arXiv:2104.08763 (2021)
18. Kokhlikyan, N., et al.: Captum: a unified and generic model interpretability library for PyTorch. arXiv preprint arXiv:2009.07896 (2020)

19. Liu, Y., et al.: Roberta: a robustly optimized BERT pretraining approach. arXiv preprint arXiv:1907.11692 (2019)
20. Loshchilov, I., Hutter, F.: Fixing weight decay regularization in Adam. arXiv preprint arXiv:2011.08042v1 (2018)
21. Madry, A., Makelov, A., Schmidt, L., Tsipras, D., Vladu, A.: Towards deep learning models resistant to adversarial attacks. arXiv preprint arXiv:1706.06083 (2017)
22. Mikolov, T., Sutskever, I., Chen, K., Corrado, G.S., Dean, J.: Distributed representations of words and phrases and their compositionality. In: Advances in Neural Information Processing Systems, pp. 3111–3119 (2013)
23. Miyato, T., Dai, A.M., Goodfellow, I.: Adversarial training methods for semi-supervised text classification. arXiv preprint arXiv:1605.07725 (2016)
24. Mohammad, S.: Obtaining reliable human ratings of valence, arousal, and dominance for 20,000 English words. In: Proceedings of the 56th Annual Meeting of the Association for Computational Linguistics (Volume 1: Long Papers), pp. 174–184 (2018)
25. Pan, L., Hang, C.W., Sil, A., Potdar, S., Yu, M.: Improved text classification via contrastive adversarial training. arXiv preprint arXiv:2107.10137 (2021)
26. Parker, R., Graff, D., Kong, J., Chen, K., Maeda, K.: English gigaword fifth edition ldc2011t07 (tech. rep.). Technical report, Linguistic Data Consortium, Philadelphia (2011)
27. Peters, M.E., et al.: Deep contextualized word representations. arXiv preprint arXiv:1802.05365 (2018)
28. Shafahi, A., et al.: Adversarial training for free! Adv. Neural Inf. Process. Syst. **32** (2019)
29. Song, D., et al.: Physical adversarial examples for object detectors. In: 12th {USENIX} Workshop on Offensive Technologies ({WOOT} 2018) (2018)
30. Sun, C., Qiu, X., Xu, Y., Huang, X.: How to fine-tune BERT for text classification? In: Sun, M., Huang, X., Ji, H., Liu, Z., Liu, Y. (eds.) CCL 2019. LNCS (LNAI), vol. 11856, pp. 194–206. Springer, Cham (2019). https://doi.org/10.1007/978-3-030-32381-3_16
31. Sundararajan, M., Taly, A., Yan, Q.: Axiomatic attribution for deep networks. In: International Conference on Machine Learning, pp. 3319–3328. PMLR (2017)
32. Vaswani, A., et al.: Attention is all you need. Adv. Neural Inf. Process. Syst. **30** (2017)
33. Xie, C., Wang, J., Zhang, Z., Zhou, Y., Xie, L., Yuille, A.: Adversarial examples for semantic segmentation and object detection. In: Proceedings of the IEEE International Conference on Computer Vision, pp. 1369–1378 (2017)
34. Yang, Z., Dai, Z., Yang, Y., Carbonell, J., Salakhutdinov, R.R., Le, Q.V.: Xlnet: generalized autoregressive pretraining for language understanding. In: Advances in Neural Information Processing Systems, pp. 5754–5764 (2019)
35. Zbontar, J., Jing, L., Misra, I., LeCun, Y., Deny, S.: Barlow twins: self-supervised learning via redundancy reduction. In: International Conference on Machine Learning, pp. 12310–12320. PMLR (2021)
36. Zhu, C., Cheng, Y., Gan, Z., Sun, S., Goldstein, T., Liu, J.: FreeLB: enhanced adversarial training for natural language understanding. arXiv preprint arXiv:1909.11764 (2019)

Adaptive Knowledge Distillation for Efficient Relation Classification

Haorui He, Yuanzhe Ren, Zheng Li, and Jing Xue[✉]

School of Computer Science, Nanjing University of Posts and Telecommunications,
Nanjing 210003, People's Republic of China
xuejing@njupt.edu.cn

Abstract. Knowledge Distillation (KD) methods are widely adopted to reduce the high computational and memory costs incurred by large-scale pre-trained models. However, there are currently no researchers focusing on KD's application for relation classification. Although directly leveraging traditional KD methods for relation classification is the easiest way, it should not be neglected that the concept of "relation" is highly ambiguous so machine learning models are likely to give uncertain predictions of relations. Moreover, the label smoothing progress in KD would result in further uncertainty in supervision, leading to bad student model performances. In this work, we propose a confusion-based KD method through which the uncertainty in supervision can be adaptively adjusted based on how confused teacher models are in relation classification. In addition, we propose a new knowledge adjustment method called logit replacement, which can adaptively fix teachers' mistakes to avoid genetic errors. We conducted comprehensive experiments on the basis of the SemEval-2010 Task 8 relation classification benchmark. Test results demonstrate the effectiveness of the proposed methods.

Keywords: Knowledge distillation · Relation classification · Natural language processing

1 Introduction

In many applications such as Question Answering, Information Retrieval, and Knowledge Graph, relation classification is a key step in extracting information from a lot of digital texts in every day's news articles, research publications, blogs, social media, etc. The objective of this task is to predict semantic relations between entity nouns. For example, if a sentence S with an annotated pair of entities mentions e1 and e2 given, the aim is to identify the semantic relation between e1 and e2 among a set of candidate relation types [8]. Take a data sample as an example, in which e1 and e2 show Component-Whole(e1,e2) relation: "The

Supported in part by the Major Project of Philosophy and Social Science Research in Jiangsu Universities of China (2020SJZDA102).

<e1>macadamia nuts</e1>in the <e2>cake</e2>also make it necessary to have a very sharp knife to cut through the cake neatly."

With recent success in deep learning, a wide range of methods have been proposed to address the relation classification task [2,11,17,19,24,26,28,29]. However, like other natural language processing (NLP) tasks, the evolution of neural networks for relation classification, became unending but predictable that new models continue to outperform previous architectures in both performance and complexity [22]. This trend became extremely obvious after the famous pre-trained BERT [5] model was proposed. [24,26] are the existing methods based on BERT to address relation classification tasks. Although BERT-based methods [24,26] lead to improved relation classification accuracy, the great complexity in their model architectures reduce the speed of inference and increases the memory cost of the model file, which restricts their use in real-time applications and on mobile devices that have limited memory.

To address these issues, Knowledge Distillation (KD) [1,9] method has been widely studied. KD guides the training process of a student model to imitate the teacher model so that it can achieve a competitive or even better performance [6]. Inspired by research on the application of knowledge distillation methods in both CV [3,12,23] and NLP [4,7,13,22], this work focuses on fine-tuning the knowledge distillation method based on the features of relation classification task to improve knowledge distillation.

Amongst several features of relation classification tasks, the most important is the inherent ambiguity of the concept of "relation" and what a relationship "means", which is usually reflected in the human's difficulty in distinguishing two kinds of relations [15]. Mathematically, this property would be reflected as unapparent distinctiveness in the logits (the output values of the final layer) by a deep learning model. Nevertheless, in the KD method, the logits computed by the teacher model are required to be softened in the label smoothing process [9,21]. This operation further increases uncertainty in supervision and may lead to excessive supervision. Although moderate uncertainty in supervision was proved to be beneficial to the student model [1,9,18], excessive uncertainty may lead to confusion in student models. Without appropriate control, it is difficult for the student model to obtain useful knowledge from the teacher's uncertain supervision, which will ultimately result in incorrect predictions.

According to [9], the degree of label smoothing is directly related to a "temperature" parameter (a higher temperature leads to softer logits), so we propose a confusion-based Dynamic Temperature Distillation (CDTD) method to dynamically adjust this distillation temperature parameter according to the degree of confusion the teacher model: the more confused the teacher model is, the lower the temperature. In this way, when the teacher finds it extremely difficult to determine a data sample's relation type, the effect of the label smoothing will be reduced accordingly. In addition, relation classification is extremely challenging as it requires detecting mentioned entities and the type of their relations [15]. Therefore, the performance of the teacher model is unlikely to be perfect so it may give incorrect predictions. When the student model imitates incorrect predictions in the teacher model, errors will be repeated, which is named "genetic error" [25]. To alleviate genetic error, Wen et al. [25] proposed two kinds of Knowledge Adjustment (KA) methods, namely Label Smooth Regularization and Probability Shift, to find and correct the teacher's wrong predictions based on corresponding ground truth labels. Unlike the Probability Shift operation, which preserves the values of rest classes in the original error logits, we suppose that when the teacher is wrong, the probabilities of rest classes given by the teacher model shouldn't be trusted. Therefore, we present another KA method called "logits replacement" to stabilize the training of the student model and avoid genetic errors. In this method, all logits of each training sample generated by the well-trained teacher model are cached first. When it goes wrong, the incorrectly given logits would be replaced by the average vector of logits of samples in the ground-truth class.

Our contributions can be summarized as follows:

a) A novel confusion-based dynamic temperature distillation method is proposed to help the student model challenge of learning from uncertain supervision in the relation classification task.
b) A logit replacement knowledge adjustment strategy is proposed to help avoid genetic errors and stabilize the training of the student model.
c) Extensive experiments on SemEval2010-Task8 [8] dataset are conducted to explore the effectiveness of the proposed methods. Specifically, applying the proposed method, an LSTM-based model [29] achieved significant F1-score improvement by 2.35%. Though it is still 2.9% lower than the BERT-based teacher model [26], the used network parameters, the inference time, and the memory cost are reduced by 2.5 times, 20.6 times, and 63%, respectively.

2 Related Work

2.1 Relation Classification

Deep learning methods [2,11,17,19,24,26,28,29] have been widely studied to address the relation classification task. Zeng et al. [28] addressed relation classification by incorporating both word embedding and position features as the input of a CNN model. Santos et al. [17] addressed the relation classification task by a ranking CNN. Their optimization goal is based on pairwise ranking. Shen et al. [19] proposed another CNN architecture with two levels of attention mechanism to capture the patterns in heterogeneous contexts for relation classification. Besides, there are also many approaches built on RNN. One of the most representative works [29] is to combine an attention mechanism with a BLSTM. Lee et al. [11] applied an end-to-end RNN model which incorporated an entity-aware attention mechanism with a potential entity typing to classify relations. With the recent development of NLP, relation classification methods [24,26] took advantage of the pre-trained language model BERT. These models surpass previous architectures in both performance and complexity.

2.2 Knowledge Distillation

Knowledge Distillation approaches [10,16,20,22] have demonstrated their advantages in reducing computational and memory costs of pre-trained language models and avoiding a sharp decline in accuracy over the past few years. In these methods, helpful knowledge from a well-trained teacher model is transferred to a student model. Ba and Caruana [1] first proposed the idea that a shallow neural network can improve its performance by mimicking a deeper network. Later Hinton et al. [9] proposed the definition of knowledge distillation and a systematic framework, in which the output of a teacher model is used as the training target for the student neural network. In addition to learning from the teacher's output, other methods [10,16] have also been proposed to learn from the intermediate knowledge representations of deep neural networks. As we expect to transfer the knowledge in a BERT-based model to a simple but completely different Bi-LSTM architecture in this work, we focus on the former method. Although KD methods [3,4,7,12,13,22,23] have been widely studied and applied in other NLP and CV tasks, to our best knowledge, there are not any researchers focusing on KD's application in relation to classification. We present our proposed method in the following section.

3 Methods

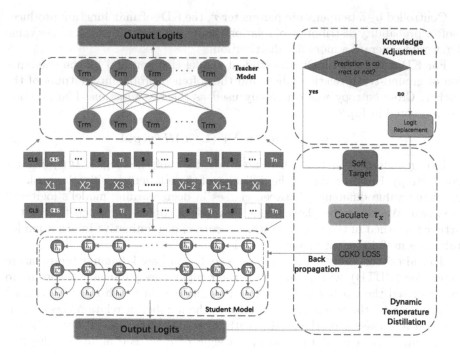

Fig. 1. Framework of adaptive knowledge distillation.

In this section, a novel distillation algorithm that focuses on Confusion-based Dynamic Temperature Distillation (CDTD) and Logit Replacement for Knowledge Adjustment (LRKA) are presented. The main aim of CDTD is to relatively minimize the temperature parameter to reduce the degree of label smoothing when the teacher network is uncertain and avoid excessive supervision uncertainty. The main purpose of LRKA is that when the teacher network goes wrong, the correctly-classified average logits value of the data sample of the same relation category would replace the logits of the incorrectly predicted samples by the teacher. Using CDTD and LRKA simultaneously can ensure that the student model can acquire rich and correct knowledge from the teacher. The framework of Confusion-based Dynamic Temperature Distillation is demonstrated in Fig. 1.

3.1   Confusion-Based Dynamic Temperature Distillation

Although appropriate uncertainty in supervision [1,9,18] was proved to be beneficial to the student model, excessive uncertainty may also lead to interrelation confusion. This issue is explored from the perspectives of soft targets and distillation temperature τ.

First, the method using soft target for KD is reviewed. Neural network typically converts its logit, z_i, to class probability, q_i, by a "softmax" output layer:

$$q_i = \text{softmax}_{\text{KD}}(z_i) = \frac{\exp(z_i)/\tau}{\sum_j \exp(z_j)/\tau}. \tag{1}$$

Controlled by a temperature parameter τ, the KD softmax function produces a softer probability distribution of relation classes, i.e., soft targets. A larger value of τ would generate a more flat distribution.

For KD using soft target, the student model is supervised by the combination of ground-truth relation labels and the softened probability outputs of the teacher. Cross entropy was commonly used as the loss function. The function was presented in Eq. 2:

$$L_{\text{KD}} = \alpha\tau^2 H(q_\tau, p_\tau) + (1-\alpha)H(y, p_\tau). \tag{2}$$

Here q_τ and p_τ denote teacher and student's τ softened logits. $H(\cdot)$ denotes cross entropy. However, due to the difficulty of the relation classification task, no significant value differences between classes in deep learning model's logit will be shown. We name the phenomenon as model's confusion. When the logit is further smoothed in the label smoothing process, discriminative information for training a useful student model will be lost.

To address this problem, we propose a confusion-based dynamic temperature distillation (CDTD), which can change the temperature parameter according to how confused the teacher is. Given a data sample x, in which $s_x = [s_1, \ldots, s_n]$ is logit given by the teacher model and n is the number of relation classes. x is classified into class a by the model, with s_a being the top possibility, followed by the value s_b of class b, the confusion weight of x, w_x is computed as Eq. 3:

$$w_x = s_a - s_b, \tag{3}$$

where a smaller value of w_x indicates that the teacher model is more confused in classifying the data sample into class a or class b. Then a batch-wise dynamic temperature is computed as Eq. 4:

$$\tau_x = \tau_0 + \left(\frac{w_x - w_{\min}}{w_{\max} - w_{\min}} - \frac{\frac{\sum_j w_j}{N} - w_{\min}}{w_{\max} - w_{\min}} \right) \beta, \tag{4}$$

where β is a bias parameter, τ_0 denotes the base temperature and N is the batch size. $w_{\min}$ and $w_{\max}$ denote the minimum and maximum weight in a same mini-batch. The loss of KD using CDTD is computed as Eq. 5:

$$L_{\text{CDTD}} = \alpha \tau_x^2 H\left(q_{\tau_x}, p_{\tau_x}\right) + (1 - \alpha)H\left(y, p_{\tau_x}\right). \tag{5}$$

3.2 Logit Replacement for Knowledge Adjustment

In traditional knowledge distillation, the student model is trained to mimic the prediction of the teacher model, but whether the prediction is correct is ignored. In this way, when the teacher model goes wrong, the student model will be misled by those mistakes and repeat the mistakes. Such phenomenon was noted as "genetic error" in [25] and two knowledge adjustment methods namely Label Smooth Regularization (LSR) and Probability Shift (PS) were proposed to avoid genetic errors. The Label Smooth Regularization directly replaces the incorrect soft target with a softened hot label, while the Probability Shift operation directly swaps the value of the ground truth relation class (the authentic maximum) and the value of the incorrectly predicted relation class (the predicted maximum) to ensure the maximum degree of confidence of the ground-truth label.

Though these methods modify a part of the prediction with reference to the ground-truth label, the rest parts of the distribution could still be noisy and affect the student models. We assume that when the teacher model gives an incorrect prediction, the overall probability distribution presented in the logit couldn't be trusted.

Intuitively, it is believed that data samples belonging to the same relation class are very similar in both textual form and logits outputted by the teacher model, so we raise the logit replacement knowledge adjustment (LRKA). First of all, the training set is input into the well-trained teacher model and cache the logits outputted of correctly-classified data samples. In the KD process, when a prediction of the teacher model is incorrect, the wrong logits will be replaced by the average value of logits of the data samples in the ground-truth class. Formally, given a data sample x, which belongs to class c_p but is mistakenly classified into c_q, the logits z_x by teacher model is replaced by z_p, which is computed as Eq. 6:

$$z_p = \frac{\sum_i^m z_i}{m}, \tag{6}$$

where z_i denotes each logits of data samples which are correctly classified into c_p and m is the number of those data samples. To express the role of LRKA mathematically, a knowledge adjusting function KA $(\cdot)$ is defined. Unlike Eq. 5, the loss of KD using LRKA is expressed with KL divergence:

$$L_{\text{LRKA}} = \tau^2 \text{KL} \left(\text{KA} \left(\boldsymbol{q}_\tau \right), \boldsymbol{p}_\tau \right). \tag{7}$$

3.3 Combination

In this sub-section, LRKA and CDTD are combined. The final loss function of the adaptive knowledge distillation solution L_{AKD} is formulated as Eq. 8.

$$L_{\text{AKD}} = \tau_x^2 KL \left(KA \left(\boldsymbol{q}_{\tau_x} \right), \boldsymbol{p}_{\tau_x} \right) \tag{8}$$

This equation is very similar to Eq. 7, but CDTD method is involved: τ is replaced by the τ_x computed with CDTD method. It should be noted that the ground truth labels are discarded in Eq. 8 because the $KA(\cdot)$ function has already made use of the ground truth information.

To demonstrate the combination method more intuitively, the pipeline in Algorithm 1 is described. LRKA is conducted after CDTD to improve the KD process in our settings, but actually, their order is completely flexible.

Algorithm 1 Computation of AKD loss.

Input: teacher logits $\boldsymbol{t}$; student logits $\boldsymbol{s}$; ground truth label y; data sample i;
Output: Loss L_{AKD}
 1: compute confusion weights $\boldsymbol{w}_i$ with Eq. 3 according to $\boldsymbol{t}$;
 2: compute dynamic temperature τ_i with Eq. 4;
 3: calculate teacher softened logits t_{τ_i} and student softened logit s_{τ_i} using Eq. 1 function with τ_i;
 4: **if** prediction of sample i whose t_{τ_i} does not match y **then:**
 5:     replace t_{τ_i} with the result of Eq. 6;
 6: **end if**
 7: compute L_{AKD} with Eq. 8;
 8: **return** L_{AKD}

---

4 Experiment Results and Discussions

4.1 Dataset and Evaluation Metrics

In our experiments, we use the relation classification benchmark: SemEval-2010 Task 8 dataset [8]. The dataset includes ten classes of relations and focuses on classifying the semantic relation of two entities in a sentence. The training set consists of 8,000 sentences, and 2,717 sentences are used for testing. Table 1 demonstrates specific statistics about the dataset. Please note that the relation classes are directional, for example, Cause-Effect(e1, e2) is different from Cause-Effect(e2, e1). To evaluate the models, the SemEval-2010 Task 8 official scorer script is used. It takes directions of relation classes into account and computes macro-averaged F1 scores for the nine actual relations (excluding the "Other" relation).

Table 1. SemEval-2010 Task 8 dataset statistic.

Relation	Frequency
Cause-effect	1331 (12.4%)
Component-whole	1253 (11.7%)
Entity-destination	1137 (10.6%)
Entity-origin	974 (9.1%)
Product-producer	948 (8.8%)
Member-collection	923 (8.6%)
Message-topic	895 (8.4%)
Content-container	732 (6.8%)
Instrument-agency	660 (6.2%)
Other	1864 (17.4%)
Total	10717 (100%)

4.2 Experimental Setting

The knowledge distillation framework enjoys great flexibility in the choice of teacher and student models. In our setting, a fine-tuned end-to-end R-BERT model [26] is used as the teacher model, and an Attention-Bi-LSTM [29] model is used as the student model. The experiments were implemented with the PyTorch [14] library and Text-Brewer [27] toolkit. Please refer to [26,29] for more implementation details for our teacher and student model.

On a single Tesla P100-PCIE-16GB GPU, our experiments were performed with a batch size of 16. To distill knowledge from the teacher model to the student model, the base temperature parameter τ_0 is set at 3. In the preliminary experiment, it was found the student model performs better when the bias parameter β was equal to τ_0. The performance of models is computed as an average value of five repeated experiments.

4.3 Model Performance Comparison

To evaluate our proposed methods, three configurations are created to explore the specific contributions: The Direct Distillation configuration directly leveraged the original KD methods [9]; the CDTD configuration used only the CDTD method, and the CDTD+LRKA configuration used both the proposed operation. Table 2 presents the experiment results. Interestingly, the student model trained under the supervision of the teacher model performs even worse by 1.48% F1-score than training with ground truth labels. Such results showed that the teacher failed to transfer helpful knowledge to students, which validates the concerns raised in the previous sections that excessive supervision uncertainty and genetic errors may mislead students. Scores of the student model using the CDTD method are 2.27% higher than that of the Direct Distillation and 0.79%

higher than the original student model. The results proved that CDTD can alleviate the misleading effect of excessive supervision uncertainty. The highest score (86.35%) was achieved by the distilled student using both the CDTD and LRKA methods, which is 3.83% higher than that of the Direct Distillation and 2.35% higher than the original student model. The result indicates that LRKA also made a great contribution to the performance of the student.

Table 2. Relation classification test results.

Architecture	Methods	Test score
Teacher model	R-BERT [26]	89.25
Student model	Attention Bi-LSTM [29]	84.00
Distilled student	Direct Distillation [9]	82.52
	CDTD	84.79
	CDTD+LRKA	86.35

4.4   Model Efficiency Comparison

The statistics of the inference time and model file size are shown in Table 3. # of Par. denotes the number of millions of parameters, inference time is measured in seconds and file size is measured in MBs.

Distilled by our method, the distilled student used 2.5 times fewer network parameters and is about 20.6 times faster. The memory occupied is only about 37% of that of the teacher model R-BERT. Such efficiency improvement and memory save are achieved only sacrifices the model performance of 2.9%, which is 2.35% less than using the traditional KD method.

Table 3. Comparison of model efficiency.

Methods	# of Par.	Inference time	File size	Test score
R-BERT	101.71 (2.5X)	34.80 (20.6X)	422.32 (2.7X)	89.25 (+2.90)
Attention Bi-LSTM	40.16 (1X)	1.69 (1X)	153.21 (1X)	84.00 (−2.35)
Distilled Student	40.16 (1X)	1.69 (1X)	153.21 (1X)	86.35 (+0.00)

5   Conclusions

In this paper, we explored adaptive knowledge distillation methods for relation classification. Using the proposed CDTD and LRKA methods, the knowledge from R-BERT was adaptively distilled into an Attention-Bi-LSTM model, which achieves a significant improvement of 2.35%. It achieved comparable results with transformer-based teacher models while using fewer parameters, less inference time, and less memory. In the future, more teacher-student pairs will be explored to further evaluate the robustness of the proposed CDTD and LRKA methods. Another important work is to explore more potential knowledge adjustment methods.

References

1. Ba, J., Caruana, R.: Do deep nets really need to be deep? Adv. Neural Inf. Process. Syst. **27** (2014)
2. Cai, R., Zhang, X., Wang, H.: Bidirectional recurrent convolutional neural network for relation classification. In: Proceedings of ACL (2016)
3. Chen, W.C., Chang, C.C., Lee, C.R.: Knowledge distillation with feature maps for image classification. In: Proceedings of ACCV (2018)
4. Chen, Y.C., Gan, Z., Cheng, Y., Liu, J., Liu, J.: Distilling knowledge learned in BERT for text generation. arXiv preprint arXiv:1911.03829 (2019)
5. Devlin, J., Chang, M.W., Lee, K., Toutanova, K.: BERT: pre-training of deep bidirectional transformers for language understanding. arXiv preprint arXiv:1810.04805 (2018)
6. Gou, J., Yu, B., Maybank, S.J., Tao, D.: Knowledge distillation: a survey. Int. J. Comput. Vision **129**(6), 1789–1819 (2021). https://doi.org/10.1007/s11263-021-01453-z
7. Hahn, S., Choi, H.: Self-knowledge distillation in natural language processing. arXiv preprint arXiv:1908.01851 (2019)
8. Hendrickx, I., et al.: SemEval-2010 Task 8: multi-way classification of semantic relations between pairs of nominals. arXiv preprint arXiv:1911.10422 (2019)
9. Hinton, G., Vinyals, O., Dean, J., et al.: Distilling the knowledge in a neural network. arXiv preprint arXiv:1503.02531 2(7) (2015)
10. Jiao, X., et al.: TinyBERT: distilling BERT for natural language understanding. arXiv preprint arXiv:1909.10351 (2019)
11. Lee, J., Seo, S., Choi, Y.S.: Semantic relation classification via bidirectional LSTM networks with entity-aware attention using latent entity typing. Symmetry **11**(6), 785 (2019)
12. Li, Z., Hoiem, D.: Learning without forgetting. IEEE Trans. Pattern Anal. Mach. Intell. **40**(12), 2935–2947 (2017)
13. Liu, J., Chen, Y., Liu, K.: Exploiting the ground-truth: an adversarial imitation based knowledge distillation approach for event detection. In: Proceedings of AAAI (2019)
14. Paszke, A., et al.: PyTorch: an imperative style, high-performance deep learning library. Adv. Neural Inf. Process. Syst. **32** (2019)
15. Pawar, S., Palshikar, G.K., Bhattacharyya, P.: Relation extraction : a survey. arXiv preprint arXiv:1712.05191 (2017)
16. Sanh, V., Debut, L., Chaumond, J., Wolf, T.: DistilBERT, a distilled version of BERT: smaller, faster, cheaper and lighter. arXiv preprint arXiv:1910.01108 (2019)
17. Santos, C.N.d., Xiang, B., Zhou, B.: Classifying relations by ranking with convolutional neural networks. arXiv preprint arXiv:1504.06580 (2015)
18. Sau, B.B., Balasubramanian, V.N.: Deep model compression: distilling knowledge from noisy teachers. arXiv preprint arXiv:1610.09650 (2016)
19. Shen, Y., Huang, X.J.: Attention-based convolutional neural network for semantic relation extraction. In: Proceedings of COLING (2016)

20. Sun, S., Cheng, Y., Gan, Z., Liu, J.: Patient knowledge distillation for BERT model compression. arXiv preprint arXiv:1908.09355 (2019)
21. Szegedy, C., Vanhoucke, V., Ioffe, S., Shlens, J., Wojna, Z.: Rethinking the inception architecture for computer vision. In: Proceedings of CVPR (2016)
22. Tang, R., Lu, Y., Liu, L., Mou, L., Vechtomova, O., Lin, J.: Distilling task-specific knowledge from BERT into simple neural networks. arXiv preprint arXiv:1903.12136 (2019)
23. Wang, X., Fu, T., Liao, S., Wang, S., Lei, Z., Mei, T.: Exclusivity-consistency regularized knowledge distillation for face recognition. In: Vedaldi, A., Bischof, H., Brox, T., Frahm, J.-M. (eds.) ECCV 2020. LNCS, vol. 12369, pp. 325–342. Springer, Cham (2020). https://doi.org/10.1007/978-3-030-58586-0_20
24. Wei, Z., Su, J., Wang, Y., Tian, Y., Chang, Y.: A novel cascade binary tagging framework for relational triple extraction. arXiv preprint arXiv:1909.03227 (2019)
25. Wen, T., Lai, S., Qian, X.: Preparing lessons: improve knowledge distillation with better supervision. Neurocomputing **454**, 25–33 (2021)
26. Wu, S., He, Y.: Enriching pre-trained language model with entity information for relation classification. In: Proceedings of CIKM (2019)
27. Yang, Z., et al.: TextBrewer: an open-source knowledge distillation toolkit for natural language processing. In: Proceedings of ACL, pp. 9–16 (2020)
28. Zeng, D., Liu, K., Lai, S., Zhou, G., Zhao, J.: Relation classification via convolutional deep neural network. In: Proceedings of COLING (2014)
29. Zhou, P., et al.: Attention-based bidirectional long short-term memory networks for relation classification. In: Proceedings of ACL (2016)

An Adversarial Multi-task Learning Method for Chinese Text Correction with Semantic Detection

Fanyu Wang[iD] and Zhenping Xie[(✉)][iD]

School of Artificial Intelligence and Computer Science, Jiangnan University,
Wuxi 214122, China
xiezp@jiangnan.edu.cn

Abstract. Text correction, especially the semantic correction of more widely used scenes, is strongly required to improve, for the fluency and writing efficiency of the text. An adversarial multi-task learning method is proposed to enhance the modeling and detection ability of character polysemy in Chinese sentence context. Wherein, two models, the masked language model and scoring language model, are introduced as a pair of not only coupled but also adversarial learning tasks. Moreover, the Monte Carlo tree search strategy and a policy network are introduced to accomplish the efficient Chinese text correction task with semantic detection. The experiments are executed on three datasets and five comparable methods, and the experimental results show that our method can obtain good performance in Chinese text correction task for better semantic rationality.

Keywords: Chinese text correction · Adversarial learning · Multi-task learning · Text semantic modeling

1 Introduction

1.1 Bottlenecks and Defects

Text correction is an essential process for daily writing, also, has been widely developed in current office software products [9, 20, 22]. However, the complexity and flexibility of natural language especially for Chinese, cause huge obstacles to developing a high-quality text correction method. For Chinese, its finest process level of parsing sentences is character-level containing over 20,000 commonly used vocabulary characters. Usually, each sentence is composed of several phrases, and there is no characteristic separator between phrases, in which each phrase also contains several characters. Hence, the syntax in Chinese is complicated and easy to be misunderstood.

Traditionally, the two aspects in Chinese error correction are divided into CSC (Chinese Spelling Check) and CGEC (Chinese Grammatical Error Correction) which accord to their processing level as character-level and phrase-level respectively. The complexity syntax determines that there are few robust

E. Pimenidis et al. (Eds.): ICANN 2022, LNCS 13530, pp. 159–173, 2022.
https://doi.org/10.1007/978-3-031-15931-2_14

Table 1. An example of correction results at different levels

Sentence type	Sentence example
Original correct sentence	他上周去了金字塔。 He went to the pyramid last week
Incorrect sentence	他上周取了金字。 He got golden character last week
Character-level correction	他上周取了金子。 He got gold last week
Phrase-level correction	他上周取了金字塔。 He got the pyramid last week

logic and adequate features for checking the grammar errors at phrase-level. At present, the pertained models like BERT (Bidirectional Encoder Representations from Transformers [7]) is considered to represent the sentence semantics, and CRF (Conditional Random Field [14]) can be introduced to realize the effective grammatical error correction [15,18]. For the character-level processing, the visual and phonological similarities is employed to generate the confusion set for Chinese Spelling Check [16,27]. Moreover, the additional feature is also integrated into BERT to enhance the consistency of the Spelling Check methods [3,11,12,26]. It reflects that the semantic feature is unreliable for Chinese Spelling Check, and the auxiliary verification methods utilized the the additional features is reasonably introduced.

For example, the correction process from the semantic perspective is vulnerable for the subtle errors at character-level. For a pair of correct and incorrect sentences shown in Table 1, the incorrect sentence contains a grammatical error (金字 /gold character of 金字塔 /pyramid) at phrase-level and a spelling error (取 /take of 去 /went with a similar pronunciation) at character-level. Moreover, the corrected results at character-level and phrase-level, in which both the corrected sentences are still incorrect in semantic logic, cannot be completely corrected even by further correction process.

The example of the correction results demonstrates that the reliable detection process is significant for the correction method at phrase-level. As the error detection methods used at character-level [31,32], the semantics-based error detection network is also adequate for grammar error correction. Besides, the example also reflects the inconsistency of different processing level, the Chinese text correction process cannot be regarded as a simple combination of above two aspects of correction procedures because of the semantic polysemy of different parsing. Recently, the unified method of the above two aspects of strategies has developed. Malmi proposed the LaserTagger method by tagging characters with base tags and added phrases [19]. Wherein, the base tag process is like error detection mentioned before, and the added phrase is analyzed based on the constructed semi-dynamic vocabulary at both character-level and phrase-level. LaserTagger tends to break the boundary between the character-level and phrase-level, even if the completely dynamic vocabulary list is closely related to the minimum k-union problem, which is NP-hard.

1.2 Motivation and Contributions

In this study, we proposed a novel correction strategy by taking the character-level and phrase-level correction as a unified semantic correction process, and in which, an adversarial multi-task learning method is introduced to effectively model the unified semantics of a sentence. Here, the masked character prediction and token scoring tasks are considered a couple of learning tasks in the multi-task learning method [2]. Moreover, their generative adversarial learning [10] relation, the masked language model as the generator, and the scoring language model as the discriminator, is also newly introduced to improve task robustness.

In addition, for the automatic poetry writing area [8,30,33], inspired by the polishing process [6,29], we also introduce the polishing concept to realize the text correction based on the trained masked language model and scoring language model. Besides, because the sentence length of the common text is flexible which is different from poetry writing, the MCTS (Monte Carlo tree search [1,13]) strategy is introduced to our method inspired by the idea in AlphaGo [25].

1.3 Achievements

Thanks to the newly innovated adversarial multi-task learning strategy, the following contributions can be gained.

- A new Chinese text correction framework with a unified correction process of character-level and phrase-level is proposed by means of a more robust sentence semantic modeling strategy.
- Two core models for text correction, masked language model and scoring language model, are designed as a group of adversarial multi-task learning models.
- Our experimental analysis indicates that the MCTS strategy should be valuable to improve the text correction quality for those sentences with multiple positions and character errors (or needing complex editing correction).

2 Methodology

2.1 Task Formulation

Given a sentence $\mathbb{S} = (c_1, \ldots, \dot{c}_i, \dot{c}_{i+1}, \ldots, c_k)$ with some character errors $(\dot{c}_i, \dot{c}_{i+1})$ originated from the correct sentence $S = (c_1, \ldots, c_i, \ldots, c_k)$. The correction task can be defined as a prediction task of generating a corrected sentence $\hat{S}$ from the wrong sentence $\mathbb{S}$ with minimum semantic deviation.

2.2 Adversarial Multi-task Learning

Structure of Adversarial Multi-task Learning. We consider that adversarial multi-task learning is a model training strategy for two adversarial and cooperative model tasks. For Chinese text correction, two core task models, including

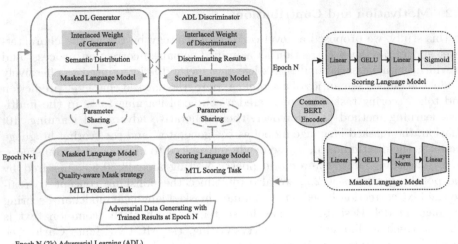

Fig. 1. The framework of adversarial multi-task learning method (Best view in color).

the masked language model and the scoring language model, are considered in this study. Wherein, the masked language model is to predict reasonable characters in the masked position of a sentence, and the scoring language model is to examine the semantic quality of every character in its sentence context.

As shown in Fig. 1, a BERT [7] encoder is introduced as the common encoder for scoring language model and masked language model. The adversarial multi-task learning is composed of the adversarial learning phase and multi-task learning phase. The multi-task learning aims to find the optimal semantic representation using the common encoder for different down-stream tasks. While, the adversarial learning is to enhance the robustness of classifier in distinguishing similar tokens in a sentence.

The Multi-task Learning Phase. Benefits from the structure of multi-task learning paradigm, the common encoder effectively prevent the model from the overfitting problem and the general semantic representation can enhance the modeling ability of the method. However, the general semantic representation from the encoder is vulnerable to adversarial attacks from the generative tokens which are semantic similar to original tokens [24]. Besides the introduction of the following adversarial learning phase, an additional adversarial data generation strategy is introduced in this phase.

Adversarial Data Generating Strategy. As shown in Fig. 2, the trained masked language model is firstly used to generate a group of ordered candidate token (character) sequence according to their confidence distributions on given masked positions in a sentence. Moreover, an index function is defined as following for-

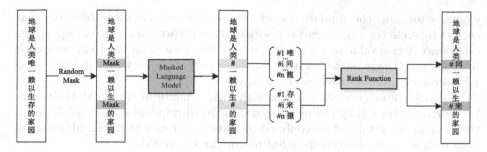

Fig. 2. Adversarial data generating strategy.

mula to select a token in a candidate token sequence

$$Ik_t(\cdot) = e^{randI()\cdot ln(Ct)} \tag{1}$$

where, $Ik_t(\cdot)$ denotes an index value generation function, and $randI()$ is a uniform random function on $[0, 1]$. Ct is a constant, and the value 1000 is considered as default in this study. The generated tokens less than the threshold 20 are considered as positive token (has reasonable semantic), otherwise as negative token.

The Adversarial Learning Phase. In this part, the masked language model and the scoring language model are respectively considered as the generator and the discriminator in standard adversarial learning method. However, when the vanilla generative adversarial method is applied to natural language process problem, the excessive precision of the generator will lead to training confusion of the discriminator [4]. Therefore, in order to keep the increasing balance with the training execution, the interlaced weights between the generator and the discriminator are introduced in our framework. The interlaced weights are used to dynamically adjust the learning strengths of different generated samples and discriminated samples according to the semantic similarity of the predicted tokens to correct tokens.

Interlaced Weights Definitions. Here, we use W_G to denote the interlaced weight matrix from the generator to the discriminator, and W_D to denote the interlaced weight matrix from the discriminator to the generator. For W_G, it is used to adjust the training strength of the discriminator for different generative tokens, and lower values will be calculated for those generative tokens with higher semantic similarity to their correct original tokens. Concretely, the following equations can be defined.

$$W_{\mathcal{G}}[i] = \begin{cases} \text{sigmoid}(s_i) + 0.5 & \text{if } s_i \geq 0 \\ \tanh(s_i) & \text{if } s_i \leq 0 \end{cases} \tag{2}$$

$$s_i = \frac{d_i[0] - d_i[Ik_t]}{d_i[Ik_t]} - S_g \tag{3}$$

where, s_i denotes the similarity score values of generative token from original correct token in the i-th character position in a sentence, and d_i is corresponding confidence degree value vector related to the generative candidate token sequence by masked language model. Besides, S_g is a hyperparameter with a default value 1.15 according to our experimental analysis.

Thus, for those generative tokens with high semantic similarity to their original correct tokens, they will be weakened in the discriminator training. That is, the discriminator will not be confused by those generative (adversarial) samples with high semantic reasonability but not originally correct.

For W_D, it is used to adjust the training strength of the generator, and the lower values will be determined that the discriminator cannot effectively distinguish the generated tokens and their original correct tokens. In this study, the following equations can be defined.

$$W_{\mathcal{D}}[i] = \frac{score_g[i]}{score_o[i]} \tag{4}$$

For the i-th character in S, $score_g$ and $score_o$ denote the score vector of different positions respectively for the generative sentence and the original sentence predicted by the discriminator.

Therefore, $W_{\mathcal{D}}$ also reversely indicates the generative performance of the generator, and can subtly raise the training strength of those prediction tokens with high semantic similarity to original tokens but low discrimination scores.

Training for Adversarial Multi-task Learning. For the loss functions of adversarial multi-task learning, the objective of generative adversarial learning and the objective of multi-task learning should be respectively considered.

Objectives of Adversarial Learning. According to the above discussions and standard entropy loss function, the following objectives are introduced.

$$L_{\mathcal{G}} = L_{\mathcal{D} \sim \mathcal{G}} = \sum_{i \in R} W_{\mathcal{D}}[i] \{ -x [\text{ class }_i] + \log(\sum_{j=0}^{vs} e^{x[j]}) \} \tag{5}$$

$$L_{\mathcal{D}} = L_{\mathcal{G} \sim \mathcal{D}} + L_{\mathcal{D} \sim \mathcal{D}} \tag{6}$$

$$L_{\mathcal{G} \sim \mathcal{D}} = \sum_{i=1}^{k} W_{\mathcal{G}}[i] \left[y_i \log(x_i) + (1 - y_i) \log(1 - x_i) \right] \tag{7}$$

$$L_{\mathcal{D} \sim \mathcal{D}} = \frac{\sum_{i \in C} \text{sigmoid}(x_i)}{\sum_{j \in R} \text{sigmoid}(x_j)} \tag{8}$$

where, k denotes the number of the total token (character) in a given sentence, and R and C are the index sets with generated tokens and original tokens. Besides, $L_{\mathcal{D} \sim \mathcal{G}}$ and $L_{\mathcal{G} \sim \mathcal{D}}$ reflect the interlaced loss objectives between the generator and discriminator. And, $L_{\mathcal{D} \sim \mathcal{D}}$ is the loss function of discriminating the generative tokens from original correct tokens. For these objectives, all parameters except in the common encoder should be optimized.

Algorithm 1 Basic Correction Process with Adversarial Multi-task Learning

---

Input: Sentence $\mathbb{S} = c_1, c_2, ..., \dot{c}_i, \dot{c}_{i+1}, ..., c_k$ with errors $\dot{c}_i, \dot{c}_{i+1}$

Output: Corrected sentence $\hat{\mathbb{S}}_{MCST} = c_1, ..., c_i, , ..., c_{k-1}$

1: Perform the **Scoring Language Model** on $\mathbb{S}$ to get the $score_\mathbb{S} = s_1, \ldots, s_{k+1}$ and the character position with the maximum score p_m

2: **for** $p_s \leftarrow p_m$ and $p_e \leftarrow p_m$ to $p_m - width$ and $p_m + width$ **do**

3:     **for** $num \leftarrow 0$ to $depth$ **do**

                                      $\overbrace{num*[\text{MASK}]}$

4:         Replace $\{p_s, ..., p_e\}$ with $\{[\text{MASK}], ..., [\text{MASK}]\}$ to get $\mathbb{S}_{p_s,p_e}$

5:         Perform the **Masked Language Model** on $\mathbb{S}_{p_s,p_e}$ to get $\hat{\mathbb{S}}_{p_s,p_e} = c_1, ..., \hat{c}_i, \hat{c}_{i+num-1}, ..., c_{k-1}$

6:         Perform the **Scoring Language Model** on $\hat{\mathbb{S}}_{p_s,p_e}$, $score_{\hat{\mathbb{S}}} = \text{SLM}(\hat{\mathbb{S}}_{p_s,p_e})/k$

7:         Append $score_{\hat{\mathbb{S}}}$ to $list_{\hat{\mathbb{S}}}$

8:     **end for**

9: **end for**

10: Return $\hat{\mathbb{S}}_{MCST} | score_{\hat{\mathbb{S}}} = min(list_{\hat{\mathbb{S}}})$

Objectives of Multi-task Learning. The general objectives are introduced as follows

$$L_{MTL} = L_{PS} + L_{ML} \tag{9}$$

$$L_S - \sum_{i=1}^{k} y_i \log(x_i) + (1 - y_i) \log(1 - x_i) \tag{10}$$

$$L_{ML} = \sum_{i=1}^{k} -x[\text{class}_i] + \log(\sum_{j=0}^{vs} e^{x[j]}). \tag{11}$$

where L_{PS} and L_{ML} are the objectives of the masked language model and the scoring language model respectively. Similarly, k denotes the total token (character) numbers in a given sentence, vs is the size of the vocabulary list.

2.3   Chinese Text Correction with Semantic Error Detection

In order to realize the correction of a sentence with possible errors, the Monte Carlo tree search (MCTS) strategy is introduced to find and correct possible error characters. Wherein, all possible positions with error characters can be found by means of the trained scoring language model, and the most reasonable (correct) sentence can be recommended based on the combined use of the trained masked language and scoring language models. In summary, the following Algorithm 1 can be proposed.

In above Algorithm 1, the two-fold scoring and prediction searching[1] has to be executed, so the computing efficiency will not satisfy the practical requirements.

---

[1] In Algorithm 1, the default values of width (step 2) and depth (step 3) are set as 2 and 4.

Furthermore, a policy network inspired by the idea of AlphaGo is introduced to speed up the error position searching computation. In our policy network, the most possible error range in a sentence is defined as the network output.

In our policy network, the network output is considered to be the most possible error range for a wrong sentence. Here, all wrong sentences are generated by randomly replacing multiple character strings (with a maximum length of 4) in original correct sentences, in which the lengths of the original and replaced character strings may be different. Moreover, the corrected sentences of those wrong sentences can be predicted according to Algorithm 1. Thus, for a generated wrong sentence, the most possible error character can be recognized based on the trained scoring language model. Then we may introduce $(Is_{w \sim o}, Ie_{w \sim o})$ to denote the start and end position index values of the error string containing the most possible error character in the wrong sentence. Similarly, $(Is_{w \sim cw}, Ie_{w \sim cw})$ is used to indicate the start and end position index values of the corresponding string in the wrong sentence of the corrected string in the corrected sentence by Algorithm 1, in which the corresponding string still contains that most possible error character.

Moreover, for a wrong sentence and its most error character string containing the most possible error character evaluated by the trained scoring language model, the following computations can be defined as

$$[S_l, S_h] = [\min(Is_{w \sim o}, Is_{w-cw}), \max(Is_{w \sim o}, Is_{w \sim cw})] \tag{12}$$

$$[E_l, E_h] = [\min(Ie_{w \sim o}, Is_{w-cw}), \max(Ie_{w \sim o}, Ie_{w \sim cw})] \tag{13}$$

here, $[S_l, S_h]$ and $[E_l, E_h]$ as possible position range indicators of an error character string are introduced to make the policy network can output a reasonable error position range for a detected sentence.

In addition, an extra loss coefficient is introduced to indicate the performance on error recognition coverage and corresponding correction accuracy of Algorithm 1, which is calculated by the following formula

$$\mu = \frac{\text{len}(\text{char}_{IS_{W \sim CW} - Ie_{W \sim CW}} \cap \text{char}_{Is_{W \sim O} - Ie_{W \sim O}})^2}{\text{len}(\text{char}_{Is_{W \sim CW} - Ie_{W \sim CW}}) \, \text{len}(\text{char}_{IS_{W \sim O} - Ie_{W \sim O}})} \tag{14}$$

where, $char_{Is_{W \sim cw} - Ie_{W \sim cw}}$ and $char_{Is_{W \sim o} - Ie_{W \sim o}}$ are strings in range of $Is_{w \sim cw} - Ie_{w \sim cw}$ and $Is_{w \sim o} - Ie_{w \sim o}$, $len(\cdot)$ function is used to calculate the character-length of the string. Based on the loss coefficient μ and the position ranges of start and end labels, we can jointly learn the start position prediction task and end position prediction task to train the policy network by minimizing the following objectives.

$$L = 0.5 L_{R_S} + 0.5 L_{R_e} \tag{15}$$

$$L_{R_s} = \mu \left[\text{sam}(x_s) - S_l\right]^2 e^{S_l - \text{sam}(x_s)} + (1 - \mu)\left[\text{sam}(x_s) - S_h\right]^2 e^{\text{sam}(x_s) - S_h} \tag{16}$$

$$L_{R_e} = \mu \left[\text{sam}(x_e) - E_l\right]^2 e^{E_l - \text{sam}(x_e)} + (1 - \mu)\left[\text{sam}(x_e) - E_h\right]^2 e^{\text{sam}(x_e) - E_h} \tag{17}$$

where x_{start} and x_{end} are the prediction results of the policy network, and $\text{sam}(\cdot)$ function is soft-argmax function [21]. The policy network faster in prediction compared to the standard MCTS correction process. Additionally, the policy network is semantic sensitive, which results in a more flexible usage scenario.

3   Experimental Result

3.1   Dataset

The datasets in our experiments are CLUE (Chinese Language Understanding Evaluation Benchmark [28]), CGED-2018 (Chinese Grammatical Error Diagnosis [23]), and our Xuexi dataset.

Table 2. Ablation results

Dataset	Method	MLM				SLM
		Acc.	Prec.	Rec.	F1.	Acc.
CLUE	Normal supervised-learning	58.5	42.2	42.0	40.3	69.8
	Multi-task learning	61.3	42.7	44.7	**44.0**	74.1
	Generative adversarial learning	52.9	34.5	37.4	35.4	73.6
	Adversarial multi-task learning	**62.9**	**45.0**	**44.9**	43.3	**75.7**
Xuexi	Normal supervised-learning	49.2	33.1	33.2	31.8	71.9
	Multi-task learning	59.3	42.7	41.6	40.3	72.9
	Generative adversarial learning	51.4	33.1	32.7	31.3	64.9
	Adversarial multi-task learning	**61.1**	**44.3**	**43.1**	**41.9**	**74.8**

The corpora in CGED-2018 were taken from the testing result of HSK (Pinyin of Hanyu Shuiping Kaoshi, Test of Chinese Level). The dataset contains different types of grammar errors, which can ideally reflect the situation of the writing errors faced in our daily. CLUE is the largest language understanding corpus in Chinese, in which the Chinese Wikipedia dataset is selected and is mixed with multiple languages characters representing a complex semantic environment. Xuexi dataset are collected by ours from the most prominent Chinese political news website "学习强国 /Xuexi Qiangguo"[2], which is managed by the Central Propaganda Department of the Communist Party of China. Xuexi dataset can reflect the usage scenario for people in daily working.

For model training, 200,000 sentences are randomly selected from Xuexi and CLUE datasets. In the main evaluation experiment, we randomly select 1,000 samples from each dataset mentioned above. In addition, for those 1,000 selected sentences from Xuexi and CLUE corpus, corresponding wrong sentences are constructed by using a similar strategy of generating wrong sentences for policy network training.

3.2   Training Settings

Our experimental environment is built on NVIDIA Tesla V100 (16 GB GPU RAM), using a Transformer Package based on PyTorch. The pretrained BERT-base model for Chinese is employed to initialize the language models. The model

---

[2] https://www.xuexi.cn/.

Table 3. Main results

Dataset	Method	Founder detection	Baidu PPL	Baidu DNN	BLEU
Xuexi	MacBERT	78	0.320	0.638	0.703
	ERNIE	105	0.262	0.560	0.687
	ELECTRA	103	0.257	0.561	0.694
	TtT	122	0.252	0.557	0.694
	Our method	**7**	**0.813**	**0.929**	**0.738**
CLUE	MacBERT	61	0.498	0.707	**0.685**
	ERNIE	119	0.559	0.694	0.663
	ELECTRA	84	0.507	0.714	0.678
	TtT	98	0.528	0.717	0.679
	Our method	**6**	**0.814**	**0.958**	0.629
CGED	MacBERT	22	**0.846**	0.920	0.720
	ERNIE	41	0.795	0.921	0.712
	ELECTRA	36	0.774	0.916	**0.819**
	TtT	44	0.766	0.914	0.818
	Our method	**5**	0.766	**1.021**	0.643

is trained using AdamW [17]. We set the initial learning rate to 0.00002 and set the first 10k adjustments to the warm-up stage, and then linearly adjusted the learning rate. For the application scenarios of the text correction, the parameters in the original BERT-Base model are partly customized. We set the length to 64 Chinese and English characters, keeping the remaining hyperparameters consistent with BERT-base. In the training process of the policy network, we set the dropout rate to 0.5 to train the generalization ability of the model.

3.3   Ablation Results

We set up an ablation experiment on CLUE Dataset and Xuexi Dataset to evaluate the performance of the adversarial multi-task learning method. For evaluating the scoring language model, we sort the score sequence of the sentence and extract the first K positions with high rank, then the scoring accuracy is calculated by comparing with the error positions in the sentence.

As shown in Table 2, the result of the adversarial multi-task learning method has a significant improvement compared with other models, which indicates that our adversarial multi-task learning method is efficient in modeling ability improvement.

3.4   Main Results

Here, several open-source Chinese detection and correction tools are introduced to examine the correction performance of different methods. The Founder detection tool as a classical technique in Chinese proofreading is performed to detect

Table 4. Examples of the correction methods

Num.	Method	E.g.
1	Original	试着在国际竞争中掌握更大话语权。
		Trying to control a greater power in international competition
2	Wrong	试着在国际竞争力具己更大话语权。
		Trying to 'juji' a greater power international competitiveness
3	MacBERT	试着在国际竞争力具有更大话语权。
		Trying to have a great status international competitiveness
4	ERNIE	试着在国际竞争力具己更大话语权。
		Trying to 'juji' a greater power international competitiveness
5	ELECTRA	试着在国际竞争力具己更大话语权。
		Trying to 'juji' a greater power international competitiveness
6	TtT	试着在国际竞争力具己更大话语权。
		Trying to 'juji' a greater power international competitiveness
7	Our Method	试着在国际竞争力中争得更大话语权。
		Striving for a greater voice in international competitiveness

the number of errors in corrected sentences. The number of errors reflects the error correction capability of the methods. The NLP tools from Baidu's artificial intelligence platform are also used, in which the language perplexity (PPL) computation can evaluate the fluency of sentences based on every word in the sentences, and the DNN score can evaluate the possibility of every word in the sentence. Wherein, the normalized performance values in illustrated results are calculated by the ratio with respect to PPL and DNN score values of original sentences. BLEU is a classical evaluation matrix, which is widely used in the evaluation of translation task. It reflects the ability of restoring an error sentence to its original sentence for text correction methods.

In our correction performance analysis, the hard mode named as VarLen scenario [15] is also considered, in which the two length values of a wrong sentence and its ideal correct sentence are different. However, some of the existing text correction methods can only perform the correction for the FixLen scenario. So, the following methods are adopted as comparison including ELECTRA [4], ERNIE [34], MacBERT [5], and TtT [15] as a state-of-the-art method in variable-length correction as the baseline.

As shown in Table 3, our method gained better performance compared to the baseline in various evaluation indexes. Even so, because the structure and length of the wrong sentences are not much different from the original sentences, our method did not get a significant improvement in BLEU (for restoring ability evaluation). But in Founder detection performance, our method has an overwhelming advantage over all other methods, which represents that our method can effectively discover the semantic errors in the sentences and correct them under appropriate semantics.

In Table 4, an example is presented including an original correct sentence, a typical wrong sentence generated in our experiment, and five corrected results by four comparable correction methods and our method. For the above different corrected results, the corrected result of our method might be the most reasonable in sentence semantics. Concretely, for the character string with wave underlines in sentences, our method accurately understands the emotion of the given wrong sentence and finds similar words (争得 /strive for). Similarly, for the character string with straight under-lines, only our method can give a correction solution that the (中 /in) is added. Of course, the last result of our method still has not completely repaired the wrong sentence to the ideal result (original correct sentence), which also reflects the complexity and hardness of the Chinese text correction task.

4   Conclusion

For Chinese text correction task with complex semantic errors, we proposed a novel correction method by introducing an adversarial multi-task learning strategy. The proposed method can model Chinese sentences into a unified semantic feature and effectively resolve the modeling confusion of similar characters in semantics. In addition, a policy network is introduced to gain the high searching quality and efficiency of error positions. The experimental results on three datasets clearly indicate the significant advantages of our method in the VarLen scenario.

In the future, we plan to enhance the explainable modeling ability for Chinese text correction by developing explainable scoring language models.

Acknowledgements. This work was supported in part by the grants from National Natural Science Foundation of China (Grant no. 61872166) and Six Talent Peaks Project of Jiangsu Province of China (2019 XYDXX-161).

References

1. Browne, C.B., et al.: A survey of Monte Carlo tree search methods. IEEE Trans. Comput. Intell. AI Games **4**(1), 1–43 (2012). https://doi.org/10.1109/TCIAIG. 2012.2186810
2. Caruana, R.: Multitask learning. Mach. Learn. **28**(1), 41–75 (1997)
3. Cheng, X., et al.: SpellGCN: incorporating phonological and visual similarities into language models for Chinese spelling check. In: Proceedings of the 58th Annual Meeting of the Association for Computational Linguistics, pp. 871–881. Association for Computational Linguistics, Online, July 2020. https://doi.org/10.18653/v1/ 2020.acl-main.81
4. Clark, K., Luong, T., Le, Q.V., Manning, C.: Electra: pre-training text encoders as discriminators rather than generators. In: ICLR (2020). https://openreview.net/ pdf?id=r1xMH1BtvB
5. Cui, Y., Che, W., Liu, T., Qin, B., Wang, S., Hu, G.: Revisiting pre-trained models for Chinese natural language processing. In: Findings of the Association for Computational Linguistics: EMNLP 2020, pp. 657–668. Association for Computational Linguistics, Online, November 2020. https://doi.org/10.18653/v1/2020. findings-emnlp.58

6. Deng, L., et al.: An iterative polishing framework based on quality aware masked language model for Chinese poetry generation. In: Proceedings of the AAAI Conference on Artificial Intelligence, vol. 34, no. 05, pp. 7643–7650 (2020). https://doi.org/10.1609/aaai.v34i05.6265

7. Devlin, J., Chang, M.W., Lee, K., Toutanova, K.: BERT: pre-training of deep bidirectional transformers for language understanding. In: Proceedings of the 2019 Conference of the North American Chapter of the Association for Computational Linguistics: Human Language Technologies, Volume 1 (Long and Short Papers), pp. 4171–4186. Association for Computational Linguistics, Minneapolis, June 2019. https://doi.org/10.18653/v1/N19-1423

8. Ghazvininejad, M., Shi, X., Choi, Y., Knight, K.: Generating topical poetry. In: Proceedings of the 2016 Conference on Empirical Methods in Natural Language Processing, pp. 1183–1191. Association for Computational Linguistics, Austin, November 2016. https://doi.org/10.18653/v1/D16-1126

9. Ghufron, M.A., Rosyida, F.: The role of grammarly in assessing English as a foreign language (EFL) writing. Lingua Cultura **12**(4), 395–403 (2018)

10. Goodfellow, I., et l.: Generative adversarial nets. In: Ghahramani, Z., Welling, M., Cortes, C., Lawrence, N., Weinberger, K. (eds.) Advances in Neural Information Processing Systems, vol. 27. Curran Associates, Inc. (2014). https://proceedings.neurips.cc/paper/2014/file/5ca3e9b122f61f8f06494c97b1afccf3-Paper.pdf

11. Hong, Y., Yu, X., He, N., Liu, N., Liu, J.: FASPell: a fast, adaptable, simple, powerful Chinese spell checker based on DAE-decoder paradigm. In: Proceedings of the 5th Workshop on Noisy User-generated Text (W-NUT 2019), pp. 160–169. Association for Computational Linguistics, Hong Kong, November 2019. https://doi.org/10.18653/v1/D19-5522

12. Ji, T., Yan, H., Qiu, X.: SpellBERT: a lightweight pretrained model for Chinese spelling check. In: Proceedings of the 2021 Conference on Empirical Methods in Natural Language Processing, pp. 3544–3551. Association for Computational Linguistics, Online and Punta Cana, Dominican Republic, November 2021. https://doi.org/10.18653/v1/2021.emnlp-main.287

13. Kocsis, L., Szepesvári, C.: Bandit based Monte-Carlo planning. In: Fürnkranz, J., Scheffer, T., Spiliopoulou, M. (eds.) ECML 2006. LNCS (LNAI), vol. 4212, pp. 282–293. Springer, Heidelberg (2006). https://doi.org/10.1007/11871842_29

14. Lafferty, J.D., McCallum, A., Pereira, F.C.N.: Conditional random fields: probabilistic models for segmenting and labeling sequence data. In: Proceedings of the Eighteenth International Conference on Machine Learning. ICML 2001, pp. 282–289. Morgan Kaufmann Publishers Inc., San Francisco (2001)

15. Li, P., Shi, S.: Tail-to-tail non-autoregressive sequence prediction for Chinese grammatical error correction. In: Proceedings of the 59th Annual Meeting of the Association for Computational Linguistics and the 11th International Joint Conference on Natural Language Processing (Volume 1: Long Papers), pp. 4973–4984. Association for Computational Linguistics, Online, August 2021. https://doi.org/10.18653/v1/2021.acl-long.385

16. Liu, C.L., Lai, M.H., Tien, K.W., Chuang, Y.H., Wu, S.H., Lee, C.Y.: Visually and phonologically similar characters in incorrect Chinese words: analyses, identification, and applications. ACM Trans. Asian Lang. Inf. Process. **10**(2) (2011). https://doi.org/10.1145/1967293.1967297

17. Loshchilov, I., Hutter, F.: Decoupled weight decay regularization. In: International Conference on Learning Representations (2018)

18. Luo, Y., Bao, Z., Li, C., Wang, R.: Chinese grammatical error diagnosis with graph convolution network and multi-task learning. In: Proceedings of the 6th Workshop on Natural Language Processing Techniques for Educational Applications, pp. 44–48. Association for Computational Linguistics, Suzhou, December 2020. https://aclanthology.org/2020.nlptea-1.6

19. Malmi, E., Krause, S., Rothe, S., Mirylenka, D., Severyn, A.: Encode, tag, realize: high-precision text editing. In: Proceedings of the 2019 Conference on Empirical Methods in Natural Language Processing and the 9th International Joint Conference on Natural Language Processing (EMNLP-IJCNLP), pp. 5054–5065. Association for Computational Linguistics, Hong Kong, November 2019. https://doi.org/10.18653/v1/D19-1510

20. Napoles, C., Sakaguchi, K., Tetreault, J.: JFLEG: a fluency corpus and benchmark for grammatical error correction. In: Proceedings of the 15th Conference of the European Chapter of the Association for Computational Linguistics: Volume 2, Short Papers, pp. 229–234. Association for Computational Linguistics, Valencia, April 2017. https://aclanthology.org/E17-2037

21. Nibali, A., He, Z., Morgan, S., Prendergast, L.: Numerical coordinate regression with convolutional neural networks. arXiv preprint arXiv:1801.07372 (2018)

22. Omelianchuk, K., Atrasevych, V., Chernodub, A., Skurzhanskyi, O.: GECToR - grammatical error correction: tag, not rewrite. In: Proceedings of the Fifteenth Workshop on Innovative Use of NLP for Building Educational Applications, pp. 163–170. Association for Computational Linguistics, Seattle, July 2020. https://doi.org/10.18653/v1/2020.bea-1.16

23. Rao, G., Gong, Q., Zhang, B., Xun, E.: Overview of NLPTEA-2018 share task Chinese grammatical error diagnosis. In: Proceedings of the 5th Workshop on Natural Language Processing Techniques for Educational Applications, pp. 42–51. Association for Computational Linguistics, Melbourne, July 2018. https://doi.org/10.18653/v1/W18-3706

24. Ruder, S.: An overview of multi-task learning in deep neural networks. arXiv preprint arXiv:1706.05098 (2017)

25. Silver, D., et al.: Mastering the game of go without human knowledge. Nature **550**(7676), 354–359 (2017)

26. Tan, M., Chen, D., Li, Z., Wang, P.: Spelling error correction with BERT based on character-phonetic. In: 2020 IEEE 6th International Conference on Computer and Communications (ICCC), pp. 1146–1150 (2020). https://doi.org/10.1109/ICCC51575.2020.9345276

27. Wang, D., Song, Y., Li, J., Han, J., Zhang, H.: A hybrid approach to automatic corpus generation for Chinese spelling check. In: Proceedings of the 2018 Conference on Empirical Methods in Natural Language Processing, pp. 2517–2527. Association for Computational Linguistics, Brussels, October–November 2018. https://doi.org/10.18653/v1/D18-1273

28. Xu, L., et al.: CLUE: a Chinese language understanding evaluation benchmark. In: Proceedings of the 28th International Conference on Computational Linguistics, pp. 4762–4772. International Committee on Computational Linguistics, Barcelona (Online), December 2020. https://doi.org/10.18653/v1/2020.coling-main.419

29. Yan, R.: I, poet: automatic poetry composition through recurrent neural networks with iterative polishing schema. In: Proceedings of the Twenty-Fifth International Joint Conference on Artificial Intelligence. IJCAI 2016, pp. 2238–2244. AAAI Press (2016)

30. Yi, X., Li, R., Sun, M.: Chinese poetry generation with a salient-clue mechanism. In: Proceedings of the 22nd Conference on Computational Natural Language Learning, pp. 241–250. Association for Computational Linguistics, Brussels, October 2018. https://doi.org/10.18653/v1/K18-1024

31. Zhang, R., et al.: Correcting Chinese spelling errors with phonetic pre-training. In: Findings of the Association for Computational Linguistics: ACL-IJCNLP 2021, pp. 2250–2261. Association for Computational Linguistics, Online, August 2021. https://doi.org/10.18653/v1/2021.findings-acl.198

32. Zhang, S., Huang, H., Liu, J., Li, H.: Spelling error correction with soft-masked BERT. In: Proceedings of the 58th Annual Meeting of the Association for Computational Linguistics, pp. 882–890. Association for Computational Linguistics, Online, July 2020. https://doi.org/10.18653/v1/2020.acl-main.82

33. Zhang, X., Lapata, M.: Chinese poetry generation with recurrent neural networks. In: Proceedings of the 2014 Conference on Empirical Methods in Natural Language Processing (EMNLP), pp. 670–680. Association for Computational Linguistics, Doha, October 2014. https://doi.org/10.3115/v1/D14-1074

34. Zhang, Z., Han, X., Liu, Z., Jiang, X., Sun, M., Liu, Q.: ERNIE: enhanced language representation with informative entities. In: Proceedings of the 57th Annual Meeting of the Association for Computational Linguistics, pp. 1441–1451. Association for Computational Linguistics, Florence, July 2019. https://doi.org/10.18653/v1/P19-1139

An Unsupervised Sentence Embedding Method by Maximizing the Mutual Information of Augmented Text Representations

Tianye Sheng[✉], Lisong Wang, Zongfeng He, Mingjie Sun, and Guohua Jiang

Nanjing University of Aeronautics and Astronautics, Nanjing, China
{tysheng,jianggh}@nuaa.edu.cn

Abstract. For natural language processing tasks with unlabeled or partially labeled datasets, it is vital to learn sentence representations in an unsupervised manner. However, unsupervised methods pale by comparison to supervised ones on many tasks. Recently, some unsupervised methods propose to learn sentence representations by maximizing the mutual information between text representations of different levels, such as global MI maximization: global and global representations, local MI maximization: local and global representations. Among these methods, local MI maximization encourages the global representations to capture useful information that shared across the local contexts. Despite this advantage, this method suffers from the inherent gap of semantic information contained in the global representations and the local representations. Consequently, the performance is inferior to models using global MI maximization as well as supervised ones. In this paper, we propose an unsupervised sentence embedding method by maximizing the mutual information of augmented text representations. Experimental results show that our model achieves an average of 73.36% Spearman's correlation on a series of semantic text similarity tasks, a 7 points improvement compared to the previous best model using local MI maximization. Furthermore, our model outperforms models using global MI maximization and close the gap to supervised methods to 1.5 points.

Keywords: Natural language processing · Unsupervised sentence embedding · Semantic text similarity

1 Introduction

Learning high-quality sentence representations is vital for many NLP tasks. Although BERT [7] has achieved good results on many NLP tasks, it cannot learn good sentence representations that are suitable for sentence pair regression tasks [22]. One of the reasons is that the calculation is too time-consuming. It takes 49995000 inference calculations to find the sentence pair with the highest similarity among 10000 sentences, which costs 65 h on a V100 GPU [19]. The

© The Author(s), under exclusive license to Springer Nature Switzerland AG 2022
E. Pimenidis et al. (Eds.): ICANN 2022, LNCS 13530, pp. 174–185, 2022.
https://doi.org/10.1007/978-3-031-15931-2_15

other reason is that, without fine-tuning, BERT produces an anisotropic word embedding space: the word embeddings are biased to word frequency, leading to corrupted semantic information [13]. For example, when directly using sentence embeddings generated by BERT to evaluate on the semantic text similarity (STS) tasks, one can find almost all sentence pairs obtain a score between 0.6 to 1.0, despite the fact that some sentence pairs are not semantically related [21].

Sentence-BERT (SBERT) [19] proposed to employ siamese network structures to map the input sentence pair into two fixed-length vectors, and then calculate their cosine similarity. This model can reduce the time consumption of tens of hours to 5 s, solving the problem of time-consuming. However, SBERT is trained on high-quality labeled datasets by supervised methods. As is well known, manual labeling of data is expensive. For many tasks that do not have labeled data or have only partially labeled data, the ability of SBERT is limited. Therefore, it is particularly significant to use unsupervised methods to learn good sentence representations on unlabeled datasets.

Based on BERT, Zhang et al. [22] proposed an unsupervised sentence embedding method: IS-BERT, alleviating the problem of native BERT word embeddings. This model utilizes the idea of mutual information (MI) maximization. By maximizing the MI of the global sentence embedding and its corresponding local word embeddings, semantically meaningful sentence representations can be learnt. Similarly, Yan et al. [21] proposed an unsupervised method based on a contrastive framework: ConSERT, which essentially utilizes the idea of MI maximization as well. But not like IS-BERT, it maximizes the MI between two views of global sentence embeddings obtained through different data augmentation strategies. In other words, IS-BERT uses the "local-global" architecture and ConSERT uses the "global-global" architecture.

As pointed out in [22], the "local-global" architecture can capture the unique information shared across the local contexts of sentences. Additionally, [9] indicated that compared with global MI maximization, local MI maximization makes the encoder avoid passing the specific and limited part of the global embeddings to the final sentence representations. However, the result is that the "global-global" architecture performs better than the "local-global" architecture on STS tasks.

In this paper, we analyze the "global-global" architecture and the "local-global" architecture from the angle of mutual information maximization. Then we propose an unsupervised sentence embedding method by maximizing mutual information of augmented text representations, still under the "local-global" architecture. The "augmented" means richer contextual information. It is achieved by the cross selection of text representations from two pipelines and the multi-head attention mechanism. Specifically, we construct two pipelines to generate word embeddings for each input sentence. In the fist pipeline, the input sentence first passes through a data augmentation module and then is encoded by BERT, while in the second pipeline, the sentence is directly encoded by BERT. After that, we employ the multi-head attention mechanism to enhance the extraction of semantic information over the local word representations, so that each word can obtain contextual information of all words within a sentence. Finally, we cross select the global representations in the second pipeline and the local representations in the first pipeline to form sample pairs to compute scores for MI estimation. Experimental results show that our proposal is effective. On a series of STS tasks, we achieve a 7% average relative improvement and further narrow the gap to supervised models. On most STS tasks, we also outperform the model using the "global-global" architecture. To sum up, we make the following contributions: 1) We propose to using augmented text representations to enhance the performance of unsupervised sentence embedding methods and close the gap to supervised methods. 2) We show the superiority of local MI maximization, compared with global MI maximization. 3) We make the interpretability and ablate some design choices for our proposal.

2   Related Work

2.1   Unsupervised Sentence Embedding

Early unsupervised sentence embedding methods are inferior to supervised methods. According to whether the input sentences are in order, unsupervised sentence embedding methods are divided into two categories. The first one has no order requirements for input sentences, and this method is more versatile. The paragraph vector model [11] can learn sentence representations and documents representations respectively. Sequential Denoising Auto-Encoder (SDAE) [12] stacks multiple DAE together to form a deep architecture for variable length sentences processing.

The other one requires ordered input sentences. Skip-thought [10] promotes the idea of skip-gram in word2vec [16]: using a sentence to predict its last or next sentence since it is related to its context. FastSent [8] improves Skip-thought. They replace the RNN with the BOW (bag-of-words) model, which greatly accelerates the training speed. Quick-thought [14] uses a classifier to learn sentence representations. Faster than Skip-thought and simpler than FastSent, Quick-thought performs better than the former two on multiple tasks.

2.2   Mutual Information and Representation Learning

People have used MI for representation learning for a long time. The infomax principle proposes to maximize the MI between input and output of neural network for feature learning. Auto Encoder uses the back propagation algorithm to make the output value of the neural network equal to the input value for high-dimensional complex data processing. This idea is very similar to maximizing the MI of the input and output.

However, since MI is very difficult to calculate, people later proposed MI estimator to estimate the lower bound of MI, so that the purpose of MI maximization is indirectly achieved. MINE [2] uses the Donsker-Varadhan representation based on KL divergence to give the lower bound definition of MI. [9] proposes that since the precise value of MI is not concerned, relying on non-KL divergences is possible. Hence Jensen-Shannon MI estimator [17] and infoNCE [18] are given.

3   Model

In this section, we first give a description of sentence representation learning using MI maximization between global sentences and local words, then we analyze the shortcomings existing in the "local-global" architecture, and finally give the improved model architecture and details.

3.1   Description

Given a set of sentences $S = \{s_1, s_2, s_3, \ldots, s_m\}$, we encode every sentence to get a sequence of word embeddings $F \in \mathbb{R}^{l \times d}$, where l is the number of words in the longest sentence in current batch and d is the dimension of every word embedding. Then we get the global sentence embedding G from $\mathbb{R}$ via pooling. Words in current sentence are denoted as the positive sample corresponding to current sentence, and words in other sentences in current batch are denoted as the corresponding negative sample. Then we compute the score of the positive pairs and the negative pairs for MI estimation. The end-goal learning objective is to maximize the lower bound of MI. This way, similar sentences in the semantic space become close to each other, and dissimilar sentences become far away from each other, eventually good sentence representations can be obtained.

3.2   Analysis

For the learning objective $L(G, F)$, where G is the global sentence representations and F is the local word representations, our end goal is to maximize the MI between G and F. As we know, the more similar the two variables, the greater the value of MI. Assuming that G' is the another view of the corresponding sentence representations obtained through some data augmentation skills, then G' is close to G in the semantic space for we only give a little perturbation to G. However, as a single word in G, F contains limited part of semantic information in G. Accordingly, the distance between F and G is greater than that between G' and G in the semantic space, i.e., $MI(G, G') > MI(G, F)$. Due to the inherent gap, the "global-global" architecture is in an advantageous position when narrowing the distance between the positive sample pairs compared with the "local-global" architecture.

Based on the consideration that the "local-global" architecture can avoid the final sentence representations being limited to certain noise information that is useless for downstream tasks [9], we decide to retain the "local-global" architecture and try to augment the contextual information contained in the text representations. So we need to increase the MI between the global representation and the corresponding local representation to narrow their distance.

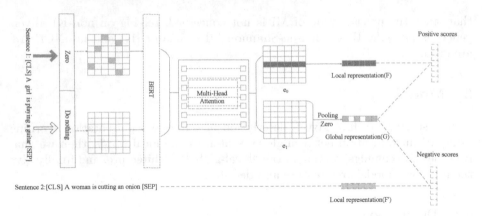

Fig. 1. Model architecture

3.3   Model Architecture

The model architecture is illustrated in Fig. 1. Different from previous local MI maximization methods that using a single pipeline, such as IS-BERT [22], we construct two pipelines for every sentence to go through. In the first pipeline, as shown in Fig. 1, Sentence 1 passes through the data augmentation module and then is encoded by BERT. Simultaneously, it is directly encoded by BERT in the second pipeline. Inspired by [21], here we choose the regularization method dropout, which is originally used to avoid overfitting, as our data augmentation strategy. Specifically, we randomly select a certain ratio of dimensions in the token embedding layer to make the value to zero. As shown in Fig. 1, the yellow blocks are dimensions that are set to zero.

Then we employ the multi-head attention mechanism over the word embeddings to extract contextual information from the whole sentence for each word. The calculation of the self-attention mechanism is given below.

Given a sentence $s = \{w_1, w_2, w_3, \ldots, w_n\}$, where n is the number of words in s, $w \in \mathbb{R}^d$. Multiply each w by matrices $Q^{d \times d}$, $K^{d \times d}$, $V^{d \times d}$ to get a set of vectors q, k, v. Taking the word w_j as an example, the calculation process of the result vector β_j is as follows:

$$q_j = Q \cdot w_j \qquad k_i = K \cdot w_i \qquad v_i = V \cdot w_i,$$

$$\alpha_j^i = softmax(\sum_{i=1}^{n} q_j \cdot k_i),$$

$$\beta_j = \sum_{i=1}^{n} \alpha_j^i \cdot v_i. \tag{1}$$

In actual practice, we divide the matrix $\mathbb{R}^{d \times d}$ into a tensor $\mathbb{R}^{d \times d \times (d/k)}$, where k is the number of heads, to complete the calculation of the multi-head attention mechanism.

After that, we get two sequences of word embeddings: the e_0 and the e_1 in Fig. 1. Now e_0 has his work done and the word embeddings in e_0 are exactly our positive samples corresponding to Sentence 1, denoted as the local representations F. As for e_1, we employ average pooling over it to get a temporary global representation, denoted as g. Afterwards, we operate dropout again to make some dimensions of g to zero and obtain the final global sentence representation, denoted as G. In this way, F and G form the positive sample pairs, while F', the local representations obtained from Sentence 2 in the first pipeline (as shown in Fig. 1, the dotted line means that Sentence 2 goes through the same operation as Sentence 1), form the negative sample pairs with G.

Finally, we compute scores of positive pairs and negative pairs for MI estimation. The end-goal learning objective is to maximize lower bound of MI between the global representation G and each local representation F. Here we use the Jensen-Shannon estimator the same as IS-BERT [22]. The Jensen-Shannon estimator is defined as

$$L_{JSD}(F_i, G) := E_p[-sp(-T(F_i, G))] - E_{p \times \tilde{p}}[-sp(T(F'_i, G))], \qquad (2)$$

where T is the function that measures the distance between F and G. Here we use the dot product. F_i is the words in current sentence(e.g. Sentence 1), forming a positive sample pair with G. F'_i are words in other sentences (e.g. Sentence 2) within current batch, forming a negative sample pair with G. sp is the softplus function, which is defined as $sp(z) = log(1 + e^z)$. The learning objective over the whole dataset S is defined as

$$\Theta = argmax \frac{1}{|S|} (\sum_{s \in S} \sum_{i=1}^{l} L_{JSD}(F_i, G)), \qquad (3)$$

where Θ is the optimum, $|S|$ is the number of sentences in the dataset, l is the length of the sentence. By maximizing L, G is encouraged be closer to F and far away from F', so that the final sentence representations are more characteristic and find the more appropriate place in the semantic space.

4   Experiment

In order to verify the effectiveness of our proposed approach, we conduct experiments on the semantic text similarity tasks. The model training is performed on the NLI dataset, and the evaluation is performed on a series of STS tasks.

We use two groups of baseline models for comparison. The first group includes a set of models trained with unlabeled data. Following IS-BERT, we select unigram-TFIDF, Paragraph Vector [11], SDAE [12], SkipThought [10], Fast-Sent [8], the Avg. GloVe embeddings (the average of Glove embeddings), the Avg. BERT embeddings (the average of representations of BERT's last hidden layer) and the BERT CLS-vector (the [CLS] embedding of BERT). Additionally, IS-BERT [22] and ConSERT [21], which represent the local MI maximization and the global MI maximization respectively, are added in. The second group includes a set of models trained with labeled data. We select InferSent [6], USE [5], and SBERT [19].

4.1   Dataset and Setups

Following IS-BERT, our model is trained on the combination of the Stanford Natural Language Inference dataset (SNLI) [3] and the Multi-Genre NLI (MultiNLI) dataset [20]. We exclude the gold labels and mix them with a total of about one million sentences. The model is evaluated on the STS tasks: STS2012-2016 [1], STS benchmark (STSb) [4] and SICK-Relatedness (SICK-R) [15]. These datasets are composed of pairs of sentences with a gold label indicating the score about their semantic relatedness. The gold label is set from 0 to 5, where the label 0 represents that the sentence pair has completely different meaning while the label 5 represents that the sentence pair has exactly the same meaning.

In experiments, we use the cosine similarity to calculate the similarity of the two sentence embeddings after encoding. The Spearman rank correlation between the cosine similarity and the normalized gold labels of the sentence pairs is given as the evaluation metric. The value of dropout for the word embedding matrix and the global representations is set to 0.1. The learning rate is set to 5e-6 and the batch size is 32.

4.2   Results

The results are shown in Table 1. We first compare our model with unsupervised baselines. In can be observed that our model achieves a 4.6% relative improvement on the STSb dataset compared to the previous best model using local MI maximization: IS-BERT, and performs better on the other six datasets as well. In general, on all seven datasets our model outperforms IS-BERT with a 7% relative performance gain on average. Moreover, on the STSb dataset, we have equal shares with ConSERT, which uses global MI maximization, and surpass it on the other six datasets. Besides, our model performs better than other unsupervised baselines. Among them, it is worth mentioning that the Avg. BERT embeddings and the BERT CLS-vector perform poorly on all tasks, even worse than the average of Glove embeddings, which reflects the problem of the anisotropic word embedding space generated by BERT.

Then we compare our model with supervised baselines. It can be observed that although IS-BERT surpasses InferSent on five tasks, it is still a bit inferior to USE and SBERT, especially to SBERT. This is because both the two models are trained on datasets with high-quality labels. Yet it can be seen that our model surpasses USE on five datasets: STS2012-2016, and trails by less than one point on STSb. Furthermore, we surpass SBERT on three datasets: STS2013, STS2015, STS2016, and bridge the gap on other datasets (1.5% fall behind on average). This indicates that our model is competitive even among supervised models. For many downstream tasks lacking annotated datasets, our model will be more valuable.

Table 1. Spearman rank correlation (multiply by 100) between the cosine similarity of sentence representations and the gold labels for seven STS tasks. Results are extracted from [8,19,21,22].

Model	STS12	STS13	STS14	STS15	STS16	STSb	SICK-R	Avg.
Unsupervised Methods								
Unigram-TFIDF	-	-	58.00	-	-	-	52.00	-
SDAE	-	-	12.00	-	-	-	46.00	-
ParagraphVec DBOW	-	-	43.00	-	-	-	42.00	-
ParagraphVec DM	-	-	44.00	-	-	-	44.00	-
SkipThought	-	-	27.00	-	-	-	57.00	-
FastSent	-	-	63.00	-	-	-	61.00	-
Avg.GloVe embeddings	55.14	70.66	59.73	68.25	63.66	58.02	53.76	61.32
Avg.BERT embeddings	38.78	57.98	57.98	63.15	61.06	46.35	58.40	54.81
BERT CLS-vector	20.16	30.01	20.09	36.88	38.08	16.50	42.63	29.19
ConSERT	64.64	78.49	69.07	79.72	75.95	73.97	67.31	72.74
IS-BERT	56.77	69.24	61.21	75.23	70.16	69.21	64.25	66.58
Ours	**65.96**	**79.53**	**70.85**	**79.88**	**76.07**	**73.83**	**67.38**	**73.36**
Supervised Methods								
InferSent - GloVe	52.86	66.75	62.15	72.77	66.87	68.03	65.65	65.01
USE	64.49	67.80	64.61	76.83	73.18	74.92	76.69	71.22
SBERT-NLI	70.97	76.53	73.19	79.09	74.30	77.03	72.91	74.89

5   Qualitative Analysis

5.1   Analysis of Multi-head Attention

We replace the attention layer with the CNN layer to make further understanding of the role the attention mechanism plays in our model. The Spearman rank correlation on the STSb dataset in two scenarios are given. The results are shown in Table 2.

Table 2. Spearman rank correlation for STS tasks in two different scenarios.

Layer	STS12	STS13	STS14	STS15	STS16	STSb	SICK-R
CNN	63.29	76.62	67.97	78.65	73.39	72.15	67.06
Attention	65.96	79.53	70.85	79.88	76.07	73.83	67.38

It can be observed that on all seven datasets, the performance of Attention is better than CNN. Intuitively, we make the following analysis. For a sequence of word embeddings $h_i \in \{\mathbb{R}^d\}_{i=1}^l$, supposing that applying several CNNs with different window sizes (denoted as k, such as 1, 3, 5) to the word embeddings for feature extracting. The final representation of every word $c_i = f(w \cdot h_{i:i+k-1} + b)$, where $h_{i:i+k-1}$ is the concatenation of the word embeddings within a window. Obviously, contextual information that can be captured by c_i is limited by the size of the convolution kernel k. If the sentence length is longer, contextual information beyond the size of the convolution kernel cannot be captured. But the attention mechanism gets rid of the distance limitation. In the attention mechanism, $c_i = Attention(h_1, h_2, h_3, \ldots, h_l)$, the local representation can obtain the information of all words in the current sentence. This is exactly the augmentation of text representations on one hand, which means richer information contained.

5.2   Analysis of Dropout

To make further understanding of what the role the operation of dropout plays, we collect the dot product of the positive sample pairs in different pipelines to visualize the data. As shown in Fig. 2.

Specifically, the green points are the dot product of global representations and the corresponding local representations in a single pipeline (without dropout) like IS-BERT. The blue points are the dot product of local presentations in the first pipeline (with dropout) and the global representations in the second pipeline (with second dropout). Every point is the average dot product of all positive sample pairs within a batch. It can be seen from Fig. 2 that compared using a single pipeline, cross selecting different representations from two pipelines makes bigger values. According to formula 2, increasing dot product between local representations and global representations makes contribution to a bigger $L_{JSD}(F_i, G)$. Hence, by performing dropout, we successfully bring the global representations and the corresponding local representations closer. This will help the achievement of high-quality text representations, which is exactly the augmentation on the other hand.

6   Ablation Study

6.1   Dropout for Global Embeddings

Here we discuss the effect of applying the second dropout for the global embeddings. Our idea is that the MI between local representations and global representations can be increased by appropriate perturbation. Since the operation object of the dot product is the local representation and the global representation, in which the former is obtained in the first pipeline(with dropout) while the latter is obtained in the second pipeline (without dropout), we try zeroing the global representation again to see if the distance to local representations can be further narrowed. We make the comparative experiment and the results are shown in Table 3.

It can be found that although the effect on STSb is not obvious, there are obvious effect on the five datasets of STS2012-2016. This indicates that we can give some extra perturbation to the global representation to further narrow the distance between the local representation and the global representation.

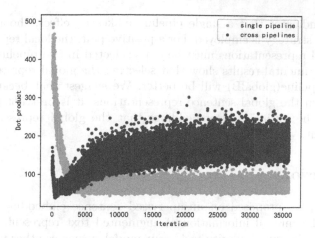

Fig. 2. The change of dot product.

Table 3. Spearman rank correlation for STS tasks in two different scenarios.

Setting	STS12	STS13	STS14	STS15	STS16	STSb	SICK-R
Without dropout	63.91	77.23	67.69	77.11	73.24	73.59	65.99
With dropout	65.96	79.53	70.85	79.88	76.07	73.83	67.38

6.2   Combination Experiments

We also try combining different global representations and local representations in two pipelines to conduct some combination experiments. Specifically, the local representation in the first pipeline is denoted as localA(with dropout, e_0 in Fig. 1) and the global representation via pooling over localA is denoted as globalA. Samely, we get the localB(without dropout, e_1 in Fig. 1) in the second pipeline and the corresponding globalB. Eventually, we have the following three groups: localA and globalA, localA and globalB, localB and globalA. For brevity, experimental results on the STSb dataset are given. As shown in Table 4.

Table 4. Spearman rank correlation for STSb in three different scenarios.

Combinations	STSb
localA and globalA	69.74
localA and globalB	73.83
localB and globalA	72.46

It can be found that the first group makes the relative worst performance, similar to IS-BERT's 69.21. The third group is slightly inferior to the second group. This indicates that a single pipeline makes no effect, though the data augmentation strategy is employed. For a positive pair, the local representations and the global representations must be cross selected in two pipelines. In addition, the experimental results show that selecting the global representations in the second pipeline(globalB) will be better. We suggest that because our end goal is to learn the global sentence representations, it is best not to give perturbation to the initial word embeddings that the global representations are generated from.

7   Conclusion

In this paper, we proposed an unsupervised sentence embedding method by maximizing the mutual information of augmented text representations. On a series of semantic text similarity tasks, our model surpasses other unsupervised methods, and is comparable to supervised methods. We also gave intuitive and visual explanations of our proposed method and ablated some design choices to consummate our work. In the next work, we hope to explore the application of our unsupervised sentence embedding method on more downstream tasks.

References

1. Agirre, E., Cer, D., Diab, M., Gonzalez-Agirre, A.: Semeval-2012 task 6: a pilot on semantic textual similarity. In: * SEM 2012: The First Joint Conference on Lexical and Computational Semantics-Volume 1: Proceedings of the main conference and the shared task, and Volume 2: Proceedings of the Sixth International Workshop on Semantic Evaluation (SemEval 2012), pp. 385–393 (2012)
2. Belghazi, M.I., et al.: Mutual information neural estimation. In: International Conference on Machine Learning, pp. 531–540. PMLR (2018)
3. Bowman, S.R., Angeli, G., Potts, C., Manning, C.D.: A large annotated corpus for learning natural language inference. arXiv preprint arXiv:1508.05326 (2015)
4. Cer, D., Diab, M., Agirre, E., Lopez-Gazpio, I., Specia, L.: Semeval-2017 task 1: semantic textual similarity-multilingual and cross-lingual focused evaluation. arXiv preprint arXiv:1708.00055 (2017)
5. Cer, D., et al.: Universal sentence encoder for English. In: Proceedings of the 2018 Conference on Empirical Methods in Natural Language Processing: System Demonstrations, pp. 169–174 (2018)
6. Conneau, A., Kiela, D., Schwenk, H., Barrault, L., Bordes, A.: Superv.sied learning of universal sentence representations from natural language inference data. In: Proceedings of the 2017 Conference on Empirical Methods in Natural Language Processing, pp. 670–680 (2017)
7. Devlin, J., Chang, M.W., Lee, K., Toutanova, K.: Bert: pre-training of deep bidirectional transformers for language understanding. In: NAACL-HLT (1) (2019)
8. Hill, F., Cho, K., Korhonen, A.: Learning distributed representations of sentences from unlabelled data. In: HLT-NAACL (2016)
9. Hjelm, R.D., et al.: Learning deep representations by mutual information estimation and maximization. In: International Conference on Learning Representations (2018)

10. Kiros, R., Zhu, Y., Salakhutdinov, R.R., Zemel, R., Urtasun, R., Torralba, A., Fidler, S.: Skip-thought vectors. In: Advances in Neural Information Processing Systems, pp. 3294–3302 (2015)
11. Le, Q., Mikolov, T.: Distributed representations of sentences and documents. In: International Conference on Machine Learning, pp. 1188–1196. PMLR (2014)
12. Vincent, P., Larochelle, H., Lajoie, I., Bengio, Y., Manzagol, P.-A., Bottou, L.: Stacked denoising autoencoders: learning useful representations in a deep network with a local denoising criterion. J. Mach. Learn. Res. **11**(12) (2010)
13. Li, B., Zhou, H., He, J., Wang, M., Yang, Y., Li, L.: On the sentence embeddings from pre-trained language models. arXiv preprint arXiv:2011.05864 (2020)
14. Logeswaran, L., Lee, H.: An efficient framework for learning sentence representations. In: International Conference on Learning Representations (2018)
15. Marelli, M., Menini, S., Baroni, M., Bentivogli, L., Bernardi, R., Zamparelli, R., et al.: A sick cure for the evaluation of compositional distributional semantic models. In: Lrec, pp. 216–223. Reykjavik (2014)
16. Mikolov, T., Chen, K., Corrado, G., Dean, J.: Efficient estimation of word representations in vector space. arXiv preprint arXiv:1301.3781 (2013)
17. Nowozin, S., Cseke, B., Tomioka, R.: f-gan: training generative neural samplers using variational divergence minimization. In: Proceedings of the 30th International Conference on Neural Information Processing Systems, pp. 271–279 (2016)
18. Oord, A.v.d., Li, Y., Vinyals, O.: Representation learning with contrastive predictive coding. arXiv preprint arXiv:1807.03748 (2018)
19. Reimers, N., Gurevych, I.: Sentence-bert: sentence embeddings using siamese bert-networks. In: Proceedings of the 2019 Conference on Empirical Methods in Natural Language Processing and the 9th International Joint Conference on Natural Language Processing (EMNLP-IJCNLP), pp. 3982–3992 (2019)
20. Williams, A., Nangia, N., Bowman, S.R.: A broad-coverage challenge corpus for sentence understanding through inference. In: 2018 Conference of the North American Chapter of the Association for Computational Lingusitics: Human Language Technologies, NAACL HLT 2018, pp. 1112–1122. Association for Computational Lingu.sitics (ACL) (2018)
21. Yan, Y., Li, R., Wang, S., Zhang, F., Wu, W., Xu, W.: Consert: a contrastive framework for self-supervised sentence representation transfer. arXiv preprint arXiv:2105.11741 (2021)
22. Zhang, Y., He, R., Liu, Z., Lim, K.H., Bing, L.: An unsupervisied sentence embedding method by mutual information maximization. In: Proceedings of the 2020 Conference on Empirical Methods in Natural Language Processing (EMNLP), pp. 1601–1610 (2020)

Analysis of COVID-19 5G Conspiracy Theory Tweets Using SentenceBERT Embedding

Or Elroy and Abraham Yosipof[✉] [iD]

Faculty of Information Systems and Computer Science, College of Law and Business,
Ramat-Gan, Israel
aviyo@clb.ac.il

Abstract. Twitter is a popular major social media platform with a central role in the distribution of information, and as such a fertile land for the growth of conspiracy theories in different subjects, with COVID-19 conspiracies among them. In this research, we collected a dataset of 331,448 tweets related to the COVID-19 5G conspiracy theory. We present a workflow to collect, classify, and analyze conspiracy related tweets as supporting or opposing the conspiracy theory. We hand labeled 4,291 tweets and trained a classifier using a novel approach containing two sets of features: a set of sentence embeddings produced by Covid-Twitter-BERT and Sentence-BERT, and a set of external features. We used five different classifiers and ensemble learning to combine them. We classified the dataset and analyzed the classified dataset to conclude that opponents of the conspiracy dominate the conversation on Twitter.

Keywords: Conspiracy Theory · 5G · COVID-19 · Classification · CT-BERT · Sentence BERT

1 Introduction

Social media platforms, including Twitter, have a key role in the distribution of information regarding the COVID-19 pandemic, including communicating reliable news, updates and medical instructions. In addition, social media has been a fertile ground for the growth and distribution of misinformation and conspiracy theories regarding the COVID-19 pandemic. The director-general of the World Health Organization named that an infodemic: "A global epidemic of misinformation—spreading rapidly through social media platforms and other outlets—poses a serious problem for public health" [1]. People's belief in conspiracy theories is motivated by the desire for information and the need to rationalize events. Conspiracy theories offer people with explanations and a sense of control over the situation [2]. The Pew research center found that 36% of American adults think that conspiracy theories are probably true [3]. One of the main COVID-19 conspiracy theories is the 5G conspiracy.

The 5G technology is the fifth-generation technology standard for broadband cellular networks, aiming to meet various quality-of-service (QoS) requirements, with higher

© The Author(s), under exclusive license to Springer Nature Switzerland AG 2022
E. Pimenidis et al. (Eds.): ICANN 2022, LNCS 13530, pp. 186–196, 2022.
https://doi.org/10.1007/978-3-031-15931-2_16

bandwidth. 5G achieves this by using a large number of antennas, radios, multi-layer networks and spectrum handling [4, 5].

The COVID-19 5G conspiracy theory tries to create a fictitious connection between the 5G technology and the creation or spreading of COVID-19, and other harmful effects on human health, such as that 5G towers are weakening the immune system [6]. In response, people have been burning down expensive infrastructure, such as communication towers, out of fear for their health [6, 7].

In this paper, we present a workflow to support an ongoing research project in emergency management and disaster science, by investigating the discussion on COVID-19 conspiracy theories in social media. The workflow was developed to collect, classify and analyze conspiracy related tweets as supporting or opposing a conspiracy. In this study, we concentrate on the COVID-19 5G conspiracy theory. We collected tweets related to the 5G conspiracy theory, and metadata of the users who posted the tweets. We combined word embeddings of Covid-Twitter-BERT, a Bidirectional Encoder Representations from Transformers (BERT) model that was pre-trained and fine-tuned on COVID-19 tweets [8], with Sentence-BERT (SBERT), a transformer to sentence embedding [9]. We enhanced the sentence embeddings with features that are external to the text, applied different classification models to the data, and analyzed the results.

2 Related Work

Following recent development in the field of Natural Language Processing (NLP), several research papers used word embedding methods to investigate tweets related to COVID-19 misinformation and conspiracy theories [2, 10]. There are multiple methods available to embed text, from basic Word2Vec and TF-IDF [11], to more sophisticated models such as Global Vector for Word Representation (GloVe) and BERT [12].

Batzdorfer et al. [2] investigated the motifs and temporal dynamics of COVID-19 conspiracy theory tweets by comparing between tweets from a group of users who tweeted about the conspiracy and general tweets about COVID-19 from a group of users who did not tweet about the conspiracy. In that work, the authors used GloVe word embeddings to identify semantically similar expressions about conspiracy theories.

A key task in analyzing conspiracy or misinformation tweets is to label and classify the tweets. A set of embeddings and labels are needed for the training of a classifier. BERT provides superior results for different NLP tasks, including word embedding [13, 14]. Micallef et al. [10] used BERT embeddings to investigate and counter misinformation in tweets related to COVID-19 over a period of five months. In that work, the authors trained a classifier and classified a dataset of 150K COVID-19 related tweets using BERT embeddings, and analyzed the results.

Different metadata and characteristics of tweets and their authors were proven to be useful for classification tasks and were previously used to enhance classification models. Beskow and Carley [15] used the number of users that follow the author and the number of users the author follows as an indication of whether the author is a robot or not. O'Donovan et al. [16] and Gupta et al. [17] found that metadata of tweets, such as URLs, mentions, retweets and tweet length may serve as indicators for credibility.

3 Problem Definition and Challenges

Following the literature review, and to the best of our knowledge, this study is the first to attempt classifying tweets related to the COVID-19 5G conspiracy theory into supporters and opponents of the conspiracy theory and analyzing the results.

A study of conspiracy theory tweets presents several challenges, such as the collection of enough relevant data over a long time period for the classifiers, but at the same time not collecting too much irrelevant data. Another challenge is to embed the semantic meaning of the tweets in vectors of features, labeling, and classifying the data. Finally, an analysis of the tweets is needed in order to gain insights about how the conspiracy evolves.

Our objective is to develop a workflow to collect and classify tweets as supporting, opposing, or neutral of a conspiracy theory, in order to analyze the discussion on COVID-19 conspiracy theories on Twitter. We therefore suggest the following workflow as described in Fig. 1:

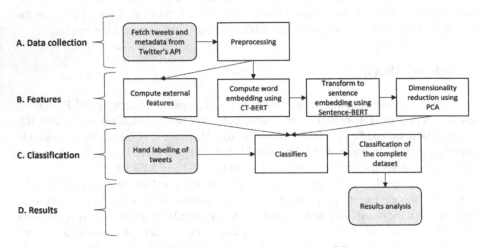

Fig. 1. COVID-19 conspiracy analysis workflow.

(A) Data collection: collect tweets related to the COVID-19 5G conspiracy theory over a period of two years; (B) Features: compute a set of word embedding features using CT-BERT, transform to sentence embeddings using SBERT, and compute a set of external features; (C) Classification: develop a classifier based on the sentence embeddings and external features to classify tweets as supporting or opposing of the conspiracy; and (D) Results analysis of the classified dataset.

4 Dataset

The data was collected using Twitter API's v2 full search endpoint which is limited to Academic Research. According to the API documentation, a full search query retrieves tweets matching the specified criteria throughout Twitter's history from March 2006 when the first tweet was published on the platform.

The search criteria included all tweets written in English that contain one or more COVID-19 related keywords, and 5G, and excluded retweets. The full search query we used is: {covid OR coronavirus OR corona} AND {5G}. The criteria aim to provide all tweets within the scope of the conspiracy theory that are either supporting, opposing, or neutral/irrelevant of the conspiracy theory. The keywords maintain that we only collect tweets that are in some way related to the topic.

We collected 331,448 tweets related to the discussion on the COVID-19 5G conspiracy theory, and metadata of the users that posted the tweets, over a period of two years from January 1, 2020, shortly after the pandemic emerged, to December 31, 2021. The dataset was saved in a relational database.

We hand labeled 4,291 tweets as belonging to one of three categories: 2,147 supporters, 676 opponents, and 1,468 neutral/irrelevant of the conspiracy theory. Table 1 displays example tweets and their manual classification.

Table 1. Examples of tweets and their manual classification.

Tweet	Classification
"5G is killing people. Covid was a cover. Now the jab is a cover."	Supporter
"You can get COVID through 5G."	Supporter
"#lie: 5G mobile networks DO NOT spread COVID-19. #coronavirus"	Opponent
"I can't believe there's people out there that actually think 5G causes covid"	Opponent
"Check out: Ericsson Revival Rides 5G, R&D "One critical factor, COVID, has been present in almost all discussions during the year," CEO Börje Ekholm said."	Neutral/ Irrelevant
"5G, AI, cybersecurity and renewable energy set for investment boost under EU coronavirus recovery plan"	Neutral/ Irrelevant

5 Features

In this study, we computed two sets of features for each tweet. First, the sentence embedding using CT-BERT and SBERT. Second, external features that we computed or extracted from the tweets, authors, or their metadata.

5.1 Embedding

BERT is a Bidirectional Encoder Representations from Transformers [18], that provides state of the art performance when pre-trained and fine-tuned on data that is relevant to specific NLP tasks [19]. Covid-Twitter-BERT (CT-BERT) is a model based on BERT Large, that was pre-trained and fine-tuned on a corpus of 160M tweets about the coronavirus [8]. The data on which CT-BERT was pre-trained and fine-tuned fits the scope of this work. BERT Large, and thus CT-BERT, yields 1,024 features for each word in the tweet.

Sentence-BERT (SBERT) is a modification of the pre-trained BERT network that uses siamese and triplet network structures on top of the BERT model and fine-tuned based on high quality sentence interface data to learn more sentence level information [9]. SBERT transforms the CT-BERT word embedding into a single sentence embedding with 1,024 features.

In this work, we computed the embedding of each tweet in the dataset using the CT-BERT model for the word embedding and used SBERT to transform it into sentence embedding. To avoid overfitting of the classification models, we used Principal Component Analysis (PCA) to reduce the number of features. We selected the new principal components with eigenvalues greater than 0.1, which explain 82% of the variance of the 1,024 original features. The final vector of each sentence embedding consists of 211 features.

5.2 External Features

In addition to the sentence embedding, we computed and extracted six additional features from the metadata of tweets and their authors. Table 2 presents descriptive statistics of the external features.

The six features include the sentiment score of each tweet as computed by VADER (Table 2, VADER), a parsimonious rule-based model for general sentiment analysis [20]. The sentiment score of each tweet is between -1 and 1, for negative and positive sentiment, respectively. We also used features based on the metadata of each tweet and author. These include the total number of tweets the author has posted (Table 2, Tweets), the average VADER of all of the conspiracy tweets we collected by the user (Table 2, Author avg. VADER), the presence of a URL in the tweet (Table 2, URL), the author's number of followers (Table 2, Followers), and how many users they are following (Table 2, Following). The external features were standardized using Z-score to prevent bias of the models toward high numbers.

Table 2. Descriptive statistics of the external features.

Feature	Min	Max	Mean	Std
Tweets	1	7,613,045	47,132.8	139,928.9
Author avg. VADER	−1	1	−0.12	0.39
Followers	0	55,462,408	28,056.6	531,498.2
Following	0	594,127	1,865.2	9,439.1
VADER	−1	1	−0.12	0.46
	Min	Max	#0	#1
URL	0	1	168,435	163,013

6 Classification

We used five classification methods to classify each tweet as supporting, opposing, or neutral/irrelevant of the conspiracy theory.

The five methods are XGBoost with a learning rate of 0.3, Random Forest (RF) with 1,000 trees, Support Vector Machine (SVM) with a linear kernel function, K-Nearest Neighbors (KNN) with nine nearest neighbors, and Naïve Bayes. We further used voting ensemble learning to combine the results of all five methods.

In order to evaluate the performance of each model over the different sets of features, each classifier was trained on the embedding-based features (211 features), on the external features (6 features), and on the embedding and the external features together (217 features).

We evaluated the models using stratified 10-folds cross validation on the hand labeled tweets. The performance of each model was evaluated using the weighted F1, precision, and recall scores.

7 Results

The hand labeled training set was assigned to each of the classifiers as detailed in the classification section. Table 3 presents the classification performance for each model with the corresponding standard deviation when using the embedding features, the external features, and both sets of features together.

Table 3 shows that the Voting Ensemble model provided the best results using the embedding features and the external features together, with weighted F1, precision and recall scores of 0.904, 0.907, and 0.903, respectively. The Voting Ensemble also performed well when only the embedding features were used, but with lower results compared to the combination of the embedding features and the external features. The models that were trained on the external features alone, provided poorer results compared to embedding features alone and both sets of features together.

Voting Ensemble with both sets of features is therefore the best method for the classification of the complete dataset. Following these results, we applied the Voting Ensemble model with both sets of features to classify the unlabeled dataset.

Table 3. Classification performance metrics.

Model	F1	Precision	Recall
Embedding + External Features			
XGBoost	0.895 ± 0.02	0.896 ± 0.02	0.894 ± 0.02
Random Forest	0.891 ± 0.02	0.893 ± 0.02	0.891 ± 0.02
KNN	0.878 ± 0.02	0.889 ± 0.01	0.876 ± 0.02
SVM	0.877 ± 0.02	0.877 ± 0.02	0.877 ± 0.02
Naive Bayes	0.742 ± 0.02	0.791 ± 0.02	0.736 ± 0.02
Voting Ensemble	**0.904** ± 0.02	**0.907** ± 0.02	**0.903** ± 0.02
Embedding Features			
XGBoost	0.890 ± 0.02	0.892 ± 0.02	0.890 ± 0.02
Random Forest	0.888 ± 0.02	0.890 ± 0.02	0.889 ± 0.02
KNN	0.879 ± 0.02	0.890 ± 0.02	0.877 ± 0.02
SVM	0.881 ± 0.02	0.882 ± 0.02	0.881 ± 0.02
Naive Bayes	0.737 ± 0.02	0.787 ± 0.01	0.732 ± 0.02
Voting Ensemble	**0.902** ± 0.02	**0.904** ± 0.02	**0.901** ± 0.02
External Features			
XGBoost	**0.597** ± 0.02	**0.595** ± 0.02	**0.614** ± 0.02
Random Forest	0.594 ± 0.02	0.591 ± 0.02	0.608 ± 0.02
KNN	0.531 ± 0.03	0.527 ± 0.03	0.557 ± 0.03
SVM	0.515 ± 0.03	0.534 ± 0.03	0.565 ± 0.02
Naive Bayes	0.516 ± 0.02	0.506 ± 0.04	0.561 ± 0.02
Voting Ensemble	0.564 ± 0.02	0.585 ± 0.03	0.599 ± 0.02

Table 4 presents the results of the classification of the unlabeled dataset. The results show that 64,080 of the tweets support the conspiracy theory, 108,175 oppose the conspiracy theory, and 159,193 are neutral or irrelevant. Noticeably, there are 69% more tweets opposing the conspiracy theory than there are tweets supporting it. Examining the number of tweets per user in each category reveals that for each user supporting the conspiracy theory, there are 2.53 users opposing it. On the other hand, supporters of the conspiracy theory posted significantly more tweets per user, with an average of 1.82 tweets while opponents posted only 1.22 tweets on average.

Table 4. The number of tweets and users in each category.

Category	# Tweets	# Users	Tweets/User
Supporters	64,080	35,169	1.822
Opponents	108,175	89,030	1.215
Neutral/Irrelevant	159,193	100,298	1.587

Following the classification of the complete dataset, we analyzed the textual properties and frequency over time of the supporters and opponents of the conspiracy. We begin with examining the distribution of the classification categories by the sentiment of their tweets. Figure 2 presents a histogram with the density of tweets per classification category by their sentiment scores. The results show that the majority of the tweets in both categories have had a neutral sentiment score between 0 and 0.1. It can further be noticed that the frequency is denser with negative sentiments for both opponents and supporters of the conspiracy.

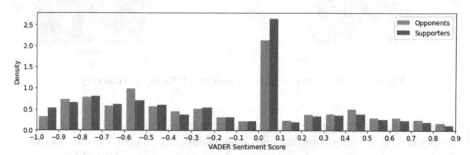

Fig. 2. Density histogram of tweets' sentiment scores per classification category.

Figure 3 presents the monthly frequency of tweets per classification category. The conspiracy theory is noticeably declining over time in both categories. The monthly frequency of tweets per category emphasizes that when the conspiracy theory emerged around February 2020, there were substantially more tweets from supporters of the conspiracy theory. However, the balance changed in April 2020 when opponents have possibly started to confront the conspiracy theory. Since April 2020, there have been more tweets from opponents than supporters, which may indicate users have been educated.

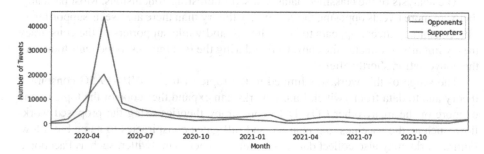

Fig. 3. The monthly frequency of tweets per category.

The presence of a URL in a tweet, which is also one of the external features used in the classification process, shows how supporters and opponents use online resources to reinforce their opinions.

Figure 4 shows the number of tweets with and without a URL in each category. The analysis shows that only 28% of the tweets posted by opponents of the conspiracy theory linked a URL.

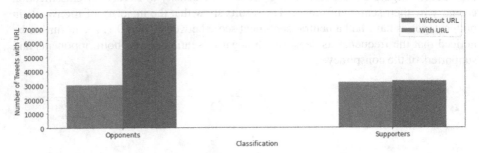

Fig. 4. Number of tweets with and without a URL in each category.

This finding that opponents of the conspiracy theory include less evidence to refute the conspiracy, is not surprising and lines with Micallef et al. [10]. On the other hand, 49% of the tweets supporting the conspiracy theory did include a URL, likely to serve as evidence or to support the content of the tweet.

8 Conclusion

In this study, we focused on the COVID-19 5G conspiracy theory on Twitter. Our work presents a workflow to collect, classify, and analyze tweets related to COVID-19 conspiracy theories. The classification process uses two sets of features: sentence embeddings using CT-BERT and SBERT, and external features, and classifies each tweet as supporting the conspiracy, opposing the conspiracy, or neutral/irrelevant.

The analysis of the classified dataset raised interesting conclusions. Most basically, there are more tweets opposing the conspiracy theory than there are tweets supporting it. The conspiracy theory appears to be declining, and while supporters of the conspiracy theory initially dominated the conversation during the first months, opponents took over the conversation shortly after.

The scope of this work was limited to the topic of the COVID-19 5G conspiracy theory and to data from Twitter. Future works can expand the scope of the topic to one or more of the many other COVID-19 conspiracy theories using the proposed workflow, such as the vaccines, big pharma, and bill gates conspiracies to name but a few. Future works may also collect data from sources other than Twitter, such as Facebook, Instagram, and TikTok.

Acknowledgements. This research has received funding from the European Union's Horizon 2020 research and innovation program under grant agreement No. 101021746, CORE (science and human factor for resilient society).

References

1. Zarocostas, J.: How to fight an infodemic. The lancet **395**, 676 (2020)
2. Batzdorfer, V., Steinmetz, H., Biella, M., Alizadeh, M.: Conspiracy theories on Twitter: emerging motifs and temporal dynamics during the COVID-19 pandemic. Int. J. Data Sci. Anal. **13**, 1–9 (2021). https://doi.org/10.1007/s41060-021-00298-6
3. Basu, T.: How to Talk to Conspiracy Theorists—And Still be Kind. MIT Technology Review (2020)
4. Gupta, A., Jha, R.K.: A survey of 5G network: architecture and emerging technologies. IEEE access **3**, 1206–1232 (2015)
5. Osseiran, A., et al.: Scenarios for 5G mobile and wireless communications: the vision of the METIS project. IEEE Commun. Mag. **52**, 26–35 (2014)
6. Elmousalami, H.H., Darwish, A., Hassanien, A.E.: The truth about 5G and COVID-19: basics, analysis, and opportunities. Digital Transformation and Emerging Technologies for Fighting COVID-19 Pandemic: Innovative Approaches, pp. 249–259 (2021)
7. Ahmed, W., Vidal-Aaball, J., Downing, J., Seguí, F.L.: COVID-19 and the 5G conspiracy theory: social network analysis of Twitter data. J. Med. Internet Res. **22**, e19458 (2020)
8. Müller, M., Salathé, M., Kummervold, P.E.: Covid-Twitter-BERT: a natural language processing model to analyse covid-19 content on Twitter. arXiv preprint arXiv:2005.07503 (2020)
9. Reimers, N., Gurevych, I.: Sentence-bert: sentence embeddings using siamese bert-networks. arXiv preprint arXiv:1908.10084 (2019)
10. Micallef, N., He, B., Kumar, S., Ahamad, M., Memon, N.: The role of the crowd in countering misinformation: a case study of the COVID-19 infodemic. In: 2020 IEEE International Conference on Big Data (Big Data), pp. 748–757. IEEE (2020)
11. Jalilifard, A., Caridá, V.F., Mansano, A.F., Cristo, R.S., da Fonseca, F.P.C.: Semantic sensitive TF-IDF to determine word relevance in documents. In: Thampi, S.M., Gelenbe, E., Atiquzzaman, M., Chaudhary, V., Li, KC. (eds.) Advances in Computing and Network Communications, pp. 327–337. Springer, Singapore (2021). https://doi.org/10.1007/978-981-33-6987-0_27
12. Kalyan, K.S., Sangeetha, S.: SECNLP: A survey of embeddings in clinical natural language processing. J. Biomed. Inform. **101**, 103323 (2020)
13. Piskorski, J., Haneczok, J., Jacquet, G.: New benchmark corpus and models for fine-grained event classification: to BERT or not to BERT? In: Proceedings of the 28th International Conference on Computational Linguistics, pp. 6663–6678 (2020)
14. González-Carvajal, S., Garrido-Merchán, E.C.: Comparing BERT against traditional machine learning text classification. arXiv preprint arXiv:2005.13012 (2020)
15. Beskow, D.M., Carley, K.M.: Bot-hunter: a tiered approach to detecting & characterizing automated activity on Twitter. In: Conference paper. SBP-BRiMS: International Conference on Social Computing, Behavioral-Cultural Modeling and Prediction and Behavior Representation in Modeling and Simulation, p. 3 (2018)
16. ODonovan, J., Kang, B., Meyer, G., Höllerer, T., Adalii, S.: Credibility in context: an analysis of feature distributions in Twitter. In: 2012 International Conference on Privacy, Security, Risk and Trust and 2012 International Confernece on Social Computing, pp. 293–301. IEEE (2012)
17. Gupta, A., Kumaraguru, P., Castillo, C., Meier, P.: Tweetcred: Real-time credibility assessment of content on Twitter. In: Aiello, L.M., McFarland, D. (eds.) International Conference on Social Informatics, pp. 228–243. Springer, Cham (2014). https://doi.org/10.1007/978-3-319-13734-6_16

18. Devlin, J., Chang, M.-W., Lee, K., Toutanova, K.: Bert: Pre-training of deep bidirectional transformers for language understanding. arXiv preprint arXiv:1810.04805 (2018)
19. Kovaleva, O., Romanov, A., Rogers, A., Rumshisky, A.: Revealing the dark secrets of BERT. arXiv preprint arXiv:1908.08593 (2019)
20. Hutto, C., Gilbert, E.: VADER: A parsimonious rule-based model for sentiment analysis of social media text. In: Proceedings of the International AAAI Conference on Web and Social Media, pp. 216–225 (2014)

Chinese Named Entity Recognition Using the Improved Transformer Encoder and the Lexicon Adapter

Mingjie Sun, Lisong Wang, Tianye Sheng, Zongfeng He, and Yuhua Huang[✉]

School of Computer Science and Technology,
Nanjing University of Aeronautics and Astronautics, Nanjing, China
{smj_2020,wangls,hezongfeng}@nuaa.edu.cn, hyuhua2k@163.com

Abstract. As a basic work of natural language processing (NLP), named entity recognition (NER) has attracted wide attention. Many methods of fusing the potential word representations in a Chinese sentence into the corresponding Chinese character representations have been applied to the Long-Short Term Memory (LSTM) model with good results in the Chinese NER task. However, the structure of LSTM cannot take full advantage of the parallelism of GPUs. Hence, we design a character-word attention adapter in the embedding layer to accelerate information fusion. Recently, the Transformer encoder has been popular in NLP for its parallel computing performance and the advantage of modeling the long-distance context. Nevertheless, the native Transformer encoder performs poorly on the NER task. We have deeply analyzed some of the shortcomings of the Transformer encoder. On these bases, we have further refined the position embedding and the self-attention calculation method in the Transformer encoder. Finally, we propose a new architecture of Chinese NER using the improved Transformer encoder and the lexicon adapter. On the four datasets of the Chinese NER task, our model achieves better performance than other models.

Keywords: Chinese NER · Character-word attention adapter · Position embedding · Transformer

1 Introduction

Named entity recognition (NER) is a basic task of natural language processing. It plays an important role in relation extraction [9], information retrieval [3], knowledge question answering [16], and machine translation [13]. NER mainly includes the accurate recognition of the entity boundaries and the correct classification of entity categories. For NER, the sentence needs to be segmented to obtain words, and then the words are represented as word vectors. Next, put them into a model to learn context information. There are natural blank spaces between English words, but there are no such marks in Chinese. For the word segmentation processing of Chinese sentences, manual word segmentation can

© The Author(s), under exclusive license to Springer Nature Switzerland AG 2022
E. Pimenidis et al. (Eds.): ICANN 2022, LNCS 13530, pp. 197–208, 2022.
https://doi.org/10.1007/978-3-031-15931-2_17

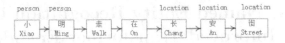

Fig. 1. Relative position information in a sentence

obtain high-quality words, but it will be time-consuming and labor-intensive. In different contexts, the words obtained by the automatic tokenizer may not conform to the current semantics. They will affect the subsequent operations. In NER, the boundaries of the word and the named entity are usually the same, which is very important for recognition performance. Another strategy, to avoid the problem of word segmentation errors, a Chinese sentence is segmented into a sequence of Chinese characters. The Chinese character vectors are used as the input of a model. Some studies have shown that a model may learn the word-formation information between a small number of characters in different contexts. The actual effect of this strategy is better than the automatic tokenizer. It can be seen the importance of word information in Chinese named entity recognition. Therefore, some methods of fusing information between characters and words have been presented.

In NER, entities are sensitive to position information. Figure 1 shows the importance of relative position information in a sentence to NER. A person's name usually appears before the verb "walk"; a place's name usually appears after the preposition "on"; Chinese characters on both sides of "on" do not form a named entity. This point is crucial to the classification and the boundary of an entity. This paper proposes a new Chinese NER architecture. The model achieves outstanding performance on benchmark datasets of Chinese NER with higher efficiency. In summary, the contributions of this work are:

(1) In the embedding layer, we design a lexicon adapter to dynamically fuse the potential word information of a sentence into the characters with an attention algorithm.
(2) We abandon the original position embedding and propose a relative position embedding with relative direction information.
(3) At the same time, we improve the calculation method of the self-attention mechanism to better model semantic information and position information.

2   Background

In this section, we first briefly explain the well-known attention mechanism and the absolute position embedding [14].

2.1   Self-attention

The Transformer can well model context information in parallel. Even if sentences are long, it will not weaken the modeling information, which benefits from the self-attention mechanism. The Transformer encoder takes in a matrix $I \in \mathbb{R}^{l \times d}$, where l is the sentence length and d is the input dimension. Then there are three trainable parameter matrices W_q, W_k, and W_v in the model to project the input I into different spaces. The dimensions of three matrices are usually $\mathbb{R}^{d \times d_m}$, where d_m is the dimension of the hidden layer. The attention score is calculated as follows:

$$Q, K, V = IW_q, IW_k, IW_v$$

$$Attention(Q, K, V) = softmax(\frac{QK^T}{\sqrt{d_m}})V \tag{1}$$

Here, Q, K, and V represent query vectors, key vectors, and value vectors, respectively. QK^T is used to calculate the attention scores between characters in a sentence. Then the *softmax* function performs a normalization operation in the last dimension to get the attention weights.

2.2   Absolute Position Embedding

There is no position information in the self-attention calculation. To introduce position information, the absolute position embedding is proposed and added to the character embedding before self-attention calculation [14]. The position embedding is defined as follows:

$$PE_{t,2x} = \sin(t/10000^{2x/d})$$

$$PE_{t,2x+1} = \cos(t/10000^{2x/d}) \tag{2}$$

Here, t is the index of a character in a sentence. $2x$ and $2x+1$ are dimensions with even and odd subscripts in the position embedding vector, respectively.

3   Related Work

In recent years, many character-word information fusion methods [4,8,20] have been proposed in Chinese NER. The most representative is the Lattice LSTM, which adds gate structures controlling word information flow based on LSTM. The structure of recurrent neural networks has a sequential dependency, resulting in low modeling efficiency. And the Lattice LSTM captures potential words that end with the current character. The words captured in a sentence are insufficient with this method.

Another is to find words containing the current character by multi-layer CNN networks with different size convolution kernels [4]. In this way, there will be sufficient related words. And through a feedback mechanism to assign different weights to each word. This method also has the problem of low efficiency, but it has been greatly improved compared to Lattice LSTM.

In the definition of Eq. 2, this absolute position embedding method is used to define the position information for each character in a sentence. Let's use

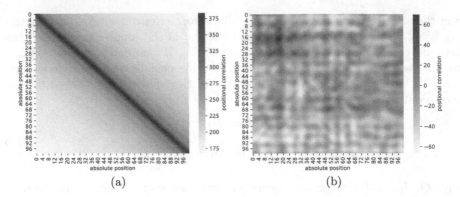

Fig. 2. The visualization of correlation between absolute positions. (a): $PE_{t1}PE_{t2}^T$. (b): $PE_{t1}W_qW_k^TPE_{t2}^T$

the following derivation to calculate the positional relationship between any two characters in a sentence:

$$PE_tPE_{t+dis}^T = \sum_{x=0}^{\frac{d}{2}-1}[sin(\frac{t}{10000^{\frac{2x}{d}}})sin(\frac{t+dis}{10000^{\frac{2x}{d}}}) + cos(\frac{t}{10000^{\frac{2x}{d}}})cos(\frac{t+dis}{10000^{\frac{2x}{d}}})]$$

$$= \sum_{x=0}^{\frac{d}{2}-1}cos(\frac{t}{10000^{\frac{2x}{d}}} - \frac{t+dis}{10000^{\frac{2x}{d}}}) = \sum_{x=0}^{\frac{d}{2}-1}cos(-\frac{dis}{10000^{\frac{2x}{d}}}) = \sum_{x=0}^{\frac{d}{2}-1}cos(\frac{dis}{10000^{\frac{2x}{d}}})$$

$$(3)$$

Here, dis represents the relative position between any two characters. $+dis$ represents dis units to the right of the current character, and $-dis$ is the opposite. It can be seen that the final result of the derivation is an even function, only related to the distance, not to the directionality. The visualization result calculated by the absolute position embedding between any two characters in a sentence is shown in Fig. 2(a). Obviously, the calculation result is a symmetric matrix. The further along the leading diagonal, the lower the correlation. It also shows that the correlation between any two positions represented by the absolute position embedding is only related to the distance.

Recently, some researchers [17] have proposed a kind of relative position embedding, which alleviates the problem of position relativity to a certain extent. However, the relativity of position is not fully reflected in the embedding but half of the dimensions.

In the native Transformer, character embeddings and absolute position embeddings are added together to calculate attention scores, as follows:

$$score_{a,b} = [c^e(a) + p^e(a)]W_qW_k^T[c^e(b) + p^e(b)]^T = c^e(a)W_qW_k^Tc^e(b)^T$$
$$+ p^e(a)W_qW_k^Tc^e(b)^T + c^e(a)W_qW_k^Tp^e(b)^T + p^e(a)W_qW_k^Tp^e(b)^T \quad (4)$$

Here, $score_{a,b}$ represents the calculation score of the attention for a-th and b-th characters with position information. c^e and p^e represent the character

Fig. 3. An example of semantic and position information independence

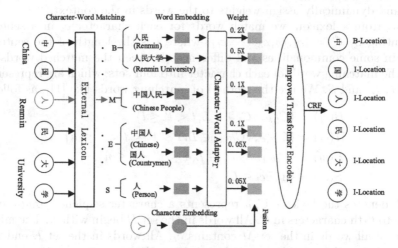

Fig. 4. Our model structure for Chinese NER tasks. For a sentence, each character matches relevant candidate words from the lexicon. According to the position feature of the character in words, the candidate words are divided into four sets. The model uses the adapter to learn weights to fuse word information. Finally, the context information is learned through the improved Transformer.

embedding and the absolute position embedding. It is not hard to find that the character embedding and the absolute position embedding are projected with the shared W_q and W_k matrix parameters. Character embeddings contain the meaning of semantic level, while position embeddings are only related to position information and should not be affected by semantic information. As shown in Fig. 3, at the semantic level, "it" and "cat" should be very close rather than "it" and "road." Two words may be very similar in semantic space but not necessarily in position space.

We use the W_q and W_k matrix parameters of training completion. It is found from Fig. 2(b) that these distributions tend to be uniform compared with Fig. 2(a). Distance information has also become more obscure.

To deal with the above issues, we design a character-word information fusion adapter using the attention mechanism to perform information fusion more effectively and quickly. A relative position embedding with complete relative information is proposed, and the attention modeling mechanism is improved.

4 Our Model

An overview of our proposed architecture is shown in Fig. 4.

4.1 Attention Adapter for Character-word Fusion

At present, there are many character-word fusion methods to achieve information enhancement. We design a trainable attention adapter to realize the parallel fusion and dynamically assign weights to the words in the context.

First, from a lexicon, we match words for each character c_t in a sentence representing by $C = \{c_1, c_2, c_3, \cdots, c_l\}$, where l is the length of the sentence. To retain some commonalities and differences between the matched words, we divide the matching words of each character into four sets, which are represented as B, M, E, and S. We use the method of matching words like [11], as follows:

$$
\begin{aligned}
B(c_t) &= \{C_{t,t'}, \forall C_{t,t'} \in L, t < t' \le l\} \\
M(c_t) &= \{C_{t'',t'}, \forall C_{t'',t'} \in L, 1 \le t'' < t < t' \le n\} \\
E(c_t) &= \{C_{t'',t}, \forall C_{t'',t} \in L, 1 \le t'' < t \le n\} \\
S(c_t) &= \{c_t, \exists c_t \in L\}
\end{aligned}
\tag{5}
$$

Here, L denotes the lexicon. $C_{t,t'}$ represents a character sequence composed of the t-th to t'-th characters in C. All words in the set B begin with c_t. The middle position of all words in the set M contains c_t. All words in the set E end with c_t. The word in the set S is formed by c_t alone. When a set is empty, a special word "None" is added to it. By now, we have got four word-sets corresponding to each character.

Secondly, in the embedding layer, use the attention adapter to fuse character-word information as follows,

$$
\begin{aligned}
H(c_t) &= c^e(c_t) \\
T(O) &= w^e(O) \qquad O \in \{B(c_t), M(c_t), E(c_t), S(c_t)\}
\end{aligned}
\tag{6}
$$

c^e and w^e represent the character embedding and word embedding, respectively. H and $T(O)$ are the vector representations obtained after embedding. We first embed each character c_t of the sentence to get the character vector and then embed the words of the four sets corresponding to each character to get the word vector.

Perform one linear transformation and a *tanh* activation function for the word vectors in each word-set to get $J(B(c_t))$, $J(M(c_t))$, $J(E(c_t))$, and $J(S(c_t))$ in Eq. 7.

$$
J(O) = tanh(T(O)X + b) \qquad O \in \{B(c_t), M(c_t), E(c_t), S(c_t)\}
\tag{7}
$$

Then we calculate attention scores for the current character and the words in each word-set belonging to it and normalize the scores to obtain the weights in Eq. 8.

$$
W(O) = softmax(H(c_t)J(O)^T) \qquad O \in \{B(c_t), M(c_t), E(c_t), S(c_t)\}
\tag{8}
$$

$$
\begin{aligned}
F = [&H(c_t); W(B(c_t))T(B(c_t)); W(M(c_t))T(M(c_t)); \\
&W(E(c_t))T(E(c_t)); W(S(c_t))T(S(c_t))]
\end{aligned}
\tag{9}
$$

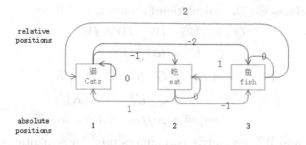

Fig. 5. An example of relative positions in a sentence

In Eq. 9, [;] indicates that the tensor is spliced in the last dimension. In each word-set, the weights of the character and words are used to aggregate word information of this word-set. To preserve the semantic independence of the four word-sets as much as possible, we use the splicing method to fuse the character and word information. Finally, F is the vector representation of the character-word information fusion.

4.2 Our Relative Position Embedding

We propose a new kind of definition of relative position embedding to solve the problem of representation.

$$R_{t1-t2}^{(2x)} = sin(\frac{t1-t2}{10000^{\frac{2x}{d}}})$$

$$R_{t1-t2}^{(2x+1)} = \frac{t1-t2}{|t1-t2|} cos(\frac{t1-t2}{10000^{\frac{2x}{d}}}) \qquad (10)$$

In a sentence, any two characters' positions can be represented by absolute positions such as $t1$ and $t2$. To some extent, using $t1-t2$ can reflect the relativity between the two positions. There are $2(l-1)+1$ relative positions in a sentence with l characters as shown in Fig. 5. We need to encode each relative position in a sentence as a vector with relative information. The dimensional information of even-numbered subscripts is encoded with sin. Because sin is an odd function, the information encoded for the relative positions $t1-t2$ and $t2-t1$ is also opposite to each other. The dimensional information of odd-numbered subscripts is encoded with cos. Because cos is an even function, $\frac{t1-t2}{|t1-t2|}$ is used in front of cos to ensure that the relative positions $t1-t2$ and $t2-t1$ have opposite encoding information. The information encoded with this method for two opposite relative positions will be reflected in all dimensions.

4.3 Our Attention Algorithm

We improve the attention calculation method to better model semantic and position information. Semantic and position parameters are trained in two independent subspaces. The calculation formula is as follows:

$$Q^c, K^c, V^c = IW_q^c, IW_k^c, IW_v^c$$
$$Q^p, K^p = RW_q^p, RW_k^p$$
$$Attention(c_t, c_{t'}) = Q_{c_t}^c K_{c_{t'}}^{c\ T} + Q_{t-t'}^p K_{c_{t'}}^{c\ T} \qquad (11)$$
$$+ Q_{c_t}^c K_{t-t'}^{p\ T} + uK_{t-t'}^{p\ T}$$
$$Output = softmax(Attention)V^c$$

Here, W_q^c, W_k^c, and W_v^c are matrix parameters used for semantic projection. Q^c, K^c, and V^c are the query vector, key vector, and value vector obtained by projecting the semantic vector. W_q^p and W_k^p are matrix parameters used for position projection. Q^p and K^p are the query vector and key vector obtained by projecting the position vector. c_t and $c_{t'}$ represent the t-th character and the t'-th character in a sentence, respectively. u is a trainable parameter.

It can be seen in Eq. 11 that the parameters of semantic and position projection are independent, which makes their representations in the respective projection spaces independent of each other. Ensure the independence of semantics and position information. Finally, the joint attention scores are calculated on the semantics and position of the characters in a sentence through *Attention*. *Output* is the character vector representation with contextual semantic information and positional information.

Then we only take the character representation into the conditional random field (CRF) layer for the tag prediction.

5   Experiments

5.1   Datasets

In this section, we describe four benchmark datasets in Chinese NER, including OntoNotes [15], MSRA [7], Weibo NER [5,12], and Resume NER [20]. [15] released OntoNotes 4.0. We adopt the same pre-process followed [1] in Chinese parts. The Chinese NER datasets OntoNotes and MSRA came from the news domain. Weibo NER was from Chinese social media Sina Weibo. The Resume NER came from social media. For OntoNotes, gold segmentation is available for the train, development, and test data. The gold segmentation refers to the high-quality word segmentation. However, gold segmentation is not provided in most datasets.

5.2   Experimental Settings

Most experimental settings in our work followed the protocols of Lattice-LSTM. In the embedding layer, the character and word embedding sizes are set to 50 and the hidden dimension of attention in the character-word adapter to 50. The final output dimension after the fusion of characters and words is 250. In the improved Transformer, the number of attention heads is set to 4. The dimension of each head is set to 64. We use one layer of the Transformer. The initial learning rate is set to 0.001 with an Adamax optimizer.

Table 1. Main results on OntoNotes.

Input	Models	P	R	F1
Gold seg	[18]	65.59	71.84	68.57
	Word-based (LSTM)	76.66	63.60	69.52
	+char+bichar	**78.62**	**73.13**	**75.77**
Auto seg	Word-based (LSTM)	72.84	59.72	65.63
	+char+bichar	**73.36**	**70.12**	**71.70**
No seg	Lattice LSTM [20]	76.35	71.56	73.88
	LR-CNN [4]	76.40	72.60	74.45
	SoftLexicon (LSTM) [11]	77.28	74.07	75.64
	DS-attention+ID-CNN [19]	**77.97**	71.64	74.67
	Adapter+Transformer	73.14	73.01	73.07
	Ours	75.81	**76.90**	**76.35**

5.3 Comparison with Previous Models

We compare our model with several competing models on four Chinese NER datasets. The overall results are shown in the tables below. Note that the experimental results of all baseline models are derived from the original papers.

Table 1 shows three different sets of settings. "Gold seg" refers to high-quality word segmentation. "Auto seg" refers to automatic word segmentation through a tokenizer. "No seg" refers to the input on the Chinese character level without word segmentation. The method we propose is based on the character level. Gold word segmentations were provided for the training, validation, and test data on the OntoNotes dataset. In the word-based group, we can make several observations. First, adding the single character and double characters to words can enhance the representations of words. Secondly, due to the word segmentation boundary error mentioned above, the F1 score is reduced from 75.77% to 71.70% when automatically generated word segmentation replaces gold word segmentation. "Adapter" refers to our proposed method of using the attention to fuse word information into character-based input. We can find that the effect of semantic enhancement using the "Adapter" on the native Transformer is not even as good as Lattice LSTM. But, in the last line, our approach has achieved excellent results in terms of model performance. The improved Transformer delivers consistent gain on Chinese NER.

The comparative performances of the models on the Resume/MSRA/Weibo datasets are shown in Tables 2, 3, and 4, respectively. We make the comparison between state-of-the-art models and the classic models including leveraging rich handcrafted features [2] and character embedding features [10]. From the comparative data, our proposed method has achieved good results compared with other models.

For Weibo, all baseline models only provide F1 in the experiment. From the dataset type and absolute F1 score improvements, since Resume and MSRA have

Table 2. Main results on Resume.

Models	P	R	F1
Word-level LSTM	93.72	93.44	93.58
Char-level LSTM	93.66	93.31	93.48
Lattice LSTM [20]	94.81	94.11	94.46
LR-CNN [4]	95.37	94.84	95.11
[11]	95.30	95.77	95.53
Adapter+Transformer	94.29	94.23	94.26
Ours	**95.60**	**95.89**	**95.74**

Table 3. Main results on MSRA.

Models	P	R	F1
[2]	91.22	81.71	86.20
[10]	-	-	87.94
Lattice LSTM [20]	93.57	92.79	93.18
LR-CNN [4]	94.50	92.93	93.71
[11]	94.63	92.70	93.66
Adapter+Transformer	93.42	92.09	92.75
Ours	**94.69**	**92.95**	**93.81**

much larger samples, the boosting performance of the model is relatively small. In other words, the number of samples in the dataset is critical to the performance improvement of models. Our model takes the characters of a Chinese sentence as the input to avoid automatic word segmentation errors. Character-word information dynamic fusion is achieved by an attention adapter. It achieves the effect of semantic enhancement. The improvement of relative position embedding and attention mechanism alleviates the shortcomings of the native Transformer to a certain extent. This enables the model to better deal with semantic and position information. These are very important for Chinese NER. This is why our proposed model achieves good results.

Table 5 shows the relative test-time speed comparison of different models with the same batch size (=1). Our proposed model achieves the best performance on the inference speed.

Our model is mainly divided into the module of character-word information fusion and sentence information encoding. On the one hand, in the character-word information fusion module, we can use the attention mechanism to learn the weights between characters and words in parallel. On the other hand, in the sentence information encoding module, we also use the attention mechanism to model the context information in parallel. These factors cause our model to have a faster inference speed than other models.

Table 4. Main results on Weibo. NE, NM and Overall denote F1 scores for named entities, nominal entities (excluding named entities) and both, respectively.

Models	NE	NM	Overall
[12]	51.96	61.05	56.05
[6]	54.50	62.17	58.23
Lattice LSTM [20]	53.04	62.25	58.79
LR-CNN [4]	57.14	**66.67**	59.92
SoftLexicon (LSTM) [11]	**59.08**	62.22	61.42
Adapter+Transformer	47.46	58.40	55.23
Ours	58.00	65.32	**62.58**

Table 5. Relative test-time speed of different models.

Datasets	Models		
	[20]	[4]	Ours
OntoNotes	1×	2.23×	**5.35×**
MSRA	1×	1.57×	**4.56×**
Weibo	1×	2.41×	**5.10×**
Resume	1×	1.44×	**5.62×**

6   Conclusion and Future Work

In this paper, we present a very effective method for Chinese named entity recognition. This method is mainly composed of a character-word information fusion adapter and one layer of the improved Transformer. The character-word information fusion mechanism can effectively avoid the problem of word segmentation errors and fully use the words in Chinese named entity recognition. The proposed position embedding with relative position information is used with the improved attention calculation so that the model can better capture the position information in a sentence. In this process, we also give full play to the parallel computing capabilities of attention. In the future, we intend to apply this method to the follow-up tasks of natural language processing to coordinate the completion of the information extraction goal.

References

1. Che, W., Wang, M., Manning, C.D., Liu, T.: Named entity recognition with bilingual constraints. In: Proceedings of the 2013 Conference of the North American Chapter of the Association for Computational Linguistics: Human Language Technologies, pp. 52–62 (2013)
2. Chen, A., Peng, F., Shan, R., Sun, G.: Chinese named entity recognition with conditional probabilistic models. In: Proceedings of the Fifth SIGHAN Workshop on Chinese Language Processing, pp. 173–176 (2006)
3. Chen, Y., Xu, L., Liu, K., Zeng, D., Zhao, J.: Event extraction via dynamic multi-pooling convolutional neural networks. In: Proceedings of the 53rd Annual Meeting of the Association for Computational Linguistics and the 7th International Joint Conference on Natural Language Processing (Volume 1: Long Papers), pp. 167–176 (2015)
4. Gui, T., Ma, R., Zhang, Q., Zhao, L., Jiang, Y.G., Huang, X.: CNN-based Chinese NER with lexicon rethinking. In: IJCAI, pp. 4982–4988 (2019)
5. He, H., Sun, X.: F-score driven max margin neural network for named entity recognition in Chinese social media. In: Proceedings of the 15th Conference of the European Chapter of the Association for Computational Linguistics: Volume 2, Short Papers, pp. 713–718 (2017)
6. He, H., Sun, X.: A unified model for cross-domain and semi-supervised named entity recognition in Chinese social media. In: Proceedings of the AAAI Conference on Artificial Intelligence, vol. 31 (2017)
7. Levow, G.A.: The third international Chinese language processing bakeoff: word segmentation and named entity recognition. In: Proceedings of the Fifth SIGHAN Workshop on Chinese Language Processing, pp. 108–117 (2006)
8. Li, X., Yan, H., Qiu, X., Huang, X.: Flat: Chinese NER using flat-lattice transformer. arXiv preprint arXiv:2004.11795 (2020)
9. Lin, Y., Shen, S., Liu, Z., Luan, H., Sun, M.: Neural relation extraction with selective attention over instances. In: Proceedings of the 54th Annual Meeting of the Association for Computational Linguistics (Volume 1: Long Papers), pp. 2124–2133 (2016)
10. Lu, Y., Zhang, Y., Ji, D.: Multi-prototype Chinese character embedding. In: Proceedings of the Tenth International Conference on Language Resources and Evaluation (LREC 2016), pp. 855–859 (2016)

11. Peng, M., Ma, R., Zhang, Q., Huang, X.: Simplify the usage of lexicon in Chinese NER. In: ACL (2020)
12. Peng, N., Dredze, M.: Named entity recognition for Chinese social media with jointly trained embeddings. In: Proceedings of the 2015 Conference on Empirical Methods in Natural Language Processing, pp. 548–554 (2015)
13. Sutskever, I., Vinyals, O., Le, Q.V.: Sequence to sequence learning with neural networks. In: Advances in Neural Information Processing Systems, pp. 3104–3112 (2014)
14. Vaswani, A., et al.: Attention is all you need. In: Advances in Neural Information Processing Systems, pp. 5998–6008 (2017)
15. Weischedel, R., et al.: Ontonotes release 4.0. LDC2011T03. Linguistic Data Consortium, Philadelphia (2011)
16. Wu, P., Zhang, X., Feng, Z.: A survey of question answering over knowledge base. In: Zhu, X., Qin, B., Zhu, X., Liu, M., Qian, L. (eds.) CCKS 2019. CCIS, vol. 1134, pp. 86–97. Springer, Singapore (2019). https://doi.org/10.1007/978-981-15-1956-7_8
17. Yan, H., Deng, B., Li, X., Qiu, X.: Tener: adapting transformer encoder for named entity recognition. arXiv preprint arXiv:1911.04474 (2019)
18. Yang, J., Teng, Z., Zhang, M., Zhang, Y.: Combining discrete and neural features for sequence labeling. In: Gelbukh, A. (ed.) CICLing 2016. LNCS, vol. 9623, pp. 140–154. Springer, Cham (2018). https://doi.org/10.1007/978-3-319-75477-2_9
19. Zhang, D., Chi, C., Zhan, X.: Leveraging lexical features for Chinese named entity recognition via static and dynamic weighting. IAENG Int. J. Comput. Sci. **48**(1) (2021)
20. Zhang, Y., Yang, J.: Chinese NER using lattice LSTM (2018)

Concatenating BioMed-Transformers to Tackle Long Medical Documents and to Improve the Prediction of Tail-End Labels

Vithya Yogarajan[1]([✉]) [iD], Bernhard Pfahringer[2] [iD], Tony Smith[2] [iD], and Jacob Montiel[2] [iD]

[1] Strong AI Lab, School of Computer Science, University of Auckland,
Auckland, New Zealand
vithya.yogarajan@auckland.ac.nz
[2] Department of Computer Science, University of Waikato,
Hamilton, New Zealand

Abstract. Multi-label learning predicts a subset of labels from a given label set for an unseen instance while considering label correlations. A known challenge with multi-label classification is the long-tailed distribution of labels. Many studies focus on improving the overall predictions of the model and thus do not prioritise tail-end labels. Improving the tail-end label predictions in multi-label classifications of medical text enables the potential to understand patients better and improve care. The knowledge gained by one or more infrequent labels can impact the cause of medical decisions and treatment plans. This research presents a variation of concatenated domain-specific language models, multi-BioMed-Transformers, to achieve two primary goals: first, to improve F1 scores of infrequent labels across multi-label problems, especially with long-tail labels; second, to handle long medical text and multi-sourced electronic health records (EHRs), a challenging task for standard transformers designed to work on short input sequences. A vital contribution of this research is new state-of-the-art (SOTA) results obtained using TransformerXL for predicting medical codes. A variety of experiments are performed on the Medical Information Mart for Intensive Care (MIMIC-III) database. Results show that concatenated BioMed-Transformers outperform standard transformers in terms of overall micro and macro F1 scores and individual F1 scores of tail-end labels, while incurring lower training times than existing transformer-based solutions for long input sequences.

Keywords: Multi-label · Transformers · Long documents · Medical text · Tail-end labels · SOTA

1 Introduction

Multi-label text classification techniques enable predictions of treatable risk factors in patients, aiding in better life expectancy and quality of life [2]. The goal of multi-label learning is to predict a subset of labels for an unseen instance

E. Pimenidis et al. (Eds.): ICANN 2022, LNCS 13530, pp. 209–221, 2022.
https://doi.org/10.1007/978-3-031-15931-2_18

from a given label set while considering label correlations [25]. One of the known challenges with multi-label classification is the long-tailed distribution of labels. In general, with multi-label problems, a small subset of the labels are associated with a large number of instances, and a significant fraction of the labels are associated with a small number of instances.

There are some examples of studies that focus on exploiting label structure [26] and label co-occurrence patterns [15]. In studies especially relating to medical text, the focus is on improving the overall performance of the model instead of individual tail-end labels [18]. However, prediction of infrequent labels in order to understand all aspects of a patient's prognosis is as crucial as predicting frequent labels [8]. The knowledge gained by one or more infrequent labels can impact the cause of medical decisions, treatments and patient care.

This research explores the opportunity to improve predictions of tail-end labels using transformers for medical-domain specific tasks by exploiting models pre-trained on health data. We show concatenated BioMed-Transformers improve tail-end predictions compared to other neural networks and single transformers. In addition, we demonstrate concatenated domain-specific transformer models are a solution for handling text data with extended text and multi-sources of texts. Given that most transformer models are limited to a maximum sequence length of 512 tokens, with some exceptions, there is still a gap in alternative solutions for long documents. Transformer models such as Longformer [3] and TransformerXL [6] can handle longer sequences and perform better than other language models for long documents. Unfortunately, these models require considerable amounts of memory and processing time. In contrast, concatenated domain-specific transformers require fewer resources.

We compare concatenated domain-specific transformer models with standard language models for increasingly larger multi-label problems with 30, 50, 73, 158 and 923 labels. The multi-label problems considered in this paper are: predicting ICD-9 codes for ICD-9 hierarchy levels, most frequent 50 ICD-9 codes, cardiovascular disease and systemic fungal or bacterial disease. The contributions of this work are:

1. analyse the effectiveness of using concatenated domain-specific language model –multi-BioMed-Transformers– for predicting medical codes from EHRs for multiple document lengths, multi-sources of texts and number of labels;
2. show that multi-BioMed-Transformers improve both F1 scores of infrequent labels and overall micro and macro F1 scores, using fewer resources;
3. present new SOTA results for predicting medical codes from EHRs.

2   Related Work

In the last two to three years, there have been considerable advancements in transformer models, which have shown substantial improvements in many NLP tasks, including BioNLP tasks [10]. With minimum effort, transfer learning of pre-trained models by fine-tuning on downstream supervised tasks achieves very good results [1].

Table 1. Statistics of multi-label classification problems.

Multi-label problems	q	# Inst	LCard	LDens	LFreq $\geq 1\%$	LFreq $< 1\%$
MIMIC-III Level 3	923	52,722	14.43	0.02	244	679
MIMIC-III Level 2	158	52,722	11.61	0.07	100	58
MIMIC-III Top50	50	50,957	5.60	0.11	50	0
Fungal or Bacterial	73	30,814	2.06	0.03	34	39
Cardiovascular	30	28,154	2.51	0.08	16	14

A significant obstacle for transformers is the 512 token size limit they impose on input sequences [9]. Gao et al. (2021) [9] presents evidence showing BERT-based models under-perform in clinical text classification tasks with long input data, such as MIMIC-III [12], when compared to a CNN trained on word embeddings that can process the complete input sequences. Si and Roberts (2021) [20] presents an alternative system to overcome the issue of long documents, where transformer-based encoders are used to learn from words to sentences, sentences to notes and notes to patients, progressively. However, it requires considerable computational resources [20]. Chalkidis et al. (2020) [4] proposes a similar hierarchical version using SCI-BERT to deal with long documents for predicting medical codes from MIMIC III. Unfortunately, HIER-SCI-BERT performed poorly compared to other neural networks [4]. One possible reason for poor results is the use of a continuously pre-trained BERT model [4]. The continuous training approach would initialise with the standard BERT model, pre-trained using Wikipedia and BookCorpus. It then continues the pre-training process with a masked language model and next-sentence prediction using domain-specific data. In this case, the vocabulary is the same as the original BERT model, which is considered a disadvantage for domain-specific tasks [10]. For our research, PubMedBERT [10], a domain-specific BERT based model trained solely on biomedical text, is used.

Our research focuses on automatically predicting medical codes from medical text as the multi-label classification task. Studies relating to predicting medical codes using transformers, such as [24], restrict themselves to (1) truncated text sequences of <512 tokens and (2) predicting frequent labels [1]. MIMIC-III consists of many infrequent labels, where most codes only occur in a small number of clinical documents. This research focuses on improving the predictive accuracy for infrequent labels and using long medical texts. SOTA methods for automatically predicting medical codes from EHRs include Convolutional Attention for Multi-Label classification (CAML) [19], and most recently (Nov 2021) EffectiveCAN [16] an effective convolution attention network. We provide evidence to show TransformerXL outperforms CAML and EffectiveCAN for predicting medical codes.

3   Data and Labels

Medical Information Mart for Intensive Care (MIMIC-III) is one of the most extensive publicly available medical databases [12] with more than 50,000 patient EHRs. Among the available free-form medical text, more than 90% of the hospital admissions contain at least one discharge summary (dis). Other text summaries include categories ECG (ecg) and Radiology(rad). As with most free form EHRs, MIMIC-III text data includes acronyms, abbreviations, and spelling errors. For example (data as presented in MIMIC III with errors):

82 yo M with h/o CHF, COPD on 5 L oxygen at baseline, tracheobron-chomalacia s/p stent, presents w acute dyspnea over several days...

MIMIC-III data includes long documents, where dis ranges from 60 to 9,500 tokens with an average of 1,513 tokens and rad with an average of 2,500 tokens. The document lengths of ecg are short with an average of 84 tokens. In this research, MIMIC-III text is pre-processed by removing tokens that contain non-alphabetic characters, including all special characters and tokens that appear in less than three training documents.

The discharge summary is split into equal segments for a given hospital admission, and each section is labelled text $1, ..., 4$. For multi-BioMed-Transformers where the maximum sequence length is 512, each of text $1, ..., 4$ is truncated to 512 tokens. This research presents results for the following configurations:

Op-0. $dis_{1 \, of \, 2} + dis_{2 \, of \, 2}$	Op-3. $dis_{1 \, of \, 2} + dis_{2 \, of \, 2} + rad$	Op-6. $dis + ecg$
Op-1. $dis_{1 \, of \, 3} + dis_{2 \, of \, 3} + dis_{3 \, of \, 3}$	Op-4. $dis_{1 \, of \, 2} + dis_{2 \, of \, 2} + ecg + rad$	Op-7. $dis + rad$
Op-2. $dis_{1 \, of \, 2} + dis_{2 \, of \, 2} + ecg$	Op-5. $dis_{1 \, of \, 4} + dis_{2 \, of \, 4} + dis_{3 \, of \, 4} + dis_{4 \, of \, 4}$	

We consider predicting ICD-9 codes (standards for International statistical Classification of Diseases and related health problems) from EHRs as flat multi-label problems. ICD codes are used to classify diseases, symptoms, signs, and causes of diseases. Manual assigning of medical codes requires expert knowledge and is very time-consuming. Thus, the ability to predict and automate medical coding is vital. ICD-9 codes are grouped in a hierarchical tree-like structure by the World Health Organisation. In this research, we focus on levels 2 and 3 for MIMIC-III data containing 158 labels and 923 labels respectively, with associated medical text for the patient. We also consider case studies cardiovascular disease, and systemic fungal or bacterial infections, where commonly used medical codes are used as labels. For the purposes of direct comparison with the recently published SOTA, the most frequent 50 ICD-9 codes in MIMIC-III are also considered.

Table 1 provides a summary of the multi-label problems used in this research. For multi-label problems, the notations as per Tsoumakas et al. (2009) [21] are used, where $L = \{\lambda_j : j = 1...q\}$ refers to the finite set of labels and $D = \{(x_i, Y_i), i = 1...m\}$ refers to set of multi-label training examples. Here x_i is the feature vector, and $Y_i \subseteq L$ is the set of labels of the i-th example. Label cardinality ($LCard$) is the average number of labels of the examples in a dataset, and label density ($LDens$) is cardinality divided by q. Table 1 provides

---

Algorithm 1 Multiple BioMed-Transformer

1: **Input:** Fixed length multi-sourced or long document text input with set of labels
   $Y \subseteq L$, domain specific pre-trained transformer models x_i with parameters $\theta_{1,2,\ldots,n}$,
   Linear layer (FC) with L number of output units having θ_l parameters and loss
   function Binary-cross-entropy (BCE).
2: **for** each mini-batch **do**
3:     pooled_$features$ = []
4:     **for** each document i **do**
5:         x_i = BioMed-Transformer(document$_i$)
6:         pooled_features.append(AVG_POOL(x_i))
7:     **end for**
8:     combined_features = CONCATENATE(pooled_features)
9:     drop_output = DROPOUT(combined_features)
10:    output = FC$_{\theta_l}$(drop_output)
11:    $\mathcal{L} = \mathcal{L}_{BCE}$(output, targets)
12:    $\theta = [\theta_1, \theta_2, \theta_3, \ldots, \theta_n, \theta_l]$
13:    $\theta = \theta - \nabla_\theta \mathcal{L}$
14: **end for**

---

the number of labels selected for experiments presented in this paper, with the
frequency of occurrences <1%, tail-end labels, and the number of labels ≥1%.

4   Language Models

This research mainly focuses on transformer models, with CNNText [13] and
CAML [19] used for comparison. Transformers are feed-forward models based
on the self-attention mechanism with no recurrence. Self-attention takes into
account the context of a word while processing it. Transformer models take all
the tokens in the sequence at once in parallel, enabling the capture of long-
distance dependencies. Vaswani et al. (2017) [22] provides an introduction to
the transformer architecture.

BERT (Bidirectional Encoder Representations from Transformers) [7] is a
transformer models that applies bidirectional training of encoders [22] to language modelling. The 12-layer BERT-base model with a hidden size of 768,
12 self-attention heads, 110M parameter neural network architecture, was pre-
trained from scratch on BookCorpus and English Wikipedia. PubMedBERT [10]
uses the same architecture, and is domain-specifically pre-trained from scratch
using abstracts from PubMed and full-text articles from PubMedCentral to better capture the biomedical language [10]. BioMed-RoBERTa-base [11] is based
on the RoBERTa-base [17] architecture. RoBERTa-base, originally trained using
160GB of general domain training data, was further continuously pre-trained
using 2.68 million scientific papers from the Semantic Scholar corpus.

TransformerXL [6] is an architecture that enables the representation of
language beyond a fixed length. It can learn dependency that is longer than
recurrent neural networks and vanilla transformers. The Longformer [3] model
is designed to handle longer sequences without the limitation of the maximum token size of 512. Longformer reduces the model complexity from

quadratic to linear by reformulating the self-attention computation. Compared to Transformer-XL [6], Longformer is not restricted to the left-to-right approach of processing documents.

5 Concatenated Language Models

Multi-BioMed-Transformers use an architecture where two or more domain-specific transformer models are concatenated together to enable the usage of multiple text inputs. Algorithm 1 presents an outline of multi-Bio-Med-Transformer models concatenated together. We explore the options of two to four PubMed-BERT models that are concatenated together. Concatenated transformer models enable the processing of longer sequences, where the longer input sequence is split into multiple smaller segments with a maximum length of 512 tokens. The average length of discharge summaries in MIMIC-III is approximately 1, 500 tokens, hence the choice to concatenate two to four PubMedBERT models. Moreover, as indicated in Sect. 3, MIMIC-III contains text from other categories, such as ecg and rad. Multi-BioMed-Transformers provides the option to explore using these other available texts as additional input text.

In addition to concatenated transformer models, we experimented with other variations such as concatenating multiple CNNText networks and concatenating CNNText with transformers. Unfortunately, these variations did not perform as well as Multi-BioMed-Transformers and due to space restrictions we do not present results for these variations.

6 Experiments

We present overall micro and macro F1 scores and individual label F1 scores for the multi-label problems outlined in Table 1. Critical difference plots are presented as supportive statistical analysis. The Nemenyi posthoc test (95% confidence level) identifies statistical differences between learning methods. CD graphs show the average ranking of individual F1 scores obtained using various language models. The lower the rank, the better it is. The difference in average ranking is statistically significant if there is no bold line connecting the two settings. All experimental results are obtained from a random seeds training-testing scheme and averaged over three runs. The variation of these three independent runs are within a range of ±0.015. We explore several different transformer models and compare the performance to concatenated BioMed-Transformers.

Transformer implementations are based on the open-source PyTorch transformer repository (HuggingFace). Transformer models are fine-tuned on all layers without freezing. For the optimiser, we use Adam [14] with learning rates between 9e−6, and 1e−5. Training batch sizes were varied between 1 and 16. A non-linear sigmoid function $f(z) = \frac{1}{1+e^{-z}}$, with a range of 0 to 1 is used as the activation function. Binary-cross-entropy [5] loss, $Loss_{BCE}(X, y) = -\sum_{l=1}^{L}(y_l log(\hat{y}_l) + (1 - y_l)log(1 - \hat{y}_l))$, over each label is used for multi-label classification. Domain-specific fastText embeddings [23] of a 100-dimensional skipgram model are used for neural networks.[1]

7 Results

Results are presented in three parts. First we present the overall performance of the language models, followed by SOTA comparison, and finally we present tail-end performance.

7.1 Overall Performance

Table 2 presents the results for various language model variations for cardiovascular disease, using MIMIC-III data with 28,154 hospital admissions of patients and 30 labels. Multi-PubMedBERT and multi-BioMed-RoBERTa show a consistent improvement of 3% to 7% in micro-F1 scores over single PubMedBERT and BioMed-RoBERTa, respectively. The macro-F1 score of TriplePubMed-BERT option is better than other language models presented with at least 3% improvement, except for TransformerXL with 3,072 tokens. For cardiovascular disease, incorporating ecg and rad does show some improved overall results, especially with TriplePubMedBERT options. Table 2 shows that TransformerXL with dis 3,072 tokens is the best option. However, multi-BioMed-Transformers show improvements, especially when compared to single-BioMed-Transformers.

Micro and macro F1 scores for various language model variations for systemic fungal or bacterial infection are presented in Table 3. Multi-PubMedBERT show improvements of 12% to 19 % in micro-F1, and 2% to 10% in macro-F1 scores over single PubMedBERT, except for TriplePubMedBERT with rad and ecg, where the macro-F1 score is on par with single PubMedBERT. Contrary to the case of cardiovascular disease, here the additional inputs of ecg and rad do not

Table 2. Micro-F1 and Macro-F1 of cardiovascular disease among various language models and input text for MIMIC-III data. **Best results for each grouping in the table; <u>overall best results</u>.** Results are averaged over three runs.

Neural network details		Micro F1	Macro F1	Neural network details		Micro F1	Macro F1
BioMed-RoBERTa	(dis 512)	0.69	0.30	Dual-Bio-RoBERTa	(Op-0: 512)	0.72	0.28
PubMedBERT	(dis 512)	0.70	0.30	DualPubMedBERT	(Op-0: 512)	0.72	0.30
TransformerXL	(dis 1,536)	0.75	0.28	Triple-BioMed-RoBERTa	(Op-1: 512)	0.72	0.29
TransformerXL	(dis 3,072)	**0.78**	**0.32**	TriplePubMedBERT	(Op-1: 512)	0.73	0.29
Longformer	(dis 3,000)	0.74	0.30	TriplePubMedBERT	(Op-2: 512)	0.73	**0.31**
CAML	(dis 3,000)	0.77	0.24	TriplePubMedBERT	(Op-3: 512)	0.73	0.30
CNNText	(dis 3,000)	0.74	0.30	QuadruplePubMedBERT	(Op-4: 512)	**0.74**	0.28

---

[1] https://github.com/vithyayogarajan/Medical-Domain-Specific-Language-Models/tree/main/Concatenated-Language-Models-Multi-label.

Table 3. Micro-F1 and Macro-F1 of systemic fungal or bacterial infection, levels 2 and 3 of ICD-9 codes among various language models. Results are averaged over three runs. Time per epoch is in seconds.

Neural network details		Fungal or Bacterial			MIMIC-III Level 2 codes		MIMIC-III Level 3 codes		
		Micro-F1	Macro-F1	Time[a]	Micro-F1	Macro-F1	Micro-F1	Macro-F1	Time[a]
PubMedBERT	(dis 512)	0.48	0.39	2,940	0.65 [24]	0.41 [24]	0.55	0.18	3,393
BioMed-RoBERTa	(dis 512)	0.45	0.39	2,554	0.64 [24]	0.40 [24]	0.53	0.18	4,877
TransformerXL	(dis 3,072)	**0.64**	**0.46**	43,200	**0.73**	**0.46**	-	-	-
Longformer	(dis 3,000)	0.58	0.43	13,500	0.72	0.45	0.62	0.19	16,889
CAML	(dis 3,000)	0.62	0.38	**47**	0.72	0.43	**0.64**	**0.26**	64
DualPubMedBERT	(Op-0: 512)	**0.57**	**0.43**	4,020	**0.68**	**0.45**	0.57	**0.20**	4,750
DualBioMed-RoBERTa	(Op-0: 512)	-	-	-	0.66	0.43	0.56	0.19	6,842
TriplePubMedBERT	(Op-1: 512)	0.56	0.40	5,580	0.66	0.43	-	-	-
TriplePubMedBERT	(Op-2: 512)	0.54	0.39	5,580	-	-	-	-	-
TriplePubMedBERT	(Op-3: 512)	0.54	0.39	5,580	-	-	-	-	-
QuadruplePubMedBERT	(Op-4: 512)	0.54	0.40	7,080	-	-	-	-	-
QuadruplePubMedBERT	(Op-5: 512)	**0.57**	0.40	7,080	-	-	-	-	-

[a]Average times (in seconds) per epoch is based on experiments run on 12 core Intel(R) Xeon(R) W-2133 CPU @ 3.60 GHz, GPU device GV100GL [Quadro GV100].

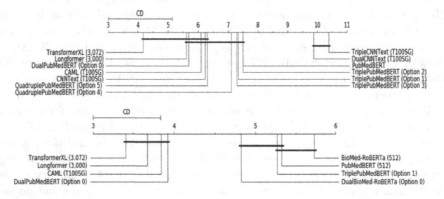

Fig. 1. Critical difference plots for Systemic fungal or bacterial infections (top) and MIMIC-III Level 2 codes (bottom). Critical difference is calculated for individual label F1 scores presented in Table 3.

result in better performance. It is likely that ecg and rad are not that relevant for coding fungal or bacterial infections.

Both case studies show that TransformerXL with dis 3,072 tokens is the top performer in terms of predictive performance. However, concatenated BioMed-Transformers show improvements, especially when compared to single BioMed-Transformers. Table 3 also presents the time per epoch in seconds for systemic fungal or bacterial infection to provide a direct comparison among the language models. TransformerXL (3,072) requirements are much greater than that of other language models, including multi-PubMedBERT, for example, needing 240 h (for dis 3,072) when DualPubMedBERT only requires 22 h.

Table 3 presents micro and macro F1 scores for levels 2 and 3 of ICD-9 codes. As mentioned above, due to the processing time required by TransformerXL (3,072), we only use Longformer for encoding long documents for ICD-9 level 3. For MIMIC-III Level 2 codes, TransformerXL with dis 3,072 tokens is the top performer. DualPubMedBERT shows improvements in both micro and macro F1 scores by 3% to 5% over other PubMedBERT variations, and macro-F1 of DualPubMedBERT and Longformer are equal and only marginally behind TransformerXL. For MIMIC-III Level 3 codes, the macro-F1 score of DualPub-MedBERT is better than other transformer models, including Longformer. However, CAML outperforms all variations of transformer models.

Figure 1 presents the critical difference plots for results presented in Table 3. The Nemenyi posthoc test (95% confidence level) shows statistical differences between learning methods. TransformerXL (3,072) and Longformer (3,000) are the overall top performers. However, the difference between them and DualPub-MedBERT is not statistically significant.

7.2   SOTA Results

Both Tables 2 and 3 show that TransformerXL outperforms CAML across all multi-label problems for predicting medical codes. In addition, there are other language models, including concatenated models, that perform on par with or above CAML, especially when macro-F1 scores are compared.

Table 4. MIMIC-III Top 50 ICD-9 codes: with published results for comparison and the **overall best results**. Our results are averaged over three runs.

Models	Micro-F1	Macro-F1
CAML [19]	0.614	0.532
Description regularized-CAML [19]	0.633	0.576
EffectiveCAN^a (sum-pooling attention) [16]	0.702	0.644
EffectiveCAN^a (multi-layer attention) [16]	0.717	0.668
DualPubMedBERT (Op-0: 512)	0.640	0.576
TriplePubMedBERT (Op-1: 512)	0.641	0.583
Longformer (3,000)	0.703	0.654
TransformerXL (3,072)	**0.723**	**0.677**

^{a} See Liu et al. (2021) [16] for details of EffectiveCAN variations and architectures.

Table 4 provides the overall micro and macro F1 scores of the most frequent 50 ICD-9 codes in MIMIC III with discharge summary. In this particular case, for direct comparison, the labels and input data are all matched to the exact specifications of the compared published methods. This is the only section in this research where Top 50 ICD-9 codes are used for experimental evaluations. Evidently TransformerXL (3,072) with a learning rate of 1e−5 presents new SOTA results.

7.3 Tail-End Labels

This section presents a comparison of individual label F1 scores for the multi-label problems presented in Sect. 7.1. The focus here is to show the differences and the improvements in F1 scores of tail-end labels with multi-BioMed-Transformers compared to single transformer models including Longformer and TransformerXL. Table 1 presents the number of labels with frequency ≥1%, and tail-end labels (with label frequency <1%).

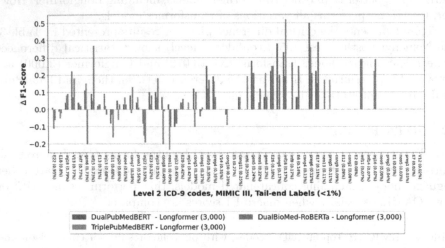

Fig. 2. MIMIC-III Level 2 codes, where the difference between F1 scores of dual/triple language model variations and Longformer (3,000 tokens) is presented. Negative values indicate better F1 scores for Longformer (3,000).

Figure 2 presents the difference in F1 scores for level 2 ICD-9 codes. Due to space restrictions only one example of tail-end labels is presented. However, it is important to note that for frequent labels, smaller differences in F1 scores arise among the most frequent labels, and occasional dual and triple models perform slightly better than Longformer for specific labels. In general, Longformer has the most wins over other models for label frequency ≥1%. This pattern is reversed for tail-end labels, with Longformer losing more to the dual and triple models where the difference in F1 scores is noted. For some tail-end labels, these differences are noticeably higher than other labels.

Table 5 presents the number of per-label wins, draws, and losses for levels 2 and 3 ICD-9 codes. For multi-label problems, F1-scores of many infrequent labels are zero. This observation is also evident in Fig. 2. To quantify the observations, differences of F1 scores are presented as wins, draws and losses. For most cases, draws are where the F1 scores are zero. We acknowledge that there is a need for further analysis to understand the behaviour observed in Table 5.

As observed in Fig. 2 for tail-end labels, more wins are observed for concatenated models. DualPubMedBERT is the best performing option with the fewest

Table 5. The number of wins, draws and losses of concatenated language models compared to Longformer (LF) and TransformerXL (TXL).

Models	Freq $\geq$ 1%			Freq $<$ 1%		
	Wins	Draws	Losses	Wins	Draws	Losses
MIMIC-III Level 2 codes, 158 labels						
DualPubMedBERT - TXL	26	0	74	26	16	16
DualBioMed-RoBERTa - TXL	25	0	75	28	16	14
TriplePubMedBERT - TXL	20	1	79	27	14	17
DualPubMedBERT - LF	19	11	70	30	22	6
DualBioMed-RoBERTa - LF	12	5	83	28	21	9
TriplePubMedBERT - LF	13	2	85	26	20	12
MIMIC-III Level 3 codes, 923 labels						
DualPubMedBERT -LF	92	17	135	160	476	43
DualBioMed-RoBERTa -LF	83	21	144	181	454	40

losses among the more frequent label groups and most wins among the tail-end labels. For MIMIC-III Level 3 codes, the results in Table 5 show Longformer losing more to dual transformers at tail-end labels. For frequent labels for systemic fungal or bacterial infection, the F1 scores of TransformerXL are consistently better than the PubMedBERT variations and a clear winner. For infrequent labels, multi-PubMedBERT variations perform better than TransformerXL for many labels.

8   Discussion

We presented concatenated domain-specific language model variations to improve the overall performance of the many infrequent labels in multi-label problems with long input sequences. Although TransformerXL and Longformer can encode long sequences, and in general, TransformerXL outperforms other models setting new SOTA results, the required computational resources are prohibitive. Concatenated PubMedBERT models outperformed single BioMed-Transformers. There was a noticeable improvement in micro-F1 for multi-BioMed-transformers with cardiovascular disease and systemic fungal or bacterial infection. For larger multi-label problems, dualPubMedBERT, TransformerXL and Longformer achieve the same macro-F1 for MIMIC-III Level 2, but dualPubMedBERT wins for MIMIC-III Level 3.

We also study the impact on predictive performance for less frequent labels. Label frequency is highly biased by the hospital/department where the data were collected. If the data were from a fertility ward, the label frequency of pregnancy-related medical codes would be high, while for the cardiovascular ward this may not be the case. However, only being able to predict highly frequent labels well poses risks to a patient's health and well being. Hence, this research also compared individual label F1 scores for multi-label problems focusing on tail-end labels. For larger multi-label problems with long tail-end labels, such as level 2 and 3 ICD-9 codes, multi-BioMed-transformers had more wins than Longformer and TransformerXL.

The experimental evidence provided in this study shows that, with fewer resources, concatenated BioMed-Transformers can improve overall micro and macro F1 scores for multi-label problems with long medical text. In addition, for multi-label problems with many tail-end labels, multi-BioMed-Transformers outperform other language models when F1 scores of tail-end labels are compared directly.

There are many avenues of research that arise directly from this research. If processing time or resources are not an issue, then continuous training of TransformerXL and Longformer on health-related data might improve prediction accuracy possibly even for tail-end labels. Concatenating TransformerXL or Longformer is also a possibility. ICD-9 codes have a tree-like hierarchy nature. Hence, predicting ICD-9 codes as a hierarchical multi-label classification problem using transformers to encode medical text is another relevant avenue to explore.

References

1. Amin-Nejad, A., Ive, J., Velupillai, S.: Exploring transformer text generation for medical dataset augmentation. In: LREC, pp. 4699–4708 (2020)
2. Aubert, C.E., et al.: Patterns of multimorbidity associated with 30-day readmission: a multinational study. BMC Publ. Health 19(1), 738 (2019)
3. Beltagy, I., Peters, M., Cohan, A.: LongFormer: the long-document transformer. arXiv preprint arXiv:2004.05150 (2020)
4. Chalkidis, I., Fergadiotis, M., Kotitsas, S., Malakasiotis, P., Aletras, N., Androutsopoulos, I.: An empirical study on large-scale multi-label text classification including few and zero-shot labels. In: Proceedings of the 2020 Conference on Empirical Methods in Natural Language Processing (EMNLP), pp. 7503–7515 (2020)
5. Cox, D.R.: The regression analysis of binary sequences. J. Roy. Stat. Soc. Ser. B (Methodol.) 20(2), 215–232 (1958)
6. Dai, Z., Yang, Z., Yang, Y., Carbonell, J., Le, Q., Salakhutdinov, R.: TransformerXL: attentive language models beyond a fixed-length context. In: ACL (2019)
7. Devlin, J., Chang, M., Lee, K., Toutanova, K.: BERT: pre-training of deep bidirectional transformers for language understanding. In: NAACL-HLT (2019)
8. Flegel, K.: What we need to learn about multimorbidity. CMAJ 190(34) (2018)
9. Gao, S., et al.: Limitations of transformers on clinical text classification. IEEE J. Biomed. Health Inform. 1–12 (2021). https://doi.org/10.1109/JBHI.2021.3062322
10. Gu, Y., et al.: Domain-specific language model pretraining for biomedical natural language processing. arXiv preprint arXiv:2007.15779 (2020)
11. Gururangan, S., et al.: Don't stop pretraining: adapt language models to domains and tasks. In: Proceedings of ACL (2020)
12. Johnson, A.E., et al.: MIMIC-III, a freely accessible critical care database. Sci. Data 3, 160035 (2016)
13. Kim, Y.: Convolutional neural networks for sentence classification. In: EMNLP, pp. 1746–1751. Association for Computational Linguistics (2014)

14. Kingma, D.P., Ba, J.: Adam: a method for stochastic optimization. In: International Conference on Learning Representations (ICLR) (2015)
15. Kurata, G., Xiang, B., Zhou, B.: Improved neural network-based multi-label classification with better initialization leveraging label co-occurrence. In: Proceedings of the 2016 Conference of the North American Chapter of the Association for Computational Linguistics: Human Language Technologies, pp. 521–526 (2016)
16. Liu, Y., Cheng, H., Klopfer, R., Schaaf, T., Gormley, M.R.: Effective convolutional attention network for multi-label clinical document classification. EMNLP 2021 (2021)
17. Liu, Y., et al.: RoBERTa: a robustly optimized BERT pretraining approach. arXiv preprint arXiv:1907.11692 (2019)
18. Moons, E., Khanna, A., Akkasi, A., Moens, M.F.: A comparison of deep learning methods for ICD coding of clinical records. Appl. Sci. **10**(15), 5262 (2020)
19. Mullenbach, J., Wiegreffe, S., Duke, J., Sun, J., Eisenstein, J.: Explainable prediction of medical codes from clinical text. In: Proceedings of the 2018 Conference of the North American Chapter of the Association for Computational Linguistics: Human Language Technologies, vol. 1. ACL, New Orleans (2018)
20. Si, Y., Roberts, K.: Hierarchical transformer networks for longitudinal clinical document classification. arXiv preprint arXiv:2104.08444 (2021)
21. Tsoumakas, G., Katakis, I., Vlahavas, I.: Mining multi-label data. In: Maimon, O., Rokach, L. (eds.) Data Mining and Knowledge Discovery Handbook, pp. 667–685. Springer, Boston (2009). https://doi.org/10.1007/978-0-387-09823-4_34
22. Vaswani, A., et al.: Attention is all you need. Adv. Neural Inf. Process. Syst. **30**, 5998–6008 (2017)
23. Yogarajan, V., Gouk, H., Smith, T., Mayo, M., Pfahringer, B.: Comparing high dimensional word embeddings trained on medical text to bag-of-words for predicting medical codes. In: Nguyen, N.T., Jearanaitanakij, K., Selamat, A., Trawiński, B., Chittayasothorn, S. (eds.) ACIIDS 2020. LNCS (LNAI), vol. 12033, pp. 97–108. Springer, Cham (2020). https://doi.org/10.1007/978-3-030-41964-6_9
24. Yogarajan, V., Montiel, J., Smith, T., Pfahringer, B.: Transformers for multi-label classification of medical text: an empirical comparison. In: Tucker, A., Henriques Abreu, P., Cardoso, J., Pereira Rodrigues, P., Riaño, D. (eds.) AIME 2021. LNCS (LNAI), vol. 12721, pp. 114–123. Springer, Cham (2021). https://doi.org/10.1007/978-3-030-77211-6_12
25. Zhang, M.L., Zhou, Z.H.: A review on multi-label learning algorithms. IEEE Trans. Knowl. Data Eng. **26**(8), 1819–1837 (2013)
26. Zhang, W., Yan, J., Wang, X., Zha, H.: Deep extreme multi-label learning. In: ACM on International Conference on Multimedia Retrieval, pp. 100–107 (2018)

Eliciting Knowledge from Pretrained Language Models for Prototypical Prompt Verbalizer

Yinyi Wei, Tong Mo[✉], Yongtao Jiang, Weiping Li, and Wen Zhao

Peking University, Beijing, China
wyyy@pku.edu.cn, motong@ss.pku.edu.cn

Abstract. Recent advances on prompt-tuning cast few-shot classification tasks as a masked language modeling problem. By wrapping input into a template and using a verbalizer which constructs a mapping between label space and label word space, prompt-tuning can achieve excellent results in few-shot scenarios. However, typical prompt-tuning needs a manually designed verbalizer which requires domain expertise and human efforts. And the insufficient label space may introduce considerable bias into the results. In this paper, we focus on eliciting knowledge from pretrained language models and propose a prototypical prompt verbalizer for prompt-tuning. Labels are represented by prototypical embeddings in the feature space rather than by discrete words. The distances between the embedding at the masked position of input and prototypical embeddings are used as classification criterion. To address the problem of random initialization of parameters in zero-shot settings, we elicit knowledge from pretrained language models to form initial prototypical embeddings. Our method optimizes models by contrastive learning. Extensive experimental results on several many-class text classification datasets with low-resource settings demonstrate the effectiveness of our approach compared with other verbalizer construction methods. Our implementation is at https://github.com/Ydongd/prototypical-prompt-verbalizer.

Keywords: Prompt-tuning · Few-shot text classification · Contrastive learning · Prototypical networks

1 Introduction

In recent years, pretrained language models (PLMs) have shown excellent performance for language understanding and language generation in NLP tasks [13]. The most widely used method for using PLMs is fine-tuning [9]. By adding a classifier on the top of PLMs, fine-tuning has achieved remarkable results on supervised tasks compared with traditional methods. However, since the parameters of the classifier in fine-tuning are randomly initialized, it needs sufficient

This work was supported by the Research on Intelligent Text Understanding Technology of Green Development on Big Data (No. DM202002).

E. Pimenidis et al. (Eds.): ICANN 2022, LNCS 13530, pp. 222–233, 2022.
https://doi.org/10.1007/978-3-031-15931-2_19

labeled data for training, thus fine-tuning is hard to obtain satisfactory results in scenarios with little labeled data. And the gap between pretraining objective and downstream tasks will hinder the transfer of knowledge in PLMs.

To alleviate this issue, prompt-tuning, a new paradigm for using PLMs, has been proposed for low-resource works to narrow the gap between pretraining objective and downstream tasks [15]. The main idea of prompt-tuning is to transfer a downstream task into a cloze question, which is consistent with the pretraining process of PLMs. Take text classification for an example, the input sentence is wrapped into a task-specific template, e.g.,"[Category: [MASK]] [SENTENCE]", where [SENTENCE] is filled with the input sentence and [MASK] is served as the set of predicted words. After constructing a verbalizer, a mapping between label space and label word space, a predicted word from [MASK] can be easily transformed into the corresponding label. Since a verbalizer directly determines the effectiveness of classification, how to construct a good verbalizer becomes a very important issue in prompt-tuning.

The traditional verbalizer construction methods construct an one-to-one mapping [14,15] or one-to-many mapping [7] by manually or automatically selecting label words. Methods which use discrete words to build verbalizers can't summarize the semantics of a label well and make the coverage of a label vulnerable. And deciding which label words to choose to represent a particular task's label requires a lot of domain expertise and human efforts.

To eliminate the impact of discrete words, soft prompt verbalizers have been proposed [6,19]. Soft prompt verbalizers treat labels as trainable tokens and the optimization objective is set to a cross entropy loss between output of [MASK] token and label tokens. Such methods are difficult to form highly representational and meaningful label embeddings, and are also hard to apply in zero-shot scenarios because both label tokens and classifiers are randomly initialized.

In this paper, we propose prototypical prompt verbalizer to address the above issues. By using prototypical networks, we generate prototypical embeddings for different labels in the feature space to summarize the semantic information of labels. We select the label corresponding to the prototypical embedding closest to the embedding of [MASK] token as the classification result. To overcome the difficulties of application in scenarios with few labeled training samples when training from scratch, we use the word corresponding to each label in the instruction document and a small number of sentences containing this word in the unlabeled corpus to form initial prototypical embeddings by a manual template. Note that although we also use some of the label words here, we do not need to do operations such as filtering and expansion, we only use the label words to form initial prototypical embeddings, not to select the final label. Even though there is a lot of noise in the selected sentences containing specific words, the semantics of labels can still be extracted to some extent. Based on contrastive learning, we devise three different objective functions to optimize the models. In summary, the main contributions of our work are:

- We design a method which can generate prototypical embeddings for labels as semantic representations in the feature space and use contrastive learning

at instance-instance and instance-label level to learn meaningful and interpretable prototypical embeddings.
- For zero-shot scenario, we use some unlabeled sentences containing specific words to generate initial prototypical embeddings.
- Results of extensive experiments on three many-class text classification datasets with low-resource settings demonstrate the effectiveness of our approach.

2 Related Work

Verbalizer Construction. In prompt-tuning, there are two key factors: template and verbalizer. When in low-resource settings, how to construct a good verbalizer becomes an essential factor in improving the efficiency of prompt-tuning. Current verbalizers are divided into two main categories: word-based verbalizers [7,14,15] and embedding-based verbalziers [6,19]. The former may lead to weak label coverage and the construction of such verbalizers may require domain expertise and human efforts. While the latter is hard to apply in zero-shot settings and it is a challenging issue to form meaningful and interpretable label embeddings with current methods.

Contrastive Learning. Contrastive learning [5], aiming to learn good representations by constructing positive instances and negative instances, is widely used for self-supervised representation learning mainly in domain of computer vision [18]. As for natural language processing, some well-known works also apply the idea of contrastive learning, such as Word2Vec [12] and BERT [9]. In NLP tasks, contrastive learning is usually used for generating high-quality text representations based on the construction of positive and negative samples [4].

Prototypical Networks. In few-shot classification tasks, a classifier needs to generate label representations with insufficient instances. To address this issue, some works [8,16] have proposed to use prototypical networks to learn representations for labels in the feature space. In contrast to traditional approaches, prototypical networks can learn a metric space where classification can be performed by computing distances from the input representation to prototypical representations of labels. The approach introduces a semantic generalization of labels, which can achieve excellent results with limited data. Some works have applied prototypical networks to other domains, e.g., information extraction [3].

3 Method

In this section, we present our method to construct a prototypical prompt verbalizer. Firstly, we describe general paradigm of prompt-tuning. Secondly, we elaborate our prototypical prompt verbalizer in detail. Finally, we introduce the different settings in zero-shot and few-shot scenarios.

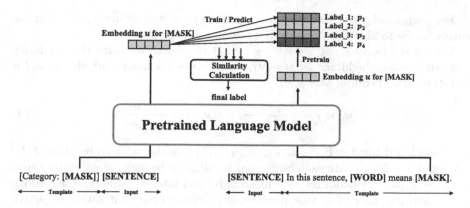

Fig. 1. Overview of our method. The right side shows the pretraining process, where the model knowledge is elicited through a manual template combined with a specific word. The left side is the training process. Both pretraining and training process are trained with contrastive objective function.

3.1 Overview

General Prompt-Tuning. Formally, denote $\mathcal{M}$, $\mathcal{T}$ and $\mathcal{V}$ as pretrained language model, template function and verbalizer function, respectively. Given an input x, template function $\mathcal{T}$ inserts pieces of texts into x to convert it into the corresponding input of $\mathcal{M}$ which has a [MASK] token in it, i.e., $x_p = \mathcal{T}(x)$. Let V be the label words set, Y be the label set. $\mathcal{V} : Y \to V$ is a mapping from label space to label word space, $\mathcal{V}(y)$ represents label words corresponding to label y. Then for input x, the probability of label y is

$$P(y|x) = \sigma(P_{\mathcal{M}}([\text{MASK}] = v|x_p)|v \in \mathcal{V}(y)) \tag{1}$$

where $\sigma(\cdot)$ determines which aggregation function to be used for labels with several different label words, such as *max* or *average*.

With prompt-tuning, a classification problem can be transferred into a masked language modeling problem by filling the [MASK] token in the input.

Prototypical Prompt Verbalizer. In prototypical prompt verbalizer, instead of directly predicting the corresponding label words from [MASK] token, we first generate prototypical embeddings which capture the main semantic information of labels, then use them to conduct classification.

Given an input x, we first convert it into a template-based input with a [MASK] token: $x_p = \mathcal{T}(x)$, then we feed x_p into pretrained language model $\mathcal{M}$ and obtain the last layer's hidden state of output $h = \mathcal{M}(x_p)$. Like general prototypical networks, We put the embedding of the [MASK] token $h_{[\text{MASK}]} \in \mathbb{R}^M$ through an embedding function $f : \mathbb{R}^M \to \mathbb{R}^D$ to get a mask embedding:

$$f(h_{[\text{MASK}]}) = u \tag{2}$$

For each label $y \in Y$, we generate a prototypical embedding $p_y \in \mathbb{R}^D$ in the feature space to abstract the essential semantics of y.

Cosine similarity $s : \mathbb{R}^D \times \mathbb{R}^D \to [-1, 1]$ is used to measure the similarity between mask embeddings as $s(u_i, u_j)$ and between a mask embedding and a prototypical embedding as $s(p, u)$:

$$s(u_i, u_j) = \frac{u_i \cdot u_j}{\|u_i\| \, \|u_j\|}, \quad s(p, u) = \frac{p \cdot u}{\|p\| \, \|u\|} \tag{3}$$

A batch is defined as $\mathcal{B} = \{u_0, u_1, \ldots, u_{N-1}\}$, u_i is the mask embedding of the i-th input x_i, $|\mathcal{B}| = N$. In each batch, our intuition is to make mask embeddings and prototypical embeddings have meaningful and interpretable representations in the feature space. For this purpose, we define three contrastive objective functions and all three objective functions are used in a batch $\mathcal{B}$.

The first objective function aims to keep embeddings of the same kind close to each other and embeddings of different kinds away from each other. Inspired by [17] and [3], we define it as:

$$\mathcal{L}_s = -\frac{1}{N^2} \sum_{i,j} \log \frac{\Theta(i, j)}{\Theta(i, j) + \sum_{j', \pi(j') \neq \pi(i)} \exp(s(u_i, u'_j))} \tag{4}$$

where $\Theta(i, j) = \exp(\varphi(i, j) s(u_i, u_j))$, $\varphi(i, j)$ is a function to indicate whether u_i and u_j having the same label, i.e., given two embeddings u_i and u_j, if they have the same label, then $\varphi(i, j) = 1$, otherwise 0. $\pi(i)$ denotes the label of u_i.

The second and third objective functions aim at learning meaningful prototypical embeddings. Given a label y and its prototypical embedding p_y, the second objective function keeps a embedding labeled y close to p_y and away from $p_{y'}$ where $y' \neq y$. While the third objective function keeps p_y close to the embeddings labeled y and away from the embeddings labeled y' where $y' \neq y$.

$$\mathcal{L}_{p_1} = -\frac{1}{N} \sum_i \log \frac{\exp(s(u_i, p_{\pi(i)}))}{\sum_k \exp(s(u_i, p_k))} \tag{5}$$

$$\mathcal{L}_{p_2} = -\frac{1}{N} \sum_i \log \frac{\exp(s(p_{\pi(i)}, u_i))}{\sum_{j, j = i | \pi(j') \neq \pi(i)} \exp(s(p_{\pi(i)}, u_j))} \tag{6}$$

Finally, combining the above three objective functions with hyperparameters $\lambda_1, \lambda_2, \lambda_3$, the full objective function is computed as:

$$\mathcal{L} = \lambda_1 \mathcal{L}_s + \lambda_2 \mathcal{L}_{p_1} + \lambda_3 \mathcal{L}_{p_2} \tag{7}$$

Given an input x, u is the mask embedding for x, then the probability for label y is:

$$p(y|x) = \frac{\exp(s(u, p_y))}{\sum_k \exp(s(u, p_k))} \tag{8}$$

Our method is shown in Fig. 1, we will detail the use in zero-shot and few-shot scenarios with pretraining and training process in following sections.

3.2   Few-Shot Settings

Given the set of templates $\mathcal{T}_{\mathcal{D}}$ for dataset $\mathcal{D}$. For $\mathcal{T}_i \in \mathcal{T}_{\mathcal{D}}$, we wrap input sentence into $\mathcal{T}_i$ and take the embedding of [MASK] token to form prototypical embeddings as mentioned above. By taking advantage of mask embeddings and prototypical embeddings, we can efficiently get the label of input sentence. We name this process training in our method.

3.3   Zero-Shot Settings

In zero-shot settings, it is challenging to initialize prototypical embeddings for labels. To alleviate this issue, we use a manually designed template to elicit knowledge from $\mathcal{M}$ to form initial prototypical embeddings for labels.

For a specific label y, we use its corresponding literal word v in the instruction document and sample a small amount of unlabeled sentences $\mathcal{Q} = \{q_1, q_2, \ldots, q_Q\}$ containing v from the training set with labels removed. Having the word v and a sentence q_i, we wrap them into a template $\mathcal{T}_z$: "[SENTENCE] In this sentence, [WORD] means [MASK]." where [SENTENCE] is filled with q_i and [WORD] is filled with v.

Then we take the embedding of [MASK] token as the mask embedding and perform process as mentioned in the previous subsection. In this way, the initial prototypical embeddings can be obtained and we name this process pretraining in our method. Randomly sampled sentences may be very noisy due to different meanings of a specific word, however, the probability of a specific word with different meanings appearing in one sampling is relatively small, and to the purpose of simplicity, we do not prune them.

After getting the initialized prototypical embeddings, we can experiment with zero-shot settings by wrapping input sentence into template $\mathcal{T}_i \in \mathcal{T}_{\mathcal{D}}$ as stated in the previous subsection.

4   Experiments

In this section, we conduct experiments on three many-class text classification datasets to empirically demonstrate the effectiveness of our prototypical prompt verbalizer.

4.1   Datasets and Templates

We evaluate our proposed method on three widely-used topic classification datasets: AG's News, Yahoo Answers [20] and DBPedia [10]. Statistics of these datasets are shown in Table 1.

Table 1. Statistics for AG's News, Yahoo Answers and DBPedia.

Name	#Class	Test Size	Label Word
AG's News	4	7600	World, sports, business, technology&science
Yahoo Answers	10	60000	Society & culture, science & mathematics, health, Education & reference, computers & internet, sports, Business & finance, entertainment & music, Family & relationships, politics & government
DBPedia	14	70000	Company, school & university, artist, athlete, Politics, transportation, building, book & publication Village, animal, plant & tree, album, Film, river & mountain & lake

Due to the rich semantics and the high adaptability to different datasets, manual templates have an advantage over automatically generated templates in zero-shot and few-shot scenarios. To alleviate the bias in the results caused by different templates, we use four manual templates for each datasets as in [15] and [7].

4.2   Baselines

In this subsection, we introduce the baselines we use, including fine-tuning, general prompt-tuning and soft prompt verbalizer. We compare the baselines with our prototypical prompt verbalizer in both with pretraining and without pretraining cases. Since our approach focuses on verbalizer for prompt-tuning, we compare with some recent and relevant prompt verbalizers rather than other self-supervised methods and meta-learning frameworks.

Fine-Tuning (FT). As the most popular paradigm for using pretrained language models, fine-tuning feeds the embedding in the last layer's hidden state of [CLS] token to a classifier to obtain the final label of input. We do not conduct zero-shot tests on fine-tuning, since the parameters of its classifier are randomly initialized.

Prompt-Tuning (PT). As mentioned previously, prompt-tuning, a new paradigm that has emerged recently, can work well with little training data with the help of pretrained masked language head. For each label, we use the words from the instruction document as its label words and test it in zero-shot and few-shot settings. In our implementation, there may be multiple label words corresponding to one label, so the verbalizer here is not a simple one-to-one mapping but one-to-many mapping for some labels.

Soft Prompt Verbalizer (SPV). Soft prompt verbalizer treats labels as trainable tokens to mitigate the impact of discrete words. Since the parameters of the classifier are randomly initialized, the approach is also not suitable for zero-shot scenario.

Table 2. Micro-F1 and standard deviation on AG's News, Yahoo Answers and DBPedia in zero- and few-shot scenarios. The best Micro-F1 scores are shown in the brackets. The best results among all methods for the same k-shot experiment are marked in bold. $w/\,p$ and $w/o\,p$ are whether to apply pretraining process for prototypical prompt verbalizer respectively. We conduct experiments on three different random seeds for four templates. In zero-shot scenario, the average results of all random seeds and the best results of one random seed are shown as avg and max respectively.

k	Method	AG's news	Yahoo answers	DBPedia
0	PT	71.84 ± 5.82 (**80.36**)	50.68 ± 10.43 (59.90)	65.10 ± 4.43 (71.10)
	$PPV_{w/\,p}$(avg)	67.12 ± 9.07 (77.00)	51.84 ± 11.41 (**59.93**)	78.86 ± 3.41 (**83.14**)
	$PPV_{w/\,p}$(max)	**72.14** ± 6.61 (77.00)	**53.85** ± 7.91 (**59.93**)	**80.65** ± 2.05 (**83.14**)
1	FT	38.38 ± 5.79 (45.23)	16.50 ± 3.09 (20.80)	30.67 ± 2.38 (33.56)
	PT	**77.69** ± 8.16 (**85.72**)	57.77 ± 3.39 (**62.19**)	93.97 ± 1.18 (**95.96**)
	SPV	35.82 ± 6.82 (47.00)	20.83 ± 3.43 (25.68)	64.77 ± 11.17 (76.67)
	$PPV_{w/\,p}$	74.29 ± 5.52 (80.27)	**57.79** ± 1.54 (60.16)	**94.21** ± 0.50 (94.96)
	$PPV_{w/o\,p}$	57.10 ± 6.34 (70.85)	24.21 ± 3.23 (28.84)	61.06 ± 4.47 (70.99)
5	FT	62.56 ± 16.02 (75.03)	56.09 ± 0.41 (56.65)	94.48 ± 0.87 (95.68)
	PT	**83.76** ± 2.08 (**86.88**)	61.61 ± 1.94 (**65.70**)	95.90 ± 0.77 (96.85)
	SPV	57.81 ± 7.51 (68.96)	46.67 ± 8.37 (57.61)	94.54 ± 2.01 (**97.49**)
	$PPV_{w/\,p}$	81.49 ± 1.59 (83.52)	**63.06** ± 1.55 (65.28)	**96.54** ± 0.41 (97.22)
	$PPV_{w/o\,p}$	79.00 ± 5.13 (84.03)	56.95 ± 5.45 (63.77)	95.46 ± 1.00 (96.95)
10	FT	82.76 ± 0.35 (83.07)	62.57 ± 1.16 (63.75)	97.61 ± 0.41 (98.05)
	PT	84.27 ± 2.02 (**87.30**)	64.19 ± 1.46 (65.94)	97.06 ± 0.80 (98.10)
	SPV	73.08 ± 5.25 (80.48)	59.68 ± 2.29 (62.86)	97.22 ± 0.38 (97.87)
	$PPV_{w/\,p}$	84.39 ± 1.11 (86.25)	65.05 ± 1.36 (**67.40**)	97.76 ± 0.25 (98.32)
	$PPV_{w/o\,p}$	**84.73** ± 1.15 (86.28)	**65.41** ± 0.71 (66.39)	**97.89** ± 0.29 (**98.34**)
20	FT	85.23 ± 0.18 (85.44)	66.85 ± 0.34 (67.29)	98.01 ± 0.19 (98.15)
	PT	86.23 ± 1.28 (88.03)	67.11 ± 0.66 (68.61)	98.11 ± 0.18 (98.32)
	SPV	82.52 ± 2.69 (85.48)	65.78 ± 1.28 (68.00)	98.01 ± 0.26 (98.44)
	$PPV_{w/\,p}$	86.84 ± 0.92 (**88.40**)	67.80 ± 0.73 (69.00)	98.25 ± 0.23 (98.48)
	$PPV_{w/o\,p}$	**86.92** ± 0.79 (88.11)	**68.22** ± 0.91 (**69.87**)	**98.34** ± 0.19 (**98.63**)

4.3 Implementation Details

In zero-shot scenario, models evaluate on the entire test set without training on the labeled training data and we cut sentences from unlabeled corpus by nltk [1]. While in few-shot scenario, we carry out 1, 5, 10 and 20-shot experiments. For a k-shot experiment, we randomly select k instances of each class from the training set as the new training set and test the model on the entire test set.

When pretraining a prototypical prompt verbalizer, we sample 60 sentences for AG's News, 40 sentences for Yahoo Answers, 30 sentences for DBPedia.

For all experiments, we use RoBERTa-large [11] as backbone to keep in line with previous works and use Micro-F1 as test metrics. For fine-tuning, prompt-tuning and prototypical prompt verbalizer, we use our own framework. For soft prompt verbalizer, we use OpenPrompt framework [2]. We select AdamW with the learning rate of $3e - 5$. The size of embedding function is set to 256 and the max sequence length is set to 512. We train the model for 10 epochs with the batchsize setting to 8 in each experiment. For objective functions, we set

$\lambda_1 = \lambda_2 = \lambda_3 = 0.5$. We conduct experiments on three different random seeds for four templates, that means twelve experiments are performed for each result.

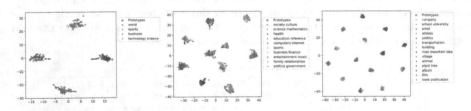

Fig. 2. Prototypical embeddings and mask embeddings on three datasets after 20-shot training with prototypical prompt verbalizer and visualized after dimension reduction by t-SNE.

4.4 Results and Analysis

Experimental Results. In this subsection, we detail the results of our method and perform an insightful analysis. Experimental results are shown in Table 2.

In zero-shot settings, since the randomly sampled sentences used for pretraining are noisy, which leads to unexpected deviations in the semantics of the generated initial prototypical embeddings, the results of pretraining on various sentences differ to some extent. However, the results still indicate effectiveness. On average, our method works better on DBPedia and Yahoo Answers compared with prompt-tuning. In terms of the best results, our method outperforms prompt-tuning on all three datasets. The results show that the pretraining process can elicit knowledge from pretrained language model well, and to some extent matches the masked language model head trained on large-scale corpora.

In few-shot settings, our method is proven to be powerful. Prototypical prompt verbalizer without pretraining beats fine-tuning and soft prompt verbalizer on 1-shot and 5-shot experiments, but the results are weaker than prompt-tuning due to insufficient samples for contrastive learning. Comparison with soft prompt verbalizer demonstrates that our method can generate high quality, meaningful and interpretable prototypical embeddings in the feature space. With pretraining process, prototypical prompt verbalizer can obtain initial prototypical embeddings for labels and achieve better results in comparison to prompt-tuning except on AG's News. We attribute the reason why our method do not work as well as prompt-tuning in 1-shot and 5-shot scenarios on AG's News to too few categories and training samples which result in inadequate contrastive learning. When in 10-shot and 20-shot scenarios, our method outperforms prompt-tuning with and without pretraining, however, the unpretrained one can attain better results with respect to the pretrained one. The major reason is that the semantics of initial prototypical embeddings generated in the pretraining process are a bit different from the real prototypical embeddings, which takes more time to reach the global optimum and also has a higher probability of falling

Table 3. Results on Yahoo Answers with trainable parameters after freezing the pretrained language model. Since the mask language head of prompt-tuning has parameters tied to the input layer which do not participate in the optimization process, we list it in the brackets. Results are obtained from three random seeds for four templates.

Method	5-shot	20-shot	# Param ($\times 10^4$)
SPV	18.66 ± 2.88	37.06 ± 4.11	1.024
PT	58.49 ± 5.42	62.82 ± 3.88	110.2 (5147.1)
$PPV_{w/o\,p}$	11.91 ± 2.37	17.74 ± 6.39	26.4
$PPV_{w/\,p}$	59.13 ± 1.94	61.02 ± 1.99	26.4

Table 4. Results on Yahoo Answers with different combination of losses. Results are obtained from one random seed for four templates.

Loss	0-shot	5-shot	20-shot
$\mathcal{L}_s$	11.62 ± 2.35	9.12 ± 2.64	6.27 ± 0.85
$\mathcal{L}_{p1} + \mathcal{L}_{p2}$	39.63 ± 17.38	59.51 ± 2.86	67.88 ± 0.46
$\mathcal{L}_s + \mathcal{L}_{p1}$	45.77 ± 17.11	59.58 ± 2.42	68.32 ± 0.45
$\mathcal{L}_s + \mathcal{L}_{p2}$	41.89 ± 17.35	58.02 ± 2.48	68.27 ± 0.41
$\mathcal{L}_s + \mathcal{L}_{p1} + \mathcal{L}_{p2}$	48.64 ± 16.72	60.70 ± 2.31	68.55 ± 0.45

into the local optimum. Prototypical embeddings and mask embeddings after 20-shot training are visualized in Fig. 2.

The pretrained prototypical prompt verbalizer performs worse than the one without pretraining when the number of training samples increases, which also indicates from another perspective that the semantics of the label words are still some distance away from the semantics of the generated prototypical embeddings which can better abstract the semantics of labels.

Freezing the Pretrained Language Model. We further freeze the pretrained language model and conduct experiments on Yahoo Answers as illustrated in Table 3 with the number of head parameters. The goal of prototypical prompt verbalizer is to form prototypical embeddings, where limited trainable parameters will make it hard to train. Soft prompt verbalizer, on the other hand, only needs to construct a mapping from the output embeddings to the label space and is therefore easier to train. After pretraining, prototypical prompt verbalizer basically forms prototypical embeddings, so it obtains fine results. However, due to the numerous parameters of mask language head, prompt-tuning will achieve better results when the size of training set increases.

Effect of Objective Function. To illustrate the effectiveness of our objective function, we conduct experiments with different combination of losses. As shown in Table 4, $\mathcal{L}_{p1}$ and $\mathcal{L}_{p2}$ are used to form prototypical embeddings while $\mathcal{L}_s$

allows embeddings with identical labels to be aggregataed and embeddings with different labels to be dispersed in the feature space.

Table 5. Results on three datasets in zero-shot settings with pretraining on different data sources. Results are obtained from three random seeds for four templates.

Source	AG's news	Yahoo answers	DBPedia
Unlabeled Set	67.12 ± 9.07	51.84 ± 11.41	78.86 ± 3.41
Wikidata	64.19 ± 6.67	49.95 ± 6.21	76.57 ± 7.18

Pretraining on Other Data Sources. To explore whether the pretraining process works on other sources as well, we conduct experiments with unlabeled training set and a small part of Wikidata as shown in Table 5. It is notable that DBPedia is also derived from Wikidata. The results illustrate that pretraining is also valid on other data sources. And no matter what data source is used, fluctuations can be significant due to the large noise in the pretraining process.

5   Conclusion

In this paper, we propose prototypical prompt verbalizer to enhance the semantic scope of labels by forming prototypical embeddings and construct a mapping from output of pretrained language models to the feature space. To obtain meaningful and interpretable embeddings, we optimize models with contrastive objective functions. In order to solve the problem of poor results caused by parameter initialization in zero-shot scenarios, we propose to conduct pretraining on a small amount of unlabeled training set. The experiments show the effectiveness and potential of our method. However, the existence of large noise in randomly sampled sentences may seriously affect the pretraining results, and we will mitigate this issue in the future with denoising and self-supervision measures.

References

1. Bird, S., Klein, E., Loper, E.: Natural language processing with Python: analyzing text with the natural language toolkit (2009)
2. Ding, N., et al.: OpenPrompt: aopen-source framework for prompt-learning. In Proceedings of the 60th Annual Meeting of the Association for Computational Linguistics: System Demonstrations (ACL-SD) (2022)
3. Ding, N., et al.: Prototypical representation learning for relation extraction. In: International Conference on Learning Representations (ICLR) (2021)
4. Gao, T., Yao, X., Chen, D.: SimCSE: simple contrastive learning of sentence embeddings. In: Proceedings of the 2021 Conference on Empirical Methods in Natural Language Processing (EMNLP) (2021)

5. Hadsell, R., Chopra, S., LeCun, Y.: Dimensionality reduction by learning an invariant mapping. In: Proceedings of the IEEE Computer Society Conference on Computer Vision and Pattern Recognition (CVPR) (2006)
6. Hambardzumyan, K., Khachatrian, H., May, J.: Warp: word-level adversarial reprogramming. In: Proceedings of the 59th Annual Meeting of the Association for Computational Linguistics and the 11th International Joint Conference on Natural Language Processing (ACL-IJCNLP) (2021)
7. Hu, S., et al.: Knowledgeable prompt-tuning: incorporating knowledge into prompt verbalizer for text classification. In: Proceedings of the 60th Annual Meeting of the Association for Computational Linguistics (ACL) (2022)
8. Ji, Z., Chai, X., Yu, Y., Pang, Y., Zhang, Z.: Improved prototypical networks for few-shot learning. Pattern Recogn. Lett. (2020)
9. Devlin, J., Kenton, M.-W.C., Toutanova, L.K.: BERT: pre-training of deep bidirectional transformers for language understanding. In: Proceedings of the 2019 Conference of the North American Chapter of the Association for Computational Linguistics: Human Language Technologies (NAACL-HLT) (2019)
10. Lehmann, J., et al.: DBpedia - a large-scale, multilingual knowledge base extracted from Wikipedia. Semantic Web (2015)
11. Liu, Y., et al.: RoBERTa: a robustly optimized BERT pretraining approach. arXiv preprint arXiv:1907.11692 (2019)
12. Mikolov, T., Chen, K., Corrado, G., Dean, J.: Efficient estimation of word representations in vector space. In: International Conference on Learning Representations (ICLR) (2013)
13. Roberts, A., Raffel, C., Shazeer, N.: How much knowledge can you pack into the parameters of a language model? In: Proceedings of the 2020 Conference on Empirical Methods in Natural Language Processing (EMNLP) (2020)
14. Schick, T., Schmid, H., Schütze, H.: Automatically identifying words that can serve as labels for few-shot text classification. In: Proceedings of the 28th International Conference on Computational Linguistics (COLING) (2020)
15. Schick, T., Schütze, H.: Exploiting cloze-questions for few-shot text classification and natural language inference. In: Proceedings of the 16th Conference of the European Chapter of the Association for Computational Linguistics (EACL) (2021)
16. Snell, J., Swersky, K., Zemel, R.: Prototypical networks for few-shot learning. Adv. Neural Inf. Process. Syst. (2017)
17. Soares, L.B., Fitzgerald, N., Ling, J., Kwiatkowski, T.: Matching the blanks: distributional similarity for relation learning. In: Proceedings of the 57th Annual Meeting of the Association for Computational Linguistics (ACL) (2019)
18. Wu, Z., Xiong, Y., Yu, S.X., Lin, D.: Unsupervised feature learning via nonparametric instance discrimination. In: Proceedings of the IEEE Computer Society Conference on Computer Vision and Pattern Recognition (CVPR) (2018)
19. Zhang, N., et al.: Differentiable prompt makes pre-trained language models better few-shot learners. arXiv preprint arXiv:2108.13161 (2021)
20. Zhang, X., Zhao, J., LeCun, Y.: Character-level convolutional networks for text classification. Adv. Neural Inf. Process. Syst. (2015)

Integrating Label Semantic Similarity Scores into Multi-label Text Classification

Zihao Chen, Yang Liu, Baitai Cheng, and Jing Peng[✉]

Wuhan University of Technology, No. 122 Luosi Road, Wuhan, Hubei, China
{305306,271790,chengbaitai,pengjing}@whut.edu.cn

Abstract. The target of multi-label text classification (MLTC) is to annotate texts with the most relevant labels from a candidate label set. In MLTC models, representing a true label as a one-hot vector is a common practice. However, the inadequate one-hot representation may ignore the similar predicted scores between semantically relevant labels that share the same text information in the same document. To overcome this challenge and improve the performance of multi-label text classification tasks, we propose a model for learning label embedding to calculate the semantic **S**imilarity **S**cores between label embeddings and document dense vector. Then adaptively integrate them with the **O**ne-hot **V**ector predicted score (SSOV). SSOV has two parts, one using a transformer model to extract the text information to build a one-hot vector to improve the performance of each label predict score. The other part feeds the document word embeddings to a deep learning network and generates a dense vector to learn label embeddings, which can explicitly measure the similarity score with the document's dense vector by cosine similarity. Meanwhile, we construct a new loss function that can **A**daptively **W**eighted above two parts' score to calculate loss value (AWLoss). Furthermore, AWLoss can also assign weights to labels to eliminate the limitation of BCELoss. SSOV outperforms the state-of-the-art methods on all three benchmark datasets.

Keywords: Text classification · Multi label · Label relevance

1 Introduction

Multi-label text classification, a significant task in natural language processing, has been widely applied in topic recognition [1], question answering [2], sentimental analysis [3] and so on. In the MLTC dataset, each training sample contains multiple labels, so these labels have similar semantic information. Moreover, some datasets have most of the training samples belonging to a few head labels, while a large number of tail labels only contain rarely positive samples.

Nowadays, in machine learning and natural language processing, researchers have made great efforts to investigate various methods to improve the performance of models for multi-label text classification. Among them, deep learning-based approaches have been successful. They can fully extract the semantic information of the text to construct a classifier, such as XML-CNN [4] and BERT

© The Author(s), under exclusive license to Springer Nature Switzerland AG 2022
E. Pimenidis et al. (Eds.): ICANN 2022, LNCS 13530, pp. 234–245, 2022.
https://doi.org/10.1007/978-3-031-15931-2_20

[5]. However, they simply encode the labels as one-hot vectors, which ignores the dependencies of label-document and label-label.

In order to explore the association between labels, some researchers have proposed some classification models that focus on how to exploit label structure [6], label content meaning [7] and [8], or label co-occurrence patterns [9]. Nevertheless, these methods ignore the unbalanced distribution of the labels. Recently, HTTN [10] used semantic relevance between labels and transferred the knowledge learned from data-rich labels to help data-poor labels. However, this knowledge migration ignores the independence between labels, which can easily cause redundancy of information, and negatively affect classification performance. Furthermore, all the above multi-label text classification models use BCELoss with limitations on tail labels.

In this paper, thus, we propose the SSOV for multi-label classification tasks. Depending on different learning tasks, our model is designed in two parts, and constructing AWLoss to adaptive weighted different part score to calculate loss value. A part of SSOV is called one-hot vector scoring network, and we employ a transformer model that can fully capture the semantic information of the raw text to construct a one-hot vector to predict probability score, aiming to improve the accuracy of each label's score. The other part is named label similarity scoring network. It is well known that cosine similarity can be used to measure the semantic relevance between word embeddings, so we feed document word embeddings into a network to generate dense vectors, aiming to learn label embeddings similar to word embeddings for efficiently computing label semantic similarity scores. Furthermore, learned label embedding will help to explore the label-label dependencies since labels that have similar semantics have a close score to each other. The contributions of our work can be summarized as follows.

- SSOV is proposed to adaptively combine one-hot vector predicted scores and label semantic similarity scores, which improve the accuracy of each label and take into account the correlation between labels that enhance label generalization performance.
- We construct a deep learning network to generate a dense vector from document word embeddings to learned label embedding that can help to explore the label-document and label-label dependencies.
- We construct a new loss function AWLoss that adaptive weighted different part scores to calculate loss values in SSOV and assigned weights to labels to eliminate the limitation of BCELoss.

2   Related Work

With the development of NLP, deep learning-based methods have shown significant advancement in MLTC because it can learn better text representations from the text, such as CNN [11], RNN [12], attention mechanism Attentionxml [13], large pre-trained language models like ELMO [14] and BERT. These models share the same learning paradigm: a deep learning model for text representation, a simple one-hot classifier for predicting labels, and BCELoss between the predicted probability distribution and the one-hot label vector. However, this learning paradigm has many shortcomings. One-hot label representation in the general text classification task assumes that all categories are independent. In MLTC, each training sample is annotated with multiple labels; thus, these labels are semantically or statistically linked. Simply representing labels with one-hot vectors cannot consider the semantic connections.

To learn the dependencies between labels, JointEO [15] introduces an attention framework that measures the compatibility of embeddings between text sequences and labels. SGM [16] proposed to view the MLTC task as a sequence generation problem and apply a sequence generation model with a novel decoder structure to solve it. LSAN uses label semantic information to determine the semantic connection between labels and documents for constructing label-specific document representation. Although these models change the learning paradigm of traditional deep learning-based methods by considering the semantic information of labels, which improves the classification performance, they do not consider the unbalance distribution of the label set and the text representation model is too simple to extract enough information. Recently, HTTN taking advantage of semantic relationships between labels, transfer the knowledge learned from data-rich classes to data-poor classes, which alleviates the negative impact caused by the poor tail label's training samples. Nevertheless, such knowledge migration easily causes redundancy of information and negatively affects classification performance.

3   Methodology

This section will introduce SSOV and AWLoss, as shown in Fig. 1. SSOV consists of two parts: Part I is a one-hot classifier scoring network, which constructs a one-hot vector by fully capturing the semantic information of the raw text through the pre-training model BERT; Part II is label similarity scoring network, which generates dense vector through a deep learning network to learn label embedding. AWLoss can adaptive weighted different part scores to calculate loss values in SSOV and assign exponentially weighted moving average to labels to eliminate the limitation of BCELoss in tail labels.

3.1   Problem Definition

Given a training set with N samples $\{(x_i, y_i)\}_{i=1}^{N}$, where x_i represents the original text, $y_i \in \{0,1\}^l$ represents the corresponding label set, and l is the total number of labels, and each training sample contains many words $x_i = \{w_1, \ldots, w_q, \ldots, w_n\}$, if x_i feed into deep learning model $w_q \in R^k$ denotes the qth word vector that encoded by word2vec [17], or as a input for transformer models w_q is the qth token based on the pre-trained model, and n denotes the length of the training text. SSOV contains two parts. One is used to construct a one-hot vector $C \in R^l$ to get each label predict score and the other generates a dense vector $V \in R^k$ to calculate the cosine similarity with the initialized label

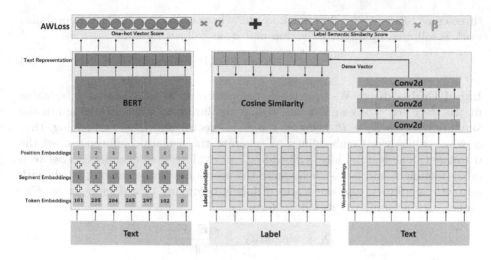

Fig. 1. An overview of SSOV

embedding that loaded by word2vec $E \in R^{l \times k}$ to obtain a semantic relevance score $D_i \in R^l$.

3.2   One-Hot Vector Scoring Network

Text Representation: Transformer models have shown excellent performance in fully extracting semantic information, so we chose the pre-trained model BERT for our text representation model. In order to make full use of the BERT, we concatenate the [CLS] token in the hidden state of the last five layers as text representation. The formula is as follows:

$$H_i = \text{BERT}\left(\theta_{BERT}, x_i\right) = [h_1, \cdots, h_5] \tag{1}$$

x_i denotes the ith training sample, and θ_{BERT} denotes pre-trained model BERT parameters.

One-Hot Vector Scoring: This layer consists of a fully connected layer, which predicts each label's score. We drop out high-dimensional text vector representation to prevent overfitting. We input the textual representation Hi to the fully connected layer:

$$C_i = W_h H_i + b_h \tag{2}$$

$W_h \in R^{5t*l}$, C_i is the one-hot vector of dimension l for the ith training sample.

3.3   Label Similarity Scoring Network

Dense Vector: In order to sufficiently extract the word embeddings of the document to generate a dense vector $V_i \in R^k$ to learn label embedding, we employ three convolutional neural network layers, where each convolutional neural network is followed by a relu activation unit σ, as follows formula:

$$V_i = (W\sigma(\text{Conv2d}(x_i)) + b) \tag{3}$$

Label Embedding: We load labels embedding from word2vec as a trainable matrix $E \in R^{l \times k}$, so we can use cosine similarity to efficiently compute the similarity scores $D_i \in R^l$ between the dense vector and label embedding, that is why we use word embeddings to generate the semantic information of the document. The learned label embedding can explore the dependencies between label-document and label-label, where the scores are similar among labels with semantic similarity, and the scores of labels belonging to a document are also higher. Cosine similarity as follows formula:

$$D_i = \text{similarity} = \frac{E \cdot V_i}{\|E\| \, \|V_i\|} \tag{4}$$

3.4 Adaptive Weighted Loss

To enable the model to automatically learn different weights assigned to the one-hot vector score and label embedding score, AWLoss sets two adaptive parameters α and β, multiple different part scores separately, and then calculates the loss value. Moreover, in BCELoss, because tail labels lack positive training samples in the whole dataset, the model is overfitting the head labels with considerable loss value and underfitting the tail labels with small loss value when parameters update, so the positive tail labels will be selectively ignored by the model. Thus, to balance the loss value of different frequency labels, we assign exponentially weighted moving average to smoothly scale up the loss value of the tail labels in different frequencies. The formula is as follows:

$$L = \sum_{i=1}^{l} \alpha * [\omega_i y_i * \log \sigma(c_i) + (1 - y_i) * \log(1 - \sigma(c_i))] + \beta * [y_i * (1 - d_i) + (1 - y_i) * d_i] \tag{5}$$

In AWLoss, we sort the labels based on occurrences in the training set, and optional occurrences o are chosen as the threshold to tail labels. σ is sigmoid function. c_i is the predicted score of the ith label in the one-hot vector $C \in R^l$. ω_i is the weight of the tail label base on ω_o as following formula, where δ is a hyperparameter and $\omega_{o+1} = 1$.

$$\omega_{o-j} = \sum_{j=0}^{o-1} \delta * \omega_{o+1-j} + (1 - \delta) * (j + 1) \tag{6}$$

4   Experiment Setup

4.1   Datasets

We uses three benchmark datasets that commonly used for multi-label text classification, RCV1, AAPD, and EUR-Lex. They are described in the following.

RCV1 [18]: Reuters Corpus Volume I contains 103 classes and over 80,000 manually categorized news.

AAPD: Collecting abstracts of 55,840 papers from the arXiv computer science domain, and containing 54 classes.

EUR-Lex [19]: Dataset from the EU legal domain has 3956 tag categories, 11585 training sets, and 3856 test sets.

4.2 Baseline Models

SSOV is a deep learning-based model. Thus the current state-of-the-art deep learning-based MLTC methods are selected as baselines, including traditional deep learning model XML-CNN, BERT, and label relationship learning model SGM, LSAN, and meta-knowledge transfer model HTTN.

4.3 Parameter Setting

The training and testing sample sets are consistent with LSAN. BERT model has 12 layers and 768 hidden dimensions h. We select 300 convolutional kernels of size 3 for maximum pooling of size 3 and step of size 2 in Conv2d. The dimension of label embedding is 300. Our model is trained with a constant learning rate of 1e-4 weight decay for bias and layer norm weight.

4.4 Evaluation Metrics

We use two kinds of metrics, precision at top K ($P@k$) and the Normalized Discounted Cumulated Gains at top K ($nDCG@k$), to evaluate prediction performance as follows.

$$P@k = \frac{1}{k} \sum_{l \in \text{rank}_k(\hat{y})} y_l \tag{7}$$

$$DCG@k = \sum_{l \in \text{rank}_k(\hat{y})} \frac{y_l}{\log(l+1)} \tag{8}$$

$$nDCG@k = \frac{DCG@k}{\sum_{l=1}^{\min(k, \|y\|_0)} \frac{1}{\log(l+1)}} \tag{9}$$

where $\hat{y}$ denotes predicted score vector, $\text{rank}_k(y)$ is the label indexes of the top k highest scores of the current prediction result, $\|y\|_0$ counts the number of relevant labels in the ground truth label vector y.

5 Experimental Results

5.1 Comparison Results and Discussion

This section compares the SSOV model on three benchmark datasets with five baseline models. Evaluation methods are $P@K$ and $nDCG@K$ (K = 1, 3, 5) as

Table 1. Comparing SSOV with five baselines in terms of $P@K$

Datasets	Metrics	XML-CNN	BERT	SGM	LSAN	HTTN	SSOV (ours)
RCV1	P@1	95.75%	97.01%	95.37%	96.81%	95.86%	**97.50%**
	P@3	78.63%	82.31%	81.36%	81.89%	78.92%	**82.95%**
	P@5	54.94%	57.38%	53.06%	56.92%	55.27%	**57.61%**
AAPD	P@1	74.38%	85.32%	75.67%	85.28%	83.84%	**86.70%**
	P@3	53.84%	61.22%	56.75%	61.12%	59.92%	**61.53%**
	P@5	37.79%	41.56%	35.65%	41.84%	40.79%	**41.98%**
EUR-Lex	P@1	70.40%	82.64%	70.45%	79.17%	81.14%	**84.50%**
	P@3	54.98%	69.82%	60.37%	64.99%	67.62%	**71.80%**
	P@5	44.86%	57.92%	43.88%	53.67%	56.38%	**59.85%**

Table 2. Comparing SSOV with five baselines in terms of $nDCG@K$

Datasets	Metrics	XML-CNN	BERT	SGM	LSAN	HTTN	SSOV (ours)
RCV1	nDCG@3	89.89%	93.38%	91.76%	92.83%	89.61%	**93.86%**
	nDCG@5	90.77%	93.87%	90.69%	93.43%	90.86%	**94.39%**
AAPD	nDCG@3	71.12%	81.09%	72.36%	80.84%	79.27%	**82.12%**
	nDCG@5	75.93%	84.31%	75.35%	84.78%	82.67%	**85.61%**
EUR-Lex	nDCG@3	58.62%	73.11%	60.72%	68.32%	70.89%	**74.65%**
	nDCG@5	53.10%	66.76%	55.24%	62.47%	64.42%	**68.55%**

described above. Tables 1 and 2 show the best results of each model on the test texts. In all three datasets, the traditional deep learning model XML-CNN does not work as well as the non-transformer models SGM, LSAN, and HTTN that have learned the relationship between labels, which indicates that the incorporation of the relationship between labels has enhanced the classification effect when the semantic extraction models are comparable. BERT that based on a pre-trained transformer model achieves better results than other baselines, which shows that BERT can fully extract semantic information to construct a one-hot vector and improve the prediction performance; however, it ignores the relationship between labels, and the improvement is concentrated on the head labels, which is also proved by the subsequent experiments. However, in the EUR-Lex dataset, there are thousands of labels, most of which are tail labels, and HTTN achieves better results than the non-transformer model. It is shown that moderating the long-tail problem is beneficial for performance improvement. LSAN achieves better results than HTTN in AAPD and RCV1 datasets because there are enough training samples and few labels in the AAPD and RCV1 dataset, the semantic connection between labels is weak and long-tailed problem is not prominent. However, HTTN knowledge migration may cause redundancy of information.

SSOV constructs a one-hot vector based on the BERT model, which can fully extract semantic information to maintain the excellent performance of the transformer model in scoring head labels. Therefore, our model improves more than 2% over the non-transformer model. SSOV also consider similarity score between labels by employing label embedding to calculate semantic similarity score, which improves the generalization performance of label prediction. Improving 1% compare to the BERT model without considering the label relationship. Furthermore, we also proposed AWLoss to adaptive weighted different part scores to calculate loss values in SSOV and assign exponentially weighted moving average to labels to eliminate the limitation of BCELoss, so that our model has good performance on the tail tab as well. In the EUR-Lex dataset, we outperformed HTTN by 3%.

5.2   Ablation Test

SSOV consists of two parts integrated by AWLoss, so we designed four ablation experiments. The first is a traditional text representation model BERT without label similarity scoring network for constructing a one-hot vector scoring network and BCELoss function for calculating loss value, and we denote it as B+B. The second one uses BERT for constructing a one-hot vector scoring network and Conv2d to construct a label similarity scoring network, and BCELoss for loss value calculation, which we denote as B+C+B. The third one is using BERT to construct a one-hot vector scoring network and learn label embedding at the same time with AWLoss, and we denote it as B+Λ; the last one is to use BERT for constructing one-hot vector scoring network and Conv2d to construct label similarity scoring network and AWLoss for calculating loss value, which we denote as B+C+A. The experimental results are shown in Table 3.

Table 3. Result of the ablation test

Datasets	Metrics	B+B	B+C+B	B+A	B+C+A (ours)
RCV1	P@1	97.01%	97.06%	97.10%	**97.50%**
	P@3	82.31%	82.46%	82.76%	**82.95%**
	P@5	57.38%	57.23%	57.40%	**57.61%**
AAPD	P@1	85.32%	85.40%	85.70%	**86.70%**
	P@3	61.22%	60.53%	60.93%	**61.53%**
	P@5	41.56%	41.06%	40.98%	**41.98%**
EUR-Lex	P@1	82.64%	83.41%	83.50%	**84.50%**
	P@3	69.82%	70.70%	71.37%	**71.80%**
	P@5	57.92%	59.14%	59.53%	**59.85%**

B+B does not consider the relationship between labels and uses BCELoss, which is limited on the tail labels, so the effect is worse than other models, and it shows that ignoring the label relationship will have a negative impact on the classification performance. B+C+B takes into account the relationship between labels. However, we only sum the one-hot vector score and label similarity score since the BCELoss cannot calculate the loss value by adaptively integrating them according to the different weights of the score, and BCEloss is not suitable for calculating the label similarity score. So we designed AWLoss can eliminate this problem, and our model is improved by about 1% compared to B+C+B. B+A only uses BERT to construct a one-hot vector and learn label embedding simultaneously. However, the semantic information extracted by BERT fails to learn label embedding properly because the label embedding is loaded from word2vec, while BERT is trained based on token embedding. That is why our model constructs a network for extracting document word embeddings information to learn label embedding.

5.3 Comparison on Tail Labels

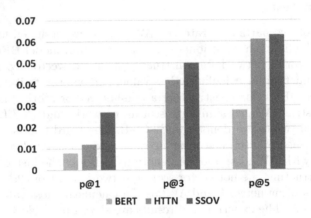

Fig. 2. Precision@k for tail labels with label occurrences less than 5 in EUR-Lex

To validate the performance of SSOV on tail labels, we evaluate them with label occurrences less than 5 in EUR-Lex. Figure 2 shows the prediction results in terms of P@1, P@3, and P@5 obtained by BERT, HTTN, and SSOV. The figure shows that the SSOV model improves nearly 300% over BERT and HTTN on P@1, which indicates that our model has excellent prediction performance on tail labels than baseline. The SSOV has a weak improvement on P@5, because P@5 require 5 predicted labels for evaluation; the number of true labels is usually smaller than this, which has adverse effects on the improvement of the results. BERT achieves poor results on tail labels since it will over-fit the head labels.

5.4 Different Hyperparameters of AWLoss

In order to investigate the effect of different values of hyperparameters δ in AWLoss, we selected three values: $\delta = 0.90$, $\delta = 0.95$ and $\delta = 0.98$ for experiments on the EUR-Lex dataset. The experimental results are shown in Fig. 3. It can be observed that the best results are obtained by assigning an exponentially weighted moving average weight of $\delta = 0.95$ to labels.

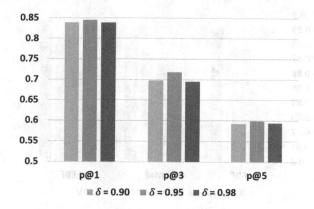

Fig. 3. Different values of hyperparameters δ in AWLoss.

5.5   Applications in COVID-19 Literature Multi-label Classification

Since the beginning of the novel coronavirus (COVID19), the scientific community has been focused on the fight against this disease. In this context, the National Institutes of Health (NIH) has implemented the LitCovid platform [20], a literature database of COVID-19-related articles in PubMed, which has accumulated more than 180,000 articles, with millions of accesses each month by users worldwide. Moreover, the number of COVID-19-related articles in LitCovid grows by about 10,000 articles per month. The rapid literature growth significantly increases the burden of LitCovid curation. Therefore, a system that can automatically annotate COVID-19-related articles with relevant topics would greatly minimize manual costs, speed up the efficiency of article annotation, and make the document's retrieval easier for scientists, policymakers, healthcare professionals, or even the general public.

The LitCovid platform provides a dataset to train and test our models. The training, development, and testing sets contain 24,960, 6,239, and 2,500 PubMed articles in LitCovid. The topic classification step assigns 8 topics to the COVID-19 related articles. We use SSOV for the COVID-19 literature multi-label classification task. As shown in Fig. 4. We compared the performance of our model with the baseline model using the test dataset provided by LitCovid with the evaluation metrics Micro F-Measure (MiF), Macro F-Measure (MaF), and Example Based F-Measure (EBF). Our model improves by more than 1% compared to the baseline in the three evaluation metrics.

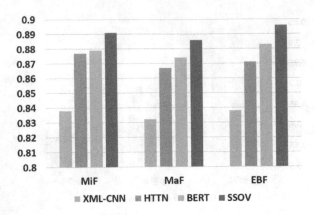

Fig. 4. Compare the performance of SSOV with the baseline model on the test set provided by LitCovid

6   Conclusion

We propose the SSOV construct a one-hot vector and integrate label similarity score for multi-label classification. We also construct a new loss function AWLoss, to adaptively weight different parts' predict scores to calculate loss value and assign exponentially weighted moving average to labels. Therefore, AWLoss can smoothly scale up the loss value of the tail labels in different frequencies and eliminate the limitation of BCELoss. The advantages of SSOV are demonstrated by extensive experiments with state-of-the-art methods on three benchmark datasets.

References

1. Yang, Z., Yang, D., Dyer, C., He, X., Smola, A., Hovy, E.H.: Hierarchical attention networks for document classification. In: NAACL (2016)
2. Kumar, A.J.R., et al.: Ask me anything: dynamic memory networks for natural language processing. In: ICML (2016)
3. Cambria, E., Olsher, D.J., Rajagopal, D.: SentiUet 3: a common and common-sense knowledge base for cognition-driven sentiment analysis. In: AAAI (2014)
4. Liu, J., Chang, W.-C., Wu, Y., Yang, Y.: Deep learning for extreme multi-label text classification. In: Proceedings of the 40th International ACM SIGIR Conference on Research and Development in Information Retrieval (2017)
5. Devlin, J., Chang, M.-W., Lee, K., Toutanova, K.: BERT: pre-training of deep bidirectional transformers for language understanding. In: NAACL (2019)
6. Huang, X., Chen, B., Xiao, L., Jing, L.: Label-aware document representation via hybrid attention for extreme multi-label text classification. arXiv:1905.10070 (2019)
7. Pappas, N., Henderson, J.: Gile: a generalized input-label embedding for text classification. Trans. Assoc. Comput. Linguist. **7**, 139–155 (2019)
8. Xiao, L., Huang, X., Chen, B., Jing, L.: Label-specific document representation for multi-label text classification. In: EMNLP (2019)

9. Kurata, G., Xiang, B., Zhou, B.: Improved neural network-based multi-label classification with better initialization leveraging label co-occurrence. In: NAACL (2016)
10. Xiao, L., Zhang, X., Jing, L., Huang, C., Song, M.: Does head label help for long-tailed multi-label text classification. arXiv, abs/2101.09704 (2021)
11. Kim, Y.: Convolutional neural networks for sentence classification. In: EMNLP (2014)
12. Liu, P., Qiu, X., Huang, X.: Recurrent neural network for text classification with multi-task learning. arXiv, abs/1605.05101 (2016)
13. You, R., Dai, S., Zhang, Z., Mamitsuka, H., Zhu, S.: AttentionXML: extreme multi-label text classification with multi-label attention based recurrent neural networks. arXiv, abs/1811.01727 (2018)
14. Peters, M.E., et al.: Deep contextualized word representations. In: NAACL (2018)
15. Wang, G., et al.: Joint embedding of words and labels for text classification. arXiv, abs/1805.04174 (2018)
16. Yang, P., Sun, X., Li, W., Ma, S., Wei, W., Wang, H.: SGM: sequence generation model for multi-label classification. In: COLING (2018)
17. Mikolov, T., Chen, K., Corrado, G.S., Dean, J.: Efficient estimation of word representations in vector space. In: ICLR (2013)
18. Lewis, D.D., Yang, Y., Rose, T.G., Li, F.: RCV1: a new benchmark collection for text categorization research. J. Mach. Learn. Res. **5**, 361–397 (2004)
19. Luttinen, J., Raiko, T., Ilin, A.: European conference on machine learning and knowledge discovery in databases (2014)
20. Chen, Q., Allot, A., Zhiyong, L.: LitCovid: an open database of Covid-19 literature. Nucleic Acids Res. **49**, D1534–D1540 (2021)

Learning Flexible Translation Between Robot Actions and Language Descriptions

Ozan Özdemir[(✉)], Matthias Kerzel, Cornelius Weber, Jae Hee Lee, and Stefan Wermter

Knowledge Technology, Department of Informatics, University of Hamburg, Hamburg, Germany
{ozan.oezdemir,matthias.kerzel,cornelius.weber,jae.hee.lee, stefan.wermter}@uni-hamburg.de
http://www.knowledge-technology.info

Abstract. Handling various robot action-language translation tasks flexibly is an essential requirement for natural interaction between a robot and a human. Previous approaches require change in the configuration of the model architecture per task during inference, which undermines the premise of multi-task learning. In this work, we propose the paired gated autoencoders (PGAE) for flexible translation between robot actions and language descriptions in a tabletop object manipulation scenario. We train our model in an end-to-end fashion by pairing each action with appropriate descriptions that contain a signal informing about the translation direction. During inference, our model can flexibly translate from action to language and vice versa according to the given language signal. Moreover, with the option to use a pretrained language model as the language encoder, our model has the potential to recognise unseen natural language input. Another capability of our model is that it can recognise and imitate actions of another agent by utilising robot demonstrations. The experiment results highlight the flexible bidirectional translation capabilities of our approach alongside with the ability to generalise to the actions of the opposite-sitting agent.

Keywords: Language grounding · Autoencoders · Multimodal fusion · Robot language learning · Embodiment

1 Introduction

Learning language involves multiple modalities such as audio, vision and proprioception. For example, a colour word refers to a visual concept; sensing the weight of an object is related to the concept of force; the concept of position such as left and right can be learnt with proprioception and vision. More modalities can be enumerated that help with learning language but the essential component of language learning pertains to embodiment (i.e. having a body and interacting in the environment) [4]. The embodied language learning or language grounding

The original version of this chapter was revised: this chapter was previously published non-open access. The correction to this chapter is available at
https://doi.org/10.1007/978-3-031-15931-2_67

E. Pimenidis et al. (Eds.): ICANN 2022, LNCS 13530, pp. 246–257, 2022.
https://doi.org/10.1007/978-3-031-15931-2_21

has recently been a topic of interest at the crossroads between natural language processing (NLP) and robotics [1,4,13,17].

Inspired by the early language development in children in which interactions in the environment are paired with language, language grounding approaches have achieved learning representations, forming of abstractions, sequence-to-sequence learning and bidirectional learning of action and language. However, these approaches are not designed to endow a robot with the autonomy to understand and choose the appropriate action to carry out during an interaction with a human. They are either designed

Fig. 1. Our object manipulation scenario: a) an example action ('push cyan slowly') undertaken by NICO [10] b) the same action undertaken by the opposite agent as seen by NICO. (Color figure online)

to carry out a single task such as recognising an instruction and executing it [7,13,16,17] or they can handle multiple tasks but they require the task mode in advance to know what is expected of them [14,18,19]. In contrast, a truly autonomous agent must be able to decide whether to produce language or execute an action according to the verbal instruction given by its human partner. Therefore, end-to-end multimodal and multi-task models, which do not require adaptation to new tasks by the experimenter, are desired.

Fig. 2. The abstract architecture with four different tasks: 'describe', 'execute', 'repeat action' and 'repeat language'. The PGAE architecture consists of encoders, decoders and a GMU bottleneck. Each column shows our architecture with the information flow (indicated by the arrows) per task. The thick green arrows denote the main information flow in the respective signal's task.

In this work, we address the problem of flexible bidirectional translation between robot actions and language. We define flexibility as translating between the two modalities without having to reconfigure the model for a specific task during inference. According to our scenario (Fig. 1), we expect our agent to flexibly translate from action to language and vice versa, viz. given textual descriptions, joint angle values and visual features, our agent must either manipulate an object or describe the object manipulation act carried by itself or the second agent depending on the situation. To this end, we introduce the paired gated autoencoders (PGAE) architecture for flexible translation between robot actions and language, realised by our humanoid robot NICO [9,10] in the simulation environment. PGAE includes an attention mechanism in its bottleneck which allows the model to directly exchange information between the action and language modalities. The attention mechanism, which is adopted from the gated multimodal units (GMU) [3], acts as a filter to pick information between the modalities across all dimensions. Moreover, we signal the task by prepending a phrase to the language input and ensure that our model recognises the task and is trained accordingly. Thus, during inference, our model is able to do each of the translation tasks (Fig. 2) according to user input without having to configure the model in advance. Further, we test a realistic setup in which the NICO robot can describe and repeat the actions of the opposite-sitting second agent. Our experiment results show that PGAE performs competitively in terms of translations between language and action with the previous approaches [18,19] that implicitly bind the two modalities and in turn could use only some parts of the network, which is set a priori according to the given translation task. Our contributions can be summarised as:

1. introducing an end-to-end neural network (NN) architecture that can flexibly handle various action-language translation tasks during inference, consistent with the training conditions,
2. enabling the robot to recognise and imitate both the self-performed actions and the actions of an opposite-sitting agent.

2   Related Work

Translation between language and action has been a topic of interest: there are approaches that learn the general mapping between objects and language as well as attributes like colour, texture and size [7,17], and there exist approaches that learn complex manipulation concepts [13,16]. However, these approaches can only translate from language to action as their focus is not on bidirectional translation. Other approaches can translate from action to language [6,8]. Only few approaches [1,2,14,18,19] are capable of bidirectional translation, i.e. they have the ability to translate a given action into language as well as to translate a given language description into an action.

Abramson et al. [1] propose a complex paradigm combining supervised learning, reinforcement learning (RL) and imitation learning in order to solve the problem of intelligently interacting in an abstract 3D play environment while using language. In the environment, two agents communicate with each other as one agent (setter) asks questions to or instructs the other (solver) that answers questions and interacts with objects according to a given instruction. However, the scenario is abstract as the objects are interacted with unrealistically. Hence, proprioception is not used as the actions are abstract. Therefore, the transfer of the approach from simulation to the real world is non-trivial.

Ogata et al. [14] propose an RNN-based model to enable bidirectional translation between compound sentences and robotic arm motions. Artificial bias vectors are used to bind the two modalities, which have separate RNNs, to enable flexible translation between them. Yamada et al. [18] introduce the paired recurrent autoencoders (PRAE) approach which can bidirectionally translate between robot actions and language in a one-to-one manner: each action has exactly one description. Similar to [14], PRAE consists of independent action and language networks and uses a binding loss to align the hidden representations of the paired actions and descriptions. PRAE cannot handle one-to-many mapping between action and language, i.e. when an action can be described by multiple descriptions. Moreover, it cannot flexibly change the direction of the translation during inference. For instance, to translate from action to language, PRAE accepts joint values and visual features through its action encoder and uses its description decoder alone to output a description - it practically excludes its description encoder and action decoder. Inspired by the PRAE architecture, we proposed the paired variational autoencoders (PVAE) [19] that can translate between a robot action and its multiple descriptions - we enabled one-to-many translation between actions and descriptions by utilising the stochastic gradient variational Bayes-based sampling (SGVB) [12] that randomises the hidden representation space so that descriptions that are equivalent in meaning are represented tightly together, whereas those that have different meanings are represented far from each other. Like PRAE, PVAE employs the binding loss to map descriptions and actions. Therefore, due to its artificial nature in its multimodality fusion, PVAE too must be in a certain configuration according to the desired translation direction. The aim of our work is therefore to lift this constraint and allow flexible use of the model triggered by a verbally provided signal.

3   Proposed Method: PGAE

Our paired gated autoencoders approach (PGAE) is a bidirectional translation model between robot actions and language. As can be seen in Fig. 3, PGAE consists of two autoencoders, namely language and action. It is intended to associate simple robot actions like pushing a cube on the table with their corresponding language descriptions. PGAE accepts as input language descriptions, visual features extracted from images and joint angle values. PGAE outputs language descriptions and joint angle values conditioned on visual features. Moreover, PGAE is trained end-to-end with a signal prepended to the language input indicating the expected output of the training iteration. Five different signals are randomly chosen during training at each iteration: 'describe', 'execute', 'repeat action', 'repeat both' and 'repeat language'.

Language Autoencoder. The language autoencoder (AE) accepts as input one-hot encoded words of a description (or the whole description at once when BERT is used as language encoder) and produces a description by outputting a word at each time step. The language AE has an encoder, a decoder and hidden layers (in the bottleneck) that contribute to the common hidden representations. The language encoder embeds a description of length $N + 1$, $(x_1, x_2, ..., x_{N+1})$, including the signal, into the final state f_{N+1} as follows:

$$h_t^{enc}, c_t^{enc} = \text{LSTM}(x_t, h_{t-1}^{enc}, c_{t-1}^{enc}) \quad (1 \leq t \leq N + 1),$$
$$f_{N+1}^{enc} = [h_{N+1}^{enc}; c_{N+1}^{enc}],$$

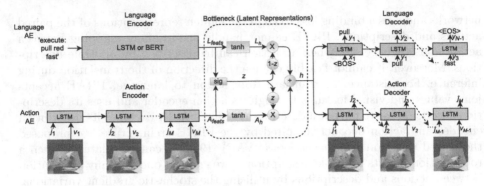

Fig. 3. The architecture of the PGAE model: Language encoder is either an LSTM or the BERT model. The action encoder and both decoders are LSTMs - we show unfolded versions of the LSTMs. The bottleneck, where the two streams are connected, is based on the GMU; z is the gating vector, whilst h is the shared representation vector.

where h_t^{enc} and c_t^{enc} are the hidden and cell state of the LSTM at time step t respectively. h_0^{enc} and c_0^{enc} are set as zero vectors, whereas x_1 is the signal word. The square brackets $[.;.]$ denote the concatenation operation. The LSTMs we use here and the action encoder and both decoders are a peephole LSTM [15] following [18,19]. The language encoder LSTM can also be replaced by a pretrained language model to recognise unconstrained user instructions. Specifically, we use the pretrained BERT Base model [5] as the language encoder. This variation of the model is called PGAE-BERT.

The language decoder autoregressively generates the descriptions word by word by expanding the shared latent representation vector h:

$$h_0^{dec}, c_0^{dec} = W^{dec} \cdot h + b^{dec},$$
$$h_t^{dec}, c_t^{dec} = \text{LSTM}(y_{t-1}, h_{t-1}^{dec}, c_{t-1}^{dec}) \quad (1 \leq t \leq N-1),$$
$$y_t = \text{soft}(W^{out} \cdot h_t^{dec} + b^{out}) \quad (1 \leq t \leq N-1),$$

where soft represents the softmax activation function. y_0 is the vector for the symbol indicating the beginning of the sentence, the <BOS> tag.

Action Autoencoder. The action autoencoder (AE) accepts a sequence of joint angle values and visual features as input and generates the appropriate joint angle values. It consists of an encoder, a decoder and latent layers (in the bottleneck) that contribute to the common latent representations. The action encoder encodes a sequence of length M, $((j_1, v_1), (j_2, v_2), ..., (j_M, v_M))$ that is the combination of joint angles j and visual features v. The visual features are extracted by the channel-separated convolutional autoencoder (CAE) in advance. The action encoder can be defined as[1]:

$$h_t^{\text{enc}}, c_t^{\text{enc}} = \text{LSTM}(v_t, j_t, h_{t-1}^{\text{enc}}, c_{t-1}^{\text{enc}}) \quad (1 \leq t \leq M),$$
$$f_M^{\text{enc}} = [h_M^{\text{enc}}; c_M^{\text{enc}}],$$

where h_t^{enc} and c_t^{enc} are the hidden and cell state of the LSTM at time step t. h_0^{enc}, c_0^{enc} are set as zero vectors. f_M^{enc} is the final state of the action encoder.

The action decoder generates the joint angles at each time step by recursively expanding the shared latent representation vector h:

$$h_0^{\text{dec}}, c_0^{\text{dec}} = W^{\text{dec}} \cdot h + b^{\text{dec}},$$
$$h_t^{\text{dec}}, c_t^{\text{dec}} = \text{LSTM}(v_t, \hat{j}_t, h_{t-1}^{\text{dec}}, c_{t-1}^{\text{dec}}) \quad (1 \leq t \leq M - 1),$$
$$\hat{j}_{t+1} = \tanh(W^{\text{out}} \cdot h_t^{\text{dec}} + b^{\text{out}}) \quad (1 \leq t \leq M - 1),$$

where tanh is the hyperbolic tangent activation function and $\hat{j}_1$ is equal to j_1, i.e. joint angle values at the initial time step. Visual features v are used as in teacher forcing.

Bottleneck. The language and action streams connect at the bottleneck, which is situated between the encoders and decoders of the model. We use a Gated Multimodal Unit (GMU) to fuse the language and action (joints, images) modalities. Thanks to its learned gating mechanism, GMU allows our model to flexibly learn multiple tasks according to the given command such as 'describe' or 'execute'. This way, our approach works in different translation directions using the whole model during inference without having to put the model in a specific mode. Our bottleneck can be defined with the following equations:

$$L_{\text{feats}} = f_{N+1}, A_{\text{feats}} = f_M,$$
$$L_h = \tanh(W^{\text{L}} \cdot L_{\text{feats}} + b^{\text{L}}),$$
$$A_h = \tanh(W^{\text{A}} \cdot A_{\text{feats}} + b^{\text{A}}),$$
$$z = \sigma(W^z \cdot [A_{\text{feats}}; L_{\text{feats}}] + b^z),$$
$$h = z \odot A_h + (1 - z) \odot L_h,$$

where σ denotes the sigmoid activation function, whilst tanh stands for the hyperbolic tangent activation function and $\odot$ is the Hadamard product. h represents the shared hidden representation vector and is used as input to both language and action decoders.

Signals. Five different signals are used during training. Four of them can be used during inference. According to the given signal, the input and output of the model change.

---

[1] Some symbols in the equations coincide with the symbols used for the language AE.

- **Describe** tells the model to describe the given action sequence, i.e. action-to-language translation. With this signal, the model accepts as input the sequence of visual features and joint angle values for the action as well as the <EOS> tag for language. The model is then trained to output the correct description and the static joint angle values corresponding to the final time step of the action sequence.
- **Execute** signals the model to execute the given language description, i.e. language-to-action translation. With this signal, the model expects to be fed with the whole description sentence, and joint angle values and visual features corresponding to the first time step of the action sequence. The model is then expected to output the joint angle values of the action sequence from the action decoder and the <EOS> from the language decoder.
- **Repeat Action** is the signal for reconstructing the sequence of joint angle values. PGAE expects as input the sequence of joint angle values and visual features for the action encoder and the <EOS> tag in addition to the signal for the language encoder. The action decoder reconstructs the joint values and the language decoder outputs the <EOS> tag.
- **Repeat Both** signal demands the paired language and action input to be present. With this signal, PGAE is trained similar to PVAE [19] end-to-end. The language encoder accepts the full description in addition to the phrase 'repeat both', whilst the action encoder accepts the corresponding action sequence (joint values and visual features). The language decoder and action decoder outputs the full description and joint angle values correspondingly. This signal is intended to be used only during training, since it is implausible to expect the robot to repeat an action and its description at the same time.
- **Repeat Language** is used for reconstructing the full description. The full description and the first time step of the action sequence are fed as input to the encoders. As output, the language decoder reconstructs the description and the action decoder outputs the joint angle values of the first time step.

Visual Feature Extraction. Following the previous work [19], we employ the channel-separated convolutional autoeconder architecture (CAE) to extract the visual features from images captured by the NICO robot. Instead of processing all three channels together, we train an instance of the CAE for each colour channel (red, green and blue) – i.e. channel separation. The channel separation technique has been shown to distinguish between the colours of the objects more accurately [19]. Each channel of 120×160 RGB images fed into the channel-separated CAE at a time. The channel-separated CAE consists of a convolutional encoder, a fully-connected bottleneck and a deconvolutional decoder. After training for the RGB channels separately, the channel-specific visual features are extracted from the bottleneck and then concatenated. The resulting visual features v are used as input to PGAE. For more details of the channel-separated CAE, please refer to the PVAE paper [19].

Loss Function. The overall loss is calculated by adding up the reconstruction losses, i.e. language loss and action loss. The language loss, L_{lang}, is defined as the cross entropy loss between input and output words, whereas the action loss, L_{act}, is defined as the mean squared error (MSE) between original and predicted joint values:

$$L_{\text{lang}} = \frac{1}{N-1} \sum_{t=1}^{N-1} \left(- \sum_{i=0}^{V-1} w^{[i]} x_{t+1}^{[i]} \log y_t^{[i]} \right),$$

$$L_{\text{act}} = \frac{1}{M-1} \sum_{t=1}^{M-1} \| j_{t+1} - \hat{j}_{t+1} \|_2^2,$$

where V is the vocabulary size, N is the number of words per description, M is the sequence length for an action trajectory and w is the weight vector used to counter the imbalance in the frequency of words. The overall loss is the sum of the language and action loss:

$$L_{\text{all}} = \alpha L_{\text{lang}} + \beta L_{\text{act}}$$

where α and β are weighting factors for language and action terms in the loss function. In our experiments, we set α and β to 1.

Training Details. To train PGAE and PGAE-BERT, we first extract visual features using our channel-separated CAE. The visual features are used to condition the actions depending on the cube arrangement, i.e., the action execution according to a given description is dependent on the position of the target cube. Both PGAE and PGAE-BERT are trained end-to-end. PGAE and PGAE-BERT are trained for 6,000 epochs with the gradient descent algorithm and Adam optimiser [11]. In our experiments, h has 50 dimensions, x has 28 dimensions, j has 5 dimensions, N is equal to 5 and M is 50 for fast and 100 for slow actions. We take the learning rate as 10^{-5} with a batch size of 6 samples after determining them as optimal hyperparameters. After a few trials, we have decided to freeze the weights of BERT during training as fine-tuning it reduces the performance of our model. Since BERT has millions of parameters, fine-tuning it leads to overfitting.

4   Experiment Results

We train and test our model on the paired robot actions and descriptions dataset [19] that involves 864 samples of sequences of images, joint values and textual descriptions. The dataset consists of simple manipulation of two cubes of different colours on the table by the humanoid NICO robot. The NICO robot is a child-size humanoid robot with a camera in each of its two eyes. The dataset was created using the Blender software[2]. According to our scenario, using its left arm,

---

[2] https://www.blender.org/.

NICO manipulates one of the two cubes on the table for each sample utilising the inverse kinematics solver provided on Blender. Each sample includes a sequence of first-person view images and joint angle values from NICO's left arm alongside a textual description of the action. In total, the dataset includes 12 distinct actions, 6 cube colours, 288 descriptions and 144 patterns (action-description-cube arrangement combinations). We slightly vary the 144 patterns six times randomly in terms of action execution in simulation. Out of 864 samples, we exclude 216 samples that involve every unique description and action type and use them as the test set. By carefully selecting the test samples, we ensure that the combinations of descriptions, action types and cube arrangements in the test set are not seen during training. For more details on the dataset, please consult the PVAE paper [19]. Additionally, we introduce a second agent that does the same actions and include the resulting images from the NICO's perspective. We use the visual features extracted from these images as additional input, and randomly select between them and the images that show NICO doing the actions. These cases are shown in Table 1, with the '-opposite' suffix for describing or repeating the action of the second agent, and with the '-self' suffix for describing or repeating the action of NICO. Therefore, PGAE-self and PGAE-opposite are the same model trained on the same dataset – the former is tested with self-agent (NICO's own) actions, while the latter with the second-agent actions. PGAE and PGAE-BERT are trained on the previous dataset as PVAE [19]. We test the models on action-to-language, language-to-action, action-to-action and language-to-language translations as shown in Table 1.

Table 1. Translation results for test set. Green background denotes the main output of the respective task (e.g., description for the action-to-language translation). As the opposite-sitting agent data is irrelevant for 'repeat language' and 'execute' tasks, PGAE-self and PGAE-opposite share those results.

	Describe Act.→Lang.	Repeat Lang. Lang.→Lang.	Execute Lang.→Act.	Repeat Act. Act.→Act.
Approach	Descr. Acc.	Descr. Acc.	Descr. Acc.	Descr. Acc.
PGAE	93.05%	96.30%	100%	100%
PGAE-BERT	94.91%	99.07%	100%	100%
PGAE-self	80.56%	93.98%	100%	100%
PGAE-opposite	65.28%			100%
Approach	J. Err. (nRMSE)	J. Err. (nRMSE)	J. Err. (nRMSE)	J. Err. (nRMSE)
PGAE	0.23%	0.37%	0.44%	0.44%
PGAE-BERT	0.21%	0.33%	0.44%	0.42%
PGAE-self	0.58%	0.73%	0.79%	0.89%
PGAE-opposite	2.40%			0.80%

Action-to-Language Translation. PGAE and its variants use the 'describe' signal as input to the language encoder to translate from action to language. The first result column of Table 1 reports the accuracy of predicted test descriptions for different approaches. In order for a generated description to be accepted as correct, all of its words must match the ground truth description according to our predefined grammar, i.e. action-colour-speed-<EOS>. Moreover, the second half of the table shows the normalised root-mean-square error (nRMSE) between the generated and ground truth joint values. We calculate nRMSE values by dividing the square root of the MSE (which is used as the action loss L_{act}) by the observed range of joint values. Accordingly, PGAE is competitive with the earlier approach, PVAE (achieves 100%, not given in the table), that has to be set in the specific configuration, which includes using only the action encoder and language decoder while bypassing the language encoder and action decoder by avoiding feeding any language input and not outputting the final joint values. Therefore, PVAE cannot output joint values when it is configured to be used for action-to-language translation. Both PGAE and PGAE-BERT, however, recognise the task from the signal in the language input and generate both the description and the joint values for all different tasks. Both PGAE and PGAE-BERT achieve near perfect joint value prediction. Moreover, PGAE-BERT performs slightly better than PGAE in terms of description accuracy. However, its main advantage over PGAE is that it has the potential to recognise unconstrained natural language due to the use of a pretrained language model.

In the setting where we demand the model to describe the action done by the opposite agent, our model achieves 65% accuracy (PGAE-opposite). It achieves 80% accuracy when describing NICO's own actions (PGAE-self). Moreover, the joint value error also increases slightly to over 2% for the case opposite-agent case, whereas it is comparable with the original approaches for PGAE-self. The decrease in the action-to-language accuracy is expected as introducing the second-agent actions makes the problem more challenging, e.g., pulling an object by the second agent might be interpreted as pushing the object by NICO itself. Moreover, this is an extra capability demonstrated by our approach.

Language-to-Action Translation. PGAE and its variants use the 'execute' signal prepended to the description for the translation from language to action. The description accuracy (whether <EOS> is outputted by the language decoder) and nRMSE between predicted and ground truth joint values for language to action translation are given in Column 'Lang.→Act.'. All of the approaches are able to generate near perfect joint values (less than 1% nRMSE). However, PVAE is not trained to generate descriptions (<EOS> in this case) when it is configured to execute descriptions (N.A.). This highlights the superiority of using signals as part of the language input and having a common hidden representation vector over the artificial use of a loss term to align two separate streams. Training PGAE with the demonstrations from the opposite-sitting agent does not significantly affect the action-to-language performance (0.79% for PGAE-self/PGAE-opposite).

Language-to-Language & Action-to-Action Translations. PGAE and PGAE-BERT are competitive with PVAE (achieves 100%, not given in the table) in terms of the description accuracy for language-to-language translation and slightly better in terms of the joint value prediction for the action-to-action translation. PVAE does not have the capacity to output joint values for language-to-language and descriptions for action-to-action translations, whereas PGAE and PGAE-BERT almost perfectly output the initial time-step joint values for language-to-language translation and achieves perfect description accuracy in action-to-action translation. Training PGAE with the additional opposite-sitting agent demonstrations slightly increases the joint value error in action-to-action translation for both the actions executed by NICO (PGAE-self) and by the second agent (PGAE-opposite).

5 Conclusion

We have introduced an end-to-end NN approach that can flexibly perform translation between robot actions and language descriptions in multiple directions, some of which involving both first-person actions and opposite-sitting agent actions. By integrating the task signal in the language input, our approach can recognise the given task and output the suitable descriptions and joint values during inference. Our approach, PGAE, exhibits competitive performance in all four translation tasks while having a consistent configuration across learning and inference. With the additional demonstrations from a second agent, our model can not only recognise and imitate its own actions but also the actions of the second agent despite the challenging nature of the task. To our knowledge, this skill set has not been modelled by previous approaches. In summary, PGAE can perform various translation tasks robustly without any change in the use of the architecture between learning and test time, which the previous approaches lacked, through its attention-based explicit multimodal fusion mechanism and the insertion of the task signal to the language input. Furthermore, the realism in our simulation promises sim-to-real transfer, which we will tackle in the future. Another avenue is to embed our model into a continuous human-robot dialogue framework in a closed-loop. Finally, we can utilise RL for more dexterous object manipulation with diverse ways to execute an action.

Acknowledgements. The authors gratefully acknowledge support from the German Research Foundation DFG under Project CML (TRR 169).

References

1. Abramson, J., et al.: Imitating interactive intelligence. arXiv preprint arXiv:2012.05672 (2020)
2. Antunes, A., Laflaquiere, A., Ogata, T., Cangelosi, A.: A bi-directional multiple timescales LSTM model for grounding of actions and verbs. In: 2019 IEEE/RSJ International Conference on Intelligent Robots and Systems (IROS), pp. 2614–2621 (2019)

3. Arevalo, J., Solorio, T., Montes-y-Gómez, M., González, F.A.: Gated multimodal networks. Neural Comput. Appl. **32**(14), 10209–10228 (2019). https://doi.org/10.1007/s00521-019-04559-1
4. Bisk, Y., et al.: Experience grounds language. In: Proceedings of the 2020 Conference on Empirical Methods in Natural Language Processing, pp. 8718–8735. Association for Computational Linguistics, November 2020
5. Devlin, J., Chang, M.-W., Lee, K., Toutanova, K.: BERT: pre-training of deep bidirectional transformers for language understanding. In: NAACL-HLT, no. 1 (2019)
6. Eisermann, A., Lee, J.H.: Weber, C., Wermter, S.: Generalization in multimodal language learning from simulation. In: Proceedings of the International Joint Conference on Neural Networks (IJCNN 2021), July 2021
7. Hatori, J., et al.: Interactively picking real-world objects with unconstrained spoken language instructions. In: 2018 IEEE International Conference on Robotics and Automation (ICRA), pp. 3774–3781. IEEE (2018)
8. Heinrich, S., et al.: Crossmodal language grounding in an embodied neurocognitive model. Front. Neurorobot. **14**, 52 (2020)
9. Kerzel, M., Pekarek-Rosin, T., Strahl, E., Heinrich, S., Wermter, S.: Teaching NICO how to grasp: an empirical study on crossmodal social interaction as a key factor for robots learning from humans. Front. Neurorobot. **14**, 28 (2020)
10. Kerzel, M., Strahl, E., Magg, S., Navarro-Guerrero, N., Heinrich, S., Wermter, S.: NICO-neuro-inspired COmpanion: a developmental humanoid robot platform for multimodal interaction. In: 2017 26th IEEE International Symposium on Robot and Human Interactive Communication (RO-MAN), pp. 113–120. IEEE (2017)
11. Kingma, D.P., Ba, J.: Adam: a method for stochastic optimization. In: 3rd International Conference on Learning Representations, ICLR, San Diego, CA, USA, 7–9 May 2015
12. Kingma, D.P., Welling, M.: Auto-encoding variational Bayes. In: Proceedings of International Conference on Learning Representations (ICLR), Banff, AB, Canada, 14–16 April 2014
13. Lynch, C., Sermanet, P.: Language conditioned imitation learning over unstructured data. Robot. Sci. Syst. (2021)
14. Ogata, T., Murase, M., Tani, J., Komatani, K., Okuno, H.G.: Two-way translation of compound sentences and arm motions by recurrent neural networks. In: 2007 IEEE/RSJ International Conference on Intelligent Robots and Systems, pp. 1858–1863 (2007)
15. Sak, H., Senior, A., Beaufays, F.: Long short-term memory recurrent neural network architectures for large scale acoustic modeling. In: Proceedings of InterSpeech 2014, pp. 338–342 (2014)
16. Shao, L., Migimatsu, T., Zhang, Q., Yang, K., Bohg, J.: Concept2Robot: learning manipulation concepts from instructions and human demonstrations. In: Proceedings of Robotics: Science and Systems (RSS) (2020)
17. Shridhar, M., Mittal, D., Hsu, D.: INGRESS: interactive visual grounding of referring expressions. Int. J. Robot. Res. **39**(2–3), 217–232 (2020)
18. Yamada, T., Matsunaga, H., Ogata, T.: Paired recurrent autoencoders for bidirectional translation between robot actions and linguistic descriptions. IEEE Robot. Autom. Lett. **3**(4), 3441–3448 (2018)
19. Ozan Özdemir, M.K., Wermter, S.: Embodied language learning with paired variational autoencoders. In: 2021 IEEE International Conference on Development and Learning (ICDL), pp. 1–6, August 2021

Learning Visually Grounded Human-Robot Dialog in a Hybrid Neural Architecture

Xiaowen Sun[✉], Cornelius Weber, Matthias Kerzel, Tom Weber, Mengdi Li,
and Stefan Wermter

Department of Informatics, Knowledge Technology, University of Hamburg,
Hamburg, Germany
{xiaowen.sun,cornelius.weber,matthias.kerzel,tom.weber,
stefan.wermter}@uni-hamburg.de, mli@informatik.uni-hamburg.de
http://www.knowledge-technology.info

Abstract. Conducting a dialog in human-robot interaction (HRI)
involves complexities that are hard to reconcile by individual research or
engineering works. Towards the development of a robotic dialog agent,
we develop a verbal and visual instruction scenario in which a robot
needs to enter into a dialog to resolve ambiguities. We propose a novel
hybrid neural architecture to learn the robotic part of the interaction.
A neural dialog state tracker learns to process the user input depending
on visual inputs and dialog instances. It uses variables to allow certain
generality to generate the robot's physical or verbal actions. We train it
on a new visual dialog dataset, test different forms of input representations, and validate the robot agent on unseen examples. We evaluate our
hybrid neural network approach in handling an HRI conversation scenario that is extendable to a real robot. Furthermore, we demonstrate
that the hybrid approach allows generalization to a large range of unseen
visual inputs and verbal instructions.

Keywords: Human-robot interaction · Visual dialog generation ·
Natural language processing · Computer vision · Recurrent neural
networks

1 Introduction

Human-robot interaction (HRI) utilizing dialog is a challenge for neural network
research. Open-domain dialog agents produce dialog actions of reasonable quality, but they do not pursue any specific goal [27]. In contrast, for real-world applications, dialog is usually domain-specific and goal-oriented. Task-oriented dialog
systems show good performance in specific tasks helping in our daily lives, such
as for making a restaurant reservation, receiving orders, getting technical support, or giving smart-home commands [2]. Beyond these language-based systems,

The original version of this chapter was revised: this chapter was previously published
non-open access. The correction to this chapter is available at
https://doi.org/10.1007/978-3-031-15931-2_67

E. Pimenidis et al. (Eds.): ICANN 2022, LNCS 13530, pp. 258–269, 2022.
https://doi.org/10.1007/978-3-031-15931-2_22

(a) Conversational scenario.

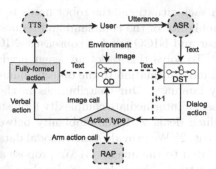

(b) Hybrid neural architecture.

Fig. 1. (a) Visually grounded human-robot conversational scenario. The user is talking to the NICO robot about objects on the table. (b) Hybrid neural architecture. White boxes: Object Detection (OD) and Dialog State Tracker (DST) are both trained components. Yellow boxes: Automatic Speech Recognition (ASR), Text to Speech (TTS) and Robotic Arm Planner (RAP) are pre-trained components. Blue boxes represent Human-Robot Interaction Policy (HRIP). The dashed arrows denote conditional input. (Color figure online)

visually grounded human-robot interaction is usually situated in an environment that can be perceived visually and with other sensors, and in which a robot can interact, or execute commands. Verbal interaction usually involves multi-turn dialog. Due to ambiguities in language or complex scenarios, if one person wants to instruct another person to perform a certain task, this often requires multiple turns to unambiguously determine the goal. Conducting a dialog that requires disambiguation remains a scientific challenge in visually grounded human-robot interaction.

The development of visually grounded dialog requires suitable multimodal datasets. Related areas like Visual Question Answering [10], Visual Dialog [6], Visual Dialog Generation [7], Image-Grounded Conversations [25], and CLEVR-dialog [18] are mainly focussed on understanding the image information, not the interaction within an environment. A seller-buyer interaction in a virtual shop is covered in the Situated and Interactive MultiModal Conversations (SIMMC) dataset [24], where the focus is however on fashion and furniture, but not HRI.

To address this gap, we designed the conversational scenario shown in Fig. 1a, presenting a new task and dataset in the area of robotic manipulation research. The robot, Neuro-Inspired COmpanion (NICO) [16], sits at a table on which there are some common household objects. The user uses natural language to instruct NICO to pick or point to one of those objects. We assume there are always three different objects on the table and the robot cannot point to two objects at once. Sometimes, the user's command may be ambiguous. For example, the user instruction could contain two targets (e.g. Show me the lemon and apple). NICO can understand that this is an ambiguous instruction and give feedback. Another situation is that the user gives an unambiguous instruction (e.g. Point to the red object), but multiple objects have the same color.

In such situations, the robot needs to use visual information to understand the ambiguity of the command and request the user for additional input. Once, the user and NICO reach a consensus, NICO will execute the appropriate action.

To solve this task, our agent needs to recognize the objects and relate the visual information to the objects' names, colors, and positions as communicated by language. Our contributions in the HRI domain are: 1) we propose a new task of intermediate complexity for visually grounded human-robot conversation, which deals with the ambiguity between human instructions and the environment. 2) We provide a multimodal dataset including images and dialog instances related to the images. 3) We propose a new architecture, a hybrid neural model that tracks the dialog state for the visually grounded human-robot conversation and evaluates the model's performance.

2   Background and Related Work

The Situated and Interactive Multimodal Conversations (SIMMC) incorporates multimodal inputs (e.g., vision, memories of previous interactions, and users' utterances) for multimodal actions (e.g., representing the search results while generating the agent's next utterance) [24]. The next generation of SIMMC 2.0 is still focussed on a shopping scenario [17], which is devised of four main benchmark tasks: Multimodal Disambiguation, Multimodal Coreference Resolution, Multimodal Dialog State Tracking, and Response Generation [17]. The primary task of SIMMC is dialog state tracking. To solve this task, many studies focus on transformer architecture, such as Bidirectional Encoder Representations from Transformers (BERT) [8], Bidirectional Auto Regressive Transformers (BART) [19] and Generative Pre-trained Transformer (GPT) [29] to solve this task recently [13,14,28].

Visual Question Answering (VQA) [10] and Visual Dialog (VisDial) [6] are used for common-sense learning of visual-language representations, which are both based on Microsoft Common Objects datasets [21]. In contrast, Guess-What? [7] is a two-player guessing game, which aims to find an unknown object in a rich image scene by question-answering strategies based on reinforcement learning. The CLEVR-dialog [18] dataset focuses on multi-round reasoning learning in visual dialog, which constructs a dialog grammar that is grounded in the scene graphs of the images from the CLEVR dataset. Lu et al. [22] present Vision-and-Language BERT (VilBERT) which extends BERT [8] to process visual and linguistic input. Murahari et al. [26] pretrained the VilBERT on the VQA [10] dataset and fine-tuned it on the VisDial dataset, then created the VisDial-BERT for multi-turn visually grounded conversations. The augmented extended train robots dataset [15], which expands the extended train robots dataset [1], offers tasks for a robotic agent to reach for objects in three-dimensional space based on augmented reality and a simulation environment. However, in all above approaches, no dialog studies focus on the visually grounded human-robot interaction domain.

A traditional dialog pipeline usually contains natural language understanding, a dialog manager, and natural language generation. The core part of a dialog

Table 1. List of instruction utterances. The parts left and right of the slash can be substituted for each other. An ambiguous instruction refers to multiple objects. An unambiguous instruction refers to one specific object. Show me: SM, Where is: WI, Point to: PT, Where are: WA.

Unambiguous instructions	`SM/ WI/ PT the [name].`
	`SM/ WI/ PT the [color] object/ [name].`
	`SM/ PT the [position] object/ [name].`
	`SM/ PT the [color] object/ [name] on the [position].`
Ambiguous instructions	`SM/ PT the object on the table.`
	`SM/ WA the [color1] and [color2] objects.`
	`SM/ WA the [name1] and [name2].`

system is the dialog manager, including a dialog state tracker and dialog policy [4,27]. Recurrent neural networks (RNNs) are usually trained in an end-to-end fashion to match an observable dialog history to output sentences [11]. A hybrid approach is also attractive for task-oriented dialog modelling, since it can combine multiple approaches, such as rule-based and data-driven [9]. Hybrid-code networks combine an RNN with domain-specific knowledge, which perform well on the bAbI dataset [3], and are applied to a real customer support domain [31].

Inspired by the lack of robotic visually grounded datasets, we generated an artificial multimodal dataset for our HRI domain, which mainly focuses on human use of language, including naturally occurring ambiguities, to instruct the humanoid robot to point to an object in the environment. Learning from the principle of the Hybrid-code networks, we train an RNN for dialog state tracking and define an HRI policy for our scenario.

3   Multimodal Dataset for Human-Robot Interaction

We propose a dataset consisting of two modalities, visual scenes and conversations in text form. The visual scenes were generated with Blender[1] and CoppeliaSim[2]. The user and NICO use language to talk about objects' characteristics in the scene, such as an object's position, color, and name.

3.1   Human-Robot Conversation Task Definition

The task is set in the context of robot manipulation with human instruction, which requires understanding user utterances, using symbols and recognizing objects, and using the acquired knowledge. The subtasks are:

Subtask 1: Opening greetings. The greeting is the start of the conversation.

---

[1] https://www.blender.org/.
[2] https://www.coppeliarobotics.com/.

Table 2. List of dialog actions.

Tasks	No	Content
Subtask 1	$a_1 \sim a_4$	[Greeting], what can I do for you
Subtask 2	a_5, (UOI)	Please give me a specific target instruction
	a_6, (AIR)	I cannot point to multiple things at once
	a_7, (UIR)	Ok, let me check
	a_8, (IC)	image_call
Subtask 3	a_9, (NC)	Do you mean the [name]?
	a_{10}, (PC)	Do you mean the one on the [position]?
	a_{11}, (OI)	Ok, let me show you the [name]
	a_{12}, (SAR)	There is more than one object you ask for
	a_{13}, (VRF)	I cannot see anything
Subtask 4	a_{14}	arm_action_call
	a_{15}	Am I wrong, or do you want to change your mind?
	a_{16}	It is fine, You can try again by saying hello
	a_{17}	Sorry, I am still learning
	a_{18}	Here it is
	a_{19}	Do you want to try again, start by saying hello.
	a_{20}	You are welcome, See you

Subtask 2: Receiving user requests. We assume that the user request is always related to the objects on the table. Nevertheless, there are still two types of ambiguities: ambiguous instructions from user utterances and ambiguous scenes that contain multiple objects with the same characteristic (e.g. color). In this subtask, the agent clarifies ambiguous instructions from the user. If an instruction does not contain enough information to identify any object on the table. NICO will, therefore, ask the user to specify and include more detailed information, which we call Unspecified Object Instruction (UOI, a_5). If the user's instructions contain multiple names or colors, NICO will announce his inability to point to multiple objects at once. We term this action Ambiguous Instruction Recognition (AIR, a_6). When the robot receives unambiguous instructions, it will confirm the valid instruction. We term this action Unambiguous Instruction Recognition (UIR, a_7). After this, NICO will detect the relevant objects using the camera command Image Call (IC, a_8). Table 1 shows all ambiguous and unambiguous instructions in this subtask.

Subtask 3: Confirming user requests. Upon receiving results from OD, the robot confirms the user's request. The main challenge of this subtask is matching an unambiguous instruction with the environment, so the model can find a corresponding dialog action (refer to Table 2 for a list of all dialog actions). NICO tackles this matching problem with one of the following approaches. If the user asks for the position, he replies with the name. We term this action Name Confirmation (NC, a_9). If the user's instructions contain a name and/or a color, NICO replies with the position. We term this action Position Confirmation (PC, a_{10}). If the user requests an object by its color, name, and position, NICO replies with the name. We term this action Object Identification (OI, a_{11}). If the user's request contains ambiguous information in relation to the environment, so that the matching task cannot be fulfilled, the robot should recognize this ambiguity. An action we term Scene Ambiguity Recognition (SAR, a_{12}). The robot can also automatically detect if an image capture failure within the camera occurred, henceforth called Visual Recognition Failure (VRF, a_{13}).

Subtask 4: Issuing *Arm_action_calls*. After getting the confirmed information, the user either gives a negative or an affirmative answer. For the negative response, the robot will ask for the reason and guide the user to restart the conversation. When receiving an affirmative response, the robot will call for the arm motor to execute the specific action.

3.2   Visual Scenes

We selected a subset of objects from the Yale-CMU-Berkeley (YCB) objects [5], representing objects that often occur in everyday situations. We use 28 objects each for both, the training and test set, where each set contains 9 colors (red (8 objects), blue (3 objects), yellow (5 objects), brown (2 objects), green (1 objects), orange (3 objects), black (2 objects), white (3 objects), purple (1 objects)). We selected three different objects out of 28 objects for every scene. Following the combination formula, we generate 3276 scenes for every set. An ambiguous scene means objects have the same color. An unambiguous scene means the objects have three different colors. For each set there are 1136 ambiguous scenes and 2140 unambiguous scenes. The test and training set contain the same number of objects and the same color balance to let the percentage of ambiguous scenes be the same (34.7%).

3.3   Conversations

Based on the task that we define in Sect. 3.1 and the visual scenes, we generate a dialog instance dataset, which is inspired by Bordes and Weston's work [3, 30]. We use 15 unambiguous instruction utterances (see Table 1) and create 15 templates for every visual scene. Every template also includes some ambiguous instructions. Overall, we have 147420 dialog instances for both, the training and test set. For the training set, there are 117936 dialog instances for training and 29484 dialog instances for validation.

4   Approach

An overview of our hybrid neural architecture is shown in Fig. 1b. Its six components are Automatic Speech Recognition (ASR), Text-to-Speech (TTS), Object

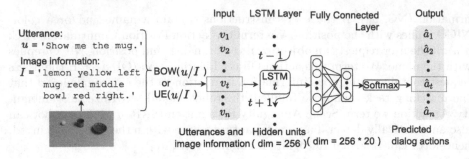

Fig. 2. Dialog State Tracker (DST). We use bag of words (BOW) or utterance embeddings (UE) to represent utterances and image information. These are fed as input v_t at time step t into the network. The output $\hat{a}_t$ at time step t denote the predicted dialog action. n is the number of the conversational turns of the person as well as of the agent.

Detection (OD), Robotic Arm Planner (RAP), Human-robot interaction policy (HRIP), and Dialog State Tracker (DST). The cycle begins when the user starts with a greeting. The very first action of the architecture is to process the user input with its ASR. The ASR result is then fed into the DST, which classifies the dialog action (Table 2 states all the dialog actions used in this study). In addition to the user's utterance, the DST potentially has two other input modalities, depending on the situation. One is from the OD containing the scene's visual information. The other is its previous dialog action. Based on the classified action, the HRIP determines NICO's behavior. The behavior entails detecting the object with its camera (OD), pointing to a target (RAP) or forming appropriate verbal responses and using TTS to generate a vocal response. The main contribution of this work is that the DST can handle the ambiguity in a user's language input and in the environment the input pertains to. The OD and DST are both neural models trained on our datasets. In this paper, the focus is mainly on OD, DST, and HRIP. Inspired by [31], we call our combination of learning-based DST and a code-based HRIP a hybrid-code dialog manager.

4.1   Object Detection (OD)

Our object detection is realized with the single-stage object-detector RetinaNet [20]. The neural architecture backbone of RetinaNet is formed by a Feature Pyramid Network (FPN) and a connected deep residual network. In essence, it constructs a semantic feature map at different scales and thus compensates for the CNN's low resolution on high-level feature maps. The FPN regression and classification subnetworks perform the actual object detection. In this work, the RetinaNet is trained on a corpus of one thousand images like the one shown in Fig. 2. The images are generated using Blender and automatically annotated with bounding boxes. During the dialog, the OD is invoked by the robot and supplied with an image of the scene. The RetinaNet subsequently detects the objects and returns the object names, positions and colors. These attributes can then be used to formulate appropriate responses through the DST.

4.2 Dialog State Tracker (DST)

Multimodal Feature Representation. As shown in Fig. 1b, the whole visually grounded human-robot dialog is based on multimodal, audio-visual input, being the user's utterance and an image of the environment. However, the DST receives pure text input (see Fig. 2, image I and utterances $U = [u_1, \ldots, u_n]$). The two modalities, therefore, have to be processed into text format, so that the DST can make use of it. Representing natural language can be done in manifold ways. We decided to use the bag of words (BOW) for its simplicity and utterance embeddings (UE) for its successful applications in other natural language tasks. In order to create a vector of inputs, we build a vocabulary dictionary for the training set. For the BOW, we create a vector from the sum of the individual one-hot vectors of this dictionary. For the UE, we employ a word2vec model [23] that has been pre-trained on the Google News corpus to obtain word vector representations, and then, we calculate the mean vector of these representations. These representations are applied to both, utterances and image descriptions. Moreover, each dialog instance d_j combines user utterances, image information and labeled dialog actions ($d_j = [(u_1, a_1), \ldots, (I, a_i), \ldots, (u_n, a_n)]$, i is the position of an image reading within a dialog instance, n is the number of conversational turns). There is a total of m dialog instances ($D = [d_1, \ldots, d_m]$).

LSTM + FCL. Besides the user's utterances U and image I, which both are represented by BOW or UE, the previous action (PA) is an additional input to the DST. Every utterance u_i of the dialog instance, its image information I and its previous action a_{i-1} are concatenated to form a feature vector. They are fed into an RNN, specifically, a long short-term memory (LSTM) network [12]. The output of the LSTM is passed to a fully connected layer (FCL), after which the softmax function is applied. The output of the model are predicted dialog actions ($\hat{a}_1, \ldots, \hat{a}_n$).

4.3 Human-Robot Interaction Policy (HRIP)

A dialog manager usually contains a dialog state tracker and a dialog policy. Here, we train a neural network for the state tracking. Additionally, rules for knowledge extraction and decision-making are needed. When the DST recognizes that the user gives a specific instruction, HRIP extracts the user's target and matches it with the output of the OD. With the matched information, a decision will be made. Based on the predicted dialog action of the DST, rules determine the robot's behavior. Possible robot behavior includes calling for the camera to get image information, calling for the robot's arm to execute the specific action (e.g. point to the object), using the OD result to formulate correct verbal answers and generating speech to respond to the user.

Table 3. Average test accuracy of labeled actions in subtask 2 and subtask 3. Unspecified Object Instruction (UOI), Ambiguous Instruction Recognition (AIR), Unambiguous Instruction Recognition (UIR), Image Call (IC), Name Confirmation (NC), Position Confirmation (PC), Object Identification (OI), Scene Ambiguity Recognition (SAR), Visual Recognition Failure (VRF).

Labeled actions	Average accuracy (%)±Standard deviation					
	BOW	(BOW, PA)	UE	(UE, PA)	(BOW, UE)	(BOW, UE, PA)
UOI	100 ± 0	100 ± 0	100 ± 0	100 ± 0	100 ± 0	100 ± 0
AIR	100 ± 0	100 ± 0	73.98 ± 12.19	77.50 ± 10.45	100 ± 0	100 ± 0
UIR	100 ± 0	100 ± 0	98.33 ± 0.85	99.58 ± 0.63	100 ± 0	100 ± 0
IC	100 ± 0	100 ± 0	98.72 ± 1.94	99.91 ± 0.26	100 ± 0	100 ± 0
NC	78.24 ± 5.84	78.96 ± 6.08	98.09 ± 2.18	99.99 ± 0.02	95.51 ± 3.93	97.96 ± 3.29
PC	100 ± 0	99.94 ± 0.18	97.76 ± 1.54	99.48 ± 1.52	100 ± 0	96.64 ± 9.44
OI	99.56 ± 0.75	100 ± 0	89.24 ± 12.99	98.15 ± 2.64	99.81 ± 0.55	97.63 ± 4.40
SAR	91.65 ± 6.3	90.98 ± 7.84	55.79 ± 22.32	42.70 ± 15.85	74.17 ± 7.47	67.40 ± 9.97
VRF	100 ± 0	100 ± 0	97.38 ± 6.32	99.83 ± 0.48	100 ± 0	100 ± 0

5   Experiments

During training, each dialog instance constituted its own minibatch, and updates were computed on full rollouts (i.e., non-truncated backpropagation through time). Because it is a multi-class classification task, categorical cross-entropy (CCE) was used to calculate the error terms. We selected the AdaDelta optimizer [32] to minimize the loss function. We evaluate six different variants of inputs to the RNN of the DST: bag of words only BOW, utterance embeddings UE only, bag of words and utterance embeddings (BOW, UE) together, and the previous action added to all those combinations. Each combination was trained 9 times with different sampling order for 30 epochs to reduce noise and avoid biases.

5.1   Results

Subtask 1 (*Opening greetings*) and subtask 4 (*Issuing Arm_action_calls*) are both essential parts of our visual grounded human-robot dialog. Since they are not the focus of our research, we define them in a simple fashion, using the same data in training and test sets. The DST successfully predicts the correct dialog action with an accuracy of 100% for all action classes belonging to these subtasks. Table 3 only shows the results for subtask 2 (*Issuing user requests*) and subtask 3 (*confirming user requests*). Mean and standard deviation of the accuracy are computed from 9 runs. The challenge of subtask 2 is to deal with an ambiguous instruction from the user, and the challenge of subtask 3 is to correctly combine the user's instruction and image input.

Action AIR responds to a type of ambiguous instructions (see Table 1). Compared with variants BOW and (BOW, UE) that can predict the dialog action with 100% of accuracy, variants UE cannot properly react to a user's unspecific instruction, achieving only accuracy of 73.98%. Action SAR responds to an ambiguous scene. The variant BOW performs better than UE and (BOW, UE) in situations when SAR is the expected dialog action. In unambiguous situations when action NC is expected, utterance embedding cannot help the model handle ambiguous situations, but it helps the model perform well in unambiguous situations. Comparing variant BOW with (BOW, UE), a striking difference is that the addition of UE helps in NC but has a negative effect in SAR.

5.2 Discussion

The results indicate that using BOW to represent the inputs for the DST model can be a worthwhile option to tackle visually grounded human-robot dialog state tracking. For the BOW, we found that one problem is the multiple meanings of the word *orange*, which can be either a color or an object name, but is represented the same via BOW. For the UE in subtask 2, DST may predict a wrong dialog action, e.g. for *Show me the [name1] and [name2]*, it incorrectly predicts UIR. The reason is that the UE uses word2vec that does not have a representation of stop words like *and*. Furthermore, the pretraining of the UE on a non-related corpus could explain some issues. For the action SAR in subtask 3, the predicted dialog action is NC, which means the model misunderstood the user's instruction for a position. These limitations of our model are related to the simple utterance representations, which might be remedied in future work by more sophisticated sentence embeddings.

6 Conclusion and Future Work

Integrating visual information into a dialog is an essential necessity for robots to interact and cooperate with humans naturally. To this end, we propose a visually grounded human-robot dialog task along with a dataset. Moreover, we designed a novel hybrid neural architecture to solve this task, entailing a neural model to track the dialog state and a knowledge-based policy for the robot behavior. The hybrid nature of the architecture allows integrating state-of-the-art neural modules for vision and language processing with symbolic reasoning mechanisms. We explored how to represent user utterance and visual scene inputs to let the dialog model learn interaction skills. The results show that the simple bag of words (BOW) method can solve this task better than utterance embeddings (UE) based on a pre-trained word2vec model. Notably, the model generalizes to objects in the test set that were never shown in training, indicating that the model can generalize to any unseen object, provided the OD can recognize it. Moreover, although the number of dialog actions are fixed, they are dependent on the scenario and not on the model architecture, thereby allowing adaptation and application to a multitude of different scenarios and domains.

   In future work, we plan to use ill-formed utterances where the user language does not strictly follow a correct grammar, to train the model and to improve the model's robustness. Also, we plan to deploy the model on the real NICO robot, making the model cooperate with its camera and robot arm (RAP), and to evaluate our architecture in the real world, including ASR and TTS. Furthermore, more variations in the table scene, like a random number of objects, might increase the robustness and applicability of the model in the real world.

Acknowledgment. The authors gratefully acknowledge support from the China Scholarship Council (CSC) and the German Research Foundation DFG under project CML (TRR 169). We thank Alexander Sutherland for his advice on the experimental design.

References

1. Alomari, M., Dukes, K.: Extended train robots (2016). https://doi.org/10.5518/32
2. Bagaskara, A., Naufal, A.R., Dhojopatmo, I.E., Abdurrab, A., Budiharto, W.: Development of smart restaurant application for dine-in. In: Conference on Computer Science and Artificial Intelligence, vol. 1, pp. 230–235 (2021)
3. Bordes, A., Boureau, Y.L., Weston, J.: Learning end-to-end goal-oriented dialog. Preprint arXiv:1605.07683 (2016)
4. Brabra, H., Báez, M., Benatallah, B., Gaaloul, W., Bouguelia, S., Zamanirad, S.: Dialogue management in conversational systems: a review of approaches, challenges, and opportunities. IEEE Trans. Cogn. Dev. Syst. (2021)
5. Calli, B., Walsman, A., Singh, A., Srinivasa, S., Abbeel, P., Dollar, A.M.: Benchmarking in manipulation research: the YCB object and model set and benchmarking protocols. Preprint arXiv:1502.03143 (2015)
6. Das, A., et al.: Visual dialog. In: IEEE Conference on Computer Vision and Pattern Recognition (2017)
7. De Vries, H., Strub, F., Chandar, S., Pietquin, O., Larochelle, H., Courville, A.: GuessWhat?! Visual object discovery through multi-modal dialogue. In: IEEE Conference on Computer Vision and Pattern Recognition (2017)
8. Devlin, J., Chang, M.W., Lee, K., Toutanova, K.: BERT: pre-training of deep bidirectional transformers for language understanding. arXiv:1810.04805 (2018)
9. Goel, R., Paul, S., Hakkani-Tür, D.: HyST: a hybrid approach for flexible and accurate dialogue state tracking. Preprint arXiv:1907.00883 (2019)
10. Goyal, Y., Khot, T., Summers-Stay, D., Batra, D., Parikh, D.: Making the V in VQA matter: elevating the role of image understanding in visual question answering. In: IEEE Conference on Computer Vision and Pattern Recognition (2017)
11. Henderson, M., Thomson, B., Young, S.: Word-based dialog state tracking with recurrent neural networks. In: 15th Annual Meeting of the Special Interest Group on Discourse and Dialogue, pp. 292–299 (2014)
12. Hochreiter, S., Schmidhuber, J.: Long short-term memory. Neural Comput. **9**(8), 1735–1780 (1997)
13. Huang, X., et al.: Joint generation and bi-encoder for situated interactive multimodal conversations. In: AAAI 2021 DSTC9 Workshop (2021)
14. Jeong, Y., Lee, S.J., Ko, Y., Seo, J.: TOM: end-to-end task-oriented multimodal dialog system with GPT-2. In: AAAI 2021 DSTC9 Workshop (2021)
15. Kerzel, M., Abawi, F., Eppe, M., Wermter, S.: Enhancing a neurocognitive shared visuomotor model for object identification, localization, and grasping with learning from auxiliary tasks. IEEE Trans. Cogn. Dev. Syst. 1–13 (2020)

16. Kerzel, M., Strahl, E., Magg, S., Navarro-Guerrero, N., Heinrich, S., Wermter, S.: NICO-neuro-inspired COmpanion: a developmental humanoid robot platform for multimodal interaction. In: IEEE International Symposium on Robot and Human Interactive Communication, pp. 113–120 (2017)

17. Kottur, S., Moon, S., Geramifard, A., Damavandi, B.: SIMMC 2.0: a task-oriented dialog dataset for immersive multimodal conversations. arXiv:2104.08667 (2021)

18. Kottur, S., Moura, J.M., Parikh, D., Batra, D., Rohrbach, M.: CLEVR-dialog: a diagnostic dataset for multi-round reasoning in visual dialog. Preprint arXiv:1903.03166 (2019)

19. Lewis, M., et al.: BART: denoising sequence-to-sequence pre-training for natural language generation, translation, and comprehension. Preprint arXiv:1910.13461 (2019)

20. Lin, T.Y., Goyal, P., Girshick, R.B., He, K., Dollár, P.: Focal loss for dense object detection. IEEE International Conference on Computer Vision (2017)

21. Lin, T.-Y., et al.: Microsoft COCO: common objects in context. In: Fleet, D., Pajdla, T., Schiele, B., Tuytelaars, T. (eds.) ECCV 2014. LNCS, vol. 8693, pp. 740–755. Springer, Cham (2014). https://doi.org/10.1007/978-3-319-10602-1_48

22. Lu, J., Batra, D., Parikh, D., Lee, S.: ViLBERT: pretraining task-agnostic visiolinguistic representations for vision-and-language tasks. In: Advances in Neural Information Processing Systems, vol. 32 (2019)

23. Mikolov, T., Chen, K., Corrado, G., Dean, J.: Efficient estimation of word representations in vector space (2013)

24. Moon, S., et al.: Situated and interactive multimodal conversations. Preprint arXiv:2006.01460 (2020)

25. Mostafazadeh, N., et al..: Image-grounded conversations: multimodal context for natural question and response generation. Preprint arXiv:1701.08251 (2017)

26. Murahari, V., Batra, D., Parikh, D., Das, A.: Large-scale pretraining for visual dialog: a simple state-of-the-art baseline. In: Vedaldi, A., Bischof, H., Brox, T., Frahm, J.-M. (eds.) ECCV 2020. LNCS, vol. 12363, pp. 336–352. Springer, Cham (2020). https://doi.org/10.1007/978-3-030-58523-5_20

27. Ni, J., Young, T., Pandelea, V., Xue, F., Adiga, V., Cambria, E.: Recent advances in deep learning based dialogue systems: a systematic survey. Preprint arXiv:2105.04387 (2021)

28. Qian, K., et al.: Database search results disambiguation for task-oriented dialog systems. Preprint arXiv:2112.08351 (2021)

29. Radford, A., Narasimhan, K., Salimans, T., Sutskever, I.: Improving language understanding by generative pre-training (2018)

30. Weston, J., et al.: Towards AI-complete question answering: a set of prerequisite toy tasks. Preprint arXiv:1502.05698 (2015)

31. Williams, J.D., Asadi, K., Zweig, G.: Hybrid code networks: practical and efficient end-to-end dialog control with supervised and reinforcement learning. Preprint arXiv:1702.03274 (2017)

32. Zeiler, M.D.: ADADELTA: an adaptive learning rate method. Preprint arXiv:1212.5701 (2012)

MTHGAT: A Neural Multi-task Model for Aspect Category Detection and Aspect Term Sentiment Analysis on Restaurant Reviews

Liang Ge and Jun Li[✉]

College of Computer Science, Chongqing University, Chongqing, China
{geliang,lijun1997}@cqu.edu.cn

Abstract. Aspect-based sentiment analysis (ABSA) is one of the fundamental task in text sentiment analysis which aims to analyze the sentiment polarity of a specific aspect (terms or categories) in a given sentence. Aspect category detection (ACD) and aspect term sentiment analysis (ATSA) are both sub-task of ABSA. However, most of the previous methods regard them as two separate tasks, and ignore the potential relationship between them. In this paper, we propose a multi-task hierarchical graph attention network (MTHGAT) which contains two levels of graph attention networks, a sentence level and a document level. The former is built based on the reshaped dependency parse tree, the latter is built to gather information between sentences in a document. Extensive experiments are conducted on the two restaurant datasets in SemEval-2015 and SemEval-2016. The results show that our proposed model performs better than most baseline methods.

Keywords: Aspect based sentiment analysis · Graph attention network · Joint learning

1 Introduction

Aspect-based sentiment analysis (ABSA) is a fine-grained sentiment classification task in the natural language processing [1] that try to analyze the sentiment polarity for each aspect discussed in a given sentence. We focus on two sub-tasks in ABSA: aspect category detection (ACD) and aspect term sentiment analysis (ATSA). Given a predefined set of aspect categories, ACD aims to identify all the aspect categories discussed in a given sentence, while ATSA is to recognize the sentiment polarities for aspect term. For example, give a sentence *"The restaurant downstairs has delicious food but the service is quite bad."*, the aspect category for **food** is "FOOD#GENERAL" and sentiment polarity is positive. For aspect **service**, the aspect category is "SERVICE#GENERAL" and the sentiment polarity is negative.

Intuitively, associating aspect terms with their corresponding sentiment opinion words is the focus of solving ATSA. Therefore, many methods usually use

E. Pimenidis et al. (Eds.): ICANN 2022, LNCS 13530, pp. 270–281, 2022.
https://doi.org/10.1007/978-3-031-15931-2_23

LSTM to encode words vector [18,23], then adopt various attention mechanisms to find the correlation between the context and the aspect. However, because of the complexity of language syntax and syntactic structure, these attention-based methods are always unsuccessful. For example, *"So great was the service but bad food"*, in this sentence sequence, the opinion word **great** of aspect term **service** is farther than another opinion word **bad**. In this case, the attention mechanisms will be ineffective due to the long-distance word dependencies.

Some studies have shown that dependency-based parse trees can effectively resolve the problem and provide more comprehensive syntactic structure information [28]. As presented in Fig. 1, we can regard the dependency-based parse tree as a special graph. Recently, many works have used graph neural networks (GNNs) to learn the sentence representation from the dependency tree [9,27]. But these graph neural networks just work on a single sentence and ignore the contextual information in the document. It's difficult for these methods to predict aspect sentiment polarity when individual sentences are short or incomprehensible, e.g., *"$170 down the toilet."*. Without contextual information, it would be hard for models to know that this sentence was a bad review for a restaurant.

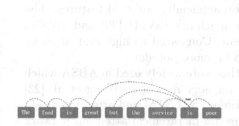

S1 : Everytime I decide to try another place on the UES, I get angry that I didn't just go to Zucchero Pomodori.
Opinion: aspect ="Zucchero Pomodori"
category="RESTAURANT#GENERAL" polarity="positive"

S2 : This is by far my favorite place in the neighborhood.
Opinion: aspect ="place"
category="RESTAURANT#GENERAL" polarity="positive"

S3 : I'm partial to the Gnocchi.
Opinion: aspect ="Gnocchi"
category="RESTAURANT#GENERAL" polarity="positive"

Fig. 1. The dependency-based parse tree of a sentence.

Fig. 2. A document from Rest16 [2] datasets.

For another detailed example shown in Fig. 2, there is an obvious phenomenon that the aspect words with the same category are likely to have the same polarity of sentiment. For example, in the document shown in Fig. 2, sentence S1 involves aspect **Zucchero Pomodori**, S2 and S3 involve aspects **place** and **Gnocchi** respectively, and their aspects have the same category **RESTAURANT#GENERAL**. Obviously, it's difficult to infer the positive sentiment for the aspect **Zucchero Pomodori** through the clause *"I get angry that I didn't just go to Zucchero Pomodori"* in S1. However, we can infer the aspect sentiment of S1 may be positive according to S2 and S3. In sentence S2, it's easier to infer positive for aspect **place** through the phrase *"my favorite place"*. In sentence S3, we also can easily infer positive for the aspect through the clause *"I'm partial"*. Therefore, the contextual information between sentences in a document is helpful to predict the sentiment of the target aspect word.

Unlike previous methods to infer sentiment polarity by a single sentence, we proposed a MTHGAT model to gather the sentiment features from the sentence level and the document level. In addition, we consider ACD and ATSA task together under a multi-task setting.

The detailed evaluation shows that MTHGAT effectively resolves both limitations of the current aspect-based sentiment classification approaches and achieves higher performance than many benchmark methods.

Major contributions from our work include:

- We propose a joint learning model which has a share encoding layer and an independent layer to solve the ACD task and ATSA task. To the best of our knowledge, this is the first work using joint learning framework for ACD and ATSA simultaneously.
- We propose MTHGAT to capture the contextual information from both sentence-level and document-level for aspect term sentiment analysis.
- By conducting experiments with public datasets, it verifies the importance of the document-level contextual information.

2   Related Work

Aspect-based sentiment analysis (ABSA) is a branch of sentiment analysis [15]. Early traditional methods are often based on artificially designed features, then train classifier models like support vector machines (SVM) [20] and opinion lexicon [6] to identify given aspect sentiment. Compared to high-cost artificial engineering, deep learning methods tend to be more popular.

Subsequently, neural network-based methods are widely used in ABSA which mainly include attention mechanisms and memory networks. Wang et al. [23] proposed an ATAE-LSTM model that combined the LSTM and attention mechanism. In another work, Wang et al. [21] used a hierarchical attention network to learn from words and clauses information. Besides, some researchers have also used CNN to resolve this task [8,25]. CNN can control the information flow generated from the aspect in a sentence [25]. Khalil et al. [11] used CNN in ACD task. Researchers have made great strides in many natural language processing tasks by BERT including ABSA. For example, Xu et al. [24] used additional in-domain corpus to post-train BERT [5] and then fine-tuned it, this study proved the effectiveness of the pre-trained model on this task. However, these methods always lay emphasis on words features and ignore the syntactic structure information. Recently, graph neural networks (GNNs) have been attempted to learn representations from the dependency parse trees so that learn the syntactic structure information. Zhang et al. [27] was the first to deploy graph convolutional network (GCN) [13] on this task, Huang et al. [9] proposed a TD-GAT model based on graph attention network (GAT) [19] to explicitly establish the dependency relations between words.

The above previous studies either focus on aspect category detection or aspect term sentiment analysis, to the best of our knowledge, no study is found to jointly implements the two tasks. Unlike all the above studies, we are no longer limited to a single task and propose a new multi-task hierarchical graph attention network (MTHGAT) to solve the two tasks simultaneously.

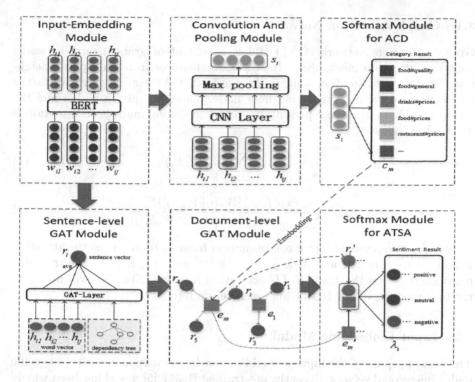

Fig. 3. The framework of MTHGAT.

3   Multi-task Hierarchical Graph Attention Network

In this section, we'll elaborate on the details of MTHGAT. Firstly, the aspect-based sentiment analysis task is formulated as follows. Given a document D with sentences $\{s_1, s_2, ..., s_I\}$, each sentence $s_i = \{w_i1, w_i2, ..., w_{ij}\}, i \in \{1, 2, ..., I\}, j \in \{1, 2, ..., N_i\}$ contains N_i words, w_{ij} represents j-th word in the i-th sentence in D. Then sentence has aspect a_m the purpose of the ATSA task is to infer the sentiment polarity λ for aspect a_m automatically, the purpose of the ACD task is to infer its aspect category c_m.

In our study, we propose a MTHGAT approach which contains two kinds of graph attention network (GAT) to gather the two-level sentiment preference information respectively. Figure 3 gives an overview of the HGAT which consists of six major modules: (1) Input-Embedding Module; (2) Sentence-level GAT Module; (3) Document-level GAT Module; (4) Convolution And Pooling Module; (5) Softmax Module For ACD; (6) Softmax Module For ATSA. Next, we will first illustrate the basic graph attention network (GAT) then introduce the other four modules.

3.1 Graph Attention Network

Graph Attention Network (GAT) [19] is a variant of graph neural networks including attention mechanisms. It aggregates features from an aspect's neighbors by different attention weights. In addition, GAT can also propagate the information of the node to its neighbor node. Therefore, give a node i and the node's neighbors $n[i]$, the representation of node i using multi-head attention is updated as follows:

$$h_i = \|_{k=1}^{K} \sigma(\sum_{j \in n[i]} \alpha_{ij} W_k h_j) \tag{1}$$

$$\alpha_{ij} = \frac{exp(f(w^\top [W_k h_i \| W_k h_j]))}{\sum_{t \in n[i]} exp(f(w^\top [W_k h_i \| W_k h_t]))} \tag{2}$$

where $\|_{k=1}^{K} x_i$ represents vector concatenation from x_1 to x_k, α_{ij} is the attention weight between node i and node j. $W_k \in \mathbb{R}^{d \times d}$ and $w \in \mathbb{R}^{2d}$ are the trainable parameters, $f()$ is the *LeakyReLU* activation function. Next, we will illustrate the four modules of our HGAT approach separately.

3.2 Input-Embedding Module

The main purpose of the input-embedding module is mapping words to specific high-dimensional vectors. Recently, pre-trained BERT [5] model has been widely used on many natural language processing tasks such as sentiment analysis and named entity recognition. For each sentence, we use BERT to covert the j-th word in the i-th sentence w_{ij} into the embedding vector $h_{ij} \in \mathbb{R}^{d \times 1}$. We also covert the category of aspect c_m into $e_m \in \mathbb{R}^{d \times 1}$ by BERT.

3.3 Sentence-level GAT Module

This module aims to learn the information from words and syntactic structure information based dependency tree. In the document D, h_{ij} is the representation of j-th word in the i-th sentence. We follow the method processed by Wang et al. [22], l_{jk} represents the relation embedding between j-th word and k-th word in the reshaping dependency tree [22]. We construct the graph on the dependency tree, each edge is marked by the matching dependence type between the two connected words. We update h_{ij} as follows:

$$g_{jk} = \sigma(relu(l_{jk} W_{m1} + b_{m1}) W_{m2} + b_{m2}) \tag{3}$$

$$\beta_{jk}^m = \frac{exp(g_{jk}^m)}{\sum_{k \in n[j]} exp(g_{jk}^m)} \tag{4}$$

$$h_{ij} = \|_{m=1}^{M} \sum_{k \in n[j]} \beta_{jk} W_m h_{ik} \tag{5}$$

where $\|_{m=1}^{M}$ represents M attentional heads, β_{jk} is the attention weight, $n[j]$ is the neighbours of word j, W_m, W_{m1}, W_{m2}, b_{m1} and b_{m2} are the trainable parameters. Then r_i is the representation of i-th sentence in the document D and is updated as follows:

$$r_i = \frac{\sum_{j=1}^{N_i} h_{ij}}{N_i} \tag{6}$$

which is the averaging of words vectors.

3.4 Convolution and Pooling Module

This module aims to get the sentence representation s_i' for aspect category detection. After the input-embedding module, we get the word representation h_{ij}. We follow the method processed by Yoon Kim [4], a convolution operation involves a filter w, which is applied to a window of h words to produce a new feature. For example, a feature t_j is generated from a window of words $h_{ij:j+h-1}$ by

$$t_j = f(w * h_{ij:j+h-1} + b) \tag{7}$$

This filter is applied to each possible window of words in the sentences and get a feature map $T = [t_1, t_2, t_3, \ldots, t_{j-h+1}]$. We then apply a max-over-time pooling operation $\hat{T} = max\{T\}$ and after a fully connected layer, we can get the sentence representation s_i'.

3.5 Document-level GAT Module

This module aims to learn the information from other sentences in the document. Given a document D with sentences $\{s_1, s_2, ..., s_I\}$, the sentences representations are $\{r_1, r_2, ..., r_I\}$ after the sentence-level GAT module. After the softmax module for ACD, we can get the aspect categories $\{c_1, c_2, ..., c_m\}$, and $\{e_1, e_2, ..., e_m\}$ are the aspect corresponding category embedding representations. For these sentences, we build a graph that connecting the sentences representations with their aspect categories. As shown in Fig. 3, the sentence vertices $\{r_1, r_2, ..., r_{I'}\}$ share the same aspect category e_m in the same document. In the graph G, aspect category is the center vertex, sentences representations are edge vertices. According to Eq. (1) and Eq. (2), We update r_i and e_m as follows:

$$v_i = \|_{k=1}^{K} \sigma\left(\sum_{j \in n[i]} \alpha_{ij} W_k v_j\right) \tag{8}$$

where v_i represents the vertices in graph G such as r_i or e_m. Finally, after document-level GAT module, we get the new sentence representation r_i' and new aspect category e_m'.

3.6　Softmax Module for ACD

For ACD task, after obtaining the sentence representation s_i' by convolution module, we feed s_i' to a softmax classifier to generate the probability distribution $P \in \mathbb{R}^{d_p}$ of the sentiment polarity space as follows:

$$P = softmax(W_p s_i' + b_p) \tag{9}$$

where W_p and b_p are the trainable parameters. Finally, the highest probability label represent for the predicted aspect category c_m.

3.7　Softmax Module for ATSA

For ATSA task, after obtaining the final sentence representation r_i' and aspect category e_m', we concatenate r_i' and e_m', the final vector is computed by $x_i = r_i' \| e_m'$. Then we feed x_i to a softmax classifier to generate the probability distribution $P \in \mathbb{R}^{d_p}$ of the sentiment polarity space as follows:

$$P = softmax(W_p x_i + b_p) \tag{10}$$

where W_p and b_p are the trainable parameters. Note that the dimension of d_p is the same as sentiment polarities. Finally, the highest probability label represent for the predicted sentiment polarity of the aspect.

3.8　Model Training

We trained the model by standard cross-entropy and the sub-task loss function as $loss_{1.2} = -\sum_{d \in S_D} \sum_{f=1}^{F} Y_{df} log(P_{df})$, the final loss function computed as follows:

$$Loss = \alpha loss_1 + \beta loss_2 \tag{11}$$

where $\alpha + \beta = 1$, $loss_1, loss_2$ represent the loss functions ACD and ATSA respectively.

4　Experimentation

In this section, the experimental data sets and benchmark methods are presented first. After that, we will show the experimental results using our method from various angles.

4.1　Datasets and Experimental Settings

We conduct experiments on two public datasets: Rest15 and Rest16 are restaurant review datasets come from SemEval-2015 task 12 and SemEval-2016 task 5 respectively. Statistics of the two datasets can be showed in Table 1 respectively.

For our HGAT approach, we adopt Adam [12] optimizer with learning rate of 10^{-5}. We use Biaffine Parser [7] to parse the dependency tree, the dimension of

Table 1. The statistics of the two restaurant review datasets

dataset	Positive		Neutral		Negative	
	Train	Test	Train	Test	Train	Test
Rest15	1198	460	53	45	405	348
Rest16	1663	615	101	44	753	206

dependency relation embeddings is 300. The parameters of BERT are the same as Wang et al. [22], the dimension of each word vector is 768. For the multi-head attention mechanism, the number of heads is set to 6. The parameters of BERT are the same as the method processed by Yoon Kim [4]. In our study, all the trainable weights and biases are initialized by xavier uniform distribution. As usual, accuracy and Macro-F1 are used by us to evaluate the performance of our model.

4.2   Baseline Methods

Because the ATSA task is the main task in our model, and no study is found to jointly implements ACD and ATSA tasks. We can only select the single-task methods which aim to solve the ATSA, including:

- **TD-LSTM** [18]: This approach used two LSTM networks that contains a forward one and a backward one to select context sentiment information.
- **ATAE-LSTM** [23]: This approach proposes an attention-based LSTM to learn the word embedding representation.
- **RAM** [3]: This approach combines RNN and multiple attention mechanisms to capture the context information for the aspect and resolve the problem of long-distance word representation.
- **IAN** [14]: This approach is an interactive learning approach, which employs two attention mechanisms to interactively learn attentions between contexts and aspects.
- **AOA** [10]: This approach proposes an attention-based LSTM to model aspects and texts at the same time and the two representations interact with each other by an attention-over-attention module.
- **BERT-QA** [17]: This approach constructs an auxiliary sentence from the aspect and converts ABSA to a sentence-pair classification task, such as question answering (QA).
- **Sentiue** [16]: This is the most efficient approach of SemEval-2015 Task 12. It achieved the best accuracy scores in *restaurant15*.
- **XRCE** [2]: This is the most efficient approach of SemEval-2016 Task 5. It achieved the best accuracy scores in *restaurant16*.
- **ASGCN-DG** [27]: This approach proposes a novel aspect-specific GCN model that is the first using graph convolutional network in this task.
- **R-GAT** [22]: This approach proposes a novel relational graph attention network model that is the first using relation information in this task.

4.3   Experimental Results

Table 2. Comparison results of the different approaches. The results with † are retrieved from the original papers. All methods with BERT used BERT-base as words encoder in our study.

Approaches	Rest15		Rest16	
	Acc	F1	Acc	F1
TD-LSTM	0.741	0.497	0.860	0.547
ATAE-LSTM	0.791	0.533	0.855	0.552
RAM	0.767	0.645	0.839	0.661
IAN	0.755	0.639	0.836	0.652
AOA	0.781	0.572	0.875	0.662
BERT-QA	0.824	0.65	0.896	0.715
Sentinue	$0.787^\dagger$	$0.66^\dagger$	–	–
XRCE	–	–	$0.881^\dagger$	–
ASGCN-DG	$0.799^\dagger$	$0.619^\dagger$	$0.89^\dagger$	$0.675^\dagger$
R-GAT	0.831	0.671	0.894	0.752
MTHGAT	**0.859**	**0.701**	**0.901**	**0.771**
MTHGAT w/o sentence-level GAT	0.853	0.609	0.897	0.73
MTHGAT w/o document-level GAT	0.842	0.687	0.898	0.76

Table 2 showed the experimental results of the various approaches. The table shows that all approaches based on attention mechanisms such as **ATAE-LSTM, RAM, IAN** and **AOA**, perform better than **TD-LSTM**. Although **TD-LSTM** considered the role of aspect term, it cannot make full use of the correlation information between aspect term and context [26]. The experimental result proved the effectiveness of the attention mechanism for the ABSA task. On these two datasets, the **BERT-QA** based BERT technique outperforms the above approaches. The experiment results proved the effectiveness of the pre-trained model BERT as the word and sentence encoder for this NLP task. In particular, the three approaches **ASGCN-DG** and **R-GAT** based GNN, all perform better than most approaches. The main reason may be that learning the syntactic structure information is helpful for this task. In addition, the approach **R-GAT** perform better than **ASGCN-DG** because the method consider various types of relations in the dependency tree and uses BERT as the word encoder.

Furthermore, our approach **MTHGAT** performs better than all the above state-of-the-art approaches. It approved the effectiveness of our method using the multi-task framework and hierarchical graph attention network learning sentence structure information and document contextual feature. On the one hand, the sentence-level and document-level sentiment features are both helpful for this task, on the other hand, the multi-task learning method can make multiple related sub-tasks share parameters and improve each other's performance.

4.4 Ablation Study

To further examine the actual influence of each module in MTHGAT brings to the performance, we conduct an ablation study on **MTHGAT w/o sentence-level GAT** and **MTHGAT w/o document-level GAT**. We also present the results of **R-GAT** as a baseline.

First, we remove the sentence-level GAT module (i.e. MTHGAT w/o sentence-level GAT) and use the averaging of word vectors as the sentence representation. Then enter the sentence representation into the document-level GAT module. As Table 2 showed that this removal leads to performance drops on both two datasets. This result proved the effectiveness of syntactic structure information.

Furthermore, we remove the document-level GAT module (i.e. MTHGAT w/o document-level GAT) and use the output of sentence-level GAT module as the final output. As Table 2 showed that this removal also leads to a significant drop in performance. This result proved that the contextual information in a document is helpful for our model. However, **MTHGAT w/o sentence-level GAT** and **MTHGAT w/o document-level GAT** is still slightly better than baseline **R-GAT**. To sum up, the **MTHGAT** with two modules capture multiple level information more effectively.

4.5 Error Analysis

To analyze the limitations of our model, we randomly select 100 error examples from Rest15 and Rest16. After looking into these bad cases, we roughly categorized them into 4 classes as follows. (1) **24%** of errors are due to the negation expression, e.g., *"Not a very fancy place but very good chinese style indian food."*. MTHGAT incorrectly predicts negative polarity for aspect **food**. (2) **42%** of errors are due to misleading neutral reviews, e.g., *"The menu looked great, and the waiter was very nice, but when the food came, it was average."*. It's hard to recognize neutral instances because of the shortage of neutral training examples. (3) **18%** of errors are caused by too short sentences, e.g., *"What a hassle!."*. (4) The fourth category, **16%** of errors are due to the difficulty to understand when there are no clues in sentences, e.g., *"This place has ruined me for neighborhood sushi."*. The third and fourth categories inspire us to incorporate more external information.

Through the above error analysis, we can learn that because of the complexity of language, there are still some complicated sentences that our model cannot correctly predict the sentiment polarity. For these sentences, more training corpus and more efficient sentiment information extraction methods are necessary.

5   Conclusion

In this paper, we proposed a novel hierarchical graph attention network (MTH-GAT) approach to aspect-based sentiment analysis (ABSA). We first use the pre-trained BERT model as the word encoder and employ the aspect-oriented dependency tree raised by Wang et al. [22] to build the sentence-level GAT. Afterwards, we develop the document-level GAT based on the same aspect categories of sentences. When the sentence-level sentiment information is lacking to predict aspect sentiment polarity, we use document-level information as a supplement. Several comparative experimental results show that the proposed model is simple and effective, and can be applied to solve aspect category detection and aspect term sentiment analysis simultaneously.

Then we conducted an ablation study to confirm the actual influence of sentence-level GAT and document-level GAT modules. At last, an error analysis was conducted on the examples of mispredictions, which allowed for a better understanding of the MTHGAT. In our future work, we would consider how to capture more structure information of sentences. One potential solution is to consider the clauses' information.

References

1. Bakshi, R.K., Kaur, N., Kaur, R., Kaur, G.: Opinion mining and sentiment analysis. In: 2016 3rd international conference on computing for sustainable global development (INDIACom), pp. 452–455. IEEE (2016)
2. Brun, C., Perez, J., Roux, C.: XRCE at SemEval-2016 task 5: feedbacked ensemble modeling on syntactico-semantic knowledge for aspect based sentiment analysis. In: Proceedings of the 10th International Workshop on Semantic Evaluation (SemEval-2016), pp. 277–281 (2016)
3. Chen, P., Sun, Z., Bing, L., Yang, W.: Recurrent attention network on memory for aspect sentiment analysis. In: Proceedings of the 2017 Conference on Empirical Methods in Natural Language Processing, pp. 452–461 (2017)
4. Chen, Y.: Convolutional neural network for sentence classification. Master's thesis, University of Waterloo (2015)
5. Devlin, J., Chang, M.W., Lee, K., Toutanova, K.: Bert: pre-training of deep bidirectional transformers for language understanding. arXiv preprint arXiv:1810.04805 (2018)
6. Ding, X., Liu, B., Yu, P.S.: A holistic lexicon-based approach to opinion mining. In: Proceedings of the 2008 International Conference on Web Search and Data Mining, pp. 231–240 (2008)
7. Dozat, T., Manning, C.D.: Deep biaffine attention for neural dependency parsing. arXiv preprint arXiv:1611.01734 (2016)
8. Huang, B., Carley, K.M.: Parameterized convolutional neural networks for aspect level sentiment classification. arXiv preprint arXiv:1909.06276 (2019)
9. Huang, B., Carley, K.M.: Syntax-aware aspect level sentiment classification with graph attention networks. arXiv preprint arXiv:1909.02606 (2019)
10. Huang, B., Ou, Y., Carley, K.M.: Aspect level sentiment classification with attention-over-attention neural networks. In: Thomson, R., Dancy, C., Hyder, A., Bisgin, H. (eds.) SBP-BRiMS 2018. LNCS, vol. 10899, pp. 197–206. Springer, Cham (2018). https://doi.org/10.1007/978-3-319-93372-6_22
11. Khalil, T., El-Beltagy, S.R.: Niletmrg at semeval-2016 task 5: deep convolutional neural networks for aspect category and sentiment extraction. In: Proceedings of the 10th International Workshop on Semantic Evaluation (SEMEVAL-2016), pp. 271–276 (2016)

12. Kingma, D.P., Ba, J.: Adam: a method for stochastic optimization. arXiv preprint arXiv:1412.6980 (2014)
13. Kipf, T.N., Welling, M.: Semi-supervised classification with graph convolutional networks. arXiv preprint arXiv:1609.02907 (2016)
14. Ma, D., Li, S., Zhang, X., Wang, H.: Interactive attention networks for aspect-level sentiment classification. arXiv preprint arXiv:1709.00893 (2017)
15. Pang, B., Lee, L.: Opinion mining and sentiment analysis. Comput. Linguist **35**(2), 311–312 (2009)
16. Pontiki, M., Galanis, D., Papageorgiou, H., Manandhar, S., Androutsopoulos, I.: Semeval-2015 task 12: aspect based sentiment analysis. In: Proceedings of the 9th International Workshop on Semantic Evaluation (SemEval 2015), pp. 486–495 (2015)
17. Sun, C., Huang, L., Qiu, X.: Utilizing bert for aspect-based sentiment analysis via constructing auxiliary sentence. arXiv preprint arXiv:1903.09588 (2019)
18. Tang, D., Qin, B., Feng, X., Liu, T.: Effective LSTMs for target-dependent sentiment classification. arXiv preprint arXiv:1512.01100 (2015)
19. Veličković, P., Cucurull, G., Casanova, A., Romero, A., Lio, P., Bengio, Y.: Graph attention networks. arXiv preprint arXiv:1710.10903 (2017)
20. Wagner, J., et al.: DCU: aspect-based polarity classification for semeval task 4 (2014)
21. Wang, J., et al.: Aspect sentiment classification with both word-level and clause-level attention networks. In: IJCAI, vol. 2018, pp. 4439–4445 (2018)
22. Wang, K., Shen, W., Yang, Y., Quan, X., Wang, R.: Relational graph attention network for aspect-based sentiment analysis. arXiv preprint arXiv:2004.12362 (2020)
23. Wang, Y., Huang, M., Zhu, X., Zhao, L.: Attention-based LSTM for aspect-level sentiment classification. In: Proceedings of the 2016 Conference on Empirical Methods in Natural Language Processing, pp. 606–615 (2016)
24. Xu, H., Liu, B., Shu, L., Yu, P.S.: Bert post-training for review reading comprehension and aspect-based sentiment analysis. arXiv preprint arXiv:1904.02232 (2019)
25. Xue, W., Li, T.: Aspect based sentiment analysis with gated convolutional networks. arXiv preprint arXiv:1805.07043 (2018)
26. Yin, C., Zhou, Q., Ge, L., Ou, J.: Multi-hop Syntactic Graph Convolutional Networks for Aspect-Based Sentiment Classification. Knowledge Science, Engineering and Management (2020)
27. Zhang, C., Li, Q., Song, D.: Aspect-based sentiment classification with aspect-specific graph convolutional networks. arXiv preprint arXiv:1909.03477 (2019)
28. Zhang, Y., Qi, P., Manning, C.D.: Graph convolution over pruned dependency trees improves relation extraction. arXiv preprint arXiv:1809.10185 (2018)

Multi-task Alignment Scheme for Span-level Aspect Sentiment Triplet Extraction

Zefang Zhao[1,2], Yuyang Liu[1,2], HaiBo Wu[2], Zhaojuan Yue[2], and Jun Li[2(✉)]

[1] University of Chinese Academy of Sciences, Beijing 100049, China
[2] Computer Network Information Center, Chinese Academy of Sciences, Beijing 100190, China
{zhaozefang,liuyuyang,yuezhaojuan,lijun}@cnic.cn,
wuhaibo@cstnet.cn

Abstract. Aspect Sentiment Triplet Extraction (ASTE) aims to extract aspect terms, opinion terms, and the corresponding sentiments from the target sentence, which is a universal subtask in the field of aspect-based sentiment analysis. Recent models achieve considerable performance in a joint learning manner but still suffer from significant limitations, such as the inability to capture span representations accurately and redundant triples are extracted due to ignoring syntactic dependencies. To tackle these issues, we propose a novel multi-task alignment scheme (MAS) for the ASTE task to tackle these issues. Particularly, we explore the aspect/opinion semantic composition module to obtain the aspect candidate set and the opinion candidate set at span-level. Moreover, the pointer-specific tagging strategy is designed to characterize internal associations between aspects and opinions by incorporating syntactic dependencies. Furthermore, a triplet alignment scheme is designed to generate triplets by aligning aspects and corresponding opinions with the position of specific pointers. Experimental results on four benchmark datasets demonstrate that our proposed model outperforms other representative ones in terms of Precision, Recall and Macro-Averaged F1.

Keywords: Span-level triplet extraction · Multi-task learning · Position alignment · Syntactic dependency · Pointer-specific tagging

1 Introduction

Aspect-based sentiment analysis (ABSA) is an essential task in the field of sentiment analysis, which contains two core subtasks: aspect sentiment classification (ASC) and Aspect Sentiment Triplet Extraction (ASTE). Previous research has revolved around the ASC subtask, but it only fucuses on the sentiment tendency of a given aspect, which is difficult to apply in real-world scenarios. In this work, we focus on the universal task - ASTE, which aims to distill the triplets (*aspect, opinion, sentiment*) of the target sentence. For example, in the sentence "*The*

E. Pimenidis et al. (Eds.): ICANN 2022, LNCS 13530, pp. 282–293, 2022.
https://doi.org/10.1007/978-3-031-15931-2_24

cream cheeses are out of this world and I love that coffee", it is evident that the sentence contains two triples: (*cream cheeses, out of this world, positive*) and (*coffee, love, negative*).

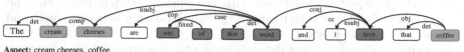

Aspect: cream cheeses, coffee

Triplet: (cream cheeses, out of this world, positive); (coffee, love, positive)

Fig. 1. An example of triplets (*aspect, opinion, sentiment*). The blue block represents the span of aspects, the orange block represents the span of opinions, and the line represents syntactic dependence at the word level. (Color figure online)

Early researches on ASTE adopted a pipeline approach to separate aspect extraction and sentiment classification. However, this strategy leads to superposition of error propagation, which affects the accuracy of triple extraction. Recently, the end-to-end joint models have been proposed to address the shortcomings of pipeline models. There are some advanced works [1,6,21] utilizing tagging strategy to capture the corresponding tagging of triplet through the relationship between words. However, it is not sufficient to determine triples merely according to the relationship at word-level. As shown in Fig. 1, the word-level representation is difficult to capture multi-word terms accurately, such as *"cream cheeses"* and *"out of this world"*.

Besides, a sentence may contain overlapping and multi-word aspect terms and opinion terms, which pose new challenges for triple extraction. [10] adopted an encoder-decoder architecture to generate an entire opinion triplet at each time step. Moreover, an interactive model based on span representation is proposed by [22], which captures the span-to-span interactions for the first time. Although these methods have achieved relatively well performance, they ignore the importance of syntactic information for exploring the relationships between aspects and opinions. Figure 1 presents the syntactic dependency of the example sentence, it is obvious that there is a syntactic dependency between the aspect term and the corresponding opinion term, such as *"nsubj: world-cheeses"*, which imposes a great effect on the search for the *"aspect-opinion"* pair.

In this paper, we propose a novel multi-task alignment scheme (MAS) for ASTE task to alleviate the disadvantages of above issues. Particularly, inspired by Span-ASTE [22], we construct aspect/opinion semantic composition module to obtain span-based aspect and opinion candidate sets. Moreover, in pointer-specific tagging module, we first integrate syntactic dependency into sentence representation using graph convolutional networks (GCN), after which two specific pointers, i.e., *"aspect_head → opinion_head"*, *"aspect_tail → opinion_tail"*, are constructed to the correspondence between apsect and opinion. Furthermore, a triplet alignment scheme is designed to further extract triples by aligning aspects and corresponding opinions with the position of specific pointers. The main contributions are summarized as follows:

- A novel pointer-specific tagging strategy is proposed to capture internal associations between aspect terms and opinion terms by the syntactic dependencies.
- We propose a novel triplet alignment sheme to align the corresponding positions of the aspect candidate set with the opinion candidate set. Such an approach is capable of better capturing the relationship between aspect and opinion by pointer tagging.
- Experimental results on five datasets show that the proposed model outperforms state-of-the-art models. Moreover, ablation studies confirm the effectiveness of each module in our model.

2   Related Work

The core tasks of Aspect-based sentiment analysis (ABSA) can be divided into two types, namely aspect sentiment classification (ASC) and aspect sentiment triplet extraction (ASTE).

The ASC task is a popular research direction in recent years, which aims to identify the corresponding sentiment tendencies through the given aspect terms. Existing methods [4,7,9,18] mainly model relationships between the aspect and context by neural networks and attention mechanism. Moreover, considering the importance of syntactic dependencies for sentiment judgment, models based on convolutional neural networks (GCN) have gained more attention. [17,24] updated the nodes in the dependency tree through the GCN for sentiment analysis. [19,25] took into account the impact of different dependency types on sentiment classification, which gain promising performance. Although relatively mature results have been obtained, these methods lack universality and are difficult to apply to real scenarios.

Recently, sentiment triplet extraction, which combines the extraction task with the aspect sentiment classification task, has received extensive attention due to its competence in various scenarios. [12] presented a two-stage triplet extraction model, which first extracts the *"aspect-sentiment"* pair and opinion information, then applys an MLP-based classifier to identify corresponding opinion for each aspect. [1,21] proposed the strategy of location tagging to obtain the associated information of aspect and opinion. [10] adapted an encoder-decoder architecture to generate an entire opinion triplet at each time step. Moreover, an interactive model based on span representation was proposed by [22], which captures the span-to-span interactions for the first time. Unlike previous studies, we propose a novel multi-task alignment scheme (MAS) for the ASTE task, which aligns aspect terms and opinion terms at corresponding positions to capture more accurate triplets.

3   Proposed Model

In this section, we present the proposed MAS model. Given a sentence of n-words, $S = [w_1, w_2, ..., w_n]$, the goal of our model is to extract all triples (*aspect, opinion, sentiment*) in the sentence. As shown in Fig. 2, the model consists of four

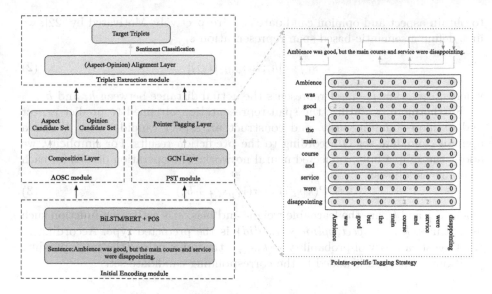

Fig. 2. The overview of our model. (Color figure online)

modules, including Initial Encoding Module, Aspect/Opinion Semantic Composition module, Specific Pointer Tagging Module and Triplet Alignment Module. These modules of MAS will be introduced separately in the rest of this section.

3.1 Initial Encoding Module

In this module, we use the BiLSTM model [5] and the pretrained BERT model [3] to obtain the encoded representation of each word.

BiLSTM. We fristly use the pretrained embedding matrix GloVe [13] to obtain the initial embedding representation $E^s = [e_1, e_2, ..., e_n] \in R^{n*d}$, where d denotes the dimension of word embeddings. Then, we set up a bidirectional LSTM model after Glove embedding, The initial representation of each word obtained by BiLSTM model is as follows:

$$h_l^{(i)} = [h_1^{(i)}, h_2^{(i)}, ..., h_n^{(i)}] \in R^{N*2d} \tag{1}$$

where $h_j^{(i)} = [\overrightarrow{h_j^{(i)}}; \overleftarrow{h_j^{(i)}}]$, $[\Delta; \Delta]$ denotes the vector concatenation operation.

BERT. We utilize the pre-trained BERT model to generate the sentence-depth bidirectional linguistic representations $h_r = [h_1, h_2, ..., h_n]$. Additionally, we use an embedding layer to obtain part-of-speech (POS) feature representations h_{pos}.

3.2 Aspect/Opinion Semantic Composition Module

In the Aspect/Opinion Semantic Composition (AOSC) module, we implement aspect extraction and opinion extraction subtasks from the semantic perspective to obtain aspect and opinion candidate sets, respectively. Motivated by [22], we first define a semantic-based span representation $s_{i,j}$:

$$s_{i,j} = [h_i; h_j; f_{dis}(i, j)] \tag{2}$$

where $f_{dis}(i, j) = j - i + 1$ represents the actual distance between h_i and h_j.

Furthermore, we utilize the span representation obtained to predict aspect and opinion simultaneously, and construct an aspect candidate set A and a opinion candidate set O according to the prediction results. For simplicity, we adopt the simple fully connected neural network. The operation details for each span are as follows:

$$P(k|s_{i,j}) = \sigma(W_p s_{i,j} + b_p) \tag{3}$$

where W_p and b_p are the learnable weight and bias. σ is activation function such as softmax. $k \in \{aspect, opinion, invalid\}$ is the predicted type. According to the largest category of probability $P(k|s_{i,j})$, the index pair of the corresponding position of the span is added to the corresponding candidate set.

3.3   Pointer-specific Tagging Module

As depicted in Fig. 2, the Pointer-specific Tagging (PST) module consists of two component: GCN layer and Pointer-specific Tagging Layer, and the main goal is to capture the relevance between aspects and opinions through syntactic dependency information.

GCN Layer. As aforementioned, syntactic dependencies are crucial for capturing the relationship between aspects and opinions. Before pointer tagging, we utilize a graph convolutional network to incorporate syntactic dependency into sentence representations. The construction of the syntactic dependency graph A and the text representation h_i^l with syntactic dependency are computed as follows:

$$A[i, j] = \begin{cases} 1, & \text{if node } i \text{ is connected to node } j \\ 0, & \text{otherwise} \end{cases} \tag{4}$$

$$h_i^l = \sum_{j=1}^{n} \xi_i A_{ij}^c W^l \widetilde{h}_j^{l-1} + b^l \tag{5}$$

where $\widetilde{h}_j^{l-1}$ is the output representation of the previous GCN layer, the initial input h_0 is the output of BiLSTM or BERT model, $\xi_i = 1/(d_i + 1)$ to normalize the matrix, W^l and b^l indicate learnable weights and bias.

Pointer-specific Tagging Layer. In order to consider the correlation between aspects and opinions, enabling the matching of information in aspect sets and opinion sets, we formulate a new specific pointer marking scheme. Specifically, we construct two pointer types, namely "*aspect_head → opinion_head*" (AH-OH), "*aspect_tail → opinion_tail*" (OT-AT). As shown on the right of Fig. 2, we construct a specific pointer marker matrix, in which the blue part represents the AH-OH pointer and the green part represents the OT-AT pointer. Our proposed model aims to predict the position matrix and analytically combine the resulting specific pointer-marker matrix to extract "*aspect-opinion*" pairs. Symbolically, we can calculate the predicted probability distribution $r_{i,j}$ of the "*aspect-opinion*" pair (w_i, w_j) as follows:

$$r_{i,j} = \text{argmax}(\text{softmax}(W_q[h_i^l; h_j^l] + b_q)) \tag{6}$$

where $r_{i,j} \in \{\text{AH-OH, OT-AT, NULL}\}$ represents pointer type, W_q, b_q are the learnable weights and bias.

3.4 Triplet Alignment Module

Alignment Strategy. We construct a novel triplet alignment strategy to align semantic modules with information obtained from specific pointer-labeled modules, reducing the problem of invalid or incorrect matching between candidate sets. Specifically, we use the AH-OH pointer and the OT-AT pointer as guidelines to match the candidates in the aspect candidate set and the opinion candidate set, respectively. Moreover, we fuse the same pairs in the obtained aspect-opinion pairs:

$$z = [h_{a,b}; h_{c,d}; g_{\text{num}}(a, b, c, d)] \tag{7}$$

where $(h_{a,b}, h_{c,d})$ represents the "*aspect-opinion*" pair finally extracted by the AOSC module and the PST module, $g_{num}(a, b, c, d)$ is a discriminant function that judges whether the extracted "*aspect-opinion*" is a repeated pair.

Sentiment Classifier. We utilize the final representation to predict the final sentiment orientation $P(y|z)$ through the full connected layer:

$$P(y|z) = \sigma(W_f z + b_f) \tag{8}$$

where W_f and b_f are the learnable weights and bias, σ is activation function such as softmax, and $y \in \{Positive, Neutarl, Negative, Invalid\}$ is the predicted label.

3.5 Training Loss

We train three modules jointly, the three tasks complement each other and optimize performance by sharing the parameters. The total loss consists of the following three parts:

$$\zeta_1 = \sum_{s_{i,j} \in S} k_{i,j}^t \log(P(k_{i,j}^t | s_{i,j})) \tag{9}$$

$$\zeta_2 = -\sum_{i=1}^{n} \sum_{j=1}^{n} r_{i,j}^t \log(r_{i,j}^t) \tag{10}$$

$$\zeta_3 = -\sum_{z \in G} y^t \log(P(y^t|z)) \tag{11}$$

where k^t, r^t, y^t represent the ground truth of the type, relation and label of "*aspect-opinion*", respectively. S denotes the span candidate set. G indicates the "*aspect-opinion*" pair candidate set. The total loss function is defined as:

$$\zeta_{total} = \alpha\zeta_1 + \beta\zeta_2 + \gamma\zeta_3 \tag{12}$$

where α, β, γ is a hyper-parameter that controls the importance of each subtask. In the experiment, we set α, β, γ to 1 for simplicity.

Table 1. Statistics of triples in ASTE-Data-V2

Dataset	Lap14			Rest14			Rest15			Rest16		
	Train	Test	Dev	Train	Test	Dev	Train	Test	Dev	Train	Test	Dev
Pos	817	364	169	1692	773	404	783	185	317	1015	407	252
Neg	517	116	141	480	155	119	205	143	53	329	78	76
Neu	126	63	36	166	66	54	25	25	11	50	29	11

4   Experiments

4.1   Datasets and Experimental Setting

For the convenience to compare our model with previous work, we evaluate our model on the ASTE-Data-V2 dataset created by [21], which contains two categories, i.e., laptop and restaurant. This dataset originated from the SemEval Challenge tasks [14–16], and extended the overlapping aspect sentiment triples based on the aspect and opinion annotation information in the ASTE-Data-V1 dataset [12]. The statistics of datasets are show in Table 1.

Settings. We implement our experiments in Pytorch [11] on an NVIDIA Tesla V100 GPU. The hidden dimension is 300. The batch size is 16. All the weights are randomly initialized by Xavier normal distribution. The dropout rate is 0.5 in our model. Adam [8] is employed to train the model, and the learning rate is set to be $1e^{-3}$ for Glove and $2e^{-5}$ for BERT. Moreover, we use an existing toolkit (Stanford CoreNLP[1]) to extract the syntactic relationship of the sentence. In additional, Precision (P), Recall (R) and Macro-Averaged F1 (F1) are adopted as the performance evaluation metrics for the sentiment triplet extraction task.

4.2   Baselines

To comprehensively evaluate the performance of the proposed MAS model, we compare our model with the following representative models.

---

[1] We use the tool of version 4.3.0 from https://stanfordnlp.github.io/CoreNLP/.

- **CMLA+** [20] adopts a multilayer attention network to co-extract apsect and opinion without requiring any syntactic dependency parsers to generate additional information as input.
- **RINANTE+** [2] proposes a BiLSTM-CRF-based neural model for joint extraction of aspect and opinion.
- **TSF** [12] proposes a two-stage framework for triplet extraction. The first stage use a unified model to predicts aspect, sentiment and opinion; the second stage couples the extracted and corresponding opinion.
- **JET** [23] utilizes a novel position-aware tagging scheme to jointly extract the triplets in end-to-end approach.
- **GTS** [21] designs a novel grid tagging scheme to address the opinion pair extraction task and the aspect-oriented opinion triplet extraction task, with one unified tagging approach.
- **PASTE** [10] adapts an encoder-decoder architecture with a position-based scheme that generates an entire opinion triplet at each time step.
- **Span-ASTE** [22] proposes a span-level approach to explicitly consider the span-to-span interactions for the ASTE task. Moreover, a dual-channel spanning pruning strategy is designed to reduce computational cost.

4.3   Experimental Results

Table 2 reports the experimental results of our model and other baselines for all the datasets. To keep in line with previous works, we compare BiLSTM-based models and BERT-based models respectively. From Table 2, we achieve the following observations.

Table 2. Experimental results on five datasets (%). The best proformances of BiLSTM-based models and BERT-based models are shown separately in bold.

Model	Lap14			Rest14			Rest15			Rest16		
	P	R	F1	P	R	F1	P	R	F1	P	R	F1
CMLA+	30.1	36.9	33.2	39.2	47.1	42.8	34.6	39.8	37.0	41.3	42.1	41.7
RINANTE+	21.7	18.7	20.1	31.4	39.4	35.0	29.9	30.1	30.0	25.7	22.3	23.9
TSF	49.6	41.1	44.8	62.7	57.1	59.7	55.6	42.5	48.0	61.0	53.4	56.8
TET	53.0	33.9	41.4	61.5	55.1	58.1	64.4	44.3	52.5	70.9	57.0	63.3
GTS	53.4	41.0	46.3	66.1	57.9	61.7	60.1	46.9	52.7	63.3	58.6	60.8
PASTE	53.7	48.6	51.0	62.4	61.8	62.1	54.8	53.4	54.1	62.2	62.8	62.5
Span-ASTE	59.9	45.7	51.8	72.5	62.4	67.1	64.3	52.1	57.6	67.3	61.8	64.4
MAS	60.5	47.1	**53.0**	70.7	64.2	**67.3**	64.7	53.7	**58.7**	67.4	63.3	**65.3**
GTS-BERT	57.8	51.3	54.4	67.8	67.3	67.5	62.6	57.9	60.2	66.1	69.9	67.9
JET-BERT	55.4	47.3	51.0	70.6	55.9	62.4	64.5	52.0	57.5	70.4	58.4	63.8
PASTE-BERT	55.0	51.6	53.2	64.8	63.8	64.3	58.3	56.7	57.5	65.5	64.4	65.0
Span-ASTE	63.4	55.8	59.4	72.9	70.9	**71.9**	62.2	64.5	63.3	69.5	71.2	70.3
MAS-BERT	65.1	56.8	**60.7**	71.6	70.3	70.8	62.0	67.5	**64.6**	70.5	71.8	**71.1**

Compared with all BiLSTM-based models, our proposed model achieves state-of-the-art performance over Twitter, Lap14, Rest14, and Rest16 datasets while achieving approximately optimal results over Rest15 dataset, which verifies the effectiveness of our model for triplet extraction task. To be specific, the end-to-end based models, such as CMLA+, RINANTE+, and TSF, have better performance than the pipeline method, which shows that the end-to-end methods (GTS, PASTE, Span-ASTE) effectively solves the issue of error propagation. Besides, our model has a significant improvement over the PASTE model. The main reason may be that the span representation of our model has a significant effect on extracting aspects and opinion terms. Furthermore, compared with Span-ASTE that is also based on span representation, our model improved by 1% in F1 score. This is mainly caused by that the specific pointer captures the intrinsic association between aspect and opinion.

We can observe that the BERT-based models have a significant improvement compared to the BiLSTM-based models. The primary reason is that BERT can obtain more richer semantic information. Moreover, compared to the BERT-based variant models of JET, GTS, PASTE, and SPAN-ASTE, our model achieves significant improvements except on the REST14 dataset, which indicates that the BERT model is indiscriminatel adapted to our model. It is noteworthy that the BERT-base-uncased pre-trained model is used for all BERT-based models.

4.4   Ablation Study

We design an ablation study to examine the effects of each component of our model on Lap14 and Rest14 datasets. Specifically, we evaluate the effect of three ablation models on the experimental results: 1) MAS w/o AOSC module. 2) MAS w/o PST module. 3) MAS w/o syntactic relation.

Table 3. Experimental results of ablation study on Lap14 and Rest14 datasets.

Model	Lap14			REST14		
	P	R	F1	P	R	F1
w/o AOSC	59.7	45.0	51.3	70.6	62.9	66.5
w/o PST	60.1	46.2	52.3	69.3	64.1	66.7
w/o syntactic relation	55.7	39.3	46.1	64.3	59.3	61.7
MAS	60.5	47.1	53.0	70.7	65.2	67.3

Effect of AOSC Module. In the absence of the AOSC module, we only use pointer-specific tagging to extract *"aspect-opinion"* pairs. As shown in Table 3, the F1 score significantly decreases without this component, because the model's ability to extract multi-word aspects/opinions decreases. Through this experiment, the effectiveness of AOSC module that aims to extract multi-word span representation is proved, which significantly improves the accuracy of triple extraction.

Effect of PST Module. To compare the impact of PST modules, we utilize the random matching principle to combine the *"aspect-view"* pair which is used by [22]. As shown in Table 3, the F1 score of this ablation model drops about 0.7% compared with our model over the LAP14 and REST14 datasets. This verifies that PST module has a great impact on the capture of aspect and corresponding opinion and the localization of span boundaries.

Effect of Syntactic Dependency. As shown in Table 3, after removing the syntactic dependency, the F1 score of our model decrease about 6% over the LAP14 and REST14 datasets, which indicates that considering the syntactic dependency further improves the ability to capture the relationship between aspects and corresponding opinions.

4.5   Case Study and Error Analysis

In this section, to intuitively understand our model and gain some insights about how we can further improve it, we conduct a case study and analyze the error examples. Some examples are listed in Table 4.

Table 4. Case study for the ASTE task

No.	Text	Ground truth	Prediction
1	He cream cheeses are out of this world and I love that coffee !!	(Cream cheeses, out of this world, POS) (coffee, love, POS)	(Cream cheeses, out of this world, POS) ✓ (coffee, love, POS)✓
2	Ambience was good, but the main course and service were disappointing	(Ambience, good, POS) (main course, disappointing, NEG) (service, disappointing, NEG)	(Ambience, good, POS) ✓ (main course, disappointing, NEG) ✓ (service, disappointing, NEG) ✓
3	The brioche and lollies as party favors is a cute and sweet touch to a most memorable meal	(Brioche and lollies, cute, POS) (brioche and lollies, sweet, POS) (meal, memorable, POS)	(Brioche and lollies, cute, POS) ✓ (brioche and lollies, sweet touch, POS) ✗ (meal, memorable, POS)
4	I would definitely go back – if only for some of those exotic martinis on the blackboard	(Martinis, exotic, POS)	((Martinis, exotic, NEU) ✗

In the first sentence, our model not only predicts single-word based triplets, but also accurately captures multi-word based triples. Moreover, for texts with overlapping triples, such as the second sentence, the overlapping opinion (*"disappointing"*) corresponding to aspects (*"main course"* and *"service"*) is accurately extracted. In brief, our model has significant performance on multi-word and overlapping triplet issues.

However, there are also some bad cases. In the third sentence, although our model correctly predicts the aspect and corresponding sentiment tendency, the opinion *"sweet"* is incorrectly captured as *"sweet touch"*. In the last example, the sentiment orientation of the *"aspect-opinion"* pair is predicted incorrectly. To make the right prediction, the model should understand *"definitely go back"*, which is far away from aspect and opinion.

5 Conclusion

In this paper, a multi-task learning framework is presented for aspect sentiment triplet extraction, which effectively solves the multi-word aspect/opinion and triplet overlapping challenges. Specifically, a semantic composition module is adopted to build the aspect candidate set and opinion candidate set at the span level. Moreover, a novel syntactic-based pointer tagging module is proposed to capture the correlation between aspects and opinions. Furthermore, a novel alignment scheme is designed, which fuses the information of candidate sets and pointer tagging to extract triplet. Experimental results show that our model significantly outperforms several baselines in the public datasets and successfully handles multi-word and overlapping triplets scenarios.

Acknowledgements. This work was supported by the National Key Research and Development Project of China (Grant No. 2019YFB1405801).

References

1. Chen, Z., Huang, H., Liu, B., Shi, X., Jin, H.: Semantic and syntactic enhanced aspect sentiment triplet extraction. arXiv preprint arXiv:2106.03315 (2021)
2. Dai, H., Song, Y.: Neural aspect and opinion term extraction with mined rules as weak supervision. arXiv preprint arXiv:1907.03750 (2019)
3. Devlin, J., Chang, M.W., Lee, K., Toutanova, K.: Bert: pre-training of deep bidirectional transformers for language understanding. arXiv preprint arXiv:1810.04805 (2018)
4. Fan, F., Feng, Y., Zhao, D.: Multi-grained attention network for aspect-level sentiment classification. In: Proceedings of the 2018 Conference on Empirical Methods in Natural Language Processing, pp. 3433–3442 (2018)
5. Hochreiter, S., Schmidhuber, J.: Long short-term memory. Neural Comput. **9**(8), 1735–1780 (1997)
6. Huang, L., et al.: First target and opinion then polarity: enhancing target-opinion correlation for aspect sentiment triplet extraction. arXiv preprint arXiv:2102.08549 (2021)
7. Jiang, B., Hou, J., Zhou, W., Yang, C., Wang, S., Pang, L.: Metnet: a mutual enhanced transformation network for aspect-based sentiment analysis. In: Proceedings of the 28th International Conference on Computational Linguistics, pp. 162–172 (2020)
8. Kingma, D.P., Ba, J.: Adam: a method for stochastic optimization. arXiv preprint arXiv:1412.6980 (2014)
9. Ma, D., Li, S., Zhang, X., Wang, H.: Interactive attention networks for aspect-level sentiment classification. arXiv preprint arXiv:1709.00893 (2017)
10. Mukherjee, R., Nayak, T., Butala, Y., Bhattacharya, S., Goyal, P.: Paste: a tagging-free decoding framework using pointer networks for aspect sentiment triplet extraction. arXiv preprint arXiv:2110.04794 (2021)

11. Paszke, A., et al.: Pytorch: An imperative style, high-performance deep learning library. CoRR **abs/1912.01703** (2019). http://arxiv.org/abs/1912.01703
12. Peng, H., Xu, L., Bing, L., Huang, F., Lu, W., Si, L.: Knowing what, how and why: a near complete solution for aspect-based sentiment analysis. In: Proceedings of the AAAI Conference on Artificial Intelligence, vol. 34, pp. 8600–8607 (2020)
13. Pennington, J., Socher, R., Manning, C.D.: Glove: global vectors for word representation. In: Proceedings of EMNLP, pp. 1532–1543 (2014)
14. Pontiki, M., et al.: Semeval-2016 task 5: aspect based sentiment analysis. In: International Workshop on Semantic Evaluation, pp. 19–30 (2016)
15. Pontiki, M., Galanis, D., Papageorgiou, H., Manandhar, S., Androutsopoulos, I.: Semeval-2015 task 12: aspect based sentiment analysis. In: Proceedings of the 9th International Workshop on Semantic Evaluation (SemEval 2015), pp. 486–495 (2015)
16. Pontiki, M., Papageorgiou, H., Galanis, D., Androutsopoulos, I., Pavlopoulos, J., Manandhar, S.: Semeval-2014 task 4: aspect based sentiment analysis. SemEval **2014**, 27 (2014)
17. Sun, K., Zhang, R., Mensah, S., Mao, Y., Liu, X.: Aspect-level sentiment analysis via convolution over dependency tree. In: Proceedings of the 2019 Conference on Empirical Methods in Natural Language Processing and the 9th International Joint Conference on Natural Language Processing (EMNLP-IJCNLP), pp. 5679–5688 (2019)
18. Tang, D., Qin, B., Feng, X., Liu, T.: Effective LSTMs for target-dependent sentiment classification. In: Proceedings of COLING, pp. 3298–3307 (2016)
19. Tian, Y., Chen, G., Song, Y.: Aspect-based sentiment analysis with type-aware graph convolutional networks and layer ensemble. In: Proceedings of the 2021 Conference of the North American Chapter of the Association for Computational Linguistics: Human Language Technologies, pp. 2910–2922 (2021)
20. Wang, W., Pan, S.J., Dahlmeier, D., Xiao, X.: Coupled multi-layer attentions for co-extraction of aspect and opinion terms. In: Proceedings of the AAAI Conference on Artificial Intelligence, vol. 31 (2017)
21. Wu, Z., Ying, C., Zhao, F., Fan, Z., Dai, X., Xia, R.: Grid tagging scheme for aspect-oriented fine-grained opinion extraction. arXiv preprint arXiv:2010.04640 (2020)
22. Xu, L., Chia, Y.K., Bing, L.: Learning span-level interactions for aspect sentiment triplet extraction. arXiv preprint arXiv:2107.12214 (2021)
23. Xu, L., Li, H., Lu, W., Bing, L.: Position-aware tagging for aspect sentiment triplet extraction. arXiv preprint arXiv:2010.02609 (2020)
24. Zhang, C., Li, Q., Song, D.: Aspect-based sentiment classification with aspect-specific graph convolutional networks. arXiv preprint arXiv:1909.03477 (2019)
25. Zhang, M., Qian, T.: Convolution over hierarchical syntactic and lexical graphs for aspect level sentiment analysis. In: Proceedings of EMNLP, pp. 3540–3549 (2020)

SSMFRP: Semantic Similarity Model for Relation Prediction in KBQA Based on Pre-trained Models

Ziming Wang, Xirong Xu[✉], Xinzi Li, Xiaoying Song, Xiaopeng Wei,
and Degen Huang

School of Computer Science and Technology, Dalian University of Technology,
Dalian, China
xirongxu@dlut.edu.cn

Abstract. Pre-trained Relation Extraction (RE) models are widely employed in relation prediction in Knowledge Base Question Answering (KBQA). However, pre-trained models are usually optimized and evaluated on datasets (e.g. GLUE) which contain various Natural Language Processing (NLP) tasks except a RE task. As a result, it is difficult to select a best pre-trained model for relation prediction unless we evaluate all available pre-trained models on a relation prediction dataset. As the Semantic Similarity (SS) task in GLUE is similar to a RE task, a Semantic Similarity Model for Relation Prediction (SSMFRP) is proposed in this paper to convert a RE task in relation prediction to a SS task. In our model, a relation candidate in a RE model is converted into the corresponding question which contains a relation candidate. Then a modified SS model is employed to find the best-matched relation. Experimental results show that the effectiveness of our proposed model in relation prediction is related to the effectiveness of the original pre-trained model in SS and GLUE. Our model achieves an average accuracy of 91.2% with various pre-trained models and outperforms original models by an average margin of 1.8% with the similar training cost. In addition, further experiments show that our model is robust to abnormal input and outperforms original models by an average margin of 1.0% on datasets of abnormal input.

Keywords: Knowledge base question answering · Relation prediction · Semantic similarity · Pre-trained model

1 Introduction

In the relation prediction task in Knowledge Base Question Answering (KBQA), it is a common way to employ a Relation Extraction (RE) model which is based

---

Supported by the Natural Science Foundation of China under Grant No. U21A20491, No. U1936109, No. U1908214.

on pre-trained models such as BERT [5]. In a BERT-based RE model, question-relation pairs (e.g. "what city was alex golfis born in"-"people person place of birth") are inputted and scored. The best-matched relation with the highest score is considered as the result for the relation prediction. Compared to traditional methods, such models achieve better performance. In addition, there are many researchers which focus on further improving such models by adding more parameters, training with more data or employing larger pre-trained models. However, although a higher accuracy could be achieved, more time, energy and storage space cost would also be required

Besides BERT, there are various pre-trained models with different structure and size. In general, employing a pre-trained model with larger size would lead to a slightly higher accuracy but much more time, energy and storage space cost. In addition, a model may be effective with a certain pre-trained model, but ineffective with another one. As a result, it is significant for a practical model to be compatible with pre-trained models with different structure and size.

In fact, pre-trained models are usually evaluated on datasets (e.g. GLUE [16]) which contain various Natural Language Processing (NLP) tasks except a RE task. If a RE model based on a pre-trained model which is effective in GLUE is simply employed in relation prediction, worse performance may be achieved. For example, ELECTRA [3] outperforms BERT in GLUE, but it show worse performance in relation prediction in our experiments. As there are various pre-trained models, it is impractical to evaluate each model on a relation prediction dataset to select a best one.

Among various tasks in GLUE, Semantic Similarity (SS) is a task which is similar to a RE task. In a SS task, a pair of sentences are fed to a pre-trained SS model and a score would be outputted based on the similarity between them. For example, to a sentence pair "An animal is chewing on something"-"An animal is chewing on a key chain", a score of 3.2 (out of 5.0) is outputted because "a key chain" is a reasonable interpretation for "something". If a SS model could be employed in a relation prediction task and achieve a better performance, it would be easier to select per-trained models for relation prediction and it would be hopeful to achieve further better performance because pre-trained models have often been optimized in GLUE tasks by researchers.

In this paper, a Semantic Similarity Model for Relation Prediction (SSM-FRP) is proposed and a RE task in relation prediction could be converted to a SS task. In our model, a sentence with a relation candidate inserted ahead of the subject entity to the question is generated as the replacement to a relation candidate in a RE model. Then the similarity between it and the original question with subject entity replaced by a placeholder "x" is scored by a pre-trained SS model. The relation in the generated sentence with the highest score is considered as the result for relation prediction.

The contributions of this paper are summarized as follow:

- We propose a model to convert a RE task in relation prediction to a SS task, so SS models could be employed in relation prediction. Experimental results show that our model achieves better performance than the baseline with similar training cost.

- Our model is more robust to abnormal input. Experimental results show that it outperforms the baseline on two datasets of abnormal input.
- Our model is compatible with various pre-trained models. Experimental results show that our model with BERT-base, BERT-small, ELECTRA-base or ELECTRA-small outperforms the corresponding original model.

2   Related Work

In KBQA, it is a common way to employ a Named Entity Recognition (NER) model for subject recognition and a RE model for relation prediction. Recently, a unified generative framework for various NER subtasks is proposed to recognize flat, nested, and discontinuous entities [18]. In RE, several researchers focus on RE for different levels such as bag-level [7], sentence-level [13] and document-level [9]. However, many of them require more training cost.

In SS tasks (e.g. STS-B in GLUE [16]), a model is supposed to score a pair of sentences, paragraphs or dialogs based on the similarity between them. Recently, many effective SS models for various tasks are proposed. For example, some researchers focus on SS models for other languages [6], some researchers propose models to learn concept representations from the perspective of the entire text corpus [19], and a cross-encoder-based metric is also proposed to estimate the SS in a paragraph-Level QA task [15]. If a SS model could be employed in relation prediction, it might be able to achieve a better performance.

Pre-trained models, such as BERT [5], ALBERT [11] and ELECTRA [3], are widely employed in various NLP tasks. BERT and other pre-trained models have shown excellent performance in relation classification [20], SS [8], KBQA [12], etc. As pre-trained models vary in structure and size, it would be better for a model to be compatible with different pre-trained models.

3   Approach

3.1   Overview

A KB (e.g. Freebase [1]) contains three components: a set of entities E, a set of relations R, and a set of facts $F = \{< s, r, o > | s, o \in E, r \in R\} \subseteq E \times R \times E$, where $< s, r, o >$ are subject-relation-object tuples. In KBQA, to an input question q, a best-matched subject $s' \in E$ is found by a NER model or other approaches. Then a set of relation candidate $R' = \{r | r \in R, < s', r > \in F\}$ is generated and a best-matched relation r' would be found in relation prediction. In general, if s' and r' are both golden ones, the golden object o' could be retrieved from F as the answer and the question is considered to be answered correctly.

In relation prediction, pre-trained RE models (e.g. BERT) have shown good performance in recent researches. In these models, tokens of a question and a relation candidate are fed to the model. After calculation, a tuple (p_0, p_1) would be outputted, representing the probability that the question is unmatched (p_0) or matched (p_1) to the candidate.

In fact, pre-trained models can be employed not only in RE, but also in other NLP tasks such as SS, interpretation and entailment tasks. In these tasks, pre-trained models are employed in a similar way, as shown in Fig. 1.

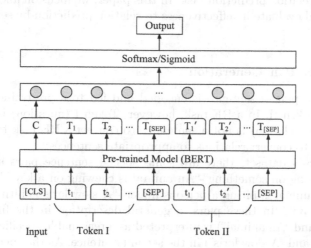

Fig. 1. A pre-trained model employed in NLP tasks

In a pre-trained model, two sentence (or phrase) are encoded into a token pair and inputted to the model. Then the similarity (or other relevance) between them is calculated by the model. The output of the model is a tuple as $(p_0, p_1, ..., p_{n-1})$. In the tuple, n could be set as the unit of the Softmax or Sigmoid layer for classification, and p_i represents a probability (or score) to evaluate whether this token pair is matched to Class i. We can also calculate

$$s = \sum_{i=0}^{n-1} (i \cdot p_i) \tag{1}$$

as the composite score to evaluate the relevance between two tokens.

In relation prediction, it is a common way to employ a general RE model: choose Softmax as the layer for classification, $n = 2$ as its unit and "question-relation" pairs as token pairs. In this way, to a question q and a set of relation candidate $R = \{r_1, r_2, ..., r_x\}$. x question-relation pairs are generated and fed to the model and then a prediction set Pre would be outputted:

$$Pre = \{(p_{1,0}, p_{1,1}), \ldots, (p_{x,0}, p_{x,1})\} \tag{2}$$

In the equation, $p_{i,0}$ is the probability that pair (q, r_i) belongs to Class 0 (Unmatched) and $p_{i,1}$ is the probability that this pair belongs to Class 1

(Matched). Then the best-matched relation r_m, which has the highest score $p_{i,1}$, could be found by the following equation:

$$m = \arg\max_{p \in Pre} p_{m,1} \qquad (3)$$

However, it is uncertain whether the above-mentioned method is the best choice for the relation prediction task. In this paper, we focus on another choice: a SS model and evaluate its effectiveness to relation prediction by several experiments.

3.2 Sentence Pair Generation

In a SS task, a pair of sentence is encoded and fed to a pre-trained model as Token I and Token II. In a RE task, however, Token I (question) is a sentence while Token II (relation) is not a sentence. To convert a RE task to a SS task, it is necessary to convert relations to appropriate sentences.

In the STS-B dataset, there are some special sentence pairs such as "An animal is chewing on something"-"An animal is chewing on a key chain" (Score 3.2) and "An animal is biting a persons finger"-"A slow loris is biting a persons finger" (Score 3.0). In these pairs, a general description in the first sentence ("something" and "An animal") is interpreted as a reasonable specific description ("a key chain" and "A slow loris") in the second sentence. As the specific description is matched to the general description as well as the whole sentence, their scores are comparatively high. If a description is interpreted in a inappropriate way, a low score is expected. For example, the score of "A woman is reading"-"A woman is kneading dough" is only 1.0, because "reading" is interpreted as a inappropriate description "kneading dough".

Obviously, in relation prediction, there are not such general descriptions to be interpreted in a question, so a SS model cannot be employed directly. In fact, researches have shown that the subject entity in a question is almost irrelevant in relation prediction, and it is a common way to replace it with a placeholder [4]. As a result, to get a Token I, we replace the subject entity in a question with a placeholder "x" which represents a general description "something" or "somebody", so that it could be interpreted as any entities.

To get a Token II, a sentence with a specific description is required. Relations in the KB, which are organized as hierarchical structure "domain type topic", could be considered as specific descriptions. In relation prediction, a golden relation is supposed to be synonymous to the whole sentence and relevant to the subject entity. Therefore, the golden "domain type topic subject" should be a reasonable interpretation of the "x", and Token II could be generated by inserting (ahead the subject entity) the relation into the question, as shown in Table 1. For example, to a question "what city was alex golfis born in", the golden relation "people person place of birth" has the same meaning "birthplace" as the whole question. To the subject entity "alex golfis", it is a "people" as well as "person", and have a "place of birth". As a result, Token II "what city was people person

Table 1. Examples of Token I and Token II in different models

Model	Token I	Token II
RE	What city was alex golfis born in	People person place of birth
SS	An animal is chewing on **something**	An animal is chewing on **a key chain**
SSMFRP	What city was **x** born in	What city was **people person place of birth alex golfis** born in

place of birth alex golfis born in" should be the interpretation of Token I "what city was x born in" with a high score of similarity.

In this way, a question-relation pair could be converted to a sentence pair, so a RE task in relation prediction could be converted to a SS task. Then a SS model could be employed to find the best-matched relation.

3.3 Score Calculation

In a RE model for relation prediction, a "question-relation" pair is classified into two categories: Class 0 (Unmatched) and Class 1 (Matched). However, in a SS model, the similarity between two sentences should be quantified and different scores are expected for sentences with different similarity. For example, pair (from STS-B) "A little boy is vacuuming the floor"-"A boy is vacuuming" (Score 3.8) has a higher score than pair "Someone is greating a carrot"-"A woman is grating an orange food" (Score 2.5). As there are no quantification standards in the KBQA dataset, we propose a method to calculate scores based on the similarity between a relation candidate and a golden relation.

As relations in the KB are organized as "domain type topic", there could be several relation candidates which contain a golden domain but a wrong topic, a golden topic but a wrong domain, or a golden domain and topic but a wrong type. Obviously, they have different similarity to the golden relation, and sentences with them also have different similarity to the question. In a relation, "domain" generally describes what the question talks about, "topic" specifically describes what the question actually asks, and "type" is often a supplementary description. As a result, a relation candidate would be scored based on the difference between it and the golden relation as follow:

- Score 0: a different domain and topic.
- Score 1: only the same domain.
- Score 2: only the same topic.
- Score 3: the same domain and topic, but a different type.
- Score 4: the same domain, topic and type.

In the set of relation candidates to a question, it is often difficult to find enough candidates with all these scores. As a result, to a question, we generate 1 sample with Score 4, several samples with Score 3 and 2 (all available candidates with Score 3 and 2), at most 2 samples with Score 1 and at most 2 samples with Score 0 (randomly selected from candidates with Score 1 and 0). Then a pre-trained model with $n = 5$ and Softmax would be fine-tuned by these samples.

Compared to the general method, which generates 1 positive sample (golden relation) and at most 5 negative samples (randomly selected from all candidates) for each question, fewer samples are generated (281,113 in our method and 313,515 in the general method). In addition, samples could be retrieved from the KB automatically and time cost for retrieval is much less than that for training. As a result, the total training cost in our model is similar as the general RE model.

During predicting, to a Token I-Token II pair, score s could be calculated by Eq. 1. To a question q and a set of relation candidates $R = \{r_1, r_2, ..., r_x\}$. x Token I-Token II pairs are generated and fed to the model and then a prediction set Pre would be outputted:

$$Pre = \{\sum_{i=0}^{4}(i \cdot p_{1,i}), ..., \sum_{i=0}^{4}(i \cdot p_{x,i})\} = \{s_1, ..., s_x\} \qquad (4)$$

In the equation, s_j is the score of the pair generated by the question and r_j. Then the best-matched relation r_m, which has the highest score, could be found by the following equation:

$$m = \arg\max_{s \in Pre} s_m \qquad (5)$$

In addition, as the value of n could be 2 or 5, either of Softmax and Sigmoid could be the layer for classification in the pre-trained model and Pre could be generated by either of Eq. 2 and 4, several experiments are conducted and results show that the strategy with $n = 5$, Softmax and Eq. 4 achieves the best performance.

4   Experiments

4.1   Dataset

We conduct experiments on the SimpleQuestions dataset [2]. It provides 108,442 single-relation questions with their answer facts, which are organized as subject-relation-object tuples in Freebase. We eliminate ineffective pairs where the golden subject is unmatched to FB5M or all n-grams which could be generated from the question [4]. In this way, we get a training set with 69,399 pairs, a validation set of 10,215 pairs and a testing set (Dataset I) of 20,302 pairs. Samples for training are generated by the method in Sect. 3.3.

To evaluate the robustness of the model, two extra datasets (Dataset II and III) are generated by randomly deleting at most 1 or 2 words (not a part of the subject entity) in each question from Dataset I.

4.2   Experiment Setting

Our model is based on pre-trained models achieved by bert4keras[1] in following experiments. Among various pre-trained models, BERT-base is a representative

---
[1] https://github.com/bojone/bert4keras.

one which is chosen as the default pre-trained model in our experiments. In this model, the number of Transformer blocks is 12, the hidden size is 768, and the number of self-attention heads is 12. Parameters are trained by an Adam optimizer [10] with a learning rate of 5e-5, a loss function of sparse categorical crossentropy, an activation function of tanh and a batch size of 64. In addition, a dropout layer with 0.1 dropout rate and a SoftMax layer with n units are appended to prevent overfitting and output results respectively. Experiments are conducted with an AMD R9-5950X CPU and a GeForce RTX 3090 GPU. Both of our model and the baseline model are trained in 3 epochs.

4.3 Experimental Results

Our SSMFRP based on different pre-trained models and corresponding pre-trained RE models (also achieved by bert4keras) are evaluated on Dataset I, II and III. With subject entities known, results for accuracies (%) in relation prediction are shown in Table 2.

Table 2. Experimental results for accuracies (%) in relation prediction

Method		Dataset I	Dataset II	Dataset III
BERT-base	Baseline	90.7	83.8	73.9
	SSMFRP	91.4	84.5	74.3
	Outperform	0.7	0.7	0.4
BERT-small	Baseline	88.5	82.9	72.2
	SSMFRP	90.7	83.3	72.7
	Outperform	2.2	0.4	0.5
ELECTRA-base	Baseline	89.5	84.0	73.9
	SSMFRP	91.4	84.9	74.9
	Outperform	1.9	0.9	1.0
ELECTRA-small	Baseline	89.1	83.0	71.8
	SSMFRP	91.3	83.6	73.0
	Outperform	2.2	0.6	1.2

As shown in the table, on Dataset I, SSMFRP achieves an average accuracy of 91.2% and outperforms the baseline by an average margin of 1.8%. On Dataset II and III, SSMFRP outperforms the baseline by an average margin of 1.0%, which shows the higher robustness of our model. Besides our appropriate strategies, another possible reason for the outperformance could be that a pre-trained model has been already optimized in SS and GLUE tasks (except a RE task). Among all pre-trained models in the table, SSMFRP with BERT-base or ELECTRA-base achieves the highest accuracy of 91.4%, and SSMFRP with ELECTRA-base shows the highest robustness to abnormal input. In addition, to BERT-large and

ELECTRA-large (not shown in the table), they fail to achieve a similar accuracy as a base model after fine-tuning in 3 epochs. In fact, large pre-trained models have much more parameters to train than base models so it would take much more time and epochs to fine-tune them. In practical applications, a base or small pre-trained model is usually employed to balance the cost and accuracy. As a result, models based on a large pre-trained model are abandoned in our experiments.

In addition, baseline RE models based on ELECTRA, which is more effective in SS and GLUE, shows worse performance in many experiments, while SSMFRP based on ELECTRA shows better performance in all experiments in the table. In other words, the effectiveness of our proposed model in relation prediction is related to the effectiveness of the original pre-trained model in SS and GLUE.

To get the subject entity in a question, a NER model could be employed. In the case that the subject entity and the relation are both correct, the answer would be correct. BERT-CRF, GlobalPointer[2] and Efficient GlobalPointer[3] are general models which have achieved good performances in general NER tasks, and all of them are based on a BERT-base model are achieved by bert4keras in our experiments. Experiments are conducted on the whole SimpleQuestions dataset to evaluate integrated models based on different NER models and relation prediction methods (general BERT-based RE model and our SSMFRP) and results for overall accuracies (%) are shown in Table 3.

Table 3. Experimental results for overall accuracies (%)

Method	Accuracy (%)
MemNN-Ensemble [2]	63.9
CFO [4]	75.7
BiLSTM-CRF+BiLSTM [14]	78.1
Structure Attention+MLTA [17]	82.3
Bert-CRF+RE	**82.6**
GlobalPointer+RE	81.3
Efficient GlobalPointer+RE	81.4
BERT-CRF+**SSMFRP**	**83.0**
GlobalPointer+**SSMFRP**	81.7
Efficient GlobalPointer+**SSMFRP**	81.8

As shown in the table, Bert-CRF achieves the best performance. In addition, Bert-CRF with our SSMFRP (based on BERT-base) outperforms that with a general RE model (also based on BERT-base) by a margin of 0.4%.

---

[2] https://kexue.fm/archives/8373.
[3] https://kexue.fm/archives/8377.

4.4   Ablation Experiments

Our SSMFRP contains 2 components: Sentence Pair Generation (SPG) and Score Calculation (SC). Ablation experiments on Dataset I are conducted to evaluate each component and results for accuracies (%) in relation prediction are shown in Table 4.

Table 4. Results for ablation experiments

Method	Accuracy (%)
Baseline	90.7
SPG	91.0
SC	90.5
SPG+SC (SSMFRP)	**91.4**

As shown in the table, compared to the baseline, SPG achieves a better performance and SSMFRP performs further better. However, SC fails to achieve a good performance alone. In fact, in a RE model for relation prediction in KBQA, few researches employ a multi-classification strategy or a quantification score strategy, while these strategies are widely employed in SS models. As a result, in this task, SC is inapplicable to a RE model, but applicable to a SS model (our SSMFRP).

In Sect. 3.2, the subject entity in Token I is replaced with a placeholder "x" and it would be restored in Token II. To evaluate this strategy, following experiments on Dataset I are conducted and results for accuracies (%) in relation prediction are shown in Table 5.

Table 5. Experimental results for different strategies in Sect. 3.2

Strategy	Accuracy (%)
Token I with entity, Token II with entity	91.1
Token I with placeholder, Token II with placeholder	90.3
Token I with placeholder, Token II with entity (SSMFRP)	**91.4**

As shown in the table, although the subject entity in a question is almost irrelevant in a RE model, it is significant in a SS model. Among these strategies, the strategy in our SSMFRP achieves the best performance.

In Sect. 3.3, the value of n could be 2 or 5, the layer for classification could be Softmax or Sigmoid, and Pre could be generated by Eq. 2 or 4. Especially, in the case of $n = 2$, to sentence pairs, normalization is applied to scores as their labels and Eq. 2 and 4 would lead to a same result ($p_{j,1} = s_j$ is the normalized score of

Table 6. Experimental results for different strategies in Sect. 3.3

Strategy	Accuracy (%)
$n = 2$, Softmax	91.1
$n = 2$, Sigmoid	91.1
$n = 5$, Sigmoid, Eq. 2	90.9
$n = 5$, Sigmoid, Eq. 4	86.8
$n = 5$, Softmax, Eq. 2	91.3
$n = 5$, Softmax, Eq. 4 (SSMFRP)	**91.4**

r_j). Following experiments on Dataset I are conducted to evaluate each strategy and results for accuracies (%) in relation prediction are shown in Table 6.

As shown in the table, the strategy with $n = 5$, Softmax and Eq. 4 has the best performance, which is applied in our SSMFRP.

5 Conclusion

In this paper, we propose a Semantic Similarity Model for Relation Prediction (SSMFRP) to convert a RE task in relation prediction to a SS task, so a SS model could be employed in relation prediction. In our model, the subject entity in a question is replaced with a placeholder "x" as Token I and a relation candidate is inserted (ahead of the subject entity) into the question as Token II. Then such sentence pairs would be scored based on the difference between the relation candidate and the golden relation. Then a pre-trained model would be fine-tuned by Token I, Token II and their scores, and the best-matched relation with the highest score could be found. Experimental results show that our model outperforms the baseline by an average margin of 1.8% with similar training cost and it is more robust to abnormal input.

Our SSMFRP is not only a more effective and robust model for relation prediction in KBQA, but also a general method of converting a RE task in relation prediction to a SS task. By our method, a dataset for KBQA (e.g. SimpleQuestions) could be converted to a dataset for SS, which has the similar structure and contents as STS-B dataset. As a result, countless methods (present and future) for SS tasks (especially for STS-B) could be easily employed in relation prediction, and it would be hopeful to achieve further better performance by employing a certain SS method. This is also our future work.

References

1. Bollacker, K., Evans, C., Paritosh, P., Sturge, T., Taylor, J.: Freebase: a collaboratively created graph database for structuring human knowledge. In: Proceedings of the 2008 ACM SIGMOD International conference on Management of Data, pp. 1247–1250 (2008)

2. Bordes, A., Usunier, N., Chopra, S., Weston, J.: Large-scale simple question answering with memory networks. arXiv preprint arXiv:1506.02075 (2015)

3. Clark, K., Luong, M.T., Le, Q.V., Manning, C.D.: Electra: pre-training text encoders as discriminators rather than generators. In: Proceedings of The International Conference on Learning Representations (2020)

4. Dai, Z., Li, L., Xu, W.: Cfo: conditional focused neural question answering with large-scale knowledge bases. In: Proceedings of Annual Meeting of the Association for Computational Linguistics, pp. 800–810 (2016)

5. Devlin, J., Chang, M.W., Lee, K., Toutanova, K.: Bert: pre-training of deep bidirectional transformers for language understanding. In: Proceedings of the 2019 Conference of the North American Chapter of the Association for Computational Linguistics: Human Language Technologies, pp. 4171–4186 (2019)

6. Fikri, F.B., Oflazer, K., Yanikoglu, B.: Semantic similarity based evaluation for abstractive news summarization. In: Proceedings of the 1st Workshop on Natural Language Generation, Evaluation, and Metrics, pp. 24–33 (2021)

7. Hu, Z., Cao, Y., Huang, L., Chua, T.S.: How knowledge graph and attention help? a qualitative analysis into bag-level relation extraction. In: Proceedings of the 59th Annual Meeting of the Association for Computational Linguistics. p. 4662–4671 (2021)

8. Huang, B., Bai, Y., Zhou, X.: Hub at semeval-2021 task 2: word meaning similarity prediction model based on roberta and word frequency. In: Proceedings of the 15th International Workshop on Semantic Evaluation, pp. 719–723 (2021)

9. Huang, K., Qi, P., Wang, G., et al.: Entity and evidence guided document-level relation extraction. In: Proceedings of the 6th Workshop on Representation Learning for NLP, pp. 307–315 (2021)

10. Kingma, D.P., Ba, J.: Adam: a method for stochastic optimization. In: Proceedings of the 3rd International Conference on Learning Representations (2015)

11. Lan, Z., Chen, M., Goodman, S., et al.: Albert: a lite bert for self-supervised learning of language representations. arXiv preprint arXiv:1909.11942 (2019)

12. Luo, D., Su, J., Yu, S.: A bert-based approach with relation-aware attention for knowledge base question answering. In: Proceedings of International Joint Conference on Neural Networks, pp. 1–8 (2020)

13. Ma, R., Gui, T., Li, L., et al.: Sent: Sentence-level distant relation extraction via negative training. In: Proceedings of the 59th Annual Meeting of the Association for Computational Linguistics, pp. 6201–6213 (2021)

14. Petrochuk, M., Zettlemoyer, L.: Simplequestions nearly solved: a new upperbound and baseline approach. In: Proceedings of the 2018 Conference on Empirical Methods in Natural Language Processing, pp. 554–558 (2018)

15. Risch, J., Möller, T., Gutsch, J.: Semantic answer similarity for evaluating question answering models. In: Proceedings of the 3rd Workshop on Machine Reading for Question Answering, pp. 149–157 (2021)

16. Wang, A., Singh, A., Michael, J., et al.: Glue: A multi-task benchmark and analysis platform for natural language understanding. In: Proceedings of the 7th International Conference on Learning Representations (2019)

17. Wang, R., Ling, Z., Hu, Y.: Knowledge base question answering with attentive pooling for question representation. IEEE Access **7**, 46773–46784 (2019)

18. Yan, H., Gui, T., Dai, J., et al.: A unified generative framework for various NER subtasks. In: Proceedings of the 59th Annual Meeting of the Association for Computational Linguistics, pp. 5808–5822 (2021)

19. Zhang, X., Zong, B., Cheng, W., et al.: Unsupervised concept representation learning for length-varying text similarity. In: Proceedings of the 2021 Conference of the North American Chapter of the Association for Computational Linguistics: Human Language Technologies, pp. 5611–5620 (2021)
20. Zhu, W.: Autorc: improving BERT based relation classification models via architecture search. In: Proceedings of the 59th Annual Meeting of the Association for Computational Linguistics and the 11th International Joint Conference on Natural Language Processing: Student Research Workshop, pp. 33–43 (2021)

SubCrime: Counterfactual Data Augmentation for Target Sentiment Analysis

Wei Chen[1], Lulu Wang[1], Jinglong Du[2(✉)], and Zhongshi He[1]

[1] College of Computer Science, Chongqing University, Chongqing, China
mlg_cwei@cqu.edu.cn
[2] College of Medical Informatics, Chongqing Medical University, Chongqing, China
jldu@cqu.edu.cn

Abstract. The goal of Target Sentiment Analysis (TSA) is to predict the users' sentiment towards specific targets from review sentences. However, the predicting results may not perform well due to the sparsity of training data. Data augmentation is a fruitful technology to alleviate the influence of imperfect training data, which obtains additional data by transforming the original samples. Unfortunately, there is hardly a particular data augmentation approach for TSA. To address this problem, in this paper, we propose a low-cost and effective data augmentation method called **SubCrime**, which constructs auxiliary sentences in two steps: <u>Sub</u>stitute and dis<u>Crime</u>inate. The former aims to substitute reasonable targets for the observed sentences through the masked language model, while the latter discriminates the restructured sentences via the constrained objective. SubCrime does not require extra knowledge and tedious manual annotation. We design SubCrime to answer the key counterfactual question: "If the review target in the sentence changed, would its sentiment be different ?". Experiments show SubCrime improves on average 2 to 4 points in F1 scores on four datasets compared to methods without enhancement. Moreover, SubCrime also outperforms other data augmentation methods widely used in other Natural Language Processing (NLP) tasks.

Keywords: Target Sentiment Analysis · Counterfactual · Data augmentation

1 Introduction

Target Sentiment Analysis (TSA) is a fine-grained task in the field of sentiment analysis, which aims at identifying the sentiment polarities (i.e., positive, neutral, and negative) of the certain targets given in reviews. For example, in a restaurant review "The food is delicious, but the service is dreadful.", here, the reviewer mentions two targets (also called aspects): "food" and "service", but expresses two different sentiments: positive sentiment towards the former and negative sentiment towards the latter.

E. Pimenidis et al. (Eds.): ICANN 2022, LNCS 13530, pp. 307–319, 2022.
https://doi.org/10.1007/978-3-031-15931-2_26

Many early efforts are devoted to manually designing rule-based features and building sentiment classifiers [10]. With the flourishing development of Neural Network (NN), some advanced architectures have been applied to the TSA, like Recurrent Neural Networks (RNNs) [3,16], Convolution Neural Networks (CNNs) [9,13], Memory Networks (MN) [14,23], Graph Neural Network (GNN) [1] and Bidirectional Encoder Representation from Transformers (BERT) [11,22]. Currently, most studies that achieve the state-of-the-art performances rely on efficient representations of pre-training networks. However, they neglect a major challenge that the benchmark dataset is sparse. Specifically, the sentences are limited and the target words are unbalanced in benchmark dataset. On the one hand, these limited sentences may cause the model cannot generalize well in real-world testing data once the representation ability of network reaches the bottleneck. On the other hand, due to the target words exhibit a long-tail distribution, some tail target words usually converge to an inferior state without sufficient sample exposure during the training phase. To mitigate this problem, some researchers leverage transfer learning [4] to enhance the domain knowledge from other similar domains. Although this approach can achieve some impressive results, it requires external resources and some strict assumptions. Data augmentation is an alternative way, which focuses on increasing the diversity of available data by making transformations on the original data. Such strategy is intuitive and effective and has been employed in some NLP tasks successfully. such as machine translation [6] and text classification [24]. Hence, in this work we explore how data augmentation techniques can help TSA task.

From the perspective of language expression, people have their preferences for expressing feelings about a certain object, e.g., "I enjoy a very much.", "It would be better if the b was cheaper", and "Oh, I'm so pleased with the c.". If we collect a user's review for product a, we speculate the user may have similar expressions for related products purchased before (e.g., b or c). Although such potential review sentences were not recorded in the training data, they were intuitively reasonable and consistent with people's speech. From the perspective of causal inference, these potential sentences are counterfactual data, which provide the answer to a key counterfactual question: **"If the review target in the sentence changed, would its sentiment be different?"**. Therefore, for the given m user's reviews including m different targets (i.e., suppose each user gives a review for one target), we can potentially acquire $m \cdot (m-1)$ review sentences based on these existing targets. As an important complementary resource in the observed sentences, counterfactual sentences can recompense for the sparse sentences and alleviate the unbalance of target distribution, thus benefiting to train a sentiment classification model with good accuracy and robustness.

On the other hand, sentiment prediction relies on both the context and the target words. For example, in the sentences "The **computer** is large." and " The **hard disk** is large.", the same sentimental word "large" expresses different sentiments due to the different targets: positive sentiment towards "hard disk" but negative attitude to "computer". This actually shows that targets also play a key role in predicting the sentiment. Hence, it is unreasonable to blindly expand the sentences and ignore the sentiment changes brought by the targets.

Motivated by the above analysis, in this paper, we propose a simple but effective framework **SubCrime** to achieve counterfactual data augmentation for the TSA task, which contains two main steps: substitute and discriminate. First the SubCrime substitutes some reasonable candidate targets based on existing targets sets for each sentence. Then, we leverage a discriminator to filter some enhanced sentences complete in content but semantically unreasonable. We conduct many experiments on four benchmark datasets and the results show SubCrime's effectiveness.

2   Related Work

Target Sentiment Analysis. Target Sentiment Analysis (TSA) falls in the broad scope of fine-grained sentiment analysis. And it is basically formulated as mining sentiment polarity of given targets or aspects in the sentence, which has attracted increasing attention from the academic and industrial communities. Most studies pay attention to designing various architectures like RNNs [16], CNNs [9,13], MN [14,23], GNN [1] and BERT [11,22] to train the sentiment classification model based on available data. However, as mentioned above, there exists a critical issue in TSA that the benchmark dataset is sparse. We know a machine learning problem includes two key aspects: "algorithm" and "data". Currently, most researchers are focused on designing complex network models to achieve promising performances. Considering TSA is a classification task of relatively simple, the improvement of effect is more dependent on efficient pre-training model representation. Once the training data is limited, the results are difficult to substantially improve. Therefore, we aim to improve the sentiment classification performance from the data perspective.

Counterfactual Thinking. Counterfactual thinking refers to the thinking activity that negates and reproduces the facts happened in the past, thereby constructing a possible hypothesis, and its typical example is: "what would ... if ...?". Recently, many researchers leverage counterfactual thinking to design explainable, robust, and fair models in some machine learning problems [7,8], which have achieved promising results. In addition, counterfactual thinking can also be applied to augment the data-scarce tasks [2], obviously, our work falls into this research category. Counterfactual thinking has been widely used to augment training targets in some neural language processing (NLP) tasks, e.g., language bias [27], neural machine translation [15], and name entity recognition [25], but has to the best of our knowledge not yet been used in the TSA. Hence, in this paper, we propose to apply the counterfactual thinking to TSA.

Data Augmentation. Data augmentation aims to increase the diversity of data by applying constrained transformation on the observed data, which has been widely used in the NLP tasks. A commonly used manner [26] in data augmentation is to replace local words with synonyms from WordNet or Word2Vec. Inspired by this strategy, the authors in [24] proposed some Easy Data Augmentation (EDA) operations (i.e., synonyms replace, randomly insert, randomly

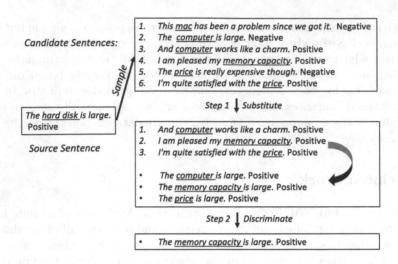

Fig. 1. A simple example of SubCrime for "The hard disk is large".

swap, and randomly delete) to further boost the performance on text classification [24] and receive substantial attention from the research community. Later, some researchers [20] generate the data by using back-translation in machine translation task, this strategy first translates the English sentence into another language (e.g., French) and then translates it back to English.

Recently, a more advanced generative approach [12] that using a bidirectional language model to predict the word given the context surrounding the original word, has also achieved promising results. Different augmentation strategies have their own advantages, the replacement-based method is easy to implement and can maintain the sentence consistency (i.e., replacing words with synonyms in sentences), while the generative-based manner (i.e., replacing words with related words in sentences using language model) can enhance the semantic diversity. In this work, we combine both the replacement-based and generative-based methods, which can enhance the consistency and diversity of training data simultaneously.

3   SubCrime Model

In TSA task, given a training dataset $D_{train} = \{(\boldsymbol{x}_i, \boldsymbol{t}_i, \boldsymbol{p}_i)\}_{i=1}^{N}$, where N is the number of training samples. Each sentence and target in it can be respectively denoted by $X = \{x_1, x_2, \cdots, x_n\}$ and $T = \{t_1, t_2, \cdots, t_m\}$, where T is the substring of $X(T \in X)$, n and m refer to the length of sentence and target. TSA focuses on detecting the sentiment polarity about the target T, which can be formalized as: $\hat{y} = \arg\max_{y \in S} \mathcal{A}(y \mid X, T)$, where S denotes the sentiment types for y and $\hat{y}$ represents the predicted sentiment.

3.1   Step 1: Substitute Target Words

For the first step, we require a Language Model (LM) for calculating the target probability based on its context, the context is a sequence of words surrounding an original target T in a sentence X. The calculated probability is:

$$\mathcal{F} = \mathrm{LM}(\cdot \mid X - T) \tag{1}$$

where $\mathcal{F} = \{(t_0, p_0), (t_1, p_1), (t_2, p_2), \cdots\}$ is the target set, $t_{\{\cdot\}}$ is the target indexes and $p_{\{\cdot\}}$ is the corresponding probabilities of appearing in the sentence. In other words, for each sentence X, we can generate a series of candidate targets $\{t_0, t_1, \cdots\}$ for it. $\{X - T\}$ denotes the sentence without the target words, LM is a large-scale language model pre-trained on 2500M Wikipedia corpus [5], since our training data is small, we directly use the pre-trained model with the same model configuration with BERT-large. For predicting the words at the position of the original target, the model encodes the surrounding words individually forward and backward. The outputs from both directions are concatenated and fed into the following feed-forward neural network, which produces targets with a probability distribution over the vocabulary.

We know that the number of target words generated by LM is huge, although we only select some existing target words, there are still some redundant words in $\mathcal{F}$, hence in this step, we need to sample some appropriate targets to substitute the original targets and construct counterfactual sentences. To this end, we define the following constraints:

- Firstly, we address the issue that augmentation sentences are not always compatible with annotated sentiment labels. Considering the sentence in Fig. 1 "The **hard disk** is large." and the labeled target "**hard disk**", the sentiment polarity is annotated with positive label. A LM often assigns high probabilities to words such as "computer", "Windows 7", or "memory" in the laptop domain, although some of them are mutually contradictory to the annotated labels of positive. Such a simple augmentation may generate sentences that are implausible with respect to their original labels and harmful for model training. We notice that if the two sentences have the same sentiment label and the targets are highly related, then the sentences formed by swapping the targets are more reasonable. Hence, in our approach, we choose the targets of the sentence with the same polarity as the original sentence, which can alleviate this problem of inconsistent labels to some extent.
- Secondly, in the source training datasets, the number of target words is inherently uneven, if we evenly sample each target, the distribution of the targets is even more lopsided, so it is necessary to balance the target distribution. To achieve this goal, we assume the proportion of target t presented in the source training set is q, the probability of it being selected by each sentence is $1 - q$.
- Finally, to achieve the goal of controlling the rationality and numbers of synthetic sentences, we set a threshold ϵ to judge the probability gap between the source target words and the candidate targets, if $\epsilon \geq \|p_s - p_c\|$, (i.e., p_s is the probability of source target and p_c denotes the probability of candidate

target), we remain candidate target. This constraint can help to find more semantically similar target words.

During the generative process, we use a simple strategy, where we generate 4 extra sentences for each sentence. After this step, we synthesize a set of labeled sentences, which is denoted by D_{mid}.

3.2 Step 2: Discriminate Synthesized Sentence

Actually, one obstacle in using synthesized sentences is the noise and error it may introduce. For example, in Fig. 1, the candidate sentence 2: "The computer is large." is filtered for labeling reason after step 1, but the remaining sentence 3: "And computer works like a charm." may still cause unreasonable synthetic sentences. Moreover, we also need further inspection for these sentences with possibly unreasonable semantics, such as "The price is large.", since the quality of data basically determines the performance of the model.

In this work, we believe a generated sentence that is high quality should at least meet two basic demands: (1) the sentence should maintain the fluency of the source sentence, (2) sentiment polarity should be consistent with the given context. To achieve these ends as much as possible, independently we propose an automatic filter method, which trains a baseline co-extractor using D_{train}. More specifically, we use the D_{train} to label two tasks: (1) target extraction (i.e., start indexes and end indexes of target words); (2) sentiment extraction (i.e., neutral, positive, and negative). Then, for target extraction, two classifiers are applied to predict the start score g_s and end score g_e of each token at both positions, respectively. For sentiment classification, the BERT classifier is applied to predict the sentiment score $\hat{y}_{i,j}$. The parameters are estimated by minimizing the following loss function $\mathcal{J}$, that is:

$$\mathcal{J} = -\sum_{i=1}^{n}\{\boldsymbol{p}_s^i \log(\boldsymbol{g}_s^i) + \boldsymbol{p}_e^i \log(\boldsymbol{g}_e^i)\} - \sum_{i=1}^{N}\sum_{j=1}^{K} y_{i,j} \log \hat{y}_{i,j} \qquad (2)$$

where $\boldsymbol{p}_s^i$ and $\boldsymbol{p}_e^i$ are the ground truths of the targets' boundaries. n is the sentence's length. In second term, N and K are the total training samples and sentiment types, respectively, $y_{i,j}$ refers to the corresponding ground truth.

Thus, during the testing phase, if the discriminator successfully extracts the correct target and sentiment in D_{mid}, we keep the sample; otherwise, we discard it. This results in a synthesized dataset $D_{sysnt} \subset D_{mid}$, consisting of labeled sentences and with the same structure as $D_{training}$, which is the outcome of Sub-Crime. Finally, we mix the $D_{training}$ and D_{sysnt} as the augmentation datasets to help the model achieve superior accuracy and robustness.

4 Experiments

4.1 Datasets

We conduct experiments on four benchmark datasets, i.e., *Laptop*14 [17] and *Restaurant*14 [17], *Restaurant*15 [19], *Restaurant*16 [18]. More specially,

Table 1. For the statistics on the four datasets, the upper part is the polarity frequency statistics, and the lower part is the target frequency statistics. "Rank -1" represents the least target type.

Frequencies of polarities								
Polarity	Laptop14		Restaurant14		Restaurant15		Restaurant16	
	Train	Test	Train	Test	Train	test	Train	Test
Positive	994	180	2164	318	912	163	1240	234
Neutral	464	122	637	122	36	19	69	12
Negative	870	87	807	80	256	70	439	43
Total	2328	389	3605	520	1204	252	1748	280
Frequencies of categories								
Category	Laptop14		Restaurant14		Restaurant15		Restaurant16	
	Target	Number	Target	Number	Target	Number	Target	Number
Rank 1	#screen	61	#food	361	#food	146	#food	214
Rank 2	#price	56	#service	225	#service	116	#service	146
Rank 3	#use	54	#prices	63	#place	78	#place	116
Rank 4	#battery life	53	#place	59	#restaurant	28	#restaurant	43
Rank 5	#keyboard	50	#menu	56	#staff	27	#staff	39
Rank -1	#repair	1	#pictures	1	#patis	1	#pasta	1

*Laptop*14 is the user's reviews that collected from the electronic product domain and *Restaurant* datasets contain different reviews about restaurant from SemEval2014, SemEval2015, and SemEval2016. For all datasets, we use the original train/test splits and clean them by filtering out the target words with the conflict label as well as the sentences without a target. However, since the source testing datasets have an imbalanced target distribution and we aim to train a robustness model that can be applied to inputs of any target words, we build a new testing set from the source testing set for each dataset. Specially, we make sure that the amount of each target words in the sentence is equal. The statistics of the processed four datasets are reported in Table 1, it can be seen that each dataset has the most positive reviews, and the number of neutral reviews is significantly lower than the number of positive reviews in *Restaurant*15 and *Restaurant*16, while the training samples are more than the other two datasets in *Laptop*14 and *Restaurant*14.

4.2 Evaluation Metrics and Settings

To evaluate the performance, we use the commonly-used accuracy (Acc) and macro F1-score (F1) as the metrics. Since there is no validation set, we report the average results using the ten-fold cross-validation method.

In step 1, we use the BERT-large model to estimate the probability of target occurring in the original sentence. In step 2, we train a co-extractor to discriminate the synthesized sentence and choose the BERT-base model as the backbone network. The batch size is 16 and the learning rate is 2e-5. In classifier $\mathcal{A}$, the hyper-parameters are determined with grid search. In specific, the learning rate and batch size are tuned in the ranges of [1e–5,2e–5,3e–5,4e–5,5e–5,]

Table 2. Performance (%) comparisons of employing different models on original and enhanced datasets, respectively. "Aug." and "Ori." represent whether we use our method for the augmentation or not. "Change" denotes the changes of performance on overall datasets, "↑" is for improvement, and "↓" is for decline.

Model			Laptop14 (%)		Restaurant14 (%)		Restaurant15 (%)		Restaurant16 (%)	
			Acc	F1	Acc	F1	Acc	F1	Acc	F1
RNN	TNet-LF [13]	Ori.	67.22	63.49	74.69	64.73	76.03	51.11	86.78	57.10
		Aug.	68.24	65.22	75.67	66.30	76.07	52.28	88.03	59.78
		Change	1.02↑	1.73↑	0.98↑	1.57↑	0.04↑	1.17↑	1.25↑	2.68↑
	AEN-Glove [21]	Ori.	65.45	62.42	74.35	64.13	77.94	55.63	86.27	55.80
		Aug.	67.10	63.95	74.48	65.02	78.17	55.14	87.58	57.03
		Change	1.65↑	1.53↑	0.13↑	0.89↑	0.23↑	0.49↓	1.31↑	1.23↑
BERT	BERT-SPC [5]	Ori.	73.88	71.20	75.40	62.02	82.58	63.79	90.55	65.40
		Aug.	75.37	72.83	80.25	73.27	82.82	64.80	91.11	68.90
		Change	1.49↑	1.63↑	4.85↑	11.25↑	0.24↑	1.01↑	0.56↑	3.50↑
	AEN-BERT [21]	Ori.	74.45	71.45	77.77	69.23	82.30	59.22	90.76	63.91
		Aug.	76.61	74.13	78.52	71.60	83.10	64.98	91.14	68.24
		Change	2.16↑	2.68↑	0.75↑	2.37↑	0.80↑	5.76↑	0.38↑	4.33↑

Table 3. Performance (%) comparisons of applying different augmentation methods to the BERT-base model on four datasets. For all the baseline we use the same number of augmentation sentences. Texts in **bold** represent the best results and texts underlined indicate the second best results.

Model		Laptop14 (%)		Restaurant14 (%)		Restaurant15 (%)		Restaurant16 (%)	
		Acc	F1	Acc	F1	Acc	F1	Acc	F1
AEN-BERT	Original	74.45	71.45	77.77	69.23	<u>82.30</u>	59.22	<u>90.76</u>	<u>63.91</u>
	Random deletion	73.60	70.49	77.48	69.02	81.71	**65.27**	88.90	57.02
	Random insertion	73.57	70.47	77.73	69.42	82.07	61.68	88.10	60.67
	Random swap	73.78	70.42	76.83	68.71	81.99	61.21	89.52	60.80
	Synonym replacement	74.24	71.21	77.89	69.80	81.35	62.51	89.86	61.33
	Target replacement	<u>74.86</u>	<u>71.90</u>	<u>78.49</u>	<u>70.50</u>	82.02	61.95	88.41	58.10
	SubCrime	**76.61**	**74.13**	**78.52**	**71.60**	**83.10**	<u>64.98</u>	**91.14**	**68.24**
BERT-SPC	Original	<u>73.88</u>	<u>71.20</u>	75.40	62.02	<u>82.58</u>	<u>63.79</u>	<u>90.55</u>	<u>65.40</u>
	Random deletion	70.00	64.14	77.34	68.97	75.83	52.44	89.21	60.36
	Random insertion	72.16	69.31	77.58	69.15	75.67	51.38	90.14	64.81
	Random swap	72.96	69.85	77.42	69.17	72.70	47.35	88.37	62.02
	Synonym replacement	70.41	67.22	<u>78.12</u>	<u>70.46</u>	72.38	44.81	86.99	56.81
	Target replacement	73.62	70.89	77.29	69.37	76.43	53.26	89.03	59.04
	SubCrime	**75.37**	**72.83**	**80.25**	**73.27**	**82.82**	**64.80**	**91.11**	**68.90**

and [16,32,64], respectively, and the maximum sentence length is 85. For the baselines, we set the parameters as tuned them in the same ranges as ours.

4.3 Experimental Results

Results on Original and Augmentation Datasets. We first report the results (Acc and F1 score) obtained from four models on the source and augmentation datasets in Table 2. We can see:

SubCrime basically achieves consistent improvement over the source datasets on four TSA-related models, which shows the effectiveness of our proposed method. In addition, compared with RNN-based models, BERT-based models can achieve better results in four datasets, which can be improved by 5% to 10% on average, since BERT has stronger feature representation capability than RNN. Furthermore, it can be observed that the improvement effects of BERT-based models are generally higher than these of RNN-based models, we speculate the reasons come from two aspects, on the one hand, the RNN-based models may learn some shallow features and don't make full use of the augmentation data, which just increase the amount of the training data, hence, there is no competitive performance. On the other hand, since BERT has an efficient representation, the counterfactual samples we generated could enhance the richness of the context and reduce the imbalance of the training data.

Table 2 also shows that the AEN-Glove achieves lower results than source dataset in *Restaurant*15. Intuitively, the number of the training data in *Restaurant*15 is the least among all datasets (see Table 1), which possibly led to the glove model could not learn sufficient representation from the mixed dataset. Similarly, among all datasets, we observe that there is the smallest improvement space (1.01% vs 2.68%, 2.37%, and 3.50%) on the *Restaurant*15, which also verified our expectation.

Results on Different Augmentation Models. We further compare the proposed method SubCrime with other typical data augmentation methods using BERT-based models and the results are shown in Table 3.

It can be observed that our method achieves the best performances on all baselines and datasets, considering the datasets span a wide range of TSA, these results demonstrate the generality of SubCrime. We summarize these outstanding performances into the following two reasons: one is the generated data relieves the imbalanced problem of the target in training, which raises the exposure of a few targets, and another reason is that we increase the diversity of training data, which promotes the establishment of association between content features and target representations.

Target Replacement, which randomly chooses a target and replaces the original target appearing in the sentence, is most similar to SubCrime among all the baselines and achieves the best results in *Laptop*14 and *Reataurant*14 based on AEN-BERT, this basically shows the utility of our approach for TSA.

4.4 Case Study

In this section, to provide an intuitive understanding of our proposed method SubCrime, we present some case studies in Table 4.

- SubCrime can check the rationality of the generated sentence from two aspects: (1) fluency checking, (2) sentiment checking. To ensure the quality of the generated sentences. In the first example, it is obvious that "music" does not match "delicious", which leads to generating an unreasonable sentence.

Table 4. Examples generated by different augmentation methods. ⊗ means this sentence is discarded by the SubCrime, instead, ⊙ denotes the sentence is preserved by the model. The true sentences and false sentences are marked with ✓ and ✗.

Target:	Meal	
Polarity:	Positive	
Source:	I just wonder how you can have such a delicious **meal** for such little money the latin food here is	
SubCrime 1:	I just wonder how you can have such a delicious **music** for such little money the latin food here is	⊗
SubCrime 2:	I just wonder how you can have such a delicious **latin food** for such little money the latin food here is	⊙
Target:	Computer	
Polarity:	Negative	
Source:	I really didn't expect the **computer** is so large	
SubCrime 1:	I really didn't expect the **disk capacity** is so large	⊗
SubCrime 2	I really didn't expect the **mouse** is so large	⊙
Target:	Motherboard	
Polarity:	Negative	
Source:	After about a week i finally got it back and was told that the **motherboard** had failed and so they installed a new motherboard	
RD:	About a week I it was the **motherboard** had failed and so they installed new motherboard	✗
RI:	After about a plunk for just about week I finally just about got it back and plunk for was told that the **motherboard** had failed and so they installed a new information technology motherboard	✗
RS:	After about a I finally back it got the week installed that and **motherboard** had failed and so they told a new motherboard was	✗
SR:	After about a week iodin finally got it plump for and was severalize that the **motherboard** had conk out and so they instal a new motherboard	✓
TR:	After about a week i finally got it back and was told that the **keyboard** had failed and so they installed a new motherboard	✗
SubCrime:	After about a week i finally got it back and was told that the **charger unit** had failed and so they installed a new motherboard	✓

Similarly, in the second sentence, when target word "computer" is changed to "disk capacity", the sentiment is also changed, but our discriminator is able to filter out these extreme unreasonable examples and remain counterfactual examples that may occur in the sentence.

- In the third sentence, we show five examples of augmentation methods, i.e., Random Deletion (**RD**), Random Insertion (**RI**), Random Swap (**RS**), Synonym Replacement (**SR**), Target Replacement (**TR**). While the first four are operationally sound, they lack some semantic coherence and richness, some operations even pollute the source data and degrade performance. For example, the sentence "About a week I it was the **motherboard** had failed and so they installed new motherboard" in **RD**, although this operation may not change the sentiment polarity of the output, it is semantically unreasonable and affects the representation of the sentence and model robustness (e.g., the model may learn the shallow features of the word "motherboard" association with positive sentiment). In this sentence, from common sense we know that the battery cannot be charged may be caused by the battery itself, yet it may be also caused by the damaged motherboard. As expected, our method changes the target "motherboard" to "charger unit", which is clear that it is more reasonable in terms of semantic richness when compared with other baselines.

5   Conclusion

This paper proposes a novel data augmentation strategy SubCrime by leveraging counterfactual thinking for target sentiment analysis. SubCrime contains two steps: substitute and discriminate. Experiments show SubCrime improves on average 2 to 4 points in F1 scores on four public datasets compared to the setting without data augmentation. In fact, from the perspective of algorithm, it is difficult to increase the model by 1 to 2 points, but our SubCrime has increased by 2.68%, 2.37%, 5.76%, 4.33% based on the most advanced BERT-based method on the four public datasets, respectively, which shows the advanced nature of our method. In addition, SubCrime also achieves better results on several datasets compared to other augmentation baselines.

Acknowledgments. This work was supported in part by the Natural Science Foundation of Chongqing, China under Grant cstc2021jcyi-bshX0168, the Intelligent Medical Project of Chongqing Medical University under Grant ZHYXQNRC202101, and Graduate Research and Innovation Foundation of Chongqing, China (Grant No.CYC21072).

References

1. Bai, X., Liu, P., Zhang, Y.: Investigating typed syntactic dependencies for targeted sentiment classification using graph attention neural network. In: IEEE/ACM Transactions on Audio, Speech, and Language Processing, pp. 503–514 (2020)
2. Chen, L., Zhang, H., Xiao, J., He, X., Pu, S., Chang, S.F.: Counterfactual critic multi-agent training for scene graph generation. In: Proceedings of the IEEE/CVF International Conference on Computer Vision, pp. 4613–4623 (2019)
3. Chen, W., et al.: Target-based attention model for aspect-level sentiment analysis. In: Gedeon, T., Wong, K.W., Lee, M. (eds.) ICONIP 2019. LNCS, vol. 11955, pp. 259–269. Springer, Cham (2019). https://doi.org/10.1007/978-3-030-36718-3_22
4. Chen, Z., Qian, T.: Transfer capsule network for aspect level sentiment classification. In: Proceedings of the 57th Annual Meeting of the Association for Computational Linguistics, pp. 547–556. Association for Computational Linguistics, Florence, Italy, July 2019
5. Devlin, J., Chang, M.W., Lee, K., Toutanova, K.: Bert: pre-training of deep bidirectional transformers for language understanding. In: Proceedings of the 2019 Conference of the North American Chapter of the Association for Computational Linguistics: Human Language Technologies, pp. 4171–4186 (2019)
6. Edunov, S., Ott, M., Auli, M., Grangier, D.: Understanding back-translation at scale. In: Proceedings of the 2018 Conference on Empirical Methods in Natural Language Processing, pp. 489–500 (2018)
7. Garg, S., Perot, V., Limtiaco, N., Taly, A., Chi, E.H., Beutel, A.: Counterfactual fairness in text classification through robustness. In: Proceedings of the 2019 AAAI/ACM Conference on AI, Ethics, and Society, pp. 219–226 (2019)

8. Goyal, Y., Wu, Z., Ernst, J., Batra, D., Parikh, D., Lee, S.: Counterfactual visual explanations. In: International Conference on Machine Learning, pp. 2376–2384 (2019)
9. Huang, B., Carley, K.M.: Parameterized convolutional neural networks for aspect level sentiment classification. In: Proceedings of the 2018 Conference on Empirical Methods in Natural Language Processing, pp. 1091–1096 (2018)
10. Jiang, L., Yu, M., Zhou, M., Liu, X., Zhao, T.: Target-dependent twitter sentiment classification. In: Proceedings of the 49th annual meeting of the association for computational linguistics: human language technologies, pp. 151–160 (2011)
11. Ke, Z., Xu, H., Liu, B.: Adapting bert for continual learning of a sequence of aspect sentiment classification tasks. In: Proceedings of the 2021 Conference of the North American Chapter of the Association for Computational Linguistics: Human Language Technologies, pp. 4746–4755 (2021)
12. Kobayashi, S.: Contextual augmentation: data augmentation by words with paradigmatic relations. arXiv preprint arXiv:1805.06201 (2018)
13. Li, X., Bing, L., Lam, W., Shi, B.: Transformation networks for target-oriented sentiment classification. In: Proceedings of the 56th Annual Meeting of the Association for Computational Linguistics, pp. 946–956 (2018)
14. Lin, P., Yang, M., Lai, J.: Deep mask memory network with semantic dependency and context moment for aspect level sentiment classification. In: Proceedings of the 28th International Joint Conference on Artificial Intelligence, pp. 5088–5094 (2019)
15. Liu, Q., Kusner, M., Blunsom, P.: Counterfactual data augmentation for neural machine translation. In: Proceedings of the 2021 Conference of the North American Chapter of the Association for Computational Linguistics: Human Language Technologies, pp. 187–197 (2021)
16. Ma, D., Li, S., Zhang, X., Wang, H.: Interactive attention networks for aspect-level sentiment classification. In: Proceedings of the 26th International Joint Conference on Artificial Intelligence, pp. 4068–4074 (2017)
17. Pontiki, M., Galanis, D., Pavlopoulos, J., Papageorgiou, H., Androutsopoulos, I., Manandhar, S.: Semeval-2014 task 4: aspect based sentiment analysis. In: Proceedings of the 8th International Workshop on Semantic, pp. 27–35 (2014)
18. Pontiki, M., et al.: Semeval-2016 task 5: aspect based sentiment analysis. In: Proceedings of the 10th International Workshop on Semantic Evaluation, pp. 19–30 (2016)
19. Pontiki, M., Galanis, D., Papageorgiou, H., Manandhar, S., Androutsopoulos, I.: Semeval-2015 task 12: aspect based sentiment analysis. In: Proceedings of the 9th International Workshop on Semantic Evaluation, pp. 486–495 (2015)
20. Sennrich, R., Haddow, B., Birch, A.: Improving neural machine translation models with monolingual data. In: Proceedings of the 54th Annual Meeting of the Association for Computational Linguistics, pp. 86–96 (2016)
21. Song, Y., Wang, J., Jiang, T., Liu, Z., Rao, Y.: Attentional encoder network for targeted sentiment classification. arXiv preprint arXiv:1902.09314 (2019)
22. Sun, C., Huang, L., Qiu, X.: Utilizing bert for aspect-based sentiment analysis via constructing auxiliary sentence. arXiv preprint arXiv:1903.09588 (2019)
23. Tang, D., Qin, B., Liu, T.: Aspect level sentiment classification with deep memory network. arXiv preprint arXiv:1605.08900 (2016)
24. Wei, J., Zou, K.: Eda: easy data augmentation techniques for boosting performance on text classification tasks. In: Proceedings of the 2019 Conference on Empirical Methods in Natural Language Processing and the 9th International Joint Conference on Natural Language Processing (EMNLP-IJCNLP) (2019)

25. Zeng, X., Li, Y., Zhai, Y., Zhang, Y.: Counterfactual generator: a weakly-supervised method for named entity recognition. In: Proceedings of the 2020 Conference on Empirical Methods in Natural Language Processing (EMNLP) (2020)
26. Zhang, X., Zhao, J., LeCun, Y.: Character-level convolutional networks for text classification. In: Advances in Neural Information Processing Systems, pp. 649–657 (2015)
27. Zmigrod, R., Mielke, S.J., Wallach, H., Cotterell, R.: Counterfactual data augmentation for mitigating gender stereotypes in languages with rich morphology. In: Proceedings of the 57th Annual Meeting of the Association for Computational Linguistics, pp. 1651–1661 (2019)

Word Embeddings with Fuzzy Ontology Reasoning for Feature Learning in Aspect Sentiment Analysis

Asmaa Hashem Sweidan[1]([✉]), Nashwa El-Bendary[2], and Haytham Al-Feel[3]

[1] Faculty of Computers and Information, Fayoum University, Fayoum, Egypt
aha07@fayoum.edu.eg
[2] College of Computing and Information Technology,
Arab Academy for Science, Technology and Maritime Transport, Aswan, Egypt
nashwa.elbendary@aast.edu
[3] College of Community, Computer Science Department,
Imam AbdulRahman Bin Faisal University, Dammam, Kingdom of Saudi Arabia
Htaalfeel@iau.edu.sa

Abstract. In this paper, a hybrid feature learning approach is proposed to employ aspect sentiment analysis on sentence level through contextual discovery of unstructured text data. The proposed approach joins sentiment lexicon with pre-trained BERT (Bidirectional Encoder Representations from Transformers) word embeddings model for feature deep learning and prediction of context words. In addition, fuzzy ontology reasoning is employed for supporting more in-depth feature extraction through representing semantic knowledge by forming relationships between aspects. Subsequently, the extracted sentiment indicators in online user reviews are classified using Bi-LSTM (Bi-directional Long Short-Term Memory) deep learning model so that the context around words are learned and the corresponding meanings are captured both syntactically and semantically. According to the obtained results, the proposed approach outperforms other related feature learning approaches through improving sentence aspect sentiment analysis and accordingly boosting the overall accuracy of sentiment classification. An average accuracy of 96%, AUC score of 94.5%, and F-score of 95% are achieved by the proposed approach considering five public social media datasets of online reviews. The significance of this study is investigating enrichment of extracted features through using BERT transformer with fuzzy ontology in order to improve the performance of aspect-based sentiment analysis while adding the contextual meanings to the prediction task, and extracting the indirect relationships embedded in social data of user reviews.

Keywords: Sentiment analysis · Feature learning · BERT · Natural Language Processing · Fuzzy ontology

E. Pimenidis et al. (Eds.): ICANN 2022, LNCS 13530, pp. 320–331, 2022.
https://doi.org/10.1007/978-3-031-15931-2_27

1   Introduction

Sentiment Analysis (SA), also known as Opinion Mining (OM), is one of the most active research fields in Natural Language Processing (NLP). As the unstructured nature of social media text data places a key challenge for data analysis, SA applies contextual mining and computational analysis for systematically detecting, extracting, and investigating subjective information in social media data. Moreover, sentiments are expressed in different ways with a prerequisite to discover sentiments that are related to each aspect stated in user reviews before determining the polarity of the corresponding sentence [1]. Consequently, SA is utilized for categorizing opinions expressed in user online reviews for entities in order to determine user polarity [2,3].

The recent state-of-the-art in aspect based sentiment analysis indicates the noteworthy growing in researches addressing aspects in unstructured text along with recognizing the corresponding sentiment. In the next paragraphs, a review of several related research work proposed recently is presented with a focus on studies considering opinion mining of drug reviews related aspects in order to match the case study of Adverse Drug Reaction (ADR) topic mining that is considered in this paper. In [4], the authors developed a system based on feature selection from drug reviews dataset for retrieving important features and eliminating noise. In order to extract features, the proposed system used Term Frequency-Inverse Document Frequency (TF-IDF) algorithm based on the Bag of Words (BoW) model. Afterwards, the system utilized fuzzy based rough sets to reduce features dimension as well as using several machine learning classifiers. Experimental results in that study showed enhancement in feature selection using the proposed system. Also, in [5], the authors proposed an approach to classify the medical relationships in clinical records based on in-depth studies. The proposed approach used Word2vec word embeddings method for feature extraction including word position features. The proposed approach in that study employed Convolutional Neural Network (CNN) through generating local features in the convolution layer and developing more local features from every sentence through multi-pooling operations. The proposed approach in that study examined a dataset of clinical records and achieved significant values of accuracy, recall, and F-score of 72.9%, 66.7%, and 69.6%, respectively. Moreover, in [6], the authors developed a system that employs opinion mining for detecting drugs side effects. The proposed system used a rule-based system to estimate the drug side effects based on user opinion. The proposed system is implemented on data collected from m www.drugratingz.com, which is a website where users may provide ratings, reviews and recommendations for drugs and medications. An F-score of 57% was achieved by the proposed approach. Furthermore, in [7], the authors proposed a model based on ontology combined with deep learning algorithm for monitoring system to assist travel. The proposed model used ontology with Word2vec as feature extraction. An F-score of 80% was achieved by the proposed system, which was experimented on data collected from TripAdvisor, Facebook, and Twitter.

This paper aims to integrate the power of BERT word embeddings transformer model and fuzzy ontology based semantic knowledge. The BERT deep learning model is employed for extracting strong relationships within the context around a word in order to capture the corresponding contextual meaning [8]. Moreover, fuzzy ontology is utilized for representing semantic knowledge that enriches the designed approach through relationship formation between aspects [9,10]. Then, the extracted aspect features are combined and used as an input of Bi-directional Long Short-Term Memory (Bi-LSTM) model to classify aspect sentiment. Accordingly, the proposed approach learns sentence-level contextual meaning in unstructured text data.

The remaining part of this paper is organized as follows. Section 2 explains the phases of the proposed approach. In Sect. 3, the utilized datasets are described, the performance evaluation metrics are listed, and a discussion for the obtained experimental results is presented. Section 4 summarizes conclusions and discusses points for future work.

2   The Proposed Aspect-Based Sentiment Analysis Approach

This section describes the phases of the proposed approach, which are: Pre-processing, Feature polarity identification, Feature extraction, and Aspect sentiment classification, as depicted in Fig. 1.

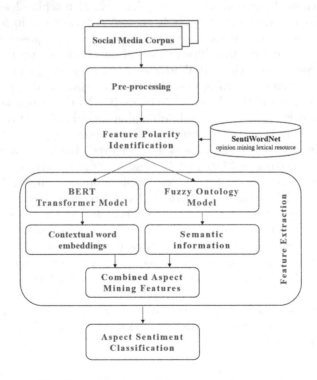

Fig. 1. Architecture of the proposed approach

2.1   Pre-processing

The major steps of pre-processing phase are detailed as follows:

1. *Tokenization:* presents each word in the input social media text as smaller units (tokens) and remove the blank spaces.
2. *Deleting stop words and punctuation:* uses Natural Language ToolKit (NLTK) for deletion.
3. *Slang words conversion:* converts slang workds from the current form into their standard form.
4. *Stemming and lemmatization:* restores the derived words to their word stem/base form or dictionary word format and removing inflectional endings using the NLTK suffix-dropping algorithm.
5. *Change negative reference text:* applies changes according to different views of negativity.
6. *Spelling correction:* generates all keywords for lexical variants using Levenshtein distance then applies filters for misspelling keyword.
7. *Part Of Speech (POS) tagging:* identifies the label (tag) of each word using Stanford POS tagger.

Completing the last step of pre-processing phase should enable obtaining context lexical for each word.

2.2   Feature Polarity Identification

During the feature polarity identification phase, the proposed approach uses the tagged POS resulted from the pre-processing phase for dimensionality reduction of the matrix and accordingly for topic mining model improvement. After detecting each word property by the POS, it's used in order to find the word polarity score. Furthermore, word frequencies in each document is an additional output of the pre-processing phase. Thus, the POS is utilized to recognize word property and calculate the score for word polarity. Consequently, SentiWordNet (SWN) [11] opinion mining lexical resource is searched for each POS, the corresponding features polarity are calculated, and one score is assigned to each sentiment word. A score = 0 is assigned to the opinion word that are not existing in the SWN lexical resource.

2.3   Feature Extraction

During feature extraction phase, the proposed approach uses BERT model to generate (predict) a set of contextual word embeddings. Moreover, it uses fuzzy ontology technique for more in-depth semantic information discovery. Thus, after completing feature polarity identification phase, the proposed approach utilizes BERT model to predict words of the context in each sentence. The BERT [12] model generates meaningful sentence embeddings through calculating sentence words that are linked with each word embeddings. The main training functionality of BERT model depends on randomly (but partially) masking tokens in an input sentence and predicting/reconstructing the original sentence only based on those masked tokens. Thus, BERT suffers from the downside of not fully considering the interdependence between masked positions, which sometimes causes loss of important information about basic semantics of the features. Thus, along with applying BERT word embeddings transformer, fuzzy ontology method is utilized by the proposed approach for describing semantic knowledge that provides semantic relationships between words to obtain more specific features.

Protégé-OWL is used to generate a classical ontology. Fuzzy OWL plug-in is then implemented to extend the classical ontology to a vague one. The proposed approach uses fuzzy ontology, based on the efficiently categorized tagged POS in user reviews and the calculated polarity, for retrieving the most related words for each aspect query. Then, the membership degree between concepts is calculated in order to extract the corresponding features based on the extracted opinion words. The major steps of feature extraction with fuzzy ontology are presented in Algorithm 1. The main output of the feature extraction phase is a vector that consists of a combination of aspect mining features. After completing the feature extraction phase, the resulted feature word vectors, which are extracted using BERT and ontology methods, are passed to Bi-LSTM model for deriving qualitative topics.

Algorithm   1.   Feature   extraction   with   fuzzy   ontology
INPUT: POS   and   feature   polarity   scores
OUTPUT: Feature vectors of ontology (concepts, relationships)

1: Build ontology (concept (class), corresponding relationship (property)).
2: Search ontology and extract features
3: Compute feature weights using TF-IDF algorithm [4], as shown in Eq. (1):

$$tf - idf_{t,d} = (1 + \log tf_{t,d}) \cdot \log \frac{N}{df_t} \tag{1}$$

where t refers to the terms; d is the document, D is the collection of documents.
4: Select the top N feature based on TF-IDF algorithm.
5: Use similarity metric (Cosine similarity) to compute similarity between concept as shown in Eq. (2):

$$Sim(onto, topic) = \sum_{t=1}^{T} fonto, t_i * tf - idf_{t,d} \tag{2}$$

where $fonto$ refers to ontology feature, $topic$ is topic keyword, and i is feature importance.
6: Apply ontology with fuzzy reasoner to retrieve the most related words for each query.
7: Measure similarity between the query words.
8: Calculate the membership value between concepts based on the relationship weights and edge weights mapped on SentiWordNet sentiment analysis lexical resource.
9: Extract the opinion words used for finding features.

2.4   Sentiment Classification

During sentiment classification phase, the extracted sentiment indicators, using BERT with fuzzy ontology models in the previous phase, are passed to the Bi-LSTM deep learning model to be classified through having the context around words learned and capturing the corresponding meanings both syntactically and semantically. The main deliverable of sentiment classification phase is a set of detected aspects, from users' reviews, along with their corresponding predicted sentiment. Moreover, words in social media reviews may exist before and after a specific term in order to determine certain semantic significance. Thus, the proposed approach processes text forward and backward in order to deal with long document text.

One main advantage of the LSTMs is the ability to capture sequential data through taking the previous data into account.

The LSTM layer is built as a memory cell to store the preceding information. Each LSTM unit involves a memory cell that holds an input gate I_t, a forget gate F_t, and an output gate O_t to manage updating and usage of previous information [13]. The final output of the LSTM is h_t that determined through utilizing the cell-state input matrix as well as the result of the output gate's feature matrix at a specific time. Afterwards, the LSTM output layer determines the probability value of $(0,1)$ that accordingly indicates the polarity (negative, positive) of the feature found in the social text using the Softmax function [12]. Consequently, the sentiment label inside the entered text is predicted.

3   Experimental Results and Discussion

This section illustrates obtained experimental results of the proposed BERT-fuzzy ontology feature learning approach in the light of the Adverse Drug Reaction (ADR) topic as a case study for aspect sentiment analysis. Also, the performance of the proposed approach is investigated through conducting comparative analysis against other implemented state-of-the-art related approaches for sentence-level aspect sentiment analysis. Simulation experiments are implemented on a PC with 2.7 GHz Intel Core i7 CPU and 32 GB memory with 16 GB GPU. The proposed approach is developed using TensorFlow Deep Learning framework with Keras Python libraries and Protégé OWL tool for ontology creation with fuzzy reasoner.

The proposed approach is tested using five social media datasets based on publicly available real-world online user reviews. The selected datasets for experimental work, which are related to the ADR case study considered in this paper, are constructed from real drug-related reviews on five health-related online forums/platforms, as follows:

1. **AskaPatient:** The AskaPatient dataset consists of 63,782 positive, neutral, and negative drug reviews, with positive/negative reviews are detected based on feature polarity.

2. **WebMD:** The WebMD dataset contains 241,980 positive, neutral, and negative drug reviews associated with approximately 14,000 crawled drugs.
3. **DrugBank:** The DrugBank dataset contains a list of 215,063 reviews on drug conditions, effectiveness, and side effects considering around 6345 drugs.
4. **Twitter:** The Twitter dataset consists of 267,215 Twitter posts including drug conditions and ADRs, indications, and positive/negative reactions, with tweets accessed using Tweepy Python API.
5. **n2c2 2018:** The n2c2 2018 benchmark dataset includes 505 summaries from the MIMIC-III health care database, and is divided into 0.7 training and 0.3 testing sets.

For evaluating the performance of the proposed approach, aspect sentiment classification is basically assessed using *accuracy* metric, according to Eq. (3), where *TP* refers to *True Positives*, *TN* refers to *True Negatives*, *FP* refers to *False Positive*, and *FN* refers to *False Negatives*. However, as the accuracy metric can be misleading, with high accuracy alone doesn't mean high model performance, *F-score* metric is also computed according to Eq. (4) as the harmonic mean that combines the effect of both *recall (sensitivity)* and *precision* metrics, as shown in Eqs. (5) and (6), respectively. Moreover, Root Mean Square Error (RMSE) measure, defined as the average magnitude of variations (errors) *e* in a set of predictions, is considered for performance assessment as shown in Eq. (7).

$$accuracy = \frac{TP + TN}{TP + TN + FP + FN} \tag{3}$$

$$F - score = \frac{2 \cdot Precision \cdot Recall}{Precision + Recall} \tag{4}$$

$$recall = \frac{TP}{TP + FN} \tag{5}$$

$$precision = \frac{TP}{TP + FP} \tag{6}$$

$$MAE = \frac{1}{n} \sum_{t=1}^{n} |e_t| \tag{7}$$

3.1   Experimental Results

For implementation of the proposed approach, fuzzy ontology features are extracted and joined with BERT word embeddings learned features. In addition, the proposed approach employs Bi-LSTM model with 10-fold cross validation for sentiment classification.

Figure 2 depicts the ROC (receiver operating characteristic curve) for the proposed approach. The applied approach investigates each dataset against the remaining tested datasets based on the Area Under Curve (AUC) metric, which is commonly used to evaluate unbalanced datasets. From Fig. 2, it's noticed that the proposed approach performs in a manner that keeps the ROC curve closer to the Y-axis. That is interpreted as a fair attainment of the most suitable ratio of TPR against FPR. Moreover, as shown from the ROC curve in Fig. 2, the proposed approach obtained AUC scores of 0.942, 0.935, 0.92, 0.89, and 0.94 considering AskaPaint, WebMD, DrugBank, Twitter, and n2c2 2018 datasets, respectively. That is to say, the proposed approach ranks the randomly selected positive reviews more powerfully against the randomly selected negative reviews with an average probability of 98.2%. Based on that observation, it's noticeable that the proposed aspect sentiment analysis model shows an improved performance. However, this observation also may not be sufficient for fair assessment. Therefore, the other previously stated performance metrics are used to evaluate the performance of the proposed approach.

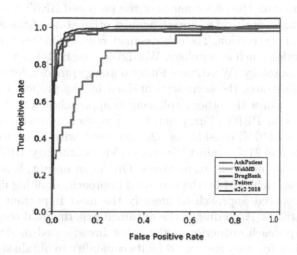

Fig. 2. Comparative area under the ROC curve for the proposed approach

Table 1 shows the performance of the proposed approach using different datasets. As observed from Table 1, the most significant values of performance metrics are achieved on AskaPatient dataset, which is the most balanced among the 5 tested datasets, with 95.1%, 94.2%, 94%, and 96% for precision, recall, F-score, and accuracy, respectively.

In general, it's observed from the obtained experimental results that the proposed approach sufficiently detects and retrieves semantic and sentiment relations among objects from social data.

Table 1. Performance measures of the proposed approach using different datasets

Measurement	Dataset				
	AskaPatient	WebMD	DrugBank	Twitter	n2c2 2018
Precision	95.1%	94.1 %	88.3%	84.8%	94.4%
Recall	94.2%	90.1 %	89.5%	84.3%	94.2%
F-score	94%	93.8%	90.8%	84.5%	93.4%
Accuracy	96%	95.5%	91.7%	92.9%	97.2%

3.2 Comparative Analysis

This section compares the performance of the proposed BERT with fuzzy ontology (BERT+Fuzzy ontology) approach against other state-of-the-art approaches in terms of feature extraction. The other considered approaches employed several independent models, such as ontology, Word2vec, and BERT, as well as a hybrid Word2vec with ontology (Word2vec+Fuzzy ontology) model, for feature extraction. Figure 3 illustrates the accuracy obtained by the proposed BERT+Fuzzy ontology model against the other implemented approaches. The results depicted in Fig. 3 clarify that BERT+Fuzzy ontology proposed approach achieved a significant accuracy of 97%, considering n2c2 datasets, with an average increase of 10%, 7.5%, 14%, and 21%, against Word2vec+Fuzzy ontology, BERT, Word2vec, and Fuzzy ontology methods, respectively. One main insight, based on the considerable accuracy achieved by the proposed approach, shall highlight the capability of the proposed approach to identify the most important features from various text datasets. Accordingly, the obtained experimental results show that the proposed approach outperforms the other investigated models in terms of feature extraction accuracy supported by its capability to obtain significant word semantics and sentiment relations.

As observed from Table 2, the most significant results are achieved using AskaPatient dataset. Thus, comparing the proposed approach with other related approaches, it's noticed that the proposed approach of BERT with fuzzy ontology (BERT+Fuzzy ontology) for feature extraction achieved the values of 95.1%, 94.2%, and 94.6% for precision, recall, and F-score, respectively. Whereas, Word2vec with fuzzy ontology approach (Word2vec+Fuzzy ontology) achieved results of 89.1%, 90.28%, and 91.9% for precision, recall, and F-score, respectively. Based on the measured performance metrics, it's also noticed that the proposed approach outperformed both Word2vec with Fuzzy ontology and BERT models. Moreover, considering significant findings of studies proposed in relevant literature, the scientific merit of the work proposed in this paper has been clearly revealed. In [1], the authors proposed a model based on ontology combined with Word2vec embeddings feature extraction algorithm for developing a monitoring system to assist travelers. The proposed model achieved an F-score of 80%. Also, in [6], the authors used word2vec with CNN model and achieved significant values of accuracy, recall, and F-score of 72.9%, 66.7%, and 69.6%, respectively.

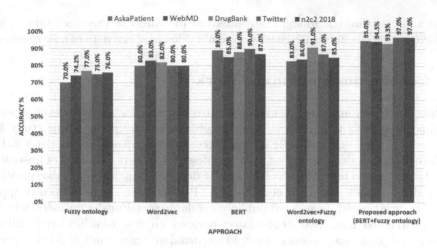

Fig. 3. Accuracy of the proposed BERT+Fuzzy ontology model against the other implemented approaches

Table 2. Comparative analysis of the proposed model performance against other tested approaches

Method	Measurement	Dataset				
		AskaPatient	WebMD	DrugBank	Twitter	n2c2 2018
Fuzzy ontology	Precision	72%	70%	72.3%	76%	74%
	Recall	72.4%	72.4%	89.1%	70.3%	79%
	F-score	72.6%	74%	71%	72%	76%
	MAE	0.36	0.43	0.37	0.376	0.352
Word2vec	Precision	81%	80.3 %	80%	78%	81%
	Recall	80.28%	78.9%	80.1%	80	81%
	F-score	81.1%	78.9%	79.2%	78.5%	80%
	MAE	0.37	0.36	0.36	0.388	0.397
BERT	Precision	92%	90.5%	91.2%	93%	90.2%
	Recall	94.4 %	92.4%	89.1%	90.3%	89%
	F-score	92.6%	94%	90.81%	91.7%	92%
	MAE	0.22	0.23	0.27	0.26	0.239
Word2vec+Fuzzy ontology	Precision	89.1%	85.3%	83%	81%	85%
	Recall	90.28%	89%	76.01%	80%	81 %
	F-score	91.9%	79%	89.2%	85%	90%
	MAE	0.27	0.26	0.25	0.28	0.27
Proposed approach	Precision	**95.1%**	**94.1%**	**88.3%**	84.8%	94.4%
(BERT+Fuzzy ontology)	Recall	**94.2%**	90.1%	**88.3%**	**84.3%**	94.2%
	F-score	**94.6%**	**92.9%**	**88%**	84.5%	94%
	MAE	0.14	**0.13**	0.14	0.15	**0.13**

Thus, the results presented in Table 2 in addition to the results reported in relevant literature highlighted the support provided to the proposed approach by the enrichment of extracted features, using BERT transformer with fuzzy ontology. Furthermore, it's concluded that applying BERT+Fuzzy ontology approach for extracting hybrid features improves the performance of aspect-based sentiment analysis through adding the contextual meanings to the prediction task, and extracting the indirect relationships embedded in social data of user reviews.

4   Conclusions and Future Work

In this paper, an approach of hybrid feature learning for sentence-level aspect sentiment analysis is developed. The tangible scientific merit of this study is achieved through employing BERT contextual word embeddings model jointly with sentiment lexicon as well as fuzzy ontology for feature discovery of unstructured social media text. Moreover, Bi-LSTM deep learning model is subsequently utilized for aspect sentiment classification. Performance of the proposed approach is investigated on selected publicly available social media datasets, which are constructed from real drug-related reviews on five health-related online forums and platforms, in order to serve the considered case study of ADR aspect sentiment analysis. The most significant observations of the current study show that the proposed hybrid BERT with fuzzy ontology feature learning approach for aspect sentiment analysis outperformed other state-of-the-art related methods, such as fuzzy ontology, Word2vec, BERT, and Word2vec with fuzzy ontology, with an achieved average accuracy of 96%, AUC score of 94.5%, F-score of 95%, and MAE of 0.13. Also, it's noticed that the resulted sentiment classification is positively affected while using properly balanced datasets (AskaPatient dataset) against the clear negative impact of poorly balanced datasets on sentiment classification (Twitter dataset). Generally, it's concluded that the proposed approach that implemented BERT sentence embeddings transformer jointly with fuzzy ontology reasoning features is capable of collecting greater elements of sentiment and semantic in comparison to other related approaches and models proposed in relevant literature. Accordingly, the proposed approach improves sentence-level aspect sentiment analysis. For future research work, a wide domain is available for improvements in aspect sentiment classification performance through analyzing various text content and utilizing more novel feature discovery approaches.

References

1. Kharde, V.A., Sonawane, S.: Sentiment analysis of twitter data: a survey of techniques. Int. J. Comput. Appl. **139**(11), 5–15 (2016)
2. Injadat, M., Saloa, F., BouNassif, A.: Data mining techniques in social media: a survey. Neurocomputing **214**(19), 654–670 (2016)
3. Gupta, S., Gupta, M., Varma, V., Pawar, S., Ramrakhiyani, N., Palshikar, G.K.: Co-training for extraction of adverse drug reaction mentions from tweets. In: Pasi, G., Piwowarski, B., Azzopardi, L., Hanbury, A. (eds.) ECIR 2018. LNCS, vol. 10772, pp. 556–562. Springer, Cham (2018). https://doi.org/10.1007/978-3-319-76941-7_44
4. Rezaeinia, S.M., Rahmani, R., Ghodsi, A., Veisi, H.: Sentiment analysis based on improved pre-trained word embeddings. Expert Syst. Appl. **117**, 139–147 (2019)

5. He, B., Guan, Y., Dai, R.: Classifying medical relations in clinical text via convolutional neural networks. Artif. Intell. Med. **93**, 43–49 (2019)
6. Ebrahimi, M., Yazdavar, A.H., Salim, N., Eltyeb, S.: Recognition of side effects as implicit-opinion words in drug reviews. Online Inf. Rev. **40**(7), 1018–1032 (2016)
7. Ali, F., El-Sappagh, S., Kwak, D.: Fuzzy ontology and LSTM-based text mining: a transportation network monitoring system for assisting travel. Sensors **19**(2), 234 (2019)
8. Devlin, J., Chang, M.W., Lee, K., Toutanova, K.: BERT: pre-training of deep bidirectional transformers for language understanding. arXiv preprint arXiv:1810.04805 (2018)
9. Jayawardana, V., Lakmal, D., de Silva, N., Perera, A.S., Sugathadasa, K., Ayesha, B.: Deriving a representative vector for ontology classes with instance word vector embeddings. In: 2017 Seventh International Conference on Innovative Computing Technology (INTECH), pp. 79–84. IEEE (2017)
10. Nicola, G., Daniel, O., Rudi, S.: What is an ontology? In: Staab, S., Studer, R. (eds.) Handbook on Ontologies, pp. 1–17 (2009)
11. Baccianella, S., Esuli, A., Sebastiani, F.: SentiWordNet 3.0: an enhanced lexical resource for sentiment analysis and opinion mining. In: LREC, vol. 10, pp. 2200–2204 (2010)
12. Sweidan, A.H., El-Bendary, N., Al-Feel, H.: Aspect-based sentiment analysis in drug reviews based on hybrid feature learning. In: Sanjurjo González, H., Pastor López, I., García Bringas, P., Quintián, H., Corchado, E. (eds.) SOCO 2021. AISC, vol. 1401, pp. 78–87. Springer, Cham (2022). https://doi.org/10.1007/978-3-030-87869-6_8
13. Yu, Y., Si, X., Hu, C., Zhang, J.: A review of recurrent neural networks: LSTM cells and network architectures. Neural Comput. **31**(7), 1235–1270 (2019)

3D Face Reconstruction with Geometry Details from a Single Color Image Under Occluded Scenes

Dapeng Zhao[1] and Yue Qi[1,2,3(✉)]

[1] State Key Laboratory of Virtual Reality Technology and Systems,
School of Computer Science and Engineering at Beihang University,
Beijing, China
qy@buaa.edu.cn
[2] Peng Cheng Laboratory, Shenzhen, China
[3] Qingdao Research Institute of Beihang University, Qingdao, China

Abstract. 3D face reconstruction technology aims to generate a face stereo model naturally and realistically. Previous deep face reconstruction approaches are typically designed to generate convincing textures and cannot generalize well to multiple occluded scenarios simultaneously. By introducing bump mapping, we successfully added mid-level details to coarse 3D faces. More innovatively, our method takes into account occlusion scenarios. Thus on top of common 3D face reconstruction approaches, we in this paper propose a unified framework to handle multiple types of obstruction simultaneously (e.g., hair, palms and glasses *et al.*). Extensive experiments and comparisons demonstrate that our method can generate high-quality reconstruction results with geometry details from captured facial images under occluded scenes.

Keywords: 3D face reconstruction · Face parsing · Occluded scenes

1 Introduction

High-quality 3D face reconstruction is a fundamental problem in computer graphics [31] that is related to various applications such as digital animation [32], video editing [32] and face recognition [40,41]. Since Vetoer's first 3D face [35], 3D reconstruction methods have rapidly advanced enabling applications. However, these methods all perform poorly in terms of face geometry details. To make the problem tractable, most proposed methods introduce existing statistical models or prior knowledge. These models are unable to reconstruct expression-dependent wrinkles, which are essential for analyzing human expression.

Several methods recover detailed facial geometry that lacks robustness to occlusions [1,9]. We introduce a novel face geometry detail generation method, which learns bump maps (simulate geometry changes) from in-the-wild face images with occlusion. In contrast to prior work (estimating mid-level features often breaks down), our method generates bump maps from a low-dimensional representation containing subject-specific detail parameters and

E. Pimenidis et al. (Eds.): ICANN 2022, LNCS 13530, pp. 332–344, 2022.
https://doi.org/10.1007/978-3-031-15931-2_28

expression parameters. Our detailed model builds upon this separation design. This design is fundamental, as it allows estimating a robust global shape, even under occluded scenes.

The main contributions are summarized as follows:

- We propose a novel Face Image Synthesis Network, a simple yet effective diversity promoting face image regeneration approach. The regenerated eyeglasses removal face without glasses will guide the generation of a 3D model.
- We have improved the loss function of our 3D reconstruction system for occluded scenes with eyeglasses. Our results are more accurate than other approaches. As a result of our method, we are able to obtain state-of-the-art qualitative performance in real-world images.

2 Related Work

2.1 Single Image 3D Face Reconstruction

Since the first 3DMM model was proposed by Blanz and Vetter [2], single image based 3D face reconstruction has become a hot research topic and considerable progress have been made in the field. Richardson *et al.* [25] presented a method based on CNN that can reconstruct 3D face based on synthetic data. As training deep neural networks usually demand a large amount of data to get acceptable results, Deng *et al.* [5] proposed an approach that can achieve accurate 3D face reconstruction with weakly supervised learning based on less training data. Kemelmacher-Shlizerman and Basri [11] recovered 3D faces by exploiting the similarity of faces based on a single 3D reference model of a different person. Liu *et al.* [19] built a 3D face model that can exploit both faces with fully labeled 3D landmarks and unlimited unlabeled in-the-wild face images. Lee *et al.* [16] employed an uncertainty-aware encoder and a fully nonlinear decoder model for realistic 3D face reconstruction. Cheng *et al.* [3] solved the 3D face reconstruction problem based on graph convolutional networks obtaining good results without scarifying speed. Shang *et al.* [30] proposed a self-supervised training architecture that is accurate and robust, even under large variations of expressions, poses, and illumination conditions. Li *et al.* [17] publicized an end-to-end framework and designed an efficient network model that can apparently increase the accuracy of face alignment and 3D face reconstruction. Li *et al.* [18] presented a multi-attribute regression reconstruction network that can work well in complex cases when provided with 2D images including severe poses, extreme expressions, and partial occlusions.

2.2 Generative Adversarial Networks

Generative adversarial networks (GANs) was first proposed by Goodfellow *et al.* to study the generative model. Classical GANs consist of a generator and a discriminator. The aim of the generator is to generate data samples that can confuse the discriminator. The generator and the discriminator must improve themselves to win the 'game' until a Nash equilibrium is achieved; then generator success-fully learns the distribution of the real dataset. GANs have been applied in many fields, including face image synthesis. Zhan *et al.* [39] proposed Spatial Fusion GAN (SF-GAN), which can obtain better results in both geometry and appear-ance spaces utilizing a geometry synthesizer and an appearance synthesizer. A triple-translation GAN (TTGAN) is proposed for face image synthesis by Ye *et al.* [38]. TTGAN adopts a triple translation consistency loss to translate from a rendered original input image to the desired output image. Sangloy *et al.* [28] proposed an adversarial image synthesis architecture that can extract informa-tion from sketched boundaries and parse color strokes and output realistic face images.

2.3   Face Image Synthesis

Deep pixel-level face generating has been studied for several years. Many meth-ods achieve remarkable results. Context encoder [23] is the first deep learning network designed for image inpainting with encoder-decoder architecture. Nev-ertheless, the networks do a poor job in dealing with human faces. Following this work, Yang *et al.* used a modified VGG network to improve the result of the context-encoder, by minimizing the feature difference of photo background. Dolhansky *et al.* demonstrated the significance of exemplar data for inpainting. However, this method only focuses on filling in missing eye regions of the frontal face, so it does not generalize well. EdgeConnect [21] shows impressive proceeds which disentangling generation into two stages: edge generator and image com-pletion network. Contextual Attention takes a similar two-step approach. First, it produces a base estimate of the invisible region. Next, the refinement block sharpens the photo by background patch sets. The typical limitations of current face image generate schemes are the necessity of manipulation, the complexity of fundamental architectures, the degradation in accuracy, and the inability of restricting modification to local region.

3   Proposed Approach

We propose a detailed 3D face reconstruction method (as shown in Fig. 1) based on a single photo that consists of two steps:

- in response to the occlusion area, synthesizing the 2D face with complete facial features.
- detailed 3D shape reconstruction module based on unobstructed frontal images.

3.1   Face Parsing Map Generation

Our goal is to realize detailed 3D face shape reconstruction under occluded scenes using our method. Pixel-level recognition of eyeglasses areas serves as a key

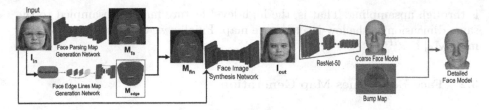

Fig. 1. Method overview. At first, as input for our face image synthesis network, we need the target image $\mathbf{I_{in}}$ and map $\mathbf{M_{fin}}$. We utilize the face parsing map generation module and edge lines map generation module to obtain the map $\mathbf{M_{fa}}$ and $\mathbf{M_{edge}}$. Then we obtain the final face parsing map $\mathbf{M_{fin}}$ following Zhao *et al.*'s Algorithm [42]. After obtaining the face image $\mathbf{I_{out}}$ with eyeglasses removed, in step two, we leverage ResNet-50 and texture refinement network to reconstruct the final 3D model.

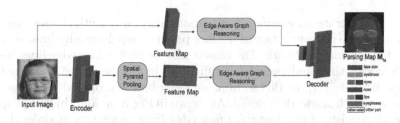

Fig. 2. The overview of the proposed face parsing network.

step for our framework to ensure accuracy. Face parsing is a fundamental facial analysis task. Recently, methods based on Fully Convolutional Networks have achieved remarkable results on this task [8,20,36]. As shown in Fig. 2, given a squarely resized face image $\mathbf{I_{in}} \in \mathbb{R}^{H \times W \times 3}$, we aim to apply a modified encoder-decoder network $\mathcal{N}_{fa}$ as the backbone frame for face parsing. We take $\mathcal{N}_{fa}$ to extract features at different levels for multi-scale illustration. In the structure of $\mathcal{N}_{fa}$, high-level features contain semantic information while low-level features show local details, both of which are essential for face parsing. We feed the feature map with multi-scale information into the Edge Aware Graph Reasoning module, targeting to learn fundamental graph illustration for the characterization of the relations between vertices. The reasoning module consists of three components: graph projection operation, graph reasoning operation and graph reprojection operation. Let us make it clear. The graph projection operation projects the initial information onto vertices. The graph reasoning operation reasons the relational expression between regions over the graph and projects the acquired graph interpretation back to previous pixel grids. The graph reprojection operation leads to an optimized feature map with the same dimension and size. We implemented the reasoning module following the method of Gusi *et al.* [31]. Let us explain the last step of the network. We transmit the optimized features into a decoder to estimate the final pixel labels. In our network, two different level feature maps are concatenated into the decoder. The two feature maps are concatenated by the 1×1 convolution layer. The specific fusion method is through upsampling. That is, the high-level feature map is upsampled to the same dimension as the low-level feature map. Finally, we obtain the face parsing map $\mathbf{M_{fa}} \in \mathbb{R}^{H \times W \times 1}$.

3.2   Face Edge Lines Map Generation

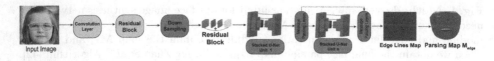

Fig. 3. The overview of the proposed face edge lines map generation approach.

In order to generate an accurate face parsing map, our method uses face edge lines to guide the reconstruction of the face parsing map. Face edge lines is closely related to the facial landmark. The reason why we choose face edge lines instead of landmarks is that landmarks have difficulties in presenting the accurate facial features structure [37]. In this section, we describe the proposed face edge lines map generation framework in detail. As shown in Fig. 3 (a) and (b), the proposed framework consists of two parts: (a) face edge lines generation module; (b) face edge lines effectiveness discriminator.

As shown in Fig. 3 (a), stacked U-Nets is the core part of the face edge lines generation module. More than piecemeal landmarks, face edge lines can well describe the geometry structure of a face. Most of the previous convolutional networks only use the convolutional features of the last layer. Image information at other scales will be lost. Unlike the previous network, the main contribution of the stacked U-Nets unit [22, 26] is to use multi-scale features to represent image information. We Leverage the mean squared error (MSE) between the estimated Face edge lines map and the ground-truth map. The presence of obstructions (this paper focuses on eyeglasses) will significantly affect the accuracy of edge lines generation. In order to relieve the loss of image information due to eyeglasses, we introduce message passing layers to pass information between face edge lines. It is proposed in this implementation that the feature map at the end of each stack should be divided into M (the number) areas. We implemented the message passing approach following the method of Chu et al. [4]. This process is visualized in Fig. 3.

Intra-level Message Passing Layer. Among the steps involved in dealing with the problem of occlusion of eyeglasses, the intra-level message passing plays a crucial role. A layer such as this one is used at the end of each U-Nets stack in order to transmit information between visible edge lines and eyeglasses areas. Consequently, in the process of designing eyeglasses, the prediction of the eyeglasses areas can be improved through the visible edge lines data.

Inter-level Message Passing Layer. It is true that there are various U-Nets stacks that focus on different dimensions of facial information, but in the case of multiple stacks, the facial information is transferred in the different stacks by performing communication between the former stacks and the latter stacks. When stacking more hourglass subnets, inter-level message passing is adopted to ensure that the face edge lines map maintains the quality when messages are passed from the lower stacks to the higher stacks.

Adversarial Learning for Edge Lines Effectiveness. Poor face edge lines map will adversely affect the accuracy of the 3D face model. When training, we use adversarial learning between the estimated edge lines map and the ground-truth map in order to guarantee the effectiveness of the edge lines map obtained in the generation stage. Using the Face edge lines map generator, the edge lines map $\mathbf{M_{edge}} \in \mathbb{R}^{H \times W \times 1}$ is generated with the coordinate set S_{coor}; the mapping between the generated coordinate set and the ground-truth distance matrix $\mathbf{MA_{gt}}$. In order to determine whether a generated edge line map is fake or not, the ground truth d_{gt} can be calculated as:

$$d_{gt}(\mathbf{M_{edge}}, S_{coor}) = \begin{cases} 0, Est_{s \in S_{coor}}(d_{gt} < \theta) < \delta \\ 1, \text{other cases} \end{cases} \tag{1}$$

where Est denotes the probability value calculation function, θ denotes the distance threshold to ground truth edge lines, δ denotes the probability threshold.

In order to combine the edge lines effectiveness discriminator D and the face edge lines map estimator G, we apply the concept of adversarial learning. The loss function of the discriminator D can be calculated as:

$$\mathcal{L}_D = \mathbb{E}[\log(1 - |D(G(\mathbf{I_{in}})) - d_{gt}|)] - \mathbb{E}[\log D(\mathbf{M_{gt}})] \tag{2}$$

where $\mathbf{M_{gt}}$ denotes the ground truth face edge lines map. A discriminator is trained to predict an edge lines map on the ground truth as well as predict the generated edge lines map according to d_{gt}. With effectiveness discriminator, the adversarial loss can be calculated as:

$$\mathcal{L}_{adv-loss} = \mathbb{E}\left[\log(1 - D(G(\mathbf{I_{in}})))\right] \tag{3}$$

3.3 Recovering 3D Face Geometric Details

We obtain the final face parsing map $\mathbf{M_{fin}}$ following Zhao *et al.*'s Algorithm [42]. We synthesize the face photo $\mathbf{I_{out}}$ by existing methods [15]. Given $\mathbf{I_{out}}$, we used the ResNet to regress the corresponding coefficient y. Due to the collection of large scale high-resolution 3D texture datasets is still very costly and scarce, the ResNet was trained under weakly supervised. The corresponding loss function consists of four parts [2,5]:

$$\mathcal{L}_{shape} = \lambda_{feat}\mathcal{L}_{feat} + \lambda_{regu}\mathcal{L}_{regu} + \lambda_{phot}\mathcal{L}_{phot} + \lambda_{land}\mathcal{L}_{land} \tag{4}$$

Here we set $\lambda_{feat} = 0.2, \lambda_{regu} = 3.6e-4, \lambda_{phot} = 1.4, \lambda_{land} = 1.6e-3$ respectively in all our experiments.

The addition of human face geometric details is the core of our method. We choose to add a bump map on the base shape $\mathbf{S_{basi}}$. Inspired by the method of image-to-image translation method, we define the displacements of the depth map as the distances through the pixels of $\mathbf{I_{out}}$ to the 3D face surface. Generally, we define the bump map $\Phi(\mathbf{b})$ as:

$$\Phi(\mathbf{b}) = \begin{cases} \phi(0) & \text{othercases} \\ \phi(d'(\mathbf{b}) - d(\mathbf{b})) & \text{face projects to } \mathbf{b} \end{cases} \tag{5}$$

where $\phi(\cdot)$ denotes an encoding function that converts the depth value to the linear range $[0, \ldots, 255]$, $\mathbf{b}$ denotes the pixel coordinate $[x, y]$ in $\mathbf{I_{out}}$, $d'(\mathbf{b})$ denotes the depth, which is the distance from the surface of the detailed face shape to $\mathbf{b}$ along the line of sight, $d(\mathbf{b})$ denotes the depth of the basic shape.

Thus, Given a bump map Φ and the depth of the basic shape, we can compute the detailed depth follows $d'(\mathbf{b}) = d(\mathbf{b}) + \phi^{-1}(\Phi(\mathbf{b}))$. In order to increase geometric details and to suppress noise, we define the loss function as follows:

$$\mathcal{L}_{geo} = \left\| \tilde{\Phi} - \Phi \right\| + \left\| \frac{\partial \tilde{\Phi}}{\partial x} - \frac{\partial \Phi}{\partial x} \right\| + \left\| \frac{\partial \tilde{\Phi}}{\partial y} - \frac{\partial \Phi}{\partial y} \right\| \tag{6}$$

where $\|\cdot\|$ denotes the L_1 norm, $\tilde{\Phi}$ denotes the ground truth and $\frac{\partial \tilde{\Phi}}{\partial x}$, $\frac{\partial \tilde{\Phi}}{\partial y}$ denotes the 2D gradient of the bump map. After the 3D face is reconstructed, it can be projected onto the image plane with the perspective projection:

$$V_{2d}(\mathbf{P}) = f * \mathbf{P_r} * \mathbf{R} * \mathbf{S_{mod}} + \mathbf{t_{2d}} \tag{7}$$

where $V_{2d}(\mathbf{P})$ denotes the projection function that turned the 3D model into 2D face positions, f denotes the scale factor, $\mathbf{P_r}$ denotes the projection matrix, $\mathbf{R} \in SO(3)$ denotes the rotation matrix and $\mathbf{t_{2d}} \in \mathbb{R}^3$ denotes the translation vector.

Therefore, we approximated the scene illumination with Spherical Harmonics (SH) [24] parameterized by coefficient vector $\gamma \in \mathbb{R}^9$. In summary, the unknown parameters to be learned can be denoted by a vector $y = (\alpha_{id}, \beta_{exp}, \beta_t, \gamma, \mathbf{p}) \in \mathbb{R}^{239}$, where $\mathbf{p} \in \mathbb{R}^6 = \{\mathbf{pitch}, \mathbf{yaw}, \mathbf{roll}, f, \mathbf{t_{2D}}\}$ denotes face poses. In this work, we used a fixed ResNet-50 network to regress these coefficients.

We found that by adding these last two terms of loss function and we reduce bump map noise by favoring smoother surfaces. At the same time, the final effect shows that high-frequency details are preserved.

4   Implementation Details

All the networks were trained using the Adam solver [12]. To train our face parsing map generation network, we collected two sources dataset: Helen dataset [14] and CelebAMask-HQ dataset [15]. The Helen dataset contains 2330 images with 11 categories: background, skin, paired lips, paired eyes, paired brows,

paired mouth and hair. The CelebAMask-HQ dataset is a large-scale face parsing datasets which includes 30000 high-resolution portrait images. The dataset
contains 19 categories. In addition to the facial unit, the components such as
eyeglass, earring, necklace, neck, and cloth are also annotated.

In the face parsing map generation stage, our backbone is a modified version
of the trained parsing model [31]. We made the parsing model exclude the average
pooling layer. For the pyramid pooling module, we follow the implementation of
the method of Te et $al.$ [31] with exploiting global contextual information. We
leveraged the fixed parsing model to generate M_{fa}. In the face edge lines map
generation stage, all training images are cropped and resized to 512×512. We
obtained M_{edge} according the lines map generation network. We implemented
message passing module following naturally obtains face features in different
sizes. In the above two stages, we train our network on four datasets including
300W (3148 sample images) [27] and AFLW (24386 sample images) [13].

5   Experimental Results

In this work, we aim to generate a wide range of diverse and yet realistic 3D
detailed reconstructions from occluded face images. Our approach should be
characterized by the following three qualities: 1) the reconstructed geometry
should fit as convincingly as possible to the visible regions, 2) the reconstructed
model texture should not include eyeglasses, which is the essential requirement
for the accuracy of the reconstruction.

5.1   Qualitative Comparisons with Recent Art

Figure 4 shows our results compared with the other arts. The last columns show
our results. The remaining columns demonstrate the results of Sela et $al.$ [29],
PRNet [6] and 3DDFA [7]. Our results show that our results have better han-
dled the occlusion area than other methods. Figure 4 shows that our method
can reconstruct a complete face shape with geometry details under occlusion
scenes such as glasses, food and fingers. The approach of 3DDFA was aimed at
extremely large poses. Therefore, it cannot reconstruct a detailed face model
under occluded scenes. Its shape lacks details. Other methods focused on generating high-resolution face textures instead of geometry details. At the same
time, it must also be pointed out, the other methods cannot effectively deal with
occluded scenes.

5.2   Quantitative Comparison with Recent Art

Our choice of using the ResNet-50 to regress the shape coefficients is motivated
by the unique robustness to extreme viewing conditions in the paper of Deng
et $al.$ [5]. To fully support the application of our method to occluded face images,
we test our system on the Labeled Faces in the Wild datasets (LFW) [10]. We
used the same face test system from Anh et $al.$ [34], and we refer to that paper
for more details.

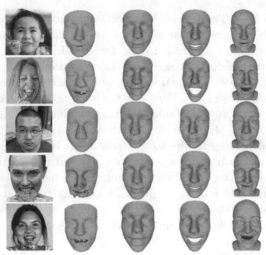

Input Sela *et al.*'17 PRNet'18 3DDFA'20 Ours

Fig. 4. Comparison of qualitative results. Baseline methods from left to right: Sela *et al.*, PRNet, 3DDFA and our method.

Figure 5 (left) shows the sensitivity of the method of Sela *et al.* [29]. Their result clearly shows the outline of the eyeglasses. Their failure may be due to more focus on local details, which weakly regularizes the global shape. However, our method recognizes and regenerates the occluded area. Our method much robust provides a natural face shape under eyeglasses scenes. Though 3DMM also limits the details of shape, we use it only as a foundation and add refined texture separately.

We further quantitatively verify the robustness of our method to eyeglasses. Table 1 (top) reports verification results on the LFW benchmark with and without eyeglasses (see also ROC in Fig. 5-right). Though eyeglasses clearly impact recognition, this drop of the curve is limited, demonstrating the robustness of our method.

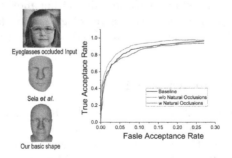

Fig. 5. Reconstructions with eyeglasses. Left: qualitative results of Sela *et al.* [29] and our shape. Right: LFW verification ROC for the shapes, with and without eyeglasses.

Table 1. Quantitative evaluations on LFW.

Method	100%-EER	Accuracy	nAUC
Tran *et al.* [33]	89.40 ± 1.52	89.36 ± 1.25	95.90 ± 0.95
Ours (w/ Gla)	84.37 ± 1.44	85.79 ± 0.42	92.87 ± 1.09
Ours (w/o Gla)	87.69 ± 1.01	89.02 ± 0.89	95.37 ± 0.65

6   Conclusions

In this work, we describe a 3D face detailed reconstruction framework that can run efficiently under occluded scenes. Our method enables unobstructed face image synthesis by concatenating the original face parsing map with the face edge lines map which both are extracted from the input face image in the encoder-decoder network. The experiments on 3D face reconstruction using various datasets have shown that our method can effectively remove eyeglasses with equivalent quality and better accuracy control than the existing methods.

Acknowledgements. This paper is supported by National Natural Science Foundation of China (No. 62072020) and the Leading Talents in Innovation and Entrepreneurship of Qingdao (19-3-2-21-zhc).

References

1. Abrevaya, V.F., Boukhayma, A., Torr, P.H., Boyer, E.: Cross-modal deep face normals with deactivable skip connections. In: Proceedings of the IEEE/CVF Conference on Computer Vision and Pattern Recognition, pp. 4979–4989 (2020)
2. Blanz, V., Vetter, T.: A morphable model for the synthesis of 3D faces. In: Siggraph, vol. 99, pp. 187–194 (1999)
3. Cheng, S., Tzimiropoulos, G., Shen, J., Pantic, M.: Faster, better and more detailed: 3D face reconstruction with graph convolutional networks. In: Proceedings of the Asian Conference on Computer Vision (2020)
4. Chu, X., Ouyang, W., Li, H., Wang, X.: Structured feature learning for pose estimation. In: Proceedings of the IEEE Conference on Computer Vision and Pattern Recognition, pp. 4715–4723 (2016)
5. Deng, Y., Yang, J., Xu, S., Chen, D., Jia, Y., Tong, X.: Accurate 3D face reconstruction with weakly-supervised learning: from single image to image set. In: Proceedings of the IEEE Conference on Computer Vision and Pattern Recognition Workshops (2019)
6. Feng, Y., Wu, F., Shao, X., Wang, Y., Zhou, X.: Joint 3d face reconstruction and dense alignment with position map regression network. In: Proceedings of the European Conference on Computer Vision (ECCV). pp. 534–551 (2018)
7. Guo, J., Zhu, X., Yang, Y., Yang, F., Lei, Z., Li, S.Z.: Towards fast, accurate and stable 3D dense face alignment. arXiv preprint arXiv:2009.09960 (2020)
8. Guo, T., et al.: Residual encoder decoder network and adaptive prior for face parsing. In: Thirty-Second AAAI Conference on Artificial Intelligence (2018)

9. Guo, Y., Cai, J., Jiang, B., Zheng, J.: CNN-based real-time dense face reconstruction with inverse-rendered photo-realistic face images. IEEE Trans. Pattern Anal. Mach. Intell. **41**(6), 1294–1307 (2018)

10. Huang, G.B., Mattar, M., Berg, T., Learned-Miller, E.: Labeled faces in the wild: a database for studying face recognition in unconstrained environments. In: Workshop on faces in 'Real-Life' images: detection, alignment, and recognition (2008)

11. Kemelmacher-Shlizerman, I., Basri, R.: 3D face reconstruction from a single image using a single reference face shape. IEEE Trans. Pattern Anal. Mach. Intell. **33**(2), 394–405 (2010)

12. Kingma, D.P., Ba, J.: Adam: a method for stochastic optimization. arXiv preprint arXiv:1412.6980 (2014)

13. Koestinger, M., Wohlhart, P., Roth, P.M., Bischof, H.: Annotated facial landmarks in the wild: a large-scale, real-world database for facial landmark localization. In: 2011 IEEE International Conference on Computer Vision Workshops (ICCV workshops), pp. 2144–2151. IEEE (2011)

14. Le, V., Brandt, J., Lin, Z., Bourdev, L., Huang, T.S.: Interactive facial feature localization. In: Fitzgibbon, A., Lazebnik, S., Perona, P., Sato, Y., Schmid, C. (eds.) ECCV 2012. LNCS, vol. 7574, pp. 679–692. Springer, Heidelberg (2012). https://doi.org/10.1007/978-3-642-33712-3_49

15. Lee, C.H., Liu, Z., Wu, L., Luo, P.: MaskGAN: towards diverse and interactive facial image manipulation. In: Proceedings of the IEEE/CVF Conference on Computer Vision and Pattern Recognition, pp. 5549–5558 (2020)

16. Lee, G.H., Lee, S.W.: Uncertainty-aware mesh decoder for high fidelity 3d face reconstruction. In: Proceedings of the IEEE/CVF Conference on Computer Vision and Pattern Recognition, pp. 6100–6109 (2020)

17. Li, K., et al.: Joint face alignment and 3D face reconstruction with efficient convolution neural networks. In: 2020 25th International Conference on Pattern Recognition (ICPR), pp. 6973–6979. IEEE (2021)

18. Li, X., Wu, S.: Multi-attribute regression network for face reconstruction. In: 2020 25th International Conference on Pattern Recognition (ICPR), pp. 7226–7233. IEEE (2021)

19. Liu, P., Han, X., Lyu, M., King, I., Xu, J.: Learning 3D face reconstruction with a pose guidance network. In: Proceedings of the Asian Conference on Computer Vision (2020)

20. Masi, I., Mathai, J., AbdAlmageed, W.: Towards learning structure via consensus for face segmentation and parsing. In: Proceedings of the IEEE/CVF Conference on Computer Vision and Pattern Recognition, pp. 5508–5518 (2020)

21. Nazeri, K., Ng, E., Joseph, T., Qureshi, F.Z., Ebrahimi, M.: EdgeConnect: generative image inpainting with adversarial edge learning. arXiv preprint arXiv:1901.00212 (2019)

22. Newell, A., Yang, K., Deng, J.: Stacked hourglass networks for human pose estimation. In: Leibe, B., Matas, J., Sebe, N., Welling, M. (eds.) ECCV 2016. LNCS, vol. 9912, pp. 483–499. Springer, Cham (2016). https://doi.org/10.1007/978-3-319-46484-8_29

23. Pathak, D., Krahenbuhl, P., Donahue, J., Darrell, T., Efros, A.A.: Context encoders: feature learning by inpainting. In: Proceedings of the IEEE Conference on Computer Vision and Pattern Recognition, pp. 2536–2544 (2016)

24. Ramamoorthi, R., Hanrahan, P.: An efficient representation for irradiance environment maps. In: Proceedings of the 28th Annual Conference on Computer Graphics and Interactive Techniques, pp. 497–500 (2001)

25. Richardson, E., Sela, M., Kimmel, R.: 3D face reconstruction by learning from synthetic data. In: 2016 Fourth International Conference on 3D Vision (3DV), pp. 460–469. IEEE (2016)
26. Ronneberger, O., Fischer, P., Brox, T.: U-net: convolutional networks for biomedical image segmentation. In: Navab, N., Hornegger, J., Wells, W.M., Frangi, A.F. (eds.) MICCAI 2015. LNCS, vol. 9351, pp. 234–241. Springer, Cham (2015). https://doi.org/10.1007/978-3-319-24574-4_28
27. Sagonas, C., Tzimiropoulos, G., Zafeiriou, S., Pantic, M.: 300 faces in-the-wild challenge: the first facial landmark localization challenge. In: Proceedings of the IEEE International Conference on Computer Vision Workshops, pp. 397–403 (2013)
28. Sangkloy, P., Lu, J., Fang, C., Yu, F., Hays, J.: Scribbler: controlling deep image synthesis with sketch and color. In: Proceedings of the IEEE Conference on Computer Vision and Pattern Recognition, pp. 5400–5409 (2017)
29. Sela, M., Richardson, E., Kimmel, R.: Unrestricted facial geometry reconstruction using image-to-image translation. In: Proceedings of the IEEE International Conference on Computer Vision, pp. 1576–1585 (2017)
30. Shang, J., et al.: Self-supervised monocular 3D face reconstruction by occlusion-aware multi-view geometry consistency. arXiv preprint arXiv:2007.12494 (2020)
31. Te, G., Liu, Y., Hu, W., Shi, H., Mei, T.: Edge-aware graph representation learning and reasoning for face parsing. In: Vedaldi, A., Bischof, H., Brox, T., Frahm, J.-M. (eds.) ECCV 2020. LNCS, vol. 12357, pp. 258–274. Springer, Cham (2020). https://doi.org/10.1007/978-3-030-58610-2_16
32. Thies, J., Zollhofer, M., Stamminger, M., Theobalt, C., Nießner, M.: Face2face: real-time face capture and reenactment of RGB videos. In: Proceedings of the IEEE Conference on Computer Vision and Pattern Recognition, pp. 2387–2395 (2016)
33. Tuan Tran, A., Hassner, T., Masi, I., Medioni, G.: Regressing robust and discriminative 3D morphable models with a very deep neural network. In: Proceedings of the IEEE Conference on Computer Vision and Pattern Recognition, pp. 5163–5172 (2017)
34. Tuan Tran, A., Hassner, T., Masi, I., Paz, E., Nirkin, Y., Medioni, G.: Extreme 3D face reconstruction: seeing through occlusions. In: Proceedings of the IEEE Conference on Computer Vision and Pattern Recognition, pp. 3935–3944 (2018)
35. Vetter, T., Blanz, V.: Estimating coloured 3D face models from single images: an example based approach. In: Burkhardt, H., Neumann, B. (eds.) ECCV 1998. LNCS, vol. 1407, pp. 499–513. Springer, Heidelberg (1998). https://doi.org/10.1007/BFb0054761
36. Wei, Z., Liu, S., Sun, Y., Ling, H.: Accurate facial image parsing at real-time speed. IEEE Trans. Image Process. 28(9), 4659–4670 (2019)
37. Wu, W., Qian, C., Yang, S., Wang, Q., Cai, Y., Zhou, Q.: Look at boundary: a boundary-aware face alignment algorithm. In: Proceedings of the IEEE Conference on Computer Vision and Pattern Recognition, pp. 2129–2138 (2018)
38. Ye, L., Zhang, B., Yang, M., Lian, W.: Triple-translation GAN with multi-layer sparse representation for face image synthesis. Neurocomputing 358, 294–308 (2019)
39. Zhan, F., Zhu, H., Lu, S.: Spatial fusion GAN for image synthesis. In: Proceedings of the IEEE/CVF Conference on Computer Vision and Pattern Recognition, pp. 3653–3662 (2019)
40. Zhang, Y., Zhang, H., Wu, G., Li, J.: Spatio-temporal self-supervision enhanced transformer networks for action recognition. In: IEEE International Conference on Multimedia and Expo (ICME). IEEE (2022)

41. Zhang, Y., Zhang, H., Wu, G., Xu, Y., Shi, Z., Li, J.: TMN: temporal-guided multiattention network for action recognition. In: 2022 26th International Conference on Pattern Recognition (ICPR). IEEE (2022)

42. Zhao, D., Qi, Y.: Generative face parsing map guided 3D face reconstruction under occluded scenes. In: Magnenat-Thalmann, N., et al. (eds.) CGI 2021. LNCS, vol. 13002, pp. 252–263. Springer, Cham (2021). https://doi.org/10.1007/978-3-030-89029-2_20

A Transformer-Based GAN for Anomaly Detection

Caiyin Yang[1] , Shiyong Lan[1]([✉]), Weikang Huang[1], Wenwu Wang[2],
Guoliang Liu[1], Hongyu Yang[1], Wei Ma[1], and Piaoyang Li[1]

[1] College of Computer Science, Sichuan University, Chengdu 610065, China
lanshiyong@scu.edu.cn
[2] University of Surrey, Guildford GU2 7XH, UK
w.wang@surrey.ac.uk

Abstract. Anomaly detection is the task of detecting outliers from normal data. Numerous methods have been proposed to address this problem, including recent methods based on generative adversarial network (GAN). However, these methods are limited in capturing the long-range information in data due to the limited receptive field obtained by the convolution operation. The long-range information is crucial for producing distinctive representation for normal data belonging to different classes, while the local information is important for distinguishing normal data from abnormal data, if they belong to the same class. In this paper, we propose a novel Transformer-based architecture for anomaly detection which has advantages in extracting features with global information representing different classes as well as the local details useful for capturing anomalies. In our design, we introduce self-attention mechanism into the generator of GAN to extract global semantic information, and also modify the skip-connection to capture local details in multi-scale from input data. The experiments on CIFAR10 and STL10 show that our method provides better performance on representing different classes as compared with the state-of-the-art CNN-based GAN methods. Experiments performed on MVTecAD and LBOT datasets show that the proposed method offers state-of-the-art results, outperforming the baseline method SAGAN by over 3% in terms of the AUC metric.

Keywords: Anomaly detection · Transformer · Generative advertise network

1 Introduction

Anomaly detection is an important field in computer vision. The detection of abnormal images plays an increasingly important role due to the growing demand

This work was funded in part by the Key R&D Project of Sichuan Science and Technology Department, China (2021YFG0300), and in part by 2035 Innovation Pilot Program of Sichuan University, China.
C. Yang and W. Huang—Equal contribution.

E. Pimenidis et al. (Eds.): ICANN 2022, LNCS 13530, pp. 345–357, 2022.
https://doi.org/10.1007/978-3-031-15931-2_29

in various applications, such as video surveillance, risk management and damage detection [8,14]. Current state of the art methods in this area are based on deep learning methods such as Deep-anomaly [17] and ADCNN [10]. However, the performance of these methods is limited by the lack of labelled data. On the one hand, it is hard to collect abnormal images due to unbalanced distribution of normal and abnormal data. On the other hand, abnormal data is difficult to be defined clearly [15]. To solve these problems, a number of abnormal detection methods have been proposed based on unsupervised learning which consider anomaly detection as a one-class classification problem [20]. These methods learn the feature distribution of normal data and the data whose distribution is substantially different from the learned distribution in terms of a predefined threshold is regarded as containing abnormal objects.

A recent method for anomaly detection is based on unsupervised learning with generative adversarial network (GAN) [9]. The adversarial learning process facilitates the generator to learn normal data distribution [6]. AnoGAN [19] is the first GAN-based representation learning method for anomaly detection [16]. In EBGAN [25] and Fast-AnoGAN [18], a network is built to learn feature representations in a latent space with an inverse of the generator. GANomaly [1] introduced an encoder-decoder-encoder network for the generator to learn image representations within the latent space of images. Skip-GANomaly [2] uses an U-net structure as the generator to improve detection performance. SAGAN [12] uses an attention module in skip connection to capture additional local information. However, due to the limited receptive field induced by the convolution operation, the aforementioned methods can only model local information but are limited in capturing long-range information within the data, thus are ineffective in detecting the abnormal information distributed both locally and globally.

The self-attention mechanism in transformer has been widely used in computer vision tasks, offering state-of-the-art performance. The attention module in a transformer can associate the input sequence to learn long range information globally. ViT [7] firstly applied a transformer to computer vision tasks by directly processing image as patch sequences. Swin Transformer [13] proposed a method to calculate the attention in local windows to reduce its computational complexity. U-shaped transformers which are similar to SwinUnet [4] and Uformer [23] have also been proposed. These models take advantage of the self-attention mechanism in capturing long range dependency that CNN lacks for representation learning.

In this paper, we propose a novel anomaly detection framework to address the limitation of CNN in modelling the long-range information within the data by leveraging the strength of the transformer model. We build our model based on GAN, and introduce the self-attention mechanism to capture long-range information within the image data. The key idea of our framework is that we build an Unet-Shaped Encoder-Decoder structure with Transformer-based blocks. A limitation with the transformer model is that it may ignore local information while learning long-range dependencies. To address this issue, we propose to modify the skip-connection for capturing multi-scale information from local features.

Experimental results show that our method outperforms state-of-the-art anomaly detection methods on datasets such as CIFAR10 [11], and STL10 [22] on outer-class task, LBOT [12] and MVTecAD [3] considering inter-class task, additionally. The main contributions of this paper are summarized as follows:

- We propose a novel anomaly detection framework AnoTrans which combines the Transformer-based module with existing GAN-based method to address the limitation of the CNN encoder used in GAN-based method for modelling the long range information within image data.
- We design a new method for fusing the global attention with the local attention, which enables the global and local information to be captured simultaneously when performing anomaly detection.
- Experimental results on four datasets, CIFAR10, STL10, LBOT and MVTecAD, respectively, demonstrate the superiority of our method over the state-of-the-art CNN-based methods in anomaly detection.

2   Proposed Method

2.1   Model Overview

To enhance the feature representation with global information as well as the local details, we propose AnoTran (Fig. 1) based on SAGAN [12], where an attention module (i.e., CBAM [24]) is incorporated into the depth-wise CNN-based encoder of GAN to enhance the latent representation of input images. To introduce long-range dependency within the representation, we replace the convolution block by the self-attention module as used in the encoder of the transformer.

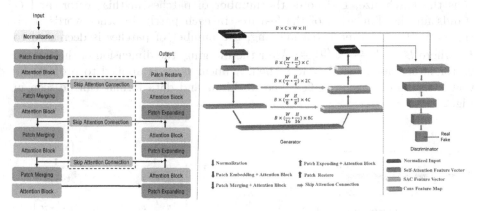

Fig. 1. The structure of our proposed model, where the attention block is used to replace the convolution module. The left part is the logical composition of the generator, and the right part is the overall network structure of our model.

In addition, we design a new skip attention connection, which introduces an attention mechanism to modify skip connections in SAGAN. In our proposed attention connection, the global dependencies captured by the Transformer-based module can be used to relate each local feature, so as to enhance the feature representation of the input image. Moreover, we add a batch normalization in the beginning of the input, which can mitigate the impact of the overall offset of each batch of the input data, thus facilitate the generator to learn a better representation for normal data.

As shown in Fig. 1, our model is composed of a generator and discriminator. The generator is implemented by a U-shaped encoder-decoder structure which will be described in detail in Sect. 2.2. The Transformer-based self attention module is used to replace the convolution in the encoder of the generator, as discussed in Sect. 2.3. The improved skip connection module with self-attention mechanism is introduced, as discussed in Sect. 2.4. The loss function used in our model and the criteria for calculating the anomaly score will be described in Sects. 2.5 and 2.6, respectively. The discriminator which is the same as that in SAGAN is used in our model to distinguish the label of the extracted latent representation of the input image.

2.2   U-Shape Generator

To simulate the convolution operation, inspired by [13] and [4], we use a reshape operation to change the dimension of the feature vector from the transformer. Patch merging and expanding are applied to change the scales of the vector obtained from the patch embedding of the input image. The operation retains the same data as the input features, but with a new specified shape to achieve the scale transformations.

In our model, the feature vector plays the same role as feature map in the convolution network. The feature vector has three dimensions $B \times L \times C$, where B is the batch size, L denotes the number of patches in this vector, and C stands for the dimension of the features in each patch. In other words, $L = W_{patch} \times H_{patch}$. After patch merging, the number of patches is decreased to L', where $L' = \frac{W_{patch}}{2} \times \frac{H_{patch}}{2}$. After the merging, the dimension of the feature vector is increased to $C' = 4C$. Then, a linear layer is applied to project the vector to the dimension of $2C$. The workflow and data format can be seen in Fig. 2.

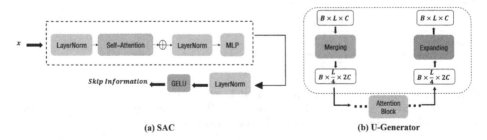

(a) SAC   (b) U-Generator

Fig. 2. (a) Transformer-based module in Skip Attention Connection (SAC) which provides multi-scale information through self-attention. (b) The workflow and data format in the U-shape Generator.

2.3 Swin Transformer Block

Transformer captures long-range dependency within image data while increasing the number of tokens at the same time. When the images are represented in high-resolution, the tokens may lead to high computational complexity. To reduce the complexity, we introduce Swin Transformer [13] by replacing the conventional multi-head self-attention module with shifted windows, and calculating the self-attention within the local windows. The Swin Transformer blocks in our model are computed as:

$$\hat{x}^l = W\text{-}MSA(LN(x^{l-1})) + x^{l-1} \tag{1}$$

$$x^l = MLP(LN(\hat{x}^l)) + \hat{x}^l \tag{2}$$

$$\hat{x}^{l+1} = SW\text{-}MSA(LN(x^l)) + x^l \tag{3}$$

$$x^{l+1} = MLP(LN(\hat{x}^{l+1})) + \hat{x}^{l+1} \tag{4}$$

where $\hat{x}^l$ and x^l represent the outputs of the Window Multihead Self-Attention (i.e., W-MSA) and the MLP of the l-th block, respectively. $\hat{x}^{l+1}$ is output of the Sift Window Multihead Self-Attention (i.e., SW-MSA).

2.4 Skip Attention Connection

The Transformer-based structure offers promising results, as demonstrated in Sect. 3. However, we empirically found (in Table 5) that the Transformer-based U-Generator is not effective in capturing some critical local information in feature representation. Inspired by SAGAN [12] where the CBAM module is incorporated into the skip connection to capture local information, we propose a Skip Attention Connection (SAC) to further improve the performance of our method.

CBAM is a mixed attention mechanism involving convolution operation which can be limited in the receptive field. The work in [5] illustrates the benefit of using positional encoding in a single multi-head self-attention layer. This inspired us to employ the SAC as the module in skip-connection to replace the CBAM module. In the self-attention module, different heads can pay attention to different pixels and areas in the image via the attention mechanism during training. Thus, our improved skip-connection can capture the local information to complement the Transformer-based structure, without being limited by the convolution receptive field as in CBAM.

As shown in Fig. 2, we incorporate self-attention into the output of the encoder in each layer to obtain a feature vector. The feature vector can focus on pixels in different areas in multi-scale by self-attention blocks. The output of each self-attention block will be sent to an MLP followed by a layer normalization. Finally, the vector is passed through a GELU activation function and transferred to the decoder. Therefore, our proposed skip connection block with self-attention can offer multi-scale local information without using the transforms (e.g. reshape operation and convolution) as performed in the CBAM module. Our empirical results in Sect. 3 show that it performs better than the original CBAM module.

2.5   Loss Function

The aim of our GAN-based anomaly detection method is to train the model on normal data and correctly reconstruct the normal data on both image and latent space. On the contrary, the model should fail to reconstruct the abnormal data as if it is never trained on the abnormal data. Thus we use the loss from [2] in our model as follows.

Adversarial Loss: $\mathcal{L}_{adv}$ is the standard loss used in GAN to optimize the generator G and discriminator D in the adversarial process which ensures the generated image from G to be as realistic as possible with the help of classification result from D.

$$\mathcal{L}_{adv} = E_{x \sim p_x}[log D(x)] + E_{x \sim p_x}[log(1 - D(G(x)))] \tag{5}$$

where $E_{x \sim p_x}[.]$ indicates expectation.

Contextual Loss: Contextual loss $\mathcal{L}_{con}$ is defined as the error between the generated image $G(x)$ and the input image x, as follows:

$$\mathcal{L}_{con} = E_{x \sim p_x} ||x - G(x)||_1 \tag{6}$$

where $|| \cdot ||_1$ is an L_1 norm. This loss helps the algorithm learn contextual information from images.

Latent Loss: The latent loss aims to reduce the reconstruction loss in latent representation. We choose the feature in the last layer of D to get the latent representation. The latent loss $\mathcal{L}_{lat}$ is formulated as:

$$\mathcal{L}_{lat} = E_{x \sim p_x} ||f(x) - f(G(x))||_2 \tag{7}$$

where $|| \cdot ||_2$ is an L_2 norm, the $f(x)$ and $f(G(x))$ are the latent representation of the input image x and the generated image $G(x)$, respectively. The final loss function is shown as a weighted sum of the loss functions mentioned above.

$$\mathcal{L} = \lambda_{adv} \mathcal{L}_{adv} + \lambda_{con} \mathcal{L}_{con} + \lambda_{lat} \mathcal{L}_{lat} \tag{8}$$

where λ_{adv}, λ_{con}, and λ_{lat} are the weighting parameters chosen empirically in our experiments.

2.6   Inference

Anomaly score is often used to determine whether a test image is an anomaly or not. Image with a score higher than a predefined threshold is considered as an anomaly. We use the method in SAGAN [12] and Skip-Anomaly [2] to obtain the anomaly score as follows:

$$A(x) = \lambda R(x) + (1 - \lambda)L(x) \tag{9}$$

where x represents the test image, $A(x)$ is the raw anomaly score of x, $R(x)$ is the reconstruction score between x and the generated image x', $L(x)$ is the difference between the latent representations of x and x' which are obtained from the discriminator, and λ is the weight that controls the relative importance of $R(x)$ and $L(x)$ in $A(x)$. After calculating the raw anomaly score for all the test images in the test set and denoting them as a vector A, we use the equation below to normalize the scores to the range of $[0, 1]$. Thus, the final anomaly score for an individual test image is obtained as:

$$A'(x) = \frac{A(x) - min(A)}{max(A) - min(A)} \tag{10}$$

3 Experiment

We evaluate our model[1] in a way of leave-one-class-out anomaly detection, with datasets CIFAR10 [11], STL10 [22], LBOT [12] and MVTecAD [3]. We use SAGAN[2] and Skip-Anomaly as baseline methods in our comparison. The area under the curve (AUC) of the receiver operating characteristic (ROC) is used as the performance metric.

3.1 Dataset

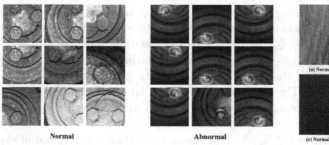

(a) Examples on the left are from normal data, and those on the right are abnormal data with red boxes containing damaged or missing bolts.

(b)   Examples   in MVTecAD   with   slight abnormal part which can be detected by SAC

Fig. 3. Examples in the dataset.

CIFAR10: CIFAR10 is a benchmark dataset which consists of color images in 32×32 pixels from 10 classes. We choose one class of images as anomaly and the other images as normal data. Then we train our model on the normal data and test on both normal data and abnormal data.

---

[1] https://github.com/SYLan2019/Transformer-Gan-Anomaly-Detection.
[2] https://github.com/SYLan2019/Skip-Attention-GAN.

STL10: STL10 is a dataset similar to CIFAR10. The difference between them is that STL10 has less labeled training data than CIFAR10 in each class. In addition, image resolution in STL10 is 96×96 pixels. We train our model on STL10 in the same way as CIFAR10.

LBOT: The LBOT dataset is used in [12] which focuses on the inspection of axle bolts. The dataset includes 5,000 image patches of the train axle bolt status extracted by the 128×128 overlapping sliding window method. In training, we define the missing or damaged bolts as anomalies. We split the LBOT dataset into 4,000 training images and 1,000 test images. The training images are all normal bolt images, and the 1,000 test images contain 500 normal bolt images and 500 abnormal bolt images.

MVTecAD: MVTecAD is a benchmark anomaly detection method which focuses on industrial inspection. It contains 5000 images of fifteen different objects and texture categories. The abnormal images in MVTecAD have partial differences from the normal ones in terms of details. We select the images in certain classes as abnormal data and others as normal data.

3.2 Training Details

Our experiments are performed on an NVIDIA GeForce RTX 3090 GPU with 24 Gb Memory. In the training process, the objective function is optimized by Adam optimizer with momentum $\beta_1 = 0.5$, $\beta_2 = 0.999$ and initial learning rate $l_r = 2 \times 10^{-4}$. We set $\lambda = 0.1$ in Eq. 9 when calculating the anomaly score, $\lambda_{adv} = 1$, $\lambda_{con} = 50$ and $\lambda_{lat} = 1$ in Eq. 8 when calculating the loss function. We use a patch size of 2×2 in the patch embedding with positional encoding and a four-head self-attention. The window size in the windowed attention is set to 2 with a shift size of 1. Data augmentation is applied to increase the amount of training data.

Due to the instability of GAN, our Transformer-based model may not always converge on the dataset. To alleviate this issue, we introduce a training strategy where in each epoch, we would train the generator once but the discriminator twice. This strategy can help the model to get a relatively strong discriminator first, which helps guide the optimization of the generator in the right direction. The loss function in Fig. 4 shows our model converges faster with this training strategy.

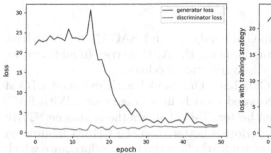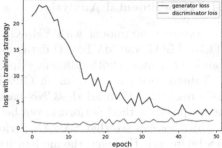

Fig. 4. Convergence of the loss functions. The left plot shows the loss curve on the CIFAR10 with cat as the abnormal class, while the right plot shows that our training strategy can help the model converge faster.

3.3 Encoder of Our Transformer-Based Structure

We tested two different self-attention modules of the transformer as our encoder block, respectively, the self-attention module from classical ViT [7] and the window attention of Swin Transformer [13]. The results are shown in Table 1. It can be seen that the shifted windows in Swin Transformer reduce the complexity on computation and also improve the performance over the ViT, as the Swin Transformer performs the self-attention in parallel. In the following experiments, we use the window attention module of Swin Transformer as the encoder in our proposed method for its computational efficiency.

Table 1. The average AUC with different transformer-based blocks

Module	Dataset	Average AUC
Self-attention of [7]	CIFAR10	0.963
Window attention of [13]	CIFAR10	0.978
Self-attention of [7]	STL10	0.946
Window attention of [13]	STL10	0.982

Table 2. The AUC results on the LBOT dataset.

Model	AUC
GANomaly [1]	0.900
Skip-GANomaly [2]	0.840
SAGAN [12]	0.960
Proposed with SAC	**0.996**

Table 3. The AUC results on the CIFAR10 dataset.

Model	Frog	Bird	Cat	Deer	Dog	Horse	Ship	Truck	Average
GANomaly [1]	0.512	0.523	0.466	0.467	0.502	0.387	0.534	0.579	0.496
Skip-GANomaly [2]	0.955	0.611	0.670	0.845	0.706	0.666	0.909	0.857	0.777
SAGAN [12]	0.996	**0.957**	0.951	0.998	**0.975**	0.891	0.990	0.980	0.967
Proposed with CBAM module	**1.000**	0.932	**0.977**	0.998	0.940	0.941	**1.000**	0.969	0.970
Proposed with SAC	**1.000**	0.944	0.960	**0.999**	0.968	**0.949**	0.999	**0.990**	**0.976**

3.4   Experimental Analysis

We compare our model with Skip-GAnomaly [2] and SAGAN on CIFAR10, STL10, LBOT and MVTecAD datasets, using the AUC metric. In addition, we evaluate our model with different skip-connection modules.

Table 3 shows our results on CIFAR10. Our model with modified CBAM performs better than all the CNN-based models in average score. With SAC, the proposed method performs even better. Table 4 shows the results on STL10 in which we can see that SAGAN performs better than the CBAM module on 96 × 96 images. However, the model with SAC offers the best performance which shows that our proposed SAC can adapt to the resolution change better than the CBAM module.

Table 4. The AUC results on STL10.

Model	Bird	Car	Cat	Deer	Dog	Horse	Monkey	Ship	Truck	Average
SAGAN [12]	0.929	**1.000**	0.963	0.996	0.859	0.947	0.979	**0.999**	**0.998**	0.963
Skip-GANomaly [2]	0.588	0.902	0.556	0.664	0.581	0.726	0.590	0.568	0.770	0.661
Proposed with CBAM module	0.916	0.999	0.937	0.991	0.821	0.922	0.938	0.993	0.997	0.951
Proposed with SAC	**0.966**	**1.000**	**0.985**	**0.998**	**0.942**	**0.975**	**0.980**	**0.999**	0.997	**0.984**

The experimental results on both CIFAR10 and STL10 show that our proposed method performs better in detecting a certain class as an anomaly. This can be attributed to the long-term dependencies within the image that help obtain a more accurate feature representation, in which local details are associated with global information. In addition, the results on MVTecAD (which is mainly used for local texture anomalies) are also greatly improved as compared to SAGAN, further demonstrating that our Transformer-based method outperforms CNN-based methods.

Table 5. The AUC results on MVTecAD dataset.

Model	Bottle	Capsule	Carpet	Grid	Leather	Nut	Pill	Screw	Brush	Transistor	Wood	Zipper	Average
SAGAN	0.873	0.951	0.966	0.918	0.984	0.922	0.806	0.991	0.824	0.832	0.931	0.742	0.896
Skip-GANomaly	0.882	0.869	0.964	**0.966**	0.955	0.954	0.862	0.976	0.900	0.956	0.930	0.898	0.926
Proposed	1.000	**0.988**	0.959	0.945	0.928	**0.991**	0.994	**0.992**	**0.999**	0.984	0.769	1.000	0.962
Proposed with SAC	**1.000**	0.978	**0.974**	0.938	**0.991**	0.965	**1.000**	0.986	0.981	**0.989**	**0.970**	1.000	**0.981**

Table 5 shows the results on the MVTecAD dataset. From this table, we can see that our proposed Transformer-based method gives better performance than the SAGAN due to its effectiveness in capturing the long range dependency in image data. However, the table also shows our proposed method with pure skip connection gives relatively low accuracy in some types (such as wood in Table 5). By inspecting the images in these images, we found that the defects in them are so small that the standard skip connection may miss the subtle details. In contrast, with the skip connection method described in Sect. 2.4, the results can be significantly improved on MVTecAD. Experiments on MVTecAD and LBOT datasets show that the proposed method outperforms the baseline SAGAN by over 3% in terms of AUC metric (e.g. see details in Table 2 and Table 5).

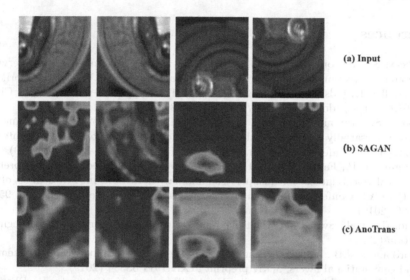

(a) Input

(b) SAGAN

(c) AnoTrans

Fig. 5. The heat-map from attention features in our proposed model AnoTrans and SAGAN.

We also train the model with skip attention connection on LBOT, which is a real anomaly dataset. The results are shown in Table 2. We can see that the proposed model with transformer has a stronger representation ability than the convolution model. Figure 5 visualizes the attention features on LBOT using Grad-Cam [21]. We can observe that our Transformer-based method has a wider horizon on image detection. Compared to the SAGAN which focuses on the local area when detecting anomalies, our method picks the abnormal area at a larger scale through the long-range dependency. The result shows that a wider horizon with long-range dependency can produce a better representation and locate the anomaly more precisely considering the semantic of the whole image.

4   Conclusion

In this paper, we have presented a Transformer-based method for anomaly detection from images. The experiments show that the proposed method outperforms the CNN-based methods in capturing long-range dependency, and the limited receptive field of CNN can be effectively mitigated by the self-attention mechanism of the transformer. In addition, using the modified skip connection with self-attention in our Transformer-based encoder can further improve the performance, due to the advantage of skip connection in exploiting the multi-scale information. Compared with the state-of-the-art CNN-based anomaly detection methods, our method achieves better results on four datasets evaluated. In the future, we will further study representation enhancement in anomaly detection from images.

References

1. Akcay, S., Atapour-Abarghouei, A., Breckon, T.P.: GANomaly: semi-supervised anomaly detection via adversarial training. In: Jawahar, C.V., Li, H., Mori, G., Schindler, K. (eds.) ACCV 2018. LNCS, vol. 11363, pp. 622–637. Springer, Cham (2019). https://doi.org/10.1007/978-3-030-20893-6_39
2. Akçay, S., Atapour-Abarghouei, A., Breckon, T.P.: Skip-ganomaly: skip connected and adversarially trained encoder-decoder anomaly detection. In: 2019 International Joint Conference on Neural Networks (IJCNN), pp. 1–8. IEEE (2019)
3. Bergmann, P., Fauser, M., Sattlegger, D., Steger, C.: Mvtec ad - a comprehensive real-world dataset for unsupervised anomaly detection. In: Proceedings of the IEEE/CVF Conference on Computer Vision and Pattern Recognition, pp. 9592–9600 (2019)
4. Cao, H., et al.: Swin-Unet: Unet-like pure transformer for medical image segmentation (2021)
5. Cordonnier, J.B., Loukas, A., Jaggi, M.: On the relationship between self-attention and convolutional layers. arXiv preprint arXiv:1911.03584 (2019)
6. Creswell, A., White, T., Dumoulin, V., Arulkumaran, K., Sengupta, B., Bharath, A.A.: Generative adversarial networks: an overview. IEEE Sig. Process. Mag. **35**(1), 53–65 (2018)
7. Dosovitskiy, A., et al.: An image is worth 16x16 words: transformers for image recognition at scale. arXiv preprint arXiv:2010.11929 (2020)
8. Ghazal, M., Vázquez, C., Amer, A.: Real-time automatic detection of vandalism behavior in video sequences. In: 2007 IEEE International Conference on Systems, Man and Cybernetics, pp. 1056–1060. IEEE (2007)
9. Goodfellow, I., et al.: Generative adversarial nets. In: Advances in Neural Information Processing Systems, vol. 27 (2014)
10. Kwon, D., Natarajan, K., Suh, S.C., Kim, H., Kim, J.: An empirical study on network anomaly detection using convolutional neural networks. In: 2018 IEEE 38th International Conference on Distributed Computing Systems (ICDCS), pp. 1595–1598. IEEE (2018)
11. Li, H., Liu, H., Ji, X., Li, G., Shi, L.: Cifar10-DVS: an event-stream dataset for object classification. Front. Neurosci. **11**, 309 (2017)
12. Liu, G., Lan, S., Zhang, T., Huang, W., Wang, W.: SaGAN: skip-attention GAN for anomaly detection. In: 2021 IEEE International Conference on Image Processing (ICIP), pp. 2468–2472. IEEE (2021)
13. Liu, Z., et al.: Swin transformer: hierarchical vision transformer using shifted windows. arXiv preprint arXiv:2103.14030 (2021)
14. Mould, N., Regens, J.L., Jensen, C.J., III., Edger, D.N.: Video surveillance and counterterrorism: the application of suspicious activity recognition in visual surveillance systems to counterterrorism. J. Policing Intell. Counter Terror. **9**(2), 151–175 (2014)

15. Pang, G., Shen, C., Cao, L., Hengel, A.V.D.: Deep learning for anomaly detection: a review. ACM Comput. Surv. (CSUR) **54**(2), 1–38 (2021)

16. Radford, A., Metz, L., Chintala, S.: Unsupervised representation learning with deep convolutional generative adversarial networks. arXiv preprint arXiv:1511.06434 (2015)

17. Sabokrou, M., Fayyaz, M., Fathy, M., Moayed, Z., Klette, R.: Deep-anomaly: fully convolutional neural network for fast anomaly detection in crowded scenes. Comput. Vis. Image Underst. **172**, 88–97 (2018)

18. Schlegl, T., Seebӧck, P., Waldstein, S.M., Langs, G., Schmidt-Erfurth, U.: f-AnoGAN: fast unsupervised anomaly detection with generative adversarial networks. Med. Image Anal. **54**, 30–44 (2019)

19. Schlegl, T., Seebӧck, P., Waldstein, S.M., Schmidt-Erfurth, U., Langs, G.: Unsupervised anomaly detection with generative adversarial networks to guide marker discovery. In: Niethammer, M., et al. (eds.) IPMI 2017. LNCS, vol. 10265, pp. 146–157. Springer, Cham (2017). https://doi.org/10.1007/978-3-319-59050-9_12

20. Schölkopf, B., Williamson, R.C., Smola, A.J., Shawe-Taylor, J., Platt, J.C., et al.: Support vector method for novelty detection. In: NIPS, vol. 12, pp. 582–588. Citeseer (1999)

21. Selvaraju, R.R., Cogswell, M., Das, A., Vedantam, R., Parikh, D., Batra, D.: Gradcam: Visual explanations from deep networks via gradient-based localization. In: Proceedings of the IEEE International Conference on Computer Vision, pp. 618–626 (2017)

22. Singh, H., Swagatika, S., Venkat, R.S., Saxena, S.: Justification of stl-10 dataset using a competent CNN model trained on cifar-10. In: 2019 3rd International conference on Electronics, Communication and Aerospace Technology (ICECA), pp. 1254–1257. IEEE (2019)

23. Wang, Z., Cun, X., Bao, J., Liu, J.: Uformer: a general U-shaped transformer for image restoration. arXiv preprint arXiv:2106.03106 (2021)

24. Woo, S., Park, J., Lee, J.Y., Kweon, I.S.: CBAM: convolutional block attention module. In: Proceedings of the European Conference on COMPUTER VISION (ECCV), pp. 3–19 (2018)

25. Zenati, H., Foo, C.S., Lecouat, B., Manek, G., Chandrasekhar, V.R.: Efficient GAN-based anomaly detection. arXiv preprint arXiv:1802.06222 (2018)

AMMUNIT: An Attention-Based Multimodal Multi-domain UNsupervised Image-to-Image Translation Framework

Lei Luo$^{(\boxtimes)}$ and William H. Hsu

Kansas State University, Manhattan, KS 66502, USA
{leiluoray,bhsu}@ksu.edu

Abstract. We address the open problem of unsupervised multimodal multi-domain image-to-image (I2I) translation using a generative adversarial network with attention mechanism. Previous works, such as Cycle-GAN, MUNIT, and StarGAN2 are able to translate images among multiple domains and generate diverse images, but they often introduce unwanted changes to the background. In this paper, we propose a simple yet effective attention-based framework for unsupervised I2I translation. Our framework not only translates solely objects of interests and leave the background unaltered, but also generates images for multiple domains simultaneously. Unlike recent studies on unsupervised I2I with attention mechanism that require ground truth for learning attention maps, our approach learns attention maps in an unsupervised manner. Extensive experiments show that our framework is superior than the state-of-the-art baselines.

Keywords: Image-to-image translation · Attention learning · Unsupervised learning

Image-to-image (I2I) translation refers to translating images from one domain to another featuring different styles, which are visually distinctive among different domains. An example is the task of turning images of cartoon sketches into real-life photographs. Many tasks in computer vision can be viewed as I2I translation, such as image inpainting [1], style transfer as in StyleGAN2 [2], and super-resolution [3]. Supervised I2I translation tasks need paired data sets that are costly to obtain, and such tasks are relatively easier to solve than their unsupervised counterpart. Under paired data supervision, I2I translation can be done by taking a regression approach [4] or using conditional generative models [5]. Our work addresses the more challenging unsupervised I2I translation task without access to paired data sets. Most of works on unsupervised I2I translation draw inspiration from CycleGAN [6] using the cycle consistency constraint, and have achieved impressive results. More recent studies, such as MUNIT [7] and StarGAN2 [8], have improved upon on CycleGAN and are able to translate images

Supported by Kansas State University.

among multiple domains. These works, however, introduce unwanted changes to both objects of interest and the background, which is undesired. In our study we propose a simpler yet effective approach. Our framework only consists of one generator-discriminator pair and a mapping network, which enable multimodal and multi-domain translation. Moreover, our framework learns attention maps by using a attention module, which allows translating objects of interest and leave the background intact. Extensive experiments show that our framework is superior or comparable to state-of-the-art (SOTA) baselines. The contributions of our work can be summarized as follows:

- We propose a novel framework for unsupervised I2I translation with attention mechanism, which allows for image translation at instance level.
- Our framework learns attention maps with an unsupervised manner, which does not require segmentation annotations. Our attention module could be used as a plug-and-play add-on for existing pre-trained I2I translation frameworks, making them capable of learning attention maps at lower cost than training an attention module and its generator from scratch.
- Unlike previous works, such as MUNIT and DRIT [9], that require training $n(n-1)$ generators for translating images for n domains, we propose a novel framework architecture, which requires training only one generator-discriminator pair and achieves multimodal multi-domain I2I translation.
- Extensive experiments on publicly available data sets show that our framework is superior than SOTA baselines.

1   Related Work

Generative Adversarial Networks. Ideally, generative models learn how data is distributed, thus allowing data synthesis from the learned distribution. Since the advent of GANs [10], generative models have achieved impressive results in various tasks like image editing [11] and style transfer as in Style-GAN2. GANs try to learn the data distribution by approximating the similarity of distributions between the training data and the fake data produced by the learned model. GANs usually comprise a generator and a discriminator. The entire model learns by playing a minimax game: the generator tries to fool the discriminator by gradually generating realistic data samples, and the discriminator, in turn, tries to distinguish real samples from fake ones. GANs have been improved in various ways. To produce more realistic samples, an architecture of stacked GANs has been proposed: the laplacian pyramid of GANs [12]; layered, recursive GANs [13]; and style-based GANs (StyleGAN and StyleGAN2). Several studies have attempted to solve the instability training of GANs using energy-based GANs [14] and Wasserstein GANs [15]. In this study, we use GANs with their improved techniques to learn the distribution of data and how to translate among different domains.

Unsupervised I2I Translation. Unsupervised I2I translation translates images from one domain to another without paired data supervision. Much success in unsupervised I2I translation is due to the cycle consistency constraint, proposed in three earlier works: CycleGAN, DiscoGAN [16], and DualGAN [17]. To translate more than two domains, MUNIT and DRIT are proposed. These methods, however, sample style codes from a standard normal distribution, which leads to inferior translation results. Moreover, they require training $n(n-1)$ generators and n discriminators for translating images among n domains, which is computationally expensive and time-consuming. Our method proposes a simpler yet more effective approach that requires only one set of generator-discriminator. Recent systems such as StarGAN2 and ModularGAN [18] are developed to perform multimodal image-to-image translation to produce images with the same content but different contexts. All the aforementioned methods, however, introduce undesired changes to the background while translating images.

Attention Learning. Motivated by human attention mechanism, attention has been successfully applied in various computer vision and natural language processing tasks, such as machine translation [19], visual question answering [20], and image and video captioning [21]. Attention improves the performance of all these tasks by encouraging the model to focus on the most relevant parts of the input. In order to focus on the most discriminative semantic part and retain the background of images during translation, attention mechanism has been introduced into I2I. ConstrastGAN [22] takes a supervised approach and uses segmentation mask annotations as extra input data. Similar to our approach that learns attention masks without using extra annotation, AttentionGAN [23], ATAGAN [24], and AGGAN [25] add an attention module to each generator to locate the object of interest in image-to-image translation tasks. Thus, the background can be excluded from I2I translation. All these mentioned methods, however, are only able to translate two domains at a time. In order to remedy the drawbacks mentioned above, we propose an unified I2I translation framework with attention mechanism. Instead of having to train $n(n-1)$ generator-discriminator pairs for learning to translate among n domains, our methods only requires training one such pair. Thus, our framework reduces training time and memory footprint with better or comparable translation performance.

2 Methods

2.1 Preliminaries

Let x be an image that belongs to one of many domains. The diagram (a) in Fig. 1 shows an overview of our model. We start from a latent vector z that is sampled from a standard normal distribution. z goes through a mapping network, which learns style codes s of a specific domain, where m is a domain label and $s = M(z, m)$. Meanwhile, we employ a content encoder E_c to extract content codes c from image inputs. The decoder D takes content and style codes to generate reconstructed images x', which are then used by style encoder E_s to produce reconstructed style codes s'. We compute two L1 losses using the reconstructed images and style codes. Finally, we use a multi-task discriminator to distinguish real images from generated ones. During the translation phase, we keep the same content codes but use the style codes of target domains. Attention maps are learned using the attention module. Take translating a horse image x_m to a zebra image as an example, shown in the diagram (b) of Fig. 1. The horse image is processed by the encoder, resulting in style codes s_m and content codes c_m. In the meantime, the attention module extracts attention maps att from the horse image. The style codes of the zebra image s_n are exchanged with that of the horse image. Then, the decoder uses the content codes c_m and style codes s_n to generate an intermediate fake zebra image, whose background contains unwanted changes. We incorporate the attention map with the intermediate fake zebra image by $att \times D(c_m, s_n) + (1 - att) \times x_m$, which results in the final fake zebra image. Note that we only show the attention branch for translating horse to zebra due to space limitation, the other direction of translation is similar.

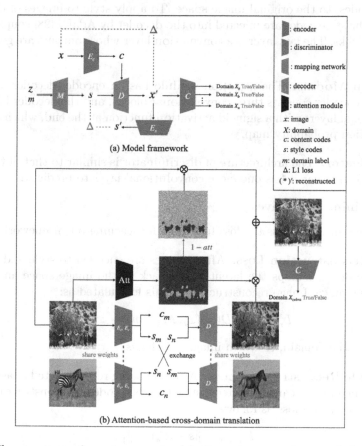

Fig. 1. The structure of our framework. (a) Shows how our framework learns, and (b) shows cross-domain translation within the horse and zebra domain. The attention branch of translating zebra2horse is similar to horse2zebra, and thus is not shown.

2.2 Framework Architecture

In this section, we outline the architecture of different modules in our framework.

Encoder. Our encoder has two sub-encoders: the style encoder and the content encoder. Both start with a convolution layer. The content encoder consists of six residual blocks [26]. All the layers are downsampled by average pooling operation (except for the last two layers) and are followed by an instance normalization (IN) [27]. The style encoder also comprises six residual blocks but without any activation function expect for the last residual block. Lastly, the style encoder consists of a convolution layer with leaky ReLU and a reshape operation before outputting style codes by the linear layer.

Mapping Network. Style codes of domains are modelled by a mapping network, which consists of eight linear layers with ReLU activation function expect for the last layer.

Decoder. The decoder maps latent codes, which consist of style codes and content codes, to the original image space. To apply style to images of different domain, the style codes are injected into the decoder by AdaIN [28] coupled with residual blocks. The last layer is a convolution layer whose outputs are generated images.

Attention Module. The attention module has an encoder-decoder architecture. The encoder consists three convolutional blocks, and the decoder has three convolutional layers with a sigmoid activation function at the end, which outputs the attention probability map.

Discriminator. The architecture of discriminator is similar to that of the style encoder except that it has one more convolutional layer to predict domains.

2.3 Training Objectives

In this section, we discuss the loss functions for learning our framework.

Image Reconstruction Loss. After images are encoded to style and content codes, the decoder maps the latent space back to the image space and reconstructs the image. Image reconstruction loss is formulated as:

$$L_{recon}^{x} = \|D(E_c(x), M(z,m)) - x\|_1,$$ (1)

where m is the domain, to which image x belongs.

Style Code Reconstruction Loss. After encoding reconstructed images using the style encoder, we can obtain reconstructed style codes. We construct the style code reconstruction loss as follows:

$$L_{recon}^{s} = \|s - E_s(x')\|_1,$$ (2)

where $x' = D(E_c(x), M(z,m))$ and $x \in X_m$.

Attention Consistency Loss. Images before and after translation should have the same attention maps. Thus, the attention consistency loss is defined as:

$$L_{att} = \|att(x_{mn}) - att(x_m)\|_1, \tag{3}$$

where x_{mn} is the translated image, which is obtained by $att \times D(c_m, s_n) + (1 - att) \times x_m$. c_m is the content information of x_m and s_n is the style information of image x_n.

Regularization on Style and Content Codes. To further encourage style codes being domain-variant and content codes being domain-invariant, we add regularizers on style and content encoders. The style regularizer forces style codes of different domains to be different by minimizing L_{regu}^s, which is calculated as:

$$L_{regu}^s = - \|D(c_m, s_m) - D(c_m, s_n)\|_1 - \|D(c_n, s_m) - D(c_n, s_n)\|_1, \tag{4}$$

where $(c_m, s_m) = (E_c(x_m), E_s(x_m))$ and $(c_n, s_n) = (E_c(x_n), E_s(x_n))$. c_m and s_m are content and style codes of image $x_m \in X_m$. c_n and s_n are content and style codes of image $x_n \in X_n$.

The content regularizer encourages content codes of different domains to be similar by minimizing L_{regu}^c, which is formulated as:

$$L_{regu}^c = \|D(c_m, s_m) - D(c_n, s_m)\|_1 + \|D(c_m, s_n) - D(c_n, s_n)\|_1. \tag{5}$$

Inspired by StarGAN2, we calculate style diversity as:

$$L_{ds} = \|E_s(x_1) - E_s(x_2)\|_1, \tag{6}$$

where $x_1 = D(E_c(x), M(z_1, m))$, and $x_2 = D(E_c(x), M(z_2, m))$, and z_1 and z_2 are two random latent vectors.

Adversarial Loss. GANs are used to match the distribution of translated results to real image samples, so the discriminator finds real and fake samples indistinguishable. We use two adversarial losses with one for learning latent-guided translation and the other for reference-guided translation. Latent-guided translation refers to using the mapping network to obtain target style codes, and reference-guided translation uses the style encoder to extract style codes of target domains. The adversarial loss for learning the discriminator C_m with latent-guided translation is formulated as:

$$L_{adv}^l = \mathop{\mathbb{E}}_{z \sim N(0,I), x_n \sim p(X_n)} [log(1 - C_m(att \times D(c_n, M(z, m)) + (1 - att) \times x_n))]$$
$$+ \mathop{\mathbb{E}}_{x_m \sim p(X_m)} [log(C_m(x_m))], \tag{7}$$

where m is the target domain label and the adversarial loss for learning the discriminator C_m with reference-guided translation is constructed as:

$$L_{adv}^r = \mathop{\mathbb{E}}_{x_m \sim p(X_m), x_n \sim p(X_n)} [log(1 - C_m(x_{nm}))] + \mathop{\mathbb{E}}_{x_m \sim p(X_m)} [log(C_m(x_m))], \tag{8}$$

where the discriminator C_m tries to tell if images are from the domain m, and x_{nm} is obtained by $att \times D(c_n, E_s(x_m)) + (1 - att) \times x_n$.

Full Objective. Our full objective is formulated as follows:

$$\min_{M,E,D} \max_{C} \lambda_1 L_{recon}^x + \lambda_2 L_{recon}^s + \lambda_3 (L_{regu}^s + L_{regu}^c)$$
$$+ \lambda_4 (L_{adv}^l + L_{adv}^r) - \lambda_5 L_{ds} + \lambda_6 L_{att}, \tag{9}$$

where λ_1 to λ_6 are hyperparameters for each loss term.

Model Training Scheme. We find it difficult for the model to converge when training the generator and the attention module simultaneously. Therefore, we first train the generator and the discriminator using $1e^{-4}$ as learning rate for 100,000 iterations, which is empirically calibrated. Then, we freeze the parameters of the generator when training the attention module for 30,000 iterations with the same learning rate. Lastly, we jointly train the entire framework for another 10,000 iterations using a smaller learning rate $5e^{-5}$.

3   Experiments

In this section we talk about the data sets, baselines, and evaluation metrics.

Baselines and Data Set. We compare our framework against four baseline models developed in recent years. CycleGAN is one of the pioneer work in unsupervised I2I, which is used as a baseline model. MUNIT and StarGAN2 achieve impressive results in unsupervised multimodal I2I translation, against which, thus, we compare our framework. For the sake of fair comparison, we compare our approach to AGGAN that is a recently proposed attention-based I2I translation framework.

We evaluate our framework on the *horse2zebra*, *AFHQ*, and *map2aerial* data sets. The *horse2zebra* data set contains images of horses and zebras, and it is downloaded from ImageNet using keywords wild horse and zebra. There are in total 1,067 horse images and 1,334 zebra images are used for training, and 120 horse images and 140 zebra images are for testing. The *AFHQ* data set contains images of house cats, dogs, and wild animals (e.g. tigers, foxes, and lions). Similar to StarGAN2, we divide the *AFHQ* data set into domains of cats, dogs, and wild animals. The *map2aerial* data set are scraped from Google Maps, and images were sampled from in and around New York City. All images are of size 256×256.

Evaluation Metrics. We evaluate the visual quality of translation using the Amazon Mechanical Turk (AMT), which is based on user preferences given results of different models. To seek a quantitative measure that does not require human participation, Structural Similarity Index (SSIM) and Peak Signal-to-Noise Ratio (PSNR) are employed similar to Chen et al. in AttentionGAN and AGGAN.

4   Results

In this section, we show the qualitative and quantitative results of the experiments. Ablation study is also carried out to evaluate the effectiveness of several key design choices.

Qualitative Results. We utilize the Amazon Mechanical Turk (AMT) to compare our results against the baselines based on user preferences. Given a source image and a reference image, we instruct AMT workers to select the best transfer result among all models. We ask 50 questions for all ten workers. As shown in Table 1, our method outperforms all the baseline models, especially for MUNIT, CycleGAN, and StarGAN2 that are not attention based I2I translation framework. Similar to MUNIT and StarGAN2, our model is also able to perform latent-guided and reference-guided translation. We illustrate examples of latent-guided translation in (a) of the Fig. 2, and Fig. 3 shows examples of I2I translation guided by reference images of all models. We can see that our model and AGGAN are capable of preserving the background information and only translating the objects of interests. CycleGAN and AGGAN are only able to perform reference-guided translation, thus their latent-guided translation results are not shown. We present two examples of attention maps of our model comparing against AGGAN in (b) of the Fig. 2, which shows that our attention maps are more accurate than AGGAN. From the results we argue that there should be a clear definition on what "undesired changes" are. It is clear that when performing translation, such as transferring a map into an aerial photo, we would assume the attention mask to be the entire image (See the attention map in figure (b) of the Fig. 2). We think it is probably more appropriate to apply such separation of background and background on domains of *horse2zebra* instead of *map2aerial*.

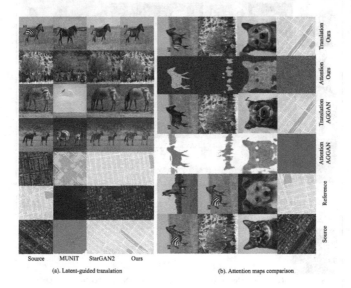

Source   MUNIT   StarGAN2   Ours

(a). Latent-guided translation   (b). Attention maps comparison

Fig. 2. (a) Are examples of latent-guided I2I translation results, and (b) compares attention maps generated by our framework and AGGAN.

Table 1. Votes from ATM workers for most preferred translation results.

Models	User preference (↑)
CycleGAN	8.31 %
MUNIT	2.55 %
StarGAN2	3.13 %
AGGAN	40.93 %
Ours	**45.08 %**

| Source | Reference | CycleGAN | MUNIT | StarGAN2 | AGGAN | Ours |

Fig. 3. Examples of reference-guided I2I translation by different models.

Source Reference Naive w/ style, content regu w/ style, content regu
                                                        w/ attention mask

Fig. 4. An example of reference-guided translation by incrementally adding modules.

Quantitative Results. Similar to MUNIT and StarGAN2, our model is able to perform latent-guided and reference-guided translation. We evaluate all models using SSIM and PSNR, which require ground truth attention maps of images. Similar to AttentionGAN, we obtain attention maps using the DeepLab semantic image segmentation model [29] pretrained on MSCOCO [30] data set. Note that we only provide quantitative results on the *horse2zebra* data set because the DeepLab model is not trained on the *map2aerial* data set, and no ground truth attention maps are available for calculating SSIM and PSNR. As Table 2 and Table 3 show, our framework outperforms all baseline models, especially for CycleGAN, MUNIT, and StarGAN2 for a large margin. Again, CycleGAN and AGGAN are not capable of performing latent-guided translation. Therefore, quantitative results on these two models are not reported.

Table 2. Quantitative comparison on reference-guided translation.

Models	horse2zebra		zebra2horse	
	SSIM(↑)	PSNR (↑)	SSIM(↑)	PSNR (↑)
CycleGAN	0.7313	21.96	0.8453	26.31
MUNIT	0.1176	14.89	0.3664	15.29
StarGAN2	0.3281	16.86	0.4729	19.43
AGGAN	0.9686	33.16	0.9843	43.02
Ours	**0.9699**	**36.12**	**0.9851**	**44.11**

Table 3. Quantitative comparison on latent-guided translation.

Models	horse2zebra		zebra2horse	
	SSIM(↑)	PSNR (↑)	SSIM(↑)	PSNR (↑)
MUNIT	0.1925	11.66	0.3901	13.88
StarGAN2	0.3353	18.87	0.4953	19.92
Ours	**0.9712**	**33.76**	**0.9857**	**43.14**

Ablation Studies. To further validate effects of key design choices in our framework, we carry out ablation studies on the *horse2zebra* data set, whose results are shown in Table 4 and Fig. 4. Let the model without style, content regularizer, and attention module be the naive model. We can see that adding attention greatly helps increase translation results.

Table 4. SSIM and PSNR results of incrementally adding modules to our framework for reference-guided translation on the *horse2zebra* data set.

Modules	SSIM ($\uparrow$)	PSNR ($\uparrow$)
Naive model	0.3062	12.73
+ style, content regularizer	0.3511	19.04
+ attention masks	**0.9699**	**36.12**

5 Conclusions and Discussion

In this research, we present a simple yet effective attention-based framework for unsupervised I2I translation. Our framework not only translates solely objects of interests and leave the background unaltered, but also generates images for multiple domains simultaneously. Unlike similar studies on unsupervised I2I with attention mechanism that require ground truth for learning attention maps, our approach learns attention maps in an unsupervised manner. The qualitative and quantitative results show that our framework is superior than the SOTA baselines.

References

1. Wang, Y., Tao, X., Qi, X., Shen, X., Jia, J.: Image inpainting via generative multi-column convolutional neural networks. In: Advances in Neural Information Processing Systems, pp. 331–340. Curran Associates Inc., Montréal (2018)
2. Karras, T., Laine, S., Aittala, M., Hellsten, J., Lehtinen, J., Aila, T.: Analyzing and Improving the Image Quality of StyleGAN. In: Proceedings of the Conference on Computer Vision and Pattern Recognition (CVPR), Seattle, WA, pp. 8110–8119 (2020)
3. Wang, Z., Chen, J., Hoi, S.C.H.: Deep learning for image super-resolution: a survey. IEEE Trans. Pattern Anal. Mach. Intell. 1 (2020)
4. Chen, Q.-F., Koltun, V.: Photographic image synthesis with cascaded refinement networks. In: Proceedings of the Conference on Computer Vision and Pattern Recognition (CVPR), pp. 1511–1520. IEEE, Honolulu (2017)
5. Isola, P., Zhu, J.-Y., Zhou, T.-H., Efros, A.A.: Image-to-image translation with conditional adversarial networks. In: Proceedings of the Conference on Computer Vision and Pattern Recognition (CVPR), Honolulu, Hawaii, pp. 5967–5976 (2017)
6. Zhu, J.-Y., Park, T., Isola, P., Efros A.A.: Unpaired image-to-image translation using cycle-consistent adversarial networks. In: 2017 IEEE International Conference on Computer Vision (ICCV), pp. 2242–2251. IEEE, Venice (2017)

7. Huang, X., Liu, M.-Y., Belongie, S., Kautz, J.: Multimodal unsupervised image-to-image translation. In: Ferrari, V., Hebert, M., Sminchisescu, C., Weiss, Y. (eds.) Multimodal Unsupervised Image-to-Image Translation. LNCS, vol. 11207, pp. 179–196. Springer, Cham (2018). https://doi.org/10.1007/978-3-030-01219-9_11

8. Choi, Y., Uh, Y.-J., Yoo, J., Ha, J-W.: StarGAN v2: diverse image synthesis for multiple domains. in: Proceedings of the Conference on Computer Vision and Pattern Recognition (CVPR), pp. 8185–8194. IEEE, Seattle (2020)

9. Lee, H.-Y., Tseng, H.-Y., Huang, J.-B., Singh, M., Yang, M.-H.: Diverse image-to-image translation via disentangled representations. In: Ferrari, V., Hebert, M., Sminchisescu, C., Weiss, Y. (eds.) ECCV 2018. LNCS, vol. 11205, pp. 36–52. Springer, Cham (2018). https://doi.org/10.1007/978-3-030-01246-5_3

10. Goodfellow, I. J., et al.: Generative adversarial nets. In: Proceedings of the 27th International Conference on Neural Information Processing Systems, pp. 2672–2680. MIT Press, Montreal (2014)

11. Zhu, J.-Y., Krähenbühl, P., Shechtman, E., Efros, A.A.: Generative visual manipulation on the natural image manifold. In: Leibe, B., Matas, J., Sebe, N., Welling, M. (eds.) ECCV 2016. LNCS, vol. 9909, pp. 597–613. Springer, Cham (2016). https://doi.org/10.1007/978-3-319-46454-1_36

12. Denton, E.L., Chintala, s., Szlam, A., Fergus, B.: Deep generative image models using a Laplacian pyramid of adversarial networks. In: Proceedings of the 28th International Conference on Neural Information Processing Systems, pp. 1486–149. MIT Press, Montreal (2015)

13. Yang, J.-W., Kannan, A., Batra, D., Parikh, D.: LR-GAN: layered recursive generative adversarial networks for image generation. In: 5th International Conference on Learning Representations (ICLR), OpenReview.net, Toulon, France (2017)

14. Zhao, T., Mathieu, M., LeCun, Y.: Energy-based generative adversarial networks. In: 5th International Conference on Learning Representations (ICLR), OpenReview.net, Toulon, France (2017)

15. Arjovsky, M., Chintala, S., Bottou, L.: Wasserstein generative adversarial networks. In: Proceedings of the 34th International Conference on Machine Learning (ICML), pp. 214–223. PMLR, Stockholm (2017)

16. Kim, T., Cha, M., Kim, H., Lee, J.-K., Kim, J.: Learning to discover cross-domain relations with generative adversarial networks. In: Proceedings of the 34th International Conference on Machine Learning (ICML), pp. 1857–1865. PMLR, Sydney (2017)

17. Yi, Z.-L., Zhang, H., Tan, P., Gong, M.-L.: DualGAN: unsupervised dual learning for image-to-image translation. In: 2017 IEEE International Conference on Computer Vision (ICCV), pp. 2868–2876. IEEE, Venice (2017)

18. Zhao, B., Chang, B., Jie, Z., Sigal, L.: Modular generative adversarial networks. In: Ferrari, V., Hebert, M., Sminchisescu, C., Weiss, Y. (eds.) Computer Vision – ECCV 2018. LNCS, vol. 11218, pp. 157–173. Springer, Cham (2018). https://doi.org/10.1007/978-3-030-01264-9_10

19. Bahdanau, D., Cho, K., Bengio, Y.: Neural machine translation by jointly learning to align and translate. In: 3rd International Conference on Learning Representations (ICLR), OpenReview.net, San Diego, CA, USA (2015)

20. Yang, Z.-C., He, X.-D., Gao, J.-F., Deng, L., Smola, A.-J.: Stacked attention networks for image question answering. In: Proceedings of the Conference on Computer Vision and Pattern Recognition (CVPR), pp. 21–29. IEEE, Las Vegas (2016)

21. Xu, K., et al.: Show, attend and tell: Neural image caption generation with visual attention. In: Proceedings of the 32nd International Conference on Machine Learning (ICML), Lille, France, pp. 2048–2057 (2015)

22. Liang, X., Zhang, H., Lin, L., Xing, E.: Generative semantic manipulation with mask-contrasting GAN. In: Ferrari, V., Hebert, M., Sminchisescu, C., Weiss, Y. (eds.) ECCV 2018. LNCS, vol. 11217, pp. 574–590. Springer, Cham (2018). https://doi.org/10.1007/978-3-030-01261-8_34

23. Chen, X., Xu, C., Yang, X., Tao, D.: Attention-GAN for object transfiguration in wild images. In: Ferrari, V., Hebert, M., Sminchisescu, C., Weiss, Y. (eds.) ECCV 2018. LNCS, vol. 11206, pp. 167–184. Springer, Cham (2018). https://doi.org/10.1007/978-3-030-01216-8_11

24. Kastaniotis, D., Ntinou, I., Tsourounis, D., Economou, G., Fotopoulos, S.: Attention-aware generative adversarial networks (ATA-GANs). In 13th IEEE Image, Video, and Multidimensional Signal Processing Workshop (IVMSP), Aristi Village, Zagorochoria, Greece, pp. 1–5 (2018)

25. Tang, H., Xu, D., Sebe, N., Yan, Y.: Attention-guided generative adversarial networks for unsupervised image-to-image translation. In: International Joint Conference on Neural Networks (IJCNN), Budapest, Hungary, pp. 1–8 (2019)

26. He, K.-M., Zhang, X.-Y., Ren, S.-Q., Sun, J.: Deep residual learning for image recognition. In: Proceedings of the Conference on Computer Vision and Pattern Recognition (CVPR), pp. 770–778. IEEE, Las Vegas (2016)

27. Ulyanov, D., Vedaldi, A., Lempitsky, V.S.: Improved texture networks: maximizing quality and diversity in feed-forward stylization and texture synthesis. In: Proceedings of the Conference on Computer Vision and Pattern Recognition (CVPR), pp. 4105–4113. IEEE, Honolulu (2017)

28. Huang, X., Belongie, S.-J.: Arbitrary style transfer in real-time with adaptive instance normalization. In: 2017 IEEE International Conference on Computer Vision (ICCV), pp. 1510–1519. IEEE, Venice (2017)

29. Chen, L.-C., Papandreou, P., Kokkinos, I., Murphy, K., Yuille, A.-L: DeepLab: semantic image segmentation with deep convolutional nets, atrous convolution, and fully connected CRFs. IEEE Pattern Anal. Mach. Intell. 834–848 (2018)

30. Lin, T.-Y., Maire, M., Belongie, S., Hays, J., Perona, P., Ramanan, D., Dollár, P., Zitnick, C.L.: Microsoft COCO: common objects in context. In: Fleet, D., Pajdla, T., Schiele, B., Tuytelaars, T. (eds.) ECCV 2014. LNCS, vol. 8693, pp. 740–755. Springer, Cham (2014). https://doi.org/10.1007/978-3-319-10602-1_48

Continual Learning by Task-Wise Shared Hidden Representation Alignment

Xu-hui Zhan, Jian-wei Liu$^{(\boxtimes)}$ (iD), and Ya-nan Han

Department of Automation, College of Information Science and Engineering,
China University of Petroleum, Beijing, China
liujw@cup.edu.cn

Abstract. One of the goals of machine learning is learning a sequence of tasks more naturally. Continual learning imitates the real learning mode of human beings and continually learns new knowledge without forgetting old knowledge at the same time. In the past decades, considerable attention has been paid to this learning method. However, avoiding forgetting old knowledge in the process of learning new knowledge remains an ongoing challenge due to catastrophic forgetting. Therefore, it is desirable to exploit a new method to improve the stability in a continual learning scenario. In this paper, we specifically focus on the shared feature extraction between two consecutive tasks. To this end, we explore a continual learning paradigm by using the task-wise shared hidden representation alignment module, which contrasts shared representations from the current task and shared representations from reconstruction pseudo samples of previous tasks. Our proposed TSHRA model grasps similarity features provided by the alignment module to learn shared representations more consummately when the model is learning the current task. To verify our proposed model, we conduct experiments on Split-MNIST and Fashion-MNIST. The experimental results show that our proposed TSHRA's performance is outstanding which justify that the alignment module has a positive effect on learning shared representations among different tasks for the continual learning scenario.

Keywords: Continual learning · The task-wise shared hidden representation · Catastrophic forgetting · Alignment

1 Introduction

Human beings constantly learn from the changing dynamic world, adapt, finetune the learned knowledge. The setting scene of continual learning (CL) is similar to exploring the dynamic world, i.e., learning new knowledge in upcoming series of data [1]. The agent of CL updates the parameters and weights in the continuously input data, rather than learning once in the fixed data. Similar to the biological characteristics of human beings, the CL intelligent agent will also have the problem of forgetting during the learning

J. Liu—This work was supported by the Science Foundation of China University of Petroleum, Beijing (No. 2462020YXZZ023).

process. The learning of a new task will modify the weight of the net-work, thereby forgetting the previous learning task, which is manifested as the agent will completely forget the previously learned task when learning the current task. This phenomenon is called catastrophic forgetting [2].

In recent years, the theoretical and experimental research on alleviating cata-strophic forgetting has increased tremendously [3–8]. Continual learning strategies can be divided into four forms [9]. [7] defines several subnetworks corresponding to training without tasks to avoid forgetting caused by parameter changes. [6, 8] use different regularization parameters for training different parts of the network. [4] and [5] 'reprocess' the previously trained samples and put them into a sample batch in current training. [3] selects specific samples from previously trained samples to save and also adopts a replay strategy.

These different strategies all need to learn the underlying hidden representations of the training samples from sequent different tasks. We will optimize the stability of CL from the perspective of learning shared representations. Non-contrastive learning is mostly used for self-supervised paradigm, which finds visual similarity or weak information in unlabeled samples, and compares the cosine similarity [10] after random enhancement of the input images [11]. Inspired by the non-contrastive learning [12], we propose a conjecture: the process of extracting latent representations be-tween different tasks at the same time step by CL model can be seen as an encoder extracting two randomly augmented views. According to this conjecture, we propose a CL model based on the Task-wise Shared Hidden Representation Alignment (TSHRA). Our proposed TSHRA can compare the similarity of latent representations, extract the shared features of input examples from different tasks more accurately. This model adopts self-supervised training and the memory replay strategy from the CL scenario. Memory replay pseudo samples are used to extract latent representations for two batches of samples which are from different labels. We adopt memory reconstruction strategy to strengthen the TSHRA's capability of extracting shared representations.

We validate our contributions on two benchmark datasets Split-MNIST and Fashion-MNIST. Our TSHRA model achieved acceptable performance on two data sets. We also proved that the influence of the non-contrastive learning on the extraction of shared features from different tasks is positive. The main contributions of our study are as follows:

1) We establish the task-wise shared hidden representation alignment module by replay pseudo samples, which can effectively extract shared representations for the different tasks and alleviate the impact of catastrophic forgetting.
2) Our proposed framework TSHRA fills the gap between CL and non-contrastive learning. We introduce non-contrastive learning into CL scenarios and avoid the model relying on positive and negative sample pairs during contrastive learning, which facilitates the CL model to compare the latent representations from the current and previous batch of training samples belonging to different classes.
3) We conduct comprehensive empirical studies using two public benchmark datasets under the commonly-used evaluation protocol. TSHRA consistently outperforms existing approaches.

2   Related Works

In this section, we briefly summarize BYOL, Simsiam, contrastive learning, deep generative model, and continual learning.

BYOL and Simsiam. BYOL [12] uses a Siamese network structure, one of its network branches is a momentum encoder. BYOL can directly predict the two types of images without using positive and negative samples. [13] believes that although the momentum encoder can improve the accuracy, it cannot prevent the gradient from collapsing. [13] removes the momentum encoder of the branch network and adds a gradient stop on this side. On this basis, the Simple Siamese (Simsiam) model is established, which effectively avoided the gradient collapse that may occur in the Siamese network. Simsiam can carry out contrastive learning without positive and negative sample pairs. Therefore, we guess that Simsiam structure can be used in CL scenarios to carry out latent contrastive learning for the input samples of the current batch.

Contrastive Learning. Contrastive learning is widely used in computer vision [14, 15], natural language processing [16] and recommendation system [17]. Contrastive learning's main idea is attracting positive sample pairs and repelling negative sample pairs. However, in the CL scenario, it is difficult to divide the input samples into positive and negative pairs. Our proposed TSHRA can avoid relying on positive and negative sample pairs in contrastive learning. We optimize the similarity metric between the input examples of current task and the pseudo examples of previous task. The idea is similar to non-contrastive learning thought. What is significantly different from comparative learning and non-contrastive learning is, in place of optimizing the conditional probability on positive and negative samples or constraining the similarity of multiple views of one sample, we utilize the examples of current task and pseudo examples of preceding seen tasks to implement quasi-non-contrastive learning, we regard the set of previous seen tasks as super-task or super-class, each subclass or task must possess common super-class characteristics. By introducing similarity constraints, the agents are prompted to obtain the common hidden representation of the superclass, the common hidden representation is shared by all seen tasks, therefore, we call this procedure as common representation alignment between multiple tasks.

Deep Generative Model. Deep generative model uses deep neural networks to approximate probability distributions. At present, the well-known deep generative models are Variational Autoencoder (VAE) [18] and Generative Adversarial Nets (GANs) [19]. Conditional Variational Autoencoder (cVAE) [20] adds sample's label to VAE to maximize log likelihood. Our proposed TSHRA model combines the task-wise shared hidden representation alignment module with cVAE model.

Continual Learning. CL has a high degree of attention in the deep learning community. The regularization-based method protects the old knowledge from being covered by the new knowledge by imposing constraints on the loss function of the new task [6, 8]. The replay method retains or reconstructs a part of the representative old data and uses it for the model to review the old knowledge what has been learned. While learning new tasks to reduce forgetting, these previous task samples will be replayed. They are either replay as model inputs for rehearsal, or constrain the loss of new tasks to prevent interference from previous tasks [4, 5, 21]. The parameter isolation method sets a network with independent parameters for different tasks. When learning a new network, the parameters of the old network will not be changed. Therefore, the performance of the old task will not be degraded. This method specifies different model parameters for each task to prevent any possible forgetting. When there is no constraint on the size of the architecture, new branches can be added for new tasks, while the previous task parameters can be frozen, or a model copy can be specified for each task. Or, the network structure remains static and a fixed part is assigned to each task. During the training of the new task, parts of the previous task will be masked or applied at the parameter level or unit level. [7] However, at present, no literature has proposed a method to make Siamese networks join the CL scenario for contrastive learning of latent representations. Our proposed model focuses on enhancing the model's ability to learn shared representations and introducing a Siamese network to achieve this goal.

3   Task-Wise Shared Hidden Representation Alignment (TSHRA)

In this section, we will describe in detail how we apply the task-wise shared hidden representation alignment to CL scenarios, and introduce the network structure of TSHRA. Our pivot idea is to grasp the consecutive inter-task dependencies. When training current task, we not only extract the specific hidden features for current task, but also build the shared hidden representations for current and previous all trained tasks. We argue that to subdue the catastrophic forgetting, and remember the learned knowledge, we need to learn the shared hidden representations for all trained tasks. Although each task belongs to different classes, if the same model wants to learn well for all tasks belonging to different classes, it should grasp the common characteristics of all tasks. In particular, by considering the constraints and relations between two successive tasks we will point out how TSHRA can learn the shared hidden representations from samples belonging to different tasks through the task-wise shared hidden representation alignment technique.

3.1   Problem Setting

First, we define the class incremental learning setup with memory buffers, which contains a series of N tasks φ^1, φ^2, $\ldots$, φ^N. Each task φ^i corresponds to a sample set σ^i containing only the i-th class. σ^i consists of all input samples $\left\{ x_j^i \in R^F \right\}_{j=1}^{m_i}$ belonging to task φ^i and corresponding one-hot encoding labels $\left\{ y_j^i \in \{0, 1\} \right\}_{j=1}^{m_i}$, which satisfies the hypothesis: $y^i \cap y_{i \in \{i|1 \leq i \leq N\}, j \in \{j|1 \leq j \leq N, j \neq i\}}^j = \emptyset$. . The Class Incremental Model (CIL) will learn each task in turn from φ^1 to φ^N. We allocate $N - 1$ memory buffers $\mathcal{B}^1, \ldots, \mathcal{B}^{N-1}$ to store reconstruction examples of decoder of cVAE when the CIL model is trained from φ^1 to φ^{N-1} tasks. More specifically, When the CIL model trains the samples $\left\{ x_j^i, y_j^i \right\}_{j=1}^{m_i}$ for the task φ^i, the reconstruction samples the reconstruction samples stored in the buffers

$\mathcal{B}^1, \cdots, \mathcal{B}^{i-1}$ will also participate in the training. The buffers $\mathcal{B}^1, \cdots, \mathcal{B}^{i-1}$ are composed of the reconstruction samples labeled from 1 to $i - 1$. The reconstruction samples are as follows:

$$\left\{ \left\{ \hat{x}_k^1, y_k^1 \right\}_{k=1}^{r_1}, \left\{ \hat{x}_k^2, y_k^2 \right\}_{k=1}^{r_2}, \cdots, \left\{ \hat{x}_k^{i-1}, y_k^{i-1} \right\}_{k=1}^{r_{i-1}} \right\}. \quad (1)$$

3.2 Our Proposed Model

More specifically, our proposed model constitutes six components: encoder of cVAE, which extracts the shared hidden features; the task-wise shared hidden representation alignment module, which enforces the similarity constraint between the shared hidden features of current task and the previous task, and deduces the shared hidden representation among current task φ^i and previous tasks $\varphi^1, \cdots, \varphi^{i-1}$ that have been trained; decoder of cVAE, which generates the replay samples of previous task which has been trained on; the buffers $\mathcal{B}^1, \cdots, \mathcal{B}^{i-1}$, which are composed of the reconstruction samples for rehearsal labeled from 1 to $i - 1$; specific encoder for current task φ^i, which introduces the specific hidden features for current task; The classifier, which utilize the shared hidden representations and the specific hidden features as inputs to construct the classifier to estimate the class labels from 1 to $i - 1$. Figure 1 shows the structure of our TSHRA model.

For the CL scenario, samples will enter the agent in batches, and then the latent representation of the batch of samples will be learned. If we want to add the task wise

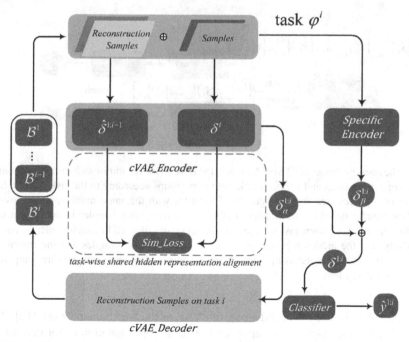

Fig. 1. Structure of our TSHRA model and the training process of TSHRA on task.

shared hidden representation alignment architecture to the CL scenario, the agent needs to generate two batches of latent representations at the same time. Our goal is to enable the agent to better obtain the shared hidden representations between different tasks, so the two batches of samples for comparison should belong to different tasks. Based on this viewpoint, we choose the memory replay method as the basic learning scenario for our proposed TSHRA model. In the light of this basic learning scenario, to meet the conditions for building the hidden representation alignment, we regard the samples of the previous task and the current task as two batches. We call the latent representation generated through the hidden representation alignment as shared representation. We also consider that the replay samples should have more shared features. Obviously, by reconstructing the shared representations generated by the agent, the reconstructed samples are more suitable as the replay samples. Based on the above considerations, we choose to use the cVAE [18] as the main subnetwork for our proposed TSHRA model.

We believe that the process of the encoder extracting the latent representations of the reconstruction samples $\left\{ \{\hat{x}_k^1, y_k^1\}_{k=1}^{r_1}, \{\hat{x}_k^2, y_k^2\}_{k=1}^{r_2}, \cdots, \left\{\hat{x}_k^{i-1}, y_k^{i-1}\right\}_{k=1}^{r_{i-1}} \right\}$ from buffers $\mathcal{B}^{1:i-1}$ and the current task examples $\left\{ x_j^i, y_j^i \right\}_{j=1}^{m_i}$ can be regarded as the encoder extracting two randomly augmented views. According to this idea, we can compare the latent representations $\delta^i \left\{ \{x_k^i\}_{k=1}^p \right\}$ of the current task input examples with the pseudo latent representations $\hat{\delta}^{1:i-1} \left\{ \{\hat{x}_k^1\}_{k=1}^{q_1}, \{\hat{x}_k^2\}_{k=1}^{q_2}, \cdots, \left\{\hat{x}_k^{i-1}\right\}_{k=1}^{q_{i-1}} \right\}$ of the previous task samples, so that we can better learn the task-wise shared hidden representation for the task φ^i. Figure 2 shows the training process of TSHRA on task φ^i.

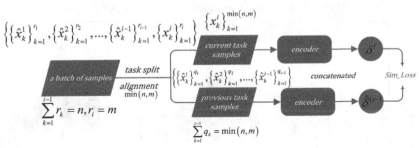

Fig. 2. The learning process of TSHRA model. TSHRA divide the mini-batch samples containing the ones of current tasks and previous tasks into two groups according to the task indices. Since the alignment process requires two groups of samples with the same number, we remove the redundant samples based on the smaller number of the two group samples in the current mini-batch. Specifically, the current task samples and the previous task pseudo samples enter the encoder respectively, and the hidden representations of the previous task samples and the current task samples are obtained after encoder process. Next, the two hidden representations are compared to obtain the similarity loss.

Specifically, we use the encoder part of cVAE as the backbone network [12]. After the training samples input to the encoder, the latent representation δ^i for current task φ^i, and pseudo latent representation $\hat{\delta}^{1:i-1}$ from pervious tasks are obtained. Then we define the negative cosine similarity to be minimized, as alignment objective function:

$$\theta\left(\delta^i, \hat{\delta}^{1:i-1}\right) = -\frac{\delta^i}{\left\|\delta^i\right\|_2} \cdot \frac{\hat{\delta}^{1:i-1}}{\left\|\hat{\delta}^{1:i-1}\right\|_2} \tag{2}$$

where $\|\cdot\|_2$ is the L2-norm. For the encoder part of cVAE, we use the mean square error to define the reconstruction loss:

$$\mathcal{L}\_re = \left\|x^i - \hat{x}^i\right\|^2 \tag{3}$$

For the decoder part, in order to minimize the distance between the distributions, we use KL divergence as a constraint:

$$\mathcal{L}\_kl = KL\left(q\left(\delta|\sigma^{1:i}\right)||p(\delta^{1:i})\right) \tag{4}$$

Finally, the loss function of our cVAE combined with the alignment objective function can be expressed as:

$$\mathcal{L}\_cVAE = \mathcal{L}\_kl + \mathcal{L}\_re - \mathcal{L}\_sim$$

$$= KL\left(q\left(\delta|\sigma^{1:i}\right)||p(\delta^{1:i})\right) + \left\|x^i - \hat{x}^i\right\|^2$$

$$- \frac{\delta^i}{\left\|\delta^i\right\|_2} \cdot \frac{\hat{\delta}^{1:i-1}}{\left\|\hat{\delta}^{1:i-1}\right\|_2} \tag{5}$$

We also need to extract the specific representations δ_β of the input samples. We define a specific encoder whose function is to extract the specific representations of the input samples. We use the cross-entropy loss to constrain the encoder. Finally, the shared representations and specific representations are added and sent to the classifier to get the predicted output.

4 Experiments

In this section, we first introduce the details of datasets, and then evaluate the proposed TSHRA model on two benchmarks datasets. We compare our TSHRA with the current advanced CL methods. We analyze the impact of joining the task-wise shared hidden representation alignment architecture on the model learning shared representation and visualized the example after the cVAE reconstruction. Finally, we compare with the results. Our experimental code is inspired by [22].

4.1 Datasets

We use two benchmark datasets, Split-MNIST and Fashion-MNIST, which are widely used in continuous learning scenarios. We define 5–10 epochs for training, and visualize the reconstructed samples in each epoch.

Split MNIST. Split-MNIST splits the MNIST dataset [23] into 5 different tasks, each of task has two non-overlapping classes. The Split-MNIST data set contains handwritten forms ranging from digits 0 to 9, divided into 10 Class, consisting of 60,000 samples and 10,000 test samples, and each sample is a 28 × 28-pixel grayscale picture.

Fashion-MNIST. Fashion-MNIST [24] contains 28 × 28 grayscale images of 70,000 fashion products from 10 categories, each with 7000 images. The training set has 60,000 images, and the test set has 10,000 images. Fashion MNIST is higher than MNIST in sample complexity.

4.2 The CL Baseline

We selected three different CL methods as the baseline. LWF [4], DGR [5] and IRCL [22] are three different reconstruction memory replay methods. EWC [6] is a representative CL method with the regularization strategy.

LWF. LWF [4] uses the previously trained model as a teacher model, and adopts the knowledge distillation scheme to constrain the student model for training new tasks. So as to achieve the purpose of not forgetting the previous task.

DGR. DGR [5] includes a deep generative model and a task solving model. The deep generative model is used to generate samples from the past tasks, task solving model is trained to couple the inputs and targets drawn. Through these two models, the training data of the previous task can be easily crossed with the training data of the new task.

IRCL. Similar to DGR, IRCL [22] uses a deep generative model to generate pseudo samples in CL scenarios.

EWC. As a classical CL method with the regularization strategy, EWC [6] adds elastic weight to the regularization item and revises the parameters of each task in combination with the Fisher information matrix of the training task. The punishment of each parameter for each task depends on the importance of the parameter to the task, and the penalty for more important parameters is higher.

4.3 Experimental Results and Comparison

We compare our proposed TSHRA model with the current CL baseline model. First, we use average accuracy (ACC) [25] to evaluate the average classification accuracy of the model for each task after learning all the tasks. We use backward transfer (BWT) [25] as another evaluation criterion. BWT will harm the performance of the model in the previous task. The large backward transfer is also called catastrophic forgetting. We define an accuracy P, which represents the classification accuracy of the previous task after the model finishes training on current task φ^i, ACC and BWT can be expressed as:

$$ACC = \frac{1}{N} \sum_{i=1}^{N} P_{N,i}$$

$$BWT = \frac{1}{N-1} \sum_{i=2}^{N} P_{N,i} - P_{i,i} \qquad (6)$$

As shown in Fig. 3 and Table 1 the Average Accuracy value of TSHRA is significantly better than other CL methods. On Split-MNIST our TSHRA has a 3.6 increase in accuracy compared to DGR and has a 41.3 increase in accuracy compared to LWF. On Fashion-MNIST, our TSHRA has a 1.8 increase in accuracy compared to DGR, which shows that the performance of TSHRA is better than the existing baseline model. We think it is because TSHRA adopts the method of memory reconstruction and replay. This method can effectively avoid the model's forgetting of previous tasks. We believe that the use of ACC alone is not enough to judge whether the task-wise shared hidden representation alignment architecture has improved the model's learning level of shared features. The regularization method EWC has only 20 ACC on both two datasets. We think EWC completely forgets the previous tasks.

Table 1. The value of ACC on the test datasets for different models

Method	Split-MNIST	Fashion-MNIST
EWC	19.9%	19.6%
LWF	44.9%	45.6%
DGR	82.6%	74.4%
IRCL	85.0%	75.9%
TSHRA	**86.2%**	**76.2%**

Table 2. The value of BWT on the test datasets for different models

Method	Split-MNIST	Fashion-MNIST
EWC	−100	−100
LWF	−6.0	−22.8
DGR	−15.4	−22.6
IRCL	−12.8	−19.2
TSHRA	**−11.6**	−19.2

From Table 2, we can intuitively understand that the negative impact of TSHRA is much less than other baseline methods. Compared with DGR and LWF, our TSHRA has dropped 3.8 and 5.6 respectively on Split-MNIST, and 3.5 and 3.3 respectively on Fashion-MNIST. We identify it is because we combine the task-wise shared hidden representation alignment architecture in the CL scenario. The regularization method EWC has almost close to −100 on both two datasets. That means EWC completely forgets the previous tasks. We think TSHRA has capability to promote the CL model to extract the shared representation of the input example more effectively, thereby effectively alleviating catastrophic forgetting.

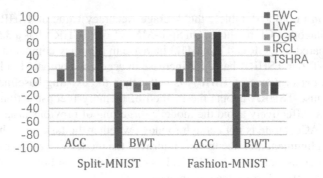

Fig. 3. Experimental results on two datasets.

We removed the task-wise shared hidden representation alignment module and compared the model with TSHRA. We found that the accuracy of the model decreased, and the impact on the previous task increased. We visualized the reconstructed samples of the model after removing the similarity loss and compared it with TSHRA. Figure 4 visualizes the reconstruction samples generated by TSHRA at different epochs in Task 5. We can see that compared to the model which does not use the task-wise shared hidden representation alignment architecture. TSHRA produces a further complete sample reconstruction image. We believe that the addition of the task-wise shared hidden representation alignment architecture makes the model extract more valuable shared representation and obtain stronger robustness, which shows that TSHRA remembers the characteristics of the previous task sample more stable, and is not affected by the current task.

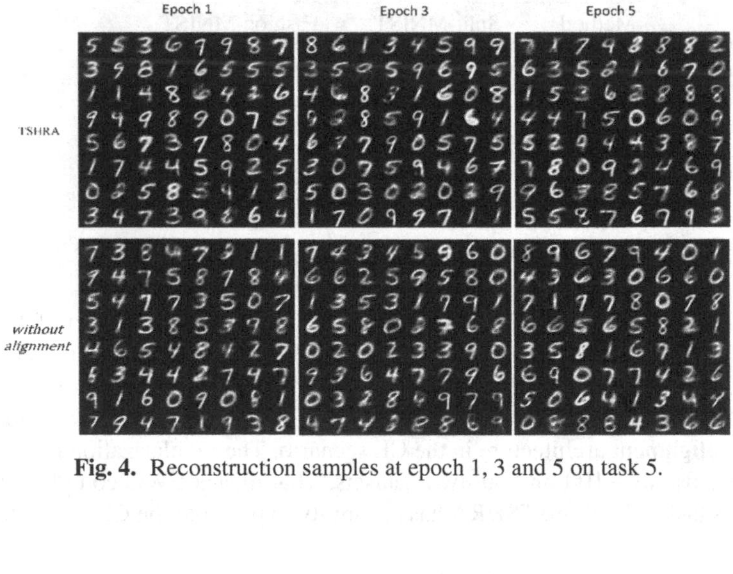

Fig. 4. Reconstruction samples at epoch 1, 3 and 5 on task 5.

5 Conclusions and Future Work

In this paper, we propose TSHRA, a task-wise shared hidden representation alignment architecture for continual learning by reconstructed pseudo samples. We con-sider the process of extracting latent representations between different tasks by CL model can be seen as an encoder extracting two randomly augmented views for task-wise shared hidden representation. We added a task-wise shared hidden representation alignment architecture to the CL scenarios to compare the similarities of shared hidden represen-tations between different classes of input examples on the successive tasks. We add similarity loss based on cVAE and constrain the encoder to extract more similar shared representations between sequential tasks. The experimental rsults verified our conjecture that the task-wise shared hidden representation alignment structure can help CL model to extract better shared representations.

In the future, we can incorporate the other non-contrastive learning networks for self-supervised learning into CL scenarios. Finally, we hope that this research can inspire further exploration of the combination of self-supervised learning and CL.

References

1. Ring, M.: Continual learning in reinforcement environment, Ph. D. thesis, University of Texas, Austin (1994)
2. French, R.M.: Catastrophic forgetting in connectionist networks. Trends Cogn. Sci. 3(4), 128–135 (1999)
3. Shim, D., et al.: Online class-incremental continual learning with adversarial shapley value. In: Proceedings of the AAAI Conference on Artificial Intelligence, vol. 35. no. 11 (2021)
4. Li, Z., Hoiem, D.: Learning without forgetting. IEEE Trans. Pattern Anal. Mach. Intell. 40(12), 2935–2947 (2017)
5. Shin, H., et al.: Continual learning with deep generative replay. arXiv preprint arXiv:1705.08690 (2017)
6. Kirkpatrick, J., et al.: Overcoming catastrophic forgetting in neural networks. Proc. Nat. Acad. Sci. 114(13), 3521–3526 (2017)
7. Fernando, C.: Evolution channels gradient descent in super neural networks. arXiv preprint arXiv:1701.08734 1–16 (2017)
8. Zenke, F., Poole, B., Ganguli, S.: Continual learning through synaptic intelligence. In: International Conference on Machine Learning, PMLR (2017)
9. Van de Ven, G.M., Tolias, A.S.: Three scenarios for continual learning. arXiv preprint arXiv: 1904.07734 (2019)
10. Bromley, J., et al.: Signature verification using a "siamese" time delay neural network. Int. J. Pattern Recognit. Artif. Intell. 7(4), 669–688 (1993)
11. Ye, M., et al.: Unsupervised embedding learning via invariant and spreading instance feature. In: Proceedings of the IEEE/CVF Conference on Computer Vision and Pattern Recognition (2019)
12. Grill, J.-B., et al.: Bootstrap your own latent: a new approach to self-supervised learning. arXiv preprint arXiv:2006.07733 (2020)
13. Chen, X., Kaiming, H.: Exploring simple siamese representation learning. In: Proceedings of the IEEE/CVF Conference on Computer Vision and Pattern Recognition (2021)
14. Chen, T., et al.: A simple framework for contrastive learning of visual representations. In: International Conference on Machine Learning, PMLR (2020)

15. He, K., et al.: Momentum contrast for unsupervised visual representation learning. In: Proceedings of the IEEE/CVF Conference on Computer Vision and Pattern Recognition (2020)
16. Wu, Z., et al.: Clear: contrastive learning for sentence representation. arXiv preprint arXiv: 2012.15466 (2020)
17. Wu, J., et al.: Self-supervised graph learning for recommendation. In: Proceedings of the 44th International ACM SIGIR Conference on Research and Development in Information Retrieval (2021)
18. Kingma, D.P., Welling, M.: Auto-encoding variational Bayes. arXiv preprint arXiv:1312. 6114 (2013)
19. Goodfellow, I.J., et al.: Generative adversarial nets. In: Advances in Neural Information Processing systems 27 (2014)
20. Kingma, D.P., et al.: Semi-supervised learning with deep generative models. In: Advances in Neural Information Processing Systems (2014)
21. Rebuffi, S.-A., et al.: iCaRL: incremental classifier and representation learning. In: Proceedings of the IEEE Conference on Computer Vision and Pattern Recognition (2017)
22. Sokar, G., Mocanu, D.C., Pechenizkiy, M.: Learning invariant representation for continual learning (2021)
23. LeCun, Y.: The MNIST database of handwritten digits. http://yann.lecun.com/exdb/ mnist/ (1998)
24. Xiao, H., Rasul, K., Vollgraf, R.: Fashion-MNIST: a novel image dataset for benchmarking machine learning algorithms. arXiv preprint arXiv:1708.07747 (2017)
25. Lopez-Paz, D., Ranzato, M.: Gradient episodic memory for continual learning. Adv. Neural. Inf. Process. Syst. **30**, 6467–6476 (2017)

Contrast and Aggregation Network for Generalized Zero-shot Learning

Bin Li, Cheng Xie$^{(\boxtimes)}$, Jingqi Yang, and Haoran Duan

Yunnan University, Kunming, Yunnan, China
xiecheng@ynu.edu.cn, {flyingsheep,yangjingqi,duanhaoran}@mail.ynu.edu.cn

Abstract. Generalized zero-shot learning (GZSL) aims to classify both seen classes and unseen classes by training seen classes and the semantic information shared by seen and unseen classes. Some methods try to synthesize unseen samples by unseen semantic information; however, the performance of the GZSL is limited as the distribution of synthesized samples and of real samples is misalignment. To tackle this problem, we propose a Contrast and Aggregation Network (CAN). CAN employs a feature and contrast module to align the real and synthesized feature, which maps the real and synthesized visual feature to a new space and aggregates both real and synthesized features to the centroid of real visual features. Since the semantic information may be lost during the generating and mapping stage, we designed a semantic feature alignment module to project the mapped feature into semantic space. We evaluate our proposed CAN on four benchmark datasets to demonstrate that our method is against the state-of-the-art GZSL methods. The source code is available at https://github.com/fesfa/CAN.

Keywords: Zero-shot learning · Image classification · Visual computing · Generative adversarial networks

1 Introduction

Recently, Zero-Shot Learning (ZSL) [14,20] has attracted more and more attention, which aims to classify the unseen classes by training seen classes and the shared semantic information. In the future, ZSL is expected to provide a solution to the problem of difficult data collection and training in the image classification task.

Early ZSL approaches focused on finding a relation between visual and semantic. Some methods [1,7] project visual features to semantic space in training and expect to transfer the relations to unseen classes. However, mapping from higher dimensions to lower dimensions may lead to the collapse of the visual feature space. And a hubness problem [4] has been found in these methods. Some

Supported by National Natural Science Foundation of China (No. 62106216 and 62162064), Science and Technology Planning Project of Yunnan Province, China, No. 202001BB050035.

methods [13,15] alleviated the hubness problem by projecting semantic descriptions to visual feature space. Nevertheless, the semantic information may not be sufficient to classify different classes. Some methods [7,12] that project semantic descriptions and visual features to a shared embedding space work well for the ZSL task, which balanced the above two problems. However, in Generalized Zero-shot Learning (GZSL) which test classes contain both seen and unseen classes, those above methods bias to classify unseen classes into seen classes, the problem is called the "Domain-Shift Problem". This problem owns to data imbalance as samples of unseen classes are not available.

Recently, generative methods [2,9,10,19,31] were proposed to mitigate the data imbalance problem that existed in GZSL. GAZSL [31] applies the Generative Adversarial Network (GAN) [8] to synthesize unseen visual features, which transform the GZSL task into a supervised classification task. GAZSL significantly improved the performance of GZSL. TFVAEGAN [19] developed this idea and introduced a feedback loop, from a semantic embedding decoder, that iteratively refines the generated features during both the training and feature synthesis stages to enforce semantic description consistency. RFF-GZSL [10] believes that the image is redundant and applied mutual information to remove the redundant information. CE-GZSL [9] integrates the generation model with the embedding model and proposes a contrastive embedding, yielding a hybrid GZSL framework, which achieves the state-of-the-art. However, the performance of the generative methods is limited as the distribution of synthesized visual features is different from the distribution of real visual features; it is especially obvious in unseen classes. This problem is called the "misalignment problem".

In this paper, we proposed a Contrast and Aggregation Network based on GAN to tackle the misalignment problem. Firstly, we design a Feature Contrast and Aggregation (FCA) module, which maps the real visual feature and synthesized visual feature to a new space, then aggregate the mapped feature to the centroid of the real visual feature in each class. It helps to make the distribution of real features and of synthesized features more consistent. Since there still exist some hard samples that are difficult to move to the centroid of real visual features, inspired by contrastive learning, we leverage the contrastive loss to align the hard sample. Secondly, as the semantic information may be lost during generating and mapping stage, we design a semantic feature alignment to project both real and synthesized mapped features to semantic space. The experiments on four benchmark datasets indicate that our CAN achieves state-of-the-art.

The contributions are summarized as follows:

- We propose a contrast and aggregation network for generalized zero-shot learning to tackle the misalignment problem that existed in generative methods. Extensive experiments results on four benchmarks indicate our CAN achieves the state-of-the-art.
- We design a feature contrast and aggregation module to solve the "misalignment" problem. Quantitative and qualitative experiments show that we can mitigate this problem.

– We designed a semantic feature alignment module to map the visual feature to semantic space, which helps to prevent semantic information lost during the generating and mapping stage. The ablation study demonstrates the performance of GZSL benefited from the module.

2   Related Work

2.1   Embedding Methods

Early ZSL works focus on building a bridge between the visual feature domain and the semantic domain. DAP [14] maps the visual features into semantic space, which trains a nonlinear support vector machine for each binary semantic, then applies the trained SVM with Platt scaling to each test image. The method was found time-consuming by training each attribute classifier independently. [1] solves this problem by using all attributes as a whole semantic description. However, the hubness problem [4] was found in the group of methods. Shigeto et al. [23] formulated the ZSL as a regression problem of finding a mapping from the target space to the source space to tackle the emergence of hubs in the subsequent nearest neighbor search step. SAE [13] takes the encoder-decoder paradigm, the decoder aims to project back a semantic vector into the visual feature space. The other methods project both visual features and semantics to a shared embedding space. DEVISE [7] used the ranking loss to learn the bilinear compatibility function between the semantic embedding and visual feature spaces. Inspired by the idea of contrastive learning, TCN [12] learned a network to calculate the similarity of all of the semantic features and the seen visual features and calculate the similarity using ridge regression. Those embedding methods perform well on the ZSL task but fail in the more challenging GZSL task. In GZSL, the above methods generally classify unseen classes as seen classes due to data imbalance in that unseen samples are not available. In more recent times, the embedding methods have achieved better performance, but this problem was never solved.

2.2   Generative Methods

To solve the data imbalance problem, GAZSL [31] combines the GAN to synthesize the visual features of the unseen class using attributes, thus the GZSL task has been transformed into a supervised classification task. TFVAEGAN [19] improves the GAN network and designed a feedback network, which improves the performance of GZSL. Cycle-CLSWGAN [6] maps visual features back to semantic descriptions to ensure the consistency of generated visual features and semantics. RFF-GZSL [10], inspired by mutual information(MI), believe that the image is redundant, so they apply MI to cut the redundant information by adding a mapping network based on GAN. CE-GZSL [9] projected the synthesized visual features and real visual features into an embedding space and compared semantic knowledge with embedding features to design a complex network to achieve state-of-the-art results. However, the performance of GAN generating visual features of unseen classes is limited since the distribution of real features and of the synthesized features are misalignment.

To tackle this misalignment problem, we propose a Contrast and Aggregation Network(CAN). Inspired by the supervised classification methods that aggregate the visual feature to the centroid in each class, we designed a feature contrast and aggregation module. In this module, we mapped both real and synthesized visual features to a new space, in which the mapped features are aggregated to the centroid of real visual features in each class. And inspired by contrastive learning, we apply a contrast loss to aggregate the hard samples. In addition, since the semantic information may be lost during generating and mapping stage, we designed a semantic feature alignment module, which projects the mapped feature to semantic space with a semantic alignment loss to align the mapped semantic vector with the original semantic vector.

3   Methodology

This section is divided into four subsections. The definition of ZSL and GZSL is given in Section III-A. In Section III-B, we will introduce the Visual Feature Generation module, and then the Feature Contrast and Aggregation module will be introduced in Section III-C. Finally, the Semantic Feature Alignment module will be introduced in Section III-D.

3.1   Problem Setting

ZSL aims to classify the unseen classes by learning seen classes, while semantics shared by seen classes and unseen classes are available. Formally, let $\mathcal{S} = \{(x_i, a_i, y_i)|x_i \in \mathcal{X}^s, a_i \in \mathcal{A}^s, y_i \in \mathcal{Y}^s\}_{i=1}^N$ denote seen classes which consist of N instance, where $\mathcal{X}^s$ represents the visual feature space of seen classes, $\mathcal{A}^s$ denotes the semantic space of seen classes, $\mathcal{Y}^s$ is the label set of seen classes. Similarly, we denoted the unseen class as $\mathcal{U} = \{(x_i, a_i, y_i)|x_i \in \mathcal{X}^u, a_i \in \mathcal{A}^u, y_i \in \mathcal{Y}^u\}_{i=N+1}^{N+M}$, where $\mathcal{X}^u$ represents the visual feature space of unseen classes, $\mathcal{A}^u$ represents the semantic space of unseen classes, $\mathcal{Y}^u$ is the label set of unseen classes, where $\mathcal{Y}^s \cap \mathcal{Y}^u = \emptyset$. $\mathcal{X}^s$ and $\mathcal{X}^u$ shared a common visual feature space $\mathcal{X}$, $\mathcal{A}^s$ and $\mathcal{A}^u$ share a common attribute space $\mathcal{A}$. The training set is $D_t = \{\mathcal{X}^s, \mathcal{A}, \mathcal{Y}\}$, where $\mathcal{Y} = \mathcal{Y}^s \cup \mathcal{Y}^u$. ZSL aims to learn a function $f : \mathcal{X}^u \to \mathcal{Y}^u$. More challengingly, GZSL is to learn a function $f : \mathcal{X} \to \mathcal{Y}$, where the search space is the whole label space $\mathcal{Y}$.

3.2   Visual Feature Generation

As shown in Fig. 1(a), we generate the synthesized visual feature x' at first. Given a semantic vector a (from attribute or textual descriptions) and a Gaussian noise ϵ, x' is generated by $x' = G(a, \epsilon)$. At the same time, a real image is fed into ResNet-101 and output a real visual feature x. Then we apply a synthesized

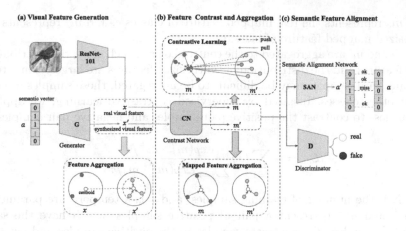

Fig. 1. Illustration of the proposed CAN. In the first module (a), we generate synthesized visual feature x' from attribute a and extract real visual feature x from images by ResNet101 [11], x' is aggregated into the centroid of x. Module (b) maps x and x' into a new space, in which m and m' are aggregated to the centroid of x to align the m with m' and hard samples are aligned by contrastive learning. Finally, in module(c), a discriminator D is to classify m and m' as real or fake. At the same time, m and m' are projected to semantic space to align a' with a.

feature aggregation loss $\mathcal{L}_{sfa}$ to aggregate x' to the centroid of x in each class, which keeps the feature inter-class aggregated and out-class repelled:

$$\mathcal{L}_{sfa} = \frac{1}{C} \sum_{c=1}^{C} \| \frac{1}{\tilde{N}_c} \sum_{i=1}^{\tilde{N}_c} \tilde{x}_c^i - \frac{1}{N_c} \sum_{i=1}^{N_c} x_c^i \| \tag{1}$$

where C is seen class number, $\tilde{x}_c$ represents the synthesized visual feature of class c, $\tilde{N}_c$ is the number of $\tilde{x}_c$, x_c represents the real visual feature of classes c, and N_c is the number of x_c.

3.3 Feature Contrast and Aggregation

In this section, we apply contrastive learning and aggregation to align real features and synthesized features, which can be seen in Fig. 1(b).

Different from the former methods of mapping visual features to a small embedding space, we map x and x' to a new space by Contrast Network (CN). In the space, real mapped feature m and synthesized mapped feature m' have the same dimensions as x and x'. Then we aggregate m and m' to the centroid of x in each class:

$$\mathcal{L}_a = \frac{1}{C} \sum_{c=1}^{C} (\| \frac{1}{N_c} \sum_{i=1}^{N_c} m_c^i - \frac{1}{N_c} \sum_{i=1}^{N_c} x_c^i \| + \| \frac{1}{\tilde{N}_c} \sum_{i=1}^{\tilde{N}_c} m'^i_c - \frac{1}{N_c} \sum_{i=1}^{N_c} x_c^i \|) \tag{2}$$

where m_c represents the real mapped feature of classes c, and m'_c represents the synthesized mapped feature of class c.

As m and m' are aggregated to the centroid of x in each class, the distribution of real features and the distribution of synthesized features are largely consistent. But some hard samples may be difficult to be aggregated, these samples are still around other classes. Inspired by supervised contrastive learning, we apply a contrast loss to contrast the positive pair samples and negative pair samples:

$$\mathcal{L}_{cr} = -\sum_{i=1}^{N} \log \frac{exp(m_i^T \cdot m^+ / \tau)}{\sum_{j=1}^{N} exp(m_i^T \cdot m_j / \tau)} \tag{3}$$

where N is the number of training samples, and τ is a temperature parameter. The m_i^T and m^+ represent a pair of positive samples, which have the same class label. The loss $\mathcal{L}_{cr}$ contrasts samples to the positive samples and negative samples, which makes the samples with the same label closer and samples with different labels far away, and temperature τ is helpful to control the weight when optimizer the loss.

3.4 Semantic Feature Alignment

Finally, as shown in Fig. 1(c), the mapped features m and m' are fed into discriminator(D) and Semantic Alignment Network(SAN).

The discriminator judge m and m' is synthesized or real. Combined network Generator(G), CN, and D, the adversarial loss is formulated as below:

$$\begin{aligned} V(D, CN \circ G) &= \mathbf{E}_{x \sim p_{data}}[\mathbf{E}_{m \sim p_{cn}(m|x)}[logD(m)]] \\ &+ \mathbf{E}_{x' \sim p_g(x')}[\mathbf{E}_{m' \sim p_{cn}(m'|x')}[log(1 - D(m'))]] \end{aligned} \tag{4}$$

where $CN \circ G$ is a composite generator, and $p_{cn}(m'|x')$ is the distribution of synthesized mapped feature m' conditioned on the synthesized visual feature x'.

The original semantic vector a is mapped by G and CN, there is some semantic information that may be lost, so we projected m and m' back to semantic vector a'. The semantic alignment loss is computed by the following:

$$\mathcal{L}_{sa} = ||a - SAN(m)||_2^2 + ||a - SAN(m')||_2^2 \tag{5}$$

To this end, the overall loss function is written as:

$$\mathcal{L} = V(D, CN \circ G) + \lambda_{sfa}\mathcal{L}_{sfa} + \lambda_a\mathcal{L}_a + \lambda_{cr}\mathcal{L}_{cr} + \lambda_{sa}\mathcal{L}_{sa} \tag{6}$$

where λ_{sfa}, λ_a, λ_{cr}, and λ_{sa} are hyper-parameters for synthesized feature aggregation loss, visual feature alignment loss, contrastive loss, and semantic feature alignment loss.

Table 1. Statistics for APY, AWA1, CUB, and SUN.

Datasets	Seen	Unseen	Attr	All samples	train+val
APY [5]	15+5	12	64	15399	5932
AWA1 [14]	27+13	10	85	30475	19832
CUB [25]	100+50	50	1024	11788	7057
SUN [21]	580+65	72	102	14340	10320

4 Experiments

4.1 Datasets

We evaluate our method on four widely used benchmark datasets for GZSL, including APascal-aYahoo (**aPY**) [5], Animal with Attributes 1 (**AWA1** [14]), Caltech-UCSD Birds-200-2011 (**CUB** [25]), and Scene UNderstanding (**SUN** [21]). The 2,048-dimensional CNN features are extracted for all datasets with the ResNet-101 [11] network which is not fine-tuned. For aPY, AWA1, and SUN, the semantic descriptions are annotated with attributes. The class-level semantic descriptors are generated from textual descriptions [22] for CUB. Moreover, the Proposed-Split(PS) methods proposed in [26] are adopted to divide all classes into seen and unseen classes on each dataset, which are summarized in Table 1.

4.2 Evaluation Protocols

For GZSL, the test set is composed of seen classes and unseen classes. We evaluate the performance of our method by per-class Top-1 accuracy on both, denoted as S and U, respectively. Furthermore, the harmonic mean $H = 2 \times U \times S/(U+S)$ is computed to evaluate the GZSL performance.

4.3 Implementation Details

We implement our CAN with PyTorch. The adam solver with $\beta_1 = 0.5$ and $\beta_2 = 0.999$ is used for all networks. Moreover, we set batch size = 512 for aPY, and AWA1, batch size = 2048 on CUB and SUN. Finally, the CAN model is trained on 4× GTX-2080Ti GPUs.

4.4 Performance on Generalize Zero-shot Learning

Comparison with State-of-the-Art: Since CAN is an inductive method, other inductive state-of-the-art methods are compared for a fair comparison. We simply divide the methods into nongenerative methods and generative methods. The results are shown in Table 2.

The results show that our CAN model achieves the best performance for harmonic mean on three benchmark datasets, i.e., 50.6 on APY, 69.2 on AWA1,

Table 2. GZSL results on APY, AWA1, CUB, and SUN. U and S represent the Top-1 accuracies tested on unseen classes and seen classes, respectively. H is the harmonic mean of U and S. The best and second-best results are marked in red and blue, respectively.

	Method	APY			AWA1			CUB			SUN		
		U	S	H	U	S	H	U	S	H	U	S	H
NON-Generative	MLSE [3]	12.7	74.3	21.7	-	-	-	22.3	71.6	34.0	20.7	36.4	26.4
	AREN [27]	9.2	76.9	16.4	-	-	-	38.9	78.7	52.1	19.0	38.8	25.5
	TCN [12]	24.1	64.0	35.1	49.4	76.5	60.0	52.6	52.0	52.3	31.2	37.3	34.0
	VSE-S [30]	24.5	72.0	36.6	-	-	-	33.4	87.5	48.4	-	-	-
	GAFE [18]	-	-	-	25.5	76.6	38.2	22.5	52.1	31.4	19.6	31.9	24.3
	CN-ZSL [24]	-	-	-	63.1	73.4	67.8	49.9	50.7	50.3	44.7	41.6	43.1
Generative	MGA-GAN [28]	-	-	-	-	-	-	46.6	58.3	51.8	45.6	37.3	41.0
	GMN [29]	-	-	-	55.3	78.2	64.8	58.8	60.7	59.7	46.3	38.4	42.0
	MFGN [17]	40.8	52.4	45.9	-	-	-	49.1	59.5	53.8	49.7	36.0	41.7
	AMAZ(weighted-soft) [16]	-	-	-	64.4	63.6	64.1	58.2	55.7	56.9	42.0	35.1	38.3
	RFF-GZSL [10]	-	-	-	59.8	75.1	66.5	52.6	56.6	54.6	45.7	38.6	41.9
	CE-GZSL [9]	35.5	65.4	46.0	65.3	73.4	69.1	63.9	66.8	65.3	48.8	38.6	43.1
	FREE [2]	-	-	-	62.9	69.4	66.0	55.7	59.9	57.7	47.4	37.2	41.7
	Ours	42.2	63.0	50.6	63.5	76.0	69.2	66.0	62.6	64.2	48.4	39.0	43.2

Table 3. Efficiency comparison. This is the result of CAN versus CE-GZSL in terms of time spent in training, *time* represents the average time (second) required to train an epoch, and *epoch* represents the training epochs required to achieve the best results.

Method	APY		AWA1	
	time/s	epoch	time/s	epoch
CE-GZSL	2.69	58	15.67	67
Ours	0.39	73	0.56	171

and 43.2 on SUN, respectively. To the best of our knowledge, our result on APY is the first method that obtains a performance >50.0 on H among the state-of-the-art GZSL methods and is ahead of the best method CE-GZSL by 4.6 points. This indicates that our CAN is efficient on both coarse- and fine-grained datasets. We also compare the speed of CE-GZSL and our model achieves the best epoch on APY and AWA1 datasets in Table 3; the result shows that our training time is much less than CE-GZSL. This indicates our method is better than CE-GZSL and more efficient.

Ablation Study: As shown in Table 4, we conduct ablation studies to evaluate the effect on different components. Firstly, we train a baseline that contains a Generator and a Discriminator with adversarial loss. Then we add Semantic Alignment(SA) module with $\mathcal{L}_{sa}$ loss to the baseline. Next, the Feature Contrast and Aggregation(FCA) module with $\mathcal{L}_{cr}$ and $\mathcal{L}_a$ losses is added to the baseline. Finally, we add both the SA module and the FCA module at the same time. The result shows that the baseline gain a poor performance. When the SA and FCA modules are added to the baseline, the performance of GZSL has been significantly

Table 4. Result (%) of GZSL ablation study on APY, AWA1, CUB, and SUN. The *base* is GAN method, the *base* + *SA* is *base* with SA module, the *base* + *FCA* is *base* with FCA module, *CAN* is our final model.

Method	APY			AWA1			CUB			SUN		
	U	S	H	U	S	H	U	S	H	U	S	H
base	24.4	**65.1**	35.5	7.3	72.1	13.3	0.0	0.0	0.0	0.0	0.0	0.0
base + *SA*	27.8	59.4	37.9	42.8	53.1	47.4	35.7	36.2	36.0	25.8	31.9	28.5
base + *FCA*	40.8	61.9	49.2	**63.7**	74.6	68.7	63.5	63.6	63.5	48.4	38.5	42.9
CAN	**42.2**	63.0	**50.6**	63.5	**76.0**	**69.2**	**66.0**	62.6	**64.2**	48.4	39.0	**43.2**

improved, which indicates the model benefit from SA and FCA module. A large improvement is gained by adding only the FCA module, which indicated the feature alignment is helpful on the GZSL task, and the misalignment is alleviated.

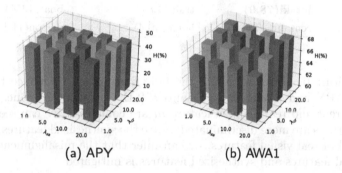

(a) APY   (b) AWA1

Fig. 2. The influence of λ_{cr} and λ_{sa} hyperparameters on H in APY, and AWA1 datasets.

Hyper-Parameters Analysis: In Fig. 2, we cross-validate the influence of hyper-parameters λ_{sa} and λ_{cr} on APY and AWA1 datasets. The result shows that the H result on different datasets changes slightly when λ_{sa} changed, the best result was achieved on $\lambda_{sa} = 10.0$. The λ_{cr} is more sensitive to different datasets. For APY, we achieve the best result on $\lambda_{cr} = 5.0$. For AWA1, the best result was achieved on $\lambda_{cr} = 10.0$.

Domain-Shift Problem: The traditional methods suffer from the bias that misclassified the unseen instance into seen classes. In Table 5, we analyze the misclassification of the APY dataset. The result shows that the test unseen instances are not biased to be classified as seen classes; this indicates our CAN model can balance the seen and unseen classes.

Table 5. Statistic of misclassification on APY datasets. The target class represents the test unseen classes. T1 indicates the proportion is top-1 in test images classification. The correct classification is indicated in bold. And the seen classes are underlined.

target class	T1	T2	T3
cow	goat(25.3%)	sheep(24.9%)	horse(22.3)
horse	**horse(58.5%)**	sheep(8.8%)	centaur(6.2%)
motorbike	**motorbike(78.5%)**	bicyle(8.4%)	jetski(5.7%)
person	pottedplant(28.4%)	tvmonitor(13.4%)	sheep(8.4%)
pottedplant	tvmonitor(61.2%)	**pottedplant(22.5%)**	sheep(4.4)
sheep	**sheep(44.0%)**	goat(20.5%)	cow(12.0%)
train	**train(79.5%)**	tvmonitor(5.7%)	building(5.1%)
tvmonitor	**tvmonitor(76.3%)**	pottedplant(10.4%)	train(6.4%)
donkey	horse(33.1%)	goat(29.5%)	**donkey(12.2%)**
goat	sheep(32.5%)	**goat(30.7%)**	cow(13.5)
jetski	**jetski(78.9)**	train(4.8)	boat(4.5%)
statue	centaur(30.9)	horse(30.4)	person(11.1)

Visualization: In Fig. 3, we apply the t-SNE approach to reduce the visual feature of APY and AWA1 datasets into a 2-D visualization plane. The real visual feature x and real mapped feature m are compared, we can see that the mapped features are more discriminated. Since the synthesized features surround the centroid of real visual features, we can infer that the misalignment problem between real features and synthesized features is mitigated.

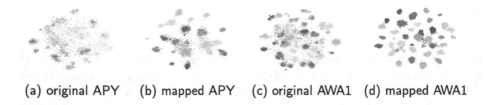

(a) original APY　　(b) mapped APY　　(c) original AWA1　(d) mapped AWA1

Fig. 3. The visualization of APY and AWA1. (a) and (c) are the real visual features extracted by ResNet-101. (b) and (d) are the real mapped features.

5　Conclusion

In this work, we propose a Contrast and Aggregation Network to solve the misalignment problem which normally exists in generative methods. To tackle this problem, we designed a feature contrast and aggregation module and a semantic feature alignment module. The former module leverage feature aggregation and contrastive learning to align the distribution of real features and of the synthesized features. In the semantic feature alignment module, we project both real and synthesized mapped features to semantic space, which prevents the semantic information from being lost during generating and mapping stage. Extensive experiments show that our method has achieved state-of-the-art on three benchmark datasets and achieved the second-best on one benchmark dataset. Qualitative and quantitative experiments show that our method can mitigate the misalignment problem.

References

1. Akata, Z., Reed, S., Walter, D., Lee, H., Schiele, B.: Evaluation of output embeddings for fine-grained image classification. In: Proceedings of the IEEE Conference on Computer Vision and Pattern Recognition, pp. 2927–2936 (2015)
2. Chen, S., et al.: Free: feature refinement for generalized zero-shot learning. In: Proceedings of the IEEE/CVF International Conference on Computer Vision, pp. 122–131 (2021)
3. Ding, Z., Liu, H.: Marginalized latent semantic encoder for zero-shot learning. In: Proceedings of the IEEE/CVF Conference on Computer Vision and Pattern Recognition, pp. 6191–6199 (2019)
4. Dinu, G., Lazaridou, A., Baroni, M.: Improving zero-shot learning by mitigating the hubness problem. arXiv preprint arXiv:1412.6568 (2014)
5. Farhadi, A., Endres, I., Hoiem, D., Forsyth, D.: Describing objects by their attributes. In: 2009 IEEE Conference on Computer Vision and Pattern Recognition, pp. 1778–1785. IEEE (2009)
6. Felix, R., Reid, I., Carneiro, G., et al.: Multi-modal cycle-consistent generalized zero-shot learning. In: Proceedings of the European Conference on Computer Vision (ECCV), pp. 21–37 (2018)
7. Frome, A., et al.: Devise: a deep visual-semantic embedding model. In: Advances in Neural Information Processing Systems 26 (2013)
8. Goodfellow, I., et al.: Generative adversarial nets. In: Advances in Neural Information Processing Systems 27 (2014)
9. Han, Z., Fu, Z., Chen, S., Yang, J.: Contrastive embedding for generalized zero-shot learning. In: Proceedings of the IEEE/CVF Conference on Computer Vision and Pattern Recognition, pp. 2371–2381 (2021)
10. Han, Z., Fu, Z., Yang, J.: Learning the redundancy-free features for generalized zero-shot object recognition. In: Proceedings of the IEEE/CVF Conference on Computer Vision and Pattern Recognition, pp. 12865–12874 (2020)
11. He, K., Zhang, X., Ren, S., Sun, J.: Deep residual learning for image recognition. In: Proceedings of the IEEE Conference on Computer Vision and Pattern Recognition, pp. 770–778 (2016)
12. Jiang, H., Wang, R., Shan, S., Chen, X.: Transferable contrastive network for generalized zero-shot learning. In: Proceedings of the IEEE/CVF International Conference on Computer Vision, pp. 9765–9774 (2019)
13. Kodirov, E., Xiang, T., Gong, S.: Semantic autoencoder for zero-shot learning. In: Proceedings of the IEEE Conference on Computer Vision and Pattern Recognition, pp. 3174–3183 (2017)

14. Lampert, C.H., Nickisch, H., Harmeling, S.: Learning to detect unseen object classes by between-class attribute transfer. In: 2009 IEEE Conference on Computer Vision and Pattern Recognition,pp. 951–958. IEEE (2009)

15. Li, K., Min, M.R., Fu, Y.: Rethinking zero-shot learning: a conditional visual classification perspective. In: Proceedings of the IEEE/CVF International Conference on Computer Vision, pp. 3583–3592 (2019)

16. Li, Y., Liu, Z., Yao, L., Chang, X.: Attribute-modulated generative meta learning for zero-shot learning. IEEE Trans. Multimed. (2021)

17. Liu, J., Bai, H., Zhang, H., Liu, L.: Beyond normal distribution: More factual feature generation network for generalized zero-shot learning. IEEE MultiMed., 1 (2022). https://doi.org/10.1109/MMUL.2022.3155541

18. Liu, Y., Xie, D.Y., Gao, Q., Han, J., Wang, S., Gao, X.: Graph and autoencoder based feature extraction for zero-shot learning. In: IJCAI, vol. 1, p. 6 (2019)

19. Narayan, S., Gupta, A., Khan, F.S., Snoek, C.G.M., Shao, L.: Latent embedding feedback and discriminative features for zero-shot classification. In: Vedaldi, A., Bischof, H., Brox, T., Frahm, J.-M. (eds.) ECCV 2020. LNCS, vol. 12367, pp. 479–495. Springer, Cham (2020). https://doi.org/10.1007/978-3-030-58542-6_29

20. Palatucci, M., Pomerleau, D., Hinton, G.E., Mitchell, T.M.: Zero-shot learning with semantic output codes. Advances in neural information processing systems 22 (2009)

21. Patterson, G., Xu, C., Su, H., Hays, J.: The sun attribute database: Beyond categories for deeper scene understanding. Int. J. Comput. Vision 108(1), 59–81 (2014)

22. Reed, S., Akata, Z., Lee, H., Schiele, B.: Learning deep representations of fine-grained visual descriptions. In: Proceedings of the IEEE Conference on Computer Vision and Pattern Recognition, pp. 49–58 (2016)

23. Shigeto, Y., Suzuki, I., Hara, K., Shimbo, M., Matsumoto, Y.: Ridge regression, hubness, and zero-shot learning. In: Appice, A., Rodrigues, P.P., Santos Costa, V., Soares, C., Gama, J., Jorge, A. (eds.) ECML PKDD 2015. LNCS (LNAI), vol. 9284, pp. 135–151. Springer, Cham (2015). https://doi.org/10.1007/978-3-319-23528-8_9

24. Skorokhodov, I., Elhoseiny, M.: Class normalization for (continual)? generalized zero-shot learning. In: International Conference on Learning Representations (2021). https://openreview.net/forum?id=7pgFL2Dkyyy

25. Wah, C., Branson, S., Welinder, P., Perona, P., Belongie, S.: The caltech-ucsd birds-200-2011 dataset (2011)

26. Xian, Y., Lampert, C.H., Schiele, B., Akata, Z.: Zero-shot learning-a comprehensive evaluation of the good, the bad and the ugly. IEEE Trans. Pattern Anal. Mach. Intell. 41(9), 2251–2265 (2018)

27. Xie, G.S., et al.: Attentive region embedding network for zero-shot learning. In: Proceedings of the IEEE/CVF Conference on Computer Vision and Pattern Recognition, pp. 9384–9393 (2019)

28. Xie, G.S., et al.: Generalized zero-shot learning with multiple graph adaptive generative networks. IEEE Trans. Neural Networks Learning Syst. (2021)

29. Xu, B., Zeng, Z., Lian, C., Ding, Z.: Generative mixup networks for zero-shot learning. IEEE Trans. Neural Networks Learn. Syst. (2022)

30. Zhu, P., Wang, H., Saligrama, V.: Generalized zero-shot recognition based on visually semantic embedding. In: Proceedings of the IEEE/CVF Conference on Computer Vision and Pattern Recognition, pp. 2995–3003 (2019)

31. Zhu, Y., Elhoseiny, M., Liu, B., Peng, X., Elgammal, A.: A generative adversarial approach for zero-shot learning from noisy texts. In: Proceedings of the IEEE Conference on Computer Vision and Pattern Recognition, pp. 1004–1013 (2018)

DT2I: Dense Text-to-Image Generation from Region Descriptions

Stanislav Frolov[1,2(✉)], Prateek Bansal[1], Jörn Hees[2], and Andreas Dengel[1,2]

[1] Technical University of Kaiserslautern, Kaiserslautern, Germany
stanislav.frolov@dfki.de
[2] German Research Center for Artificial Intelligence, Kaiserslautern, Germany

Abstract. Despite astonishing progress, generating realistic images of complex scenes remains a challenging problem. Recently, layout-to-image synthesis approaches have attracted much interest by conditioning the generator on a list of bounding boxes and corresponding class labels. However, previous approaches are very restrictive because the set of labels is fixed a priori. Meanwhile, text-to-image synthesis methods have substantially improved and provide a flexible way for conditional image generation. In this work, we introduce dense text-to-image (DT2I) synthesis as a new task to pave the way toward more intuitive image generation. Furthermore, we propose DTC-GAN, a novel method to generate images from semantically rich region descriptions, and a multi-modal region feature matching loss to encourage semantic image-text matching. Our results demonstrate the capability of our approach to generate plausible images of complex scenes using region captions.

1 Introduction

In the last few years, deep generative image modelling has experienced remarkable progress [4,33]. Current models can produce realistic results when trained on single-domain datasets such as human faces, birds or flowers, but struggle when trained on complex datasets with multiple objects such as COCO [25] and Visual Genome [20]. While learning the natural image distribution via unconditional image synthesis is interesting, controlling the image generation process is important for many practical applications such as image editing, computer-aided design, and visual storytelling.

Strong supervision in the form of segmentation masks often leads to impressive visual results [29], but they are difficult and time-consuming to create from a user's perspective. Recently, layout-to-image methods [37,46] have attracted much interest by conditioning on a spatial layout of bounding boxes and class labels to allow the user to create a complex scene of multiple objects. To gain control over the specific appearance of objects, [6,27] further improved the methods by providing additional attributes to the corresponding objects (e.g. "red bus").

S. Frolov and P. Bansal—Equal contribution.

© The Author(s), under exclusive license to Springer Nature Switzerland AG 2022
E. Pimenidis et al. (Eds.): ICANN 2022, LNCS 13530, pp. 395–406, 2022.
https://doi.org/10.1007/978-3-031-15931-2_33

Table 1. Overview of tasks and their corresponding input. Brackets indicate optional implicit information. L2I methods use a spatial layout of bounding boxes and class labels, while T2I methods use single captions. We propose DT2I as a new task with the goal to produce realistic images from multiple localized free-form region descriptions.

Input	Layout-to-Image (L2I)	Text-to-Image (T2I)	Dense Text-to-Image (DT2I)
Spatial layout	✓	(✓)	✓
Class labels	✓	(✓)	(✓)
Free-form text	–	✓	✓
Dense captions	–	–	✓

However, the set of class labels and attributes is fixed a priori which strongly limits their expressiveness. In contrast to labels, text is much more flexible, intuitive and can carry rich semantic information about the object's appearance and relationship to other objects [5].

In this paper, we introduce dense text-to-image (DT2I) synthesis as a new task with the goal to generate realistic images using multiple region descriptions. See Table 1 for an overview of tasks and corresponding inputs. To solve this task, we propose a novel method based on a state-of-the-art adversarial layout-to-image [37] model and incorporate best practices from the text-to-image literature (e.g. triplet [33] and DAMSM [42] losses), and propose a novel multi-modal region feature matching loss between real and generated image-text pairs. We create a synthetic dataset to validate the effectiveness of our approach. Finally, we extensively evaluate our model on a challenging real-world dataset to demonstrate the capability of our method. Our model outperforms previous methods on several metrics while allowing free-form region descriptions as input.

2   Related Work

Layout-to-Image Synthesis: The layout-to-image (L2I) task was first studied in [45] using a VAE [18] by composing object representations into a scene before producing an image. It was further improved in [46] with an object-wise attention mechanism to predict a map of object details. Adversarial approaches [36,37] were able to produce higher-resolution images and provide better control of individual objects by using a reconfigurable layout with separate latent style codes. Recent developments focused on better instance representations [38], context-awareness [9], and improving the mask prediction of overlapping and nearby objects [24]. Recently, [6,27] enabled more explicit appearance control of individual objects by conditioning on attributes. However, the set of attributes is limited and lacks the ability to model complex interactions between objects. In contrast, our model generates an image from free-form region descriptions.

Text-to-Image Synthesis: Generating images from text descriptions (T2I) is a challenging but fascinating problem with remarkable progress in recent years [5]. Compared to labels, they can carry dense semantic information about the appearance of objects and scenes. Initial approaches [33] conditioned on a sentence embedding and trained the discriminator to distinguish between real, matching, and generated, non-matching image-text pairs. Stacked architectures [44] were further improved by using attention mechanisms [42], contrastive losses [43] and transformers [31]. However, all previous approaches are either applied on single-object datasets or aim to generate an image from one short text description which lacks fine-grained details.

Combinations of Location & Text: In [32], the location of one object can be specified by a bounding box or keypoints, while the appearance is described by a text description. Generating complex scenes from a single description is challenging, as it requires modelling multiple objects. To alleviate this problem, [14,23] used a text-to-layout-to-image framework to first predict a layout of bounding boxes which are subsequently refined into shapes before producing the output image. In [12,13], an object pathway is added to both generator and discriminator which uses bounding boxes and class labels to focus on the individual objects in the scene. Sparse semantic masks are used in [22,29] to define the position of objects, while an input text can be used to control the style. In [19], the Localized Narratives [30] dataset is used to generate images from mouse traces and paired descriptions. Different from all previous works, our model takes free-form captions and corresponding locations as input and hence allows rich expression of individual image regions.

3   Method

The goal of our method is to produce realistic images of complex scenes depicting multiple objects from localized region descriptions (which can be seen as the inverse of dense image captioning). To address this challenging task, we propose a novel framework consisting of the following key components: 1) Dense-Text-Conditional GAN, and 2) Regional Semantic Image-Text Matching. See Fig. 1 for an illustration of our DTC-GAN architecture.

3.1   Dense-Text-Conditional GAN

Generator: Our DTC-GAN builds upon a state-of-the-art L2I model [37]. The generator consists of a linear layer to process the global image latent code $z_{\text{img}} \sim \mathcal{N}(0,1)$ and multiple ResNet [8] based generator blocks with upsampling to produce an image. To condition our generator on a layout of region descriptions, we adapt the feature normalization technique proposed in [36]. Given a layout $L = \{(b_i, t_i)_{i=1}^m\}$ of m regions as input, where each region is described by a bounding box b_i and text description t_i, we first embed t_i using a pre-trained fixed BERT [3] model. Next, we concatenate regional latent codes $Z_{\text{r}} = \{z_i\}_{i=1}^m$ sampled from $\mathcal{N}(0,1)$, and text embeddings $E_{\text{r}} = \{e_i\}_{i=1}^m$ to produce the embedding matrix $\mathcal{S} = (Z_{\text{r}}, E_{\text{r}})$ of size $m \times (d_z + d_e)$, with the dimensions $d_z = 128$ and $d_e = 768$. As in [37], we use the embedding matrix $\mathcal{S}$ to regress masks for each region using a sub-network. Finally, we predict affine transformation parameters γ and β at each generator layer to modulate the visual feature maps

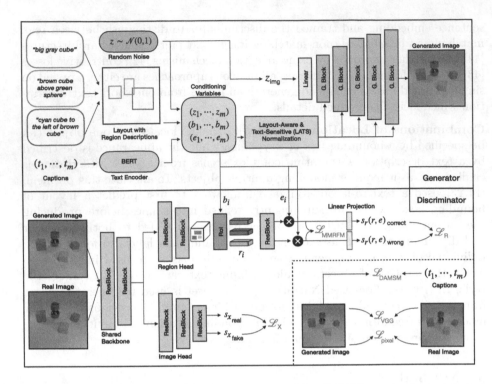

Fig. 1. Given region descriptions as input, our novel DTC-GAN is trained to minimize several losses which encourage both image quality as well as image-text alignment.

in the generator after normalizing them as in BatchNorm [15]. Using the bounding boxes b_i, we unsqueeze γ and β to their corresponding bounding boxes and weight them by the predicted region masks. Please refer to [37] for more details on this normalization technique. Given that we use text embeddings, our γ and β parameters are now *Layout-Aware & Text-Sensitive (LATS)*.

Discriminator: The architecture of the discriminator remains largely unchanged from [37] and consists of multiple ResBlocks. A shared backbone takes images as input to extract coarse features, while two classification heads are used for adversarial training to encourage realism on the image and region level. More specifically, the region head extracts region features using the bounding boxes and RoIAlign operation [7], and adopts projection-based conditioning [1,28] to compute a region-embedding score s_r. The image head continues processing the full image without any semantic knowledge to produce an image score s_x. Both image and region-embedding scores are used for adversarial training.

3.2 Regional Semantic Image-Text Matching

The goal of a good DT2I model is not only to produce realistic images but also such that correctly reflect the semantic meaning of the input captions at the corresponding locations. Inspired by the T2I literature, we adapt two main techniques to learn semantic image-text matching and apply them on the regional level. Furthermore, we propose a multi-modal region feature matching loss to guide the region classification head of our discriminator.

Regional Triplet Loss: The region-embedding classification head in the discriminator takes pairs of extracted region features and corresponding text embeddings as input and is trained to distinguish real from generated pairs. However, even if the generator produces realistic image regions, there is another kind of possible error, namely, non-matching. Similar to [33], we construct another pair of real image regions and randomly chosen captions to encourage semantic image-text matching and penalize mismatching pairs.

Regional DAMSM Loss: The Deep Attentional Multimodal Similarity Model (DAMSM) proposed in [42] computes the similarity between an image and global sentence as well as word features using an attention mechanism to improve semantic matching. We first fine-tune an Inception-v3 [39] image encoder that was pre-trained on ImageNet [2], and a pre-trained BERT text encoder to map matching image regions and text features into a common embedding space. The encoder networks can then be used to provide a fine-grained learning signal to our generator. We follow the procedure in [42], but in contrast to traditional T2I methods, our captions describe specific regions in the image which leads to better alignment between individual regions and corresponding captions.

Multi-Modal Region Feature Matching (MMRFM): The regional triplet and DAMSM losses encourage images with matching captions. However, adversarial losses can lead to adversarial examples and DAMSM lacks proper localization. Because of the complexity of natural language and diversity of real images, our task is an inherent one-to-many mapping problem between input conditions and output images which pixel-wise losses alone can not handle. Inspired by the perceptual feature loss [21], which maximizes similarity at the intermediate feature space, we propose a Multi-Modal Region Feature Matching (MMRFM) loss on the semantics-enriched region features denoted as $\mathcal{L}_{\mathrm{MMRFM}}(r_{\mathrm{real}}, r_{\mathrm{fake}}, t)$. More precisely, we use the resulting region features after projection-based conditioning and minimize the distance between corresponding real and generated image-text features at the region level, see Fig. 2.

3.3 Training Objectives and Implementation Details

We combine multiple loss functions during training of our model. Given an image x and corresponding layout L with text descriptions t_i and regions r_i, the discriminator predicts a score for the full image $s_x = D_X(x)$, and matching-aware region-embedding scores $s_r = D_R(r_i, t_i)$. We consider (r_i, t_i) to be correct if r_i is a real image region with corresponding and matching caption t_i, and wrong if a) r_i is generated, or b) (r_i, t_i) is a non-matching pair. Using an adversarial hinge loss [1,36,40], we get $\mathcal{L}_X(x)$ as our (unconditional) image loss, $\mathcal{L}_R(r, t)$ as our (conditional) regional triplet loss, and the discriminator objective as:

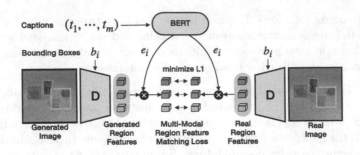

Fig. 2. Overview of our Multi-Modal Region Feature Matching loss $\mathcal{L}_{\mathrm{MMRFM}}$. We first extract region features using bounding boxes b_i. Next, we multiply individual region features with corresponding text embeddings and minimize L1 distance between real and generated multi-modal region features to improve semantic image-text matching.

$$\mathcal{L}_X = \mathbb{E}[\max(0, 1 - D_X(x_{\mathrm{real}})] + \mathbb{E}[\max(0, 1 + D_X(x_{\mathrm{fake}})] \tag{1}$$

$$\begin{aligned} \mathcal{L}_R = \ &\mathbb{E}[\max(0, 1 - D_R(r_{\mathrm{real}}, t_{\mathrm{match}})] \\ &+ \mathbb{E}[\max(0, 1 + D_R(r_{\mathrm{fake}}, t_{\mathrm{match}})] \\ &+ \mathbb{E}[\max(0, 1 + D_R(r_{\mathrm{real}}, t_{\mathrm{non\text{-}match}})] \end{aligned} \tag{2}$$

$$\mathcal{L}_D = \lambda_1 \mathcal{L}_X + \lambda_2 \mathcal{L}_R \tag{3}$$

To train the generator, we maximize fooling the discriminator. Additionally, we extract image features and corresponding text features using the pre-trained encoders and compute the DAMSM loss $\mathcal{L}_{\mathrm{DAMSM}}(x, t)$ as proposed in [42] for an additional learning signal on a per-region level of generated images. Following [37], we also employ the perceptual loss [21] using extracted VGG [35] features and pixel loss for improved image quality. With our multi-modal region feature matching loss, the generator objective becomes:

$$\begin{aligned} \mathcal{L}_G = \ &-\lambda_1 \mathbb{E}[D_X(x_{\mathrm{fake}})] - \lambda_2 \mathbb{E}[D_R(r_{\mathrm{fake}}, t_{\mathrm{match}})] \\ &+ \mathcal{L}_{\mathrm{DAMSM}}(x_{\mathrm{fake}}, t_{\mathrm{match}}) \\ &+ \mathcal{L}_{\mathrm{MMRFM}}(r_{\mathrm{real}}, r_{\mathrm{fake}}, t_{\mathrm{match}}) \\ &+ \mathcal{L}_{\mathrm{VGG}}(x_{\mathrm{real}}, x_{\mathrm{fake}}) + \mathcal{L}_{\mathrm{pixel}}(x_{\mathrm{real}} - x_{\mathrm{fake}}) \end{aligned} \tag{4}$$

Our code is based on the official repositories of [6,36,37], and we use the pre-trained BERT model from [41] as our text encoder. For training, we use the Adam [17] optimizer with $\beta_1 = 0.0$ and $\beta_2 = 0.999$. The learning rates are set to $10e^{-4}$, and weights are fixed as in [36] to $\lambda_1 = 0.1, \lambda_2 = 1.0$. We train our models using a batch size of 128 on 4 NVIDIA V100-32GB GPUs for 200 epochs which takes roughly 12 d using an image resolution of 128×128.

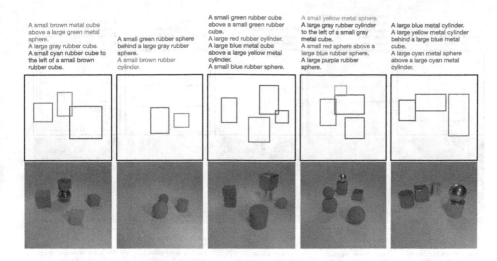

Fig. 3. Results on CLEVR. Our model can faithfully produce image regions with correct objects, attributes and relationships. (Color figure online)

4 Experiments

4.1 Synthetic Images

Dataset: We first create a synthetic dataset similar to [26] based on CLEVR [16] to qualitatively validate our approach. To that end, we render 50,000 images each depicting 3–8 objects where each object consists of four different attributes including color, shape, size, and material. Using these attributes, we can create simple text descriptions of localized objects (e.g. "a small red cube"). To simulate complex image regions with multiple objects, we randomly group nearby objects and additionally use spatial relationship annotations to describe them (e.g. "a small yellow sphere *behind* a small green cylinder").

Results: Figure 3 shows input layouts with text descriptions and the corresponding images as generated by our model. As can be seen, the image quality is high as every object is clearly visible and generated according to the input description. Our model learned to faithfully produce image regions that describe two objects in a spatial relationship. In contrast to [26], our model allows to precisely define the location of generated objects and in particular generates only what is specified as input.

4.2 Real Images

Dataset: We use the Visual Genome (VG) [20] dataset, which contains complex images with multiple, interacting objects and region descriptions that describe localized portions of the image. The region descriptions in the VG dataset are very noisy, repetitive and contain many small regions. We remove regions smaller

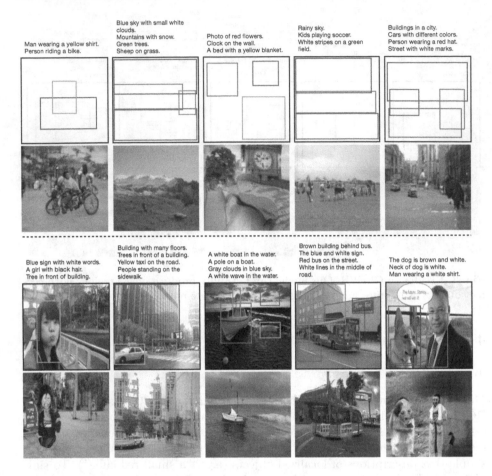

Fig. 4. Results on Visual Genome. Images generated by manual annotation (top), and from the test set with real images for comparison (bottom). Our model can often generate plausible images, correctly respecting the input descriptions.

than 32×32 pixels and only keep images that contain 3–30 region descriptions with a minimum description length of 5 words. During training, we select a maximum of 10 regions randomly. Next, we find and remove similar region descriptions if they are overlapping for more than 30% and have similar area size. In summary, we get 85,414 train, 6,206 validation, 6,173 test images, and a total of 1,117,766 region descriptions.

Evaluation Metrics: A good DT2I model should produce realistic images and image regions that reflect the semantic meaning of the input captions. Using several commonly used measures, we extensively evaluate our model in terms of image quality and image-text alignment.

Table 2. Quantitative results on Visual Genome. Our model benefits from combining all discussed losses and outperforms previous layout-to-image methods on several metrics while allowing free-form region descriptions as input. Both [24] and [9] are recent improvements which could also be applied to our backbone generator.

Method 128×128	IS ↑	SceneIS ↑	FID ↓	SceneFID ↓	R-prec. ↑	CLIP-S ↑
LostGAN [36]	11.10	–	29.65	13.17	–	–
LostGANv2 [37]	10.71	–	29.00	–	–	–
AttrLostGANv2 [6]	10.81	**9.46**	31.57	**7.78**	–	–
OC-GAN [38]	12.30	–	28.26	9.63	–	–
LAMA [24]	–	–	23.02	8.28	–	–
CAL2IM [9]	12.69	–	**21.78**	–	–	–
DTC-GAN (our base)	8.65	8.00	39.80	9.58	55.93	63.98
+ triplet	8.41	7.89	44.39	11.86	59.97	66.56
+ MMRFM	8.43	8.30	47.08	13.63	58.50	66.19
+ DAMSM (our final)	**13.80**	**9.46**	27.67	<u>7.85</u>	**89.07**	**68.20**
Method 256×256	IS ↑	SceneIS ↑	FID ↓	SceneFID ↓	R-prec. ↑	CLIP-S ↑
LostGANv2 [37]	14.10	–	47.62	–	–	–
AttrLostGANv2 [6]	14.25	11.96	35.73	14.76	–	–
OC-GAN [38]	14.70	–	40.85	–	–	–
LAMA [24]	–	–	**31.63**	13.66	–	–
DTC-GAN (our final)	**15.96**	**12.03**	<u>35.29</u>	**9.32**	**77.68**	**67.98**

Image Quality: The Inception Score (IS) [34] uses a pre-trained image classifier to measure recognizability as well as image diversity of generated images. We also compute the Fréchet Inception Distance (FID) [11] which measures the distance between feature distributions of real and generated images. Following [6,38], we evaluate the visual fidelity of individual image regions by applying the IS and FID on image crops, denoted as SceneIS [6] and SceneFID [38].

Image-Text Alignment: To evaluate the semantic matching between input captions and generated images, we adopt the R-precision [42] by concatenating all captions per image as a full-scene description. We report top-5 accuracy given that our task requires distinguishing between multiple text-described regions which is much more challenging when compared to traditional T2I methods. Furthermore, we use the recently proposed CLIP-Score [10] to assess global image-text compatibility using a general-purpose model trained on a large dataset.

Results: Figure 4 shows images generated by our model. Our method provides an unprecedented interface for the user to communicate what image should be generated. Despite the very challenging task, it is able to produce images which match the input region descriptions with objects at the correct location. Furthermore, the model respects color attributes and compositions such as "man wearing a yellow shirt" and "mountains with snow". Next, we evaluate and compare our model with several recent methods, see Table 2. A naive replacement of labels with text embeddings (our base) leads to low scores across all metrics. Although adding the MMRFM loss results in slightly lower scores, we observed faster and stable convergence during training and better performance when combining all losses. Combining two techniques from the T2I literature with our proposed MMRFM loss outperforms previous methods on several metrics while allowing free-form region descriptions as input.

Limitations: Generating images of complex scenes is a very challenging task. As all current approaches, our model still struggles to produce highly realistic images. From a training perspective, our model relies on dense captions, which are time-consuming to collect. The used dataset mostly contains rather short captions, and it would be interesting to expand towards longer descriptions with more details. During testing, we observed that details such as positional and numerical information is often ignored during image generation, which is also currently a problem in the wider T2I literature [5]. Improved mask prediction [24, 38] and context awareness [9], both of which are recent improvements of the generator, may as well improve the image quality for our application. While our method produces promising results, it is merely the first step in this direction and further research efforts are required to improve the image quality to enable practical applications.

5   Conclusion

In this paper, we introduced dense text-to-image (DT2I) synthesis as a new task and proposed DTC-GAN, a novel method that generates images from multiple free-form region descriptions. To address this challenging task, our method successfully combines recent layout-to-image and text-to-image techniques. Furthermore, we proposed a multi-modal region feature matching loss to improve semantic image-text matching between real and generated image regions and stabilize training. From a user's perspective, our model is the first of a new kind of image generation methods which are intuitive, flexible, and not restricted by a fixed set of labels. In terms of future work, enhancing the quality of generated images is required for practical applications and can for example be achieved by scaling up the networks and using contrastive losses.

Acknowledgments. This work was supported by the BMBF projects ExplAINN (Grant 01IS19074), XAINES (Grant 01IW20005), the NVIDIA AI Lab (NVAIL) and the TU Kaiserslautern PhD program.

References

1. Brock, A., Donahue, J., Simonyan, K.: Large scale gan training for high fidelity natural image synthesis. In: ICLR (2018)
2. Deng, J., Dong, W., Socher, R., Li, L.J., Li, K., Fei-Fei, L.: Imagenet: a large-scale hierarchical image database. In: CVPR, pp. 248–255 (2009)
3. Devlin, J., Chang, M.W., Lee, K., Toutanova, K.: Bert: pre-training of deep bidirectional transformers for language understanding. In: NAACL (2019)

4. Esser, P., Rombach, R., Ommer, B.: Taming transformers for high-resolution image synthesis. In: CVPR, pp. 12873–12883 (2021)
5. Frolov, S., Hinz, T., Raue, F., Hees, J., Dengel, A.: Adversarial text-to-image synthesis: a review. Neural Networks (2021)
6. Frolov, S., Sharma, A., Hees, J., Karayil, T., Raue, F., Dengel, A.: Attrlost-gan: attribute controlled image synthesis from reconfigurable layout and style. In: GCPR (2021)
7. He, K., Gkioxari, G., Dollár, P., Girshick, R.: Mask R-CNN. In: ICCV, pp. 2961–2969 (2017)
8. He, K., Zhang, X., Ren, S., Sun, J.: Deep residual learning for image recognition. In: CVPR, pp. 770–778 (2016)
9. He, S., et al.: Context-aware layout to image generation with enhanced object appearance. In: CVPR, pp. 15049–15058 (2021)
10. Hessel, J., Holtzman, A., Forbes, M., Bras, R.L., Choi, Y.: CLIPScore: a reference-free evaluation metric for image captioning. In: EMNLP (2021)
11. Heusel, M., Ramsauer, H., Unterthiner, T., Nessler, B., Hochreiter, S.: Gans trained by a two time-scale update rule converge to a local nash equilibrium. In: NeurIPS, pp. 6626–6637 (2017)
12. Hinz, T., Heinrich, S., Wermter, S.: Generating multiple objects at spatially distinct locations. In: ICLR (2019)
13. Hinz, T., Heinrich, S., Wermter, S.: Semantic object accuracy for generative text-to-image synthesis. IEEE TPAMI (2020)
14. Hong, S., Yang, D., Choi, J., Lee, H.: Inferring semantic layout for hierarchical text-to-image synthesis. In: CVPR, pp. 7986–7994 (2018)
15. Ioffe, S., Szegedy, C.: Batch normalization: accelerating deep network training by reducing internal covariate shift. In: ICML, pp. 448–456 (2015)
16. Johnson, J., Hariharan, B., Van Der Maaten, L., Fei-Fei, L., Lawrence Zitnick, C., Girshick, R.: Clevr: a diagnostic dataset for compositional language and elementary visual reasoning. In: CVPR, pp. 2901–2910 (2017)
17. Kingma, D.P., Ba, J.: Adam: a method for stochastic optimization. In: ICLR (2014)
18. Kingma, D.P., Welling, M.: Auto-encoding variational bayes. In: ICLR (2013)
19. Koh, J.Y., Baldridge, J., Lee, H., Yang, Y.: Text-to-image generation grounded by fine-grained user attention. In: WACV, pp. 237–246 (2021)
20. Krishna, R., et al.: Visual genome: connecting language and vision using crowd-sourced dense image annotations. Int. J. Comput. Vis. (2017)
21. Ledig, C., et al.: Photo-realistic single image super-resolution using a generative adversarial network. In: CVPR, pp. 4681–4690 (2017)
22. Li, B., Qi, X., Torr, P.H., Lukasiewicz, T.: Image-to-image translation with text guidance. arXiv:2002.05235 (2020)
23. Li, W., et al.: Object-driven text-to-image synthesis via adversarial training. In: CVPR, pp. 12166–12174 (2019)
24. Li, Z., Wu, J., Koh, I., Tang, Y., Sun, L.: Image synthesis from layout with locality-aware mask adaption. In: ICCV, pp. 13819–13828 (2021)
25. Lin, T.Y., et al.: Microsoft coco: common objects in context. In: ECCV, pp. 740–755 (2014)
26. Liu, N., Li, S., Du, Y., Tenenbaum, J., Torralba, A.: Learning to compose visual relations. In: NeurIPS (2021)
27. Ma, K., Zhao, B., Sigal, L.: Attribute-guided image generation from layout. In: British Machine Vision Virtual Conference (2020). arXiv:2008.11932
28. Mirza, M., Osindero, S.: Conditional generative adversarial nets. arXiv:1411.1784 (2014)

29. Pavllo, D., Lucchi, A., Hofmann, T.: Controlling style and semantics in weakly-supervised image generation. In: Vedaldi, A., Bischof, H., Brox, T., Frahm, J.-M. (eds.) ECCV 2020. LNCS, vol. 12351, pp. 482–499. Springer, Cham (2020). https://doi.org/10.1007/978-3-030-58539-6_29

30. Pont-Tuset, J., Uijlings, J., Changpinyo, S., Soricut, R., Ferrari, V.: Connecting vision and language with localized narratives. In: Vedaldi, A., Bischof, H., Brox, T., Frahm, J.-M. (eds.) ECCV 2020. LNCS, vol. 12350, pp. 647–664. Springer, Cham (2020). https://doi.org/10.1007/978-3-030-58558-7_38

31. Ramesh, A., et al.: Zero-shot text-to-image generation. In: ICML, pp. 8821–8831 (2021)

32. Reed, S.E., Akata, Z., Mohan, S., Tenka, S., Schiele, B., Lee, H.: Learning what and where to draw. In: NeurIPS, pp. 217–225 (2016)

33. Reed, S.E., Akata, Z., Yan, X., Logeswaran, L., Schiele, B., Lee, H.: Generative adversarial text to image synthesis. In: ICML, pp. 1060–1069 (2016)

34. Salimans, T., Goodfellow, I., Zaremba, W., Cheung, V., Radford, A., Chen, X.: Improved techniques for training gans. In: NeurIPS, pp. 2234–2242 (2016)

35. Simonyan, K., Zisserman, A.: Very deep convolutional networks for large-scale image recognition. In: ICLR (2014)

36. Sun, W., Wu, T.: Image synthesis from reconfigurable layout and style. In: ICCV, pp. 10531–10540 (2019)

37. Sun, W., Wu, T.: Learning layout and style reconfigurable gans for controllable image synthesis. arXiv:2003.11571 (2020)

38. Sylvain, T., Zhang, P., Bengio, Y., Hjelm, R.D., Sharma, S.: Object-centric image generation from layouts. In: AAAI (2021)

39. Szegedy, C., Vanhoucke, V., Ioffe, S., Shlens, J., Wojna, Z.: Rethinking the inception architecture for computer vision. In: CVPR, pp. 2818–2826 (2016)

40. Tran, D., Ranganath, R., Blei, D.M.: Hierarchical implicit models and likelihood-free variational inference. In: NeurIPS (2017)

41. Wolf, T., et al.: Transformers: state-of-the-art natural language processing. In: EMNLP: System Demonstrations, pp. 38–45 (2020)

42. Xu, T., et al.: Attngan: fine-grained text to image generation with attentional generative adversarial networks. In: CVPR, pp. 1316–1324 (2017)

43. Zhang, H., Koh, J.Y., Baldridge, J., Lee, H., Yang, Y.: Cross-modal contrastive learning for text-to-image generation. In: CVPR, pp. 833–842 (2021)

44. Zhang, H., et al.: Stackgan++: realistic image synthesis with stacked generative adversarial networks. IEEE TPAMI (2017)

45. Zhao, B., Meng, L., Yin, W., Sigal, L.: Image generation from layout. In: CVPR (2019)

46. Zhao, B., Yin, W., Meng, L., Sigal, L.: Layout2image: image generation from layout. IJCV (2020)

Image Inpainting Based Multi-scale Gated Convolution and Attention

Hualiang Jiang, Xiaohu Ma$^{(\boxtimes)}$, Dongdong Yang, Jiaxin Zhao, and Yao Shen

School of Machine Learning, University of Soochow, Suzhou, China
xhma@suda.edu.cn

Abstract. For image inpainting tasks, details and semantics are very important. Most methods based deep learning will make the result lack structure and texture features or even lose rationality. Additionally, many algorithms are step-by-step inpainting algorithms, which complicates the whole process. To avoid these, following the previous work, we propose an end-to-end inpainting model based on a multi-scale residual convolutional network, using MSGC to replace the conventional convolutional layer in encoder. This method combines multi-scale information and expands the receptive field, which can capture long-term information. In addition, we exploit SAB, a new scale attention block to capture important features from previous scale. At the same time, for getting richer detailed information, various loss functions are used to constrain the model during the training process. The test results of CelebA-HQ and Paris street view show that our proposed method is superior to other classic image inpainting algorithms.

Keywords: Image inpainting · Gated convolution · Multi-scale connection · Generative adversarial network

1 Introduction

Image inpainting is a technology that utilize the known area of the image to inference the unknown area [1]. In recent years, it has been widely used in image defogging, cultural relics protection, mural restoration, image denoising and other fields. Traditional algorithms mainly include partial differential equations [2] and diffusion methods [3]. These methods can inpaint relatively simple areas, such as the background. But when the scene is particularly complex, the synthetic results are often unsatisfying. In addition, most of these methods are passive, in other words, they lack of initiative. At the same time, the limitation of hardware resources brought a lot of time overhead.

In recent years, convolutional neural networks (CNNs) and generative adversarial networks(GANs) [4] have made significant progress in computer vision tasks [5–7]. CNN is characterized by active learning and strong spatial perception ability, while GAN is characterized by confrontation. Many previous methods use these two structures as inpainting models to process images of complex

© The Author(s), under exclusive license to Springer Nature Switzerland AG 2022
E. Pimenidis et al. (Eds.): ICANN 2022, LNCS 13530, pp. 407–418, 2022.
https://doi.org/10.1007/978-3-031-15931-2_34

scenes [8–10]. These methods can achieve better results than before, but most of them do not take into account the very important feature that this task requires a larger receptive field. One solution is to use dilated convolution [11]. [12] proposed a Dense Multi-scale Fusi-on Block (DMFB), which expands the receptive field by superimposing multiple DMFBs. This method is currently a better image inpainting algorithm, but the details are not well processed, and it does not make full use of the feature information of each layer of the decoder. And this convolution method will lose some more important textures. Some other methods use a large convolution kernel to form a parallel network. Yi et al. [13] proposed a multi- column convolution structure, using multiple branches to extract the features of different receptive fields, and then introduce the dilated convolution in the low-resolution layer to expand the receptive field. But this method does not consider the importance of information brought by each channel, only connects features on the channel.

The above method will also bring about the loss of detailed information. In order to solve these problems, we propose a multi-scale connection method to expand the receptive field while extracting rich details. Specifically, we use multiple branches to extract information, and each branch is composed of convolution kernels of different sizes. In addition, we use element-wise addition to fuse multi-scale information, which helps the neural network to extract fine-grained features. And we also use a scale attention block(SAB) to capture previous features.

The model we proposed has been qualitatively and quantitatively evaluated on CelebA-HQ and Paris street view). Experimental results show that the proposed algorithm outperforms other algorithms on the subjective level and objective indicators. The main contributions of this paper can be summarized as follows:

- We propose a novel multi-scale gated convolution structure(MSGC) combined with channel attention(CA) [14], which can help the model extract a larger receptive field and fuse different levels of information.
- We introduce a new scale attention block to actively emphasize or suppress the features from the previous scale.
- Our proposed method can achieve better structural and semantic results than other image inpainting models, especially in the processing of edges and details.

2   Related Work

2.1   Image Inpainting

Traditional image inpainting algorithms are mainly based on diffusion and sample block methods. [1] proposed a diffusion- based algorithm to spread the characterization information from the known area to the unknown area. [2] used a fast search algorithm to search for patches from known space and paste them into unknown space. These mathematics-based methods often only consider low-level information and are suitable for simple images. But when the features of the picture is especially complicated, such as a street scene, the final result often lacks semantic features.

Recently, inpainting algorithms using deep learning have achieved better results. Most of the current methods use U-Net and GAN as the generation skeleton. Pathak et al. [8] proposed a auto-encoder inpainting algorithm (Context Encoder, CE), which is also the basis of the current mainstream algorithm. However, this method has great limitations: the method is too simple to apply to large-area missing images. Yan et al. [9] introduced a shift connection layer in the decoder, combining the traditional patch-based method with the existing deep learning technology. [10] proposed a gated convolution structure to solve the problem of edge blur in partial convolution [15], which can automatically learn the effectiveness of pixels through parameters. This method can extract rich information, but the final results still lack details information, and there is also a problem of non-smooth edge transition. Zeng et al. [16] proposed a pyramid structure pyramid context encoder network (PENNet). PENNet uses the pyramid structure to transfer high-level semantic features to the lower layers, so that the inpainting results are visually and semantically consistent. [17] proposes an edge-guided learnable two-way attention map to further improve the method of updating mask in [15]. [18] proposed a two-stage progressive network, which is suitable for high-resolution images. Zhu et al. [19] proposed a dynamic filtering module to extract multiple Scale characteristics, because the missing area is random in practice.

2.2 Gated Convolution

For an image with mask, it is inaccurate to extract features by methods of sliding windows. Li et al. [15] believes that each pixel of the window is not all valid. When the window contains the known area filled with 1 and the area filled with 0, the pixels in the occluded area are not valid pixels. Based on this phenomenon, a partial convolution (PConv) method is proposed to replace ordinary convolution. PConv can occlude invalid areas, which will make the model pay more attention to valid information. Then the mask will be dynamically updated according to the mask value. This method can make up for the shortcomings of ordinary convolution, but its effect on edge area is not satisfying, because partial convolution uses a hard occlusion method, which directly shields the invalid pixel space, which is not flexible.

Yu et al. [10] proposed a gated convolution (GC) module to solve the problem brought by partial convolution. Unlike PConv, GC is a soft occlusion, which can automatically learn parameters in the network and has greater flexibility.

3   Method

3.1   Inpainting Network

Our overall network (see Fig. 1) includes a generator to inpainting broken image and a discriminator for adversarial training. In the training phase, a variety of loss functions are used to train the model. In the testing phase, only the generator is used. In addition, a pre-trained VGG-19 [20] network is use to achieve better results.

Our network consists of multiple up-sampling and down-sampling blocks. First, an image with a regular mask is input into the network together with the mask. Before the MSGC module extract the features, the features are passed through a convolution of size 3. Then, when features are extracted by multiple down sampling modules, the features will be compressed into a small laten space, and finally enter the decoder. The decoder consists of multiple transposed convolutions, each of which is followed by a residual group convolution (RGC). RGC is a common residual block, but it is a important part of our model. In order to solve the problem of information loss, we directly connect the middle layer of the decoder and the corresponding layer of the encoder.

For fine-grained inpainting tasks, the network needs to pay close attention to the instance itself and cannot be affected by other distributions in one batch. Based this, after each convolutional layer, we use instance normalization instead of batch normalization. To avoid the over-fitting problem, we use convolution with a group number of 2 in RGC to reduce the parameters. This trick is very effective for deep residual networks and can be strongly proven by our experiments. We use ELU activation instead of ReLU because the former has negative values, which make the mean of output close to 0.

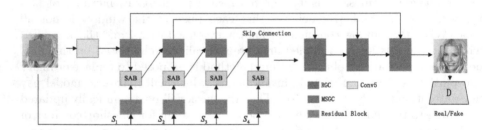

Fig. 1. The overall network of our inpainting network. We exploit skip connection to concat the encoder and decoder. $S_k(k = 1, 2, 3, 4)$ is the scaled features of original scale.

3.2   Multi-scale Gated Convolution

We now give the details of MSGC (see Fig. 2). This network consists of three parts: gated convolution, residual layer and attention module. This multi-scale feature extraction method can make the inpainting result has more details.

Image inpainting tasks require a larger receptive field to capture long-term information. Simply increasing the size of the convolution kernel may increase network performance, but there will be greater parameter overhead. To alleviate this problem, we first divide the input feature into two groups in the channel direction. One of the branches is superimposed by multiple 3×3 convolutions, and the other branch uses a larger convolution kernel to increase the field of view of the network. This method is different to the traditional way of directly using larger kernel size .

The above-mentioned fusion features include multiple feature maps. Simply connecting cannot make good use of these information, so we use CA mechanism to weight these information. Finally, we can obtain the output

$$Y' = Y \odot \sigma(W_{M2}\varphi W_{M1}H_{GP}(Y)) \tag{1}$$

where H_{GP} is the global pooling operation, W_{M1} and W_{M2} are the different parameters of fully connected layers, φ is the activation function, and Y is the result of multi branches. $\odot$ means the element-wise multiply. σ is the sigmoid function.

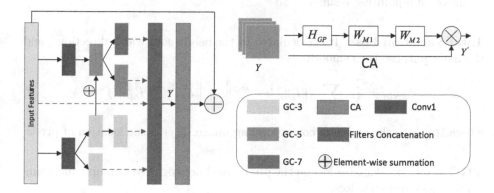

Fig. 2. The multi-scale gated convolution of ours. GC-K (K=3,5,7) is K $\times$ K gated convolution.

3.3   Scale Attention Block

We make multi-scale features and output of MSGC as the input of next layer by SAB. First, scaled features are extracted by a residual block, here we use GC as convolution layer. The output of the MSGC at the kth layer is denoted as $MSGC_k^{out}$. Then we adopt attention method to fuse features (see Fig. 3).

3.4   Loss Functions

Reconstruction Loss. It is calculated between the target image I_{gt} and the inpainting result I_{out}.

$$\zeta_{rec} = \|I_{gt} - I_{out}\|_1 \tag{2}$$

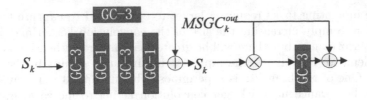

Fig. 3. The scale attention block

Adversarial Loss. In order to improve the authenticity and sensory effect of the inpainting image, we introduce the adversarial loss. We use SN-PatchGAN [10] for adversarial training. It is defined as:

$$\zeta_{adv} = \min_G \max_D E_{I_{gt} \sim P_{data}} \log[D(I_{gt})] + E_{I_{out} \sim P_z} \log[1 - D(G(I_{out} \odot M))] \quad (3)$$

where $G(\cdot)$ and $D(\cdot)$ means the generator and discriminator. M is the mask designed by us. P_{data} is the distribution of training dataset, and P_z is the distribution of inpainting results.

Total Variation Loss. It is calculated in the height and width directions, and the main purpose is to smooth.

$$\zeta_{tv} = \frac{1}{N} \sum_{(i,j) \in \Omega} (\left\| I_{out}^{i,j+1} - I_{gt}^{i,j} \right\|_1 + \left\| I_{out}^{i+1,j} - I_{gt}^{i,j} \right\|_1) \quad (4)$$

where Ω means the region of corresponding image. (i, j) is the location of pixels.

VGG Loss. It calculates loss on the pre-trained network layer, mainly including content loss and style loss.

We select specific feature maps produced by the pre-trained VGG-19. We select relu4_2, relu3_2 and relu2_2 layers to calculate the style loss.

$$\zeta_{sty} = \frac{1}{N} \sum_{l=1}^{N} \frac{1}{C_l \cdot C_l} \left\| \Psi^l(I_{out})(\Psi^l(I_{out}))^T - \Psi^l(I_{gt})(\Psi^l(I_{gt}))^T \right\|_2 \quad (5)$$

where C_l denotes the channel numbers at the lth layer of selected three layers in the VGG-19. $\Psi(\cdot)$ is the output of selected layers .

To obtain more advanced semantic features, we introduce content loss, we use the output of relu4_2 layer to calculate.

$$\zeta_{con} = \frac{1}{N} \sum_{l=1}^{N} \left\| \Psi^l(I_{out}) - \Psi^l(I_{gt}) \right\|_1 \quad (6)$$

Final Objective. We use multiple loss functions to constrain the model. During the training process, we set a weight for each loss function. The overall loss is given by:

$$\zeta_{total} = \lambda_{rec}\zeta_{rec} + \lambda_{adv}\zeta_{adv} + \lambda_{tv}\zeta_{tv} + \lambda_{sty}\zeta_{sty} + \lambda_{con}\zeta_{con} \qquad (7)$$

where λ_{rec}, , λ_{tv}, λ_{adv} , λ_{sty} and λ_{con} are the trade-off factors to balance the effects and set as 1.0, 0.01, 0.0002, 10.0 and 1.0 respectively.

4   Experiments

4.1   Experiments Settings

The training procedure is optimized by Adam optimizer [22] with β_1 =0.5 and β_2=0.9. We set learning rate to 0.0002 and in the last 10 epochs it is set to 0.0001. The batchsize is 12. We apply TensorFlow framework to implement our model and train them using TITAN Xp GPU. For training, the input image I_{in} is obtained by the real image I_{gt} and set as $I_{in} = I_{gt} \odot (1-M)$. We use the center mask(0 for known pixels) M , and the size is 128×128. We take $[I_{in}, M]$ as input. All input and output are scaled to [-1, 1]. We use images of resolution 256×256 to start our training. For CelebA-HQ, images are directly scaled to 256×256. For Paris street view, we first randomly crop patches with size 537×537 and then we scale down them to 256×256. All the results produced by our model are not post-processed.

4.2   Qualitative Comparisons

We compare our method with other classic methods in structure and texture coherence. As shown in Fig. 4, based on the fusion of multi-scale information, our method can generate pictures with better visibility and authenticity. It can be seen that Shift-Net [9], GMCNN [13], PENNEet [16], DMFN [12] tend to generate blurred or unsmooth results. On the whole, these methods are difficult to ensure that the structure and semantics are consistent at the same time. In contrast, our method pays more attention to details, so the subjective effect of the generated image is better. For the face dataset, our method can ensure that the main features are not deformed or distorted, such as glasses, nose, etc.; for the street view dataset, our algorithm can make the overall structure more consistent, such as doors, windows, and tree.

4.3   Quantitative Comparisons

To objectively verify the superiority of our proposed method, we introduce a number of objective indicators to conduct experiments on the datasets. The peak signal-to-noise ratio (PSNR), structural similarity (SSIM), Fr-échet Inception Distance (FID) and Learned perceptual image patch similarity (LPIPS) [23] are used.

PSNR compares the difference in pixels, while SSIM compares the overall structural consistency. FID compares the distance between two distributions, the smaller the distance, the better the inpainting result. LPIPS is a new metric that can better evaluate the perceptual similarity between two images.

For CelebA-HQ, we chose 2000 images for the evaluation. For Paris street view, we use the standard validation set. Table 1 shows the performance of our method against other methods. It is clear that our method is superior to others in four metrics.

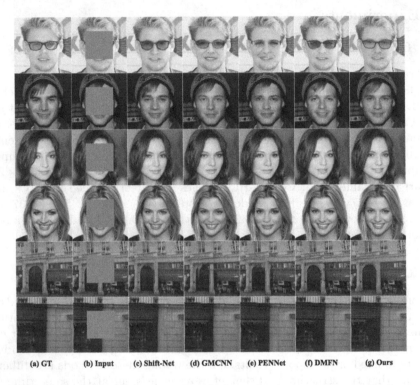

(a) GT   (b) Input   (c) Shift-Net   (d) GMCNN   (e) PENNet   (f) DMFN   (g) Ours

Fig. 4. Qualitative results compared with four classic inpainting methods on two datasets. k. (c), (d), (e), (f) and (g) are the results generated by shift-net [9], GMCNN [13], PENNet [16], DMFN [12] and our method respectively from left to right. (a) is the ground truth.

4.4   Ablation Stud

We conducted experiments on CelebA-HQ to analyze the effectiveness of each component of our method: MSGC, SAB, RGC. We tested our model without MSGC, RGC, and SAB. For comparison, a baseline model was trained without using any of the three components. As shown in Table 2, each of the three parts can improve the PSNR.

Table 1. Quantitative results (center regular mask) on two datasets.

Method	CelebA-HQ (2000)				Paris street view			
	PSNR	SSIM	LPIPS	FID	PSNR	SSIM	LPIPS	FID
Shift-Net [9]	24.13	0.8661	0.0724	6.99	24.97	0.8425	0.1056	46.22
GMCNN [13]	25.72	0.8804	0.0535	9.48	24.65	0.8483	0.1202	48.11
PENNet [16]	25.50	0.8810	0.0676	10.72	23.59	0.8204	0.1404	63.82
DMFN [12]	26.43	0.8952	0.0465	6.20	24.98	0.8526	0.1141	47.18
Ours	**26.85**	**0.8973**	**0.0425**	**6.06**	**25.39**	**0.8563**	**0.1078**	**45.63**

Table 2. Ablation studies on CelebA-HQ.

MSGC	RGC	SAB	PSNR
			25.84
✓			26.21
	✓		25.99
		✓	26.13
✓	✓		26.74
✓		✓	26.52
	✓	✓	26.36
✓	✓	✓	**26.85**

4.5 Additional Results

For image inpainting, the inpainting of irregular mask is also worthy of attention. Therefore, we used random and irregular mask for additional evaluation of the model. The inpainting results can be seen in Fig. 5. Obviously, when the missing region is more complicated, our model still generate high quality results.

We also investigate the effectiveness of different loss functions of our method, because each loss has a different degree of contribution to the model. We select five models to conduct experiments on the CelebA-HQ dataset. Four of them remove one loss respectively, and the last model uses all the loss functions for training. The final objective results can be seen in Table 3. It clearly demonstrates that each loss function is critical.

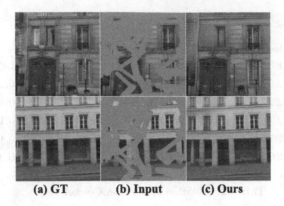

(a) GT   (b) Input   (c) Ours

Fig. 5. Inpainting results with irregular masks

Table 3. Investigation on different loss functions On CelebA-HQ .

ζ_{rec}	ζ_{adv}	ζ_{tv}	$\zeta_{sty} + \zeta_{con}$	PSNR	SSIM	LPIPS	FID
%				25.37	0.8674	0.0505	23.15
	%			25.25	0.8721	0.0491	21.28
		%		26.39	0.8818	0.0460	6.96
			%	26.68	0.8954	0.0745	15.76
				26.85	**0.8973**	**0.0425**	**6.06**

5   Conclusion

In this paper, we propose a novel end-to-end network which uses multi-scale gated convolution a to replace normal convolution layer. Further we introduce scale attention block to obtain more information from previous scale. With the assistance of our approach, our model generate smoother results with obvious structure features and rich textures than other methods. Additionally, we apply attention mechanism and some tricks to improve the ability of our network . Experiments on CelebA-HQ and Paris street view certify the superiority of our method in generating richer, more fine-detailed results. Subsequentially, our work will focus on diverse image restoration.

References

1. Bertalmio, M., Sapiro, G., Caselles, V., Ballester, C.: Image inpainting. In: Proceedings of the 27th Annual Conference on Computer Graphics and Interactive Techniques, pp. 417–424 (2000)
2. Barnes, C., Shechtman, E., Finkelstein, A., et al.: PatchMatch: a randomized correspondence algorithm for structural image editing. ACM Trans. Graph. **28**(3, article 24) (2009)

3. Bertalmio, M., Sapiro, G., Caselles, V., et al.: Image inpainting. In: Proceedings of the 27th Annual Conference on Computer Graphics and Interactive Techniques, pp. 417–424. ACM Press, New York (2000)
4. Goodfellow, I.J., et al.: Generative adversarial nets. In: Advances in NeuralInformation Processing Systems (NeurIPS), pp. 2672–2680 (2014)
5. Finn, C., Abbeel, P., Levine, S.: Model-agnostic meta-learning for fast adaptation of deep networks. arXiv preprint arXiv:1703.03400 (2017)
6. Cao, J., Hu, Y., Zhang, H., He, R., Sun, Z.: Learning a high fidelity pose invariant model for high-resolution face frontalization. In: Advances in Neural Information Processing Systems, pp. 2867–2877 (2018)
7. Huang, H., He, R., Sun, Z., Tan, T.: Wavelet domain generative adversarial network for multi-scale face hallucination. Int. J. Comput. Vision **127**(6–7), 763–784 (2019)
8. Pathak, D., Krahenbuhl, P., Donahue, J., et al.: Context encoders : feature learning by inpainting. In: Proceedings of the 2016 IEEE Conference on Computer Vision and Pattern Recognition, Piscataway, pp. 2536–2544. IEEE (2016)
9. Yan, Z., Li, X., Li, M., Zuo, W., Shan, S.: Shift-Net: image inpainting via deep feature rearrangement. In: Ferrari, V., Hebert, M., Sminchisescu, C., Weiss, Y. (eds.) Computer Vision – ECCV 2018. LNCS, vol. 11218, pp. 3–19. Springer, Cham (2018). https://doi.org/10.1007/978-3-030-01264-9_1
10. Yu, J., Lin, Z., Yang, J., et al.: Free- form image Inpainting with gated convolution. arXiv:1806.03589 (2018)
11. Yu, F., Koltun, V.: Multi-scale context aggregation by dilated convolutions. In: ICLR (2016)
12. Hui, Z., Li, J., Wang, X., et al.: Image fine-grained inpainting. arXiv:2002.02609v2 (2020)
13. Wang, Y., Tao, X., Qi, X.J., et al.: Image inpainting via generative multi-column convolutional neural networks. In: Proceedings of the Advances in Neural Information Processing Systems, pp. 329–338. MIT Press, Cambridge (2018)
14. Hu, J., Shen, L., Sun, G.: Squeeze-and-excitation networks. In: Proceedings of the IEEE Conference on Computer Vision and Pattern Recognition, pp. 7132–7141. IEEE Computer Society Press, Los Alamitos (2018)
15. Liu, G., Reda, F.A., Shih, K.J., Wang, T.-C., Tao, A., Catanzaro, B.: Image inpainting for irregular holes using partial convolutions. In: European Conference on Computer Vision (ECCV), pp. 85–100 (2018)
16. Zeng, Y.H., Fu, J.L., Chao, H.Y., et al.: Learning pyramid-context encoder network for high-quality image inpainting. In: Proceedings of the IEEE Conference on Computer Vision and Pattern Recognition, pp. 1486–1494. IEEE Computer Society Press, Los Alamitos (2019)
17. Wang, D., Xie, C., Liu, S., et al.: Image inpainting with edge-guided learnable bidirectional attention maps. arXiv:2104.12087v1 (2021)
18. Moskalenko, A., Erofeev, M., Vatolin, D.: Deep two-stage high-resolution image inpainting. arXiv: 2104.13464v1 (2021)
19. Zhu, M., et al.: Image inpainting by end-to-end cascaded refinement with mask awareness. IEEE Trans. Image Process. **30**, 4855–4866 (2021). https://doi.org/10.1109/TIP.2021.3076310
20. Simonyan, K., Zisserman, A.: Very deep convolutional networks for large-scale image recognition. In: International Conference for Learning Representations (ICLR) (2015)
21. Karras, T., Aila, T., Laine, S., Lehtinen, J.: Progressive growing of GANs for improved quality, stability, and variation. In: International Conference for Learning Representations (ICLR) (2018)

22. Kingma, D.P., Ba, J.: Adam: a method for stochastic optimization. In: International Conference for Learning Representations (ICLR) (2015)
23. Zhang, R., Isola, P., Efros, A.A., Shechtman, E., Wang, O.: The unreasonable effectiveness of deep features as a perceptual metric. In: IEEE Conference on Computer Vision and Pattern Recognition (CVPR), pp. 586–595 (2018)

Pancreatic Image Augmentation Based on Local Region Texture Synthesis for Tumor Segmentation

Zihan Wei[1], Yizhou Chen[1], Qiu Guan[1(✉)] ⓘ, Haigen Hu[1], Qianwei Zhou[1], Zhicheng Li[2], Xinli Xu[1], Alejandro Frangi[3], and Feng Chen[4(✉)]

[1] College of Computer Science and Technology,
Zhejiang University of Technology, Hangzhou, China
gq@zjut.edu.cn
[2] Shenzhen Institutes of Advanced Technology,
Chinese Academy of Sciences, Shenzhen, China
[3] School of Computing, University of Leeds, Leeds, UK
[4] The First Affiliated Hospital,
Zhejiang University School of Medicine, Hangzhou, China
chenfenghz@zju.edu.cn

Abstract. High-accuracy segmentation of lesions in pancreatic images is essential for computer-aided precision diagnosis and treatment. The segmentation accuracy of deep learning-based segmentation models depends on the number of annotated pancreatic tumor images. Due to the high cost of labeling, the size of the training set for segmentation models is usually small. This paper proposes an image augmentation model based on local region texture generation. For pancreas images (background) and tumor images (foreground) with ablated regions, the model can generate image textures for the remaining blank areas after combining the two images to obtain new samples. To improve the texture continuity between the tumor region and surrounding tissues in the generated image, this paper constructs a three-level loss function to constrain the training of the augmented model. Simulation experiments on the pancreatic tumor image set provided by the partner hospital show that the Dice coefficient of the segmentation model trained on the dataset augmented by the proposed model improves by 2.4% compared with the current optimal method when the number of real images is sparse, which proves its effectiveness and feasibility.

Keywords: Pancreatic tumor · Image segmentation · Image texture generation · Data augmentation · Adversarial learning

This work is supported in part by the National Natural Science Foundation of China (U20A20171, 61802347, 61972347, 62106225), and the Natural Science Foundation of Zhejiang Province (LY21F020027, LGF20H180002, LGG20F020017, LY20H18006, LSD19H180003).

1   Introduction

Pancreatic cancer is the fourth leading cause of cancer death worldwide, and the one-year survival rate for patients is less than 20%, and the five-year survival rate is only 9% [1]. Therefore, the segmentation of pancreatic tumor images has essential clinical value and practical significance in disease research and imaging diagnosis and treatment. The medical image segmentation model can automatically or semi-automatically outline the target region in medical images, vital for the subsequent computer-aided diagnosis and physician treatment [2]. The segmentation accuracy of the medical image segmentation model based on deep learning has been dramatically improved in recent years. With sufficient training samples, the performance of such segmentation models is significantly better than that of traditional segmentation models. However, for pancreatic tumor images, where the shape of the lesion is irregular, and edge information is challenging to confirm, producing a divided training set with expert knowledge is costly. Therefore, it is imperative to develop augmentation models for pancreatic tumor images to provide sufficient training samples for segmentation models.

Affine transformations such as flip and rotate are the most classical image augmentation methods, which can significantly increase the number of training samples. However, due to the high similarity between the new samples obtained by this method and the original samples in the data set, the diversity of the data set after augmented has not been substantially improved. Therefore, researchers would prefer to obtain new samples with significant content differences from the original illustrations. Generative adversarial networks (GANs) [3] are networks that can generate new images that are "Mix the spurious with the genuine" realistic and have received widespread attention and application since their introduction, becoming one of the most critical research hotspots in artificial intelligence. Many medical image augmentation methods based on GAN have been proposed [4–6].

Lin et al. [7] incorporated the actual image of the area where the lesion was located into the specified location of the background area without the lesion to obtain the composite image. In this case, the lesion representation in the composite image is usually accurate. However, when the performance of the augmentation model is poor, the texture continuity between the lesion and the surrounding area may be shown as the small amount of unreasonable texture. In contrast, Wu et al. [8] selected a target region on an accurate image of the healthy organ and generated it as the image with the lesion. The textural continuity between the generate area and the surrounding region is enhanced. However, the images generated by this method are difficult to determine whether the synthesized area has the characteristics of the lesion.

Guan et al. [9] combined the above two methods, and the augmentation dataset allows for the more extraordinary performance of the downstream model when the training samples are relatively abundant. However, when the number of training samples is reasonably limited, the performance of this method does not outperform the above two methods. Therefore, when the number of pancreatic tumor images with annotations is too small, the method is challenging to achieve the desired results.

Xing et al. [10] constructed the method to generate background images based on foreground lesion images to address the challenge of too few training samples. The method can only generate background images with relatively simple textures and a relatively small percentage of the global vision to ensure. However, the anatomical structures in the abdominal images are complex, especially in the pancreatic area, where the imaging texture is refined. Therefore, generating the realistic global image of the abdomen with a few training samples is difficult to achieve.

We build on existing work to construct a Two-Channel Supervision of Texture Generation GAN (TSTG-GAN) for pancreatic image augmentation based on local region texture generation. The model begins by ablating selected areas and transposing a tumor image from another patient into the blank area. This step ensures that the composite image will be differentiated from the original sample and have accurately characterized tumor regions. The model in this paper performs texture generation on the remaining blank area to make it texturally contiguous with the adjacent tumor region and the background region, thus enhancing the realism of the synthesized site. The contributions of this paper are summarized as follows:

(1) This paper constructs the pancreatic image augmentation model based on local region texture generation, which can augment abdominal images where the number of samples is scarce. The pancreatic tumor region is a small proportion of the global image. The resulting images can be used for the training of downstream segmentation models.
(2) To improve the texture continuity of the synthetic image, this paper designs image reconstruction loss (pixel level) and local image texture confrontation loss (texture level) to provide supervised and unsupervised learning-based training constraints for the generator.
(3) To improve the labeling accuracy of the synthesized image, this paper constructs the gradient map-based adversarial loss (label level) in the training phase of the model to ensure that the image texture of the synthesized region does not have the lesion characterization.

2 Proposed Method

2.1 The Overall Framework of TSTG-GAN

The overall framework of TSTG-GAN is shown in Fig. 1. Where the framework diagram shows the two-channel supervised generative adversarial network and its training loss term based on rational generation of local area textures, divided into two channels, supervised and unsupervised learning.

After the sample data set pre-processing session, the original lesion x_n is weighted with the ablated image y_n to form a blank area. The resulting image $x_n \oplus y_n$ is fed into the multi-channel edge information constraint local generator

(LG) to generate the reconstructed image z_n of the ablated blank area of the original lesion as the supervised training channel. The randomly sampled lesion to be fused X_n is filled into the border area X_n' and fused with y_n to produce the weighted image $X_n \oplus X_n' \oplus y_n$ input to LG to generate composite image Z_n as the unsupervised training channel (the process of fusing the new lesion is detailed in Sect. 2.2).

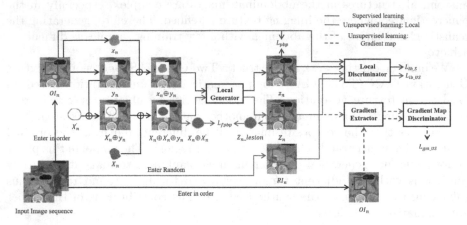

Fig. 1. The overall framework of TSTG-GAN.

2.2   The Process of Fusing the New Lesion

As shown in Fig. 2, fusing the new lesion consists of a simple operation that follows two steps, while referring to Yao et al. [11] for the process of synthesizing the new lesion.

a) **Generating lesion border shapes:** There may be lesions with different shapes and textures of varying sizes in CT scans. To form multiple similar

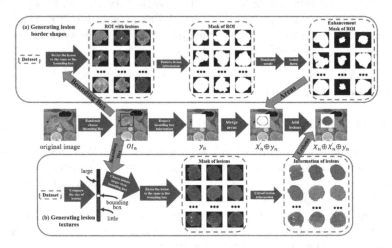

Fig. 2. Schematic representation of the process of fusing new lesions.

lesions, we obtained the outline of the existing lesion based on its label. They were deformed by random flip and zoom operations, and a lesion contour was randomly selected to be added to the y_n.

b) Generating lesion textures: Generating lesion textures can be challenging due to the diversity of lesion texture patterns. We use the original lesion texture for the generation operation, which significantly avoids this challenge and satisfies the diversity condition. We sort the lesion size and select the image larger than the original lesion resizes into y_n blank area size. Then, one kind of lesion information is extracted and randomly chosen to fill into the lesion contour of a).

It is worth noting that there is still room for optimization of our method, but it is operationally effective for generating new lesions.

2.3 Optimization Objectives of TSTG-GAN

2.3.1 Optimisation Objectives for Supervised Learning Channels

In the supervised training channel, the reconstruction image z_n are generated. The pixel-by-pixel reconstruction loss $\mathcal{L}_{pbp}$ generated between z_n and the original image OI_n provides pixel-level supervision for network training:

$$\mathcal{L}_{pbp} = ||z_{n\_L} - OI_{n\_L}||_1 \tag{1}$$

where $_L$ represents the blank area. By minimizing $\mathcal{L}_{pbp}$, LG is optimized.

To make the texture representation of the region around the z_n lesion realistic, we designed to reconstruct the local image texture against the loss term $\mathcal{L}_{lb\_S}$. The region trained in LD is the generated background region, and the loss in the iterative training phase is shown below:

$$\mathcal{L}_{lb\_S} = \left| \frac{1}{m} \sum_{n=1}^{m} [\log(LD(OI_{n\_L})) + \log(1 - LD(LG(x_n \oplus y_n)_{\_L}))] \right| \tag{2}$$

By minimizing $\mathcal{L}_{lb\_S}$, LD is optimized. By maximizing $\mathcal{L}_{lb\_S}$, LG is optimized.

2.3.2 Optimization Objectives for Unsupervised Learning Channels

Similarly, the synthetic image Z_n was generated in the unsupervised training channel. To further constrain the lesion profile of the new lesion $X_n \oplus X_n'$, the pixel-by-pixel fusion loss $\mathcal{L}_{fpbp}$ developed between extracting the lesion Z_n_lesion in the Z_n and $X_n \oplus X_n'$ provides pixel-level differences for network training.

$$\mathcal{L}_{fpbp} = ||Z_n\_lesion - X_n \oplus X_n'||_1 \tag{3}$$

By minimizing $\mathcal{L}_{fpbp}$, LG is optimized.

In the next step, to enhance the texture continuity between the lesion and the surrounding region, input Z_n and Randomly enter image RI_n into LD for adversarial training to obtain the blend of surrounding textures against loss $\mathcal{L}_{lb\_US}$. The loss in the iterative training phase is shown below:

$$\mathcal{L}_{lb\_US} = \left| \frac{1}{m} \sum_{n=1}^{m} [\log(LD(RI_{n\_L})) + \log(1 - LD(LG((X_n \oplus X_n' \oplus y_n)\_L)))] \right| \tag{4}$$

Similarly, LD is optimized by minimizing $\mathcal{L}_{lb\_US}$, and LG is optimized by maximizing $\mathcal{L}_{lb\_US}$.

Also, in the unsupervised learning channel, to improve the labeling accuracy of the synthesized image, we designed to introduce the gradient map-based adversarial loss term $\mathcal{L}_{gm\_US}$ (shown in Fig. 3) to ensure that the image texture of the synthesized region does not have the lesion characterization.

The Gradient Extractor (GE) performs gradient processing for Z_{n_L} and OI_{n_L}:

$$Ge\_Z_{n\_L} = GE(Z_{n\_L}), Ge\_OI_{n\_L} = GE(OI_{n\_L}) \tag{5}$$

where $GE()$ represents the Extract Gradient Map operation.

The operation obtains $Mask\_X_n'$ and $Mask\_OI_{n\_L}$ in Fig. 2a. During the GmD training phase, the LG parameters are fixed. To make GmD accurately identify the imaging features of the lesion, it is expected that GmD is optimized so that it can treat $Ge\_OI_{n\_L}$ and $Mask\_OI_{n\_L}$ as positive, $Ge\_Z_{n\_L}$ and $Mask\_X_n'$ as negative samples. During the LG training phase, the GmD parameters are fixed. It is expected that LG will be optimized to generate Z_n that is more realistic and consistent with the imaging representation of the lesion. Therefore, $Ge\_Z_{n\_L}$ can be considered the positive sample by GmD. The loss in the iterative training phase are shown below:

$$\mathcal{L}_{gm\_US} = | \log(GmD(Ge\_OI_{n\_L})) + \log(GmD(Mask\_OI_{n\_L}))$$
$$+ \log(1 - GmD(Ge\_Z_{n\_L})) + \log(1 - GmD(Mask\_X_n'))| \tag{6}$$

By minimizing $\mathcal{L}_{gm\_US}$, GmD is optimized. By maximizing $\mathcal{L}_{gm\_US}$, LG is optimized.

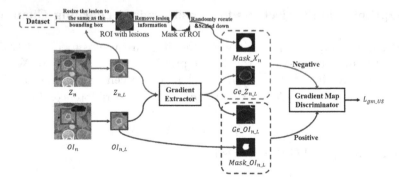

Fig. 3. Schematic diagram of the calculation process of the gradient map-based loss function $\mathcal{L}_{gm\_US}$.

2.3.3 Overall Optimisation Objectives

Since the pixel-by-pixel reconstruction loss and the pixel-by-pixel fusion loss have better optimization performance for the TSTG-GAN network, LG was first optimized according to $\mathcal{L}_{pbp}$ and $\mathcal{L}_{fpbp}$. Referring to the network training model of Ambita et al. [12], the discriminator was optimized first and the generator second. The LG parameters were fixed first, and $\mathcal{L}_{lb\_S}$, $\mathcal{L}_{lb\_US}$ and $\mathcal{L}_{gm\_US}$ were optimized for LD and GmD, respectively. Conversely, the parameters of LD and GmD are fixed, and the loss terms are again computed. Thus, our complete training objective consists of:

$$\mathcal{L}_{all} = \lambda_1 * \mathcal{L}_{pbp} + \lambda_2 * \mathcal{L}_{fpbp} + \lambda_3 * \mathcal{L}_{lb\_S} + \lambda_4 * \mathcal{L}_{lb\_US} + \lambda_5 * \mathcal{L}_{gm\_US} \qquad (7)$$

where λ_1, λ_2, ..., λ_5 are the weight parameters. Optimize the TSTG-GAN network by minimizing $\mathcal{L}_{all}$.

2.4   TSTG-GAN Network and Application of Synthetic Samples

After the TSTG-GAN network has been trained and optimized, LG is fixed while inputting X_n, X_n', and y_n to generate an augmented pancreatic tumor dataset that meets expectations. The generated dataset was then used in the classical segmentation network U-net [13] to train its segmentation performance. To improve its segmentation performance, we also introduce a migration learning mechanism, i.e., after the U-net is trained on the augmented sample set, the U-net is then fine-tuned with the actual sample image set.

The U-net is trained to optimize its segmentation performance through the above steps.

3   Experiments and Results

3.1   Datasets and Pre-processing

Our proposed method was experimented with and evaluated on the partner hospital's CT dataset of pancreatic tumors. The clinical pancreatic tumor CT dataset from the partner hospital consists of 1066 2D CTs of pancreatic tumors. Pancreatic tumors on each CT are contour-labeled by a medical professional. We created a bounding box of pancreatic tumors based on the pathological contour annotation of the tumors, with the largest bounding box being approximately 150 * 150 pixels and the smallest bounding box being approximately 20 * 20 pixels. By downsampling operation, we obtained 1066 images of pancreatic tumors of size 30 * 30 pixels X_n $(n = 1, 2, ..., 1066)$.

In the training process of TSTG-GAN, we set different sample sizes for the training set of the augmentation model, i.e., 50, 200, and 1000 samples for the training set, respectively, and the remaining samples were used for testing. The above operation demonstrates that this method can achieve effective and reliable augmentation on minimal data.

The image pixel intensity values were normalized during the execution of each network module [14]. This experiment used the bilinear interpolation algorithm for the image resize operation, using a conv downsampling operation with stride=2. This method experiment's training and testing processes were executed on NVIDIA GeForce GTX 2080Ti 11G GPU.

3.2 Comparison Methods and Evaluation Indicators

To evaluate the effectiveness of this paper's method, we applied it to the pancreatic tumor image segmentation task (U-Net) to segment pancreatic tumors from CT images. To test the data augmentation effect of the method in this paper, the proposed method was compared with the benchmark without any changes, the affine transform based on operations such as flip and rotation, and five typical and novel deep learning augmentation methods. Among them, Lin et al. [7] is the fusion generation method, Wu et al. [8] is the foreground generation method, Xing et al. [10] is the background generation method, Chen et al. [15] is the FTN reconstruction generation method (Fast Thinking Network (FTN) learns decoupled image features and shape features to generate images with lesions). Gilbert et al. [16] is the annotation generation method (using GANs to generate images with lesions from existing high-quality annotations to generate images with foci).

For the establishment of evaluation metrics, we refer to Chen et al. [15] and Gilbert et al. [16] to indirectly evaluate the quality and effectiveness of synthetic images using downstream segmentation tasks. For the evaluation metrics, we used the mainstream metrics Precision, Sensitivity, Intersection Over Union (IOU), and Dice Score in the field of image segmentation, calculated as follows:

$$Precision = TP/(TP + FP), Sensitivity = TP/(TP + FN)$$
$$IOU = tp/(tp + fn + fp), Dice\ Score = (2 * tp)/[(tp + fn) + (tp + fp)] \tag{8}$$

where TP represents the part of the tumor region accurately segmented, FP represents the part of the non-tumor region incorrectly segmented by the network, and FN represents the part of tumor region unsegmented by the network. A represents the labeled tumor and B represents the network segmentation result, then tp represents the overlapping part of A and B (correct segmentation), fn represents the part of A with tp removed (missed segmentation), and fp represents the part of B with tp removed (incorrect segmentation). So an alternative formula for the IOU is as follows:

$$IOU = Dice\ Score/(2 - Dice\ Score) \tag{9}$$

3.3 Experimental Results and Analysis

3.3.1 Comparative Experiments

The synthetic images of the pancreatic tumor generated by the various enhancement methods are shown in Fig. 4 (the "Sample size" refers to the sample size of the training set). Since various augmentation methods only operate on the pancreatic site for synthesis, the qualitative map only shows the pancreas's area, and local enlargement shows the area containing the pancreatic tumor and its surroundings to verify the augmentation effect.

Firstly, the background map generated by Xing et al. [10] clearly shows distortions. The synthetic tumor contours generated by Wu et al. [8] did not include the tumor region. The synthetic tumor generated by Lin et al. [7] was highly similar to the surrounding region, and we could not determine whether it matched the imaging features of the pancreatic tumor. The reconstructed pancreatic images generated by Chen et al. [15] had the high degree of reproduction. Still, they had the problem that the size and shape of the tumor did not correspond to the original image. The image of the pancreas generated by Gilbert et al. [16] has the textural abruptness from the neighboring regions.

The pancreatic image generated by TSTG-GAN, in which the tumor site is highly similar to the actual lesion in shape and characteristics. The overall brightness of the tumor and the texture are consistent with the surrounding area. The surface of the generated tumor peripheral area is constant and continuous with the periphery of the original image's blue frame.

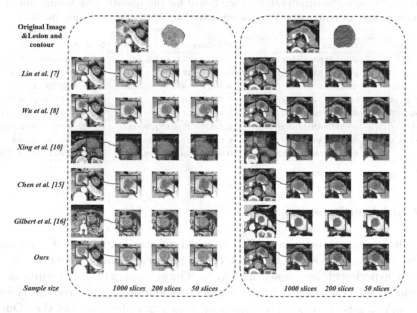

Fig. 4. Various enhancement methods generate synthetic images of the pancreatic tumor. The blue bounding box indicates the area around the tumor generated by our method, and the yellow outline shows the label of the tumor generated by each augmentation method. (Color figure online)

By analyzing Table 1, it can be seen that the evaluation metrics of Wu et al. [8] and Xing et al. [10] were significantly lower than the benchmark metrics, probably because these two methods could not effectively augmentation the pancreatic sites with complex and variable imaging structures. The evaluation indexes of Lin et al. [7] and Chen et al. [15] are slightly better than those of benchmark and affine transformation. The evaluation metrics of Gilbert et al. [16] perform the best among the five comparison methods, thanks to its unique annotation generation method. But are not even as good as the other comparison methods in solving the diversity problem. When the training set sample is reduced, the effect of each comparison method is exhausted, i.e., the significant decline in evaluation indicators.

The evaluation indicators "Ours" is significantly better than that of the comparison method. The increase is significant, showing that TSTG-GAN is more suitable for enhancing pancreatic tumor image sets than the existing enhancement methods. The evaluation index of "Ours" was similar to that of the optimal comparison method with the sample size of 1000 slices, even for the sample size of 50 slices. This result demonstrates that our method can provide augmentation even when the sample size is minimal.

Table 1. Precision/Sensitivity/IOU/Dice Score for the quantitative evaluation of the synthetic images of pancreatic tumors generated by each augmentation method.

Sample size	50 slices	200 slices	1000 slices
Original	0.821/0.835/0.668/0.801	0.821/0.835/0.668/0.801	0.821/0.835/0.668/0.801
Affine	0.825/0.839/0.672/0.804	0.828/0.842/0.675/0.806	0.833/0.851/0.679/0.809
Lin et al. [7]	0.797/0.809/0.633/0.775	0.813/0.818/0.647/0.786	0.859/0.867/0.692/0.818
Wu et al. [8]	0.724/0.741/0.574/0.729	0.733/0.758/0.589/0.741	0.796/0.814/0.629/0.772
Xing et al. [10]	0.701/0.724/0.552/0.711	0.718/0.744/0.577/0.732	0.743/0.790/0.612/0.759
Chen et al. [15]	0.827/0.840/0.669/0.802	0.834/0.849/0.682/0.811	0.867/0.876/0.706/0.828
Gilbert et al. [16]	0.836/0.842/0.676/0.807	0.849/0.857/0.695/0.820	0.870/0.882/0.723/0.839
Ours	**0.867/0.888/0.721/0.838**	**0.875/0.894/0.735/0.847**	**0.883/0.902/0.759/0.863**

3.3.2 Ablation Experiments

The ablation experiments were all performed on the sample size of 1000 slices.

The results of the synthetic image of the pancreatic tumor generated by the ablation experiment are shown in Fig. 5. "$Ours_1$" indicates the results of the ablation study experiment with the supervised learning reconstruction channel removed, i.e., missing $\mathcal{L}_{pbp}$. The generated tumor periphery area of the "$Ours_1$" display image is significantly different from the original image. "$Ours_2$" indicates the results of the ablation study with the unsupervised learning gradient map discriminator removed, i.e., $\mathcal{L}_{gm\_US}$ is missing. "$Ours_2$" shows the fused tumor with severe distortion and texture discontinuity. "$Ours_3$" indicates the ablation study experiment with the migration learning mechanism removed from the U-net training phase, i.e., only the U-net is pre-trained with the augmented dataset. The "$Ours_3$" and "Ours" display images are visually indistinguishable.

Table 2 demonstrates the impact of ablation experiments on segmenting pancreatic tumors. When ablation experiments were performed, the evaluation metrics of the downstream segmentation tasks were all reduced, i.e., each step reflected its unique value when TSTG-GAN augmented the pancreatic tumor dataset. The sharp decline in segmentation performance in "Ours$_2$" may be due to the lack of $\mathcal{L}_{gm\_US}$, which is used to constrain the contours of the fused tumors and causes severe deformation of the fused tumors. The segmentation performance in "Ours$_1$" is slightly lower than that of the optimal comparison method Gilbert et al. [16]. The lack of texture information in the $\mathcal{L}_{pbp}$ constrained generation region prevents the generator from encoding and decoding correctly. The segmentation performance of "Ours$_3$" is lower than that of "Ours", which indicates that the migration learning mechanism can improve U-net's segmentation performance.

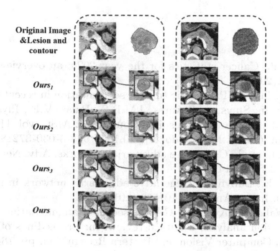

Fig. 5. Synthetic images of pancreatic tumors generated from ablation experiments. (Color figure online)

Table 2. Effect of modular ablation experiments on segmentation index of pancreatic tumor.

	Precision	Sensitivity	IOU	Dice Score
Original	0.821	0.835	0.668	0.801
Affine	0.833	0.851	0.679	0.809
Ours$_1$	0.871	0.879	0.715	0.834
Ours$_2$	0.834	0.849	0.686	0.814
Ours$_3$	0.874	0.890	0.732	0.845
Ours	**0.883**	**0.902**	**0.759**	**0.863**

4 Discussions and Conclusions

In this research, we propose a two-channel supervised generative adversarial network TSTG-GAN based on the rational generation of textures in the neighboring regions of tumors, using actual pancreatic tumor transplants fused to authentic pathological images and generating textures that match the transplanted tumors and their surrounding areas. Our synthetic image-labeling could allow other researchers to build models with only a small amount of labeled patient data and will greatly facilitate research in this area.

We will conduct further experiments on other datasets with similar characteristics in the future. Also, we will introduce the Rubikąŕs Cube+ pre-training mechanism into the generator pre-training module of TSTG-GAN to ensure reasonable image texture generation and more accurate generation of textures in the background region of the tumor to be fused.

References

1. Ferlay, J., et al.: Cancer statistics for the year 2020: an overview. Int. J. Cancer **149**, 778–789 (2021)
2. Sindhu, A., Radha, V.: Pancreatic tumour segmentation in recent medical imaging – an overview. In: Smys, S., Tavares, J.M.R.S., Balas, V.E., Iliyasu, A.M. (eds.) Computational Vision and Bio-Inspired Computing. AISC, vol. 1108, pp. 514–522. Springer, Cham (2020). https://doi.org/10.1007/978-3-030-37218-7_58
3. Goodfellow, I.J., et al.: Generative adversarial networks. Adv. Neural. Inf. Process. Syst. **3**, 2672–2680 (2014)
4. Yi, X., Walia, E., Babyn, P.: Generative adversarial network in medical imaging: a review. Med. Image Anal. **58**, 101552 (2019)
5. Bissoto, A., Valle, E., Avila, S.: GAN-based data augmentation and anonymization for skin-lesion analysis: a critical review. In: Proceedings of the IEEE/CVF Conference on Computer Vision and Pattern Recognition, pp. 1847–1856 (2021)
6. Chen, Y., et al.: Generative adversarial networks in medical image augmentation: a review. Comput. Biol. Med. **144**, 105382 (2022)
7. Lin, C., et al.: Breast mass detection in mammograms via blending adversarial learning. In: Burgos, N., Gooya, A., Svoboda, D. (eds.) Simulation and Synthesis in Medical Imaging. LNCS, vol. 11827, pp. 52–61. Springer, Cham (2019). https://doi.org/10.1007/978-3-030-32778-1_6
8. Wu, E., Wu, K., Cox, D., Lotter, W.: Conditional infilling GANs for data augmentation in mammogram classification. In: Stoyanov, D., et al. (eds.) Image Analysis for Moving Organ, Breast, and Thoracic Images. LNCS, vol. 11040, pp. 98–106. Springer, Cham (2018). https://doi.org/10.1007/978-3-030-00946-5_11
9. Guan, Q., et al.: Medical image augmentation for lesion detection using a texture-constrained multichannel progressive GAN. Comput. Biol. Med. **145**, 105444 (2022)
10. Xing, Y., et al.: Adversarial pulmonary pathology translation for pairwise chest X-ray data augmentation. In: Shen, D., et al. (eds.) Medical Image Computing and Computer Assisted Intervention – MICCAI 2019. LNCS, vol. 11769, pp. 757–765. Springer, Cham (2019). https://doi.org/10.1007/978-3-030-32226-7_84

11. Yao, Q., Xiao, L., Liu, P., Zhou, S.K.: Label-free segmentation of COVID-19 lesions in lung CT. IEEE Trans. Med. Imaging **40**, 2808–2819 (2021)

12. Ambita, A.A.E., Boquio, E.N.V., Naval, P.C.: COViT-GAN: vision transformer for COVID-19 detection in CT scan images with self-attention GAN for data augmentation. In: Farkaš, I., Masulli, P., Otte, S., Wermter, S. (eds.) Artificial Neural Networks and Machine Learning – ICANN 2021. LNCS, vol. 12892, pp. 587–598. Springer, Cham (2021). https://doi.org/10.1007/978-3-030-86340-1_47

13. Ronneberger, O., Fischer, P., Brox, T.: U-Net: convolutional networks for biomedical image segmentation. In: Navab, N., Hornegger, J., Wells, W.M., Frangi, A.F. (eds.) Medical Image Computing and Computer-Assisted Intervention – MICCAI 2015. LNCS, vol. 9351, pp. 234–241. Springer, Cham (2015). https://doi.org/10.1007/978-3-319-24574-4_28

14. Liu, Y., Jia, X., Shen, L., Ming, Z., Duan, J.: Local normalization based BN layer pruning. In: Tetko, I.V., Kůrková, V., Karpov, P., Theis, F. (eds.) Artificial Neural Networks and Machine Learning – ICANN 2019: Deep Learning. LNCS, vol. 11728, pp. 334–346. Springer, Cham (2019). https://doi.org/10.1007/978-3-030-30484-3_28

15. Chen, C., Hammernik, K., Ouyang, C., Qin, C., Bai, W., Rueckert, D.: Cooperative training and latent space data augmentation for robust medical image segmentation. In: de Bruijne, M., et al. (eds.) Medical Image Computing and Computer Assisted Intervention – MICCAI 2021. LNCS, vol. 12903, pp. 149–159. Springer, Cham (2021). https://doi.org/10.1007/978-3-030-87199-4_14

16. Gilbert, A., Marciniak, M., Rodero, C., Lamata, P., Samset, E., Mcleod, K.: Generating synthetic labeled data from existing anatomical models: an example with echocardiography segmentation. IEEE Trans. Med. Imaging **40**, 2783–2794 (2021)

Phenotype Anomaly Detection for Biological Dynamics Data Using a Deep Generative Model

Eisuke Ito[1], Takaya Ueda[1], Ryo Takano[1], Yukako Tohsato[1], Koji Kyoda[2], Shuichi Onami[2], and Ikuko Nishikawa[1]

[1] Ritsumeikan University, Shiga 525–8577, Japan
is0448fs@ed.ritsumei.ac.jp, nishi@ci.ritsumei.ac.jp
[2] RIKEN Center for Biosystems Dynamics Research, Kobe 650–0047, Japan

Abstract. Unsupervised anomaly detection is applied to biological dynamics data using a deep generative model. Phenotype anomaly detection for gene function identification has been successfully used in the reverse genetics, where the anomaly is conventionally characterized by a large number of pre-defined handcrafted features. The latest database of three-dimensional cell division data for the early development process of a model animal *Caenorhabditis elegans* (*C. elegans*) enables the present data-driven approach. A variational auto-encoder (VAE) was trained by 59 wild type (WT) data to acquire the normal individual features, and used to detect phenotypic anomalies in individuals resulting from selective RNA interference (RNAi) gene knockdown. Morphological anomalies were detected using the reconstruction error, whereas temporal anomalies were characterized by the time development trajectory in the VAE latent space. RNAi data corresponding to 97 essential genes on chromosome III in the two-cell period were studied by computational experiments, and several genes were suggested to be responsible for morphological or temporal anomalies, including genes with well-known functions in asymmetric cell division or cytoskeleton organization.

Keywords: Unsupervised anomaly detection · Variational auto-encoder · Biological time series · *C. elegans* · Gene function analysis

1 Introduction

Unsupervised anomaly detection [1,2] approaches are considered a practical choice as only normal data are used to obtain an anomaly detector and these normal data are easier to collect than abnormal data. In addition, abnormal data can greatly vary and are not known completely in advance. Generative models [3,4] trained using normal data effectively acquire data features in their latent space and thus reconstruct any normal data. Then, data anomalies are detected as any feature that cannot be reconstructed by those normal features.

The present study uses a variational auto-encoder (VAE) [4] generative model for unsupervised anomaly detection of three-dimensional biological cell division dynamics data. Normal data in biological systems will often follow a particular statistical distribution, and anomalies can be characterized by a deviation from this distribution. Therefore, the unsupervised approach is suitable to characterize anomalies using both data reconstruction and data distribution in the latent space of VAE.

The gene function identification is an important problem in biology, and phenotype anomaly detection has been used in the reverse genetics. Observed anomalies are conventionally characterized by a large number of handcrafted features, whereas the recent accumulation of the biological experimental data enables an alternative approach using unsupervised learning. Thus, we apply an unsupervised approach to the latest comprehensive database [5] of the early embryonic cell division dynamics for a model animal *Caenorhabditis elegans* (*C. elegans*). Wild type (WT) data, i.e., data of untreated individuals of the standard strain, is used as the normal dataset, whereas the detection targets are phenotype anomalies observed in RNA interference (RNAi) data, i.e., data of individuals one of whose essential embryonic genes is specifically knocked down by RNAi technique.

The paper is organized as follows: Sect. 2 describes the target problem for the three-dimensional time series data of cell division of *C. elegans*, Sect. 3 explains the proposed approach for morphological and temporal anomaly detection in RNAi data, Sect. 4 presents the results of computational experiments, and Sect. 5 summarizes the current results.

2   Biological Time Series Data of Cell Division

2.1   Gene Function Identification Through Knocking-Down a Gene

Gene function identification is a fundamental problem in biology. Reverse genetics is one solution approach, where a target gene is knocked down and the resulting phenotype is investigated to identify any anomalies. If detected, any phenotype anomalies are considered to be caused by the gene knockdown, suggesting gene function.

C. elegans is a nematode that has been extensively investigated as a major model animal in embryology. In particular, the *C. elegans* developmental cell lineage from fertilized egg to adult has been clarified, and the cell division processes for the formation of each organ in adults are known. Moreover, many genes present in *C. elegans* are conserved in other animal species. Thus, gene function analysis of *C. elegans* is expected to contribute to clarifying the general mechanism of three-dimensional multicellular structure formation in animals.

2.2   Developmental Dynamics Data of *C. elegans* as a model animal

The Worm Developmental Dynamics Database 2[a] (WDDD2) [5] is a public open database. It provides three-dimensional time series data of *C. elegans* cell division for its early embryo from the fertilization (single cell) up to the eight-cell stage. Three-dimensional data are provided as a set of slice images at different depths taken by a Nomarski differential interference contrast (DIC) microscope, with segmentation of cell nucleus areas. The time series has a sample rate of 20 s while gray scale images are provided for slice interval 0.5016 μm. Each slice is 600×600 pixels, and the pixel size is 0.1015 μm. The nucleus and spindle are detected as nucleus area using an automated system [6].

WDDD2 provides data appropriate for reverse genetics, as the dataset includes fair numbers of both WT and RNAi embryos. In the WT embryos, gene function is retained as normal, whereas in the RNAi embryos, a specific gene is knocked down using the RNA interference technique. Therefore, if any phenotype anomalies are observed in RNAi data during the developmental process, they can be assumed to be caused by the malfunction due to the gene knockdown. Our study intends to detect phenotype anomalies in RNAi data without using any predefined handcrafted features for anomaly characterization.

The data of 59 WT embryos and 1,142 RNAi embryos are registered in WDDD2. Each RNAi datapoint corresponds to one knocked-down gene, with a total of 350 genes that are all those known to be essential for *C. elegans* embryogenesis. Our proposed study focuses on 226 RNAi datapoints corresponding to 97 genes on chromosome III, one of six chromosomes in *C. elegans*. Each knocked-down gene is featured in between one to five RNAi datapoints.

Two cells are obtained after the first cell division, and each of them is again divided into two in the next division. The WDDD2 dataset contains the one-to eight-cell periods. Our study focuses on the two-cell period due to relatively simple shape of the smaller number of cells, although the proposed method is expected to be applicable also for later stages given sufficient available data. Based on the nucleus segmentation registered in the database, we define two-cell period as follows: the two-cell period starts from the moment at which a gap is observed between two nucleus areas for the first time. The two nuclei correspond to two cells, named AB and P_1, which are located on the anterior (head) and posterior (tail) sides, respectively. As the next cell division in the WT embryo starts earlier at AB than P_1, the two-cell period ends just before the moment at which a gap is observed between the two nucleus areas in AB.

A more detailed definition of the period in the mitotic cell division can be given using the relatively longer and stabler *interphase*, during which the nucleus retains its spherical shape, and the relatively shorter Mitotic phase (*M phase*), during which the nucleus shape deviates greatly from a sphere. At a certain moment during the M phase, the nucleus area becomes divided into two. Our definition of two-cell period uses this moment to define its beginning and ending, simply because it is well-defined and observable by the segmentation. Conversely, the definition of the interphase is given by a threshold of the sphericity

---

[a] https://wddd.riken.jp.

of nucleus area, and used for a time normalization descried later. Therefore, the time series of the two-cell period analyzed in the following experiments comprises three dynamic stages defined by the sphericity of the nucleus: before interphase, interphase, and after interphase.

2.3   Representation of Three-Dimensional Nucleus Data

Cubic voxel data are obtained by preprocessing the original data. As described in the previous section, the slice interval 0.5016 μm is longer than the liner size of a pixel on a slice 0.1015 μm. Therefore, the original data are transformed by linear interpolation to a voxel of size 0.5016 μm × 0.5016 μm × 0.5016 μm.

It should be noted that two-cell period, on which our study focuses, has a proper spatial symmetry. Though the first cell division breaks the spatial symmetry of anterior and posterior (head and tail), the rotational symmetry around the head to tail axis remains, and this axis is denoted anterior-posterior or AP axis. In other words, the dorsal and ventral (DV) i.e., back and front and left and right (LR) axes are still undefined. This is not because of lack of information, but is due to the developmental stage in which symmetry breaks. This rotational symmetry around the AP axis is broken by the next cell division. The AP axis is derived from each 3-dimensional datapoint as follows: the center of AB and P_1 is obtained from the center of gravity (COG) for each nucleus area, and the line connecting both centers is defined as AP axis. The direction of AP axis is also available in the database. The center of the data is also registered for each datapoint, given by COG of the whole embryo. Then, the position and angle of the three-dimensional data are normalized by setting the center to the origin, and aligning the AP axis to the direction of x-axis. Finally, the data size is normalized to 150 × 150 × 150 voxels by deleting the peripheral empty area. Further preprocessing to obtain the input data for the VAE is described next.

Voxel Data. The voxel data size is decreased from 150×150×150 to 58×40×40 by further trimming the empty peripheral area and by down-sampling using the nearest neighbor interpolation. To consider rotational symmetry, the original data are rotated around the AP axis by $\pi/6$ to obtain 12 datapoints from one original. This is necessary because the original data cannot be compared with each other, as their rotation angles are not aligned.

Set of Multiple Cross Section Images. For computational cost reduction, a set of cross section images is used in place of voxel format to express the 3-dimensional shape of the nucleus area. Here again, considering rotational symmetry around the AP axis, conventional parallel cross sections are unavailable. Instead, a set of cross sections, which intersect each other along the AP axis, are obtained as shown on the left in Fig. 1, while twelve sections rotated by $\pi/6$ around the AP axis are shown on the right.

As two sections rotated by π are simply mirror images, a set of six consecutive sections are used to express one original datapoint. The nucleus area is shown by white pixels in the figure, with the background in black. Each section image contains the AP axis at the center along a vertical direction. To consider rotational symmetry around the AP axis, the data are again rotated around AP axis by $\pi/6$ to obtain 12 sets of six sections.

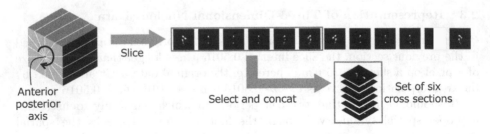

Fig. 1. Set of six cross section images expressing 3-dimensional data which possess a rotational symmetry in two-cell period

Examples of the original voxel data for each stage are shown in the upper row of Fig. 2; (a) before interphase, (b) interphase, and (c) after interphase, whereas the lower row shows each corresponding set of six images.

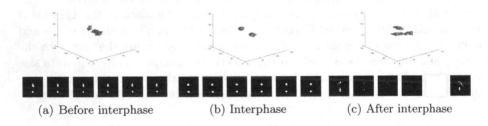

(a) Before interphase   (b) Interphase   (c) After interphase

Fig. 2. Visualization of a WT datapoint as voxel data (upper) and a set of six cross section data (lower) in (a) before interphase, (b) interphase, and (c) after interphase

3   Anomaly Detection by Variational Auto-Encoder

This section briefly reviews unsupervised anomaly detection using AE or VAE, then describes our study to detect the phenotype anomaly of RNAi data in WDDD2. Two types of phenotype anomaly of the RNAi embryo are investigated. The first type is morphological anomalies in the nucleus area, i.e., anomalies in the 3-dimensional shape and location at each time step. The second type is temporal anomalies of time development in the nucleus area, i.e., a temporal change of the shape and location during the two-cell period. Each anomaly is detected as shown in Fig. 3. First, the morphological anomaly is characterized by the reconstruction error of AE or VAE methods. Then, the temporal anomaly is characterized by a latent space trajectory for the data which did not feature reconstruction errors in the first step.

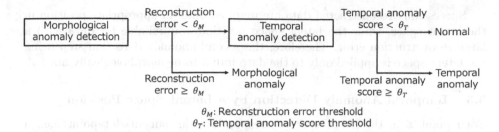

θ_M: Reconstruction error threshold
θ_T: Temporal anomaly score threshold

Fig. 3. Stepwise detection of the morphological and the temporal anomaly for each data

3.1 Auto-encoder and Variational Auto-Encoder

Auto-encoder (AE) [7] is a neural network trained to output data identical to the input data. The middle layer is a feature space, which gives a latent representation of the input data. The training loss of AE is given by the mean square error (MSE) or binary cross entropy (BCE).

VAE [4] is a neural network that both reconstructs each input data as AE and contains the data distribution in the latent space in a preliminary given functional form. Thus, the middle layer is expected to acquire the data distribution in addition to latent data representation. Therefore, the VAE training loss is given by Eq. (1), as the summation of the second term corresponding to the reconstruction error, and the first term corresponding to KL-divergence between (the log of) latent space distribution of the data $q_\phi(\mathbf{z})$ and preliminary given distribution $p_\theta(\mathbf{z})$:

$$Loss = D_{KL}[\log q_\phi(\mathbf{z}|\mathbf{x})|| \log p_\theta(\mathbf{z})] - \mathbb{E}_{q_\phi(\mathbf{z}|\mathbf{x})}[\log p_\theta(\mathbf{x}|\mathbf{z})] , \qquad (1)$$

where ϕ and θ are the encoder and decoder parameters, respectively. The obtained encoder is expected to be a continuous mapping in that a close neighbor data pair in the original data space retain close neighbor status in VAE after mapping, whereas in AE this is often broken by a strongly nonlinear mapping. This leads to our proposed idea to characterize the data by its position in the VAE latent space.

Both AE and VAE have effective reconstruction ability to detect data possessing features outside the latent space. First, a set of normal data with a certain distribution is used to train AE or VAE to acquire the features necessary to reconstruct the normal data. Then, the input data reconstruction error is used to indicate data anomalies or the deviation from the normal data distribution. The application to phenotype anomaly detection for RNAi data in WDDD2 will now be described.

3.2 Morphological Anomaly Detection by a Reconstruction Error

WT data are used as normal data to train AE or VAE. After training, the reconstruction error is used to characterize morphological anomalies in the RNAi data. The threshold of the anomaly is derived from the WT test data.

Successfully reconstructed data are mapped onto an appropriate position in the latent space, while the latent space position is unreliable for data with a large reconstruction error. Therefore, the second anomaly detection step using the latent space is applied only to the data found to be morphologically normal.

3.3 Temporal Anomaly Detection by a Latent Space Position

Each point z in the latent space corresponds to an output datapoint, i.e., a 3-dimensional nucleus area of WT embryo found during the two-cell period. Therefore, the development of each embryo can be expressed by a trajectory in the latent space. Continuous trajectory was observed through a visualization of WT data distribution in an obtained latent space as will be shown in Fig. 5 in the next section.

Let us define a morphological time t^* for each point z by

$$t^*(z) = \operatorname{argmax}_t p(t|z) , \qquad (2)$$

where t is a normalized time of WT data, with the start and end of interphase set to $t = 0$ and $t = 1$, respectively for each WT data. Morphological time t^* indicates a (normalized) physical time in two-cell period corresponding to the shape z based on the standard growth rate of WT. Approximate calculation of $t^*(z)$ from finite number of WT data is done as follows. When the dimension of z is relatively low and distribution $p(t|z)$ can be estimated from the WT data distribution, the distribution is approximately obtained by discretization. The z space is discretized into a fine mesh space, the histogram of t over all WT data in each mesh is obtained, and t^* given by the mode of the histogram. This approach works well for 2-dimensional z in our experiments. Otherwise, for higher dimensions of z or when insufficient WT data are available in each mesh, the k nearest neighbor approach is used instead, with t^* given by the average t over k WT data in the neighborhood of z.

The temporal anomaly is characterized by the deviation from morphological time t^* at each physical time t for data $z(t)$. Equation (3) calculates the temporal anomaly score S for time series data of one embryo. The score S is defined by the linear deviation $|t^* - t|$ averaged over all time t during two-cell period with length T, and over 12 rotation angles around AP axis:

$$S = \frac{1}{12T} \sum_t^T \sum_\theta^{12} |t^*_{t,\theta} - t| . \qquad (3)$$

4   Computational Experiments of Morphological and Temporal Anomaly Detection on RNAi Embryos

Two computational experiment settings are presented in this paper. The first experiment used VAE owing to the reliability of its latent space positions, and a set of cross section images was used as input data owing to the lower computational cost. The second experiment used AE and 3-dimensional voxel input.

Thus, 3-dimensional convolution and deconvolution layers were used in AE. Both experiments used the same WT data for training and RNAi data for anomaly detection, and the obtained results were compared to study the effectiveness of each latent space and data format.

4.1 Anomaly Detection by VAE Using a Set of Cross Section Data

VAE Model Structure and Parameter Settings Figure 4 shows the VAE model used in our experiments, with an encoder and a decoder each comprising three convolution and deconvolution layers, respectively. Batch normalization [8] is attached to all but the final layer. The rectified linear (ReLU [9]) activation function is used, except for the final decoder layer, which uses a sigmoidal function to output a grayscale image expressing the nucleus density on a cross section. The latent space z has six dimensions, which was found the lowest possible for reconstruction.

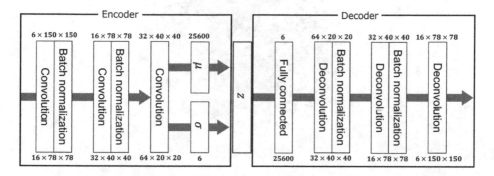

Fig. 4. Convolutional layered structure of VAE

Fifty-nine WT data registered in WDDD2 were divided into 52 training datapoints and seven test datapoints. The 52 training time-series comprised 2,432 time step data in total, with each rotated by 12 angles to produce 29,184 three-dimensional datapoints, with varying embryo, times and angles of rotation. Similarly, 3,444 datapoints were obtained from the seven test time-series. Furthermore, the after-interphase data from the single-cell period was added to the training data to support the before-interphase data in two-cell period. However, the effect on reconstruction was found to be limited in the experimental results.

Training is stopped at 330 epochs to avoid over-fitting, the batch size is 64, and Adam optimization is used. The parameter k for obtaining morphological time t^* is set to 15, as smaller k values produce a larger anomaly score S for WT data.

The anomaly threshold θ is given by

$$\theta = m + 3\sigma , \tag{4}$$

where m is an average and σ is a standard deviation over seven WT test data of the reconstruction error and of score S, for the morphological and temporal anomalies, respectively. No WT data was found abnormal by this threshold.

Visualization of an Obtained Latent Space. Figure 5 shows an example visualized data distribution in an obtained latent space. Fifty-nine WT data at all time points and all rotation angles are plotted in the latent space and visualized by t-SNE. The prior distribution is 6-dimensional standard normal distribution, and t-SNE perplexity is 30. It is observed that any pair of data in a similar shape or at consecutive time points are plotted in a close neighbor in the latent space.

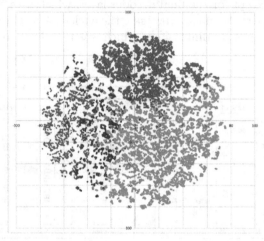

Fig. 5. Distribution of WT data in each developmental stage in 6-dimensional latent space visualized by t-SNE. The blue, orange, gray, and yellow data points represent the data after interphase in single-cell period, before interphase, during interphase, and after interphase in two-cell period, respectively. (Color figure online)

Results of Morphological Anomaly. A list of RNAi data detected as morphologically abnormal is given in Table 1. The table shows gene names and the number of abnormal datapoints in descending ratio order. Twenty-six RNAi datapoints corresponding to 12 genes are listed.

Table 1. List of RNAi data detected as abnormal in morphology by VAE

Locus	Abnormal/Total	Locus	Abnormal/Total
sas-4	5/5	cls-2	2/5
par-3	5/5	mel-32	1/5
rpl-23	1/1	gop-2	1/5
cyk-1	1/1	cpf-2	1/5
par-2	4/5	ucr-1	1/5
pola-1	3/5	hcp-3	1/5

Of the genes in the table, *par-2*, *par-3* are well known to have functions in asymmetric cell division [10], while *sas-4*, *cyk-1* are known for cytoskeleton organization [11]. Resultant anomalies are detected in the two-cell period.

Results of Temporal Anomaly. Table 2 lists the RNAi data detected as temporally abnormal with the gene name and number of abnormal datapoints. Twenty RNAi datapoints corresponding to 17 genes are listed.

Table 2. List of RNAi data detected as abnormal in the time development by VAE

Locus	Abnormal/Total	Locus	Abnormal/Total
pola-1	2/3	*rpb-8*	1/5
eif-3.D	1/1	*rnp-1*	1/5
pcf-11	1/1	*ccdc-55*	1/5
tufm-1	3/5	*mcm-5*	1/5
mlc-5	1/2	*bud-31*	1/5
cls-2	1/3	*rsp-3*	1/5
C26E6.4	1/3	C34C12.8	1/5
klp-19	1/4	*ykt-6*	1/5
ucr-1	1/4		

cls-2, *klp-19* are known as the protein for kinetochore and the mitotic chromosome, respectively [11], and the silencing of these genes could cause temporal anomalies during the mitotic period. Our study is anticipated to detect such anomalies in two-cell period.

Next, the temporal development of two RNAi datapoints listed as temporally abnormal in Table 2 is studied in more detail. Figure 6 shows normalized physical time t versus morphological time t^* for (b) *ykt-6* and (c) *bud-31*. The line $t^* = t$ is shown in orange, and the anomaly is quantified by the deviation from the line. The WT data show a small deviation indicating a normal growth rate, whereas deviation is large for (b) before ($t \leq 0$) and after interphase ($t \geq 1$) indicating a slower growth rate. While (c) shows a large deviation after interphase, with t^* decreasing before interphase, indicating the presence of a morphological anomaly, as there is no time reversal in the growth.

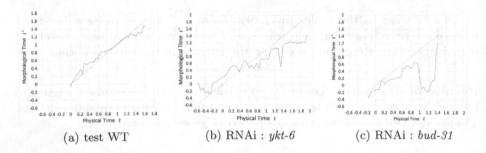

(a) test WT   (b) RNAi : *ykt-6*   (c) RNAi : *bud-31*

Fig. 6. Temporal development of each embryo characterized by morphological time t^*

4.2 Anomaly Detection by AE Using Voxel Data

AE Model Structure and Parameter Settings. AE is composed of an encoder and a decoder comprising five convolution and deconvolution layers, respectively. Batch normalization and activation were set as in VAE. The dimension of latent space z was also six. The same data was prepared as for VAE for both training and testing. The training was stopped at 30 epochs to prevent overfitting, the batch size was 12, and Adam optimization was used. The parameter k for obtaining t^* was set to 12. The anomaly threshold is given by Eq. (4).

Results of Morphological and Temporal Anomaly. Table 3 lists the RNAi data detected as morphologically abnormal. Thirty-six RNAi datapoints for 18 genes are listed.

Table 3. List of RNAi data detected as abnormal in morphology by AE

Locus	Abnormal/Total	Locus	Abnormal/Total
sas-4	5/5	*tost-1*	1/2
par-3	5/5	*taf-9*	1/4
rpl-23	1/1	*ani-1*	1/4
cyk-1	1/1	*pal-1*	1/5
par-2	4/5	*cpf-2*	1/5
pola-1	4/5	*dcn-1*	1/5
C23G10.8	3/5	*baf-1*	1/5
glp-1	2/5	*chc-1*	1/5
cls-2	2/5	*gop-2*	1/5

Table 4 lists the RNAi data detected as abnormal in temporal development, with 11 RNAi data corresponding to 11 genes.

Table 4. RNAi data detected as abnormal in the time development by AE

Locus	Detection/Total	Locus	Detection/Total
rpb-2	1/3	rnp-4	1/5
ykt-6	1/4	cls-2	1/5
bud-31	1/5	mcm-5	1/5
C34C12.8	1/5	pola-1	1/5
cpf-2	1/5	rpb-8	1/5
ucr-1	1/5		

Comparison of Two Experimental Settings. The two settings use different models (VAE and AE), and different data formats (section image and voxel). The obtained anomaly detection results have similar anomaly indices for both reconstruction error and anomaly score S. Corresponding pairs of Tables 1 and 3, and Tables 2 and 4 show some difference, most of which are caused by thresholding. The latent space visualization for AE also follows a similar structure to that of Fig. 5 obtained for VAE. Moreover, the morphological time development shown by $t^* - t$ graphs in Fig. 6 is similar for each RNAi datapoint. Therefore, the latent space positions from AE are reliable for anomaly detection in our experiments. In addition, a set of cross section data is sufficient to express the 3-dimensional structure as voxel data. However, a cross section is more vulnerable to experimental data loss in an original DIC slice, which may lead to a false morphological anomaly detection.

5   Summary

A variational auto-encoder is used for anomaly detection in biological dynamics data for cell division in the early developmental process. Comprehensive WT and RNAi data of a model animal *C. elegans* were acquired from the public database WDDD2, which enabled our unsupervised approach requiring no handcrafted features. Computational experiments suggested several genes responsible for morphological or temporal anomalies in the two-cell period, including some genes with well-known functions. In future work, we intend to compare our unsupervised approach results with those produced using handcrafted features on the same data. The proposed method may requires more number of the WT data for more complex morphology in the later stage with more than two cells.

Acknowledgment. This work was supported in part by JSPS KAKENHI Grant No. 19K12164.

References

1. An, J., Cho, S.: Variational autoencoder based anomaly detection using reconstruction probability. Technical Report SNU Data Mining Center (2015)

2. Schlegl, T., Seeböck, P., Waldstein, S.M., Schmidt-Erfurth, U., Langs, G.: Unsupervised anomaly detection with generative adversarial networks to guide marker discovery. In: Niethamme, M., et al. (eds.) Information Processing in Medical Imaging. LNCS, vol. 10265, pp. 146–157. Springer, Cham (2017). https://doi.org/10.1007/978-3-319-59050-9_12

3. Goodfellow, I. et al.: Generative adversarial nets. In: NIPS, pp. 2672–2680 (2014). https://doi.org/10.48550/arXiv.1406.2661

4. Kingma, D.P., Welling, M.: Auto-encoding varitational Bayes. In: ICLR (2014). https://doi.org/10.48550/arXiv.1312.6114

5. Kyoda, K., Okada, H., Itoga, H., Onami, S.: Deep collection of quantitative nuclear division dynamics data in RNAi-treated *Caenorhabditis elegans* embryos. bioRxiv (2020). https://doi.org/10.1101/2020.10.04.325761

6. Hamahashi, S., Kitano, H., Onami, S.: A system for measuring cell division patterns of early *Caenorhabditis elegans* embryos by using image processing and object tracking. Syst. Comput. Jpn. **38**(11), 12–24 (2007)

7. Hinton, G.E., Salakhutdinov, R.R.: Reducing the dimensionality of data with neural networks. Science **313**(5786), 504–507 (2006)

8. Ioffe, S., Szegedy, C.: Batch normalization: accelerating deep network training by reducing internal covariate shift. In: ICML, pp. 448–456 (2015)

9. Nairand, V., Hinton, G.E.: Rectified linear units improve retricted Boltzmann machines. In: ICML, pp. 807–814 (2010)

10. Rose, L., Gönczy, P.: Polarity establishment, asymmetric division and segregation of fate determinants in early *C. elegans* embryos. In: WormBook, pp. 1–43, 30 December 2014

11. Oegema, K., Hyman, A.A.: Cell division. In: WormBook, pp. 1–40, 19 January 2006

Progressive Image Restoration with Multi-stage Optimization

Jiaming Yang⬛, Weihua Zhang$^{(\boxtimes)}$, and Yifei Pu

School of Computing, Sichuan University, Chengdu 610065, Sichuan, China
zhangweihua@scu.edu.cn

Abstract. With the recent development of deep learning technology, researchers have achieved significant results in small-scale image inpainting. However, when the missing area is large, undesirable artifacts and noise are introduced into the inpainting area. Hence, we present a multi-stage progressive image inpainting framework based on the well-known generative adversarial network(GAN) to solve this problem. In our MOPR-GAN method, generator uses a progressive inpainting module(PIM) and an image optimization module(IOM), while discriminator combines a patchGAN with an attention mechanism and a globalGAN. The PIM can gradually repair the image loss area and generate an attention map simultaneously. The IOM optimizes the details of the generated image based on the information provided by the attention map. The discriminator can capture the local continuity and universal global features of the image better. When comparing the test results with the latest research, the model showed a significant effect in both qualitative and quantitative analyses.

Keywords: Progressive image inpainting · Attention map · GAN

1 Introduction

Image inpainting aims to fill in the missing areas of damaged images to achieve the maximum possible authenticity. These algorithms are usually used for picture editing tasks, such as filtering unwanted objects [2,16] or repairing old pictures [22]. When the missing area of the image is large, less information can be obtained; thus, increasing the available information of the image is critical to the restoration task. Moreover, the generated portion of the image may not have the same style as the real image; consequently, restorations tasks require both partial continuity and overall similarity.

Most traditional image inpainting methods diffuse the background data to the missing area using a differential operator [4]. Subsequently, with the explosive growth in data volume, patch-based inpainting methods were introduced, where

Supported by the Key Research and Development Program of the Sichuan Province (Grant No. 2022YFQ0047).

CelebA   Paris StreetView   Place365

Fig. 1. Some inpainting results using the proposed framework on different datasets. Among them, (Up) Input image with missing areas. The missing areas are shown in white. (Down) Repaired picture using MOPR-GAN(ours).

the algorithm identifies patches in several source pictures to fill in the missing areas, to obtain the maximum similarity [10]. However, these methods perform poorly when restoring a complex detailed texture in a missing area.

Recently, with the rapid development of deep learning technologies, deep convolutional networks have begun to demonstrate extraordinary capabilities in the field of image inpainting. These methods replace the missing parts of the content through continuous learning of existing data, thereby generating a coherent structure in the missing area, which is difficult to achieve using traditional methods. However, images generated by these method are often blurred or have artifacts, which are dissatisfying in terms of visual performance.

To solve this challenging problem, in 2014, Goodfellow et al. proposed a generative adversarial network (GAN) [9], which is a network model composed of two deep convolutional networks called generator and discriminator. The generator uses data to generate images to deceive the discriminator, whereas the discriminator learns the difference between the real and generated images to efficiently identify the generated image, and returns an adversarial loss to improve the generator. Subsequently, several GAN-based models [7,17] have been developed, many of which use encoder-decoder architectures as their generator.

Researchers began to make bolder attempts. They identified that global inpainting does not directly conform to the way in which the human brain thinks; therefore, they developed several model frameworks for multi-stage inpainting [14,20]. For example, the EdgeConnect framework, which was proposed by Kamyar et al. [14], divides the task into two stages: edge prediction and edge-based repair. Although using the edge as the pre-information for repairing the image has a good effect, obtaining a good edge is a difficult task. Almost all these algorithms have similar shortcomings.

In this paper, we propose an image inpainting network called Multi-Stage Optimized Progressive Restoration with GAN (MOPR-GAN). The framework follows the basic principles of GAN, and is divided into generators and discriminators. The generator consists of two parts: (1) a Progressive Inpainting Module (PIM) and (2) an Image Optimization Module (IOM). The PIM is responsible for progressively repairing the missing area and generating an attention map. The IOM refers to the attention map to optimize the details of the initial repaired image, so that it can generate high-quality images. The discriminator is a hybrid of a local discriminator (patchGAN) and a global discriminator (globalGAN). In contrast to the discriminator model proposed by Iizuka et al. [17], we added the attention map generated by the PIM and the IOM; consequently, the discriminator can identify the repaired area more efficiently.

We verified the performance of our model using three standard datasets CelebA [21], Paris Street View [5], and Place365 [3] (certain results are shown in Fig. 1), and compared our method with some of the most advanced frameworks. The primary contributions of this paper are as follows:

- We propose an Image Optimization Module (IOM), that uses a form of competition within the region to extract the best matching distribution of the real image.
- An attention mechanism, called Global Adaptive Attention (GAA), is developed, which acts on the entire network. Under the joint constraints of structure and texture, it gradually updates the attention score following the progress of the network to obtain finer details, thereby enhancing the potential and efficiency of the network.
- We propose a Multi-Stage Optimized Progressive Restoration GAN (MOPR-GAN) framework, which can generate images with better results in terms of details and overall performance; the framework has achieved good performance in both qualitative and quantitative analysis.

Moreover, we performed certain ablation experiments to verify the accuracy of the contributions.

2   Method

In this section, we first introduce the structure of each part of the proposed network framework. And then, we introduce the GAA scheme based on a multi-stage network. Finally, we explain the loss function. The pipeline of our network model is shown in Fig. 2.

2.1   Generator

The generator comprises two modules: 1) PIM, which is used for preliminary image restoration, and 2) IOM, which is used for updating image details. Meanwhile, the generator of the entire network is divided into two forms in the two phases: (1) contains only PIM modules; (2) contains PIM and IOM modules. We will introduce specific training strategy in Sect. 3.1. Here, we explain the two modules in detail.

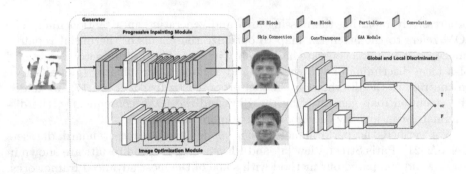

Fig. 2. The overall architecture of the proposed network model is divided into two phases, which we use the red line to represent the first stage and the green line to represent the second one in the diagram(the specific process is described in Sect. 3.1). And then, the network inputs are images and masks, Progressive Inpainting Module (PIM) is used to generate pre-inpainting images recursively, the Image Optimization Module (IOM) optimizes details, and the global and local discriminator (Up is local, Down is global) enhances the network repair potential. (Color figure online)

PIM. The design idea for PIM is derived from RFR [13], which using recursive reasoning to achieve a gradual inpainting process from the edge to the center of the missing area. The difference is that we modified the reasoning network structure and used our own attention mechanism. The details of this part are as follows:

Referring to the network architecture proposed by Johnson et al. [11], we built an encoding-decoding network for the reasoning network. The encoder is composed of three convolutions. The decoder is composed of three deconvolutions with strides of 1/2, 1/2, and 1. Three residual blocks, a GAA and a convolution were added to the middle. The residual blocks are used to avoid the disappearance of the gradient, and the GAA is used to calculate the current attention score and update the feature map. The GAA calculation process is described in Sect. 2.3. Furthermore, the role of the convolutional layer is concatenating the reconstructed feature map with the input one in order to get the final feature.

In general, the PIM iterates multiple times until the feature map is completely filled. Thus, a good pre-inpainting image can be generated.

IOM. Because of the limitation of the repair method based on the partial progressive algorithm, it is inevitable that the output of the preliminary repair image will have a certain degree of local artifacts or chromatic aberration especially the center of the missing area, even though we adaptively mix the previous attention score when computing the new one. Therefore, we launched the IOM to resolve this problem effectively, and generate images with good performance in terms of both details and overall.

Inspired by the multi-scale convolutional fusion block proposed by Yu et al. [19], the IOM of this paper is divided into three parts.

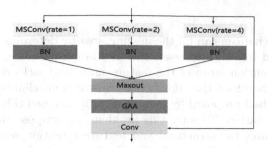

Fig. 3. The main part of the IOM. It can improve the image details in the feature space.

The first stage is the initial extraction of the image which comes from PIM. Through three convolutional layers, it can learn the basic feature information. We retained this current feature map for later use.

The second stage comprises four MIE blocks. The MIE block is shown in Fig 3, whose main body is a multi-scale competitive convolution with a scale of 3. Multi-scale convolution allows the convolution calculations to have a wider field of view, and can capture longer dependencies so that we can improve the network capability. Meanwhile, using Maxout prevents overfitting and provides a lightweight constraint, as well as selects the best feature value of the current position in multiple feature regions. Subsequently, we added a GAA and concatenate the resulting feature map with the input one through a convolution. The role of GAA is the same as in PIM, responsible for calculating the attention score and updating the feature map. The GAA calculation process is described in Sect. 2.3.

Finally, we skip concatenating the feature maps after multiple multi-scale convolutions with the retained feature map in the first stage, which can strengthen the consistency of the image structure and prevent the gradient from disappearing after optimization.

2.2   Discriminator

Iizuka et al. [17] proposed a multi-scale discriminator architecture including a local discriminator and global discriminator, which can enhance the detailed performance of the repaired area and improve the global consistency of the image. Therefore, the discriminator of our network also uses this scheme. The local discriminator uses four convolutional layers and one fully connected layer, whereas the global discriminator uses five convolutional layers and one fully connected layer. Spectral normalization and LeakyReLU [1] with a slope of 0.2 were added to each layer of the two discriminators. In addition, we also added the attention mechanism to the discriminator, which is mainly manifested in the loss function as shown in Sect. 2.4.

2.3 GAA

The attention mechanism can fill the missing area by determining the similarity in the background texture. However, the traditional attention mechanism only calculates the attention score of the feature map, and lacks direct supervision of the attention; therefore, the information learned is unreliable. Conversely, the self-attention method proposed by Peng et al. [15] specified this, but ignored the rich texture information. To solve this problem, we propose the GAA module, which first calculates the structural and texture attention scores, makes them constrain each other, and then performs adaptive accumulation.

Our attention mechanism is divided into two parts: attention calculation and attention transfer. First, in the attention calculation step, we calculate the truncated distance similarity [18] of structure attention with 3×3 patches in the input structure feature ($\bar{d}^s$) and the cosine similarity of texture attention ($\bar{d}^i$).

$$\bar{d}^s_{(x,y,x',y')} = \tanh(-(\frac{d^s_{(x,y,x',y')} - v}{\sigma})), \tag{1}$$

where $d^s_{(x,y,x',y')}$ is the Euclidean distance between the patches at (x,y) and (x',y'); v and σ are the mean value and standard deviation of $d^s_{(x,y,x',y')}$, respectively.

$$\bar{d}^i_{(n,m,n',m')} = \frac{\sum_{i,j\in(-k,...,k)} d^i_{(n+i,m+j,n',m')}}{k^2} \tag{2}$$

where $d^i_{(n,m,n',m')}$ is the cosine similarity of each part of the feature pixels between (n,m) and (n',m').

Then, we used the softmax function to generate structure and texture attention score maps respectively, which are referred to as $score^s$ and $score^i$.

$$score^s_{(x,y,x',y')} = softmax(\lambda \bar{d}^s_{(x,y,x',y')}) \tag{3}$$

$$score^i_{(n,m,n',m')} = softmax(\lambda \bar{d}^i_{(n,m,n',m')}) \tag{4}$$

where λ is set to 50. After that, we used $score^s$ as a constraint to adjust the value of $score^i$. The calculation process is as follows:

$$score'_{(n,m,n',m')} = softmax(2score^i_{(n,m,n',m')} score^s_{(x,y,x',y')}) \tag{5}$$

where $pixel(n,m) \in patch(x,y)$, $pixel(n',m') \in patch(x',y')$. At this point, we can calculate the final attention map. If $s\bar{c}ore^{i-1}_{(n,m,n',m')}$ represents the attention score computed at the previous iteration, λ is a learnable parameter, so the final attention map $score_{(n,m,n',m')}$ is:

$$score_{(n,m,n',m')} = \begin{cases} \lambda score'_{(n,m,n',m')} + (1-\lambda)s\bar{c}ore^{i-1}_{(n,m,n',m')} & if \quad \exists s\bar{c}ore^{i-1} \\ score'_{(n,m,n',m')}, & otherwise \end{cases} \tag{6}$$

In particular, $s\bar{c}ore^{i-1}_{(n,m,n',m')}$ in the first MIE submodule equals to the attention scores generated by the last iteration of PIM.

The next step is attention transfer. We used the score map to reconstruct the feature map. If f represents the input feature and f' represents the reconstructed feature, the formula is

$$f'_{(n,m)} = \sum_{n' \in 1,...W \, m' \in 1,...H} score_{(n,m,n',m')} f_{(n',m')} \qquad (7)$$

Finally, we reserve the attention score calculated for the next iteration.

2.4   Loss Function

Because our network is a GAN-based model, the loss function is divided into two parts: the loss of the discriminator and the generator. The first we calculated is the loss of the discriminator. Because the attention mechanism is added to it to increase the accuracy when identifying the authenticity of the image, this part is composed of adversarial and attention losses. If D is the discriminator, G is the generator, A is the attention map, I_R represents the real image, and I_G represents the generated image, then its loss function(L_D) is calculated as follows:

$$L_{attention} = L_{MSE}(D(I_R), 0) + L_{MSE}(D(I_G), A); \qquad (8)$$

$$L_D = -log(D(I_R)) - log(1 - D(I_G)) + \lambda_{att} L_{attention}, \qquad (9)$$

where $\lambda_{att} = 0.2$ in our experiments. Meanwhile, the attention map A will be explained in Sect. 3.1.

Refer to the idea in [14], our generator is trained using a joint loss comprising $l1$, adversarial, perceptual, and style losses. The $l1$ loss is normalized by the mask size, while the adversarial loss is provided by the mapping output of the generated image in the discriminator, which is a part of L_D, as

$$L_{adv} = log(1 - D(I_G)). \qquad (10)$$

The perceptual loss L_{per} and style loss L_{style} are two loss functions that were proposed by Johnson et al. [11]. Finally, the overall loss function of our generator is

$$L_G = \lambda_{l_1} L_{l_1} + \lambda_{adv} L_{adv} + \lambda_{per} L_{per} + \lambda_{style} L_{style}. \qquad (11)$$

We finally set $\lambda_{l_1} = 1$, $\lambda_{adv} = 0.01$, $\lambda_{per} = 0.2$, and $\lambda_{style} = 200$. The generator's loss function combination in our model is similar to [14] and has been shown to be effective.

3   Experiments

In this section, we elaborately explain certain related settings and strategies to facilitate the reproduction of the network.

3.1 Training Setting and Strategy

We trained our model with a batch size of six. As this is a GAN-based archi-tecture, there is a generator and discriminator that must be updated; therefore, we used the Adam optimizer. The entire network design strategy is divided into two steps: (1)We only use PIM as the generator Until PIM converges. In this case, the attention map in the discriminator loss function is the one generated by the last iteration of the PIM. (2)We join IOM and make PIM and IOM work together as generator. At this time, the attention map becomes the one gener-ated by IOM's last MIE. During each step, we both used learning rates of $2e^{-4}$ and $2e^{-5}$ to train the generator and discriminator, respectively. Then, we used $5e^{-5}$ to fine-tune the generator, while the discriminator used $5e^{-6}$. During the fine-tuning, we did not want to relearn all other network parameters; therefore, we froze all the batch normalization layers of our generator. It is worth noting that we don't unfreeze PIM's batch normalization layers during the second step. All experiments were performed using Python 3.7 on an Ubuntu 20.04 system, with an 11 G NVIDIA GeForce RTX 2080 GPU and Intel Xeon E5-1650 v4 3.60 GHz CPU.

3.2 Datasets

We used datasets CelebA [21], Paris StreetView [5] and Place365 [3] to verify our model. Meanwhile, the irregular masks are automatically generated by scripts.

3.3 Comparison Models

We compared our experimental results with those of certain state-of-the-art methods, both qualitatively and quantitatively. These methods include CA [12], GLCIC [17], PIC [6], EC(EdgeConnect) [14], FE [8], and RFR [13].

4 Results

We conducted experiments on the three datasets, and compared the results with the methods mentioned in the previous section both qualitatively and quanti-tatively. Moreover, we conducted ablation tests to verify the necessity of the proposed module.

4.1   Qualitative Comparison

Figure 4, 5, and 6 show the visualization of our approach when compared to the four state-of-the-art methods on the three datasets. In comparison, our model showed excellent visual effects, and when the missing area became larger, the effect was more apparent. This shows the superiority of our Network.

| Masked | Gate | PIC | FE | EC | MOPR(ours) |

Fig. 4. Results on Place365 [3]

| Masked | CA | PIC | EC | RFR | MOPR(ours) |

Fig. 5. Results on CelebA [21]

| Masked | PIC | EC | FE | RFR | MOPR(ours) |

Fig. 6. Results on Paris StreetView [5]

Table 1. Quantitative results over three standard datasets with six models: Contextual Attention(CA) [12], Globally and Locally Consistent Image Completion(GLCIC) [17], Pluralistic Image Completion(PIC) [6], EdgeConnect(EC) [14], Recurrent Feature Reasoning(RFR) [13], MOPR-GAN(Ours). The best result of each group is bolded. *Higher is better. †Lower is better.

Dataset		Place365			CelebA			Paris Street View		
Mask ratio		10%-20%	30%-40%	50%-60%	10%-20%	30%-40%	50%-60%	10%-20%	30%-40%	50%-60%
SSIM*	CA	0.893	0.739	0.502	0.888	0.750	0.614	0.905	0.766	0.625
	GLCIC	0.862	0.686	0.535	0.865	0.689	0.560	0.878	0.724	0.588
	PIC	0.932	0.786	0.494	0.965	0.881	0.672	0.930	0.785	0.519
	EC	0.933	0.802	0.553	0.975	0.915	0.759	0.950	0.849	0.646
	RFR	0.939	0.819	0.596	0.981	0.934	0.819	0.954	0.862	0.681
	MOPR(Ours)	**0.941**	**0.825**	**0.744**	**0.988**	**0.942**	**0.862**	**0.966**	**0.901**	**0.732**
PSNR*	CA	24.36	19.13	16.56	25.32	19.94	17.18	26.09	20.74	18.17
	GLCIC	23.49	18.50	16.06	24.09	18.50	16.24	25.72	21.02	18.71
	PIC	27.14	21.72	17.17	30.67	24.74	19.29	29.35	23.97	19.52
	EC	27.17	22.18	18.35	32.48	26.62	21.49	31.19	26.04	21.89
	RFR	27.75	22.63	18.92	33.56	**27.76**	22.88	**31.71**	26.44	22.40
	MOPR(Ours)	**29.15**	**24.60**	**20.77**	**34.81**	27.75	**24.79**	31.54	**26.67**	**23.44**
Mean $l1$†	CA	0.0241	0.0615	0.0991	0.0248	0.0564	0.0921	0.0210	0.0553	0.0906
	GLCIC	0.0266	0.0678	0.1096	0.0253	0.0695	0.1121	0.0220	0.0558	0.0902
	PIC	0.0161	0.0441	0.0944	0.0111	0.0314	0.0749	0.0140	0.0379	0.0799
	EC	0.0157	0.0408	0.0821	0.0088	0.0247	0.0572	0.0110	0.0286	0.0582
	RFR	0.0142	0.0381	0.0761	**0.0075**	0.0212	0.0470	**0.0110**	0.0275	0.0546
	MOPR(Ours)	**0.0129**	**0.0359**	**0.0736**	0.0082	**0.0150**	**0.0383**	0.0113	**0.0269**	**0.0503**

4.2   Quantitative Comparisons

We also performed quantitative comparisons from three aspects: 1) structural similarity index (SSIM), 2) peak signal-to-noise ratio (PSNR), and 3) mean $l1$ loss, to evaluate our model and compare the results with other methods. Table 1 lists the results of the six methods for different irregular mask ratios for the three standard datasets. It can be observed from the table that our method shows superior results under different irregular mask ratios on the Places2, CelebA, and Paris StreetView datasets in most cases, particularly for large holes. The data of CA [12] and RFR [13] in the table were obtained from their papers, and the remaining data were obtained using the pre-model provided by their author.

4.3   Ablation Studies

The preceding content illustrates the effectiveness of the overall architecture of our model. In this section, we present a verification of the validity of our proposed contributions. Here, we describe the proposed IOM and GAA.

Masked Image   Without IOM   With IOM

Fig. 7. Qualitative comparison of the two methods on the Paris Streetview dataset: 1)without IOM, 2)with IOM.

Table 2. Quantitative comparison of the two methods on the Paris Streetview dataset with different irregular mask ratios: 1)without IOM, 2)with IOM.

Dataset	Without IOM		With IOM	
Mask ratio	20%–30%	40%–50%	20%–30%	40%–50%
SSIM	0.910	0.799	0.917	0.839
PNSR	28.14	23.80	28.30	24.72
Mean l1	0.0254	0.0375	0.0246	0.0332

Capabilities of the IOM. To demonstrate the function of the IOM, we compared the network repair effects of using and deprecating this module. It can be observed from Fig. 7 that it is lacking in details, although an almost complete image can be repaired without the IOM. The addition of the IOM can significantly improve the local performance of the image. From the perspective of a quantitative comparison, as shown in Table 2, we tested two cases with different sizes of irregular masks, and identified that IOM can improve the network performance significantly. Furthermore, the missing area is larger, the more pronounced the effect.

(1)   (2)   (3)   (4)

Fig. 8. The comparison results with different attention. (1) Masked Image; (2) Traditional Attention; (3) Existing Progressive Attention; (4)GAA(ours)

Capabilities of the GAA. As mentioned in Sect. 2.3, our GAA module is a progressive attention mechanism with equal emphasis on the structure and texture. We compared it with other existing attention mechanisms, and the results are shown in Fig. 8. From this, we can determine that the progressive accumulation of the attention mechanism is more suitable with global consistency, which can make it more deceiving to the eye, particularly for large holes. Further, allowing the structure to constrain the details (shown in Eq. 5) can effectively prevent local artifacts and generate a more realistic image.

5 Conclusion

In this paper, we built a new GAN-based image inpainting framework (MOPR-GAN), which first repairs the missing areas from the outside to the inside step by step, and then, uses the proposed IOM to correct the details of the generated pre-repair images to obtain more accurate results. Moreover, we proposed a GAA module that acts on the entire network. Through qualitative and quantitative analyses on three standard datasets, plus several ablation experiments, the superiority of our network was proved.

References

1. Maas, A.L., Hannun, A.Y., Ng, A.Y.: Rectifier nonlinearities improve neural network acoustic models. In: Proceedings of ICML, vol. 30 (2013)
2. Antonio Criminisi, P.P., Toyama, K.: Region filling and object removal by exempeler based image inpainting. IEEE TIP **13**(9), 1200–1212 (2004)
3. Bolei Zhou, Agata Lapedriza, A.K.A.O., Torralba, A.: Places: a 10 million image database for scene recognition. IEEE TPAMI **40**(6), 1452–1464 (2018)
4. C. Ballester, M. Bertalmio, V.C.G.S., erdera, J.V.: Filling-in by joint interpolation of vector fields and gray levels. IEEE TIP **10**(8), 1200–1211 (2001)
5. Doersch, C., Singh, S., Gupta, A., Sivic, J., Efros, A.: What makes Paris look like Paris? ACM TOG **31**(4) (2012)
6. Zheng, C., Cham, T.J., Cai, J.: Pluralistic image completion. In: Proceedings of CVPR, pp. 1438–1447 (2019)
7. Pathak, D., Krahenbuhl, P., Donahue, J., Darrell, T., Efros, A.A.: Context encoders: feature learning by inpainting. In: Proceedings of CVPR, pp. 2536–2544 (2016)
8. Liu, H., Jiang, B., Song, Y., Huang, W., Yang, C.: Rethinking image inpainting via a mutual encoder-decoder with feature equalizations. In: Vedaldi, A., Bischof, H., Brox, T., Frahm, J.-M. (eds.) ECCV 2020. LNCS, vol. 12347, pp. 725–741. Springer, Cham (2020). https://doi.org/10.1007/978-3-030-58536-5_43
9. Goodfellow, I., et al.: Generative adversarial nets. In: Proceedings of NIPS, vol. 27, pp. 2672–2680 (2014)
10. Huang, J.B., Kang, S.B., Ahuja, N., Kopf, J.: Image completion using planar structure guidance. ACM TOG **33**(4), 1–10 (2014)
11. Johnson, J., Alahi, A., Fei-Fei, L.: Perceptual losses for real-time style transfer and super-resolution. In: Leibe, B., Matas, J., Sebe, N., Welling, M. (eds.) ECCV 2016. LNCS, vol. 9906, pp. 694–711. Springer, Cham (2016). https://doi.org/10.1007/978-3-319-46475-6_43
12. Yu, J., Lin, Z., Yang, J., Shen, X., Lu, X., Huang, T.S.: Generative image inpainting with contextual attention. In: Proceedings of CVPR (2018)

13. Li, J., Wang, N., Zhang, L., Du, B., Tao, D.: Recurrent feature reasoning for image inpainting. In: Proceedings of CVPR, pp. 7760–7768 (2020)
14. Nazeri, K., Ng, E., Joseph, T., Qureshi, F.Z., Ebrahimi, M.: Edgeconnect: generative image inpainting with adversarial edge learning. In: Proceedings of ICCV (2019)
15. Peng, J., Liu, D., Xu, S., Li, H.: Generating diverse structure for image inpainting with hierarchical VQ-VAE. In: Proceedings of CVPR (2021)
16. Song, L., Cao, J., Song, L., Hu, Y., He, R.: Geometry-aware face completion and editing. CoRR (2008)
17. Iizuka, S., Simo-Serra, E., Ishikawa, H.: Globally and locally consistent image completion. ACM TOG 36(4), 1–14 (2017)
18. Min-cheol, S., Shin, Y.-G., Kim, S.-Wk., Park, S., Ko, S.-J.: Pepsi: fast image inpainting with parallel decoding network. In: Proceedings of CVPR, pp. 11360–11368 (2019)
19. Yu, F., Koltun, V.: Multi-scale context aggregation by dilated convolutions. In: Proceedings of ICLR, pp. 23–32 (2016)
20. Xiong, W., et al.: Foreground-aware image inpainting. In: Proceedings of CVPR (2019)
21. Liu, Z., Luo, P., Wang, X., Tang, X.: Deep learning face attributes in the wild. In: Proceedings of ICCV, pp. 3730–3738 (2015)
22. Wan, Z., et al.: Bringing old photos back to life. In: Proceedings of CVPR, pp. 2747–2757 (2020)

A Unified View on Self-Organizing Maps (SOMs) and Stochastic Neighbor Embedding (SNE)

Thibaut Kulak[✉], Anthony Fillion, and François Blayo

NeoInstinct S.A., Rue Traversière 3, 1018 Lausanne, Switzerland
`thibaut.kulak@neoinstinct.com`

Abstract. We propose a unified view on two widely used data visualization techniques: Self-Organizing Maps (SOMs) and Stochastic Neighbor Embedding (SNE). We show that they can both be derived from a common mathematical framework. Leveraging this formulation, we propose to compare SOM and SNE quantitatively on two datasets, and discuss possible avenues for future work to take advantage of both approaches.

Keywords: Data visualization · Stochastic Neighbor Embedding · Self-Organizing Map · Auto organization · Representation learning

1 Introduction

Self-organizing Maps (SOMs) [5] have been widely used over the last decades on diverse applications [11], and have emerged as a very efficient biologically-inspired method for learning organized representations of data. More recently, the Stochastic Neighbor Embedding (SNE) algorithm [4] has been proposed to visualize a set of datapoints in a two-dimensional space, hence creating a map. This algorithm, and notably its extension t-distributed Stochastic Neighbor Embedding (t-SNE) [6] has become very popular for visualizing large datasets. The goal of this work is to propose a unified view over those two algorithms.

We will show that both SOM and SNE algorithms can be seen in the context of a general mathematical formulation that attempts to find points in a 2D space associated to weights in an observation space, where the weights represent the data, and where neighborhood relations in the 2D space and the observation space are respected (points that are close in the map should be close in the observation space, and vice versa). In the context of this optimization problem, we will see that SOM's algorithm fixes the points in the 2D space, and then optimizes the weights of the neurons, while SNE fixes the weights of the neurons, and optimizes the positions of the points in the 2D space.

Such a unified view of those algorithms brings several contributions: for SOMs, this sheds light on what is actually minimized and on how we might be able to assess the quality of a map both in terms of organization and representation, which remains so far non-trivial [1,2]. For SNE, we propose a formulation that showcases the fact that SNE is not only a visualization technique

© The Author(s), under exclusive license to Springer Nature Switzerland AG 2022
E. Pimenidis et al. (Eds.): ICANN 2022, LNCS 13530, pp. 458–468, 2022.
https://doi.org/10.1007/978-3-031-15931-2_38

but is also learning a representation of the data. Moreover, the number of neuron weights can be different from the number of datapoints in our formulation, which goes beyond the standard SNE approach that assumes one neuron per datapoint. Most importantly, as we will discuss later, we hope that bridging those algorithms will open the way to future works leveraging their respective advantages.

Our paper is organized as follows: first, we introduce the mathematical framework, and show that the SOM and SNE algorithms can be derived from it. Then, we exploit the fact that both algorithms pursue a very similar objective to compare their results quantitatively on two different datasets. Finally, we conclude and discuss interesting avenues for future work leveraging our unified formulation.

1.1   Notations and Definitions

We assume there are N points $\{z_i\}_{i=1}^{N}$ in a 2D space (visualization space), corresponding to N weights (neuron weights) $\{w_i\}_{i=1}^{N}$ in a d-dimensional space (observation space). We introduce two conditional distributions $p(i|x)$ and $q(i|x)$ defined for a datapoint (stimulus) x. Those distributions are defined over the discrete set $[\![1; N]\!]$:

$$p(i|x) = \frac{\exp\left(-\frac{||x-w_i||^2}{\sigma^2}\right)}{\sum_{j=1}^{N} \exp\left(-\frac{||x-w_j||^2}{\sigma^2}\right)} \quad \text{and} \quad q(i|x) = \frac{\exp\left(-||z_i - z_{i^*(x)}||^2\right)}{\sum_{j=1}^{N} \exp\left(-||z_j - z_{i^*(x)}||^2\right)},$$

$$\tag{1}$$

where σ is an hyperparameter[1], and $i^*(x) = \arg\max_{i=1}^{N} p(i|x)$ is the index of the winning neuron (the neuron that responds the most to the stimulus x).

We can interpret those conditional distributions qualitatively:

- $p(i|x)$ increases with the proximity of the weights to the stimulus **in the observation space**, i.e., which neurons respond to the stimulus.
- $q(i|x)$ increases with the proximity of the points to the stimulus **in the 2D (visualization) space**

To give further intuition on those conditional distributions, we show in Fig. 1 those distributions for two different maps, one organized map that was obtained using SOM's algorithm and one non-organized map (that was obtained by randomly permuting the indices of the neurons weights of the organized map). We can see that when the map is organized $p(i|x)$ and $q(i|x)$ are close to each other, which is not the case for the non-organized map. More precisely, if we look at $p(i|x)$ and $q(i|x)$ in the visualization space, $q(i|x)$ looks like a Gaussian distribution no matter if the map is organized or not, but $p(i|x)$ looks like a Gaussian

---

[1] Note that $p(i|x)$ has been obtained from Bayes rule by choosing $p(x|i) = \mathcal{N}(w_i, \sigma^2)$ and a uniform prior over the discrete space $p(i) = 1/N$, so σ is actually the chosen standard deviation of $p(x|i)$. Such model also defines a probability distribution on the observation space $p(x) = \sum_{i=1}^{N} p(x|i)p(i) = 1/N \sum_{i=1}^{N} p(x|i)$.

only if the map is organized, which indeed means that points around the winning neuron also respond to the stimulus. Similarly, if we look at $p(i|x)$ and $q(i|x)$ in the observation space, $p(i|x)$ looks like a Gaussian distribution no matter if the map is organized or not, but $q(i|x)$ looks like a Gaussian only if the map is organized, which indeed means that the points that respond to the stimulus are those that are close in the visualization space. We will see in the next sections that both SOMs and SNE methods attempt to make these distributions close to each other, while representing the data.

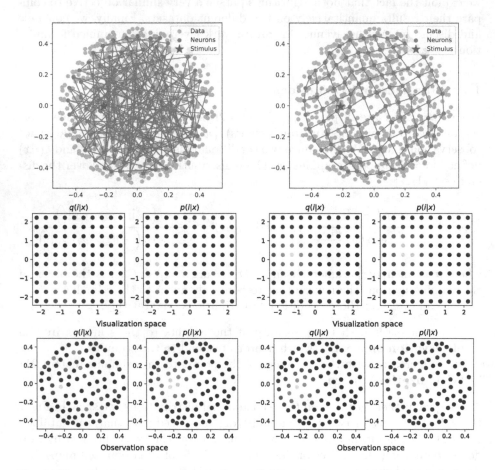

Fig. 1. Visualization of an unorganized map (left) and an organized map (right), along with the conditional distributions $p(i|x)$ and $q(i|x)$, both in visualization space (points $\{z_i\}$ colored by the probabilities, middle row) and observation space (weights $\{w_i\}$ colored by the probabilities, bottom row). Purple color corresponds to low probabilities and yellow to high probabilities (Color figure online)

1.2   SOMs in This Framework

Let us assume that stimulus x's are samples from an unknown density $p^{\text{data}}(x)$. We propose the following objective function, that is a trade-off between organization (in the sense of making $p(i|x)$ and $q(i|x)$ close) and representation (maximizing $p(x)$):

$$J^{\text{SOM}}\left(\{z_i\}_{i=1}^N, \{w_i\}_{i=1}^N\right) = \int_x \left(\mathcal{D}_{KL}(q(i|x), p(i|x)) - \ln p(x)\right) p^{\text{data}}(x)\, dx \quad (2)$$

The standard SOM algorithm (non-batch version) is a stochastic algorithm that updates the neuron weights as a stimulus x is presented. For a stimulus x coming from $p^{\text{data}}(x)$, we can get the objective function for this stimulus x by removing the integral over the unknown density function $p^{\text{data}}(x)$ (stochastic gradient descent):

$$J^{\text{SOM}}\left(\{z_i\}_{i=1}^N, \{w_i\}_{i=1}^N \mid x\right) = \mathcal{D}_{KL}(q(i|x), p(i|x)) - \ln p(x) \quad (3)$$

Differentiating with respect to the neuron weights and negating gives us the following update rule of the neuron weights:

$$-\frac{\partial J^{\text{SOM}}\left(\{z_i\}_{i=1}^N, \{w_i\}_{i=1}^N \mid x\right)}{\partial w_i} = \frac{2}{\sigma^2}(x - w_i)q(i|x) \quad (4)$$

We can see that this is exactly the update rule of SOM's algorithm, where neuron weights get moved towards the stimulus x if they are in the neighborhood of the winning neuron.

In SOM's algorithm, there is typically a neighborhood parameter that is monotically decreasing. In our framework we did not put a neighborhood parameter on $q(i|x)$, because we can alternatively see it[2] as a scaling of the points $\{z_i\}_{i=1}^N$ typically chosen on a grid. Choosing a monotically decreasing neighborhood parameter is equivalent to scaling monotically the points $\{z_i\}_{i=1}^N$ from a small to a big grid with fixed neighborhood parameter.

In our view, the SOM algorithm is performing an optimization over a set of points in a 2D space and their corresponding weights, and is supposing a particular time-dependent form for the points locations in the 2D space (from a small to a big grid). Viewing it this way will make it easier to compare with SNE in the next section, which does not use any neighborhood parameter in the visualization space.

1.3   SNE in This Framework

In this section, we will show that the SNE algorithm can be derived from our framework, hence show that both SOMs and SNE algorithms are solving the same mathematical problem, and exhibit their differences.

---

[2] Trivially: $\frac{||z_i - z_{i*}(x)||^2}{\sigma_z^2} = ||\frac{z_i}{\sigma_z} - \frac{z_{i*}(x)}{\sigma_z}||^2$.

Let us define for a stimulus x the following objective function:

$$J^{\text{SNE}}\left(\{z_i\}_{i=1}^N, \{w_i\}_{i=1}^N \mid x\right) = \mathcal{D}_{KL}(p(i|x), q(i|x)) - \ln p(x) \qquad (5)$$

This objective is very similar to Eq. 3, the only difference is the use of the forward KL divergence instead of the reverse KL divergence. Given that the KL divergence is not symmetric, Eq. 3 and Eq. 5 differ only by the way they measure the difference between $p(i|x)$ and $q(i|x)$.

Differentiating with respect to the 2D points locations gives us the following update rule of the points:

$$-\frac{\partial J^{\text{SNE}}\left(\{z_i\}_{i=1}^N, \{w_i\}_{i=1}^N \mid x\right)}{\partial z_i} = 2(z_{i^*(x)} - z_i)(q(i|x) - p(i|x)) \qquad (6)$$

This update rule is very similar from the SNE algorithm and can be interpreted as such: if a neuron weight w_i is far from the stimulus x (i.e., $p(i|x)$ small), but is close to the winning neuron in the 2D visualization space (i.e., $q(i|x)$ big) then the point is moved towards the location of the winning neuron in the 2D space. Reversely, if a neuron weight w_i is close from the stimulus x (i.e., $p(i|x)$ big), but is far from the winning neuron in the 2D visualization space (i.e., $q(i|x)$ small) then the point is moved away from the location of the winning neuron in the 2D space.

We have presented here the update rule equations for any set of neuron weights. In the standard SNE algorithm, usually the neuron weights are equal to the datapoints, because the number of neurons chosen is equal to the number of datapoints to visualize. In that case, a stimulus x is therefore a weight w_j, and trivially $i^*(x) = j$, which gives us the usual SNE formulation.[3]

It is important to note that Eq. 5 differs from the standard SNE objective function by the addition of a representation term $-\ln p(x)$, which only depends on the neuron weights $\{w_i\}_{i=1}^N$ and not on the 2D points, which is why we recover the same update rule as SNE. If, similarly to our interpretation of SOM's algorithm, we interpret SNE as an optimization over both the neuron weights and the 2D points, this term makes a lot of sense because the first step in SNE consists in choosing as many neurons as the number of datapoints and putting a Gaussian $p(x|i)$ around it. This can be seen as a kernel density estimation method, and hence as a minimization of $-\ln p(x)$

We have shown that SOMs and SNE are two dual algorithms sharing the same global objective function over the neuron weights and 2D points, the main difference being in the way they approach this optimization. SOMs fix the 2D points (typically, on a grid) and optimize the neuron weights, while SNE fixes the neuron weights (typically one for each datapoint) and optimizes the 2D points locations. We outline their differences in Table 1.

---

[3] In practice, the SNE formulation is slightly different because it is done in batch mode (using all datapoints x for each update), the conditional distributions $p(i|w_j)$ and $q(i|w_j)$ are set to zero for $i = j$, and a different σ_i is used for each stimulus $x = w_i$ to account for different local variations in the data.

Table 1. Main differences between SOM and SNE

	SOM	SNE
Objective	Reverse KL + Data fitting $\mathcal{D}_{KL}(q(i|x), p(i|x)) - \ln p(x)$	Forward KL + Data fitting $\mathcal{D}_{KL}(p(i|x), q(i|x)) - \ln p(x)$
Given	2D points $\{z_i\}_{i=1}^N$ are given (typically on a grid)	Neuron weights $\{w_i\}_{i=1}^N$ are given (typically one for each datapoint)
Optimized	Neuron weights $\{w_i\}_{i=1}^N$ are learned (with stochastic gradient descent)	2D points $\{z_i\}_{i=1}^N$ are learned (with gradient descent)

2 Quantitative Comparisons

We have shown previously that the SOM and SNE algorithms pursue a very similar objective: making the conditional distribution of the neurons response to a stimulus $p(i|x)$ and the neighborhood of the winning neuron $q(i|x)$ close to each other, and fitting the data. Such unified view permits to compare quantitatively the quality of maps learned with SOM and SNE, and shed light on their performances. This section is organized as follows: first, we detail in more details our approach for comparing those techniques. Then we compare them on a toy two-dimensional dataset. Finally, we compare them on a more realistic real-world dataset, the Fashion-MNIST dataset.

2.1 Comparison Approach

The objectives J^{SOM} and J^{SNE} we have introduced in previous section depend on the hyperparameter σ governing what it means to be close in the observation space, and on the scaling of the 2D points governing what it means to be close in the visualization space. We propose to take inspiration from [12] and [3] to choose those parameters in a meaningful way. The entropies in bits of the conditional distributions $p(i|x)$ and $q(i|x)$ are continuous approximations of the number of neighbors of the stimulus x (a.k.a. perplexities [6]), respectively in the observation and the visualization spaces. The method proposed in [12] for comparing the organization of maps was to look at k neighbors in the observation space, and look if they are indeed the k neighbors in the visualization space, and vice versa, for a varying number of neighbors k. We propose to take a similar approach and, for a stimulus x and a given perplexity Perp (continuous number of neighbors), choose σ so that $2^{H(p(i|x))} = $ Perp, and scale the points $\{z_i\}_{i=1}^N$ so that $2^{H(q(i|x))} = $ Perp. We will monitor J^{SOM} and J^{SNE} for different perplexities averaged over the datasets, to assess the quality of the map at different scales. Such approach is therefore a continuous equivalent of the topographic function introduced in [12] for assessing the quality of a map organization, but quantifies the data representation at the same time because the objectives we proposed contain not only an organization term but also a data fitting term.

In all experiments, we have used an exponential decay for the neighborhood parameter (inverse of the scaling parameter) and the learning rate[4] for the SOM algorithm as suggested in [9]. For SNE, we used the open-source implementation of t-SNE [8] with a number of degrees of freedom equal to 10000 (hence, considering a Gaussian distribution instead of a t-distribution, as in SNE) and the other default hyperparameters.

2.2   Toy 2D Datasets

We compare here quantitatively the SOM and SNE algorithms on a toy two-dimensional dataset of 1000 points: the **moons** dataset. A visualization of the maps learned (in visualization and observation space) is shown in Fig. 2. A grid of 10×10 was used in these experiments[5], for a fair comparison between SOM and SNE we did use also 100 neurons for SNE (and not one neuron per datapoint), those neuron weights have been learned using kMeans [7] with 100 clusters.

We can see in Fig. 3 that SNE clearly outperforms SOM for both objectives and all perplexities. We believe that this sheds light on the fact that assuming the points to lie on a grid is a very strong assumption of SOM's algorithm that drastically limits its performance capabilities in terms of the objectives defined above.

2.3   Fashion-MNIST Dataset

We propose here to compare quantitatively the SOM and SNE algorithms on a more realistic dataset: a subset of 10k images taken randomly from the Fashion-MNIST dataset [13]. We believe that SOM's assumption of the points lying on a grid might be less restrictive when using a very large number of neurons, which would be coherent with [10] arguing that large maps must be used for an interesting representation to emerge. We learn a 100×100 SOM[6] on the Fashion-MNIST dataset, and as we chose 10k images from the original dataset we can use standard SNE with 10k neurons (one for each datapoint), and hence propose a clear and fair comparison between standard SOM and standard SNE with the same number of neurons.

We can see qualitatively that our maps have been learned properly for both methods in Fig. 4, as they have grouped similar images into clusters (note that the labels used for coloring the points have not been used for training, but merely for this qualitative visualization). It is interesting to observe that the maps learned with SOM and SNE share similarities. The yellow and light green clusters are adjacent and well separated, and are also close to the two darker green clusters, that are more interrelated. (see left part of the maps in Fig. 4). Except for the purple cluster that is clearly separated in both maps, the other clusters on the right hand sides of the maps learned seem very interrelated in

---

[4] $\sigma(t) = \sigma_i \left(\frac{\sigma_f}{\sigma_i}\right)^{t/t_{\max}}$ and $\lambda(t) = \lambda_i \left(\frac{\lambda_f}{\lambda_i}\right)^{t/t_{\max}}$.

[5] We chose $\sigma_f = 10^{-10}$, $\sigma_i = 100$, $\lambda_f = 10^{-10}$, $\lambda_i = 1$ and $t_{\max} = 100000$.

[6] We chose $\sigma_f = 10^{-3}$, $\sigma_i = 10$, $\lambda_f = 10^{-3}$, $\lambda_i = 1$ and $t_{\max} = 120000$.

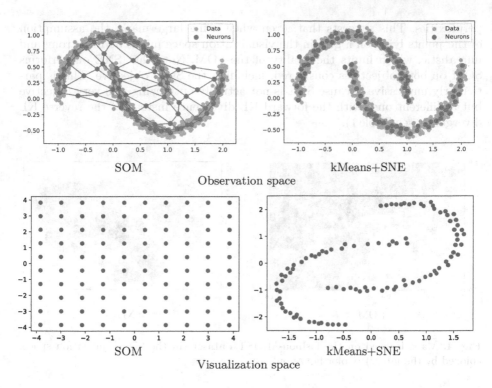

Fig. 2. Maps learned on the **moons** dataset for the SOM and kMeans+SNE algorithms

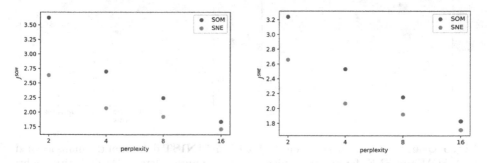

Fig. 3. Quantitative comparisons on the **moons** dataset of the maps learned with SOM and SNE, for the two objectives we proposed (left: SOM objective, right: SNE objective)

both SOM and SNE maps. Such a qualitative evaluation shows that both maps are coherent with each other, which also supports our view that both approaches optimize a similar objective function.

We show the quantitative comparison in Fig. 5, where we can see that the SNE algorithm outperforms the SOM algorithm for both objectives for all perplexities. This suggests that, even when using large maps, the assumption of the points lying on a grid in the visualization space might be too strong and unrealistic, which limits the quality of the SOM. Note that SNE outperforms SOM on both objectives considered, including the SOM objective. This is particularly impressive because SNE is not actually optimizing this very objective but a different one (with the forward KL divergence instead of the reverse KL divergence, see Table 1).

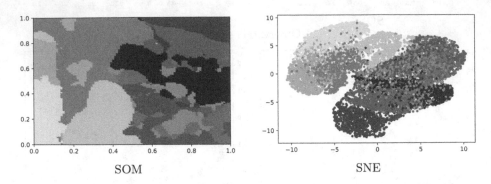

SOM   SNE

Fig. 4. Maps learned on the fashion-MNIST dataset (in the 2D visualization space, colored by the labels) (Color figure online)

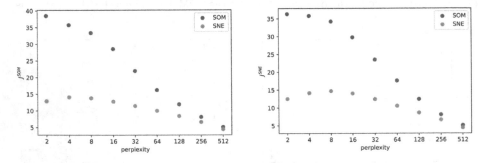

Fig. 5. Quantitative comparisons on the **Fashion-MNIST** dataset of the maps learned with SOM and SNE, for the two objectives we proposed (left: SOM objective, right: SNE objective)

3   Conclusion

In this work, we have proposed a unified view on the two widely used algorithms: Self-Organizing Maps (SOMs) and Stochastic Neighbor Embedding (SNE). We have shown that both approaches can be seen as the minimization of a very similar objective function attempting to organize the map and fit the data, the main difference being that the SOM algorithm fixes the 2D points (typically on a grid) and learns the neuron weights, while SNE fixes the neuron weights (typically, one for datapoint) and learns the 2D points. They can therefore be seen as dual algorithms, and can be compared quantitatively.

We proposed to compare them quantitatively on two datasets: a toy 2D dataset and the more realistic Fashion-MNIST dataset. In both experiments, we have observed that SNE significantly outperforms SOM for both objectives considered. We believe this is due to the SOM assumption that the 2D points are on a grid, which is very strong assumption that limits the quality of the map organization.

Most importantly, we hope that our work will inspire methods to combine the advantages of both approaches. SOMs are bio-inspired, have a fixed number of neurons, but are not biologically plausible due to the infinite neighborhood in the beginning. SNE, in its standard form, has as many neurons as the number of data points, which is not biologically plausible and might pose some problems in terms of complexity if it were to be applied online on infinitely growing datasets, but the perplexity is fixed throughout learning and no neighborhood parameter is required, which alleviates one of the fundamental drawbacks of SOM's algorithm: the need to tune and decay the neighborhood parameter carefully. Also, as we proposed in some of the experiments, our formulation of the SNE algorithm can be applied on a fixed number of neurons whose weights have been learned previously (e.g., using the kMeans algorithm).

Methods jointly learning both the positions in 2D and the neuron weights could definitely be worth considering, and open an interesting avenue for future work.

References

1. Bauer, H.U., Pawelzik, K.R.: Quantifying the neighborhood preservation of self-organizing feature maps. IEEE Trans. Neural Networks 3(4), 570–579 (1992)
2. De Bodt, E., Cottrell, M., Verleysen, M.: Statistical tools to assess the reliability of self-organizing maps. Neural Netw. 15(8–9), 967–978 (2002)
3. Demartines, P., Hérault, J.: Curvilinear component analysis: a self-organizing neural network for nonlinear mapping of data sets. IEEE Trans. Neural Networks 8(1), 148–154 (1997)
4. Hinton, G.E., Roweis, S.: Stochastic neighbor embedding. In: Advances in Neural Information Processing Systems, vol. 15 (2002)
5. Kohonen, T.: The self-organizing map. Proc. IEEE 78(9), 1464–1480 (1990)
6. Van der Maaten, L., Hinton, G.: Visualizing data using t-SNE. J. Mach. Learn. Res. 9(11), 2579–2605 (2008)
7. Pedregosa, F., et al.: Scikit-learn: machine learning in python. J. Mach. Learn. Res. 12, 2825–2830 (2011)
8. Poličar, P.G., Stražar, M., Zupan, B.: Opentsne: a modular python library for t-SNE dimensionality reduction and embedding. bioRxiv (2019)
9. Rougier, N., Boniface, Y.: Dynamic self-organising map. Neurocomputing 74(11), 1840–1847 (2011)
10. Ultsch, A., Mörchen, F.: Esom-maps: tools for clustering, visualization, and classification with emergent som. Technical Report No. 46, Department of Mathematics and Computer Science, University of Marburg, Germany (2005)

11. Van Hulle, M.M.: Self-organizing maps. Handbook of Natural Computing, pp. 585–622 (2012)
12. Villmann, T., Der, R., Herrmann, M., Martinetz, T.M.: Topology preservation in self-organizing feature maps: exact definition and measurement. IEEE Trans. Neural Networks $8(2)$, 256–266 (1997)
13. Xiao, H., Rasul, K., Vollgraf, R.: Fashion-mnist: a novel image dataset for benchmarking machine learning algorithms. arXiv (2017)

Decoupled Representation Network for Skeleton-Based Hand Gesture Recognition

Zhaochao Zhong[1], Yangke Li[2(✉)], and Jifang Yang[3]

[1] Xuzhou Xinzhi Science and Technology Co., Ltd., Xuzhou, China
[2] Xi'an Jiaotong University, Xi'an, China
liyangke@stu.xjtu.edu.cn
[3] Nanjing LES Information Technology Co., Ltd., Nanjing, China

Abstract. Skeleton-based dynamic hand gesture recognition plays an increasing role in the human-computer interaction field. It is well known that different skeleton representations will have a greater impact on the recognition results, but most methods only use the original skeleton data as input, which hinders the improvement of accuracy to a certain extent. In this paper, we propose a novel decoupled representation network (DR-Net) for skeleton-based dynamic hand gesture recognition, which consists of temporal perception branch and spatial perception branch. For the former, it uses the temporal representation encoder to extract short-term motion features and long-term motion features, which can effectively reflect contextual information of skeleton sequences. Besides, we also design the temporal fusion module (TFM) to capture multi-scale temporal features. For the latter, we use the spatial representation encoder to extract spatial low-frequency features and spatial high-frequency features. Besides, we also design the spatial fusion module (SFM) to enhance important spatial features. Experimental results and ablation studies on two benchmark datasets demonstrate that our proposed DR-Net is competitive with the state-of-the-art methods.

Keywords: Dynamic hand gesture recognition · Skeleton representation · Feature fusion

1 Introduction

In recent years, the human-computer interaction field has owned increasing diverse interaction methods, including speech recognition [16], hand gesture recognition [3] and touch recognition [20]. Hand gesture, as the second mainstream human communication method, provides solutions for interactive environments that use non-touch interfaces. Currently, it has been applied in many application fields, such as virtual reality systems [6], somatosensory games [22], sign language communication [25], and so on. Meanwhile, the increasing demand for intuitive interaction promotes research on hand gesture recognition.

© The Author(s), under exclusive license to Springer Nature Switzerland AG 2022
E. Pimenidis et al. (Eds.): ICANN 2022, LNCS 13530, pp. 469–480, 2022.
https://doi.org/10.1007/978-3-031-15931-2_39

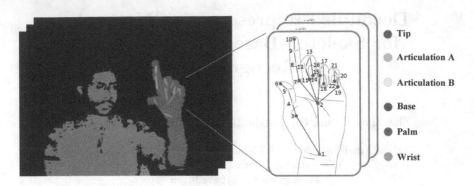

Fig. 1. Captured depth images and hand skeleton images. Each hand skeleton consists of 22 joints, including: one joint for the center of the palm, one joint for the position of the wrist and four joints for each finger.

At present, the related research on hand gesture recognition can be divided into two categories: static hand gesture recognition and dynamic hand gesture recognition. The former is mainly to recognize hand gestures from a single image, while the latter has more extensive application value, which is mainly to understand the information conveyed by hand gesture sequences. In recent years, low-cost depth sensors can capture the hand pose with reasonably good quality and provide the precise 3D hand skeleton. As shown in Fig. 1, we present the depth images and hand skeleton images captured by Intel RealSense. Compared to original RGB images, hand skeleton data can provide more intuitive information, and it is more robust to varying lighting conditions and occlusions. Therefore, skeleton-based dynamic hand gesture recognition has gradually become a current research hotspot.

The hand is an object with complex topology and has no fixed variation period, which makes skeleton-based dynamic hand gesture recognition still a challenging topic. Original skeleton data can not effectively reflect temporal motion features and spatial structure features. Meanwhile, most methods do not make full use of multi-scale features to provide the discriminative basis for hand gesture recognition. To solve these problems, we propose a novel DR-Net to realize dynamic hand gesture recognition. On the one hand, it uses the temporal representation encoder to obtain short-term motion features and long-term motion features, which have lower intra-class variance and higher inter-class variance. Meanwhile, it also introduces the TFM to perceive multi-scale temporal features, which can effectively reduce time dependency. On the other hand, it uses the spatial representation encoder to obtain low-frequency spatial features and high-frequency spatial features, which reduces the impact of location-viewpoint variation on the recognition result. Besides, it uses the SFM to enhance important spatial features. The DR-Net uses the cross-entropy loss function as the loss term, which effectively improves the recognition results.

In summary, our main contributions are summarized as follows:

- We propose a temporal representation encoder and a spatial representation encoder to enrich original skeleton data, which makes DR-Net use short-term motion features, long-term motion features, low-frequency spatial features, and high-frequency spatial features as input sources.
- We design an efficient feature fusion module for DR-Net in the temporal and spatial domains, respectively. Specifically, our proposed TFM can effectively capture multi-scale temporal features, while SFM can effectively enhance important spatial features.
- We conduct comprehensive experiments on two public benchmark datasets to verify the effectiveness of our method. Related experimental results demonstrate that DR-Net is competitive with the state-of-the-art methods.

2   Related Works

2.1   Skeleton Representations

Different skeleton representations can have an important impact on hand gesture recognition and human action recognition. Li et al. [17] proposed to use the Lie group to model the skeleton representation, which can effectively describe the three-dimensional geometric relationship between joints. Jiang et al. [15] proposed a spatial-temporal skeleton transformation descriptor, which describes the relative transformations of skeletons, including the rotation and translation during movement. Wei et al. [30] proposed a novel high order joint relative motion feature to describe the instantaneous status of the skeleton joint, which consists of the relative position, velocity, and acceleration. Caetano et al. [2] proposed to encode the temporal dynamics by explicitly computing the magnitude and orientation values of the skeleton joints. Liu et al. [19] proposed to use 3D hand posture evolution volume and 2D hand movement map to represent hand posture variations and hand movements, respectively.

2.2   Deep Neural Networks

In recent years, deep neural networks have been widely used in dynamic hand gesture recognition and achieved satisfactory results. Nguyen et al. [23] presented a new neural network for hand gesture recognition that learns a discriminative SPD matrix encoding the first-order and second-order statistics. Chen et al. [4] proposed a novel motion feature augmented network for hand gesture recognition. Guo et al. [10] proposed a novel spatial-based GCNs called normalized edge convolutional networks for hand gesture recognition. Nunez et al. [24] proposed a deep learning approach based on a combination of a convolutional neural network and a long short-term memory network for hand gesture recognition. Chen et al. [5] proposed a dynamic graph-based spatial-temporal attention network for skeleton-based hand gesture recognition. Hou et al. [11] proposed an end-to-end spatial-temporal attention residual temporal convolutional network for hand gesture recognition. Weng et al. [31] proposed a deformable pose traversal convolution network for dynamic hand gesture recognition.

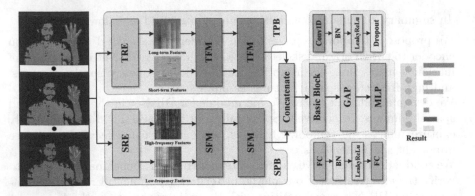

Fig. 2. The overall architecture of our proposed DR-Net. The temporal perception branch (TPB) consists of the temporal representation encoder (TRE) and the temporal fusion module (TFM). The spatial perception branch (SPB) consists of the spatial representation encoder (SRE) and the spatial fusion module (SFM).

3   Our Approach

3.1   Overview

As shown in Fig. 2, our proposed DR-Net mainly contains temporal perception branch and spatial perception branch. For the former, it uses the TRE to extract long-term motion features and short-term motion features. Besides, it uses the TFM to effectively capture and fuse multi-scale temporal features. For the latter, it uses the SRE to extract high-frequency spatial features and low-frequency spatial features. Besides, we propose the SFM to effectively enhance and fuse important spatial features. To balance the model size and recognition accuracy, the DR-Net adopts two continuous TFMs and SFMs.

3.2   Temporal Perception Branch

As we all know, dynamic hand gesture recognition not only needs to obtain the spatial information between the joints in the frame, but also needs to extract the temporal information of each joint between the frames. To solve the above problems, we propose the temporal representation encoder to process original skeleton data. In this paper, we assume the total frame number is T and the number of joints included in each frame is J. For the j-th skeleton joint of the t-th frame, in the 3D Cartesian coordinate system, it can be expressed as $S_j^t = (x_j^t, y_j^t, z_j^t)$. The set of all skeleton joints in the t-th frame of the k-th hand gesture can be expressed as: $G_k^t = \{S_1^t, S_2^t, S_3^t, \cdots, S_J^t\}$. Our proposed temporal representation encoder designs two different temporal skeleton representations as input sources. As shown in Fig. 3, short-term motion features refer to the difference between adjacent frames, while long-term motion features mean computing the difference between all other frames and the first skeleton frame.

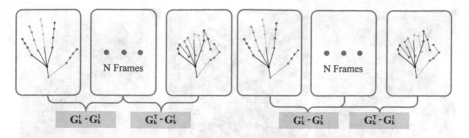

Fig. 3. Illustration of the temporal representation encoder. The left figure shows the acquisition method of short-term motion features, and the right figure shows the acquisition method of long-term motion features.

To effectively fuse short-term motion features and long-term motion features, we design the temporal fusion module, which can help DR-Net obtain multi-scale motion features. As shown in Fig. 4, the TFM has two input sources and two output sources. For two consecutive TFMs, the output of the former will be the input of the latter, and the latter will use the concatenation operation to fuse the output result. Besides, the TFM processes motion features by using different convolution kernels with different scales of receptive fields, which can tolerate a variety of temporal extents in a complex hand gesture. Specifically, we fuse short-term motion features and long-term motion features, and send them into three different branches. Their convolution kernel sizes are all 3, and the dilation rates are 1, 3, and 5, respectively. We do not use the addition method to aggregate the results of multi-scale perception, but adopt the concatenation method, which can avoid the loss of information. Finally, we use the average pooling operation to process the aggregated motion features.

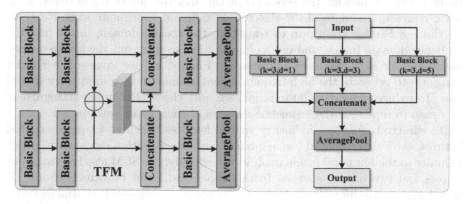

Fig. 4. The left figure shows the overall architecture of the TFM. The right figure shows the internal details of the TFM.

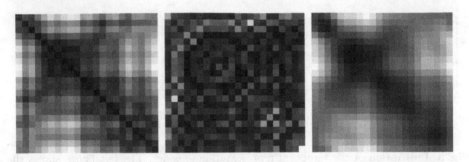

Fig. 5. Images generated by the spatial representation encoder. The left figure is the original spatial map. The middle figure is the high-frequency spatial map. The right figure is the low-frequency spatial map.

3.3   Spatial Perception Branch

To enhance the generalization ability of the model, we often need to perform extra operations such as translation, flipping, and rotation. However, the Cartesian coordinate feature is very sensitive to these data enhancement operations. Meanwhile, geometric features can fully reflect the spatial relationship of the skeleton joints. Therefore, we design an effective spatial representation encoder to extract geometric features. As shown in Fig. 5, the SRE can generate three different skeleton maps. For each skeleton frame, the original spatial map is generated by computing the Euclidean distance between any two joints, its specific calculation formula is as follows:

$$D_{i,j}^t = \sqrt{\left(x_i^t - x_j^t\right)^2 + \left(y_i^t - y_j^t\right)^2 + \left(z_i^t - z_j^t\right)^2} \tag{1}$$

where i and j represent the serial ID of the skeleton joints respectively. x, y, and z represent the data of the skeleton on different coordinate axes. Next, we use the fast Fourier transform to transform the spatial domain image into the frequency domain image, and use a circular filter to filter out the low-frequency information or high-frequency information. Finally, we use inverse fast Fourier transform to generate the high-frequency spatial map and low-frequency spatial map. To reduce redundant information, we only choose the upper triangular of each map to represent the geometric features of each hand skeleton.

To effectively fuse low-frequency spatial features and high-frequency spatial features, we design a spatial fusion module with the attention mechanism, which is similar to the temporal fusion module. Specifically, the SFM also has two input sources and two output sources. In the upper and lower branches, we use 1D convolutions with different dilation rates to perceive multi-scale spatial features, and use the concatenation operation to fuse them. In addition, we subtract the low-frequency features from the high-frequency features to obtain the significant difference features. Meanwhile, we take the difference feature as the input of the middle layer, and use the basic block and full connection layer to obtain the attention weight, so as to obtain the weighted features by multiplication.

4   Experiments

In this section, we evaluate our method on two public datasets: FPHA dataset and SHREC'17 Track dataset. Extensive ablation studies and comparative results show the effectiveness of our model.

4.1   Datasets

SHREC'17 Track Dataset. The SHREC'17 Track Dataset [27] is a public dynamic hand gesture dataset, which contains 2800 sequences. 28 participants perform each gesture between 1 and 10 times in two ways: using one finger and the whole hand. The depth images and hand skeletons are captured at 30 frames per second, with a resolution of 640×480. The length of hand gestures ranges from 20 to 50 frames. Each skeleton frame provides the coordinates of 22 hand joints in the 3D world space, which forms a full hand skeleton.

FPHA Dataset. The FPHA dataset [9] is a challenging 3D hand pose dataset, which provides first-person dynamic hand gestures interacting with 3D objects. The dataset contains 1,175 action videos corresponding to 45 different action categories and performed by 6 actors in 3 different scenarios. It provides the 3D coordinates of 21 hand joints except for the palm joint. We used the 1:1 setting with 600 sequences for training and 575 sequences for testing.

4.2   Implementation Details

We perform all our experiments on an NVIDIA GeForce GTX 2080Ti with Keras using the TensorFlow backend. The learning rate is initially set to be 0.001. If the loss remains unchanged after 25 iterations, we set it to 0.5 times the current learning rate. The minimum learning rate is set to be $1e^{-8}$. The batch size is set to be 64 and the network train 400 epochs. We employ the Adam algorithm with default parameters to optimize the network. Besides, we use median filtering operations to preprocess the original skeleton data and use linear interpolation to adjust the skeleton sequence with different lengths to 32 frames. To avoid over-fitting, we set the dropout rate to 0.5.

4.3   Ablation Study

Different Network Branches. To examine the influence of different network branches on hand gesture recognition accuracy, we conduct related ablation experiments according to different input sources. As shown in Table 1, the performance of the temporal perception branch is significantly better than that of the spatial perception branch. In addition, compared with long-term motion features, short-term motion features can provide a more discriminative recognition basis for the network. Meanwhile, we can get better recognition results by fusing SPB and TPB, which can achieve 96.31% and 93.21% recognition accuracy on 14 hand gestures and 28 hand gestures, respectively.

Table 1. Recognition accuracy (%) of our method for different network branches on the SHREC'17 Track dataset.

Network branches	14 Gestures(%)	28 Gestures(%)
TPB(short-term)	95.71	91.19
TPB(long-term)	95.48	89.88
SPB(low-frequency)	72.14	67.38
SPB(high-frequency)	71.31	65.36
TPB + SPB	**96.31**	**93.21**

Table 2. Recognition accuracy (%) of our method for different joint distances on the SHREC'17 Track dataset.

Joint distances	14 Gestures(%)	28 Gestures(%)
Correlation distance	95.48	89.52
Cosine distance	95.95	91.43
Cityblock distance	96.07	92.86
Euclidean distance	**96.31**	**93.21**

Different Joint Distances. To investigate the influence of different joint distances on recognition accuracy, we design four related ablation experiments. As shown in Table 2, using Euclidean distance as the metric can obtain the best recognition performance, which can reach 96.31% and 93.21% on 14 hand gestures and 28 hand gestures, respectively. Besides, we find that the recognition result of using Correlation distance as the metric is the worst. This is mainly because it reduces the inter-class variance to a certain extent. Besides, we find that Cityblock distance also can obtain satisfactory results, which reflects the spatial position relationship of skeleton joints.

4.4   Comparison with the State-of-the-Art

In this section, we compare our method with the state-of-the-art methods on the SHREC'17 Track dataset [27] and FPHA dataset [9]. For the former, we use 1960 sequences for training and 840 sequences for testing. As shown in Table 3, our proposed DR-Net achieves 96.31% and 93.21% recognition accuracy for 14 hand gestures and 28 hand gestures, respectively. The DR-Net adopts temporal skeleton representation and spatial skeleton representation as input sources, which effectively improves recognition results. For the latter, we quote related results of compared methods from this paper [23] to demonstrate the effectiveness of our proposed DR-Net. As shown in Table 4, our approach outperforms the state-of-the-art methods. Besides, ST-TS-HGR-NET [23] uses SVM for hand gesture recognition, which is not suitable for larger datasets. HMM+HPEV [19] uses deep neural networks to recognize hand gestures, which performs poorly on smaller datasets. The related experimental results demonstrate that our method is suitable for datasets of various sizes.

Table 3. Comparison of recognition accuracy (%) with the state-of-the-art methods on the SHREC'17 Track dataset.

Method	14 Gestures(%)	28 Gestures(%)
Key-Frame CNN [27]	82.90	71.90
SoCJ+Dir+Rot [26]	86.90	84.20
3D PAT [1]	90.50	80.50
Two-stream 3DCNN [28]	83.45	77.43
SEM-MEM+WAL [18]	90.83	85.95
Res-TCN [11]	91.10	87.30
STA-Res-TCN [11]	93.60	90.70
MFA-Net [4]	91.31	86.55
DG-STA [5]	94.40	90.70
DD-Net [33]	94.60	91.90
DeepGRU [21]	94.50	91.40
ST-GCN [32]	92.70	87.70
ST-TS-HGR-NET [23]	94.29	89.40
HMM+HPEV [19]	94.88	92.26
NC-CNN [10]	94.80	92.90
Ours	**96.31**	**93.21**

Table 4. Comparison of recognition accuracy (%) with the state-of-the-art methods on the FPHA dataset (**C**, **D**, **S** represent color images, depth images and skeleton data).

Method	C	D	S	45 Gestures(%)
JOULE-color [12]	✓	✗	✗	66.78
JOULE-depth [12]	✗	✓	✗	60.17
JOULE-pose [12]	✗	✗	✓	74.60
JOULE-all [12]	✓	✓	✓	78.78
1-layer LSTM [36]	✗	✗	✓	78.73
2-layer LSTM [36]	✗	✗	✓	80.14
Moving Pose [34]	✗	✗	✓	56.34
Lie Group [29]	✗	✗	✓	82.69
HBRNN [7]	✗	✗	✓	77.40
Gram Matrix [35]	✗	✗	✓	85.39
TF [8]	✗	✗	✓	80.69
Riemannian-Net [13]	✗	✗	✓	84.35
Grassmann-Net [14]	✗	✗	✓	77.57
ST-TS-HGR-NET [23]	✗	✗	✓	93.22
HMM+HPEV [19]	✗	✗	✓	90.96
NC-CNN [10]	✗	✗	✓	87.60
Ours	✗	✗	✓	**94.09**

5   Conclusion

In this paper, we propose a novel DR-Net for skeleton-based dynamic hand gesture recognition, which decouples the original skeleton data into different skeleton representations as input. For the temporal perception branch, we use short-term motion features and long-term motion features as the temporal skeleton representation. Meanwhile, we design the TFM to capture multi-scale temporal features. For the spatial perception branch, we use spatial low-frequency features and spatial high-frequency features as the spatial skeleton representation. Besides, we also propose the SFM to enhance important spatial features. On the two public benchmark datasets, related experimental results demonstrate that our proposed DR-Net is competitive with the state-of-the-art methods. At present, our method cannot adaptively learn spatial geometric relationships, which leads to unsatisfactory performance for the spatial perception branch. In the future, we intend to use GCN to automatically learn the spatial geometric relationship between joints.

References

1. Boulahia, S.Y., Anquetil, E., Multon, F., Kulpa, R.: Dynamic hand gesture recognition based on 3d pattern assembled trajectories. In: 2017 Seventh International Conference on Image Processing Theory, Tools and Applications (IPTA), pp. 1–6. IEEE
2. Caetano, C., Sena, J., Brémond, F., Dos Santos, J.A., Schwartz, W.R.: Skelemotion: a new representation of skeleton joint sequences based on motion information for 3d action recognition. In: 2019 16th IEEE International Conference on Advanced Video and Signal Based Surveillance (AVSS), pp. 1–8. IEEE (2019)
3. Cao, W.: Application of the support vector machine algorithm based gesture recognition in human-computer interaction. Informatica **43**(1), 123–127 (2019)
4. Chen, X., Wang, G., Guo, H., Zhang, C., Wang, H., Zhang, L.: Mfa-net: motion feature augmented network for dynamic hand gesture recognition from skeletal data. Sensors **19**(2), 239 (2019)
5. Chen, Y., Zhao, L., Peng, X., Yuan, J., Metaxas, D.N.: Construct dynamic graphs for hand gesture recognition via spatial-temporal attention. In: 30th British Machine Vision Conference, pp. 103–116 (2019)
6. Côté, S., Beaulieu, O.: VR road and construction site safety conceptual modeling based on hand gestures. Front. Robot. AI **6**, 15 (2019)
7. Du, Y., Wang, W., Wang, L.: Hierarchical recurrent neural network for skeleton based action recognition. In: Proceedings of the IEEE Conference on Computer Vision and Pattern Recognition, pp. 1110–1118 (2015)
8. Garcia-Hernando, G., Kim, T.K.: Transition forests: learning discriminative temporal transitions for action recognition and detection. In: Proceedings of the IEEE Conference on Computer Vision and Pattern Recognition, pp. 432–440 (2017)
9. Garcia-Hernando, G., Yuan, S., Baek, S., Kim, T.K.: First-person hand action benchmark with RGB-d videos and 3d hand pose annotations. In: Proceedings of the IEEE Conference on Computer Vision and Pattern Recognition, pp. 409–419 (2018)

10. Guo, F., He, Z., Zhang, S., Zhao, X., Fang, J., Tan, J.: Normalized edge convolutional networks for skeleton-based hand gesture recognition. Pattern Recogn. **118**, 108044 (2021)

11. Hou, J., Wang, G., Chen, X., Xue, J.-H., Zhu, R., Yang, H.: Spatial-temporal attention res-tcn for skeleton-based dynamic hand gesture recognition. In: Leal-Taixé, L., Roth, S. (eds.) ECCV 2018. LNCS, vol. 11134, pp. 273–286. Springer, Cham (2019). https://doi.org/10.1007/978-3-030-11024-6_18

12. Hu, J.F., Zheng, W.S., Lai, J., Zhang, J.: Jointly learning heterogeneous features for RGB-d activity recognition. In: Proceedings of the IEEE Conference on Computer Vision and Pattern Recognition, pp. 5344–5352 (2015)

13. Huang, Z., Gool, L.V.: A riemannian network for SPD matrix learning. In: Proceedings of the Thirty-First AAAI Conference on Artificial Intelligence, pp. 2036–2042 (2017)

14. Huang, Z., Wu, J., Van Gool, L.: Building deep networks on grassmann manifolds. In: Proceedings of the Thirty-Second AAAI Conference on Artificial Intelligence (AAAI-18), pp. 3279–3286. AAAI Press (2018)

15. Jiang, X., Xu, K., Sun, T.: Action recognition scheme based on skeleton representation with ds-LSTM network. IEEE Trans. Circ. Syst. Video Technol. **30**(7), 2129–2140 (2019)

16. Lee, M., Lee, J., Chang, J.H.: Ensemble of jointly trained deep neural network-based acoustic models for reverberant speech recognition. Digital Sig. Process. **85**, 1–9 (2019)

17. Li, Y., Guo, T., Liu, X., Xia, R.: Skeleton-based action recognition with lie group and deep neural networks. In: 2019 IEEE 4th International Conference on Signal and Image Processing (ICSIP), pp. 26–30. IEEE (2019)

18. Liu, H., Tu, J., Liu, M., Ding, R.: Learning explicit shape and motion evolution maps for skeleton-based human action recognition. In: 2018 IEEE International Conference on Acoustics, Speech and Signal Processing (ICASSP), pp. 1333–1337. IEEE (2018)

19. Liu, J., Liu, Y., Wang, Y., Prinet, V., Xiang, S., Pan, C.: Decoupled representation learning for skeleton-based gesture recognition. In: Proceedings of the IEEE/CVF Conference on Computer Vision and Pattern Recognition, pp. 5751–5760 (2020)

20. Liu, J., Liu, N., Wang, P., Wang, M., Guo, S.: Array-less touch position identification based on a flexible capacitive tactile sensor for human-robot interactions. In: 2019 IEEE 4th International Conference on Advanced Robotics and Mechatronics (ICARM), pp. 458–462. IEEE (2019)

21. Maghoumi, M., LaViola, J.J.: DeepGRU: deep gesture recognition utility. In: Bebis, G., et al. (eds.) ISVC 2019. LNCS, vol. 11844, pp. 16–31. Springer, Cham (2019). https://doi.org/10.1007/978-3-030-33720-9_2

22. Nasri, N., Orts-Escolano, S., Cazorla, M.: An semg-controlled 3d game for rehabilitation therapies: real-time time hand gesture recognition using deep learning techniques. Sensors **20**(22), 6451 (2020)

23. Nguyen, X.S., Brun, L., Lézoray, O., Bougleux, S.: A neural network based on SPD manifold learning for skeleton-based hand gesture recognition. In: 2019 IEEE/CVF Conference on Computer Vision and Pattern Recognition (CVPR), pp. 12028–12037. IEEE (2019)

24. Nunez, J.C., Cabido, R., Pantrigo, J.J., Montemayor, A.S., Velez, J.F.: Convolutional neural networks and long short-term memory for skeleton-based human activity and hand gesture recognition. Pattern Recogn. **76**, 80–94 (2018)

25. Rastgoo, R., Kiani, K., Escalera, S.: Sign language recognition: a deep survey. Expert Syst. Appl. **164**, 113794 (2021)

26. de Smedt, Q.: Dynamic hand gesture recognition-From traditional handcrafted to recent deep learning approaches. Ph.D. thesis, Université de Lille 1, Sciences et Technologies; CRIStAL UMR 9189 (2017)
27. de Smedt, Q., Wannous, H., Vandeborre, J.P., Guerry, J., Le Saux, B., Filliat, D.: Shrec 2017 track: 3d hand gesture recognition using a depth and skeletal dataset. In: 3DOR-10th Eurographics Workshop on 3D Object Retrieval, pp. 1–6 (2017)
28. Tu, J., Liu, M., Liu, H.: Skeleton-based human action recognition using spatial temporal 3d convolutional neural networks. In: 2018 IEEE International Conference on Multimedia and Expo (ICME), pp. 1–6. IEEE Computer Society (2018)
29. Vemulapalli, R., Arrate, F., Chellappa, R.: Human action recognition by representing 3d skeletons as points in a lie group. In: Proceedings of the IEEE Conference on Computer Vision and Pattern Recognition, pp. 588–595 (2014)
30. Wei, S., Song, Y., Zhang, Y.: Human skeleton tree recurrent neural network with joint relative motion feature for skeleton based action recognition. In: 2017 IEEE International Conference on Image Processing (ICIP), pp. 91–95. IEEE (2017)
31. Weng, J., Liu, M., Jiang, X., Yuan, J.: Deformable pose traversal convolution for 3d action and gesture recognition. In: Proceedings of the European Conference on Computer Vision (ECCV), pp. 136–152 (2018)
32. Yan, S., Xiong, Y., Lin, D.: Spatial temporal graph convolutional networks for skeleton-based action recognition. In: Proceedings of the AAAI Conference on Artificial Intelligence, vol. 32 (2018)
33. Yang, F., Wu, Y., Sakti, S., Nakamura, S.: Make skeleton-based action recognition model smaller, faster and better. In: Proceedings of the ACM multimedia Asia, pp. 1–6 (2019)
34. Zanfir, M., Leordeanu, M., Sminchisescu, C.: The moving pose: an efficient 3d kinematics descriptor for low-latency action recognition and detection. In: Proceedings of the IEEE International Conference on Computer Vision, pp. 2752–2759 (2013)
35. Zhang, X., Wang, Y., Gou, M., Sznaier, M., Camps, O.: Efficient temporal sequence comparison and classification using Gram matrix embeddings on a Riemannian manifold. In: Proceedings of the IEEE Conference on Computer Vision and Pattern Recognition, pp. 4498–4507 (2016)
36. Zhu, W., et al.: Co-occurrence feature learning for skeleton based action recognition using regularized deep LSTM networks. In: Proceedings of the Thirtieth AAAI Conference on Artificial Intelligence, pp. 3697–3703 (2016)

Dual Perspective Contrastive Learning Based Subgraph Anomaly Detection on Attributed Networks

Songlin Hu[1] and Minglai Shao[1,2(✉)]

[1] School of New Media and Communication, Tianjin University, Tianjin, China
shaoml@tju.edu.cn
[2] Wenzhou Safety (Emergency) Insititute, Tianjin University, Wenzhou, China

Abstract. Network anomaly detection is widely used to discover the anomalies of complex attributed networks in reality. Existing approaches can detect independent abnormal nodes by comparing the attribute differences between nodes and their neighbors. However, in real attributed networks, some abnormal nodes are concentrated in a local subgraph, so it is difficult to find out by comparing neighbor nodes because the features within the subgraph are similar. Furthermore, most of these methods use GCN for feature extraction, which means that each node will indiscriminately aggregate its neighbors, causing the value of normal nodes to be severely affected by the surrounding abnormal nodes. In this paper, we propose an improved unsupervised contrastive learning method that is universally applicable to multiple anomaly forms. It will comprehensively compare the inside and outside of the subgraph as two perspectives and use the knowledge of the trained teacher model to adjust the sampling probability for the selectively aggregating of neighbor nodes. Experimental results show that our proposed framework is not limited by the distribution of abnormal nodes and outperforms the state-of-the-art baseline methods on all four benchmark datasets.

Keywords: Anomaly detection · Contrastive learning · Knowledge distillation

1 Introduction

Attributed networks are ubiquitous in the real world, such as social networks [17] and citation networks, in which each node is associated with a rich set of attributes or characteristics. Anomaly detection task is a vital graph analysis task. It aims to find nodes that are significantly different from the reference node, which has a broad impact on various domains such as network intrusion detection and misquotes detection [15].

Detecting anomalies effectively on attributed networks is not trivial due to the diversity of anomalies and the lack of supervision; this makes the performance of shallow mechanism methods unsatisfactory, especially when the dimension of the attribute is high. With the rapid development of deep learning, Graph Neural Network for anomaly detection attracts considerable research interest due to its outstanding performance on traditional graph tasks. Recently, various methods based on deep learning have been proposed to deal with the anomaly detection task on attributed networks, such as DOMINANT [1] and CoLA [9].

© The Author(s), under exclusive license to Springer Nature Switzerland AG 2022
E. Pimenidis et al. (Eds.): ICANN 2022, LNCS 13530, pp. 481–493, 2022.
https://doi.org/10.1007/978-3-031-15931-2_40

Although these deep methods have shown good performance in node anomaly detection, they have a common prerequisite: anomaly must exist in separate nodes rather than nodes closer to each other. This is because they focused on the most basic case of graph anomalies: node anomalies. Only when the abnormal nodes are far apart can the abnormal nodes be identified by comparing the surrounding nodes. However, in the real attributed network, some anomalies appear in groups, such as the behavior of click farming on the commodity network and the water army of the social network. These grouped nodes can also be called a subgraph. Therefore anomaly subgraphs are a more common form of anomalies in reality, including isolated anomaly nodes and dense anomaly nodes [13, 14]. Only when the algorithm is suitable for anomaly subgraph detection can it be suitable for diversified anomalies in real attributed networks.

Our experiments prove that the denser the anomaly nodes, the worse the effect of the current method. There are two main reasons. The first is that when the abnormal nodes are densely concentrated, the difference between nodes in the subgraph will decrease, causing the center node to be hidden by the surrounding abnormal nodes. The second is that the existing models use GCN [7] to extract features or randomly samples neighbor nodes as a positive example; this means that each node will aggregate information indiscriminately, which makes the value of the center node assimilated by anomaly nodes during the training process.

Inspired by CoLA, we also use contrastive learning to let the model identify nodes with similar attributes because it can fully exploit the rich information of the attributed graph for effective graph representation learning. We design a novel anomaly judgment method to overcome the above two problems. This method will comprehensively consider the anomaly scores inside the subgraph and the anomaly scores between the subgraph and the external environment as two perspectives. Inspired by distillation learning [5], we design a novel sampling module for contrastive instances. It will use the knowledge of the trained teacher model to set the probability of each neighbour node so that the sampling probability of abnormal nodes will be significantly reduced. Experimental results show that the performance of the student model will be much better than the teacher model. To summarize, the main contributions are as follows.

- We extend the task to the general subgraph anomaly detection and propose a novel dual perspective contrastive learning method, which comprehensively measures the anomalies inside and outside the subgraph.
- We use knowledge from the teacher model to improve the robustness and anti-noise ability of the student model. Through the well-designed probability sampling module, the performance of the student model can be much better.
- We conduct extensive experiments to demonstrate the effectiveness of our method. Our method achieves state-of-the-art results on various datasets.

2   Related Work

2.1   Shallow Mechanism Method

The shallow node anomaly detection method define an anomaly score function based on some characteristics of the attribute or structure and then measure the anomaly score between the current node and neighbor nodes. Typical representatives of this type of method are Radar [8] and ANOMALOUS [11].

Radar extract the residual of attribute information and the consistency of network information to detect outlier nodes. ANOMALOUS introduces CUR decomposition based on residual analysis to combine attribute selection and anomaly detection. Due to the limitation of their shallow mechanisms and the complexity and difficulty of scoring function design, when the feature dimension of the attribute network is high, the performance of these methods will be significantly reduced.

2.2 Deep Learning Method

At present, with the successful application of deep learning in the field of graphs, the mainstream subgraph anomaly detection algorithms all use graph neural networks as the basic framework of the model. DOMINANT [1] is the first to apply the graph autoencoder to node anomaly detection. By measuring the reconstruction errors of nodes from both the structure and the attribute perspectives, it can find nodes that are difficult to reproduce the structure. AnomlyDAE [3] using two autoencoders to learn attribute features and structure features separately and can do better through the cross-modality interactions between network structure and node attribute.

Although the deep methods achieve superior performance over the shallow methods by introducing deep neural networks, they also have limitations. Reconstruction mechanism with autoencoders neither directly optimizes the target of anomaly detection nor can it make full use of data.

2.3 Contrastive Learning Method

To overcome the above problems, Liu et al. apply contrastive learning to anomaly detection named as CoLA. Through comparing nodes with neighbors and building a GNN based classifier to distinguish between positive and negative samples, the model can thoroughly learn the similarity between nodes and then find anomaly nodes that are pretty different from the surrounding ones.

The above methods all find anomalies by comparing neighbor nodes, so they are not suitable for subgraph anomalies. On the contrary, our method performs well on both isolated nodes and abnormal subgraphs, thanks to the dual perspective scoring and weighted sampling modules. Our method will selectively sample the local subgraph to reduce the interference of abnormal nodes and comprehensively consider the internal and external differences of the subgraph to avoid the center nodes being concealed by the surrounding nodes. These improvements make our method no longer limited to the distribution of abnormal nodes.

3 Methods

In this subsection, we extensively detail our extension of the problem and innovation in the model. We enable our model to identify more general subgraph anomalies by sampling inside and outside of subgraphs and analyzing both inside and outside anomalies. Figure 2 shows the flow chart of our entire model.

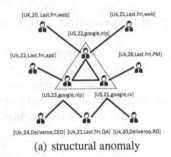

(a) structural anomaly

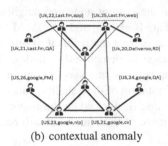

(b) contextual anomaly

Fig. 1. Examples to illustrate different types of subgraph anomalies in attributed networks. Structural subgraph anomaly can be manifested as dense edge connections between several unrelated subgraphs. Nodes in structural anomaly subgraphs will be disturbed by other structural anomaly subgraphs. For contextual subgraph anomalies, its internal structure is usually no problem, so it is difficult to find out through the internal comparison of subgraphs. But the subgraph is in the wrong environment, different from the outside.

3.1   Problem Formulation

Definition 1. Attributed Networks. *An attributed network can be denoted as an undirected graph $G = (V, E, X)$, where $V = \{v_1, ..., v_n\}$ is the set of nodes ($|V| = n$), E is the set of edges ($|E| = m$), and $X \in \mathbb{R}^{n \times f}$ is the attribute matrix. The ith row vector $X_i \in \mathbb{R}^f$ of the attribute matrix denotes the attribute information of the ith node. An binary adjacency matrix $A \in \mathbb{R}^{n \times n}$ is employed to denote the structure information of the attributed network, where $A_{i,j} = 1$ if there is a link between nodes v_i and v_j, otherwise $A_{i,j} = 0$.*

We first extend the form of anomalies into subgraph anomalies. The extended anomaly types include various anomalies from isolated abnormal nodes to dense sub-clusters. Figure 1 shows the standard form of subgraph anomaly.

Structural Subgraph Anomaly. For two nodes v_0, v_1 and node sets V_0, V_1 of subgraphs centered on v_0, v_1, the structural subgraph anomaly can be described as follows:

$$V_k = N_{v_k} \cup v_k, A_{V_0^i, V_1^j} = 1, \tag{1}$$

where $k \in [0, 1]$, N_{v_k} is the neighbor nodes of v_k, V_0^i is the ith node of subgraph V_0 and $A_{m,n}$ is the m-th row, n-th column of the adjacency matrix A.

Contextual Subgraph Anomaly. For two nodes v_0, v_1 and node sets V_0, V_1 of subgraphs centered on v_0, v_1, the contextual subgraph anomaly can be shown as follows:

$$V_k = N_{v_k}, \tag{2}$$

$$X_{v_0} = X_{v_1}, X_{V_0^i} = X_{V_1^j}. \tag{3}$$

Since subgraphs are sets of nodes, detecting anomaly subgraphs is equivalent to detecting anomaly nodes inside subgraphs. Then the subgraph anomaly detection problem on the attributed network can be stated as a ranking problem:

Problem 1. Subgraph Anomaly Detection. *Given an attributed network* $G = (V, E, X)$ *with nodes* $v_1, ..., v_n$ *, the goal is to learn an anomaly score function* f *to calculate the subgraph anomaly score* $k_i = f(v_i, N_{v_i})$ *of the subgraph consists of each node and its neighbors. The anomaly score* k_i *can represent the probability whether node* v_i *is in anomaly subgraph. By ranking all the nodes with their subgrph anomaly scores, the anomaly nodes in each subgraph can be detected according to their positions.*

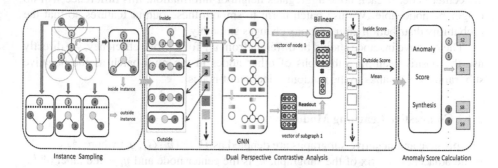

Fig. 2. The overall framework of our method. Node 1 is the node we are currently testing while node 1,2,3 is an attribute anomaly subgraph. We first sample subgraphs from two perspectives. After that, the GNN-based contrastive learning model evaluates the predicted score for each instance pair. Finally, we averaged all the external instances to obtain the outside subgraph anomaly score, and combine anomaly scores via the anomaly combination module. After performing the same operation on all nodes, we can find the abnormal nodes in the abnormal subgraph by sorting the abnormal scores.

3.2 Probability Sampling Module

In each training epoch, we randomly select k nodes as a mini-batch to generate contrastive samples and gradient descent denoted as V_{train}. To recognize similar nodes, we select neighbor nodes as positive samples and distant nodes as negative samples inspired by CoLA [9].

For each node v_i in V_{train} , the positive instance is a subgraph composed of nodes selected from the neighbor nodes of v_i with a sample weight w_{sam}. For the teacher model, the weight of each neighbor node is the same. After trained a teacher GNN model M_t, w_{sam} can be generated as follows:

$$X_t = M_t(X, A_{eye}), \tag{4}$$

$$w_{sam,j} = 1/Dis(X_t^{v_i}, X_t^{v_j}), (v_j \in N_{v_i}), \tag{5}$$

$$w_{sam} = Softmax(BatchNorm(w_{sam})), \tag{6}$$

where $X \in \mathbb{R}^{n \times f}$ is the attribute matrix of the attribute network, $A_{eye} \in \mathbb{R}^{n \times n}$ is an identity matrix, $X_t^{v_i}$ is the teacher model's output of node v_i and Dis($\bullet$) is a function of measuring the distance of attribute values. In this paper, we use $Euclidean Distance$, which can be shown as:

$$\|X_1 - X_2\|_2 = (\sum_{i=1}^{f} |X_1^i - X_2^i|^2)^{1/2}, \tag{7}$$

where f is the dimension of attributes in the attributed network and X_1 is the attribute vector of node1.

Here we do not input the adjacency matrix to the teacher model because our original intention was to give a smaller weight to neighbor nodes that are more different from the center node. If each node aggregates neighbor information, this difference will no longer be noticeable. We use batch norm to smooth these output features so that the probability distribution after softmax changes smoothly.

The negative instance should be different from v_i. To improve efficiency, we directly use the positive sample subgraphs of other nodes in the mini-batch as the negative subgraphs of v_i thanks to the random selection of nodes.

3.3 Contrastive Learning Module

The positive and negative subgraphs are denoted as $P_i = (v_i, G_i, y_i)$ where $A_i \in \mathbb{R}^{c \times c}$ is the adjacency matrix of the subgraph, v_i is the center node and y_i is the label of P_i. When P_i is a positive instance pair y_i is 1, otherwise it is 0.

Then we can use the graph neural network such as GCN [7], GAT [18] or GIN [19] to further encode the features of each node. In this paper, we use GCN as it is the most efficient with the following propagation rule:

$$\mathbf{H}_i^{(l+1)} = \sigma \left(\tilde{\mathbf{D}}_i^{-\frac{1}{2}} \tilde{\mathbf{A}}_i \tilde{\mathbf{D}}_i^{-\frac{1}{2}} \mathbf{H}_i^{(l)} \mathbf{W}^{(l)} \right). \tag{8}$$

Here, $\tilde{\mathbf{D}}_i$ is the degree matrix of the subgraph, $\tilde{\mathbf{A}}_i = \mathbf{A}_i + \mathbf{I}$ is the adjacency matrix of the subgraph with self-loop and $\mathbf{W}^{(l)}$ is a trainable parameter matrix. $\sigma(\bullet)$ represents an activation function, such as ReLU.

We choose average pooling [4] as a ReadoutFunction to generate the final vector of the local subgraph denoted as $\mathbf{h}_i^{lc}$, which can be shown as:

$$\mathbf{h}_i^{lc} = \text{Readout}(\mathbf{H}_i) = \sum_{k=1}^{n_i} \frac{(\mathbf{H}_i)_k}{n_i}, \tag{9}$$

where $(\mathbf{H}_i)_k$ is the kth row of $\mathbf{H}_i$, and n_i is the number of nodes of the local subgraph G_i.

Then we use bilinear scoring function [10] to calculate the contrastive score between v_i and G_i. The anomaly score is calculated by:

$$s_i = \text{bilinear}\left(\mathbf{h}_i^{lc}, \mathbf{h}_i^{v_i}\right) = \sigma\left(\mathbf{h}_i^{lc} \mathbf{W}^{(f)} \mathbf{h}_i^{v_i \top}\right), \tag{10}$$

where $\mathbf{W}^{(f)}$ is a trainable weight matrix, $\mathbf{h}_i^{v_i}$ is the embedding vector of v_i and $\sigma(\bullet)$ denotes the sigmoid function.

Our objective is to let the embedding of center node be similar to that of the positive instance; this is equivalent to having the model output a score close to the label of

P_i, which can be considered as a binary classification. Therefore, we adopt a standard binary cross-entropy loss to train our model, which is calculated as follows:

$$\mathcal{L} = -\sum_{i=1}^{N} y_i \log(s_i) + (1 - y_i) \log(1 - s_i). \tag{11}$$

3.4 Dual Perspective Inference Module

Let the predicted score of the positive pair be denoted as $s^{(+)}$, while the negative one is $s^{(-)}$. During inference, we first sample contrastive instances via the method illustrated in Sect. 3.2. In the inference phase, the neighbors' sampling weights are the same. The positive and negative subgraphs are denoted as $P_i = (v_i, G_i)$. Then the inside anomaly score can be calculated by:

$$S_{in}^{v_i} = s_i^{(-)} - s_i^{(+)}. \tag{12}$$

From another perspective, we need to measure the difference between P_i and the external environment. We select another pairs of contrastive instance via the method illustrated in Sect. 3.2 for each node in P_i denoted as $P_j = (v_j, G_j)$. Nodes in P_j can be also called the 2-hop neighbors of v_i. Note that during sampling for v_j, we will not choose the nodes in P_i because it can not reflect the environment outside the subgraph. For P_j and our trained model $\mathbf{M}$, the outside anomaly score can be calculated as follows:

$$s_j = \mathbf{M}(X_j, A_j), \tag{13}$$

$$S_{out}^{v_i} = \frac{1}{n_i} \sum_{j=1}^{n_i} \left(s_j^{(-)} - s_j^{(+)} \right), \tag{14}$$

where n_i is the number of nodes of the local subgraph G_i.

We will get R results by repeating the inference process denoted as $(S_{in,1}^{v_i}, ..., S_{in,R}^{v_i}), (S_{out,1}^{v_i}, ..., S_{out,R}^{v_i})$ to examine each neighbor node of v_i in consideration of the accuracy. To combine these two anomaly scores, the final anomaly score of node v_i can be calculated as follows:

$$S_{inf}^{v_i} = \frac{1}{R} \sum_{r=1}^{R} S_{in,r}^{v_i}, \tag{15}$$

$$S_{v_i} = \begin{cases} S_{inf}^{v_i} & S_{inf}^{v_i} < K_h \\ \frac{1}{R} \sum_{r=1}^{R} \text{Max}(S_{in,r}^{v_i}, S_{out,r}^{v_i}) & S_{inf}^{v_i} \geq K_h \end{cases}, \tag{16}$$

where K_h is a hyperparameter of our model. We take the larger score as the final anomaly score of v_i to recall as many abnormal nodes as possible. However, such an operation will make the normal nodes near the abnormal subgraph appear abnormal. For this reason, we will ignore the outer anomalies of nodes with particularly low inside anomaly scores. Our experiment shows that after setting K_h, the recognition effect of abnormal nodes will only slightly decrease while the prediction scores of normal nodes will drop significantly, making the overall performance better.

4   Experiments

4.1   Datasets

We evaluate the proposed framework on four widely used benchmark datasets for anomaly detection on attributed networks. The datasets include one social network datasets (BlogCatalog) and three citation network datasets (Cora, Citeseer, Pubmed) [6, 12, 16, 17]. The statistics of these datasets are demonstrated in Table 2, and the detailed descriptions are given as follows:

- **Social Networks.** BlogCatalog is a typical social network dataset acquired from the blog sharing website BlogCatalog. In social networks, nodes denote the users of websites, and links represent the relationships between users. The attribute vectors in social networks come from the interaction between users, such as blog comments, item evaluations, etc.
- **Citation Networks.** Cora, Citeseer, and Pubmed are three available public scientific paper datasets. In these networks, nodes denote the published papers while edges represent the citation relationships between papers. The attribute vector of each node is the bag-of-word representation of the content of the paper

We will inject contextual anomalies and structural anomalies with the same number of subgraphs following the generic anomaly form described in Section 3.1 [2]. We first randomly choose multiple sets of center nodes through random sampling and select the group with the largest average distance between center nodes as the final set. The number of anomaly subgraphs is 24 for Cora and Citeseer and 28 for Pubmed. As the average degree of BlogCatalog is very high (over 30), we only randomly select nodes with less than 60 neighbor nodes to inject anomalies. The number of anomaly subgraphs is 12 for BlogCatalog.

4.2   Experimental Setup

We compare our framework with five popular methods for anomaly detection : **Radar, ANOMALOUS, DOMINANT, AnomalyDAE, CoLA** introduced in Sect. 2.

To measure the performance of our proposed framework and the baselines, we employ ROC-AUC as the metric which is widely used in previous works for the evaluation of anomaly detection performance [1, 8, 9, 11]. For the Citation Networks, we

Table 1. The statistics of the datasets. NAS represents the number of anomaly subgraphs, while PAN represents the proportion of different anomaly nodes divided by the proportion of abnormal nodes in the neighbor nodes from high to low.

Dataset	Nodes	Edges	Attributes	NAS	PAN
Blogcatalog	5,196	171,743	8,189	12	0.04, 0.26, 0.7
Pubmed	19,717	44,338	500	28	0.24, 0.1, 0.66
Cora	2,708	5,429	1,433	24	0.5, 0.23, 0.27
Citeseer	3,327	4,732	3,703	24	0.53, 0.3, 0.17

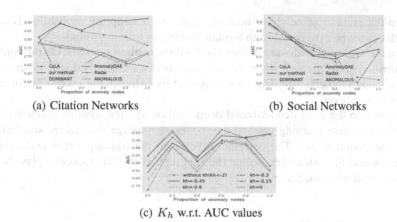

(a) Citation Networks   (b) Social Networks

(c) K_h w.r.t. AUC values

Fig. 3. Auc scores on social networks and citation networks and the influence of the parameter K_h on citation networks.

choose the total AUC for comparison, but for the Social Networks, because the number of different types of abnormal nodes is seriously unbalanced, we choose the average value of the total AUC and the AUC in each category(divided by the proportion of abnormal nodes in the neighbor nodes). This is because we want to examine the average capability of the model rather than just focusing on the category with the most nodes (Table 1).

We fix the training size of the sampled subgraph to 4 and evaluated size to 3 for Citation Networks and both 4 for Social Networks. In the contrastive learning model, all parameters are set the same as CoLA [9]. In inference phase, we sample 256 rounds to acquire accurate detection results for each dataset. K_h is −0.45 for Citation Networks and −1 for Social Networks. All the parameter settings of the student model and the teacher model are the same except for the sampling module. All baseline results are after fine-tuning. All the category labels are removed in our experiments, and the anomaly labels are only visible in the inference phase. We use an NVIDIA GeForce RTX 2080Ti (11 GB memory) for our experiments.

4.3   Anomaly Detection Results and Analysis

By calculating the area under the ROC curves, the AUC scores of the five benchmark datasets are shown in Table 2. After dividing the abnormal nodes by the proportion of abnormal nodes in the neighbor nodes, we calculate the AUC scores of each category as shown in Fig. 3. Figure 3 also shows the influence of the parameter K_h on citation networks. According to the results, we have the following observations:

– Compared with the best results of the baselines, our framework obtains a significant improvement of 5% on AUC averagely. In citation networks, the performance of the student network is better than that of the teacher network thanks to weighted sampling. For social networks, anomaly subgraphs are close due to the high degree.

When the number of neighbor nodes is large, each sampling probability is small, which cannot be distinguished in a small number of training rounds.

- When the abnormal nodes are denser, the baseline method worsens. On the contrary, our method performs well when the abnormal nodes are highly dense. After setting K_h, although the effect of dense nodes is slightly reduced, the overall performance has been improved.
- Compared to the autoencoder-based deep method and the shallow methods, GNN based contrastive learning method can better summarize the feature similarity of high-dimension nodes. The correlation between the training target and anomaly detection and the calculation within the subgraph allows the model to play the role of the neural network better.

4.4 Hyperparameter Study

We investigate the impacts of another two important parameters on the performance of the proposed framework: the size of the subgraph and the number of sampling rounds. As the degree of social networks is too high to study the model's performance, we only conduct experiments on citation networks.

Subgraph Size. As shown in Fig. 4, when the training subgraph size is larger than 3, the final results are similar. The inference subgraph size shouldn't exceed 3; otherwise, the performance will be greatly reduced. As the average degree of the center anomaly node is small, so small-scale sampling is more helpful to distinguish abnormal neighbor nodes.

Sample Rounds. In inference process, as the anomaly label is invisible, we need to sample multiple times to find nodes that are quite different. Therefore, the more rounds of sampling, the more accurate the result will be. Subfigure(b) of Fig. 4 also confirms this. However, when the number of sampling rounds exceeds a certain value, the improvement of the effect is not obvious. Based on this, we set R = 256 in experiments to balance performance and efficiency.

Table 2. Auc scores on four benchmark datasets. OOM means the issue out-of-memory is incurred.

Methods	Blogcatalog	Pubmed	Cora	Citeseer
Radar	0.5917	OOM	0.7218	0.7021
ANOMALOUS	0.5824	OOM	0.7316	0.7442
DOMINANT	0.6504	OOM	0.7496	0.7099
AnomalyDAE	0.5602	OOM	0.6546	0.6613
CoLA	0.5531	0.8122	0.8167	0.7847
Teacher(without K_h)	0.6404	0.8245	0.8598	0.8228
Teacher	**0.6524**	0.8414	0.8682	0.8346
Student(without K_h)	0.5824	0.8260	0.8842	0.8526
Student	0.6059	**0.8443**	**0.8967**	**0.8599**

Table 3. Effect of different score computation functions and distillation learning methods on AUC values. WSS, WSN, PSN represent weight setting within subgraph, weight setting within neighbor nodes, probabilities setting within neighbor nodes, respectively.

Methods	Pubmed	Cora	Citeseer
Inside	0.8145	0.8390	0.7956
Outside	0.3731	0.6898	0.6767
Mean	0.7380	0.8541	0.8186
Max	**0.8245**	**0.8598**	**0.8228**

Methods	Pubmed	Cora	Citeseer
Teacher	0.8245	0.8598	0.8228
WSS	0.7982	0.8145	0.7926
WSN	0.8117	0.8624	0.8340
PSN	**0.8260**	**0.8842**	**0.8526**

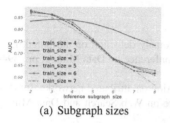

(a) Subgraph sizes

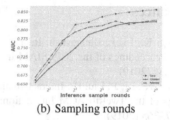

(b) Sampling rounds

Fig. 4. The experimental results for parameter study. The subfigure (a) and (b) shows the impact of different subgraph sizes and sampling rounds w.r.t. AUC values, respectively.

4.5 Ablation Study

In this subsection, we study the effect of changing different anomaly score computation functions and methods of introducing prior knowledge on citation networks.

Anomaly Combining Method. In inference phase, we can focus on only one anoamly score, average the two scores, or take the maximum value. The results in Table 3 show that selecting the maximum value has the best performance. The mean value does not represent the anomaly degree of subgraphs, because the inside and outside anomaly scores are weakly correlated. At the same time, if we only pay attention to one of the values, some specific types of outliers will be ignored.

Methods of Introducing Prior Knowledge. We designed three ways to utilize prior knowledge. The results are shown in Table 3. The weights set in the sampling subgraph are only relative and can't reflect the real difference between neighbor nodes. Although setting weights for neighbor nodes can play a certain role, when the outliers are dense, they will be sampled more times and still affect the normal nodes. When the sampling probabilities of anomaly nodes are set to be minor, in the limited number of training rounds, the improvement is often the largest.

5 Conclusion

In this paper, we show through experiments that existing node anomaly detection methods are not suitable for subgraph anomalies. Then, we propose the dual perspective contrastive learning method. By investigating the internal and external aspects of the subgraph, our method is competent for the task of anomaly subgraph detection. We also make the first attempt to combine distillation learning into the method to reduce the interference of surrounding abnormal nodes. In future work, we will study more reasonable abnormal forms of subgraphs and improve the method so that the model can perform well when the degree of the network is high.

Acknowledgements. This work was supported by China Postdoctoral Science Foundation (2021M702448) and the Scientific Research Translational Foundation of Wenzhou Safety (Emergency) Institute of Tianjin University (TJUWYY2022012).

References

1. Ding, K., Li, J., Bhanushali, R., Liu, H.: Deep anomaly detection on attributed networks. In: Proceedings of the 2019 SIAM International Conference on Data Mining, pp. 594–602. SIAM (2019)
2. Ding, K., Li, J., Liu, H.: Interactive anomaly detection on attributed networks. In: Proceedings of the Twelfth ACM International Conference on Web Search and Data Mining, pp. 357–365 (2019)
3. Fan, H., Zhang, F., Li, Z.: Anomalydae: dual autoencoder for anomaly detection on attributed networks. In: ICASSP 2020–2020 IEEE International Conference on Acoustics, Speech and Signal Processing (ICASSP), pp. 5685–5689. IEEE (2020)
4. Hassani, K., Khasahmadi, A.H.: Contrastive multi-view representation learning on graphs. In: International Conference on Machine Learning, pp. 4116–4126. PMLR (2020)
5. Hinton, G., Vinyals, O., Dean, J.: Distilling the knowledge in a neural network. arXiv preprint arXiv:1503.02531 (2015)
6. Hu, W., et al.: Open graph benchmark: datasets for machine learning on graphs. arXiv preprint arXiv:2005.00687 (2020)
7. Kipf, T.N., Welling, M.: Semi-supervised classification with graph convolutional networks. arXiv preprint arXiv:1609.02907 (2016)
8. Li, J., Dani, H., Hu, X., Liu, H.: Radar: residual analysis for anomaly detection in attributed networks. In: IJCAI, pp. 2152–2158 (2017)
9. Liu, Y., Li, Z., Pan, S., Gong, C., Zhou, C., Karypis, G.: Anomaly detection on attributed networks via contrastive self-supervised learning. IEEE Trans. Neural Netw. Learn. Syst. **33**, 2378–2392 (2021)
10. Oord, A.V.d., Li, Y., Vinyals, O.: Representation learning with contrastive predictive coding. arXiv preprint arXiv:1807.03748 (2018)
11. Peng, Z., Luo, M., Li, J., Liu, H., Zheng, Q.: Anomalous: a joint modeling approach for anomaly detection on attributed networks. In: IJCAI, pp. 3513–3519 (2018)
12. Sen, P., Namata, G., Bilgic, M., Getoor, L., Galligher, B., Eliassi-Rad, T.: Collective classification in network data. AI Mag. **29**(3), 93–93 (2008)
13. Shao, M., Li, J., Chen, F., Chen, X.: An efficient framework for detecting evolving anomalous subgraphs in dynamic networks. In: IEEE INFOCOM 2018-IEEE Conference on Computer Communications, pp. 2258–2266. IEEE (2018)
14. Shao, M., Li, J., Chen, F., Huang, H., Zhang, S., Chen, X.: An efficient approach to event detection and forecasting in dynamic multivariate social media networks. In: Proceedings of the 26th International Conference on World Wide Web, pp. 1631–1639 (2017)
15. Shi, C., Hu, B., Zhao, W.X., Philip, S.Y.: Heterogeneous information network embedding for recommendation. IEEE Trans. Knowl. Data Eng. **31**(2), 357–370 (2018)

16. Tang, J., Zhang, J., Yao, L., Li, J., Zhang, L., Su, Z.: Arnetminer: extraction and mining of academic social networks. In: Proceedings of the 14th ACM SIGKDD International Conference on Knowledge Discovery and Data Mining, pp. 990–998 (2008)
17. Tang, L., Liu, H.: Relational learning via latent social dimensions. In: Proceedings of the 15th ACM SIGKDD International Conference on Knowledge Discovery and Data Mining, pp. 817–826 (2009)
18. Veličković, P., Cucurull, G., Casanova, A., Romero, A., Lio, P., Bengio, Y.: Graph attention networks. arXiv preprint arXiv:1710.10903 (2017)
19. Xu, K., Hu, W., Leskovec, J., Jegelka, S.: How powerful are graph neural networks? arXiv preprint arXiv:1810.00826 (2018)

GCMK: Detecting Spam Movie Review Based on Graph Convolutional Network Embedding Movie Background Knowledge

Hao Cao[1], Hanyue Li[1], Yulin He[1], Xu Yan[2], Fei Yang[1], and Haizhou Wang[1(✉)]

[1] School of Cyber Science and Engineering, Sichuan University, Chengdu, China
{caohao,lihanyue,heyulin,yanxu}@stu.scu.edu.cn, whzh.nc@scu.edu.cn
[2] College of Computer Science, Sichuan University, Chengdu, China
Yangfei@stu.scu.edu.cn

Abstract. In recent years, the movie industry is booming and many consumers regard movie reviews as an important reference for choosing movies. In the mean time, more and more movie marketing teams glorify their movies and suppress rival movies of the same period by hiring spammers to publish massive misleading reviews. It results in the existence of a large number of spam movie reviews on the online movie review platforms, which greatly misleads consumers and seriously undermines the healthy development of the movie industry. At present, there is little research on spam movie reviews, whose method of detecting spam movie reviews mainly relies on the text and statistical features of reviews, ignoring the significance of movie background knowledge such as movie characters and plots. In this paper, we propose a novel method for detecting spam movie reviews, which uses a graph convolutional neural network embedding movie background knowledge (GCMK). Specifically, we firstly construct a directed heterogeneous knowledge graph by using the movie synopsis and the high-quality long comments of movies. Then we use the graph convolutional neural network to obtain the embedded features of the movie background knowledge, use BERT (Bidirectional Encoder Representations from Transformers) model to extract the text features of reviews, and obtain the correlation vectors between these reviews and the corresponding movies by comparing the embedded features of the movie background knowledge and the text features of reviews. Finally, we fuse text features, user statistical features and correlation vectors to construct the detection model. The experimental results demonstrate our proposed GCMK method is more effective than the other state-of-the-art baselines, with an F1-score of 84.94%.

Keywords: Movie reviews · Spam detection · Movie background knowledge · Graph embedding · Features fusion

E. Pimenidis et al. (Eds.): ICANN 2022, LNCS 13530, pp. 494–505, 2022.
https://doi.org/10.1007/978-3-031-15931-2_41

1 Introduction

1.1 Background

With the continuous development of social economy, watching movies has become an important part of people's entertainment. According to the annual report[1] from the Motion Picture Association, the global box office revenue reached \$21.3 billion in 2021. At the same time, with the rapid development of Internet technology, more and more people publish and share movie reviews on online movie ticketing and review platforms (such as Maoyan[2], Douban[3], IMDB[4], Rotten Tomatoes[5]). Movie reviews and ratings have become important references for consumers to make choices on purchasing movie tickets [17]. Existing research shows that positive word of mouth of movies (including reviews and ratings) from popular online movie ticketing and review platforms will have a significant impact on movie box office [3,16]. Therefore, driven by commercial interests, a growing number of spam movie reviews are utilized to influence the movie box office on major online movie ticketing and review platforms [3]. On one hand, this phenomenon seriously misleads consumers who are going to watch movies; on the other hand, it also leads movie marketing team to invest enormous amount of money in false propaganda and other improper manipulations of movie reviews, which greatly damages users' consumption experience and undermines the healthy development of the movie industry. Hence it is extremely necessary and urgent to conduct research on the detection of spam movie reviews.

1.2 Challenges

In recent years, online movie reviews have drawn more and more attention with the popularity of online movie ticketing and review platforms. Compared with the online reviews of e-commerce [4,6,19,21] and restaurant [2,4,11,12], there is very rarely research on spam movie reviews due to its recent emergence. Although spam movie reviews are similar to the spam reviews on the online e-commerce and restaurant platforms, there are some significant differences. (1) Movie reviews often involve specific movie plots, actors, and other movie background knowledge. (2) Movie reviews can be evaluated from more abundant perspectives such as plots, special effects, actors' acting skills and movie types [3,15]. (3) The life cycle of movies is shorter compared with other products [16], so spammers will focus on the first couple of weeks after the movie released to manipulate the reputation of the movie, thereby affecting the movie box office. Due to the differences mentioned above, the existing research methods for spam reviews cannot be directly applied to the detection of spam movie reviews.

---

[1] https://www.motionpictures.org/wp-content/uploads/2022/03/MPA-2021-THEME-Report-FINAL.pdf.

[2] https://www.maoyan.com/.

[3] https://www.douban.com/.

[4] https://www.imdb.com/.

[5] https://www.rottentomatoes.com/.

At present, the main challenges of the research work on the detection of spam movie reviews are as follows: (1) As an emerging research field, there is no available benchmark dataset for researchers (Note that the only research work [3] for the detection of spam movie review did not release their dataset). (2) The existing detection model [3] for spam movie reviews ignores the fact that the content of the movie review should be closely related to the movie background knowledge such as the plot, characters, and actors. As a result, the performance of the existing model for spam movie reviews needs to be further improved. (3) Because of the differences between spam movie reviews and other spam reviews, the existing detection models for spam reviews cannot be directly transferred to the detection research of spam movie reviews, and thus new detection models against spam movie reviews need to be built.

1.3   Contributions

In order to address above problems, this paper builds and publishes a benchmark dataset on GitHub website[6] (Maoyan Dataset), and proposes a **G**raph **C**onvolution-based **M**ovie background **K**nowledge embedding model (GCMK[7]) to detect spam movie reviews. To be specific, we first collect large-scale data from one of the largest Chinese online movie ticketing and review platforms (i.e. Maoyan) and then construct a large-scale spam movie review dataset named M-Dataset using web crawlers. After that, a directed heterogeneous knowledge graph is constructed using the movie synopses and the high-quality long movie comments. The embedding features of the movie background knowledge are obtained by the graph convolutional neural network. Then, we use BERT (Bidirectional Encoder Representations from Transformers) [1] model to extract the text features of the reviews and obtain the correlation vectors between the reviews and the movies by comparing the movie background knowledge embedding vectors and the text feature vectors. Finally, we fuse text features, user statistical features, and correlation vectors to construct a spam movie review detection model.

The main contributions of this paper include the following aspects:

- To the best of our knowledge, we are the first to release large-scale benchmark dataset for detection of spam movie reviews. Specifically, we crawled a huge amount of movie review data from Maoyan (one of the largest online movie ticketing and review platforms in China), covering 2,352 movies of almost all genres, with 734,130 review records in total. A spam movie review dataset called M-Dataset containing a total of 65,696 reviews was constructed by manual annotation, which has been publicly available[8].

- We propose a novel feature extraction method for movie background knowledge based on graph convolutional neural network. First, we construct a directed heterogeneous graph containing movie synopses and real high-quality

---

[6] https://github.com/yiyepianzhounc/M-Dataset.
[7] https://github.com/yiyepianzhounc/GCMK.

long comments. Then, we use a graph convolutional neural network to obtain the embedded features containing movie background knowledge such as movie characters and plots. Moreover, we calculate the correlation vectors between the reviews and the corresponding movies by comparing the graph embedding vectors with the feature vectors of the review text. Finally, they are fused with other features to support spam movie review detection.

- We propose a novel spam movie review detection model GCMK based on deep neural network, which integrates user statistical features, text features and movie background knowledge features. Research results on large-scale experimental dataset demonstrate that our proposed model can effectively combine the above three features, improving accuracy of detecting spam movie reviews and outperforming the state-of-the-art baselines.

The rest of the paper is organized as follows. Section 2 will go through related work and achievements in the field of spam review detection. Our proposed GCMK model is elaborated in Sect. 3. In Sect. 4, we present the experimental setup and evaluation results. Finally, conclusions are drawn and future research directions are outlined in Sect. 5.

2   Related Work

Spam movie reviews are essentially a branch of spam reviews. Early research on spam review detection mainly focused on reviews in e-commerce [4,6,19,21], restaurants [2,4,11,12] and other industries [2,14]. The existing detection methods include supervised, unsupervised and semi-supervised learning methods. Among them, models based on supervised learning have been widely used in the detection of spam reviews. The methods [6,11,20] mainly apply machine learning to classify online reviews by manually extracting features. However, manual feature extraction is too time-consuming and laborious, so the existing research work [2,4,12,14,21] et al. proposed various spam review detection methods based on deep learning models, which overcomes the shortcoming that manual features can not extract the deep semantics of reviews. However, supervised learning needs to label a large amount of original data, which is also time-consuming. Besides, the model accuracy is also susceptible to the quality of labeling. Therefore, in parallel with the development of supervised learning methods, research work [3,19] used the unsupervised or semi-supervised methods to identify spam reviews.

Although a number of early studies have focused on movie reviews, they mainly concern about mining opinions in movie reviews for sentiment classification [9,18], summarization [10,13] and making box office predictions [16,17,24]. Currently, Gao et al. [3] is the only research work to study the detection of spam movie reviews. To be specific, Gao et al. [3] adopted an unsupervised learning method based on generative adversarial neural network, which is user-centric and learns textual and statistical features to distinguish the authenticity of movie reviews. However, they ignore the importance of the correlation between user reviews and movie background knowledge for the judgment of the authenticity of reviews. Moreover, they do not release a publicly available benchmark dataset.

3 Methodology

In this section, we describe our method for spam movie review detection based on graph convolution-based movie background knowledge embedding.

3.1 Dataset Construction

Currently, Maoyan is one of the largest online platforms for movie ticketing and review in China. In our research, we choose Maoyan platform to collect movie reviews to construct our dataset. Based on referring existing annotation methods[8] for spam reviews and our rigorous annotation, we construct a benchmark dataset as shown in Table 1. Among them, M-Raw-Data (Maoyan Review Raw Data) is the original collected review records without data annotation. The M-Dataset (Maoyan Review Dataset) is the benchmark dataset of review records after data cleaning and labeling. We finally obtain 65,696 review annotations from 457 movies, including 20,092 spam review records.

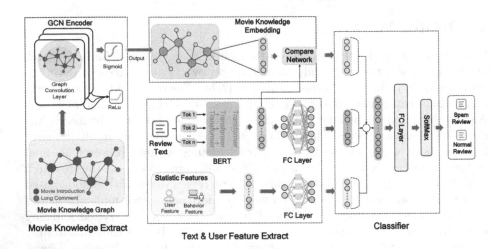

Fig. 1. GCMK model structure

3.2 Detection Model

As shown in Fig. 1, we propose a spam movie review detection model that uses graph convolutional neural network with movie background knowledge embedded. Firstly, we extract text features and user statistical features to obtain text feature vectors and user statistical feature vectors. Secondly, we use graph convolutional neural network to extract the embedded features of movie background

---

[8] https://consumerist.com/2010/04/14/how-you-spot-fake-online-reviews/.

Table 1. Dataset statistics

Name	#Movie	#Reviews	#Spam	#Non-spam	Genre	Movie Released Year
M-Raw-Data	2,352	734,130	–	–	40	2017–2021
M-Dataset	457	65,696	20,092	45,604		

knowledge, and then obtain the correlation vectors between reviews and movies through the comparison network. Finally, the three feature vectors are concatenated and fed into the fully connected layer and the Softmax layer to obtain the classification results.

Movie Background Knowledge Extraction

Building a Movie Background Knowledge Graph. We construct a directed heterogeneous graph $\delta = (V, E)$ that contains movie synopses and high-quality long comments of movies. The graph contains two types of nodes: movie synopses $S = \{V_1^s, V_2^s, ..., V_i^s, ..., V_M^s\}$ and long comments $L = \{V_1^l, V_2^l, ..., V_j^l, ..., V_N^l\}$, where M denotes the number of movie synopsis nodes and N denotes the number of long comment nodes. To be specific, V_i^s denotes the ith movie synopsis node, V_j^l denotes the jth long comment node, i.e., $V = S \cup L$. And the set of edges E include bidirectional connections and unidirectional connections. The details of constructing the graph are described as follows.

The set of M movies is denoted as $F = \{f_1, f_2, f_3, ..., f_M\}$, and one movie can belong to multiple themes. Movies of the same theme may have certain similarities in the plots, which leads to some similarities of user reviews. Firstly, we establish a bidirectional connection between the movie synopsis nodes of the same theme movies, so as to allow useful background knowledge to propagate among the same theme movies. Secondly, we establish a bidirectional connection between the long comment node and the movie synopsis node in the same movie, and expand the useful movie background knowledge through multiple high-quality long comments from the reviewers. Finally, in a long comment, the reviewer tends to compare the movie they reviewed with other movies, including the quality of the movies, the plots, the characters, etc. So we establish a connection between the long comment node and the other movie synopses. In order to avoid embedding other unrelated movie information into movie background knowledge through long comment nodes, the edges we build here are unidirectional edges.

Constructing Directed Heterogeneous Graph Convolutions. Based on the above-constructed directed heterogeneous movie background knowledge graph $\delta = (V, E)$, we design a graph convolutional neural network based on the directed heterogeneous graph. First, we use the pre-trained Chinese-BERT model to embed the node features. The vector $x_s \in R^D$ denotes the embedded feature of the node V_s. The matrix $X = \{x_1, x_2, x_3, ..., x_{|V|}\} \in R^{|V| \times D}$ contains the feature vectors of all nodes, and each row of X represents the feature vector of one node. We define A is the adjacency matrix and D is the degree matrix. Then, the heterogeneous graph convolution layer updates the $(i+1)$th layer representation of the aggregated features by aggregating the features of their adjacent nodes.

$$A' = D^{-\frac{1}{2}} \left(A + I \right) D^{-\frac{1}{2}} \tag{1}$$

$$H^{(i+1)} = \sigma \left(A' H^i W^i \right) \tag{2}$$

where I is the identity matrix of dimension $|V|$. The A' is the adjacency matrix after self-connection and normalization. The W^i is the weight matrix of the ith layer, The H^i is the feature matrix of the ith layer, σ is the nonlinear activation function (such as the $ReLU$ function), and $H^{(i+1)}$ is the next layer after aggregation feature matrix.

Feature Extraction of Review Correlation. After obtaining the embedded representation of the movie background knowledge, we compare the review feature vector T_n with the embedded vector x_n of the corresponding movie background knowledge, and get their correlation vector $S_n = f_{cmp}(T_n, x_n)$, where $f_{cmp}()$ is the comparison function. Based on [5], we design the comparison function as $f_{cmp}(x, y) = W[x - y, x \odot y]$, where W is the transformation matrix, x and y are the movie background knowledge embedding vector and the review feature vector, respectively, $\odot$ denotes element-wise multiplication for two matrixes.

Text and User Statistical Feature Extraction

Text Feature Extraction. First, we use the review r_n as the input data to the pre-trained Chinese-BERT model to get its vector representation, and then feed the vector representation into the fully connected layer to get the text feature vector T_n.

Table 2. User statistical features

Feature Name	Description
User Rating (UR)	It reflects the user's rating towards the movie
Movie Rating (MR)	It reflects the audience's average rating of the movie
Consensus of Opinion (CO)	Using $|UR - MR|$ to evaluate the consistency of opinions between one reviewer and other audience
Account Active Degree (ACD)	The level of activity of the account making the review
Review Time (RT)	The user's review time in a day
Time Span (TS)	The span between review time and movie release time

User Statistical Feature Extraction. According to the characteristics of movie reviews and the Maoyan platform, we propose six statistical features of users. The details are shown in the Table 2.

3.3 Feature Concatenation

First, we concatenate the text feature representation vector T_n, the user statistical feature vector U_n and the comment correlation vector S_n to get the vector F_n, where $F_n = concat(T_n, U_n, S_n) \in R^{|S_n|+|U_n|+|T_n|}$. Then the vector F_n is fed into the Softmax classification layer, which is simplified as $Z = Softmax(WF_n + b)$ where W is the parameter matrix of the fully connected layer, and b is the bias vector of the fully connected layer.

4 Experiments

In this section, we will evaluate the performance of our proposed GCMK method. First, we describe the experimental setup in our work. Then, we illustrate the superiority of our method in comparison with the baseline methods. Then, the effects of different modules on the model are examined by ablation experiments. Finally, we verify the robustness of our model by randomly adding different proportions of noise to the training set.

4.1 Experiment Settings

We implemented our GCMK approach and baseline model with Pytorch v1.10.1 framework. In our work, all experiments were performed on a workstation equipped with Intel (R) Core (TM) i9-10900 CPU and NVIDIA GeForce RTX 3070 GPU with 64GB of memory.

   We use the M-Dataset for training and verification. Specifically, we do not change the number of spam reviews, randomly sample the same number of spam reviews from 45,604 non-spam reviews, and construct a balanced dataset containing 40,184 reviews. We reproduce three models for comparison experiments, where addCGAN [3] is the first state-of-the-art model for spam movie review detection, and CBRNN [21] and HACL [14] are the state-of-the-art models for spam review detection. At the same time, we select a couple of very popular text classification models like TextCNN [22], FastText [8], DPCNN [7], AttBiLSTM [23] as our baseline models. Four evaluation metrics are used to quantify the effect of the models, including Accuracy, Precision, Recall, and F1-score.

4.2 Baseline Model Comparison Experiment

To demonstrate the effectiveness of our proposed GCMK method, we test our model and seven other baselines on our built M-Dataset. The results are shown in Table 3. The results show that our proposed GCMK method outperforms other baseline models on spam movie review detection in terms of Accuracy,

Precision, Recall and F1-score. Compared with these state-of-the-art detection methods, GCMK is proved to effectively extract more discriminative features of spam movie reviews (background knowledge of movies and user features) and achieves significant performance improvements in detecting spam movie reviews.

Table 3. Results for baseline model comparison experiment

Model	Accuracy	Spam			Non-Spam		
		Precision	Recall	F1-score	Precision	Recall	F1-score
TextCNN [22]	74.80	77.77	70.31	73.85	72.29	77.00	79.41
FastText [8]	76.73	80.01	73.41	76.42	73.79	80.55	77.02
DPCNN [7]	77.14	77.51	77.26	77.39	76.75	77.00	76.88
AttBiLSTM [23]	76.77	79.50	74.06	76.68	74.25	79.67	76.86
CBRNN [21]	76.77	77.91	76.71	77.31	75.60	76.84	76.22
HACL [14]	72.83	72.83	71.82	72.45	72.59	73.83	73.21
addCGAN [3]	76.08	76.95	75.96	76.45	75.19	76.21	75.70
GCMK(our model)	**85.01**	**83.22**	**86.73**	**84.94**	**86.85**	**83.38**	**85.08**

4.3 Feature Ablation Experiment

Our proposed GCMK model combines text features, user statistical features and the movie background knowledge. We explore the contribution of each proposed block by ablation experiment. Specifically, the use of ablation features is shown in Table 4, where K denotes movie background knowledge, U denotes user statistical feature. And we use Accuracy, Precision, Recall and F1-score to measure the detection effect of the model. The experimental results are shown in Fig. 2. The results show that our designed movie background knowledge embedding and user statistical feature extraction are better than merely using text features. Meanwhile, each block plays a role in the effectiveness of the GCMK model, and the ablation of both block can weaken the effect of the model. These two blocks give a comprehensive improvement to the GCMK model. Evidently, our proposed blocks can effectively help distinguish spam movie reviews.

Table 4. The description of feature sets

Feature set	Categories of features included
GCMK	Movie background knowledge, User statistical feature, Text feature
GCMK\K	User statistical feature, Text feature
GCMK\U	Movie background knowledge, Text feature
GCMK\$K\&U$	Text feature

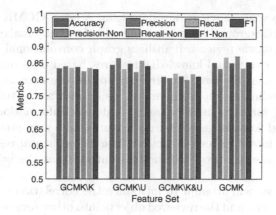

Fig. 2. Results for ablation experiment

4.4 Robustness Experiment

We randomly label the training set incorrectly according to a certain ratio (5%–45%), and train our model and the baseline models to test the robustness under different noise levels. The experimental results are shown in Fig. 3. The results show that as the noise rate continues to increase, the performances (F1-score) of all models almost decrease to varying degrees, while our model changes little.

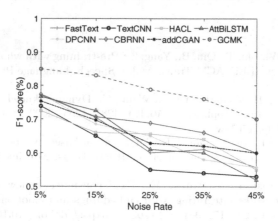

Fig. 3. Results for robustness experiment

5   Conclusion

In this paper, we construct the first publicly available Chinese spam movie review dataset (M-Dataset) for spam movie reviews detection, and innovatively propose to use graph convolutional neural network to extract movie background knowledge to help spam movie review detection. A novel GCMK model is developed with movie background knowledge embedded to truly make progress in the problem of spam movie reviews. It utilizes graph convolutional neural network to get the movie background knowledge features based on a directed heterogeneous graph and uses the text features to capture the correlations of reviews and the corresponding movie. Futhermore, we extract six features about spam movie reviews in terms of user behavior and user information. We combine movie background knowledge with text features and user statistical features to improve spam movie reviews detection. The experimental results on our M-Dataset demonstrate our proposed method outperforms the other state-of-art models.

In the future, we will attempt to introduce the correlation comparison algorithm between reviews and the reviewed objects into other review detection fields (e-commerce, restaurant, etc.).

Acknowledgments. This work is supported by the National Natural Science Foundation of China (NSFC) under grant nos. 61802271, 61802270, 81602935, and 81773548. In addition, this work is also partially supported by Joint Research Fund of China Ministry of Education and China Mobile Company (No. CM20200409), Sichuan University and Yibin Municipal People's Government University and City Strategic Cooperation Special Fund Project (No. 2020CDYB-29), Science and Technology Plan Transfer Payment Project of Sichuan Province (No. 2021ZYSF007) and The Key Research and Development Program of Science and Technology Department of Sichuan Province (No. 2020YFS0575, No. 2021YFG0159, No. 2021KJT0012-2021YFS0067).

References

1. Cui, Y., Che, W., Liu, T., Qin, B., Yang, Z.: Pre-training with whole word masking for Chinese Bert. IEEE/ACM Trans. Audio, Speech, Language Process. **29**, 3504–3514 (2021)
2. Fang, Y., Wang, H., Zhao, L., Yu, F., Wang, C.: Dynamic knowledge graph based fake-review detection. Appl. Intell. **50**(12), 4281–4295 (2020). https://doi.org/10.1007/s10489-020-01761-w
3. Gao, Y., Gong, M., Xie, Y., Qin, A.K.: An attention-based unsupervised adversarial model for movie review spam detection. IEEE Trans. Multimedia **23**, 784–796 (2020)
4. Hajek, P., Barushka, A., Munk, M.: Fake consumer review detection using deep neural networks integrating word embeddings and emotion mining. Neural Comput. Appl. **32**(23), 17259–17274 (2020). https://doi.org/10.1007/s00521-020-04757-2
5. Hu, L., et al.: Compare to the knowledge: Graph neural fake news detection with external knowledge. In: Proceedings of the 59th Annual Meeting of the Association for Computational Linguistics and the 11th International Joint Conference on Natural Language Processing, pp. 754–763 (2021)
6. Jindal, N., Liu, B.: Opinion spam and analysis. In: Proceedings of the 8th International Conference on Web Search and Data Mining, pp. 219–230 (2008)
7. Johnson, R., Zhang, T.: Deep pyramid convolutional neural networks for text categorization. In: Proceedings of the 55th Annual Meeting of the Association for Computational Linguistics, pp. 562–570 (2017)

8. Joulin, A., Grave, E., Bojanowski, P., Mikolov, T.: Bag of tricks for efficient text classification. arXiv preprint arXiv:1607.01759 pp. 1–5 (2016)
9. Kaur, G., Sharma, A.: Has: Hybrid analysis of sentiments for the perspective of customer review summarization. J. Ambient Intell. Hum. Comput. 1–14 (2022). https://doi.org/10.1007/s12652-022-03748-6
10. Khan, A., et al.: Movie review summarization using supervised learning and graph-based ranking algorithm. Comput. Intell. Neurosci. **2020**, 1–14 (2020)
11. Li, J., Ott, M., Cardie, C., Hovy, E.: Towards a general rule for identifying deceptive opinion spam. In: Proceedings of the 52nd Annual Meeting of the Association for Computational Linguistics, pp. 1566–1576 (2014)
12. Li, L., Qin, B., Ren, W., Liu, T.: Document representation and feature combination for deceptive spam review detection. Neurocomputing **254**, 33–41 (2017)
13. Liu, C.L., Hsaio, W.H., Lee, C.H., Lu, G.C., Jou, E.: Movie rating and review summarization in mobile environment. IEEE Trans. Syst. Man Cybern. **42**(3), 397–407 (2011)
14. Liu, Y., Wang, L., Shi, T., Li, J.: Detection of spam reviews through a hierarchical attention architecture with n-gram CNN and BI-LSTM. Inf. Syst. **103**, 101865 (2022)
15. Liu, Z., Sun, Q., Yang, Z., Jiang, K., Yan, J.: Fined-grained aspect extraction from online reviews for decision support. In: 2020 IEEE 19th International Conference on Trust, Security and Privacy in Computing and Communications, pp. 1536–1541 (2020)
16. Ma, H., Kim, J.M., Lee, E.: Analyzing dynamic review manipulation and its impact on movie box office revenue. Electron. Commer. Res. Appl. **35**, 100840 (2019)
17. Ma, H., Kim, J.M., Lee, E.: A 2020 perspective on "analyzing dynamic review manipulation and its impact on movie box office revenue. Electron. Commer. Res. Appl. **41**, 100950 (2020)
18. Manek, A.S., Shenoy, P.D., Mohan, M.C., et al.: Aspect term extraction for sentiment analysis in large movie reviews using GINI index feature selection method and SVM classifier. World Wide Web **20**(2), 135–154 (2017)
19. Neisari, A., Rueda, L., Saad, S.: Spam review detection using self-organizing maps and convolutional neural networks. Comput. Secur. **106**, 102274 (2021)
20. Ott, M., Choi, Y., Cardie, C., Hancock, J.T.: Finding deceptive opinion spam by any stretch of the imagination. In: Proceedings of the 49th Annual Meeting of the Association for Computational Linguistics: Human Language Technologies, pp. 309–319 (2011)
21. Soubraylu, S., Rajalakshmi, R.: Hybrid convolutional bidirectional recurrent neural network based sentiment analysis on movie reviews. Comput. Intell. **37**(2), 735–757 (2021)
22. Zhang, Y., Wallace, B.: A sensitivity analysis of (and practitioners' guide to) convolutional neural networks for sentence classification. arXiv preprint arXiv:1510.03820 (2015)
23. Zhou, P., et al.: Attention-based bidirectional long short-term memory networks for relation classification. In: Proceedings of the 54th Annual Meeting of the Association for Computational Linguistics, pp. 207–212 (2016)
24. Zhou, Y., Zhang, L., Yi, Z.: Predicting movie box-office revenues using deep neural networks. Neural Comput. Appl. **31**(6), 1855–1865 (2017). https://doi.org/10.1007/s00521-017-3162-x

Heterogeneous Graph Attention Network for Malicious Domain Detection

Zhiping Li[1,2], Fangfang Yuan[1(✉)], Yanbing Liu[1,2], Cong Cao[1], Fang Fang[1], and Jianlong Tan[1,2]

[1] Institute of Information Engineering, Chinese Academy of Sciences, Beijing, China
{lizhiping,yuanfangfang,liuyanbing,caocong,
fangfang,tanjianlong}@iie.ac.cn
[2] School of Cyber Security, University of Chinese Academy of Sciences, Beijing, China

Abstract. Domain name system(DNS) is a basic part of the Internet infrastructure, but it is also abused by attackers in various cybercrimes, making the task of malicious domain detection increasingly important. Most of previous detection methods employ feature-based methods for malicious domain detection. However, the feature-based methods can be easily circumvented by attackers. To solve this issue, some recent researches utilize associations among domains to identify malicious domains, yet without jointly considering both local neighbor's importance and global semantic information's importance. In this paper, we present HANDom, a robust and accurate malicious detection system based on a heterogeneous graph attention network. In HANDom, we first model the DNS scene as a heterogeneous information network(HIN) including domains, clients, IP addresses and their relationships, to capture implicit relationships between domains. Then, we use a hierarchical attention mechanism to learn the importance of different neighbors based meta-path as well as the importance of different meta-paths to the current domain node. Extensive experiments are carried out on the real DNS dataset and results show that our system outperforms the state-of-the-art methods.

Keywords: Malicious domain detection · Heterogeneous information network · Graph attention network

1 Introduction

As the foundation of the Internet, DNS provides a mapping relationship between domains and IP addresses to identify services, devices, or other resources in the network. At the same time, DNS is also abused by attackers, such as phishing, spam, botnets, etc., causing serious economic losses. Therefore, how to effectively detect malicious domains becomes a hot topic in cyber security research.

A simple and direct approach is maintaining blacklists to detect malicious domains. However, with the development of flexible technologies (such

E. Pimenidis et al. (Eds.): ICANN 2022, LNCS 13530, pp. 506–518, 2022.
https://doi.org/10.1007/978-3-031-15931-2_42

as Domain-Flux, Fast-Flux, Double-Flux, etc.), the blacklist-based methods become infeasible. In order to overcome the shortcomings of blacklists, much research has been devoted to developing new methods to detect malicious domains. The traditional methods [6,7,14] mainly extract multiple domain features (such as the length of domain, the number of subdomains, the number of IP addresses, etc.) and adopt a machine learning-based classifier to distinguish malicious domains from benign domains. However, these hand-crafted features can easily be altered by attackers to circumvent the detection system. In order to deal with this issue, some researchers [9,11,12,15,16] utilize associations between domains which are hard to be forged to identify malicious domains. However, these studies do not jointly consider both local neighbor's importance and global semantic information's importance, which limits the ability to learn comprehensive and fine-grained node representation to achieve more accurate detection results.

In order to solve the problems mentioned above, we propose a novel malicious domain detection system named HANDom, which jointly considers the importance of different neighbors and the different semantics reflected by meta-paths. In specific, we use a hierarchical attention mechanism to detect malicious domains, including node level attention and meta-path level attention. We use node level attention to learn the weights of neighbors and use meta-path level attention to learn the weights of meta-paths. The more important the neighbors or meta-paths are, the higher the weights we learn. In addition, we adopt a pre-trained BERT to analyze the character distribution of domain and automatically initialize the nodes of domain through fine-tuning. In this way, we can adaptively get better node initialization.

In summary, we make the following contributions:

(1) We propose a novel malicious domain detection system named HANDom, which can adaptively initialize domain nodes, learn the comprehensive and fine-grained representation of domains and capture implicit relationships between domains.
(2) We design a hierarchical attention mechanism including node level attention and meta-path level attention, which simultaneously considers the importance of different neighbors and the importance of different meta-paths.
(3) Experimental results on real-world DNS dataset show that our proposed method outperforms the state-of-the-art methods and is suitable for less-labeled data scenarios.

2   Related Work

Existing malicious domain detection methods can be roughly divided into three categories: rule-based methods, feature-based methods and association-based methods.

Rule-based methods are the most traditional detection methods, maintaining blacklists to detect malicious domains. These methods are generally simple and efficient, but with the development of flexible technologies, the rule-based methods become infeasible.

Feature-based methods analyze the DNS traffic to extract features, and then train a machine learning-based classifier [6,7,14]. Antonakakis et al. [6] calculates accurate reputation scores for new domains by analyzing network, regional and evidence characteristics. BILGE et al. [7] extracts four sets of features from DNS records to train a J48 decision tree to discover malicious domains. Schüppen et al. [14] detects DGA-based malware by monitoring non-existent domain responses in DNS traffic. However, these methods rely on hand-crafted statistical features which can be carefully altered by attackers to evade the malicious domain detection.

Association-based methods are based on the fact that an attacker cannot easily forge the natural relationship generated in the DNS. Researchers [9,11,12,15–17] utilize the association between domains to detect malicious domains. He et al. [9] constructs a domain association graph and uses DeepWalk to extract local structural features to detect malicious domains. Zhang et al. [19] exploits attribute similarity and structural correlation among domains to recognize malicious domains. Sun et al. [17] proposes a heterogeneous graph convolution network to identify malicious domains. However, the methods mentioned above only focus on the importance of different neighbors or the importance of different meta-paths, without considering the combination of the two. To solve this problem, we propose HANDom with a hierarchical attention mechanism for malicious domain detection.

3   Preliminary

In this section, we will introduce some basic concepts, including heterogeneous information network, meta-path, and meta-path based neighbors.

Definition 1. *Heterogeneous information network. We define a HIN as $\mathcal{G} = (\mathcal{V}, \mathcal{E})$, where $\mathcal{V}$ represents the set of nodes, and $\mathcal{E}$ represents the set of edges. HIN is also related to mapping functions, including nodes mapping function $\phi : \mathcal{V} \to \mathcal{A}$ and edges mapping function $\psi : \mathcal{E} \to \mathcal{R}$. $\mathcal{A}$ and $\mathcal{R}$ are defined as a set of node types and a set of edge types, where $|\mathcal{A}| + |\mathcal{R}| > 2$.*

Definition 2. *Meta-path. A meta path is defined as a path composed of a set of nodes and relationships, such as $\mathcal{A}_1 \xrightarrow{\mathcal{R}_1} \mathcal{A}_2 \xrightarrow{\mathcal{R}_2} \cdots \xrightarrow{\mathcal{R}_l} \mathcal{A}_{l+1}$, which can also be described as $\mathcal{A}_1 \mathcal{A}_2 \cdots \mathcal{A}_{l+1}$ or $\mathcal{R}_1 \circ \mathcal{R}_2 \circ \cdots \mathcal{R}_l$, where $\circ$ is defined as a combination operator on relations.*

Definition 3. *Meta-path based neighbors. Given a meta-path $\mathcal{P}$ and a node i, take node i as a starting point and perform random walks guided by the meta-path $\mathcal{P}$, and the resulting node sequence $\mathcal{N}_i^{\mathcal{P}}$ are the neighbors based on the meta-path, including node i.*

4   The System Description of HANDom

In this section, we will introduce HANDom in detail. It consists of five components: data preprocessing, HIN construction, graph pruning, meta-path based neighbors extraction and HAN classification. The system architecture of HANDom is shown in Fig. 1.

4.1   Data Preprocessing

During the recursive process of domain query, various data including DNS traffic are generated. DNS traffic reflects the communications between clients, resolvers and higher-level DNS servers. Hence, we collect DNS traffic and extract necessary information for constructing the HIN.

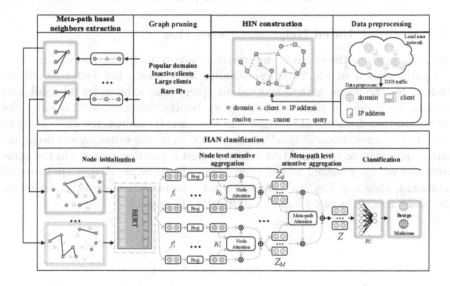

Fig. 1. The system architecture of HANDom

4.2   HIN Construction

We use the collected data to model the DNS scenario as a HIN including three types of nodes (domains, clients, IP addresses) and three kinds of relations between them (query, resolve, cname). The HIN instance and its network schema in HANDom are shown in Fig. 2(a) and Fig. 2(b).

4.3   Graph Pruning

The data we collect from the real DNS traffic is dirty and contains a lot of noise, such as popular domains, large clients, etc. Hence, we perform pruning operations on the HIN to improve the performance of HANDom. The pruning rules are as follows:

- **Popular domains.** Domains queried by a large fraction of clients are usually benign. Otherwise, it will cause significant attack events which can be detected easily. So, we remove domains queried by more than $K_a\%$ of clients.
- **Inactive clients.** Clients that query a few domains are useless on mining graph structural information. Therefore, we remove clients that query less than K_b domains.
- **Large clients.** Clients that query a large number of domains are more likely to be forwarders or proxies. To reduce noise, we remove clients that query more than K_c domains.
- **Rare IPs.** The IP addresses that map to one domain have little effect on mining graph structural information. Hence, we remove them.

In fact, attackers will try to conceal their tracks by reducing their activities. So even if malicious domains comply with the pruning rules, we still retain them.

4.4   Meta-path Based Neighbors Extraction

In order to capture the semantic information between domains, we design three meta-paths shown in Fig. 2(c). Specifically, MP1 shows the fact that clients attacked by the same attackers tend to query the similar set of malicious domains, while normal clients usually query benign domains. MP2 denotes the observation that domains which resolve to the same IP address are more likely to belong to the same owner. Therefore, they tend to be the same class of domains, namely, malicious or benign. MP3 indicates that if two domains are in the same cname record, they belong to the same class. An example of meta-path based neighbors is shown in Fig. 2(d). For meta-path domain-client-domain, the meta-path based neighbors of d3 includes d3(itself), d2 and d4.

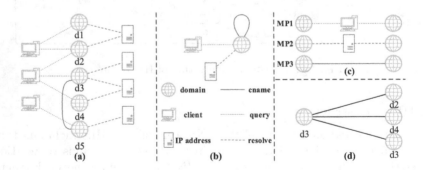

Fig. 2. The HIN instance(a) and its network schema(b) in HANDom. The designed meta-paths(c) and the example of meta-path based neighbors(d)

4.5   HAN Classification

Node Initialization. We observe that the character distribution of malicious domains has high randomness, while benign domains are readable and have some linguistic characteristics. In order to better capture character distribution patterns of domains, we introduce a pre-trained BERT containing richer priori knowledge. During training process, we fine-tune the BERT to obtain adaptive domain initial embeddings. We segment the text of domain node i by word and use its tokens as the input of BERT:

$$f_i = \text{BERT}\,(T_i)\,, \tag{1}$$

where T_i is the token sequence of domain node i, $f_i \in \mathbb{R}^x$ is the initial embedding of domain node i, x is the dimension size of domain initial embedding.

Node Level Attentive Aggregation. In malicious domains detection, the meta-path based neighbors play a different role. In order to capture the impacts of different neighbors, we use the node level attention to learn the importance of neighbors and aggregate the information of neighbors to obtain a domain node representation.

Firstly, guided by meta-paths, we extract several graphs that contain domain nodes from HIN. Then, we design a transformation matrix to map the domain node embedding to the specific feature space:

$$h_i = W_h \cdot f_i, \tag{2}$$

where $h_i \in \mathbb{R}^H$ is the projected embedding of node i, H is the dimension size of projected embedding and $W_h \in \mathbb{R}^{H \times x}$ is the transformation matrix.

Next, we calculate the similarity $e_{ij}^{\mathcal{P}}$ between target node i and its neighbor j in meta-path $\mathcal{P}$. $e_{ij}^{\mathcal{P}}$ is asymmetric which means that the node i and the node j make different contribution to each other. The similarity is calculated as follows:

$$e_{ij}^{\mathcal{P}} = \text{att}_{node}\,(h_i, h_j; \mathcal{P}) = \sigma\left(a_{\mathcal{P}}^T \cdot [h_i \| h_j]\right), \tag{3}$$

where att_{node} is the node level attention, $a_{\mathcal{P}} \in \mathbb{R}^{2H}$ is the parameter matrix and it shares parameters under each meta-path, $\mathcal{P}$ is the $\mathcal{P}$-th meta-path, $\cdot^T$ represents transposition, σ is the activation function, $\|$ denotes the concatenate operation. After that, we obtain the weight $\alpha_{ij}^{\mathcal{P}}$ by normalizing the similarity:

$$\alpha_{ij}^{\mathcal{P}} = \text{softmax}\left(e_{ij}^{\mathcal{P}}\right) = \frac{\exp\left(\sigma\left(a_{\mathcal{P}}^T \cdot [h_i \| h_j]\right)\right)}{\sum_{k \in \mathcal{N}_i^{\mathcal{P}}} \exp\left(\sigma\left(a_{\mathcal{P}}^T \cdot [h_i \| h_k]\right)\right)}. \tag{4}$$

Then, we aggregate the projected embeddings of neighbors with the corresponding weights to get the representation of node i:

$$z_i^{\mathcal{P}} = \sigma\left(\sum_{j \in \mathcal{N}_i^{\mathcal{P}}} \alpha_{ij}^{\mathcal{P}} \cdot h_j\right), \tag{5}$$

where $z_i^{\mathcal{P}} \in \mathbb{R}^H$ is the representation of node i in meta-path $\mathcal{P}$.

To reduce the high variance caused by the heterogeneity of graph data during the training process, here we extend the node level attention to multi-head attention to make the training process more stable. We repeat the node level attention aggregation K times and concatenate the embeddings:

$$z_i^P = \overset{K}{\underset{k=1}{\|}} \sigma \left(\sum_{j \in \mathcal{N}_i^P} \alpha_{ij}^P \cdot h_j \right), \tag{6}$$

where $z_i^P \in Z_P$, Z_P is the set of aggregation representation of all nodes under meta-path P.

Meta-path Level Attentive Aggregation. Meta-paths will make different contributions to malicious domain detection. In order to learn a more comprehensive domain node representation, we use the meta-path level attention to automatically assign the weights to meta-paths.

We measure the importance of meta-path as the similarity between aggregation representation and meta-path attention vector d. Furthermore, we calculate the average similarity of all nodes under a meta-path and regard it as the importance of this meta-path:

$$s_P = \text{att}_{semantic}(Z_P, d) = \frac{1}{|\mathcal{V}|} \sum_{i \in \mathcal{V}} d^T \cdot \tanh\left(W_d \cdot z_i^P + b\right), \tag{7}$$

where $\text{att}_{semantic}$ is meta-path attention that calculates importance s_P of meta-path P, $d \in \mathbb{R}^q$ is a meta-path attention vector, q is the size of the meta-path attention vector, $W_d \in \mathbb{R}^{q \times H}$ is weight matrix, b is the bias vector. Then, we calculate the weight β_P of meta-path P:

$$\beta_P = \text{softmax}(s_P) = \frac{\exp(s_P)}{\sum_{l=0}^M \exp(s_l)}, \tag{8}$$

which can be considered as the contribution of meta-path P to the detection task. The more important the meta-path is, the higher the weight β_P is.

Finally, we aggregate these meta-path level embeddings with the corresponding weights of meta-paths to get the final domain representation:

$$Z = \sum_{P=0}^M \beta_P \cdot Z_P, \tag{9}$$

where $Z = \{z_1', z_2', \cdots, z_{|\mathcal{V}|}'\}$ is the set of domain representations, $z_i' \in \mathbb{R}^H$.

Classification. With domain representations, we simplify the malicious domain detection as a binary classification task. The final domain representation Z is fed to a fully connected network to classify domains. Then, we train the HANDom in a semi-supervised paradigm and minimize the cross-entropy loss over all labeled nodes between the true labels and predictions for malicious domain detection:

$$\hat{y}_i = \text{softmax}\left(\sigma\left(W_o \cdot z_i' + b\right)\right), \tag{10}$$

$$L = -\sum_{i=1}^{|\mathcal{V}_{\mathcal{L}}|} \left(y_{i,0} \cdot \log \hat{y}_{i,0} + y_{i,1} \cdot \log \hat{y}_{i,1}\right), \tag{11}$$

where $\hat{y}_i \in \mathbb{R}^2$ is the prediction of the i-th node, $W_o \in \mathbb{R}^{2 \times H}$ is the transition matrix, y_i is ground truth of the i-th node, $|\mathcal{V}_{\mathcal{L}}|$ is the size of the labeled node.

5   Experiments

5.1   Dataset

DNS Traffic Collection. We collect real DNS traffic of a university during two weeks from 2020-08-01 to 2020-08-14. Then, we obtain necessary information including domains, clients, IP addresses and their relationships. Through the graph pruning mentioned in Sect. 4.3, we remove some unhelpful nodes. Finally, we construct the DNS HIN that contains 200,014 domains, 5,670 clients, 58,657 IP addresses and edges between them.

Domain Labeling. Since our method is based on semi-supervised learning, we need to label our domains. For whitelist, we collect the Alexa top 1M list [1]. For blacklist, we collect domains from malwaredomains [3], phishtank [4] and cybercrime [2], etc. Furthermore, we use VirusTotal [5] to validate a part of domains and identify the suspect domain. Eventually, we label 36,489 benign domains and 11,747 malicious domains and use them as the final labeled dataset. The description of experimental dataset is shown in Table 1.

We randomly split the labeled dataset into training set, validation set, and testing set with the ratio of 7:2:1, and get the average results with 10-fold cross-validations.

Table 1. The description of experimental dataset

DNS HIN		
Clients	Domains	IP addresses
5,670	200,014	58,657
Domain-Client	Domain-Domain	Domain-IP address
57,261	7,780	297,534
Labeled domains		
Benign domains	Malicious domains	
36,489(11,747 sampled)	11,747	

5.2   Comparative Methods

We first compare HANDom with four baseline methods, including two network embedding based methods and two graph neural network based methods.

- **DeepWalk** [13]: A classical network embedding based method which uses random walk and the skip-gram model to learn node representations on homogeneous graph. Here we ignore the heterogeneity of nodes.
- **Metapath2vec** [8]: A widely used network embedding based method on heterogeneous graph which exploits meta-path based random walk and the skip-gram model to learn node representations.
- **GCN** [10]: A classical graph convolution based approach which can capture high-order neighbors information. Here we ignore the heterogeneity of nodes.
- **GAT** [18]: A common method that exploits an attention mechanism on homogeneous graph. It can assign different weights to neighbors. Here we ignore the heterogeneity of nodes.

Then, we compare HANDom with three state-of-the-art malicious domain detection methods, including feature-based method and association-based methods.

- **FANCI** [14]: It extracts 21 features including three categories: structural features, linguistic features and statistical features. It trains SVM and Random Forest to detect malicious domains.
- **GAMD** [19]: It uses node type-aware feature transformation and edge type-aware attention mechanism to learn fine-grained domain representation.
- **HGDom** [17]: It extracts several homogeneous graphs guided by meta-path from heterogeneous graphs and uses convolutional neural network to fuse the domain features and graph structure.

5.3   Experimental Setting

In our experiments, we use Adam optimizer and initialize its parameters randomly. We select the best parameters by manually experimenting on multiple parameters. According to the graph pruning rules, we discard some unhelpful nodes by setting $K_a = 35$, $K_b = 4$, $K_c = 100$. For HANDom, we set the learning rate to 0.001, the regularized weight decay to 0.001, the dropout parameter to 0.6, the number of attention heads to 8, the number of neighbors to 20, the initial label fraction to 70%, and the dimension of vector d to 512. For DeepWalk and Metapath2vec, we set the random walk length to 10, window size to 4, walks per node to 2, and the number of positive samples to 2. For GCN, GAT, GAMD and HGDom, we set the node embedding dimension to 768. For a fair comparison, we use the same training set, validation set and testing set to ensure fairness.

5.4   Performance Comparisons

Comparison with Baselines. From Table 2, we can see that HANDom outperforms baselines overall. Among the baselines, Metapath2vec is the most competitive network embedding based method and GAT is the most competitive graph neural network based method. Compared with Metapath2vec, HANDom performs better. The reason is that Metapath2vec only uses the node co-occurrence relationship. In contrast, HANDom not only aggregates neighbors to capture graph structural information, but also utilizes node attributes to enrich node representation. Compared with GAT, HANDom shows its superiority. This is because HANDom in heterogeneous graph can learn the information of other types of entities than GAT in homogeneous graph. Furthermore, the meta-path level attention in HANDom can capture complex semantic information in heterogeneous graph.

Table 2. Performance(%) comparisons of HANDom with baseline methods

Method	Acc	F1	Precision	Recall
DeepWalk	62.33	74.73	75.88	73.61
Metapath2vec	70.25	82.53	70.29	99.92
GCN	86.19	91.47	85.84	97.89
GAT	88.12	92.67	86.86	99.31
HANDom	**98.88**	**99.27**	**98.59**	**99.95**

Comparison with State-of-the-Art Methods. From Table 3, we can see that HANDom outperforms all the state-of-the-art methods for all evaluation metrics. Compared with FANCI, HANDom performs better than it by a large margin. It is because HANDom utilizes the association information between domains, while FANCI takes advantage of hand-crafted features which are easily to be tampered with by attackers. In association-based methods, HGDom outperforms GAMD as HGDom exploits meta-paths to capture rich semantic information in heterogeneous graphs, which further enriches the node representation. Furthermore, HANDom is superior to HGDom. The reason is that HGDom roughly aggregates the information of neighbors, ignoring the different contributions of different nodes. However, HANDom considers the different importance of nodes and the different contributions of meta-paths to learn comprehensive and fine-grained node representation successfully.

Table 3. Performance(%) comparisons of HANDom with the state-of-the-art methods

Method	Acc	F1	Precision	Recall
FANCI	89.57	89.81	90.05	89.57
GAMD	94.96	96.76	94.30	99.34
HGDom	96.97	98.04	96.23	99.92
HANDom	**98.88**	**99.27**	**98.59**	**99.95**

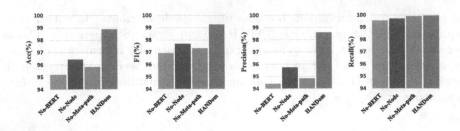

Fig. 3. Performance comparisons of HANDom with its variants

5.5 Ablation Study

We conduct ablation study to validate the effectiveness of three components, including (1)**No-BERT**: we remove the BERT layer and generate the node initial embedding by averaging its randomly initialized word embeddings. (2)**No-Node**: we apply the mean operation instead of node level attention. (3)**No-Meta-path**: we apply the mean operation instead of meta-path level attention.

From Fig. 3, we can get some conclusions as follows: (1) HANDom has better performance than No-BERT, proving the effectiveness of BERT for node initialization. The reason is that BERT can adaptively capture the character distribution of domain. (2) HANDom achieves better results than No-Node, demonstrating that node level attention is effective. It is because that node level attention can learn the important of different neighbors. (3) HANDom outperforms No-Meta-path, indicating that considering the importance of different meta-paths is useful for malicious domain detection. Finally, HANDom significantly outperforms all the variants by applying node initialization and hierarchical attention mechanism including node level attention and meta-path level attention.

5.6 Parameter Analysis

Dimension of Meta-path Attention Vector d. In our experiments, the value of d ranges from 64 to 1024. Figure 4(a) shows that the performance of HANDom achieves the best result when d is 512. When d is greater than 512, the F1 of HANDom decreases.

Number of Attention Head K. To analyze the impact of multi-head attention, we make the number of attention heads range from 2 to 10. Figure 4(b) shows that with the increase of the number of attention heads, the F1 of HANDom increases. However, when K exceeds 8, the performance of HANDom improves slightly.

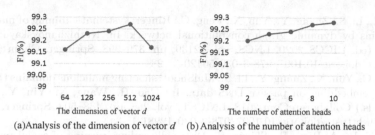

(a) Analysis of the dimension of vector d (b) Analysis of the number of attention heads

Fig. 4. Parameter sensitivity of HANDom

6   Conclusion

In this paper, we propose a novel malicious domain detection system named HANDom. Particularly, we first model the DNS scenario as a heterogeneous information network consisting of domains, clients, IP addresses and their associations. Then, with jointly consideration of the importance of different neighbors and the importance of different meta-paths, HANDom captures the key information at multiple granularity that can effectively distinguish malicious domains from benign domains. Extensive experimental results on the real DNS dataset show that our proposed approach outperforms the state-of-the-art methods.

Acknowledgements. This work was partly supported by Strategic Priority Research Program of the Chinese Academy of Sciences under Grant No. XDC02030000.

References

1. Alexa top 1 million. https://aws.amazon.com/cn/alexa-top-sites/ (2022)
2. cybercrime. https://cybercrime-tracker.net/ (2022)
3. Malware domain block list. www.malwaredomains.com (2022)
4. Phishtank. www.phishtank.com (2022)
5. Virustotal. www.virustotal.com (2022)
6. Antonakakis, M., Perdisci, R., Dagon, D., Lee, W., Feamster, N.: Building a dynamic reputation system for DNS. In: USENIX Security Symposium, pp. 273–290 (2010)
7. Bilge, L., Sen, S., Balzarotti, D., Kirda, E., Kruegel, C.: Exposure: a passive DNS analysis service to detect and report malicious domains. ACM Trans. Inf. Syst. Secur. (TISSEC) **16**(4), 1–28 (2014)
8. Dong, Y., Chawla, N.V., Swami, A.: metapath2vec: scalable representation learning for heterogeneous networks. In: Proceedings of the 23rd ACM SIGKDD International Conference on Knowledge Discovery and Data Mining, pp. 135–144 (2017)
9. He, W., Gou, G., Kang, C., Liu, C., Li, Z., Xiong, G.: Malicious domain detection via domain relationship and graph models. In: 2019 IEEE 38th International Performance Computing and Communications Conference (IPCCC), pp. 1–8. IEEE (2019)
10. Kipf, T.N., Welling, M.: Semi-supervised classification with graph convolutional networks. arXiv preprint arXiv:1609.02907 (2016)

11. Liu, Z., Li, S., Zhang, Y., Yun, X., Peng, C.: Ringer: systematic mining of malicious domains by dynamic graph convolutional network. In: Krzhizhanovskaya, V.V., et al. (eds.) ICCS 2020. LNCS, vol. 12139, pp. 379–398. Springer, Cham (2020). https://doi.org/10.1007/978-3-030-50420-5_28

12. Peng, C., Yun, X., Zhang, Y., Li, S.: MalShoot: shooting malicious domains through graph embedding on passive DNS data. In: Gao, H., Wang, X., Yin, Y., Iqbal, M. (eds.) CollaborateCom 2018. LNICST, vol. 268, pp. 488–503. Springer, Cham (2019). https://doi.org/10.1007/978-3-030-12981-1_34

13. Perozzi, B., Al-Rfou, R., Skiena, S.: Deepwalk: online learning of social representations. In: Proceedings of the 20th ACM SIGKDD International Conference on Knowledge Discovery and Data Mining, pp. 701–710 (2014)

14. Schüppen, S., Teubert, D., Herrmann, P., Meyer, U.: {FANCI}: feature-based automated nxdomain classification and intelligence. In: 27th {USENIX} Security Symposium ({USENIX} Security 18), pp. 1165–1181 (2018)

15. Sun, X., Tong, M., Yang, J., Xinran, L., Heng, L.: Hindom: a robust malicious domain detection system based on heterogeneous information network with transductive classification. In: 22nd International Symposium on Research in Attacks, Intrusions and Defenses ({RAID} 2019), pp. 399–412 (2019)

16. Sun, X., Wang, Z., Yang, J., Liu, X.: Deepdom: malicious domain detection with scalable and heterogeneous graph convolutional networks. Comput. Secur. **99**, 102057 (2020)

17. Sun, X., Yang, J., Wang, Z., Liu, H.: Hgdom: heterogeneous graph convolutional networks for malicious domain detection. In: NOMS 2020–2020 IEEE/IFIP Network Operations and Management Symposium, pp. 1–9. IEEE (2020)

18. Veličković, P., Cucurull, G., Casanova, A., Romero, A., Lio, P., Bengio, Y.: Graph attention networks. arXiv preprint arXiv:1710.10903 (2017)

19. Zhang, S., et al.: Attributed heterogeneous graph neural network for malicious domain detection. In: 2021 IEEE 24th International Conference on Computer Supported Cooperative Work in Design (CSCWD), pp. 397–403. IEEE (2021)

IA-ICGCN: Integrating Prior Knowledge via Intra-event Association and Inter-event Causality for Chinese Causal Event Extraction

Zhengming Zhao[1], Hang Yu[1(✉)], Xiangfeng Luo[1(✉)], Jianqi Gao[1], Xiao Xu[2], and Guo Shengming[2]

[1] School of Computer Engineering and Science, Shanghai University, Shanghai 200444, China
{aloha_zzm,yuhang,luoxf,gjqss}@shu.edu.cn
[2] College of Joint Operations, National Defence University, Beijing 100091, China

Abstract. Causal event extraction (CEE) is a joint extraction task of event detection and event causality discrimination, which is of great value on dialogue system, event prediction and so on. However, the ambiguity of Chinese event description and the implicit causal relationship makes the poor performance with existing models. To deal with this problem, we propose a model to incorporate domain knowledge by taking Intra-event Association and Inter-event Causality into account. We use causal indicators to obtain sentences containing causal relationships from domain texts, and use these sentences to construct event association networks and causality transition networks. To obtain complete event expressions and accurate event causality, we use graph convolutional neural networks (GCN) to encode the information of the two networks separately. Finally, all the information are fed into the Bidirectional Long Short-Term Memory networks. Experimental results on two datasets show that our method outperforms the state-of-the-art baselines.

Keywords: Event detection · Causal event extraction · Chinese event · Graph convolutional neural network

1 Introduction

Causal event extraction (CEE) [1] is a joint extraction task of event detection and event causality discrimination. It plays an important role in information extraction which has been widely applied in event prediction [2] and dialogue system [3]. CEE is defined as the combination of detecting events from plain text and determining whether there exists a causal relationship between the two events.

Causal event can be divided into explicit causal event and implicit causal event. Explicit causal event usually contains causal indicators, such as "because",

E. Pimenidis et al. (Eds.): ICANN 2022, LNCS 13530, pp. 519–531, 2022.
https://doi.org/10.1007/978-3-031-15931-2_43

Table 1. Example of explicit causal sentences and implicit causal sentence

types of causality	plain text	cause event	causal indicators	effect event
Explicit causal sentence	毛利率下滑导致公司盈利低于预期 (The decline in gross profit margin led to the company's profit being lower than expected)	毛利率下降 (decline in gross profit margin)	导致 (led to)	公司盈利低于预期 (the company's profit being lower than expected)
Implicit causal sentence	发生一起连环相撞事故，有1人在事故中死亡 (A series of collisions occurred and one person died in the accident)	连环相撞事故 (a series of collisions occurred)		1人在事故中死亡 (one person died in the accident)

"lead to", etc. Table 1 shows the example of explicit causality and implicit causality. In sentence "The decline in gross profit margin led to the company's profit to be lower than expected", the word "led to" indicates that there is a causal relationship between the cause "decline in gross profit margin" and the effect "the company's profit to be lower than expected". However, for implicit causal sentence "A series of collisions occurred and one person died in the accident", it is difficult for the model to learn the causal relationship between the event "a series of collisions occurred" and "one person died in the accident".

Causal event extraction can be divided into rule-based method, statistical machine learning method and deep learning method. For rule-based method, researchers extract causal relations from texts by constructing handcrafted linguistic patterns, such as lexical patterns, syntactic patterns and semantic patterns [4–7]. However, due to the diversity and complexity of natural language expression, it is impossible to enumerate all causal expression templates, which results in low efficiency and recall of rule-based method. For machine learning method [3,8,9], causal events are extracted by using a large number of handcrafted features. However, the features used in machine learning method are constructed by sophisticated features engineering, which costs too much time and may contain some noise.

In recent years, deep learning has gradually become the mainstream method of information extraction including causal event extraction. Researchers regard causal event extraction as a sequence labeling task and try to improve the effect by applying BiLSTM and CNN to the model [10–13]. However, the ambiguity of event description and the implicit causal relationship makes the poor performance with existing models.

The problem is more prominent in the Chinese corpus due to the difference in the labeling process and the amount of information carried by the token. We conducted statistics on three commonly used datasets of causality, including two Chinese datasets and one English dataset [14], as shown in the Table 2. The Chinese event mentions are more difficult to extract because they are usually composed of several words instead of one word, like English corpus. In addition,

Table 2. Statistical comparison between Chinese dataset and English dataset

types of causality	CEC Dataset(Chinese)	Financial Dataset(Chinese)	SemEval Dataset(English)
Average sentence length	33.16	59.92	20.84
Max sentence length	95	≥256	60
Average trigger length	4.83	6.14	1.04
(trigger length>6) / all triggers	0.21	0.31	0
Average distance between causal events	6.82	7.38	4.65
Example of Semeval Dataset	Several blocks of flats caught fire after the blaze spread from a building site in Sumner Road		
Cause event	blaze		
Effect event	fire		

the distance between causal events is longer, resulting in the long-distance dependence of causal relationship. It is difficult to improve the model's performance to extract complete events and recognize the event causality just relying on the label data.

In order to solve the above problems, in this paper, we propose a novel framework to make full use of the existing prior knowledge. To extract complete event and improve the accuracy of recognizing event causality, we use external causal data to construct Intra-event Association network and Inter-event Causality network. The above two networks are encoded by graph convolutional neural networks (GCN) [15] respectively. Finally, sentence embedding and GCN encoding are merged together, and fed into BiLSTM+CRF layer. Our contributions are summarized as follows:

- We propose a new model IA-ICGCN for causal event extraction, which integrates the prior knowledge of the two graphs of Intra-event Association and Inter-event Causality to enhance the performance of CEE.
- A method of constructing Intra-event Association network and Inter-event Causality network is proposed to improve the model to extract complete event mentions and recognize more implicit event causality.
- Our results on two Chinese causality domain datasets demonstrate that IA-ICGCN achieves state-of-the-art performance.

2   Related Work

The method of causal event extraction can be divided into pattern matching, statistical learning and neural networks. We will briefly introduce these methods in this section.

2.1   Pattern Matching for CEE

The method based on pattern matching uses template to extract event causality. Khoo et al. [6] apply linguistic cues and pattern matching to extract causal

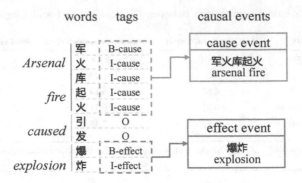

words   tags   causal events

Fig. 1. An example of CEE from Chinese emergency corpus. It extracts causal events and determine whether they are cause or effect simultaneously.

knowledge from the Wall Street Journal. Girju et al. [4] divided CEE into two parts. First, syntactic patterns were used to extract event causality, and then the candidate pair is classified into a causal pair or a non-causal pair using semantic constraints. Furthermore, Ittoo et al. [7] proposed a minimally-supervised approach for explicit and implicit causality extraction to reduce the dependence on labeled data. Pattern matching method requires a large number of manually constructed templates, and its generalization performance still needs to be improved.

2.2 Statistical Learning for CEE

Statistical learning classifies causality by manually constructing a large number of features. Girju et al. [3] used the C4.5 decision tree to discover causality in question answering, and their work shows the effectiveness of machine learning method in causality extraction. Luo et al. [8] obtained term-based causality network from large-scale English short texts based on causality clues and developed a new statistical metric to capture event causality between two short texts. Zhao et al. [9] used the Restricted Hidden Naive Bayes model to analyze the syntactic similarity of causal texts to extract causality.

2.3 Neural Networks for CEE

Due to the outstanding ability of automatic feature extraction, deep neural networks have become the most popular method in CEE. Fu et al. [10] regards CEE as a sequence labeling problem as Fig. 1 shows. Martinez et al. [12] employed Bi-directional Long Short-Term Memory (Bi-LSTM) to obtain the long-term dependence of cause and effect in the text. Furthermore, Jin et al. [13] designed a cascade network model combining Convolution Neural Network (CNN) and Bi-LSTM to extract local phrase features to extract causality, and has good performance on implicit causality. Li et al. [16] proposed a method named SCITE

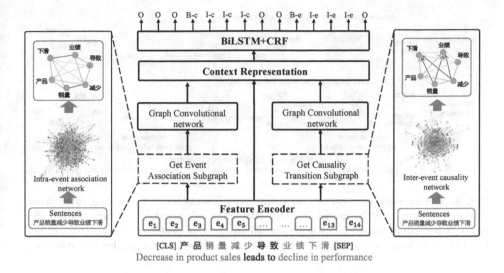

Fig. 2. Overview of our model architecture.

(Self-attentive BiLSTM-CRF wIth Transferred Embeddings), which can directly extract cause and effect and address the problem of data insufficiency. However, due to the complexity of event causality and the limited annotation data set, it is difficult to obtain complete event causality just relying on the model itself. Recently, some researchers have tried to incorporate prior knowledge into their models. Li et al. [17] integrate the knowledge into the convolution kernel to improve the accuracy of event causality extraction. Wang et al. [18] initialize convolutional filters with important n-gram knowledge, which can help the model to capture causal events and promote the training convergence.

3 Our Model

In this section, we will introduce the IA-ICGCN model and describe the process of constructing Intra-event association and Inter-event causality networks. The IA-ICGCN model was shown in Fig. 2, and Fig. 3 gives an illustration of prior knowledge networks construction.

3.1 Feature Encoder

Causal event extraction is a joint task of event extraction and causality classification. We define a sentence as $S = (w_1, w_2, w_3, ..., w_n)$. In CEE, each token w_i is assigned a label $y_i \in y = \{O, B-c, I-c, B-e, I-e\}$. The tag "O" represents the "Other" tag. The tag "B-c" and "I-c" means the token are cause event while "B-e" and "I-e" means it is effect event.

In order to extract richer text semantic features, we use BERT to encode the feature of sentence. BERT [19] is deep bidirectional representations trained

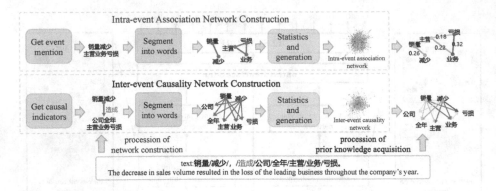

Fig. 3. The example of constructing Intra-event association network and Inter-event causality network. In the model training stage, the sub-graphs is extracted from the network according to the input sentence. In the sample sentence, the red text is the labeled event, and the green is the detected causal indicator word. (Color figure online)

from the large unlabeled text. The pre-trained BERT model can be fine-tuned through an additional output layer to adapt to a variety of tasks. Given an n-word sentence S, BERT will transform S into a fixed vector.

3.2 Intra-event Association and Inter-event Causality Networks Construction

Association Link Network (ALN) [20,21] aims to establish associated relations among various resources [20]. The Intra-event Association and Inter-event Causality Networks (IA-IC) are constructed based on ALN. Domain news is collected on the Internet and used to build IA-IC as follows:

Causal Indicator Word Recognition. The goal of causal indicator word recognition is to generate high-quality domain prior knowledge networks IA-IC. Causal indicator words (CIW) usually reflect the causality in the sentence, and they can effectively filter out sentences which not contain causal relationship.

Event Principal Component Identification. Event Nugget is defined as a semantically meaningful unit that expresses the event in a sentence, which consists of a single word (verbs, nouns, adjectives, adverbs, gerunds) or a phrase [22,23]. The event principal components are detected in the sentence through the following two steps. First of all, sentences are segmented into words and labeled the part-of-speech by Lexical Analysis of Chinese (LAC), which is a lexical analysis tool for Chinese word segmentation, part of speech tagging [24]. Then, we retain the critical words of these words, such as verbs, nouns, adjectives, which can be considered as the main part of the event mentions.

The data from the training datasets and corpus found to have implicit causality are also collected for networks construction. When dealing with the sentences from the datasets and corpus, we directly use labeled cause/effect events instead of the above procession. Figure 3 shows the construction of IA-IC. The details are as follows.

Intra-event Association Network. As Fig. 3 shown. Given sentence "销量减少造成公司全年主营业务亏损(The decrease in sales volume resulted in the loss of the leading business throughout the company's year)", the events are "销量减少(The decrease in sales volume)" and "主营业务亏损(the loss of leading business)". We segment the event mentions into "销量(sales volume)-减少(decrease)" and "主营(leading)-业务(business)-亏损(loss)", then the words ("销量", "减少") and ("主营", "业务", "亏损") can be interconnected internally. Similar operations apply to all the domain texts. The data is arranged to generate the IA network, and the edge weight between words is calculated by the following formula.

$$weight(w_i, w_j) = \frac{co(w_i, w_j)}{\sqrt{DF(w_i) * DF(w_j)}} \tag{1}$$

where $weight(w_i, w_j)$ means the weight between w_i and w_j, $co(w_i, w_j)$ means the co-occur of w_i and w_j in the entire dataset, $DF(w_i)$ means the number of trigger mentions containing the word w_i.

Inter-event Causality Network. Causal indicator words (CIW) not only reflect the causality in the sentence but also reveal the direction of event causality. We manually identify the direction of CIW and judge the direction of event causality. The inter-event causality network can be constructed as follows:

For sentence in Fig. 3, the causal indicator word "造成(resulted in)" divides the text into two parts: "销量减少" and "公司全年主营业务亏损". The causal direction revealed by "造成" is from left to right. After removing stop words and extracting keywords, we get the edges "销量/减少→ 公司/主营/业务/亏损". We do similar operations for all domain texts to construct the IC network. The calculation of causality transition between words can be summarized as follows.

$$weight(w_i{\rightarrow}w_j) = \frac{co(w_i{\rightarrow}w_j)}{\sqrt{DF(w_i) * DF(w_j)}} \tag{2}$$

where $weight(w_i{\rightarrow}w_j)$ means the weight from w_i to w_j. $co(w_i{\rightarrow}w_j)$ means the co-occur from w_i to w_j in the entire dataset, $DF(w_i)$ means the number of trigger mentions containing the word w_i.

3.3   Prior Knowledge Encodeing with GCN

Graph convolution network (GCN) has been widely used to encode graph information in NLP tasks [2,25]. In this paper, we use GCN to encode the Intra-event Association network and the Inter-event Causality network. The network is defined as a weighted graph $G = (V, E)$, where V is the set of nodes and the element is $v_i(v_i \in V)$. E is the set of edges between nodes. The element is $e_i(e_i = (v_i, v_j, w_i) \in E)$, and w_i is the weight of v_i and v_j. The input of GCN mainly consists of two parts: node embedded representation $X = \{x_i\}_{i=1}^n$ and adjacency matrix $A \in R^{N \times N}$.

For the processed sentence $S = (w_1, w_2, w_3, ..., w_n)$, we can get the sub-graph of S from Intra-event Association (IA) and Inter-event Causality (IC) Networks, and convert them into adjacency matrix A_{ia} and A_{ic}. Then the (X,A_{ia}) and (X,A_{ic}) are feed into GCN respectively. The propagation rules of multi-layer GCN is:

$$X^{(l+1)} = f(X^{(l)}, A) = \sigma(\tilde{D}^{-1/2} \tilde{A} \tilde{D}^{-1/2} X^{(l)} W^l), (l \in 0, 1, ...L) \qquad (3)$$

where $X^{(l)}$ is the feature matrix of layer i, A is the adjacency matrix of A_{ia} or A_{ic}, L is the number of layers of GCN, $\tilde{A} = A + I_N$ and I_N is the unit matrix, $\tilde{D}$ is the degree matrix of $\tilde{A}$, W^l is a trainable weight matrix, and $\sigma(\cdot)$ indicates sigmoid activation function.

3.4   Causality Extracting with BiLSTM+CRF

LSTM is a recurrent neural network (RNN) that solves the problems of gradient vanishing in the traditional RNN model [30]. BiLSTM uses two LSTM layers to learn the past and future context information in the sentence, and has a better effect in solving the long-distance dependence of information extraction.

Conditional random field (CRF) [31] can obtain labels in the global optimal chain of a given input sequence, and consider the relevant relationship between neighbor labels. For sentences $S = \{s_1, s_2, s_3, ..., s_n\}$ and predicted tag sequences $y = \{y_1, y_2, y_3, ..., y_n\}$, the scores of CRF can be calculated as follows:

$$score(S, y) = \sum_{i=1}^{n+1} A_{y_{i-1}, y_i} + \sum_{i=1}^{n} P_{i, y_i} \qquad (4)$$

Finally, we minimize the loss function until the model converges.

$$E = log \sum_{y \in Y} exp^{s(y)} - score(s, y), \qquad (5)$$

where Y is a set of all possible tag sequences of an input sentence.

4   Experiment

4.1   Datasets

We conduct our experiments on two datasets. The first dataset is the Chinese emergency corpus[1], which is a publicly available event corpus, including six types

---

[1] https://github.com/shijiebei2009/CEC-Corpus.

of events: disease outbreak, earthquake, fire, traffic accident, terrorist attack, and food poisoning. The other is the Financial dataset, which is collected from Chinese financial news reports, such as Jinrongjie[2] and Hexun[3]. After screening, we annotate 1026 causal sentences from CEC corpus, and 2070 causal sentences from financial corpus.

4.2   Experimental Setting

For all datasets, We use Bert as the embedded coding of sentences. The maximum length of sentences to 256, the size of batches to 8, Adam's learning rate to 0.0001, and the training batch to 50. To prevent overfitting, we set the dropout rate to 0.4.

For the CEC dataset, we collect 11331 sentences containing event causality to construct the IA-IC network. For the financial dataset, 100,000 sentences containing causal relations are found to construct the IA-IC.

4.3   Baseline Methods

To demonstrate the effectiveness of our method, we compared our method with the following baseline.

IDCNN+CRF (2017) [26]: An improved CNN model uses iterate dilated convolution to extract text features with full consideration of context, and use CRF to obtain the label of a given sequence in the global optimal chain.

BiLSTM+CRF (2015) [27]: A classic sequence labeling model, which use BiLSTM layers to learn the past and future context information.

CNN+BiLSTM+CRF (2016) [28]: The model uses CNN to extract n-gram features, and use BiLSTM to learn the dependency of each feature.

CSNN (2020) [13]: The model uses CNN, attention mechanism and BiLSTM simultaneously to obtain different levels of semantic information.

CISAN (2021) [18]: This model applies convolutional semantic-infused filters and key-query attention into CEE and gets sequential tags by BiLSTM+CRF.

SCITE (2021) [29]: This is a BiLSTM+CRF model that introduces self-attention mechanism to learn the dependencies between causal words.

IC-IA-GCN: Our model uses GCN to encode Intra-event Association and Inter-event Causality Networks, and feeds the obtained features and text embedding representation into BiLSTM+CRF layer.

4.4   Comparison with Baseline Methods

We compared our model with the above five baselines and used F1-score as the evaluation metrics. Table 3 shows the experimental results of these models on CEC and Financial datasets. Experimental data show that our model achieves

---

[2] http://www.jrj.com.cn/.
[3] http://www.hexun.com/.

Table 3. Average F1-scores of our methods on two datasets compared with other baselines.

Model	CEC	Financial
IDCNN+CRF (2017)	68.26%	71.81%
BiLSTM+CRF (2015)	68.74%	74.75%
CNN+BiLSTM+CRF (2016)	71.68%	74.31%
CSNN (2020)	73.91%	74.67%
BERT+CSNN (2020)	74.61%	76.23%
CISAN (2021)	72.49%	75.99%
BERT+CISAN (2021)	75.93%	77.09%
SCITE (2021)	74.13%	78.2%
IC-IA-GCN	78.5%	79.12%

the best results on both datasets. Although IDCNN+CRF uses iterated dilated convolution to extract event causality with full consideration of context, it is difficult to capture the sequence information. Compared with IDCNN+CRF, BiLSTM+CRF can capture the sequence information and long-distance dependence between texts. However, the ambiguity of the Chinese event description leads to the poor performance of BiLSTM+CRF. CNN+BiLSTM+CRF and CSNN extract n-gram features, which is more suitable for extracting event causality. SCITE model proves the excellent performance of self-attention in causal event extraction, which is why we use Bert model with 12 self-attention layers. CISAN can improve the model's performance by initializing convolutional kernel with n-gram knowledge.

Though relevant studies get success by mining text features through combination of CNN and LSTM, due to the complexity of event causality, it is difficult to achieve the best effect on the limited annotation data just rely on the model itself. We can see that our model is 2.57% and 2.03% higher than the optimal baseline BERT+CISAN, proving that the introduction of external knowledge is helpful to improve the performance of extracting event causality.

4.5   Comparison w.r.t. Epoch

We further compared the convergence speed and performance of our model with other baselines on the Financial dataset as shown in Fig. 4. We can see that our model is better than other baselines after the fifth epoch and achieved the best result at the 29th epoch. It can be seen that the performance of the non-BERT model is worse than that BERT-based model, which may be caused by the lack of training data and the complexity of event causality. Our model takes advantage of external knowledge to enhance the model from the perspectives of event completeness and causality information transmission, which can solve the above problems to a certain extent.

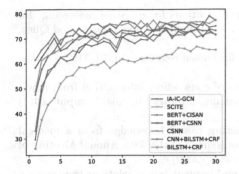

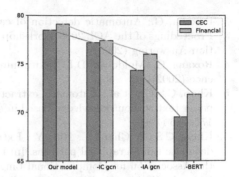

Fig. 4. F1-score on test dataset of financial w.r.t training epoch.

Fig. 5. Ablation analysis of our model in three datasets.

4.6   Ablation Experiments

In order to prove the effectiveness of each part in our proposed model, we delete IC-GCN, IA-GCN and Bert in turn. The experimental results are shown in the Fig. 5. It can be seen that each part of the model plays a positive role, and the removal of BERT has the greatest impact on the model. The base model with BERT gets 74.32% and 75.99% F1 score in CEC dataset and Financial dataset. When adding IA-GCN structure, these two values increased by 2.87 and 1.41. Then, when IC-GCN is added, they increased by 1.31 and 1.72. Inter-event causal network and Intra-event Association Network can improve the effectiveness of the model by 4.18 and 3.13% points in CEC and Financial dataset respectively, proving the effectiveness of prior knowledge construction and its integration into the model.

5   Conclusion

In this paper, we propose a causal event extraction framework based on Intra-event Association Network and Inter-event Causal Network. We collect domain texts containing event causality, and construct the prior knowledge of Intra-event Association Network and Inter-event causality network, and encode the prior knowledge through GCN. Our model achieved significant improvement in CEE task compared with the baseline model. In the future, we will try to extract multiple causal pairs from text to solve the problem of overlapping in event causality extraction.

References

1. Nabiha, A.: Automatic extraction of causal relations from natural language texts: a comprehensive survey. arXiv preprint arXiv:1605.07895 (2016)
2. Li, Z., Xiao, D., Liu, L.: Constructing narrative event evolutionary graph for script event prediction. arXiv preprint arXiv:1805.05081 (2018)

3. Roxana, G.: Automatic detection of causal relations for question answering. In: Proceedings of the ACL 2003 Workshop on Multilingual Summarization and Question Answering (2003)
4. Roxana, G., Moldovan, D.I.: Text mining for causal relations. In: FLAIRS Conference (2002)
5. Khoo, C.S.G., et al.: Automatic extraction of cause-effect information from newspaper text without knowledge-based inferencing. Literary Linguist. Comput. **13**(4) 177–186 (1998)
6. Khoo, C.S.G., Chan, S., Niu, Y.: Extracting causal knowledge from a medical database using graphical patterns. In: Proceedings of the 38th Annual Meeting of the Association for Computational Linguistics (2000)
7. Ittoo, A., Bouma, G.: Extracting explicit and implicit causal relations from sparse, domain-specific texts. In: Muñoz, R., Montoyo, A., Métais, E. (eds.) NLDB 2011. LNCS, vol. 6716, pp. 52–63. Springer, Heidelberg (2011). https://doi.org/10.1007/978-3-642-22327-3_6
8. Luo, Z., et al.: Commonsense causal reasoning between short texts. In: Fifteenth International Conference on the Principles of Knowledge Representation and Reasoning (2016)
9. Zhao, S., et al.: Event causality extraction based on connectives analysis. Neurocomputing **173**, 1943–1950 (2016)
10. Fu, J., et al.: Event causal relation extraction based on cascaded conditional random fields. Pattern Recogn. Artif. Intell. **24**(4), 567–573 (2011)
11. Tirthankar, D., et al.: Automatic extraction of causal relations from text using linguistically informed deep neural networks. In: Proceedings of the 19th Annual SIGdial Meeting on Discourse and Dialogue (2018)
12. Eugenio, M., et al.: Neural disambiguation of causal lexical markers based on context. In: IWCS 2017–12th International Conference on Computational Semantics-Short papers (2017)
13. Jin, X., Wang, X., Luo, X., Huang, S., Gu, S.: Inter-sentence and implicit causality extraction from Chinese corpus. In: Lauw, H.W., Wong, R.C.-W., Ntoulas, A., Lim, E.-P., Ng, S.-K., Pan, S.J. (eds.) PAKDD 2020. LNCS (LNAI), vol. 12084, pp. 739–751. Springer, Cham (2020). https://doi.org/10.1007/978-3-030-47426-3_57
14. Hendrickx, I., Kim, S.N., Kozareva, Z., et al.: Semeval-2010 task 8: multi-way classification of semantic relations between pairs of nominals. arXiv preprint arXiv:1911.10422 (2019)
15. Thomas, N.K., Welling, M.: Semi-supervised classification with graph convolutional networks. arXiv preprint arXiv:1609.02907 (2016)
16. Li, Z., et al.: Causality extraction based on self-attentive BiLSTM-CRF with transferred embeddings. Neurocomputing **423**, 207–219 (2021)
17. Li, P., Mao, K.: Knowledge-oriented convolutional neural network for causal relation extraction from natural language texts. Expert Syst. Appl. **115**, 512–523 (2019)
18. Wang, Z., Wang, H., Luo, X., Gao, J.: Back to prior knowledge: joint event causality extraction via convolutional semantic infusion. In: Karlapalem, K., et al. (eds.) PAKDD 2021. LNCS (LNAI), vol. 12712, pp. 346–357. Springer, Cham (2021). https://doi.org/10.1007/978-3-030-75762-5_28
19. Jacob, D., et al.: Bert: pre-training of deep bidirectional transformers for language understanding. arXiv preprint arXiv:1810.04805 (2018)
20. Luo, X., et al.: Building association link network for semantic link on web resources. IEEE Trans. Autom. Sci. Eng. **8**(3), 482–494 (2011)

21. Liu, Y., et al.: Association link network based core events discovery on the web. In: IEEE 16th International Conference on Computational Science and Engineering. IEEE (2013)

22. Teruko, M., et al.: Event nugget annotation: processes and issues. In: Proceedings of the The 3rd Workshop on EVENTS: Definition, Detection, Coreference, and Representation (2015)

23. Jun, A., Mitamura, T.: Open-domain event detection using distant supervision. In: Proceedings of the 27th International Conference on Computational Linguistics (2018)

24. Jiao, Z., Shuqi, S., Ke, S.: Chinese lexical analysis with deep Bi-GRU-CRF network. arXiv preprint arXiv:1807.01882 (2018)

25. Liu, X., Luo, Z., Huang, H.: Jointly multiple events extraction via attention-based graph information aggregation. arXiv preprint arXiv:1809.09078 (2018)

26. Emma, S., et al.: Fast and accurate entity recognition with iterated dilated convolutions. arXiv preprint arXiv:1702.02098 (2017)

27. Huang, Z., Xu, W., Yu, K.: Bidirectional LSTM-CRF models for sequence tagging. arXiv preprint arXiv:1508.01991 (2015)

28. Tao, C., et al.: Improving sentiment analysis via sentence type classification using BiLSTM-CRF and CNN. Expert Syst. Appl. **72**, 221–230 (2017)

29. Li, Z., Li, Q., Zou, X., et al.: Causality extraction based on self-attentive BiLSTM-CRF with transferred embeddings. Neurocomputing **423**, 207–219 (2021)

30. Hochreiter, S., Schmidhuber, J.: Long short-term memory. Neural Comput. **9**(8), 1735–1780 (1997)

31. John, L., McCallum, A., Pereira, F.: Conditional random fields: probabilistic models for segmenting and labeling sequence data. (2001)

Knowledge Graph Bidirectional Interaction Graph Convolutional Network for Recommendation

Zengqiang Guo[1], Yan Yang[1,2(✉)], Jijie Zhang[1], Tianqi Zhou[1],
and Bangyu Song[1]

[1] School of Computer Science and Technology, Heilongjiang University,
Harbin, China
`2201831@s.hlju.edu.cn, yangyan@hlju.edu.cn`
[2] Key Laboratory of Database and Parallel Computing of Heilongjiang Province,
Harbin, China

Abstract. Recently, the recommended method based on the Knowledge Graph (KG) has become a hot research topic in modern recommendation systems. Most researchers use assistive information such as entity attributes in KG to improve recommendation performance and alleviate Collaborative Filtering (CF) sparsity and cold start problems. The most recent technical trend is to develop end-to-end models based on the Graph Convolutional Network (GCN). In this paper, we propose a Knowledge Graph Bidirectional Interaction Graph Convolution Network for recommendation (KBGCN). This method is used to refine the embedded representation of node by recursively delivering messages from the neighbors (attributes or items) of the node (entity) and applies the knowledge aware attention mechanism to distinguish the contributions of different neighbors based of the same node. It uses neighbors of each entity in KG as the view of this entity, which can be extended by expanding the view of Multi-hop neighbors to mine high-order connectivity information existing in KG automatically. We apply the proposed method to three real-world datasets. KBGCN is better than seven KG-based baselines in recommendation accuracy and the two state-of-the-art GCN-based recommendations frameworks.

Keywords: Recommender systems · Knowledge graph · Graph convolutional networks

1 Introduction

With the success of the recommendation system, people can search for a large number of interesting content in various applications on the network, such as searching for commodities [12] on E-commerce platforms, news [23] on news portals, and movies [3] on video websites. Early recommendation systems were devoted to collaborative filtering [5,7]. Product based on the ID of the user and

E. Pimenidis et al. (Eds.): ICANN 2022, LNCS 13530, pp. 532–543, 2022.
https://doi.org/10.1007/978-3-031-15931-2_44

the item itself or trained through the neural network. The main disadvantage of collaborative filtering [2, 4, 24] is that it cannot effectively model user's and items' assistive information (attributes and context). Researchers have turned to bring recommendations into richer scenarios in recent years, such as building Knowledge Graph. The assistive information in KG can be used to model the user and item sides. Compared with the KG free method, the KG method can deeply mine the high-order information of users and items, and the path information based on KG improves the accuracy of the recommendation system. But at the same time, the heterogeneity and high dimensionality of the KG make it difficult to combine with the recommendation system. A feasible method is to use the *Knowledge Graph Embedding* (KGE) [16] method to pretrain the KG to obtain the embedding vector. For example, CKE [22] uniformly collects various types of assistive information such as entity attributes and text information and uses the TransE [1] algorithm to encode latent vectors and extract features. MKR [14] combines KGE and recommendation to learn the potential representation of items on the one hand and the semantic matching of entities related to items on the other hand. However, KGE is more often used in graph classification tasks, such as link prediction. HeteRec [21] uses meta path similarity to enrich the user-item interaction matrix so as to extract a more comprehensive representation of users and items. Both the above embedding-based and path-based approaches utilize only one aspect of the information in the graph. The idea of embedding-based propagation that combines the semantic representation of relationships and connection information is proposed to make full use of the information in KG.

In this paper, inspired by the idea of message passing in GCN, We propose Knowledge graph Bidirectional interaction Graph Convolutional Network for recommendation (KBGCN). Our purpose is to automatically capture the high-order connected information in the KG to enrich the representation of entities. The core idea of KBGCN is to have biased aggregation of neighborhood information in the knowledge graph, learn item representations of distant neighbors inward, and aggregate higher-order information using a bidirectional interaction module. We release the codes and datasets at https://github.com/zq816/KBGCN.

Our contributions in this paper are summarized as follows:

- We propose a simple yet effective GCN-based knowledge graph recommendation framework. We use the bidirectional interaction which can better aggregate neighborhood information to obtain good entity representation.
- We design a novel neural knowledge aware attention mechanism to learn the knowledge-based weights of entities in the same entity set and generates weighted representation of entities.
- Experimental results on three public benchmark datasets have demonstrated that the KBGCN outperforms recent state-of-the-art models.

2   Related Work

Knowledge Graph based RS (KGRS) usually constructs KG based on external knowledge (such as edge information), explores the implicit or high-order connection relationship between users or items. Due to the use of assistive knowledge, KGRS can better understand user behaviour and item characteristics. RippleNet [12] is the first method to use preference propagation. It uses KG to spread information and get the embedded representation of high-order neighbors. The AKUPM [10] model is combined with the TransR [6] algorithm to simulate users' click history and spread users' preferences for different entities. Like RippleNet, our work can be viewed as a KG-based neighborhood propagation method.

Graph Convolution Network (GCN) usually learns how to use graph structure and node feature information and uses neural network to iteratively aggregate feature information from local graph neighborhoods. For example, GCN are used for influence diffusion on social graphs in social recommendations [19]. Mining the user-item connection information hidden in the user-item interaction graph to alleviate the problem of data sparsity in collaborative filtering [11]. KGCN [15] first samples the neighbors of the candidate items in KG and then aggregates the information of multi-hop neighbors and propagates it inward to the candidate items. KGNN-LS [13] further adds a label smoothing (LS) mechanism to the KGCN model. Our method also connects to KGCN [15] and CKAN [18]. But the major difference between our work and the literature is the use of a bidirectional interaction method to aggregate entity neighbors and the design of a novel neural knowledge-aware attention mechanism to learn knowledge-based entity weights.

3   Methodology

We introduce the framework of the proposed KBGCN in detail. As shown in Fig. 1, the model framework consists of four main parts: (1) Embedded Layer. (2) Knowledge Graph Awareness Propagation Layer. This is divided into neighborhood view propagation and knowledge awareness attention embedding. (3) BI-Interactional Aggregation Layer. (4) The Prediction Layer.

3.1   Problem Formulation

In a typical recommendation scene, we have a set of users $U = \{u_1, u_2, u_3 \ldots u_m\}$, and a set of items $V = \{v_1, v_2, v_3 \ldots v_n\}$. We get the user-item interaction matrix $Y(Y \in R^{m \times n})$ based on user's implicit feedback (click or purchase), the user's implicit feedback is defined as $Y_{uv} = \{y(u, v) | u \in U, v \in V\}$, where $y(u, v)$ equals 0 or 1. Knowledge Graph G consists of triples $\{(h, r, t) | t \in E, r \in R\}$. for example, in the triplet (The Avengers, film.film.actor, Robert Downey Jr.), the actor of The Avengers is Robert Downey Jr. In most recommended scenes, items are represented in KG with the corresponding entities. Our goal is to learn a prediction function $\hat{y}_{uv} = F(u, v)$ to predict whether user u will click the item i that has never been clicked, where $\hat{y}_{uv}$ is a probability value.

$$Y_{uv} = \begin{cases} 1 & \text{if (u,v) has an interaction} \\ 0 & \text{else} \end{cases} \tag{1}$$

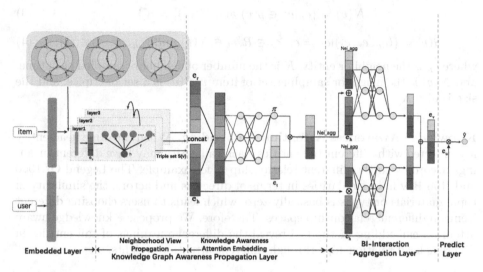

Fig. 1. The KBGCN framework consists of four main parts: (1) Embedded layer (2) Knowledge graph awareness propagation layer (3) BI-Interaction aggregation layer (4) Prediction layer.

3.2   Embedded Layer

We take the one-layer structure as an example. Assuming a pair of user-item pairs (u, v), we use $p(v)$ to represent all the direct neighbors of item v, $r(a, b)$ represents the relationship between a and b. Firstly, initialize the user embedding vector $e_u \in R^d$, the entity embedding vector E and relationship embedding vector R in the knowledge graph G, the initialization embedding vector of the item is mapped from the knowledge graph G.

$$e_v = E * v_v, \tag{2}$$

where $E \in R^d$ is the entity embedding matrix, v_v is the ID representation of item v, and $e_v \in R^d$ represents the initial embedding representation of item v.

3.3   Knowledge Graph Awareness Propagation Layer

As shown in Fig. 1, the Knowledge Graph Awareness Propagation Layer is mainly composed of two modules: Neighborhood View Propagation for entities seeking information about their neighbors in the view. Knowledge Awareness Attention Embedding provides a novel neural knowledge aware attention mechanism to learn the knowledge-based weights of entities in the view.

Neighborhood View Propagation. In the real world KG, each entity will not have only one neighbor node. That is, $P(v)$ is greater than or equal to 1. In order to ensure the computational efficiency and space utilization of the model, the number of neighbors of each entity takes a fixed size during model training. We set the number of neighbors K as a hyperparameter.

$$N(v) = \{e_n | e_n \in p(v) \text{ and } |N(v)| = K\}, \tag{3}$$

$$S(v) = \{(e_h, e_r, e_t) | e_h = e_v, e_r \in R, e_t \in N(v) \text{ and } (e_h, e_r, e_t) \in G\}, \tag{4}$$

where e_n is the neighbor entity, K is the number of neighbors sampled each time, and $N(v)$ is the neighbor sampling set of item v. $S(v)$ is a set of triples, and the size is also K.

Knowledge Awareness Attention Ambedding. When the same head entity is connected with different tail entities, each tail entity may have different meanings according to the different relationship r. for example, The Legend Of 1900 and Rob Roy have similarities in terms of directors and actors, the similarity in topic materials or types is basically zero, which leads to users choosing different items in different relationship spaces. Therefore, We propose a knowledge aware attention embedding method to reveal the different meanings of tail entities in different head relationships through different attention weights.

$$A_i = \pi \left(e_i^h, e_i^r \right) e_i^t, \tag{5}$$

where e_i^h is the header entity embedding, e_i^r is the relational embedding, e_i^t and A_i are the tail entity embedding and weighted representation of the $i-th$ triplet. π is a matrix controlling the impact of the weights generated by the head entity and related entity on the tail entity. We design such a neural network function similar to the attention mechanism to realize π :

$$c_0 = \text{ReLU} \left(w_0 \left(e_i^h \| e_i^r \right) + b_0 \right), \tag{6}$$

$$\pi \left(e_i^h, e_i^r \right) = \sigma \left(w_2 \, \text{ReLU} \left(w_1 c_0 + b_1 \right) + b_2 \right), \tag{7}$$

we use a three-layer depth neural network model to generate the weight of the tail entity. e_i^h and e_i^r are first concat operated, the activation function is relu, and the last layer is sigmoid. $w_0 \in R^{d \times 2d}$, $w_1 \in R^{2d \times 2d}$ and $w_2 \in R^{2d \times d}$ are all trainable parameters. Finally, we normalize the weight score:

$$\pi \left(e_i^h, e_i^r \right) = \frac{\exp \left(\pi \left(e_i^h, e_i^r \right) \right)}{\sum_{(h', r', t') \in S_{(v)}} \exp \left(\pi \left(e_i^{h'}, e_i^{r'} \right) \right)}. \tag{8}$$

Finally, we sum the representations of the K triples obtained:

$$neighbor_{agg} = \sum_{i=1}^{K} A_i. \tag{9}$$

3.4 BI-Interaction Aggregation Layer

The final stage is to reaggregate the header entity and neighborhood representation into a new entity representation, that is, the final representation of the item. Here, we propose a new aggregator, the BI-Interactional aggregator:

$$
\begin{aligned}
f_{\text{BI-Interactional}} &= \text{LeakyReLU}\left(w_3\left(e_h + neighbor_{agg}\right)\right) \\
&\quad + \text{LeakyReLU}\left(w_4\left(e_h \odot neighbor_{agg}\right)\right),
\end{aligned}
\tag{10}
$$

where $w_3 \in R^{d \times d}$ and $w_4 \in R^{d \times d}$ is the trainable parameter matrix, and $\odot$ is the element product. The BI-Interactional aggregator consists of two parts: the sum of head entity and neighborhood information and the other part is the element product of head entity and neighborhood information. Adding the two parts, we realize bidirectional interaction, breaking the previous aggregation methods such as concat or addition. Achieved a significant improvement.

3.5 Predict Layer

$$
\hat{y}_{uv} = e_u^{\top} f_{\text{BI-Interactional}},
\tag{11}
$$

where e_u and $f_{\text{BI-Interactional}}$ are the final vector representation of user and item, and $\hat{y}_{uv}$ is the prediction probability value.

3.6 Optimization

We train all user-item pairs. During the training, we adopt the negative sampling strategy, and the loss function is as follows:

$$
\mathcal{L} = \sum_{u \in U}\left(\sum_{v:y(u,v)=1} \mathcal{J}\left(y_{uv}, \hat{y}_{uv}\right) - \sum_{i=1}^{N^u} \mathcal{J}\left(y_{uv_i}, \hat{y}_{uv_i}\right)\right) + \lambda\|\mathcal{W}\|_2^2,
\tag{12}
$$

where $\mathcal{J}$ is the cross entropy loss, $N^u = |v : y(u,v) = 1|$ is the number of user negative samples, and the last item is L2-regulator.

4 Experiments

In this section, we evaluate the performance of KBGCN through three real-world datasets.

4.1 Datasets

- **MovieLens-20M** is a data set widely used in the field of movie recommendation, including 138000 users and 20 million ratings for 27000 movies. The rating is 1–5.

- **Book-Crossing** contains more than 1 Million Book rating information. The rating ($'Book - Rating'$) is either explicit, expressed in a rating of 1–10, or implicit, expressed in 0.
- **Last.FM** contains 92,800 artist recordings from 1,872 users.

The basic information of the three datasets is shown in Table 1:

Table 1. Basic statistics for the three datasets

		MovieLens-20M	Book-Crossing	Last.FM
User-Item interaction	#Users	138159	17860	1872
	#Items	16954	14967	3846
	#Interactions	13501622	139746	42346
Knowledge graph	#Entities	102569	77903	9366
	#Relations	32	25	60
	#Triplets	499474	151500	15518

4.2 Baselines

- **PER** [20] is a path based method that uses the relationship heterogeneity to disperse user preferences to different meta paths in the information network.
- **CKE** [22] introduces structural information, text data, image data and other information in the knowledge base to improve the quality of the recommendation system.
- **BPRMF** [9] is a classical CF method, which proposes the sampling of positive and negative samples (triples) in the recommendation field, and then trains the model through BPR loss.
- **LibFM** [8] + **TransE** [1] is a feature-based factorization model for CTR scene takes user ID, item ID and corresponding entities learned through TransE algorithm as the input of the model.
- **RippleNet** [12] is a classic recommendation method based on propagation, which enriches the user representation by propagating the user's potential preferences in the knowledge graph.
- **KGCN** [15] applies the graph convolutional networks to the recommendation system, aggregates the neighborhood information with deviation in combination with the knowledge graph, and refines the embedding of items.
- **KGNN-LS** [13] transforms heterogeneous KG into user specific weighted graph, and adds label smoothing mechanism to KGCN framework to calculate personalized item embedding.
- **KGAT** [17] is a state-of-the-art propagation-based method that collectively refines embeddings of users, items, and KG entities via training interaction and KG embeddings jointly.
- **CKAN** [18] is another state-of-the-art propagation-based method employing a heterogeneous propagation strategy to encode diverse information for better recommendation.

4.3   Experiments Settings

In the experiment, we divide the data set according to the ratio of 6:2:2. We provide two actual recommended scenario predictions: (1) CTR prediction: we use AUC and F1 scores as the evaluation indexes. (2) Top-K recommendation, we use the recall@k Index evaluation model. Adam optimizer is used to optimize all trainable parameters. The hyperparameters are set as shown in Table 2, where d is the feature vector dimensions, K is the number of randomly sampled neighbor nodes, H is the view size in the neighborhood aggregation, and BS is the batch size, η is learning rate, λ is L2 regularization coefficient.

Table 2. Hyperparameter settings for three datasets

Datasets	d	K	H	BS	η	λ
MovieLens-20M	32	4	1	65536	5×10^{-3}	1.8×10^{-7}
Book_Crossing	4	8	1	256	1.5×10^{-4}	4.5×10^{-5}
Last.FM	8	8	1	128	2×10^{-4}	1×10^{-4}

4.4   Results

Table 3 and Fig. 2 show the results of CTR prediction and Top-K recommendation for two recommended scenarios respectively. We have the following conclusions:

Table 3. The results of AUC and $F1$ in CTR prediction

Model	MovieLens-20M		Book-Crossing		Last.FM	
	AUC	F1	AUC	F1	AUC	F1
PER	0.832	0.788	0.617	0.562	0.633	0.596
CKE	0.924	0.871	0.677	0.611	0.744	0.673
BPRMF	0.958	0.914	0.658	0.611	0.756	0.701
LibFM+TransE	0.966	0.917	0.659	0.622	0.777	0.709
RippleNet	0.968	0.912	0.672	0.625	0.780	0.702
KGCN	0.970	0.923	0.651	0.613	0.780	0.702
KGNN-LS	0.975	0.929	0.676	0.631	0.803	0.722
KGAT	0.976	0.928	0.652	0.619	0.805	0.725
CKAN	0.971	0.922	**0.711**	0.634	0.811	0.731
KBGCN	**0.983**	**0.942**	0.695	**0.660**	**0.825**	**0.747**

- Compared with these state-of-the-art baselines, KBGCN achieves competitive performance on all three datasets, especially in movie and music datasets, which shows that KBGCN is better at dealing with datasets with strong sparsity.

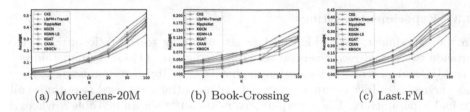

(a) MovieLens-20M   (b) Book-Crossing   (c) Last.FM

Fig. 2. The results of Recall@K in Top-K recommendation

- The performance of KBGCN compared to RippleNet demonstrates the effectiveness of the knowledge-aware attention mechanism. Comparative results with KGAT indicate the importance of explicitly bidirectional interactions.
- CKAN has a more prominent result on the Book-Crossing dataset. In the Top-K recommendation, when the k value is larger, KBGCN effect is equal to CKAN. It can be inferred that CKAN will introduce more noise when the dataset becomes larger and sparser, while KBGCN's bidirectional interaction aggregation method will be more effective.
- In the Top-K recommendation, no matter what the K value is, the experimental effect of KBGCN is superior to all baseline models. With the increase of the K value, the value of recall tends to rise. The $recall@K$ of KBGCN on the three datasets is higher than KGAT and CKAN. This illustrates the effectiveness of bidirectional interactions aggregation and knowledge-aware attention mechanism.

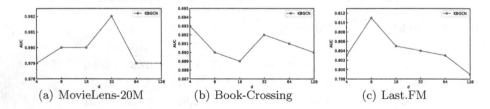

(a) MovieLens-20M   (b) Book-Crossing   (c) Last.FM

Fig. 3. The influence of embedding vector dimensions d

The Influence of Embedding Vector Dimensions. As shown in Fig. 3, when the dimension is increased with a certain range in the lower dimension, the performance of KBGCN will improve, but when it exceeds a certain threshold, the performance will decline. We guess that too large d value will encode more entity information to a certain extent, resulting in a slight improvement in performance, but it will also cause overfitting.

The Influence of Neighbor Sampling Size. As shown in the Table 4. We find that the K value is relatively average in all datasets, and the promotion effect of the model is the best when it is in the middle position ($k = 4$ or 8). On the one hand, because the small number of samples can not provide sufficient information, the large number will bring unnecessary noise interference to the model.

Table 4. AUC result of KBGCN with different neighbor sampling size K.

K	2	4	8	16	32
MovieLens-20M	0.980	**0.983**	0.980	0.980	OOM
Book-Crossing	0.690	0.690	**0.695**	0.690	0.689
Last.FM	0.804	0.805	**0.825**	0.804	0.806

Table 5. AUC result of KBGCN with different view size H.

H	1	2	3	4
MovieLens-20M	**0.983**	0.978	0.977	0.899
Book-Crossing	**0.695**	0.689	0.689	0.678
Last.FM	**0.825**	0.795	0.594	0.586

The Influence of View Size. As shown in the Table 5. On the music dataset, the influence of the model on the view size fluctuates greatly. The model effect decreases sharply when the view size is high-level. With the increase of view size, the effect of other datasets also decreases to varying degrees. As the path becomes longer, the information too late is meaningless to the head entity but will mislead the original entity representation.

5 Conclusions

In this paper we propose knowledge graph bidirectional interaction graph convolutional network for recommendation. Through knowledge-based deep propagation and utilizes a knowledge-aware attention mechanism to discriminate the contribution of different knowledge-based neighbors. The knowledge based high-order interaction information of item is successfully captured, effectively improves the model's ability to represent item with latent vectors. Experimental results on three public benchmark datasets the KBGCN is superior to state-of-the-art models.

References

1. Bordes, A., Usunier, N., García-Durán, A., Weston, J., Yakhnenko, O.: Translating embeddings for modeling multi-relational data. In: Advances in Neural Information Processing Systems 26: 27th Annual Conference on Neural Information Processing Systems 2013. Proceedings of a meeting held December 5–8, 2013, Lake Tahoe, Nevada, United States, pp. 2787–2795 (2013)
2. Cheng, H., et al.: Wide & deep learning for recommender systems. In: Proceedings of the 1st Workshop on Deep Learning for Recommender Systems, DLRS@RecSys 2016, Boston, MA, USA, 15 September 2016, pp. 7–10 (2016)
3. Diao, Q., Qiu, M., Wu, C., Smola, A.J., Jiang, J., Wang, C.: Jointly modeling aspects, ratings and sentiments for movie recommendation (JMARS). In: The 20th ACM SIGKDD International Conference on Knowledge Discovery and Data Mining, KDD 2014, New York, NY, USA - 24–27 August 2014, pp. 193–202 (2014)
4. He, X., Chua, T.: Neural factorization machines for sparse predictive analytics. In: Proceedings of the 40th International ACM SIGIR Conference on Research and Development in Information Retrieval, Shinjuku, Tokyo, Japan, 7–11 August 2017, pp. 355–364 (2017)
5. Juan, Y., Zhuang, Y., Chin, W., Lin, C.: Field-aware factorization machines for CTR prediction. In: Proceedings of the 10th ACM Conference on Recommender Systems, Boston, MA, USA, 15–19 September 2016, pp. 43–50 (2016)
6. Lin, Y., Liu, Z., Sun, M., Liu, Y., Zhu, X.: Learning entity and relation embeddings for knowledge graph completion. In: Proceedings of the Twenty-Ninth AAAI Conference on Artificial Intelligence, 25–30 January 2015, Austin, Texas, USA, pp. 2181–2187 (2015)
7. Rendle, S.: Factorization machines. In: ICDM 2010, The 10th IEEE International Conference on Data Mining, Sydney, Australia, 14–17 December 2010, pp. 995–1000 (2010)
8. Rendle, S.: Factorization machines with libfm. ACM Trans. Intell. Syst. Technol. **3**, 57:1–57:22 (2012)
9. Rendle, S., Freudenthaler, C., Gantner, Z., Schmidt-Thieme, L.: BPR: bayesian personalized ranking from implicit feedback. In: UAI 2009, Proceedings of the Twenty-Fifth Conference on Uncertainty in Artificial Intelligence, Montreal, QC, Canada, 18–21 June 2009, pp. 452–461 (2009)
10. Tang, X., Wang, T., Yang, H., Song, H.: AKUPM: attention-enhanced knowledge-aware user preference model for recommendation. In: Proceedings of the 25th ACM SIGKDD International Conference on Knowledge Discovery & Data Mining, KDD 2019, Anchorage, AK, USA, 4–8 August 2019, pp. 1891–1899 (2019)
11. Wang, H., Lian, D., Ge, Y.: Binarized collaborative filtering with distilling graph convolutional network. In: Proceedings of the Twenty-Eighth International Joint Conference on Artificial Intelligence, IJCAI 2019, Macao, China, 10–16 August 2019, pp. 4802–4808 (2019)
12. Wang, H., et al.: Ripplenet: propagating user preferences on the knowledge graph for recommender systems. In: Proceedings of the 27th ACM International Conference on Information and Knowledge Management, CIKM 2018, Torino, Italy, 22–26 October 2018, pp. 417–426 (2018)
13. Wang, H., et al.: Knowledge-aware graph neural networks with label smoothness regularization for recommender systems. In: Proceedings of the 25th ACM SIGKDD International Conference on Knowledge Discovery & Data Mining, KDD 2019, Anchorage, AK, USA, 4–8 August 2019, pp. 968–977 (2019)

14. Wang, H., Zhang, F., Zhao, M., Li, W., Xie, X., Guo, M.: Multi-task feature learning for knowledge graph enhanced recommendation. In: The World Wide Web Conference, WWW 2019, San Francisco, CA, USA, 13–17 May 2019, pp. 2000–2010 (2019)
15. Wang, H., Zhao, M., Xie, X., Li, W., Guo, M.: Knowledge graph convolutional networks for recommender systems. In: The World Wide Web Conference, WWW 2019, San Francisco, CA, USA, 13–17 May 2019, pp. 3307–3313 (2019)
16. Wang, Q., Mao, Z., Wang, B., Guo, L.: Knowledge graph embedding: a survey of approaches and applications. IEEE Trans. Knowl. Data Eng. **29**, 2724–2743 (2017)
17. Wang, X., He, X., Cao, Y., Liu, M., Chua, T.: KGAT: knowledge graph attention network for recommendation. In: Proceedings of the 25th ACM SIGKDD International Conference on Knowledge Discovery & Data Mining, KDD 2019, Anchorage, AK, USA, 4–8 August 2019, pp. 950–958 (2019)
18. Wang, Z., Lin, G., Tan, H., Chen, Q., Liu, X.: CKAN: collaborative knowledge-aware attentive network for recommender systems. In: Proceedings of the 43rd International ACM SIGIR conference on research and development in Information Retrieval, SIGIR 2020, Virtual Event, China, 25–30 July 2020, pp. 219–228 (2020)
19. Wu, L., Sun, P., Fu, Y., Hong, R., Wang, X., Wang, M.: A neural influence diffusion model for social recommendation. In: Proceedings of the 42nd International ACM SIGIR Conference on Research and Development in Information Retrieval, SIGIR 2019, Paris, France, 21–25 July 2019, pp. 235–244 (2019)
20. Yu, X., et al.: Personalized entity recommendation: a heterogeneous information network approach. In: Seventh ACM International Conference on Web Search and Data Mining, WSDM 2014, New York, NY, USA, 24–28 February 2014, pp. 283–292 (2014)
21. Yu, X., et al.: Recommendation in heterogeneous information networks with implicit user feedback. In: Seventh ACM Conference on Recommender Systems, RecSys 2013, Hong Kong, China, 12–16 October 2013, pp. 347–350 (2013)
22. Zhang, F., Yuan, N.J., Lian, D., Xie, X., Ma, W.: Collaborative knowledge base embedding for recommender systems. In: Proceedings of the 22nd ACM SIGKDD International Conference on Knowledge Discovery and Data Mining, San Francisco, CA, USA, 13–17 August 2016, pp. 353–362 (2016)
23. Zheng, G., et al.: DRN: a deep reinforcement learning framework for news recommendation. In: Proceedings of the 2018 World Wide Web Conference on World Wide Web, WWW 2018, Lyon, France, 23–27 April 2018, pp. 167–176 (2018)
24. Zhou, G., et al.: Deep interest network for click-through rate prediction. In: Proceedings of the 24th ACM SIGKDD International Conference on Knowledge Discovery & Data Mining, KDD 2018, London, UK, 19–23 August 2018, pp. 1059–1068 (2018)

Learning Hierarchical Graph Convolutional Neural Network for Object Navigation

Tao Xu[1,2] , Xu Yang[1,2], and Suiwu Zheng[1,2,3]( )

[1] State Key Laboratory of Management and Control for Complex Systems, Institute of Automation, Chinese Academy of Sciences, Beijing, China
{xutao2020,xu.yang,suiwu.zheng}@ia.ac.cn
[2] University of Chinese Academy of Sciences, Beijing, China
[3] Huizhou Zhongke Advanced Manufacturing Limited Company, Huizhou, China

Abstract. The goal of object navigation is to navigate an agent to a target object using visual input. Without GPS and the map, one challenge of this task is how to locate the target object in the unseen environment, especially when the target object is not in the field of view. Previous works use relation graphs to encode the concurrence relationships among all the object categories, but these relation graphs are usually too flat for the agent to locate the target object efficiently. In this paper, a Hierarchical Graph Convolutional Neural Network (HGCNN) is proposed to encode the object relationships in a hierarchical manner. Specifically, the HGCNN consists of two graph convolution blocks and a graph pooling block, which constructs the hierarchical relation graph by learning an area-level graph from the object-level graph. Consequently, the HGCNN based framework enables the agent to locate the target object efficiently in the unseen environment. The proposed model is evaluated in the AI2-iTHOR environment, and the performance of object navigation shows a significant improvement.

Keywords: Object navigation · Hierarchical relation graph · AI2-iTHOR

1 Introduction

Object navigation [2,5,18] provides a fundamental capability for robots and other unmanned systems, which has attracted great attention in the past few years with the development of various embodied AI simulators.

The goal of object navigation is to navigate an agent to a specified target using the first-view visual input such as RGB image. To achieve this goal, the agent should learn about visual representation and navigation policy. For instance, when an agent is asked to find an apple in an unseen environment, it should know the appearance of the apple and how to search it in the environment. Furthermore, the agent should also be able to reason, especially in the unseen environment, because targets are often out of sight at the first location.

© The Author(s), under exclusive license to Springer Nature Switzerland AG 2022
E. Pimenidis et al. (Eds.): ICANN 2022, LNCS 13530, pp. 544–556, 2022.
https://doi.org/10.1007/978-3-031-15931-2_45

Recently, to learn an informative visual representation and gain the ability of reasoning, Graph Convolutional Network (GCN) has been introduced into this task to construct relation graphs [5, 11] among the object categories in the environment. However, almost all existing relation graphs used in this task are inherently flat, which means that they can only encode the local object-level relationships among the object categories and ignore the hierarchical structure of the relation graphs. On the other hand, the hierarchical architecture of knowledge is key for humans to learn how to navigate to a target. For example, when a person is asked to find a plunger in a house, he may first recall that the plunger, toilet paper and toilet always appear in the same area. Then he will search for that area in the house because it is easier to find the area than the plunger in the big house. Finally, when he gets to the area, he will search for the plunger in the area and find it eventually. The example shows that the hierarchical architecture of knowledge makes human's decision-making more efficient, which inspires us to design the agent acting like that.

The main challenge is how to learn the hierarchical architecture of the relationships among the object categories in the environment. Specifically, the model needs to extract the area-level concepts from the existing object categories and encode the relationships among them in the area-level relation graph. Learning how to utilize the hierarchical relation graph to navigate is another challenge. We notice that Zhang et al. [22] implement a Hierarchical Object-to-Zone (HOZ) graph to learn hierarchical relationships among the object categories, which makes a significant improvement over the baseline. However, the HOZ graph is limited by setting the so-called current zone, sub-goal zone and target zone by rules, for the agent to get an efficient navigation policy. And the HOZ graph uses a heuristic method to generate the area-level graph rather than a learning scheme.

In this paper, a novel Hierarchical Graph Convolutional Neural Network (HGCNN) is proposed to encode the hierarchical relationships among the object categories for navigation. Specifically, the HGCNN consists of two graph convolution blocks and a graph pooling block, where the graph convolution blocks encode the relationships among the nodes, and the graph pooling block provides a way to cluster the nodes in the object-level relation graph together and then extract the area-level concepts as new nodes. After that, an area-level relation graph with the new nodes can be constructed. Besides, an LSTM layer is implemented as the navigation policy module to learn to utilize the hierarchical relation graph to navigate in the unseen environment. By end-to-end reinforcement learning, the agent is able to utilize the hierarchical object relationships to reason and navigate to the target efficiently.

The proposed model is evaluated in the AI2-iTHOR [9] environment, and the experiment shows a significant improvement over the baseline. The main contributions of this paper can be summarized as follows:

- A novel Hierarchical Graph Convolutional Neural Network (HGCNN) is proposed to encode the hierarchical relation graph for object navigation.

- This paper modifies the DIFFPOOL [21] layer and introduces it into the HGCNN, which facilitates the task a lot.
- With the implementation of the HGCNN, the performance of object navigation shows a significant improvement.

2 Related Work

Visual Navigation. According to the different ways of setting goals, target-driven visual navigation can be divided into ImageGoal navigation [11,23], Point-Goal navigation [17] and object navigation. This paper focuses on object navigation, which aims to navigate an agent to a target object in the unseen environment. Conventional works usually treat visual navigation as a geometric problem. Oriolo *et al.* [14] use a given map to navigate the robots. Gupta *et al.* [6] divide it into two parts: mapping and planning, which makes it more interpretable. However, these approaches usually have problems in dealing with complex environments or situations. So reinforcement learning (RL, *e.g.*, A3C [13] and DDPPO [17]) is introduced into this task to learn the complex policy [23]. However, instead of relying on the map or focusing on the training algorithm, this paper proposes the HGCNN to learn an visual representation to provide more prior knowledge for navigation.

Object Navigation. Recent works improve generalization to unknown environment with different strategies. Chaplot *et al.* [2] build an episodic semantic map to explore the environment. Maksymets *et al.* [12] propose a data augmentation technique to address overfitting in object navigation. Ye *et al.* [20] add auxiliary learning tasks to improve the generaliazation to unknown environment. This line of works have achieved great results but they also rely on other inputs besides RGB image, such as depth image and GPS coordinate. In this paper, we propose a novel method to navigate the agent to the target object only using the RGB input.

Learning Visual Representation Based on Graph. Learning visual representation aims to extract an informative feature vector from the visual input. Moreover, many works use graphs to encode prior knowledge to facilitate visual navigation. Du *et al.* [5] introduce an Object Relation Graph (ORG) which can be learned during end-to-end training to encode the concurrence relationships among object categories. Yang *et al.* [19] leverage a knowledge graph to encode the semantic scene priors. Lv *et al.* [11] use a relation graph to encode the 3D spatial relationships among object categories. Taniguchi *et al.* [16] propose a graph-based memory to encode the topological memory for navigation. However, the graphs this line of works construct are mostly flat, which means that the visual representation they learn can only encode the local feature of the environment. In this paper, the HGCNN is proposed to construct the hierarchical relation graph, which contains a subset of global object relationships.

Graph Pooling. The goal of graph pooling is to extract the global feature from the original graph. In particular, there are three different mechanisms for graph

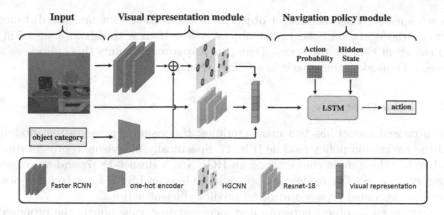

Fig. 1. Model overview. The proposed model includes two main modules: the visual representation module and the navigation policy module. The visual representation module takes the current first-view image and the target object category as input and generates a visual representation. Given the visual representation, previous action probability and hidden state, the navigation policy module outputs the current action probability.

pooling, and they are mechanisms based on graph coarsening [21], mechanisms based on edge contraction [4] and mechanisms based on TopK [10] respectively. In this paper, the HGCNN focuses on mechanisms based on graph coarsening (*e.g.*, DIFFPOOL [21]). Different from the conventional graph pooling, in this paper, the standard DIFFPOOL is modified according to the task specificity and introduced into the HGCNN, which facilitates the task a lot.

3   Model

In this section, the task definition of object navigation is introduced at the beginning. Then this paper provides an overview of the proposed model. Finally, the HGCNN and how it works to construct the hierarchical relation graph are expatiated.

3.1   Task Definition

Given an object category, the goal of the task in this paper is to navigate an embodied agent to a specified target only using the first-view visual input such as RGB image, while the conventional navigation input is not available such as GPS. At the beginning of each episode, the agent is initialized at a random state $S = \{x, y, \theta_r, \theta_h\}$ in a random scene, where x and y represent the location of the agent, θ_r and θ_h represent the point of view of the agent. With the first-view visual input, the agent should select a series of actions from $\Lambda = \{MoveAhead, RotateLeft, RotateRight, LookDown, LookUp, Done\}$ to navigate to the object which belongs to the given object category. At the end of each episode, when the target object is in the field of view and the distance between the agent and the target object is less than a threshold(*e.g.*, 1.5 m) and the agent chooses the action *Done*, the experiment counts this episode as a successful episode, otherwise it is a failure one.

3.2   Model Overview

The proposed model has two main modules: the visual representation module and the navigation policy module (Fig. 1). Specifically, the visual representation module has three main components: an HGCNN, a Resnet-18 [7] and an object category encoder. The navigation policy module is an LSTM layer to learn how to utilize the visual representation to predict efficient actions.

First, given an object category and a current first-view image, the proposed model employs a Faster RCNN [15] to get the local detection feature which consists of the bounding box positions and detection confidence. After that, the model concatenates it with the object embedding as location-aware feature (LAF) following [5]. And then the HGCNN encodes the hierarchical relationships among the object categories, the Resnet-18 which is pretrained on ImageNet [3] embeds the current first-view image to extract the visual feature, and the object category encoder uses a one-hot vector to encode the target object category. After that, three new embeddings are generated and they are concatenated as a visual representation vector. Finally, the model inputs the visual representation vector, the previous action and the hidden state to the LSTM layer to predict efficient actions.

3.3   HGCNN

Similar to Convolutional Neural Network (CNN), the proposed HGCNN consists of two main components: the graph convolution block and the graph pooling block (Fig. 2).

Graph Convolution Block. The goal of the graph convolution block is to learn the object representation embedding. Consider such a graph $G = (N, A)$, each node $n \in N$ denotes the LAF extracted from the current first-view image, and each edge $a \in A$ denotes the relationship among different nodes. The graph convolution block uses a multi-layer GCN to learn the object representation embedding, and a GCN layer is expressed as:

$$Z = f(AXW_{conv}) \tag{1}$$

where A denotes the adjacent matrix, X denotes all the nodes, W_{conv} denotes the embedding matrix and $f(\cdot)$ denotes the ReLU activation function. After that, an object representation embedding Z is generated.

Graph Pooling Block. The graph pooling block provides a way to cluster the nodes in the object-level graph together and then extract the area-level concepts as new nodes (Fig. 3). After that, an area-level graph can be constructed. In

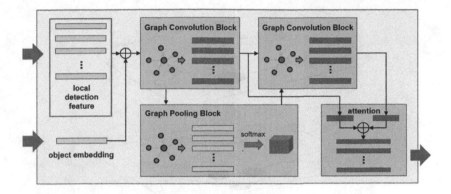

Fig. 2. Detailed structure of the HGCNN. The HGCNN consists of two main components: the graph convolution block and the graph pooling block. The graph convolution block aims to learn the object representation embedding. And the goal of the graph pooling block is to cluster the nodes in the object-level relation graph to extract the area-level concepts as new nodes and then construct the area-level relation graph. Additionally, at the end of the HGCNN, a graph attention layer is introduced to obtain the final feature.

the graph pooling block, a modified DIFFPOOL [21] layer is implemented to achieve this goal. Specifically, the graph pooling block first uses a multi-layer GCN to learn a cluster assignment matrix S from the object-level graph and then constructs a new area-level graph using the cluster assignment matrix S. The number of columns of S is a hyperparameter that corresponds to the number of areas. In particular, the following equations are applied:

$$S = \text{softmax}(f(AXW_{pool})) \tag{2}$$

$$X' = S^T Z \tag{3}$$

$$A' = S^T A S^T \tag{4}$$

where W_{pool} denotes the pooling embedding matrix, S denotes the assignment matrix, X' denotes all the nodes in the area-level graph, and A' denotes the new adjacent matrix. After that, a new coarsened area-level graph can be constructed. Then the HGCNN uses the other graph convolution block to learn an area-level object representation embedding.

In the standard DIFFPOOL [21] layer, the cluster assignment matrix S provides an assignment of each node at the low layer to the new cluster at the high layer. Each row of S corresponds to a node at the low layer, and each column of S corresponds to a cluster at the high layer. Therefore, each row of S should be close to a one-hot vector because each node at the low layer can only cluster to one node at the high layer. However, in this work, the distribution of objects in the environment always changes, which means that an object not always clusters to an area. In other words, each row of S does not need to be close to a one-hot vector. So this constraint is removed in the model.

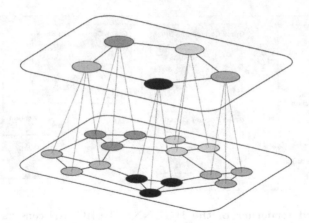

Fig. 3. Graph pooling block. The goal of the graph pooling block is to cluster the nodes in the object-level relation graph to extract the area-level concepts as new nodes and then construct the area-level relation graph.

Model Details. In the HGCNN, the first graph convolution block uses two GCN layers to learn the object-level representation embedding. Then the graph pooling block uses two GCN layers to learn the assignment matrix S. Finally, the second graph convolution block uses another two GCN layers to learn the area-level representation embedding.

After the graph convolution blocks, two new embeddings Z_1 and Z_2 are generated. Following [5], a graph attention layer is introduced to obtain the attended location-aware appearance feature. By concatenating it with LAF, the HGCNN outputs the final feature.

4   Experiments

4.1   Environment Settings

The proposed model is evaluated on AI2-iTHOR v1.0.1, which contains four types of scenes, and each of them contains 30 rooms. Following [18], a subset of 22 object categories are selected from the four types of scenes to ensure that there are more than 4 objects in each scene. Moreover, the rooms from each scene are divided into three parts, 20 as the training set, 5 as the validation set, and the remaining 5 as the testing set.

4.2   Evaluation

In this paper, the experiment uses success rate (SR) and success weighted by path length (SPL) [1] to evaluate the proposed methods. SR is the success rate of the agent finding the target objects, which is defined as the ratio of the number of successful episodes and the number of all the episodes. SPL aims to evaluate the proximity between the actual path and the optimal path, which is formulated as $SPL = \frac{1}{N}\Sigma_{i=1}^{N}\delta(i)\frac{L_i^{opt}}{\max(L_i,L_i^{opt})}$, where N denotes the number of episodes, L_i^{opt} and L_i represent the optimal path length and the actual path length in episode i respectively, and $\delta(i)$ is a binary indicator to indicate whether the episode i is successful. We report results for all targets (ALL) and a subset of targets ($L \geq 5$) whose length of optimal path is no less than 5.

4.3   Implementation Details

In this paper, a fundamental model which simply inputs the feature extracted by the Faster RCNN to the LSTM layer to predict the actions is chosen as the baseline. The A3C algorithm is introduced to train the proposed model for 6M episodes with 12 asynchronous workers. In each episode, the agent is penalized every step with -0.01, which forces the agent to learn the most efficient policy. At the end of each episode, the agent will get a reward of 5 if the episode is successful. The Faster RCNN in the model is pretrained and finetuned on AI2-iTHOR dataset. To update the network, the experiment employs Adam optimizer [8] with a learning rate of 10^{-4}.

Besides, all the models are evaluated in the validation set for 250 episodes in each scene type, and the model with the highest success rate is selected. Due to the stochasticity of the inference, the experiment performs each model 5 times in the testing set and calculates the average of all metrics as the final result.

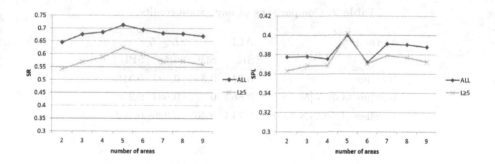

Fig. 4. Impact of the number of areas.

4.4   Ablation Study

Impact of the Number of Areas. In this paper, the number of objects is set to 22, and the number of areas is a hyperparameter that determines the size of the area-level relation graph. In theory, whether the number of areas is too large or too small, the HGCNN will be less effective, which can be proved in Fig. 4. As indicated in Fig. 4, the optimal number of areas in the experiment is 5. So the number of areas in the remaining experiments is set to 5.

Table 1. Comparisons of different graph pooling block.

Method	ALL		$L \geq 5$	
	SR	SPL	SR	SPL
NO pooling	0.663	0.377	0.564	0.368
Standard DIFFPOOL	0.678	0.386	0.587	0.381
Modified DIFFPOOL	0.713	0.400	0.626	0.402

Impact of the Graph Pooling Block. In the proposed model, the HGCNN uses the graph pooling block to cluster the nodes and extract the area-level concepts as new nodes. According to the task specificity, the DIFFPOOL layer is modified and introduced into the HGCNN. Table 1 indicates that the model with modified DIFFPOOL layer outperforms the model with standard DIFF-POOL layer and the model without graph pooling block. So in the remaining experiments, the modified DIFFPOOL layer is introduced to cluster the nodes and extract the area-level nodes.

Table 2. Comparisons of navigation results.

Method	ALL		$L \geq 5$	
	SR	SPL	SR	SPL
baseline	0.618	0.345	0.494	0.316
baseline+ORG [5]	0.663	0.377	0.564	0.368
baseline+HGCNN (ours)	0.713	0.400	0.626	0.402

4.5   Quantitative Results

The quantitative results are shown in Table 2. As seen in Table 2, the proposed model outperforms the baseline and the baseline with ORG in all four metrics, which justifies the effect of the HGCNN. The baseline simply inputs the detection results to the navigation policy module, which means that it can not utilize the object relationships to reason and locate the target object. Moreover, the baseline with ORG uses an object-level graph to encode the concurrence relationships, which ignores the hierarchical architecture of relation graph. Compared with them, the model with HGCNN encodes the hierarchical relationships among object categories, which is more efficient for the agent to locate the target object. Specifically, as shown in Fig. 5, when the environment is complex and the target

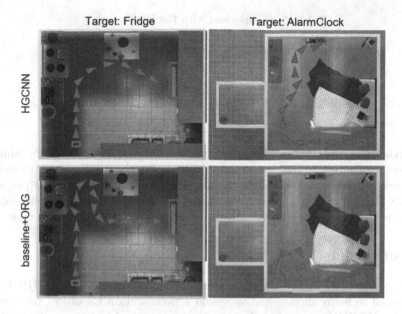

Fig. 5. Visual results of different models. We compare the HGCNN model with the baseline with ORG. The target objects are highlighted by red bounding boxes and the blue squares represent the initial position of agent.

object is not in the field of view, the baseline with ORG often takes more steps or even fails to reach the target object while the HGCNN model can always provide efficient policy based on the hierarchical relation graph.

Besides, this paper also compares the proposed model with the HOZ graph and shows the results in Table 3. As indicated in Table 3, the proposed model achieves better results especially in SPL($L \geq 5$) metric. Moreover, the experiment shows that the HOZ graph uses average 36.5 steps to reach the target object while the HGCNN only uses average 17.1 steps to achieve it, which means that compared to the HOZ graph, the HGCNN model provides more efficient navigation policy rather than rotating on the spot. It may be caused by the rules the HOZ graph uses to set the current zone, sub-goal zone and target zone during navigation, which is too limited for the agent to learn an efficient policy. Moreover, the HOZ graph uses a heuristic method to generate the area-level graph while the HGCNN uses a learnable graph pooling block to achieve it.

Table 3. Comparison with the HOZ graph.

Method	ALL		$L \geq 5$	
	SR	SPL	SR	SPL
baseline+HOZ [22]	0.706	0.400	0.628	0.392
baseline+HGCNN (ours)	0.713	0.400	0.626	0.402

Furthermore, in theory, when the environment is complex and the number of object categories is too large, it is difficult for the HOZ graph to extend the layers of the hierarchical graph to enhance the effect. However, the proposed HGCNN can simply stack the graph convolution blocks and graph pooling blocks to construct a multi-layer hierarchical relation graph to facilitate the task.

5   Conclusion

In this paper, a Hierarchical Graph Convolutional Neural Network (HGCNN) is proposed to learn an informative visual representation for object navigation. With the HGCNN, the agent can locate the target object more efficiently in the unseen environment. Moreover, a DIFFPOOL layer is modified according to the task specificity and introduced into the HGCNN, which facilitates the task a lot. The experiment shows a significant improvement over the baseline. In future work, fusing the features extracted from different graph layers better and applying the model to more complex environments are two areas of concern.

Acknowledgement. This work was supported by the National Key Research and Development Program of China under Grant 2020AAA0105900, partly by National Natural Science Foundation (NSFC) of China (grants 91948303, 61973301, 61972020), partly by Youth Innovation Promotion Association CAS, and partly by Beijing Science and Technology Plan Project (grant Z201100008320029).

References

1. Anderson, P., et al.: On evaluation of embodied navigation agents. arXiv preprint arXiv:1807.06757 (2018)
2. Chaplot, D.S., Gandhi, D.P., Gupta, A., Salakhutdinov, R.R.: Object goal navigation using goal-oriented semantic exploration. In: Advances in Neural Information Processing Systems, pp. 4247–4258 (2020)
3. Deng, J., Dong, W., Socher, R., Li, L.J., Li, K., Fei-Fei, L.: Imagenet: a large-scale hierarchical image database. In: Proceedings of the IEEE conference on Computer Vision and Pattern Recognition, pp. 248–255 (2009)
4. Diehl, F.: Edge contraction pooling for graph neural networks. arXiv preprint arXiv:1905.10990 (2019)
5. Du, H., Yu, X., Zheng, L.: Learning object relation graph and tentative policy for visual navigation. In: Vedaldi, A., Bischof, H., Brox, T., Frahm, J.-M. (eds.) ECCV 2020. LNCS, vol. 12352, pp. 19–34. Springer, Cham (2020). https://doi.org/10.1007/978-3-030-58571-6_2

6. Gupta, S., Davidson, J., Levine, S., Sukthankar, R., Malik, J.: Cognitive mapping and planning for visual navigation. In: Proceedings of the IEEE Conference on Computer Vision and Pattern Recognition, pp. 2616–2625 (2017)

7. He, K., Zhang, X., Ren, S., Sun, J.: Deep residual learning for image recognition. In: Proceedings of the IEEE Conference on Computer Vision and Pattern Recognition, pp. 770–778 (2016)

8. Kingma, D.P., Ba, J.: Adam: A method for stochastic optimization. In: International Conference on Learning Representations (Poster), pp. 1–15 (2015)

9. Kolve, E., et al.: Ai2-thor: An interactive 3d environment for visual ai. arXiv preprint arXiv:1712.05474 (2017)

10. Lee, J., Lee, I., Kang, J.: Self-attention graph pooling. In: International Conference on Machine Learning, pp. 3734–3743 (2019)

11. Lv, Y., Xie, N., Shi, Y., Wang, Z., Shen, H.T.: Improving target-driven visual navigation with attention on 3d spatial relationships. arXiv preprint arXiv:2005.02153 (2020)

12. Maksymets, O., et al.: Thda: treasure hunt data augmentation for semantic navigation. In: Proceedings of the IEEE/CVF International Conference on Computer Vision, pp. 15374–15383 (2021)

13. Mnih, V., et al.: Asynchronous methods for deep reinforcement learning. In: International Conference on Machine Learning, pp. 1928–1937 (2016)

14. Oriolo, G., Vendittelli, M., Ulivi, G.: On-line map building and navigation for autonomous mobile robots. In: Proceedings of 1995 IEEE International Conference on Robotics and Automation, pp. 2900–2906 (1995)

15. Ren, S., He, K., Girshick, R., Sun, J.: Faster R-CNN: towards real-time object detection with region proposal networks. In: Advances in Neural Information Processing Systems, pp. 91–99 (2015)

16. Taniguchi, A., Sasaki, F., Yamashina, R.: Pose invariant topological memory for visual navigation. In: Proceedings of the IEEE/CVF International Conference on Computer Vision, pp. 15384–15393 (2021)

17. Wijmans, E., et al.: DD-PPO: learning near-perfect pointgoal navigators from 2.5 billion frames. In: International Conference on Learning Representations, pp. 1–21 (2019)

18. Wortsman, M., Ehsani, K., Rastegari, M., Farhadi, A., Mottaghi, R.: Learning to learn how to learn: Self-adaptive visual navigation using meta-learning. In: Proceedings of the IEEE/CVF conference on Computer Vision and Pattern Recognition, pp. 6750–6759 (2019)

19. Yang, W., Wang, X., Farhadi, A., Gupta, A., Mottaghi, R.: Visual semantic navigation using scene priors. In: International Conference on Learning Representations, pp. 1–13 (2019)

20. Ye, J., Batra, D., Das, A., Wijmans, E.: Auxiliary tasks and exploration enable objectgoal navigation. In: Proceedings of the IEEE/CVF International Conference on Computer Vision, pp. 16117–16126 (2021)

21. Ying, R., You, J., Morris, C., Ren, X., Hamilton, W.L., Leskovec, J.: Hierarchical graph representation learning with differentiable pooling. In: Advances in Neural Information Processing Systems, pp. 4805–4815 (2018)

22. Zhang, S., Song, X., Bai, Y., Li, W., Chu, Y., Jiang, S.: Hierarchical object-to-zone graph for object navigation. In: Proceedings of the IEEE/CVF International Conference on Computer Vision, pp. 15130–15140 (2021)
23. Zhu, Y., Mottaghi, R., Kolve, E., Lim, J.J., Gupta, A., Fei-Fei, L., Farhadi, A.: Target-driven visual navigation in indoor scenes using deep reinforcement learning. In: Proceedings of the IEEE International Conference on Robotics and Automation, pp. 3357–3364 (2017)

Low-Level Graph Convolution Network for Point Cloud Processing

Hongyu Yan[1] , Zhihong Wu[1], and Li Lu[2](✉)

[1] National Key Laboratory of Fundamental Science on Synthetic Vision,
Sichuan University, Chengdu, China
hongyuyan@stu.scu.edu.cn, wuzhihong@scu.edu.cn
[2] College of Computer Science, Sichuan University, Chengdu, China
luli@scu.edu.cn

Abstract. Enlightened by the success of graph neural network, recent graph-based methods achieve impressive performance in point cloud processing. However, these methods usually employ high-level semantic edge features to update the central point feature. Less attention has been paid to the low-level geometric edge information that provides the geometric structure to enhance the model's robustness for the coordinates and rigid transformation. To solve this drawback, we propose a novel graph convolution, named Low-level Graph Convolution (LGConv), for point cloud processing. Specifically, LGConv combines semantic and geometric edge features to update the central point feature. In addition, we propose a Divisible Attention Mechanism (DAM) to our LGConv to weigh the contributions of different neighbor nodes. With the proposed LGConv, we design our LGCNet for 3D shape classification and part segmentation. Extensive experiments demonstrate the superiority of LGCNet compared with previous graph convolution methods.

Keywords: Point clouds processing · Low-level Graph Convolution · Divisible Attention Mechanism

1 Introduction

As the fundamental representative of 3D data, the point cloud has attracted great extensive attention. A large variety of applications (e.g., autonomous driving) have begun to use the point cloud as their vision data since the point cloud can provide additional spatial information compared with 2D images. Therefore, it is vital to reach a better understanding of the 3D point cloud.

PointNet [13] firstly proposed a point-based method to process point cloud, which learns a global view by point-wise multi-layer perceptrons (MLP) followed by a max-pooling operation. To exploit local structure, PointNet++ [14] introduced a set abstraction to process a set of points in a hierarchical fashion. Subsequently, several graph-based methods [1,4,8,11,15,18,20,23] leveraged the graph-liked structures to dynamically build the relations between disorder

© The Author(s), under exclusive license to Springer Nature Switzerland AG 2022
E. Pimenidis et al. (Eds.): ICANN 2022, LNCS 13530, pp. 557–569, 2022.
https://doi.org/10.1007/978-3-031-15931-2_46

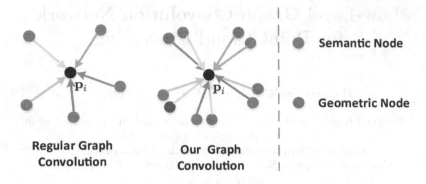

Fig. 1. Visualization of graph convolution in the point cloud. Compared with regular graph convolution, our graph convolution (LGConv) additionally considers the features of low-level geometric neighbor nodes.

point clouds. Inspired by the graph attention mechanism [16], other graph-based works [17,19,28] attempted to weigh the contributions of different neighboring points. For instance, the recent method AdaptConv [28] proposed an adaptive graph convolution to learn semantic features by generating adaptive kernels.

However, these graph-based methods mentioned above ignore the low-level geometric edge feature in their convolution blocks. As shown in Fig. 1, regular graph-based methods only focus on the features of semantic edge nodes for the central point. To solve this drawback, we propose a novel graph convolution operation, named Low-level Graph Convolution (LGConv). Different from other graph-based methods, LGConv combines the low-level geometric edge feature and high-level semantic edge feature to update the central feature (see Fig. 1). With the low-level geometric feature, our LGConv captures the diverse local feature more effectively and precisely, thereby improving the accuracy of classification and segmentation tasks. In addition, an attention mechanism is introduced to our LGConv to weigh the contributions of different neighbor nodes. To achieve this, we propose a Divisible Attention Mechanism (DAM) to simultaneously generate the attention maps of geometric edge features and semantic edge features from learned semantic and geometric relations.

Compared with the previous graph-based method, our LGConv is able to adaptively observe and extract richer structural information from the semantic features and geometric features. With the LGConv, we construct the graph-based network LGCNet. We further evaluate the proposed LGCNet on the datasets of ModelNet40 (for object classification) and ShapeNetPart (for object part segmentation). The result shows the superiority and effectiveness of LGCNet compared with existing graph-based methods.

The main contributions are listed as follows:

- We propose a novel Low-level Graph Convolution (LGConv) to process point cloud, which combines the low-level geometric edge feature and high-level semantic edge feature to update the central point feature. Besides, we propose a Divisible Attention Mechanism (DAM) to weigh the contribution of the geometric and semantic nodes.

- With the low-level graph convolution LGConv, we further propose a novel graph-based network LGCNet for point cloud classification and segmentation.
- Extensive experiments on the benchmarks of classification and segmentation demonstrate that our LGCNet achieves the best performance compared with previous graph-based methods.

2 Related Work

Point-Based Methods. In order to handle the irregularity and disorder of point clouds, the pioneering method PointNet [13] leveraged point-wise multi-layer perceptrons (MLP) to learn on points independently and utilized a symmetric function (e.g., max-pooling operation) to gain a global view. Following the PointNet [13], PointNet++ [14] further introduced a local aggregator to process a set of points sampled in a metric space in a hierarchical neural network. Likewise, various methods [5,9,25,27] have been beginning to study how to capture richer local features. Point2Sequence [9] proposed a novel deep learning model to learn 3D shape features by capturing fine-grained contextual information in a novel implicit way. PointWeb [27] presented an adaptive feature adjustment module to find the interaction between points.

Convolution-Based Methods. In order to achieve traditional convolution on the irregularity and disorder point clouds, many convolution-based approaches [6,7,10,21,24] employed dynamic strategies of transformation to support the normal work of convolution. By learning $\mathcal{X}$-transformations to simultaneously weigh and permute the input features, PointCNN [6] applied a typical convolution on the point cloud to learn the local feature. PointConv [21] directly designed weight and density functions to fully approximate the 3D continuous convolution on any set of 3D points.

Graph-Based Methods. Inspired by the graph neural network [3], several graph-based methods [1,4,8,11,15,18,20,23] utilized graph-liked structure to construct relations between points. Benefiting from the capability of the graph structure for local representation, these methods also obtained notable performance in point cloud classification and segmentation tasks. DGCNN [20] learned local geometric features by dynamically building the relations between the node and its neighbors. By assigning proper attention weights to different neighboring points, GACNet [19] selectively focuses on the most relevant part of them according to their dynamically learned features. The most recent method Adaptconv [28] proposed to adaptively establish the relationship between a pair of points by learning an adaptive convolution kernel.

3 Graph on Point Clouds

In this section, we first present the background of the graph-based methods in point clouds. Then, we explore how LGConv learns context features from both

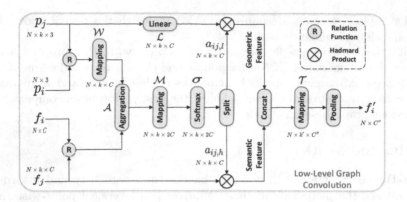

Fig. 2. Low-level Graph Convolution (LGConv). For an input point p_i, f_i and its neighbor p_j, f_j, we firstly obtain the semantic relation $f_j - f_i$ and geometric relation $\mathcal{W}(p_i - p_j)$. The $\mathcal{W}$ is a mapping function (e.g., MLPs). Then, we generate the attention map via a non-linearity function $\mathcal{M}$ and a $Softmax$ function σ. Following, we employ a channel-wise split operation to divide the attention map. The high-level semantic attention weight $a_{ij,h}$ and the low-level geometric attention weight $a_{ij,l}$ respectively are used to weigh the contribution of semantic neighbor node f_j and geometric neighbor node p_j. Finally, after concatenation operation for the semantic edge feature $(a_{ij,h} * f_j)$ and geometric edge feature $(a_{ij,l} * p_j)$, we generate the new central point feature f_i' by a updating function $\mathcal{T}$ and a pooling operation. $\mathcal{A}$ is a aggregation function (e.g., subtraction, concatenation). The N denotes number of point. The C denotes channel dimensions. The k is number of neighbor nodes.

semantic edge features and geometric edge features. Moreover, we introduce how to generate attention maps in our LGConv. Finally, we present the detailed designs of network architectures for object classification and part segmentation.

3.1   Background

A traditional graph convolution [3] aims to extract central node features from the product between the feature matrix and edge adjacency matrix. The adjacency matrix can help the network to find the edge features related to the central node. However, due to the disorder and irregularity of the point cloud, the predefined adjacency matrix can not directly be applied to identify the neighbor edges of central points. To solve this problem, DGCNN [20] exploited a dynamic way to construct relations between points. Based on a dynamic query, DGCNN proposed a graph-based convolution method, called EdgeConv, for point cloud processing.

We denote the input point clouds as $P = \{p_1, \ldots, \mathbf{p}_n\} \subseteq \mathbb{R}^{N \times 3}$ with the corresponding features defined as $F = \{f_i \mid i = 1, 2, \ldots, N\} \in \mathbb{R}^{N \times D}$. N is the total number of the input point clouds. A undirected graph $\mathcal{G}(\mathcal{V}, \mathcal{E})$ is build from the given point clouds by grouping method, e.g., k-nearest neighbors (kNN), Ball Query [14], where $\mathcal{V} = \{1, \ldots, N\}$ and $\mathcal{E} \subseteq \mathcal{V} \times \mathcal{V}$ represents the set of edges. In the EdgeConv, the output feature of the i-th point can be formulated as:

$$\mathbf{f}_i' = \max_{j:(i,j)\in\mathcal{E}} \{\mathcal{W}\left([\mathbf{f}_j - \mathbf{f}_i, \mathbf{f}_i]\right)\} \tag{1}$$

where $\mathbf{f}_i$ is the feature of central points. $[\cdot]$ is the operation of concatenation. $\mathcal{M}$ is a non-linearity function, i.e., $\{MLP \to ReLU\}$. "max" is an max-pooling function over all the edge features in the neighborhood.

Although dynamic graph convolution gained better performance compared with previous point-based methods [13,14], it assigns the contribution of each neighbor node equally. With the success of Graph Attention Network (GAT) [16], the methods [8,19,28] based on graph attention were proposed. The general purpose of the graph attention network is to learn the weight matrix of neighbor nodes. In the Graph Attention Convolution (GAC [19]), the output feature f_i' of the i-th point can be defined as:

$$f_i' = \sum_{j:(i,j)\in\mathcal{E}} a_{ij} * M_g\left(f_j\right) + b_i \tag{2}$$

where a_{ij} indicates the attention weight of vertex j to vertex i, which is computed by a relation function (e.g., MLP) applied on both coordinate and feature relation between vertex j to vertex i. M_g is a multi-layer perceptron.

In this case, GAC leverage a simple relation function to obtain the weight matrix of the edge feature. Other methods based on graph attention, such as AdaptConv [28] and 3DGCN [8], employ the adaptive or deformable kernels to establish the relationship between a pair of points, which are effective attempts and achieves the surprise performance. However, all of these graph-based methods mentioned above ignore the low-level geometric edge feature in updating central point features, which leads them to a lack of representation capacity for the spatial structure.

3.2   Our Low-Level Graph Convolution

Different from the previous graph-based methods [8,19,20,28], our LGConv combines semantic edge features and geometric edge features to update the central point feature, as shown in Fig. 2.

In our LGConv, we first use the linear function to transform the point feature F into a hidden space, which can reduce the model's complexity. Finally, the output feature of the i-th point in our LGConv can be formulated as:

$$\mathbf{f}_i' = \max_{j:(i,j)\in\mathcal{E}} \{\mathcal{T}\left([a_{ij,h} * f_j, a_{ij,l} * \mathcal{L}(p_j)]\right)\} \tag{3}$$

where $[\cdot]$ is the operation of channel-wise or point-wise concatenation. The mapping function $\mathcal{T}$ is used to update the semantic and geometric edge feature, which can be implemented as a series of shared MLPs. $\mathcal{L}$ is a linear function, which transforms the channel-wise features of geometric neighbor points to a high-level space. The $a_{ij,h}$ and $a_{ij,l}$ are attention maps of high-level semantic

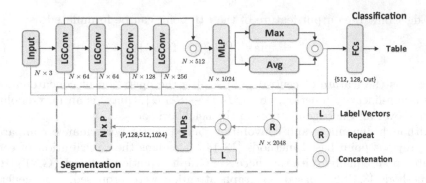

Fig. 3. The architectures of our LGCNet for classification (top) and segmentation (bottom). N denotes the number of points. The label vector is a one-hot vector representing category types for each point.

edge features and low-level geometric edge features, respectively. In this case, the concatenation operation can provide more information to the max-pooling operation, which will expand the model's reception field. Note that, for the consistency between semantic edge feature and geometric edge feature, we use the geometric similarity to construct graph structure $\mathcal{G}(\mathcal{V}, \mathcal{E})$ in both semantic edges and geometric edges.

The attention mechanism plays an important role in the graph attention network. Previous graph attention networks [19,28] trend to generate a single attention map to the high-level semantic edge features. However, there are semantic edge features and geometric edge features in our LGConv. To simultaneously generate a semantic attention map and a geometric attention map from learned relations, we design a Divisible Attention Mechanism (DAM). Specifically, we employ the geometric relationships and semantic relationships between points and their neighbors to learn the attention weights. Hence, in our LGConv, the attention weights $a_{ij,h}$ and $a_{ij,l}$ are defined as:

$$a_{ij,h}, a_{ij,l} = Split(\sigma(\mathcal{M}(\mathcal{A}(\mathcal{R}_h, \mathcal{R}_l)))) \tag{4}$$

where $\mathcal{R}_h$ and $\mathcal{R}_l$ are semantic edge relation and geometric edge relation, respectively. The semantic edge relation is $\mathcal{R}_h = f_i - f_j$. The geometric edge relation is $\mathcal{R}_l = \mathcal{W}(p_i - p_j)$, here $\mathcal{W}$ is a mapping function (e.g., MLPs). $\mathcal{A}$ is a aggregation function (e.g., subtraction, concatenation). The mapping function $\mathcal{M}$ is a nonlinear function (e.g., $\{MLP \rightarrow LeakyReLU\}$). σ is a $Softmax$ function. The $Split$ is a split operation in terms of channel, which is used to divide attention maps.

3.3 Network Architecture

We design the network architectures for point cloud classification and segmentation with the proposed LGConv. The network architectures are shown in Fig. 3.

Table 1. Classification results on ModelNet40 dataset. Our network achieves the best results. The * denotes voting strategy same as pointnet++ [14].

Methods	Points	mAcc	OA
Point-based methods			
PointNet [13]	1k	86.2	89.2
PointNet++ [14]	1k	–	91.9
So-Net [5]	5k	–	93.4
Point-Web [27]	1k	89.4	92.3
Point2Sequence [9]	1k	90.4	92.6
PointASNL [25]	1k	–	92.9
Convolution-based methods			
PointCNN [6]	1k	88.1	92.2
SpiderCNN [24]	1k	–	92.4
RS-CNN [10]	1k	–	92.9
PointConv [21]	1k	–	92.5
Graph-based methods			
SpecGCN [18]	1k	–	92.1
DGCNN [20]	1k	90.2	92.9
Grid-GCN [23]	1k	–	93.1
3D-GCN [8]	1k	–	92.1
AdaptConv [28]	1k	90.7	93.4
LGCNet (Ours)	1k	**91.0**	**93.6**
LGCNet (Ours) *	1k	**91.2**	**93.8**

We leverage four cascaded LGConv layers with dimensions (64, 64, 128, 256) to extract the geometric and semantic features of point clouds. One shared multi-layer perceptron is used to get a 512-dimensional feature via aggregate multi-scale features generated by the previous four LGConv layers. We then concatenate features from the max pooling and avg pooling to obtain the global features.

For the classification task (see the top of Fig. 3), three fully-connected layers (512, 128, C) are used to transform the global feature and predict the final category.

For the segmentation task (see the bottom of Fig. 3), we concatenate the global feature, the original inputs, the point feature from the four LGConv layers, and the label vectors to generate the final point feature. Finally, a series of shared MLPs (1024, 512, 128, P) are employed to transform the point feature and predict the categories of each point.

4   Experiments

In this section, we use the widely adopted ModelNet40 [22], and ShapeNet-Part [26] dataset to verify our method's effectiveness in the 3D shape classification and part segmentation.

Table 2. Part segmentation results on ShapeNetPart dataset evaluated as the mean class IoU (mcIoU) and mean instance IoU (mIoU).

Methods	Points	mcIou	mIou
Point-based methods			
PointNet [13]	2k	80.4	83.7
PointNet++ [14]	2k	81.9	85.1
So-Net [5]	1k	81.0	84.6
Point2Sequence [9]	2k	–	85.2
PointASNL [25]	2k	–	86.1
Convolution-based methods			
PointCNN [6]	2k	84.6	86.1
SpiderCNN [24]	2k	81.7	85.3
RS-CNN [10]	2k	–	86.2
PointConv [21]	2k	82.8	85.7
Graph-based methods			
SpecGCN [18]	2k	–	85.4
DGCNN [20]	2k	82.3	85.2
3D-GCN [8]	2k	82.1	85.1
AdaptConv [28]	2k	83.4	86.4
LGCNet (Ours)	2k	**85.0**	**86.5**

4.1   Shape Classification

Data. We conduct experiments on ModelNet40 [22] on classification through our LGCNet network. The ModelNet40 dataset contains 12311 CAD models with 40 object categories. The 9843 models are used to train and 2468 to test. We apply the mean accuracy within each category (mAcc) and the overall accuracy (OA) as evaluation metrics. In the ModelNet40 dataset, we select 1024 points without normal vectors as our inputs.

Setting. We implement the LGCNet in PyTorch [12] and CUDA. We use the Adam [2] optimizer with $\beta_1 = 0.9$ and $\beta_2 = 0.999$ on two V100 GPUs. The initial learning rate is set to 0.001 and it decays by a factor of 0.7 every 20 epochs. The batch size is set to 32 for all training models. We do not use weight decay. All LGConv layers use the LeakyReLU and batch normalization, other layers are with ReLU. We set the k number of neighbors to 20. Similar to [10,14], we apply augmentation strategy including the following components: random scaling in the range [0.8, 1.25], random shift in the range [−0.1, 0.1], random dropout points with the ratio of the range [0, 87.5%].

Results. The results are shown on Table 1. We compare our LGCNet with previous classification methods on the ModelNet40 dataset. The overall accuracy of LGCNet is 93.6%, and 93.8% (with voting strategy), which outperforms all graph-based models (e.g., AdaptConv [28]) as well as point-based and convolution-based methods.

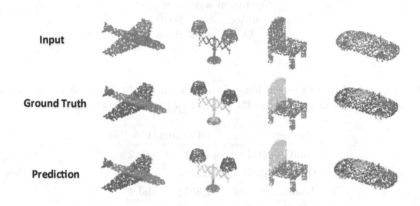

Fig. 4. Visualized results of part segmentation on ShapeNetPart dataset.

4.2 Shape Part Segmentation

Data. We further validate our method on ShapeNetPart dataset [26] for the 3D shape part segmentation task. The ShapeNetPart dataset consists of 16881 models from 16 shape categories. Most objects in the dataset have been labeled with less than 6 parts, resulting in a total number of 50 different parts. Following the split scheme of methods [14,28], the 14006 models are used to train while 2874 models are used to validate our experiment. We apply the mean class intersection of union (mcIoU) and mean intersection of union (mIoU) as the evaluation metric to verify the segmentation performance. In this dataset, we select 2048 points with normal vectors as our inputs.

Setting. Similar to [28], we introduce a one-hot vector representing category types for each point, which is stacked with the point-wise features to compute the segmentation results. Other training parameters are set the same as in our classification task.

Results. The Table 2 shows that our model achieves state-of-the-art performance compared with other methods. In addition, we visualize the results for the part segmentation in Fig. 4.

5   Ablation Study

In this section, we conduct ablation studies on the ModelNet40 dataset to evaluate the design of our LGConv, including the geometric edge features, concatenation operation between semantic edge features and geometric edge features, and mapping function $\mathcal{L}$.

The Geometric Edge Features. We ablate the effectiveness of geometric edge features (with and without) in the following:

Operation	w/o	/w
mAcc	89.7	**91.0**
OA	93.3	**93.6**

Table 3. Comparison of the previous methods with our LGCNet on complexity and overall accuracy. "#Params" means the number of parameters in a model.

Methods	#Params	OA (%)
PointNet [13]	3.5M	89.2
DGCNN [20]	1.81M	92.9
AdaptConv [28]	1.85M	93.4
LGCNet (Ours)	2.02M	**93.6**

The table indicates that the performance of the model with geometric edge features is higher than without. This suggests that the geometric edge features is essential for our LGConv to learn the point features.

The Concatenation Type. We study the type of concatenation (channel-wise concatenation compared with point-wise) in the following:

Operation	Point-wise	Channel-wise
mAcc	89.7	**91.0**
OA	93.3	**93.6**

The results demonstrate that channel-wise concatenation is more expressive compared with point-wise concatenation. we argue that channel-wise concatenation can enrich the model's ability to represent neighboring edge features but the point-wise concatenation just provides more edge nodes.

The Mapping Function $\mathcal{T}$. We further explore the designs of depths (three MLPs compared with single MLP) in the following:

Operation	Single layer	Multi layer
mAcc	90.0	**91.0**
OA	93.3	**93.6**

The results show that multi-layer works the best on mAcc and OA metrics. we argue that multi-layer enlarges the depth of the model, which can enhance the fitting capability as well as expand the receptive field.

6   Complexity Analysis

In this section, we analyze the complexity and corresponding classification results of prior methods as well as our LGCNet in the classification task on the ModelNet40 dataset. As shown in Table 3, our LGCNet has fewer parameters yet higher overall accuracy (OA) compared with Pointnet [13]. Compared to the latest graph-based methods DGCNN [20] and AdaptConv [28], our LGCNet achieves the best performance with a small growth of parameter.

7   Conclusion

In this paper, we explore the effectiveness of low-level geometric features for the graph convolution network. For that, we propose a Low-level Graph Convolution (LGConv) for point clouds analysis. In our LGConv, we combine the geometric edge feature and the semantic edge feature to update the central feature. Besides, to weigh the high-level semantic edge feature and low-level geometric edge feature, we propose a Divisible Attention Mechanism (DAM) to simultaneously generate a semantic attention map and a geometric attention map from learned semantic and geometric relations. Finally, with the proposed LGConv, we design our LGCNet for 3D shape classification and part segmentation. The extensive experiments demonstrate that our LGCNet outperforms previous graph-based methods.

Acknowledgements. This work was supported by the Sichuan Science and Technology Program (NO: 2021YFG030).

References

1. Hua, B.S., Tran, M.K., Yeung, S.K.: Pointwise convolutional neural networks. In: Proceedings of the IEEE Conference on Computer Vision and Pattern Recognition, pp. 984–993 (2018)
2. Kingma, D.P., Ba, J.: Adam: a method for stochastic optimization. arXiv preprint arXiv:1412.6980 (2014)
3. Kipf, T.N., Welling, M.: Semi-supervised classification with graph convolutional networks. arXiv preprint arXiv:1609.02907 (2016)

4. Lei, H., Akhtar, N., Mian, A.: Spherical Kernel for efficient graph convolution on 3D point clouds. IEEE Trans. Pattern Anal. Mach. Intell. **43**(10), 3664–3680 (2020)
5. Li, J., Chen, B.M., Lee, G.H.: SO-Net: self-organizing network for point cloud analysis. In: Proceedings of the IEEE Conference on Computer Vision and Pattern Recognition, pp. 9397–9406 (2018)
6. Li, Y., Bu, R., Sun, M., Wu, W., Di, X., Chen, B.: PointCNN: convolution on X-transformed points. Adv. Neural. Inf. Process. Syst. **31**, 820–830 (2018)
7. Lin, Y., et al.: FPConv: learning local flattening for point convolution. In: Proceedings of the IEEE/CVF Conference on Computer Vision and Pattern Recognition, pp. 4293–4302 (2020)
8. Lin, Z.H., Huang, S.Y., Wang, Y.C.F.: Convolution in the cloud: learning deformable Kernels in 3D graph convolution networks for point cloud analysis. In: Proceedings of the IEEE/CVF Conference on Computer Vision and Pattern Recognition, pp. 1800–1809 (2020)
9. Liu, X., Han, Z., Liu, Y.S., Zwicker, M.: Point2Sequence: learning the shape representation of 3D point clouds with an attention-based sequence to sequence network. In: Proceedings of the AAAI Conference on Artificial Intelligence, vol. 33, pp. 8778–8785 (2019)
10. Liu, Y., Fan, B., Xiang, S., Pan, C.: Relation-shape convolutional neural network for point cloud analysis. In: Proceedings of the IEEE/CVF Conference on Computer Vision and Pattern Recognition, pp. 8895–8904 (2019)
11. Monti, F., Boscaini, D., Masci, J., Rodola, E., Svoboda, J., Bronstein, M.M.: Geometric deep learning on graphs and manifolds using mixture model CNNs. In: Proceedings of the IEEE Conference on Computer Vision and Pattern Recognition, pp. 5115–5124 (2017)
12. Paszke, A., et al.: PyTorch: an imperative style, high-performance deep learning library. Adv. Neural. Inf. Process. Syst. **32**, 8026–8037 (2019)
13. Qi, C.R., Su, H., Mo, K., Guibas, L.J.: PointNet: deep learning on point sets for 3D classification and segmentation. In: Proceedings of the IEEE Conference on Computer Vision and Pattern Recognition, pp. 652–660 (2017)
14. Qi, C.R., Yi, L., Su, H., Guibas, L.J.: PointNet++: deep hierarchical feature learning on point sets in a metric space. arXiv preprint arXiv:1706.02413 (2017)
15. Shen, Y., Feng, C., Yang, Y., Tian, D.: Mining point cloud local structures by Kernel correlation and graph pooling. In: Proceedings of the IEEE Conference on Computer Vision and Pattern Recognition, pp. 4548–4557 (2018)
16. Veličković, P., Cucurull, G., Casanova, A., Romero, A., Lio, P., Bengio, Y.: Graph attention networks. arXiv preprint arXiv:1710.10903 (2017)
17. Verma, N., Boyer, E., Verbeek, J.: FeaStNet: feature-steered graph convolutions for 3D shape analysis. In: Proceedings of the IEEE Conference on Computer Vision and Pattern Recognition, pp. 2598–2606 (2018)
18. Wang, C., Samari, B., Siddiqi, K.: Local spectral graph convolution for point set feature learning. In: Proceedings of the European conference on computer vision (ECCV), pp. 52–66 (2018)
19. Wang, L., Huang, Y., Hou, Y., Zhang, S., Shan, J.: Graph attention convolution for point cloud semantic segmentation. In: Proceedings of the IEEE/CVF Conference on Computer Vision and Pattern Recognition, pp. 10296–10305 (2019)
20. Wang, Y., Sun, Y., Liu, Z., Sarma, S.E., Bronstein, M.M., Solomon, J.M.: Dynamic graph CNN for learning on point clouds. ACM Trans. Graph. (TOG) **38**(5), 1–12 (2019)

21. Wu, W., Qi, Z., Fuxin, L.: PointConv: deep convolutional networks on 3D point clouds. In: Proceedings of the IEEE/CVF Conference on Computer Vision and Pattern Recognition, pp. 9621–9630 (2019)
22. Wu, Z., et al.: 3D ShapeNets: a deep representation for volumetric shapes. In: Proceedings of the IEEE Conference on Computer Vision and Pattern Recognition, pp. 1912–1920 (2015)
23. Xu, Q., Sun, X., Wu, C.Y., Wang, P., Neumann, U.: Grid-GCN for fast and scalable point cloud learning. In: Proceedings of the IEEE/CVF Conference on Computer Vision and Pattern Recognition, pp. 5661–5670 (2020)
24. Xu, Y., Fan, T., Xu, M., Zeng, L., Qiao, Y.: SpiderCNN: deep learning on point sets with parameterized convolutional filters. In: Proceedings of the European Conference on Computer Vision (ECCV), pp. 87–102 (2018)
25. Yan, X., Zheng, C., Li, Z., Wang, S., Cui, S.: PointASNL: robust point clouds processing using nonlocal neural networks with adaptive sampling. In: Proceedings of the IEEE/CVF Conference on Computer Vision and Pattern Recognition, pp. 5589–5598 (2020)
26. Yi, L., et al.: A scalable active framework for region annotation in 3D shape collections. ACM Trans. Graph. (TOG) **35**(6), 1–12 (2016)
27. Zhao, H., Jiang, L., Fu, C.W., Jia, J.: PointWeb: enhancing local neighborhood features for point cloud processing. In: Proceedings of the IEEE/CVF Conference on Computer Vision and Pattern Recognition, pp. 5565–5573 (2019)
28. Zhou, H., Feng, Y., Fang, M., Wei, M., Qin, J., Lu, T.: Adaptive graph convolution for point cloud analysis. In: Proceedings of the IEEE/CVF International Conference on Computer Vision, pp. 4965–4974 (2021)

Low-Resource Similar Case Matching in Legal Domain

Jingxin Fang[✉], Xuwei Li, and Yiguang Liu

College of Computer Science, Sichuan University, Chengdu, China
fangjingxin@stu.scu.edu.cn, {lixuwei,liuyg}@scu.edu.cn

Abstract. Automatically finding similar cases in legal domain plays can benefit the legal system a lot. However, the annotation of legal document similarities can be time-consuming and expensive. In this study, we focus on low-resource similar case matching in the legal domain, checking which two cases are more similar among a triplet. We propose specifically designed data augmentation techniques for contrastive learning including Truncation, Double-dropout and Prompt, and consider document-level information and corpus-level information in our model. The experiment result shows that our model achieves the best performance compared with state-of-art models in different low-resource training set settings.

Keywords: Contrastive learning · Prompt · Graph neural network

1 Introduction

Similar Case Matching (SCM), aiming at automatically finding the most similar case among all other cases, is meaningful in the legal system. For example, in the common law legal system, previous similar cases will have a huge impact on the judgement result and people sometimes spend lots of time on finding the most similar case. Therefore, an automatic method for finding similar cases is needed. CAIL2019-SCM [24] is a dataset related to Private Lending provided in Chinese AI and Law Challenge (CAIL). To simplify the problem, each sample contains three documents: one anchor document (A), two candidate documents (B and C) and the task is to determine which candidate document is more similar to the anchor document. Formally, the target is to predict whether $sim(A, B) > sim(A, C)$ or $sim(A, C) > sim(A, B)$, which can be considered as a supervised contrastive learning problem. However, the annotation of this kind of dataset requires experienced experts and is quite time consuming and expensive. A model which requires fewer labelled data is useful. Therefore, our research question is: "What will be the best model for Low-Resource Similar Case Matching in Legal Domain?"

Data augmentation [3] has been proved helpful in NLP tasks especially when the labelled data is limited. Contrastive learning in NLP also introduced some

Supported by National Key R&D Program of China 2020YFC0832404.

data augmentation techniques [4,21]. Meanwhile, recent studies on prompt show good performance in few shot settings [1]. A few people tried to use prompt as a data augmentation method, but only for the generation of new samples [10,22]. Meanwhile, TextGCN [26] shows great performance in the text classification field especially when the labelled data is limited because it considers the corpus global structure information, but no effort has been used on supervised contrastive learning. In this study, we proposed a new method which is designed for Low-Resource Similar Case Matching in Legal Domain, and our main contributions are as follows:

- We propose three different data augmentation methods including truncation, dropout and prompt. As far as we know, we are the first ones who apply prompt on masked language model for data augmentation.
- We combine BERT and TextGCN for contrastive learning in a simple yet effective way that does not require carefully fine-tuning.
- We split CAIL2019-SCM into three different training sets to mimic few-resource settings and show that our model achieves the best performance compared with other state-of-art models.

2   Related Work

Contrastive learning can work well with suitable data augmentation techniques. Traditional NLP data augmentation methods like word deletion, substitution, switching, back-translation are used [2,21,23]. SimCSE [4] constructs postive pairs simply using dropout and ConSERT [2] uses adversarial attack techniques.

Prompt came to public view since the introduction of GPT3 [1] and showed great performance in few shot learning settings. Following that, numerous prompt-based methods have been applied in NLP field. The prompt template can be either manually designed by using domain knowledge [1,18] or auto generated [20], or even soft prompt template as continuous embedding [11]. The pre-trained models can be either generative models like BART [12] or masked language models like BERT [6].

During the rapid development of pre-trained models in NLP field, graph neural networks are also widely applied. TextGCN [26] applies graph convolutional neural networks [8] on transductive text classification tasks. Similarly, [27] applies GCN on sentiment analysis tasks. Recently, graph attention neural networks have also been applied in text classification tasks [17,25] but require more computation resources. Others combine pre-trained models like BERT with TextGCN by feeding BERT output into TextGCN [14] or feeding TextGCN output into BERT [16]. Both methods require large memory and carefully fine-tuning to train BERT and GCN model together.

3   Methodology

3.1   Data Augmentation

In contrastive learning, there is never a lack of methods for sampling negative examples, such as offline random sampling, or online in-batch sampling [4], etc., the relatively difficult point is to find positive examples. In our work, we use several data augmentation methods to help us mine positive data. For convenience, we use DA to refer to data augmentation in this paper.

Different Truncations. One of the major challenges in natural language understanding of legal instruments is that the length of the body of legal instruments is often very variable. With some cases being relatively simple and the instruments being short and concise, and others being relatively complex and the instruments being very diverse and long. This makes it difficult for NLP practitioners to find a suitable general approach to semantically understand and encode diverse legal documents.

Unlike other work that attempts to counteract the effects of this feature of legal instruments, in our work we use the aforementioned feature for data augmentation, relying on different excerpts of the same instrument to assist us in augmenting the semantic positive examples of the instrument.

More specifically, if there is an instrument which contains over L tokens, we would take the last L tokens as the main part of this instrument as it would be able to contain relatively critical information - the outcome of the verdict. And to make the data pair as different as possible, we intercept the L tokens at its beginning as the result of data augmentation, i.e., the positive example.

$$S_{main} = S[-L :], \ S_{cut} = S[: L], \ \text{if } len(S) > L \tag{1}$$

And S_{main} and S_{cut} will be used randomly. The workflow is also shown in Fig. 1a.

Dropout. SimCSE [4] feeds the same input twice into the model with dropout, and uses the obtained outputs as positive example pairs for each other, thus achieving unsupervised comparative learning. R-Drop [13] is a plug-and-play regular method in which each data sample is passed through the model with dropout twice in each mini-batch, and the KL-divergence constraint is used to make the output consistent between them. It's not difficult to find that, dropout is used as a simple and effective way to augment data to promote regularity. In our work, we use dropout to provide an easy-to-use means of obtaining positive example data for legal document data. As shown in Fig. 1b, the same text $Text_A$ is fed twice into the model with dropout to obtain two different outputs E_{A1} and E_{A2}, which are natural positive examples; at the same time, the other output E_B is enhanced and can be used as the negative example data for E_A.

BERT with Prompts. Prompt learning [20] refers to the processing of input textual information according to a specific template, reconstructing the task into a form that makes better use of pre-trained language models, which takes the form of pre-training, adding prompts, and making inference predictions, and its aim is to make better use of pre-trained knowledge by adding indicated information, so it is usually very effective in scenarios with cold starts and limited annotation resources, and its cost is the need to design templates and answer

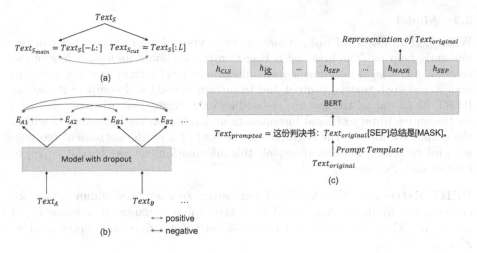

Fig. 1. Workflow of data augmentation. (a) Different truncations as DA. (b) Dropout as DA. (c) Prompt with BERT as DA.

mappings for downstream tasks. In general, prompt learning is performed in three steps to reason about the most appropriate downstream answer. The first step is the addition of instructions, a mapping function $f_{prompt}(\cdot)$ is used to transform the input text T into $T' = f_{prompt}(T)$. This usually uses a template that contains two slots, an input slot $[T]$ and an answer slot $[A]$, and then the input text T is filled into $[T]$. For example, for sentiment analysis, the template could be "[T], I am in a [A] mood." , and input x is "I got a scholarship.", then T' is "I got a scholarship, I'm in a [A] mood." . The second step is the answer search, where we need to find the $\hat{a}$ that gets the highest score from the language model. We start by defining A as the set of possible answers, and A can be either the entire language range (e.g., in a language generation task) or a limited range (e.g., in a classification task). In the above example, $A = [$"good", "bad"$]$. The answer that best fits into $[A]$, i.e. $\hat{a}$, is then can be found in A.

Considering the premise of limited resources, in our work, the idea of prompt learning is used by us to better mine the knowledge of pre-trained models. Given that our goal when using BERT is to obtain semantic embedding for legal documents, we refer to PromptBERT [5] and use a prompt template commonly used for summarization that contains the [MASK] special token and use the hidden vector of that special token as the semantic representation of the input. In this case, the prompt serves to guide the BERT to a summary representation of the preceding text at the [MASK] position. Formally, $E_{prompt} = h_{[MASK]}$.

The workflow is shown in Fig. 1c. In using this kind of DA, we first compare the performance of different prompt templates based on the public weight of BERT without fine-tune, and then select the relatively most suitable prompt template for DA in the subsequent fine-tune of BERT.

3.2 Model

When performing SCM tasks, there are two types of information that can significantly help us. The first one is based on the semantic understanding of the content of the legal instrument itself (document-level information), in order to understand such textual content and to further encode and compare it, we use BERT [6] as one of the feature embedding extractors. The other one is based on the entire library of legal instruments and relies on the information within the corpus to improve the cognition of the text of a single instrument (corpus-level information), in order to exploit this information, we use TextGCN [26] to extract such features.

BERT Extractor. For the BERT extractor, we adopt the common practice of using the hidden vector of [CLS] as the global semantic representation of the input. This will work as document-level information and represented as $E_{BERT} = h_{[CLS]}$.

TextGCN Extractor. TextGCN [26] is one kind of GCN-based models which is designed to do text classification tasks. We extend TextGCN as a feature extractor. We use all the documents in the corpus and the words within the documents for modelling the nodes in the graph, and connects the nodes in this heterogeneous graph using word-to-word and word-to-document edges, and then enables the information in the corpus to interact by GCN learning, thus utilizing the overall structural information at the corpus-level.

Formally, the graph $G = (V, E, A)$ is constructed by its node set V, edge set E, and adjacency matrix A. Each document in the corpus will have a document node in the GCN graph, and words that appear in the corpus no less than K times will have a word node in the GCN graph, $V = \{word\ nodes, document\ nodes\}$. Each document node is connected to the word nodes it contains using edges with Term Frequency-Inverse Document Frequency (TF-IDF) weights, and each word node is connected to other co-occurring word nodes by edges with point-wise mutual information (PMI) weights, $E = \{word_{to}word\ edges, word_{to}document\ edges\}$. This heterogeneous graph will be used as the initial graph of a two-layer GCN, with one-hot embedding as the initial node embedding. Then GCN learning would perform as $H^{(l+1)} = f(H^{(l)}, A) = \sigma(\hat{A}H^{(l)}W^{(l)})$, where $H^{(l+1)}$ denotes the $(l+1)_{th}$ layer's hidden states; $\hat{A} = \tilde{D}^{-\frac{1}{2}}\tilde{A}\tilde{D}^{-\frac{1}{2}} = A + I$ denotes the normalized symmetric adjacency matrix; σ is a non-linear activation function which may change with the layer; $W^{(l)} \in \mathcal{R}^{d_l \times d_{l+1}}$ denotes the l_{th} layer's weight matrix; d_i denotes the feature dimension of the i_{th} layer.

We deformed TextGCN for SCM tasks to adapt to new downstream tasks. We set the second layer's hidden dimension the same as the hidden dimension and use the second layer's embedding of the document node to calculate loss by comparing the distance of these vectors with the similar information label of the training data. With such a change, the hidden vectors of document nodes in the second layer of GCN can then be used as GCN feature vectors of legal documents.

3.3   Training and Inference

During the training, we train the BERT and TextGCN separately. After obtaining a batch of data, we randomly select some data to generate more triplets using the DA method described in Sect. 3.1, and then feed those triplets into the model to get the representation of each document and compute the loss using the triplet loss.

Formally, for a triplet (x, x_1, x_2) where x, x_1, x_2 are the document context and $similarity(x, x_1) > similarity(x, x_2)$, the triplet loss is defined as:

$$l = max(dis(x, x_1) - dis(x, x_2) + margin, 0) \tag{2}$$

where $dis()$ denotes a distance function to calculate the distance between two input documents, $margin$ is a hyperparameter that is used to control the distance difference between (x, x_1) and (x, x_2). For the distance function, we use euclidean distance for BERT and cosine distance for TextGCN.

$$Dis_{BERT}(a, b) = \sqrt{\sum_{i=0}^{d}(E_{ai} - E_{bi})^2} \tag{3}$$

$$Dis_{TextGCN}(a, b) = 1 - \frac{E_a \cdot E_b}{||E_a|| \times ||E_b||} \tag{4}$$

After separated training, the distance of each anchor/positive document pair and anchor/negative document pair from BERT and TextGCN are available for the training set, validation set and test set. The joint learning and testing phase can be described as:

$$\tilde{Dis}_{BERT} = norm(Dis_{BERT}) \tag{5}$$

$$\tilde{Dis}_{TextGCN} = norm(Dis_{TextGCN}) \tag{6}$$

$$Dis_{combined} = (1 - \alpha) * \tilde{Dis}_{BERT} + \alpha * \tilde{Dis}_{TextGCN} \tag{7}$$

Since we use different Triplet loss functions in BERT and TextGCN, we apply 0-1 normalization on the Dis_{BERT} and $Dis_{TextGCN}$ using the statistics of the training set. Then, weighted sum is applied to get the combined distance, the joint weight α is decided using the grid search on training set performance. For each possible α, the correct labelled training data is calculated when $Dis_{combined}^{(A,P)}$ is smaller than $Dis_{combined}^{(A,N)}$. We choose the α when the training set accuracy is highest, and we show the influence of α in Sect. 4.4.

Table 1. Size of different data splits

Data split	Training set			Valid	Test
	D1	D2	D3		
Count	1500	1500	1500	1500	1536

4 Experiments

4.1 Setup

Dataset. The dataset named CAIL2019-SCM comes from a similar case matching task published in 2019 by Challenge of AI in Law (CAIL), whose data source is the publicly available legal instruments on the China Judicial Documents Network. For each legal instrument in the dataset, only desensitized factual descriptions are provided, and their subject matter belongs to private lending cases. The data in the dataset are in the form of a triplet (x, x_1, x_2), where x, x_1, x_2 are the factual descriptions in the three legal documents, and the case similarity between x and x_1 is greater than the case similarity between x and x_2.

Original training split has more than 5000 triplets, to simulate the low-resource environment with limited labelled data, we randomly sampled three training splits, each containing 1500 triplets, from the original dataset without overlap. For evaluation, we use the validation set and test set provided by CAIL2019-SCM. The number of triplets in different data splits is shown in Table 1.

Baseline. Our method was compared with several current baseline and state-of-the-art models:

- TextLSTM [15]: LSTM is an improved Recurrent Neural Network that can solve the problem that RNN cannot handle long-distance dependencies. We use a bi-directional LSTM and the last hidden states of the forward pass and backward pass are concated as the document representation.
- TextCNN [7]: TextCNN applies Convolutional Neural Networks(CNN) on sentence classification tasks and we extended this method to extract the whole information of each document.
- TextGCN [26]: TextGCN is introduced for semi-supervised text classification tasks. Unlike other sequential models, TextGCN builds a graph on the whole corpus and applies Graph Convolutional Networks for the global information to classify documents.
- $BERT_{base}$ [6], $BERT_{uer}$ [28]: We used pre-trained models supplied by Huggingface. "bert-base-chinese" was selected as $BERT_{base}$ and "uer/roberta-base-word-chinese-cluecorpussmall" was for $BERT_{uer}$.

Following Sect. 3.3, each model worked as a feature extractor and the embeddings of anchor documents, positive documents and negative documents were used for Triplet loss calculation.

Table 2. Comparison of accuracy(%) of our model and other baseline models

Model	Trained on D1		Trained on D2		Trained on D3	
	Valid	Test	Valid	Test	Valid	Test
TextCNN	55.27	54.56	56.87	59.90	59.80	59.51
TextLSTM	54.33	54.95	55.07	57.03	58.00	59.51
TextGCN	57.07	58.01	59.93	61.00	61.53	61.33
BERT$_{base}$	57.47	57.75	59.87	58.98	62.13	59.90
BERT$_{uer}$	58.60	58.07	61.93	61.26	63.13	64.13
Our final	**61.73**	**62.63**	**64.47**	**65.17**	**64.93**	**67.25**

Hyperparameter Settings. For our model, BERT$_{uer}$ is chosen as the BERT backbone. We fine-tuned the BERT$_{uer}$ model using 1e-5 as the learning rate. There were 10 epochs in total and we recorded fine-tuned weights of BERT$_{uer}$ when the corresponding loss increased. We used two layers of TextGCN with a learning rate 2e-3 and a dropout rate 0. To introduce another way of information, Jieba was used for tokenization in TextGCN and words showing less than 5 times were removed. We used 768 as the hidden layer and output layer dimension to align it with BERT. When combining BERT$_{uer}$ and TextGCN, $\alpha = 0.7$ is used based on the training set performance. For other baselines, we did simple hyperparameter tuning based on the default hyperparameters to find the optimal model.

4.2 Performance Evaluation

Table 2 shows the comparison of the accuracy between our model and other baseline models. Models are evaluated on the same validation and test set but trained on different training sets according to Sect. 4.1. Our model achieves the best performance across all test settings. In detail, TextLSTM achieves the lowest accuracy, although LSTM can deal with long sequence input by introducing a gate mechanism, it is still not effective when dealing with CAIL since the sequence length of each document is too long. Similarly, TextCNN also achieves bad results because it focuses on learning local consecutive words' features while SCM requires learning on the whole documents and summarizing the document information. TextGCN can achieve relatively good results without using any external resources, we believe that using global corpus information helps learn the relationships between each document. Meanwhile, BERT$_{base}$ and BERT$_{uer}$ achieves better results than sequential models like TextCNN and TextLSTM. Two factors may contribute to the high accuracy: (1) The self-attention mechanism helps the model to extract the whole document's information (2) Pre-trained models preserve some knowledge through the pre-training phase. Between the pre-trained models, BERT$_{uer}$ achieves a better result since it uses Sentence Piece Tokenizer [9] instead of Word Piece Tokenizer [6] which tokenizes the document into Chinese words instead of Chinese characters. For example, "原告 (prosecutor)" will be "原 (original) 告 (tell)" if tokenized into characters. Our model achieves better results by using proper data augmentation for SCM, and combining document-level information and corpus-level information.

Table 3. The accuracy(%) of different datasets with different prompt template without fine-tuning.

Template	D1	D2	D3	Valid	Test
{TEXT}，指的是[MASK]。 {TEXT}, means that [MASK].	51.00	52.53	52.70	50.80	51.36
{TEXT}[SEP]指的是[MASK]。 {TEXT}, means that [MASK].	50.73	54.06	**54.00**	52.27	51.63
{TEXT}，这份判决书的意思是[MASK]。 {TEXT}, this legal document means that [MASK].	51.86	52.33	51.60	50.00	51.69
{TEXT}[SEP]这份判决书的意思是[MASK]。 {TEXT} [SEP] This legal document means that [MASK].	52.26	52.60	53.13	54.40	51.30
这份判决书：{TEXT}，总结是[MASK]。 This legal document {TEXT}, the conclusion is [MASK].	49.46	52.86	52.06	**54.60**	49.61
这份判决书：{TEXT}[SEP]总结是[MASK]。 This legal document {TEXT} [SEP] the conclusion is [MASK].	**52.67**	**54.07**	51.27	51.47	**52.41**

4.3 Effect of Data Augmentation

According to Sect. 3.1, to perform data augmentation, we firstly performed experiments on the training sets and selected the best prompt template based on the training set performance and used it in the data augmentation. In this experiment, we extended this prompt template testing to validation set and test set to show the influence of different human written prompt templates. Table 3 shows the accuracy of three training sets and validation/test sets when using the prompt template without fine-tuning. Two major conclusions can be drawn: (1) Because each document is quite long, comma("，"), the most common separation sign in natural language doesn't work well. Instead, using the special token of [SEP] helps the model extract the target information. (2) Since CAIL is a dataset of legal reports, prompt designed for legal domain works better, e.g. when prompt contains "判决书 (legal reports)", the performance increases. Based on the training set performance, we use "这份判决书： TEXT[SEP]总结是 [MASK]。 " ("This legal document TEXT [SEP] the conclusion is [MASK].") as our template for data augmentation.

Table 4 shows the effectiveness of data augmentation in our model. To show the influence of each different data augmentation technique, we excluded the joint part with TextGCN extractor during the experiments. According to the testing result, using three different data augmentation together achieves the highest performance since it takes advantage of all different techniques. Among three data augmentation mechanisms, truncation achieves relatively large improvement compared with other mechanisms, which makes the model try to extract the main information of a document by using the whole document instead of focusing on some specific part such as the result of the sentence at the end of the document. The prompt template also leads to good performance because it forces the model to learn the information on different tokens in BERT attention layers. Although dropout performs well in contrastive tasks like SimCSE, it shows the least improvement on BERT model in our experiment.

Table 4. The accuracy(%) of different data augmentation methods without TextGCN extractor

Data augmentation	Trained on D1		Trained on D2		Trained on D3	
	Valid	Test	Valid	Test	Valid	Test
N/A	58.60	58.07	62.00	61.26	63.13	64.13
with Truncation	60.67	60.81	63.53	63.67	64.13	66.41
with Dropout	58.80	58.40	62.80	62.63	63.67	64.45
with Prompt	58.67	60.09	62.73	63.02	63.67	65.04
with All	61.07	61.85	64.07	63.93	64.60	66.60

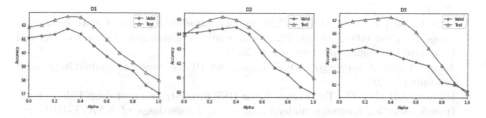

Fig. 2. The accuracy(%) of validation set and test set with different joint weight(α) when combining Dis_{BERT} and $Dis_{TextGCN}$

4.4 Effect of Global Information

Figure 2 shows the validation set and test set performance when using different joint weight(α) when combing Dis_{BERT} and $Dis_{TextGCN}$. $\alpha = 0$ means only using BERT result and $\alpha = 1$ means only using TextGCN result. By checking the experiment result, we can conclude that combining BERT and TextGCN is quite useful which achieves the best performance. Also, based on different models trained on D1, D2 and D3, the joint performance reaches the highest accuracy when α is around 0.3, indicating that the final performance mainly relies on the BERT extractor and TextGCN result helps to improve the BERT result. This conclusion also aligns with some previous works on combing BERT and TextGCN on text classification tasks where BERT contributes more to the good performance.

5 Conclusion and Future Work

In this study, we propose a pipeline model specific for low-resource similar case matching in the legal domain by introducing data augmentation techniques including truncation, prompt and dropout. Document-level information and corpus-level information are also combined in a simple yet effective way by using BERT extractor and TextGCN extractor. Our experiment result shows our proposed model achieves the best performance in three different training sets. However, with an extremely limited training set like a few shot problem, we would like to know whether generative language models like T5 [19] with soft prompt [11] can have better performance and we leave it to future work.

References

1. Brown, T., Mann, B., Ryder, N., Subbiah, M., Kaplan, J.D., Dhariwal, P., Neelakantan, A., Shyam, P., Sastry, G., Askell, A., et al.: Language models are few-shot learners. Adv. Neural. Inf. Process. Syst. **33**, 1877–1901 (2020)
2. Fang, H., Wang, S., Zhou, M., Ding, J., Xie, P.: CERT: contrastive self-supervised learning for language understanding. arXiv preprint arXiv:2005.12766 (2020)
3. Feng, S.Y., et al.: A survey of data augmentation approaches for NLP. In: Findings of the Association for Computational Linguistics: ACL-IJCNLP 2021, pp. 968–988 (2021)
4. Gao, T., Yao, X., Chen, D.: SimCSE: simple contrastive learning of sentence embeddings. In: Proceedings of the 2021 Conference on Empirical Methods in Natural Language Processing, pp. 6894–6910 (2021)
5. Jiang, T., et al.: PromptBERT: improving BERT sentence embeddings with prompts (2022)
6. Kenton, J.D.M.W.C., Toutanova, L.K.: BERT: pre-training of deep bidirectional transformers for language understanding. In: Proceedings of NAACL-HLT, pp. 4171–4186 (2019)
7. Kim, Y.: Convolutional neural networks for sentence classification. In: Proceedings of the 2014 Conference on Empirical Methods in Natural Language Processing, EMNLP 2014, pp. 1746–1751 (2014)
8. Kipf, T.N., Welling, M.: Semi-supervised classification with graph convolutional networks. In: 5th International Conference on Learning Representations, ICLR 2017, Toulon, France, April 2017, pp. 24–26. Conference Track Proceedings, OpenReview.net (2017)
9. Kudo, T., Richardson, J.: SentencePiece: a simple and language independent subword tokenizer and detokenizer for neural text processing. In: Proceedings of the 2018 Conference on Empirical Methods in Natural Language Processing: System Demonstrations, pp. 66–71 (2018)
10. Kumar, V., Choudhary, A., Cho, E.: Data augmentation using pre-trained transformer models. In: Proceedings of the 2nd Workshop on Life-long Learning for Spoken Language Systems, pp. 18–26 (2020)
11. Lester, B., Al-Rfou, R., Constant, N.: The power of scale for parameter-efficient prompt tuning. In: Proceedings of the 2021 Conference on Empirical Methods in Natural Language Processing, pp. 3045–3059 (2021)

12. Lewis, M., et al.: BART: denoising sequence-to-sequence pre-training for natural language generation, translation, and comprehension. In: Proceedings of the 58th Annual Meeting of the Association for Computational Linguistics, pp. 7871–7880 (2020)
13. Liang, X., et al.: R-Drop: regularized dropout for neural networks. arXiv preprint arXiv:2106.14448 (2021)
14. Lin, Y., et al.: BertGCN: transductive text classification by combining GNN and BERT. In: Findings of the Association for Computational Linguistics: ACL-IJCNLP 2021, pp. 1456–1462 (2021)
15. Liu, P., Qiu, X., Huang, X.: Recurrent neural network for text classification with multi-task learning. In: Kambhampati, S. (ed.) Proceedings of the Twenty-Fifth International Joint Conference on Artificial Intelligence, IJCAI 2016, New York, NY, USA, 9-15 July 2016, pp. 2873–2879. IJCAI/AAAI Press (2016)
16. Lu, Z., Du, P., Nie, J.-Y.: VGCN-BERT: augmenting BERT with graph embedding for text classification. In: Jose, J.M., et al. (eds.) Advances in Information Retrieval, ECIR 2020. LNCS, vol. 12035, pp. 369–382. Springer, Cham (2020). https://doi.org/10.1007/978-3-030-45439-5_25
17. Mei, X., Cai, X., Yang, L., Wang, N.: Graph transformer networks based text representation. Neurocomputing **463**, 91–100 (2021)
18. Petroni, F., et al.: Language models as knowledge bases? In: Proceedings of the 2019 Conference on Empirical Methods in Natural Language Processing and the 9th International Joint Conference on Natural Language Processing (EMNLP-IJCNLP), pp. 2463–2473 (2019)
19. Raffel, C., et al.: Exploring the limits of transfer learning with a unified text-to-text transformer. J. Mach. Learn. Res. **21**, 1–67 (2020)
20. Shin, T., Razeghi, Y., Logan IV, R.L., Wallace, E., Singh, S.: AutoPrompt: eliciting knowledge from language models with automatically generated prompts. In: Proceedings of the 2020 Conference on Empirical Methods in Natural Language Processing (EMNLP), pp. 4222–4235 (2020)
21. Wang, D., Ding, N., Li, P., Zheng, H.: CLINE: contrastive learning with semantic negative examples for natural language understanding. In: Proceedings of the 59th Annual Meeting of the Association for Computational Linguistics and the 11th International Joint Conference on Natural Language Processing (Volume 1: Long Papers), pp. 2332–2342 (2021)
22. Wang, Y., et al.: PromDA: prompt-based data augmentation for low-resource NLU tasks. arXiv preprint arXiv:2202.12499 (2022)
23. Wu, Z., Wang, S., Gu, J., Khabsa, M., Sun, F., Ma, H.: CLEAR: contrastive learning for sentence representation. arXiv preprint arXiv:2012.15466 (2020)
24. Xiao, C., Zhong, H., Guo, Z., Tu, C., Liu, Z., Sun, M., Zhang, T., Han, X., Hu, Z., Wang, H., et al.: CAIL2019-SCM: a dataset of similar case matching in legal domain. arXiv preprint arXiv:1911.08962 (2019)
25. Yang, T., Hu, L., Shi, C., Ji, H., Li, X., Nie, L.: HGAT: heterogeneous graph attention networks for semi-supervised short text classification. ACM Trans. Inf. Syst. **39**(3), 1–29 (2021). https://doi.org/10.1145/3450352
26. Yao, L., Mao, C., Luo, Y.: Graph convolutional networks for text classification. In: Proceedings of the AAAI Conference on Artificial Intelligence, vol. 33, pp. 7370–7377 (2019)

27. Zhang, C., Li, Q., Song, D.: Aspect-based sentiment classification with aspect-specific graph convolutional networks. In: Proceedings of the 2019 Conference on Empirical Methods in Natural Language Processing and the 9th International Joint Conference on Natural Language Processing (EMNLP-IJCNLP), pp. 4568–4578 (2019)
28. Zhao, Z., et al.: UER: an open-source toolkit for pre-training models. In: EMNLP-IJCNLP 2019, p. 241 (2019)

Message Passing Neural Networks for Hypergraphs

Sajjad Heydari[✉][iD] and Lorenzo Livi[iD]

Computer Science, Univeristy of Manitoba, Winnipeg, Canada
heydaris@myumanitoba.ca

Abstract. Hypergraph representations are both more efficient and better suited to describe data characterized by relations between two or more objects. In this work, we present a new graph neural network based on message passing capable of processing hypergraph-structured data. We show that the proposed model defines a design space for neural network models for hypergraphs, thus generalizing existing models for hypergraphs. We report experiments on a benchmark dataset for node classification, highlighting the effectiveness of the proposed model with respect to other state-of-the-art methods for graphs and hypergraphs. We also discuss the benefits of using hypergraph representations and, at the same time, highlight the limitation of using equivalent graph representations when the underlying problem has relations among more than two objects.

Keywords: Graph neural network · Hypergraph · Message passing

1 Introduction

Graphs perfectly capture structured data, not only representing data points, but also relations amongst them. Recently, Graph Neural Networks have been employed as a tool to directly process graph data with huge success in various tasks, such as node classification in citation network labeling [1,8,11], link predictions in recommender networks [18], and state prediction in traffic prediction or weather forecasting via sensory networks [4,12,16,17].

Graph Neural Networks have provided a significant reduction in numbers of trainable parameters in a machine learning model with input that could be represented as graphs, much like Convolutional Neural Networks have done for tensors. This reduction in parameters allows complex problems to be addressed with much smaller datasets. However there still remains a set of problems that could benefit from a change in representation, namely the hypergraph representation.

Hypergraphs constitute a natural generalization of graphs, where relations are not restricted to represent the interaction of two objects: hypergraphs can

---

Supported by The Canada Research Chairs program.

E. Pimenidis et al. (Eds.): ICANN 2022, LNCS 13530, pp. 583–592, 2022.
https://doi.org/10.1007/978-3-031-15931-2_48

encode higher-order relations, i.e. relations between two or more objects. Formally, a hypergraph $H = (V, \mathcal{E})$ is composed by a set of vertices, V, and a set of hyperedges, $\mathcal{E} \subset \mathcal{P}(V)$, where $\mathcal{P}(V)$ is the power set of V. Accordingly we may refer to the vertices composing a hyperedge as $v \in e, e \in \mathcal{E}$. In a citation network, for example, there are pair-wise relations between cited work and citing work. However, there are also bigger relations among multiple works that have been cited together in a single publication, which require hyperedges to be properly modeled.

Higher-order relations could still be encoded in a graph by performing suitable transformations (e.g. using line graphs). However, we find that none of the currently used encodings are as effective as directly processing hypergraphs. We note that well-established graph neural networks [6] fail to apply to hypergraphs due to their more complex structure. Therefore, newer methods for processing hypergraphs with neural networks have been introduced in the literature [5].

Here we introduce the Hypergraph Message Passing Neural Network (HMPNN), a Message Passing Neural Network model [6] that can process hypergraph-structured data of variable size. The main contributions of this paper can be summarized as follows:

– We develop a new message passing neural network model for hypergraph-structured data;
– We show that hypergraph convolution methods from the literature can be seen as a special case of HMPNN;
– We show that the proposed model significantly outperforms other existing methods from the literature on a common node classification benchmark.

The reminder of this paper is structured as follows. Section 2 contextualizes the paper. In Sect. 3, we show that common approaches for transforming a hypergraph into a graph inevitably lead to loss of structural information, hence preventing the correct functioning of any machine learning method operating on them. Section 4 presents the main contribution of this paper, namely a novel hypergraph neural network model. In Sect. 5 we show experimental results on a common hypergraph benchmark used in the literature. Finally, Sect. 6 concludes the paper.

2   Related Work

Gilmer et al. [6] reformulated existing graph neural networks in a framework called Message Passing Neural Networks. There are two phases in MPNN, the message passing and readout, which corresponds to convolutions and pooling operations, respectively. The convolutional layer consists of updating the hidden state of node V at layer t (h_v^t), based on the previous state of v and their neighbors. The model reads:

$$m_v^{t+1} = \sum_{w \in N(v)} M_t(h_v^t, h_w^t, e_{vw})$$
$$h_v^{t+1} = U_t(h_v^t, m_v^{t+1}) \tag{1}$$

The function M prepares messages from each node to each of its neighbours, which are then aggregated together to form the incoming message for each node. M can utilize the sender's features, the receiver features, or the weight of the edge between them. The incoming message is then processed with function U along with the internal feature, to form the next feature of each node.

2.1   Graph Design Space

You et al. [15] introduced a design space for graph neural networks. Their contributions involves a similarity metric and an evaluation method for GNNs. Their design space consists of three parts: intra-layer, inter-layer, and training configuration.

The intra-layer is responsible for creation of various GNN convolutions, while also considering dropout and batch normalization. It is described as follows:

$$h_v^{(k+1)} = AGG(ACT(DROPOUT(BN(W^{(k)}h_u^{(k)} + b^{(k)})))), u \in \mathcal{N}(v))$$

The inter-layer is responsible for the interconnection of the various layers. These includes choices for *layer connectivity, pre-process layers, mp-layers* and *post-process layers*; with layer connectivity having options such as *stack, skip-sum* and *skip-cat*.

Finally, training configuration includes choices for batch size, learning rate, optimizer and number of epochs.

2.2   Hypergraph Neural Networks and Hypergraph Representation

The literature on graph neural networks for hypergraph-structured data is sparse. Jiang et al. [7] introduce dynamic hypergraph neural networks, a neural network that both updates the structure of the underlying hypergraph as well as performing a two phase convolution, a vertex convolution and a hyperedge convolution. Feng et al. [5] introduce hypergraph neural networks, a spectral convolution operation on hypergraphs, that considers weights of the hyperedges as well as the incident matrix. Yi and Park [14] introduce a method to perform hypergraph convolutions with recurrent neural networks. Chien et al. [3] introduce an extension to message passing operation for hypergraphs based on composition of two multiset functions.

3   Graph Expansions and Loss of Structural Information

Here, we consider the process of mapping hypergraph representations into graph representations. There are various ways of encoding hyperedges involving three or more vertices in graphs. We consider some popular approaches and show that they all have drawbacks that lead to loss of relevant structural information, thus highlighting the importance of processing hypergraph-structured data.

Clique expansion is an approach in which each hyperedge of size k is substituted with $k * (k-1)$ edges amongst pairs of its members [10]. This approach cannot distinguish between pairwise relations amongst k vertices and a hyperedge of size k, as shown in Fig. 1. In fact, they are both mapped to the same structure, and therefore lose structural information.

Fig. 1. A hyperedge of size 3 (left) and a clique with 3 vertices (right).

Star expansion is another approach of encoding a hypergraph in a simple graph, in which the hyperedge h is replaced with a new vertex v_h, and edges between h_v and original vertices of h are added [19]. An example could be seen in Fig. 2. The resulting graph is bipartite, with one partition representing the original hyperedges and the other partition representing the original vertices. This conversion is not one to one because without further encoded information it is not possible to figure out which partition is representing the hyperedges. Another downside is that due to change in neighborhoods, in order to pass messages from previously neighbouring vertices, we now have to pass messages twice to reach the same destination.

Fig. 2. A hyperedge of size 3 (left) and its star expansion (right).

Line conversions (also known as edge conversion and edge expansion) creates a simple graph, and for any hyperedge h creates a vertex v_h in it. Two vertices v_h and v_h' are connected if and only if the intersection between h and h' is not empty [9]. An example is shown in Fig. 3. Plain line conversions are not a one to one mappings, and hence we loose various kind of information, from data stored on the vertices, to size of the higher order relations, neighbourhoods and many other types of structural information.

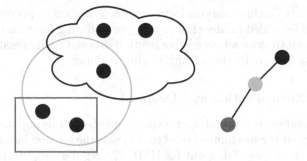

Fig. 3. A hypergraph (left) and its line conversion (right).

4 The Proposed Hypergraph Message Passing Neural Networks

The computation in the proposed Hypergraph Message Passing Neural Network (HMPNN) consists of two main phases: (1) sending messages from vertices to hyperedges and (2) sending messages from hyperedges to vertices. The operations performed by the proposed HMPNN model can be formalized as follows:

$$M_v = f_v(X_v^{(t)}) \tag{2}$$

$$W_e^{(t+1)} = g_w(W_e^{(t)}, \Box_{v \in e} M_v) \tag{3}$$

$$M_e = f_w(W_e^{(t)}, \Box'_{v \in e} M_v) \tag{4}$$

$$X_v^{(t+1)} = g_v(X_v^{(t)}, \diamond_{e, v \in e} M_e) \tag{5}$$

$X_v^{(t)}$ is the representation of vertex v at layer t, $W_e^{(t)}$ is the representation of hyperedge e at layer t, f_v and f_w are vertex and hyperedge messaging functions, respectively, g_v and g_w are vertex and hyperedge updating functions, respectively, and finally $\Box$, $\Box'$, and $\diamond$ are aggregating functions.

The choice for messaging and updating functions includes identity function, linear and non-linear functions, or MLP. The choice for aggregation functions includes mean aggregation, sum aggregation and concatenation.

We can therefore define an instance of hypergraph message passing operation by specifying what follows:

- Choice of messaging functions over vertices f_v and hyperedges f_w
- Choice of updating function over vertices g_v and hyperedges g_w
- Choice of aggregation operation over incoming messages to hyperedges $\Box$
- Choice of aggregation operation over outgoing messages to vertices $\Box'$
- Choice of aggregation operation over incoming messages to vertices $\diamond$

These choices allow us to describe a wide range of hypergraph convolutions, which can be used as an intra-layer design space for hypergraphs, in a similar fashion to You et al. [15] for graphs.

It is possible to include various forms of regularization to prevent overfitting. Dropout could be added to any of messaging or updating functions f and g. It is also possible to introduce adjacency connection dropout to aggregation functions $\square\square'\diamond$, allowing for a reduction of bias during training.

4.1   Batch Normalization and Dropout

Batch normalization is a useful operation to speed-up training and reduce bias. Similarly, dropout is a mechanism used to decrease the learned bias of the system. We introduce two types of dropout for HMPNN: regular dropout and adjacency dropout. During regular dropout, random cells in the feature vector of nodes or hyperedges are set to zero; the other cells are scaled by $\frac{n+k}{n}$, where n is the total number of cells in that vector and k is the number of cells that were zeroed. Adjacency dropout randomly removes hyperedges in a convolution step.

Adjacency dropout must be applied in neighborhood creation steps of Eq. 3 through 5. Regular dropout can follow a batch normalization right before updating functions in Eqs. 3 and 5, as part of the corresponding g functions.

4.2   Equivalency Between Hypergraph Convolutions and HMPNN

Following the spirit of the graph design space mentioned in Sect. 2.1, here we show that, by including appropriate search parameters, HMPNN can mimic the behaviour of existing hypergraph neural network convolutions, which are thus special cases of HMPNN.

In order to compare different models based on hypergraph convolutions, we need to define a notion of equivalency among models. We define two models m_1, m_2 to be equivalent if and only if for any weights w_1 there exists w_2 such that for any input hypergraph x the model outputs correspond, i.e. $m_1(w_1, x) = m_2(w_2, x)$; in other words we can translate the weights of one network to the other one.

Dynamic hypergraph neural network's convolution (DHNN) [7] operates according to algorithm 1 1. In other words, for each hyperedge containing u, they sample all members of u and capture their feature set (1st outgoing message), stacking them in X_u (hyperedge aggregation), processing them via the vertex convolution (hyperedge updating), aggregating all such hyperedge messages via stacking (incoming messages to vertices), performing edge convolution on the stacked aggregation and applying the activation function on it (vertex update function).

These steps can be directly described in terms of message passing, with specific functions for each phase of message passing operation. HMPNN can thus directly emulate this model.

Hypergraph neural networks (HNN) [5] convolution performs the following operations:

$$X^{(l+1)} = \sigma(D_v^{-1/2} H W D_e^{-1} H^T D_v^{-1/2} X^{(l)} \Theta^{(l)}) \tag{6}$$

Algorithm 1. Dynamic Hypergraph Neural Network Convolution

input: Sample x_u, hypergraph structure $\mathcal{G}$
output: Sample y_u
xlist = Φ
for e do in Adj(u) do
    X_u = VertexSample($X, \mathcal{G}$)
    X_e = 1-dconv($MLP(X_v), MLP(X_v)$) or VertexConvolution(X_v)
    xlist.insert(X_e)
end for
X_e = stack(xlist)
$X_u = \sum_{i=0}^{|Adj(u)|}$ softmax$(x_e W + b)^i x_e^i$ or edgeConv(X_e)
$y_u = \sigma(x_u W + b)$

---

where $X^{(l)}$ describes the node feature on layer l, D_v and D_e describe the diagonal matrices of node and edge degrees, respectively, W is the weights of each hyperedge, H is the incidence matrix, Θ are the learnable parameters of the layer and finally σ is the non-linear activation function. Note that this convolution assumes that hyperedge features are numbers (weights).

Given any Θ, we construct the following equivalent HMPNN where the outgoing node message is node features multiplied by inverse square root of their degree, i.e. $D_v^{-1/2} X^{(l)}$; the hyperedge aggregation is the average, i.e. $D_e^{-1} H^T$; there is no hyperedge updating; the hyperedge outgoing message is multiplied by their weight (or feature); the node aggregation function is sum of input multiplied by the inverse square root of their degree, i.e. $D_v^{-1/2} H$; and finally the node updating function is $\sigma(X\Theta^{(l)})$.

Multiset learning for hypergraphs (AllSet) [3] construct their message passing according to the following equations:

$$f_{\mathcal{V}\to\mathcal{E}}(S) = f_{\mathcal{E}\to\mathcal{V}}(S) = LN(Y + MLP(Y)), \tag{7}$$

$$Y = LN(\theta + MH_{h,\omega}(\theta, S, S)), MH_{h,\omega}(\theta, S, S) = ||_i = 1^h O^{(i)}, \tag{8}$$

$$O^{(i)} = \omega(\theta^{(i)}(K^{(i)})^T)V^{(i)}, K^{(i)} = MLP^{(K,i)}(S), V^{(i)} = MLP^{(V,i)}(S). \tag{9}$$

LN is the normalization layer, $||$ is concatenation and θ are the learnable weights, $MH_{h,w}$ denotes an h-multihead with activation function ω. It is clear that the AllSet is a special case of the proposed HMPNN with the above mentioned functions used as the updating mechanism and the identity function used for messaging. Moreover, we note that there is a direct translation of weights from a trained AllSet model to the equivalent HMPNN.

5 Experiments

In this section, we look at the semi-supervised task of node classification in citation networks, which offer a suitable playground to benchmark graph and hypergraph representations and related processing methods.

5.1   Experiment Setup

Dataset. To provide direct comparison with state-of-the-art methods [2,5,7, 8,11], we use the Cora dataset [13] which includes 2708 academic papers and 5429 citation relations amongst them. Each publication contains a bag of word feature vector, where a binary value indicates presence or absence of that word in the publication. Finally, each publication belongs to one of the 7 categories.

For train-test split, we follow the protocol described in [2,13]. We randomly select: 20 items from each category, totaling 140 for training; 70 items from each category, totaling 490 for validation; the remaining items are used for testing.

Hypergraph Construction. Citation networks are often represented as simple graphs with publications that cite each other connected via simple edges. This representation fails to appreciate documents that are cited together, and only captures them in terms of a second neighborhood. Bai et al. [2] provide an alternate representation in which documents are simultaneously treated as vertices and hyperedges at the same time, with hyperedges of a publication grouping all of its related work together. Each vertex is then characterized by a boolean matrix of their representative words acting as its feature set.

Implementation Details. Our model uses two layers of HMPNN with sigmoid activation and a hidden representation of size 2. We use sum as the message aggregation functions, with adjacency matrix dropout with rate 0.7, as well as dropout with rate 0.5 for vertex and hyperedge representation.

5.2   Results and Analysis

Table 1 shows a comparison with respect to different models taken from the state-of-the-art. As shown in the table, the proposed method (HMPNN) significantly outperforms all other methods.

Table 1. Classification accuracy on Cora dataset.

Method	Accuracy
GCN [8]	81.5
HGNN [5]	81.60
GAT [11]	82.43
DHGNN [7]	82.50
HGC+Atten [2]	82.61
HMPNN	**92.16**

Analysis of Adjacency Dropout. In order to verify the benefits of adjacency dropout, we perform a test with various different values of adjacency dropout rate used during training and report the obtained accuracy on test set. The results are shown in Table 2. Results show that, regardless of the use of activation dropout, the accuracy increases when we introduce adjacency dropout. We conclude that adjacency dropout is a useful mechanism to decrease the bias of the proposed neural network model.

Table 2. Accuracy test for various values of adjacency dropout. Test 1 had 0.5 activation dropout whereas test 2 did not have any activation dropout.

Adjacency dropout rate	Accuracy test 1	Accuracy test 2
90%	79.35%	65.51%
70%	92.16%	89.90%
50%	91.14%	83.26%
30%	89.94%	76.18%
0%	81.76%	54.11%

6   Conclusion and Future Work

We investigate the use of hypergraph representations in machine learning and showed their superiority over graph representations with respect to capturing structural information for data characterized by n-ary relations (i.e. relations involving two or more vertices). Moreover, we introduced the Hypergraph Message Passing Neural Network as a novel neural network layer to process hypergraph-structured data. We showed that HMPNN can emulate existing convolution methods for hypergraphs, and therefore could be used to search over the space of architectures for hypergraph-structured data. Finally, we investigated using HMPNN on the task of node classification over the Cora citation network, in which we employed the adjacency dropout as well as activation dropout as mechanisms of controlling the bias. Our model outperformed various state-of-the-art methods for this task.

References

1. Atwood, J., Towsley, D.: Diffusion-convolutional neural networks. In: Advances in Neural Information Processing Systems, pp. 1993–2001 (2016)
2. Bai, S., Zhang, F., Torr, P.H.: Hypergraph convolution and hypergraph attention. Pattern Recogn. **110**, 107637 (2021)
3. Chien, E., Pan, C., Peng, J., Milenkovic, O.: You are AllSet: a multiset function framework for hypergraph neural networks. arXiv preprint arXiv:2106.13264 (2021)

4. Cui, Z., Henrickson, K., Ke, R., Wang, Y.: Traffic graph convolutional recurrent neural network: a deep learning framework for network-scale traffic learning and forecasting. IEEE Trans. Intell. Transp. Syst. **21**(11), 4883–4894 (2019)
5. Feng, Y., You, H., Zhang, Z., Ji, R., Gao, Y.: Hypergraph neural networks. In: Proceedings of the AAAI Conference on Artificial Intelligence, vol. 33, pp. 3558–3565 (2019)
6. Gilmer, J., Schoenholz, S.S., Riley, P.F., Vinyals, O., Dahl, G.E.: Neural message passing for quantum chemistry. In: International Conference on Machine Learning, PMLR, pp. 1263–1272 (2017)
7. Jiang, J., Wei, Y., Feng, Y., Cao, J., Gao, Y.: Dynamic hypergraph neural networks. In: International Joint Conference on Artificial Intelligence, pp. 2635–2641 (2019)
8. Kipf, T.N., Welling, M.: Semi-supervised classification with graph convolutional networks. In: International Conference on Learning Representations, Toulon, France (2017)
9. Pu, L., Faltings, B.: Hypergraph learning with hyperedge expansion. In: Flach, P.A., De Bie, T., Cristianini, N. (eds.) Machine Learning and Knowledge Discovery in Databases, ECML PKDD 2012. LNCS (LNAI), vol. 7523, pp. 410–425. Springer, Heidelberg (2012). https://doi.org/10.1007/978-3-642-33460-3_32
10. Sun, L., Ji, S., Ye, J.: Hypergraph spectral learning for multi-label classification. In: Proceedings of the 14th ACM SIGKDD International Conference on Knowledge Discovery and Data Mining, pp. 668–676 (2008)
11. Veličković, P., Cucurull, G., Casanova, A., Romero, A., Lio, P., Bengio, Y.: Graph attention networks. arXiv preprint arXiv:1710.10903 (2017)
12. Yan, S., Xiong, Y., Lin, D.: Spatial temporal graph convolutional networks for skeleton-based action recognition. In: Thirty-Second AAAI conference on Artificial Intelligence (2018)
13. Yang, Z., Cohen, W., Salakhudinov, R.: Revisiting semi-supervised learning with graph embeddings. In: International Conference on Machine Learning, PMLR, pp. 40–48 (2016)
14. Yi, J., Park, J.: Hypergraph convolutional recurrent neural network. In: Proceedings of the 26th ACM SIGKDD International Conference on Knowledge Discovery & Data Mining, pp. 3366–3376 (2020)
15. You, J., Ying, Z., Leskovec, J.: Design space for graph neural networks. Adv. Neural. Inf. Process. Syst. **33**, 17009–17021 (2020)
16. Yu, B., Yin, H., Zhu, Z.: Spatio-temporal graph convolutional networks: a deep learning framework for traffic forecasting. arXiv preprint arXiv:1709.04875 (2017)
17. Zhang, J., Shi, X., Xie, J., Ma, H., King, I., Yeung, D.Y.: GaAN: gated attention networks for learning on large and spatiotemporal graphs. arXiv preprint arXiv:1803.07294 (2018)
18. Zhang, M., Chen, Y.: Link prediction based on graph neural networks. Adv. Neural Inf. Process. Syst. **31** (2018)
19. Zien, J.Y., Schlag, M.D., Chan, P.K.: Multilevel spectral hypergraph partitioning with arbitrary vertex sizes. IEEE Trans. Comput. Aided Des. Integr. Circuits Syst. **18**(9), 1389–1399 (1999)

Multiscale Spatial and Temporal Learning for Human Motion Prediction

Pengxiang Su, Xuanjing Shen, and Haipeng Chen[✉]

College of Computer Science and Technology, Jilin University, Changchun, China
chenhp@jlu.edu.cn

Abstract. Human motion prediction is a classic computer vision task that has numerous applications in the field of autonomous driving, human-computer interaction and motion synthesis. Recently, a large number of motion prediction methods employ graph convolutional networks to encode the spatial relationships among joints within a pose, which ignore the impact of adjacent poses in the encoding process, resulting in unsatisfactory extraction of spatial information. Moreover, the recurrent neural network is difficult to capture long-term temporal dependencies. To solve these challenges, we design a prediction model that consists of two crucial components. Firstly, A novel spatio-temporal graph convolution module utilizes multi-graph convolution layers to capture the spatial correlation information of the current frame and adjacent frames simultaneously. Secondly, a multiscale temporal encoding module consists of a series of temporal convolutions with different dilation rates to establish various temporal relationships between poses at both short-term and long-term temporal distance. We evaluate the proposed method on the largest 3D human motion capture dataset (*i.e.*, Human 3.6 Million). Extensive experimental results show that our model achieves state-of-the-art performance in both short and long-term predictions compared with existing methods.

Keywords: Human motion prediction · Spatio-temporal graph convolution network · Multiscale temporal context encoding

1 Introduction

Human motion prediction is a typical task in the field of computer vision, which predicts future action sequences by detecting the input human action sequence. With the fast development of robotics technology, it is becoming common that robots and human work collaboratively. Human-robot collaboration allows a clever combination of the advantages of fast robots and the adaptability of humans. Furthermore, a great number of researchers aim to utilize the transfer relationships between actions to predict subsequent actions by analyzing discrete actions of humans and robots executing tasks, including the prediction of handshake actions and the assisting human-robot interaction.

© The Author(s), under exclusive license to Springer Nature Switzerland AG 2022
E. Pimenidis et al. (Eds.): ICANN 2022, LNCS 13530, pp. 593–604, 2022.
https://doi.org/10.1007/978-3-031-15931-2_49

Conventional human action prediction algorithms, such as hidden Markov models (HMM) [11], Gaussian process dynamical models (GPDM) [22], and Bilinear spatiotemporal basis models [1], require a large number of parameters to be set manually and are difficult to encode complex movements.

With the advent of large motion capture datasets, more and more deep learning models have been devised and have shown excellent performance. Recently, graph convolutional networks (GCN) have received extensive attention due to their powerful spatial joint modeling capabilities and achieved superior performances, including LTD [17], LDR [7], DM-GNN [13], MT-GCN [5], MPT [15], LMC-GCN [23], and DA-GCN [14]. Unfortunately, these models only focus on modeling the spatial relationships within each pose, which ignoring the temporal dependencies that exist in human motion sequences. Therefore, we design a novel spatio-temporal graph convolution module to capture spatial dependent contexts from mulitiple adjacent poses.

Furthermore, human motion prediction models widely employ recurrent neural networks (RNN) to encode temporal context information, such as ERD [8], Res-GRU [18], and MPT [15]. However, these traditional recurrent units access motion information sequentially, frame by frame, to update the hidden state. Many crucial historical motion dynamics tend to be overwhelmed by the recent input, so it is difficult for the models to capture long-term temporal dependencies. To tackle this challenge, we propose a multiscale temporal encoding module to fuse motion dynamics from related frames at different temporal distances, including both short-term and long-term.

Following the success of existing works [9,15,19], we use inter-frame displacements of joints instead of traditional 3D coordinates to describe human motion. This method can significantly reduce the dimensionality of the motion sequence and improve the continuity between the predicted poses.

The main contributions of this paper are as follows:

(1) A novel spatio-temporal graph convolution module is designed to extract the spatial relationship of the current frame while also considering the position information of the two adjacent frames.
(2) A multiscale temporal encoding module is proposed to aggregate information from different temporal distance frames through a series of temporal convolutions with various dilation rates.
(3) Extensive experiments show that our method achieves state-of-the-art performance on both short and long term predictions.

2   Related Work

2.1   Human Motion Prediction

The input of the motion prediction task is a sequence of observed 3D poses, which outputs a sequence of predicted future poses. Human motion prediction is mainly divided into traditional methods and deep learning-based methods. Traditional methods mainly use shallow models to deal with the task of human motion prediction. RBM [21] tackled the human action prediction issue using a Conditional Restricted Boltzmann Machine (CRBM) model, which retains its most significant computational properties. HMM [11] offered simple Markov methods for modeling, using non-linear and non-parametric interactions to preserve an extremely expressive dynamic model. In [22], a Gaussian process dynamical model (GPDM) for nonlinear time series analysis is proposed, which includes a low-dimensional latent space with correlated dynamics and a mapping from the latent space to the observation space. Additionally, convolutional neural networks are naturally applied to human motion prediction due to their strong feature extraction ability. For instance, Res-GRU [18] employed a deep recurrent neural network to model human motion, which simulated both short-term motion prediction and long-term motion prediction. LDR [7] proposed a model based on graph networks and adversarial learning, which generated skeleton poses as a new dynamic graph where the natural connections of joint pairs are exploited explicitly, and the links of geometrically separated joints can also be learned implicitly. Moreover, ConSeq2Seq [12] applied an encoder-decoder model to human motion prediction, in which the encoder designs the entire motion sequence as a long-term hidden variable, while the decoder turns shorter sequences into short-term hidden variables. HMR [16] utilized the Li algebra to model their skeleton to explicitly encode anatomical constraints and a hierarchical recurrent network structure to encode both the local and global contextual information. MPT [15] proposed a semi-constrained graph to generate encoded skeletal connections and prior knowledge while learning implicit dependencies between joints adaptively.

2.2 GCN Based Spatial Relationship Modeling

Since each vertex in a topological map may have a different number of neighboring vertices, it is not possible to perform convolution operations with a convolution kernel of the same size. Therefore, CNN cannot handle data with non-Euclidean structure and cannot maintain translation invariance. GCN can effectively extract spatial features on such topological graphs for machine learning, so it has become the focus of research. LTD [17] designed a feed-forward deep network for motion prediction by exploiting the temporal smoothness and spatial dependencies between human joints, which encode temporal information by working in trajectory space instead of pose space. DM-GNN [13] used a multiscale graph to model the internal relationships, which can predict 3D skeleton-based human motions. The graph was trained to be adaptive and the motion features were learned dynamically between network layers. In addition, a multiscale graph computation unit (MGCU) was used to extract features at each scale [13]. MT-GCN [5] proposed a multi-task graph convolutional network to predict future 3D human actions and repair missing values of incomplete observations. These two tasks were fused together to achieve a shared spatio-temporal representation, which improves the performance of the network.

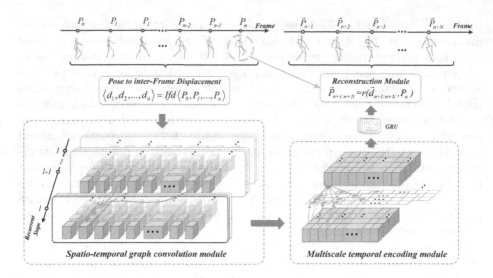

Fig. 1. Overall structure of our proposed method, which consists of a novel spatio-temporal graph convolution module, multiscale temporal encoding module, a GRU layer, a human motion encoding module, and a reconstruction module.

3   Our Approach

In the human prediction problem, a human is represented by a series of 3D coordinates of joints. A motion sequence contains a large number of successive poses. We input a historical pose sequence $\langle P_0, P_1, ..., P_n \rangle$ to the model which captures the hidden temporal relationships to generate a future motion sequence $\langle P_{n+1}, P_{n+2}, ..., P_{n+N} \rangle$. $P_n \in \mathbb{R}^{3 \times J}$ denotes a pose at n frame and J is the number of joints.

Our proposed method consists of three key steps. Firstly, the motion dynamic context of each joint is explicitly encoded as an inter-frame displacement sequence. Then, these features are fed into a novel spatio-temporal graph convolution module which can capture the adequately spatial dependent information from the current frame and two adjacent frames. Finally, a multiscale temporal information encoding module is employed to aggregate motion context information at different temporal distances.

3.1   Human Motion Encoding Module

Recent works [9,16,17,19] have demonstrated that it is challenging to capture the hidden temporal evolution from a sequence of 3D coordinates. Following existing methods [9,15,19], we utilize inter-frame displacement in trajectory space instead of traditional pose space to encode motion information. Focusing research on each joint rather than the entire pose reduces the dimensionality of motion information and improves continuity between future poses. On the other hand, the aim of motion prediction shifts from forecasting future position coordinates to predicting the dynamic evolution of joint position changes, which can significantly improve the discontinuity between predicted poses. Therefore, we select the inter-frame displacement as input to the model.

Formally, given a sequence of observed poses, a series of inter-frame displacement vectors are calculated by:

$$\langle d_1, d_2, ..., d_n \rangle = Ifd \langle P_0, P_1, ..., P_n \rangle \tag{1}$$

where $Ifd\langle \cdot \rangle$ is the transform function, $d_n \in \mathbb{R}^{3 \times J}$ denotes the inter-frame displacement vector of P_n with respect to P_{n-1}. In this way, the position change of each joint from the previous frame to the current frame can be explicitly encoded.

3.2 Spatio-Temporal Graph Convolution Module

The 3D human skeleton in these datasets is a series of individual 3D coordinate nodes recorded by the motion capture system. However, human motion is a synergistic movement involving multiple joints, and ignoring the spatial dependencies between joints would leave out some crucial cues. Recently, GCN-based methods have been widely used to solve motion prediction problems due to their capability to encode non-Euclidean structured data. For example, LTD [17] designed a trainable graph to flexibly capture the relationships between joints, LDR [7] trained two learnable graphs in two stages to encode the joint dependencies, and MPT [15] considers physical connections and prior semantic information in modeling the relationship graph. Unfortunately, these models ignore the fact that there are significant temporal connections hiddened in the pose sequence. It is unreasonable to ignore information in adjacent poses when capturing spatial-related features.

Specifically, the process of traditional graph convolutional network is defined as:

$$P_{n-1}^l = \varsigma \left(A, P_{n-1}^{l-1} \right) \tag{2}$$

where $A \in \mathbb{R}^{J \times J}$ represents the spatial relationship between joints in P_{n-1}. P_{n-1}^{l-1} and P_{n-1}^l are the input and output of the $(n-1)^{th}$ pose in the lth layer of the graph convolution network, respectively. From Eq. 2, we can observe that the model fuses information from merely one pose.

To solve this problem, we propose a novel spatio-temporal graph convolution module to capture the spatial related information from the current frame and adjacent frames. Specifically, we expand the conventional spatial relationship graph into three layers, which enlarges the receptive field in the temporal dimension.

Firstly, we construct a multi-order adjacency matrix:

$$\bar{A} = \left\{ \begin{array}{cccc} W_{1,1} & W_{1,2} & \cdots & W_{1,J} \\ W_{2,1} & W_{2,2} & \cdots & W_{2,1} \\ \vdots & \vdots & \ddots & \vdots \\ W_{J,1} & W_{J,2} & \cdots & W_{J,J} \end{array} \right\}_{\times 3} \tag{3}$$

where $\bar{A} \in \mathbb{R}^{3 \times (J \times J)}$, $W_{1,J} \in \mathbb{R}$ denotes the spatial dependence weight between joint 1 and joint J. Then, we use the multi-order adjacency matrix to capture spatial correlated information:

$$\bar{d}_{n-1}^l = \varsigma\left(\bar{A}, (d_{n-2}^{l-1}, d_{n-1}^{l-1}, d_n^{l-1})\right) \tag{4}$$

However, $\bar{d}_{n-1}^l \in \mathbb{R}^{3 \times (J \times 3)}$, we need to aggregate them together via a 2D convolutional network with a convolutional kernel of 1×3.

Finally, the process of our proposed spatio-temporal graph convolution module is denoted as:

$$\hat{d}_{n-1}^l = Conv2d(\varsigma\left(\bar{A}, (d_{n-2}^{l-1}, d_{n-1}^{l-1}, d_n^{l-1})\right)) \tag{5}$$

where $\hat{d}_{n-1}^l \in \mathbb{R}^{J \times 3}$ represents the final output that fuses the spatial dependent information contained in the three pose of d_{n-2}^{l-1}, d_{n-1}^{l-1}, and d_n^{l-1}. However, it is important to note that this graph convolution module fuses the first and last frames of the input sequence after each iteration, so the number of iterations needs to be set appropriately.

3.3   Multiscale Temporal Encoding Module

Recently, RNN has been widely adopted to capture temporal relationships, but it needs to be read data frame by frame and update its hidden state. As a result, it is challenging to capture long-term and encode multiple temporal dependencies. However, multiple temporal evolution patterns are hidden in the human motion sequences. Modeling adequate temporal context features can help the model improve prediction accuracy.

To tackle this problem, we propose a novel multiscale temporal encoding module to capture temporal information between different temporal distances. Then, these extracted features are resized by a series of designed linear mapping modules. Finally, these information are fuse together. The process can be expressed as:

$$\left\langle \tilde{d}_2, \tilde{d}_3, ..., \tilde{d}_{n-2} \right\rangle = \sum_0^T Lin_t(MTE_t(\left\langle \hat{d}_2, \hat{d}_3, ..., \hat{d}_{n-2} \right\rangle)) \tag{6}$$

where $\tilde{d}_{n-2} \in \mathbb{R}^{J \times 3}$ is the inter-frame displacement that fuses multiple time-dependent information. T is the number of sub-modules. $Lin_t(\cdot)$ and $MTE_t(\cdot)$ denote the linear mapping module and the temporal encoding module contained in the tth sub-module, respectively.

3.4   Loss Function

The existing models [8, 18] employ a simple L2 loss function to train the model. Since the position of the joints in the kinematic chain and the movement range is remarkably different, it is unreasonable to treat each joint equally. We use a weighted inter-frame displacement loss to train the model that allows it to these joints with a large range of motion. The loss function is defined as:

$$\ell = \sum\nolimits_{j=1}^{J} b^j \left\| \boldsymbol{d}_{n+N}^j - d_{n+N}^j \right\|_2 \tag{7}$$

where $b^j \in \mathbb{R}$ is the weight corresponding to the joint j. $\boldsymbol{d}_{n+N}^j$ and d_{n+N}^j denote the predicted inter-frame displacement and the corresponding ground truth of joint j in the $(n+N)^{th}$ pose, respectively.

4   Experiments

4.1   Dataset and Preprocessing

Human 3.6 Million. Human3.6M is currently the largest 3D human Mocap dataset containing 3.6 million pose and corresponding images. There are a large number of complex motion sequences, such as Directions, Smoking, Sitting, and Walk Dog. Following existing works [4,7,15], each skeleton is represented by 17 joints. We down-sample the motion sequence to 25 frames per second. Finally, the S1, S6, S7, S8, S9, and S11 have been used for training, and S5 for testing.

4.2   Implementation Details

The overview of our model is shown in Fig. 1. Ten frames (400 ms) were fed into the model to generate 25 frames (1,000 ms) of predictions. The size of the convolution kernel for the graph convolution is set to 17×17. The number of layers for the spatio-temporal graph convolution is set to 3. The multiscale temporal coding module is set to 3 layers, the convolution kernel is 1×3, and the dilation rate is 1,2 and 3. The GRU is set to 3 layers, each containing 128 neurons. The batch size is set to 16, the model has been trained for 70 epochs. We use ADAM to optimize the model, the initial learning rate is set to 0.001, and the reduction is 10% every 10 epochs.

4.3   Results

As in previous works [15,19], we use the mean joint position error (MPJPE) in millimeters to evaluate the performance of the model. The predictions are divided into short-term predictions (0–400 ms) and long-term predictions (400–1,000 ms).

Human3.6M. The motion prediction results of our proposed method are stated in Table 1, in which we compare our model with 9 kinds of state-of-the-art

Table 1. Comparisons of MPJPE for both short-term and long-term predictions on Human3.6M dataset.

	Directions					Discussion					Eating				
	80	160	320	400	1000	80	160	320	400	1000	80	160	320	400	1000
LSTM3LR [8]	46.6	52.3	87.0	101.6	135.1	29.9	49.4	85.5	105.8	135.1	21.3	38.8	78.1	91.4	121.1
Res-GRU [18]	21.6	41.3	72.1	84.1	129.1	25.7	47.8	80.0	91.3	131.8	16.8	31.5	53.5	61.7	98.0
HP-GAN [2]	80.9	101.3	148.6	168.8	234.6	71.4	91.3	105.2	129.7	150.4	64.1	78.4	99.9	113.7	136.2
Bi-GAN [10]	22.0	37.5	58.9	72.0	114.7	19.2	39.0	67.7	75.3	122.5	13.6	26.1	51.4	63.1	74.1
ConSeq2Seq [12]	22.0	37.2	59.6	73.4	118.3	18.9	39.3	67.7	75.7	123.9	13.7	25.9	52.5	63.3	74.4
HMR [16]	23.3	25.0	47.2	61.5	116.9	19.0	38.8	67.3	75.0	121.5	13.2	26.0	51.1	62.6	74.0
MA-GAN [4]	11.1	20.9	38.8	47.0	83.5	11.9	22.7	44.8	54.6	102.2	9.0	15.9	29.1	**35.0**	65.3
AM-GCN [20]	7.6	16.7	30.1	43.5	103.5	9.3	21.1	41.7	48.3	94.3	8.9	12.9	43.5	50.0	80.1
STCM [9]	9.8	18.4	34.8	43.5	90.8	10.1	20.8	40.5	48.4	116.7	8.3	13.6	32.1	39.8	72.9
Our	**7.2**	**15.1**	**29.8**	**42.4**	**82.3**	**8.7**	**20.7**	**39.6**	**48.3**	**91.8**	**8.0**	**12.1**	**27.5**	35.9	**64.5**

	Greeting					Posing					Purchases				
	80	160	320	400	1000	80	160	320	400	1000	80	160	320	400	1000
LSTM3LR [8]	21.0	61.5	73.1	78.2	177.6	46.1	72.0	130.1	156.7	176.5	39.1	78.6	88.0	104.1	142.9
Res-GRU [18]	31.2	58.4	96.3	108.8	153.9	29.3	56.1	98.3	114.3	183.2	28.7	52.4	86.9	100.7	154.0
HP-GAN [2]	81.5	118.8	178.4	200.1	258.6	75.5	107.4	168.3	178.0	250.1	42.4	88.9	95.0	120.2	170.2
Bi-GAN [10]	24.6	45.8	89.9	103.0	148.1	16.8	35.0	86.4	105.6	187.0	29.0	54.1	82.2	92.4	139.0
ConSeq2Seq [12]	24.5	46.2	90.0	103.1	191.2	16.1	35.6	86.2	105.6	163.9	29.4	54.9	82.2	93.0	139.3
HMR [16]	17.9	38.7	72.1	82.5	143.2	13.6	23.5	62.5	114.1	183.6	15.3	30.6	64.7	73.9	142.7
MA-GAN [4]	19.6	35.1	64.0	78.2	126.8	13.7	25.9	50.0	61.1	137.7	14.2	26.5	48.3	58.1	120.8
AM-GCN [20]	15.8	30.6	63.4	77.8	**124.6**	11.5	21.5	56.3	72.5	130.4	12.4	23.3	48.5	62.1	114.7
STCM [9]	18.2	32.3	63.2	75.0	125.6	12.6	23.9	47.1	60.2	130.1	12.2	23.8	44.1	52.9	114.7
Our	**14.7**	**30.1**	**61.1**	**74.4**	139.4	**10.9**	**20.7**	**45.5**	**56.1**	**128.5**	**11.5**	**22.1**	**43.3**	**49.2**	**108.3**

	Smoking					Sitting					Sitting Down				
	80	160	320	400	1000	80	160	320	400	1000	80	160	320	400	1000
LSTM3LR [8]	26.5	42.3	88.9	99.2	129.2	34.0	57.1	115.0	111.3	142.1	36.9	63.0	88.1	121.3	198.6
Res-GRU [18]	18.9	34.7	57.5	65.4	102.1	23.8	44.7	78.0	91.2	152.6	31.7	58.3	96.7	112.0	187.4
HP-GAN [2]	67.2	88.6	100.1	123.9	140.4	36.3	60.0	120.0	123.1	168.2	39.9	65.9	92.1	130.0	200.2
Bi-GAN [10]	11.0	21.0	33.1	38.2	50.1	19.9	41.0	76.3	88.2	120.5	17.0	34.8	66.5	76.9	152.0
ConSeq2Seq [12]	11.1	21.0	33.4	38.3	52.2	19.8	42.4	77.0	88.4	132.5	17.1	34.9	66.3	77.7	163.9
HMR [16]	10.3	20.5	33.0	37.2	69.1	12.6	25.6	44.7	60.7	118.4	18.6	38.6	61.1	77.7	148.3
MA-GAN [4]	7.9	14.3	25.2	30.4	63.4	10.4	17.9	33.1	40.7	97.7	15.8	28.2	52.9	64.5	125.2
AM-GCN [20]	7.2	13.9	22.2	30.1	62.5	9.9	20.9	40.7	48.9	99.3	12.5	26.4	50.6	61.5	116.4
STCM [9]	6.5	13.5	23.1	27.7	61.3	9.0	16.2	31.7	43.3	96.4	13.7	25.5	44.5	60.0	114.6
Our	**6.2**	**12.6**	**20.3**	**27.4**	**60.7**	**8.1**	**15.7**	**31.6**	**41.0**	**96.4**	**12.5**	**24.6**	**43.2**	**56.3**	**110.9**

	Taking Photo					Walking Dog					Averge				
	80	160	320	400	1000	80	160	320	400	1000	80	160	320	400	1000
LSTM3LR [8]	35.4	47.5	71.1	74.0	155.6	77.1	80.1	160.1	190.0	230.3	37.6	58.4	96.8	112.1	158.6
Res-GRU [18]	21.9	41.4	74.0	87.6	153.9	36.4	64.8	99.1	110.6	164.5	26.0	48.3	81.1	93.4	146.4
HP-GAN [2]	38.0	49.3	79.9	83.8	160.4	83.1	92.1	170.0	198.4	238.8	61.8	85.6	123.4	142.7	191.6
Bi-GAN [10]	14.2	27.1	53.5	66.1	128.0	41.2	78.3	116.2	130.1	210.5	20.8	40.0	71.1	82.8	131.5
ConSeq2Seq [12]	14.0	27.2	53.8	66.2	151.2	40.6	74.7	116.6	138.7	185.4	20.7	39.9	71.4	83.9	136.0
HMR [16]	8.9	19.0	31.5	57.3	128.6	38.2	63.6	109.3	125.6	190.0	17.4	31.8	58.6	75.3	130.6
MA-GAN [4]	8.8	16.0	32.4	40.9	98.9	19.3	34.2	65.6	77.5	117.8	12.9	23.4	44.0	53.5	103.6
AM-GCN [20]	8.5	17.1	34.5	41.8	102.9	19.0	33.4	66.8	79.8	**115.7**	11.1	21.6	45.3	56.0	104.0
STCM [9]	**7.5**	**13.4**	31.5	**40.5**	126.3	17.5	30.7	57.8	74.8	136.6	11.4	21.1	40.9	51.5	107.8
Our	7.9	17.9	**30.4**	45.3	**98.7**	**16.7**	**28.2**	**56.2**	**72.4**	121.9	**10.2**	**20.0**	**39.0**	**49.9**	**100.3**

approaches, including LSTM3LR [8], Res-GRU [18], HP-GAN [2], Bi-GAN [10], Conseq2seq [12], HMR [16], MA-GAN [4], AM-GCN [20], and STCM [9]. From the table 1, it can be observed that our model achieves state-of-the-art performance in both short-term and long-term predictions. Compared with STCM, we emphasize that the prediction accuracy of the model has achieved a large improvement at 80ms and 160ms. For slighter movements such as "Eating", our model is able to capture the long-distance temporal dependencies hidden in the movement sequence and produce better long-term predictions. Compared to STCM, our model improves by 6.1% in terms of average accuracy.

To further verify the performance of our model. We visualize the prediction results of the model as shown in Fig. 2. The ground truth is shown in the top of the figure, followed by the prediction results of Res-GRU, AM-GCN, STCM and our model. Visually, our prediction results are more similar to ground truth. Specifically, Res-GRU does not explicitly encode the spatial information between joints and generates unnatural future poses that display longer or shorter hands and feet. At 1,000ms of "Greeting", Res-GRU shows a significant difference compared to ground truth, while our model produces more accurate results. In "Walk Dog", which has a large range of motion, the predictions of our model do not show any significant difference compared to ground truth. These results evidence the performance of our proposed method.

Fig. 2. The visual results on Human3.6M dataset.

Table 2. Ablation studies for the Spatio-Temporal graph convolution module (ST) and Multiscale Temporal encoding module (MT).

ST	MT	80	160	320	400	1,000
	✓	15.3	33.1	53.8	67.2	125.4
✓		12.7	24.6	49.3	65.7	131.6
✓	✓	**10.2**	**20.0**	**39.0**	**49.9**	**100.3**

4.4 Ablation Study

To further investigate the impact of the proposed module, an ablation analysis is conducted on the Human3.6M dataset. The results of the experiments are shown in Table 2.

Spatio-Temporal Graph Convolution Module: We use the original graph convolution module in place of the proposed module. As shown in the first and third rows of Table 2, when this module is replaced, short-term prediction performance decreases. This result clearly indicates that there is critical spatially relevant information hidden in the adjacent pose. When this information is ignored, it is difficult for the model to capture short-term time evolution trends, resulting in degraded performance.

Multiscale Temporal Encoding Module: We remove this module directly from the proposed method. From the results, it can be seen that the long-term prediction performance of the model is significantly reduced, and the short-term prediction performance is also slightly reduced. This result proves that it is difficult to model long-range temporal dependencies using only RNNs. The multi-scale temporal information captured by the module can effectively improve the long and short-term prediction performance of the model.

5 Conclusion

In this paper, we design a novel human motion prediction model. Specifically, a new spatio-temporal graph convolution module is designed to capture the spatial dependency information hidden in adjacent poses. To further enhance the prediction performance of the model, the multiscale temporal coding module is proposed to model the motion context information of various temporal distances. Finally, extensive experiments on the Human3.6M dataset demonstrate that our model achieves state-of-the-art performance compared to existing methods.

Acknowledgements. This research is supported by the National Key Research and Development Program of China (2018YFB0804202, 2018YFB0804203), Regional Joint Fund of NSFC(U19A2057), and the National Natural Science Foundation of China (61876070).

References

1. Akhter, I., Simon, T., Khan, S., Matthews, I.A., Sheikh, Y.: Bilinear spatiotemporal basis models. ACM Trans. Graph. **31**(2), 1–12 (2012)
2. Barsoum, E., Kender, J., Liu, Z.: HP-GAN: probabilistic 3D human motion prediction via GAN. In: International Conference on Computer Vision and Pattern Recognition, pp. 1418–1427 (2018)
3. Cai, Y., et al.: Learning Progressive Joint Propagation for Human Motion Prediction. In: Vedaldi, A., Bischof, H., Brox, T., Frahm, J.-M. (eds.) Computer Vision – ECCV 2020. LNCS, vol. 12352, pp. 226–242. Springer, Cham (2020). https://doi.org/10.1007/978-3-030-58571-6_14
4. Chopin, B., Otberdout, N., Daoudi, M., Bartolo, A.: Human motion prediction using manifold-aware Wasserstein GAN. In: FG, pp. 1–8 (2021)
5. Cui, Q., Sun, H.: Towards accurate 3D human motion prediction from incomplete observations. In: International Conference on Computer Vision and Pattern Recognition, pp. 4801–4810 (2021)
6. Cui, Q., Sun, H., Kong, Y., Zhang, X., Li, Y.: Efficient human motion prediction using temporal convolutional generative adversarial network. Inf. Sci. **545**, 427–447 (2021)
7. Cui, Q., Sun, H., Yang, F.: Learning dynamic relationships for 3D human motion prediction. In: International Conference on Computer Vision and Pattern Recognition, pp. 6518–6526 (2020)
8. Fragkiadaki, K., Levine, S., Felsen, P., Malik, J.: Recurrent network models for human dynamics. In: International Conference on Computer Vision, pp. 4346–4354 (2015)
9. Jiao, Y., Chen, H., Yao, C., Su, P., Fu, C., Wang, X.: Spatial-temporal correlation modeling for motion prediction. In: International Conference on Multimedia and Expo, pp. 1–6 (2022)
10. Kundu, J.N., Gor, M., Babu, R.V.: BiHMP-GAN: bidirectional 3D human motion prediction GAN. In: The Thirty-First Innovative Applications of Artificial Intelligence Conference, pp. 8553–8560 (2019)
11. Lehrmann, A.M., Gehler, P.V., Nowozin, S.: Efficient nonlinear Markov models for human motion. In: International Conference on Computer Vision and Pattern Recognition, pp. 1314–1321 (2014)
12. Li, C., Zhang, Z., Lee, W.S., Lee, G.H.: Convolutional sequence to sequence model for human dynamics. In: Conference on Computer Vision and Pattern Recognition, pp. 5226–5234 (2018)
13. Li, M., Chen, S., Zhao, Y., Zhang, Y., Wang, Y., Tian, Q.: Dynamic multiscale graph neural networks for 3D skeleton based human motion prediction. In: International Conference on Computer Vision and Pattern Recognition, pp. 211–220 (2020)
14. Li, Q., Chalvatzaki, G., Peters, J., Wang, Y.: Directed acyclic graph neural network for human motion prediction. In: International Conference on Robotics and Automation, pp. 3197–3204 (2021)
15. Liu, Z., et al.: Motion prediction using trajectory cues. In: International Conference on Computer Vision, pp. 13299–13308 (2021)
16. Liu, Z., et al.: Towards natural and accurate future motion prediction of humans and animals. In: International Conference on Computer Vision and Pattern Recognition, pp. 10004–10012 (2019)

17. Mao, W., Liu, M., Salzmann, M., Li, H.: Learning trajectory dependencies for human motion prediction. In: International Conference on Computer Vision, pp. 9488–9496 (2019)
18. Martinez, J., Black, M.J., Romero, J.: On human motion prediction using recurrent neural networks. In: International Conference on Computer Vision and Pattern Recognition, pp. 4674–4683 (2017)
19. Su, P., Liu, Z., Wu, S., Zhu, L., Yin, Y., Shen, X.: Motion prediction via joint dependency modeling in phase space. In: ACM Multimedia Conference, pp. 713–721 (2021)
20. Su, P., Shen, X., Shi, Z., Liu, W.: Adaptive multi-order graph neural networks for human motion prediction. In: International Conference on Multimedia and Expo, pp. 1–6 (2022)
21. Taylor, G.W., Hinton, G.E.: Factored conditional restricted Boltzmann machines for modeling motion style. Int. Conf. Mach. Learn. **382**, 1025–1032 (2009)
22. Wang, J.M., Fleet, D.J., Hertzmann, A.: Gaussian process dynamical models. In: Advances in Neural Information Processing Systems, pp. 1441–1448 (2005)
23. Zhou, H., Guo, C., Zhang, H., Wang, Y.: Learning multiscale correlations for human motion prediction. In: International Conference on Development and Learning, pp. 1–7 (2021)

Multi-view Cascading Spatial-Temporal Graph Neural Network for Traffic Flow Forecasting

Zibo Liu[1]([✉]), Kaiqun Fu[2], and Xiaotong Liu[3]

[1] Virginia Tech, Falls Church, VA 22043, USA
zbliu@vt.edu
[2] South Dakota State University, Brookings, SD 57007, USA
Kaiqun.Fu@sdstate.edu
[3] George Washington University, Washington, DC 20052, USA
liuxiaotong2017@gwu.edu

Abstract. Spatial-temporal patterns have been applied in many areas, such as traffic forecasting, skeleton-based recognition, and so on. In such areas, researchers can convert the prior knowledge into graphs and combine the latent graph dependencies into original features to get better representation. However, few works focus on the underlying pattern in the original feature, and they cannot capture the flexible interaction both spatially and temporally. What is more, they often ignore the heterogeneity in spatial-temporal data. In this paper, we solve this problem by designing a novel model, Multi-view Cascading Spatial-temporal Graph Neural Network. Our model has a cascading structure to enhance interaction and capture heterogeneity. Also, it takes the differencing orders of flow data into account to get a better representation and contains specific coupled graphs designed based on the sliding window technique. Extensive experiments are conducted on four real-world datasets, demonstrating that our method achieves state-of-the-art performance and outperforms other baselines.

Keywords: Traffic forecasting · Multi-view · Spatio-temporal · Attention · Graph neural network · Graph Convolutional Network

1 Introduction

With the urban expansion and increasing number of vehicles, intelligent transportation systems are developed to make our trips more efficient and safe. Using data like traffic flow/speed/density, there are many real-world applications such as optimal route and estimated arrival time [17,18], abnormal traffic behavior detection [15] and so on. Given the broad applications of traffic data, we focus on traffic flow forecasting, which is a technology based on the past traffic flow to predict the future traffic flow. It is challenging due to the complex intra-dependencies (i.e., temporal correlations within one traffic series) and inter-dependencies (i.e., spatial correlations among huge correlated traffic series) [12]

E. Pimenidis et al. (Eds.): ICANN 2022, LNCS 13530, pp. 605–616, 2022.
https://doi.org/10.1007/978-3-031-15931-2_50

generated from different sources such as the different traffic detectors in the intersections and various vehicles' data.

Researchers first used the traditional machine learning method to solve problems, like ARIMA [3]. Then when the outbreak of deep learning, they use Convolutional Neural Network (CNN) and some graph-based CNN, get >10% performance improvement compared with machine learning methods. The capstone work was STGCN [21] in 2017. It achieved better performance because it facilitated spatial and temporal dependencies and combined them with the CNN layers. Then is STSGCN [12], they divide the whole time series data into data pieces to capture the heterogeneity between different time stamps, designed a new pattern.

However, there are several disadvantages to the prior models: 1) The graph's topology is static and predefined based on the location map. It can not be guaranteed as optimal for traffic flow tasks. For example, when we concern with two nodes, A, B. A, B are big cities on the highway, but it is not connected due to the long distance. However, there are a great number of tracks to deliver groceries from A to B. It is difficult to capture this dependency through predefined graphs. Also, some models use the 0/1 spatial graphs instead of distance graphs. It is not fair to treat the node pair with a relatively high distance and the one with a low distance as the same (the distances are under the threshold). 2) The prior models use an entire network to deal with the entire spatial-temporal data flow. They could miss some essential dependencies like heterogeneity and homogeneity. For example, if a car accident happened on the road an hour ago, the current flow would be lower because the drivers always choose a faster route, not this road, which is more likely to be jammed. Nevertheless, if the car accident happened 10 h ago, we cannot say whether now it is jammed or not because the road is probably back to normal. 3) In the aggregation step and final output transformation step, exist model structure is relatively simple to extract the complete and higher dimensional information. Our work overcomes these shortages, and the contributions are as follows:

- We propose a novel spatial-temporal graph neural network to capture local and global spatial-temporal correlations. We discover that the various differencing orders of original data are additional support for feature representation in the traffic flow task. Based on that, we build our paralleled modules on the sliding window technique to find the same or different patterns, instead of using a single module to deal with the whole time series.
- We also build the hierarchical and temporal cascading structures to keep long-term dependencies and flexible interactions by learnable parameters to decide the weight of information to communicate through modules.
- Meanwhile, we developed a delicate graph block to aggregate the graph features, which could capture the subtle relationships of features. Extensive experiments are conducted on four real-world datasets, and the experimental results show that our model consistently outperforms all the baseline methods.

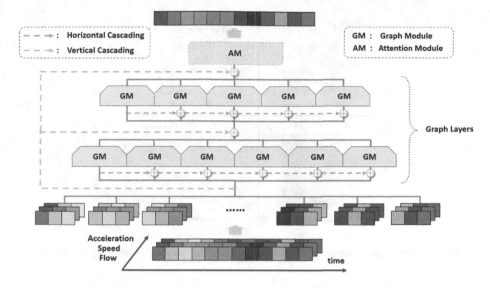

Fig. 1. This is a diagram of the whole model. The bottom color rows represent the three channels, flow, speed, and acceleration. Then the data is divided into several windows to feed into each Graph Module. Between layers and between Graph Modules are cascading connections. After a few Graph Layers, the Attention Module is the final part of getting the output. (Color figure online)

2 Related Work

2.1 Machine Learning and Convolutional Method

Like K-Nearest Neighbor (KNN) [4], they calculate the center of cluster and assign each data point to the specific cluster. ARIMA used the differencing function to find the fit pattern. The derivation of it, SARIMA [16] adds a specific ability to recognize the seasonal pattern. The machine learning models are designed by human-set rules and are sensitive to outliers. It is challenging for them to learn the actual relationship of features. But the deep learning methods could work well because millions of neurons and kernels could learn the higher dimensional features. CNN/RNN based models and their derivation could be transferred to solve time series, such as ConvLSTM [20], ST-LSTM [11], STCNN [7].

2.2 Graph Method

Graph-based methods could be summed up into three parts. First, constructing the data into the nodes and finding their neighbors based on the latent relationship. Second, using the developing method to upgrade the information of the node. Third, merging the upgraded information and using the aggregation method to reach the final output. For example, Graph Convolutional Network

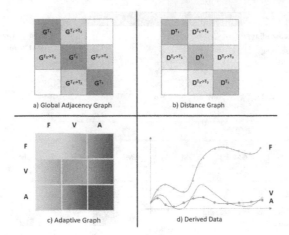

Fig. 2. This figure contains key components in our model. (Color figure online)

(GCN) [9] is a derivation of Graph Neural Network (GNN), using the Convolutional Network to get node representation. Recent work like GAT [14], which introduces attention mechanism into the graph field, and GraphSAGE [6], which generates node embeddings by sampling and aggregating features.

2.3 Traffic Flow Prediction

For this topic, the deep network could learn higher-dimensional features of data. AGCRN [1] uses the recurrent network as the main structure to obtain long-term relationships through time and automatically form a graph based on the data. STSGCN [12] divides the data into data pieces, takes the heterogeneities in spatial-temporal dependencies into account. STGODE [5] focuses on Ordinary Differential Equations to mimic the trajectory of traffic flow. STFGNN [10] is a work derived from STSGCN, used the Dynamic Time Warping algorithm [2] to gain a unique temporal graph.

3   Problem Formulation

We denote graph set as $\mathcal{G} = \{V, E, G, D, \mathcal{A}\}$, V is the set of nodes, E is set of edges, G is a global graph, D is a distance graph, $\mathcal{A}$ is set of data-based graph, $\mathcal{A} = (A^1, A^2, ..., A^T)$. The problem of spatial-temporal forecasting can be described as: learning a mapping function f which maps the current spatial-temporal data series $\mathcal{X} = (X_{t-T+1}, X_{t-T+2}, ..., X_t)$ into the future spatial-temporal data series $\mathcal{Y} = (X_{t+1}, X_{t+2}, ..., X_{t+T'})$, where T and T' denotes the length of historical and the target time series to forecast respectively. $\hat{\mathcal{X}} = f(\mathcal{X}, \mathcal{G})$, $\hat{\mathcal{X}}$ is the model output, we want the $\hat{\mathcal{X}}$ as close to $\mathcal{Y}$ as possible.

4   Model

The followings are three general characteristics of our model. 1) Differencing and multi-view: We derive the different orders of original flow data to enrich the model input. Furthermore, we design three graphs from different views. The first two are static graphs, which are global and distance graphs. And the third one is an adaptive graph. It has an independent graph for each data piece and provides extra hidden patterns for the model. 2) Cascading: The model has two types of cascading. One is temporal, which transfers the information from the previous data piece to the current data piece with a weight value, which captures data heterogeneity by paralleled modules. The other is hierarchical, which transfers the complete features to the following graph layer with a weight value. 3) In the aggregation step and final output transformation step, we borrow the idea of attention [13] to capture both global and local features better.

4.1   Differencing Process

The latent feature could be inconspicuously hidden in the original data. And it can be a great help for the model to have a better performance. Later in the ablation study, it was proved. In our opinion, this traffic flow data $F \in \mathbb{R}^{N*T*1}$ is not powerful enough to provide the learning features. Here, we borrow the concept in Physics, using speed and acceleration to express first-order differencing and second-order differencing information in traffic flow data, as shown in Fig. 2d). We use S_1, S_2, S_3 to represent the flow, speed, and acceleration channels, respectively. S_1, S_2, $S_3 \in \mathbb{R}^{T*N*1}$. We concatenate all three dimensions together in the last dimension, $S \in \mathbb{R}^{N*T*3}$. In Fig. 1, the three-color row on the bottom represents the flow, speed, and acceleration channel.

4.2   Graph

Global Graph G. The size of Global Graph is $\mathbb{R}^{3N*3N}$, here we set the 3 as the window size, the sliding window goes along the time axis. The diagonal of the adjacency matrix are three same $N \times N$ spatial graphs. For example in Fig. 2 a), the Global Graph contains three timestamps T_1, T_2, T_3, if v_i and v_j are connected in the navy blue squares, this pair of nodes is also connected in four shallow blue squares $T_1 - T_2, T_2 - T_1, T_2 - T_3$, and $T_3 - T_2$.

$$G_{i,j} = \begin{cases} 1, & if\ v_i\ and\ v_j\ are\ neighbors \\ 0, & otherwise \end{cases} \tag{1}$$

Distance Graph D. Even though the global graph gives the connection information among nodes, it still lacks the meaning of distance. Here, we provide the specific value between each connected node, instead of 0/1 in the Global Graph.

We follow what we did in Global Graph, using the distance between node i and j, E_{ij}. The size of the Distance Graph is $\mathbb{R}^{3N*3N}$, shown as Fig. 2b).

$$D_{i,j} = \begin{cases} \frac{\sigma}{E_{ij}}, & if\ G_{i,j} = 1 \\ 0, & otherwise \end{cases} \tag{2}$$

Adaptive Graph A. Considering the previous track-highway example, we propose this well-designed graph to capture the hidden patterns. This graph aggregates S_1, S_2, S_3 based on the sliding window strategy. It is a data-driven graph that learns one unique graph for each window. We use the multiplication among S_1, S_2, S_3 to emphasize the underlying correlation and to determine how strong the connection is. Figure 2c) is a diagram of the Adaptive Graph. In Eq. 3., the multiplication is to obtain an $\mathbb{R}^{N*N}$ relevance matrix. The diagonal of the matrix A is the node similarity of S_1, S_2, S_3 from top to bottom. The side of this diagonal line is the relevance among them. We take a Softmax on the $3N$ dimension.

$$A_{i,j} = S_i^T \otimes S_j, A_{i,j} \in \mathbb{R}^{N*N}, A \in \mathbb{R}^{3N*3N}, i/j \in \{0,1,2\} \tag{3}$$

Mask. We apply a learnable mask and multiply it into the adjacency matrix to enhance the matrix learning ability and latent feature expression. Here, we multiply a Global Mask G_{mask} to a data-driven graph to give the Adaptive Graph more spatial restriction and let the model learn the underlying relationship between the static graphs and the adaptive graph. Here $\times$ represents the Hadamart product.

$$G' = G_{mask} \times G, \ D' = D_{mask} \times D, \ A' = G_{mask} \times A \tag{4}$$

4.3   Graph Layer

In the Graph Layer, we capture the hierarchical and temporal dependencies through the cascading structure. The whole model contains J cascading Graph Layers. Each Graph Layer contains several paralleled Graph Modules, Fig. 1 provides a general structure. This paralleled structure captures the unique pattern for different data pieces. Before the data was fed into the first Graph Layer, we first map the input S into higher embedding space $S' \in \mathbb{R}^{N*T*C}$, the input of the first Graph Layer $L^1 = S'$. The j-th Graph Layer $L^j = \|(M_1^j, M_2^j, M_3^j, ..., M_{T-(j\times2)}^j), j \in \{1, 2, .., J\}, \|$ means the concatenation on the time dimension. The i-th Graph Module $M_i^j \in \mathbb{R}^{N*t*C}$, here t = 3 is the length of sliding window. For example, the first Graph Layer has $10 = 12 - (1 \times 2)$ paralleled Graph Modules.

$$M_{i+1}^j = \alpha * M_i^j + M_{i+1}^j, \ L^{j+1} = \beta * AdpAvgPool(L^j) + L^{j+1} \tag{5}$$

To save the long-term information hierarchically and temporally, we combine the input of the last layer with the current layer to make the final input and add the previous Graph Module input to the current one. We add control variables α and β to control the value. $AdpAvgPool$ is an Adaptive Average Pool to adjust the tensor shape.

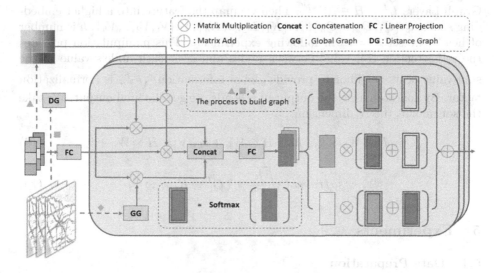

Fig. 3. The diagram of the Graph Block.

4.4   Graph Module and Graph Block

We develop delicate Graph Blocks to aggregate and capture the subtle relationships of features. Figure 3 shows the structure of Graph Block. Each Graph Module contains B Graph Blocks. In each Graph Block, we have K copied input, here $K = 3$, the input of the Graph Module M_i^j is the input of the first Graph Block P^1. These copies are multiplied with masked graphs, respectively. Next, these parts are concatenated together and mapped to a higher embedding space. Then the feature is divided into K branches on the channel dimension, $\{p_1^{g'}, p_2^{g'}, p_3^{g'}, ..., p_K^{g'}\} = P^{g'}$, each branch is multiplied by the sum of other branches, which are normalized by the softmax function. The output of P^1 is the input of P^2, after B iterations of Eqs. 6 to 7, we get P^1 to P^B. By using the MaxPool, we get the output of the Graph Module M_i^j, which is the input of Graph Module M_i^{j+1}. The input of (j+1)-th Graph Layer $L^{j+1} = \|(M_1^{j+1}, M_2^{j+1}, M_3^{j+1}, ..., M_{T-(j\times2)}^{j+1})$. $g \in \{1, 2, .., B\}$ means the g-th Graph Block.

$$P^{g'} = W^i \otimes \|(A'P^g, D'P^g, G'P^g) + b^g, \tag{6}$$

$$P^{g+1} = \frac{1}{2K} \sum_{m}^{K} \sum_{n \neq m}^{K} p_m^{g'} \otimes softmax(p_n^{g'}) \tag{7}$$

$$M_i^{j+1} = MaxPool(P^1, P^2, ..., P^B) \tag{8}$$

4.5   Attention Module

The Attention Module is designed to replace the simple Fully Connected Layer to capture the global feature from previous Graph Layers. We got the output of Graph Layers $L^J = H \in \mathbb{R}^{N*F'}$. Then we map the feature into a higher embedding space. $Q:\{Q_1, Q_2, .., Q_h\}$, $K:\{K_1, K_2, .., K_h\}$, $V:\{V_1, V_2, .., V_h\}$, h is number of heads, we set $h = 12$ in following experiments. This manipulation provides the self-attention [14] value between nodes and lever each node's value to the sum value of its neighbor to provide global information. $\sqrt{\frac{h}{F''}}$ is normalization factor. By concatenating the output of h heads, we get the final output. We take the softmax at the N dimension.

$$Q = H \otimes W_q + b_q, \ K = H \otimes W_k + b_k, \ V = H \otimes W_v + b_v \tag{9}$$

$$\hat{Y}_i = softmax\left(\sqrt{\frac{h}{F''}} * (Q_i^T \otimes K_i)\right) \otimes V_i \tag{10}$$

5   Experiments

5.1   Data Preparation

We use public traffic datasets PEMS03, PEMS04, PEMS07, and PEMS08 released by STSGCN [12]. The gap among time steps is 5 min. The whole day has 288 points in total. It has flow, occupation, and speed values at every time step on every location point. In this work, we followed previous work [10,12], only using the traffic flow value to forecast future traffic flow. More specifically, we use past 1 h, 12 continuous data to predict future 1 h, 12 continuous data. The spatial adjacency networks for each dataset is constructed by existing road network based on connectivity and distance.

5.2   Experiment Settings

The best model on these four datasets consists of $J = 4$ Graph layers, each Graph Module contains $B = 3$ Graph Blocks. The σ in the Distance Graph is 1. Before the input data is fed into the first Graph Layer, the channel has been increased from 3 to 64, $S' \in \mathbb{R}^{N*12*64}$, N is the number of nodes, it depends on datasets. In the Graph Block, W^i is $\mathbb{R}^{192*192}$. In Attention module, W_q and W_k are $\mathbb{R}^{256*864}$, W_v is $\mathbb{R}^{256*12}$. We choose Huber loss [8] as the loss function. To evaluate the effectiveness of the proposed model, Mean Absolute Error (MAE), Mean Absolute Percentage Error (MAPE), and Root Mean Squared Error (RMSE).

Table 1. Performance evaluation results

Dataset	Metric	ARIMA [3]	STGCN [21]	GraphWaveNet [19]	STSGCN [12]	STGODE [5]	STFGNN [10]	Our model
PEMS03	MAE	33.51	17.49	19.85	17.48	16.50	16.77	**15.88**
	MAPE (%)	33.78	17.15	19.31	16.78	16.69	16.30	**15.77**
	RMSE	47.59	30.12	32.94	29.21	27.84	28.34	**26.81**
PEMS04	MAE	33.73	22.70	25.45	21.19	20.84	19.83	**19.47**
	MAPE (%)	24.18	14.59	17.29	13.90	13.77	13.02	**12.47**
	RMSE	48.80	35.55	39.70	33.65	32.82	31.88	**31.51**
PEMS07	MAE	38.17	25.38	26.85	24.26	22.99	22.07	**21.95**
	MAPE (%)	19.46	11.08	12.12	10.21	10.14	**9.21**	9.28
	RMSE	59.27	38.78	42.78	39.03	37.54	35.80	**35.53**
PEMS08	MAE	31.09	18.02	19.13	17.13	16.81	16.64	**16.49**
	MAPE (%)	22.73	11.40	12.68	10.96	10.62	10.60	**10.43**
	RMSE	44.32	27.83	31.05	26.80	25.97	26.22	**25.73**

5.3 Experiment Result

In Table 1, we find that our model outperforms other models on four datasets with different metrics, except the MAPE in PEMS07, which is slightly larger than that of STFGNN.

The traditional machine learning method ARIMA does not consider spatial dependency, whereas deep learning models can take advantage of spatial-temporal information. The relatively poor performance of GraphWaveNet reveals its struggle because it can not stack its spatial-temporal layers and enlarge receptive fields of 1D CNN concurrently. STGCN repeatedly use ten layers of Graph Convolution operations to capture the feature, we believe it could cause missing features and it's feature extraction part is not so strong compared with attention-based model. STGODE focuses on a relatively new aspect, the whole model is built on the ordinary equation function to simulate the time series. Due to the unique and effective tensor-based manipulation, it reaches a good performance. Among the deep learning baselines, STSGCN and STFGNN utilize paralleled modules to model spatial-temporal flow data and capture heterogeneity of temporal information, they outperform other models. But they only concentrate on localized spatial-temporal correlations and do not focus on global dependencies enough.

6 Ablation Study

To understand the effectiveness of different techniques in this model, we design seven models. First, the base is a plain model without any techniques. We then add them one by one to the model. Then, we tune the parameters to reach their best performance.

(1) Base: This model only contains the flow channel as an input and then maps it into three channels. In the Graph Block, it only has one branch, $K = 1$. This branch is multiplied by the masked Global Graph, which is the only graph in this model. Also, it does not have intra-interaction, which is the knowledge from previous modules or layers. (e.g., The dashed line in Fig. 1) In the output layer, it uses a simple Fully Connected Layer instead of the Attention Module.

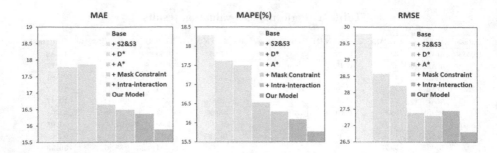

Fig. 4. The result of Ablation Study.

(2) +S2& S3: Beyond (1), we derive the first-order and second-order differencing of flow data and concatenate them to three channels as input.

(3) +D*: We add the masked Distance Graph and have two branches in the Graph Block.

(4) +A*: We add the non-masked Adaptive Graph and have three branches in the Graph Block.

(5) +Mask Constraint: Beyond (4), we multiply the mask of the Global Graph to the Adaptive Graph to get mask constraint.

(6) +Intra-interaction: We add intra-interaction hierarchically and temporally, which is knowledge from previous modules or layers.

(7) Our Model: We replace the simple Fully Connected Layer with the Attention Module.

Figure 4 is the result. We can find out that the various differencing orders of flow data are additional support for feature representation in the traffic flow task. One channel of flow data is not so informative to provide learning features. The first-order and second-order differencing of flow data gives a considerable performance improvement to the model.

The Distance Graph can only provide limited help compared with the previous model. However, the Adaptive Graph provides excellent help. Compared with the static Distance Graph, the adaptive graph find the hidden patterns inside the feature.

The mask constraint between the Global Mask and the Adaptive Graph can improve the model's performance and enhance the matrix learning ability. Even though the Adaptive Graph success in this model, the guide of spatial information is still essential. The spatial information comes from the Global Mask, which contains the real-world location for features. It gives the Adaptive Graph a rational direction to learn.

The hierarchical and temporal intra-interaction between Graph Layers and Graph Modules is also necessary for the model. In most metrics, it improves the performance of this cascading structure. The attention mechanism can obtain features based on the context, but the simple Fully Connected Layer is not strong enough.

7   Conclusion

We propose a novel model that could effectively capture the localized spatial-temporal correlations and take the underlying physical meaning into account by the differencing method. Meanwhile, to solve the problems shown in prior models, we design an adaptive graph for each sliding window, generate a robust graph feature extraction operation, and enhance the interaction between graph modules. Extensive experiments on four real-world datasets show that our model is superior to the existing models. Our proposed model is a general framework for spatial-temporal network data forecasting. It can be applied in many related applications.

References

1. Bai, L., Yao, L., Li, C., Wang, X., Wang, C.: Adaptive graph convolutional recurrent network for traffic forecasting. arXiv preprint arXiv:2007.02842 (2020)
2. Berndt, D.J., Clifford, J.: Using dynamic time warping to find patterns in time series. In: KDD Workshop, Seattle, WA, USA, vol. 10, pp. 359–370 (1994)
3. Box, G.E., Pierce, D.A.: Distribution of residual autocorrelations in autoregressive-integrated moving average time series models. J. Am. Stat. Assoc. **65**(332), 1509–1526 (1970)
4. Cover, T., Hart, P.: Nearest neighbor pattern classification. IEEE Trans. Inf. Theory **13**(1), 21–27 (1967)
5. Fang, Z., Long, Q., Song, G., Xie, K.: Spatial-temporal graph ode networks for traffic flow forecasting. In: Proceedings of the 27th ACM SIGKDD Conference on Knowledge Discovery and Data Mining, pp. 364–373 (2021)
6. Hamilton, W.L., Ying, R., Leskovec, J.: Inductive representation learning on large graphs. In: Proceedings of the 31st International Conference on Neural Information Processing Systems, pp. 1025–1035 (2017)
7. He, Z., Chow, C.Y., Zhang, J.D.: STCNN: a spatio-temporal convolutional neural network for long-term traffic prediction. In: 2019 20th IEEE International Conference on Mobile Data Management (MDM), pp. 226–233. IEEE (2019)
8. Huber, P.J.: Robust estimation of a location parameter. In: Kotz, S., Johnson, N.L. (eds.) Breakthroughs in Statistics. Springer Series in Statistics, pp. 492–518. Springer, New York (1992). https://doi.org/10.1007/978-1-4612-4380-9_35
9. Kipf, T.N., Welling, M.: Semi-supervised classification with graph convolutional networks. arXiv preprint arXiv:1609.02907 (2016)
10. Li, M., Zhu, Z.: Spatial-temporal fusion graph neural networks for traffic flow forecasting. arXiv preprint arXiv:2012.09641 (2020)
11. Liu, J., Shahroudy, A., Xu, D., Wang, G.: Spatio-temporal LSTM with trust gates for 3D human action recognition. In: Leibe, B., Matas, J., Sebe, N., Welling, M. (eds.) ECCV 2016. LNCS, vol. 9907, pp. 816–833. Springer, Cham (2016). https://doi.org/10.1007/978-3-319-46487-9_50
12. Song, C., Lin, Y., Guo, S., Wan, H.: Spatial-temporal synchronous graph convolutional networks: a new framework for spatial-temporal network data forecasting. In: Proceedings of the AAAI Conference on Artificial Intelligence, vol. 34, pp. 914–921 (2020)
13. Vaswani, A., et al.: Attention is all you need. In: Advances in Neural Information Processing Systems, pp. 5998–6008 (2017)

14. Veličković, P., Cucurull, G., Casanova, A., Romero, A., Lio, P., Bengio, Y.: Graph attention networks. arXiv preprint arXiv:1710.10903 (2017)
15. Wang, H., Xu, M., Zhu, F., Deng, Z., Li, Y., Zhou, B.: Shadow traffic: a unified model for abnormal traffic behavior simulation. Comput. Graph. **70**, 235–241 (2018)
16. Williams, B.M., Hoel, L.A.: Modeling and forecasting vehicular traffic flow as a seasonal Arima process: theoretical basis and empirical results. J. Transp. Eng. **129**(6), 664–672 (2003)
17. Wu, N., Wang, J., Zhao, W.X., Jin, Y.: Learning to effectively estimate the travel time for fastest route recommendation. In: Proceedings of the 28th ACM International Conference on Information and Knowledge Management, pp. 1923–1932 (2019)
18. Wu, N., Zhao, X.W., Wang, J., Pan, D.: Learning effective road network representation with hierarchical graph neural networks. In: Proceedings of the 26th ACM SIGKDD International Conference on Knowledge Discovery and Data Mining, pp. 6–14 (2020)
19. Wu, Z., Pan, S., Long, G., Jiang, J., Zhang, C.: Graph wavenet for deep spatial-temporal graph modeling. arXiv preprint arXiv:1906.00121 (2019)
20. Xingjian, S., Chen, Z., Wang, H., Yeung, D.Y., Wong, W.K., Woo, W.C.: Convolutional LSTM network: a machine learning approach for precipitation nowcasting. In: Advances in Neural Information Processing Systems, pp. 802–810 (2015)
21. Yu, B., Yin, H., Zhu, Z.: Spatio-temporal graph convolutional networks: a deep learning framework for traffic forecasting. arXiv preprint arXiv:1709.04875 (2017)

Parallel Message Passing in Dual-space on Graphs

Zhenglin Yu and Hui Yan[✉]

School of Computer Science and Engineering, Nanjing University of Science
and Technology, Nanjing, China
{yuzhenglin,yanhui}@njust.edu.cn

Abstract. Graph neural networks (GNNs) have achieved a great success on graph-based tasks. Most existing GNNs pay attention to the message passing process, where features propagate along the topology of the graph. Recently, dimension-wise separable 2-D graph convolution (DSGC) points out that GNNs ignore the effect of interactions between the features, and specially designs a dimension-wise feature affinity matrix via predefined corpuses. Although DSGC further improves the performance, we find that it has two shortcomings. For one thing, it performs poorly on low homophily datasets. For another thing, it tends to be over-smoothing as the number of layers increases, making node embeddings indistinguishable. In our empirical analysis, these two shortcomings are caused by the serial message passing mechanism of topology and features. To solve this problem, we propose a parallel-space graph convolution (PSGC) in this paper. The central idea is that we design a parallel message passing mechanism in dual spaces including a topology space and a feature space, which can adapt to different homophily real-world datasets and alleviate the over-smoothing issue. Besides, we design the dimension-wise feature affinity matrix derived by the original node features instead of corpuses in DSGC to alleviate the severe overfitting in the feature space, where corpuses are not provided by many benchmark datasets. Our extensive experiments on benchmark datasets obviously show that PSGC achieves significant performance gain over state-of-the-art methods for semi-supervised node classification.

Keywords: Graph convolutional networks · Homophily ·
Over-smoothing

1 Introduction

Graph data is widely used in practical scenarios, such as social networks, biology networks, and citation networks [4,17]. Recently, graph neural networks (GNNs) have made attempts to apply deep learning methods to graph data and acquired high performance in downstream tasks, such as community detection, node classification, and link prediction. There is a homophily hypothesis followed by GNNs that adjacent nodes often belong to the same class or have

© The Author(s), under exclusive license to Springer Nature Switzerland AG 2022
E. Pimenidis et al. (Eds.): ICANN 2022, LNCS 13530, pp. 617–629, 2022.
https://doi.org/10.1007/978-3-031-15931-2_51

similar features ("birds of a feather flock together"). Based on such hypothesis, GNNs actually perform Laplacian smoothing on node features. Specially, GNNs update node embeddings by serially propagating and transforming node features [20] within topological neighborhoods in each convolutional layer. The graph convolution essentially pushes representations of adjacent nodes mixed with each other.

Based on above update scheme, dimension-wise separable 2-D graph convolution (DSGC) [10] firstly explores the relation between the features. DSGC proposes a basic assumption that features indicating the same class should have strong relations. Thus, they construct a dimension-wise feature affinity matrix derived from predefined corpuses to describe such relation, which can reduce the overlap of different class areas. However, the serial message passing mechanism of topology and features in DSGC has two shortcomings. For one thing, it may lead to an inferior performance on low homophily graphs, i.e., the topology in such graphs hardly satisfies the homophily hyphthesis. For another thing, as the layers deepen, DSGC suffers from the over-smoothing issue. Intuitively, the performance of message passing is affected by the quality of graph topology. For example, in Texas dataset [13], the homophily is approximately equivalent to 0.1, which means that only one of the ten edge-connected node pairs belongs to the same class. Thus, with the graph convolution in DSGC, the update of the target node embeddings absorbs much negative information from adjacent nodes, which generates a misleading trend. Over-smoothing issue is firsted introduced by Li et al. [9]. It indicates that as the layers deepen, all nodes' embeddings become more and more similar, and converge to a stationary point at last, making themselves indistinguishable.

To solve these issues, we design a parallel-space graph convolution (PSGC), a parallel message passing mechanism in dual spaces including two spaces, i.e., the topology space and the feature space, where the topology space is mainly used to process high homophily datasets and the feature space is mainly used to process low homophily datasets without interference of the topology. Depending on these spaces, PSGC can adapt to different homophily datasets. Besides, Our feature space consisting of the original node features transformed by MLP can ensure the final embeddings distinguishable by adding the original node features into the final embeddings. A detailed analysis of over-smoothness is presented in Sect. 5.4.

In our feature space, we mainly adopt multi-layer perceptron (MLP) [12] on the original features to update node embeddings. However, we find that severe overfitting in MLP causes the performance of the entire parallel message passing mechanism to degrade, even worse than the performance of classical GNNs in its topology space, which is verified in Sect. 5.3. Overfitting comes from the case when we utilize an over-parameterice model to fit a distribution with limited training data [15], where the model we learn fits the training data very well but generalizes poorly to the test data (see MLP w/o dropout in Fig. 1). Empirically, we are surprised to find that the dimension-wise feature affinity matrix F derived from original node features rather than predefined corpuses has a

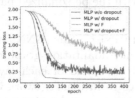

(a) Training loss on Cora.

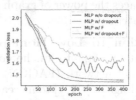

(b) Validation loss on Cora.

Fig. 1. Performance of MLP on Cora. MLP gets stuck in the over-fitting issue attaining low training error but high validation error.

dropout-like ability to alleviate overfitting issue (see MLP w/ dropout and MLP w/ F in Fig. 1), but the oscillation amplitude of loss convergence is smaller than dropout. With the transformation of feature affinity matrix, neighborhoods of the target feature tend to be the same, which indicates there exist some useless dimensions. Thus, the number of parameters can be reduced, which can alleviate the overfitting issue. Besides, at the basis of dropout, feature affinity matrix can further alleviate the overfitting issue (see in MLP w/ dropout+F in Fig. 1).

Our contributions may be summarized as follows:

- We indicate that the serial message passing mechanism in DSGC hardly adapts to low homophily datasets and tends to be over-smoothing as the layers deepen. To solve these issues, we propose a parallel-space graph convolution (PSGC) to adapt to different homophily datasets and alleviate the over-smoothing issue.
- We utilize the feature affinity matrix to alleviate the overfitting issue of MLP in the feature space, which can improve the performance of the entire model.
- We conduct extensive experiments on a variety of real-world datasets with different homophily to show that PSGC outperforms the state-of-the-art baselines. Besides, the feature space in PSGC also has the plug-and-play capability to be suitable for various GNNs.

2   Related Work

Graph Neural Networks. GNNs generalize neural techniques into graph-structure data. The essence of GNNs is a message passing mechanism, where node features aggregate in different manners. ChebyNet [3] introduces a polynomial parametrization to the convolutional kernel. Graph convolutional network (GCN) [6] only uses a localized first-order approximation based on ChebyNet. Simplifying graph convolution (SGC) [18] attempts to get rid of non-linear activation function during the process of convolution in GCN. Graph attention network (GAT) [16] adopts a strategy that each node in a GAT layer learns to weighted combine the embedding of its neighbours with an attention mechanism. Approximately personalized propagation of neural predictions (APPNP)

[7] replaces the power of graph convolutional matrix with the personalized pagerank matrix.

Adaption to Low Homophily Datasets. There exist some GNNs that attempt to adapt to low homophily datasets. Frequency adaptation graph convolutional network (FAGCN) [1] adjusts the weight threshold of each layer's embeddings to $[-1, 1]$ to increase adaptability. Graph convolutional network with homophily or heterophily (H2GCN) [21] makes GNNs adapt to low homophily datasets from three key designs, i.e., ego- and neighbor-embedding separation, higher-order neighborhoods, and combination of intermediate representations.

Ability to Alleviate Over-smoothness in GNNs. Most GNNs usually suffer from the over-smoothing issue, if we execute graph convolution numerous times [2,8,19]. SGC and APPNP commonly alleviate this issue by simplifying the architecture via decoupling propagation and transformation. Deep adaptive graph neural network (DAGNN) [11] learns weights for each layer's embedding and fuses multi layers' embeddings to update the target node embedding.

3   Problem

Given an undirected feature graph $\mathcal{G} = (\mathcal{V}, \mathcal{E}, \mathbf{X})$, where $\mathcal{V} = \{v_1, v_2, \cdots, v_n\}$ consists of a set of nodes with $|\mathcal{V}| = n$, $\mathcal{E} \subseteq \mathcal{V} \times \mathcal{V}$ is a set of edges between nodes, and $\mathbf{X} = [x_1; x_2; \cdots; x_n] \in \mathbb{R}^{n \times d}$ denotes the feature matrix of all the nodes, where $x_i \in \mathbb{R}^d$ is the real valued feature vector associated with node v_i. The topological structure of graph $\mathcal{G}$ is represented by an adjacency matrix $\mathbf{A} \in \{0, 1\}^{n \times n}$, where $\mathbf{A}_{ij} = 1$ indicates the existence of an edge between nodes v_i and v_j, otherwise $\mathbf{A}_{ij} = 0$. $\hat{\mathbf{A}}$ stands for the adjacency matrix with self-loops, $\hat{\mathbf{A}} = \mathbf{A} + \mathbf{I}_n$. $\mathbf{I}_n$ denotes the $n \times n$ sized identity matrix.

Definition 1. *The edge homophily ratio* $h = \frac{|(u,v):(u,v)\in\mathcal{E}\wedge y_u=y_v|}{|\mathcal{E}|}$ *is the fraction of edges in a graph which connect nodes that have the same class label, i.e., intra-class edges [21].*

The homophily ratio h is a measure of the graph homophily level and we have $h \in [0, 1]$. The larger the h value, the higher the homophily.

4   The Framework

4.1   Overview

To let the message passing mechanism of graph convolution essentially suitable for both high homophily and low homophily datasets, we propose a parallel-space graph convolution (PSGC). The key idea is that node features can be both utilized in two spaces, i.e., the topology space and the feature space, and the feature affinity matrix can effectively alleviate the overfitting issue in the feature space. More importantly, the weights of the topology space and the feature space do not share, which is beneficial for the two spaces to acquire better node embeddings.

4.2   Parallel Message Passing Module

On one hand, in the feature space, we construct a dimension-wise feature affinity matrix, i.e.,

$$\hat{\mathbf{F}} = kNN(\mathbf{X}^{(0)T}) \tag{1}$$

where $\hat{\mathbf{F}} \in \mathbb{R}^{d \times d}$ is a k-nearest neighbor (kNN) graph. We choose top k closest feature pairs of each target feature to set edges and finally get the feature affinity matrix $\hat{\mathbf{F}}$. $\mathbf{X}^{(0)} = \mathbf{X}$ is the original node features. We perform the symmetric normalization on $\hat{\mathbf{F}}$, i.e., $\mathbf{F} = \hat{\mathbf{D}}_f^{-1/2} \hat{\mathbf{F}} \hat{\mathbf{D}}_f^{-1/2}$, $\hat{\mathbf{D}}_f$ is the diagonal degree matrix of $\hat{\mathbf{F}}$.

Then, we apply graph-agnostic MLP with $\mathbf{F}$ to extract class-aware information, the pth layer output $\mathbf{Z}_f^{(p)}$ can be represented as:

$$\begin{aligned} \mathbf{Z}_f^{(0)} &= \mathbf{X}^{(0)} \mathbf{F} \\ \mathbf{Z}_f^{(p)} &= \sigma(\mathbf{Z}_f^{(p-1)} \mathbf{W}_f^{(p-1)}) \end{aligned} \tag{2}$$

where $\mathbf{W}_f^{(p-1)}$ is the learnable weight matrix, and σ denotes the non-linear activation function ReLU.

It is worth noting that the $\mathbf{Z}_f^{(p)}$ is only based on original node features, which are not constrained by the homophily ratios of datasets. Therefore, it is also appropriate for datasets with low homophily ratios.

On the other hand, in the topology space, we take the classical SGC [18] as the neighbor information aggregation mechanism. The lth layer output $\mathbf{Z}_t^{(l)}$ can be represented as:

$$\mathbf{Z}_t^{(l)} = \tilde{\mathbf{A}} \mathbf{Z}_t^{(l-1)} \tag{3}$$

where $\mathbf{Z}_t^{(0)} = \mathbf{X}^{(0)}$, $\tilde{\mathbf{A}}$ is the symmetric normalized $\hat{\mathbf{A}}$, i.e., $\tilde{\mathbf{A}} = \hat{\mathbf{D}}^{-1/2} \hat{\mathbf{A}} \hat{\mathbf{D}}^{-1/2}$. $\hat{\mathbf{D}}$ denotes the diagonal degree matrix of $\hat{\mathbf{A}}$.

Then, we also apply p layers' MLP to $\mathbf{Z}_t^{(l)}$ to extract class-aware information, the output can be represented as:

$$\mathbf{Z}_t^{l+p} = \sigma(\mathbf{Z}_t^{l+p-1} \mathbf{W}_t^{l+p-1}) \tag{4}$$

where $\mathbf{W}_t^{l+p-1}$ is the learnable weight matrix. We set $p = 2$ in our experiments.

Besides, we can also use GCN [6], GAT [16] and other neighbor information aggregation methods to replace SGC. The node embedding $\mathbf{Z}_f^{(p)}$ in the feature space possesses the virtue of plug-and-play capability.

At last, to make the model more effective and robust, we combine the node embeddings learning from the feature space and the topology space with an adjustable parameter as follows:

$$\mathbf{Z} = softmax(\alpha \mathbf{Z}_t^{(l+p)} + (1 - \alpha) \mathbf{Z}_f^{(p)}) \tag{5}$$

where α is a hyper-parameter to balance the importance of the node embeddings from two spaces. Softmax function is used to obtain a probability distribution of different classes.

We adopt the Cross-Entropy (CE) measurement between the predicted outputs and the one-hot ground-truth label distributions as the objective function, i.e.,

$$\mathcal{L} = - \sum_{i \in y_L} \sum_{j=1}^{c} \mathbf{Y}_{ij} ln \mathbf{Z}_{ij} \tag{6}$$

where y_L is the set of labeled nodes, $\mathbf{Y}_{ij} = 1$ if the label of node i is j, and $\mathbf{Y}_{ij} = 0$ otherwise.

4.3   Properties of PSGC

Adaptation to Different Homophily Datasets. Our PSGC consists of two spaces, i.e., the topology space and the feature space. SGC in the topology space achieves great performance on high homophily datasets, and MLP without the interference of topology in the feature space achieves great performance on low homophily datasets, which can be verified in Table 2.

Thus, we comprehensively combine both two approaches to update the node embeddings and adjust the balance parameter to adapt to different homophily datasets.

Generalization Ability. Our dimension-wise feature affinity matrix F can well alleviate the overfitting issue, which can be verified in Fig. 1. With the contribution of F, our PSGC has further performance improvements on both high homophily datasets and low homophily datasets.

Ability to Alleviate Over-smoothing Issue. Severe over-smoothness can cause nodes' embeddings to become indistinguishable. Our PSGC has a similar effect to DenseGCN [8] to alleviate over-smoothing issue, where DenseGCN proposes residual connection that combines the smoothed representation $\tilde{\mathbf{A}}\mathbf{Z}_t^{(l-1)}$ with $\mathbf{Z}_t^{(l-1)}$. Instead of using a residual connection to absorb the information from the previous layer, we employ the original node features $\mathbf{X}^{(0)}$. The original node features ensure that the final representation of each node retains at least a component of the input representation even if we stack many layers' information.

4.4   Discussion

PSGC vs. AMGCN. Adaptive multi-channel graph convolutional network (AMGCN) [17] constructs a node-wise kNN feature affinity matrix and explores the relation between the topology and features via different regularization terms. Although it also adopts two branches, we find that AMGCN performs only slightly better than GCN [6] on Citeseer, worse than many GNNs, and it overlooks the effect of the feature branch on low homophily datasets. This indicates that the node-wise kNN only works on specific datasets, while dimension-wise feature affinity matrix in PSGC can be applied universally to general benchmark datasets.

Table 1. The statistics of datasets.

	Dataset	#Nodes	#Edges	#Classes	#Features	#Homophily
Assortative	Cora	2708	5429	7	1433	0.81
	Citeseer	3327	4732	6	3703	0.74
	Pubmed	19717	44338	3	500	0.80
Disassortative	Cornell	183	298	5	1703	0.30
	Texas	183	325	5	1703	0.09
	Wisconsin	251	515	5	1703	0.19

5 Experiments

5.1 Datasets

We conduct experiments on 6 datasets including two types, i.e., assortative and disassortative, and the statistics are summarized in Table 1. In assortative datasets, graphs have high homophily ratios, while in disassortative datasets, graphs have low homophily ratios. We use 3 assortative benchmark datasets, including Cora, Citeseer, and Pubmed[1] [6]. These three datasets are citation network datasets. We employ the standard splits in previous works [6,18], where 20 labeled nodes per class are used for training, next 500 nodes and 1000 nodes are used as validation set and test set, respectively. We use 3 disassortative benchmark datasets, including Wisconsin, Cornell and Texas[2] [13]. These three datasets are the subdatasets of WebKB. These are randomly split into three parts (60%/20%/20% of nodes for training/validation/test).

5.2 Experimental Settings

To judge whether PSGC can achieve the compared performance, we compare our PSGC with three types of representative GNNs and two network embedding methods based on random walk, as well as its variants:

- Methods based on random walk include Node2vec [5] and Deepwalk [14].
- Methods focused on the topology include GCN [6], SGC [18], GAT [16], ChebyNet [3], APPNP [7], and DAGNN [11].
- Methods focused on features include MLP [12], AMGCN [17], and DSGC [10].
- Methods focused on low homophily include H2GCN [21] and FAGCN [1].
- Two PSGC variants include PSGC_GCN and PSGC_GAT. In PSGC_GCN and PSGC_GAT, we replace SGC with other classical GNNs, i.e., GCN and GAT, respectively.

---

[1] https://github.com/tkipf/gcn.
[2] https://github.com/graphdml-uiuc-jlu/geom-gcn.

Table 2. Results (%) with the state-of-the-art methods on semi-supervised node classification (- means out of memery).

Method	Assortative Datasets			Disassortative Datasets		
	Cora	Citeseer	Pubmed	Wisconsin	Cornell	Texas
Node2vec	76.7 ± 1.1	51.2 ± 1.7	76.4 ± 1.1	46.5 ± 1.7	54.1 ± 0.1	49.2 ± 2.1
Deepwalk	69.4 ± 1.4	47.1 ± 1.9	71.4 ± 1.2	45.8 ± 0.5	52.7 ± 1.1	47.3 ± 1.1
GCN	81.5 ± 0.8	68.2 ± 1.0	76.6 ± 1.5	62.7 ± 1.6	56.8 ± 1.5	64.9 ± 0.1
SGC	82.5 ± 0.4	72.7 ± 0.2	79.8 ± 0.5	72.5 ± 1.6	59.5 ± 1.2	67.5 ± 1.3
ChebyNet	80.6 ± 0.7	69.3 ± 1.2	79.0 ± 0.7	58.8 ± 0.1	54.1 ± 2.7	59.5 ± 1.6
GAT	83.1 ± 0.2	71.4 ± 0.1	-	72.5 ± 1.0	62.2 ± 0.1	67.6 ± 0.6
APPNP	83.3 ± 0.3	71.8 ± 0.4	80.1 ± 0.3	74.5 ± 1.1	62.2 ± 1.3	64.9 ± 1.6
DAGNN	83.6 ± 0.5	72.9 ± 0.1	80.1 ± 0.4	75.6 ± 2.2	69.9 ± 1.1	70.5 ± 4.1
MLP	59.5 ± 0.6	58.3 ± 1.7	72.7 ± 1.2	91.5 ± 2.5	86.5 ± 0.1	85.6 ± 3.3
AMGCN	80.8 ± 0.2	69.4 ± 0.3	-	86.9 ± 0.9	81.1 ± 2.2	78.4 ± 2.2
DSGC	81.0 ± 0.5	70.6 ± 0.8	76.6 ± 0.5	72.5 ± 0.2	67.6 ± 0.2	68.5 ± 2.5
FAGCN	83.6 ± 0.5	71.9 ± 0.8	78.4 ± 2.2	62.2 ± 1.4	81.1 ± 0.5	81.1 ± 0.3
H2GCN	82.3 ± 0.7	72.1 ± 1.1	-	86.9 ± 2.4	79.1 ± 4.4	86.5 ± 4.4
PSGC_GCN	83.2 ± 0.5	72.5 ± 1.1	80.3 ± 0.8	90.9 ± 2.5	87.1 ± 0.1	85.8 ± 2.5
PSGC_GAT	84.0 ± 0.3	72.7 ± 0.3	-	88.3 ± 4.3	87.2 ± 1.1	86.2 ± 2.2
PSGC	**84.3 ± 0.6**	**73.4 ± 0.2**	**80.7 ± 0.5**	**92.8 ± 3.4**	**89.2 ± 2.2**	**88.3 ± 2.5**
w/o F	78.5 ± 2.0	69.9 ± 1.1	77.5 ± 0.5	89.2 ± 4.1	85.6 ± 3.3	86.5 ± 2.2
w/o FS	82.5 ± 0.4	72.7 ± 0.2	79.8 ± 0.5	72.5 ± 1.6	59.5 ± 1.2	67.5 ± 1.3
w/0 TS	62.6 ± 0.8	60.5 ± 4.4	69.9 ± 0.3	88.9 ± 4.0	85.6 ± 2.5	84.7 ± 3.4

We use the Adam optimizer with 5000 epochs to optimize parameters of the proposed method and adopt early stopping with a patience of 50 epochs to control the training epochs based on validation loss. We report the mean classification accuracy and standard deviation after 10 runs. We perform grid search to select the optimal values for hyper-parameters of the methods, including the learning rate lr, the number of neighbors in kNN k, and the balance parameter α. lr, k, and α are selected within $\{0.1, 0.2, 0.5, 0.01, ..., 0.09, 0.001, ..., 0.009\}$, $\{2, 3, ..., 10\}$, and $\{0, ..., 0.5, ..., 1\}$, respectively. We set the dimension of hidden layer as 32 and the weight decay as 5e-4.

5.3   Overall Results

The node classification results are reported in Table 2, and the top accuracy is highlighted. We have the following observations:

- As shown in Table 2, our PSGC model performs better than the representative baselines by significant margins. Quantitatively, for the assortative datasets, the improvements of PSGC over the sub-optimal baseline are 0.7%, 0.5%, and 0.6% on Cora, Citeseer, and Pubmed, respectively. For the disassortative datasets, the improvements of PSGC over the sub-optimal baselines are 1.3%, 2.7%, and 1.8% on Wisconsin, Cornell, and Texas, respectively. The results demonstrate the effectiveness of PSGC.
- On assortative datasets, DSGC and AMGCN are better than GCN, but worse than SGC, indicating that the feature affinity matrix and the parallel mechanism of topology and features have certain effect, but the effect is not obvious.

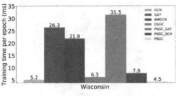
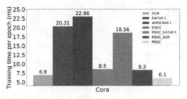

(a) Training time on Wisconsin.   (b) Training time on Cora.

Fig. 2. Training time per epoch for different methods on Wisconsin and Cora datasets. x0.1 in (b) means value here is a ten-fold reduction.

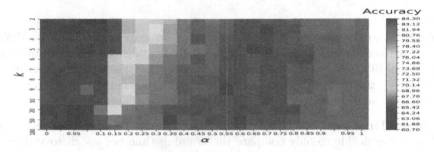

Fig. 3. The influence of hyper-parameter k and α on classification accuracy.

PSGC consistently outperforms AMGCN and DSGC on all the datasets, indicating the effectiveness of combining the advantages of both.

- On disassortative datasets, for one thing, models that rely on serial aggregation of topological neighbor information, e.g., GCN, GAT, APPNP, and so on, do not perform well, because the homophily ratios of these datasets are so low that this case misleads the prediction of nodes' labels. For another thing, models that overlook the topology to some extent, e.g., MLP, AMGCN, and H2GCN, acquire a satisfactory result. Therefore, the feature space does make for the classification prediction on disassortative datasets.
- We interpret the performance of PSGC_GCN and PSGC_GAT from two perspectives. Firstly, both PSGC_GCN and PSGC_GAT outperform the original GCN and GAT models, demonstrating the positive effects of the feature affinity matrix and the parallel message passing mechanism. Secondly, both of them are inferior to PSGC with the simple MLP in training process, indicating GCN and GAT are relatively easier to be over-smoothing than MLP.

Ablation Study. We conduct an ablation study to examine the contributions of different components in PSGC, i.e., without the feature affinity matrix (F), without the feature space (FS), and without the topology space (TS).

As shown in Table 2, we have two observations. Firstly, all PSGC variants with some components removed suffer from clear performance drops when comparing to the full model, indicating that each of the designed compoments

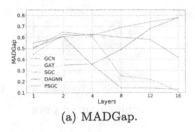

(a) MADGap.

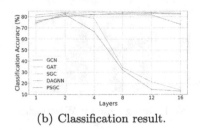

(b) Classification result.

Fig. 4. Performance (accuracy) and Over-smoothness (MADGap) of layers with different methods on Cora.

contributes to the success of PSGC. Secondly, on assortative datasets, PSGC w/o F performs worse than PSGC w/o FS, indicating the unsuccessful combination of SGC and MLP. We hold the opinion that the severe overfitting in MLP causes the performance of the entire parallel message passing mechanism to degrade and F alleviates such negative impact to a large extent.

Training Time per Epoch. We report the average training time per epoch in Fig. 2. We decide to only compare the training time per epoch to verify the efficiency of our PSGC. Obviously, comparing to the classical GNNs, related GNNs, and variants of itself, PSGC is significantly faster than them. It is owing to it puts a lot of calculation into the preprocessing outside of training. In addition, combined with Table 2, it can be seen that PSGC is the best method of aggregation among it and its variants in terms of the accuracy and training speed.

Influence of Hyper-parameter k and α. k is the number of neighbours in the kNN graph F. As k becomes larger, the range of neighboring features becomes larger, capturing more information. However, if k becomes too large, unrelated features become similar, which can cause the performance degradation. Additionally, we use α to tune the proportion of the embeddings of two spaces in the final embedding.

Figure 3 demonstrates the influence of hyper-parameters k and α on classification accuracy on Cora. Horizontally, the process of change can be divided into four stages. Firstly, when $\alpha \in [0, 0.1]$, the feature space mainly contributes to the final embedding. Next, the accuracy increases sharply when $\alpha \in (0.1, 0.35]$. Then, the accuracy reaches the peak when $\alpha \in (0.35, 0.85]$, indicating the topology space embedding and the feature space embedding can be well combined. Finally, the accuracy slowly declined until it can be on par with PSGC w/o FB when $\alpha \in (0.85, 1]$. Vertically, when the graph structure is almost overlooked, i.e., $\alpha \in [0, 0.1]$, the classification accuracy exactly increases as k becomes larger at first. However, with the continuous increase in k, the learning capacity of the model becomes weaker since some irrelevant features are associated with the target feature, which leads to a drop on accuracy. When $\alpha \in (0.1, 0.35]$, with the increase in k, the accuracy becomes larger obviously, which verifies the effectiveness of the feature affinity matrix in the same way. Then, when $\alpha \in (0.35, 1]$, the accuracy is almost stable at the same level, and different k matching the corresponding α can increase the accuracy better. Except for the first stage, the negative effects of excessive k become weaker as the proportion of topology embedding increases.

5.4   Over-Smoothing Analysis

Many GNNs inevitably face the over-smoothing issue, namely nodes with different labels will become indistinguishable at last as the depth of propagation continues to deepen. We study how PSGC is affected due to this issue by using MADGap [2], a measure of the over-smoothness of node embeddings. A smaller MADGap value indicates the more indistinguishable node embeddings and thus a more severe over-smoothing issue.

Figure 4 shows both the MADGap values of the last layer's embeddings and classification accuracy with respect to different layers. The plots indicate that as the number of layers increases, both metrics of GCN [6] and GAT [16] decrease rapidly due to the over-smoothing issue, where MADGap drops from 0.6 to 0.2 and accuracy drops from 80% to 30%. In addition, we compare PSGC with two GNNs, in which some delicate designs can alleviate the over-smoothing issue, e.g., the decoupling in SGC and the assigning weights for each layer in DAGNN [11]. The plots indicate that the capability of SGC [18] to alleviate over-smoothing issue is a little less than PSGC and DAGNN since both MADGap and accuracy decrease before than the other two, and PSGC is better than DAGNN until the 12th layer. Empirically, two-layer convolution adopted by many GNNs ignores various useful information, and there is no need for excessive-layer convolution due to the computational cost. Thus, PSGC is the best choice since it achieves the best performance during the 2nd layer and the 12th layer.

6   Conclusion

In this paper, we pay attention to two shortcomings in DSGC, and propose PSGC to overcome. PSGC consists of two key designs, i.e., a parallel message passing mechanism in dual-space and the dimension-wise feature affinity matrix constructed by the original node features. We verify that the parallel message passing mechanism can improve the adaptability to different homophily datasets and alleviate the over-smoothing issue due to its feature space, where the embeddings in the feature space are derived by the original node features. Besides, we verify that the severe overfitting in MLP in the feature space may limit the performance of the parallel message passing mechanism, even worse than its topology space, while the dimension-wise feature affinity matrix can solve the issue well. We demonstrate its performance superiority over thirteen state-of-the-art baselines on benchmark datasets. In future work, we aim to improve the scalability of PSGC on large-scale datasets.

References

1. Bo, D., Wang, X., Shi, C., Shen, H.: Beyond low-frequency information in graph convolutional networks. arXiv preprint arXiv:2101.00797 (2021)
2. Chen, D., Lin, Y., Li, W., Li, P., Zhou, J., Sun, X.: Measuring and relieving the over-smoothing problem for graph neural networks from the topological view. In: Proceedings of the AAAI Conference on Artificial Intelligence, vol. 34, pp. 3438–3445 (2020)
3. Defferrard, M., Bresson, X., Vandergheynst, P.: Convolutional neural networks on graphs with fast localized spectral filtering. Adv. Neural Inf. Process. Syst. **29**, 3844–3852 (2016)
4. Feng, W., et al.: Graph random neural networks for semi-supervised learning on graphs. Adv. Neural Inf. Process. Syst. **33**, 22092–22103 (2020)
5. Grover, A., Leskovec, J.: Node2vec: scalable feature learning for networks. In: Proceedings of the 22nd ACM SIGKDD International Conference on Knowledge Discovery and Data Mining, pp. 855–864 (2016)
6. Kipf, T.N., Welling, M.: Semi-supervised classification with graph convolutional networks. arXiv preprint arXiv:1609.02907 (2016)
7. Klicpera, J., Bojchevski, A., Günnemann, S.: Predict then propagate: graph neural networks meet personalized Pagerank. arXiv preprint arXiv:1810.05997 (2018)
8. Li, G., Muller, M., Thabet, A., Ghanem, B.: Deepgcns: can gcns go as deep as CNNs? In: Proceedings of the IEEE/CVF International Conference on Computer Vision, pp. 9267–9276 (2019)
9. Li, Q., Han, Z., Wu, X.M.: Deeper insights into graph convolutional networks for semi-supervised learning. In: Thirty-Second AAAI conference on artificial intelligence (2018)
10. Li, Q., Zhang, X., Liu, H., Dai, Q., Wu, X.M.: Dimensionwise separable 2-D graph convolution for unsupervised and semi-supervised learning on graphs. In: Proceedings of the 27th ACM SIGKDD Conference on Knowledge Discovery & Data Mining, pp. 953–963 (2021)
11. Liu, M., Gao, H., Ji, S.: Towards deeper graph neural networks. In: Proceedings of the 26th ACM SIGKDD International Conference on Knowledge Discovery & Data Mining, pp. 338–348 (2020)
12. Pal, S.K., Mitra, S.: Multilayer perceptron, fuzzy sets, classifiaction (1992)
13. Pei, H., Wei, B., Chang, K.C.C., Lei, Y., Yang, B.: Geom-GCN: geometric graph convolutional networks. arXiv preprint arXiv:2002.05287 (2020)
14. Perozzi, B., Al-Rfou, R., Skiena, S.: Deepwalk: online learning of social representations. In: Proceedings of the 20th ACM SIGKDD International Conference on Knowledge Discovery and Data Mining, pp. 701–710 (2014)
15. Rong, Y., Huang, W., Xu, T., Huang, J.: DropEdge: towards deep graph convolutional networks on node classification. arXiv preprint arXiv:1907.10903 (2019)
16. Veličković, P., Cucurull, G., Casanova, A., Romero, A., Lio, P., Bengio, Y.: Graph attention networks. arXiv preprint arXiv:1710.10903 (2017)
17. Wang, X., Zhu, M., Bo, D., Cui, P., Shi, C., Pei, J.: Am-GCN: adaptive multi-channel graph convolutional networks. In: Proceedings of the 26th ACM SIGKDD International Conference on Knowledge Discovery & Data Mining, pp. 1243–1253 (2020)
18. Wu, F., Souza, A., Zhang, T., Fifty, C., Yu, T., Weinberger, K.: Simplifying graph convolutional networks. In: International Conference on Machine Learning, pp. 6861–6871. PMLR (2019)

19. Yang, C., Wang, R., Yao, S., Liu, S., Abdelzaher, T.: Revisiting over-smoothing in deep GCNs. arXiv preprint arXiv:2003.13663 (2020)
20. Zhou, K., Dong, Y., Lee, W.S., Hooi, B., Xu, H., Feng, J.: Effective training strategies for deep graph neural networks. arXiv preprint arXiv:2006.07107 (2020)
21. Zhu, J., Yan, Y., Zhao, L., Heimann, M., Akoglu, L., Koutra, D.: Beyond homophily in graph neural networks: current limitations and effective designs. arXiv preprint arXiv:2006.11468 (2020)

Parallel Relationship Graph to Improve Multi-Document Summarization

Menghua Lu[ID], Lijia Liang[ID], and Gongshen Liu[✉][ID]

School of Electronic Information and Electrical Engineering,
Shanghai Jiao Tong University, Shanghai 200240, China
{610228633,lianglijia,lgshen}@sjtu.edu.cn

Abstract. Multi-document summarization (MDS) is an important branch of information aggregation. Compared with the single-document summary (SDS), MDS faces the problem of large search space, redundancy and complex cross-document relation. In this paper, we propose an abstractive MDS model based on Transformer, which considers the parallel information of documents with the graph attention network. During decoding, our model can utilize graph information to guide the summary generation. In addition, combined with the pre-trained language model, our model can further improve the summarization performance. Empirical results on the Multi-News and WikiSum datasets show that our model brings substantial improvements over several strong baselines, and ablation studies verify the effectiveness of our key mechanisms.

Keywords: Multi-document summarization · Graph-based summarization · Transformer

1 Introduction

The multi-document summarization (MDS) is a research challenge and hotspot in the natural language processing field. Its main task is generating a short and informative summary across a set of topic-related documents. In recent years, with the rapid development of sequence models, the research on the single-document summarization (SDS) has been well studied. Compared to SDS, the traditional encoder-decoder framework used is difficult to apply for MDS. Specifically, MDS has those challenges:

- When the encoder-decoder model is used to process MDS, cross-document relations are hard to capture, which are shown meaningful in identifying the salient information from long documents [1,2].
- The input of MDS are multiple documents, many researchers concatenate documents cluster into a flat sequence [1,3], so the overall input is always longer than SDS, and the search space is also larger.
- Documents in the same cluster usually describe the same event or topic, so different documents usually contain similar redundant information [4]. It is hard to solve the problem of redundancy.

E. Pimenidis et al. (Eds.): ICANN 2022, LNCS 13530, pp. 630–642, 2022.
https://doi.org/10.1007/978-3-031-15931-2_52

Intend to solve the above difficulties, many researchers combine graph neural network with Transformer to introduce additional information or artificially add cross-document relationship [2,5].

A common habit during completing MDS tasks is that human beings usually focus on the corresponding parts of multiple documents at different summary writing stages. Inspired by graph-based summarization works and the common habit, we design a heterogeneous graph that consists of sentence nodes and virtual nodes, and build edges from sentence similarity and sentence meaning. The graph is utilized to guide the document information encoding and summary generation process via a graph attention mechanism, which takes advantage of the graph structure and human-like summary process to help organize the summary content. During encoding, we apply the graph attention network (GAT) [6] to enable information flow between sentences nodes and get virtual nodes representation. In the decoder, the embedding of nodes and edge weights are used to guide the attention distribution to the input sentences. At this stage, we solve the problem of large search space and information redundancy.

Our contributions are as follows:

- We propose a method bordering on the habit of human beings. During summary generation, this method pays more attention to the parallel information in different documents. Thus, the generated summary has lower redundancy and is hard to be inconsistent.
- We propose a new heterogeneous graph for MDS to capture cross-document information of similar parts in different documents. In addition, the virtual node of the graph can also help the decoder adjust the attention to the input.
- Compared with other baselines, our model obtains better Rouge scores on WikiSum and Multi-News. Additional ablation experiments and manual evaluation also proved the effectiveness of the model design.

2 Related Work

2.1 Abstractive MDS

Abstractive MDS approaches have met with limited success. Extractive MDS generates summaries by selecting sentences from the original text, so it is hard to generate new words by itself, and the number of words is difficult to control. Thus the summary has low diversity and lacks flexibility, and may produce redundancy or lose some information and entities. By contrast, the process of abstractive summarization is closer to human, so the generated summary can be more fluent and have greater potential. Traditional approaches can be divided into several categories: sentence fusion-based [7], information extraction-based [8] and paraphrasing-based [9].

With the development of Transformer-based models, great achievements have been made in the study of SDS, and Transformer-based methods also became the main-stream approach for abstractive MDS. While MDS is difficult to obtain in datasets construction. Meansum [10] generated summaries by training two recurrent auto-encoders with an unsupervised method. Another way to bypass this problem is model adaptation. Zhang et al. [11] applied a hierarchical single-document summarization model to a multi-document scenario to learn the vector representation of each document input. Lebanoff et al. [12] proposed pointer generator, which adds a pointer mechanism and an overlay mechanism to solve the unknown word problem and the repeated word problem.

Some models introduce extra information or deeply mine the relationship between different documents, and take them as additional information of the encoding. Liu et al. [1] augments a Transformer architecture with the ability to encode documents in a hierarchical manner, which represents cross-document relationships via an attention mechanism allowing to share information. Pasunuru et al. [13] introduces new hierarchical encoders that enable more efficient encoding of the query together with multiple documents. Lebanoff et al. [14] generates a synopsis from each document, which serves as an endorser to identify salient content from other documents. What's more, lots of graph-based MDS also use this method.

2.2 Graph-based Summarization

Graph-based methods are originally used for extractive summarization. LexRank [15] and TextRank [16] use cosine similarity of sentences to build a graph and calculate the extraction probability of sentences based on the graph. Wan and Xiaojun [17] further propose to incorporate document-level information and sentence-to-document relations into the graph-based ranking process.

For recent methods based on graph neural networks, Tan et al. [18] reviews the difficulties of SDS and proposes a novel graph-based attention mechanism. ASGARD [19] enhances the regular document encoder with a separate graph-structured encoder, which maintains the global context and local characteristics of entities.

Some MDS tasks also introduce graph structure. Christensen et al. [20] build multi-document graphs to approximate the discourse relations across sentences based on indicators, which includes discourse cues, deverbal nouns, co-reference, and more. Fan et al. [21] construct a local knowledge graph, which is then linearized into a structured input sequence, thus the model can encode within the sequence-to-sequence setting. GraphSum [2] leverages well-known graph representations of documents such as similarity graph and discourse graph; EMSum [5] captures cross-document entity information and aggregate diverse useful information around the same entity for better summarization.

3 Model

The input of the MDS is a document cluster $\mathcal{D}$, and the output is a summary text. The original document cluster $\mathcal{D}$ cannot be directly used as the input of the model. In this paper, to get the input sequence $\{t_1, t_2, \ldots, t_n\}$, tokens (word level) form a long sequence, and different documents are segmented with a special separator [SEP] as the input of the model encoder.

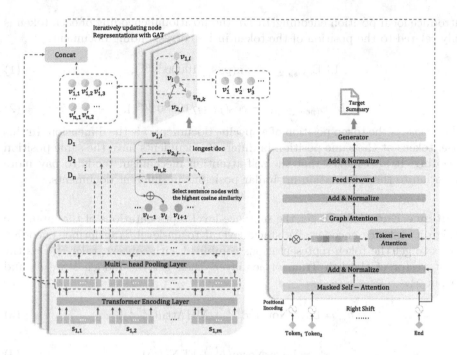

Fig. 1. Overall architecture of the model.

During encoding, we additionally calculate the embedding of the sentence, then the graph representation of documents is constructed over sentences. We take $s_{i,j}$ as the j-th sentence of the i-th document, and let $\mathbb{G}$ denotes the graph representation matrix of the input sentences.

Our model follows the Transformer-based encoder-decoder architecture [22], the specific structure is shown in Fig. 1. The input sequence is sent to several token-level Transformer encoding layers and Multi-head Pooling layers to get the token-level representations and the sentence embedding, then we build graph $\mathbb{G}$ depending on the similarities between sentence nodes. Similarly, the decoder is also composed of several graph decoding layers. These layers extend the Transformer architecture with a graph attention mechanism to guide the decoding process. In the following, we will introduce the design of encoder and decoder.

3.1 Document Encoder

Token Embedding. First, we take the input sequence $\{t_1, t_2, \ldots, t_n\}$ to an embedding layer to get the token embedding $X_w^0 = \{x_1, x_2, \ldots, x_n\}$. In this paper, we use learned embeddings to convert the input and output tokens to vectors of dimension d_t [23], in which the determination of positional encoding should be the position of the word in the long sequence. However, this method makes the output summary and the input summary order related. Thus, we introduce local position encoding(LPE), the positional encoding of each token is only related to the position of the token in its corresponding document:

$$\text{LPE}_{(pos_d, 2i)} = \sin(pos_d/10000^{2i/d_t}), \tag{1}$$

$$\text{LPE}_{(pos_d, 2i+1)} = \cos(pos_d/10000^{2i/d_t}), \tag{2}$$

where pos_d is the token position of a specific document, i is the dimension. In this case, tokens at the same position in different documents have the same position encoding. It also makes that the self-attention mechanism tends to pay more attention to the information in similar positions in different documents.

Sentence Encoder. To get the sentence-level representations of the input, we design a sentence encoder. We stack several token-level Transformer encoding layers to get the token representations combined with context, take x_w^{l-1} as the input vector of the l-th Transformer layer, then get the hidden state h_t^l and output x_t^l:

$$h_w^l = \text{LayerNorm}(x_t^{l-1} + \text{MHAttn}(x_t^{l-1})), \tag{3}$$

$$x_w^l = \text{LayerNorm}(h_t^l + \text{FFN}(h_t^l)), \tag{4}$$

where LayerNorm denotes the layer normalization [24], MHAttn denotes multi-head attention [23], FFN is a feed-forward layer with ReLU as activation function. We take the output of the last layer $\mathbf{H_t} \in \mathbb{R}^{n_t \times d_t}$ as the token-level representation matrix, where n_w means the length of the input documents and d_t means the dimension of token representation combined with context. In addition, during the encoding, our calculated self-attention is inter-document, which means a token does not focus on tokens outside its belonging document.

To get fixed length sentence representations, we introduce a multi-head pooling mechanism [1]. For each sentence, weight distributions over tokens are calculated, which allows the model to flexibly embed sentences in different representation subspaces by attending to different heads.

$$\mathbf{H_s} = \text{MHPool}(\mathbf{H_t}), \tag{5}$$

where $\mathbf{H_S} \in \mathbb{R}^{n_s \times d_h}$ is the sentence-level representation matrix, n_s is the number of the sentences and d_h is dimension of hidden state. Each row of the matrix corresponds to the embedding of a sentence $s_{i,j}$.

3.2   Graph Encoder

Our graph is based on the similarity of sentences. We first select the document with the largest number of sentences, assuming that the number of sentences is n_{dmax}, and the total sentence number of the whole document cluster is n_{all}, then we build our heterogeneous graph $\mathcal{G} = (\mathcal{V}, \mathcal{E})$. $\mathcal{V}$ includes sentence nodes

$\mathcal{V}_s$ and virtual nodes $\mathcal{V}_v$, and the number of sentence nodes $|\mathcal{V}_s|$ is n_{all}, the number of virtual nodes $|\mathcal{V}_v|$ is n_{dmax}; $\mathcal{E}$ means the undirected edges between nodes, and all the edges are between sentence nodes and virtual nodes or inside virtual nodes. For the sentence nodes $\{v_{1,1}, v_{1,2}, ...v_{1,n_{dmax}}\}$ in the longest document, we calculate their similarity with the sentence nodes in other documents, select the nodes with the highest cosine similarity in each document, establish an edge with a same virtual node, and the edge weight is set to 1. The representations of sentence nodes are the corresponding sentences' embedding, and the representations of virtual nodes are the average of the embedding of all adjacent sentence nodes. We name the virtual node having an edge with $v_{1,i}$ as v_i, add edges between all virtual nodes, and set the edge weight as the cosine similarity between nodes. The specific graph construction process is shown in Fig. 1.

After the construction of graph, we use graph attention networks(GAT) [6] to exchange semantic information between nodes. We use $\mathbf{h_i}, \mathbf{h_j} \in \mathbb{R}^{d_h}$ to denote node representations, e_{ij} to denote the edge weight, where $i, j \in \{1, 2, ..., (n_{all} + n_{dmax})\}$, and use $\mathcal{N}_i$ to denote the neighbouring nodes set. Specifically, GAT is designed as follows:

$$z_{ij} = \text{LeakyReLU}(\mathbf{W}_a[\mathbf{W}_q\mathbf{h}_i; \mathbf{W}_k\mathbf{h}_j]), \tag{6}$$

$$\tilde{z}_{ij} = e_{ij} \times z_{ij}, \tag{7}$$

$$\alpha_{ij} = \frac{\exp(\tilde{z}_{ij})}{\sum_{k \in \mathcal{N}_i} \exp(\tilde{z}_{ik})}, \tag{8}$$

$$\mathbf{u}_i = \sigma\left(\sum_{j \in \mathcal{N}_i} \alpha_{ij}\mathbf{W}_v\mathbf{h}_j\right), \tag{9}$$

where $\mathbf{W_a}, \mathbf{W_j}, \mathbf{W_k}, \mathbf{W_v}$ are learnable matrixs, σ is the sigmod function, and α_{ij} is the attention weight between node $\mathbf{h}_i$ and $\mathbf{h}_j$. Following the process of Zhou [5], we use the edge weight e_{ij} to restrict the flow of information in different nodes. Considering the gradient vanishing after iterations, we also add a residual connection following [25]:

$$\tilde{\mathbf{h}}_i = \mathbf{h}_i + \mathbf{u}_i. \tag{10}$$

We perform many operations in the GAT layer iteratively to make the sentence information flow fully and get reasonable node representations. We believe that these node representations consider the corresponding information of outer-documents and context information of inter-document. After iterating for t times, we fuse sentence representation into token representation, that is, $\mathbf{h}_i$ is spliced into the relevant token representation, then the $\mathbf{H}_t$ arrives at $\tilde{\mathbf{H}}_t \in \mathbb{R}^{n_t \times (d_t + d_h)}$.

3.3   Graph Decoder

In the decoding process, the problem of large search space is serious because of the long input sequence. Thus, we introduce the graph information obtained from the encoder to revise attention, which is specifically applied from two aspects – virtual nodes representations and sentence nodes representations.

Virtual Nodes Representations. We believe that each virtual node represents a non-repetitive section of the input documents, and all virtual nodes jointly represent the overall semantics of input documents, which are very meaningful for the generation of summary. During the decoding process, we take the state of the decoder as $\mathbf{s}$, and compute attention scores over virtual nodes $\mathbf{v}_i$(this $\mathbf{v}_i$ is different from Section Graph Encoder):

$$z_i = \mathbf{u}_0^T \text{LeakyReLU}([\mathbf{W}_{z1}\mathbf{s}; \mathbf{W}_v\mathbf{v}_i]), \tag{11}$$

where $\mathbf{u}_0^T$, $\mathbf{W}_{z1}$ and $\mathbf{W}_v$ are learnable matrix. Then we get the context vector of virtual nodes $\mathbf{c}_v$:

$$\beta_i = \frac{\exp(z_i)}{\sum_{j=1}^{n_{dmax}} \exp(z_j)}, \tag{12}$$

$$\mathbf{c}_v = \sum_{j=1}^{n_{dmax}} \beta_j \times \mathbf{v}_j. \tag{13}$$

Sentence Nodes Representations

We select the sentence nodes directly connected to the k virtual nodes with the highest attention scores β_j and sentence nodes with $0°$. Then we calculate the attention scores of the n_s tokens in these sentences:

$$z_{t_i} = \mathbf{u}_1^T \text{LeakyReLU}([\mathbf{W}_{z2}\mathbf{s}; \mathbf{W}_t\tilde{\mathbf{h}}_{t_i}]), \tag{14}$$

where $\mathbf{u}_1^T$, $\mathbf{W}_{z2}$ and $\mathbf{W}_t$ are learnable matrix, and $\tilde{\mathbf{h}}_{t_i} \in \tilde{\mathbf{H}}_t$. Then we get the context vector of sentence nodes $\mathbf{c}_s$:

$$\gamma_{t_i} = \frac{\exp(z_{t_i})}{\sum_{j=1}^{n_s} \exp(z_j)}, \tag{15}$$

$$\mathbf{c}_s = \sum_{j=1}^{n_s} \gamma_{t_j} \times \mathbf{v}_{t_j}. \tag{16}$$

Token Prediction

Finally the output is computed by concatenating and linearly transforming the state of the decoder $\mathbf{s}_t$, virtual nodes and sentence nodes:

$$P_{vocab} = \text{Softmax}(\mathbf{W}_o[\mathbf{s}_t; \mathbf{c}_v; \mathbf{c}_s]). \tag{17}$$

In addition, we introduced a pointer mechanism [26] to better solve the problem of OOV.

4   Experiments

4.1   Datasets and Experimental Settings

We evaluate our model on two datasets – Multi-News [3] and WikiSum [27].

Multi-News Dataset. Multi-News consists of news articles and human-written summaries of these articles from the site newser.com. It contains 44,972 instances for training, 5,622 for validation, and 5,622 for test.

WikiSum Dataset. Wikisum's source documents correspond to the reference for Wikipedia and the related pages retrieved from the search engine based on the title of Wikipedia. The output is the first paragraph of Wikipedia. We use the top-20 version of WikiSum dataset following the work of Zhou et al. [5]. It contains 300,000 instances for training, 38,144 for validation, and 38,205 for test.

Hyperparameters. Our model contains 4 Transformer encoding layers, and we set the hidden size as 256, the number of heads as 8, and the feed-forward hidden size as 1024. In the multi-head pooling layer, we also set the number of heads as 8. Our model contains 4 graph encoding layers, we set the hidden size as 256, the number of heads as 8. During decoding, we use beam search with beam size 5 and apply length penalty with factor 0.4. We train our model for 200,000 steps using Adam optimizers with learning rate of 0.2, $\beta_1 = 0.9$ and $\beta_2 = 0.998$. The learning rate is varied under a warmup strategy, the warmup steps and the learning rate are 20,000 and 0.002. We apply dropout with a rate of 0.1 before all linear layers and label smoothing of value 0.1.

4.2   Baseline Models

We compare our model **PGSum** with the following extractive and abstractive summarization methods. **LexRank** and **TextRank** [15,16] are two graph-based ranking methods that can be used for extractive summarization. **BaseTransformer** [23] and **CopyTransformer** [28] are models formed by the Transformer structure. BaseTransformer is the vanilla Transformer model. CopyTransformer is a 4-layer Transformer model utilizing the pointer mechanism. **Hierarchical Transformer** [1] is a 7-layer network (with 5 local attention layers at the bottom and 2 global attention layers at the top). **GraphSum** [2] and **EMSum** [5] are two latest graph-based abstractive models combined with pre-trained model.

4.3   Results

Comparison with Baselines
Table 1 lists the evaluation results of different models on the Multi-News and WikiSum datasets. Among them, BT, CT and HT represent BaseTransformer,

Table 1. ROUGE F_1 scores on Multi-News and WikiSum datasets. The results of GraphSum and EMSum are token from Zhou [5].

Model	Multi-News			WikiSum		
	R-1	R-2	R-L	R-1	R-2	R-L
LexRank	38.27	12.70	35.14	36.12	11.67	22.52
TextRank	38.44	13.10	13.50	36.09	11.73	23.16
BT	40.55	12.36	19.98	40.56	25.23	34.73
CT	43.57	14.03	23.02	41.64	26.91	35.75
HT	42.03	15.18	22.79	41.53	26.52	35.76
GraphSum	45.02	16.69	22.50	42.63	27.70	36.97
GraphSum+R	46.07	17.42	23.21	42.99	27.83	37.36
EMSum	45.57	17.71	26.43	42.40	27.97	37.28
EMSum+R	46.89	**18.26**	**27.55**	42.93	28.11	38.19
PGSum	45.66	17.51	25.27	42.87	28.01	37.45
PGSum+R	**47.00**	18.20	25.99	**43.13**	**28.22**	**38.37**

CopyTransformer and Hierarchical Transformer, models name with '+R' mean RoBERTa are used. Compared with the baseline models, our model outperforms all models except EMSum, the gap between PGSum+R and EMSum+R on ROUGE-1, ROUGE-2 and ROUGE-L are $+0.11/-0.06/-1.56(47.00$ vs 46.89, 18.20 vs 18.26, 25.99 vs 27.55). On the WikiSum dataset, our model performs better than other models, the gap between PGSum+R and the second one on ROUGE-1, ROUGE-2 and ROUGE-L are $+0.20/+0.11/+0.18(43.13$ vs 42.93, 28.22 vs 28.11, 38.37 vs 38.19). Considering all the evaluations together, the results show the effectiveness of our model. In addition, combined with RoBERTa, the results show that our model performs better on all metrics, which also proves the effectiveness of our model in the presence of the pre-trained model.

Table 2. Results of ablation experiments on dataset Multi-News and WikiSum.

Model	Multi-News			WikiSum		
	R-1	R-2	R-L	R-1	R-2	R-L
w/o LPE	45.43	17.42	24.99	42.67	27.55	37.14
w/o Graph Encoder	43.87	14.44	23.36	41.89	26.94	36.02
w/o Graph Decoder	44.92	15.61	24.41	42.43	27.06	36.95
PGSum	**45.66**	**17.51**	**25.27**	**42.87**	**28.01**	**37.45**

Model Variant Ablation Studies

Based on the Transformer architecture, PGSum adds multiple mechanisms to improve the performance. We verify the effectiveness of these mechanisms, and the evaluation results are listed in Table 2. For experiments without LPE(w/o LPE), instead of LPE, we use global position encoding, which takes the documents cluster as a long sequence to encode their positions. For the experiment without graph encoder(w/o Graph Encoder), we still calculate the virtual node representation, but we don't use GAT to exchange semantic information. For the experiment without graph(w/o Graph Decoder), we use vanilla Transformer decoder instead of graph decoder. The results show the effectiveness of our newly introduced module. The results of w/o LPE show that local location coding is meaningful for generating summaries. The results of w/o Graph Encoder and w/o Graph Decoder prove that the design of the PGSum is helpful to the flow of information in different documents, and the representation of virtual nodes and sentence nodes can guide the attention distribution of summary generation.

Experiment for Hyperparameter k

Sentence node representation is an important component during decoding. We need to focus on the sentences node related to virtual nodes with top-k attention scores, and we test the model performance at $k = 5, 10, 15, 20$. Figure 2 shows that our model performs best when k is 10. Other experiments in this paper all take k as 10.

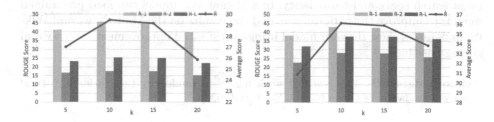

Fig. 2. Results of the experiment for hyperparameter k. The chart on the left shows the results on Multi-News, and the right shows the results on WikiSum. The ordinate value on the left corresponds to the histogram, and the ordinate value on the right corresponds to the line chart. $\dot{R}$ means the average score of R-1, R-2, and R-L.

Manual Evaluation

We selected five volunteers to evaluate the quality of the summaries generated by the PGSum, and three models (CT, HT, PGSum) are used to generate summaries. Volunteers are asked to evaluate the quality of summaries from five aspects, including grammar, non-redundancy(ND), referential clarity(RC), focus and structure & coherence(S&C). In the scoring strategy, the same Best-Worst Scaling method as Fabbri [3] is adopted.

Table 3. Results of manual evaluation on five metrics

Model	Grammar	NC	RC	Focus	S&C
CT	−0.030	−0.055	0.015	−0.120	−0.035
HT	**0.015**	−0.050	−0.040	0.030	−0.015
PGSum	**0.015**	**0.105**	**0.025**	**0.090**	**0.050**

Table 3 shows the results of human evaluation on five metrics. From the results, our model gets the best performance in all aspects (the same as HT in grammar), and the score on NC is prominent. We think that the virtual nodes revise the attention of the decoder, and reduce the redundancy of the generated summary.

5 Conclusion

In this paper, we propose an MDS model considering the parallel information of documents with a heterogeneous graph. We introduce the construction method of the graph, which helps the information of the same content between different documents have better representation; and we design an encoder and decoder structure that can use graph information. With such a novel design, our model can capture cross-document relations better, and solve the problems of large search space and redundancy. In addition, our model can load pre-trained models to improve the performance, and the results on the Multi-News and WikiSum datasets show that our model brings substantial improvements over several strong baselines.

Acknowledgments. This research work has been funded by the National Natural Science Foundation of China (Grant No. U21B2020).

References

1. Liu, Y., Lapata, M.: Hierarchical transformers for multi-document summarization. arXiv preprint arXiv:1905.13164 (2019)
2. Li, W., Xiao, X., Liu, J., Wu, H., Wang, H., Du, J.: Leveraging graph to improve abstractive multi-document summarization. arXiv preprint arXiv:2005.10043 (2020)
3. Fabbri, A.R., Li, I., She, T., Li, S., Radev, D.R.: Multi-news: A large-scale multi-document summarization dataset and abstractive hierarchical model. arXiv preprint arXiv:1906.01749 (2019)
4. Radev, D.: A common theory of information fusion from multiple text sources step one: cross-document structure. In: 1st SIGdial Workshop on Discourse and Dialogue, pp. 74–83 (2000)
5. Zhou, H., Ren, W., Liu, G., Su, B., Lu, W.: Entity-aware abstractive multi-document summarization. In: Findings of the Association for Computational Linguistics: ACL-IJCNLP 2021, pp. 351–362 (2021)

6. Veličković, P., Cucurull, G., Casanova, A., Romero, A., Lio, P., Bengio, Y.: Graph attention networks. arXiv preprint arXiv:1710.10903 (2017)
7. Banerjee, S., Mitra, P., Sugiyama, K.: Multi-document abstractive summarization using ILP based multi-sentence compression. In: Twenty-Fourth International Joint Conference on Artificial Intelligence (2015)
8. Li, W., Zhuge, H.: Abstractive multi-document summarization based on semantic link network. In: IEEE Transactions on Knowledge and Data Engineering (2019)
9. Bing, L., Li, P., Liao, Y., Lam, W., Guo, W., Passonneau, R.J.: Abstractive multi-document summarization via phrase selection and merging. arXiv preprint arXiv:1506.01597 (2015)
10. Chu, E., Liu, P.: Meansum: a neural model for unsupervised multi-document abstractive summarization. In: International Conference on Machine Learning, pp. 1223–1232. PMLR (2019)
11. Zhang, J., Tan, J., Wan, X.: Adapting neural single-document summarization model for abstractive multi-document summarization: a pilot study. In: Proceedings of the 11th International Conference on Natural Language Generation, pp. 381–390 (2018)
12. Lebanoff, L., Song, K., Liu, F.: Adapting the neural encoder-decoder framework from single to multi-document summarization. arXiv preprint arXiv:1808.06218 (2018)
13. Pasunuru, R., et al.: Data augmentation for abstractive query-focused multi-document summarization. In: Proceedings of the AAAI Conference on Artificial Intelligence, vol. 35, pp. 13666–13674 (2021)
14. Lebanoff, L., Wang, B., Feng, Z., Liu, F.: Modeling endorsement for multi-document abstractive summarization. In: Proceedings of the Third Workshop on New Frontiers in Summarization, pp. 119–130 (2021)
15. Erkan, G., Radev, D.R.: LexRank: graph-based lexical centrality as salience in text summarization. J. Artif. Intell. Res. **22**, 457–479 (2004)
16. Mihalcea, R., Tarau, P.: TextRank: bringing order into text. In: Proceedings of the 2004 Conference on Empirical Methods in Natural Language Processing, pp. 404–411 (2004)
17. Wan, X.: An exploration of document impact on graph-based multi-document summarization. In: Proceedings of the 2008 Conference on Empirical Methods in Natural Language Processing, pp. 755–762 (2008)
18. Tan, J., Wan, X., Xiao, J.: Abstractive document summarization with a graph-based attentional neural model. In: Proceedings of the 55th Annual Meeting of the Association for Computational Linguistics (Volume 1: Long Papers), pp. 1171–1181 (2017)
19. Huang, L., Wu, L., Wang, L.: Knowledge graph-augmented abstractive summarization with semantic-driven cloze reward. arXiv preprint arXiv:2005.01159 (2020)
20. Christensen, J., Soderland, S., Etzioni, O., et al.: Towards coherent multi-document summarization. In: Proceedings of the 2013 Conference of the North American Chapter of the Association for Computational Linguistics: Human Language Technologies, pp. 1163–1173 (2013)
21. Fan, A., Gardent, C., Braud, C., Bordes, A.: Using local knowledge graph construction to scale seq2seq models to multi-document inputs. arXiv preprint arXiv:1910.08435 (2019)
22. Bahdanau, D., Cho, K., Bengio, Y.: Neural machine translation by jointly learning to align and translate. arXiv preprint arXiv:1409.0473 (2014)
23. Vaswani, A., et al.: Attention is all you need. In: Advances in Neural Information Processing Systems, pp. 5998–6008 (2017)

24. Ba, J.L., Kiros, J.R., Hinton, G.E.: Layer normalization. arXiv preprint arXiv:1607.06450 (2016)
25. Wang, D., Liu, P., Zheng, Y., Qiu, X., Huang, X.J.: Heterogeneous graph neural networks for extractive document summarization. In: Proceedings of the 58th Annual Meeting of the Association for Computational Linguistics, pp. 6209–6219 (2020)
26. See, A., Liu, P.J., Manning, C.D.: Get to the point: summarization with pointer-generator networks. arXiv preprint arXiv:1704.04368 (2017)
27. Liu, P.J., et al.: Generating wikipedia by summarizing long sequences. arXiv preprint arXiv:1801.10198 (2018)
28. Gehrmann, S., Deng, Y., Rush, A.M.: Bottom-up abstractive summarization. In: Proceedings of the 2018 Conference on Empirical Methods in Natural Language Processing, pp. 4098–4109 (2018)

SNNet: Specific Node Network of Human Parsing

Zhenyang Wang, Shaoyang Wang, Pingmu Huang, and Tiejun Lv[✉]

Beijing University of Posts and Telecommunications, Beijing, China
{wangzy0403,shaoyangwang,pmhuang,lvtiejun}@bupt.edu.cn

Abstract. Recent works have made significant progress in human parsing by exploiting the hierarchical human structure. However, their modeling of human body is incomplete and how to generate adaptive contextual features for various shapes and sizes of human parts is still a challenge. In order to model more complete and specific human body, this paper proposes a novel Specific Node Network (SNNet), comprised of three modules: the node extract module, the low-high module and multi-set union module. The node extract module aims at extracting the features that represent the characteristics of each human part from backbone as a node for each human part. The low-high module aims at modeling the complex relations (including the inner and inter relations) between the human parts from the low aspect, normal aspect and high aspect, where the normal aspect means the direct modeling of connected human parts, the low aspect means the hidden modeling of human parts via less human parts than the normal aspect, and the high aspect means the hidden modeling of human parts via more human parts than the normal aspect, and we model the relations from two aspects: inner and inter. Multi-set union module aims at modeling the human parts more specific by considering the human parts as different sets such as the part set, half-body set and full-body set. Our experiments show that the node extract module can generate the node with better representations of human parts. The low-high module and multi-set union module can generate adaptive contextual features for various sizes and shapes of human parts.

Keywords: Human parsing · Graph neural network · Adaptive contextual feature

1 Introduction

Human parsing is an important branch of image segmentation, and aims to predict pixels in an image as one of the predefined categories of parts including head, torso, etc. The human parsing, as a human-oriented intelligent visual processing portal, provides the data support for higher-level tasks, widely used in various fields, such as human behavior analysis [1], person re-identification [2],

© The Author(s), under exclusive license to Springer Nature Switzerland AG 2022
E. Pimenidis et al. (Eds.): ICANN 2022, LNCS 13530, pp. 643–655, 2022.
https://doi.org/10.1007/978-3-031-15931-2_53

and human-robot interaction [3]. Although the existing studies on human parsing have made some progress in the above fields, it is still a challenging task, due to the complexity of data in instance scenarios.

The existing studies have focused on exploiting the structural features of the human body to obtain more accurate segmentation results. Ji *et al.* [4] utilized a tree structure to segment multiple semantic subregions, but only modeled the decomposition relation. The decomposition relation is one of three kinds of part relations: decomposition, composition, and dependency. For addressing this difficulty, Wang *et al.* [5] constructed the characteristic nodes of each part of the human body, then used the Graph Neural Network (GNN) to analysis all three part relations. But this work failed to generate adaptive contextual features.

Against the above backdrops, this paper proposes the Specific Node Network(SNNet), composed of the node extract module, the low-high module and the multi-set union module. The node extract module extracts the features representing the characteristics of each part of human body. Instead of separating features directly like [6], we extract different channel importance from the backbone features. Then, the low-high module, containing two hidden parts, is designed to model the relations between the body parts. Further, similar to [7], we also present the multi-set union module to directly model the relations between the parts of the human body. In this paper, the low-high module and the multi-set union module are constructed by Graph Convolutional Networks (GCNs) [13], and then can generate adaptive contextual features by calculating dynamic convolution kernels. The major contributions of this paper are summarized as follows:

1. We propose a new node extract module, which can better extract part of node features before entering the other two modules.
2. We design a new low-high module, which can characterize the relations of the human parts more explicitly and completely from the normal, low, and high aspects, and generate the dynamic convolutions for representative global features and distinguishable local features.
3. We present a new multi-set union module, which can directly model the relations of the human parts to augment the body features modeled in the low-high module.

2   Related Works

2.1   Human Parsing

Recently, the human parsing has attracted a lot of attention. To measure multi-scale features, Chen *et al.* [9] proposed an attention module, and Gong *et al.* [10] proposed a pyramid pooling module. In both studies, the human body structure was neglected. In order to take advantage of the highly structured properties of the human body, the use of pose and edge information is an effective method. Zhang *et al.* [11] proposed a non-local block to correlate the two. However, their studies to explore the structure of the human body were still insufficient.

Ji *et al.* [4] used a top-down framework, but only considered decomposition relations. In this paper, the node extract module we propose can better extract nodes. Specifically, our low-high module can not only model human relations at different levels, but also generate contextual relations. In [7], the authors explored to augment the dataset via GNN. Inspired by this, we design a multi-set union module to enhance the dataset distilled from the original dataset.

2.2 Graph Reasoning

GNNs can learn graph representations in an end-to-end manner. Recently many researches have explored to model domain knowledge as a graph, in order to find the correlations among objects in images. This approach has been proven effective in many domains like human-re-id [12]. The human body is a typical topology structure with skeleton constraints and high hierarchical feature. In [5–7], these authors made efforts to mine the relation between body parts. In this paper, both our low-high and multi-set union modules can model the relations between body parts, by leveraging GNNs, yielding superior results [13].

3 Specific Node Network

3.1 Overall Framework

The overall framework of SNNet is shown in Fig. 1. The backbone is ResNet-101 [14] (pretrained on ImageNet [15]). SNNet consists of three modules: node extraction module, low-high module and multi-set joint module. The node extraction module takes the backbone feature F_b as input, and outputs part feature, half feature and full feature respectively. Part feature is used as the input of the low-high module, and the dynamic convolution kernel θ is obtained. At the same time, the three features are jointly used as the input of the multi-set joint module, and the dynamic convolution kernel ω is calculated after processing. In order to better explore the relation between different levels of the human body, the features F_{lh} and F_m are obtained by convolution of F_b and θ, ω respectively. The features F_b, F_{lh} and F_m are concatenated to get the final segmentation result. ©️ indicates the concatenation operation. Next, the proposed node extract module, low-high module and multi-set union module are explained in detail.

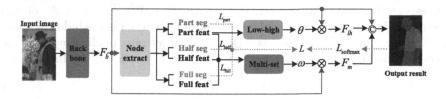

Fig. 1. Overview of the proposed specific node network.

3.2 Node Extract Module

In this module, the channel importance can be learned from the feature of backbone. We transform feature input $F_b \in \mathbb{R}^{C \times H \times W}$ into $\mathbb{R}^{C \times 6 \times 6}$ by the global average pooling (GAP) layer, and reshape $\mathbb{R}^{C \times 6 \times 6}$ to $\mathbb{R}^{C \times 36}$ by using convolution and ReLU and convolution layers. Then, based on a fully connected (FC) layer, $\mathbb{R}^{C \times 36}$ can be converted to $\mathbb{R}^{C \times 6}$. Through a softmax layer, the channel importance can be obtained from the $\mathbb{R}^{C \times 6}$. Next, we apply the normalized result to F and get two kinds of output: the node feature $\mathbb{R}^{H \times W}$, and the node output $\mathbb{R}^{2 \times H \times W}$. $\mathbb{R}^{2 \times H \times W}$ is used to constrain $\mathbb{R}^{H \times W}$ to learn the useful structure information. Figure 2 shows the process of node extract module. Then the concatenation results of all node features can be put into the low-high module.

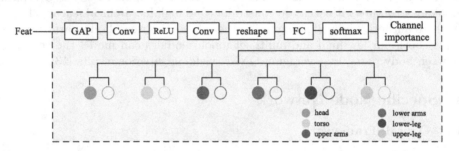

Fig. 2. The process of node extract module. The circles with different colors represent different features, and the corresponding hollow circles represent the segmentation results. (Color figure online)

3.3 Low-High Module

Unlike [5], using Message Passing Graph Networks (MPGNs) [16], this paper uses GCNs to model the relation between nodes. Usually, the GCN possesses the advantages of simple structure and low complexity (one adjacency matrix and weight matrix are enough to model the entire layer of GCN), and the modeling ability is strong.

The low-high module contains three aspects: normal aspect, low aspect and high aspect. In the normal aspect, the feature $F_i \in \mathbb{R}^{H \times W}, i \in [1, N]$ of each node is obtained from the node extraction module, where i is the index of nodes, and N is the number of body parts. By using an average pooling layer, F_i can be transformed into $F_i' \in \mathbb{R}^{h \times w}$, and reshape it to a graph node by function ϕ_n:

$$X_{ni} = \phi_n(F_i'), \tag{1}$$

where X_{ni} is the feature matrix of the ith node, and $X_n \in \mathbb{R}^{N \times D}$ is the overall feature matrix, $D = hw$ and D is the feature dimension for each category. Define the relation semantics as a graph $G(V, E)$, where V is the vertex set (human part set) and E is the edge set (relation set). Then, the adjacency matrix $A \in \mathbb{R}^{N \times N}$ can be defined as:

$$A_{ij} = \frac{e^{r_{ij}}}{\sum_{j=1}^{m} e^{r_{ij}}}, \tag{2}$$

where r_{ij} is the score of the semantic relation between two parts. The score can be calculated by using the cosine similarity f:

$$r_{ij} = f(v_i, v_j), \tag{3}$$

where $v_i, v_j \in \mathbb{R}^{1 \times D}$ are two adjacent nodes, m is the number of adjacent nodes of i. Let $W_n \in \mathbb{R}^{D \times D}$ denote the weight of graph convolution. Finally, the output of the graph convolution layer can be given by:

$$Z_n = \sigma(A X_n W_n), \tag{4}$$

where σ is the activation function such as ReLU.

In lower aspect, this paper constructs a set with less number of nodes than normal aspect. The lower aspect aims to model the relation between human body in a lower aspect (such as upper body and lower body). Let the number of nodes in lower part be N_l, the graph be $G_l(V_l, E_l)$. Define the feature matrix be $X_l \in \mathbb{R}^{N_l \times D}$, the adjacent matrix be $A_l \in \mathbb{R}^{N_l \times N_l}$ and the weight be $W_l \in \mathbb{R}^{D \times D}$. X_l is constructed from X_n:

$$X_l = M_l X_n, \tag{5}$$

where $M_l \in \mathbb{R}^{N_l \times N}$ is a learnable matrix. The adjacent matrix A_l is constructed from A:

$$A_l = P_l^T A P_l, \tag{6}$$

where $P_l \in \mathbb{R}^{N \times N_l}$ is a learnable matrix. Then the output of the graph convolution layer can be represented by:

$$Z_l = \sigma(A_l X_l W_l), \tag{7}$$

In higher aspect, this paper constructs a set with more number of nodes than normal aspect. The higher aspect aims to model the relation between human body in a higher aspect (like the more specific parts: upper torso and lower torso). It is similar to lower aspect like $X_h \in \mathbb{R}^{N_h \times D}, A_h \in \mathbb{R}^{N_h \times N_h}, W_h \in \mathbb{R}^{N_h \times D}, M_h \in \mathbb{R}^{N_h \times N}, P_h \in \mathbb{R}^{N \times N_h}$:

$$X_h = M_h X_n, \tag{8}$$

$$A_h = P_h^T A P_h, \tag{9}$$

$$Z_h = \sigma(A_h X_h W_h). \tag{10}$$

Finally, the feature $Z_f \in \mathbb{R}^{N \times D}$ can be obtained by:

$$Z_f = Z_n + Z_l + Z_h. \tag{11}$$

Feature Z_f first passes through an transform matrix with size of $N \times k^2$ and then is reshaped to $D \times k \times k$, where k is the kernel size. Finally, a convolution with size of $c_i \times k \times k$ is performed to obtain the dynamic convolution kernel θ'. Note that $c_i = C$, C is the number of channels of the original features, and define c_o as the number of channels of the output features. At last, the final kernel $\theta \in \mathbb{R}^{c_i \times c_o \times k \times k}$ can be obtained through auxiliary parameters $U \in \mathbb{R}^{c_i \times c_o \times 1 \times 1}$ and $V \in \mathbb{R}^{c_i \times c_i \times 1 \times 1}$ by:

$$\theta = U \otimes \theta'_c \otimes_c V, \tag{12}$$

where $\otimes_c$ denotes the channel-wise convolution operation. Then define the final feature be F_{lh}:

$$F_{lh} = \sigma(\theta \otimes F_b), \tag{13}$$

where F_b is the feature from backbone.

3.4   Multi-set Union Module

There is no mandatory distinction between the low and high levels modeled in the low-high module. In such implicit modeling, the boundaries between different levels are blurred, and the probability of similar features being misjudged increases. Especially in complex scenes with overlapping, the segmentation accuracy is significantly reduced. Therefore, multi-set module we proposed analyzes human body part relations directly. Multi-set is a collection of constructions from part body to half and full body.

In this paper, define the inner graph convolution represent the graph convolution inside one set, and define the inter graph convolution represent the graph convolution between one set and another set. The inner graph convolution is similar to the normal part. For inter graph convolution, the transfer matrix need to be considered, as shown in Fig. 3. Following [7], we take semantic similarity as the transfer matrix. Define A_{ij}^{ab} as the transfer value between two set a and b:

$$A_{ij}^{ab} = \frac{e^{s_{ij}}}{\sum_{j=1}^{N_b} e^{s_{ij}}}, \tag{14}$$

where s_{ij} is the cosine similarity between the word embedding vector of ith node in set a nd the jth node in set b. The word embedding vector is constructed by word2vec model [17].

Let a denote the source set and b denote the target set, the inter graph convolution is defined as:

$$Z_b = Z_b + \sigma(A^{ab} Z_a W_{ab}), \tag{15}$$

where $Z_a \in \mathbb{R}^{N_a \times D}, Z_b \in \mathbb{R}^{N_b \times D}, A^{ab} \in \mathbb{R}^{N_b \times N_a}, W_{ab} \in \mathbb{R}^{D \times D}$.

Let the part feature set X_p be the target set, and let the full-body set X_f be the source set, then the result Z_p^1 can be obtained. Let the part feature set X_p be the target set, and let the half-body set X_h be the source set, then the result Z_p^2 can be obtained. By adding Z_p^1 and Z_p^2, a new part feature set Z_p^m can be

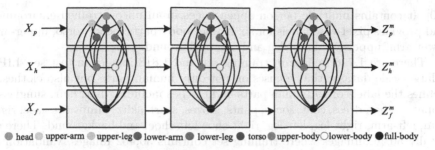

Fig. 3. The process of graph convolution in the multi-set module. The three feature sets X_p, X_h and X_f have undergone three sets of inner-graph convolution and inter-graph convolution, respectively.

obtained. Hence, we can get we get three features from three sets: Z_p^m, Z_h^m, Z_f^m belongs to part body set, half body set and full body set. Based on these three features, we have:

$$Z^m = Z_p^m + Z_h^m + Z_f^m. \tag{16}$$

By using the process similar to Eq. (12), the dynamic convolution kernel ω can be calculated from Z^m. Finally, based on F_b, the enhanced feature output by the multi-set union module can be given by:

$$F_m = \sigma(\omega \otimes F_b). \tag{17}$$

3.5 Loss Function

The node extract module has achieved the part body segmentation, half body segmentation and full body segmentation. The segmentation is the result of each part $\in \mathbb{R}^{H \times W}$ (if the pixel belongs to that part then the label is 1; otherwise 0), as for part body segmentation $\mathbb{R}^{7 \times H \times W}$, half body segmentation $\mathbb{R}^{3 \times H \times W}$, full body segmentation $\mathbb{R}^{2 \times H \times W}$. The overall loss function is:

$$L = L_{\text{softmax}} + \lambda_1 L_{\text{part}} + \lambda_2 L_{\text{half}} + \lambda_3 L_{\text{full}}, \tag{18}$$

where L_{softmax} is the softmax cross entropy between the final result and the ground truth, L_{part}, L_{half} and L_{full} are the crosses entropy between part, half, full body and the corresponding ground truth. We try to set the losses λ_1, λ_2, λ_3, and between 0 and 1. At the end of our method, $\lambda_1 = 0.5$, $\lambda_2 = 0.2$, $\lambda_3 = 0.3$ yield the best results.

4 Experiments

4.1 Datasets

We evaluate our algorithm on PASCAL-Person-Part [18] and LIP [19]. PASCAL-Person-Part dataset is a set of additional annotations from PASCAL-VOC-2010

[20]. It contains multiple person appearances in an unconstrained environment and provides pixel-wise labels for six human body parts: head, torso, upper-arm, lower-arm, upper-leg, lower-leg and one background.

There are 1,716 images in training set and 1,818 images in test set. LIP is a large-scale dataset that focuses on not only human parts but also clothes. It defines the labels of 19 human parts and clothes including hat, hair, sunglasses, upper-clothes, dress, coat, socks, pants, gloves, scarf, skirt, jumpsuits, face, right-arm, left-arm, right-leg, left-leg, right-shoe left-shoe, and background. There are totally 50,462 images where training set contains 30,462 images, validation set and test set both contain 10,000 images.

We evaluate the mean Intersection over Union(mIoU) of our network in experiments of the two datasets.

4.2   Implementation Details

We use ResNet-101 [14] (pretrained on ImageNet [15]) as baseline, and the output feature is 8× smaller than the input. For PASCAL-Person-Part, the number of nodes in node extract module is 6 for part feat, 2 for half feat and 1 for full feat. For LIP, the number of nodes in node extract module is 19 for part feat, 2 for half feat and 1 for full feat. The feature dimension D of each node is 128. Both the low-high GNN module and multi-set module have three graph convolution layers with ReLU activate function.

The input images are resized to 512×512 for PASCAL-Person-Part and 473×473 both for LIP. During the training stage, the data augmentation method is adopted, such as random scales (from 0.5 to 1.5), cropping and horizontal flipping. The batch sizes are both 8 per GPU. All the models are trained using stochastic gradient (SGD) solver with momentum 0.9 and weight decay 5×10^{-4}, and the epochs are both 150.

Table 1. Ablation study of SNNet. The result is from the val set of PASCAL-PERSON-PART. Node extract stands for node extract module. LH-1,2,3,4 means low-high module with 1,2,3,4 GCN layers. MS-1,2,3,4 represents a multi-set union module with 1,2,3,4 GCN layers.

#	Baseline	Node extract	LH-1	LH-2	LH-3	LH-4	MS-1	MS-2	MS-3	MS-4	MIoU
1	✓										67.10
2	✓	✓									69.06
3	✓	✓	✓								70.14
4	✓	✓		✓							71.53
5	✓	✓			✓						72.48
6	✓	✓				✓					72.12
7	✓	✓			✓		✓				73.14
8	✓	✓			✓			✓			73.98
9	✓	✓			✓				✓		74.76
10	✓	✓			✓					✓	74.39

4.3   Ablation Study

We conduct all our ablation study with DeeplabV3 as backbone network and report all the performances on PASCAL-Person-Part validation set.

Ablation for the Node Extract Module. We remove the low-high module and multi-set union module in Fig. 1, and concatenate part feat, half feat, full feat and F_b as the final feature. The experimental results are shown in Table 1# 2. The introduction of the node extract module increased the mIoU on the PASCAL-Person-Part validation set from 67.10 to 69.06.

Ablation for the Low-High Module. We keep the node extract module to test the low-high module of GCNs with different layers. It can be seen that mIoU increases with the number of GCN layers, but decreases when the number of layers is four. In our experiments, setting more layers keeps mIoU around 72.10. When there are three layers, the optimal mIoU is 72.48 (Table 1# 5).

Table 2. Detailed comparisons of PASCAL-Person-Part with the baseline (ResNet-101) and other networks.

Method	mIoU	FLOPs	Memory	Params
ResNet-101	67.10	190.3G	2.601G	42.4M
DeeplabV3	68.32	+62.9G	+64M	+15.2M
CE2P	69.22	+60.9G	+59M	+20M
PCNet	74.59	+42.2G	+30.1M	+11.4M
SNNet (ours)	74.76	+50.1G	+39.2M	+17.8M

Ablation for the Multi-set Union Module. In this section, we keep the node extract module and the three-layer low-high module to test the multi-set union module of GCNs with different layers. Similarly, the results show that the three-layer multi-set union module performs the best with an mIoU of 74.76 (Table 1#9). When the number of layers exceeds three, the mIoU remains around 74.40.

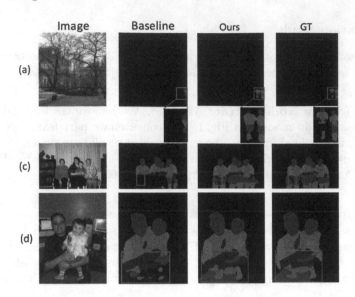

Fig. 4. Qualitative comparison SNNet results on val set of PASCAL-Person-Part.

Ablation for the Computation. Table 2 compare the computation of SNNet with DeeplabV3, CE2P [8] and PCNet [6] on validation set of PASCAL-Person-Part. Table 2 lists the mIoU, FLOPs, memory cost and parameter number. It can be seen that our SNNet has the best performance of 74.76 of mIoU among other networks.

Qualitative Comparison. The qualitative comparison results of PASCAL-Person-Part are shown in Fig. 4, SNNet segmented different human body parts more accurately. As can be seen from the figure, SNNet can perform better in images with cluttered scenes and smaller human size, and can segment human body parts more accurately. Because our low-high module and multi-set union module can generate representative global features to segment the foreground, and can also generate discriminative local features to segment human body parts.

4.4 Comparison of State of Art

Results on PASCAL-Person-Part. We compare our method with many human parsing methods including Joint [21], WSHP [22], PGN [23], Learning [24], Graphonomy [7], DPC [25] and PCNet [6]. In Table 3, our method outperforms other methods on all categories except upper-arm and background of PASCAL-Person-Part and it achieves state-of-the-art performance: 74.76.

Table 3. Performance comparison of mIoU with other methods on PASCAL-PERSON-PART.

Methods	head	torso	u-arm	l-arm	u-leg	l-leg	bkg	mIoU
Joint	85.50	67.87	54.72	54.30	48.25	44.78	95.32	64.39
WSHP	87.15	72.28	57.07	56.21	52.43	50.36	97.72	67.60
PGN	90.89	75.12	55.83	64.61	55.42	41.47	95.33	68.40
Learning	88.02	72.91	64.31	63.52	55.61	54.96	96.02	70.76
Graphonomy	-	-	-	-	-	-	-	71.14
DPC	88.81	74.54	63.85	63.73	57.24	54.55	96.66	71.34
PCNet	90.04	76.89	**69.11**	68.40	60.78	60.14	**96.78**	74.59
SNNet (ours)	**90.11**	**77.10**	68.89	**69.04**	**61.10**	**60.52**	96.55	**74.76**

Results on LIP. We compare our method with previous networks on the validation set of LIP including Attention [9], LIP [19], JPPNet [19], CE2P [19], and PCNet [6]. As shown in Table 4, our method outperforms all previous works and it achieves the mIoU of 57.72 on the LIP.

Table 4. Performance comparison of mIoU with other methods on PASCAL-PERSON-PART.

Method	Attention	LIP	MMAN	JPPNet	CE2P	Braidet	PCNet	SNNet (ours)
hat	58.87	59.75	57.66	63.55	65.29	66.8	69.32	**69.78**
hair	66.78	67.25	66.63	70.20	72.54	72.0	73.08	**74.10**
glov	23.32	28.95	30.70	36.16	39.09	42.5	44.72	**44.87**
sung	19.48	21.57	20.02	23.48	32.73	32.1	34.21	**34.97**
clot	63.20	65.30	64.15	68.15	69.46	69.8	72.59	**72.82**
dress	29.63	29.49	28.39	31.42	32.52	33.7	36.02	**37.15**
coat	49.70	51.92	51.98	55.65	56.28	57.4	60.84	**60.96**
sock	35.23	38.52	41.46	44.56	49.67	49.0	51.03	**52.34**
pant	66.04	68.02	71.03	72.19	74.11	74.9	76.66	**77.58**
suit	24.73	24.48	23.61	28.39	27.23	32.4	38.78	**39.21**
acarf	12.84	14.92	9.65	18.76	14.19	19.3	31.60	**31.87**
skirt	20.41	24.32	23.20	25.14	22.51	27.2	33.94	**34.52**
face	70.58	71.01	68.54	73.36	75.50	74.9	76.65	**76.95**
l-arm	50.17	52.64	55.30	61.97	65.14	65.5	67.07	**68.23**
r-arm	54.03	55.79	58.13	63.88	66.59	67.9	68.74	**69.31**
l-leg	38.35	40.23	51.90	58.21	60.10	60.2	60.22	**61.04**
r-leg	37.70	38.30	52.17	57.99	58.59	59.6	60.16	**61.28**
l-sh	26.20	28.08	38.58	44.02	46.63	47.4	47.65	**48.32**
r-sh	27.09	29.03	39.05	44.09	46.12	47.9	48.67	**49.65**
bkg	84.00	84.56	84.75	86.26	87.67	88.0	88.68	**89.17**
mIoU	42.92	44.73	46.81	51.37	53.10	54.4	57.03	**57.72**

5 Conclusion

In this work, we propose a novel Specific Node Network(SNNet) which significantly improves the performances on human parsing. Our method can reach the state of the art result of mIoU on both PASCAL-Person-Part and LIP. The node extract module can extract the characteristics of each human body part as the node of GCN. The low-high module models the human body parts relations in three levels and two hidden parts, generating a dynamic convolution kernel to get the capability of generating adaptive contextual features. The multi-set union module models the human body parts in visual aspect and makes two constructed sets from original set to strengthen the human body relation.

References

1. Fan, L., Wang, W., Huang, S., Tang, X., Zhu, S.-C.: Understanding human gaze communication by spatio-temporal graph reasoning (2019)
2. Farenzena, M., Bazzani, L., Perina, A., Murino, V., Cristani, M.: Person reidentification by symmetry-driven accumulation of local features. In: 2010 IEEE Computer Society Conference on Computer Vision and Pattern Recognition, pp. 2360–2367. IEEE (2010)
3. Fang, H.-S., Wang, C., Gou, M., Lu, C.: GraspNet: a large-scale clustered and densely annotated dataset for object grasping. arXiv preprint arXiv:1912.13470 (2019)
4. Ji, R., et al.: Learning semantic neural tree for human parsing. In: Vedaldi, A., Bischof, H., Brox, T., Frahm, J.-M. (eds.) ECCV 2020. LNCS, vol. 12358, pp. 205–221. Springer, Cham (2020). https://doi.org/10.1007/978-3-030-58601-0_13
5. Wang, W., Zhu, H., Dai, J., Pang, Y., Shen, J., Shao, L.: Hierarchical human parsing with typed part-relation reasoning. In: Proceedings of the IEEE/CVF Conference on Computer Vision and Pattern Recognition, pp. 8929–8939 (2020)
6. Zhang, X., Chen, Y., Zhu, B., Wang, J., Tang, M.: Part-aware context network for human parsing. In: Proceedings of the IEEE/CVF Conference on Computer Vision and Pattern Recognition, pp. 8971–8980 (2020)
7. Gong, K., Gao, Y., Liang, X., Shen, X., Wang, M., Lin, L.: Graphonomy: universal human parsing via graph transfer learning. In: Proceedings of the IEEE/CVF Conference on Computer Vision and Pattern Recognition, pp. 7450–7459 (2019)
8. Ruan, T., Liu, T., Huang, Z., Wei, Y., Wei, S., Zhao, Y.: Devil in the details: towards accurate single and multiple human parsing. In: Proceedings of the AAAI Conference on Artificial Intelligence, vol. 33, no. 01, pp. 4814–4821 (2019)
9. Chen, L.-C., Yang, Y., Wang, J., Xu, W., Yuille, A.L.: Attention to scale: scale-aware semantic image segmentation. In: Proceedings of the IEEE Conference on Computer Vision and Pattern Recognition, pp. 3640–3649 (2016)
10. Gong, K., Liang, X., Li, Y., Chen, Y., Yang, M., Lin, L.: Instance-level human parsing via part grouping network. In: Proceedings of the European Conference on Computer Vision (ECCV), pp. 770–785 (2018)
11. Zhang, Z., Su, C., Zheng, L., Xie, X.: Correlating edge, pose with parsing (2020)
12. Ye, M., Shen, J.: Probabilistic structural latent representation for unsupervised embedding. In: Proceedings of the IEEE/CVF Conference on Computer Vision and Pattern Recognition, pp. 5457–5466 (2020)

13. Kipf, T.N., Welling, M.: Semi-supervised classification with graph convolutional networks. arXiv preprint arXiv:1609.02907 (2016)
14. He, K., Zhang, X., Ren, S., Sun, J.: Deep residual learning for image recognition. In: Proceedings of the IEEE Conference on Computer Vision and Pattern Recognition, pp. 770–778 (2016)
15. Russakovsky, O., et al.: ImageNet large scale visual recognition challenge. Int. J. Comput. Vision **115**(3), 211–252 (2015)
16. Gilmer, J., Schoenholz, S.S., Riley, P.F., Vinyals, O., Dahl, G.E.: Neural message passing for quantum chemistry. In: International Conference on Machine Learning, pp. 1263–1272. PMLR (2017)
17. Pennington, J., Socher, R., Manning, C.D.: Glove: global vectors for word representation. In: Proceedings of the 2014 Conference on Empirical Methods in Natural Language Processing (EMNLP), pp. 1532–1543 (2014)
18. Chen, X., Mottaghi, R., Liu, X., Fidler, S., Urtasun, R., Yuille, A.: Detect what you can: detecting and representing objects using holistic models and body parts. In: Proceedings of the IEEE Conference on Computer Vision and Pattern Recognition, pp. 1971–1978 (2014)
19. Gong, K., Liang, X., Zhang, D., Shen, X., Lin, L.: Look into person: self-supervised structure-sensitive learning and a new benchmark for human parsing. In: Proceedings of the IEEE Conference on Computer Vision and Pattern Recognition, pp. 932–940 (2017)
20. Everingham, M., Van Gool, L., Williams, C.K., Winn, J., Zisserman, A.: The pascal visual object classes (VOC) challenge. Int. J. Comput. Vision **88**(2), 303–338 (2010)
21. Xia, F., Peng, W., Chen, X., Yuille, A.: Joint multi-person pose estimation and semantic part segmentation. IEEE (2017)
22. Fang, H.S., Lu, G., Fang, X., Xie, J., Tai, Y.W., Lu, C.: Weakly and semi supervised human body part parsing via pose-guided knowledge transfer. IEEE (2018)
23. Gong, K., Liang, X., Li, Y., Chen, Y., Yang, M., Lin, L.: Instance-level human parsing via part grouping network. In: Ferrari, V., Hebert, M., Sminchisescu, C., Weiss, Y. (eds.) ECCV 2018. LNCS, vol. 11208, pp. 805–822. Springer, Cham (2018). https://doi.org/10.1007/978-3-030-01225-0_47
24. Wang, W., Zhang, Z., Qi, S., Shen, J., Shao, L.: Learning compositional neural information fusion for human parsing. In: ICCV 2019 (2019)
25. Chen, L.C., et al.: Searching for efficient multi-scale architectures for dense image prediction (2018)

Spatial-Temporal Attention Network for Crime Prediction with Adaptive Graph Learning

Mingjie Sun[1,2], Pengyuan Zhou[1,2], Hui Tian[3], Yong Liao[1,2],
and Haiyong Xie[2,4(✉)]

[1] University of Science and Technology of China, Hefei, China
[2] Key Laboratory of Cyberculture Content Cognition and Detection, Hefei, China
mjsun@mail.ustc.edu.cn, {pzhou,yliao}@ustc.edu.cn
[3] China Mobile Xiong'an Information Communication Technologies, Ningbo, China
tianhui@cmict.chinamobile.com
[4] Advanced Innovation Center for Human Brain Protection, Capital Medical University, Beijing, China
haiyong.xie@ieee.org

Abstract. It is important but challenging to accurately predict urban crimes. Existing studies rely on domain knowledge specific, pre-defined inter-dependency graphs using extra urban data and have many disadvantages. We propose a novel framework, AGL-STAN, to efficiently capture complex spatial-temporal correlations of urban crimes with higher prediction accuracy but without extra data. In AGL-STAN, we design an adaptive graph learning method to learn the inter-dependencies among communities, and a time-aware self-attention method to accurately model the influence of time-varying crime incidents with a multi-head attention mechanism. We demonstrate the superiority of AGL-STAN over the state-of-the-art methods through extensive experiments.

Keywords: Adaptive graph learning · Time-aware self-attention · Crime prediction

1 Introduction

The rapid urbanization has led to population expansion and increasing urban crime rates. Urban crimes (*e.g.*, robbery, assault) not only seriously endanger the public safety and residential properties, but also pose tremendous risks to stable urban development, if not contained in a timely and proper manner. According to the National Violent Death Reporting System [15], more than seven people die a violent death per hour in the United States. Meanwhile, the aggregated cost of crimes in the United States remains high, with an estimated $4.9 trillion, as reported in 2021 (see, *e.g.*, [3]).

In the past decades, researchers have made significant efforts to study urban crimes. Among such efforts, how to accurately predict urban crimes has become

E. Pimenidis et al. (Eds.): ICANN 2022, LNCS 13530, pp. 656–669, 2022.
https://doi.org/10.1007/978-3-031-15931-2_54

a challenging problem. Solutions to this problem are in pressing needs by the police departments and are important for better alleviating huge losses of lives and economic losses.

Crime prediction is challenging due to its complex intra-dependencies (*i.e.*, temporal correlations within one community of an urban region) and inter-dependencies (*i.e.*, spatial correlations among different communities in an urban region within the same time slot). Researchers have made significant progress in crime prediction by designing and leveraging generative models for time series prediction, including, to name a few, Autoregressive Integrated Moving Average (ARIMA) [6], Support Vector Machine (SVM) [19], and self-exciting point process [14]. However, these models cannot effectively and accurately capture the complex non-linear correlations in the temporal evolution of crime data and do not consider the inter-dependencies among urban communities, thus failing to accurately predict the occurrence of urban crimes.

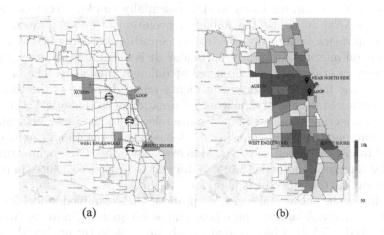

(a)   (b)

Fig. 1. (a) Major long-distance taxi flows. (b) Number of crimes in communities.

More recently, researchers have started to adopt deep learning-based methods to capture the complex spatial-temporal patterns of urban crimes. Examples of such models include but are not limited to DeepCrime [11], MiST [10], CrimeForecaster [16] and MVJGRL [21]. These models adopt different methods to capture the temporal and spatial correlations. For instance, they typically explore the complex non-linear temporal correlations using RNNs (*e.g.*, Gated Recurrent Units and Long-Short Term Memory) or Temporal Convolutional Networks, and use Convolutional Neural Networks and Graph Neural Networks (*e.g.*, Graph Convolutional Networks and Graph Attention Networks) to model the inter-dependencies of different urban communities effectively.

Compared to the generative models, the adoption of deep learning-based models has improved prediction performance in the past few years. However, there still exist many challenges with the deep learning-based models.

Firstly, such models commonly pre-define one or more inter-dependency graphs in order to capture the spatial correlations from various urban datasets (*e.g.*, community boundaries, PoIs [11], human mobilities [21], and taxi flows [18]). However, this approach requires specific domain knowledge and suitable fusion strategies, as there are many ways to capture the inter-dependencies and different choices of representative data can result in significantly different accuracies. For instance, take the Chicago crime data [1] as an example, as illustrated in Fig. 1, the community areas of Loop and Near North Side have similar crime patterns due to their geographical proximity [18]. The community areas of Loop and Austin also have similar crime patterns, which, however, clearly is not due to geographical proximity. Instead, it is caused by the major daily taxi flows [18]. Hence, it is challenging to decide what extra urban datasets are more appropriate for capturing the inter-dependencies. The manually generated inter-dependency graphs are too simplistic and incomplete to reveal the accurate spatial correlations among communities of urban crime series.

Secondly, deep learning-based models essentially employ Recurrent Neural Networks (RNNs) to model the temporal evolution of crime patterns. However, this approach is not very effective at capturing both the global and the local temporal information [17]. In particular, It is difficult to accurately model the influence of crime incidents occurred at different time slots. The impact of historical crime incidents on future incidents would decrease as the time span grows, resulting in the loss of significant information of the historical crime data. Because future crime incidents may be more relevant to historical incidents that occurred long ago than recent ones [9], RNN-based models without careful design may lead to low prediction accuracy. Moreover, since the RNN architecture is a sequential computational structure, it is difficult to process sequences in parallel and therefore its training cost is high.

To address the above challenges, we propose a novel unified model for crime prediction, namely, <u>A</u>daptive <u>G</u>raph <u>L</u>earning based <u>S</u>patial-<u>T</u>emporal <u>A</u>ttention <u>N</u>etwork (AGL-STAN), which can effectively and efficiently predict the occurrence of future crimes. More specifically, AGL-STAN consists of two core modules. We design an Adaptive Graph Learning module (AGL), dedicated to utilizing the crime data to learn the inter-dependencies among communities, by providing a unique embedding representation for each community. We also design a Time-aware Self-Attention module (TSA) to accurately model the influences of historical crime incidents occurred at different time slots in parallel, by calculating the influence scores for each pair of crime incidents with a multi-head attention mechanism. Furthermore, we conduct extensive experiments to evaluate AGL-STAN on two real-world datasets and compare it with numerous representative prediction models. The results show that AGL-STAN outperforms state-of-the-art models in terms of both prediction accuracy and computational cost. Note that the state-of-the-art models rely heavily on the auxiliary urban data such as taxi flows and human mobility to improve the accuracy, while AGL-STAN needs only the crime data itself and can still achieve better performance.

2 Related Work

Traditional Statistical Methods have been widely used in crime prediction, for instance, NBR [18], ARIMA [6] and SVR [19]. Such methods usually take advantage of feature engineering and extra data to capture inter-dependencies, in order to improve prediction accuracy.

Wang *et al.* [18] captured the inter-dependencies by using the PoIs (*e.g.*, a hospital or a bus station) and the taxi flow information, and their results demonstrated the positive effect of such inter-dependencies on improving prediction accuracy. While in [6,19], the authors used the geographic and the demographic data to improve prediction accuracy. Additionally, self-exciting point process [14] was also applied to crime prediction.

All these methods require to extract various complex features from extra, different sets of data source, so that key information such as the intra- and inter-dependencies can be leveraged to improve prediction accuracy. Therefore, they have higher costs and more noises with the increasing of data volume and diversity. More importantly, their performance heavily depend on the specific domain knowledge, the quality of the extracted features, and the availability as well as the quality of extra data sources.

Deep Learning Methods have been applied to crime prediction in recent years (see, *e.g.*, [10,11,16,21,22]) and achieve better results than traditional statistical models. In particular, Zhao *et al.* [22] proposed a novel crime prediction framework TCP to capture temporal correlations and spatial correlations into a coherent model. Huang *et al.* [11] proposed a hierarchical recurrent framework DCrime to capture the dynamic crime patterns and inherent inter-dependencies with other ubiquitous data. Furthermore, they introduced an attention mechanism for learning the important weights of crime occurrences across time frames to further improve prediction accuracy. Zhang *et al.* [21] proposed a multi-view joint learning model to learn comprehensive and representative urban community embeddings for crime prediction by leveraging both human mobility and inherent community properties.

Most of these deep learning-based methods pre-define one or more inter-dependency graphs in order to capture the spatial correlations from auxiliary datasets. The manually generated inter-dependency graphs are too simplistic and incomplete to reveal the accurate correlations of crime patterns. Moreover, those models are difficult to accurately model the long-term influence of crime incidents occurred at different time slots by RNNs.

3 Problem Formulation

Communities. An urban region is typically divided into N disconnected communities, which we denote by $R = (r_1, r_2, ..., r_n)$, where r_i represents the i-th community. As shown in Fig. 1, there are 77 communities in Chicago, and r_{32} represents the Loop community. In order to characterize the spatial correlations among communities of different crime series, we specify a weighted undirected graph $\mathcal{G} = (\mathcal{V}, \mathcal{E}, \mathcal{A})$, where $\mathcal{V}$ represents the set of communities, $|\mathcal{V}| = N$, $\mathcal{E}$ is the set of edges, and $\mathcal{A} \in \mathbb{R}^{N \times N}$ is the adjacency matrix to denote the spatial correlations among communities of crime series.

Crime Matrix. We denote by $x_{i,t} = \{x_{i,t}^1, x_{i,t}^2, ..., x_{i,t}^k\} \in \mathbb{R}^K$ the crime vector for community i during time slot t. We set $x_{i,t}^k = 1$ if a crime of category k occurs in community i during time slot t, and 0 otherwise. Then, we can denote the crime matrix for a time slot t as $X_t = \{x_{1,t}, x_{2,t}, ..., x_{n,t}\} \in \mathbb{R}^{N \times K}$.

Problem Formulation. Given the historical crime matrices $\mathcal{X}_\alpha = \{X_t, X_{t-1}, ..., X_{t-\alpha+1}\} \in \mathbb{R}^{\alpha \times N \times K}$ observed in the past α time slots, we formulate the crime prediction problem as follows: find a mapping function $\mathcal{F}_\theta$ that predicts the crime matrices $\mathcal{X}_\beta = \{X_t, X_{t+1}, ..., X_{t+\beta}\} \in \mathbb{R}^{\beta \times N \times K}$ in β future time slots (θ donates the learnable parameters):

$$\mathcal{X}_\beta = \mathcal{F}_\theta(\mathcal{X}_\alpha, \mathcal{G}). \tag{1}$$

4   Methodology

4.1   Architecture of AGL-STAN

Figure 2 illustrates the architecture of AGL-STAN. Our model mainly consists of two key modules. The first module is an Adaptive Graph Learning (AGL) module, which is devoted to modeling spatial correlations among communities

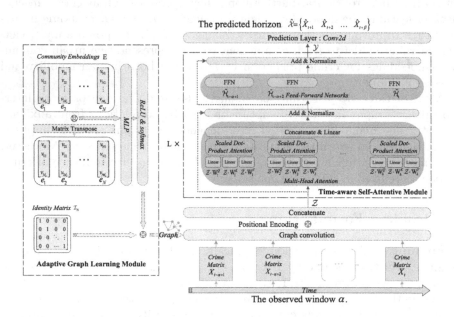

Fig. 2. The AGL-STAN framework.

from the crime data. The second module is a Time-aware Self-Attention (TSA) module, which aims to explore the complex non-linear temporal correlations of the crime data. We next describe each module in detail.

4.2 Adaptive Graph Learning Module

Many existing studies on crime prediction adopt Graph Convolutional Network (GCN) to capture the spatial correlations among multiple communities. GCN requires a pre-defined and usually manually generated graph $\mathcal{G}$ (and hence the adjacency matrix $\mathcal{A}$) derived from various urban data. Generation of such graphs requires much domain knowledge and is typically restricted and incomplete. Such approaches are difficult to reveal the inter-dependencies of crimes, lack generalizability and may even lead to biases and poor accuracy.

To address this problem, we design an Adaptive Graph Learning (AGL) module, inspired by the paper [4], to infer the hidden inter-dependency of crime series among communities.

We first define a learnable low-dimensional representation vector $e_i \in \mathbb{R}^{d_e}$ for each community, and a representation matrix $E = \{e_1, e_2, ..., e_n\} \in \mathbb{R}^{N \times d_e}$ for all communities. Note that the matrix can be either initialized randomly or pre-trained with inherent community properties (*e.g.*, PoIs).

We then define the graph convolution as the first-order approximation of localized spectral filters on graphs, as in [13]:

$$Z = (\mathcal{I}_N + \mathcal{D}^{-\frac{1}{2}} \mathcal{A} \mathcal{D}^{-\frac{1}{2}}) X \Theta, \qquad (2)$$

where $\mathcal{I}_N, \mathcal{A}, \mathcal{D} \in \mathbb{R}^{N \times N}$, $\mathcal{I}_N$ is the identity matrix for self-connections, $\mathcal{A}$ is the adjacency matrix of the graph $\mathcal{G}$, and $\mathcal{D}$ is degree matrix whose diagonal elements can be derived from $\mathcal{A}$ by summing its columns. Additionally, $X \in \mathbb{R}^{N \times K}$ and $Z \in \mathbb{R}^{N \times F}$ are input and output, and $\Theta \in \mathbb{R}^{K \times F}$ are the learnable parameters.

We next obtain the inter-dependency matrix to capture the correlations among communities. We directly replace the normalized Laplacian matrix $\mathcal{D}^{-\frac{1}{2}} \mathcal{A} \mathcal{D}^{-\frac{1}{2}}$ with the product of E and E^T, thus avoiding unnecessary repetitive calculations in the iterative training process:

$$\mathcal{D}^{-\frac{1}{2}} \mathcal{A} \mathcal{D}^{-\frac{1}{2}} = \mathtt{softmax}(\mathtt{ReLU}(\mathtt{MLP}(E \cdot E^T))), \qquad (3)$$

where ReLU is the activation function, MLP is a multi-layer perceptron, and softmax normalizes the adaptive matrix. During the iterative training process, E is automatically updated according to the crime series data, in order to fully explore the spatial correlations among communities. We finally formulate the AGL model as:

$$Z = (\mathcal{I}_N + \mathtt{softmax}(\mathtt{ReLU}(\mathtt{MLP}(E \cdot E^T)))) X \Theta. \qquad (4)$$

4.3 Time-Aware Self-attention Module

Recurrent Neural Network (RNN) has been widely used in existing studies to characterize the complex non-linear intra-dependencies in crime data. However, it may fail in capturing interactions among crime incidents over different time spans, and is computationally expensive due to RNN's sequential structure.

To address this problem, we design a Time-aware Self-Attention (TSA) module based on Transformer [17] to learn the interactions among latent representations of crime incidents at different time slots in the output of the AGL module. In particular, we consider the learned community embeddings $\mathcal{Z}$ at each time window α as the input to the TSA module. We pass $\mathcal{Z}$ through a multi-layer perceptron to obtain three matrices Q, K, and V, corresponding to the *query*, *key*, and *value* of community embeddings. The dimensions of these matrices are d_k, d_k and d_v, respectively. These matrices are then fed to an attention function. Finally we can obtain the following equation:

$$\mathcal{H} = \texttt{Attention}(\mathcal{Z} \cdot W^Q, \mathcal{Z} \cdot W^K, \mathcal{Z} \cdot W^V),$$

where $\mathcal{Z} = \{Z_1, Z_2, ..., Z_\alpha\} \in \mathbb{R}^{\alpha \times NF}$, and $Z_t = (\mathcal{I}_N + \texttt{softmax}(\text{ReLU}(\text{MLP}(E \cdot E^T))))X_t\Theta \in \mathbb{R}^{N \times F}$ is the learned community embedding from the AGL module, and $W^Q, W^K \in \mathbb{R}^{NF \times d_k}, W^V \in \mathbb{R}^{NF \times d_v}$ are learnable weights in the multi-layer perceptron. The output $\mathcal{H} \in \mathbb{R}^{\alpha \times d_v}$ is a hidden representation of the community embedding in the TSA module. We implement the attention operation using the scaled dot product attention method (see, *e.g.*, [17]) as follows:

$$\texttt{Attention}(Q, K, V) = \texttt{softmax}(\frac{QK^T}{\sqrt{d_k}})V. \tag{5}$$

Note that this attention method is computationally and spatially efficient, since it can be implemented using highly optimized matrix multiplication.

Furthermore, in order to comprehensively capture the temporal evolution of crime incidents at various time slots, we adopt a multi-head attention mechanism by replacing the single attention function with d_k-dimensional keys and d_v-dimensional values. We first perform a time-aware self-attention to yield each head, which can run in parallel; we then concatenate the multiple heads and project them with a weight matrix W^O to the new hidden representation $\widetilde{\mathcal{H}}$:

$$\widetilde{\mathcal{H}} = \texttt{MultiHead}(Q, K, V) = \texttt{Concat}(\text{head}_1, \text{head}_2, ..., \text{head}_h)W^O,$$

where $\text{head}_i = \texttt{Attention}(\mathcal{Z} \cdot W_i^Q, \mathcal{Z} \cdot W_i^K, \mathcal{Z} \cdot W_i^V)$, $W_i^Q, W_i^K \in \mathbb{R}^{NF \times d_k}$, $W_i^V \in \mathbb{R}^{NF \times d_v}$ and $W^O \in \mathbb{R}^{hd_v \times NF}$ are learnable weights, h is the number of heads, and $\widetilde{\mathcal{H}} \in \mathbb{R}^{\alpha \times NF}$ are the hidden states.

Finally, for the purpose of learning a richer embedding representation, we introduce a fully connected Feed-Forward Network (FFN) to process the hidden state $\widetilde{\mathcal{H}}_t$ at each time slot t separately. This FFN layer consists of two linear transformations and a ReLU activation:

$$\mathcal{Y} = \{Y_1, Y_2, ..., Y_\alpha\} \in \mathbb{R}^{\alpha \times NF}, \text{where } Y_t = \text{ReLU}(\widetilde{\mathcal{H}}_t W_1 + b_1)W_2 + b_2,$$

where W_1 and W_2 are the learnable weights, b_1 and b_2 are the biases.

4.4   Optimization

Prediction Layer. After stacking the AGL module and the L-layers TSA module, we obtain the output $\mathcal{Y} \in \mathbb{R}^{\alpha \times NF}$, which can be directly mapped to the probability matrix of crime occurrence $\widehat{\mathcal{X}} \in \mathbb{R}^{\beta \times NK}$:

$$\widehat{\mathcal{X}} = \{\widehat{X}_1, \widehat{X}_2, ..., \widehat{X}_\beta\} = \text{Conv2d}(\mathcal{Y}).$$

Objective Function. We adopt a commonly used objective function, namely, the Binary Cross-Entropy (BCE) function.

$$\mathcal{L}_{BCE}(\widehat{\mathcal{X}}, \theta) = -\sum_{\xi}^{\beta}(X_{t+\xi} \log(\widehat{X}_{t+\xi}) + (1 - X_{t+\xi})(1 - \log(\widehat{X}_{t+\xi}))). \qquad (6)$$

Moreover, to address the training fluctuations caused by the category imbalance problem among various crime categories, we also use the Dice Loss (DL) function (see, e.g., [20]) to balance training, which has been widely used in medical image segmentation and classification. Finally, we take the Automatic Weighted Loss (AWL) mechanism (see, e.g., [12]) to equalize the guiding effects of the above two loss functions in the process of objective optimization.

$$\mathcal{L}_{DL}(\widehat{\mathcal{X}}, \theta) = \sum_{\xi}^{\beta}(1 - \frac{2\sum X_{t+\xi}\widehat{X}_{t+\xi}}{\sum X_{t+\xi} + \sum \widehat{X}_{t+\xi}}). \qquad (7)$$

The final objective function is formulated as follows (θ: learnable parameters):

$$\mathcal{L}(\widehat{\mathcal{X}}, \theta) = \text{AWL}(\mathcal{L}_{BCE}(\widehat{\mathcal{X}}, \theta), \mathcal{L}_{DL}(\widehat{\mathcal{X}}, \theta)). \qquad (8)$$

5   Experiments

5.1   Methodology

Data Sets. We use two real-world crime datasets, the Chicago dataset [1] and the New York dataset [2]. We refer to them as CHI and NYC respectively. Both datasets are widely used in crime prediction studies and can be downloaded from their official portal. According to the administrative division plan enacted by the local governments, both Chicago and New York are divided into 77 disjointed

Table 1. Performance comparison of AGL-STAN and baselines for crime prediction

City	Month	Metrics	SVR	ARIMA	LSTM	GRU	DCrime	MiST	CF	AGL-STAN
CHI data	Aug	Macro-F1	0.6032	0.5868	0.6233	0.6399	0.6677	0.6835	0.7033	**0.7225**
		Micro-F1	0.4894	0.4656	0.5462	0.5712	0.6183	0.6293	0.6580	**0.6760**
	Sep	Macro-F1	0.5838	0.5682	0.6086	0.6075	0.6639	0.6880	0.7004	**0.7204**
		Micro-F1	0.4800	0.4635	0.5364	0.5599	0.6185	0.6373	0.6503	**0.6725**
	Oct	Macro-F1	0.5811	0.5632	0.5988	0.5963	0.6594	0.6722	0.6972	**0.7198**
		Micro-F1	0.4832	0.4629	0.5234	0.5502	0.6036	0.6300	0.6638	**0.6752**
	Nov	Macro-F1	0.5626	0.5532	0.5862	0.5803	0.6444	0.6613	0.6698	**0.6952**
		Micro-F1	0.4682	0.4580	0.5279	0.5126	0.5971	0.6283	0.6322	**0.6525**
	Dec	Macro-F1	0.5591	0.5529	0.5801	0.5761	0.6407	0.6589	0.6680	**0.6926**
		Micro-F1	0.4323	0.4421	0.5033	0.5131	0.5826	0.6127	0.6350	**0.6425**
NYC data	Aug	Macro-F1	0.6137	0.6262	0.6453	0.6599	0.6750	0.6799	0.6852	**0.7185**
		Micro-F1	0.5128	0.5377	0.5532	0.5636	0.5879	0.6063	0.6620	**0.6965**
	Sep	Macro-F1	0.6315	0.6279	0.6530	0.6486	0.6583	0.6682	0.6893	**0.7178**
		Micro-F1	0.5241	0.5345	0.5782	0.5803	0.6084	0.6237	0.6530	**0.6955**
	Oct	Macro-F1	0.6353	0.6362	0.6650	0.6530	0.6623	0.6760	0.6902	**0.7245**
		Micro-F1	0.5278	0.5514	0.5923	0.5879	0.6233	0.6241	0.6685	**0.7029**
	Nov	Macro-F1	0.6212	0.6281	0.6366	0.6316	0.6487	0.6492	0.6723	**0.6968**
		Micro-F1	0.5364	0.5478	0.5483	0.5659	0.5886	0.6026	0.6432	**0.6745**
	Dec	Macro-F1	0.6287	0.6269	0.6320	0.6354	0.6551	0.6530	0.6730	**0.6976**
		Micro-F1	0.5458	0.5451	0.5525	0.5520	0.5637	0.5911	0.6345	**0.6779**

communities. For ease of evaluations, we further split the datasets chronologically into three segments, a 6.5-month segment for training, a 0.5-month for validation and a 1-month for testing, similar to [10,11]. The validation datasets are mainly used to fine-tune the hyper-parameters. We evaluate our model separately for each month of the last five months of testing datasets.

AGL-STAN Parameters. We implement AGL-STAN using Pytorch 1.10.1 and run experiments on a server with an NVIDIA 3090 GPU. We use the Adam optimizer and a MultiStepLR scheduler with an initial learning rate of 0.0001 to dynamically update our learning rate during training. The observed sequence window α and predicted horizon β is set to 8 and 1, respectively. We set hidden state dimensionality d_w, d_k, and d_v as 1024 and the batch size as 4.

Baseline Methods. We use seven baseline models for comparisons. These baseline models can be divided into three categories, including the conventional time series prediction methods (SVR [5] and ARIMA [6]), RNN-based time series forecasting methods (LSTM [8] and GRU [7]), and spatial-temporal fusion forecasting methods (DCrime [11], MiST [10], and CrimeForecaster [16]).

Evaluation Metrics. We adopt two sets of evaluation metrics in experiments: the computational cost metrics including training time and convergence speed, and the prediction accuracy metrics including Macro-F1 and Micro-F1. Note that the higher Macro-F1 and Micro-F1 scores indicate better performance.

5.2   Prediction Accuracy

Table 1 summarizes the accuracy results of crime prediction across different time frames. We make the following observations.

Table 2. The computation cost on the CHI dataset.

Model	DCrime	MiST	CrimeForecaster	AGL-STAN
Convergence speed (number of epochs)	11	12	9	2
Training loss (each epoch)	60.77 s	75.56 s	20.66 s	1.23 s

Table 3. AGL-STAN Variants

AGL-STAN-G	AGL-STAN variant without the AGL module
AGL-STAN-T	AGL-STAN variant with GRU replacing the TSA module
AGL-STAN-M	AGL-STAN variant with a static, geographical proximity Based graph replacing AGL

Firstly, we observe that AGL-STAN outperforms the state-of-the-art baseline methods in all time frames. In particular, AGL-STAN achieves 4.97% and 5.14% improvements over the best baseline method (*i.e.*, CrimeForecaster) in terms of Macro-F1 and Micro-F1, respectively, in October on the NYC dataset. This sheds light on the benefit of AGL-STAN which can efficiently capture the intra- and inter-dependencies among urban crime incidents.

Secondly, we observe that the spatial-temporal fusion forecasting methods (*e.g.*, DCrime, MiST) outperform RNN-based methods. This is mainly because the former take inter-dependencies (*i.e.*, spatial correlations) into account by incorporating other data sources to capture the spatial correlations in the crime data. In addition, the conventional generative time series prediction models are non-parameter and based on a fixed formula, as a result, cannot effectively model the complex non-linear correlations in the temporal evolution of crime data.

Last but not least, the results suggest that compared with the spatial-temporal fusion forecasting methods, AGL-STAN is more effective in fully capturing the inter-dependencies and revealing the accurate correlations among communities of urban crime data.

5.3   Computational Cost

To evaluate this computational cost, we compare the convergence speed (the number of training epochs required to reach 90% of the final result) and training time of AGL-STAN with DCrime, MiST, and CrimeForecaster. Results are summarized in Table 2. AGL-STAN converges fast in only 2 epochs due to the addition of DL and the utilization of the AWL function to speed up convergence. Additionally, we utilize Eq. 3 in the AGL module and parallel computation in the TSA module, significantly reducing the training time by 1–2 orders of magnitude when compared with existing methods.

5.4 Model Ablation Study

We evaluate the effectiveness of each module in AGL-STAN by experimenting with the three variants defined in Table 3. Due to space limits, we summarize in Fig. 3 the results on the NYC dataset only. As we expect, the original AGL-STAN model achieves the best performance.

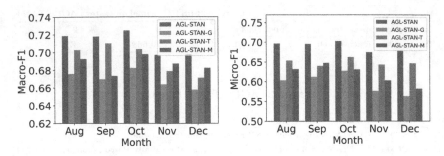

Fig. 3. Evaluation on the variants of AGL-STAN in terms of Macro-F1 and Micro-F1.

We make the following observations. Firstly, AGL-STAN outperforms AGL-STAN-G in all cases, suggesting that the adaptive graph learning can effectively capture the complex inter-dependencies to improve the prediction accuracy. In addition, AGL-STAN-G results in the worst performance of all variants, which proves that the AGL module plays the most important role in our model.

Secondly, AGL-STAN-M outperforms AGL-STAN-G in all cases, indicating that the inter-dependency of crime data plays a key role in improving the prediction accuracy. In addition, the fact that AGL-STAN outperforms AGL-STAN-M suggests that the spatio-temporal prediction approaches based on static predefined graphs fall short of revealing the underlying spatial correlations of crime data. This also suggests that the dynamically learned graph is more preferred than manually pre-defined graphs.

Last but not least, the performance gain of AGL-STAN over AGL-STAN-T suggests the TSA module effectively captures both the global and local temporal information. In particular, TSA can minimize the information loss of the historical crime data, hence improve the prediction accuracy.

5.5 Model Effectiveness

To better understand the effectiveness of AGL-STAN, we analyze the underlying spatial-correlation matrix, which AGL-STAN learns in the graph learning process, by comparing the adjacent communities of the popular community in the pre-defined graph. More specifically, we choose the Austin community as an example, as shown in Fig. 4. This community has a high crime rate in Chicago. We select from the learned graph the four communities (i.e., East Garfield Park, West Garfield Park, Lake View, and Loop) that are most relevant to Austin.

We observe that East Garfield Park and West Garfield Park share similar crime patterns with Austin, due to their close geographic proximity to each other. In contrast, Loop and Lake View are farther away from Austin but still have similar crime patterns, suggesting that other factors dominate, and such factors are not so obvious or intuitive as they can range from human mobility, population distribution (Austin and Loop have similar population), to many others such as voters' opinions (*e.g.*, Austin and Lake View are both strongly supportive of the Democratic Party). As a result, models that rely on selected auxiliary datasets to construct domain knowledge specific, manually crafted, pre-defined graphs as attempts to capture the inter-dependencies may result in low accuracy due to mis-use of datasets.

Therefore, AGL-STAN has many advantages over existing models. It not only can successfully learn the underlying multi-view spatial correlations from the crime data (thus outperforming existing models), but also can help to guide the selection, and to cross validate the effectiveness, of auxiliary data sets.

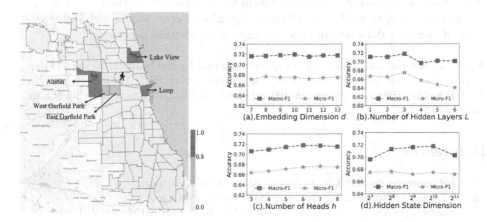

Fig. 4. Austin case study.   **Fig. 5.** Hyper-parameters on Chicago October data.

5.6   Model Hyper-Parameters

We conduct hyper-parameters studies, and due to space limit, we only report the results on October of the Chicago dataset (shown in Fig. 5). Results show that AGL-STAN is not sensitive to those parameters.

We make the following observations. Firstly, we vary the embedding dimension $d \in [7, 13]$ to evaluate how it affects the accuracy. We observe that the accuracy fluctuates only slightly as the d increases, reaching relatively good results when $d = 10$. Secondly, as shown in Fig. 5(b), increasing the number of hidden layers does not always result in higher predicting accuracy because too many layers may lead to over-fitting problems. Thirdly, as the number of attention heads increases, the prediction accuracy increases continuously, but too many heads require more parameters and result in larger cumulative errors, longer training time and a decreasing trend of accuracy. Lastly, AGL-STAN performs better as the dimension of hidden states increases and it tends to decrease when the dimension goes beyond 1024 (due to the same over-fitting problems).

6   Conclusion

In this paper, we propose a novel, unified and effective model, adaptive graph learning based spatial-temporal attention network (AGL-STAN), for crime prediction. Specifically, we design an adaptive graph learning module to reveal the accurate spatial correlations by leveraging a learning embedding representation, and a time-aware self-attention module to further capture the interactions of crime incidents occurred at different time slots in handling the complex and non-linear crime data. We conduct extensive experiments on two real-world crime datasets, and demonstrate that AGL-STAN can lean multi-view spatial correlations from the crime data and outperform state-of-the-art methods. Our model can help not only to guide the selection, but also to cross validate the effectiveness, of auxiliary data sets in order to improve prediction accuracy.

Acknowledgements. This work is supported in part by the National Key R&D Program under Grant 2021YFC3300500-02, the National Key R&D Project (Grant No. SQ2021YFC3300088 and 2020AAA0104404) and the S&T Program of Hebei (Grant No. 20470301D).

References

1. Chicago crime dataset (2022). https://data.cityofchicago.org/
2. NYC crime dataset (2022). https://data.cityofnewyork.us/
3. Anderson, D.A.: The aggregate cost of crime in the united states. J. Law Econ. **64**(4), 857–885 (2021)
4. Bai, L., Yao, L., Li, C., Wang, X., Wang, C.: Adaptive graph convolutional recurrent network for traffic forecasting. NeurIPS **33**, 17804–17815 (2020)
5. Chang, C.C., Lin, C.J.: LibSVM: a library for support vector machines. ACM Trans. Intell. Syst. Technol. **2**(3), 1–27 (2011)
6. Chen, P., Yuan, H., Shu, X.: Forecasting crime using the ARIMA model. In: International Conference on Fuzzy Systems and Knowledge Discovery, pp. 627–630 (2008)
7. Chung, J., Gulcehre, C., Cho, K., Bengio, Y.: Empirical evaluation of gated recurrent neural networks on sequence modeling. arXiv preprint arXiv:1412.3555 (2014)
8. Gers, F.A., Schmidhuber, J., Cummins, F.: Learning to forget: continual prediction with LSTM. Neural Comput. **12**(10), 2451–2471 (2000)
9. Gu, Y.: Attentive neural point processes for event forecasting. In: AAAI, pp. 7592–7600 (2021)
10. Huang, C., Zhang, C., Zhao, J., Wu, X., Yin, D., Chawla, N.: Mist: a multiview and multimodal spatial-temporal learning framework for citywide abnormal event forecasting. In: WWW, pp. 717–728 (2019)

11. Huang, C., Zhang, J., Zheng, Y., Chawla, N.V.: DeepCrime: attentive hierarchical recurrent networks for crime prediction. In: ACM CIKM, pp. 1423–1432 (2018)

12. Kendall, A., Gal, Y., Cipolla, R.: Multi-task learning using uncertainty to weigh losses for scene geometry and semantics. In: CVPR, pp. 7482–7491 (2018)

13. Kipf, T.N., Welling, M.: Semi-supervised classification with graph convolutional networks. arXiv preprint arXiv:1609.02907 (2016)

14. Mohler, G.O., Short, M.B., Brantingham, P.J., Schoenberg, F.P., Tita, G.E.: Self-exciting point process modeling of crime. J. Am. Stat. Assoc. **106**(493), 100–108 (2011)

15. NVDRS: Linking data to save lives (2021). https://www.cdc.gov/violenceprevention/datasources/nvdrs/index.html

16. Sun, J., et al.: CrimeForeCaster: crime prediction by exploiting the geographical neighborhoods' spatiotemporal dependencies. In: ECML-PKDD, pp. 52–67 (2020)

17. Vaswani, A., et al.: Attention is all you need. In: NeurIPS, pp. 5998–6008 (2017)

18. Wang, H., Kifer, D., Graif, C., Li, Z.: Crime rate inference with big data. In: ACM SIGKDD, pp. 635–644 (2016)

19. Wang, P., Mathieu, R., Ke, J., Cai, H.: Predicting criminal recidivism with support vector machine. In: International Conference on Management and Service Science, pp. 1–9 (2010)

20. Wang, Z., et al.: Spatio-temporal-categorical graph neural networks for fine-grained multi-incident co-prediction. In: ACM CIKM, pp. 2060–2069 (2021)

21. Zhang, M., Li, T., Li, Y., Hui, P.: Multi-view joint graph representation learning for urban region embedding. In: IJCAI, pp. 4431–4437 (2020)

22. Zhao, X., Tang, J.: Modeling temporal-spatial correlations for crime prediction. In: ACM CIKM, pp. 497–506 (2017)

ST^2PE: Spatial and Temporal Transformer for Pose Estimation

Yuan Wu, Yanlu Cai, Rui Feng, and Cheng Jin$^{(\boxtimes)}$

Fudan University, Shanghai Handan Road 220, Shanghai, China
{wuyuan,ylcai20,fengrui,jc}@fudan.edu.cn

Abstract. Spatial and temporal information and multi-view mutual promotion are two keys to solve depth uncertainty for 2D-to-3D Human pose estimation. However, each key requires a huge model to handle, so previous methods have to choose one of them to solve depth uncertainty. Thanks to transformer's powerful long-term relationship modeling capability and latent adaptation of one view to another, we can adopt both with an acceptable number of model parameters. To the best of our knowledge, we are the first to propose a multi-view multi-frame method for 2D-to-3D human pose estimation, called ST^2PE. The proposed method is combined with a Single-view Spatial and Temporal Transformer ($S-\mathrm{ST}^2$) and a Multiple Cross-view Transformer-based Transmission ($M-\mathrm{CT}^2$) module. Inspired by the structure of the Transformer in Transformer, the single-view spatial and temporal transformer has two nested transformer modules. The internal one extracts spatial information between joints, while the external one extracts temporal information between frames. The cross-view transformer-based transmission module extends the original encoder-decoder setting of Transformer into a multi-view setting. Experiments on three mainstream datasets (Human3.6M, HumanEva, MPI-INF-3DHP), demonstrate that ST^2PE achieves state-of-the-art performance among all the 2D-to-3D methods.

Keywords: Pose estimation · 3D · Computer vision · Machine learning

1 Introduction

2D-to-3D human pose estimation has received much attention in recent years. It aims to infer the 3D human pose based on the input 2D pose. However, multiple 3D poses can be projected to the same 2D pose, making it difficult to recover correct results. Therefore, previous methods often use multi-view 2D poses to reduce depth uncertainty and make accurate predictions.

Multi-view pose estimation methods utilize keypoint pairs in different views to restore depth information. However, these methods still have three unsolved problems.

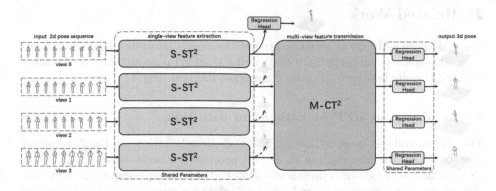

Fig. 1. The multi-view Spatial and Temporal Transformer for 2D-to-3D Pose Estimation (ST^2PE) consists of four Single-view Spatial and Temporal Transformer ($S-ST^2$) and a Multiple Cross-view Transformer-based Transmission ($M-CT^2$) module. Two series of regression heads are used for intermediate supervision and final 3D pose regression.

1. Multi-view methods suffer a lot from motion blur. Motion blur increases the deviation produced by the 2D pose detector. The deviation is amplified during triangulation, which is widely adopted in previous multi-view methods.
2. Previous methods require camera parameters as prior knowledge. This makes it necessary to calibrate the camera every time before recording a video, and the camera cannot be moved during recording.
3. Even though previous methods are called multi-view methods, most of them can only utilize information from two viewpoints. However, most of the existing datasets contain four or more viewpoints. Insufficient use of data leads to inaccurate expression of depth information.

To address the problems mentioned above, we propose a multi-view Spatial and Temporal Transformer for 2D-to-3D Pose Estimation (ST^2PE). Our contributions are three-fold:

1. To reduce the impact of 2D pose deviation caused by motion blur, we propose Single-view Spatial and Temporal Transformer ($S-ST^2$) block, which exploits spatial relationship and long-term temporal context to recover keypoints from blurred image. Experiments on three mainstream datasets (Human3.6M, HumanEva, MPI-INF-3DHP) show we achieve the state-of-the-art performance.
2. We propose Calibration-free Cross-view Transformer-based Transmission block (CT^2) to perform cross-view feature transmission and keypoint matching adaptively.
3. We propose a Multiple Cross-view Transformer-based Transmission module which is scalable with viewpoint. so that sufficient feature transmission can be carried out between every two viewpoints.

2   Related Work

Since 3D pose estimation needs to predict the depth information of the human pose, 3D pose estimation is more challenging than 2D pose estimation. We summarized the single-person 3D pose estimation method (Fig. 1).

2.1   End-to-End 3D Pose Estimation with Image

The end-to-end 3D pose estimation method directly estimates the 3D human pose based on the images. Sun et al. [13] propose a structure-aware regression method that adopts bone representation instead of joint representation to exploit the relationship between adjacent joints and define a compositional loss function to encode long-range interaction in the pose. Moon et al. [10] proposed a PoseNet, which predicts a depth value for each pixel while predicting the 2D heat map to estimate the 3D human pose directly.

The end-to-end 3D pose estimation method generally suffers from high training costs and large evaluation errors due to the large memory consumption of 3D heatmap and the lack of intermediate supervision.

2.2   Two-Stage 3D Pose Estimation with Image

The two-stage 3D pose estimation method first estimates the 2D human pose from the RGB image and then regresses the 3D human pose based on the estimated 2D human pose. Compared with the end-to-end pose estimation method, the two-stage pose estimation method takes advantage of the existing method of 2D pose estimation. It can make full use of the images in the 2D human pose dataset to train the model in the first stage. Due to the above benefits and the existence of many excellent 2D pose estimation algorithms, many researchers have devoted themselves to studying 2D-to-3D pose estimation methods.

Zhao et al. [17] proposed a semantic graph convolution network, which regards the 2D human pose as a skeleton graph, and uses the graph convolution module to extract connections between joints. Liu et al. [9] conducted a comprehensive study on the weight sharing of graph convolutional networks for 3D pose estimation.

Since the 2D pose in a single image is only a projection of the actual 3D pose on the camera plane, this projection process is bound to produce information loss, resulting in depth uncertainty. Therefore, some researchers try to leverage videos or multi-view images to solve the depth uncertainty caused by information loss to improve the accuracy and robustness of 3D pose estimation.

2.3   3D Pose Estimation with Video

Some researchers pay attention to the correlation between multi-frame pose sequences and use the neighborhood frames to guide the target frame to infer the 3D human pose from the 2D human pose.

Cai et al. [1] proposed a local to global graph convolution network to process and consolidate features across scales. Wang et al. [16] proposed a motion-guided U-shaped graph convolution network (UGCN) to captures both short-term and long-term motion information. Zheng et al. [18] employed a spatial transformer to encode local relationships between joints and a temporal transformer to represent the relationship between frames in a long sequence. Li et al. [8] proposed a strided transformer encoder with a simple intermediate supervision mechanism to extract spatial and temporal relationships by stacking strided transformer encoders.

2.4 Multi-view 3D Pose Estimation

Compared with implicitly extracting inter-frame relationships, predicting depth information from multi-view images is a more intuitive idea. However, pose estimation based on multi-view images also has some challenges, such as how to model view-invariant pose features and view-equivariant transformation features effectively and how to fuse features from different views to recover depth information.

Tome et al. [14] uses the 2D heatmaps predicted from different views to recover the 3D heat map in cascade. He et al. [4] proposed an epipolar transformer to reduce the error by passing the 3D-aware feature back to the 2D pose estimator. Reddy et al. [12] proposed a multi-task method including person detection, person tracking, Pose Estimation, and Pose Tracking using 4D CNN and Attention Aggregation to establish the 3D spatial representation.

Compared with multi-frame methods, the methods based on multi-view images generally have a lower average error, but they usually use a lot of computing resources for the explicit establishment of a 3D spatial representation, which is difficult for practical application and further optimization. Therefore, we propose a multi-view spatial and temporal transformer with multiple cross-view feature fusion for 2D-to-3D pose estimation, which implicitly performs keypoint matching and recovers depth information from the 2D pose.

3 Method

We focus on the 2D-to-3D pose estimation, which means that we employ an on-the-shelf 2D pose estimator to generate 2D pose sequences from videos in different views. We proposed a Spatial and Temporal Transformer for Pose Estimation (ST^2PE). ST^2PE consists of Single-view Spatial and Temporal Transformer $(S-ST^2)$ and Multiple Cross-view Transformer-based Transmission module $(M-CT^2)$.

3.1 Single-View Spatial and Temporal Transformer

In the past, many methods usually adopt 1D (dilated) convolution to extract the temporal relationship. However, the relationship between frames changes

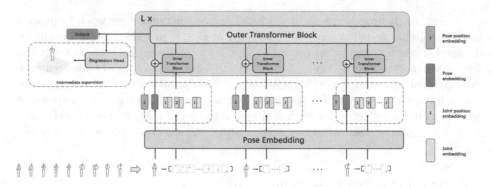

Fig. 2. Illustration of the proposed $S-\mathrm{ST}^2$. The regression head is used to generate the intermediate supervision.

drastically with the input, so it is difficult to model the temporal relationship accurately by simply stacking 1D convolution. To make matters worse, convolution is not good at extracting long-term relationships, which greatly limits the extraction of temporal relationships.

We noticed that transformer is adopted at extracting long-term relationships, so we propose a Single-view Spatial and Temporal Tramsformer $(S-\mathrm{ST}^2)$ to extract spatial and temporal features.

Nested transformer block is the core component of $S-\mathrm{ST}^2$, which contains an inner transformer block and an outer transformer block. Inspired by Han et al. [3], we treat joints as word tokens and utilize the inner transformer block to extract spatial features from joints in the same frame. Then, we treat poses as sentence tokens. The spatial features of each word in the sentence are attached to the sentence token after linear transformation. The outer block learns the spatial and temporal relationship for the whole sequence. A series of inner and outer blocks are stacked to form Single-view Spatial and Temporal Transformer $(S-\mathrm{ST}^2)$.(Fig. 2)

Pose Embedding and Position Embedding. Given the input pose sequence of T frames $\mathbb{P} = [P_1, \ P_2, \ \ldots, \ P_T]$, each frame consists of N joints' 2D-coordinates $P_i = \{P_{i,k}\}_{k=1}^N$ where $J_{i,k} \in R^2$, $i \in 1, \ 2, \ \ldots, \ T$ and $k \in 1, \ 2, \ \ldots, \ N$. To build word tokens $X_{i,k}^{(0)} \in R^{d_w}$ and sentence token $Y_i^{(0)} \in R^{d_s}$, we adopt a linear layer as pose embedding and a position embedding $E_k^X \in R^{d_w}$ or $E_i^Y \in R^{d_s}$ respectively, where d_w and d_s are the feature dimension of word and sentence separately.

$$\mathbb{X}_i^{(0)} = \|_k X_{i,k}^{(0)} \quad where \quad X_{i,k}^{(0)} = J_{i,k} W_w + b_w + E_k^X \tag{1}$$

$$\mathbb{Y}^{(0)} = \|_i Y_i^{(0)} \quad where \quad Y_i^{(0)} = \mathbb{X}_i^{(0)} W_s + b_s + E_i^Y \tag{2}$$

where $W_w \in R^{2 \times d_w}$, $b_w \in R^{d_w}$ and $W_s \in R^{(N \cdot d_w) \times d_s}$, $b_s \in R^{d_s}$ are the weights and bias of the input embedding of words and sentences. $X_i \in R^{N \times d_w}$ and $Y \in R^{T \times d_s}$ denote all the words in the i-th sentence and all the sentences. $\|$ denotes the channel-wise concatenation. The word and sentence position embedding explicitly encode the index in both spatial and temporal dimensions.

Nested Transformer Block. After obtaining the tokens, we applied a series of nested transformer blocks on these tokens. In each nested block, linear transformation and element-wise sum are applied between the outer block and the inner block to pass the spatial relationship to the sentence token.

$$X_i^{(l)} = TransformerBlock_i^X \left(X_i^{(l-1)} \right) \tag{3}$$

$$\widetilde{Y}^{(l)} = Y^{(l-1)} + \|_i \left(X_i^{(l)} W_c + b_c \right) \tag{4}$$

$$Y^{(l)} = TransformerBlock^Y \left(\widetilde{Y}^{(l)} \right) \tag{5}$$

where $W_c \in R^{(N \cdot d_w) \times d_s}$ and $b_c \in R^{d_s}$ are the weights and bias of the linear transformation.

After B_s blocks of nest transformer block, a regression head is employed to infer the single-view 3D pose sequence as intermediate supervision. The regression head is composed of a global average pooling, layer normalization, and linear transformation.

3.2 Multi-view Spatial and Temporal Transformer for Pose Estimation

Inspired by Tsai et al. [15], we realized that the primary role of the transformer in multi-modal models is cross-modal feature fusion or transmission. The intuitive idea is that the transformer takes effect in cross-modal feature transmission, which can also be efficient in cross-view feature transmission. More importantly, the Guided Attention included in the Transformer Decoder computes the correlation between features from different views and implicitly matches keypoints from different views, which significantly benefits restoring depth information from multi-view. Therefore, we utilize transformer encoder-decoder structure for multi-view feature transmission. However, there are still some problems unsolved.

The major problem is that the original transformer's encoder-decoder structure is introduced by the neural machine translation (NMT) task, which is naturally an asymmetric task, so the structure is designed to be asymmetric. However, in our task, the relationship between views is symmetrical. To solve the above problem, we design cross-view transformer-based transmission modules (CT^2), expanding the original asymmetric encoder-decoder structure into a more suitable symmetrical structure for interchangeable views. CT^2 can transmit features between two views (Fig. 3).

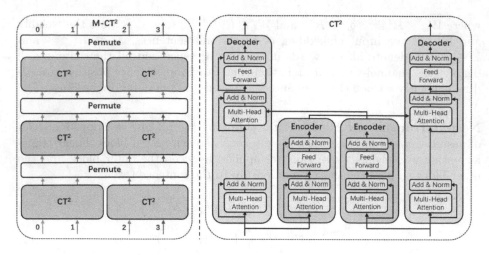

Fig. 3. $M-\mathrm{CT}^2$ (left) conducts 3 groups of CT^2 (right), and uses permute operations to rearrange the four views between groups. Four different colors mark the four views separately.

Before bringing in CT^2, we first briefly introduce the original encoder-decoder structure. The encoder and the decoder each accept one sequence as input and use the output of the decoder as the final output. The encoder is formed by simply stacking B_c blocks of the transformer blocks described above. The decoder is also formed by stacking B_c variant blocks, which adds extra guided attention between the subblock and the subblock. The guided attention performs MHA between the encoder output $Y \in R^{n \times d}$ and the decoder input $X \in R^{n \times d}$.

Guided Attention is used to find the relationship between different features, and we use it to find the high-relative keypoint pairs from different views:

$$GA(X,Y) = MHA(FC_Q(X), FC_K(Y), FC_V(Y)) \tag{6}$$

$$SubBlock_G(X,Y) = LN(X + GA(X,Y)) \tag{7}$$

Thus, the original Encoder-Decoder (ED) structure is formalized as:

$$ED(X,Y) = Decoder(X, Encoder(Y)) \tag{8}$$

The main idea of CT^2 is to let the feature between two views guide each other in parallel.

$$CT^2(X,Y)_X = ED(X,Y) \tag{9}$$

$$CT^2(X,Y)_Y = ED(Y,X) \tag{10}$$

CT^2 itself can only work with two views. In order to make full use of the four views of the Human3.6M dataset, we design an Multiple CT^2 module ($M-\mathrm{CT}^2$) which divide all views into $\frac{V}{2}$ groups of two views. Each group utilize CT^2 module to exchange features. $M-\mathrm{CT}^2$ groups $V-1$ times to ensure that any two views

Table 1. Quantitative comparisons of Mean Per Joint Position Error (MPJPE) for **2D-to-3D Pose estimation methods** between the predicted pose and the ground truth pose on the Human3.6M dataset under Protocol 1 and Protocol 2. 2D poses detected by CPN is taken as input. Best in **Bold**.

Protocol 1	Dir.	Disc.	Eat.	Greet	Phone	Photo	Pose	Purch.	Sit	SitD.	Smoke	Wait	WalkD.	Walk	WalkT.	Average
single-view method																
Zhao et al. [17]	47.3	60.7	51.4	60.5	61.1	49.9	47.3	68.1	86.2	55.0	67.8	61.0	42.1	60.6	45.3	57.6
Cai et al. [1]	44.6	47.4	45.6	48.8	50.8	59.0	47.2	43.9	57.9	61.9	49.7	46.6	51.3	37.1	39.4	48.8
Wang et al. [16]	41.3	43.9	44.0	42.2	48.0	57.1	42.2	43.2	57.3	61.3	47.0	43.5	47.0	32.6	31.8	45.6
Zheng et al. [18]	41.5	44.8	39.8	42.5	46.5	51.6	42.1	42.0	53.3	60.7	45.5	43.3	46.1	31.8	32.2	44.3
Li et al. [8]	39.9	43.4	40.0	40.9	46.4	50.6	42.1	39.8	55.8	61.6	44.9	43.3	44.9	29.9	30.3	43.6
multi-view method																
Baseline	46.5	48.6	54.0	51.5	67.5	70.7	48.5	49.1	69.8	79.4	57.8	53.1	56.7	42.2	45.4	57.0
Tome et al. [14]	43.3	49.6	42.0	48.8	51.1	64.3	40.3	43.3	66.0	95.2	50.2	52.2	51.1	43.9	45.3	52.8
Huang et al. [5]	**26.8**	**32.0**	25.6	52.1	33.3	42.3	**25.8**	**25.9**	40.5	76.6	39.1	54.5	35.9	**25.1**	**24.2**	37.5
Ours	30.9	37.2	**25.3**	**23.7**	**33.2**	**36.5**	34.4	26.5	**39.0**	**37.0**	**25.3**	**36.4**	**33.3**	28.3	26.6	**32.0**
Protocol 2	Dir.	Disc.	Eat.	Greet	Phone	Photo	Pose	Purch.	Sit	SitD.	Smoke	Wait	WalkD.	Walk	WalkT.	Average
single-view method																
Cai et al. [1]	35.7	37.8	36.9	40.7	39.6	45.2	37.4	34.5	46.9	50.1	40.5	36.1	41.0	29.6	32.3	39.0
Wang et al. [16]	32.9	35.2	33.3	35.8	35.9	41.5	33.2	32.7	44.6	50.9	37.0	32.4	37.0	25.2	27.2	35.6
Zheng et al. [18]	32.5	34.8	32.6	34.6	35.3	39.5	32.1	32.0	42.8	48.5	34.8	32.4	35.3	24.5	26.0	34.6
Li et al. [8]	32.0	35.6	32.6	35.1	35.8	40.9	33.2	31.2	44.7	48.9	36.7	33.9	35.2	23.7	25.1	34.9
multi-view method																
Tome et al. [14]	38.2	40.2	38.8	41.7	44.5	54.9	34.8	35.0	52.9	75.7	43.3	46.3	44.7	35.7	37.5	44.6
Ours	**22.5**	**27.4**	**19.6**	**17.4**	**24.2**	**28.5**	**24.8**	**19.2**	**30.9**	**30.9**	**18.5**	**25.9**	**25.4**	**22.0**	**19.5**	**23.9**

have a feature transmission. Take four views as an example. For the first time, 0 and 1 are grouped together denoted as (0, 1), and 2 and 3 are grouped together. The second time is (0, 2) and (1, 3). The third time is (0, 3) and (1, 2). This grouping strategy allows the features to be fully exchanged through $M-CT^2$, and then depth information is recovered by regression head.

The regression head here has the same structure as the regression head introduced in $S-ST^2$. However, the regression head here is used to infer the final 3D pose as output, while the regression head in $S-ST^2$ is used to generate the 3D pose for intermediate supervision.

4   Experiment

4.1   Datasets and Evaluation Metrics

We evaluate our model on the most commonly used dataset Human3.6M [6] for 3D human pose estimation and then we compare our method with Poseformer on two small datasets HumanEva and MPI-INF-3DHP to evaluate the generalizability of our method. Human3.6M is the largest and most widely used 3D human pose dataset. It has four synchronized cameras, which captured a total of 3.6 million video frames from 11 professional actors, including 17 different actions. All the 3D pose annotations are captured by a high-speed motion capture system. We follow the experiment settings consistent with previous methods for a fair comparison. The model is training and testing with the previous cross-subject setting following [11], which means that the model use five subjects (S1, S5, S6, S7, and S8) for training and two subjects (S9 and S11) for testing.

HumanEva dataset contain 7 calibrated videos from a motion capture system. 4 subjects perform 6 common actions. We follow the origin experiment setting for fair comparison.

MPI-INF-3DHP dataset contains actions performed by 8 actors from 14 viewpoints. Since the origin setting of MPI-INF-3DHP only has one view in the test set, it can not work with multi-view method. Therefore, we propose a new experiment setting for MPI-INF-3DHP dataset. We selected data from 4 chest-high perspectives for 4-fold cross-validation. Specifically, 2 performers (1 male and 1 female) are selected as the test set each time, and the remaining 6 performers (3 males and 3 females) are selected as the training set, and the final result is obtained by weighted average after 4 cycles.

Mean Per Joint Position Error (MPJPE, as Protocol 1) and Procrustes analysis MPJPE (P-MPJPE, as Protocol 2) are used to evaluate our performance with ground truth 3D pose. MPJPE uses the alignment of hips to eliminate the origin deviation between the predicted coordinate system and the ground truth coordinate system. P-MPJPE uses a rigid transformation to eliminate the deviation of the origin, direction, and scale of the two coordinate systems.

4.2   Implementation Details

Our proposed model implemented by Pytorch is trained and tested on four NVIDIA RTX 3090 GPUs. We train our model for 20 epochs with Adam optimizer and ReduceLROnPlateau scheduler. The initial learning rate is set to 1e-4. The batch size of 16 is set. Four layers of transformer block are taken in $S-ST^2$, and two layers of both encoder and decoder is used for each CT^2 module. The d_j and d_p are 32 and 544, respectively. The dimension of the MLP hidden layer is twice that of the input or output. The number of the head for Multi-head attention is set to 8. The dropout probability for the transformer module is 0.2. We take the CPN predicted pose and 2D ground truth pose respectively as the model's input to compare with existing methods.

4.3   Comparison with State-of-the-Art

We report the results of 15 actions under two evaluation protocols in Table 1. The average results of all actions are listed at the end of each row. The multi-frame methods and the multi-view methods are listed separately for the convenience of comparison. All the 2D-to-3D methods employ CPN [2] as 2D Human pose detector for a fair comparison. ST^2PE outperforms other 2D-to-3D methods by a large margin, which demonstrates ST^2PE has a good command of long-term relationship extraction and cross-view feature transmission.

Although ST^2PE is already the state-of-the-art method for 2D-to-3D pose estimation, there is still a big gap between ST^2PE and state-of-the-art image-based method [12], and the average error of A is 13.3mm higher than that of [12]. The relevant comparisons are listed in Table 2. The experiment results show that it is feasible to supplement the keypoint pairs with temporal context information, but 81-frame is still not enough, or a more effective transmission mechanism is found.

Table 2. Comparison between ST^2PE and image-based methods. With GT means that we take 2D ground truth pose as input. Best in **bold**.

Method	MPJPE	PMPJPE
Iskakov et al. [7]	20.8	**17.7**
Reddy et al. [12]	**18.7**	-
He et al. [4]	26.9	-
Ours	32.0	23.9
Ours (With GT)	26.8	20.2

4.4 Ablation Study

In order to verify the contribution of each module of ST^2PE, we take 2D ground truth as input and MPJPE as evaluation metrics and design a series of ablation experiments.

The Number of Frames. 9, 27, 81, and 243 frames are taken as input for ST^2PE. The results are listed in Table 3. The error is greatly reduced as the number of frames increases, showing that the ST^2PE module can extract long-term temporal relationships for the $M-CT^2$ module to restore depth information accurately.

The Number of Views. In this ablation experiment, we take $S-ST^2$ as the 1-view model and take ST^2PE with three layers of CT^2 as the 2-view model. The whole ST^2PE is the 4-view model. The experiment results are shown in Table 3, which show that the $M-CT^2$ structure we designed is effective for the input of more than two views.

Table 3. Ablation Experiment for the input frames and views. Ground truth 2D poses are used as input. Best in **bold**. * denotes that we replace $S-ST^2$ with PoseFormer. 81 frames with 4-view is adopted finally.

Frame/View	9	27	81	243	1	2	4
MPJPE	35.5	30.1	26.8	**25.6**	33.2	30.6	**26.8**
P-MPJPE	25.7	22.3	20.2	**19.7**	24.1	22.5	20.2

The Structure of $S-ST^2$ and $M-CT^2$. We also present the ablation experiment for the structure of $S-ST^2$ and the layers of $M-CT^2$ in Table 4. The error is greatly increased if outer block or inner block removed, showing that the ST^2PE module can extract spatial information between joints and long-term temporal relationships to restore depth information accurately. And as the number of layers increases, $M-CT^2$ can better communicate features across views.

Table 4. Ablation Experiment for the structure of $S-\mathrm{ST}^2$ and the groups of $M-\mathrm{CT}^2$. Ground truth 2D poses are used as input. Best in **bold**.

Ablation	$M-\mathrm{CT}^2$					$S-\mathrm{ST}^2$	
Method	0	1	2	3	4	w/o Outer	w/o Inner
MPJPE	33.2	32.0	29.3	26.8	25.4	37.8	41.6
P-MPJPE	24.1	23.0	21.1	20.2	18.7	29.1	32.8

4.5 Generalization Performance

We use pretrained model on Human3.6M, and train 5 epoch on HumanEva or MPI-INF-3DHP to evaluate the generalizability of our method compared with Poseformer. The result is shown in Table 5.

Table 5. Generalization Experiment. Ground truth 2D poses are used as input. Best in **bold**.

Datasets	HumanEva		MPI-INF-3DHP	
Metrics	MPJPE	P-MPJPE	MPJPE	P-MPJPE
Poseformer(27frames)	37.9	31.2	40.5	33.8
Ours(27frames)	**22.4**	**17.6**	**15.7**	**11.0**

5   Conclusion

We propose a multi-view multi-frame method for 2D-to-3D pose estimation, called ST^2PE, achieving state-of-the-art performance among all the 2D-to-3D pose estimation methods on the Human3.6M dataset.

Acknowledgment. This work was supported by National Natural Science Foundation of China under Grant (No. 62176064) and Zhejiang Lab (No. 2019KD0AB06).

References

1. Cai, Y., et al.: Exploiting spatial-temporal relationships for 3d pose estimation via graph convolutional networks. In: Proceedings of the IEEE/CVF International Conference on Computer Vision, pp. 2272–2281 (2019)
2. Chen, Y., Wang, Z., Peng, Y., Zhang, Z., Yu, G., Sun, J.: Cascaded pyramid network for multi-person pose estimation. In: Proceedings of the IEEE Conference on Computer Vision and Pattern Recognition, pp. 7103–7112 (2018)
3. Han, K., Xiao, A., Wu, E., Guo, J., Xu, C., Wang, Y.: Transformer in transformer. arXiv preprint arXiv:2103.00112 (2021)

4. He, Y., Yan, R., Fragkiadaki, K., Yu, S.I.: Epipolar transformers. In: Proceedings of the IEEE/CVF Conference on Computer Vision and Pattern Recognition, pp. 7779–7788 (2020)
5. Huang, F., Zeng, A., Liu, M., Lai, Q., Xu, Q.: Deepfuse: an imu-aware network for real-time 3d human pose estimation from multi-view image. In: Proceedings of the IEEE/CVF Winter Conference on Applications of Computer Vision, pp. 429–438 (2020)
6. Ionescu, C., Papava, D., Olaru, V., Sminchisescu, C.: Human3.6m: Large scale datasets and predictive methods for 3d human sensing in natural environments. IEEE Trans. Pattern Anal. Mach. Intell. **36**(7), 1325–1339 (jul 2014)
7. Iskakov, K., Burkov, E., Lempitsky, V., Malkov, Y.: Learnable triangulation of human pose. In: Proceedings of the IEEE/CVF International Conference on Computer Vision (ICCV), October 2019
8. Li, W., Liu, H., Ding, R., Liu, M., Wang, P.: Lifting transformer for 3d human pose estimation in video. arXiv preprint arXiv:2103.14304 (2021)
9. Liu, K., Ding, R., Zou, Z., Wang, L., Tang, W.: A comprehensive study of weight sharing in graph networks for 3d human pose estimation. In: Vedaldi, A., Bischof, H., Brox, T., Frahm, J.-M. (eds.) ECCV 2020. LNCS, vol. 12355, pp. 318–334. Springer, Cham (2020). https://doi.org/10.1007/978-3-030-58607-2_19
10. Moon, G., Lee, K.M.: I2L-MeshNet: image-to-lixel prediction network for accurate 3d human pose and mesh estimation from a single RGB Image. In: Vedaldi, A., Bischof, H., Brox, T., Frahm, J.-M. (eds.) ECCV 2020. LNCS, vol. 12352, pp. 752–768. Springer, Cham (2020). https://doi.org/10.1007/978-3-030-58571-6_44
11. Pavllo, D., Feichtenhofer, C., Grangier, D., Auli, M.: 3d human pose estimation in video with temporal convolutions and semi-supervised training. In: Proceedings of the IEEE/CVF Conference on Computer Vision and Pattern Recognition (CVPR), June 2019
12. Reddy, N.D., Guigues, L., Pishchulin, L., Eledath, J., Narasimhan, S.G.: Tessetrack: end-to-end learnable multi-person articulated 3d pose tracking. In: Proceedings of the IEEE/CVF Conference on Computer Vision and Pattern Recognition, pp. 15190–15200 (2021)
13. Sun, X., Shang, J., Liang, S., Wei, Y.: Compositional human pose regression. In: Proceedings of the IEEE International Conference on Computer Vision (ICCV), October 2017
14. Tome, D., Toso, M., Agapito, L., Russell, C.: Rethinking pose in 3d: Multi-stage refinement and recovery for markerless motion capture. In: 2018 International Conference on 3D Vision (3DV), pp. 474–483. IEEE (2018)
15. Tsai, Y.H.H., Bai, S., Liang, P.P., Kolter, J.Z., Morency, L.P., Salakhutdinov, R.: Multimodal transformer for unaligned multimodal language sequences. In: Proceedings of the Conference. Association for Computational Linguistics. Meeting, vol. 2019, p. 6558. NIH Public Access (2019)
16. Wang, J., Yan, S., Xiong, Y., Lin, D.: Motion guided 3D pose estimation from videos. In: Vedaldi, A., Bischof, H., Brox, T., Frahm, J.-M. (eds.) ECCV 2020. LNCS, vol. 12358, pp. 764–780. Springer, Cham (2020). https://doi.org/10.1007/978-3-030-58601-0_45
17. Zhao, L., Peng, X., Tian, Y., Kapadia, M., Metaxas, D.N.: Semantic graph convolutional networks for 3d human pose regression. In: Proceedings of the IEEE/CVF Conference on Computer Vision and Pattern Recognition, pp. 3425–3435 (2019)
18. Zheng, C., Zhu, S., Mendieta, M., Yang, T., Chen, C., Ding, Z.: 3d human pose estimation with spatial and temporal transformers. arXiv preprint arXiv:2103.10455 (2021)

Taking Care of Our Drinking Water: Dealing with Sensor Faults in Water Distribution Networks

Valerie Vaquet[1(✉)], André Artelt[1,2], Johannes Brinkrolf[1],
and Barbara Hammer[1]

[1] Machine Learning Group, Bielefeld University, 33501 Bielefeld, Germany
vvaquet@techfak.uni-bielefeld.de
[2] University of Cyprus, Nicosia, Cyprus

Abstract. The water supply is part of the critical infrastructure as the accessibility of clean drinking water is essential to ensure the health of the people. To guarantee the availability of fresh water, efficient and reliable water distribution networks are crucial. Monitoring these systems is necessary to avoid deterioration in water quality, deal with leakages and prevent cyber-physical attacks. While the installation of a growing amount of sensors is increasing the possibilities to monitor the system, considering the control of the senors becomes another challenge as sensor faults negatively influence the reliability of systems dealing with leakages and monitoring water quality. In this work, we aim to overcome the negative implications induced by sensor faults by using a sensor fault monitoring system based on three steps. First, established residual based fault detection is applied. In a second step, we extend this method to a fault isolation technique and finally propose fault accommodation by standard imputation techniques and different types of virtual sensors.

Keywords: Water distribution networks · Sensor faults · Data imputation

1 Introduction

Access to water is recognized as a human right by the United Nations[1]. While ensuring the water supply in some areas is already challenging, climate change will aggravate this in the future. A well working water distribution network (WDN) is crucial to ensure the availability of clean drinking water and is therefore part of the critical infrastructure. However, leakages in pipes and pollution

---

[1] https://www.unwater.org/water-facts/human-rights/.

We gratefully acknowledge funding in the frame of the BMBF project TiM, 05M20PBA; of the BMWi project KI-Marktplatz, 01MK20007E; from the VW-Foundation for the project IMPACT funded in the frame of the funding line AI and its Implications for Future Society.

are issues in the water systems, causing vast amounts of drinking water being wasted. Even in highly developed countries with a rather dry climate like Cyprus approximately 20% of the drinking water are lost through leakages[2].

With an increase in the availability of low-cost sensor technology, the possibilities of monitoring the water system are growing. Similar to other critical infrastructure, the water supply network can be realized in form of cyber-physical systems (CPS) which consist of a physical and a cyber core [8]. Considering for example modern water networks, there are pipes, pumps, and reservoirs as part of the physical system and different types of sensors enabling a monitoring of the given system. Based on the data collected by the sensors the monitoring system can observe the network, detect leakages and pollution, and enable human operators to take appropriate actions. However, since the entire monitoring system is relying on sensor information, one needs to account for all possible kinds of sensor failures as well. Usually, the process for monitoring the system for sensor faults is threefold: first, it is necessary to overall detect that a fault is present in the system. In a second step, the faulty sensor needs to be isolated before it can be finally repaired or replaced [8].

In this contribution, we propose an efficient machine learning based framework, which monitors the system by performing the three tasks. The first two steps are accomplished by a residual based anomaly detection relying on an ensemble of regression models. As usually sensors are not replaced immediately after the failure occurred and the first two steps as well as other crucial control systems rely on reasonably accurate sensor data (as will be elaborated later) our main contribution is the evaluation of different methods to reproduce the measurements of faulty sensors for the period until they are fixed. For this, we consider standard missing value imputation strategies, virtual sensors, and methods informed by the network topology.

The remainder of this paper is structured in the following way: First, we will give a brief overview of the related work in Sect. 2. Then, before presenting the three steps of our framework (Sect. 4), we will provide a short introduction on how to model WDNs (Sect. 3). Finally, we will present our experiments and results (Sect. 5) and conclude the paper (Sect. 6).

2   Related Work

Considerable research effort in the domain of WDNs lies in leakage detection. Frequently, methods rely on residuals between a prediction of some sensor data and the actual observation [3,6,12]. However, though many of these approaches rely on reasonable sensor measurements, there is little research conducted on how to address sensor faults.

While there is some work modeling fault detection and isolation in the field of control theory [9–11], to our knowledge only little work applying machine learning techniques was conducted so far. A sensor fault detection based on local

---

[2] https://www.eureau.org/resources/publications/1460-eureau-data-report-2017-1/file.

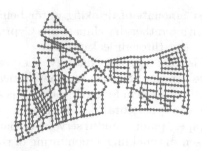

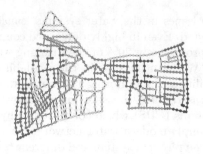

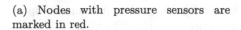

(a) Nodes with pressure sensors are marked in red.

(b) Result of neighborhood computation. Nodes belonging to the same sensor node are marked in the same color

Fig. 1. Visualization of the L-Town-Variation network. (Color figure online)

PCA was proposed by [2]. Considering fault accommodation, [7] propose a model for missing value imputation in WDNs based on combination of a forecast and a backcast model. However, they only consider sensor faults or missing values in limited time periods of few hours, which might not be realistic if a sensor is not repaired or replaced quickly. [1] propose a combination of least squares regression with Kalman filters which is evaluated on a fairly small network with regards to sensor technology. Sensor imputation is also investigated by [4]. They propose to enrich the data by temporarily installing additional sensors and to create virtual sensors based on the collected training data.

3   Water Networks

Water supply networks can be modeled as graphs consisting of nodes and undirected edges as the flow direction of the water is not pre-defined and can change over time due to different inputs and demands in the network. More precisely, the pipes can be modeled as edges and their connections and basins as nodes. As usually real world water supply systems are extended over time it is possible that multiple pipes lie parallel to each other which is why the graph needs to be realized as a multigraph allowing multiple edges between the same nodes.

Frequently, water systems also contain some sensor technology which can be installed at the connections of the pipes or in basins (e.g., level or pressure sensors) or in the pipes (e.g., flow sensors). Considering the graph representation of the water network, we can distinguish between special sensor nodes/edges and regular ones.

In this work, we consider a variation of the L-Town network [14] as an exemplary complex and realistic water supply network. Area A of the network models the water supply network in the historic center of Limassol, Cyprus containing 661 nodes and 766 edges. In this contribution, we consider 29 optimally placed pressure sensors [14], which are highlighted in red in Fig. 1a. Besides, we visualized the pressure measurements of one exemplary sensor in Fig. 2a.

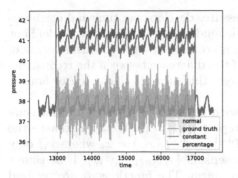
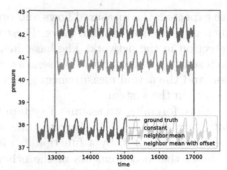

(a) Exemplary pressure measurements of one sensor (orange). Measurements with simulated sensor faults.

(b) Visualization of the imputation with neighborhood mean and neighborhood mean with offset for an exemplary sensor.

Fig. 2. Visualization of pressure sensor measurements. (Color figure online)

Some of the techniques described in the next section require the definition of a neighborhood $\mathcal{N}_i$ containing the sensor nodes in neighboring regions for each sensor node s_i. To compute the neighboring regions we incrementally assign each non-sensor node which is connected to the area of at least one sensor to the sensor area with most adjacent nodes. The obtained sensor areas are visualized in Fig. 1b. For each sensor node, the sensors of the neighboring areas are considered as its neighborhood. For the considered network, we obtain mean neighborhood sizes of 3.86 sensors ranging from 1 to 6 sensors.

4   Method

Multiple steps are required for monitoring the sensor technology in a CPS with possibly multiple sensor faults occurring in overlapping time intervals. First of all, the system is required to detect the presence of sensor faults (*fault detection*). In order to take appropriate measures, in a second step the fault needs to be isolated, i.e. the faulty sensor needs to be located (*fault isolation*). Finally, the fault needs to be dealt with. As it is costly to repair pressure sensors in the drinking water system due to pipes lying beneath the surface, frequently reparation or replacement takes time. Thus, it is necessary to either adapt the system in a way such that it can work without the sensor information or reproduce the sensor measurements (*sensor accommodation*). The latter gains special relevance if the prior two steps, as well as other monitoring and control systems rely on accurate measurements to function well. In the following sections, we describe our methodology to solve these tasks.

4.1   Fault Detection

The measurements of the different sensors in the water system are not independent. Due to the hydraulics in the system both temporal and local dependencies are expected: the measured flows and pressures develop over time and neighboring sensors measure similar flows. These dependencies can be used to model fault detection in the network: The basic idea is to reconstruct the measurements of each sensor based on the other sensors. If the difference between the reconstruction and the actual measurement gets large, this suggests that a sensor fault is present in the system.

More formally, we assume a system with n sensors $s_1, \dots s_n$ which measure data $x = [x_1 \dots x_n]_t$ at discrete time steps $t \in [1 \dots T]$. We approximate the measurements of s_i by a function $f_i : \mathbb{R}^{n-1} \to \mathbb{R}$, $f_i(x_{\setminus i}) = \hat{x}_i$ where $x_{\setminus i}$ only includes the measurements of the other sensors $\{s_j\}_{j \in \{1, \dots n\}, j \neq i}$. If at time t $\exists i : |x_i - \hat{x}_i| > \delta_i$ the system raises an alarm. The functions f_i are realized by linear regression models. The deviation thresholds δ_i are determined during the training of the models as the maximal absolute difference $\lambda \max_t |x_i^t - \hat{x}_i^t|$, where λ is a hyper-parameter of the detection scheme. Note that the functions could be also realized by more complex models, e.g. neural networks. However, we decided to apply simple linear models as we observed good approximation capabilities to the network dynamics. Besides, this model family can be trained easily and the detection algorithm runs in $\mathcal{O}(n)$ where n is the number of sensor nodes. This allows our algorithm to scale well to bigger networks.

Since we assume that the most important information for simulating a sensor comes from the physically neighboring sensors, we additionally define a localized fault detection mechanism. While the underlying idea is the same, instead of considering all sensors for simulating a sensor, we only consider sensors in neighboring regions of the water network: We approximate the measurements of s_i by a function $g_i : \mathbb{R}^{|\mathcal{N}_i|} \to \mathbb{R}$, $g(\{x_j\}_{s_j \in \mathcal{N}_i}) = \hat{x}_i$ where $\mathcal{N}_i$ includes all the neighboring sensors of s_i as obtained by the neighborhood computation described in Sect. 3. Again, the functions g_i are realized as linear regression models.

For both the local and the global fault detection method to detect a new fault, we assume that all sensors except of the faulty one yield reasonable measurements. To ensure that this is still the case after a first fault was detected, isolating the faulty sensor and repairing, replacing, or imputing it is crucial to ensure that the system can detect a second fault.

4.2   Fault Isolation

Next to the information that a sensor fault is present in the network, locating the position of the fault is necessary to take counter-measures. For our sensor isolation method, we extend the ensemble used for localized fault detection which was described in the previous section: Instead of only training one regression model g_i, we additionally train $|\mathcal{N}_i|$ functions for each sensor node s_i: for each sensor $s_j \in \mathcal{N}_i$ we estimate a function $g_{ij} : \mathbb{R}^{|\mathcal{N}_i|-1} \to \mathbb{R}$, $g(\{x_k\}_{s_k \in \mathcal{N}_i \setminus \{x_j\}}) = \hat{x}_i$ which estimates the sensor readings based on its neighborhood except for sensor s_j. Note that the number of additional models trained is small as the neighborhood for each sensor is small (see Sect. 3).

The isolation procedure itself is summarized in Algorithm 1: We first collect the set of involved sensors for each raised alarm, i.e. if f_i raises an alarm, we

---

Algorithm 1. Fault Isolation

Input: Model g_i for each sensor s_i along with neighboring sensors $\mathcal{N}_i$
Output: faulty sensor s

1: candidates = []   ▷ List of sensors involved in alarms
2: **for** $g_i \in$ models **do**   ▷ Add all sensors that were involved in alarms
3:     **if** g_i raises alarm **then**
4:         Add $\{s_i \cup \mathcal{N}_i\}$ to candidates
5:     **end if**
6: **end for**
7: suspects = $\cap$ candidates   ▷ Find sensors that were involved in all alarms
8: **for** $s \in$ suspects **do**   ▷ Figure out which sensor is responsible
9:     Return s_i as faulty sensor if all submodels $g_{ij}, s_j \in \mathcal{N}_i$ raise alarm
10: **end for**

---

add the set of s_i and $\{s_j | s_j \in \mathcal{N}_i\}$ to the set of candidate sensors. As we assume that only one sensor fault is starting to occur at the same time, we only further investigate those sensors that were involved in all alarms – they can be obtained by taking the intersection of all candidate sets.

In order to finally estimate which of the suspicious sensors is responsible for the alarm, we consider the additional functions g_{ij}. For each suspicious sensor s_i, we evaluate whether all g_{ij} for $s_j \in \mathcal{N}_i$ raise an alarm. If this is the case, we assume that s_i is responsible as we considered leaving out all other involved sensors $s_j \in \mathcal{N}_i$ – if one of them was responsible for the alarm, the according function (without this sensor) would not have raised an alarm.

Note that there exists the rare case that a sensor has only one neighbor (which is the case for one sensor in the L-Town network and assumed not very frequent in WDNs). This one is considered causing the alarm, if it is part of the set of suspicious sensors and no evidence is found for the other sensors.

4.3   Fault Accommodation

As it may be difficult and costly to repair or replace sensors in the water system (e.g. because sensors are not at the surface), it is a realistic scenario that a faulty sensor will not be repaired or replaced for quite some time. As the previously proposed fault detection and isolation methods require sensor readings from all sensors, it is necessary to simulate the sensor after the fault is detected for the first two steps of the system to work. In this work, we consider different strategies to impute the faulty sensors:

Historic mean. Missing data is imputed with the historic mean of the data: Assume that sensor s_i fails at time t_f, then the missing values are imputed by $\frac{1}{t_f - 1 - t_0} \sum_{t=t_0}^{t_f - 1} x_i^t$, where t_0 is the time step of the first measurement.
Historic median. Missing data is imputed by the historic median (similar to above description of the mean).

Table 1. Summary of considered sensor faults with the evaluated parameter choices

Fault	ϕ	a_0	a_1	Considered η
Constant	η	0.5	0.7	1, 2, 3
Drift	$\eta * (t - T_0)$	999999	1	0.01, 0.1, 1
Normal	$\mathcal{G}(0, \eta)$	100	100	0.5, 1, 2
Percentage	ηx_i^t	999999	0.7	0.01, 0.05, 0.1
Stuckzero	$-x_i^t$	999999	0.7	–

Neighborhood mean. This technique is similar to the kNN imputation strategy. Missing data for sensor s_i is imputed by $\frac{1}{|\mathcal{N}_i|} \sum_{x_j \in \mathcal{N}_i} x_j^t$ for each time step t.

Neighborhood mean with offset correction. We found in previous work that sensor differences can frequently be modeled with an offset between the sensor readings of different sensors [13]. We try this idea here and correct the previously described neighborhood mean by an offset: $\frac{1}{|\mathcal{N}_i|} \sum_{x_j \in \mathcal{N}_i} x_j^t + \theta_i$ for each time step t, where θ_i is estimated based on historical data. The difference between the neighborhood imputation with and without offset correction is visualized in Fig. 2b.

Virtual sensors. Missing data of sensor s_i is imputed based on the measurements of the other sensors by f_i as described in Sect. 4.1.

Local virtual sensors. Missing data of sensor s_i is imputed based on local virtual sensors g_i as described in Sect. 4.1.

5   Experiments

We experimentally evaluate all the previously designed steps of the fault control framework[3]. First, we will describe the data used and the type of sensor faults considered. Then, we will present and discuss our experiments and results for the three steps detection, isolation, and accommodation in the consecutive sections.

5.1   Data

For our experiments we simulate realistic networks dynamics using the Water Network Tool for Resilience (WNTR) toolbox [5]. We consider the L-Town-Variation network which was already introduced in Sect. 3. The simulation computes hydraulic measurements within the network in time steps of 5 minutes for the first three months of 2019.

We model a variety of different sensor failure types ranging from malfunctions causing noise or some offset in the measurements to a sensor failing completely in different severities. Assuming a fault happening between T_0, T_1 at sensor s_i,

---

[3] The code is available at https://github.com/vvaquet/sensor-fault-detection.

we consider the ground truth measurements $X_i = [x_i^1, \ldots, x_i^T]$. For each $x_i^t \in X_i$, we compute the faulty version

$$
\hat{x}_i^t = \begin{cases}
x_i^t & t < T_0 \\
x_i^t + (1 - \exp(-a_0(t - T_0))) \, \phi(\eta) & T_0 \le t < T_1 \\
x_i^t + ((1 - \exp(-a_0(t - T_0))) - (1 - \exp(-a_1(t - T_1)))) \, \phi(\eta) & t \ge T_1
\end{cases}
$$

where a_0, a_1 are fault specific constants describing the occurrence and disappearance evolution profile and $\phi(\eta)$ is a fault specific function.

An overview of the sensor faults with their constants, functions, and considered parameters is given in Table 1. Besides, we visualized a subset of the faults in Fig. 2a.

Table 2. Mean precision, recall, and F1 score and standard deviations for global and local fault detection (see Sect. 4.1) with $\lambda = 1.2$ for different sensor faults.

Fault	Precision	Recall	F1
Global fault detection			
Constant $\eta = 3$	0.9944 ± 0.0002	0.9998 ± 0.0	0.9971 ± 0.0001
Constant $\eta = 2$	0.9946 ± 0.0001	0.9998 ± 0.0	0.9972 ± 0.0001
Constant $\eta = 1$	0.9948 ± 0.0001	0.9998 ± 0.0	0.9973 ± 0.0001
Drift $\eta = 1$	0.9932 ± 0.0001	0.9998 ± 0.0	0.9964 ± 0.0001
Drift $\eta = 0.1$	0.9938 ± 0.0001	0.9998 ± 0.0	0.9968 ± 0.0001
Drift $\eta = 0.01$	0.9043 ± 0.0001	0.9003 ± 0.0002	0.0068 ± 0.0001
Normal $\eta = 2$	0.996 ± 0.0	0.9908 ± 0.0037	0.9934 ± 0.0019
Normal $\eta = 1$	0.996 ± 0.0	0.9815 ± 0.0064	0.9887 ± 0.0033
Normal $\eta = 0.5$	0.9959 ± 0.0001	0.9624 ± 0.0122	0.9788 ± 0.0064
percentage $\eta = 0.1$	0.9943 ± 0.0001	0.9998 ± 0.0	0.997 ± 0.0001
Percentage $\eta = 0.05$	0.9945 ± 0.0002	0.9998 ± 0.0	0.9971 ± 0.0001
Percentage $\eta = 0.01$	0.9951 ± 0.0001	0.9998 ± 0.0	0.9974 ± 0.0001
Stuckzero	0.9934 ± 0.0001	0.9998 ± 0.0	0.9966 ± 0.0001
Local fault detection			
Constant $\eta = 3$	0.9944 ± 0.0002	0.9998 ± 0.0	0.9971 ± 0.0001
Constant $\eta = 2$	0.9946 ± 0.0001	0.9998 ± 0.0	0.9972 ± 0.0001
Constant $\eta = 1$	0.9948 ± 0.0001	0.9998 ± 0.0	0.9973 ± 0.0001
Drift $\eta = 1$	0.9932 ± 0.0001	0.9998 ± 0.0	0.9964 ± 0.0001
Drift $\eta = 0.1$	0.9938 ± 0.0001	0.9998 ± 0.0	0.9968 ± 0.0001
Drift $\eta = 0.01$	0.9943 ± 0.0001	0.9993 ± 0.0002	0.9968 ± 0.0001
Normal $\eta = 2$	0.996 ± 0.0	0.9905 ± 0.004	0.9932 ± 0.002
Normal $\eta = 1$	0.996 ± 0.0	0.9817 ± 0.0061	0.9888 ± 0.0031
Normal $\eta = 0.5$	0.9959 ± 0.0001	0.9634 ± 0.0131	0.9793 ± 0.0069
Percentage $\eta = 0.1$	0.9943 ± 0.0001	0.9998 ± 0.0	0.997 ± 0.0001
Percentage $\eta = 0.05$	0.9945 ± 0.0002	0.9998 ± 0.0	0.9971 ± 0.0001
Percentage $\eta = 0.01$	0.9951 ± 0.0001	0.9998 ± 0.0	0.9974 ± 0.0001
Stuckzero	0.9934 ± 0.0001	0.9998 ± 0.0	0.9966 ± 0.0001

Table 3. Mean MSE and R^2 score with standard deviations for fault accommodation techniques.

Set-up	R2	MSE
Baseline	-208.8113 ± 162.4039	8.9962 ± 0.0
Virtual-sensor	0.9995 ± 0.0004	0.0 ± 0.0
Mean	–	0.0546 ± 0.0213
Neighbor-mean	-300.4645 ± 534.6956	9.5187 ± 10.6984
Neighbor-mean-offset	0.9339 ± 0.1615	0.0014 ± 0.0025
Median	–	0.0569 ± 0.0221

5.2 Fault Detection

For evaluating the fault detection step (Sect. 4.1) we apply the sensor faults in different intensities (see Table 2) to each sensor. All faults are occurring in the time between the 31st of January and the 28th of February. We apply our fault detection model on all generated scenarios and compute the recall and precision of the alarms reported by the model. The results are summarized in Table 2.

We observe high scores for all fault types and parameter configurations which implies that the fault detection scheme works well and there are only few false alarms or slight delays in reporting a fault. No notable differences between the global and the local detection method were found. Overall, the proposed simple methodology based on linear models works particularly well in the considered scenarios.

5.3 Fault Isolation

For evaluating our fault isolation technique, we simulated each type of sensor fault on each sensor in the time interval from the 15th of February to the 28th of February. In each scenario our method (Sect. 4.2) was able to locate the sensor fault.

5.4 Fault Accommodation

Testing the functionality of the fault accommodation strategies, we use two experimental set-ups: First, we evaluate the quality of the representation by standard metrics for regression (MSE, R^2)[4]. Thereby, we report how close the imputed values are to the ground truth measurements. Second, we evaluate how well fault detection works after sensor accommodation took place. Therefore, we again consider the recall and precision of the fault detection scheme after imputation techniques were applied to a first fault.

---

[4] MSE: $\frac{1}{n} \sum_{i=1}^{n} (y_i - \hat{y}_i)^2$, with ground truth y_i and prediciton $\hat{y}_i$; $R^2 = 1 - \frac{\sum (y_i - \hat{y}_i)^2}{\sum (y_i - \overline{y}_i)^2}$.

Representation Quality. For this experiment, we apply the accommodation strategies introduced in Sect. 4.3 to the measurements of one sensor in the time interval from the 1st of January to the 28th of February. We repeat this experiment for each sensor and report the MSE and R^2 score. Additionally, we consider the fault setting constant with $\eta = 3$ without any accommodation step as a baseline. The results for are summarized in Table 3[5].

For the historical mean and median, which perform much better than the baseline, we report an MSE of about 0.05. Considering the dynamics of the observed data (see Fig. 2a), which cannot be accurately described by a constant value, well working imputation strategies should perform better. We obtain the highest R^2 scores and the lowest MSE values for the virtual sensor approach and the neighbor mean with additional offset. In contrast, the neighbor mean without offset performs much worse than the not imputing at all. Considering an exemplary sensor in Fig. 2b, one can clearly see that the trend is approximated quite well but that the offset correction needs to be performed. Both neighborhood based mean imputations are not stable over the different sensors which is probably due to the network topology and dynamics which might cause this strategy to be more successful at certain nodes than for others.

Fault Detection Capability. To evaluate how well our detection module can detect a second failure given that the first is already accommodated, we create data sets containing two failures: the first starts at the 31st of January, the second at the 15th of February, both end at the 28th of February. We consider all possible pairs of different sensors for the failures and model the second with all the faults types defined in Table 1. In order to put the obtained results in relation, we also report results for not imputing the first sensor failure at all and for the ground truth measurements (without failure) which are not available in real world settings.

Again, we document the recall and precision of the alarms reported by the model. The mean results for the different imputation strategies are summarized in Table 4. While we report a high recall in all cases – implying that not many faulty measurements are missed, or possibly that there is still an alarm for the imputed sensor fault, the precision is quite low for this baseline because of many false alarms in the time interval where the first failure occurs. For simple imputation strategies like the mean and median we report precision scores similar to the baseline. This indicates that these simple methods are not sufficiently for the sensitive fault detection to work properly. For the neighbor based methods we find that the simple neighbor mean without offset correction is not performing any better than the baseline which was expected based on the reconstruction error. Correcting the offset enhances the precision to a score of 0.8 in the local and 0.84 in the global fault detection. Only the virtual sensor based method performs better yielding results comparable to the ground truth baseline. To sum up, virtual sensors are a solid choice for imputing missing sensor data. In case they are not working reliable in some settings, the neighborhood mean with offset correction seems to be a good starting point for designing an alternative.

---

[5] Some R^2 scores are missing as they are not defined for constant values.

Table 4. Mean precision, recall, and F1 score and standard deviations for fault detection with $\lambda = 1.2$ after different sensor accommodation techniques were applied to the first fault.

Imputation strategy	Precision	Recall	F1
Global fault detection			
No imputation	0.4814 ± 0.0001	1.0 ± 0.0	0.6499 ± 0.0001
Ground truth	0.9946 ± 0.0009	0.9948 ± 0.0112	0.9947 ± 0.0054
Historic mean	0.4814 ± 0.0001	1.0 ± 0.0	0.6499 ± 0.0001
Historic median	0.4814 ± 0.0001	1.0 ± 0.0	0.6499 ± 0.0001
Virtual sensors	0.9941 ± 0.0004	0.9948 ± 0.0112	0.9944 ± 0.0057
Local virtual sensors	0.994 ± 0.0008	0.9948 ± 0.0112	0.9944 ± 0.0057
Mean of neighborhood	0.4813 ± 0.0001	1.0 ± 0.0	0.6499 ± 0.0001
Mean of neighborhood with offset	0.8908 ± 0.1567	0.9957 ± 0.0099	0.932 ± 0.0986
Local fault detection			
No imputation	0.4814 ± 0.0001	1.0 ± 0.0	0.65 ± 0.0001
Ground truth	0.9946 ± 0.0009	0.9955 ± 0.01	0.995 ± 0.0048
Historic mean	0.4814 ± 0.0001	1.0 ± 0.0	0.65 ± 0.0001
Historic median	0.4814 ± 0.0001	1.0 ± 0.0	0.65 ± 0.0001
Virtual sensors	0.994 ± 0.0005	0.9954 ± 0.0101	0.9947 ± 0.0051
Local virtual sensors	0.9941 ± 0.0004	0.9954 ± 0.0101	0.9947 ± 0.0051
Mean of neighborhood	0.4814 ± 0.0001	1.0 ± 0.0	0.6499 ± 0.0001
Mean of neighborhood with offset	0.876 ± 0.174	0.9963 ± 0.0088	0.9219 ± 0.1103

6   Conclusion

We extended residual based fault detection to an algorithm for isolating the faulty sensor and evaluated both methods for a variety of different realistic sensor faults on data generated for the L-Town-Variation network. Besides, we proposed imputation of faulty sensor data by virtual sensors and based on the sensors neighborhood. Evaluation of the imputation was performed with respect to the deviation to ground truth measurements and to the detection capability in comparison to standard techniques. Both fault detection and fault isolation performed well for the different types of sensor faults. Besides, virtual sensors are a good choice to impute missing data until the real sensor is replaced.

Although we observed promising results in this work, we should evaluate the proposed methodology in further scenarios considering additional fault behaviors, the combination of even more faults, and different network topologies and demand patterns. These additional scenarios might make it necessary to consider more complex machine learning models in the fault detection and isolation ensemble. It would be also interesting to investigate physics-informed sensor imputation in future work.

References

1. Bennis, S., Berrada, F., Kang, N.: Improving single-variable and multivariable techniques for estimating missing hydrological data. J. Hydrol. **191**(1), 87–105 (1997). https://doi.org/10.1016/S0022-1694(96)03076-4. https://www.sciencedirect.com/science/article/pii/S0022169496030764
2. Bouzid, S., Ramdani, M.: Sensor fault detection and diagnosis in drinking water distribution networks. In: 2013 8th International Workshop on Systems, Signal Processing and their Applications (WoSSPA), pp. 378–383 (2013). https://doi.org/10.1109/WoSSPA.2013.6602395
3. El-Zahab, S., Zayed, T.: Leak detection in water distribution networks: an introductory overview. Smart Water **4**(1), 1–23 (2019). https://doi.org/10.1186/s40713-019-0017-x
4. Goldsmith, D., Preis, A., Allen, M., Whitttle, A.: Virtual sensors to improve on-line hydraulic model calibration, January 2010. https://doi.org/10.1061/41203(425)121
5. Murray, H.: An overview of the water network tool for resilience (wntr) (2018)
6. Perez, R., et al.: Leak localization in water networks: a model-based methodology using pressure sensors applied to a real network in barcelona [applications of control]. IEEE Control Syst. Mag. **34**(4), 24–36 (2014). https://doi.org/10.1109/MCS.2014.2320336
7. Quevedo, J., et al.: Validation and reconstruction of flow meter data in the Barcelona water distribution network. Control Eng. Practice **18**, 640–651 (010). https://doi.org/10.1016/j.conengprac.2010.03.003
8. Reppa, V., Polycarpou, M., Panayiotou, C.: Sensor fault diagnosis. Found. Trends Syst. Control **3**, 1–248 (2016). https://doi.org/10.1561/2600000007
9. Reppa, V., Polycarpou, M.M., Panayiotou, C.G.: Multiple sensor fault detection and isolation for large-scale interconnected nonlinear systems. In: 2013 European Control Conference (ECC), pp. 1952–1957 (2013). https://doi.org/10.23919/ECC.2013.6669349
10. Reppa, V., Polycarpou, M.M., Panayiotou, C.G.: Adaptive approximation for multiple sensor fault detection and isolation of nonlinear uncertain systems. IEEE Trans. Neural Networks Learn. Syst. **25**(1), 137–153 (2014). https://doi.org/10.1109/TNNLS.2013.2250301
11. Reppa, V., Polycarpou, M.M., Panayiotou, C.G.: Distributed sensor fault diagnosis for a network of interconnected cyberphysical systems. IEEE Trans. Control Network Syst. **2**(1), 11–23 (2015). https://doi.org/10.1109/TCNS.2014.2367362
12. Sanz, G., Pérez, R., Kapelan, Z., Savic, D.: Leak detection and localization through demand components calibration. J. Water Resour. Plan. Manag. **142**(2), 04015057 (2016). https://doi.org/10.1061/(ASCE)WR.1943-5452.0000592
13. Vaquet, V., Menz, P., Seiffert, U., Hammer, B.: Investigating intensity and transversal drift in hyperspectral imaging data. ESANN 2021 proceedings (2021)
14. Vrachimis, S.G., et al.: Battledim: Battle of the leakage detection and isolation methods (2020)

Temporal Graph Transformer for Dynamic Network

Zehong Wang[1], Qi Li[1(✉)], Donghua Yu[1,2], and Xiaolong Han[1]

[1] Department of Computer Science and Engineering, Shaoxing University,
Shaoxing 312000, China
liqi0713@foxmail.com
[2] School of Computer Science and Technology, Soochow University,
Suzhou 215000, China

Abstract. Graph neural networks (GNN) have received great attention in recent years due to their unique role in mining graph-based data. Although most work focuses on learning low-dimensional node representation in static graphs, the dynamic nature of real-world networks makes temporal graphs more practical and significant. Continuous-time dynamic graph (CTDG) is a general approach to express temporal networks in fine granularity. Owing to the high time consumption in training and inference, existing CTDG-based algorithms capture information from 1-hop neighbors, ignoring the messages from high-order neighbors, which inevitably leads to model degradation. To overcome the challenge, we propose Temporal Graph Transformer (TGT) to efficiently capture the evolving and semantic information from high-order neighborhoods in dynamic graphs. The proposed TGT consists of three modules, i.e., update module, aggregation module, and propagation module. Different from previous works that aggregate messages layer by layer, the model captures messages from 1-hop and 2-hop neighbors in a single layer. In particular, (1) the update module learns from messages derived from interactions; (2) the aggregation module aggregates 1-hop temporal neighbors to compute node embedding; (3) the propagation module re-updates the hidden state of temporal neighbors to introduce 2-hop information. Experimental results on three real-world networks demonstrate the superiority of TGT in efficacy and efficiency.

Keywords: Temporal graph · Continuous-time dynamic graph · Graph neural network · Graph embedding

1 Introduction

Owing to the capacity for learning from non-Euclidean space, graph neural network (GNN) has emerged as a ubiquitous tool in various fields, such as e-commerce [10], social network [22], recommender system [3]. In social networks, nodes denote users and edges represent the interactions between them, e.g.,

E. Pimenidis et al. (Eds.): ICANN 2022, LNCS 13530, pp. 694–705, 2022.
https://doi.org/10.1007/978-3-031-15931-2_57

having a chat, sending an e-mail, becoming friends. Existing graph neural networks aim to learn node representation that preserves topology and semantics in graphs and to perform downstream tasks, including node classification [23], link prediction [11], recommendation [3].

Most aforementioned research on graph representation learning has been done on static graphs [6,7,9,13,20], which consists of fixed nodes and edges. However, networks generally preserve complicated temporal properties in reality, which are named dynamic graphs [4,14,22]. The dynamic graph not only contains structural and semantical properties but also holds the network evolving information, indicated by the timestamp on the edges. If we directly perform static graph neural networks on dynamic graphs, the temporal property of the network will be ignored.

A common paradigm to represent the dynamic graph is called continuous-time dynamic graph (CTDG) [10,15], where the graph is represented as a sequence of time-ordered edges, maintaining fine-grained temporal information. CTDG-based graph neural networks compute and update node embedding in each timestamp [3,15]. Although temporal information [22] between timestamps is preserved, these methods still suffer from the high time consumption in training and inference. The challenge derives from the natural structure of the graph, i.e., while querying high-order neighbors, the time consumption will exponentially rise. Many works attempt to make a trade-off between the performance and the real-time requirement. These methods [10,18,22] generally aggregate messages from 1-hop neighbors, totally ignoring high-order neighbors, which inevitably impairs the performance of the model. How to efficiently capture the information from high-order neighbors is an extremely urgent challenge.

In this paper, we propose temporal graph transformer (TGT) to efficiently learn from 1-hop and 2-hop neighbors. The model composes of three modules, namely, update, aggregation, and propagation. In particular, the update module leverages gated recurrent unit (GRU) [2] to update the hidden state on the target node through the message from newly formed edges. The aggregation module leverages the transformer [19] to compute node embedding by aggregating information from 1-hop temporal neighbors. Afterward, the propagation module utilizes node embedding of the target node to re-update the hidden state on temporal neighbors. The operation in fact incorporates the 2-hop message to the temporal neighbors since the node embedding contains information from the neighbor's neighbors. By the incorporation of these three modules, TGT learns information from 1-hop and 2-hop neighbors in a layer instead of two layers [15,22], dramatically reducing the time consumption in both training and inference. We conduct extensive experiments on three real-world networks to demonstrate the superiority of TGT in efficiency and efficacy. Our contributions are summarized as follows:

- We propose a novel CTDG-based graph neural network, named temporal graph transformer (TGT), to effectively and efficiently capture the evolving and semantic information in dynamic networks.

- We propose three modules, i.e., update module, aggregation module, propagation module, to simultaneously learn messages from 1-hop and 2-hop neighbors in a single layer, dramatically reducing time consumption in training and inference.
- We conduct experiments on three real-world datasets to demonstrate the effectiveness and efficiency of TGT. Experimental results show the TGT outperforms all baselines.

2   Related Work

The temporal graph embedding technique is classified into two categories, i.e., discrete-time dynamic graph (DTDG) and continuous-time dynamic graph (CTDG). DTDG is represented as a series of snapshots obtained from different timestamps. DynGEM [5] proposes a DTDG-based graph neural network based on the deep auto-encoder to achieve stability, flexibility, and efficiency. Dyngraph2vec [4] aims to learn time dependency in inductive learning by combining auto-encoder and recurrent neural network. EvolveGCN [12] utilizes the recurrent neural network to update parameters in graph neural networks to induce temporal information as well as keep the structure of GNN. DySAT [16] introduces structural self-attention and position-aware temporal self-attention to weighted compute node embedding. Although DTDG-based algorithms can maintain time dependency between two adjacent snapshots, they fail to model temporal properties in a single snapshot.

CTDG is represented as a sequence of edges. HTNE [23] firstly applies the Hawkes process to model temporal interactions in dynamic networks. DyRep [18] considers association events and communication events to simultaneously capture immediate information and long-term information. JODIE [10] updates node memory through messages from newly formed interactions. TDGNN [14] leverage the temporal aggregator to compute node representation by aggregating temporal neighbors. TDIG-MPNN [1] utilizes the temporal point process to model the dynamics and capture the local and global dependency. TGSRec [3] models the bipartite graph to uniformly learn the sequential patterns and temporal collaborative signals by applying a novel transformer architecture. To learn from high-order neighbors, TGT [22] generalizes the vanilla GAT [20] by applying time encoding to aggregate temporal neighbors layer-by-layer. TGN [15] introduces the memory module to preserve the last node state. DGNN [11] first leverages propagation mechanism to replace the aggregation operation in [15] to model the temporal information. APAN [21] proposes a multi-layer propagation-based model, which aims to reduce the time consumption in inference. Although existing CTDG-based algorithms utilize aggregation operation or propagation operation, none of them integrate the advantages of these two mechanisms in a single model.

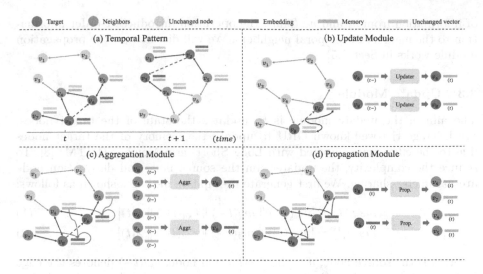

Fig. 1. An overview of the structure of TGT. (a) Temporal pattern. The figure shows edges emerged at timestamp t from v_8 to v_6 and $t+1$ from v_2 to v_3. (b) When a link is formed, update module generates messages to update memory state of target nodes. (c) Afterward, aggregation module utilizes neighbors memory to learn representation of target nodes. (d) Finally, propagation module re-updates the memory state of temporal neighbors to introduce 2-hop information.

3 Methodology

3.1 Preliminary

A dynamic graph consists of a node set $V = \{v_1, v_2, ..., v_n\}$ and a edge set $E = \{e_1, e_2, ..., e_m\}$, where n and m are the number of nodes and edges, respectively. A direct edge is represented as (v_s, v_d, t, e), where v_s is the source node, v_d is the destination node, t denotes timestamp, and e is the edge attributes.

3.2 Overall Structure

The overview structure of TGT is illustrated in Fig. 1. The model consists of three modules, namely, update, aggregation, and propagation. In Fig. 1(a), we observe an interaction emerges from v_8 to v_6 at timestamp t. Firstly, the update module (Fig. 1(b)) updates the memory of v_8 and v_6 according to the message derived from the interaction. Then, the aggregation module (Fig. 1(c)) computes node embedding by weighted aggregating temporal neighbors. At timestamp t, temporal neighbors for v_8 is $\{v_7\}$ and for v_6 is $\{v_4, v_5\}$. We aggregate them to compute node embedding for v_6 and v_8. Finally, the propagation module (Fig. 1(d)) re-updates the memory of the temporal neighbors through the embedding of the target node. For instance, at timestamp t, the memory of temporal neighbor v_4 is updated through the message from v_6, where the message consists of information from v_4 and v_5. Thus, the operation introduces 2-order information to the memory of temporal neighbors. We will discuss how the propagation module works in Sect. 3.5.

3.3   Update Module

The aim of the update module is to updates the state of the target nodes. We leverage the well-known GRU to update the memory of the target nodes due to the efficiency compared with Long Short-term Memory (LSTM) [8]. To reduce the complexity, the updaters on the source node and destination node are parameter-sharing. We first generate the update messages shown as follows:

$$msg_s(t) = [m_s(t-) \parallel m_d(t-) \parallel e_{sd}(t-) \parallel \lambda(t)] \tag{1}$$
$$msg_d(t) = [m_d(t-) \parallel m_s(t-) \parallel e_{sd}(t-) \parallel \lambda(t)] \tag{2}$$

where s is the source node, d is the destination node, $e_{sd}(t-)$ denotes the edge features, $m_s(t-)$ and $m_d(t-)$ represent the memory state of v_s and v_d before the current timestamp, respectively. $\lambda(t)$ is the time encoding, we will introduce it in Sect. 3.4.

Afterward, we leverage them to update the memory vectors of v_s and v_d. The formulas are shown as follows:

$$z_t = \sigma(W_z \cdot msg_i(t) + U_z \cdot m_i(t-)) \tag{3}$$
$$r_t = \sigma(W_r \cdot msg_i(t) + U_r \cdot m_i(t-)) \tag{4}$$
$$m_i'(t) = tanh(W_x \cdot msg_i(t) + r_t * U_m \cdot m_i(t-)) \tag{5}$$
$$m_i(t) = z_t * m_i(t-) + (1 - z_t) * m_i'(t) \tag{6}$$

where z_t is update gate, r_t is reset gate, σ is sigmoid function, $\{W_z, W_r, W_x\}$ and $\{U_z, U_r, U_m\}$ are learnable parameters.

3.4   Aggregation Module

After the memory of the target nodes is updated, we aggregate the top-k recent temporal neighbors to obtain node embedding. Figure 2 demonstrates the structure of the aggregator based on transformer [19]. The use of the transformer brings two benefits: (1) the model can be stacked to enhance expressiveness, and (2) the importance of neighbors can be learned to improve interpretability.

We first define the time encoding to replace the positional encoding in the vanilla transformer. Inspired by TGAT [22], we propose the following time encoding to capture the periodicity on the dynamic networks:

$$\lambda(t) = sin(W_t \cdot \Delta t + b_t) \tag{7}$$

where Δt is the time interval between the current timestamp and the last interaction, W_t and b_t are learnable parameters.

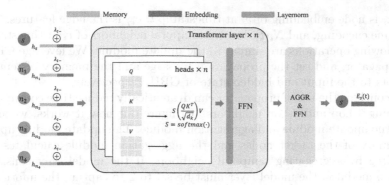

Fig. 2. The architecture of the aggregation module with three heads in the self-attention layer.

Then, we incorporate the memory vector, edge features, and time encoding to obtain the input of the transformer.

$$h_i(t-) = [m_i(t-) \parallel \frac{1}{|N_i(t)|} \sum_{j \in N_i(t)} e_{ij}(t-)] + \lambda(t) \tag{8}$$

$$h_j(t-) = [m_j(t-) \parallel e_{ij}(t-)] + \lambda_{ij}(t), \forall j \in N_i(t) \tag{9}$$

where $N_i(t)$ is the top-k recent temporal neighbors of the target node v_i, and $\parallel$ denotes the concatenation operation.

Afterward, we feed the input into the self-attention and feed-forward network (FFN) to learn the hidden state of each input in the timestamp t. In the self-attention layer, the inputs are mapped into three matrices, $Q \in \mathbb{R}^{d_h \times d_Q}$, $K \in \mathbb{R}^{d_h \times d_Q}$, and $V \in \mathbb{R}^{d_h \times d_V}$, denoting the query, key, and value matrices, respectively. We adopt the following formula to compute the output of self-attention.

$$output = Softmax\left(\frac{QK^T}{d_k}\right)V \tag{10}$$

Then, we adopt the FFN to project the outputs and obtain the hidden state of the target node and temporal neighbors in timestamp t. Finally, we utilize the aggregator (i.e., Sum-pooling or Mean-pooling) and another FNN to acquire node embedding.

3.5 Propagation Module

Following the aggregation module, we utilize the computed node embedding to generate propagation message and re-update the memory of temporal neighbors. Through the propagation module, the memory of temporal neighbors will incorporate the message from the neighbors' neighbors. We define the propagation message as follows:

$$msg_{prop}(i, j) = [z_i(t) \parallel e_{ij} \parallel \lambda_{ij}(t)], \forall j \in N_i(t) \tag{11}$$

where z_i is node embedding of v_i at timestamp t, e_{ij} is the edge features, $\lambda_{ij}(t)$ is the time encoding, and $N_i(t)$ denotes temporal neighbors of v_i at timestamp t. The following operations are similar to the update module. We leverage GRU as the propagator, and set the propagation message and the memory of temporal neighbors to the input and hidden state of GRU, respectively.

We conclude the use of propagator can dramatically reduce time consumption in learning 1-hop and 2-hop neighbors. To figure out how it works, we should review the update module and aggregation module. The update module updates the memory of the target nodes and the aggregation module calculates node embedding by aggregating temporal neighbors. If the model only consists of these two modules, the model layer must be set to 2 to capture the information from 1-hop and 2-hop neighbors. At the time, the time consumption will be high because we must query temporal neighbors in each layer.

Note that the node embedding, i.e., the output of layer 2, can be seen as the combination of the outputs of layer 1. The intuition of the propagation module is to separately combine the outputs of layer 1, decomposing the learning procedure in layer 2. In other words, the propagator aims to incrementally calculate the output of layer 2 (node embedding) in different timestamps. Therefore, we replace the operation in layer 2 with a sequence of asynchronous update operations, which is performed by the propagation module. By this means, we can learn 1-hop and 2-hop neighbors in the same layer, dramatically reducing the time consumption in querying temporal neighbors and performing corresponding numerical calculation operations.

4   Experiments

4.1   Dataset

– **UCI**[1] is a directed social network dataset, which contains 1,899 nodes and 59,835 edges. The node denotes the student from the University of California, Irvine, and the interaction represents the message communication between students where the timestamp corresponds to the time when a message is delivered.
– **MovieLens-10M**[2] is a dynamic user-tag interactions dataset, which consists of nearly 100,000 tags applied to 10,000 movies by 72,000 users. We pick the subset of the benchmark with about 1,500 nodes and 50,000 interactions.
– **Math-overflow**[3] is a temporal network of interactions on the Math Overflow. There are three types of interaction in the graph, i.e., a2q, c2q, c2a, representing the answer of a question, the comment of a question, and the comment of an answer, respectively. The dataset contains nearly 25,000 nodes and 506,550 edges.

---

[1] https://snap.stanford.edu/data/CollegeMsg.html.
[2] https://grouplens.org/datasets/movielens/10m/.
[3] https://snap.stanford.edu/data/sx-mathoverflow.html.

Table 1. Performance comparison of link prediction in terms of AUC, F1, and MRR. The **first**, <u>second</u> best performance is marked.

Baselines	UCI			MovieLen-10M			Math-overflow		
	AUC	F1	MRR	AUC	F1	MRR	AUC	F1	MRR
GCN [9]	0.9321	0.3427	0.0138	0.7324	0.3361	**0.0167**	0.9232	0.5941	0.0083
GAT [20]	0.8556	0.6934	0.0132	0.7301	0.4304	<u>0.0088</u>	0.7629	0.7242	0.0014
GSAGE [7]	0.5121	0.5815	0.0060	0.5232	0.4911	0.0020	0.5098	0.6622	0.0007
UniMP [17]	0.5509	0.6174	0.0024	0.5515	0.4910	0.0022	0.5058	0.6699	0.0007
JODIE [10]	0.8846	0.7820	0.0374	0.5915	0.5524	0.0019	0.9142	0.8158	0.2514
DyRep [18]	0.8782	0.7439	<u>0.0565</u>	0.5573	0.5160	0.0032	0.8986	0.7646	0.2580
TGAT [22]	0.7925	0.7660	0.0412	0.5823	0.4782	0.0012	0.8652	0.7824	0.2107
TGN [15]	0.9279	0.7587	0.0130	0.7509	0.6449	0.0010	0.9054	0.6337	0.1715
TGT-mean	<u>0.9689</u>	<u>0.9092</u>	0.0435	**0.8466**	**0.7393**	0.0005	<u>0.9461</u>	**0.8830**	<u>0.2634</u>
TGT-sum	**0.9707**	**0.9175**	**0.0797**	<u>0.8358</u>	<u>0.7368</u>	0.0010	**0.9496**	<u>0.8821</u>	**0.2640**

4.2   Experimental Setting

We conduct temporal link prediction and edge classification tasks to evaluate the superiority of the proposed TGT. For temporal link prediction, we set the data split as 70%~15%~15% and use AUC (Area under ROC), F1 (F1-score), MRR (Mean Reciprocal Rank) as metrics. We tune parameters on the validation set and set the early stop to 5 epochs. The number of negative sampling is the same as the positive samples. For fair comparison, we set the node embedding to 256, the number of attention heads to 2 for all baselines. For dynamic models, we set the number of temporal neighbors to 20, the batch size to 20 for UCI and MovieLen-10M, and to 50 for Math-overflow. For edge classification, we set the training ratio in {40%, 60%, 80%}, and the remaining is split equally to the validation set and testing set. We leverage AUC and F1 as metrics.

4.3   Link Prediction

In this section, we conduct experiments to evaluate the superiority of TGT on temporal link prediction. Table 1 reports the link prediction results. For UCI, all dynamic graph embedding methods outperform static graph embedding methods, showing the necessity of modeling evolving information. The TGT achieves the best performance, which demonstrates the capability of learning in small graphs. For MovieLen-10M, GCN and GAT are better than all dynamic graph learning models in terms of MRR due to the sparsity of the dataset. The proposed TGT model achieves the best performance on AUC and F1-score. We observe the mean aggregator is better than the sum. We assume in tagging networks the number of tags may not play an important role. For Math-overflow, all dynamic models achieve better performance than static methods and the proposed TGT achieves the highest score. The results show the capacity of TGT in processing large dynamic networks.

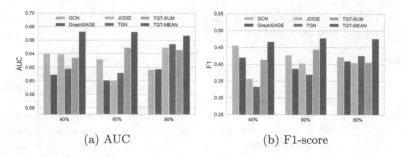

(a) AUC   (b) F1-score

Fig. 3. Performance comparison of edge classification on math-overflow dataset in terms of AUC and F1

Table 2. Ablation study of link prediction in terms of AUC, AP, and F1

Baselines	UCI			MovieLen-10M			Math-overflow		
	AUC	AP	F1	AUC	AP	F1	AUC	AP	F1
TGT-mean	0.9689	0.9708	0.9092	0.8466	0.8820	0.7393	0.9461	0.9450	0.8830
TGT-prop	0.7297	0.6996	0.7290	0.5974	0.6276	0.6599	0.7835	0.7577	0.6939
TGT-update	0.8726	0.8632	0.8082	0.5868	0.6416	0.6675	0.7691	0.7012	0.7602
TGT-aggr	0.9677	0.9702	0.9131	0.8382	0.8730	0.7485	0.9124	0.9043	0.8304

4.4 Edge Classification

For the edge classification task, Fig. 3 illustrates the performance comparison between TGT and existing models on Math-overflow. We observe that with the increase of training ratio, the performance of TGT keeps at a high score, demonstrating the generalization ability. Even though static methods outperform dynamic methods when the training ratio is low, we also observe that if the dynamic models obtain more edges in the training phase, the performance will be better than static models. The observation shows the significance of learning evolving information.

4.5 Ablation Study

In this section, we perform the ablation study to analyze the impact of each module. In particular, we define the following three variants:

TGT-update: The model drops the update module, which learns the information from newly formed interactions. The aggregator is mean aggregator.

TGT-prop: The model only consists of the update module and aggregation module. The aggregator used in the model is mean aggregator.

TGT-aggr: We evaluate the impact of aggregator by directly leveraging the output of transformer as the node embedding.

Table 2 shows the results of ablation study on link prediction. We conclude that all components are important for the model, indicating 1) the necessity

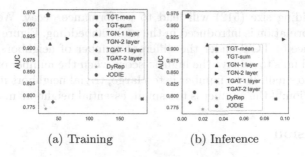

(a) Training   (b) Inference

Fig. 4. The time complexty analysis on UCI dataset. (a) Training time per epoch. (b) Inference time per batch.

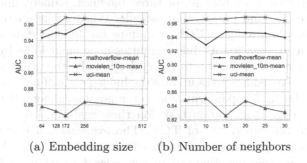

(a) Embedding size   (b) Number of neighbors

Fig. 5. Hyper-parameter analysis of TGT in three benchmarks in terms of AUC

to introduce 2-order information (i.e., propagation), (2) the information from neighbors should be aggregated, and (3) the information from newly formed interactions plays a vital role.

4.6   Efficiency and Robustness Analysis

To evaluate the efficiency and robustness of TGT, we compare the time consumption of TGT against 4 baselines and analyze the impact of two hyper-parameters, i.e., embedding size and the number of neighbors.

Figure 4a and 4b illustrates the time consumption in training and inference, respectively. Thanks to the propagation module, TGT captures 1-hop and 2-hop information in the same layer, achieving the best performance and the lowest time consumption. Note that TGT is efficient in both training and inference, showing the potential in deploying in real applications. For the other baselines, the performance of TGN and TGAT is improved when the model becomes deeper. Although the performance is improved, the time consumption also greatly increases, especially in the inference phase.

The analysis of embedding size is shown in Fig. 5a. The embedding size is set in $\{64, 128, 172, 256, 512\}$. The best performance appears when embedding size is 256 for MovieLen-10M and Math-overflow and 172 for UCI. Besides, we observe a large embedding size (512) will lead to performance decay. We assume the redundant information is introduced in the node embedding. Figure 5b illustrates the performance of TGT under the different number of neighbors. We observe that the model fails to achieve the highest score when the number of neighbors is too large or too small. If the number is too large, trivial neighbors may introduce noisy information; if the number is too small, essential neighbors may be ignored.

5   Conclusion

In this paper, we propose a novel CTDG-based graph neural network called temporal graph transformer (TGT) to learn low-dimensional node representation on dynamic graphs. TGT consists of three modules, namely, update module, aggregation module, and propagation module. When an interaction is formed, the update module leverages GRU to update the hidden state of the target node. Then, the aggregation module computes node embedding by aggregating 1-hop temporal neighbors of the target node. Finally, the propagation module utilizes the node embedding to re-update the hidden state of temporal neighbors, explicitly introducing 2-hop information to temporal neighbors. We conduct link prediction and edge classification tasks on three real-world dynamic networks to demonstrate the superiority of TGT. The experimental results show that TGT outperforms all baselines on both efficacy and efficiency. An interesting future direction is exploring other events, e.g., edge deletion, node deletion, node evolution, to capture more fine-grained properties on dynamic graphs.

Acknowledgement. This work was supported in part by Zhejiang Natural Science Foundation of China No. LY22F020003 and National Natural Science Foundation of China under Grant No. 62002226, No. 62002227.

References

1. Chang, X., et l.: Continuous-time dynamic graph learning via neural interaction processes. In: Proceedings of the 29th ACM International Conference on Information & Knowledge Management, pp. 145–154 (2020)
2. Chung, J., Gulcehre, C., Cho, K., Bengio, Y.: Empirical evaluation of gated recurrent neural networks on sequence modeling. arXiv preprint arXiv:1412.3555 (2014)
3. Fan, Z., Liu, Z., Zhang, J., Xiong, Y., Zheng, L., Yu, P.S.: Continuous-time sequential recommendation with temporal graph collaborative transformer. In: Proceedings of the 30th ACM International Conference on Information & Knowledge Management, pp. 433–442 (2021)
4. Goyal, P., Chhetri, S.R., Canedo, A.: dyngraph2vec: capturing network dynamics using dynamic graph representation learning. Knowl.-Based Syst. **187**, 104816 (2020)
5. Goyal, P., Kamra, N., He, X., Liu, Y.: Dyngem: deep embedding method for dynamic graphs. arXiv preprint arXiv:1805.11273 (2018)
6. Grover, A., Leskovec, J.: node2vec: Scalable feature learning for networks. In: Proceedings of the 22nd ACM SIGKDD International Conference on Knowledge Discovery and Data Mining, pp. 855–864 (2016)

7. Hamilton, W.L., Ying, R., Leskovec, J.: Inductive representation learning on large graphs. In: Proceedings of the 31st International Conference on Neural Information Processing Systems, pp. 1025–1035 (2017)
8. Hochreiter, S., Schmidhuber, J.: Long short-term memory. Neural Comput. **9**(8), 1735–1780 (1997)
9. Kipf, T.N., Welling, M.: Semi-supervised classification with graph convolutional networks. arXiv preprint arXiv:1609.02907 (2016)
10. Kumar, S., Zhang, X., Leskovec, J.: Predicting dynamic embedding trajectory in temporal interaction networks. In: Proceedings of the 25th ACM SIGKDD International Conference on Knowledge Discovery & Data Mining, pp. 1269–1278 (2019)
11. Ma, Y., Guo, Z., Ren, Z., Tang, J., Yin, D.: Streaming graph neural networks. In: Proceedings of the 43rd International ACM SIGIR Conference on Research and Development in Information Retrieval, pp. 719–728 (2020)
12. Pareja, A., et al.: Evolvegcn: evolving graph convolutional networks for dynamic graphs. In: Proceedings of the AAAI Conference on Artificial Intelligence, vol. 34, pp. 5363–5370 (2020)
13. Perozzi, B., Al-Rfou, R., Skiena, S.: Deepwalk: Online learning of social representations. In: Proceedings of the 20th ACM SIGKDD International Conference on Knowledge Discovery and Data Mining, pp. 701–710 (2014)
14. Qu, L., Zhu, H., Duan, Q., Shi, Y.: Continuous-time link prediction via temporal dependent graph neural network. In: Proceedings of The Web Conference 2020, pp. 3026–3032 (2020)
15. Rossi, E., Chamberlain, B., Frasca, F., Eynard, D., Monti, F., Bronstein, M.: Temporal graph networks for deep learning on dynamic graphs. arXiv preprint arXiv:2006.10637 (2020)
16. Sankar, A., Wu, Y., Gou, L., Zhang, W., Yang, H.: DYSAT: deep neural representation learning on dynamic graphs via self-attention networks. In: Proceedings of the 13th International Conference on Web Search and Data Mining, pp. 519–527 (2020)
17. Shi, Y., Huang, Z., Feng, S., Zhong, H., Wang, W., Sun, Y.: Masked label prediction: unified message passing model for semi-supervised classification. arXiv preprint arXiv:2009.03509 (2020)
18. Trivedi, R., Farajtabar, M., Biswal, P., Zha, H.: DyRep: learning representations over dynamic graphs. In: International Conference on Learning Representations (2019)
19. Vaswani, A., et al.: Attention is all you need. In: Advances in Neural Information Processing Systems, pp. 5998–6008 (2017)
20. Veličković, P., Cucurull, G., Casanova, A., Romero, A., Lio, P., Bengio, Y.: Graph attention networks. arXiv preprint arXiv:1710.10903 (2017)
21. Wang, X., et al.: APAN: asynchronous propagation attention network for real-time temporal graph embedding. In: Proceedings of the 2021 International Conference on Management of Data, pp. 2628–2638 (2021)
22. Xu, D., Ruan, C., Korpeoglu, E., Kumar, S., Achan, K.: Inductive representation learning on temporal graphs. arXiv preprint arXiv:2002.07962 (2020)
23. Zuo, Y., Liu, G., Lin, H., Guo, J., Hu, X., Wu, J.: Embedding temporal network via neighborhood formation. In: Proceedings of the 24th ACM SIGKDD International Conference on Knowledge Discovery & Data Mining, pp. 2857–2866 (2018)

Towards Understanding the Effect of Node Features on the Predictions of Graph Neural Networks

Qiming Li[1,2], Zhao Zhang[1,3(✉)], Boyu Diao[1], Yongjun Xu[1], and Chao Li[1,3(✉)]

[1] Institute of Computing Technology, Chinese Academy of Sciences, Beijing, China
{liqiming19b,zhangzhao2017,diaoboyu2012,xyj,lichao}@ict.ac.cn
[2] University of Chinese Academy of Sciences, Beijing, China
[3] Zhejiang Lab, Hangzhou, China

Abstract. Graph Neural Networks (GNNs) have shown powerful performance on various graph-related tasks. GNNs learn better knowledge representations by aggregating the features of neighboring nodes. However, the black-box representations of deep learning models make it difficult for people to understand GNN's inherent operation mechanism. To this end, in this paper, we propose a model-agnostic method called GNN Prediction Interpreter (GPI) to explain node features' effect on the prediction of GNN. Particularly, GPI first quantifies the correlation between node features and GNN's prediction, and then identifies the subset of node features that have an essential impact on GNN's prediction according to the quantitative results. Experiments demonstrate that GPI can provide better explanations than state-of-the-art methods.

Keywords: Graph Neural Networks · Node features · Interpretability

1 Introduction

Due to the superiority of graph structure in modeling rich object features and the relationships between objects, in a large number of real-world applications, data is widely represented as graphs. However, the irregularity of graphs and the interdependency between nodes degrade the performance of machine learning algorithms. To address this problem, GNNs are proposed. Because of their outstanding capability to aggregate and pass information, GNNs have achieved state-of-the-art results in various graph machine learning tasks such as node classification [5], link prediction [19], and graph classification [16]. Although GNNs have excellent discriminative ability, poor interpretability is GNN's fatal disadvantage and severely hinders its further development.

The previous works explaining GNN are mainly divided into two categories. One of them is the theoretical analysis of GNN's representative power. Considering the difficulty of training GNN with many graph convolutional layers, some

Z. Zhang—Supported by the China Postdoctoral Science Foundation under Grant No. 2021M703273.

methods explain it as a over-smoothing phenomenon [6]. For the stability of GNN, the eigenvalues of the graph convolution filters are related to the stability of the model [13]. The equivalence of GNN and Weisfeiler-Lehman (WL) graph isomorphism test has also been proved in distinguishing the graph structure [8].

The other category is the identification of the basis for GNN's prediction. Compared with theoretical analysis, recognizing the basis of prediction can provide people with a more intuitive way to understand the inherent mechanism of GNN. GNN makes a prediction based on the node features information and relational information in the graph. Therefore, it is natural to explore the influence of node features or relations on GNN's prediction. The gradient-based method directly uses the gradient value to measure the importance of the node features [1,9,15]. Nevertheless, it has the limitation of saturation problem [10]. GAT [12] trains attention weights for each edge in the graph to identify important substructures. XGNN [17] trains a graph generator to generate model-level explanations. However, GAT and XGNN are not be applied to explain the node feature. GNNExplainer [15] is proposed and recognizes substructure and subset of node features that have an important impact on GNN's prediction. However, when applied to classification tasks, GNNExplainer pays less attention to category-related features because its framework lacks a global view [18].

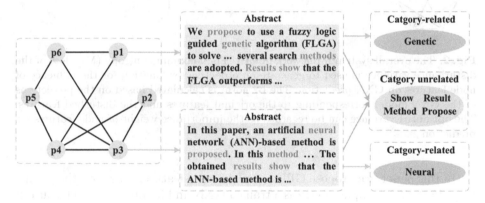

Fig. 1. Schematic diagram of some category-related and category-unrelated words in a toy citation graph.

The node features that influence the prediction should be category-related words that appear more frequently in one category but less frequently in other categories. Figure 1 shows some of the category-unrelated and category-related node features on the graph. The left part of Fig. 1 represents a toy citation graph, where nodes represent papers and edges represent citation relationships between papers. Node $p1$ is a paper in the category of *Genetic Algorithm* and Node $p3$ is a paper in the category of *Neural Network*. It can be seen from the middle part of Fig. 1, their features are composed of words in the abstracts. Considering that words *Neural* and *Generic* mainly appear in a certain category, they belong to category-related words. In contrast, words *Propose, Show, Method* and *Result* are widespread in both categories, thus belong to category-unrelated words, as shown in the right part of Fig. 1. Existing methods cannot well address the above problem. Therefore, identifying the important node features for the GNN's prediction is still an urgent challenge to be solved.

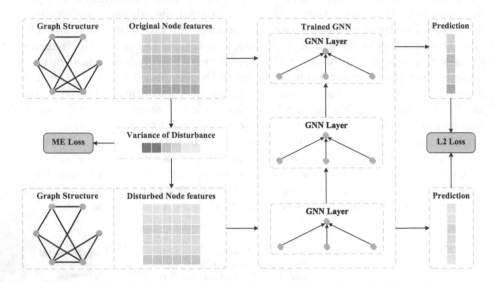

Fig. 2. The overall system framework of GPI. The maximum entropy (ME) loss of the disturbance variance is used to generate an objective explanation for the influence of node features on GNN prediction. The L2 norm is calculated based on the predictions of the GNN model corresponding to the original features and the disturbed features. The optimized variance can be regarded as the importance weight of node features for prediction.

In this paper, we propose GPI to explain node features' effect on the prediction of GNN. The input of GPI is a trained GNN and its prediction. The output is a node features' subset (some entries of the node feature vector) that is critical to the prediction. In detail, GPI first uses mutual information to quantify the correlation between each dimension of node features and the prediction. Then, to objectively explain the importance of node features for prediction, we add a set of Gaussian disturbances with trainable variance to the node features and use the maximum entropy (ME) as the optimization loss. Meanwhile, the original and disturbed node features are input into the model respectively to calculate the L2 distance between the two corresponding predictions. This term is used as a constraint loss to limit the intensity of disturbances and generate disturbances in all directions. Ultimately, GPI selects a critical subset of node features based on the quantitative results. Figure 2 is the overall system framework of GPI. GPI is model-agnostic and suitable for various graph machine learning tasks such as node classification and graph classification. Besides, GPI can make a global explanation since it considers the information from all instances. Experimental results on two real-world datasets show that GPI outperforms baselines in identifying the node features' subset that significantly impacts GNN's prediction. In summary, we highlight our contributions as follows.

– We focus on intuitively explaining GNN from understanding the effect of node features on the GNN's prediction.
– We propose a new method GNN Prediction Interpreter (GPI) to explain GNN's prediction. The goal of GPI is to identify a node features' subset that has an essential impact on the prediction of all instances.
– We conduct experiments on synthetic and real-world datasets. The results show that GPI achieves significant performance over baselines.

2   Related Works

The existing methods of interpreting GNN can be roughly divided into two groups. **(1) Analyzing the representational power of the GNN models** is one of the leading research directions. Some studies [6] have found that stacking too many convolutional layers causes the representation of different node features to be very similar, and point that residual modules [6] can be introduced to improve this phenomenon. In addition, the stability of GNNs is proved to be related to the largest absolute eigenvalue of the graph convolution filter [13]. Moreover, the power of GNN to distinguish the graph structure has been proven to be at most as powerful as the WL [8]. WL is a traditional algorithm for testing graph isomorphism. Specifically, it can be roughly regarded as a GNN model with a weight matrix replaced by a hash function. However, the above theoretical analysis methods cannot provide a reasonable and intuitive explanation for the prediction of GNN. **(2) Explaining the model by identifying the basis of GNN prediction** is the other research direction that has attracted widespread attention recently. In the gradient-based method, SA [1] adopts the square of the gradient value as a measure of the important input feature. Guided-BP [9] only keeps the positive gradient value. However, in the case of saturation [10], the gradient cannot accurately reflect the importance of the feature. Besides, GAT [12] adopts the attention mechanism to explain the GNN model, which measures the importance of edges. It cannot be applied to explain the importance of node features for model prediction. In addition, different from the method of interpreting GNN's output based on original input features, XGNN [17] introduces reinforcement learning to train a graph generator to generate subgraph for graph classification tasks. In this way, the subgraph is regarded as the explanation of the GNN's prediction, but it also cannot be applied to explain the importance of node features. GNNexplainer [15] recognizes important substructures and subsets of features by using mutual information to optimize the mask matrix of edge and node features. However, its generative explanation lacks globality to a certain extent.

3   Methods

In this section, we first briefly introduce the problem formulation of GPI. Then, we describe the process of generating a global explanation by GPI, including quantifying correlation and recognizing the subset of node features that plays a critical role in the prediction based on the quantitative results.

3.1   Problem Formulation

Let $G = (A, F)$ denote a graph, where $A \in \{0,1\}^{n \times n}$ defines the adjacency matrix and $F \in \mathbb{R}^{n \times d}$ defines the node feature matrix. n is the number of nodes and d is the dimension of a node feature vector. We denote Φ as a trained GNN model. Without loss of generality, we take the node classification task as an example to help to simplify the problem formulation. Given Φ and its prediction $Y = \Phi(A, F)$, where $Y \in \{1, \ldots, C\}^n$ and C represents the total number of categories, the goal of GPI is to explain the effect of node features on the GNN's prediction for all instances. Concretely, the explanation generation process of GPI is divided into two steps. GPI first quantifies the relevance between each dimension of the node features (every column in F) and Y. The quantified result is defined as $S \in \mathbb{R}^d$. Then GPI selects the highly correlated elements from S to form the subvector S_{imp}, which represents the subset of node features that have an important impact on the GNN's prediction.

3.2   GNN Prediction Interpreter

In information theory, mutual information I is a measure of the correlation between variables. $I(X; Z)$ reflects the amount of information that random variable X contains random variable Z, and vice versa. $I(X; Z)$ can be represented as the difference of two entropy terms:

$$I(X; Z) = H(X) - H(X|Z) \tag{1}$$

Intuitively, $I(X; Z)$ measures the information shared by X and Z. When X and Z are independent, $I(X; Z) = 0$, and when X and Z are mutually determined (for example, X and Z are two identical random variables), $I(X; Z) = H(X) = H(Z)$. Hence, we introduce mutual information to formulate the correlation between in GNN's node features F and its predictions Y. And $I(F; Y)$ is expressed as:

$$I(F; Y) = H(F) - H(F|Y) \tag{2}$$

where $H(F)$ is a constant and $H(F|Y)$ represents the amount of information that is not utilized by Y when Y is observed. Following the analysis of input features [7], $H(F|Y)$ can be calculated by disentangling the components of attribute information from node features:

$$H(F|Y) = \sum_i p(f_i|Y) \log p(f_i|Y) \tag{3}$$

where f_i represents the i-th attribute of F. Therefore, the accurate calculation of $p(f_i|Y)$ is a key for GPI to effectively recognize features that have an important impact on GNN's prediction. However, it is almost impossible to directly compute $p(f_i|Y)$ because the function represented by Φ is extremely complicated. To address this problem, we improved the perturbation-based method [3] to approximate $p(f_i|Y)$. The difference is that the above method only considers adding perturbation to a single instance, we extend it to add perturbation to multiple instances so that the framework can have a global perspective. In the first place, we randomly sample the inputs $\tilde{f}_i$ near f_i, i.e. $\tilde{f}_i = f_i + \delta_i$ where δ_i can be regarded as a random noise satisfying Gaussian distribution $\delta_i \sim \mathcal{N}(0, \sigma_i^2 I)$ and σ_i is a trainable parameter representing standard deviation. Then, we can approximate that the distribution of $\tilde{f}_i$ satisfies the Gaussian distribution $\tilde{f}_i \sim \mathcal{N}(f_i, \sigma_i^2 I)$. According to [2], the entropy $H(\tilde{F}|Y)$ of a multivariate Gaussian distribution can be calculated as:

$$H(\tilde{F}|Y) = \sum_i p(\tilde{f}_i|Y) \log p(\tilde{f}_i|Y)$$
$$= \sum_i (\log \sigma_i + \frac{1}{2} \log 2\pi e) \tag{4}$$

In order to ensure that the prediction of model only changes within a small range after adding noise, $\tilde{f}_i$ is subject to $\mathbb{E}_{\tilde{f}_i} \|\Phi(A, \tilde{F}) - Y\|^2 = \epsilon$, where $\Phi(A, \tilde{F})$ represents prediction based on the disturbed node features $\tilde{F}$ and ϵ is a small constant. The constraint term can also be equivalent to the maximum likelihood estimation of the $\tilde{f}_i$ distribution. It ensures the generation of all possible inputs. Therefore, $H(F|Y)$ can be estimated by $H(\tilde{F}|Y)$.

We expect GPI to make objective explanations that follow the truth rather than generate biased or subjective explanations by designing some heuristic assumptions. Therefore, $H(\tilde{F}|Y)$ should conform to the principle of maximum entropy. The essence of the maximum entropy principle is that when partial knowledge is known, the distribution with maximal information entropy is the most reasonable inference about the unknown distribution. To put it simply, Y may be related to multiple attributes of the node feature, rather than relying solely on a certain attribute. Therefore, we define maximizing $H(\tilde{F}|Y)$ subject to $\mathbb{E}_{\tilde{f}_i} \|\Phi(A, \tilde{F}) - Y\|^2 = \epsilon$ as the optimization objective of GPI. The loss function $\mathcal{L}$ is represented as:

$$\mathcal{L} = -H(\tilde{F}|Y) + \lambda \mathbb{E}_{\tilde{f}_i} \|\Phi(A, \tilde{F}) - Y\|^2$$
$$= -\sum_i (\log \sigma_i + \frac{1}{2} \log 2\pi e) + \lambda \mathbb{E}_{\tilde{f}_i \sim \mathcal{N}(f_i, \sigma_i^2 I)} \|\Phi(A, \tilde{F}) - Y\|^2 \tag{5}$$

where λ is a hyper-parameter. The first term can be regarded as the maximum entropy loss, which guarantees the increase in entropy $H(\tilde{F}|Y)$. The second item can be regarded as L2 loss, which restricts the intensity of the added noise and ensures that the input from all directions can be sampled. To put it simply, we want to find a maximum entropy distribution $p(\tilde{F}|Y)$ by optimizing a set of variance $S = [\sigma_1, \sigma_2, \ldots, \sigma_d]$ within a limited range. The optimized variance σ_i value can reflect the influence of the corresponding attribute f on the model's prediction. The small value of σ_i means that there is a high correlation between $\tilde{f}_i$ and Y. In other words, adding a slight disturbance to the i-th entry in node features will significantly impact the GNN's prediction. Conversely, a large variance value σ_i means that the i-th node feature have a weak influence on the prediction. It can be intuitively understood that even though adding a relatively large disturbance to the i-th entry of node features, it still cannot significantly affect the model's output.

In a nutshell, The optimized $[\sigma_1, \sigma_2, \ldots, \sigma_d]$ can be regarded as a quantified result of the importance of node features, where σ_i quantifies the correlation between the i-th entry of node features and GNN's prediction. Then we can select the σ_* with the highest relevance to form the subvector S_{imp}. It can be viewed as the subset of node features that have an essential impact on GNN's prediction. Moreover, GPI is a model-agnostic interpretation method that can be used to explain multiple GNN models. The proposed method is able to provide global feature-level explanations for various graph machine learning tasks.

4   Experiment

In this section, we first introduce the experimental settings. Then we compare the explanations generated by GPI and baselines in the node classification task and the graph classification task. Experimental results indicate that GPI can provide a more accurate explanation compared to the baselines.

4.1   Experiment Settings

Datasets. We choose a synthetic dataset BA-Community [15] and two real-world datasets: Cora [11] and Mutagenicity [14]. The details of datasets are as follows: **(1) BA-Community** is a synthetic dataset that is used for the node classification task. It contains one graph with 1400 nodes and 4460 edges. **(2) Cora** is a citation network dataset, which is used for the node classification task. Cora contains one graph with 2277 nodes and 5214 edges. Each node is labeled as one of 7 categories: Neural Network (NN), Reinforcement Learning (RL), Probabilistic Method, theory, Genetic Algorithm (GA), Casebased, and Rule Learning. **(3) Mutagenicity** is a molecular dataset, which is used for the graph classification task. Mutagenicity contains 4337 graphs. Each graph represents a molecular structure. Graphs are divided into two categories: mutagen and nonmutagen. Each node in a graph represents one of the 14 types (C, O, Cl, H, N, F, Br, S, P, I, Na, K, Li, and Ca) of atoms.

Baselines. We consider the following interpretation methods as baseline methods: GNNExplainer [15] and Grad [15], the details of the baseline methods are as follows: **(1) GNNExplainer** is currently the state-of-the-art method to explain

GNN. Specifically, GNNExplainer trains a mask matrix to measure the importance of corresponding node features. **(2) Grad** is a gradient-based method. It uses the gradient of the loss function backpropagation to measure the node features. It should note that GAT [12] and XGNN [17] are both standard methods to explain GNN's prediction. GAT interprets GNN by learning an attention weight for each edge. XGNN explains GNN by training a subgraph generator to generate a subgraph. However, neither of them can be applied to identify important node features. Therefore, we do not choose GAT and XGNN as the baseline methods.

Implementation Details of GPI. For explaining the prediction of GNN in the node classification task, we train three different GNN models on the BA-Community dataset and Cora dataset: **(1) GCN** [5] is a transductive GNN model that using convolution operators to learn node representation. **(2) Graphsage** [4] is a inductive GNN model that generates embeddings by sampling from node's neighborhood. **(3) IGCN** [15] is an improved GNN model based on GCN. It introduces new mechanisms, such as jump connection, batch normalization, etc.; For explaining the prediction of GNN in the graph classification task, we train the Diffpool on the Mutagenicity dataset: **Diffpool** [16] is a differentiable graph pooling module that can generate a hierarchical embedding of each graph. In the training process of GPI, the number of iterations is set to 500. The learning rate is set to 0.01, the weight decay is set to 0.005, and λ is set to 0.1.

4.2 Explanation Results

In this subsection, we will show that the GPI can be used for different graph machine learning tasks and does not depend on the specific GNN model. Besides, GPI can achieve state-of-the-art performance compared with existing baselines.

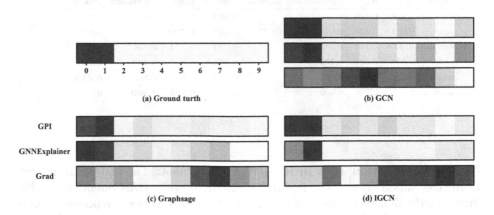

Fig. 3. Explanation results of different GNNs' prediction.

Node Classification Task in Synthetic Dataset. For three different GNNs, the global explanations generated by GPI and other baseline methods are shown in Fig. 3. For ease of understanding, the explanation is provided in the form of a heatmap. Each column of the heatmap represents a entry of the feature, and the dark color means that it significantly contributes to the model's prediction. Figure 3(a) represents the ground truth explanations. It means the first two entries of node features play the most important role in model prediction. Figure 3(b)–3(d) represent the explanations for GCN, Graphsage and IGCN. Specifically, the rows in Fig. 3(b)–3(d) correspond to the explanations generated by GPI, GNNExplainer, and Grad from top to bottom. The explanation can be seen as the visualization of importance weights, e.g., $[\sigma_1, \sigma_2, \ldots, \sigma_d]$ in GPI.

For the interpretation of GCN's and Graphsage's predictions, GPI achieves similar results to GNNExplainer, which can be seen from Figs. 3(b)–3(c). But GPI has fewer hyperparameters and trainable parameters than GNNExplainer, which shows the superiority of the GPI. It can also be seen from the interpretation of IGCN's prediction in Fig. 3(d), GPI accurately identifies the subset of node features that have an important impact on the prediction. Although GNNExplainer can indentify the first two entries as important features, it assigns a lower weight to the first entry. It shows that GPI has more tremendous advantages in interpreting GNN model with more complex structures. We can also find the Grad fails to correctly identify features that are highly correlated with the prediction in all three different GNN models. Simply using gradient values as an explanation has great limitations for the interpretation of unstructured data. In short, GPI is able to generate more accurate interpretations for various GNN models in the node classification task.

Table 1. The statistic results of the probability of all category-related words appearing in each category.

Words	NN	RL	Probabilistic method	Theory	GA	Casebased	Rule learning
reinforc	0.006	**0.605**	0	0.007	0.012	0.012	0
genet	0.011	0.041	0.011	0.007	**0.763**	0.004	0.013
neural	**0.473**	0.159	0.057	0.031	0.174	0.008	0.013
reason	0.037	0.041	0.154	0.075	0.037	**0.468**	0.058
induct	0.025	0.026	0.037	0.134	0.037	0.087	**0.413**
casebas	0	0	0.009	0.007	0.006	**0.409**	0

Node Classification Task in Real-World Dataset. The real-world dataset Cora contains richer node features compared with BA-Community. This increases the difficulty of interpretation. In Cora, each paper is represented as a node. The length of the node feature vector is the vocabulary size. Each entry is 0 or 1 which indicating whether the corresponding word is contained in the paper's abstract.

Compared to category-unrelated words, category-related words have a more important impact on the prediction of the model. Therefore, we use the category-related words as the ground truth explanations. In the experiment, we select category-related words according to the occurrence of a word in each category. A word is recognized as a category-related word if it frequently occurs in one category, and is infrequent in other categories. Specifically, we firstly calculate the probability of each word appearing in each category. The probability of the i-th word appearing in the j-th category is calculated as: $p_{ij} = t_{ij}/T_j$. t_{ij} represents the number of the papers in the j-th category containing the i-th word, and T_j represents the total number of papers in the j-th category. Then, we choose all words with a probability greater than 0.4 in a certain category and less than 0.2 in other categories as category-related words. The statistical results of category-related words are shown in Table 1. For example, *reinforc* can be regarded as a category-related word of the Reinforcement Learning category.

Table 2. The top 10 words have the most important impact on different GNN models' predictions.

Models	Interpretation methods	Top-10 words	Acc
GCN	GNNExplainer	result, network, method, algorithm, model system, present, **neural**, problem, set	1/10
	Grad	train, network, error, demonstr, random data, **neural**, form, show, given	1/10
	GPI	**genet, reinforc**, network, **neural**, learn bayesian, **casebas, reason**, train, program	**5/10**
Graphsage	GNNExplainer	network, learn, algorithm, **neural**, model system, problem, present, **genet**, result	2/10
	Grad	**neural**, train, input, consist, addit error, network, separ, demonstr, function	1/10
	GPI	**genet, reinforc**, network, **neural**, learn bayesian, train, **reason**, infer, **casebas**	**5/10**
IGCN	GNNExplainer	comput, set, perform, featur, mani process, algorithm, system, result, improv	0
	Grad	**reinforc**, bayesian, belief, converg, qlearn approxim, em, causal, markov, action	1/10
	GPI	**genet, reinforc**, bayesian, **casebas**, belief evolv, **neural**, learn, ga, **reason**	**5/10**

Considering that the length of the feature vector is too long, it is difficult to show the whole heatmap. We sort the words according to the importance weights and show the top 10 most important words provided by different interpretation methods in Table 2. Category-related words are in bold font. The accuracy represents the percentage of category-related words in the top 10 most important words. A better interpretation method should assign more important weights to the category-related words. Taking explaining the prediction of GCN as an example, GNNExplainer and Grad can only identify one category-related word *neural*. In contrast, GPI can identify five category-related words: *genet, reinfoc, neural, casebas* and *reason*. The explanations of Graphsage's and IGCN's predictions also show that for different GNN's predictions, GPI can always recognize more category-related words among the top 10 most important words than GNNExplainer and Grad. In a word, the above experimental results further prove the effectiveness of the explanation generated by GPI. At the same time, it also proves that GPI has excellent generalization performance on real-world data.

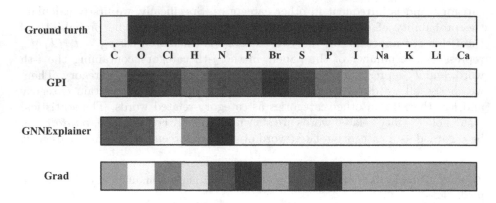

Fig. 4. Explanation results of Diffpool's prediction.

Graph Classification Task. In the Mutagenicity's example, each graph in the dataset represents a compound. Each node in the graph represents a chemical element. The length of the node feature vector is the total number of all chemical elements, and each entry is 0 or 1, indicating whether the node represents the corresponding chemical element. Considering that this dataset is to classify whether the compound has mutagenicity, we set the chemical elements (O, Cl, H, N, F, Br, S, P, and I) in the all mutagenic groups as the ground-truth explanations. The above features correspond to category-related elements. Figure 4 shows the global explanations for Diffpool's prediction. The dark color corresponding to the chemical element indicates a high correlation to the model prediction. We can see that only GPI's result is closest to the ground truth. In contrast, GNNExplainer only identifies the three category-related elements: O, H, and N. We believe that this problem lies in that the mask matrix of the GNNExplainer method is optimized for each graph individually, and it cannot generate an explanation from a global perspective. In addition, Grad not only misidentifies category-related elements but also gave some category-related elements relatively low confidence.

Overall, the above experimental results show that GPI has excellent scalability when applied to different tasks. Compared to the baseline method, GPI generates an explanation of node characteristics from a global perspective. It contributes to identifying the prediction basis of GNN accurately.

5   Conclusion

This paper proposed GPI, a novel and effective method for explaining GNN's predictions under multiple graph learning tasks without relying on specific GNN models. Particularly, GPI first quantifies the correlation between node features and prediction results, then selects the feature subset that is critical to the final result. Experimental results on benchmark datasets demonstrate the effectiveness and generalization of the proposed method.

References

1. Baldassarre, F., Azizpour, H.: Explainability techniques for graph convolutional networks. arXiv preprint arXiv:1905.13686 (2019)
2. Cover, T.M.: Elements of Information Theory. Wiley, Hoboken (1999)
3. Guan, C., Wang, X., Zhang, Q., Chen, R., He, D., Xie, X.: Towards a deep and unified understanding of deep neural models in NLP. In: ICLR (2019)
4. Hamilton, W., Ying, Z., Leskovec, J.: Inductive representation learning on large graphs. In: NIPS (2017)
5. Kipf, T.N., Welling, M.: Semi-supervised classification with graph convolutional networks. In: ICLR (2016)
6. Li, G., Muller, M., Thabet, A., Ghanem, B.: DeepGCNs: can GCNs go as deep as CNNs? In: Proceedings of the IEEE International Conference on Computer Vision, pp. 9267–9276 (2019)
7. Lundberg, S., Lee, S.I.: A unified approach to interpreting model predictions. In: NIPS (2017)
8. Morris, C., et al.: Weisfeiler and leman go neural: Higher-order graph neural networks. In: AAAI (2019)
9. Pope, P.E., Kolouri, S., Rostami, M., Martin, C.E., Hoffmann, H.: Explainability methods for graph convolutional neural networks. In: Proceedings of the IEEE/CVF Conference on Computer Vision and Pattern Recognition, pp. 10772–10781 (2019)
10. Shrikumar, A., Greenside, P., Kundaje, A.: Learning important features through propagating activation differences. In: International Conference on Machine Learning, pp. 3145–3153. PMLR (2017)
11. Tu, C., Liu, H., Liu, Z., Sun, M.: Cane: context-aware network embedding for relation modeling. In: ACL (2017)
12. Veličković, P., Cucurull, G., Casanova, A., Romero, A., Lio, P., Bengio, Y.: Graph attention networks. In: ICLR (2018)
13. Verma, S., Zhang, Z.L.: Stability and generalization of graph convolutional neural networks. In: KDD (2019)
14. Xu, K., Hu, W., Leskovec, J., Jegelka, S.: Derivation and validation of toxicophores for mutagenicity prediction. J. Med. Chem. (2005)
15. Ying, Z., Bourgeois, D., You, J., Zitnik, M., Leskovec, J.: GNNExplainer: generating explanations for graph neural networks. In: NIPS (2019)
16. Ying, Z., You, J., Morris, C., Ren, X., Hamilton, W., Leskovec, J.: Hierarchical graph representation learning with differentiable pooling. In: NIPS (2018)

17. Yuan, H., Tang, J., Hu, X., Ji, S.: XGNN: towards model-level explanations of graph neural networks. In: Proceedings of the 26th ACM SIGKDD International Conference on Knowledge Discovery and Data Mining, pp. 430–438 (2020)
18. Yuan, H., Yu, H., Gui, S., Ji, S.: Explainability in graph neural networks: a taxonomic survey. arXiv preprint arXiv:2012.15445 (2020)
19. Zhang, M., Chen, Y.: Link prediction based on graph neural networks. In: NIPS (2018)

Weight-Aware Graph Contrastive Learning

Hang Gao[1,2,3], Jiangmeng Li[1,2,3], Peng Qiao[2,3], and Changwen Zheng[2,3(✉)]

[1] University of Chinese Academy of Sciences, Zhongguancun East Road. 80,
Haidian District, Beijing 100081, China
{hang,jiangmeng}@iscas.ac.cn

[2] Science and Technology on Integrated Infomation System Laboratory,
Institute of Software Chinese Academy of Sciences, Zhongguancun South Fourth
Street, 4, Haidian District, 100083 Beijing, China

[3] Science and Technology on Integrated Infomation System Laboratory, Institute of
Software Chinese Academy of Sciences, Zhongguancun South Fourth Street, 80,
Haidian District, 100081 Beijing, China
{peng,changwen}@iscas.ac.cn
https://www.ucas.ac.cn/, http://www.iscas.cn/

Abstract. In contrastive learning, samples usually have different contributions to optimization. This inference applies to the specific downstream tasks of applying contrastive learning to graph learning. Nevertheless, the nodes, i.e., samples, are equally treated in the conventional graph contrastive learning approaches. To address such a problem and better model discriminative information from graphs, we propose a novel graph contrastive learning approach called *Weight-Aware Graph Contrastive Learning* (WA-GCL). WA-GCL first pairs up the node feature as positive and negative pairs. The weight factors of these pairs are then determined based on their similarities. WA-GCL utilizes a specific weight-aware loss to effectively and efficiently learn discriminative representations from the pairs with their corresponding weight factors. Empirically, the experiments across multiple datasets demonstrate that WA-GCL outperforms the state-of-the-art methods in graph contrastive learning tasks. Further experimental studies verified the effectiveness of different parts of WA-GCL.

Keywords: Graph neural network · Unsupervised learning · Contrastive learning · Node classification

1 Introduction

Recently, there has been a surge of interest in Graph Neural Network (GNN) approaches for graph representation learning. Such approaches have been applied to model a varieties of graph-structured data, including knowledge graphs [22], molecules [5], social networks [7], physical processes [10], and codes [1]. GNNs such as Graph Convolutional Networks (GCN) [7], Graph Attention Networks

E. Pimenidis et al. (Eds.): ICANN 2022, LNCS 13530, pp. 719–730, 2022.
https://doi.org/10.1007/978-3-031-15931-2_59

(GAT) [15], Graph Isomorphism Networks (GIN) [21] have achieved excellent results in graph learning. GNNs mostly require task-dependent labels to learn representations. However, annotating graphs is challenging compared to labeling common modalities of data, such as video, image, text, or audio. Furthermore, this task is even harder in graph node classification. A large-scale graph generally contains numerous nodes, so it is time-consuming to label each of them. To tackle such a problem, methods that can utilize unlabeled data to learn representations are desired, such as unsupervised and semi-supervised approaches.

As a powerful unsupervised learning method, contrastive learning has achieve outstanding works in computer vision [14]. Recently, some researchers further applied contrastive learning to graph learning [6]. Contrastive learning conducts unsupervised learning by comparing different views of samples. The core idea behind contrastive learning is that the views of the same sample contain consistent information, while the views of the different samples contain relatively inconsistent information. In the field of graph contrastive learning, recent works take a similar approach, i.e.: 1) performing certain augmentations on the graph to acquire different views; 2) adopting specific GNNs to learn the representations; 3) pairing the views of the same node as positive pairs and the views of the different nodes as negative pairs; 4) pushing away the representations of negative pairs and pulling together the representations of positive pairs.

However, in the task of node classification on graphs, the existing contrastive learning methods still have a solid shortcoming. Current algorithms treat features of nodes equally in optimization. Nevertheless, the features away from the optimal have more contribution to the optimization. In the field of image classification, [11] proposes that the negative samples that are similar to the anchor and the positive samples that are different from the anchor are more *important* to improve representation learning. Nevertheless, indiscriminately following such assumption to emphasize the *important* features could bring in several inevasible problems: 1) excessive emphasis leads to the learned representation becoming over-simplistic, which could cause the learned representations to lack the generalized discriminability, and therefore it is encouraged to find a balance of emphasizing the *important* pairs and the other pairs; 2) because of sampling bias [3], it is possible that the samples that are treated as negative pairs have the same label with the anchor samples, so that such incorrectly grouped negative pairs may result in a counterproductive effect and undermine the discriminability of the learned representations.

To this end, we propose *Weight-Aware Graph Contrastive Learning* (WA-GCL) to emphasize the features that contribute more to graph node classification. For encoder structures, we design a novel *Edge-Weight Sensitive Graph Attentional Layer* (EWS-GAT layer) and build the encoders based on it. Then, the features of nodes are fully explored to form positive and negative pairs in each layer of the encoder. Weight factors are then calculated to emphasize the pairs with more contribution to the optimization. We propose a novel *weight-aware loss* to calculate loss with these weight factors and sample pairs. To reduce the influence of incorrectly grouped negative pairs caused by sampling bias, we add a correction term to the weight-aware loss. The correction term uses estimation methods to approximate the distribution of the correctly grouped negative pairs. The comparisons demonstrate the effectiveness of WA-GCL, and our further experiments also validate the significance of each proposed part of WA-GCL. The main contributions of this paper are as follows:

- We design a novel edge-weight sensitive graph attentional layer, which can better adapt to node classification tasks.
- We propose a novel weight-aware loss to process all node features from all layers. Weight-aware loss emphasizes the features with greater contributions by utilizing weight factors. Several certain corrections for the problems caused by such emphasis are further explored.
- We conduct experiments to compare our method with other state-of-the-art graph learning approaches on benchmark datasets, and the results prove the superiority of our method.

2 Related Works

This section reviews some representative works on graph nodes classification and graph contrastive learning, which is related to this article.

(1) GNN. Through aggregating neighborhood information, the GNN can learn the low-dimensional representations of graphs. These representations can then be applied to various kinds of downstream tasks. Since the concept of GNN was proposed, many different GNN frameworks have been raised. Graph Convolutional Networks [7], as an extension of the convolutional neural network on graph-structured data, use convolution operation to transform and aggregate features from a node's graph neighborhood. [21] proposed Graph Isomorphism Networks with representation capability equal to the WL test [8]. GATs [15] introduced attention mechanisms into graph learning. Focusing on node classification, GATs can perceive which neighbor node's information is more important and should have greater weight during feature aggregation. Our method was built based on GAT with certain improvements to make it suitable for our tasks.

(2) Contrastive Learning. Contrastive Learning is a kind of self-supervised learning approach that measures the loss in latent space by contrasting samples from distributions that contain dependencies of interest and distributions that does not. Some methods that are based on contrastive learning use multi-view means [14] to acquire samples for contrasting. They use data augmentation on the original sample to obtain multiple views. Then, learn the self-supervised representations of the samples via minimizing the distance between different views of the same sample. In graph learning, contrastive learning has many applications. For instance, Deep Graph Infomax (DGI) [17] learns node representations through contrasting node and graph encodings. Moreover, [6] learns node-level and graph-level representations by contrasting the different structures of a graph. Our method focuses on applying contrast learning in graph node classification and tries to measure each sample's importance better.

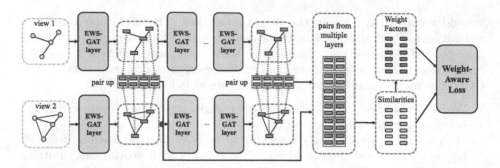

Fig. 1. The structure of our proposed WA-GCL. WA-GCL receives multiple views of the graph data as the inputs. We design a novel edge-weight sensitive graph attentional layer as our basic layer that can better adapt to graph node representation learning.

3   Methods

This section introduces the proposed weight-aware graph contrastive learning (WA-GCL) method. Figure 1 demonstrates its overall framework.

3.1   Data Augmentation

Similar to the contrastive learning methods of computer vision, graph contrastive learning also uses data augmentation to obtain multiple views of the graph. There are various ways to accomplish this task. However, our task is to learn the representation of graph nodes, so we need to keep the node features unaffected. Thus, we follow [6] and choose graph diffusion as our data augmentation method, which transforms an adjacency matrix into a diffusion matrix as a new graph view without distortion of the original node features.

3.2   Edge-Weight Sensitive Graph Attentional Layers

We designed the *Edge-Weight Sensitive Graph Attentional Layer* (EWS-GAT layer) to introduce the attention mechanism into our method, as it is proved to be more effective than other learning mechanisms in node classification [15]. We first recap the structure of the graph attentional layer as we designed our EWS-GAT layer based on it. We denote a set of input node features as $H = \{h_1, h_2, ..., h_N\}, h_i \in \mathbb{R}^F$, where N is the number of nodes, and F is the number of features in each node. For a target node i and its neighboring node j, the graph attentional layer first calculates the attention coefficients:

$$e_{ij} = LeakyReLU\{v^T[Wh_i \| h_j]\}, \tag{1}$$

where W is a weight matrix, $W \in \mathbb{R}^{F \times F'}$, F' is the number of the output features of each node. W parametrize a shared linear transformation. v is a weight vector. $\|$ is the concatenation operation. Then, the coefficient e is normalized using the softmax function:

$$\alpha_{ij} = \frac{exp(e_{ij})}{\sum_{k \in \mathcal{N}_i} exp(e_{ik})} = \frac{exp\left(LeakyReLU\{\boldsymbol{v}^T[\boldsymbol{W}\boldsymbol{h}_i\|\boldsymbol{h}_j]\}\right)}{\sum_{k \in \mathcal{N}_i} exp\left(LeakyReLU\{\boldsymbol{v}^T[\boldsymbol{W}\boldsymbol{h}_i\|\boldsymbol{h}_k]\}\right)}. \tag{2}$$

Once obtained, the normalized attention coefficients are used to compute a linear combination of the features corresponding to them:

$$\boldsymbol{h}_i^{out} = \sigma\left(\sum_{j \in \mathcal{N}_i} \alpha_{ij}\boldsymbol{W}\boldsymbol{h}_j\right), \tag{3}$$

where $\boldsymbol{h}_i^{out}$ is the output feature.

Next, We will elaborate on the architecture of our proposed EWS-GAT layer. As we select graph diffusion as our data augmentation method to keep the node features unaffected, we bring in large amounts of edge weights information generated by the graph diffusion operation. Thus, we need to consider the edge weights to utilize the diffusion matrix fully. Given the edge weight β_{ij} of the edge between node i and node j, we add β_{ij} to Eq. 2, and acquire a new attention coefficient α'_{ij}:

$$\alpha'_{ij} = \frac{exp\left(LeakyReLU\{\beta_{ij}\boldsymbol{v}^T[\boldsymbol{W}\boldsymbol{h}_i\|\boldsymbol{h}_j]\}\right)}{\sum_{k \in \mathcal{N}_i} exp\left(LeakyReLU\{\beta_{ij}\boldsymbol{v}^T[\boldsymbol{W}\boldsymbol{h}_i\|\boldsymbol{h}_k]\}\right)}. \tag{4}$$

For further emphasis on edge weights, we also add β_{ij} to the computation of the linear combination of the neighboring node features:

$$\begin{aligned}
\boldsymbol{h}_i^{out} &= \sigma\left(\sum_{j \in \mathcal{N}_i} \beta_{ij}\alpha'_{ij}\boldsymbol{W}\boldsymbol{h}_j\right) \\
&= \sigma\left(\sum_{j \in \mathcal{N}_i} \beta_{ij}\frac{exp\left(LeakyReLU\{\beta_{ij}\boldsymbol{v}^T[\boldsymbol{W}\boldsymbol{h}_i\|\boldsymbol{h}_j]\}\right)}{\sum_{k \in \mathcal{N}_i} exp\left(LeakyReLU\{\beta_{ij}\boldsymbol{v}^T[\boldsymbol{W}\boldsymbol{h}_i\|\boldsymbol{h}_k]\}\right)}\boldsymbol{W}\boldsymbol{h}_j\right).
\end{aligned} \tag{5}$$

To control the influence of edge weights, we added temperature coefficient δ as a hyperparameter:

$$\boldsymbol{h}_i^{out} = \sigma\left(\sum_{j \in \mathcal{N}_i} \beta_{ij}^\delta\frac{exp\left(LeakyReLU\{\beta_{ij}^\delta\boldsymbol{v}^T[\boldsymbol{W}\boldsymbol{h}_i\|\boldsymbol{h}_j]\}\right)}{\sum_{k \in \mathcal{N}_i} exp\left(LeakyReLU\{\beta_{ij}^\delta\boldsymbol{v}^T[\boldsymbol{W}\boldsymbol{h}_i\|\boldsymbol{h}_k]\}\right)}\boldsymbol{W}\boldsymbol{h}_j\right). \tag{6}$$

With the new EWS-GAT layer, we can build encoders that adapt to the graph diffusion augmentation method. Please see Fig. 1 for an illustration of the framework of our encoder. To obtain more pairs for training, we collect the output features of each EWS-GAT layer of our encoder and pair them up.

3.3   Weight-Aware Loss

We now introduce the mechanism of weigh-aware loss. Though we collect the output features of each layer, we do not concatenate these features as many GNNs do but treat them as different samples. As shown in Fig. 1, we first input the original graph G with n nodes into our encoder, which consists of m EWS-GAT layers. Then, we collect the outputs features of each layer. We denote these features as set $\boldsymbol{H}$. After that, we perform graph diffusion on G to get G' as another view. From G', we can get the node feature set $\boldsymbol{H'}$.

We paired the features of the node i and the layer l but under different views as positive pair: $\{\boldsymbol{h}_{il}, \boldsymbol{h}'_{il}\}$, where $\boldsymbol{h}_{il} \in \boldsymbol{H}$ and $\boldsymbol{h}'_{il} \in \boldsymbol{H'}$. With the positive pairs, we acquire the similarity set S^p by calculating the similarity between them:

$$S^p = \{similarity\,(\boldsymbol{h}_{il}, \boldsymbol{h}'_{il})\},\ (\boldsymbol{h}_{il} \in \boldsymbol{H}, \boldsymbol{h}'_{il} \in \boldsymbol{H'})\,, \tag{7}$$

where $similarity()$ is a similarity calculation function such as cosine similarity.

We randomly pick features from the different nodes under different views but belong to the same layer to form negative pair. The similarity set S^n of negative pairs can be formulated as:

$$S^n = \{similarity\,(\boldsymbol{h}_{il}, \boldsymbol{h}'_{jl})\},\ (\boldsymbol{h}_{il} \in \boldsymbol{H}, \boldsymbol{h}'_{jl} \in \boldsymbol{H'}, i \neq j)\,. \tag{8}$$

Our learning objective is to maximize the similarity between positive pairs and minimize the similarity of negative pairs. For the convenience of derivation, we abbreviate Eq. 7 and Eq. 8 into the following form:

$$S^p = \{s_i^p\}_i^{N^p}\,,\ S^n = \{s_i^n\}_i^{N^n}\,, \tag{9}$$

where s^p and s^n denote the similarity of positive and negative pairs. N^p is the number of positive pairs, $N^p = |S^p|$. N^n is the number of negative pairs, $N^n = |S^n|$.

Since we have collected the features of every layer and every node, we shall get amounts of positive and negative pairs, which will result in a considerable size of S^p and S^n. To reduce the computational complexity, we utilize a uniform way to process them. Inspired by [13], we formulate our loss function as follows:

$$\mathcal{L} = \frac{1}{\gamma}log\left[1 + \sum_{i=1}^{N^n}\sum_{j=1}^{N^p} exp\Big(\gamma(s_i^n - O^n) - \gamma(s_j^p - O^p)\Big)\right], \tag{10}$$

where O^p and O^n are the optimal values of s^n and s^p when the loss reaches minimal value, γ is a scale factor. Then, we use weight factors ω^p and ω^n to emphasize those similarities that contribute more to training. As mentioned before, [11] proposed that samples which are further away from the optimal goals contain more useful information for training. In our task, similarities that are further away from optimal goals are considered more crucial. They will be emphasized using weight factors ω^p and ω^n. We defined them as:

$$\omega_i^n = [s_i^n - O^n]_+\,,\ \omega_j^p = [O^p - s_j^p]_+\,. \tag{11}$$

With ω^p and ω^n, our loss function can be reformed as:

$$\mathcal{L} = \frac{1}{\gamma} log \left[1 + \sum_{i=1}^{N^n} \sum_{j=1}^{N^p} exp\left(\gamma \omega_i^n (s_i^n - O^n) - \gamma \omega_j^p (s_j^p - O^p) \right) \right]. \qquad (12)$$

However, this emphasis approach can also cause problems. Excessive emphasis on crucial samples will cause the learned representation to become too simplistic. Thus, a balance must be found between emphasizing a few critical samples and learning from all samples. To achieve such a goal, we add exponential parameter τ to balance the effectiveness of ω^p and ω^n:

$$\mathcal{L} = \frac{1}{\gamma} log \left[1 + \sum_{i=1}^{N^n} \sum_{j=1}^{N^p} exp\left(\gamma (\omega_i^n)^\tau (s_i^n - O^n) - \gamma (\omega_j^p)^\tau (s_j^p - O^p) \right) \right]. \qquad (13)$$

Next, we try to diminish the influence of the sampling bias that we discussed in the introduction. The weight factors ω_i^p and ω_j^n will amplify the influence of sampling bias to a certain extent, for the similarity of incorrectly grouped pairs is often rather high and will be emphasized based on our weighting mechanism. As [3] do, we want to find a way to correct such problem by simply reforming the loss function. In our task, the similarity set S^n can be divided into two sets, S^{n-} and S^{n+}. S^{n-} consists of the similarities of the pairs that truly are negative pairs. We denote these similarities as s_i^{n-}. S^{n+} consists of the similarities of the pairs that are actually positive. They are incorrectly grouped because of sampling bias. We denote these similarities as s_i^{n+}. The influence of S^{n+} needs to be eliminated, as they are miss grouped. The ideal loss function should have the following form:

$$\mathcal{L}_{Optimal} = \frac{1}{\gamma} log \left[1 + \sum_{i=1}^{N^{n-}} exp\left(\gamma (\omega_i^{n-})^\tau (s_i^{n-} - O^n) \right) \sum_{j=1}^{N^p} \left(- \gamma (\omega_j^p)^\tau (s_j^p - O^p) \right) \right],$$
$$(14)$$

where $N^{n-} = |S^{n-}|$. For the convenience of representation, we extract the summation that involves s^n in the Eq. 14 and denote it as $\mathcal{G}_{Optimal}$:

$$\mathcal{G}_{Optimal} = \sum_{i=1}^{N^{n-}} exp\left(\gamma (\omega_i^{n-})^\tau (s_i^{n-} - O^n) \right). \qquad (15)$$

As $S^n = S^{n-} \cup S^{n+}$, $\mathcal{G}_{Optimal}$ can also be formulated as:

$$\mathcal{G}_{Optimal} = \sum_{i=1}^{N^n} exp\left(\gamma (\omega_i^n)^\tau (s_i^n - O^n) \right) - \sum_{i=1}^{N^{n+}} exp\left(\gamma (\omega_i^{n+})^\tau (s_i^{n+} - O^n) \right), \qquad (16)$$

where $N^{n+} = |S^{n+}|$. Unfortunately, during unsupervised pre-training, we cannot know what elements S^{n-} contains. So $\mathcal{G}_{Optimal}$ is just an ideal goal. As an alternative, we use estimation methods to approximate the value of $\mathcal{G}_{Optimal}$. $\mathcal{G}_{Optimal}$ can be reformed as follows:

$$\mathcal{G}_{Optimal} = N^n \mathbb{E}\Big[exp\big(\gamma(\omega^n)^\tau(s^n - O^n)\big)\Big] - N^{n+}\mathbb{E}\Big[exp\big(\gamma(\omega^{n+})^\tau(s^{n+} - O^n)\big)\Big]. \quad (17)$$

When $N \to \infty$, we have:

$$N^n \mathbb{E}\Big[exp\big(\gamma(\omega^n)^\tau(s^n - O^n)\big)\Big] - N^{n+}\mathbb{E}\Big[exp\big(\gamma(\omega^n)^\tau(s^{n+} - O^n)\big)\Big] \quad (18)$$

$$\longrightarrow N^n \mathbb{E}\Big[exp\big(\gamma(\omega^n)^\tau(s^n - O^n)\big)\Big] - N^{n+}\mathbb{E}\Big[exp\big(\gamma(\omega^p)^\tau(s^p - O^n)\big)\Big]. \quad (19)$$

Thus, we could calculate the estimate of $\mathcal{G}_{Optimal}$ by replacing s^{n+} with s^p, which is easier to acquire:

$$\mathcal{G}_{Estimate} = \sum_{i=1}^{N^n} exp\big(\gamma(\omega^n)^\tau(s_i^n - O^n)\big) - \frac{N^{n+}}{N^p}\sum_{j=1}^{N^p} exp\big(\gamma(\omega^p)^\tau(s_j^p - O^n)\big) \quad (20)$$

where N^{n+} is estimated according to different datasets. Based on Eq. 14 and Eq. 20, we reform our loss function as:

$$\mathcal{L}_{Estimate} = \frac{1}{\gamma}log\Big[1 + \mathcal{G}_{Estimate}\sum_{j=1}^{N^p}\big(-\gamma(\omega^p)^\tau(s_j^p - O^p)\big)\Big]. \quad (21)$$

4 Experiments

4.1 Comparison with State-of-the-Art Methods

To demonstrate the effectiveness of our proposed WA-GCL method, we conducted extensive experiments on three widely-used benchmark datasets: Cora, CiteSeer, and PubMed [2,12]. These datasets are citation networks where documents (nodes) are connected through citations (edges). We compared our proposed WA-GCL with a variety of state-of-the-art methods, including Label Propagation (LP) [23], Chebyshev [4], GCN [7], GAT [15], SGC [19], DGI [16], GMI [9], MVGRL [6], GRACE [24], InfoGCL [20], GCA [25], and CG^3 [18]. For experimental protocol, we followed MVGRL and reported the mean classification accuracy with standard deviation on the test nodes after 50 runs of training followed by a linear model. We also adopt the same train/validation/test splits as MVGRL. Our encoder consists of two EWS-GAT layers with a hidden dimension of 512. The total epochs of pre-training are 2000 with early stop patience of 30 rounds. We set the exponential parameter τ and the scale factor γ as 0.2 and 32. We also conducted an ablation experiment by replacing the weight-aware loss of WA-GCL with the widely used InfoNCE loss [6]. The new network is named N-CGL.

Table 1. Classification accuracy of compared methods on Cora, CiteSeer, PubMed. Some of the records are not associated with standard deviations because we directly take them from [18] which did not report their standard deviations. We divided the results into two groups: supervised & semi-supervised approaches and unsupervised approaches. As demonstrated in the table, **Bold** denotes the best results in the head-to-head comparisons.

	METHOD	CORA	CITESEER	PUBMED
SUPERVISED & SEMI-SUPERVISED	LP	68.0	45.3	63.0
	CHEBYSHEVS	81.2	69.8	74.4
	GCN	81.5	70.3	79.0
	GAT	83.0 ± 0.7	72.5 ± 0.7	79.0 ± 0.3
	SGC	81.0 ± 0.0	71.9 ± 0.7	78.9 ± 0.0
	CG^3	83.4 ± 0.7	73.6 ± 0.8	80.2 ± 0.8
UNSUPERVISED	DGI	81.7 ± 0.6	71.5 ± 0.7	77.3 ± 0.6
	GMI	82.7 ± 0.2	73.0 ± 0.3	80.1 ± 0.2
	GRACE	80.0 ± 0.4	71.7 ± 0.6	79.5 ± 1.1
	MVGRL	82.9 ± 0.7	72.6 ± 0.7	79.4 ± 0.3
	GCA	82.1 ± 0.4	71.7 ± 0.2	78.9 ± 0.7
	INFOGCL	83.5 ± 0.3	73.5 ± 0.4	79.1 ± 0.2
	N-CGL	82.6 ± 0.4	72.9 ± 0.6	79.7 ± 0.3
	WA-GCL	$\mathbf{84.2 \pm 0.3}$	$\mathbf{73.7 \pm 0.5}$	$\mathbf{80.5 \pm 0.3}$

The classification results are reported in Table 1. We highlight the highest records in bold. The results show that WA-GCL achieves the best record across all datasets compared to other methods. Moreover, it is observable that WA-GCL outperforms N-CGL, proving the superiority of the weight-aware loss.

4.2 Comparison Between Different Encoders

To further evaluate the ability of our approach, we conduct a series of comparative experiments. For comparison, we build three graph learning methods with graph attentional layer, graph convolutional layer, and EWS-GAT layers and set the pre-training objective as Eq. 10. The data augmentation methods are the same as WA-GCL. Equation 10 is weight-aware loss removing weight factors and the estimate of $\mathcal{G}_{Optimal}$. The last one is the full WA-GCL with EWS-GAT layers and weight-aware loss.

Then we test them with different hidden dimensions on the Cora dataset. The results are shown in Fig. 2. As shown in the figure, with the hidden dimension size increasing, the encoder using the graph convolutional layer gradually surpasses those using the graph attentional layer. Such surpassing indicates that, in our case, the graph attentional layer cannot effectively acquire the information of multiple views and fails to use the network's representation ability fully. We solved such a problem by adopting EWS-GAT layers. By introducing edge weight information, we improved the power of the graph attention mechanism to deal with node classification problems. It can be seen that the improved network performance exceeds the previous two networks in an all-around way. On this basis, we added weight-aware loss to improve our approach's performance

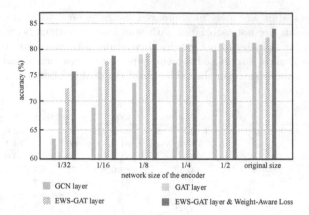

Fig. 2. The classification result of different encoders. We scaled the encoder in different proportions to the original size. The abscissa in the figure represents the size of the network. The ordinate represents the accuracy of classification.

further. The data in the figure proves that the performance of WA-GCL exceeds that of the three other networks, and it can maintain such performance when the network size changes to some extent.

4.3   Visual Analysis

In this part, we visualize the representations WA-GCL learns and analyze whether the learned representations are helpful for downstream tasks. For input data, we adopted the CiteSeer dataset. We envisioned the node features of the original dataset and the output features after processing with different methods. For comparison, we also built a GCN-based graph contrastive learning network including encoders with Graph Convolutional Layers and trained with InfoNCE loss [6]. The hidden dimension size and layer amount are the same as WA-GCL.

The results are demonstrated in Fig. 3. The original node features are not discriminatory. It is observable that there are several fuzzy horizontal lines in the figure, running through all the classes. These lines indicate that there are certain shared features among different classes. Intuitively speaking, as the CiteSeer dataset contains the vocabulary frequency in machine learning papers, some common words between classes may result in shared features. The encoder should be able to ignore these shared features. From the output representations of the GCN-based graph contrastive learning network, we can see that the vertical feature lines between different classes show more discrepancy than the original node features. We can observe some short and continuous horizontal lines in the same class. These horizontal lines represent the common features within the class. If the horizontal line is more persistent and apparent, the encoder can better identify this common feature on the data set. Compared to the former one, WA-GCL achieves much better results. We can observe that the features between classes are quite different. Furthermore, we can find multiple relatively

Original node features of
Cora dataset.

Output representations of
GCN-based contrastive
graph learning method

Output representations of
WA-GCL

Class labels

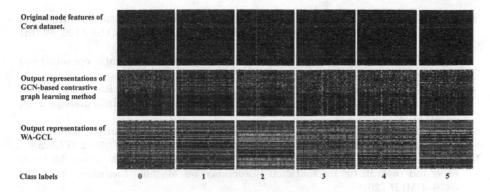

0   1   2   3   4   5

Fig. 3. The visualized node features. We visualize each feature as a vertical line. The elements in the feature vector are compressed, normalized, and then constitute the RGB component of a pixel of the vertical line. Then, we group the features belonging to the same class and put together the vertical lines representing these features.

continuous horizontal lines in the same class, indicating that the encoder can identify common features within that class. We can hardly observe any horizontal lines across multiple classes, suggesting that WA-GCL can ignore the common features of different classes.

5   Conclusions

This paper proposed a novel weight-aware contrastive learning method for graph node classification. We emphasize the nodes which possess more helpful information during training with our proposed weight-aware loss. Such emphasis enables our method to achieve better results, and we correct the problems it may bring. We designed a new edge-weight sensitive graph attentional layer to fit attention mechanism into our encoder, for they are better adapted to the task of graph node classification.

References

1. Allamanis, M., Brockschmidt, M., Khademi, M.: Learning to represent programs with graphs. In: International Conference on Learning Representations (2018)
2. Bojchevski, A., Günnemann, S.: Deep gaussian embedding of graphs: Unsupervised inductive learning via ranking. arXiv preprint arXiv:1707.03815 (2017)
3. Chuang, C.Y., Robinson, J., Yen-Chen, L., Torralba, A., Jegelka, S.: Debiased contrastive learning. arXiv preprint arXiv:2007.00224 (2020)
4. Defferrard, M., Bresson, X., Vandergheynst, P.: Convolutional neural networks on graphs with fast localized spectral filtering. Adv. Neural. Inf. Process. Syst. **29**, 3844–3852 (2016)
5. Duvenaud, D., et al.: Convolutional networks on graphs for learning molecular fingerprints. arXiv preprint arXiv:1509.09292 (2015)

6. Hassani, K., Khasahmadi, A.H.: Contrastive multi-view representation learning on graphs. In: International Conference on Machine Learning, pp. 4116–4126. PMLR (2020)
7. Kipf, T.N., Welling, M.: Semi-supervised classification with graph convolutional networks. arXiv preprint arXiv:1609.02907 (2016)
8. Leman, A., Weisfeiler, B.: A reduction of a graph to a canonical form and an algebra arising during this reduction. Nauchno-Technicheskaya Informatsiya **2**(9), 12–16 (1968)
9. Peng, Z., et al.: Graph representation learning via graphical mutual information maximization. In: Proceedings of the Web Conference 2020, pp. 259–270 (2020)
10. Sanchez-Gonzalez, A., et al.: Graph networks as learnable physics engines for inference and control. In: International Conference on Machine Learning, pp. 4470–4479. PMLR (2018)
11. Schroff, F., Kalenichenko, D., Philbin, J.: Facenet: a unified embedding for face recognition and clustering. In: 2015 IEEE Conference on Computer Vision and Pattern Recognition (CVPR) (2015)
12. Sen, P., Namata, G., Bilgic, M., Getoor, L., Galligher, B., Eliassi-Rad, T.: Collective classification in network data. AI Mag. **29**(3), 93–93 (2008)
13. Sun, Y., Cheng, C., Zhang, Y., Zhang, C., Zheng, L., Wang, Z., Wei, Y.: Circle loss: a unified perspective of pair similarity optimization. In: 2020 IEEE/CVF Conference on Computer Vision and Pattern Recognition (CVPR) (2020)
14. Tian, Y., Krishnan, D., Isola, P.: Contrastive multiview coding. In: Vedaldi, A., Bischof, H., Brox, T., Frahm, J.-M. (eds.) ECCV 2020. LNCS, vol. 12356, pp. 776–794. Springer, Cham (2020). https://doi.org/10.1007/978-3-030-58621-8_45
15. Veličković, P., Cucurull, G., Casanova, A., Romero, A., Lio, P., Bengio, Y.: Graph attention networks. arXiv preprint arXiv:1710.10903 (2017)
16. Veličković, P., Fedus, W., Hamilton, W.L., Liò, P., Bengio, Y., Hjelm, R.D.: Deep graph infomax. arXiv preprint arXiv:1809.10341 (2018)
17. Velickovic, P., Fedus, W., Hamilton, W.L., Liò, P., Bengio, Y., Hjelm, R.D.: Deep graph infomax. ICLR (Poster) **2**(3), 4 (2019)
18. Wan, S., Pan, S., Yang, J., Gong, C.: Contrastive and generative graph convolutional networks for graph-based semi-supervised learning. arXiv preprint arXiv:2009.07111 (2020)
19. Wu, F., Souza, A., Zhang, T., Fifty, C., Yu, T., Weinberger, K.: Simplifying graph convolutional networks. In: International Conference on Machine Learning, pp. 6861–6871. PMLR (2019)
20. Xu, D., Cheng, W., Luo, D., Chen, H., Zhang, X.: Infogcl: Information-aware graph contrastive learning. Advances in Neural Information Processing Systems 34 (2021)
21. Xu, K., Hu, W., Leskovec, J., Jegelka, S.: How powerful are graph neural networks? arXiv preprint arXiv:1810.00826 (2018)
22. Xu, X., Feng, W., Jiang, Y., Xie, X., Sun, Z., Deng, Z.H.: Dynamically pruned message passing networks for large-scale knowledge graph reasoning. arXiv preprint arXiv:1909.11334 (2019)
23. Zhu, X., Ghahramani, Z., Lafferty, J.D.: Semi-supervised learning using gaussian fields and harmonic functions. In: Proceedings of the 20th International Conference on Machine Learning (ICML-03), pp. 912–919 (2003)
24. Zhu, Y., Xu, Y., Yu, F., Liu, Q., Wu, S., Wang, L.: Deep graph contrastive representation learning. arXiv preprint arXiv:2006.04131 (2020)
25. Zhu, Y., Xu, Y., Yu, F., Liu, Q., Wu, S., Wang, L.: Graph contrastive learning with adaptive augmentation. In: Proceedings of the Web Conference 2021, pp. 2069–2080 (2021)

Why Deeper Graph Neural Network Performs Worse? Discussion and Improvement About Deep GNNs

Yuta Yajima[✉] and Akihiro Inokuchi

Graduate School of Science and Technology, Kwansei Gakuin University, 1 Gakuen Uegahara, Sanda 669-1330, Japan
jima971123@gmail.com, inokuchi@kwansei.ac.jp

Abstract. Many types of data can be represented by graphs consisting of nodes with features. The analysis of these graphs is facilitated by representing nodes as vectors, such that neighboring nodes and nodes with similar features have representations that are in close proximity in the vector space. Graph neural networks (GNNs) have been developed to learn such representations automatically, but their disadvantage is that the aggregation distance, which determines how many other nodes are considered relevant to each node, is fixed by the number of layers in the GNN. If the aggregation distance is too large, over-smoothing can result. This paper proposes TwinGNN for learning high-quality representations of nodes. Instead of using a fixed distance for the entire graph, TwinGNN learns the suitable distance for each node. We evaluated TwinGNN experimentally with several benchmark graph datasets. The results showed that TwinGNN successfully avoided over-smoothing. Its performance did not deteriorate as the number of GNN layers increased. Moreover, it performed better than the existing GNNs on almost all datasets.

1 Introduction

Graphs consisting of nodes with features are a fundamental type of data representation used in various applications, such as social networks, WWW, XML, chemo-informatics, bio-informatics, computer-aided design, computer vision, and software analysis. Useful knowledge can be obtained by analyzing the graphs [1]. These graphs do not have a regular grid structure, such as the pixels in images, but are geometric and contain irregular patterns. Therefore, methods of analyzing the graphs are required. In representation learning for graph analysis, nodes are represented as vectors such that nodes with similar features or nodes that are directly connected by edges are embedded in close proximity in a vector space. Having obtained vector representations of the nodes, various conventional machine learning methods—such as classification, regression, and clustering—can be applied to the vectors for graph analyses—such as node classification and link prediction—without being bound by the irregular patterns.

To learn high-quality representations of nodes, it is important to characterize each node v by features and structural properties contained in subgraphs around

© The Author(s), under exclusive license to Springer Nature Switzerland AG 2022
E. Pimenidis et al. (Eds.): ICANN 2022, LNCS 13530, pp. 731–743, 2022.
https://doi.org/10.1007/978-3-031-15931-2_60

v. To characterize the node, graph neural networks (GNNs) with L layers aggregate the features of the nodes reachable within L steps from node v [2–4]. Here, L is called the aggregation distance. Graph convolutional networks (GCNs) [2], graph attention networks (GATs) [3], and GraphSAGE [4] are representative implementations of GNNs.

Most shallow GNNs—with only two or three layers—perform better than deep GNNs because of the phenomenon known as over-smoothing. For example, in Fig. 1, if the aggregation distance is 3, the features of all nodes reachable within three steps from v are aggregated to characterize v. Because the characterization of node v has features of both classes 1 and 2, a classifier cannot classify v accurately. Because the suitable aggregation distance for each dataset is not known prior to analysis, we generally start with a small L and increase L until the classification accuracy decreases. Therefore, it would be useful to be able to learn the suitable aggregation distance from the dataset after providing a large L as input. In addition, the suitable aggregation distance differs from node to node. For example, in Fig. 1, the suitable aggregation distance for v is 1, whereas that for v' is 4 but not any value between 1 and 4 to be explained in Sect. 4.3. However, in conventional GNNs, all nodes in a graph have the same aggregation distance. To achieve high classification accuracy, we propose a method, TwinGNN, for learning node representation while learning a suitable aggregation distance for each node. The contributions of this study are as follows:

1. We propose TwinGNN, which learns a suitable aggregation distance for each node. TwinGNN can be integrated with various conventional GNNs, such as GCN, GAT, and GraphSAGE.
2. We show that TwinGNN has the ability to prevent over-smoothing and improves the performance of GNNs, by quantitative and qualitative experiments (Sect. 5.2).
3. We elucidate a basic theoretical cause of over-smoothing: a relationship between the computation of GNNs and the reproductive property of probability distributions (Sect. 4.3).

2 Preliminaries

A graph is represented as $G = (V, E, X)$, where $V = \{1, 2, \ldots, n\}$ is a set of nodes, $E \subseteq V \times V$ is a set of edges, and $X = \{\boldsymbol{x}_1, \boldsymbol{x}_2, \ldots, \boldsymbol{x}_n\}$ is a set of d-dimensional feature vectors. In this paper, we address binary node classification problems[1]. In addition, the feature vector of each node v follows a Gaussian distribution $\mathcal{N}(\boldsymbol{\mu}_i, \Sigma_i)$, where i is the label of the class to which

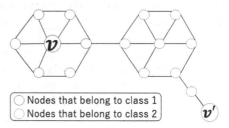

Fig. 1. Different aggregation distances

---

[1] In this paper, we address the binary classification of nodes, although the proposed method can be extended to multi-class node classification, multi-label node classification, and graph classification.

v belongs. For node v, the set of 1-neighbor nodes (including v itself) is defined as $N_v^1 = \{v\} \cup \{u \mid (v, u) \in E\}$, and the set of l-neighbor nodes of v is recursively defined as $N_v^l = \cup_{u \in N_v^1} N_u^{l-1}$. A sequence of nodes $(u_0, u_1, \ldots, u_l)$ from u_0 to u_l is called a path, and its length (number of steps) is l. A path is said to be simple if and only if it does not have repeated nodes. The paths discussed in this paper are not always simple, and we allow nodes on a path to have the property $u_i = u_{i+1}$, which means that all nodes in the graph have self-loops. The set of all possible paths of length l from v is denoted by P_v^l.

Given a graph $G = (V, E, X)$ and ground-truth class labels $y_v \in \{0, 1\}$ for a subset V' of V, the problem addressed in this paper is to learn representations $\{h_1, h_2, \ldots, h_n\}$ to classify the nodes $V \setminus V'$ accurately. According to various previous studies, classification of nodes by representation learning strongly depends on the "quality" of the representations. Intuitively, a high-quality representation is one in which h_v and h_u are similar if nodes v and u ought to be in the same class and are dissimilar otherwise. The challenge addressed in this paper is to learn a high-quality representation for the nodes in G.

3 Related Work and Drawback of GNNs

To learn high-quality representations h_v for all nodes v in G, various deep learning methods for aggregating the features of the l-neighbor nodes of v have been studied. These methods have a common structure for learning the representations: their interfaces [5], named GNNs, are formalized as

$$\left. \begin{array}{l} a_v^l = Aggregate^l(\{h_u^{l-1} \mid u \in N_v^1\}) \\ h_v^l = Combine^l(h_v^{l-1}, a_v^l) \end{array} \right\} \; l = 1, 2, \ldots, L \qquad (1)$$

$$h_v = h_v^L, \qquad (2)$$

where $h_v^0 = x_v$ and L is the number of layers. The representation h_v^l obtained in l iterations aggregates the features of nodes in N_v^l. As Eq. (2) shows, a GNN with L layers finally outputs h_v^L as the representation h_v of v after aggregating the features of the L-neighbor nodes. Thus, L refers to both the number of layers in the GNN and the aggregation distance. Since the proposal of GCN [2], various GNN implementations have been proposed to improve $Aggregate$ in Eq. (1)—such as GAT [3] and the graph isomorphism network (GIN) [5]—or to improve $Combine$—such as GraphSAGE [4] and Deeper GCN [6].

A representative model designed to improve $Aggregate$ is GAT. The $Aggregate$ operations in GCN and GAT are defined as

$$a_v^l = \text{GCN-}Aggregate^l(\{h_u^{l-1} \mid u \in N_v^1\}) = \frac{1}{|N_v^1|} \sum_{u \in N_v^1} h_u^{l-1}, \qquad (3)$$

$$a_v^l = \text{GAT-}Aggregate^l(\{h_u^{l-1} \mid u \in N_v^1\}) = \sum_{u \in N_v^1} \beta_{vu}^l h_u^{l-1}, \qquad (4)$$

respectively. GCN aggregates the features of 1-neighbor nodes equally, whereas GAT aggregates the features weighted by learnable parameters β_{vu}^l using the attention mechanism.

A representative model designed to improve *Combine* is GraphSAGE. The *Combine* operations in GCN and GraphSAGE are defined as

$$h_v^l = \text{GCN-}Combine^l(h_v^{l-1}, a_v^l) = \sigma\left(W^l a_v^l\right), \tag{5}$$

$$h_v^l = \text{SAGE-}Combine^l(h_v^{l-1}, a_v^l) = \sigma\left(W^l a_v^l + \hat{W}^l h_v^{l-1}\right), \tag{6}$$

respectively, where σ is an activation function. SAGE-*Combine*^{l} is a type of Skip-connection [4], which is widely used for image recognition tasks. When $\hat{W}^l$ is an identity matrix, SAGE-*Combine*^{l} becomes Residual-connection [7]. In contrast, when $W^l a_v^l + \hat{W}^l h_v^{l-1}$ is replaced by $(W^l a_v^l)\|h_v^{l-1}$, where the operator $\|$ denotes concatenation, it becomes Densely-connection [8]. Veit et al. [9] showed that the Skip-connection is equivalent to ensemble learning of 2^L neural networks that have various numbers of layers.

Experiments reported by Kipf and Welling [2] and those conducted in this study demonstrated that the classification accuracy is lower for deeper GNNs (with more layers). This performance degradation of GNNs is known as the over-smoothing phenomenon. This phenomenon encourages us to use shallow GNNs, with few layers. Because the suitable aggregation distance for each dataset is not known in advance of analysis, we generally start with a small L and increase L until the classification accuracy decreases. Therefore, it would be useful if the suitable aggregation distances could be learned from the dataset after providing a large L as input. In addition, the suitable aggregation distance is different for each node. For example, in Fig. 1, the suitable aggregation distance for v is 1, whereas that for v' is 4. However, in conventional GNNs, all nodes have the same aggregation distance. In this paper, we propose a method for constructing representations while learning a suitable aggregation distance l_v^* for each node v to achieve high accuracy for the classification problem.

4   Proposed Method

4.1   Derivation of the Proposed Method Using SiameseNet

Obtaining the suitable aggregation distance l_v^* for v is a discrete optimization problem: to decide whether each l $(1 \leq l \leq L)$ is suitable for aggregation for v. This is formalized as

$$h_v = Summarize\left(h_v^1, h_v^2, \ldots, h_v^L, \alpha_v\right) = \sum_{l=1}^{L} \alpha_v^l h_v^l \quad s.t. \sum_{l=1}^{L} \alpha_v^l = 1, \tag{7}$$

where $\boldsymbol{\alpha}_v = (\alpha_v^1, \alpha_v^2, \ldots, \alpha_v^L)$ is a one-hot vector whose l_*^*-th element is 1. To satisfy Eq. (7), W^l in Eq. (5) is restricted to be a square matrix. In Eq. (7), the final representation $\boldsymbol{h}_v$ is a weighted sum of representations $\boldsymbol{h}_v^l$ with learnable parameters α_v^l. In contrast, as shown in Eq. (2), conventional GNNs output $\boldsymbol{h}_v^L$— which is the representation in the last layer in the GNNs—as $\boldsymbol{h}_v$. Equation (7) employs $\boldsymbol{h}_v^{l_*}$ on the suitable aggregation distance—instead of $\boldsymbol{h}_v^L$ on the final layer—as the representation for v, thereby preventing over-smoothing.

When α_v^l is a real value between 0 and 1, the problem is relaxed to a continuous optimization problem: to predict a probability that each l is suitable for aggregation for v. We consider that the probability α_v^l is the proportion of nodes of the same class label as v that occur in N_v^l, as follows:

$$\alpha_v^l = Softmax_{1 \sim L}(\overline{\alpha}_v^l) = \frac{\exp(\overline{\alpha}_v^l)}{\sum_{l'=1}^{L} \exp(\overline{\alpha}_v^{l'})}, \tag{8}$$

$$\overline{\alpha}_v^l = \frac{1}{|N_v^l|} \sum_{u \in N_v^l} \delta(y_v, y_u), \tag{9}$$

where δ is the Kronecker delta.

Condition 1: All nodes reachable within l' steps from v belong to the same class as v and some nodes reachable with $l' + 1$ steps from v belong to distinct classes to v.

When the above condition holds, we have

$$\overline{\alpha}_v^{l'} > \overline{\alpha}_v^{l'+1}. \tag{10}$$

When Condition 1 holds, the property denoted in Eq. (10) is very important for preventing over-smoothing by Eq. (7). To calculate Eq. (9) accurately, although as many nodes as possible must have ground-truth labels, the number of nodes with labels is relatively small. Therefore, we propose an algorithm for computing Eq. (9) approximately with a small number of ground-truth labels. To design the algorithm, we assume that the representations of nodes v and $u \in N_v^l$ that belong to the same class are similar, and define

$$\overline{\alpha}_v^l = \sum_{u \in N_v^l} c_{vu} k(f_\theta^l(\boldsymbol{x}_v), f_\theta^l(\boldsymbol{x}_u)), \tag{11}$$

where f_θ^l is a linear transformation with a learnable parameter $\boldsymbol{\theta}$, k is a kernel function, and c_{vu} is a nonnegative term. $k(f_\theta^l(\boldsymbol{x}_v), f_\theta^l(\boldsymbol{x}_u))$ in Eq. (11) is known as SiameseNet [10]: it takes two inputs, transforms them with the same parameter, and returns the similarity between the two inputs. Thus, Eq. (11)—which is a linear sum of SiameseNet functions—represents the similarity between node v and the nodes around v, and can be used as an alternative to Eq. (9).

We now discuss how to learn $\boldsymbol{\theta}$ and c_{vu} from the training data. In the following discussion, the kernel function k is a dot product of two vectors.

$$\overline{\alpha}_v^l = \sum_{u \in N_v^l} c_{vu} k(f_{\boldsymbol{\theta}}^l(\boldsymbol{x}_v), f_{\boldsymbol{\theta}}^l(\boldsymbol{x}_u)) = \sum_{u \in N_v^l} c_{vu} \langle f_{\boldsymbol{\theta}}^l(\boldsymbol{x}_v), f_{\boldsymbol{\theta}}^l(\boldsymbol{x}_u) \rangle$$

$$= \left\langle f_{\boldsymbol{\theta}}^l(\boldsymbol{x}_v), \sum_{u \in N_v^l} c_{vu} f_{\boldsymbol{\theta}}^l(\boldsymbol{x}_u) \right\rangle = k \left(f_{\boldsymbol{\theta}}^l(\boldsymbol{x}_v), \sum_{u \in N_v^l} c_{vu} f_{\boldsymbol{\theta}}^l(\boldsymbol{x}_u) \right)$$

$$\risingdotseq k \left(f_{\boldsymbol{\theta}}^l(\boldsymbol{x}_v), \sum_{(v,u_1,u_2,\ldots,u_l) \in P_v^l} c_{vu_l}' f_{\boldsymbol{\theta}}^l(\boldsymbol{x}_{u_l}) \right). \tag{12}$$

By assuming that the second argument of Eq. (12) coincides with h_v^l in Eq. (1), we can rewrite Eq. (12) as

$$\overline{\alpha}_v^l = k(\overline{\boldsymbol{h}}_v^l, \boldsymbol{h}_v^l). \tag{13}$$

To clarify how to compute $\overline{\boldsymbol{h}}_v^l$ in Eq. (13), we derive the relationship between $\boldsymbol{h}_v^l$ and the second argument of Eq. (12) under the condition that the activation function σ in GCN is the identity function.

$$\boldsymbol{h}_v^l = \frac{1}{|N_v^1|} \sum_{u \in N_v^1} W^l \boldsymbol{h}_u^{l-1} = \frac{1}{|N_v^1|} \sum_{u \in N_v^1} W^l \left(\frac{1}{|N_u^1|} \sum_{u' \in N_u^1} W^{l-1} \boldsymbol{h}_{u'}^{l-2} \right)$$

$$= \sum_{u \in N_v^1} \sum_{u' \in N_u^1} \frac{1}{|N_v^1|} \frac{1}{|N_u^1|} W^l W^{l-1} \boldsymbol{h}_{u'}^{l-2}$$

$$= \sum_{(v,u_1,u_2,\ldots,u_l) \in P_v^l} \frac{1}{|N_v^1|} \frac{1}{|N_{u_1}^1|} \cdots \frac{1}{|N_{u_{l-1}}^1|} W^l W^{l-1} \cdots W^1 \boldsymbol{h}_{u_l}^0$$

$$= \frac{1}{|P_v^l|} \sum_{(v,u_1,u_2,\ldots,u_l) \in P_v^l} W^l W^{l-1} \cdots W^1 \boldsymbol{h}_{u_l}^0. \tag{14}$$

From the above discussion, we obtain $c_{vu}' = 1/|P_v^l|$, $\boldsymbol{\theta} = \{W^1, W^2, \ldots, W^l\}$, and $f_{\boldsymbol{\theta}}^l(\boldsymbol{x}) = W^l W^{l-1} \cdots W^1 \boldsymbol{x}$. Therefore, $\overline{\boldsymbol{h}}_v^l$ is expressed as $\overline{\boldsymbol{h}}_v^l = W^l W^{l-1} \cdots W^1 \overline{\boldsymbol{h}}_v^0 = W^l \overline{\boldsymbol{h}}_v^{l-1}$. That is, $\overline{\boldsymbol{h}}_v^l$ is obtained by a linear transformation only, without *Aggregate*, whereas $\boldsymbol{h}_v^l$ is obtained by the same linear transformation and *Aggregate*. Hereafter, we denote $W^l W^{l-1} \cdots W^1$ by $W_{1\sim l}$.

4.2   Pseudocode of the Proposed Method

Algorithm 1 shows the pseudocode of the feedforward procedures in the proposed method, TwinGNN. In lines 2 and 3, high-dimensional feature vectors are transformed to low-dimensional (d'-dimensional) vectors, and W^l ($1 \le l \le L$) becomes a matrix in $\mathbb{R}^{d' \times d'}$. TwinGNN can be integrated with various conventional GNNs, such as GCN, GAT, and GraphSAGE. In lines 4 and 5, the conventional GNNs to be integrated are selected. For example, when GCN-*Aggregate*

Algorithm 1. Feedfrward procedures of TwinGNN

Inputs: Graph $G = (V, E, X)$, the number of layers L, and dimension d'
Outputs: Set of representations of nodes $H = \{h_1, h_2, \ldots, h_n\}$
1: **Initialize**
2:   $h_v^0 \leftarrow Wx_v$ $\forall v \in V$ and $W \in \mathbb{R}^{d' \times d}$
3:   $\overline{h}_v^0 \leftarrow Wx_v$ $\forall v \in V$
4:   $Aggregate \leftarrow$ Selection($\{$GCN-$Aggregate$, GAT-$Aggregate$, etc.$\}$)
5:   $Combine \leftarrow$ Selection($\{$GCN-$Combine$, SAGE-$Combine$, etc.$\}$)
6: **end Initialize**
7: **for** $l \in \{1, 2, \ldots, L\}$ **do**
8:   **for** $v \in V$ **do**
9:     $a_v^l \leftarrow Aggregate^l(\{h_u^{l-1} \mid u \in N_v^1\})$
10:     $h_v^l \leftarrow Combine^l(h_v^{l-1}, a_v^l)$
11:     $\overline{a}_v^l \leftarrow \overline{h}_v^{l-1}$
12:     $\overline{h}_v^l \leftarrow Combine^l(\overline{h}_v^{l-1}, \overline{a}_v^l)$
13:   **end for**
14: **end for**
15: **for** $v \in V$ **do**
16:   **for** $l \in \{1, 2, \ldots, L\}$ **do**
17:     $\overline{\alpha}_v^l \leftarrow k(h_v^l, \overline{h}_v^l)$ //Eq. (13)
18:   **end for**
19:   $\alpha_v^l \leftarrow Softmax_{1 \sim L}(\overline{\alpha}_v^l)$ $\forall l \in \{1, 2, \ldots, L\}$ //Eq. (8)
20:   $h_v \leftarrow Summarize\left(h_v^1, h_v^2, \ldots, h_v^L, (\alpha_v^1, \alpha_v^2, \ldots, \alpha_v^L)\right)$ //Eq. (7)
21: **end for**

---

and GCN-*Combine* are selected as *Aggregate* and *Combine*, respectively, the procedures in lines 9–12 are as follows. As noted in the last paragraph of the previous subsection, h_v^l and $\overline{h}_v^l$ are obtained by the same linear transformation.

$$\left.\begin{aligned}
a_v^l &= \text{GCN-}Aggregate^l(\{h_u^{l-1} \mid u \in N_v^1\}) = \tfrac{1}{|N_v^1|}\sum_{u \in N_v^1} h_u^{l-1}, \\
h_v^l &= \text{GCN-}Combine^l(h_v^{l-1}, a_v^l) \qquad\quad = \sigma\left(W^l a_v^l\right),
\end{aligned}\right\} \; l = 1, \ldots, L$$

$$\left.\begin{aligned}
\overline{a}_v^l &= \overline{h}_v^{l-1}, \\
\overline{h}_v^l &= \text{GCN-}Combine^l(\overline{h}_v^{l-1}, \overline{a}_v^l) \qquad = \sigma\left(W^l \overline{a}_v^l\right).
\end{aligned}\right\} \; l = 1, \ldots, L$$

If Eq. (14) is computed directly, its computation time increases exponentially with l because the number of paths of length l from v increases exponentially with l. However, by integrating TwinGNN with GNNs, the procedures in lines 7–14—which form the main part of TwinGNN—are computed in $\mathcal{O}(|V|L(\overline{v}d' + d'^2))$ time, where $\overline{v}$ is the average degree (valency) of nodes.

4.3   Theoretical Discussion of the Proposed Method

Equation (13) defines the similarity $\overline{\alpha}_v^l$ between node v and the l-neighbor nodes for v. Because the similarity should satisfy Eq. (10), we now discuss theoretically whether this is the case. To do so, we partition the set P_v^l of paths of length l

from v into $P_{v,1}^l = \{(v, u_1, u_2, \ldots, u_l) \mid y_{u_l} = 1\}$ and $P_{v,0}^l = P_v^l \setminus P_{v,1}^l$. We then denote the set of paths reachable with l steps from v to u as $P_{v \rightsquigarrow u}^l$. We define an $n(= |V|)$-dimensional vector $\boldsymbol{\pi}_v^l = (|P_{v \rightsquigarrow 1}^l|, |P_{v \rightsquigarrow 2}^l|, \ldots, |P_{v \rightsquigarrow n}^l|)^T = \sum_{u \in V} |P_{v \rightsquigarrow 1}^l| \mathbb{1}_{n,u}$, each element of which represents the number of l step paths from v. Here, $\mathbb{1}_{n,u}$ is an n-dimensional one-hot vector whose u-th element is 1. We obtain a relationship $|P_v^l| = \|\boldsymbol{\pi}_v^l\|_1$. In addition, for $V^+ = \{u \in V \mid y_u = 1\}$ and $V^- = V \setminus V^+$, we also obtain a relationship $\boldsymbol{\pi}_{v,+}^l = \sum_{u \in V^+} |P_{v \rightsquigarrow u}^l| \mathbb{1}_{n,u}$.

Lemma 1. $\boldsymbol{h}_v^l$ *follows the Gaussian distribution defined below:*

$$\mathcal{N}\left(\frac{|P_{v,0}^l|}{|P_v^l|} W_{1 \sim l} \boldsymbol{\mu}_0 + \frac{|P_{v,1}^l|}{|P_v^l|} W_{1 \sim l} \boldsymbol{\mu}_1, \frac{\|\boldsymbol{\pi}_{v,-}^l\|_2^2}{|P_v^l|^2} W_{1 \sim l} \Sigma_0 W_{1 \sim l}^T + \frac{\|\boldsymbol{\pi}_{v,+}^l\|_2^2}{|P_v^l|^2} W_{1 \sim l} \Sigma_1 W_{1 \sim l}^T\right)$$
(15)

Proof. According to Eq. (14), we have $\boldsymbol{h}_v^l = \frac{1}{|P_v^l|} \sum_{(v, u_1, u_2, \ldots, u_l) \in P_v^l} W_{1 \sim l} \boldsymbol{h}_{u_l}^0$. Because the linear transformation of a Gaussian distribution is also a Gaussian distribution, we have $W_{1 \sim l} \boldsymbol{h}_{u_l}^0 \sim \mathcal{N}(W_{1 \sim l} \boldsymbol{\mu}_i, W_{1 \sim l} \Sigma_i W_{1 \sim l}^T)$ when the class of u_l is i. In addition, because $\boldsymbol{h}_v^l$ is a linear sum of random variables arising from Gaussian distributions, $\boldsymbol{h}_v^l$ follows the Gaussian distribution according to the reproductive property of Gaussian distributions [11]. Since $|P_{v \rightsquigarrow u}^l|/|P_v^l|$ is the ratio of information that $\boldsymbol{h}_v^l$ contains whose origin is $\boldsymbol{h}_u^0$, Eq. (15) holds.   □

When GNNs have many layers, that is, when l is large, the ratio of $|P_{v,1}^l|$ to $|P_{v,0}^l|$ is approximately equal to the class label ratio in the graph provided as input. In this case, representations of all nodes in GNNs with many layers follow the Gaussian distribution with the mean $\frac{|P_{v,0}^l|}{|P_v^l|} W_{1 \sim l} \boldsymbol{\mu}_0 + \frac{|P_{v,1}^l|}{|P_v^l|} W_{1 \sim l} \boldsymbol{\mu}_1$. Therefore, the representations become similar to one another, causing over-smoothing. In contrast, for each node v, there exists suitable l satisfying $|P_{v,j}^l| = 0$ which means that v belongs to class i and no nodes reachable within l steps from v belong to the other class. In this case, $\boldsymbol{h}_v^l \sim \mathcal{N}(W_{1 \sim l} \boldsymbol{\mu}_i, \frac{\|\boldsymbol{\pi}_v^l\|_2^2}{|P_v^l|^2} W_{1 \sim l} \Sigma_i W_{1 \sim l}^T)$.

If $|N_v^l|$ increases as l increases, $\frac{\|\boldsymbol{\pi}_v^l\|_2^2}{|P_v^l|^2} \Sigma_i$ which constitutes the variance of the aforementioned distribution often decreases as l increases. By decrease of the variance, the area to occur at the same time of two Gaussian distributions to be used for the binary classification are also decreased, which produces high accurate classification. Therefore, in Fig. 1, the suitable aggregation distance for v' is 4 rather than any value between 1 and 4, and the suitable aggregation distance differs from node to node.

To introduce Lemmas 2 and 3, we limit W^l to orthogonal matrices. We assume that X is initialized such as satisfying $\boldsymbol{\mu}_1 = -\boldsymbol{\mu}_0$ by using features for V' in the training dataset. In addition, we assume that class labels for all nodes in N_v^l for $l \leq l'$ are equal to one for v, $|P_{v,0}^l|/|P_{v,1}^l|$ for $l' \leq l \leq L$ increases monotonically, and it finally converges the class label ratio $|V^-|/|V^+|$ of G.

Lemma 2. *When Condition 1 holds with a certain l' and v belongs to class 1, Eq. (16) holds. (Due to lack of space, proofs for Lemmas 2 and 3 are omitted.)*

$$E[k(\overline{h}_v^l, h_v^l)] = \begin{cases} \|\mu_1\|_2^2 + \frac{|P_{v \rightsquigarrow v}^l|}{|P_v^l|} tr(\Sigma_1) & (l < l') \\ \frac{1 - |P_{v,0}^l|/|P_{v,1}^l|}{1 + |P_{v,0}^l|/|P_{v,1}^l|} \|\mu_1\|_2^2 + \frac{|P_{v \rightsquigarrow v}^l|}{|P_v^l|} tr(\Sigma_1) & (l' \le l). \end{cases} \quad \blacksquare \quad (16)$$

Because $|P_{v,0}^l|/|P_{v,1}^l|$ for $l' \le l$ monotonically increases from 0 and finally converges the class label ratio $|V^-|/|V^+|$ of G, it is expected that

$$E[\overline{\alpha}_v^{l'}] = E[k(\overline{h}_v^{l'}, h_v^{l'})] > E[k(\overline{h}_v^{l'+1}, h_v^{l'+1})] = E[\overline{\alpha}_v^{l'+1}].$$

Because $E[\overline{\alpha}_v^{l'}]$ and $E[\overline{\alpha}_v^{l'+1}]$ are normalized by the same softmax, we have

$$E[\alpha_v^{l'}] > E[\alpha_v^{l'+1}].$$

If the class labels of all nodes are known, Eq. (10) is satisfied. However, because the number of nodes whose class labels are known is limited, the property that we can introduce is limited to $E[\alpha_v^l] > E[\alpha_v^{l+1}]$. If we show that $V[\alpha_v^l]$ decreases monotonically as l increases, we conclude that $\alpha_v^l > \alpha_v^{l+1}$ for most nodes. Therefore, we introduce the following lemma.

Lemma 3. *When v belongs to class 1, $V[\overline{\alpha}_v^l]$ is expressed as*

$$\frac{\|\pi_{v,+}^l\|_2^2}{|P_v^l|^2}(\mu_1^T \Sigma_1 \mu_1 + tr(\Sigma_1^2)) + \frac{\|\pi_{v,-}^l\|_2^2}{|P_v^l|^2}(\mu_1^T \Sigma_0 \mu_1 + tr(\Sigma_1^T \Sigma_0)) + \frac{|P_{v \rightsquigarrow v}^l|^2}{|P_v^l|^2} tr(\Sigma_1^2)$$

$$+ (\frac{1 - |P_{v,0}^l|/|P_{v,1}^l|}{1 + |P_{v,0}^l|/|P_{v,1}^l|})^2 \mu_1^T \Sigma_1 \mu_1 + \frac{2|P_{v \rightsquigarrow v}^l|}{|P_v^l|} \frac{1 - |P_{v,0}^l|/|P_{v,1}^l|}{1 + |P_{v,0}^l|/|P_{v,1}^l|} \mu_1^T \Sigma_1 \mu_1. \quad \blacksquare \quad (17)$$

Equation (17) consists of $\frac{1 - |P_{v,0}^l|/|P_{v,1}^l|}{1 + |P_{v,0}^l|/|P_{v,1}^l|}$, $\frac{\|\pi_{v,i}^l\|_2^2}{|P_v^l|^2}$, $\frac{|P_{v \rightsquigarrow v}^l|}{|P_v^l|}$, and the others independent from l. $\frac{1 - |P_{v,0}^l|/|P_{v,1}^l|}{1 + |P_{v,0}^l|/|P_{v,1}^l|}$ decreases monotonically as l increases. $\frac{\|\pi_{v,i}^l\|_2^2}{|P_v^l|^2}$ and $\frac{|P_{v \rightsquigarrow v}^l|}{|P_v^l|}$ often decreases monotonically if $|N_v^l|$ increases as l increases. Therefore, it is expected that $V[\overline{\alpha}_v^l]$ and $V[\alpha_v^l]$ decrease as l increases. From these lemmas, we expect that $E[\alpha_v^l] > E[\alpha_v^{l+1}]$ holds when Condition 1 holds with l'. Therefore, for each node v, h_v is expected to be a high-quality representation in which the features of nodes within a suitable distance from v are aggregated by Eq. (7). Therefore, our method TwinGNN prevents oversmoothing.

5   Experimental Evaluation

5.1   Experimental Setting

We implemented TwinGNN[2] with PyTorch 1.9 and PyTorch Geometric. Following previous work [12–14], we divided the nodes V into V_{tr}, $V_{val} = V' \setminus V_{tr}$, and

---

[2] https://github.com/yururyuru00/TwinNet.

$V_{test} = V \setminus V'$ for training, validation, and testing, respectively. In the back-propagation procedures in TwinGNN, the following loss function is minimized:

$$- \sum_{v \in V_{tr}} [y_v \log \hat{y}_v + (1 - y_v) \log(1 - \hat{y}_v)] + C \sum_{l=1}^{L} \|W^{l^T} W^l - I\|_F^2, \qquad (18)$$

where $\hat{y}_v$ is the predicted class label for v, $C \geq 0$, and the second term is the regularization to make W^l orthogonal. The search ranges of the hyperparameters are provided in the `tuning_scripts` file in the package shown in footnote 2.

In this section, we compare TwinGNN with conventional GNNs—such as GCN, GAT, GraphSAGE, and JK (Jumping Knowledge) [12]—to evaluate whether TwinGNN can prevent over-smoothing. We calculated the percentage of the nodes that the model successfully classified (the micro-F1 score). As noted in Sect. 4.2, TwinGNN can be integrated with GAT and GraphSAGE. We denote these integrations as GAT+Twin and SAGE+Twin, respectively. Similarly to TwinGNN, JK obtains h_v from $\{h_v^1, h_v^2, \ldots, h_v^L\}$ and has three modes: JK-Cat, JK-Max, and JK-LSTM. JK-Cat returns $h_v = h_v^1 \| h_v^2 \| \cdots \| h_v^L$, JK-Max returns an elementwise maximum of $\{h_v^1, h_v^2, \ldots, h_v^L\}$, and JK-LSTM returns h_v using a bidirectional long short-term memory (LSTM) and Eq. (7). JK can also be integrated with GAT and GraphSAGE.

As summarized in Table 1, we used six datasets containing information on citation networks[3] and biochemical networks[4]. PPI and OGB-PPI are datasets for multi-label node classification, whereas each of the other datasets is for multi-class node classification. We treated citation links (of citation networks) and protein–protein interactions (of biochemical networks) as undirected edges, following the original experimental settings [2–4].

Table 1. Summary of benchmark datasets

Dataset	Nodes $|V|$	Degree $\bar{v}$	Features d	Classes c
PubMed[3]	19,717	2.2	500	3
CiteSeer[3]	3,327	1.4	3,703	6
Cora[3]	2,708	2.0	1,433	7
PPI[4]	56,944	14.4	50	121
OGB-PPI[4]	132,534	298.5	8	112
OGB-Arxiv[3]	169,343	6.9	128	40

5.2 Experimental Results

Figure 2 shows how the micro-F1 score varied with the number of layers L in learning models on PubMed. GCN and GAT did not prevent over-smoothing: their micro-F1 scores decreased significantly as the number of layers L increased, as reported in various previous studies [2–4]. The micro-F1 score of GAT+JK was almost the same for all values of L, indicating that JK has an ability to prevent over-smoothing. GAT+Twin outperformed GAT+JK significantly. The reason why GAT+Twin outperformed the other methods is that the complexity of the learnable parameters of TwinGNN (other than α_v^l and W^l) is $\mathcal{O}(cd')$ to classify one of the c classes from the d'-dimensional vector. In contrast, the complexities of JK-Cat, JK-Max, and JK-LSTM are $\mathcal{O}(cd'L)$, $\mathcal{O}(cd')$, and $\mathcal{O}(d'^2 L + cd')$, respectively, and JK requires much more training data than

TwinGNN. In Sect. 4.3, because we limited W^l to orthogonal matrices, the loss function in Eq. (18) contains the regularization in its second term. We obtained the best micro-F1 score for GAT+Twin with a C of 0. The expressive power of the model was improved by increasing the search range of W^l, although this deviates from Lemmas 2 and 3. Although similar experimental results were obtained for the other datasets, the results are omitted because of space limitations.

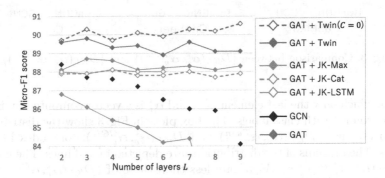

Fig. 2. Variation of micro-F1 score with number of layers L on PubMed dataset

Tables 2 and 3 show the best micro-F1 score for each learning model for each dataset. The numbers in brackets are the numbers of layers when the best micro-F1 scores were obtained. TwinGNN outperformed the other learning models for datasets other than OGB-Arxiv. The numbers of layers when the best micro-F1 scores were obtained were larger for TwinGNN and JK than for GCN, GAT, and SAGE; this is consistent with the result shown in Fig. 2. The reason why the micro-F1 scores for SAGE and SAGE+JK-Cat were greater than the score for SAGE+Twin is the low homophily of OGB-Arxiv. Homophily is the proportion of v's neighbors having the same label as v [15], and is defined as $\frac{1}{|V|}\sum_{v\in V}|\{u \mid u \in N_v^1 \setminus \{v\}, y_u = y_v\}|/|N_v^1 \setminus \{v\}|$. The homophily values of PubMed, CiteSeer, Cora, and OGB-Arxiv are 0.79, 0.71, 0.83, and 0.43, respectively.

As noted in connection with Eq. (7), TwinGNN learns the probability α_v. The probability for v by TwinGNN is denoted by α_v^{Twin}. α_v^{GCN} is a one-hot

Table 2. Best micro-F1 score for each learning model for small datasets

Model	PubMed	CiteSeer	Cora	PPI
GCN	88.4 (2)	73.4 (2)	87.3 (2)	70.5 (3)
GAT	86.8 (2)	74.4 (2)	87.4 (2)	98.1 (8)
GAT+JK-Cat	88.7 (3)	73.7 (4)	87.1 (7)	**99.3 (9)**
GAT+JK-Max	88.1 (4)	73.7 (4)	87.2 (6)	**99.3 (9)**
GAT+JK-LSTM	88.1 (4)	73.8 (8)	87.2 (6)	**99.3 (6)**
GAT+Twin	88.6 (9)	74.5 (9)	87.0 (4)	98.9 (9)
GAT+Twin ($C=0$)	**90.6 (9)**	**75.4 (9)**	**87.9 (7)**	99.2 (9)

Table 3. Best micro-F1 score for each learning model for large datasets

Model	OGB-PPI	OGB-Arxiv
GCN	72.9 (2)	71.1 (5)
SAGE	81.3 (5)	**72.1 (4)**
SAGE+JK-Cat	**82.2 (7)**	72.2 (5)
SAGE+JK-Max	**82.2 (6)**	71.8 (3)
SAGE+JK-LSTM	80.8 (7)	70.9 (2)
SAGE+Twin	77.0 (4)	66.5 (4)
SAGE+Twin ($C=0$)	**82.5 (7)**	71.8 (4)

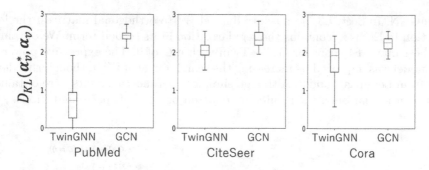

Fig. 3. Comparison between $\{D_{KL}(\boldsymbol{\alpha}_v^*, \boldsymbol{\alpha}_v^{Twin})\}$ and $\{D_{KL}(\boldsymbol{\alpha}_v^*, \boldsymbol{\alpha}_v^{GNN})\}$

vector of which only the last element is 1, and $\boldsymbol{\alpha}_v^*$ is a vector computed by Eq. (8) with all ground-truth class labels. The box plots in Fig. 3 show the distributions of KL-divergence, $D_{KL}(\boldsymbol{\alpha}_v^*, \boldsymbol{\alpha}_v^{Twin})$ and $D_{KL}(\boldsymbol{\alpha}_v^*, \boldsymbol{\alpha}_v^{GCN})$, for nodes in the 3 datasets. The medians of the distributions are depicted by red lines. The medians of $\{D_{KL}(\boldsymbol{\alpha}_v^*, \boldsymbol{\alpha}_v^{Twin}) \mid v \in V_{test}\}$ are less than those of $\{D_{KL}(\boldsymbol{\alpha}_v^*, \boldsymbol{\alpha}_v^{GCN}) \mid v \in V_{test}\}$, indicating that TwinGNN learns $\boldsymbol{\alpha}_v^{GCN}$ appropriately.

Figure 4 is a visualization of the class distribution for a certain node v and the nodes around v. Node v (depicted as a star) was selected from V_{test} in PubMed; GAT+Twin for $L = 5$ classified it accurately, whereas GCN performed less well. The nodes $N_v^{l'} \setminus N_v^{l'-1}$ that are reachable in l' steps from v are visualized on a circle of radius l', with their colors indicating their class labels. The color intensity of the nodes on the circle of radius l' is proportional to $\sum_{l=l'}^{L} \alpha_v^l$. For v, GCN aggregated the features in all nodes in Fig. 4(a) into $\boldsymbol{h}_v^5$, and output it as $\boldsymbol{h}_v$. Therefore, GCN could not classify this node accurately. In contrast, because GAT+Twin assigned a large weight α_v^1 only to the node u adjacent to v in Fig. 4(b)—even though there are many nodes around v that belong to different classes from v—most of the information in $\boldsymbol{h}_v$ consists of features $\boldsymbol{x}_v$ and $\boldsymbol{x}_u$. Therefore, GAT+Twin classified this node accurately.

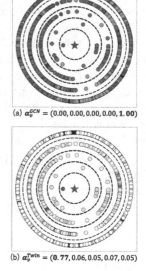

(a) $\boldsymbol{\alpha}_v^{GCN} = (0.00, 0.00, 0.00, 0.00, 1.00)$

(b) $\boldsymbol{\alpha}_v^{Twin} = (0.77, 0.06, 0.05, 0.07, 0.05)$

Fig. 4. Class distribution for node v and nodes around v

6   Conclusion

In this paper, we proposed TwinGNN, which learns the suitable aggregation distance for each node. TwinGNN can be integrated with various conventional

GNNs, such as GCN, GAT, and GraphSAGE. Through quantitative and qualitative experiments, we showed that TwinGNN prevents over-smoothing successfully and improves the performance of GNNs significantly. In addition, we theoretically elucidated a basic relationship between the computation mechanism of GNNs and the reproductive property of probability distributions under some constraints. The constraints are that (1) activation functions are identity functions, (2) feature vectors of nodes follow Gaussian distributions, and (3) the W^l matrices are orthogonal. In future work, we plan to investigate TwinGNN without these constraints.

References

1. Fortunato, S.: Community detection in graphs. Phys. Rep. **486**(3–5), 75–174 (2010)
2. Kipf, T.N., Welling, M.: Semi-Supervised Classification with Graph Convolutional Networks. arXiv preprint arXiv:1609.02907 (2016)
3. Veličković, P., et al.: Graph Attention Networks. arXiv preprint, arXiv:1710.10903 (2017)
4. Hamilton, W.L., et al.: Inductive representation learning on large graphs. In: Proceedings of Int'l Conference on Neural Information Processing Systems, pp. 1025–1035 (2017)
5. Xu, K., et al.; How Powerful are Graph Neural Networks? arXiv preprint, arXiv:1810.00826 (2018)
6. Li, G., et al.: Deepergcn: All You Need to Train Deeper GCNs. arXiv preprint, arXiv:2006.07739 (2020)
7. He, K., et al.: Deep Residual Learning for Image Recognition. In: Proceedings of the IEEE Conference on Computer Vision and Pattern Recognition, pp. 770–778 (2016)
8. Huang, G., et al.: Densely connected convolutional networks. In: Proceedings of the IEEE Conference on Computer Vision and Pattern Recognition, pp. 4700–4708 (2017)
9. Veit, A., et al.: Residual Networks Behave like Ensembles of Relatively Shallow Networks. Adv. Neural. Inf. Process. Syst. **29**, 550–558 (2016)
10. Bromley, J., et al.: Signature Verification using a "Siamese" Time Delay Neural Network. Advances in Neural Information Processing Systems, 6 (1993)
11. Yost, G.P.: Lectures on Probability and Statistics (1985)
12. Xu, K., et al.: Representation learning on graphs with jumping knowledge networks. In: International Conference on Machine Learning, pp. 5453–5462. PMLR (2018)
13. Levie, R., et al.: Cayleynets: graph convolutional neural networks with complex rational spectral filters. IEEE Trans. Signal Process. **67**(1), 97–109 (2018)
14. Hu, W., et al.: Open Graph Benchmark: Datasets for Machine Learning on Graphs. arXiv preprint, arXiv:2005.00687 (2020)
15. Pei, H., et al.: Geom-gcn: Geometric Graph Convolutional Networks. arXiv preprint, arXiv:2002.05287 (2020)

A Long and Short Term Preference Model for Next Point of Interest Recommendation

Zhaoqi Leng[1], Yanheng Liu[2,3], Xu Zhou[4(✉)] (iD), Xueying Wang[2], and Xican Wang[1]

[1] College of Software, Jilin University, Changchun 130012, China
[2] College of Computer Science and Technology, Jilin University, Changchun 130012, China
[3] Key Laboratory of Symbolic Computation and Knowledge Engineering of Ministry of Education, Jilin University, Changchun 130012, China
[4] Public Computer Education and Research Center, Jilin University, Changchun 130012, China
zhoux16@jlu.edu.cn

Abstract. The goal of next point of interest (POI) recommendation is to predict users' next location by analyzing their check-in sequence. The next POI recommendation has attracted more research attention as an important application in location based social networks. Some next POI recommendation algorithms learn spatial and time difference for modelling user check-in sequence based on recurrent neural network (RNN) and its variants. However, these methods do not take into account the difference between the users' long-term and short-term preferences, and cannot analyze the users' historical preferences accurately without considering the properties of POI about category and comment comprehensively. In order to improve the precision of recommendation result, a long and short term preference model combined with contextual information (LSPMC) is proposed for next POI recommendation in this paper. Specifically, we take geographical information, temporal influence, the category and rating comment of POI into account to construct the input embedding vector. Three long and short term memory (LSTM) networks and attention mechanism are designed for modeling user long term preference. RNN model is used to implement user short term preference. The probability of POIs that user will visit next is obtained based on the long term preference and short term preference. The experimental results on two real datasets demonstrate that the proposed method performs better than other baseline methods in terms of four commonly evaluation indicators.

Keywords: LSTM · Next POI recommendation · Contextual information · Attention mechanism · Location-based Social Networks

© The Author(s), under exclusive license to Springer Nature Switzerland AG 2022
E. Pimenidis et al. (Eds.): ICANN 2022, LNCS 13530, pp. 744–756, 2022.
https://doi.org/10.1007/978-3-031-15931-2_61

1   Introduction

Location-based social networks (LBSNs), such as Foursquare, and Gowalla are already closely related to our lives. The users of LBSNs can check-in through mobile network devices or location-based services to record their location information. Point of interest (POI) recommendation in LBSNs is to recommend personalized location for users by learning their check-in data. It can not only provide convenience for users to travel, but also explore potential POI in the city to provide auxiliary information for urban resource planning [15].

The next POI recommendation problem evolves from ordinary POI recommendation, and recommends the user's next POI through the user's historical check-in sequence [9]. Furthermore, to solve the sparisty of check-ins, constructing the network exploiting the check-in sequences and considering spatiotemporal influence of POI is to improve the user preference modelling as well. In view of the changeable patterns of users behavior, incorporating contextual factors (i.e. category, time, distance) into Recurrent Neural Network (RNN) and its variants such as long short-term memory (LSTM) can have better recommendation performance due to different contextual factors can be exploited to learn user's next movement intention [12] [4]. But those methods do not consider the influence, such as rating comment. So it reduces the accuracy of the recommendation. Moreover, a user's long-term preferences obtained by analyzing the user's overall data can express the user's general interest, and the user's short-term preference has a very fast effect on his next POI choice. It is necessary to design new method by taking advantage of those contextual information to analyze the user's long and short preference, respectively.

2   Related Work

In recent years, neural network technologies such as RNN [7] has been applied for next POI recommendation. Afterwards, a series of recommendation algorithms have integrated contextual information with the neural network technologies [11]. Liu et al. created a method named ST-RNN [3], and it takes into account time and space factors. Zhu et al. created a Time-LSTM [17] method, which adopts a variant of LSTM that adds multiple time gate structures to improve the recommendation performance. Zhang et al. created an multi-task learning method for next POI recommendation [13]. The model uses two LSTM structures for multi-task assisted prediction, and considers the type and category of POI. It is very effective in predicting POI categories. Wu et al. proposed a recommendation model named LSPL [10], it considers user's long and short-term preferences, and comprehensively considers the influence of the locations and categories of check-ins in the short-term model, but it does not consider other influence, such as rating comment. So it reduces the accuracy of the recommendation. User's previous preferences and his recent preferences should have different impact on the next POI, However, those methods do not take into account the changing in user's preferences. Furthermore, how to efficiently construct a user sequence behavior model based on the user's current context information is still need to study for recommending the user who may be interested in the next moment.

The attention mechanism has been successfully applied to next POI recommendation. It can assign different weight of user past check-ins to the next POI. Ma et al. [6] proposed a self-attention encoder-based POI recommendation model SAE-NAD, which uses a neighborhood-aware decoder to fuse the geographic impact of unchecked POIs. It is the first POI recommendation model research on the application of attention-based auto encoders. Zhou et al. [16] proposed an attention-based heterogeneous behaviors modeling framework, which uses the attention mechanism to model user behavior. Huang et al. [1] proposed a LSTM structure model with an attention mechanism to capture the impact of historical check-in data on the next POI. But this method does not consider the user's short-term preference and it will result in low recommendation accuracy and unstable performance. Combining the attention mechanism and the neural network structure can make the model more accurately to capture the user's preferences reflected in the POI check-in sequence [5], so as to achieve good personalized recommendation effect. Zhao et al. [14] studied that the sub-sequence pattern in the user's access location would have an impact on the location recommendation, and proposed a method that combines an adaptive segmentation sequence and an attention mechanism. The model uses a state-based stacked RNN to learn the latent structure of the user's check-in sequence.

3   Method

Next POI recommendation aims to recommend the user's next POI through his historical check-in information. In this section, our proposed LSPMC is described in detail. The users' check-in trajectory are splitted into long-term sequences and short-term sequences. Figure 1 describes the architecture of our LSPMC. The main structure of the model is composed of three parts including long-term preference model, short-term preference model and the recommendation model. The probability of the candidate POIs are obtained based on the user's long-short-term preference. The top-k POIs are the recommendation result for the user to visit at next time.

3.1   Long-Term Preference Model

Long-term preference model is to learn users' visiting preference from all historical check-in trajectories. It makes use of many contextual information such as the spatio-temporal influence, the category of POI and the rating comment of POI to learn user's preference. Three LSTM networks and attention mechanism are designed for modeling user long-term preference. We will describe our long-term preference modeling part in detail. abbreviations in the title or heads unless they are unavoidable.

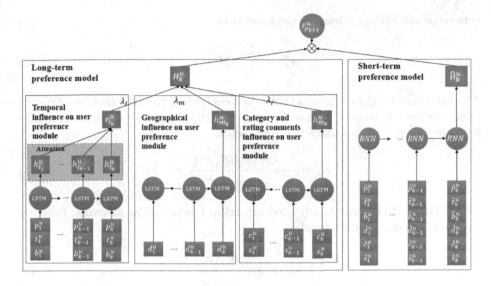

Fig. 1. The architecture of LSPMC

(1) Temporal influence on user preference module

User check-in behavior might be time dependent. It is found that the users activity trajectories on weekdays and weekends are quite different. For instance, some people would choose to go to the cafe or go home straight after get off work in the evening on weekdays, and may go to the cinema at the same time on weekends. In our proposed LSPMC model, p represents the sequence of all POI numbers of user's check-ins, the sequence t represents the sequence of all time-stamps corresponding. Besides, we differentiate the day of a week into weekday and weekend. The day sequence b represents whether it is a working day.

The input tuple is (p_k^u, t_k^u, b_k^u). Among them, p_k^u is the embedding vector representing the POI number of the kth check-in of user u, its dimension is $p_k^u \in \mathbb{R}_p^D$. t_k^u is the embedding vector representing the time-stamp of the kth check-in of user u, its dimension is $t_k^u \in \mathbb{R}_t^D$. b_k^u is the embedding vector representing if the day is a working day of the kth check-in of user u, the dimension is $b_k^u \in \mathbb{R}_b^D$. $b_k^u = 0$ represents the weekday, $b_k^u = 1$ represents weekend. The definition of the hidden state of the temporal influence on user preference module is:

$$h_{l_k}^u = LSTM(W_p p_k^u + W_t t_k^u + W_b b_k^u + b_l, h_{l_{k-1}}^u) \tag{1}$$

W_p, W_t and W_b are the parameter matrices that should be trained, b_l is bias vector of LSTM units and $h_{l_{k-1}}^u$ represents the hidden state of temporal influence on user preference module at the previous moment.

The prediction results of different check-in time may make different contribution to user's preference of POI. Then attention mechanism is utilized to capture the impact of each time-stamp t_k in the user check-in sequence on the next POI. We generated an attention weight α, the definition of weighted hidden state generated after using attention mechanism is:

$$r_{l_k}^u = \sum_{i=1}^{k} \alpha_i^u h_{l_k}^u \qquad (2)$$

The attention weight α_i^u means that how deeply does the ith check-in of user u affect the next-hop check-in in a sequence of k check-ins. Specifically, we use the following formula to calculate this parameter:

$$\alpha_i^u = \frac{exp(f(h_{l_k}^u, r^u))}{\sum_{i=1}^{k} exp(f(h_{l_k}^u, r^u))} \qquad (3)$$

where $f(h_{l_k}^u, r^u)$ is a commonly used attention function. The attention function we use is the dot product function.

$$f(h_{l_k}^u, r^u) = \frac{h_{l_k}^u (r^u)^T}{\sqrt{D}} \qquad (4)$$

In the formula, r^u represents the user's context vector.

(2) Geographical influence on user preference module

Geographical distances will also affect the user's choice of POI. Each POI has its longitude and latitude. Since users have different check-in behaviors, the activity region of each user may also be different. User will incline to decide which POI to visit next based on the distance between two POIs. In other words, we take the geographical factor into account to separately model the user's historical check-in distance difference as a geographical preference. The input of the geographical influence on user preference module is a sequence of distance difference. Each element of this sequence is donated as d_k^u, which represents the distance difference between the kth check-in and the $k - 1$th check-in of user u, while the distance differnce for the first check-in time is 0, the dimension is $d_k^u \in \mathbb{R}_d^D$. The definition of the hidden state of the user's geographical preference network is:

$$h_{m_k}^u = LSTM(W_d d_k^u + b_m, h_{m_{k-1}}^u) \qquad (5)$$

where W_d represents the parameter matrix that should be trained, b_m is bias vector of LSTM units and $h_{m_{k-1}}^u$ represents the hidden state of the temporal influence on user preference module at the previous moment.

Finally, the predicted probability of the distance between the $k+1$th check-in and the kth check-in output by the geographical influence on user preference module is:

$$r_{m_{k+1}}^u = (W_h^m h_{m_k}^u)^T (W_d d_{k+1}^u + b_m) \qquad (6)$$

where W_h^m denotes the parameter matrix that should be trained, $(W_h^m h_{m_k}^u)$ is the user representation of the geographical influence on user preference module, $W_d d_{k+1}^u + b_m$ is the representation of distance difference.

(3) Category and rating comments influence on user preference module

Except for learning the spatio-temporal information, the category of POIs, such as restaurants, stadiums, etc. and rating comment of POIs are also should be considered when we model user's preference. Since the patterns of user's preference transition over the POI categories is important to analyze user's preference of POI. In addition, each user in the LBSNs may give rating comment of the POI that reflects user's satisfaction of the POI, such as five star rating or one star rating. However, such attributes of the POI itself have always been ignored in the next POI prediction methods. We model the user preference by considering the impact of POI category and POI rating comment.

The input of user's POI preference module incoporating category and rating comments is tuple (c_k^u, s_k^u), c_k^u is the embedding vector that represents the category of POI that the kth check-in of user u, the dimension is $c_k^u \in \mathbb{R}_c^D$, s_k^u is the embedding vector that represents the rating stars of POI that the kth check-in of user u, the dimension is $s_k^u \in \mathbb{R}_s^D$. The definition of the hidden state of user's POI preference module incoporating category and rating comments is:

$$h_{r_k}^u = LSTM(W_c c_k^u + W_s s_k^u + b_r, h_{r_{k-1}}^u) \tag{7}$$

W_c and W_s are the parameter matrix that can be trained, b_r is the bias vector of LSTM units and $h_{r_{k-1}}^u$ represents the hidden state of user's POI preference module incoporating category and rating comments at the previous moment. Finally, the predicted probability of the category and rating comments of the $k+1$th check-in output by the module is:

$$r_{r_{k+1}}^u = (W_h^r h_{r_k}^u)^T (W_c c_{k+1}^u + W_s s_{k+1}^u + b_r) \tag{8}$$

W_h^r is the parameter matrix that can be trained, $(W_h^r h_{r_k}^u)$ is the user representation of the category and rating comments influence on user preference module, $W_c c_{k+1}^u + W_s s_{k+1}^u + b_r$ is the representation of POI attribute.

According to the influence of time factors, geographical distance difference, as well as the category and rating comments on user's POI preference, we can get the probability of the user's next POI predicted by the long-term model. Firstly, we concatenate the hidden states to get the overall hidden state of the long-term model as $H_k^u = [r_{l_k}^u, h_{m_k}^u, h_{r_k}^u]$. Then the predicted representation of the user's preference of next POI by the long-term model is defined as:

$$r_{p_{k+1}}^u = (W_H H_k^u)^T (W_p p_{k+1}^u + W_t t_{k+1}^u + W_b b_{k+1}^u + b_H) \tag{9}$$

W_H is the parameter matrix that should be trained, b_H is the bias vector, $(W_H H_k^u)$ is complete long-term model user representation, and the item $(W_p p_{k+1}^u + W_t t_{k+1}^u + W_b b_{k+1}^u + b_H)$ is the representation of POIs. The combination of the three long-term user preference modules will significantly improve the accuracy of prediction.

3.2   Short-Term Preference Model

Compared to choosing the whole historical check-ins to construct user's long term sequence, we have selected the user check-ins in the past six months as user's short term sequence. Due to the advantage of RNN in the memory of short sequences, RNN model is chosen to achieve the short-term preferences of users. The input tuple of short-term preference model is $(\widehat{p}_k^u, \widehat{t}_k^u, \widehat{b}_k^u, \widehat{d}_k^u, \widehat{c}_k^u, \widehat{s}_k^u)$, they are embedding vectors representing the POI number, time of day, weekday or weekend, distance difference, category, and rating comment, respectively. The dimension is $\mathbb{R}^D$. The definition of the hidden state of the short-term preference model is:

$$\widehat{H}_k^u = RNN(\widehat{W}_p\widehat{p}_k^u + \widehat{W}_t\widehat{t}_k^u + \widehat{W}_b\widehat{b}_k^u + \widehat{W}_d\widehat{d}_k^u + \widehat{W}_c\widehat{c}_k^u + \widehat{W}_s\widehat{s}_k^u + \widehat{b}) \qquad (10)$$

Among them, $\widehat{W}$ represents the trainable parameter matrices corresponding to each attribute, $\widehat{b}$ is the bias vector. The predicted representation of the user's next POI output by the short-term preference model is:

$$\widehat{r}_{k+1}^u = \widehat{r}_{sh}^u\widehat{r}_{sh}^p \qquad (11)$$

where $\widehat{r}_{sh}^u$ is denoted as the user representation of the short-term preference model, its definition is as follows:

$$\widehat{r}_{sh}^u = (\widehat{W}_H\widehat{H}_k^u)^T \qquad (12)$$

$\widehat{r}_{sh}^p$ is the representation of POIs, its definition is as follows:

$$\widehat{r}_{sh}^p = (\widehat{W}_p\widehat{p}_{k+1}^u + \widehat{W}_t\widehat{t}_{k+1}^u + \widehat{W}_b\widehat{b}_{k+1}^u + \widehat{W}_d\widehat{d}_{k+1}^u + \widehat{W}_c\widehat{c}_{k+1}^u + \widehat{W}_s\widehat{s}_{k+1}^u + \widehat{b}_H) \quad (13)$$

3.3   Recommendation Combined Long-Term and Short-Term Preference Model

After obtaining the long and short-term preferences of users, we can get the probability of the user's next POI by integrating the long-term and short-term model. The user representation combined with two models $\mathbf{R}_u$ is defined as bellow.

$$\mathbf{R}_u = \mathbf{W}_{H_{lon}}\mathbf{W}_H H_k^u + \mathbf{W}_{H_{sh}}\widehat{W}_H\widehat{H}_k^u \qquad (14)$$

$\mathbf{W}_{H_{lon}}$ and $\mathbf{W}_{H_{sh}}$ are the trainable parameter matrices, representing the respective proportions of long and short-term preference model. After combining the long and short-term models, the definition of predicted probability of the user's next POI is:

$$\widetilde{r}_{p_{k+1}^u} = (\mathbf{R}_u)^T \mathbf{R}_p \qquad (15)$$

Note that we use the following rules to select candidate POI sequences: (1) All POIs that the user has visited before are candidate POIs.(2) POIs that are close to the user's current location are also selected as candidate POIs. (3) If the candidate POI sequence is too short, POIs with high rating stars are added to the sequence until the required length is met. Where the representation vector of the candidate POIs R_p is defined as follows:

$$R_p = W_p p_{k+1}^u + W_t t_{k+1}^u + W_b b_{k+1}^u + W_t t_{k+1}^u + W_c c_{k+1}^u + W_s s_{k+1}^u + \tilde{b}_H \quad (16)$$

3.4 Model Training

Bayesian Personalized Ranking (BPR) [8] is employed to define the loss function and make parameter training. We used the method as mentioned in [1], recursively generate the check-in sequences Ω for each user. After constructing the user sequence, the negative sample set must be defined first. We select the negative samples adopting the following rules: (1) The check-in of the negative sample did not appear in the actual user trajectory. (2) The distance between the negative sample and the current position should be as close as possible to the distance between the target and the current position.

Algorithm 1: Training method of LSPMC

Require: Check-in sequence S of users U, Parameter set Θ, η, $max - iteration$
Ensure: Parameter set Θ
  1: //construct training instances
  2: **for** each $u \subset U$ **do**
  3:     **for** each check-in POI sequence $P_i \in S_u$ **do**
  4:         Select the corresponding negative sequence $P_i{}'$
  5:     **end for**
  6: **end for**
  7: //model training phase
  8: **for** each iteration $\in max - iteration$ **do**
  9:     **for** each $u \in U$ **do**
10:         Randomly choose a sequence of u
11:         **for** each $\theta \in \Theta$ **do**
12:            $\theta \leftarrow \theta - \eta * \frac{\partial \mathcal{J}}{\partial \theta}$
13:         **end for**
14:     **end for**
15: **end for**

We train the short-term model by reducing the loss function to obtain more accurate user short-term preferences. The loss function of the short-term preference model is defined as:

$$\mathcal{J}_{sh} = \sum_{(s \succ s') \in \Omega} ln(1 + e^{-(r_s^u - r_{s'}^u)}) \quad (17)$$

The loss functions of three modules of the long-term model are defined:

$$\mathcal{J}_l = \sum_{(l \succ l') \in \Omega} ln(1 + e^{-(r_l^u - r_{l'}^u)}) \tag{18}$$

$$\mathcal{J}_m = \sum_{(m \succ m') \in \Omega} ln(1 + e^{-(r_m^u - r_{m'}^u)}) \tag{19}$$

$$\mathcal{J}_r = \sum_{(r \succ r') \in \Omega} ln(1 + e^{-(r_r^u - r_{r'}^u)}) \tag{20}$$

l' represents the negative sample sequence of the temporal influence on user preference module and l is the positive sample sequence, m' represents the negative sample sequence of the geographical influence on user preference module and m is the positive sample sequence, r' represents the negative sample sequence of the category and rating comments on user's POI preference module and r is the positive sample sequence.

In the end, the overall loss function is donated as:

$$\mathcal{J} = \lambda_l \mathcal{J}_l + \lambda_m \mathcal{J}_m + \lambda_r \mathcal{J}_r + \frac{\lambda}{2} \left\| \Theta^2 \right\| \tag{21}$$

where λ_l, λ_m and λ_r parameter is to balance the weight of the three auxiliary influence on user preference predications, $\lambda_l + \lambda_m + \lambda_m = 1$. $\frac{\lambda}{2} \left\| \Theta^2 \right\|$ is a regularization term, whose purpose is to prevent the model from overfitting. λ is regularization coefficient, $\Theta = (W, p, t, b, d, c, s)$ is the set of all trainable variables. In the process of model training, Adam algorithm [2] is used for gradient optimization and parameter training.

4   Experiments

In order to illustrate the effectiveness of the proposed method LSPMC, four baseline methods named as ST-RNN [3], AT-LSTM [1], iMTL [13] and LSPL [10] are chosen to be compared with. In addtion, to validate the contribution of long-term and short-term combined structure, a variant of LSPMC named as PMC is designed. It retains the part of the long-term model, and removes the part of the user's short-term preference model. Four evaluation metrics are employed to verify the performance of the methods $P@k$(short for $Precision@k$), $R@k$(short for $Recall@k$), $F1@k$ and $MAP@k$. k is the number of POIs recommended to user. All the algorithms are coded in Python.

4.1   Datasets

The two datasets we used are the two check-ins from Charlotte(CHA) and Phoenix(PHO) that combines Foursquare and Yelp [13]. The attributes of the CHA dataset after processing consists of POI-id, User-id, TimeStamp, Latitude, Longitude, Category, Stars, Time, Date, Day. The check-in data mainly contains 20940 check-ins of 1580 users from 2012 to 2013. Among them, there are 2640

POIs and 239 categories. The PHO dataset includes 22620 check-ins. It mainly contains 1623 users, 2441 POIs and 251 categories. The attributes of PHO are the same as CHA. 80% check-ins of each dataset are taken as training set and 20% for test.

4.2 Parameter Settings

All the parameters of the baseline method are adjusted to achieve the best results. The layer size of both LSPMC long-term model and short-term model embedding is set to 256, the number of hidden-layers is 3. The long and short-term model learning rates are both 0.0002, the maximum number of iterations of the long-short-term models are both thirty, weight of loss function $\lambda_l = 0.5$, $\lambda_m = 0.1$, $\lambda_l = 0.4$. Regularization term coefficients of long-term and short-term models is set as $\lambda = 0.00005$.

4.3 Results and Analysis

Table 1 shows that comparison results of different methods on the CHA dataset and PHO dataset, the value shown in bold represents the best performance of LSPMC method.

Seen from the comparative results of six methods on the CHA dataset, LSPMC performs best and ST-RNN performs worst on $R@10$. Comparing with the experimental results of ST-RNN and AT-LSTM, it is found that the AT-LSTM algorithm based on LSTM structure and the attention mechanism has a significantly effect on the accuracy of the next POI recommendation. Through comparing the experimental results of ST-RNN with that of iMTL, it can be seen that the accuracy results of iMTL of the user's next POI prediction has increased with the consideration of the category than ST-RNN without considering the category influence. Moreover, comparing the results of LSPL with ST-RNN, AT-LSTM and iMTL, it is easily to infer that the prediction model combined with long and short-term preference has much better performance.

Table 1. Comparative results of six methods on the CHA dataset and PHO dataset

Method	CHA				PHO			
	$P@10$	$R@10$	$F1@10$	$MAP@10$	$P@10$	$R@10$	$F1@10$	$MAP@10$
ST-RNN	0.02019	0.2019	0.0367	0.0697	0.01758	0.1758	0.0319	0.0682
AT-LSTM	0.02989	0.2989	0.05454	0.078	0.02591	0.2591	0.0471	0.083
iMTL	0.02238	0.2238	0.0407	0.0558	0.03076	0.3076	0.0699	0.0842
LSPL	0.03715	0.3715	0.0675	0.0984	0.03785	0.3785	0.0688	0.1137
PMC	0.03387	0.3387	0.0615	0.0813	0.03238	0.3238	0.0588	0.0877
LSPMC	**0.0448**	**0.448**	**0.0814**	**0.1355**	**0.0417**	**0.417**	**0.0758**	**0.1221**

Specifically, the proposed LSPMC is obviously better than any other baselines in terms of four metric on the CHA dataset. It can be seen that LSPMC method has 20.6% improvement in $P@10$ and $R@10$ compared with LSPL method. The proposed LSPMC method also has 20.5% improvement over the LSPL method on $F1@10$, LSPMC has 37.7% improvement on $MAP@10$ compared with LSPL method. The improvement performance can demonstrate that LSPMC can significantly improve the prediction accuracy by using multiple auxiliary prediction tasks to make recommendation. Comparing LSPMC with PMC, it can also prove that our proposed long-term and short-term model has better performance and efficiency than other comparative methods.

In terms of performance on the PHO dataset of six methods, it is obvious to know the superiority of LSPMC for next POI recommendation on the PHO dataset. Both LSPMC and LSPL have modelled user's long and short term preference, but the proposed LSPMC has a nearly 10% improvement in the evaluation metrics $P@10$ and $R@10$ when compared with method LSPL. In the evaluation metric $MAP@10$, the proposed LSPMC has 7% improvement compared to LSPL method. In the evaluation metric $F1@10$, our proposed LSPMC has improved by 8.4% compared to the iMTL method. Compared to PMC, LSPMC improves by about 28.8%, 28.9%, and 39.2% for $R@10$, $F1@10$, and $MAP@10$ on the PHO dataset, respectively. It demonstrates that the model combined long-term and short-term preference will have better effectiveness than PMC method with only the long-term module. In a word, the experiments on two datasets show that the LSPMC method proposed by us has excellent performance in the next POI recommendation.

5   Conclusion

A long and short term preference model combined with contextual information (LSPMC) for next POI recommendation is proposed in this paper, which is a hybrid algorithm of RNN and LSTM with attention mechanism to model long-term preferences and short-term preferences of users respectively. It considers different contextual information (POI category, POI rating comment, time, geogrphical difference) and use them to construct POIs embedding representation. Moreover, three LSTM models are constructed to predict the influence of time factors, the impact of geographical distance difference, as well as the category and rating comments on user's POI preference. The experimental results on two real LBSN datasets show that the proposed method gets higher recall and MAP value than the state-of-art methods. In future work, we will improve the model by considering friendship influence in user check-in behavior.

Acknowledgements. This work is supported by the National Nature Science Foundation of China (62172186) and the Fundamental Research Funds for the Central Universities, JLU under Grant No.93K172021Z02.

References

1. Huang, L., Ma, Y., Wang, S., Liu, Y.: An attention-based spatiotemporal LSTM network for next poi recommendation. IEEE Transactions on Services Computing, pp. 1–14 (2019)
2. Kingma, D.P., Ba, J.: Adam: A method for stochastic optimization. In: 3rd International Conference on Learning Representations (2015)
3. Liu, Q., Wu, S., Wang, L., Tan, T.: Predicting the next location: a recurrent model with spatial and temporal contexts. In: Schuurmans, D., Wellman, M.P. (eds.) Proceedings of the Thirtieth AAAI Conference on Artificial Intelligence, pp. 194–200. AAAI Press (2016)
4. Liu, T., Liao, J., Wu, Z., Wang, Y., Wang, J.: Exploiting geographical-temporal awareness attention for next point-of-interest recommendation. Neurocomputing **400**, 227–237 (2020)
5. Liu, Y., Pei, A., Wang, F., Yang, Y.: An attention-based category-aware GRU model for the next POI recommendation. Int. J. Intell. Syst. **36**(7), 3174–3189 (2021)
6. Ma, C., Zhang, Y., Wang, Q., Liu, X.: Point-of-interest recommendation: exploiting self-attentive autoencoders with neighbor-aware influence. In: Proceedings of the 27th ACM International Conference on Information and Knowledge Management, pp. 697–706. ACM (2018)
7. Mikolov, T., Karafiát, M., Burget, L., Cernocký, J., Khudanpur, S.: Recurrent neural network based language model. In: INTERSPEECH 2010, 11th Annual Conference of the International Speech Communication Association, pp. 1045–1048. ISCA (2010)
8. Rendle, S., Freudenthaler, C., Gantner, Z., Schmidt-Thieme, L.: BPR: Bayesian personalized ranking from implicit feedback. In: UAI 2009, Proceedings of the Twenty-Fifth Conference on Uncertainty in Artificial Intelligence, pp. 452–461. AUAI Press (2009)
9. Shi, M., Shen, D., Kou, Y., Nie, T., Yu, G.: Next point-of-interest recommendation by sequential feature mining and public preference awareness. J. Intell. Fuzzy Syst. **40**(3), 4075–4090 (2021)
10. Wu, Y., Li, K., Zhao, G., Qian, X.: Long- and short-term preference learning for next POI recommendation. In: Proceedings of the 28th ACM International Conference on Information and Knowledge Management, pp. 2301–2304. ACM (2019)
11. Yang, C., Sun, M., Zhao, W.X., Liu, Z., Chang, E.Y.: A neural network approach to joint modeling social networks and mobile trajectories. ACM Trans. Inf. Syst. **35**(4), 36:1-36:28 (2016)
12. Zhan, G., Xu, J., Huang, Z., Zhang, Q., Xu, M., Zheng, N.: A semantic sequential correlation based LSTM model for next POI recommendation. In: 20th IEEE International Conference on Mobile Data Management, MDM, pp. 128–137. IEEE (2019)
13. Zhang, L., Sun, Z., Zhang, J., Lei, Y.: An interactive multi-task learning framework for next POI recommendation with uncertain check-ins. In: Proceedings of the Twenty-Ninth International Joint Conference on Artificial Intelligence, IJCAI 2020, pp. 3551–3557 (2020)
14. Zhao, K., et al.: Discovering subsequence patterns for next POI recommendation. In: Proceedings of the Twenty-Ninth International Joint Conference on Artificial Intelligence, pp. 3216–3222 (2020)

15. Zhao, P., Zhu, H., Liu, Y., Xu, J.: Where to go next: a spatio-temporal gated network for next POI recommendation. In: The Thirty-Third AAAI Conference on Artificial Intelligence, AAAI, pp. 5877–5884. AAAI Press (2019)
16. Zhou, C., Bai, J., Song, J., Liu, X.: ATRANK: an attention-based user behavior modeling framework for recommendation. In: Proceedings of the Thirty-Second AAAI Conference on Artificial Intelligence, pp. 4564–4571. AAAI Press (2018)
17. Zhu, Y., et al.: What to do next: modeling user behaviors by time-LSTM. In: Proceedings of the Twenty-Sixth International Joint Conference on Artificial Intelligence, pp. 3602–3608 (2017)

A Multi-stack Denoising Autoencoder for QoS Prediction

Mengwei Wu, Qin Lu(✉), and Yingxue Wang

School of Computer Science and Technology,
Qilu University of Technology (Shandong Academy of Sciences), Jinan, China
luqin@qlu.edu.cn, 54903172@qq.com

Abstract. In the era of network information overload, personalized service recommendation is paid more and more attention by researchers, and Quality of Service (QoS) is a key criterion for service selection and recommendation. QoS is described as a non-functional attribute of Web services, so the prediction of QoS with high precision is an important means to realize personalized recommendation. In this paper, a Multi-stack Denoising Autoencoder (MSDAE) model is proposed to predict QoS. Firstly, the location information and the improved Jaccard similarity coefficient are used to obtain the trusted similar neighbors of users and services. Partially missing values of sparse user-service QoS matrix are pre-populated and users' preference informations are filled. Then, MSDAE is used to learn and train the processed QoS matrix to predict the missing QoS. Finally, the experimental results on WSDream-dataset1 show that the proposed method predicts QoS with higher accuracy than other prediction methods.

Keywords: Service recommendation · QoS prediction · SDAE · Jaccard

1 Introduction

Nowadays, there exist numerous Web services with the same or similar functions on the Internet. It is more and more difficult for users to obtain better-performing Web services in such a huge set of candidate services. Traditional Web service recommendation [1] methods are limited to meeting the functional requirements of users, but ignore the non-functional attributes (QoS) of Web services [2], which makes some recommendation results do not meet the user requirements well. So many researchers have investigated services recommendation based QoS prediction. One of the earliest used and popular methods is Collaborative Filtration (CF). Based on the existing QoS information, the method predicts QoS according neighboring users or services with better similarity. For example, [3] utilized location information to improve the credibility of users' similar neighbors, and used the calculated similarity weights to predict QoS values. Huai et al. [4] used Principal Component Analysis (PCA) to reduce the dimension of the original QoS matrix, and then used K-means clustering to obtain the Top-K similar users of

---

The original version of this chapter was revised: the affiliation of the authors has been corrected. The correction to this chapter is available at https://doi.org/10.1007/978-3-031-15931-2_66

© The Author(s), under exclusive license to Springer Nature Switzerland AG 2022, corrected publication 2022
E. Pimenidis et al. (Eds.): ICANN 2022, LNCS 13530, pp. 757–768, 2022.
https://doi.org/10.1007/978-3-031-15931-2_62

target user, and predicted the missing QoS. Yang et al. [5] obtained the neighbor information of users and services according to the location information, and combined with QoS information to predict the QoS on the proposed new decomposition machine.

After that, model-based QoS prediction methods [6] and hybrid QoS prediction methods [7] have gradually emerged. Zhu et al. [8] designed a privacy-preserving strategy combined with a location-aware low-rank matrix factorization algorithm to achieve QoS prediction under privacy protection. Zou et al. [9] proposed to transition the user neighborhood through a neural network to a deep matrix decomposition to predict QoS. Ding et al. [10] combined a multi-component graph convolutional collaborative filtering method with a depth decomposition machine to predict QoS.

In recent years, the emerging deep learning has been used to predict QoS with good results. Wu et al. [11] utilized a DNM to map the contextual features of QoS information to a shared latent space for semantic representation and multi-task prediction at the perception layer. Xiang et al. [12] proposed a method of hybrid CF and RNN to predict the optimal QoS, by combining temporal attributes. Yin et al. [13] proposed a new technique of fuzzy clustering DAE and re-embedding network to solve the over-fitting problem using contextual information, thereby improving the accuracy of QoS prediction.

However, the problems of sparse QoS data and noisy data are not well solved in the above methods. So, we propose a new Multi-stack Denoising Autoencoder (MSDAE) model for predicting QoS. First, the initial QoS matrix is pre-populated with the users' trusted similar neighbors. Then, the users' preferences are obtained according to the users' invocation of the service and added to the pre-populated matrix as auxiliary information. This alleviates the data sparse problem to a certain extent. Finally, accurately predict QoS by MSDAE while solving the noise problem. The main contributions of this paper are as follows:

- The traditional Jaccard similarity coefficient is improved, and users' location informations are used to obtain the users' trusted similar neighbors, so as to pre-populate the missing values of the initial QoS matrix.
- Classify services using improved Jaccard and obtain users' preferences based on services information invoked by users.
- The MSDAE is designed to learn and train the preprocessed matrix to predict missing QoS values.
- The model is evaluated by experiments on the real dataset WSDreamd-ataset1, which verifies the effectiveness of the model.

2   QoS Prediction with MSDAE

In order to solve the data sparsity and noise problems and predict QoS more accurately, a new MSDAE model is proposed in this paper. And the model framework is shown in Fig. 1. First, the QoS matrix is pre-populated using users' location informations and users' trusted similar neighbors which are calculated with improved Jaccard. On the other hand, the users' service preferences are obtained by using the users' calling information for the service, and combined with the pre-populated QoS matrix. Finally, QoS prediction is performed by the MSDAE model.

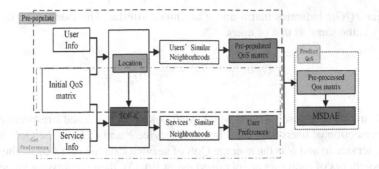

Fig. 1. QoS prediction framework based on MSDAE

2.1 Pre-populated

There are differences in the resulting QoS due to the geographic location of the users or services. We take location information as a precondition to compute similar neighbors of users and services. Take the users as an example. First, calculate the similarity of users in the same AS and country as the target user, and obtain TOP-K similar users respectively. Then take TOP-K for all similar users obtained to acquire the most credible similar neighbors of the target user. The method for obtaining trusted similar neighbors of a service is similar. The classic Jaccard has been improved by us.

Suppose users set is U, services set is S, the QoS vectors of user $u, v \in U$ are expressed as β_u and β_v, the Jaccard similarity calculation of u and v:

$$J_U(\beta_u, \beta_v) = \frac{|S_u \cap S_v|}{|S_u \cup S_v|} \tag{1}$$

where S_u and S_v are the set of services invoked by u and v. From Eq. (1), it is known that the larger value of $J_U(\beta_u, \beta_v)$, the greater possibility that v similar to u. In order to express the similarity between users in a more detailed manner, this paper introduces the difference between the QoS of the intersection part (the part that two users invoke same service and contains QoS) to improve Eq. (1). The QoS gap in the intersection of u and v invoking services is calculated:

$$QG_U = \frac{|S_{u,v}|}{\sum\limits_{i \in S_{u,v}} |I_{ui} - \bar{I}_v|} \tag{2}$$

where $S_{u,v}$ is the intersection of services invoked by u and v; I_{ui} is the QoS of service i invoked by u; $\bar{I}_v$ is the average QoS of v on the $S_{u,v}$. From Eq. (2), it can be known that the larger QG_U, the greater possibility that the two users are similar. The new similarity calculation can be obtained from Eq. (1) and Eq. (2):

$$JQG_U = J_U(\beta_u, \beta_v) + QG_U = \frac{|S_u \cap S_v|}{|S_u \cup S_v|} + \frac{|S_{u,v}|}{\sum\limits_{i \in S_{u,v}} |I_{ui} - \bar{I}_v|} \tag{3}$$

The larger JQG_U indicates that u and v are more similar. The calculation of service similarity is the same as that of users.

$$JQG_S = \frac{|U_h \cap U_k|}{|U_h \cup U_k|} + \frac{|U_{h,k}|}{\sum_{j \in U_{h,k}} |I_{hj} - \bar{I}_k|} \tag{4}$$

where U_h and U_k are the set of users who have invoked service h and k respectively; $U_{h,k}$ is the intersection of users who have invoked service h and k; I_{hj} is the QoS of user j invoking service h; and $\bar{I}_k$ is the average QoS of service k on the set of $U_{h,k}$. The TOP-K similar neighbors of each user are obtained using Eq. (3), then the missing values of the initial QoS matrix are pre-populated using the QoS of similar neighbors.

2.2   Get Users' Preferences

Define each service and its TOP-K similar neighbors obtained using Eq. (4) as homogeneous services: $es = (e_0, e_1, e_2, \cdots, e_K)$. We can get N homogeneous services: $ES = (es_1, es_2, \cdots, es_N)$. Get number of times which the user invoked services in each homogeneous service, expressed as $CN = (cn_1, cn_2, \cdots, cn_N)$. Choose the two largest numbers fn and sn in the set CN. The calculations are as follows:

$$fn = max(CN) \tag{5}$$

$$sn = max(CN - fn) \tag{6}$$

Set the QoS in each homogeneous service as the set $EQ = (eq_0, eq_1, eq_2, \cdots, eq_K)$. Calculate the weighted average of EQ:

$$\bar{eq} = \sum_{i=0}^{K} \frac{eq_i^2}{\sum_{j=0}^{K} eq_j} \tag{7}$$

where $\bar{eq}$ is the weighted average of all QoS from a certain homogeneous service. Finally, according to fn and sn, two classes of user preference services: es_f and es_s are obtained. The $\bar{eq}$ of es_f and es_s are the preferences of the user.

2.3   QoS Prediction

Based on the double-layer SDAE, MSDAE performs multiple operations on the input vector with different noise addition rates and performs multiple encoding and decoding. It is shown in Fig. 2.

Noise adding stage: MSDAE adds different degrees of Gaussian noise to the input vector x. Assuming that the additive noise rate is expressed as $q \in [0,1]$, the noise is added to x according to the number of layers of the model:

$$Q_t(\tilde{x}_t^i = x^i + \gamma) = \begin{cases} 0, t = 1 \\ 1, t > 1 \end{cases} \tag{8}$$

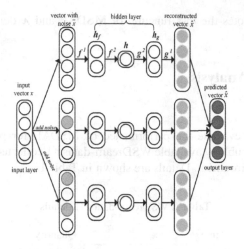

Fig. 2. Predict QoS based on MSDAE

where $Q_t(\cdot)$ denotes the noise addition rate of layer t; $\bar{x}_t^i$ denotes the value after adding noise to the $i-th$ QoS of x at layer t; x^i denotes the $i-th$ QoS of x; γ denotes Gaussian noise, which obeys the standard normal distribution and satisfies $\gamma \in [0, N(0,1)]$. In addition, the QoS without added noise in each layer input vector are scaled by $\frac{1}{1-q}$.

Encoding stage: encode the noisy QoS vector $\bar{x}$ to the low-dimensional features of the middle hidden layer:

$$h_t = f_2(w_2 f_1(w_1 \bar{x} + b_1) + b_2) \tag{9}$$

where h_t denotes the potential features at layer t after two layers of encoders; f_1, f_2 denote the activation functions at the outer and inner layer of encoders respectively; w_1, w_2 denote the feature weights at the outer and inner layer of encoders respectively; b_1, b_2 denote the bias terms at the outer and inner layer of encoders respectively.

Decoding stage: decode the h_t of the hidden layer and restore it to the same dimension as the x:

$$\hat{x}_t' = g_1(w_1' g_2(w_2' h_t + b_2') + b_1') \tag{10}$$

where $\hat{x}_t'$ denotes the reconstructed vector obtained from the output layer of layer t; g_1, g_2 denote the activation functions at the outer and inner layer of decoders respectively; w_1', w_2' denote the feature weights at the outer and inner layer of decoders respectively; b_1', b_2' denote the bias terms at the outer and inner layer of decoders respectively.

The $\hat{x}_t'$ obtained by MSDAE are averaged to obtain the final QoS prediction vector $\hat{x}$:

$$\hat{x} = \frac{1}{t} \sum_{j=1}^{t} \hat{x}_j' \tag{11}$$

The objective function for predicting missing QoS using MSDAE is expressed as:

$$Losses(x, \hat{x}) = \|x - \hat{x}\|^2 + \frac{\lambda}{2} \left(\|w_1\|^2 + \|w_2\|^2 + \|w_1'\|^2 + \|w_2'\|^2 \right) \tag{12}$$

where $Losses(\cdot)$ denotes the loss function of MSDAE and λ denotes the overfitting prevention coefficient.

3 Experiment Analysis

3.1 Dataset

To comprehensively evaluate the performance of MSDAE for predicting QoS, this experiment uses the publicly available WSDream-dataset1 collected from web services in a real network environment. Details are shown in Table 1.

Table 1. WSDream-dataset1 details

Name	Quantity
QoS record value	1,974,675
Amount of users	339
Amount of services	5825
Amount of users' countries	30
Amount of services' countries	73
Average response time	1.43 s
Average throughput	102.86 kb/s

3.2 Evaluation Indicators

For evaluating prediction models, Mean Absolute Error (MAE) and Root Mean Squared Error (RMSE) are the most important evaluation indicators of prediction accuracy. Therefore, this experiment uses MAE and RMSE to measure the experimental effect of the model. The calculation methods are as follows.

$$MAE = \frac{\sum\limits_{u,s \in R_0} |x_{us} - \hat{x}_{us}|}{|R_0|} \tag{13}$$

$$RMSE = \sqrt{\frac{\sum\limits_{u,s \in R_0} (x_{us} - \hat{x}_{us})^2}{|R_0|}} \tag{14}$$

where R_0 denotes the set of QoS for services invoked by users; x_{us} denotes the actual QoS of user u calling the service s; and $\hat{x}_{us}$ denotes the predicted QoS of user u calling the service s. If the MAE and RMSE are smaller at the same time, it indicates that the error between the predicted value and the actual value is really smaller, and the model predicted accuracy is higher.

3.3 Parameter Settings

TOP-K. The parameter TOP-K is the number of acquired similar neighbors. In this experiment, the TOP-K is selected under eight different matrix density conditions: the range of TOP-K is set to 2–10 for matrix density of 1%–4%, and the range of TOP-K is set to 10–30 for matrix density of 5%–20%. As Fig. 3 shows the impact of TOP-K on the predicted QoS under different matrix densities.

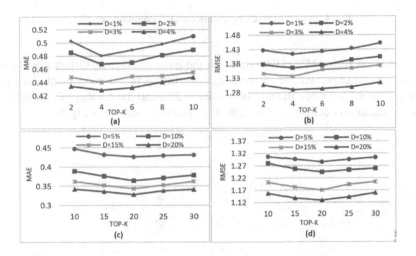

Fig. 3. Impact of TOP-K on QoS prediction results under different sparsity

In Fig. 3, it can be found that as the TOP-K increases, MAE and RSME show a decreasing trend at the beginning, but show an increasing trend when reaching a certain critical value. This indicates that the TOP-K is too large, some untrusted users will participate in the neighbor ensemble, which leads to the credibility of the trusted users to be reduced. And the inability to accurately express the outstanding features of users or services, thereby expanding the error. According to Fig. 3 (a) and (b), when the matrix density is 1%–4% and the TOP-K is taken as 4. According to Fig. 3 (c) and (d), when the matrix density is 5%–20% and the TOP-K is taken as 20.

Number of Overlays. This experiment compares the impact of different number of stacked layers on the predicted QoS under different matrix density conditions. As shown in Fig. 4.

In Fig. 4, it can be seen that MAE and RMSE are minimum for most of models stacked with 4 layers at different matrix densities. MAE and RMSE are minimized when model is stacked with 2 layers only when matrix density is 2%. Analyzing the reasons: when matrix is sparse, there are few correlations between data, the potential features extracted by model are limited, and the number of overlay layers is excessive, resulting in the extraction of irrelevant features, and outstanding features of data cannot be characterized, thus reducing accuracy of QoS prediction.

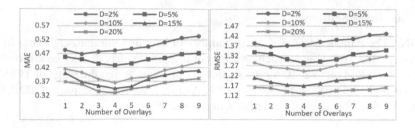

Fig. 4. Impact of stacking layers on QoS prediction results

Noise Addition Rate. MSDAE operates on the input vector with different noise addition rate, which can prevent the occurrence of overfitting. In this experiment, the number of stacked layers is 2 when the matrix density is 2%, and the number of stacked layers is 4 when the matrix density is 5%–20%. The results are shown in Fig. 5.

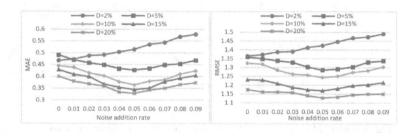

Fig. 5. Impact of noise addition rate on QoS prediction results

It can be seen from Fig. 5 that when the QoS matrix is 5%–20%, the noise addition rate is set to 0.05, and the effect of predicting QoS is optimal. Moreover, the larger matrix density, the better the predicted effect will be obtained by adding noise. The matrix density is 2% shows that the QoS prediction accuracy is reduced by the noise addition operation of the model instead. Analysis reason: when the QoS matrix density is extremely low, the correlation between the data is very weak. At this time, if noise is added, the correlation features between the data will be destroyed, and the model cannot extract prominent features, resulting in a reduced prediction effect.

Feature Dimension. The two feature vectors h_f and h in the model shown in Fig. 2 are discussed separately.

Dimension of Feature h_f. The dimension of h is set to 60. Impact of varying the dimension of feature h_f between 600 and 1100 (in steps of 50) on the predicted QoS for different matrix densities is illustrated in Fig. 6.

As can be seen in Fig. 6, with the increase of h_f dimension, MAE and RMSE both have obvious decreasing trend, but when the dimension exceeds 800, the change of

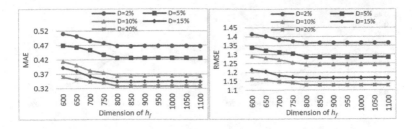

Fig. 6. Impact of dimension of h_f on QoS prediction results

MAE and RMSE tends to be flat and basically stable. Therefore, the dimension of h_f is set to 800, no need to increase it.

Dimension of Feature h. The dimension of h_f is set to 800. Figure 7 shows the impact of the change of dimension of h between 10 and 100 (with a step size of 10) on the predicted QoS under different matrix densities.

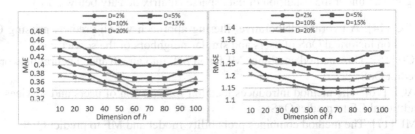

Fig. 7. Impact of dimension of h on QoS prediction results

As can be seen in Fig. 7, the change of MAE and RMSE tends to be flat when the dimension of h is set to 60–80, while the MAE and RMSE float more when it is lower than 60 or greater than 80. Analysis for reason: the lower dimension of h, the stronger ability of the model to extract features, but for decoding, it is difficult to use a suitable matrix to restore the data features, resulting in weaker correlation between the decoded data and the original data, which affects the expression of data. On the contrary, if the dimension of h is set too high, the correlation between extracted features becomes complicated, the model cannot learn well, which in turn leads to poor predicted effect.

3.4 Baseline Comparison

Impact of QoS Matrix Density on Prediction Results. It is mainly aimed at the prediction effect of the model when the matrix density is sparse. In the experiment, the matrix density is set to 2%–20% with a step size of 2%. The result is shown in Fig. 8.

It can be seen that MAE and RMSE show a decreasing trend as the matrix density increases, and the larger matrix density, the slower the decreasing trend. Analysis for

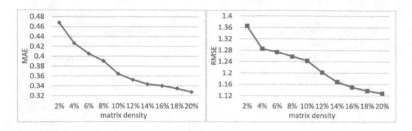

Fig. 8. Impact of matrix density on MSDAE predicted QoS results

reason: As the matrix density increases, the more QoS data that can be trained, the stronger correlation between the data. Therefore, the better model training, which in turn improves the prediction accuracy.

Baseline Comparison. In order to comprehensively evaluate the performance of the MSDAE proposed in this paper, this experiment compares the MSDAE with the following model under the condition of data sparse (matrix density below 20%):

- IPCC [14]: A hybrid collaborative filtering approach which predicts missing QoS based on historical QoS of users and similar neighbors of the services;
- NCF [15]: This method combines MLP and MF into an advanced neural network to predict QoS;
- LACF [16]: The method introduces location information of users and services into traditional CF to predict QoS;
- PMF [17]: The method combines probability model and MF to predict QoS;
- P-PMF [18]: This method is another improved form of PMF;
- LAFM [19]: The method uses CF with location information to obtain similar neighbors, and uses FM to extract features from similar neighbors to predict QoS;
- DNM [20]: The method combines contextual information of users and services with neural networks for QoS prediction.
- SDAE [21]: Predicting QoS with a simple SDAE.

The comparison results are shown in Table 2.

It can be seen that with the increase of matrix density, the MAE and RMSE of MSDAE gradually decrease, and are lower than other models in comparison. In other words, the predicted effects of MSDAE proposed in this paper is significantly better than other models. This shows that the model has a better ability to extract the potential features of data, which can alleviate the data sparsity problem to a certain extent.

4　Summary and Future Work

In this paper, we propose a MSDAE model to solve the problem of sparse QoS data and inadequate feature extraction, so as to improve the accuracy of QoS prediction. In the data preprocessing stage, the location information and improved Jaccard are used

Table 2. Results of MSDAE compared with other approaches

Model	D = 2%		D = 5%		D = 10%		D = 15%		D = 20%	
	MAE	RMSE	MAE	RMSE	MAE	RMSE	MAE	RMSE	MAE	RMSE
UIPCC	0.7368	1.5948	0.6243	1.4342	0.5892	1.3149	0.5324	1.2965	0.4136	1.2043
NCF	0.5238	1.5475	0.4400	1.3250	0.3853	1.2832	0.3724	1.2535	0.3623	1.2053
LACF	0.7011	1.6798	0.6824	1.5652	0.6545	1.4684	0.6127	1.4162	0.5825	1.3814
PMF	0.7123	1.7295	0.6473	1.5783	0.6985	1.4286	0.6081	1.4072	0.5032	1.4007
P-PMF	0.6879	1.6574	0.6116	1.4156	0.5408	1.2787	0.5056	1.2183	0.4793	1.1773
LAFM	0.5782	1.4764	0.5147	1.3053	0.4510	1.2974	0.4266	1.1484	0.4180	1.3091
DNM	0.5324	1.6389	0.4737	1.4473	0.4051	1.3804	0.4044	1.2986	0.3996	1.1862
SDAE	0.5523	1.7692	0.4963	1.4323	0.4226	1.3874	0.3873	1.2985	0.3610	1.2531
MSDAE	**0.4678**	**1.3651**	**0.4267**	**1.2853**	**0.3640**	**1.2436**	**0.3434**	**1.1695**	**0.3275**	**1.1283**

to obtain users and services trusted similar neighbors, the initial QoS matrix is prefilled and users' preferences are obtained. The MSDAE is used to train and learn the preprocessed QoS matrix predicting the missing QoS. Finally, the parametric and comparative experiments are carried out to verify the validity of the model. In the future, the impact and role of information such as user interest transfer on QoS prediction will be considered.

Acknowledgements. This work was supported in part by Shandong Province Key R&D Program (Major Science and Technology Innovation Project) Project under Grants 2020CXGC010102.

References

1. Pandharbale, P., Mohanty, S.N., Jagadev, A K.: Study of recent web service recommendation methods. In: 2020 2nd International Conference on Innovative Mechanisms for Industry Applications (ICIMIA), pp. 692–695 (2020). https://doi.org/10.1109/ICIMIA48430.2020. 9074853
2. Ma, Y., Xin, X., Wang, S.G., Li, J.L., Sun, Q.B., Yang, F.C.: QoS evaluation for web service recommendation. China Commun. **12**(4), 151–160 (2015). https://doi.org/10.1109/CC.2015. 7114061
3. Abdullah, M.N., Bhaya, W.S.: Predicting QoS for web service recommendations based on reputation and location clustering with collaborative filtering. In: 2021 7th International Conference on Contemporary Information Technology and Mathematics (ICCITM), pp. 19–25 (2021).https://doi.org/10.1109/ICCITM53167.2021.9677842
4. Yang, H., Yan, H., Dong, C.: A k-means clustering approach for PCA-based web service QoS prediction. In: 2019 IEEE International Conferences on Ubiquitous Computing & Communications (IUCC) and Data Science and Computational Intelligence (DSCI) and Smart Computing, Networking and Services (SmartCNS), pp. 129–132 (2019). https://doi.org/10.1109/ IUCC/DSCI/SmartCNS.2019.00050
5. Yang, Y., Zheng, Z., Niu, X., Tang, M., Lu, Y., Liao, X.: A location-based factorization machine model for web service QoS prediction. IEEE Trans. Serv. Comput. **14**(5), 1264–1277 (2021). https://doi.org/10.1109/TSC.2018.2876532

6. Liu, P., Liu, H., Li, C.: Research on items recommendation algorithm based on knowledge graph. In: 2020 19th International Symposium on Distributed Computing and Applications for Business Engineering and Science (DCABES), pp. 206–209 (2020).https://doi.org/10.1109/DCABES50732.2020.00061

7. Chowdhury, R.R., Chattopadhyay, S., Adak, C.: CAHPHF: context-aware hierarchical QoS prediction with hybrid filtering. IEEE Trans. Serv. Comput. (2020). https://doi.org/10.1109/TSC.2020.3041626

8. Zhu, X., et al.: Similarity-maintaining privacy preservation and location-aware low-rank matrix factorization for QoS prediction based web service recommendation. IEEE Trans. Serv. Comput. **14**(3), 889–902 (2021). https://doi.org/10.1109/TSC.2018.2839741

9. Zou, G., Chen, J., He, Q., Li, K.-C., Zhang, B., Gan, Y.: NDMF: neighborhood-integrated deep matrix factorization for service QoS prediction. IEEE Trans. Network Serv. Manag. **17**(4), 2717–2730 (2020). https://doi.org/10.1109/TNSM.2020.3027185

10. Ding, L., Kang, G., Liu, J., Xiao, Y., Cao, B.: QoS prediction for web services via combining multi-component graph convolutional collaborative filtering and deep factorization machine. In: 2021 IEEE International Conference on Web Services (ICWS), pp. 551–559 (2021). https://doi.org/10.1109/ICWS53863.2021.00076

11. Wu, H., Zhang, Z., Luo, J., Yue, K., Hsu, C.-H.: Multiple attributes QoS prediction via deep neural model with contexts*. IEEE Trans. Serv. Comput. **14**(4), 1084–1096 (2021). https://doi.org/10.1109/TSC.2018.2859986

12. Ye, X., Wang, Y., Jia, Z.: Web service quality prediction method based on recurrent neural network. In: 2021 7th Annual International Conference on Network and Information Systems for Computers (ICNISC), pp. 445–450 (2021).https://doi.org/10.1109/ICNISC54316.2021.00086

13. Yin, Y., Cao, Z., Xu, Y., Gao, H., Li, R., Mai, Z.: QoS prediction for service recommendation with features learning in mobile edge computing environment. IEEE Trans. Cogn. Commun. Networking **6**(4), 1136–1145 (2020). https://doi.org/10.1109/TCCN.2020.3027681

14. Zheng, Z., Zhang, Y., Lyu, M.R.: Investigating QoS of real-world web services. IEEE Trans. Serv. Comput. **7**(1), 32–39 (2014). https://doi.org/10.1109/TSC.2012.34

15. He, X., Liao, L., Zhang, H., Nie, L., Hu, X., Chua, T-S.: Neural collaborative filtering. roc. In: Proceedings of the 26th International Conference on World Wide Web (WWW 2017), pp. 173–182 (2017).https://doi.org/10.1145/3038912.3052569

16. Tang, M., Jiang, Y., Liu, J., Liu, X.: Location-aware collaborative filtering for QoS-based service recommendation. In: 2012 IEEE 19th International Conference on Web Services, pp. 202–209 (2012). https://doi.org/10.1109/ICWS.2012.61

17. Zheng, Z., Ma, H., Lyu, M.R., King, I.: Collaborative web service QoS prediction via neighborhood integrated matrix factorization. IEEE Trans. Serv. Comput. **6**(3), 289–299 (2013). https://doi.org/10.1109/TSC.2011.59

18. Zhu, J., He, P., Zheng, Z., Lyu, M.R.: A privacy-preserving QoS prediction framework for web service recommendation. In: 2015 IEEE International Conference on Web Services, pp. 241–248 (2015). https://doi.org/10.1109/ICWS.2015.41

19. Tang, M., Zhang, T., Yang, Y., Zheng, Z., Cao, B.: A quality-aware web service recommendation method based on factorization machine. Chin. J. Comput. **41**, 1080–1093 (2018)

20. Chen, Z., Shen, L., Li, F.: Your neighbors alleviate cold-start: on geographical neighborhood influence to collaborative web service QoS prediction. Knowl.-Based Syst. **138**, 188–201 (2017). https://doi.org/10.1016/j.knosys.2017.10.001

21. White, G., Palade, A., Cabrera, C., Clarke, S.: Autoencoders for QoS prediction at the edge. In: 2019 IEEE International Conference on Pervasive Computing and Communications (PerCom), pp. 1–9 (2019). https://doi.org/10.1109/PERCOM.2019.8767397

CKEN: Collaborative Knowledge-Aware Enhanced Network for Recommender Systems

Wei Zeng[1,2], Jiwei Qin[1,2(✉)], and Xiaole Wang[1,2]

[1] School of Information Science and Engineering, Xinjiang University,
Urumqi 830046, China
jwqin_xju@163.com
[2] Key Laboratory of Signal Detection and Processing, Xinjiang Uygur Autonomous
Region, Xinjiang University, Urumqi 830046, China

Abstract. Knowledge graph are widely used as a kind of side information to alleviate the data sparsity in collaborative filtering. However, a majority of existing recommendation methods incorporating knowledge graph emphasize how to encode knowledge associations in the knowledge graph, while ignoring the key collaboration information implied in the user-item history interactions and the shared information between the item and the knowledge graph entities, resulting in insufficient embedding representation of users and items. To that end, we propose a collaborative knowledge-aware enhanced network (CKEN). Specifically, CKEN uses a collaborative propagation approach to explicitly encode user-item collaborative information and then allows it to be propagated in the knowledge graph, and applies an attention mechanism to obtain contributions from neighbors with different knowledge during knowledge propagation. In addition, considering the association relationship between items and knowledge graph entities, this paper designs a feature interaction layer to facilitate feature sharing between items in the recommender systems and entities in the knowledge graph in order to further enrich the latent vector representation of items. Numerous experiments on several real-world scenario datasets have shown that CKEN's recommendations are significantly better than several other best-of-class baselines.

Keywords: Recommender systems · Collaborative propagation · Feature interaction · Knowledge graph

1 Introduction

Recommender systems (RS) aim to suggest certain items to users to meet their personalized preferences, thus alleviating the impact of information overload. One of the more widely used recommendation methods is collaborative filtering (CF) [5], which extracts users' preferences on items for recommendation by analyzing their historical interactions. However, collaborative filtering recommendation methods often face data sparsity and cold start problems. To tackle

E. Pimenidis et al. (Eds.): ICANN 2022, LNCS 13530, pp. 769–784, 2022.
https://doi.org/10.1007/978-3-031-15931-2_63

these problems, some researchers have introduced various types of side information in recommender systems, e.g., user social networks [4], user/item attributes features [11], and multimedia information (e.g., text [10], images [21]). Among a wide variety of side information, knowledge graph (KG) contain rich facts and connections about items have received increasing attention [1,14,17,18]. Figure 1 shows a movie recommendation scenario based on KG, the KG contains entities such as directors, actors and subject genres.

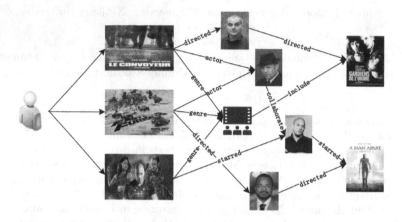

Fig. 1. Illustration of KG for movie recommendation.

Central to the combination of KG and RS is how to leverage the rich semantic information in KG to enhance the representation of users and items. For example, PER [20] and FMG [22] consider KG as heterogeneous information networks, representing the connectivity between users and items by withdrawing features of meta-paths. However, PER and FMG require manual design of meta-paths and the designed meta-paths are hardly optimal, which makes it difficult to be applied in general-purpose recommendation scenarios. DKN [13] designs a Convolutional Neural Network (CNN) framework that combines semantic and knowledge information from different channels to recommend news for users. However, since DKN are usually trained in a separate manner for entity embedding, Knowledge Graph Embedding (KGE) is not optimized for a specific task, which can lead to suboptimal results. RippleNet [12] is the first to combine entity embedding and path propagation of KG recommendation methods to propagate users' preferences in KG paths. However, RippleNet relies heavily on the representation of attributes, i.e., the construction of the KG, and the importance of the relations between entities is difficult to be described. CKE [21] extracts features from the structured knowledge, textual knowledge, and visual knowledge of the item, respectively, and then combines them with the CF module for joint learning, but the KGE module in the CKE model is more suitable for KG completion and link prediction tasks. MKR [15] is an end-to-end model that uses KGE tasks to assist recommendation tasks, which automatically share latent features between items and entities in the KG through the information sharing module designed in the model, but it ignores the user-side and item-side in the KG of propagating information, resulting in insufficient user and item embedding.

To tackle the limitations of extant knowledge graph recommendation methods, collaborative knowledge-aware enhanced network (CKEN) is proposed, which is an end-to-end model. Specifically, CKEN has two designs: 1) seamlessly combines collaborative information latent in user-item history interactions and knowledge associations in KG through the collaborative propagation layer (CPL) and the knowledge graph propagation layer (KPL), and then generates different attention weights of tail entities through a knowledge-aware attention mechanism to extract more valuable knowledge associations. 2) A feature interaction layer (FIL) is designed to explicitly model the high-level interactions between item features and entity features using a cross&compress approach and to control the knowledge transfer between item and KG entities. Through the FIL, the features of items and entities can supplement each other, which helps to obtain a richer latent vector representation of items, while avoiding fitting noise and improving generality.

In conclusion, the main contributions of CKEN are as follows :

1. We highlight the importance of the collaborative information latent in the user-item history interactions and the shared information between items and KG entities when obtaining embedding of users and items.
2. We propose CKEN, which is an end-to-end recommendation model. The design of CPL and KPL effectively combines the collaboration information latent in user-item history interactions with the side semantic associations in KG. The design of FIL enables feature sharing between items in the implicit interaction matrix and KG entities, further enhancing the latent vector representation of items.
3. We conducted extensive experiments on three realistic recommended scenarios demonstrate that CKEN surpasses compelling best-in-class baselines.

2   Problem Formulation

In the recommendation task of CKEN, we assume there exists a user set $U = \{u_1, u_2, \cdots, u_M\}$ consisting of M users and an item set $V = \{v_1, v_2, \cdots, v_N\}$ consisting of N items. Based on the implicit feedback from users in their history of actions (e.g. clicks, views and purchases), a user-item implicit feedback matrix $Y^{M \times N}$ can be obtained, where $y_{uv} = 1$ indicates that the user u has clicked or viewed the item v, otherwise $y_{uv} = 0$. In addition, this paper constructs side information in the form of KG, which is usually represented using a triple, i.e. $G = \{(h, r, t) | h, t \in E, r \in R\}$, where $E = \{e_1, e_2, \cdots, e_n\}$ and $R = \{r_1, r_2, \cdots, r_n\}$ are the sets of entities and relations in the KG, and each KG triple (h, r, t) means that the head entity h and the tail entity t are connected by the relation r. And, we use the $A = \{(v, e) | v \in V, e \in E\}$ set to represent the alignment of items and entities.

Having obtained the implicit feedback matrix $Y^{M \times N}$ and konwledge graph G, our task is to obtain the probability that user u will click on an item v that he has not interacted with. Specifically, the goal of this paper is to learn the click-through rate(CTR) prediction function $\hat{y}_{uv} = P(u, v|\theta, G)$, where $\hat{y}_{uv}$ is the probability of obtaining and θ is the parameter of the function P.

3   Method

As shown in Fig. 2, CKEN has four main design components: collaborative propagation layer, knowledge graph propagation layer, feature interaction layer, and prediction layer. In the following subsections, we will elaborate on the different parts of CKEN.

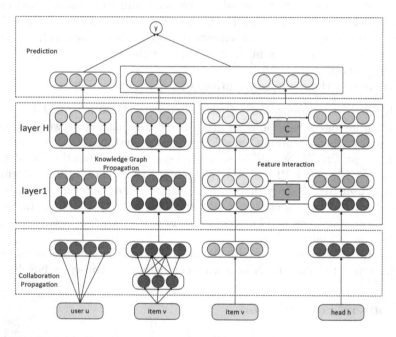

Fig. 2. Illustration of the proposed model CKEN that consists of four components: collaborative propagation layer, knowledge graph propagation layer, feature interaction layer, and prediction layer.

3.1   Collaborative Propagation Layer

According to the previous theory [19], the historical interactions of a known user u can characterize user's preferences to some extent. Therefore, we uses the set of related items V_u (first-order neighbors of the user) that user u historical interactions to represent user u, defined as follows:

$$V_u = \{v_u | v \in \{v | y_{uv} = 1\}\} \tag{1}$$

Then, we find the entities corresponding to the relevant set of items V_u based on the alignment set A of items and entities, and use them as the initial seed set for user u to propagate interest in KG. The definition is shown below:

$$\varepsilon_u^0 = \{e | (v, e) \in A \ and \ v \in V_u\} \tag{2}$$

The second-order neighbors of an item refer to other items that have been clicked by users who have generated interaction behavior with the same item v. Since user u will click on other items that are similar to the item because of their behavioral preferences, the second-order neighbors of an item can also be and are used to enhance the item representation. In this paper, we define collaborative neighbors for user history interaction items and set the set of collaborative items V_v of item v, which is defined as below:

$$V_v = \{v_u | u \in \{u | y_{uv} = 1\} \ and \ y_{uv_u} = 1\} \tag{3}$$

Based on the alignment set A between the items and KG entities, we can likewise find the set of entities corresponding to the set of collaborative items V_v of item v in KG and use it as the seed set for the propagation of item v, which is defined as shown below:

$$\varepsilon_v^0 = \{e | (v_u, e) \in A \ and \ v_u \in V_v\} \tag{4}$$

The CPL can effectively encode first-order neighbors expressing user preferences and second-order neighbors expressing item features explicitly into the seed set, thus enhancing the embedded representation of users/items.

3.2 Knowledge Graph Propagation Layer

The KPL mainly consists of two parts: knowledge graph propagation and knowledge-aware attention embedding. The knowledge graph propagation part mainly propagates knowledge associations along the links in KG in order to recursively supplement the supporting information for users and items. The knowledge-aware attention embedding part mainly learns the different weights of the same entity under different relations and generates weighted representations of the entities. They are described in detail as follows:

1) Knowledge graph propagation. The entities in KG are connected by some kind of relationship. The propagation along the connectivity of KG entities acquires extensions of the initial set of entities and triples of different distances, which can be considered as extensions of user preferences and item characteristics. The set of entities propagated by user u and item v in KG can be recursively defined as:

$$\varepsilon_*^k = \{t | (h, r, t) \in G \ and \ h \in \varepsilon_*^{k-1}\}, k = 1, 2, \cdots, H \tag{5}$$

where k denotes the distance from ε_*^0 and the symbol $*$ denotes user u or item v. Based on the above entity set definition, the set of k-th triples for user u and item v can be expressed as:

$$S_*^k = \left\{ (h,r,t) \mid (h,r,t) \in G \ and \ h \in \varepsilon_*^{k-1} \right\}, k = 1, 2, \cdots, H \tag{6}$$

The initial set of entities obtained through collaborative propagation is similar to the center of a water ripple that keeps spreading outward. After the deep propagation of the KG, the CKEN model can obtain the complementary entity information of users and items at different distances in KG, thus greatly enriching the embedding representation of users and items.

2) Knowledge-aware attention embedding. In KG, when tail entity has different implications and potential vector representations when they are connected to different entities and relations. Based on this, this paper uses a knowledge-aware attention embedding method [9,19] to produce different attention scores for the tail entities. The embedding ∂_i of the tail entities is calculated as below:

$$\partial_i = \pi \left(e_i^h, r_i \right) e_i^t \tag{7}$$

where e_i^h is the embedding of the head entity of the ith triple, r_i is the embedding of the ith triple, and e_i^t is the embedding of the ith triple tail entity. $\pi \left(e_i^h, r_i \right)$ denotes the attention scores generated by the different triples. In this paper, the implementation of the function $\pi \left(\cdot \right)$ is similar to the literature [9] and is calculated as follows:

$$O_0 = ReLU \left(W_0 \left([e_i^h, r_i] \right) + b_0 \right) \tag{8}$$

$$\pi \left(e_i^h, r_i \right) = \sigma \left(W_2 ReLU \left(W_1 O_0 + b_1 \right) + b_2 \right) \tag{9}$$

where σ denotes the Sigmoid [3] activation function, $[*]$ denotes the concatenation operation, W_* denotes the trainable weight matrix, and b_* denotes the bias vector. In this paper, the softmax [7] function is used to perform the normalization operation, which is calculated as follows:

$$\pi \left(e_i^h, r_i \right) = \mathtt{softmax}(\pi(e_i^h, r_i)) = \frac{\exp \left(\pi \left(e_i^h, r_i \right) \right)}{\sum_{(h',r',t') \in s_*^k} \exp \left(\pi \left(e_i^{h'}, r_i' \right) \right)} \tag{10}$$

where S_*^k denotes the kth level triple of the user or item. Through the knowledge-aware attention mechanism, the CKEN model can reasonably assign different weights to different neighboring tail entities, so as to capture the knowledge association more effectively. Finally, this paper obtains the latent representation of the k-th level triplet set of user/item by aggregating the attentional embedding representations of the tail entities, which is calculated as follows:

$$e_*^k = \sum_{i=1}^{|s_*^k|} \partial_i^k, k = 1, 2, \cdots, H \tag{11}$$

where $|S_*^k|$ denotes the number of triples in the set S_*^k at level k.

We know that the entities in the seed set are best used to characterize the original feature embedding of users and items. Therefore, in this paper, we add the initial entity sets for users and items, and the formula is expressed as follows:

$$e_*^0 = \frac{\sum_{e \in \varepsilon_*^0} e}{|\varepsilon_*^0|} \tag{12}$$

3.3   Feature Interaction Layer

In particular, item v itself has the key feature information of its original representation and it is related to one or more entities in KG and shares similar features in the latent feature space [6]. Therefore, in order to fully exploit the feature information of item v itself, we design FIL in CKEN model, which allows item v to interact with entity e in KG by cross&compress operation [15] to achieve feature sharing. The feature interaction matrix is shown as follows:

$$C_l = v_l e_l^T = \begin{bmatrix} v_l^{(1)} e_l^{(1)} & \cdots & v_l^{(1)} e_l^{(d)} \\ \vdots & \ddots & \vdots \\ v_l^{(d)} e_l^{(1)} & \cdots & v_l^{(d)} e_l^{(d)} \end{bmatrix} \tag{13}$$

where l is the number of layers of FIL and d is the hidden layer dimension. After calculation, the feature interaction matrix models all possible interactions $v_l^{(i)} e_l^{(i)}, \forall (i,j) \in \{1, \cdots, d\}^2$ of the item v with the entity e explicitly. The feature interaction matrix is then multiplied with the weight matrix to project them into the latent representation space, which in turn yields the input for the next level:

$$v_{l+1} = C_l W_l^{VV} + C_l^T W_l^{EV} + b_l^V = v_l e_l^T W_l^{VV} + e_l v_l^T W_l^{EV} + b_l^V \tag{14}$$

$$e_{l+1} = C_l W_l^{VE} + C_l^T W_l^{EE} + b_l^E = v_l e_l^T W_l^{VE} + e_l v_l^T W_l^{EE} + b_l^E \tag{15}$$

where $W_l^{**} \in \Re^d$ and $b_l^{**} \in \Re^d$ denote the weight matrix and bias vector. After computation, the feature interaction matrix from $\Re^{d \times d}$ space is in turn projected back into the $\Re^d$ feature space by the weight vectors. Finally, for readability, the output of FIL can be expressed as:

$$[v_{l+1}, e_{l+1}] = C(v_l, e_l) \tag{16}$$

In this paper, we denote the output items and entities in FIL by the symbols $[v]$ and $[e]$. After multiple layers of feature interactions, the final outputs of items and entities can be represented as:

$$v_e = C(v, e)[v] \tag{17}$$

$$h_e = C(v, e)[e] \tag{18}$$

With the FIL, CKEN can automatically coordinate the transfer of knowledge and fully explore the correlation between items and entities.

In CKEN, the depth of FIL should not be too large because in features tend to shift from general to specific in deep networks, and the migrability of features decreases significantly with increasing noise [15].

3.4 Prediction Layer

After knowledge-aware attention embedding and feature interaction, we set up representation sets for user u and item v that contain knowledge propagation-based attention-weighted representations and original relevant entity representations:

$$D_u = \left\{ e_u^0, e_u^1, \cdots, e_u^H \right\} \tag{19}$$

$$D_v = \left\{ v_e, e_v^0, e_v^1, \cdots, e_v^H \right\} \tag{20}$$

The representation in each layer of the propagation process can be interpreted as the potential impact of layering, which emphasizes different higher-order connectivity and preference similarities. In this paper, a summation aggregator is used to compute the final aggregation vector. Before applying the nonlinear transformation, the summation aggregator needs to sum the vectors for each layer:

$$agg_{sum}^* = \sum_{e_* \in D_*} e_* \tag{21}$$

Ultimately, e_u is used to represent the aggregation vector of users. Similarly, e_v denotes the aggregation vector of items. Then, we multiply e_v and e_u to obtain the prediction scores:

$$\hat{y}_{uv} = \sigma(e_u^T e_v) \tag{22}$$

where the activation function σ is Sigmoid [3].

3.5 Model Learning

The overall loss function for CKEN is shown below:

$$L = L_{RS} + L_{KG} + L_{REG}$$

$$= \sum_{u \in U, v \in V} J(\hat{y}_{uv}, y_{uv}) \tag{23}$$

$$-\lambda_1 \left(\sum_{(h,r,t) \in G} score(h, r, t) - \sum_{(h',r,t') \notin G} score(h', r, t') \right) + \lambda_2 \|W\|_2^2$$

where $J(\cdot)$ denotes the cross-entropy loss and the task of the second term is to add the score distance between all true and false triples. The formula for calculating the triple score is shown below:

$$score\,(h,r,t) = \sigma\,\left(t^T \hat{t}\right) = \sigma\,\left(t^T M^K\,([h_e, r_e])\right) \tag{24}$$

where t denotes the true tail entity vector, $\hat{t}$ denotes the prediction tail entity vector, r_e denotes the feature vector of the relation, $[*]$ denotes the connection operation, M^K denotes the MLP neural network with K layers, and σ is the Sigmoid [3].

The last term of the overall loss function is a regularization term for preventing overfitting, λ_1 and λ_2 are the balance parameters. And, we use the grid search method to pick parameters, with the following detailed parameter settings: $\lambda_1 = 0.1$, $\lambda_2 = 10^{-6}$.

4   Experiments

4.1   Dataset

To evaluate CKEN, we conduct experiments under several public available datasets: MovieLens-1M[1], Book-Crossing[2] and Last.FM[3]. We used MovieLens-1M dataset scores of 4 and 5 as a positive feedback signal, and all interactions in Book-Crossing and Last.FM are used as positive feedback signals. Table 1 shows the detailed statistical information.

Table 1. Detailed statistics of the three public datasets.

	MovieLens-1M	Book-Crossing	Last.FM
#users	6,036	17,860	1,872
#items	2,445	14,910	3,846
#interactions	753,772	139,746	42,346
#edge types	12	25	60
#entity	182,011	77,903	9,366
#relation	2483,990	303,000	31,036
#triplies	20,195	19,793	15,518
#sparsity level	0.948925	0.999447	0.994116

---

[1] https://grouplens.org/datasets/movielens/1m/.
[2] http://www.informatik.uni-freiburg.de/~cziegler/BX/.
[3] https://grouplens.org/datasets/hetrec-2011/.

4.2 Baselines

We have evaluated CKEN for performance comparison using the following baseline:

PER [20] uses meta-paths to characterize the relationship between users and items.

CKE [21] combines CF modules with knowledge from a variety of different sources to make recommendations.

DKN [13] combines entity and text embedding for news recommendations.

RippleNet [12] uses the user's a priori information to propagate user preferences in KG and enriches the user's representation in this way.

LibFM [8] is a feature-based decomposition model. In this paper, user IDs and item IDs, as well as related entity embeddings are concatenated as inputs to LibFM.

Wide & Deep [2] is a well-known model that trains a linear model jointly with a non-linear model to balance the overall model's ability to remember and generalise.

KGCN [16] is a recommendation model that fuses KG and GCN, which models only item-side representations.

MKR [15] is a multi-task learning framework that combines KG to assist in recommendation tasks by learning higher-order interactions between items and entities in the KG.

CKAN [19] is a recommendation model that fuses collaborative information and KG, which uses a heterogeneous propagation strategy to encode both knowledge attribute associations and user-item collaborative signals.

4.3 Experiments Setup

On the MovieLens-1M dataset, the number of FIL layers is 1, and the learning rates for the recommendation part and the knowledge graph part are 2×10^{-2} and 10^{-2}, respectively. On the Book-Crossing dataset, the number of FIL layers is 1, and the learning rates for the recommendation part and the knowledge graph part are 2×10^{-4} and 2×10^{-5}, respectively. On the Lasst.FM dataset, the number of FIL layers is 2, and the learning rates for the recommendation part and the knowledge graph part are 10^{-3} and 2×10^{-4}, respectively. In this paper, each dataset is divided into a training set, a validation set and a test set (6:2:2), and both AUC and ACC are used to evaluate the effectiveness of CTR prediction.

4.4 Performance Comparison

Table 2 shows the CTR prediction results for all models. The discussion is as follows:

- PER performs poorly because the manually designed meta-paths are hardly optimal, resulting in PER not being able to use heterogeneous information networks effectively.

Table 2. Detailed statistics of the three public datasets.

Model	MovieLens-1M		Book-Crossing		Last.FM	
	AUC	ACC	AUC	ACC	AUC	ACC
PER	0.710(−30.3%)	0.664(−28.0%)	0.623(−22.0%)	0.588(−19.4%)	0.633(−34.1%)	0.596(−30.5%)
CKE	0.801(−15.5%)	0.742(−14.6%)	0.671(−13.3%)	0.633(−10.9%)	0.744(−14.1%)	0.673(−15.6%)
DKN	0.655(−41.2%)	0.589(−44.3%)	0.622(−22.2%)	0.598(−17.4%)	0.602(−41.0%)	0.581(−33.9%)
RippleNet	0.913(−1.3%)	0.835(−1.8%)	0.729(−4.3%)	0.662(−6.0%)	0.768(−10.5%)	0.691(−12.6%)
LibFM	0.892(−3.7%)	0.812(−4.7%)	0.685(−10.9%)	0.640(−9.7%)	0.777(−9.3%)	0.709(−9.7%)
Wide&Deep	0.898(−3.0%)	0.820(−3.7%)	0.712(−6.7%)	0.624(−12.5%)	0.756(−12.3%)	0.688(−13.1%)
KGCN	0.919(−0.7%)	0.845(−0.6%)	0.694(−9.5%)	0.635(−10.6%)	0.794(−6.9%)	0.724(−7.5%)
MKR	0.917(−0.9%)	0.843(−0.8%)	0.734(−3.5%)	0.702(−0.0%)	0.797(−6.5%)	0.752(−3.5%)
CKAN	0.915(−1.1%)	0.840(−1.2%)	0.741(−2.6%)	0.655(−7.2%)	0.841(−1.0%)	0.744(−4.6%)
CKEN	0.925	0.850	0.760	0.702	0.849	0.778

- CKE outperforms PER because of the collaborative information incorporated in CKE.
- DKN performs the worst, which is because the names corresponding to the items in these datasets are too short and ambiguous, resulting in the inability to provide useful information.
- LibFM and Wide&Deep have a large improvement over PER and DKN, indicating that LibFM and Wide&Deep can better use the rich semantic relations in KG to improve the recommendation quality.
- MKR performs worse than CKEN because MKR does not take full advantage of the collaborative information as well as the propagation information in KG.
- CKAN performs less well than CKEN because the CKAN model ignores the shared information between items and knowledge graph entities. However, CKEN proposed in this paper seamlessly combines the collaborative information and knowledge associations in the KG, while further designing the FIL to mine the shared information and enrich the feature representation of items.
- Overall, our proposed CKEN performed the best on all three datasets. Specifically, the AUC increases by 0.7%, 2.6% and 1.0% in Movielens-1M, Book-Crossing and Last.FM datasets. This also proves the superiority of CKEN.

4.5   Study of CKEN

Effect of Dimension of Embedding. To facilitate the calculation, we set the embedding of entities and relationships in KG to the same dimensionality and study the effect of dimensionality on CKEN. From Fig. 3, we can see that increasing the embedding dimension in some range can enhance the recommendation effect of CKEN, but if the dimension is too large, the performance will decrease. The reason for this phenomenon is that when the dimensionality is too large, overfitting may occur.

Effect of Depths of Layer. In this paper, we choose different KPL depths to observe the variation of CKEN performance. Table 3 shows the experimental results for different depth layers, from which we can see that the model performs best when the propagation depth is 2 on MovieLens-1M and Book-Crossing

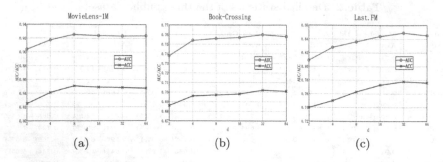

Fig. 3. The result of AU C w.r.t. different dimensions on all three datasets.

Table 3. The AUC results at different depths of layer.

Depth	MovieLens-1M	Book-Crossing	Last.FM
1	0.9248	0.7513	0.8426
2	**0.9254**	**0.7600**	0.8451
3	0.9251	0.7542	**0.8498**

Table 4. The AUC results for the effects of FIL, CPL, and knowledge perception attention mechanisms.

Model	MovieLens-1M		Book-Crossing		Last.FM	
	AUC	ACC	AUC	ACC	AUC	ACC
$CKEN_{w/o\ FIL}$	0.9239	0.8486	0.7224	0.6643	0.8160	0.7421
$CKEN_{w/o\ CPL}$	0.9242	0.8484	0.7286	0.6826	0.8115	0.7413
$CKEN_{w/o\ ATT}$	0.8775	0.7966	0.7427	0.6993	0.8069	0.7497
CKEN	**0.9254**	**0.8507**	**0.7600**	**0.7025**	**0.8498**	**0.7789**

Table 5. The AUC results for different initial entity set sizes on the Movielens-1M dataset.

User	Item				
	4	8	16	32	64
4	0.8961	0.9011	0.9002	0.9005	0.9009
8	0.9091	0.9099	0.9092	0.9116	0.9100
16	0.9151	0.9161	0.9170	0.9177	0.9171
32	0.9189	0.9204	0.9206	0.9212	0.9224
64	0.9228	0.9235	0.9229	**0.9254**	0.9251

Table 6. The AUC results for different initial entity set sizes on the Book-Crossing dataset.

User	Item				
	4	8	16	32	64
4	0.7453	0.7487	0.7476	0.7515	0.7517
8	0.7449	0.7528	0.7555	0.7564	0.7583
16	0.7468	0.7543	0.7577	0.7548	0.7559
32	0.7514	0.7548	0.7572	0.7584	**0.7600**
64	0.7516	0.7529	0.7561	0.7579	0.7589

Table 7. The AUC results for different initial entity set sizes on the Last-FM dataset.

User	Item				
	4	8	16	32	64
4	0.8314	0.8392	0.8386	0.8399	0.8434
8	0.8349	0.8415	0.8397	0.8448	0.8437
16	0.8407	0.8435	0.8461	0.8447	0.8457
32	0.8383	0.8390	0.8449	**0.8498**	0.8475
64	0.8419	0.8455	0.8477	0.8457	0.8492

datasets. On the Last.FM, the model performs best when the propagation depth is 3. This is due to the fact that deeper propagation brings in side information and also brings in a lot of noise to affect the performance of CKEN.

Effect of FIL, CPL and Knowledge-Aware Attention Mechanisms. Table 4 shows the ablation experimental results of the CKEN model, from the results in the table, we can see that the CKEN is better than the $CKEN_{w/o\ FIL}$ without FIL and the $CKEN_{w/o\ CPL}$ without CPL, the reason for this phenomenon is that the CKEN model fully captures and incorporates the collaborative information as well as the shared information between entities and items, which helps to enrich the latent vector representation of items. In addition, we replaces the knowledge-aware attention mechanism with a mean-value approach to study its effect on the experimental results of the CKEN model, and the results show that the CKEN is better than the $CKEN_{w/o\ ATT}$, which further demonstrates that the knowledge-aware attention mechanism can encode important knowledge associations into embedded representations of users and items, thus improve their representation capabilities.

Effect of Initial Entity Set Size. We change the initial entity set size of users and items to explore the upper limit of CKEN performance. Table 5, Table 6 and Table 7 show the results of AUC for MovieLens-1M dataset, Book-Crossing dataset and Last.FM dataset. We summarize the results and find that: increasing the initial entity set size can boost the performance, but if the initial entity set is too large, the results will be decreased. The reason for this phenomenon is the different number of the set of related items and the set of collaborative items, resulting in different number of entities in the KG associated with the user and the item, which is one of the key factors affecting the performance of CKEN.

5   Conclusion and Future Work

This paper proposes CKEN, a collaborative knowledge-aware enhanced network for recommender systems. Specifically, CKEN employs a collaborative propagation strategy to construct user-item collaborative relationships, which are then seamlessly combined with knowledge associations in the KG, while a feature interaction layer is designed to explicitly model the higher-order interactions between item features and KG entity features to facilitate feature sharing. Extensive experiments on multiple datasets in the real world have demonstrated that CKEN has significant performance improvement over other similar recommendation models.

In the future, we plan to untangle the user-item interaction bipartite graph to distinguish the relationship between users and items at fine-grained intent, while using dependency relationships in combination with the KG as a way to obtain fine-grained user preferences.

Acknowledgements. This work was supported by the Science Fund for Outstanding Youth of Xinjiang Uygur Autonomous Region under Grant No. 2021D01E14, the National Science Foundation of China under Grant No. 61867006, the Major science and technology project of Xinjiang Uygur Autonomous Region under Grant No. 2020A03001, the Key Laboratory Open Project of Science and Technology Department of Xinjiang Uygur Autonomous Region named Research on video information intelligent processing technology for Xinjiang regional security.

References

1. Cao, Y., Wang, X., He, X., Hu, Z., Chua, T.S.: Unifying knowledge graph learning and recommendation: towards a better understanding of user preferences. In: The World Wide Web Conference, pp. 151–161 (2019)
2. Cheng, H.T., et al.: Wide & deep learning for recommender systems. In: Proceedings of the 1st Workshop on Deep Learning for Recommender Systems, pp. 7–10 (2016)
3. Han, J., Moraga, C.: The influence of the sigmoid function parameters on the speed of backpropagation learning. In: Mira, J., Sandoval, F. (eds.) IWANN 1995. LNCS, vol. 930, pp. 195–201. Springer, Heidelberg (1995). https://doi.org/10.1007/3-540-59497-3_175
4. Jamali, M., Ester, M.: A matrix factorization technique with trust propagation for recommendation in social networks. In: Proceedings of the Fourth ACM Conference on Recommender Systems, pp. 135–142 (2010)
5. Koren, Y., Bell, R., Volinsky, C.: Matrix factorization techniques for recommender systems. Computer **42**(8), 30–37 (2009)

6. Long, M., Cao, Z., Wang, J., Yu, P.S.: Learning multiple tasks with multilinear relationship networks. In: Advances in Neural Information Processing Systems, vol. 30 (2017)

7. Memisevic, R., Zach, C., Pollefeys, M., Hinton, G.E.: Gated softmax classification. In: Advances in Neural Information Processing Systems, vol. 23 (2010)

8. Rendle, S.: Factorization machines with libfm. ACM Trans. Intell. Syst. Technol. (TIST) **3**(3), 1–22 (2012)

9. Vaswani, A., et al.: Attention is all you need. In: Advances in Neural Information Processing Systems, vol. 30 (2017)

10. Wang, H., Wang, N., Yeung, D.Y.: Collaborative deep learning for recommender systems. In: Proceedings of the 21th ACM SIGKDD International Conference on Knowledge Discovery and Data Mining, pp. 1235–1244 (2015)

11. Wang, H., Zhang, F., Hou, M., Xie, X., Guo, M., Liu, Q.: Shine: signed heterogeneous information network embedding for sentiment link prediction. In: Proceedings of the Eleventh ACM International Conference on Web Search and Data Mining, pp. 592–600 (2018)

12. Wang, H., et al.: Ripplenet: propagating user preferences on the knowledge graph for recommender systems. In: Proceedings of the 27th ACM International Conference on Information and Knowledge Management, pp. 417–426 (2018)

13. Wang, H., Zhang, F., Xie, X., Guo, M.: DKN: deep knowledge-aware network for news recommendation. In: Proceedings of the 2018 World Wide Web Conference, pp. 1835–1844 (2018)

14. Wang, H., et al.: Knowledge-aware graph neural networks with label smoothness regularization for recommender systems. In: Proceedings of the 25th ACM SIGKDD International Conference on Knowledge Discovery & Data Mining, pp. 968–977 (2019)

15. Wang, H., Zhang, F., Zhao, M., Li, W., Xie, X., Guo, M.: Multi-task feature learning for knowledge graph enhanced recommendation. In: The World Wide Web Conference, pp. 2000–2010 (2019)

16. Wang, H., Zhao, M., Xie, X., Li, W., Guo, M.: Knowledge graph convolutional networks for recommender systems. In: The World Wide Web Conference, pp. 3307–3313 (2019)

17. Wang, X., He, X., Cao, Y., Liu, M., Chua, T.S.: KGAT: knowledge graph attention network for recommendation. In: Proceedings of the 25th ACM SIGKDD International Conference on Knowledge Discovery & Data Mining, pp. 950–958 (2019)

18. Wang, X., Wang, D., Xu, C., He, X., Cao, Y., Chua, T.S.: Explainable reasoning over knowledge graphs for recommendation. In: Proceedings of the AAAI Conference on Artificial Intelligence, vol. 33, pp. 5329–5336 (2019)

19. Wang, Z., Lin, G., Tan, H., Chen, Q., Liu, X.: CKAN: collaborative knowledge-aware attentive network for recommender systems. In: Proceedings of the 43rd International ACM SIGIR Conference on Research and Development in Information Retrieval, pp. 219–228 (2020)

20. Yu, X., et al.: Personalized entity recommendation: a heterogeneous information network approach. In: Proceedings of the 7th ACM International Conference on Web Search and Data Mining, pp. 283–292 (2014)

21. Zhang, F., Yuan, N.J., Lian, D., Xie, X., Ma, W.Y.: Collaborative knowledge base embedding for recommender systems. In: Proceedings of the 22nd ACM SIGKDD International Conference on Knowledge Discovery and Data Mining, pp. 353–362 (2016)
22. Zhao, H., Yao, Q., Li, J., Song, Y., Lee, D.L.: Meta-graph based recommendation fusion over heterogeneous information networks. In: Proceedings of the 23rd ACM SIGKDD International Conference on Knowledge Discovery and Data Mining, pp. 635–644 (2017)

Conditioned Variational Autoencoder for Top-N Item Recommendation

Tommaso Carraro[1,2]([✉]) [ID], Mirko Polato[3] [ID], Luca Bergamin[1] [ID],
and Fabio Aiolli[1] [ID]

[1] Department of Mathematics, University of Padova, Padova, Italy
tommaso.carraro@studenti.unipd.it
[2] Fondazione Bruno Kessler (FBK), Trento, Italy
[3] Department of Computer Science, University of Turin, Turin, Italy

Abstract. State-of-the-art recommender systems (RSs) generally try to improve the overall recommendation quality. However, users usually tend to explicitly filter the item set based on available categories, e.g., smartphone brands, movie genres. For this reason, an RS that can make this step automatically is likely to increase the user's experience. This paper proposes a Conditioned Variational Autoencoder (C-VAE) for constrained top-N item recommendation where the recommended items must satisfy a given condition. The proposed model architecture is similar to a standard VAE in which a condition vector is fed into the encoder. The constrained ranking is learned during training thanks to a new reconstruction loss that takes the input condition into account. We show that our model generalizes the state-of-the-art Mult-VAE collaborative filtering model. Experimental results underline the potential of C-VAE in providing accurate recommendations under constraints. Finally, the performed analyses suggest that C-VAE can be used in other recommendation scenarios, such as context-aware recommendation.

Keywords: Recommender systems · Collaborative filtering · Implicit feedback · Variational autoencoder · Top-N recommendation

1 Introduction

Recommender system (RS) technologies are nowadays an essential component for e-services. Generally speaking, an RS aims at providing suggestions for items (e.g., movies, songs, news) that are most likely of interest to a particular user [18]. Since the first appearance of RSs, Collaborative Filtering (CF) [11, 22] has affirmed of being the *de facto* recommendation approach. CF exploits similarity patterns across users and items to provide personalized recommendations. Latent Factor models, in particular Matrix Factorization (MF), have dominated the CF scene [8, 14, 16, 17] for years, and this has been further emphasized with the deep learning rise [5]. A growing body of work has shown the potential of (deep) neural network approaches to face the recommendation problem. In the

© The Author(s), under exclusive license to Springer Nature Switzerland AG 2022
E. Pimenidis et al. (Eds.): ICANN 2022, LNCS 13530, pp. 785–796, 2022.
https://doi.org/10.1007/978-3-031-15931-2_64

last few years, plenty of neural network-based models have raised the bar in terms of recommendation accuracy, such as NeuCF [6], CDAE [24], and EASE [21], to name a few.

Recently, generative approaches have attracted the researchers' attention to the top-N recommendation task. The first generative models that appeared in the RS literature were based on Generative Adversarial Networks [4,23]. The GAN-based trend has been followed by a series of Variational Autoencoder-based (VAE, [10]) methods, which have soon gained much success overshadowing GAN-based ones. The seminal Variational approach for CF has been Mult-VAE [13]. After that, other VAE-based models have been proposed, such as [19], where the Mult-VAE performance is further increased thanks to a revised architecture and alternating training, and [2], which proposes an ensemble of two VAEs to learn both user and item representations jointly.

Among these VAE-based methods, [12,25], and [9] try to model user and/or item side information to deal with sparsity and cold-start. In particular, the latter work is highly related to ours since it extends the Conditional VAE [15] architecture for conditioning the latent representations based on users' style profiles (discussed in Sect. 3).

Here, we extend the Mult-VAE model [13] for conditioned recommendations in the top-N setting. Conditions are intended in a generic sense and they can be both content-based or contextual-based [1]. It is important to underline that the way conditions are treated in our training is different from the one proposed in [9]. In our setting, a condition represents a constraint, and thus the provided recommendations must satisfy the constraint to be accepted. For example, in a movie recommendation system, a user can ask for movies that belong to a specific genre.

We designed our model as a generalization of Mult-VAE, and hence if trained without the conditions, they are equivalent. Treating the conditions as we do allows the model to be versatile, making it potentially applicable as a content-based as well as a context-aware recommender. Additionally, thanks to the training process, the latent space shows nice properties that can be exploited to give a human-friendly interpretation of the model, as shown in [3]. Our experimental analyses show that C-VAE can achieve state-of-the-art performance on different benchmark data sets.

In summary, our main contributions are two-fold:

1. we propose a Conditioned VAE for top-N recommendation, dubbed C-VAE, able to manage conditioned recommendations. We define the C-VAE architecture and a new conditioned loss, with which our model is able to learn the relationships between items and conditions;
2. we provide a descriptive as well as a quantitative comparison with the state-of-the-art Mult-VAE approach.

2   Background

This section provides the notations (Sect. 2.1) and background knowledge (Sect. 2.2) useful to fully understand the rest of the paper.

2.1 Notation

We refer to the set of users of a RS with $\mathcal{U}$, where $|\mathcal{U}| = n$. Similarly, the set of items is referred to as $\mathcal{I}$ such that $|\mathcal{I}| = m$. The set of ratings is denoted by $\mathcal{R} \equiv \{(u, i) \mid u \in \mathcal{U} \wedge i \in \mathcal{I}, u \text{ rated } i\}$. Each item i is assumed to belong to a set of categories $C^{(i)} \subseteq \mathcal{C}$, where $\mathcal{C} \equiv \{C_1, C_2, \ldots, C_s\}$ is the set of all possible categories s.t. $|\mathcal{C}| = s$.

Moreover, since we face top-N recommendation tasks, we consider the binary rating matrix with $\mathbf{R} \in \mathbb{N}^{n \times m}$, where users are on the rows and items on the columns, such that $\mathbf{r}_{ui} = 1$ iff $(u, i) \in \mathcal{R}$. Given $\mathbf{R}$, $\mathbf{r}_u \in \{0, 1\}^m$ indicates the row binary vector corresponding to the user u. We add a subscript to both user and item sets to indicate, respectively, the set of items rated by a user u (i.e., $\mathcal{I}_u$) and the set of users who rated the item i (i.e., $\mathcal{U}_i$). Finally, we indicate with $\mathbf{c} = [c_1, ..., c_s]^\top$ the column binary condition vector, where $c_j = 1$ if and only if $\exists i \in \mathcal{I}_u$ such that i belongs to the category C_j.

2.2 Variational Autoencoder

The VAE is a Variational Bayesian model that assumes the input $\mathbf{x}$ is generated according to the following two-step generative process: $\mathbf{z} \sim p_{\theta^*}(\mathbf{z})$ and $\mathbf{x} \sim p_{\theta^*}(\mathbf{x}|\mathbf{z})$, where the dimensionality of $\mathbf{z}$ is (generally) much lower than $\mathbf{x}$. In other words, VAE assumes that the input vector $\mathbf{x}$ is modeled as a function of an unobserved random vector $\mathbf{z}$ of lower dimensionality. VAE aims at estimating the parameters θ^* by maximizing the likelihood of the data (Maximum Likelihood Estimation, MLE), i.e., $\hat{\theta} = \arg\max_{\theta \in \Theta} p_\theta(\mathbf{x})$. Computing the MLE requires solving

$$p_\theta(\mathbf{x}) = \int p_\theta(\mathbf{x}|\mathbf{z}) p_\theta(\mathbf{z}) d\mathbf{z}$$

which is often intractable. However, in practice, for most $\mathbf{z}$, $p_\theta(\mathbf{x}|\mathbf{z}) \approx 0$. The key idea behind VAE is to sample values of $\mathbf{z}$ that are likely to have produced $\mathbf{x}$, and compute $p_\theta(\mathbf{x})$ just from those. To do this, we need an approximation $q_\phi(\mathbf{z}|\mathbf{x})$ of the true posterior distribution $p_\theta(\mathbf{z}|\mathbf{x})$ that returns a distribution over $\mathbf{z}$ that are likely to produce the input $\mathbf{x}$. To make this problem tractable, it is assumed that q_ϕ follows a specific family of parametric distributions, usually Gaussian. The closeness between $q_\phi(\mathbf{z}|\mathbf{x})$ and the assumed posterior distribution $p_\theta(\mathbf{z}|\mathbf{x})$ is ensured by the minimization of the Kullback-Leibler divergence (KL), which can be written as:

$$\mathrm{KL}(q_\phi(\mathbf{z}|\mathbf{x}) \| p_\theta(\mathbf{z}|\mathbf{x})) = \mathbb{E}_{q_\phi(\mathbf{z}|\mathbf{x})}\left[\log q_\phi(\mathbf{z}|\mathbf{x}) - \log p_\theta(\mathbf{x}, \mathbf{z})\right] + \log p_\theta(\mathbf{x}). \quad (1)$$

After some rearrangements of Eq. (1), it is possible to write the so-called Evidence Lower BOund (ELBO) [10], which naturally defines the objective function that VAE seeks to maximize:

$$\log p_\theta(\mathbf{x}) \geq \mathbb{E}_{q_\phi(\mathbf{z}|\mathbf{x})}\left[\log p_\theta(\mathbf{x}|\mathbf{z})\right] - \mathrm{KL}(q_\phi(\mathbf{z}|\mathbf{x}) \| p_\theta(\mathbf{z}))$$
$$= \mathcal{L}(\mathbf{x}; \theta, \phi).$$

This loss can be interpreted as a reconstruction loss (first term), plus the so-called KL loss, which acts as a kind of regularization term.

In practice, p_θ and q_ϕ are parametrized by two (deep) neural networks, i.e., the decoder (f_θ) and the encoder (g_ϕ), respectively. These parameters are optimized using stochastic gradient ascent with the aid of the reparameterization trick [10], that allows to compute the gradient w.r.t. ϕ. To this end, the encoder network provides the parameters which define the distributions over each element of $\mathbf{z}$, i.e., mean $\boldsymbol{\mu}$ and variance $\boldsymbol{\sigma}$. The sampling over the Gaussian distribution is performed via an additional input $\epsilon \sim \mathcal{N}(\mathbf{0}, \mathbf{I})$, which allows the reparameterization $\mathbf{z} = \boldsymbol{\mu} + \epsilon \odot \boldsymbol{\sigma}$, where $\odot$ is the Hadamard product.

3   Related Works

In this section, we present our related works, namely Variational Autoencoder for collaborative filtering (Mult-VAE, [13]) and Style Conditioned Recommendations (SCR, [9]).

Mult-VAE. In [13], Liang et al. propose a VAE for collaborative filtering called Mult-VAE. Mult-VAE takes as input the user-item binary rating matrix and learns a compressed latent representation (the encoder) of the input. This latent representation is then used to reconstruct the input (the decoder) and impute the missing ratings. The top-N recommendation is computed by taking, for each user, the N items with the highest reconstructed ratings.

Differently from the standard VAE, Mult-VAE uses a multinomial log-likelihood rather than the classical Gaussian likelihood. Authors believe that the multinomial distribution is well suited for modeling implicit feedback [13]. Moreover, Mult-VAE employs a β-VAE loss [7] in which the hyper-parameter β is added to the loss as a trade-off parameter between the reconstruction loss and the KL loss.

SCR. In [9], a style conditioned variational autoencoder for applying *style transfer* methodologies to RSs is proposed. The conditional schema followed by SCR is similar to the standard Conditional VAE [15]. The style conditioning is achieved by adding a user style profile vector to both the input of the encoder and the decoder. This style vector representation is learned through another network using side information. The rest of the model as well as the training of the network is the same as in a standard VAE, where the input of the encoder and the decoder is the concatenation of their input with the style vector.

Once the user style profile is learned, the conditioning proposed in SCR is fixed for the user. The only way to force different styles is by acting directly in the latent space by injecting a specific style via a one-hot encoded style vector. With this trick, the decoder network is driven to reproduce inputs with a specific style. However, this is a post-training step, and hence only the decoding is influenced by the injection.

Since our conditions represent constraints, in C-VAE, the conditional vector is fed into the encoder network, and the training process guarantees that the learned latent representation depends on the given condition. In this way, different conditions map the user onto (potentially) different regions of the latent space. In [3], it has been shown that this is a nice property when it comes to interpret the model. In summary, C-VAE differs from SCR in the following main aspects:

- C-VAE is architecturally simpler than SCR (Sect. 4.1) since it does not require to pass through an additional network to compute the condition vectors;
- C-VAE is more versatile than SCR since it allows to generate diversified recommendations based on the conditioning;
- C-VAE learns the correlations between users and conditions, while SCR only learns a specific conditioning for each user.

4 Conditioned Variational Autoencoder

In this section, we present the architecture and loss function of C-VAE.

4.1 Architecture

C-VAE follows the architecture of Mult-VAE with the addition of a conditional vector to the input of the encoder network. The conditional vector is concatenated with the user rating vector after the dropout layer. The dropout layer (implemented in [13] but not reported in the paper) gives to the VAE denoising capabilities, which have shown of being effective in making recommendations [13]. The conditional vector $\mathbf{c} \in \{0,1\}^s$ is defined as a one-hot vector over the s possible conditions. It is noteworthy that the condition, differently from SCR, is not fed into the decoder network.

Figure 1 depicts the network architecture of our model.

4.2 Conditioned Loss Function

A core difference between our C-VAE and SCR is the way the training works. Since we treat the conditioning as a constraint, the reconstruction must take this into account. This means that, in general, the expected output is a filtered version of the input, where the items that do not satisfy the constraint are dropped. This is achieved by our model via a modified loss function.

The loss function we try to minimize is a conditioned version of the Mult-VAE loss [13]:

$$\mathcal{L}_\beta\left(\mathbf{r}_u, \mathbf{c}; \boldsymbol{\theta}, \boldsymbol{\phi}\right) = \mathbb{E}_{q_\phi\left(\mathbf{z}_u | \mathbf{r}_u, \mathbf{c}\right)}\left[\log p_\theta\left(\hat{\mathbf{r}}_u | \mathbf{z}_u, \mathbf{c}\right)\right] - \beta \cdot \mathrm{KL}\left(q_\phi\left(\mathbf{z}_u | \mathbf{r}_u, \mathbf{c}\right) \| p\left(\mathbf{z}_u\right)\right)$$

where $\mathbf{z}_u$ is the latent representation of the user u, and $\hat{\mathbf{r}}_u$ is $\mathbf{r}_u$ filtered by the condition $\mathbf{c}$. The filtering is directly embedded in the reconstruction loss as:

$$\log p_\theta\left(\hat{\mathbf{r}}_u | \mathbf{z}_u, \mathbf{c}\right) = \sum_{i \in \mathcal{I}} \langle \mathbf{c}, \mathbf{G}^\top \rangle_i \, \mathbf{r}_{ui} \log \pi_i(f_\theta(\mathbf{z}_u))$$

where:

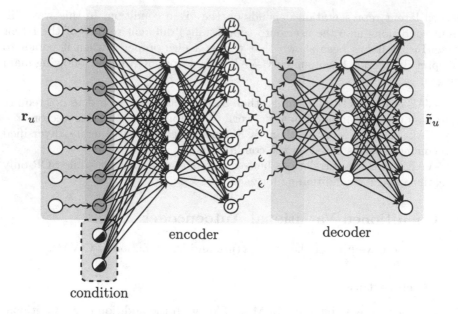

Fig. 1. High level illustration of the Conditioned VAE architecture.

- π is the softmax function;
- $\langle \cdot, \cdot \rangle$ indicates the inner-product operation;
- $\mathbf{G} \in \{0,1\}^{m \times s}$ is the item-condition matrix, where $g_{ic} = 1$ iff item i satisfies the condition c.

This reconstruction loss is what makes our model able to learn the relationship between items and conditions. When conditions are not used, then all items are assumed of satisfying the empty condition. Implementation-wise, this is achieved by removing the dot product $\langle \mathbf{c}, \mathbf{G}^\top \rangle$, which is indeed always equal to the constant vector $\mathbf{1}$. This leads the C-VAE loss to be the equal to the loss function defined in [13], making C-VAE equivalent to Mult-VAE.

It is worth to underline that the filtering part can also be dependent from both user and item. For example, in the case of context-aware recommendation [1], the conditioning can be defined in terms of the context, which is influenced by both users and items. In this case, the reconstruction loss must be modified accordingly by defining a different condition matrix $\mathbf{G}$. In this paper, we focus on conditioning defined over the items' content.

5   Experiments

In this section, we present the experiments performed on C-VAE. We compare C-VAE with Mult-VAE in terms of top-N recommendation accuracy (Sect. 5.4). A comparison with other methods is challenging since C-VAE is designed for the constrained recommendation, while the other recommenders perform general recommendations.

5.1 Datasets

We performed our experiments on three real-world data sets, chosen in such a way that they contained item side information to construct the conditions.

MovieLens 20M (ml-20m)[1]: This data set contains user-movie ratings collected from a movie recommendation service. We took the genres of the movies as conditions. We removed the rarest genres (i.e., IMAX, Film-Noir, and the neutral genre (no genres listed)) because they were poorly represented in the data set. For the rest of the pre-processing, we followed the same procedure as in [13].

Yelp[2]: This data set is a subset of Yelp's businesses, reviews, and user data. We took the categories of the businesses as conditions. We kept the 20 most popular restaurant categories as described in [20]. Afterward, since we work on implicit feedback, we binarized explicit data by keeping ratings of three or higher. Finally, we only kept users who have reviewed at least four restaurants and restaurants that have been reviewed by at least ten users.

Netflix Prize[3]: This is the official data set used in the Netflix Prize competition. As of ml-20m, we took the genres of the movies as conditions. Since the dataset does not include information about the genres, we developed a script to fetch this information from the *IMDb*[4] database. We used the title and year of the movies to query the database. Netflix dataset originally contained 17,770 movies but only 12,279 matched with *IMDb*. The retrieved movies-genres mapping is available at this URL[5]. As in movielens, we removed the rarest genres, i.e., Talk-Show, Film-Noir, Short, Reality-TV, News, and Game-Show. For the rest of the pre-processing, we followed the same procedure as in [13].

Table 1 summarizes the information about the data sets after the pre-processing presented above.

5.2 Conditions Computation

Potentially, during the training of C-VAE, it might be possible to condition each user with every possible conditions combination. However, the size of the training set would be in the order of $\mathcal{O}(n \cdot 2^s)$. We decided to limit its size by conditioning users one category at a time, i.e., $\|\mathbf{c}\|_1 = 1$. If a condition is never satisfied by the user's item set $\mathcal{I}_u$, then the condition is simply not considered

---

[1] https://grouplens.org/datasets/movielens/20m/.
[2] https://www.yelp.com/dataset.
[3] https://www.kaggle.com/netflix-inc/netflix-prize-data.
[4] https://www.imdb.com/.
[5] https://github.com/tommasocarraro/netflix-prize-with-genres.

Table 1. Composition of datasets after pre-processing.

	ml-20m	Yelp	Netflix
# of users	136,466	125,679	459,133
# of items	19,619	22,824	11,844
# of categories	17	20	21
# of interactions	19.3M	2.9M	88.8M
% of interactions	0.7	0.1	1.6
# of held-out users	10,000	9,000	40,000
# training examples	1,728,205	759,955	6,826,774
# validation examples	144,179	47,364	699,901
# test examples	143,965	46,847	700,393

in the training. In the training set we also considered the users without any condition (akin Mult-VAE).

The bottom part of Table 1 summarizes the size of the training, validation, and test sets after the computation of the conditions.

5.3 Experimental Setup

An overview of the architecture of our model is presented in Sect. 4.1. We followed the implementation as in [13], where an L^2 normalization and a dropout layer ($p = 0.5$) are applied to the input r_u before it is fed to the encoder. The encoder network is composed of a fully connected layer made of 600 neurons with $tanh$ as the activation function. The encoder outputs the mean and the standard deviation of a Gaussian distribution, that are represented with two fully connected layers made of 200 neurons and linearly activated. The decoder network is composed of a fully connected layer made of 600 neurons with $tanh$ as the activation function. Finally, the decoder linearly outputs the scores over the entire item set. Recalling that $m = |I|$ and $s = |C|$, the neural architecture of our model can be summarized as $[m + s \implies 600 \implies 200 \implies 600 \implies m]$. For Mult-VAE, we used the same architecture.

For both Mult-VAE and C-VAE, the network weights are initialized with Xavier uniform initializer, while biases are normally initialized with 0 mean and standard deviation of 0.001. We used the Adam optimizer with a learning rate of 0.001. For the tuning of the hyper-parameter β, we used the KL annealing procedure explained in [13]. In our experiments, we found that the best values for β are 0.07 for ml-20m, 0.35 for Yelp, and 0.05 for Netflix.

We used a batch size of 500 for Yelp and ml-20m, while for Netflix a batch size of 1000. We trained the models for 100 epochs on every dataset and kept the model corresponding to the best validation score in terms of nDCG@100. We used early stopping to stop the training if no improvements were found on the validation score for five consecutive epochs.

5.4   Experimental Results and Discussion

This section compares C-VAE and Mult-VAE in terms of top-N recommendation quality. We evaluated the models using recall@k and nDCG@k, two widely-used ranking-based metrics. While recall@k considers all items ranked within the first k to be equally important, nDCG@k uses a monotonically increasing discount to emphasize the importance of higher-ranked items. We did not have the chance to compare our method with SCR because the authors did not provide the implementation of their method. Experiments have been performed using the *rectorch*[6] python library. To quantitatively compare our proposed method with Mult-VAE, we used three different types of evaluation:

1. **total**: measures how well the model performs in general, that is, when the test set contains both users with conditions and users without conditions;
2. **normal**: measures how well the model performs without conditioning, that is, when the test set contains only users without conditions;
3. **conditioned**: measures how well the model performs with conditioning, that is, when the test set contains only users with conditions.

Since Mult-VAE does not directly handle the conditioning, we filtered its output according to the condition, and we computed the ranking only on those items that satisfy the condition. It is worth noticing that this filtering gives Mult-VAE a massive advantage because it dramatically narrows down the item set. Clearly, C-VAE instead performs the ranking over the whole item set.

To validate and test the models, for each validation/test user, we fed 80% of user ratings to the network and reported metrics on the remaining 20% of the rating history (for `Yelp` we used 50/50 proportions due to its sparsity). Table 2 reports the obtained results.

Table 2. Comparison between C-VAE and Mult-VAE on selected benchmark data sets. r stands for recall, while n stands for nDCG. Each metric is averaged across all test users. Standard errors are between 0.001 and 0.003.

Dataset	Method	Total			Normal			Conditioned		
		r@20	r@50	n@100	r@20	r@50	n@100	r@20	r@50	n@100
ml-20m	C-VAE	0.638	0.786	0.509	0.385	0.527	0.410	0.666	0.816	0.521
	Mult-VAE	**0.645**	**0.792**	**0.517**	**0.394**	**0.537**	**0.420**	**0.674**	**0.822**	**0.529**
Yelp	C-VAE	**0.311**	0.459	**0.238**	**0.139**	**0.235**	**0.143**	0.392	0.564	**0.282**
	Mult-VAE	**0.311**	**0.460**	**0.238**	0.134	0.233	**0.143**	**0.394**	**0.567**	**0.282**
Netflix	C-VAE	0.590	0.751	0.494	0.335	0.444	0.374	0.613	0.778	0.504
	Mult-VAE	**0.601**	**0.758**	**0.504**	**0.352**	**0.457**	**0.389**	**0.623**	**0.785**	**0.515**

From the table, it is possible to observe that C-VAE obtains state-of-the-art results, even though generally a bit lower than Mult-VAE. We want to emphasize

---

[6] https://github.com/makgyver/rectorch.

one more time that C-VAE performs the ranking over all items, while Mult-VAE only on the subset of items satisfying the condition. This shows that our method can learn the relationships between items and categories, since it is able to push the items that belong to the target category at the top of the ranking.

5.5   Analysis of the C-VAE Produced Rankings

Since we obtained promising results in terms of ranking accuracy, we decided to graphically analyze the rankings produced by C-VAE. Thanks to the conditioned loss, C-VAE learns how to filter the items in such a way to focus its attention on those belonging to the target category. To further validate this argument, we plot the distribution over the rankings produced by C-VAE for the items satisfying the conditions. The plot has been computed on the `ml-20m` training users and is shown in Fig. 2. In particular, each user has been conditioned with every possible one-hot condition vector $\mathbf{c}$, with $||\mathbf{c}||_1 = 1$, namely with one category at a time. The plot clearly shows that most of the items of the target category have been placed in the top positions, indicating that C-VAE learns to push the right items at the top. A further check has shown that in the first 100 positions of the ranking, C-VAE is always able to put only items satisfying the input condition.

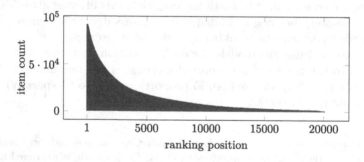

Fig. 2. Number of items of the target category per ranking position for the rankings produced by C-VAE for the training users of `ml-20m`.

6   Conclusions and Future Work

In this paper, we presented a novel method for conditioning the top-N item recommendation process. We developed a conditioned extension of Mult-VAE [13], which relies on a novel loss function that is crucial for the training of our method. We compared our method with the state-of-the-art Mult-VAE recommender, showing that C-VAE reaches similar performance in both the conditioned as well as the non-conditioned top-N recommendation tasks.

As long as we perform content-based recommendations, our model is less powerful than the filtered Mult-VAE, but in context-aware scenarios, C-VAE can capture patterns between users, items, and the interactions between them, while Mult-VAE cannot be applied since the filtering is no longer applicable. In conclusion, we intend to extend our evaluation to other open research topics, particularly context-aware recommendation systems.

References

1. Adomavicius, G., Tuzhilin, A.: Context-Aware Recommender Systems. In: Ricci, F., Rokach, L., Shapira, B. (eds.) Recommender Systems Handbook, pp. 191–226. Springer, Boston, MA (2015). https://doi.org/10.1007/978-1-4899-7637-6_6
2. Askari, B., Szlichta, J., Salehi-Abari, A.: Variational autoencoders for top-k recommendation with implicit feedback. In: Proceedings of the 44th International ACM SIGIR Conference on Research and Development in Information Retrieval. pp. 2061–2065 (2021)
3. Carraro, T., Polato, M., Aiolli, F.: A look inside the black-box: towards the interpretability of conditioned variational autoencoder for collaborative filtering. In: Adjunct Publication of the 28th ACM Conference on User Modeling, Adaptation and Personalization, pp. 233–236 (2020)
4. Chae, D.K., Kang, J.S., Kim, S.W., Lee, J.T.: Cfgan: a generic collaborative filtering framework based on generative adversarial networks. In: Proceedings of the 27th ACM International Conference on Information and Knowledge Management. CIKM 2018, New York, NY, USA, pp. 137–146. Association for Computing Machinery (2018). https://doi.org/10.1145/3269206.3271743
5. Goodfellow, I., Bengio, Y., Courville, A.: Deep Learning. MIT Press (2016). http://www.deeplearningbook.org
6. He, X., Liao, L., Zhang, H., Nie, L., Hu, X., Chua, T.S.: Neural collaborative filtering. In: Proceedings of the 26th International Conference on World Wide Web. WWW 2017. International World Wide Web Conferences Steering Committee, Republic and Canton of Geneva, CHE, pp. 173–182 (2017). https://doi.org/10.1145/3038912.3052569
7. Higgins, I., et al.: beta-vae: learning basic visual concepts with a constrained variational framework. In: ICLR (2017)
8. Hu, Y., Koren, Y., Volinsky, C.: Collaborative filtering for implicit feedback datasets. In: 2008 Eighth IEEE International Conference on Data Mining, pp. 263–272 (2008)
9. Iqbal, M., Aryafar, K., Anderton, T.: Style conditioned recommendations. In: Proceedings of the 13th ACM Conference on Recommender Systems. RecSys 2019, New York, NY, USA, pp. 128–136. Association for Computing Machinery (2019). https://doi.org/10.1145/3298689.3347007
10. Kingma, D.P., Welling, M.: Auto-encoding variational Bayes. In: Bengio, Y., LeCun, Y. (eds.) 2nd International Conference on Learning Representations, ICLR 2014, Banff, AB, Canada, 14–16 April 2014 (2014)
11. Koren, Y., Bell, R.: Advances in collaborative filtering. In: Ricci, F., Rokach, L., Shapira, B., Kantor, P.B. (eds.) Recommender Systems Handbook, pp. 145–186. Springer, Boston, MA (2011). https://doi.org/10.1007/978-0-387-85820-3_5
12. Li, X., She, J.: Collaborative variational autoencoder for recommender systems. In: Proceedings of the 23rd ACM SIGKDD International Conference on Knowledge Discovery and Data Mining. KDD 2017, New York, NY, USA, pp. 305–314. Association for Computing Machinery (2017). https://doi.org/10.1145/3097983.3098077

13. Liang, D., Krishnan, R.G., Hoffman, M.D., Jebara, T.: Variational autoencoders for collaborative filtering. In: Proceedings of the 2018 World Wide Web Conference. WWW 2018. International World Wide Web Conferences Steering Committee, Republic and Canton of Geneva, CHE, pp. 689–698 (2018). https://doi.org/10.1145/3178876.3186150

14. Ning, X., Karypis, G.: Slim: sparse linear methods for top-n recommender systems. In: 2011 IEEE 11th International Conference on Data Mining, pp. 497–506 (2011)

15. Pagnoni, A., Liu, K., Li, S.: Conditional variational autoencoder for neural machine translation. ArXiv abs/1812.04405 (2018)

16. Polato, M., Aiolli, F.: Boolean kernels for collaborative filtering in top-n item recommendation. Neurocomput. **286**(C), 214–225 (2018). https://doi.org/10.1016/j.neucom.2018.01.057

17. Rendle, S.: Factorization machines. In: 2010 IEEE International Conference on Data Mining, pp. 995–1000 (2010)

18. Ricci, F., Rokach, L., Shapira, B.: Recommender Systems Handbook, 2nd edn. Springer, New York (2015). https://doi.org/10.1007/978-1-4899-7637-6

19. Shenbin, I., Alekseev, A., Tutubalina, E., Malykh, V., Nikolenko, S.I.: Recvae: a new variational autoencoder for top-n recommendations with implicit feedback. In: Proceedings of the 13th International Conference on Web Search and Data Mining, pp. 528–536 (2020)

20. Spagnuolo, C., et al.: Analyzing, exploring, and visualizing complex networks via hypergraphs using simplehypergraphs.jl. Internet Mathematics, April 2020. https://doi.org/10.24166/im.01.2020

21. Steck, H.: Embarrassingly shallow autoencoders for sparse data. In: The World Wide Web Conference. WWW 2019, New York, NY, USA, pp. 3251–3257. Association for Computing Machinery (2019). https://doi.org/10.1145/3308558.3313710

22. Su, X., Khoshgoftaar, T.M.: A survey of collaborative filtering techniques. Adv. Artif. Intell. **2009** (2009). https://doi.org/10.1155/2009/421425

23. Wang, J., et al.: Irgan: a minimax game for unifying generative and discriminative information retrieval models. In: Proceedings of the 40th International ACM SIGIR Conference on Research and Development in Information Retrieval. SIGIR 2017, New York, NY, USA, pp. 515–524, Association for Computing Machinery (2017). https://doi.org/10.1145/3077136.3080786

24. Wu, Y., DuBois, C., Zheng, A.X., Ester, M.: Collaborative denoising auto-encoders for top-n recommender systems. In: Proceedings of the Ninth ACM International Conference on Web Search and Data Mining. WSDM 2016, New York, NY, USA, pp. 153–162. Association for Computing Machinery (2016). https://doi.org/10.1145/2835776.2835837

25. Wu, Y., Macdonald, C., Ounis, I.: A hybrid conditional variational autoencoder model for personalised top-n recommendation. In: Proceedings of the 2020 ACM SIGIR on International Conference on Theory of Information Retrieval, pp. 89–96 (2020)

Personalized Headline Generation with Enhanced User Interest Perception

Kui Zhang, Guangquan Lu$^{(\boxtimes)}$, Guixian Zhang, Zhi Lei, and Lijuan Wu

Guangxi Key Lab of Multi-Source Information Mining and Security,
Guangxi Normal University, Guilin 541004, China
lugq@mailbox.gxnu.edu.cn

Abstract. Personalized news headline generation aims to model users interests through their news browsing history, and then generate news headlines based on their preferences. Using the user representation of existing news recommendation systems to personalize news headlines has been very successful, but there are still many problems to be solved. Firstly, news recommendation and headline generation tasks have different requirements for user interest modelling. Secondly, the user interest embedding approach does not consider the redundancy of user interests and the complementarity between user interests and candidate news texts. In this paper, we propose a new personalized headline generation framework to enhance the user interest perception. It can highlight user interests related to candidate texts for accurate embedding. We further offer to improve user interest representation using entity words in the news to meet the demand for news headline personalization. Extensive experiments show that our approach achieves better performance in headline generation tasks.

Keywords: Personalized headline generation · News recommendation · Reinforcement learning

1 Introduction

Recently, personalized news headline generation [2] has become an emerging research topic. Unlike the traditional news headline generation task, it not only ensures the extraction of important information headlines in the news but also incorporates users' interests as guiding knowledge into the headline generation task [4], taking into account the reading habits and preferences of different users.

Users pay different attention to the same article and important content related to their interests. For example, as shown in Fig. 1, let U_A and U_B represent user A and user B. U_A and U_B both like basketball news, but U_A likes to read news about LeBron James, while U_B is more likely to be attracted to the Lakers. In fact, since LeBron James is a player of the Lakers, U_A may be a fan of the team, while U_B may prefer LeBron James himself. When the candidate news is about the basketball game, the personalized news headline for U_A should

© The Author(s), under exclusive license to Springer Nature Switzerland AG 2022
E. Pimenidis et al. (Eds.): ICANN 2022, LNCS 13530, pp. 797–809, 2022.
https://doi.org/10.1007/978-3-031-15931-2_65

highlight the player's performance in the game. In contrast, the headline for U_B should highlight the overall team status. The headlines generated in this way are more appealing to the user's eyes and more easily accepted by the user based on the news facts.

	User A	User B
Clicked News	LeBron James, Chris Paul and Russell Westbrook chill court side at Aces–Liberty Every Kevin Love Touchdown Pass to LeBron James! Kawhi Leonard reaches out to LeBron James, expresses interest in playing together LeBron James, Anthony Davis sit courtside for Summer League openers	NBA Finals 2020 Odds: Warriors, Lakers Headline Contenders Anthony Davis pitching in on the Lakers recruiting efforts AP Source: Lakers, Pelicans, agree on Anthony Davis trade Lakers sign Alex Caruso, Troy Daniels and Jared Dudley
Candidate News	LeBron James scored 29 points and playedexclusively at center in the second half as the Los Angeles Lakers rallied froman eight-point halftime deficit and beat the Orlando Magic 116-105 on Friday night...	LeBron James scored 29 points and playedexclusively at center in the second half as the Los Angeles Lakers rallied froman eight-point halftime deficit and beat the Orlando Magic 116-105 on Friday night...

Fig. 1. An illustrative example of personalized news headline generation. The colored bars represent the words of interest to two different users for clicking on the news headline and the candidate news body. (Color figure online)

In terms of methodology, since users' interests are aggregated from users' history of news browsing, and the headline generation task is a typical NLP task [21], it is a very challenging task considering the mutual understanding of user interest representation and headline generation information. So how to find a suitable user interest modelling approach and interest fusion approach is the main foundation.

Due to the great success of news recommendation, PENS attempts to personalize the generated headlines using existing user interest modelling in news recommendation and proposes three ways to embed user interests, essentially taking user interest representation as External knowledge to guide personalized headline generation [18]. The personalized headline generation task has achieved good results, but there are still many problems to be solved. First, the importance of features in the news recommendation task is different from that in personalized headline generation. If the user's interests are directly embedded in the text summary, it will cause a lot of information redundancy. Furthermore, the modelling of user interests differs from natural language representation, and there is a clear semantic gap between the two tasks.

In fact, when reading news headlines, users first pay attention to the specific entity words in the news headlines and then to the semantics, style, and sentiment contained in the news headlines. As shown in the example above, users' browsing history shows that two users offer different attention to LeBron James and the Lakers, the most intuitive expression of users' interests. Therefore, unlike the news recommendation, in user interest modelling, we should fully consider different users' attention to different entities and generate personalized headlines for different users in news headline generation.

In news reading, users' interests are diverse and complex rather than single [14]. For example, a user's interest in a certain topic at a specific time belongs to the user's short-term interest [1,19], such as current news like the US election. In contrast, a user's interest in a specific topic like health or sports serves as the user's long-term topic. Whether a user will click on the news recommended to him or not depends on only a small part of the historical behavior data, not all of it [20].

Through our observation and analysis of the limitations of existing methods, in this paper, we propose a personalized news headline generation model that enhances user interest perception. First, we model news embeddings and user embeddings with news topics and entities to improve the representation of user interests. Second, we also incorporate a user interest filtering module based on the correlation between candidate news and user interests, highlighting user interest information related to the candidate news context. Finally, we optimize our proposed model through reinforcement learning [16] to achieve consistency in generating titles with multiple objectives. Experimental results show that our personalized news headline generation model significantly outperforms current state-of-the-art methods on the PENS dataset.

2   Related Work

Personalized news headline generation consists of three main modules: news recommendation module, headline generation module and interest embedding module. We will present the related work in these three areas.

2.1   News Recommendation Module

The news recommendation module aims to measure how well the candidate news matches the user's interests. Most of the current news recommendation models focus on evaluating the correlation between user interests and candidate news and a unified representation of them. News modelling approaches and user modelling approaches have also emerged, such as DKN [10] using Convolutional Neural Networks (CNN) to model entities in the news to represent news.

Recently, more and more news recommendations use more news features to represent news, and NAML [12] uses CNN to model headlines and body text, and finally stitches the modelled vectors together as a news representation.

2.2   News Headline Generation Module

Title generation [3] is one of the more representative works in NLP, where extraction is mainly done by extracting a subset of sentences from the original text containing text semantics. The model is mainly based on the encoder-decode [5] framework.

Recently, Woodsend et al. [11] proposed a joint content selection and surface realization model, which formulates the title generation problem at the phrase input text. Xu et al. [17] selected keywords from functions extracted from Wikipedia and then used a keyword clustering approach to construct headlines. Rush et al. [8] trained the attention-based abstraction (ABS) model, which uses the lead (RST) sentences of each article as input for headline generation.

2.3   User Interest Embedding Module

The user interest embedding module is mainly designed to integrate user representations from news recommendations as guiding knowledge into the headline generator. Referring to existing knowledge-enhanced text generation approaches, PENS proposes to use user embedding to initialize the hidden state of the headline generator decoder. Alternatively, user interests are added to calculate the attention distribution of words in the text to distinguish how much different users pay attention to the words.

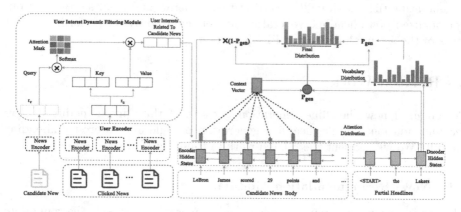

Fig. 2. The general framework of EUI-PENS, the left part is the user interest representation and user interest dynamic filtering module, the filtered user interest right part of the user interest embedding and headline generation module to realize the personalization of news headline generation.

3   Methods

In this section, we provide a personalized headline generation framework for personalized headline generation tasks based on a user interest enhancement approach named: EUI-PENS. We first describe how to enhance user interest representation with entity words, then how to use attention mechanisms to filter user interest, and finally explain a solution for the personalized title generation task based on filtered user interests. The proposed model is shown in Fig. 2.

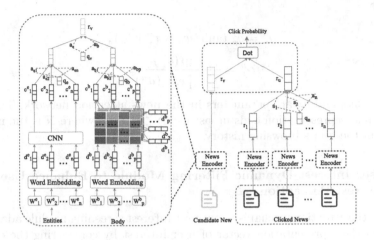

Fig. 3. News recommendation framework using entity word enhancement

3.1   User Interest Representation Using Entity Word Enhancement

The personalization of news headlines is more based on the user's interest in different entities and keywords in the news. For this reason, we improved the user interest representation to fit the headline generation task.

First, we represent entities as keywords to bridge the semantic gap between interest representations and natural language expressions. The connection between words and associated entities is also strengthened. Specifically, it is shown in Fig. 3. For the entity word encoder, we denote the entity words of the news as $[w_1^e, w_2^e, \ldots, w_n^e]$, where n is the number of entity words in the news. The word sequence is converted to a vector using the word embedding matrix as $[d_1^e, d_2^e, \ldots, d_n^e]$, and we model the entity word vector separately with CNN to represent the user's attention to the entities in the news, CNN is an effective neural structure for capturing local information. The output of the CNN layer is a sequence of entity word representations, denoted as $[c_1^e, c_2^e, \ldots, c_n^e]$, different entity keywords in the same news have different importance to the news, so we use the attention network to select the important words among the news entity words, then the final representation of the news entity words is the attention-weighted entity word context vector.

Second, we similarly treat the news body with word embedding, turning each word in the news headline into a vector, a word vector used by the multi-headed self-attentive network for feature (interaction) extraction, representing the rich news semantics using multi-headed attention modelling, and then stitching them together into a news representation using attention weights.

Finally, in the user interest encoder module, we denote the attention of news viewed by the user as a_i^n, which is calculated as:

$$a_i^n = q_n^T \tanh\left(w_n \times r_i + b_n\right), \tag{1}$$

$$\alpha_i^n = \frac{\exp\left(a_i^n\right)}{\sum_{j=1}^{N} \exp\left(a_j^n\right)}, \tag{2}$$

where q_n, w_n, and b_n are parameters in the news attention network. Then the user interest representation ends up as: $u = \sum_{i=1}^{N} \alpha_i^n r_i$, where N is the number of news in the user's browsing history.

3.2 User Interest Dynamic Filtering Module to Enhance User Interest Perception

Based on the attention mechanism, our user interest screening module adaptively calculates the representation vector of user interest by considering the correlation of historical behaviours. Specifically, by introducing a local activation unit, a weighted sum is used to obtain the representation of the user's interest about the candidate news. User interest information that is highly relevant to candidate news gets higher activation weights and dominates the entire user interest. Therefore, the filtered user interest vector varies with candidate news.

In the self-attention mechanism, given a *query*, the relevance of the *query* to the *key* is calculated, and then the most appropriate *value* is found based on the relevance of the *query* to the *key*. In the user interest filtering module, *query* is the information of candidate news (such as keywords, entities, categories, etc.), *key* is the information of user interest aggregated from user browsing history, and weighted value is the relevant information to the candidate news of user interest.

Specifically, we transform the above obtained entity-enhanced user interest vector u and candidate news vector v into the corresponding *query*, *key* and *value* matrix:

$$Q = v, \tag{3}$$

$$K = u, \tag{4}$$

Then by computing the Cross multiplication of vectors, we obtain the original attention weights. the affinity matrix is calculated as follows:

$$S_t^u = Soft\max\left(\frac{QK^T}{\sqrt{d}}\right), \tag{5}$$

The output is a correlation matrix is multiplied by this value to obtain the weighted output of the autocorrelation module: $u_t = S_t^u u$, Indicates filtered user interest related to candidate news.

3.3 User Interest Injection Module for Personalization

Using an attention mechanism, we embed the filtered user interests into the headline generation task. The user interest vector is added to the calculation of the attention distribution of words in the text. On the one hand, it is used to describe the importance of the input text to the generation process. On the other hand, the probability distribution of words copied back from the original text by the decoder is influenced to personalize the headline generation.

Specifically, we choose the pointer generator as the title generator. First, the encoder converts the candidate news text into a hidden states h_i, and for each decoding step t, the decoder receives as input the embedding of each token of the title y_t and updates its hidden state s_t, The attention distribution of the encoder hidden state h is calculated as:

$$a_t = \text{softmax} \left(V_{att}^{\top} \tanh \left(W_h h + W_s s_t + W_u u_t + b_{att} \right) \right), \tag{6}$$

where V, W_h, W_s, W_u and b_{att} are trainable parameters. u_t is the filtered user interest vector. The decoder generates the next word based on the attention distribution. Next, the attention distribution is used to generate a weighted sum of the hidden states of the encoder and thus to compute the generated vocabulary distribution:

$$P_{\text{vocab}} \left(w_t \right) = \tanh \left(V_p \left[s_t; c_t \right] + b_v \right), \tag{7}$$

$$P \left(w_t \right) = p_{gen}^t P_{vocab} \left(w_t \right) + \left(1 - p_{gen}^t \right) \sum_{j:w_j = w_t} a_{t,j}, \tag{8}$$

where V_p and b_v are learnable parameters. The context vector c_t is a fixed-size representation read from the news body at time step t, and $P_{\text{vocab}} \left(w_t \right)$ denotes the probability distribution of predicted words at time step t for all words in the vocabulary.

At decoding step t, we employ a pointer p_{gen}^t to choose whether to generate words from a vocabulary with probability $P_{\text{vocab}} \left(w_t \right)$ or to copy words from a sample of news subjects from the attention distribution.

4 Experiments

In this section, we first set up the experiment and then report and analyze the results.

4.1 Datasets

We evaluate our model with the PENS dataset, which is a personalized headline generation dataset published by MIND [15]. It contains 13,762 news articles from 115 categories, each containing news ID, headline, body and category tags. Entities were extracted from each news headline and body, and they were linked to entities in Wikidata 3. The test set invited 103 native English-speaking college students to serve as annotators, and 50 news items selected by each were considered historical click-through behaviour of the user. The 200 headlines handwritten by the annotators were reviewed for quality by professional news editors. The remaining qualified headlines were used as the gold standard for personalized news headlines for the corresponding users.

4.2   Implementation Details

Follow previous work to perform preprocessing, and we set the user's click news sequence to 50 to model the user's interest vector and set the length of the news body to 500, respectively. The word embedding is 300-dimensional and initialized by Glove, while the news body and entity embedding size are 100. the multi-headed attention network has eight heads, and the length of the user's interest vector and the candidate news vector is 64.

First, We train the user interest modelling for the news recommendation module and pre-train the user interest model with a learning rate of 10^{-4} using the user click sequences of the previous three weeks as the training set. Meanwhile, user embeddings and candidate news embeddings in the model are used as inputs to the user interest filtering module to highlight user interests associated with candidate news. Next, we embed the filtered user interests through the interest embedding module into the headline generator, which is also pre-estimated at a learning rate of 0.001.

4.3   Evaluation Metrics

Our model consists of a user interest module and a headline generation module, and we evaluate our model using two different sets of criteria. On the one hand, following previous work on news recommendations, we report the average results in terms of AUC, MRR, nDCG@5 and nDCG@10. On the other hand, we evaluate our personalized headline generation model with the standard ROUGE [7] metric, reporting ROUGE-1, ROUGE-2 and F1 scores for ROUGE-l (measuring word over) lap, double overlap and longest common sequence between the reference summary and the summary to be evaluated, respectively.

4.4   Compared Methods

For user interest modelling, we select several neural networks for news recommendation methods that perform well in personalized headline generation. All user interest modelling methods are embedded using the user interest embedding module. Personalized headline generation using the headline generation module: (1) EBNR [6]: a news recommendation system that models news representation and user representation using a sequence modelling approach. (2) DKN [10]: a deep knowledge-aware news recommendation system that uses CNN aggregated news entities to represent news and users. (3) NRMS [13]: a multi-news recommendation using multi-headed self-attentive neural networks to model news and users. (4) NAML [12]: proposes the use of different features in news to represent news as well as multi-view user representation. For non-personalized headline generation, we mainly compare the underlying model of the headline generation module in this paper: (1) Pointer-Gen [9] can select to copy from the source text or generate from the vocabulary to improve the accuracy of extracting information. (2) PG+RL-ROUGE [16] incorporates Pointer-Gen into a reinforcement learning framework to generate sensational headlines using ROUGE-L scores as rewards.

Table 1. The overall performance of compared methods. "R-1, -2, -L" indicate F scores of ROUGE-1, -2, and -L, and "NA" denotes "Not Available".

Methods	Metrics						
	AUC	MRR	NDCG@5	NDCG@10	ROUGE-1	ROUGE-2	ROUGE-L
Pointer-Gen	NA	NA	NA	NA	19.86	7.76	18.83
PG+RL_ROUGE	NA	NA	NA	NA	20.56	8.42	20.03
EBNR	63.97	22.52	26.45	32.81	25.49	9.14	20.82
DKN	65.25	24.07	26.97	34.24	27.48	10.07	21.81
NRMS	64.27	23.28	26.60	33.58	26.15	9.37	21.03
NAML	66.18	25.51	27.56	35.17	28.01	10.72	22.24
EUI-PENS	66.28	25.34	27.58	35.53	32.34	13.93	26.90

4.5   Experimental Results

As shown in Table 1, we compare our approach with the latest one-stage approach for personalized headline generation and headline generation baselines. We have the following observations.

First, we can see that personalized headline generation methods generally perform better than non-personalized headline generation methods, which indicates that incorporating user interests into headline generation leads to good performance in personalization and generates headlines that are more in line with the golden headlines of user interests. Second, we found that using entities to model user interests in news recommendation has better performance in personalized headline generation, such as DKN and our approach, which uses fewer news features in user modelling but achieves better results relative to the generation task. This suggests that users' interest is more in the extent to which they pay attention to the physical words in the news, and that strengthening the probability of copying such physical words in headline generation is an effective way to achieve personalized news headlines. Third, our model performs better results with fewer news features than NAML and other user interest modelling. We conjecture that the filtering module of user interest can filter user interest related to the candidate news for pre-embedding, highlighting the peak of user interest related to the candidate news and thus enhancing the user interest perception of the generated model. This compensates for the poor performance of the generation task when modelling user interests is complex (Table 2).

Table 2. A case study of generating personalized headers for two different users through personalized (EUI-PENS) and non-personalized (Pointer-Gen). The underlined words and coloured words represent the relevant words in the manually written headlines. Relevant words in manually written headlines, clicked news and generated headlines.

Case 1. Original Headline:	LeBron James Scores 29, Plays Center As Lakers Rally Past Magic, 116–105
Pointer-Gen:	Lakers beat the Magic 116–105
user A written headline:	LeBron James led the Lakers to a 116–105 victory over the Magic
EUI-PENS for user A:	LeBron James scored 29 points at center to led the Lakers to a 116–105 win over the Magic
Clicked News of user A:	1. LeBron James, Anthony Davis sit courtside for Summer League openers
	2. Every Kevin Love Touchdown Pass to LeBron James !
user B written headline:	Lakers play well to beat the Magic 116–105
EUI-PENS for user B:	The Lakers defeated the Magic with an outstanding 116–105 performance
Clicked News of user B:	1. Lakers sign Alex Caruso, Troy Daniels and Jared Dudley
	2. Anthony Davis pitching in on The Lakers recruiting efforts

4.6 Ablation Study

In this section, we design a different structure for Ablation study to better understand our approach. The datasets for the experiments are all PENS datasets.

To verify the importance of adding entity words to user interest modelling for both tasks, we designed a comparison experiment between user interest modelling without the addition of entity words and user representation enhanced with entity words, and the results are shown in Table 3, 4.

First, user interest modelling using entity words improves on both tasks. The method of aggregating entity words using CNN achieves AUC, MRR, NDCG@5 and NDCG@10 scores of 66.28, 25.34, 27.58 and 35.53 on the news recommendation task. The ROUGE scores for personalized headline generation reached 29.43, 11.66 and 24.96. Second, different entity word aggregation methods have different effects on performance, with the best performer being CNN, while using sequence modelling methods, such as RNN, has less performance improvement because the sequential relationships between entity words are not obvious.

To validate the usefulness of the user information filtering module, we designed the following experiments as shown in Table 5. First, the ROUGE

Table 3. News recommendation performance of modelling entity words in different ways. "Non-Entity" means no entity word is used to represent news.

Entity-Modelling approach	AUC	MRR	NDCG@5	NDCG@10
Non-Entity	64.22	23.14	26.58	33.51
Entity-Embedding	64.20	23.26	27.19	33.48
Entity-RNN	64.26	23.55	26.23	33.56
Entity-Multi-headed Attention	65.31	24.63	26.49	34.16
Entity-CNN	66.28	25.34	27.58	35.53

Table 4. Personalized headline generation performance for modelling entity words in different ways.

Entity-Modelling approach	ROUGE-1	ROUGE-2	ROUGE-L
Non-Entity	26.23	9.11	20.96
Entity-Embedding	27.86	10.24	22.21
Entity-RNN	26.15	9.38	21.17
Entity-Multi-headed Attention	28.20	10.48	22.01
Entity-CNN	29.43	11.66	24.96

Table 5. The importance of "Entity-CNN" and dynamic filtering of user interest.

Entity-CNN	Interest-filtering	ROUGE-1	ROUGE-2	ROUGE-L
		26.23	9.11	20.96
✓		29.43	11.66	24.96
	✓	31.55	11.74	25.07
✓	✓	32.34	13.93	26.90

scores of 29.43, 11.66 and 24.96 were obtained for title generation on the PENS dataset using only entity word-enhanced user representation. Then, we used the user interest filtering module without using entity-enhanced user representation to increase user prominence with user interests related to the candidate news. We found that the ROUGE scores for headline generation increased by 5.23, 2.63, and 4.11, respectively, compared to directly embedded user interests. This demonstrates the effectiveness of the user interest filtering module. Finally, we applied both the entity word-enhanced user and user interest filtering modules to achieve the final performance of our model, with personalized headline generation ROUGE scores of 32.34, 13.93 and 26.90. The results indicate that both the use of entity word-enhanced user representation and the use of interest filtering can significantly improve the model performance of personalized headline generation.

5   Conclusions

In this paper, we propose a personalized news headline generation model with enhanced user interest perception. Adding news entities to the user modelling enhances the semantic representation of news and user interests in the personalized headline generation task. Based on the relevance of candidate news and user interests, we further develop a user interest filtering module to accurately embed user interests, which solves the high redundancy of user interest information. Extensive experimental and ablation studies demonstrate the robust performance of our approach. We will consider combining the two tasks for future work to allow more interaction between news recommendation and headline generation.

Acknowledgements. This work is partially supported by the Innovation Project of Guangxi Graduate Education (YCSW2022124); and the Research Fund of Guangxi Key Lab of Multi-source Information Mining & Security (MIMS20-04, MIMS21-M-01, MIMS20-M-01, No.20-A-01-01, No.20-A-01-02).

References

1. An, M., Wu, F., Wu, C., Zhang, K., Liu, Z., Xie, X.: Neural news recommendation with long-and short-term user representations. In: Proceedings of the 57th Annual Meeting of the Association for Computational Linguistics, pp. 336–345 (2019)
2. Ao, X., Wang, X., Luo, L., Qiao, Y., He, Q., Xie, X.: Pens: a dataset and generic framework for personalized news headline generation. In: Proceedings of the 59th Annual Meeting of the Association for Computational Linguistics and the 11th International Joint Conference on Natural Language Processing (Volume 1: Long Papers), pp. 82–92 (2021)
3. Gavrilov, D., Kalaidin, P., Malykh, V.: Self-attentive model for headline generation. In: Azzopardi, L., Stein, B., Fuhr, N., Mayr, P., Hauff, C., Hiemstra, D. (eds.) ECIR 2019. LNCS, vol. 11438, pp. 87–93. Springer, Cham (2019). https://doi.org/10.1007/978-3-030-15719-7_11
4. Gu, X., et al.: Generating representative headlines for news stories. In: Proceedings of The Web Conference 2020, pp. 1773–1784 (2020)
5. Murao, K., et al.: A case study on neural headline generation for editing support. In: Proceedings of the 2019 Conference of the North American Chapter of the Association for Computational Linguistics: Human Language Technologies, Volume 2 (Industry Papers), pp. 73–82 (2019)
6. Okura, S., Tagami, Y., Ono, S., Tajima, A.: Embedding-based news recommendation for millions of users. In: Proceedings of the 23rd ACM SIGKDD International Conference on Knowledge Discovery and Data Mining, pp. 1933–1942 (2017)
7. ROUGE, L.C.: A package for automatic evaluation of summaries. In: Proceedings of Workshop on Text Summarization of ACL, Spain (2004)
8. Rush, A.M., Chopra, S., Weston, J.: A neural attention model for abstractive sentence summarization. arXiv preprint arXiv:1509.00685 (2015)
9. See, A., Liu, P.J., Manning, C.D.: Get to the point: summarization with pointer-generator networks. arXiv preprint arXiv:1704.04368 (2017)

10. Wang, H., Zhang, F., Xie, X., Guo, M.: DKN: deep knowledge-aware network for news recommendation. In: Proceedings of the 2018 World Wide Web Conference, pp. 1835–1844 (2018)
11. Woodsend, K., Feng, Y., Lapata, M.: Generation with quasi-synchronous grammar. In: Proceedings of the 2010 Conference on Empirical Methods in Natural Language Processing, pp. 513–523 (2010)
12. Wu, C., Wu, F., An, M., Huang, J., Huang, Y., Xie, X.: Neural news recommendation with attentive multi-view learning. arXiv preprint arXiv:1907.05576 (2019)
13. Wu, C., Wu, F., Ge, S., Qi, T., Huang, Y., Xie, X.: Neural news recommendation with multi-head self-attention. In: Proceedings of the 2019 Conference on Empirical Methods in Natural Language Processing and the 9th International Joint Conference on Natural Language Processing (EMNLP-IJCNLP), pp. 6389–6394 (2019)
14. Wu, C., Wu, F., Qi, T., Huang, Y.: Is news recommendation a sequential recommendation task? arXiv preprint arXiv:2108.08984 (2021)
15. Wu, F., et al.: Mind: a large-scale dataset for news recommendation. In: Proceedings of the 58th Annual Meeting of the Association for Computational Linguistics, pp. 3597–3606 (2020)
16. Xu, P., Wu, C.S., Madotto, A., Fung, P.: Clickbait? sensational headline generation with auto-tuned reinforcement learning. arXiv preprint arXiv:1909.03582 (2019)
17. Xu, S., Yang, S., Lau, F.: Keyword extraction and headline generation using novel word features. In: Twenty-Fourth AAAI Conference on Artificial Intelligence (2010)
18. Yu, W., et al.: A survey of knowledge-enhanced text generation. arXiv preprint arXiv:2010.04389 (2020)
19. Zheng, Y., et al.: Disentangling long and short-term interests for recommendation. arXiv preprint arXiv:2202.13090 (2022)
20. Zhou, G., et al.: Deep interest evolution network for click-through rate prediction. In: Proceedings of the AAAI Conference on Artificial Intelligence, vol. 33, pp. 5941–5948 (2019)
21. Lu, G., Li, J., Wei, J.: Aspect sentiment analysis with heterogeneous graph neural networks. Inf. Process. Manage. **59**(4), 102953 (2022)

Correction to: A Multi-stack Denoising Autoencoder for QoS Prediction

Mengwei Wu(iD), Qin Lu(✉)(iD), and Yingxue Wang(iD)

Correction to:
Chapter "A Multi-stack Denoising Autoencoder for QoS Prediction" in: E. Pimenidis et al. (Eds.): *Artificial Neural Networks and Machine Learning – ICANN 2022*, **LNCS 13530,**
https://doi.org/10.1007/978-3-031-15931-2_62

In the version of this paper that was originally published the affiliation of the authors was incorrect. This has now been corrected.

The updated original version of this chapter can be found at
https://doi.org/10.1007/978-3-031-15931-2_62

Correction to: Artificial Neural Networks and Machine Learning – ICANN 2022

Elias Pimenidis⬥, Plamen Angelov⬥, Chrisina Jayne⬥,
Antonios Papaleonidas⬥, and Mehmet Aydin⬥

Correction to:
E. Pimenidis et al. (Eds.): *Artificial Neural Networks*
and Machine Learning – ICANN 2022, **LNCS 13530,**
https://doi.org/10.1007/978-3-031-15931-2

Chapters, "Learning Flexible Translation Between Robot Actions and Language Descriptions", "Learning Visually Grounded Human-Robot Dialog in a Hybrid Neural Architecture" were previously published non-open access. They have now been changed to open access under a CC BY 4.0 license and the copyright holder updated to 'The Author(s)'. The book has also been updated with these changes.

The updated original version of these chapters can be found at
https://doi.org/10.1007/978-3-031-15931-2_21
https://doi.org/10.1007/978-3-031-15931-2_22

© The Author(s) 2023
E. Pimenidis et al. (Eds.): ICANN 2022, LNCS 13530, p. C2, 2023.
https://doi.org/10.1007/978-3-031-15931-2_67

Author Index

Printed in the United States
by Baker & Taylor Publisher Services

Printed in the United States
by Baker & Taylor Publisher Services